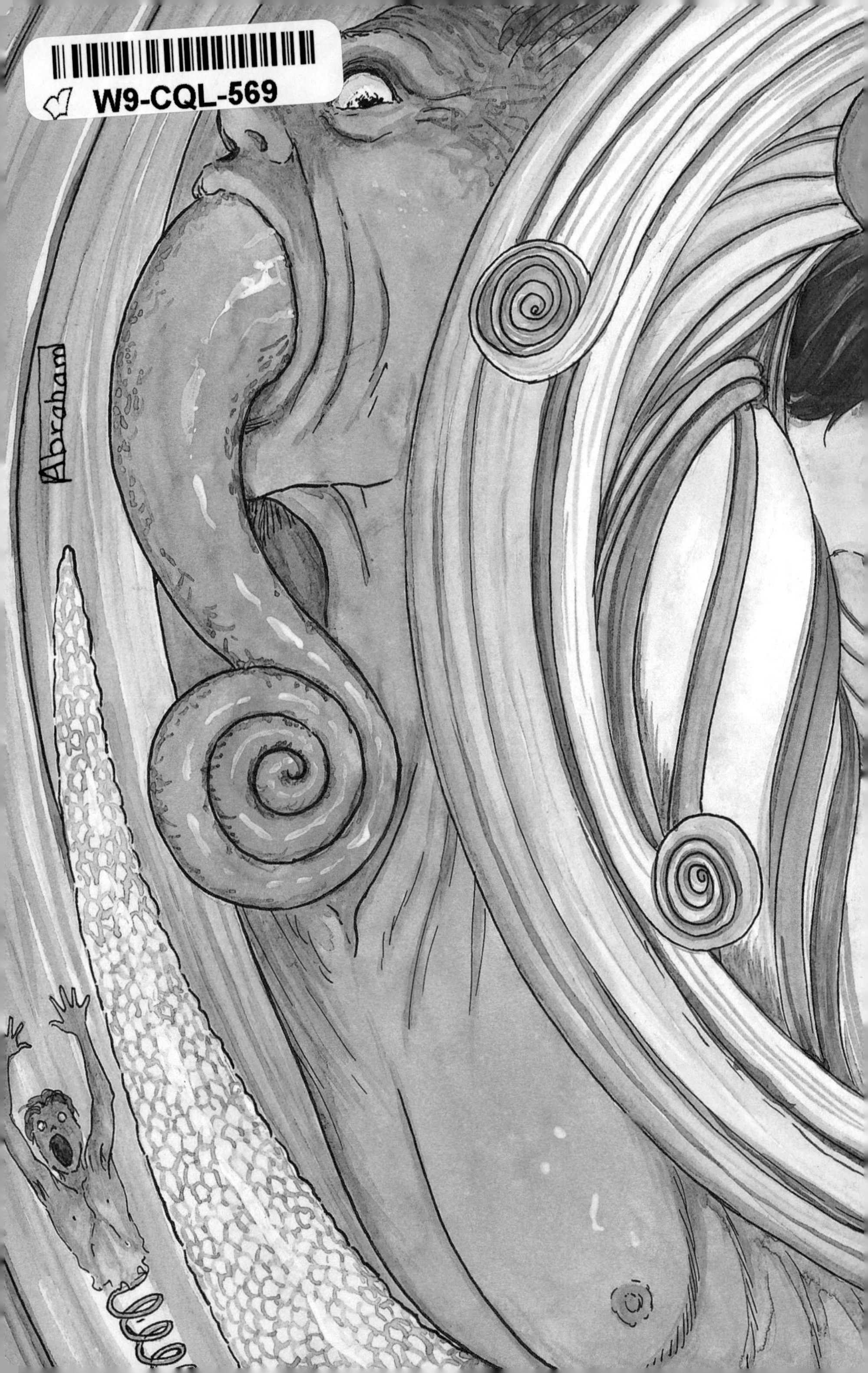
Abraham

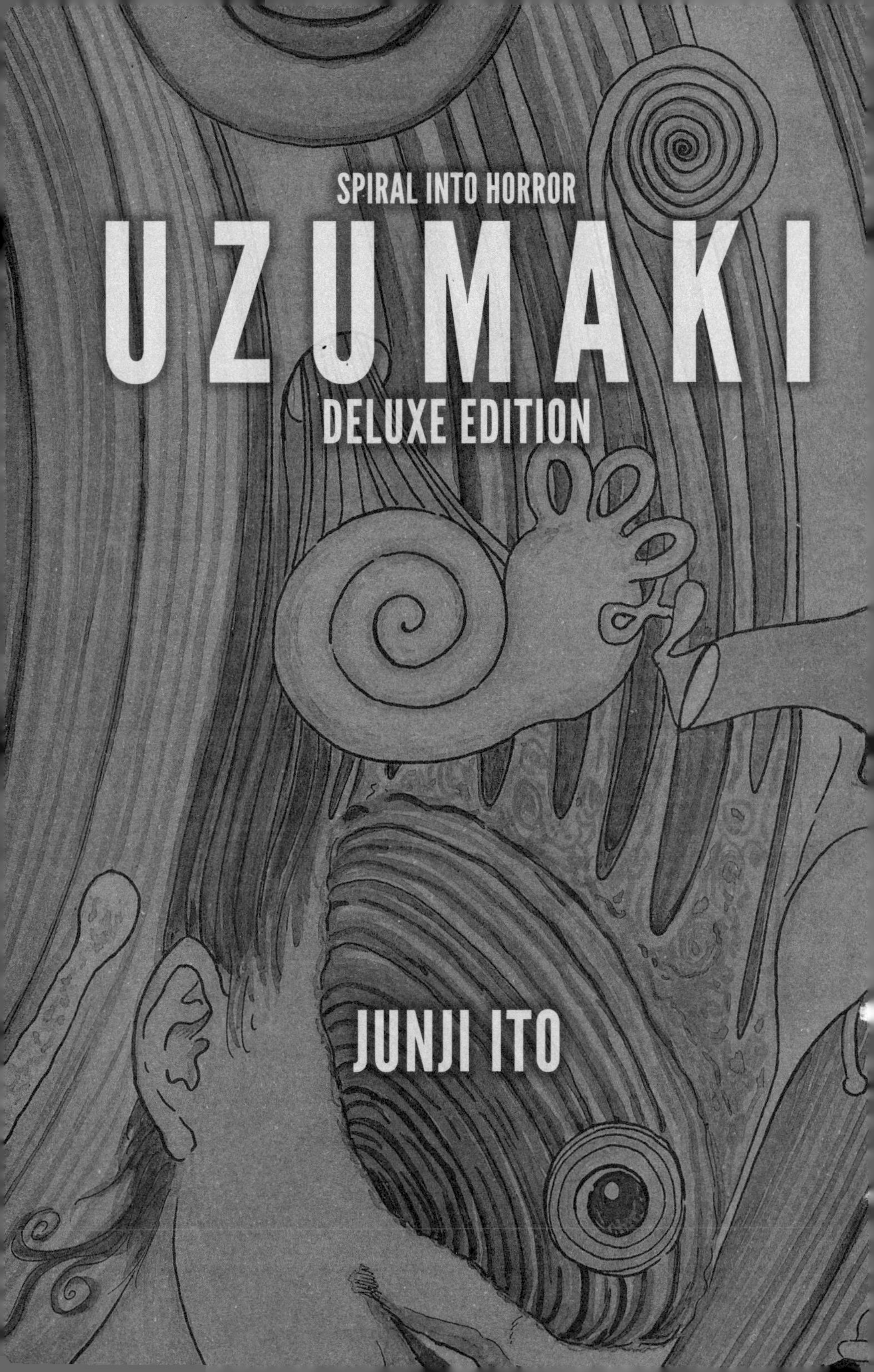
SPIRAL INTO HORROR
UZUMAKI
DELUXE EDITION
JUNJI ITO

CONTENTS

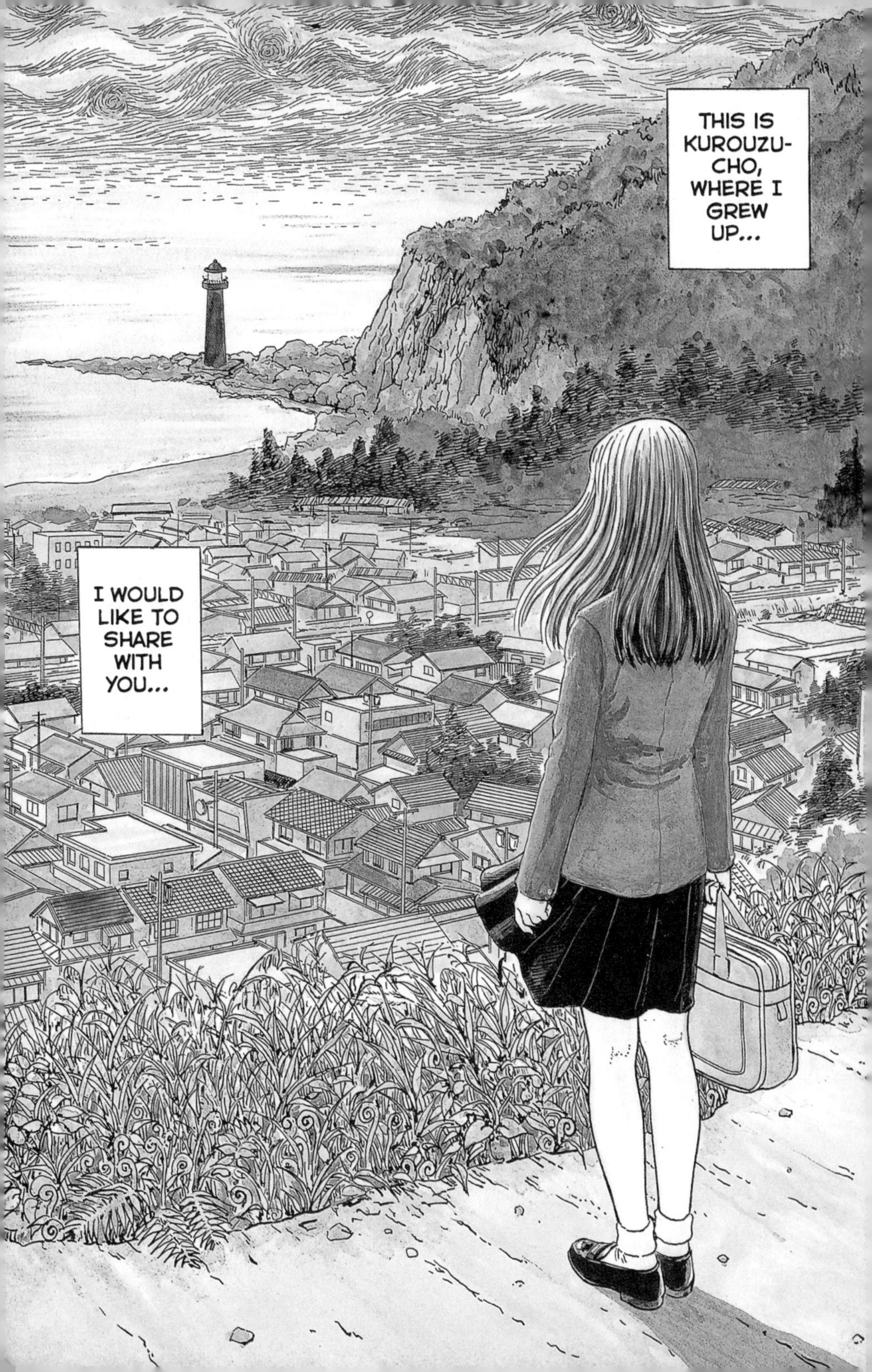
THIS IS KUROUZU-CHO, WHERE I GREW UP...
I WOULD LIKE TO SHARE WITH YOU...

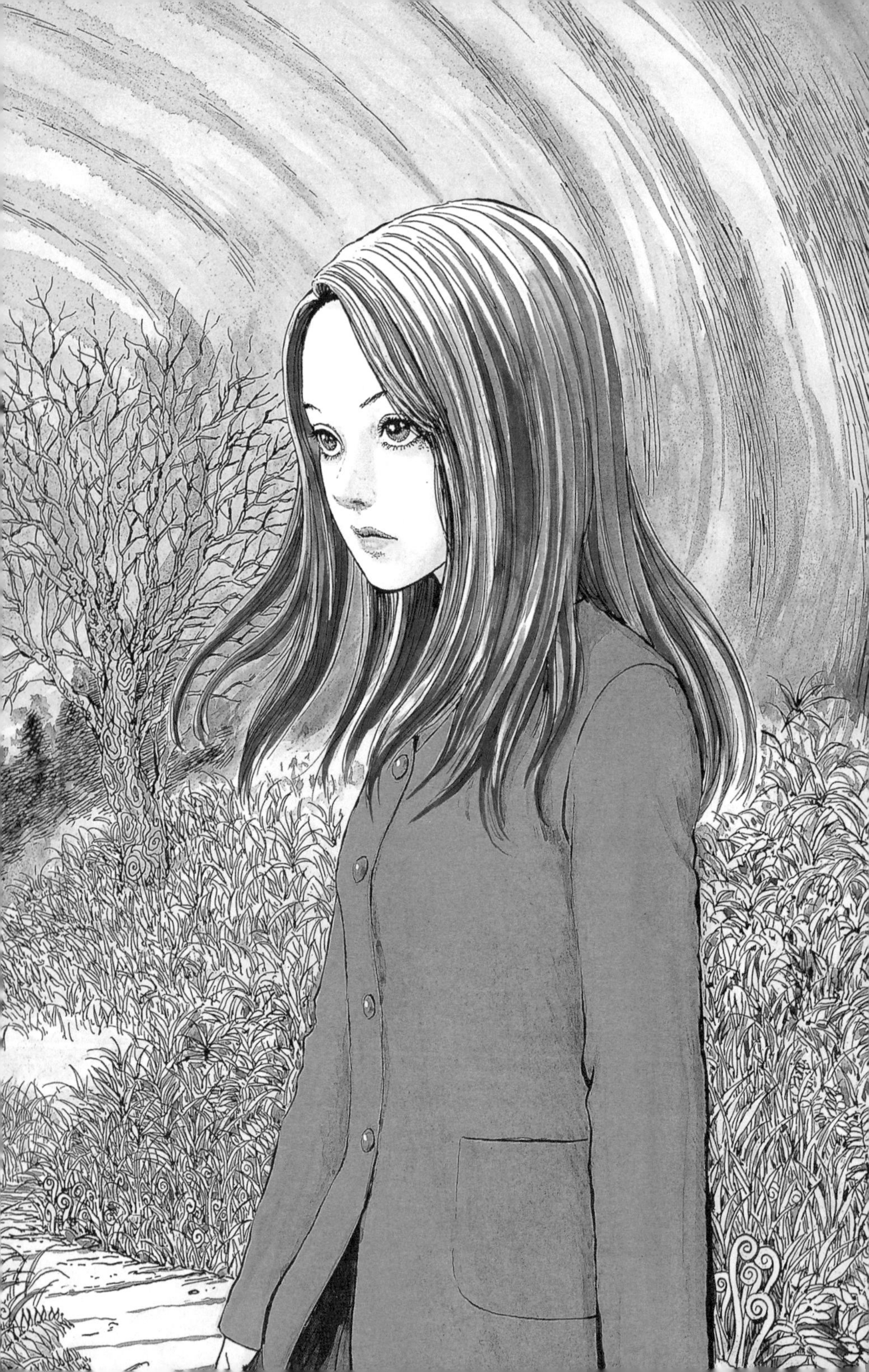

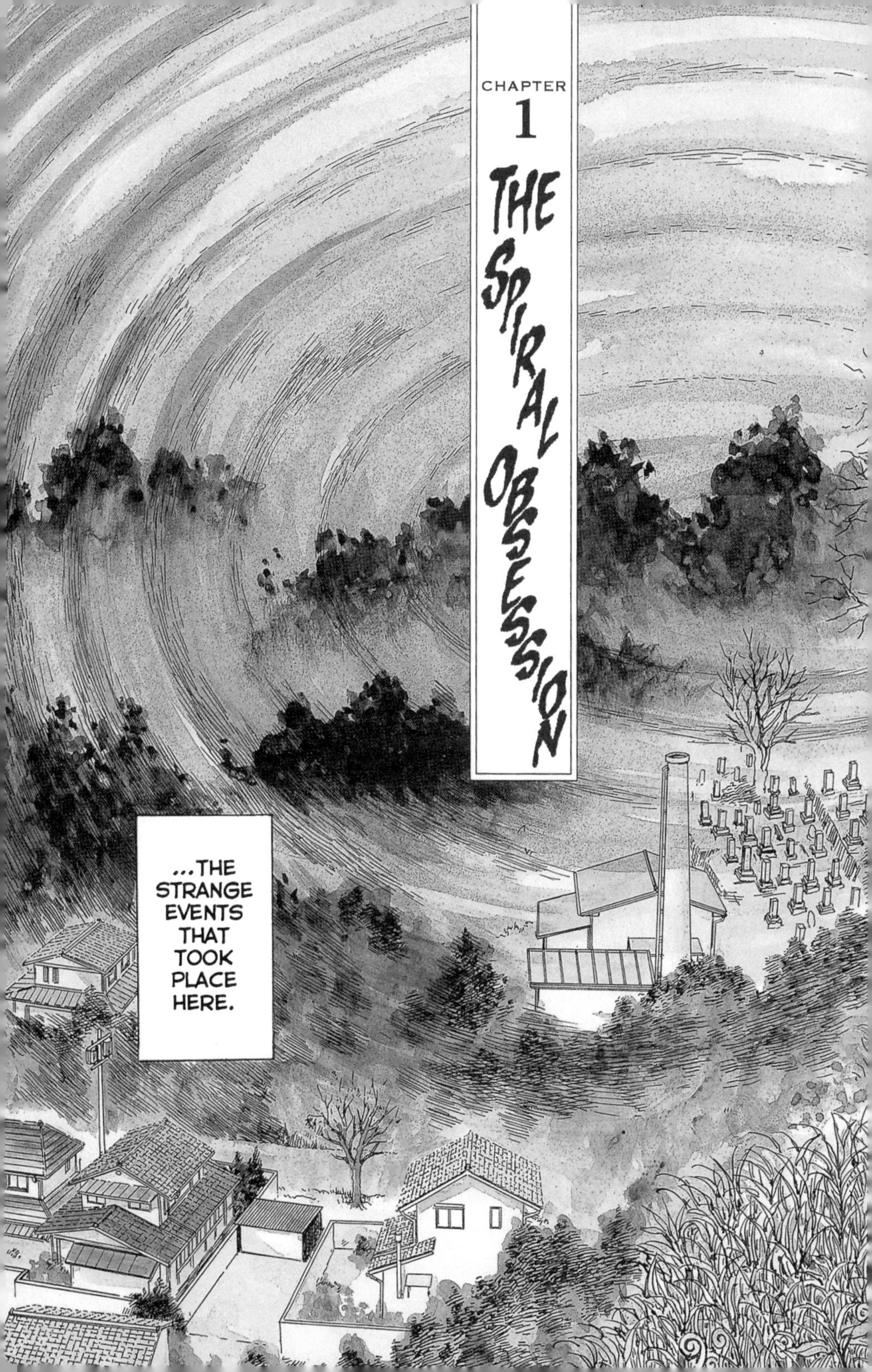
CHAPTER 1
THE SPIRAL OBSESSION
...THE STRANGE EVENTS THAT TOOK PLACE HERE.

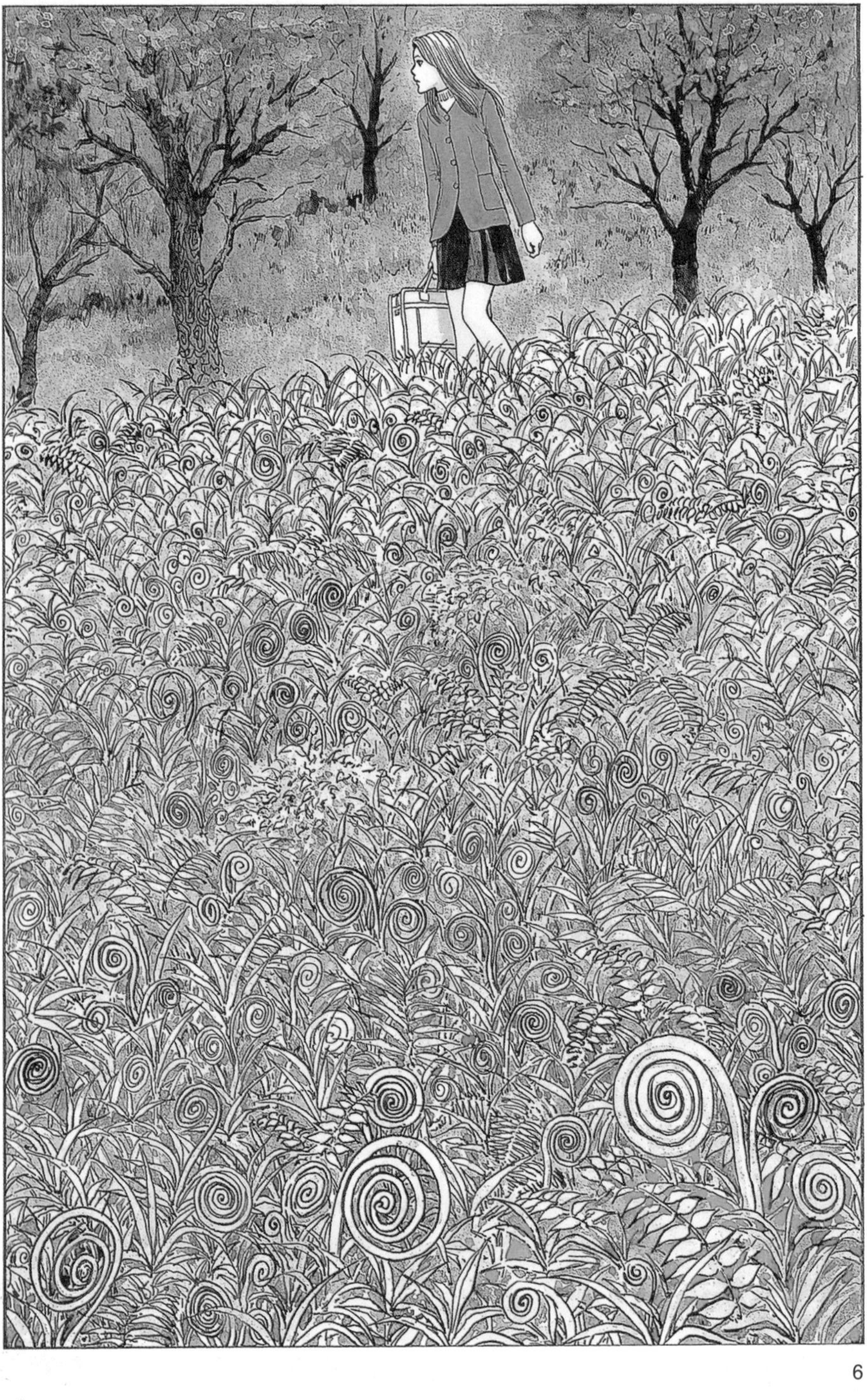

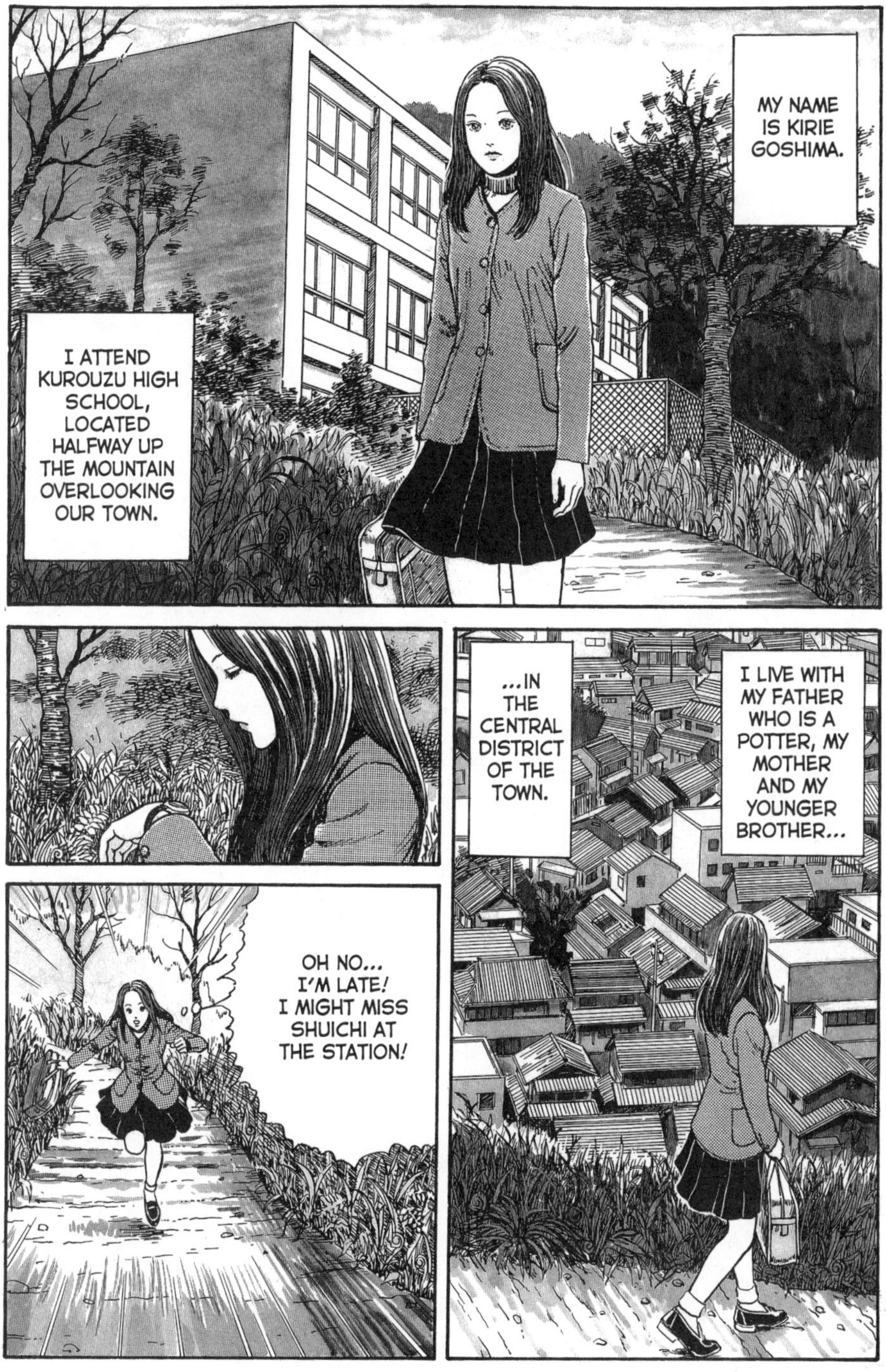
MY NAME IS KIRIE GOSHIMA.
I ATTEND KUROUZU HIGH SCHOOL, LOCATED HALFWAY UP THE MOUNTAIN OVERLOOKING OUR TOWN.
I LIVE WITH MY FATHER WHO IS A POTTER, MY MOTHER AND MY YOUNGER BROTHER...
...IN THE CENTRAL DISTRICT OF THE TOWN.
OH NO... I'M LATE! I MIGHT MISS SHUICHI AT THE STATION!

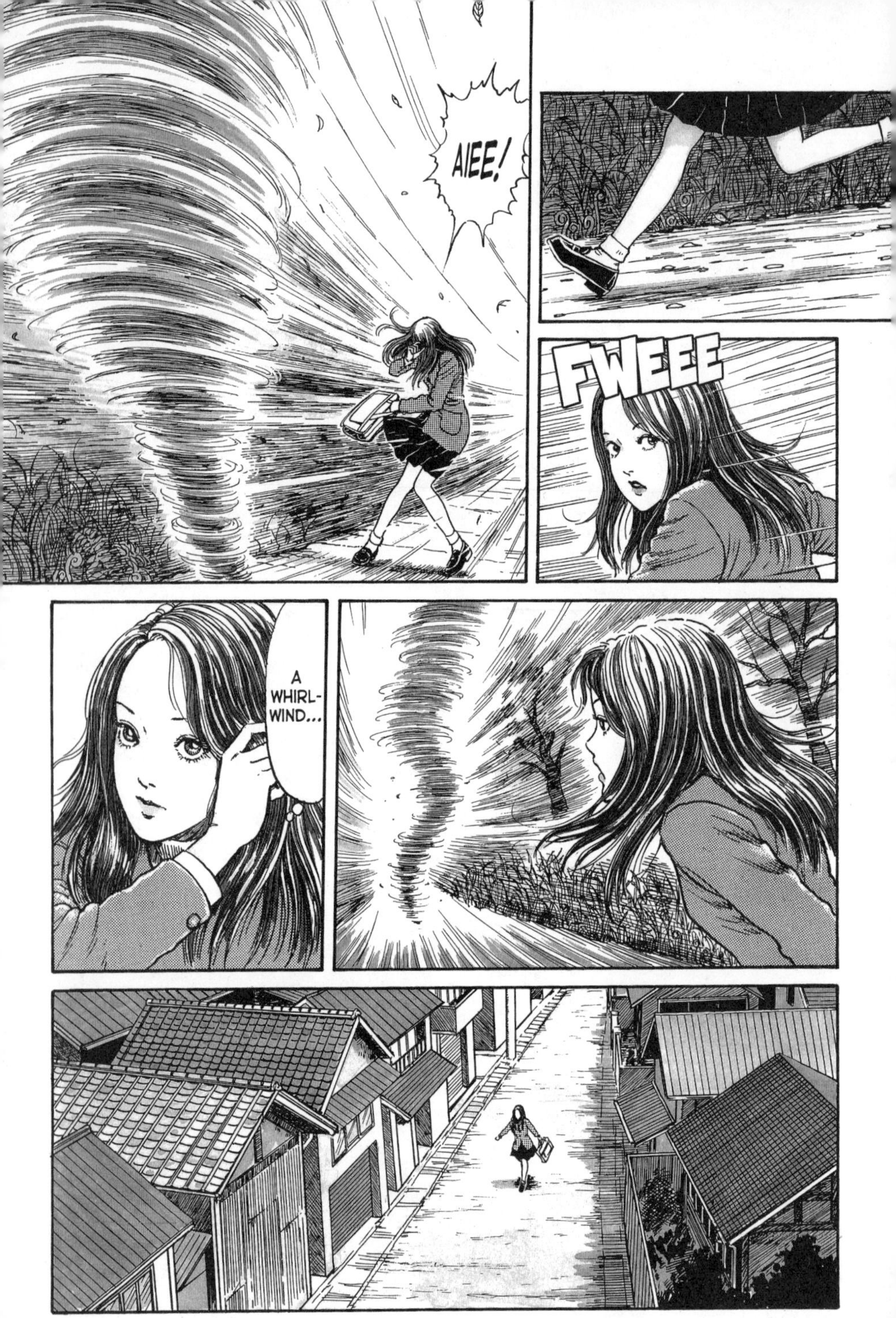
FWEEE
AIEE!
A WHIRL-WIND...

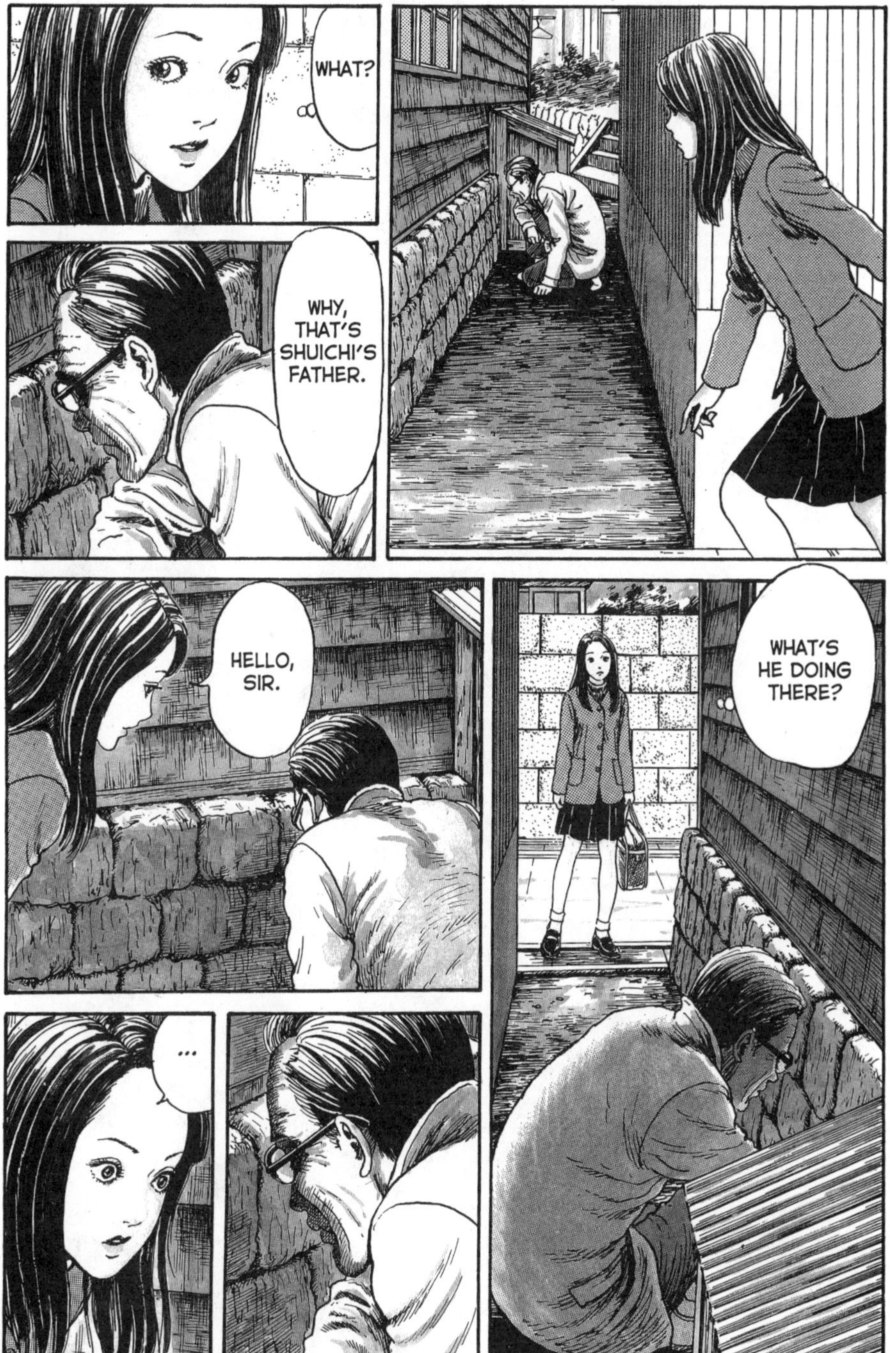
WHAT?
WHY, THAT'S SHUICHI'S FATHER.
WHAT'S HE DOING THERE?
HELLO, SIR.
...

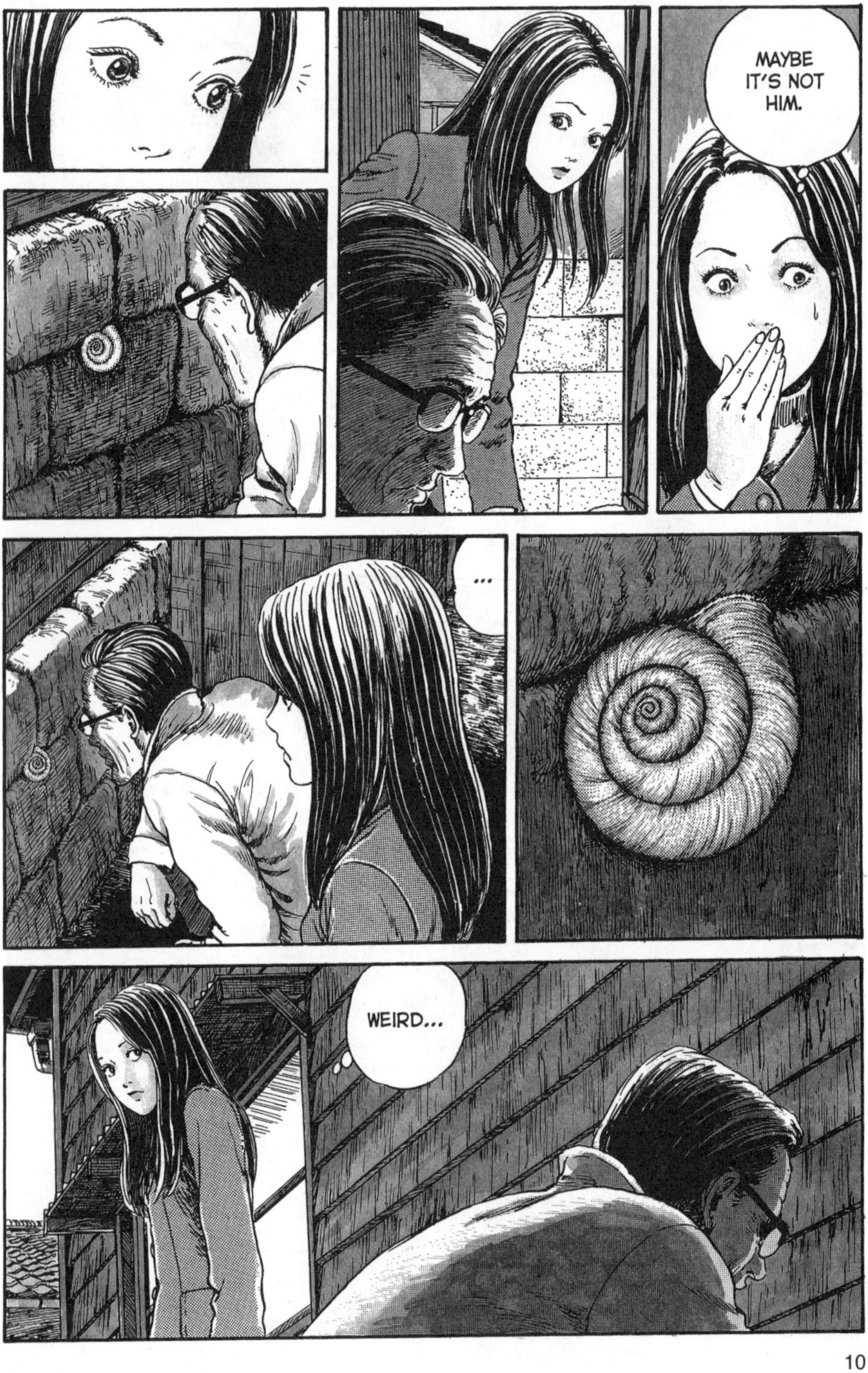
MAYBE IT'S NOT HIM.
...
WEIRD...

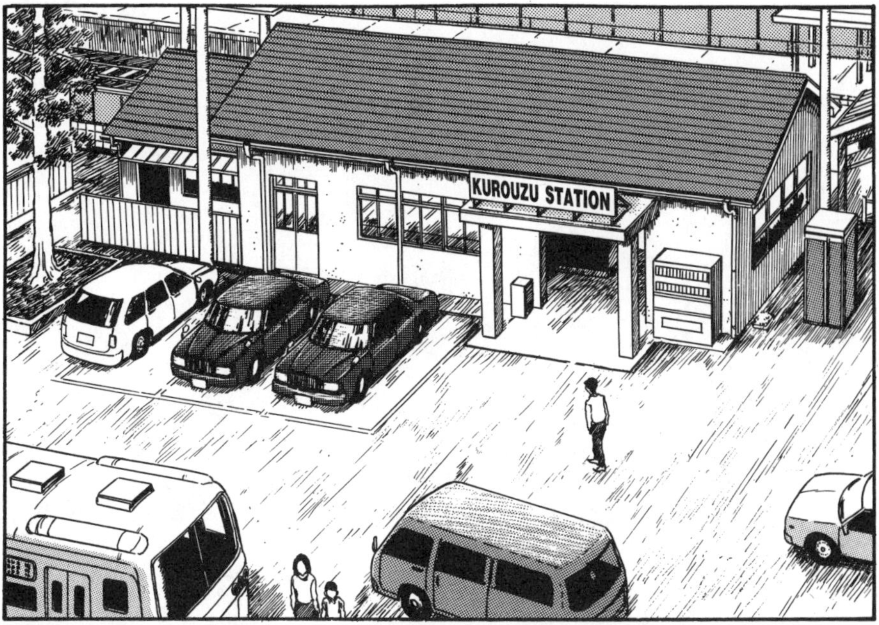
KUROUZU STATION

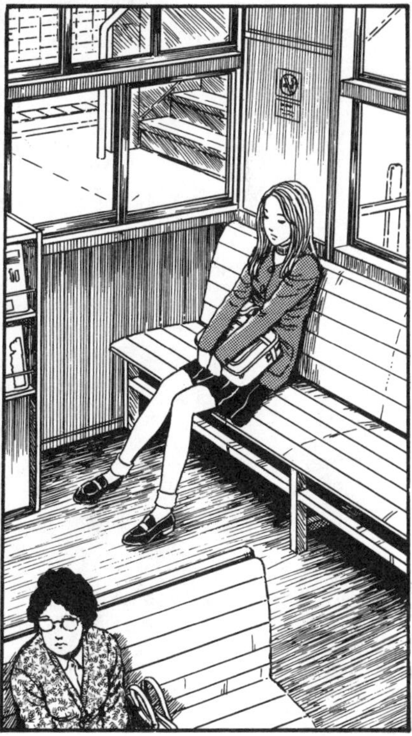

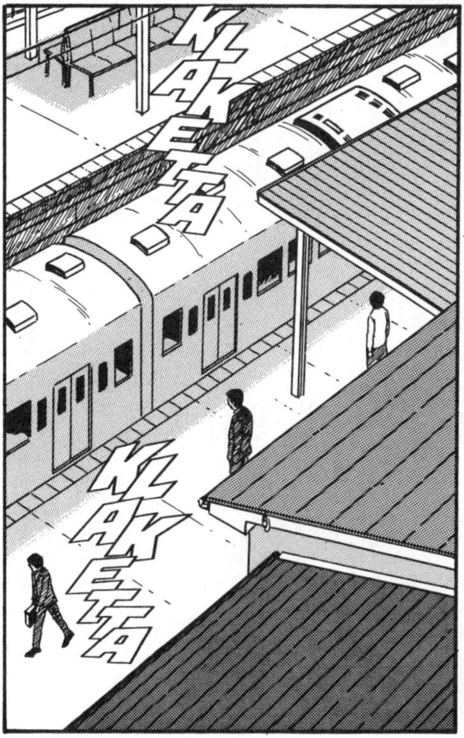
KLAKETTA
KLAKETTA

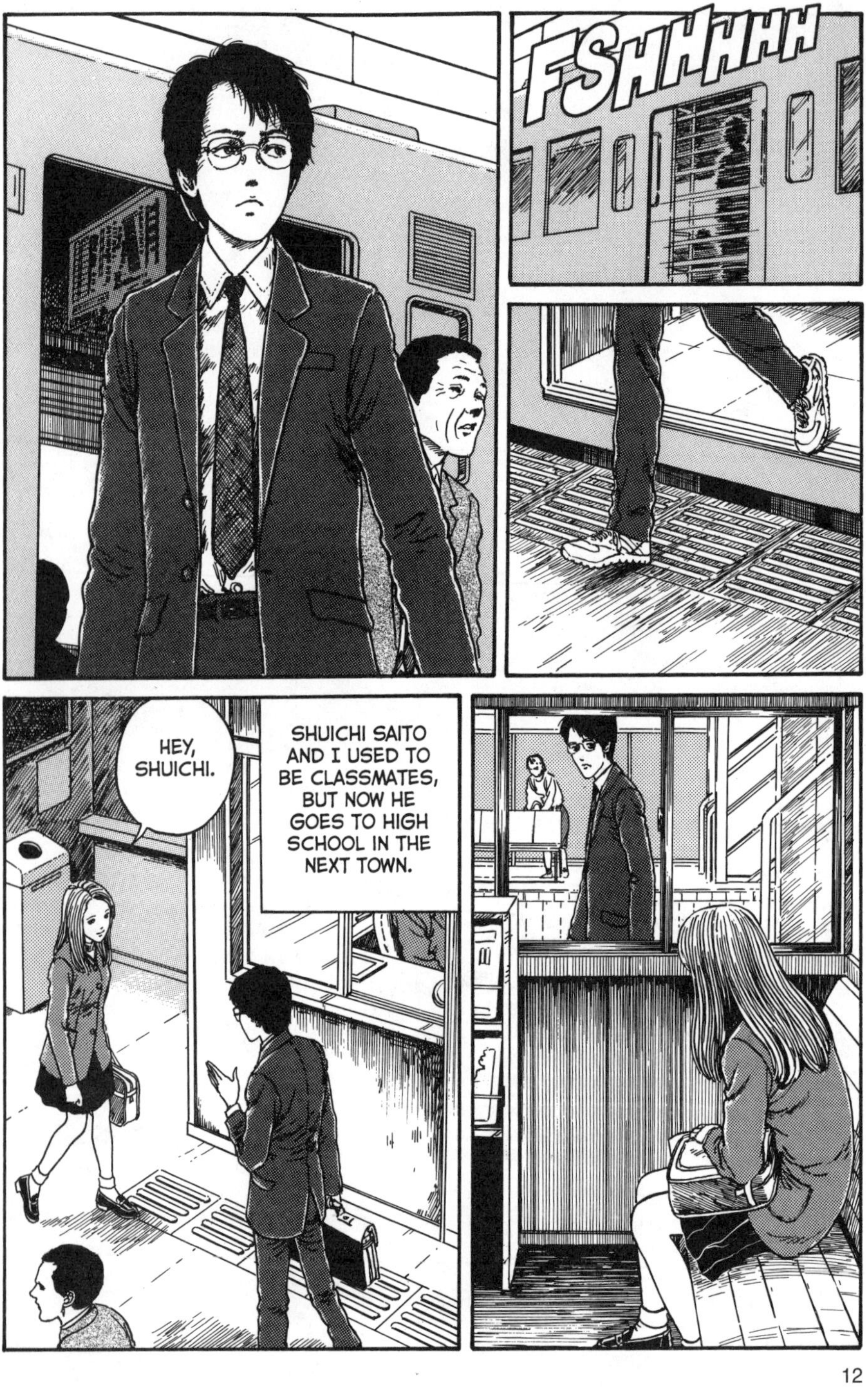
FSHHHHH
SHUICHI SAITO AND I USED TO BE CLASSMATES, BUT NOW HE GOES TO HIGH SCHOOL IN THE NEXT TOWN.
HEY, SHUICHI.

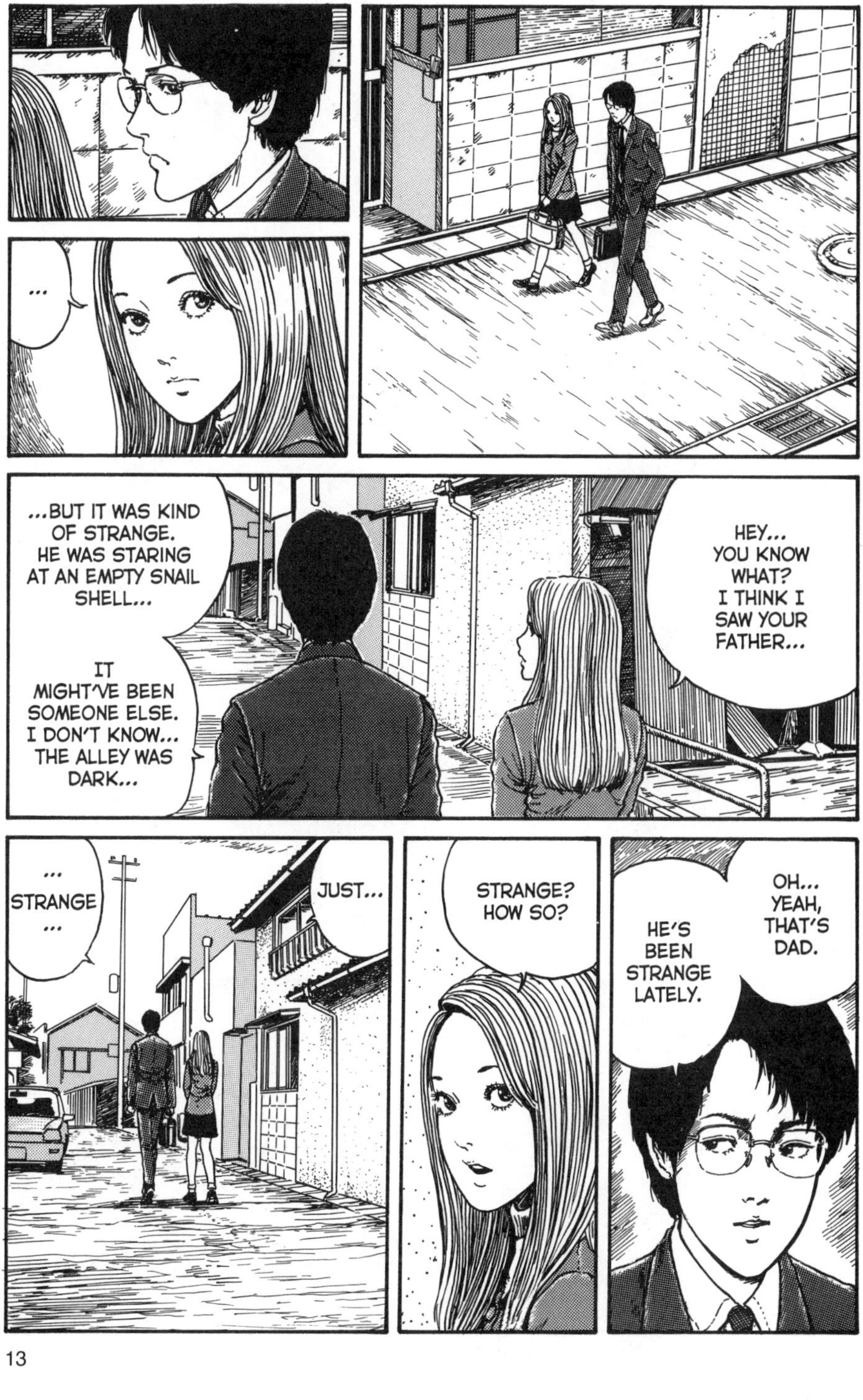
...
HEY... YOU KNOW WHAT? I THINK I SAW YOUR FATHER...
...BUT IT WAS KIND OF STRANGE. HE WAS STARING AT AN EMPTY SNAIL SHELL...
IT MIGHT'VE BEEN SOMEONE ELSE. I DON'T KNOW... THE ALLEY WAS DARK...
OH... YEAH, THAT'S DAD.
HE'S BEEN STRANGE LATELY.
STRANGE? HOW SO?
JUST...
... STRANGE ...

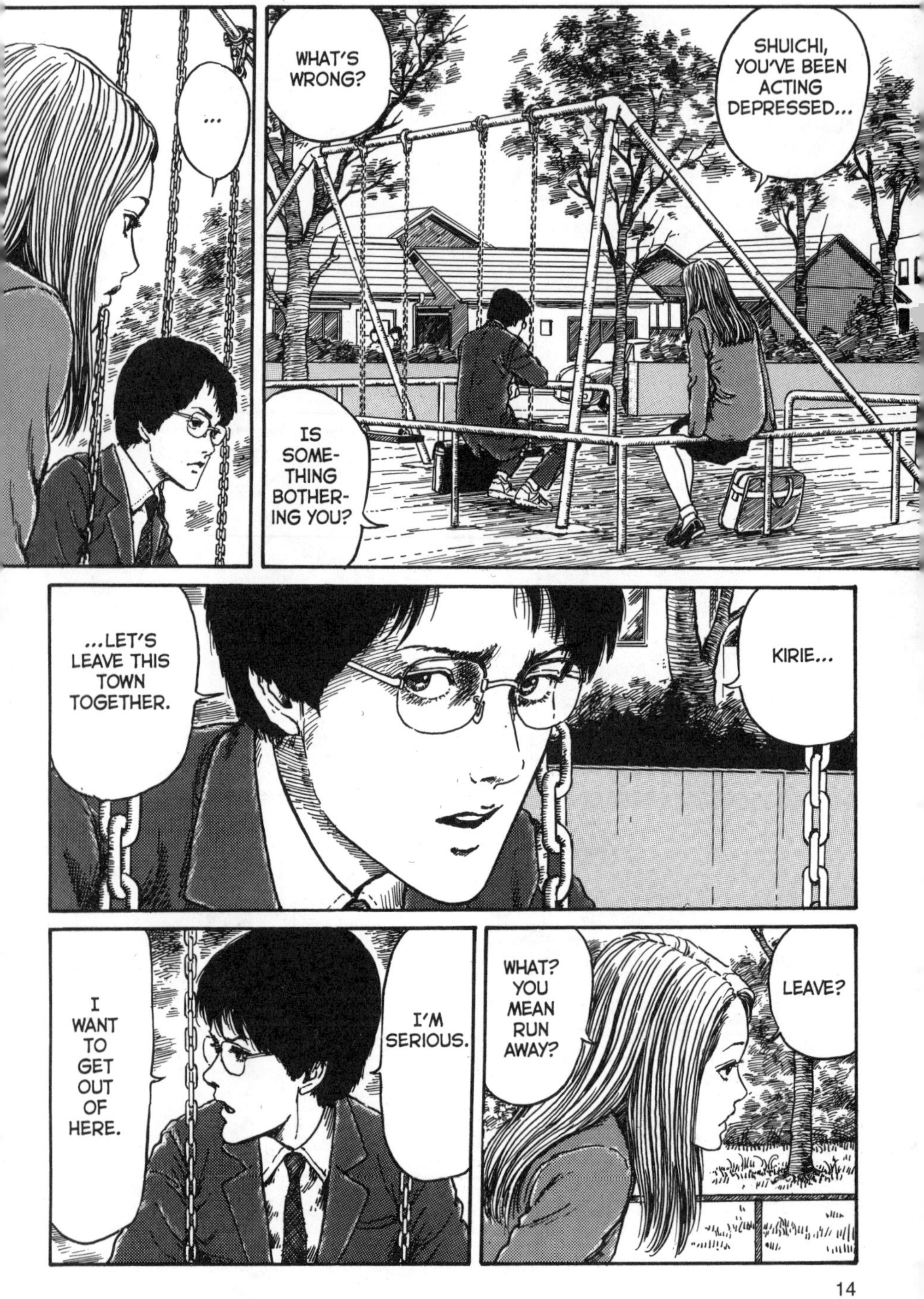
SHUICHI, YOU'VE BEEN ACTING DEPRESSED...
WHAT'S WRONG?
IS SOME-THING BOTHER-ING YOU?
...
KIRIE...
...LET'S LEAVE THIS TOWN TOGETHER.
LEAVE?
WHAT? YOU MEAN RUN AWAY?
I'M SERIOUS.
I WANT TO GET OUT OF HERE.

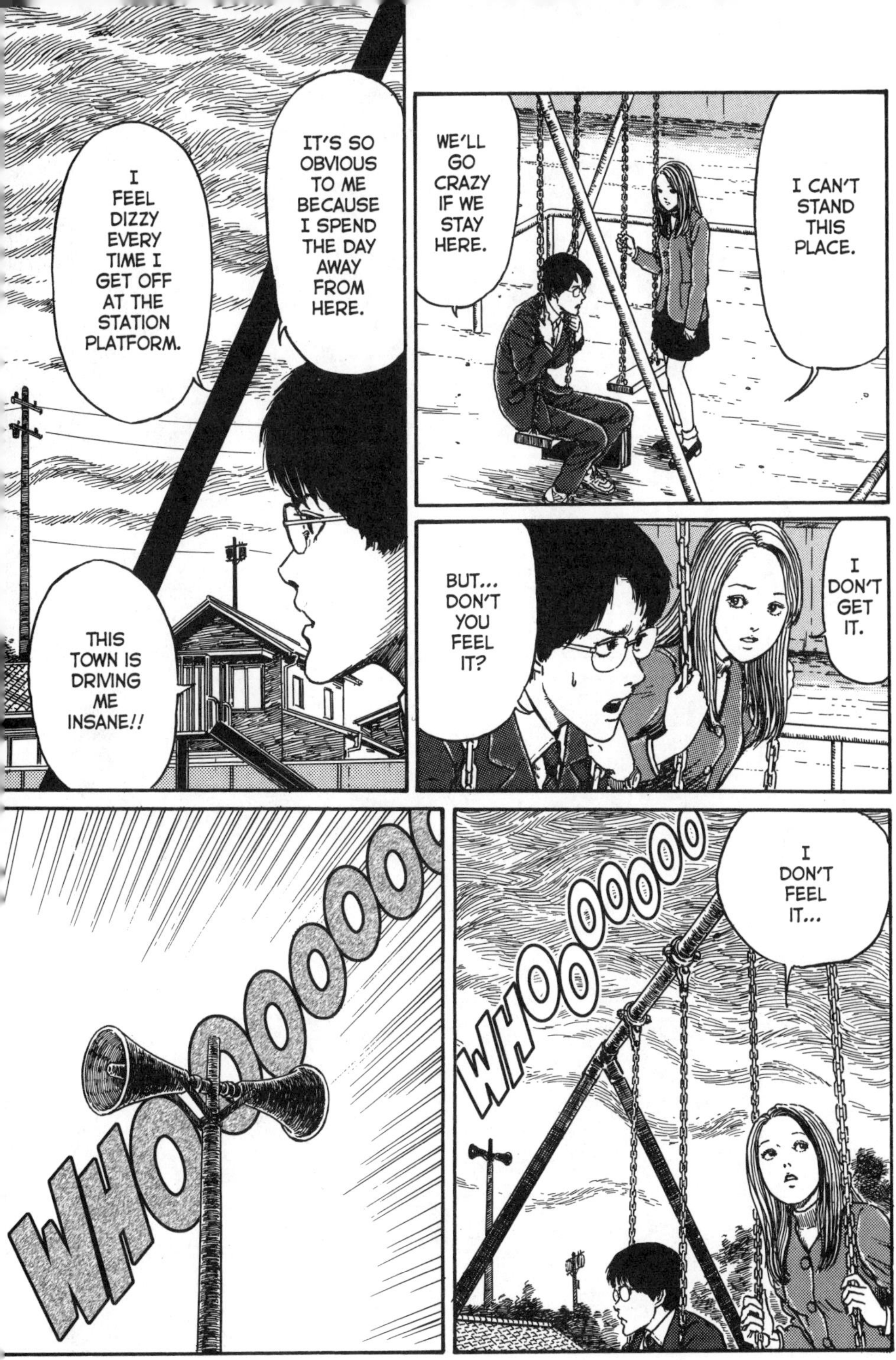
I CAN'T STAND THIS PLACE.
WE'LL GO CRAZY IF WE STAY HERE.
I DON'T GET IT.
BUT... DON'T YOU FEEL IT?
IT'S SO OBVIOUS TO ME BECAUSE I SPEND THE DAY AWAY FROM HERE.
I FEEL DIZZY EVERY TIME I GET OFF AT THE STATION PLATFORM.
THIS TOWN IS DRIVING ME INSANE!!
I DON'T FEEL IT...
WHOOOOOOO
WHOOOOOOOO

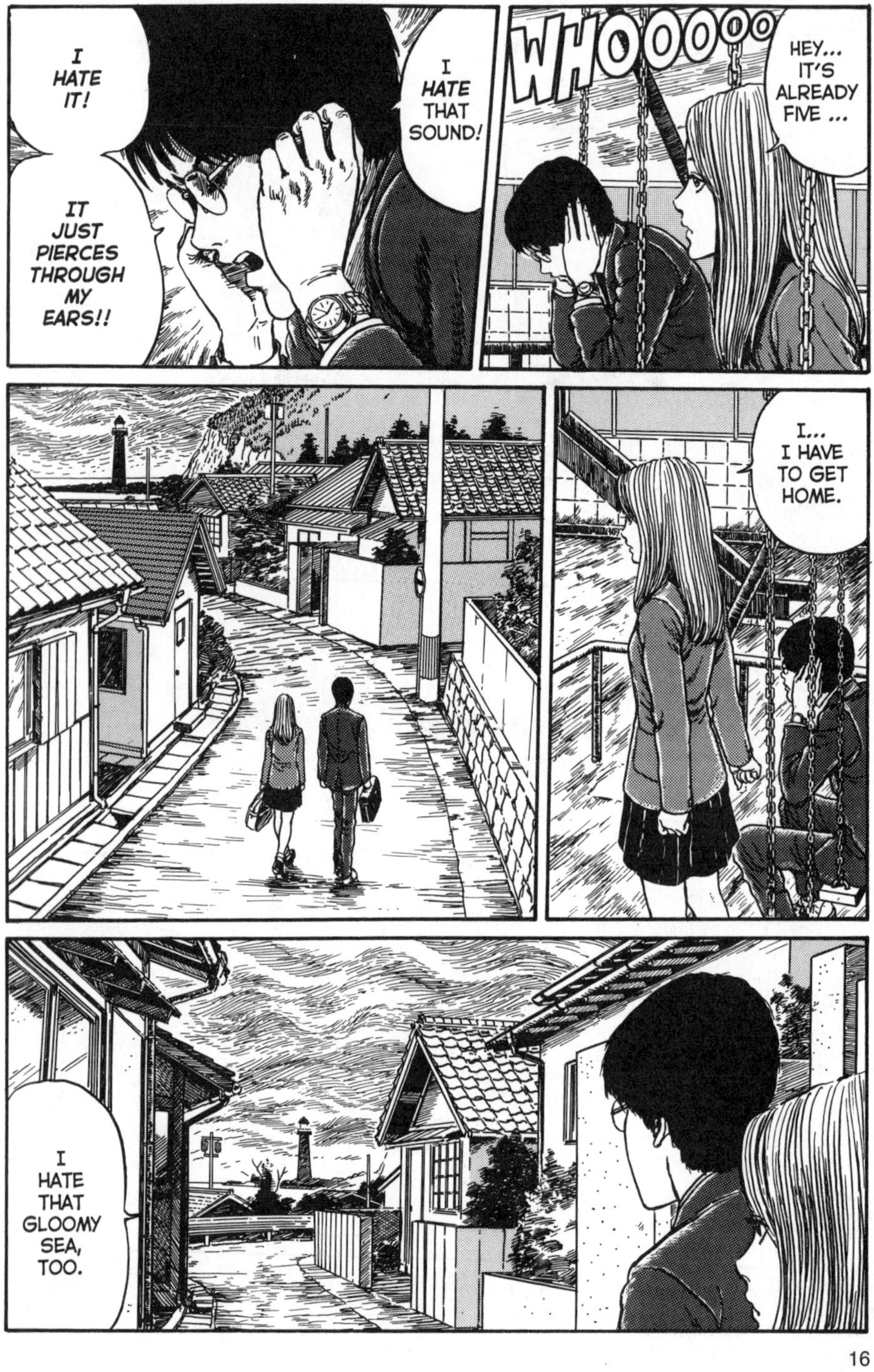
HEY... IT'S ALREADY FIVE ...
WHOOOOOO
I HATE THAT SOUND!
I HATE IT!
IT JUST PIERCES THROUGH MY EARS!!
I... I HAVE TO GET HOME.
I HATE THAT GLOOMY SEA, TOO.

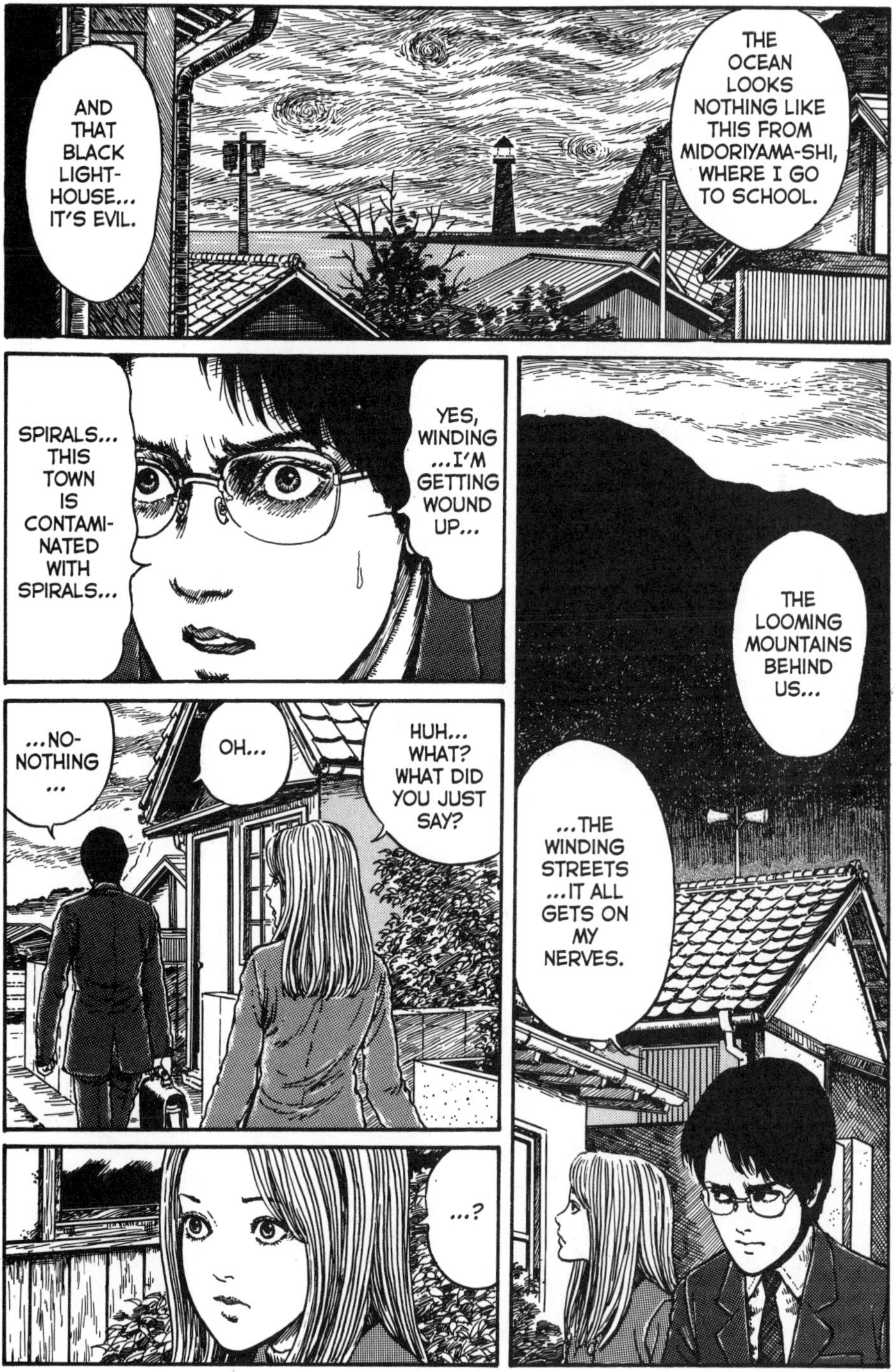
THE OCEAN LOOKS NOTHING LIKE THIS FROM MIDORIYAMA-SHI, WHERE I GO TO SCHOOL.
AND THAT BLACK LIGHT-HOUSE... IT'S EVIL.
THE LOOMING MOUNTAINS BEHIND US...
...THE WINDING STREETS ...IT ALL GETS ON MY NERVES.
YES, WINDING ...I'M GETTING WOUND UP...
SPIRALS... THIS TOWN IS CONTAMI-NATED WITH SPIRALS...
HUH... WHAT? WHAT DID YOU JUST SAY?
OH...
...NO-NOTHING...
...?

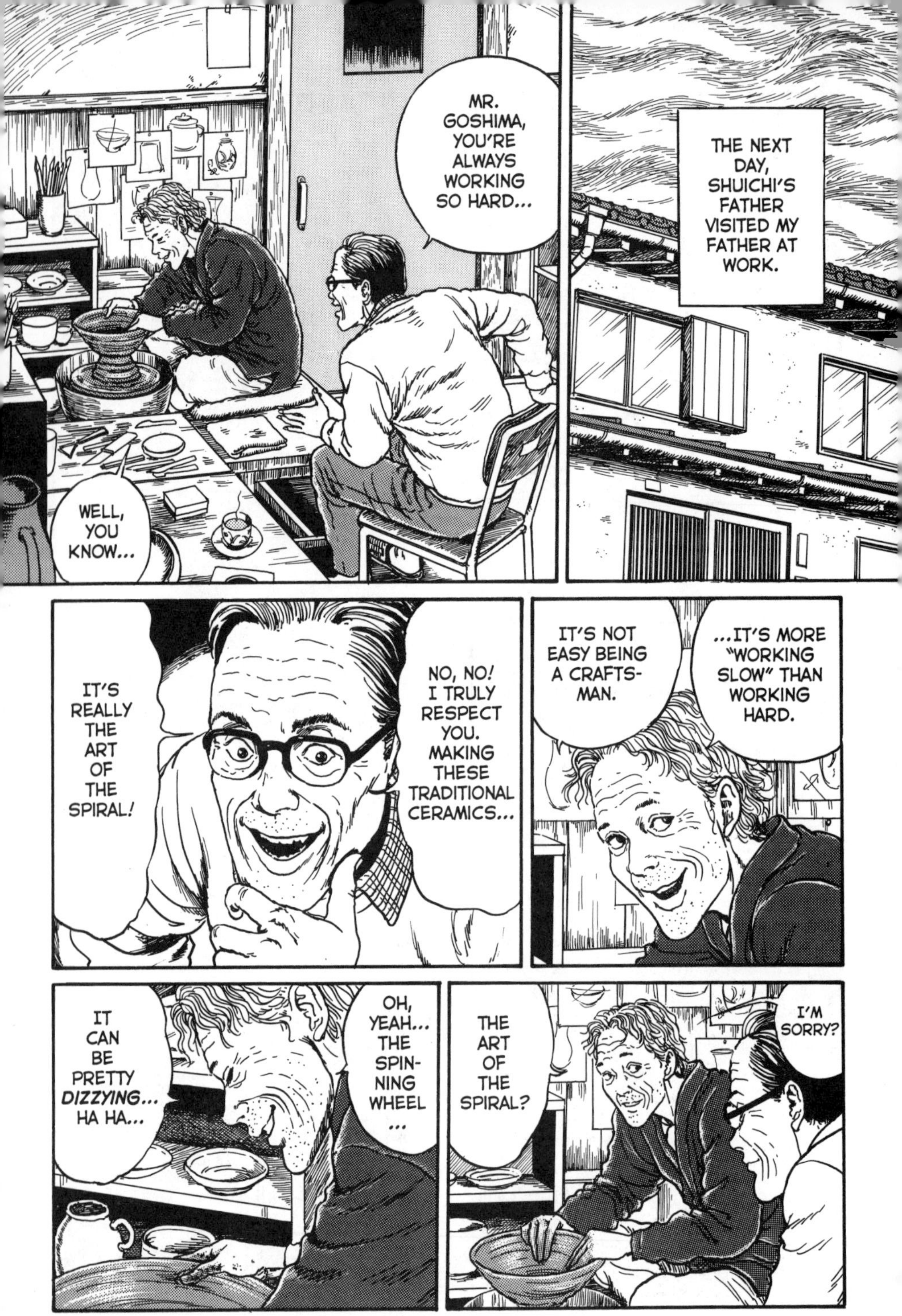
THE NEXT DAY, SHUICHI'S FATHER VISITED MY FATHER AT WORK.
MR. GOSHIMA, YOU'RE ALWAYS WORKING SO HARD...
WELL, YOU KNOW...
...IT'S MORE "WORKING SLOW" THAN WORKING HARD.
IT'S NOT EASY BEING A CRAFTSMAN.
NO, NO! I TRULY RESPECT YOU. MAKING THESE TRADITIONAL CERAMICS...
IT'S REALLY THE ART OF THE SPIRAL!
I'M SORRY?
THE ART OF THE SPIRAL?
OH, YEAH... THE SPINNING WHEEL...
IT CAN BE PRETTY *DIZZYING*... HA HA...

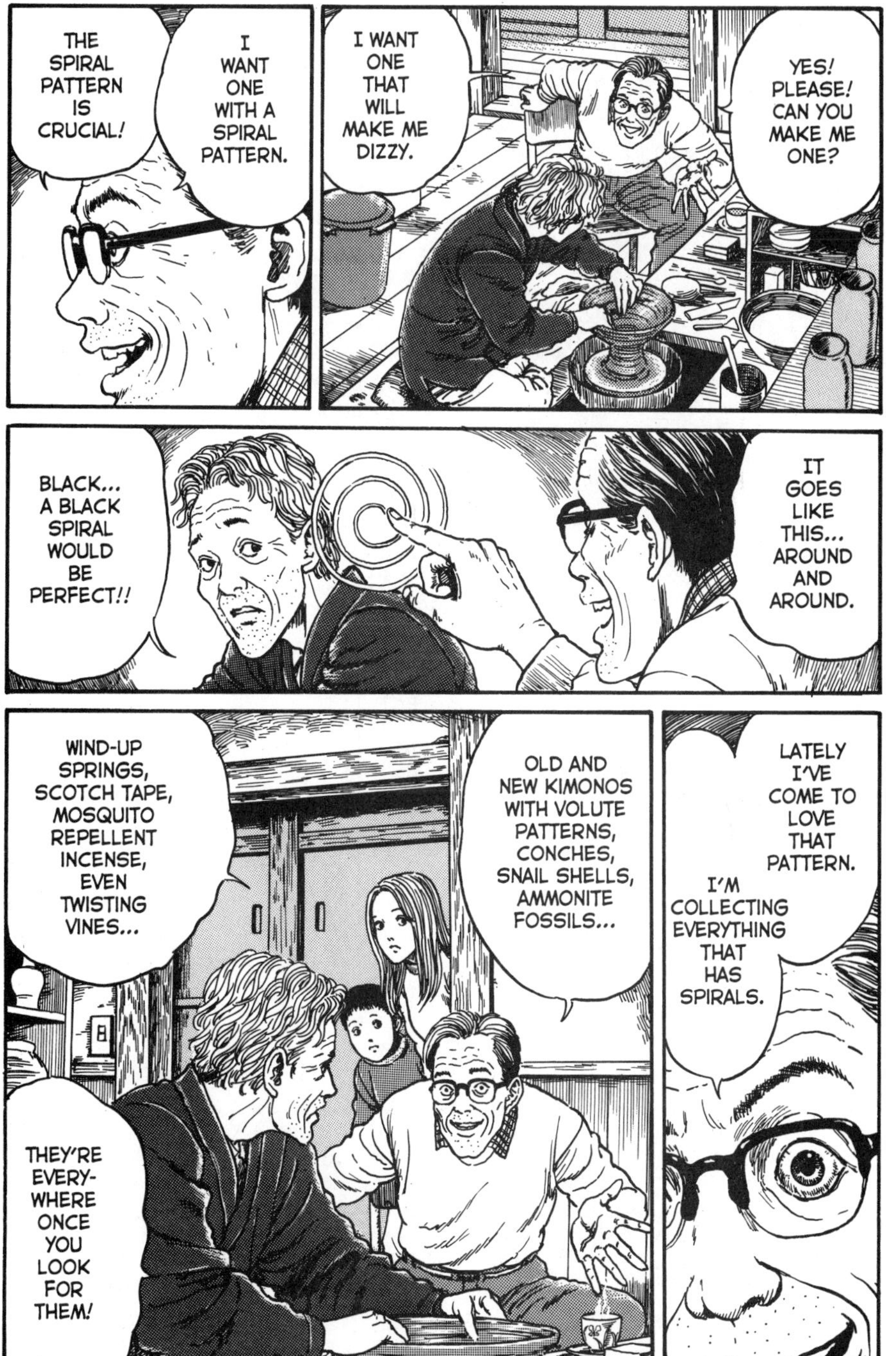
YES! PLEASE! CAN YOU MAKE ME ONE?
I WANT ONE THAT WILL MAKE ME DIZZY.
I WANT ONE WITH A SPIRAL PATTERN.
THE SPIRAL PATTERN IS CRUCIAL!
IT GOES LIKE THIS... AROUND AND AROUND.
BLACK... A BLACK SPIRAL WOULD BE PERFECT!!
LATELY I'VE COME TO LOVE THAT PATTERN.
I'M COLLECTING EVERYTHING THAT HAS SPIRALS.
OLD AND NEW KIMONOS WITH VOLUTE PATTERNS, CONCHES, SNAIL SHELLS, AMMONITE FOSSILS...
WIND-UP SPRINGS, SCOTCH TAPE, MOSQUITO REPELLENT INCENSE, EVEN TWISTING VINES...
THEY'RE EVERY-WHERE ONCE YOU LOOK FOR THEM!

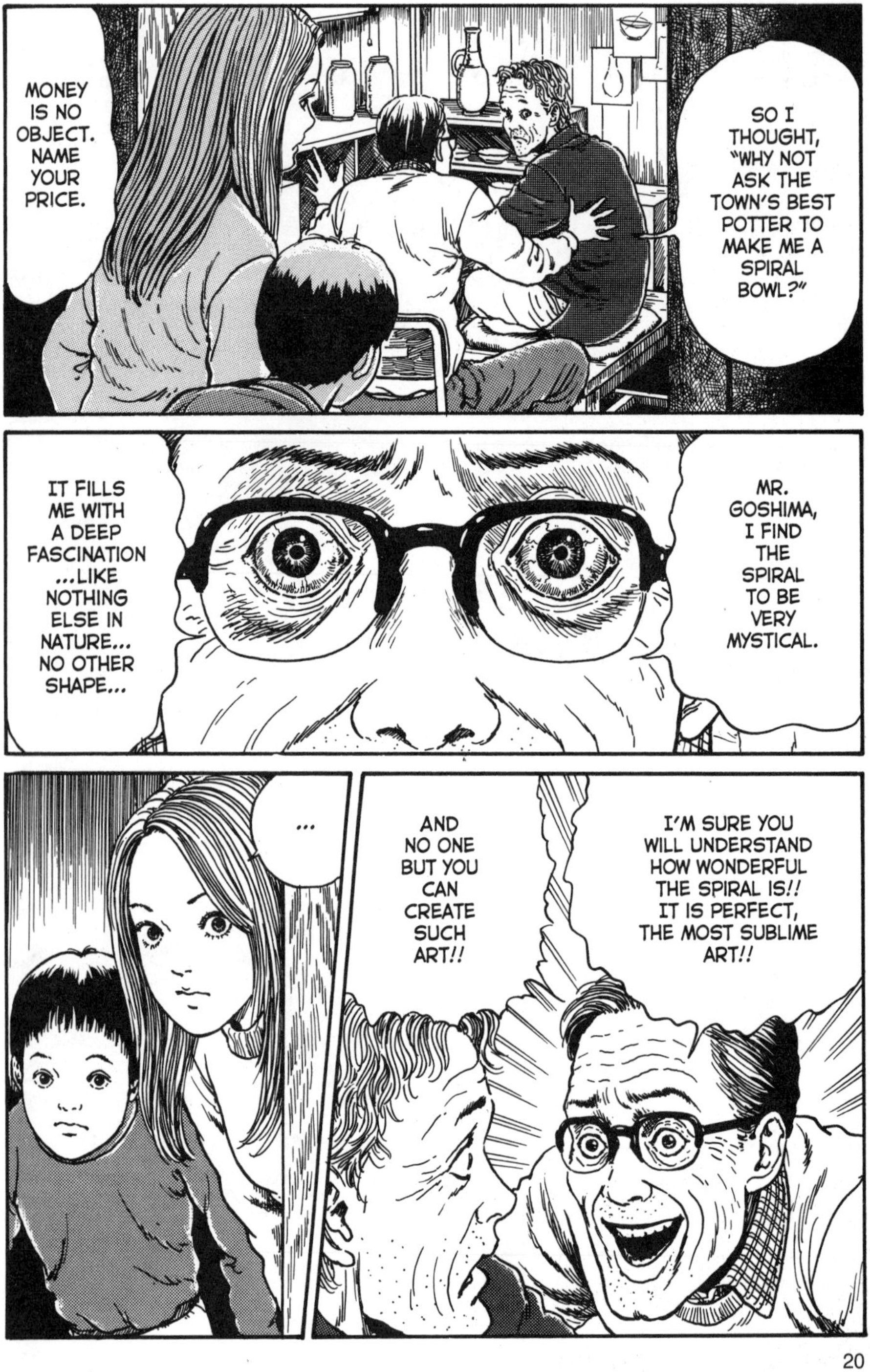
SO I THOUGHT, "WHY NOT ASK THE TOWN'S BEST POTTER TO MAKE ME A SPIRAL BOWL?"
MONEY IS NO OBJECT. NAME YOUR PRICE.
MR. GOSHIMA, I FIND THE SPIRAL TO BE VERY MYSTICAL.
IT FILLS ME WITH A DEEP FASCINATION ...LIKE NOTHING ELSE IN NATURE... NO OTHER SHAPE...
I'M SURE YOU WILL UNDERSTAND HOW WONDERFUL THE SPIRAL IS!! IT IS PERFECT, THE MOST SUBLIME ART!!
AND NO ONE BUT YOU CAN CREATE SUCH ART!!
...

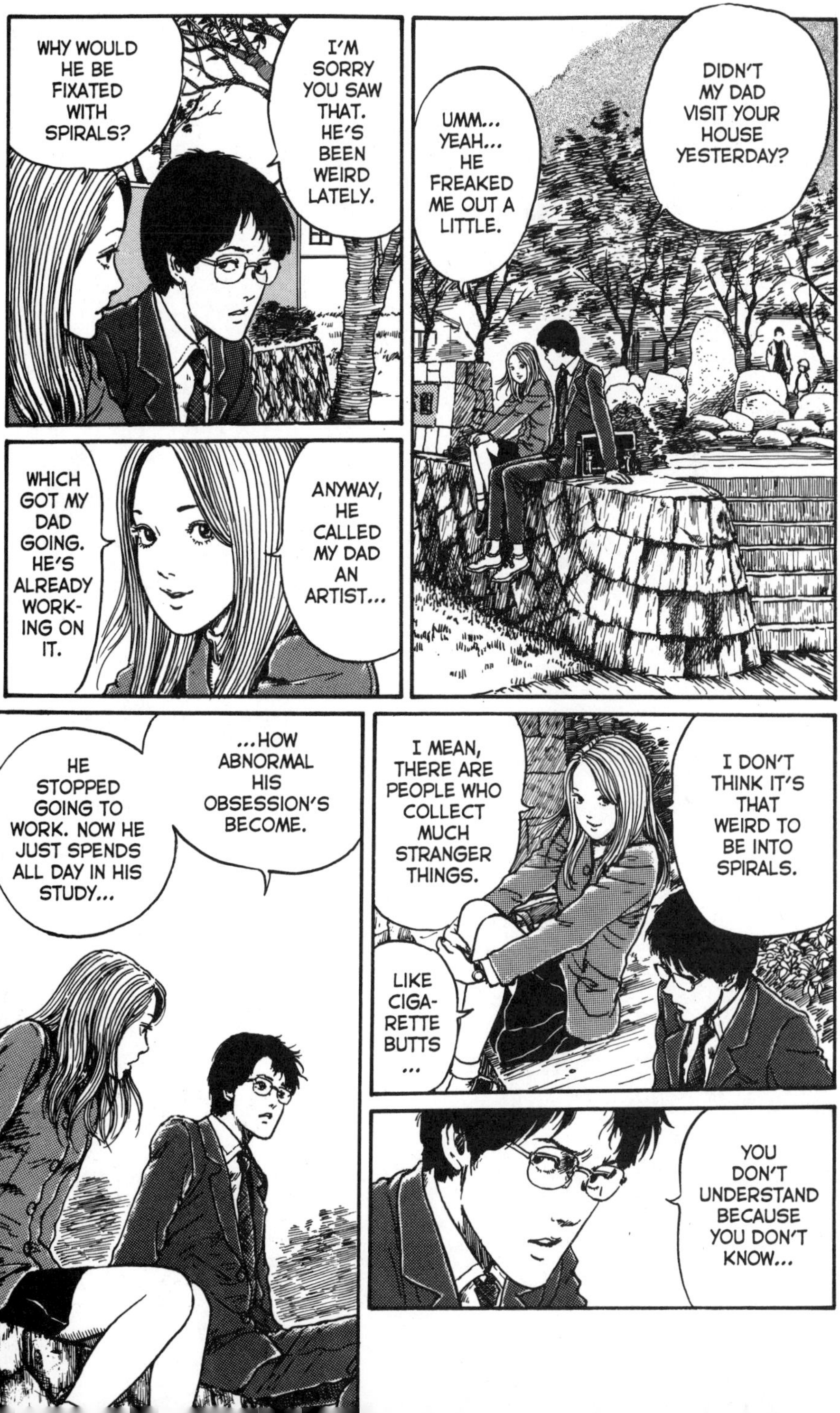
DIDN'T MY DAD VISIT YOUR HOUSE YESTERDAY?
UMM... YEAH... HE FREAKED ME OUT A LITTLE.
I'M SORRY YOU SAW THAT. HE'S BEEN WEIRD LATELY.
WHY WOULD HE BE FIXATED WITH SPIRALS?
ANYWAY, HE CALLED MY DAD AN ARTIST...
WHICH GOT MY DAD GOING. HE'S ALREADY WORKING ON IT.
I DON'T THINK IT'S THAT WEIRD TO BE INTO SPIRALS.
I MEAN, THERE ARE PEOPLE WHO COLLECT MUCH STRANGER THINGS.
LIKE CIGARETTE BUTTS...
YOU DON'T UNDERSTAND BECAUSE YOU DON'T KNOW...
HE STOPPED GOING TO WORK. NOW HE JUST SPENDS ALL DAY IN HIS STUDY...
...HOW ABNORMAL HIS OBSESSION'S BECOME.

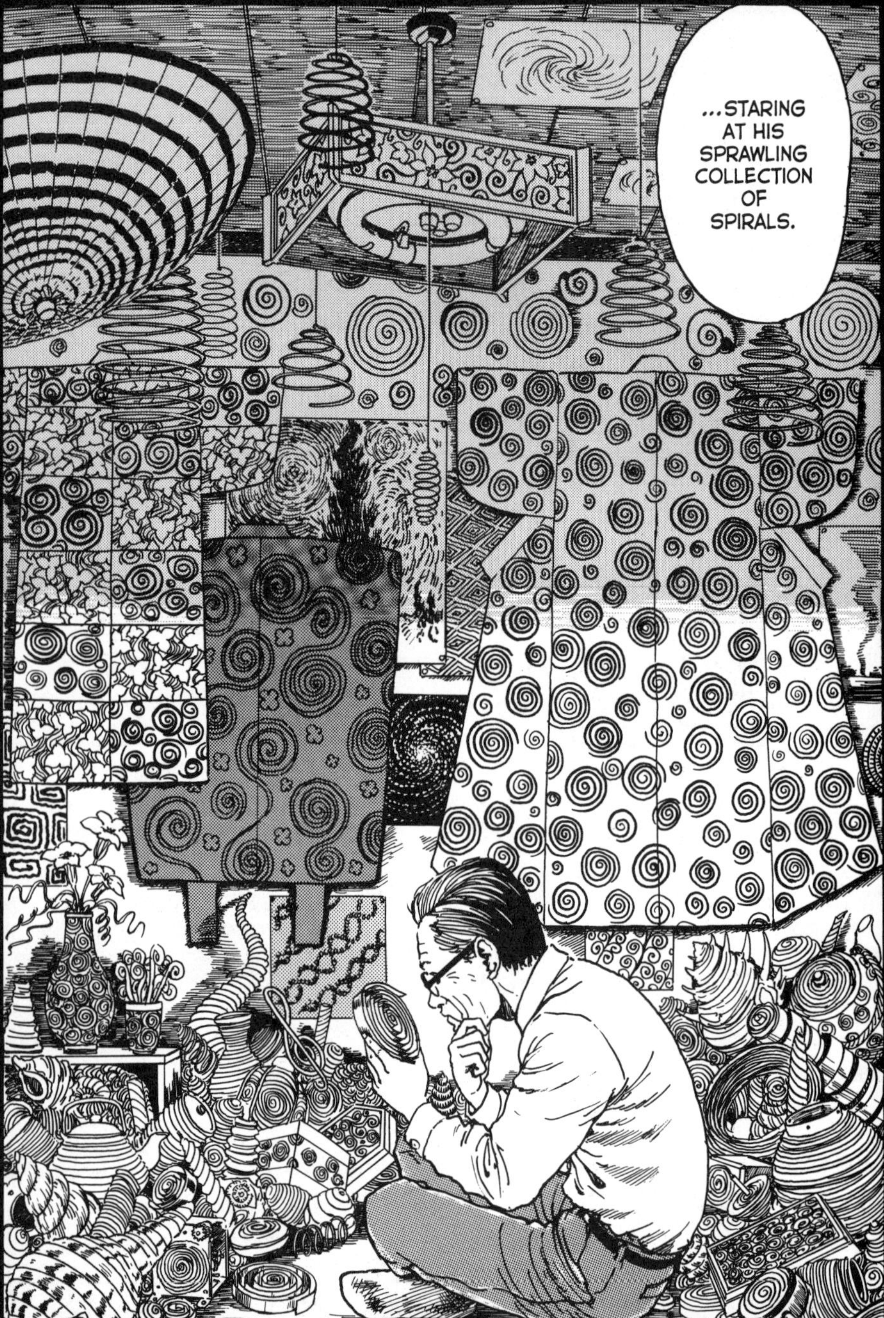
...STARING AT HIS SPRAWLING COLLECTION OF SPIRALS.

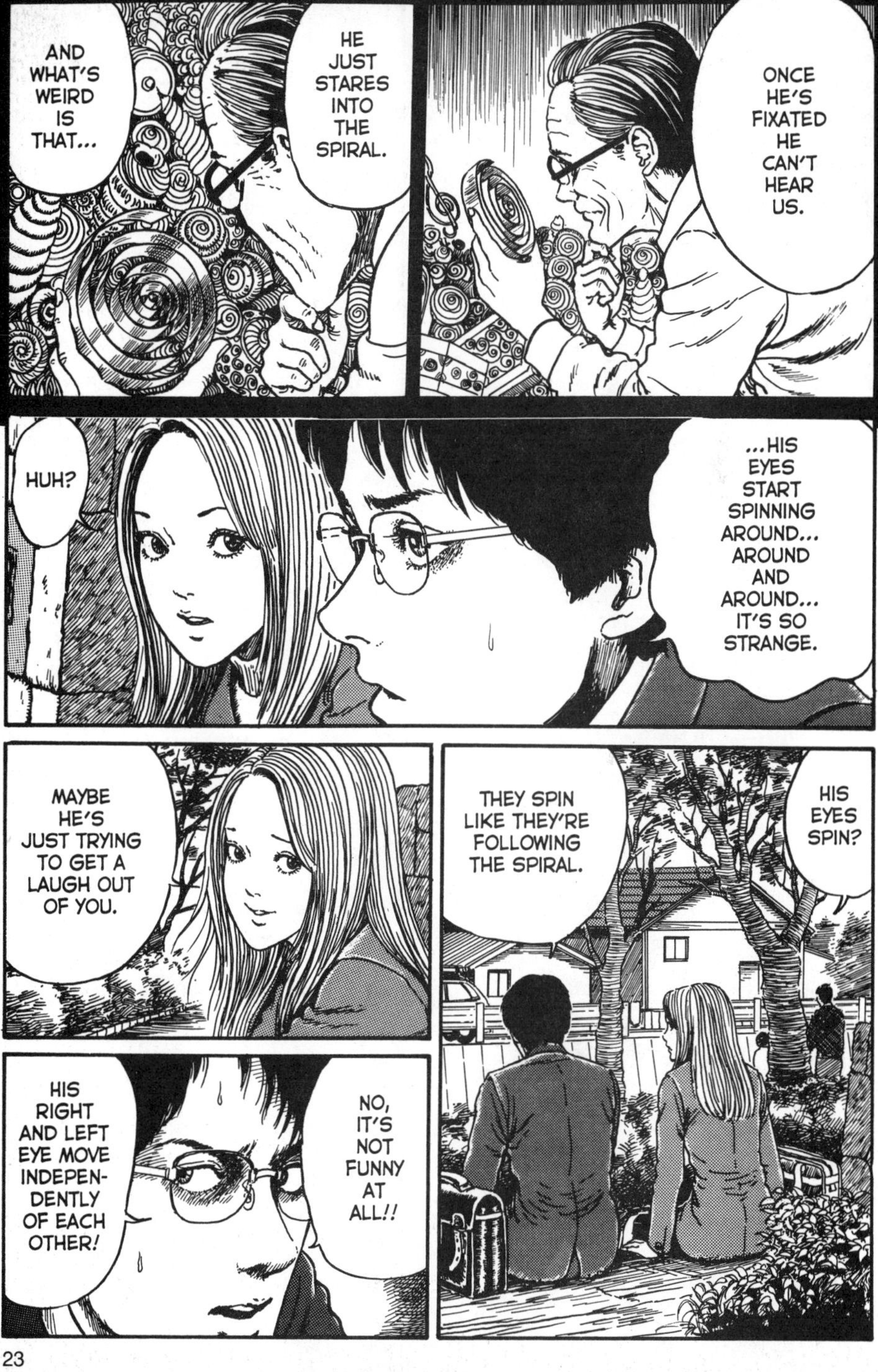
ONCE HE'S FIXATED HE CAN'T HEAR US.
HE JUST STARES INTO THE SPIRAL.
AND WHAT'S WEIRD IS THAT...
...HIS EYES START SPINNING AROUND... AROUND AND AROUND... IT'S SO STRANGE.
HUH?
HIS EYES SPIN?
THEY SPIN LIKE THEY'RE FOLLOWING THE SPIRAL.
MAYBE HE'S JUST TRYING TO GET A LAUGH OUT OF YOU.
NO, IT'S NOT FUNNY AT ALL!!
HIS RIGHT AND LEFT EYE MOVE INDEPEN-DENTLY OF EACH OTHER!

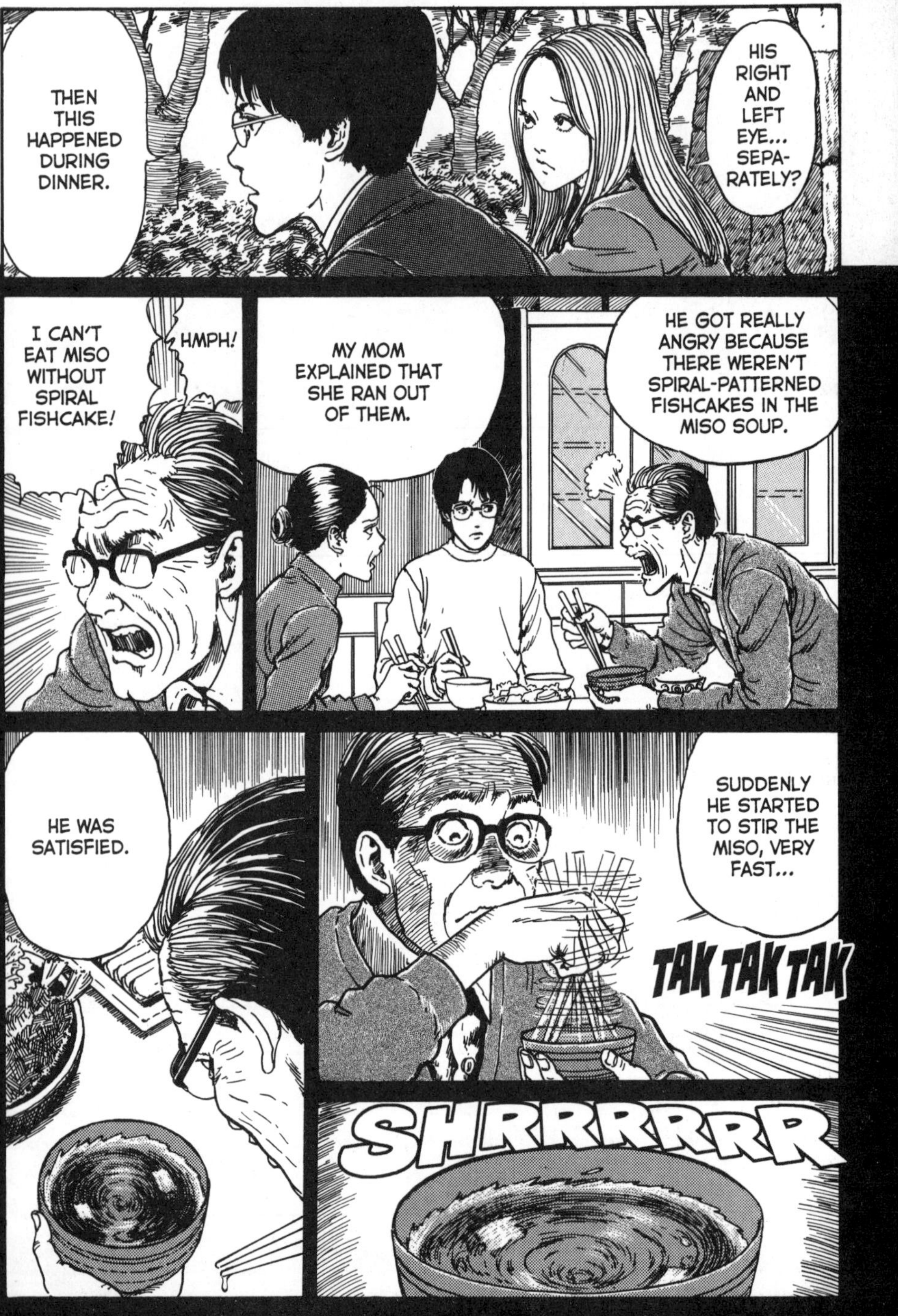
HIS RIGHT AND LEFT EYE... SEPA-RATELY?
THEN THIS HAPPENED DURING DINNER.
HE GOT REALLY ANGRY BECAUSE THERE WEREN'T SPIRAL-PATTERNED FISHCAKES IN THE MISO SOUP.
MY MOM EXPLAINED THAT SHE RAN OUT OF THEM.
HMPH!
I CAN'T EAT MISO WITHOUT SPIRAL FISHCAKE!
SUDDENLY HE STARTED TO STIR THE MISO, VERY FAST...
TAK TAK TAK
SHRRRRRR
HE WAS SATISFIED.

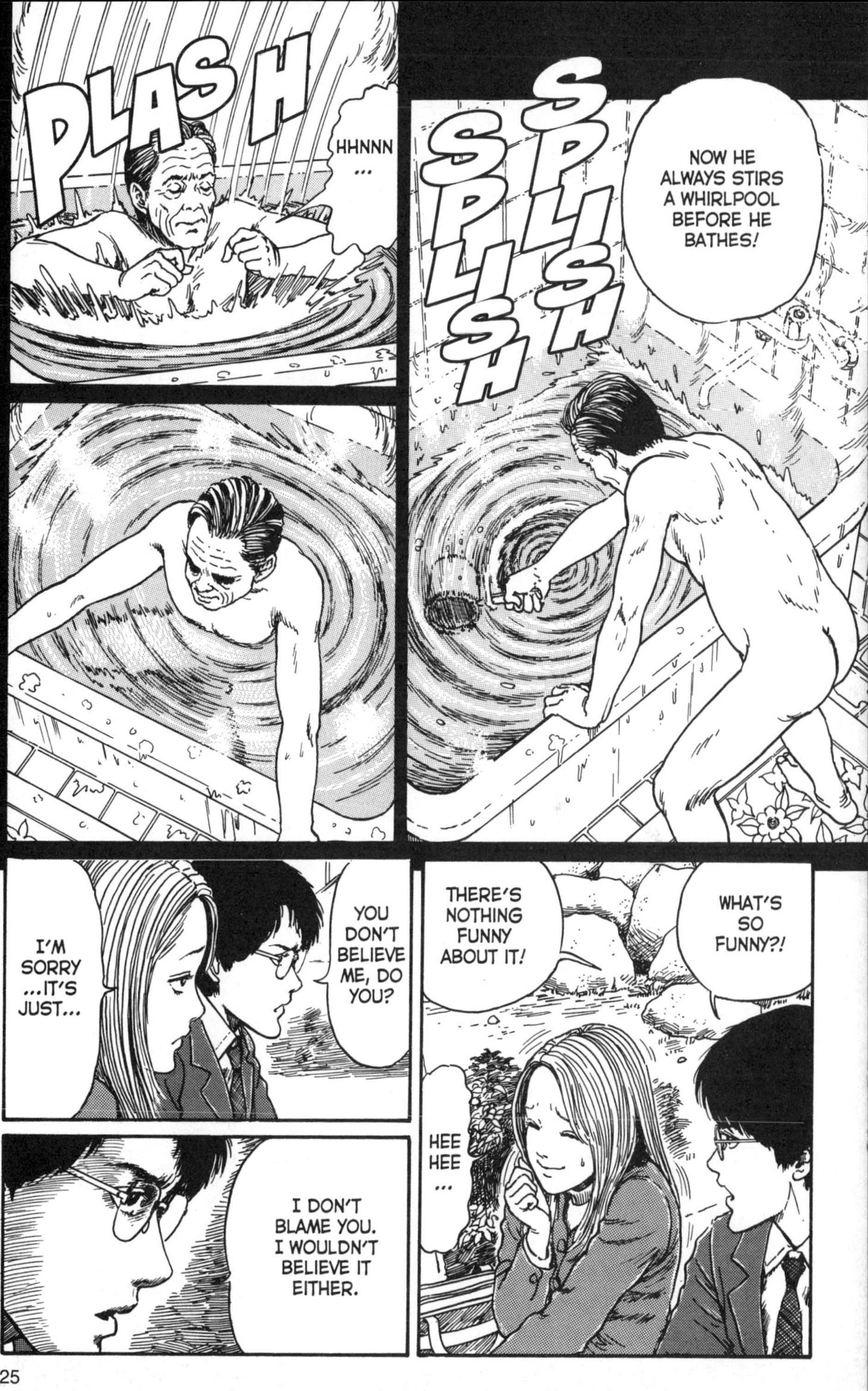
SPLISH SPLISH
NOW HE ALWAYS STIRS A WHIRLPOOL BEFORE HE BATHES!
PLASH
HHNNN ...
WHAT'S SO FUNNY?!
THERE'S NOTHING FUNNY ABOUT IT!
HEE HEE ...
YOU DON'T BELIEVE ME, DO YOU?
I'M SORRY ...IT'S JUST...
I DON'T BLAME YOU. I WOULDN'T BELIEVE IT EITHER.

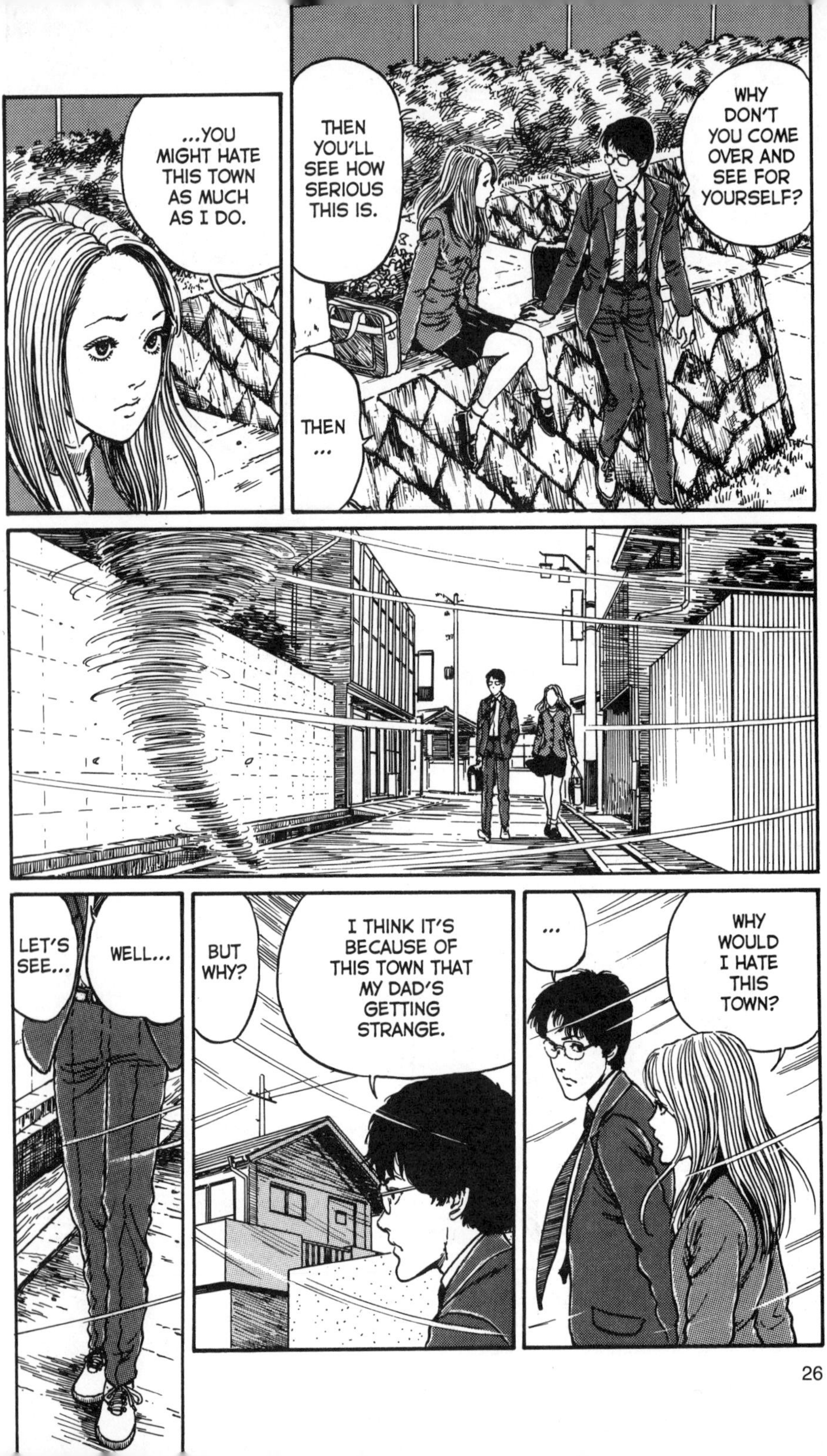
WHY DON'T YOU COME OVER AND SEE FOR YOURSELF?
THEN YOU'LL SEE HOW SERIOUS THIS IS.
THEN ...
...YOU MIGHT HATE THIS TOWN AS MUCH AS I DO.
WHY WOULD I HATE THIS TOWN?
...
I THINK IT'S BECAUSE OF THIS TOWN THAT MY DAD'S GETTING STRANGE.
BUT WHY?
WELL...
LET'S SEE...

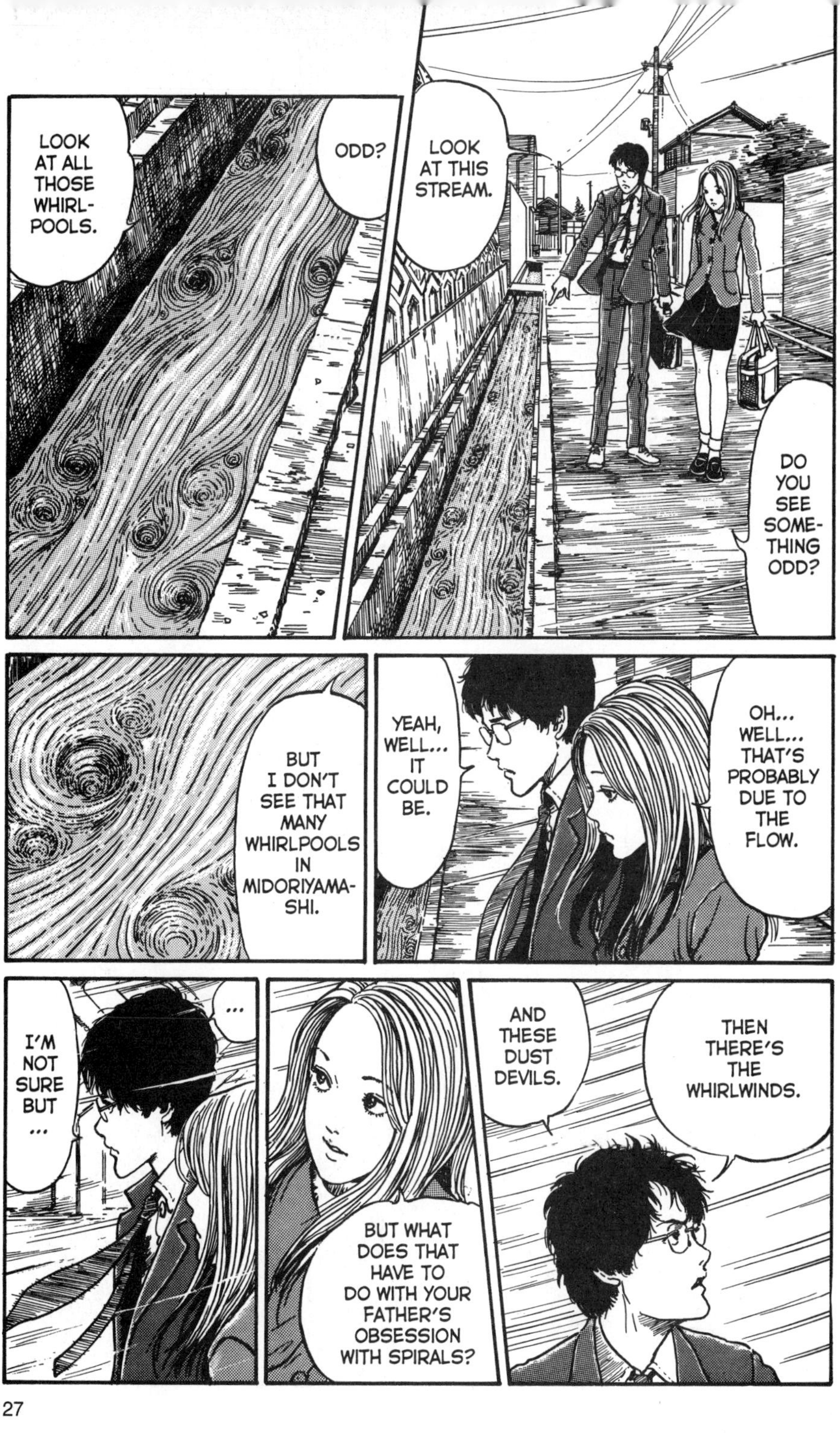
DO YOU SEE SOME-THING ODD?
LOOK AT THIS STREAM.
ODD?
LOOK AT ALL THOSE WHIRL-POOLS.
OH... WELL... THAT'S PROBABLY DUE TO THE FLOW.
YEAH, WELL... IT COULD BE.
BUT I DON'T SEE THAT MANY WHIRLPOOLS IN MIDORIYAMA-SHI.
THEN THERE'S THE WHIRLWINDS.
AND THESE DUST DEVILS.
BUT WHAT DOES THAT HAVE TO DO WITH YOUR FATHER'S OBSESSION WITH SPIRALS?
...
I'M NOT SURE BUT ...

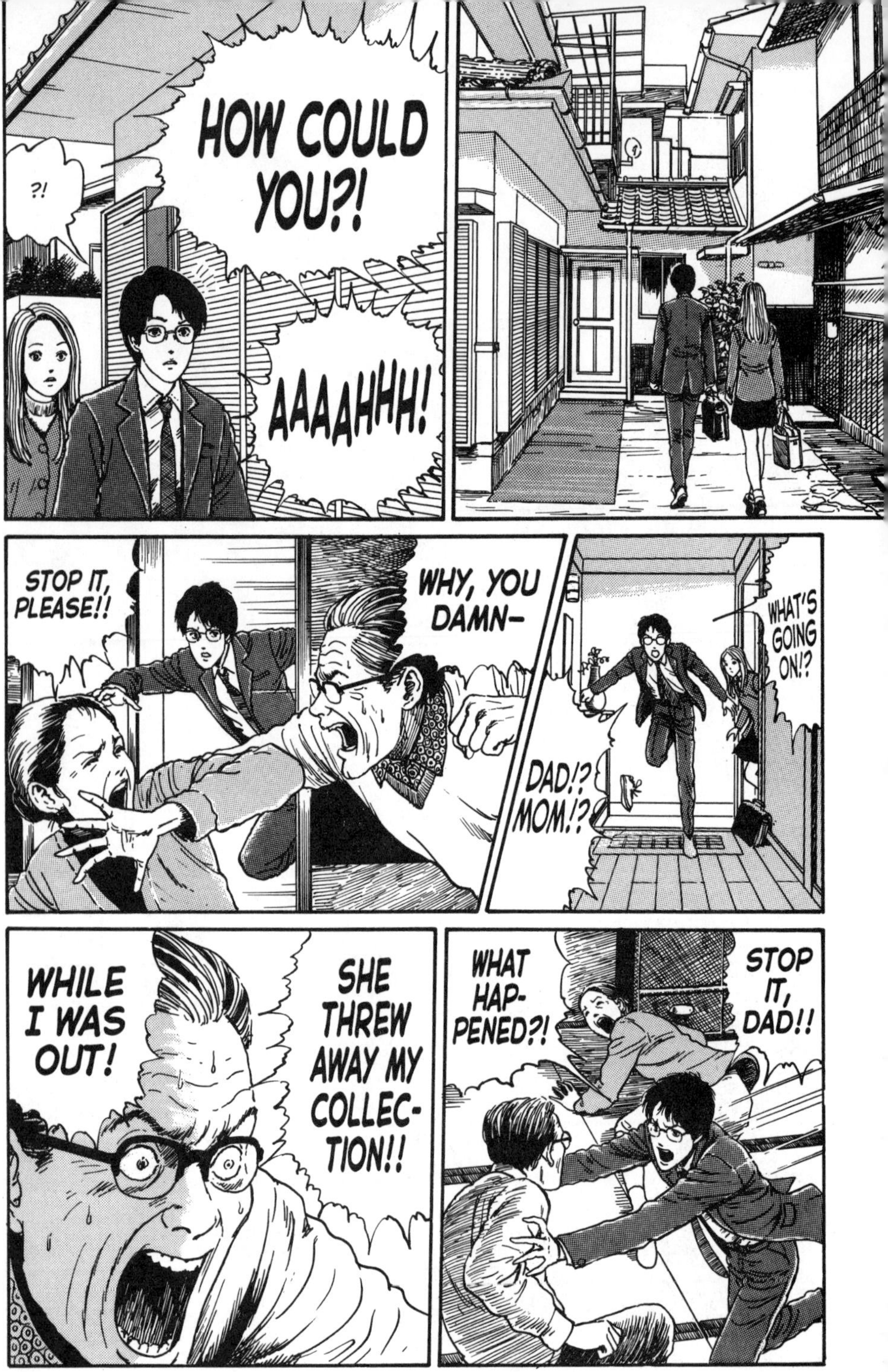
HOW COULD YOU?!
?!
AAAAHHH!
WHAT'S GOING ON!?
DAD!? MOM!?
WHY, YOU DAMN-
STOP IT, PLEASE!!
STOP IT, DAD!!
WHAT HAP-PENED?!
SHE THREW AWAY MY COLLEC-TION!!
WHILE I WAS OUT!

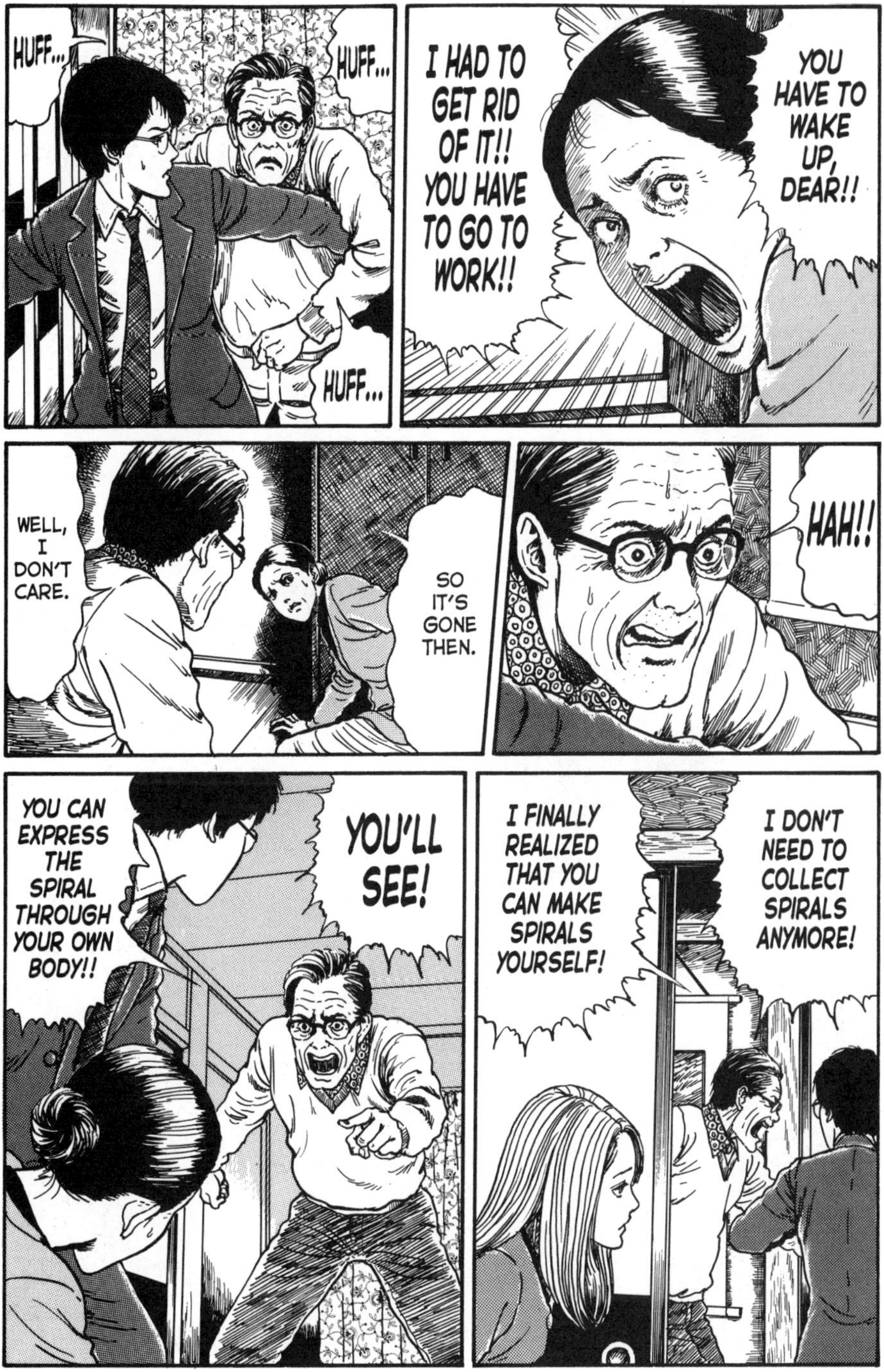
YOU HAVE TO WAKE UP, DEAR!!
I HAD TO GET RID OF IT!! YOU HAVE TO GO TO WORK!!
HUFF...
HUFF...
HUFF...
HAH!!
SO IT'S GONE THEN.
WELL, I DON'T CARE.
I DON'T NEED TO COLLECT SPIRALS ANYMORE!
I FINALLY REALIZED THAT YOU CAN MAKE SPIRALS YOURSELF!
YOU'LL SEE!
YOU CAN EXPRESS THE SPIRAL THROUGH YOUR OWN BODY!!

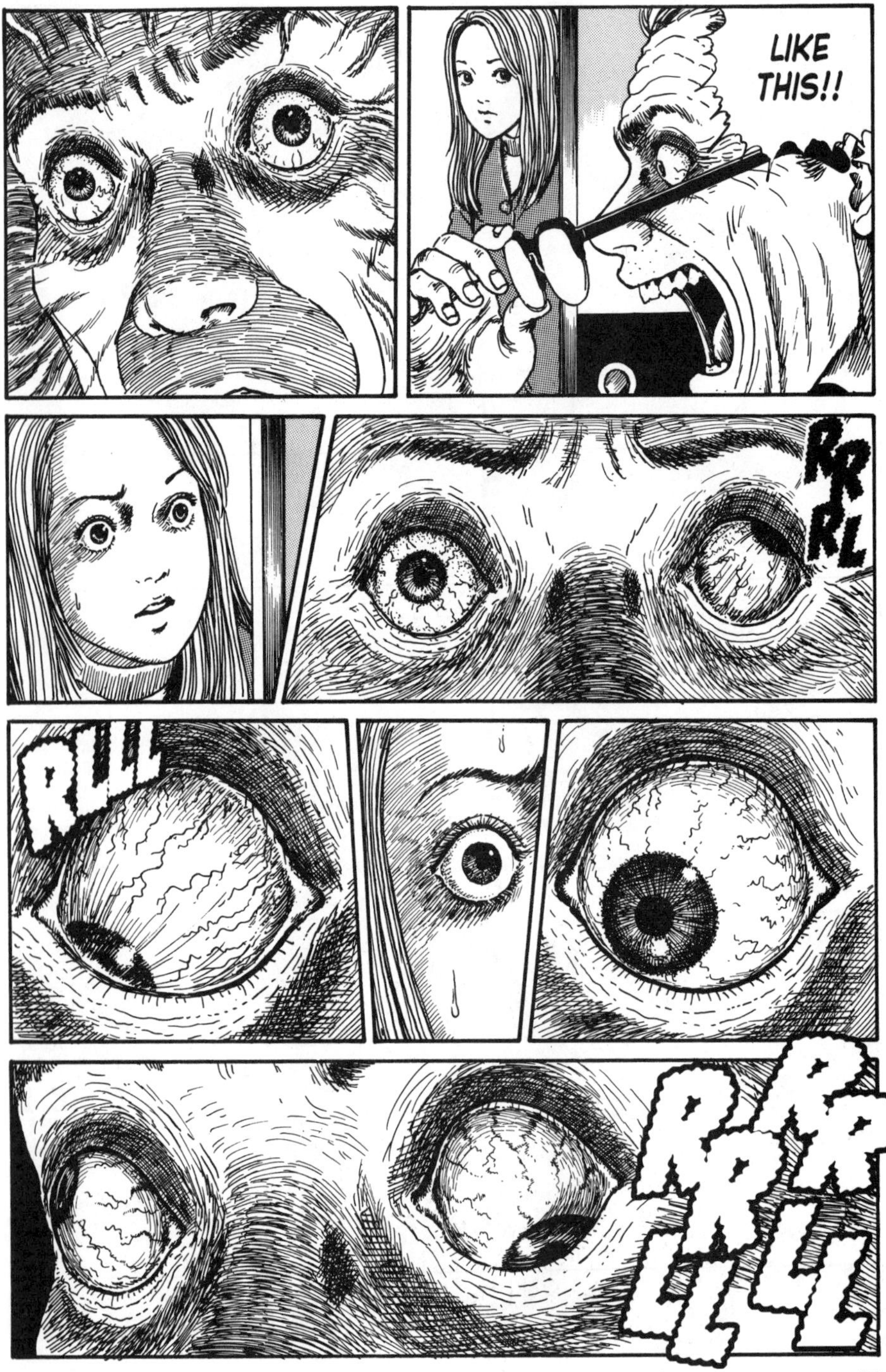
LIKE THIS!!
RRRL
RLL
RRRRLLLL

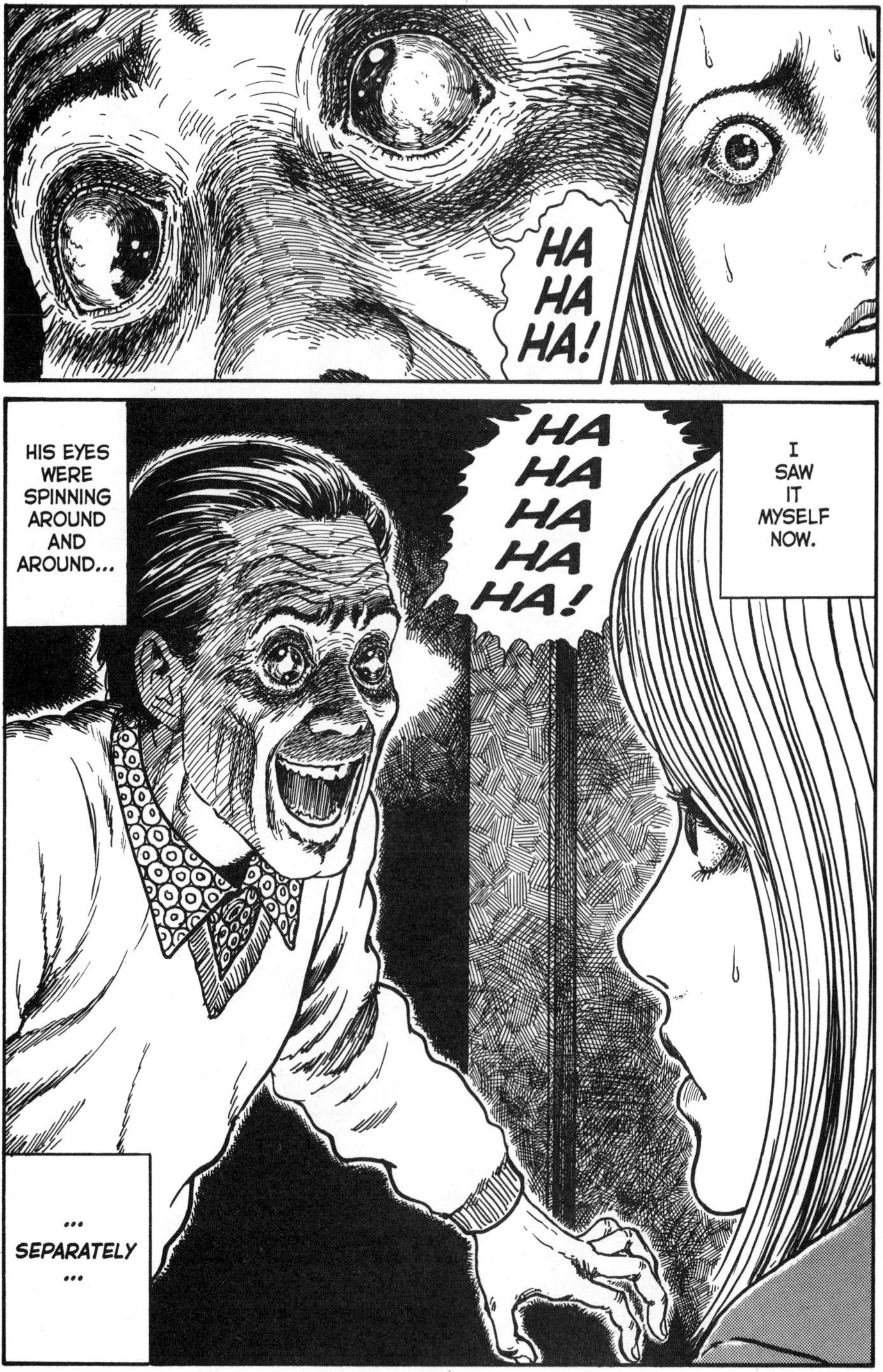
HA HA HA!
I SAW IT MYSELF NOW.
HA HA HA HA HA HA!
HIS EYES WERE SPINNING AROUND AND AROUND...
... SEPARATELY ...

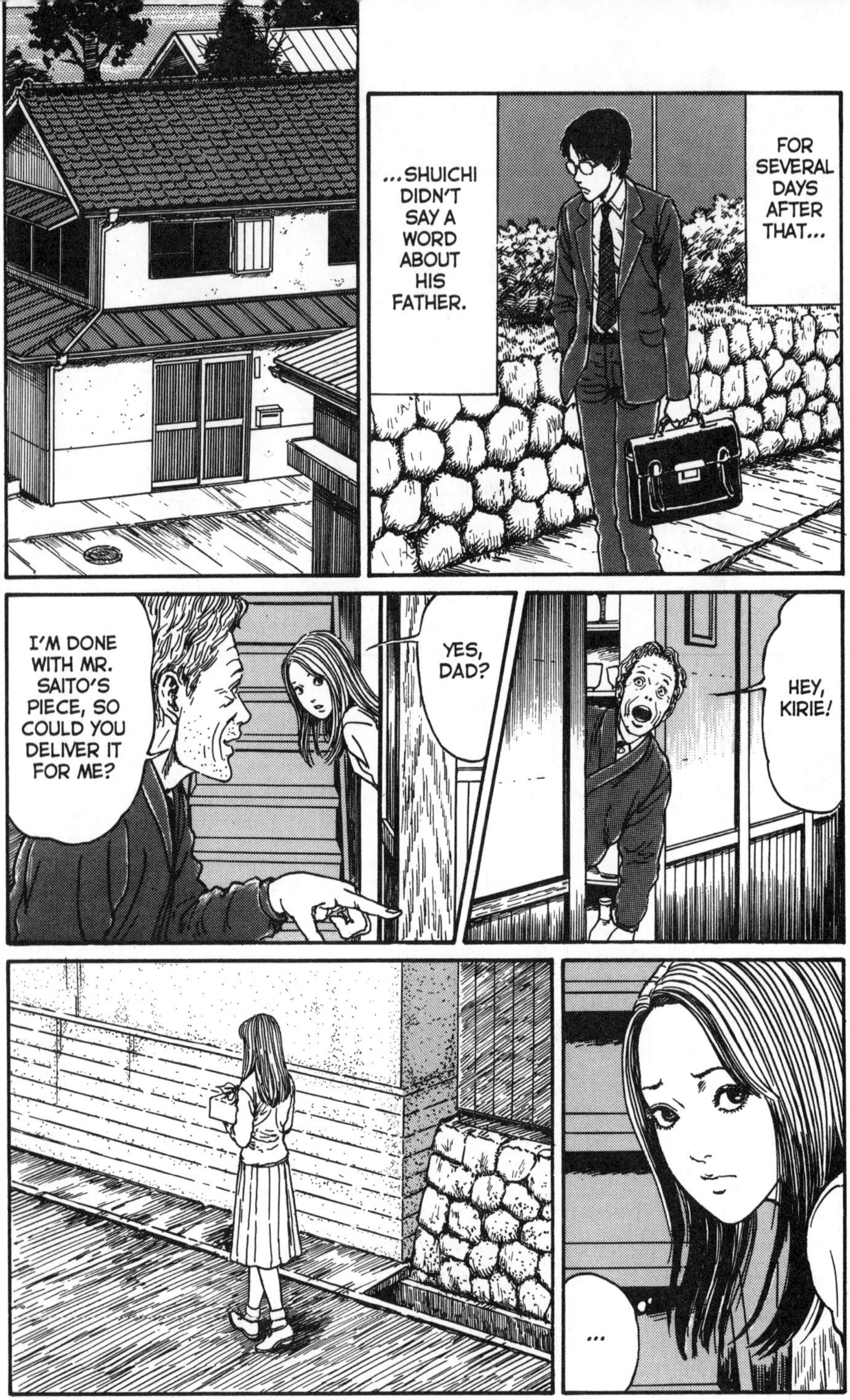
FOR SEVERAL DAYS AFTER THAT...
...SHUICHI DIDN'T SAY A WORD ABOUT HIS FATHER.
HEY, KIRIE!
YES, DAD?
I'M DONE WITH MR. SAITO'S PIECE, SO COULD YOU DELIVER IT FOR ME?
...

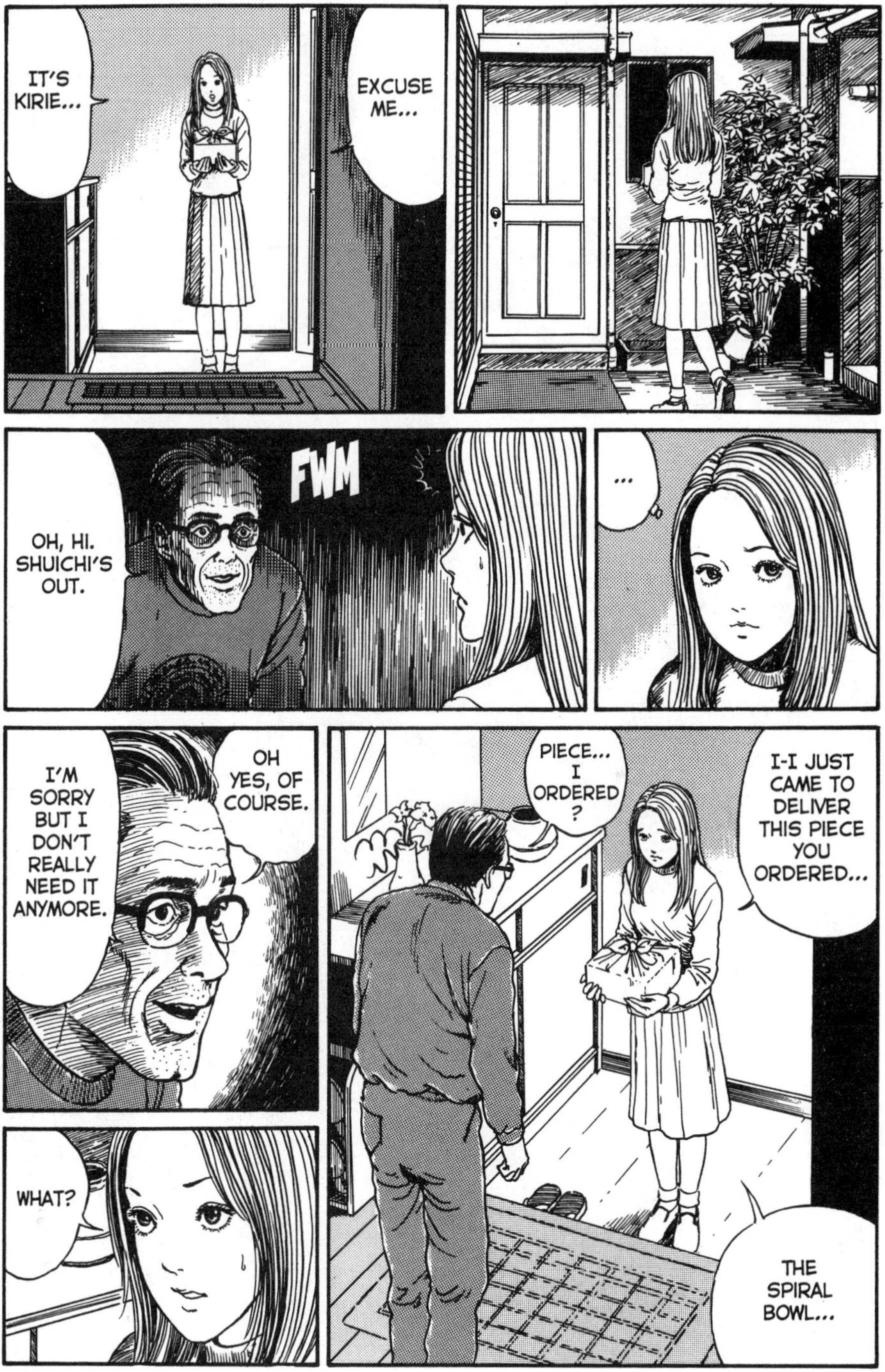
EXCUSE ME...
IT'S KIRIE...
...
FWM
OH, HI. SHUICHI'S OUT.
I-I JUST CAME TO DELIVER THIS PIECE YOU ORDERED...
PIECE... I ORDERED?
THE SPIRAL BOWL...
OH YES, OF COURSE.
I'M SORRY BUT I DON'T REALLY NEED IT ANYMORE.
WHAT?

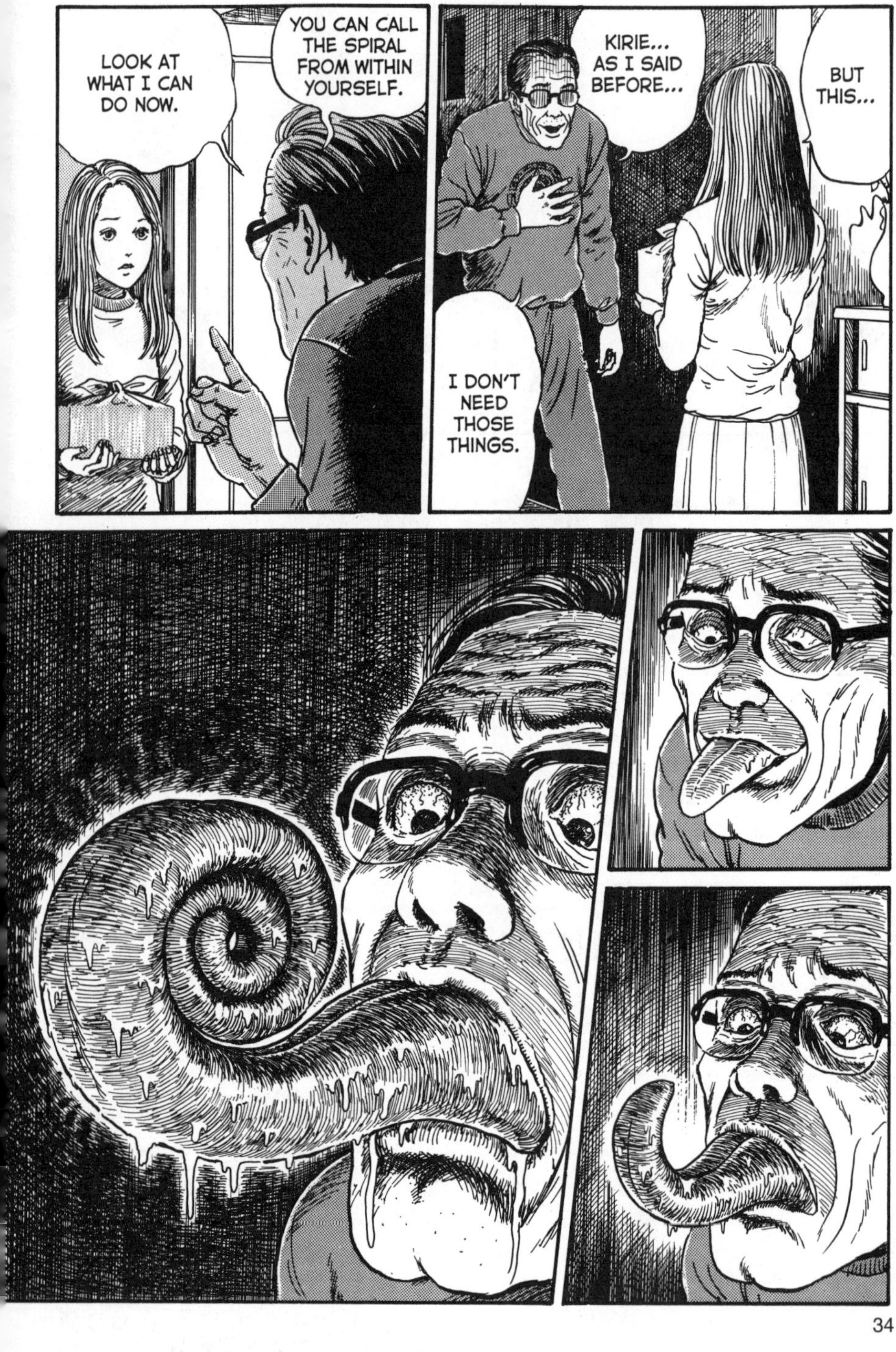
BUT THIS...
KIRIE... AS I SAID BEFORE...
I DON'T NEED THOSE THINGS.
YOU CAN CALL THE SPIRAL FROM WITHIN YOURSELF.
LOOK AT WHAT I CAN DO NOW.

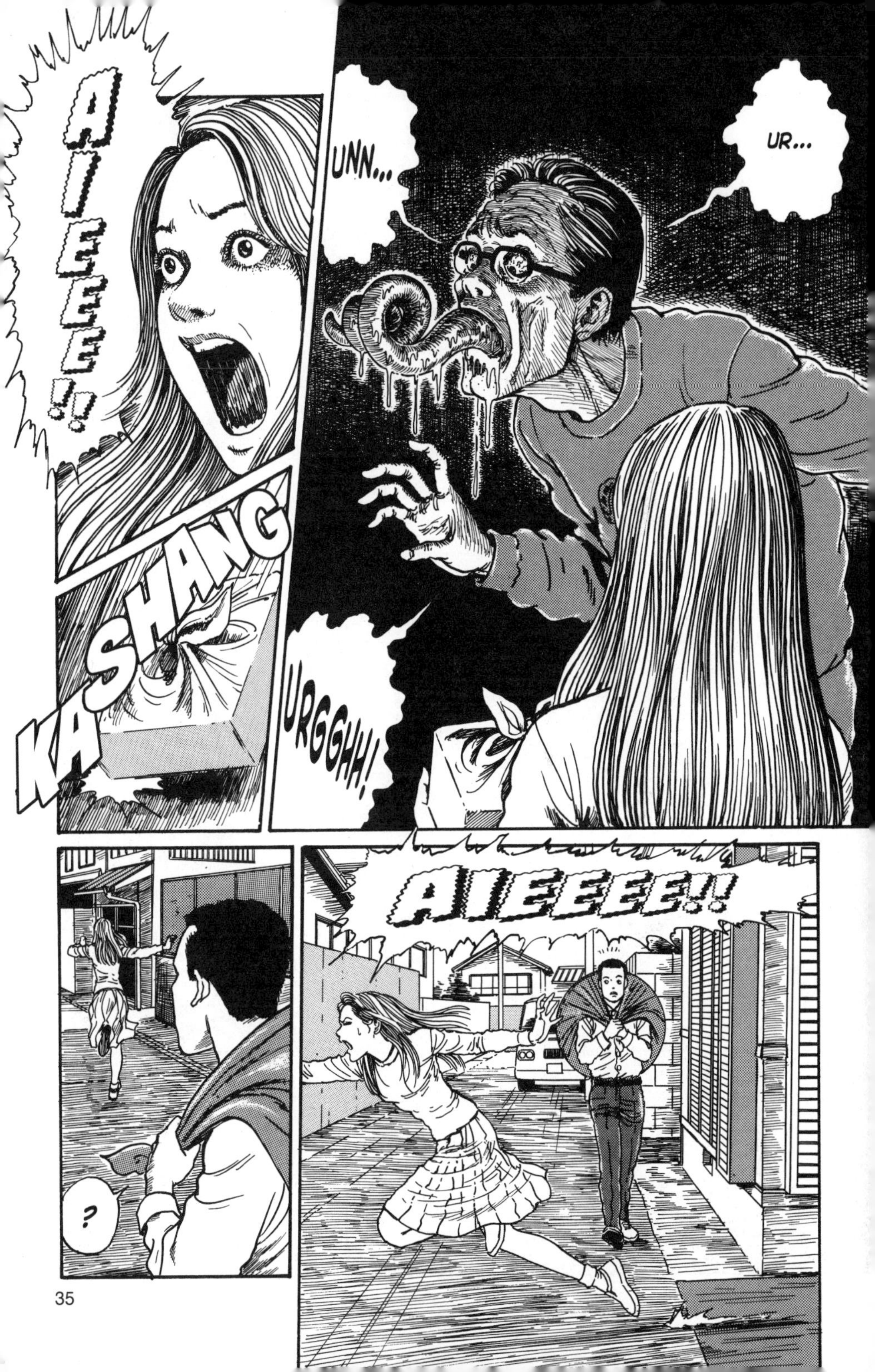
UR...
UNN...
URGGHH!
AIEEEE!!
KASHANG
AIEEEE!!
?

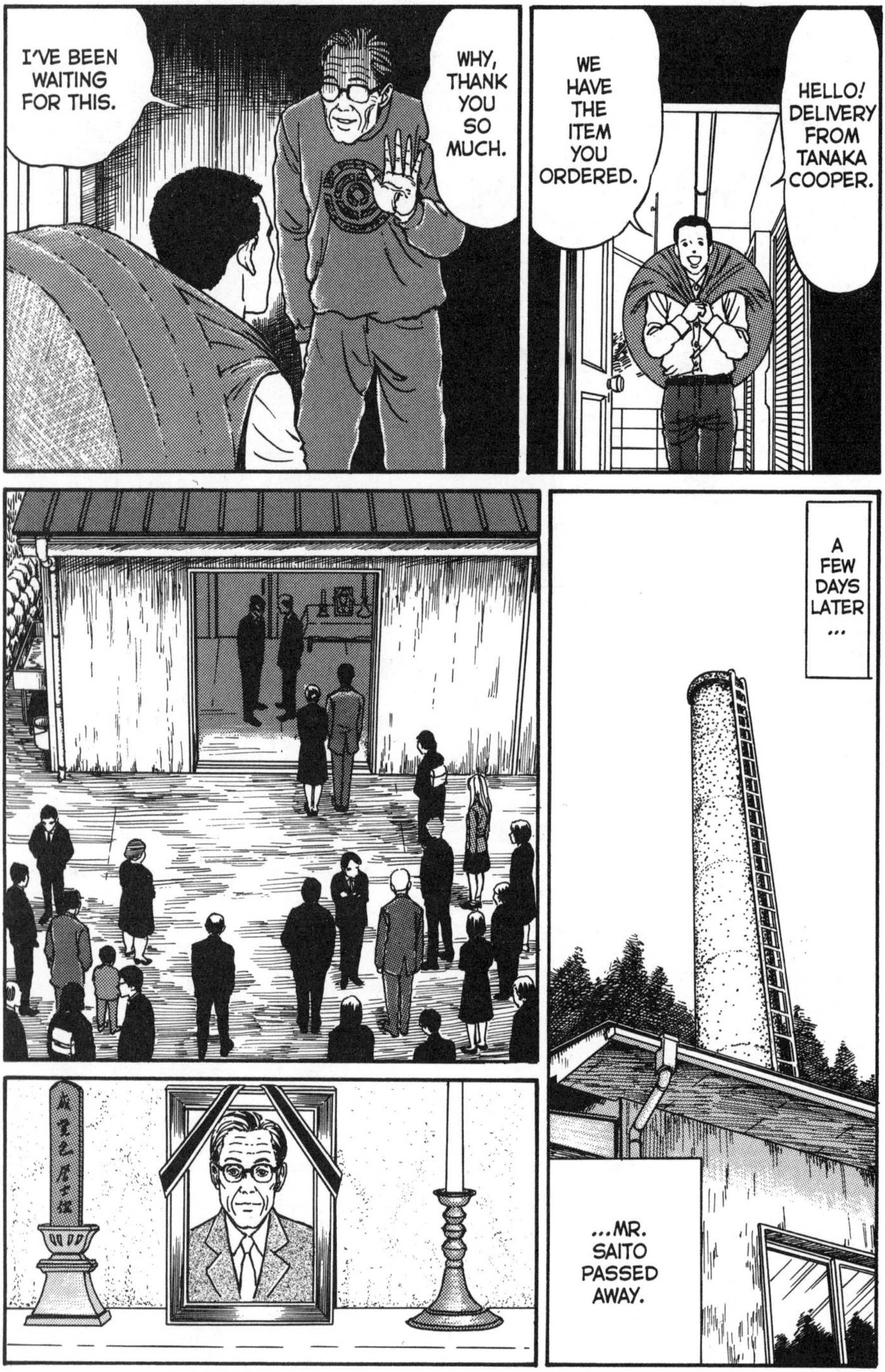
HELLO! DELIVERY FROM TANAKA COOPER.
WE HAVE THE ITEM YOU ORDERED.
WHY, THANK YOU SO MUCH.
I'VE BEEN WAITING FOR THIS.
A FEW DAYS LATER ...
...MR. SAITO PASSED AWAY.

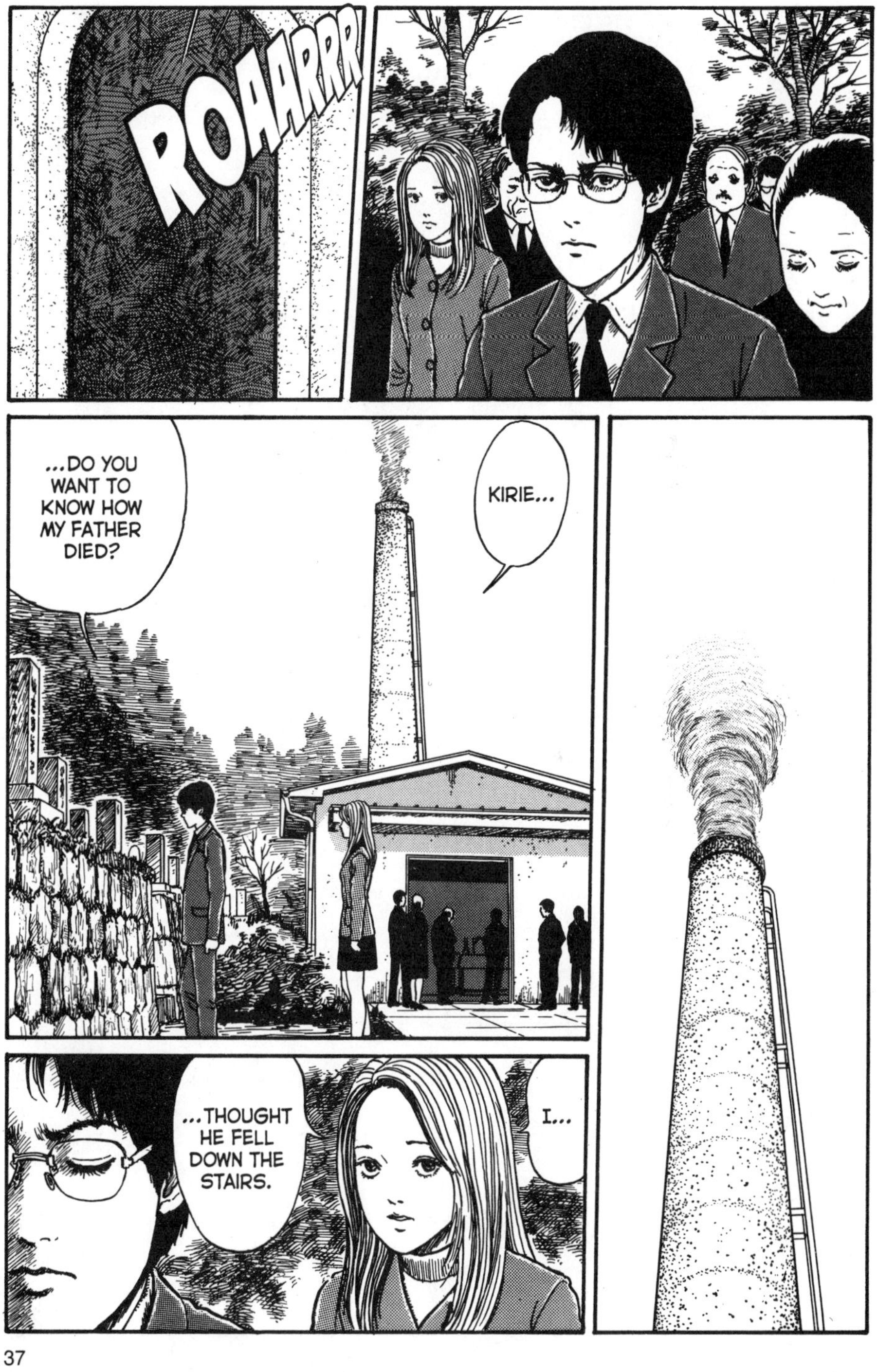
ROAARRR
KIRIE...
...DO YOU WANT TO KNOW HOW MY FATHER DIED?
I...
...THOUGHT HE FELL DOWN THE STAIRS.

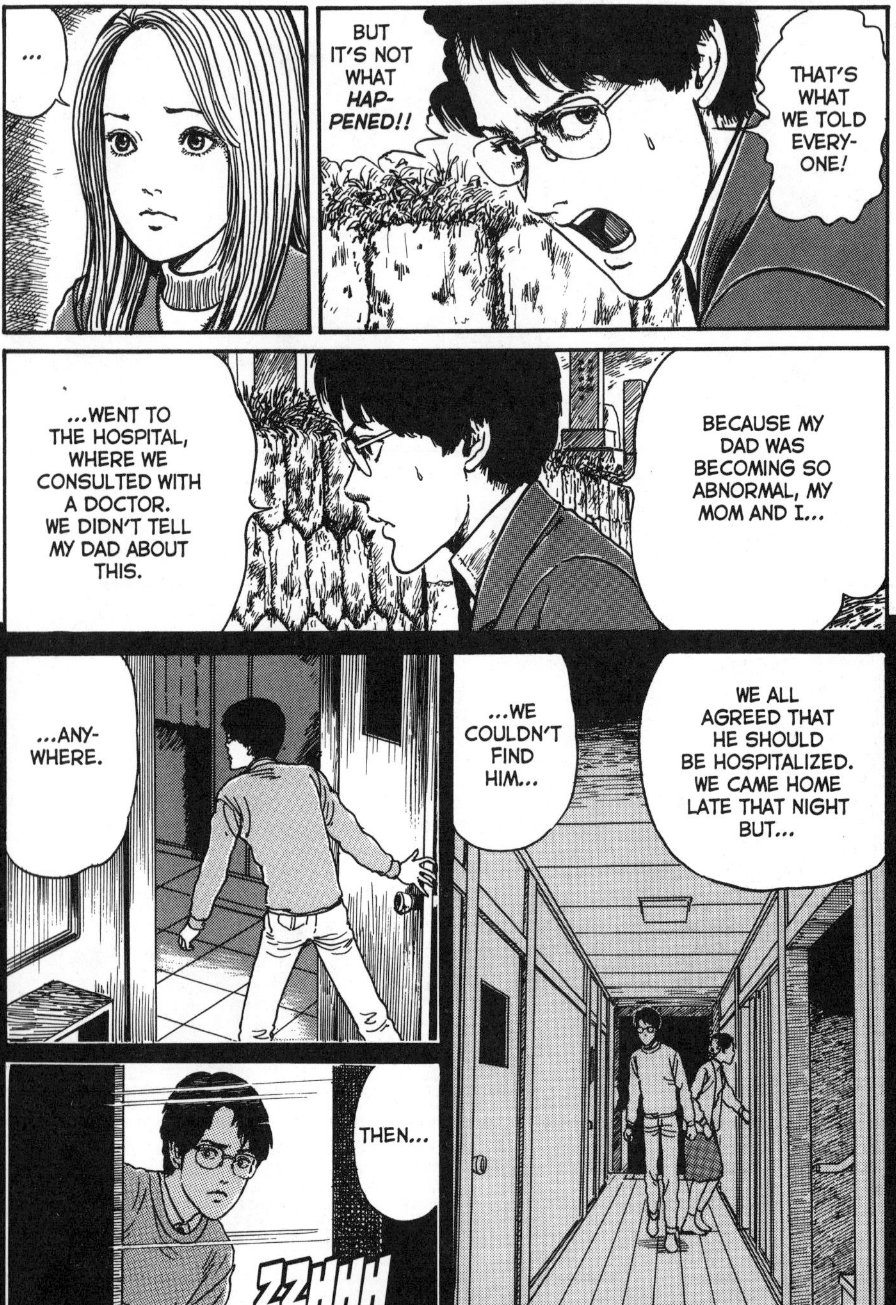
THAT'S WHAT WE TOLD EVERY-ONE!
BUT IT'S NOT WHAT HAP-PENED!!
...
BECAUSE MY DAD WAS BECOMING SO ABNORMAL, MY MOM AND I...
...WENT TO THE HOSPITAL, WHERE WE CONSULTED WITH A DOCTOR. WE DIDN'T TELL MY DAD ABOUT THIS.
WE ALL AGREED THAT HE SHOULD BE HOSPITALIZED. WE CAME HOME LATE THAT NIGHT BUT...
...WE COULDN'T FIND HIM...
...ANY-WHERE.
THEN...
ZZHHH

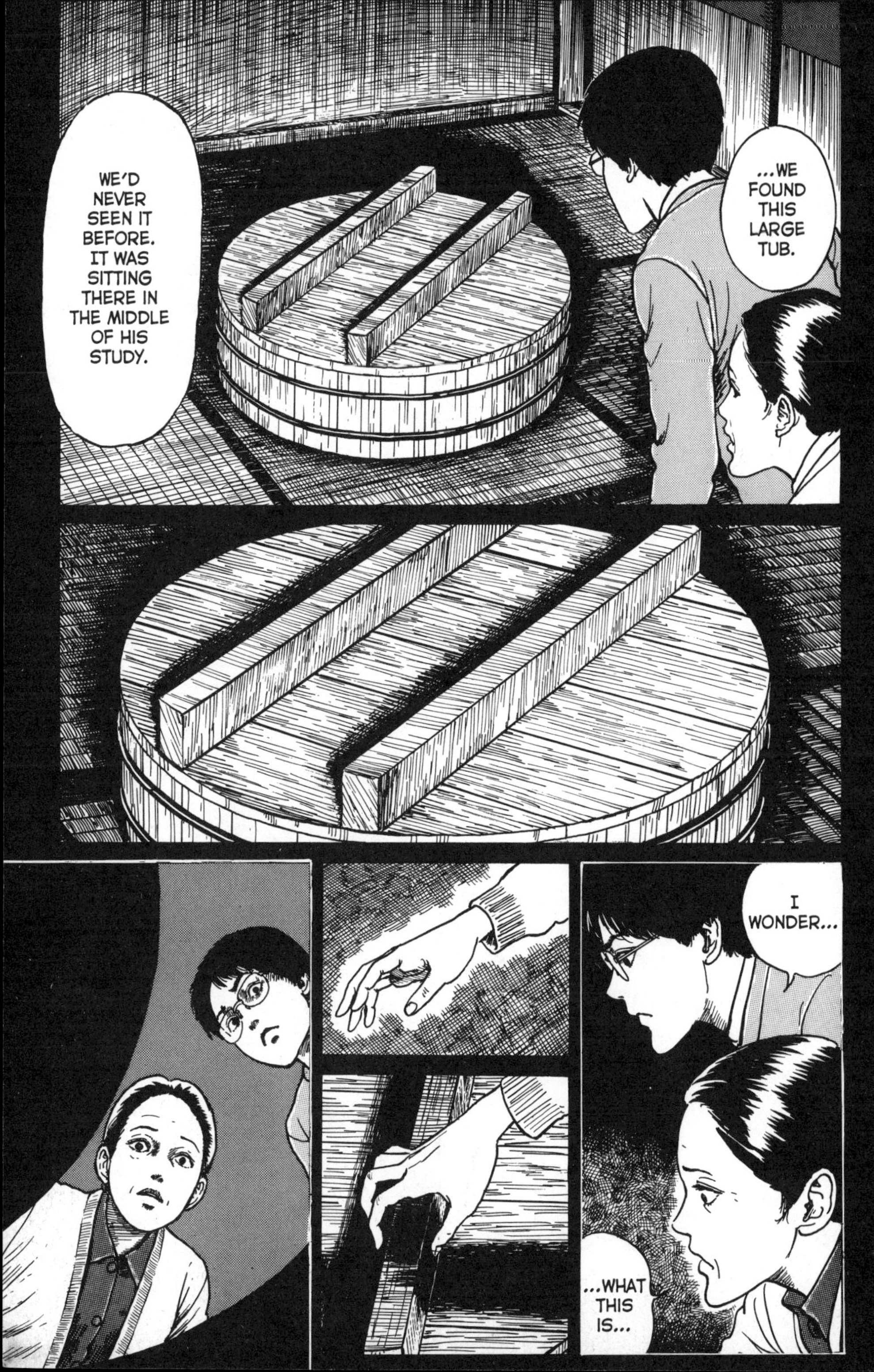
...WE FOUND THIS LARGE TUB.
WE'D NEVER SEEN IT BEFORE. IT WAS SITTING THERE IN THE MIDDLE OF HIS STUDY.
I WONDER...
...WHAT THIS IS...

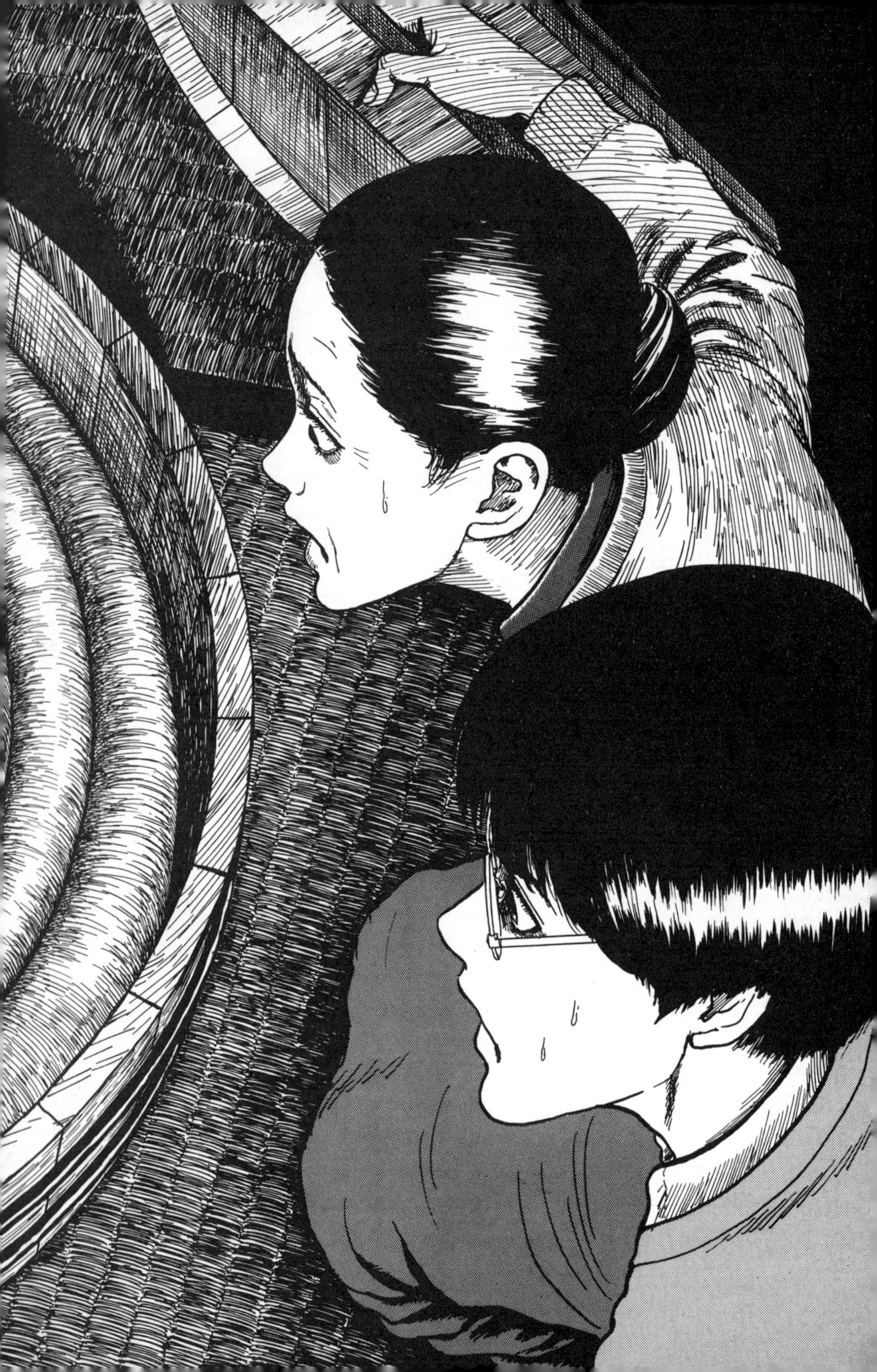

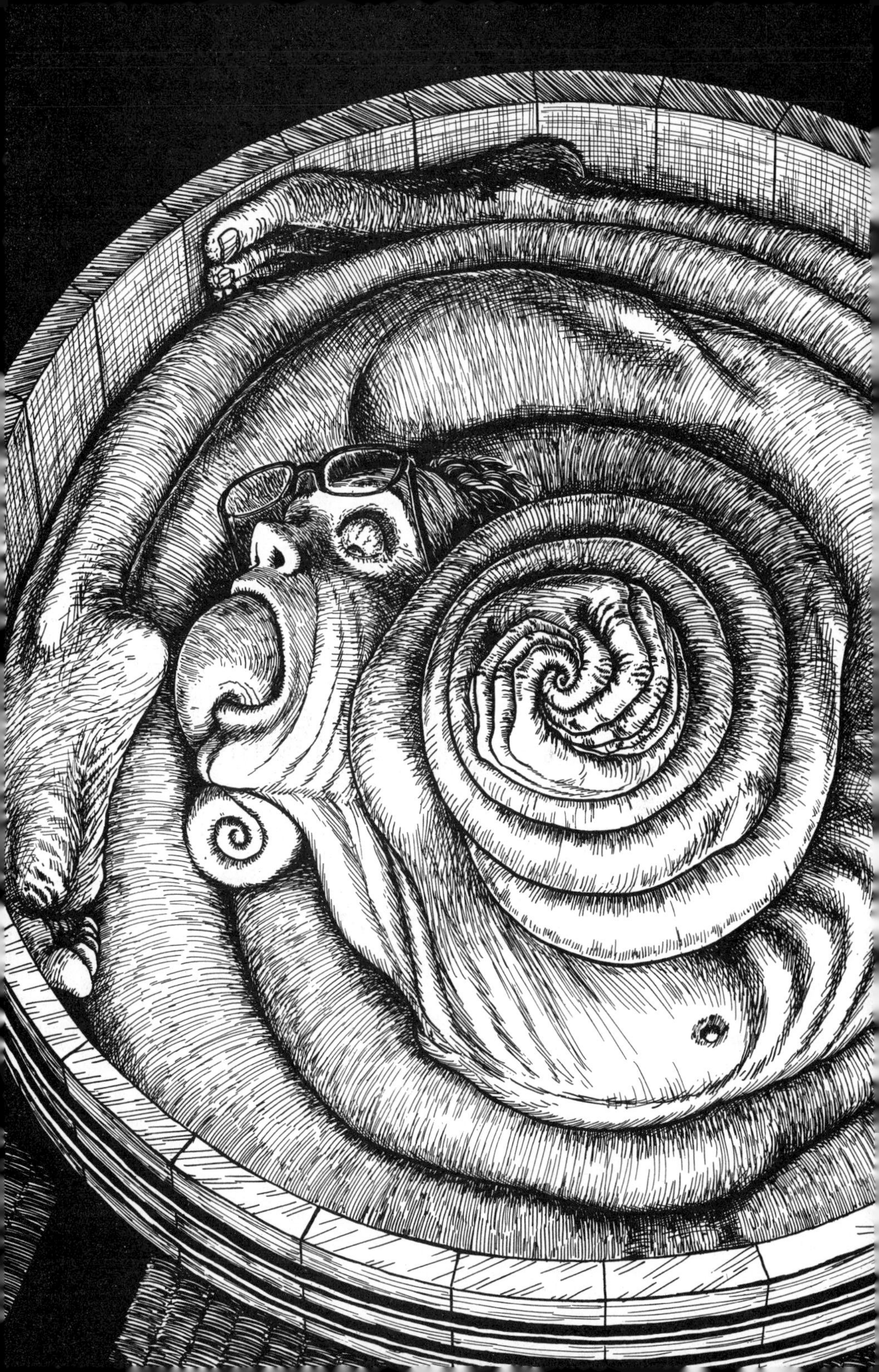

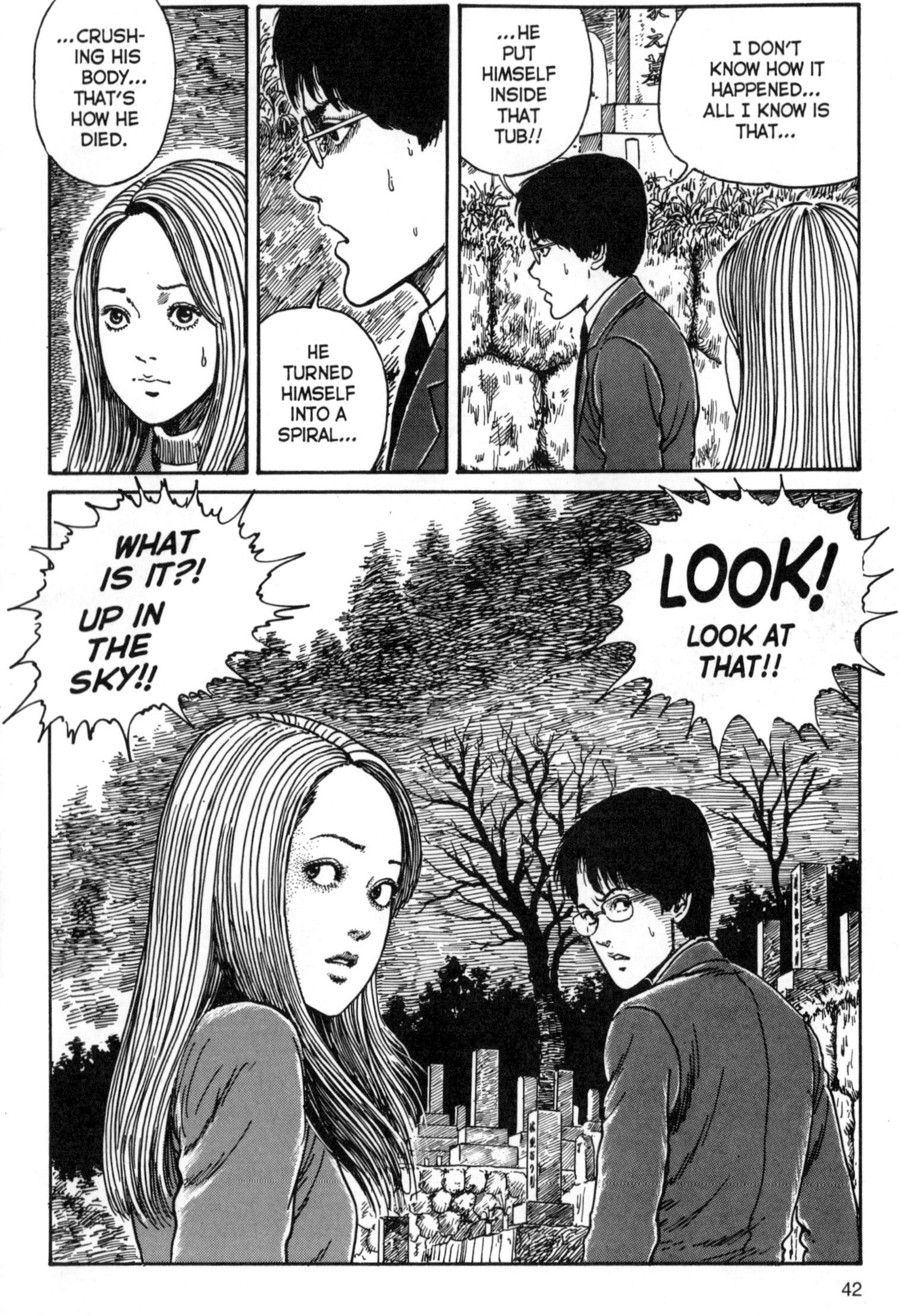
I DON'T KNOW HOW IT HAPPENED... ALL I KNOW IS THAT...
...HE PUT HIMSELF INSIDE THAT TUB!!
HE TURNED HIMSELF INTO A SPIRAL...
...CRUSHING HIS BODY... THAT'S HOW HE DIED.
LOOK!
LOOK AT THAT!!
WHAT IS IT?!
UP IN THE SKY!!

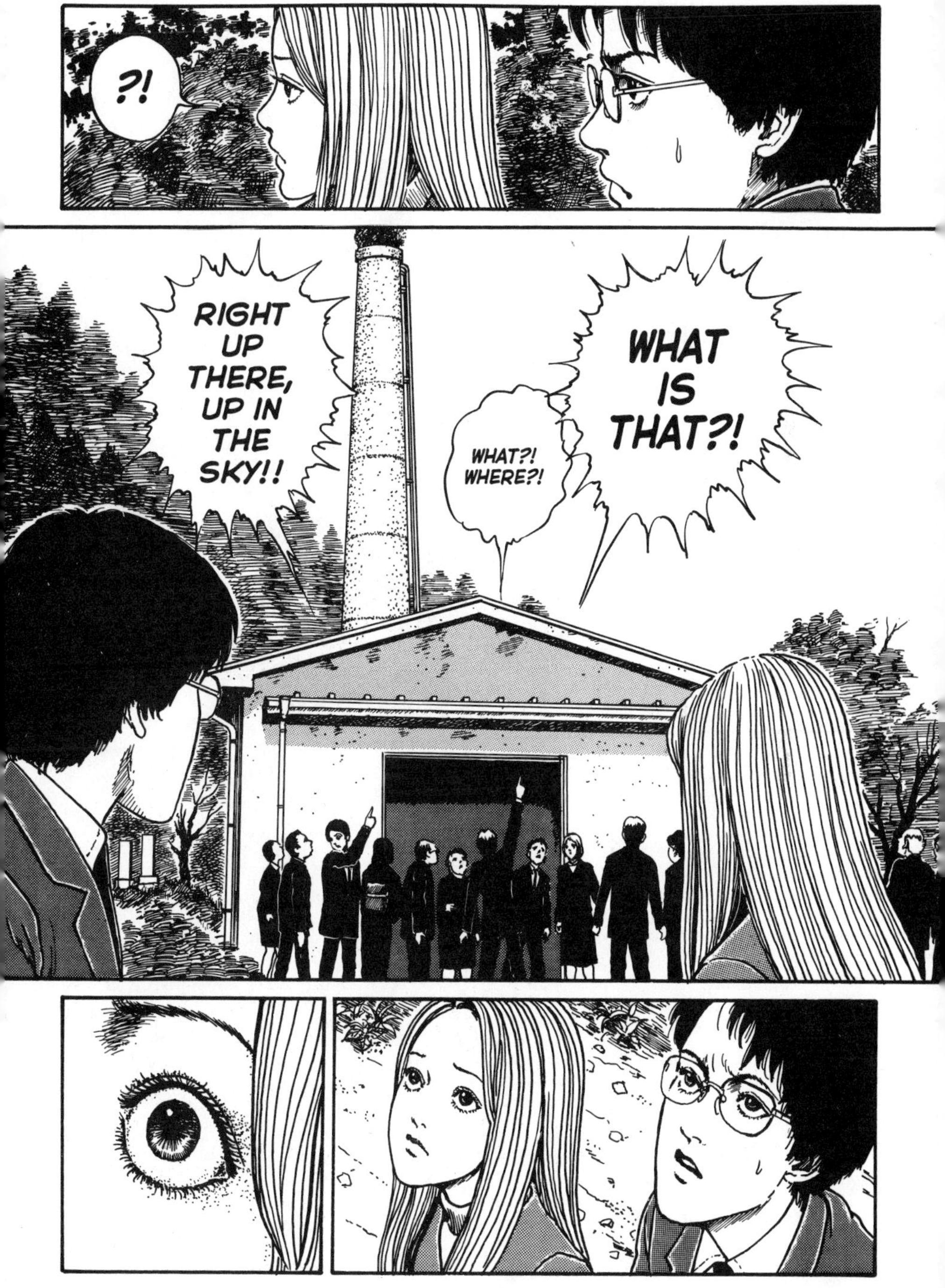
?!
WHAT IS THAT?!
WHAT?! WHERE?!
RIGHT UP THERE, UP IN THE SKY!!

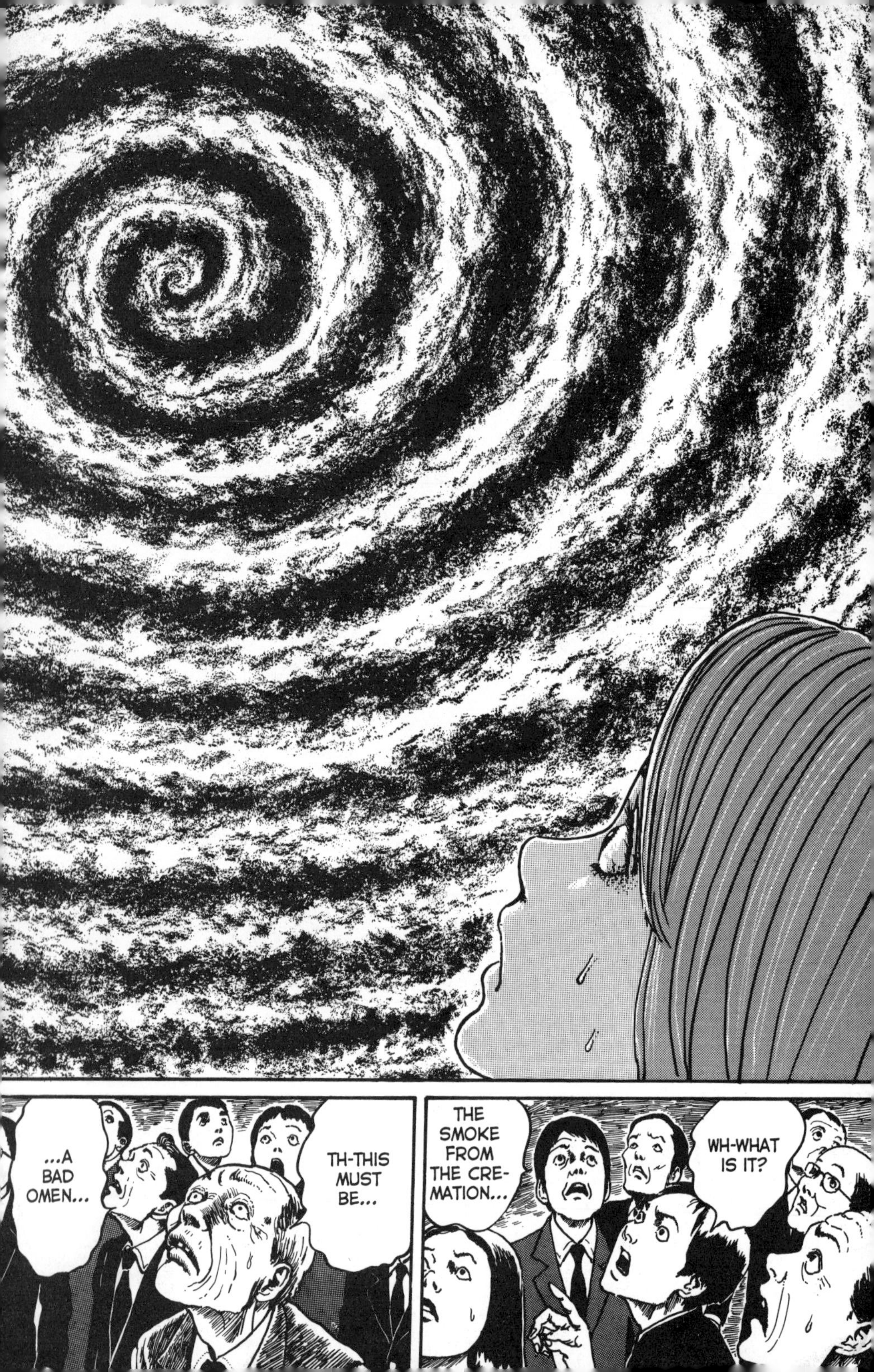
WH-WHAT IS IT?
THE SMOKE FROM THE CRE- MATION...
TH-THIS MUST BE...
...A BAD OMEN...

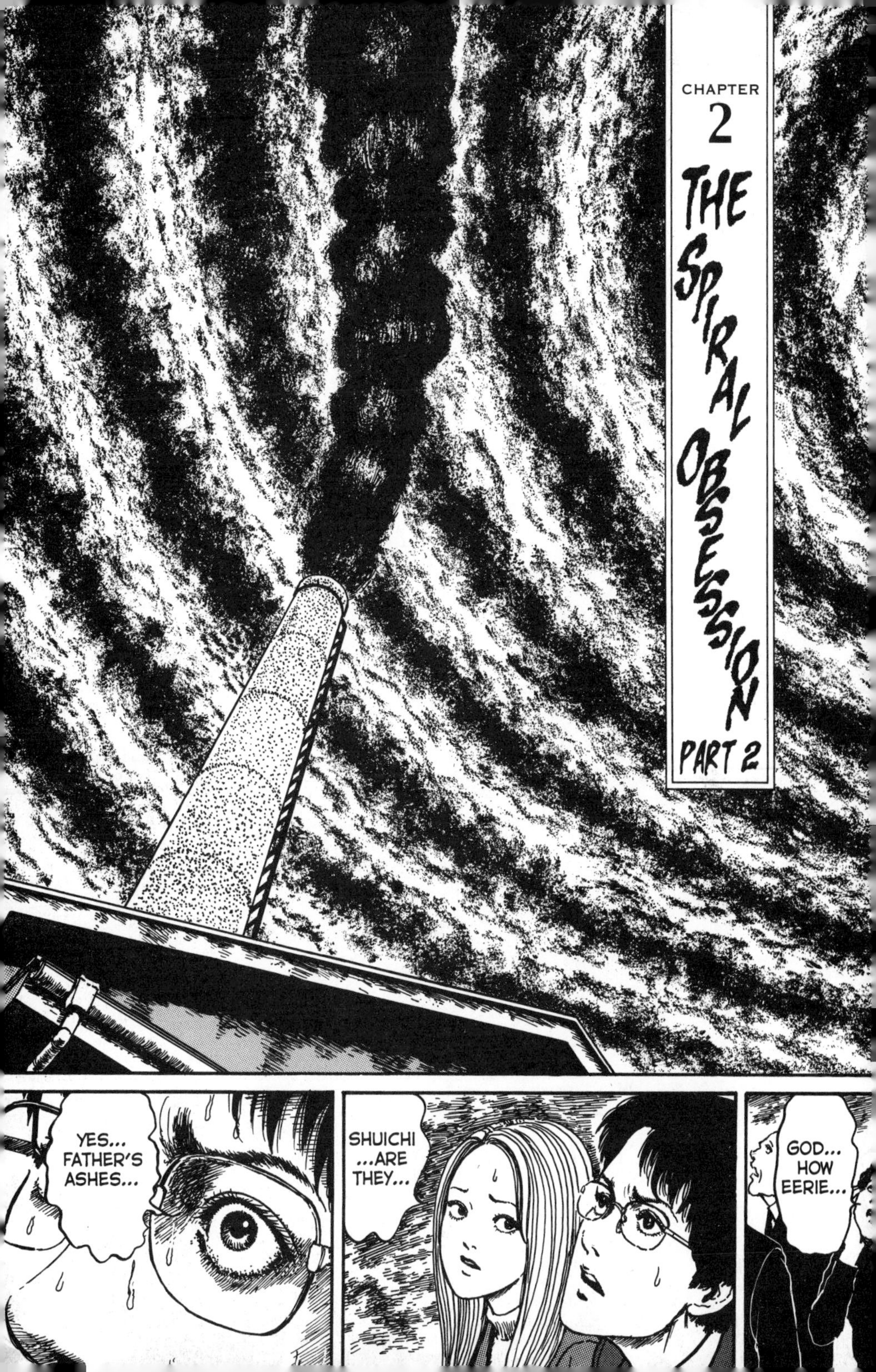
CHAPTER 2
THE SPIRAL OBSESSION PART 2
GOD... HOW EERIE...
SHUICHI ...ARE THEY...
YES... FATHER'S ASHES...

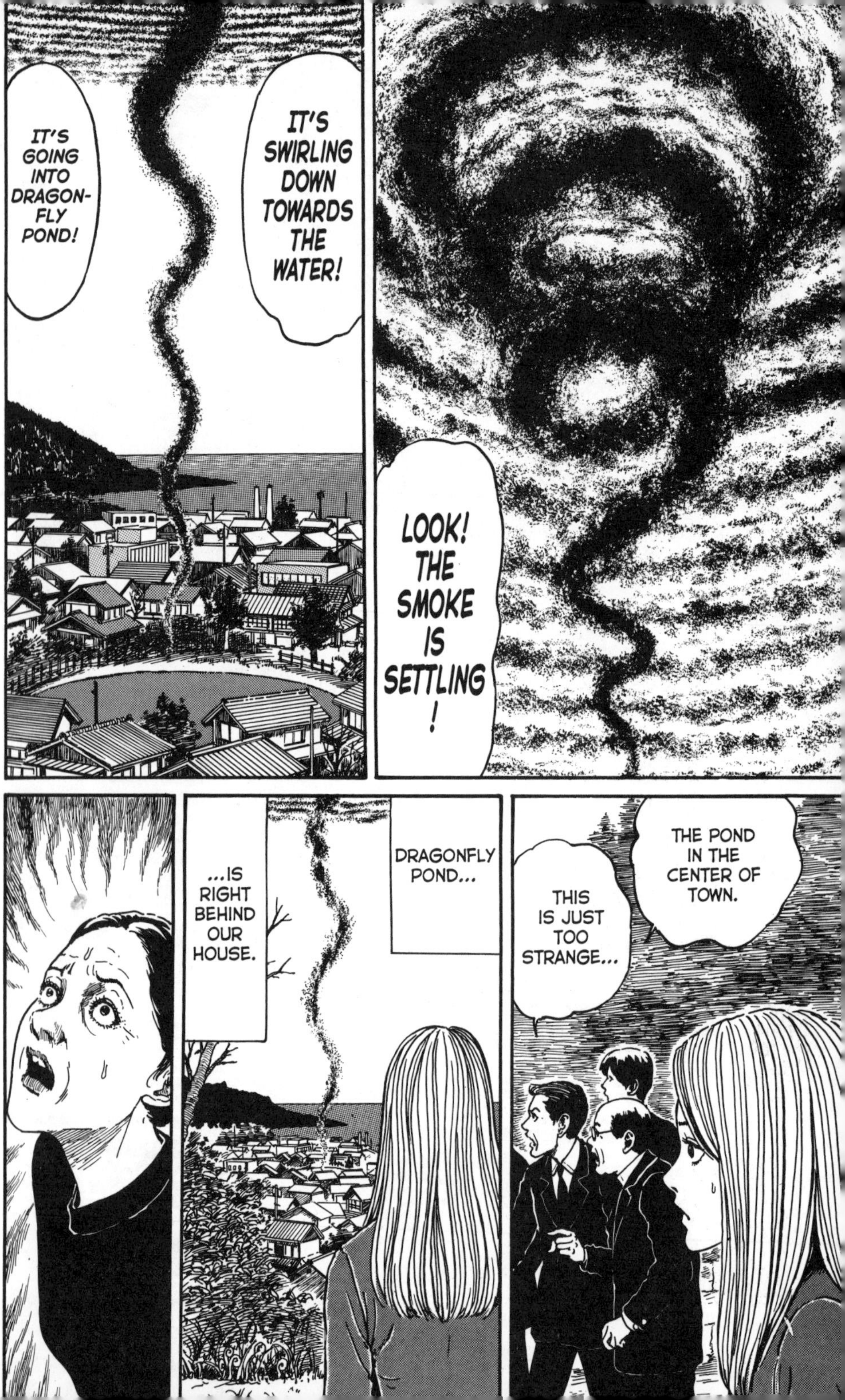
LOOK! THE SMOKE IS SETTLING!
IT'S SWIRLING DOWN TOWARDS THE WATER!
IT'S GOING INTO DRAGON-FLY POND!
THE POND IN THE CENTER OF TOWN.
THIS IS JUST TOO STRANGE...
DRAGONFLY POND...
...IS RIGHT BEHIND OUR HOUSE.

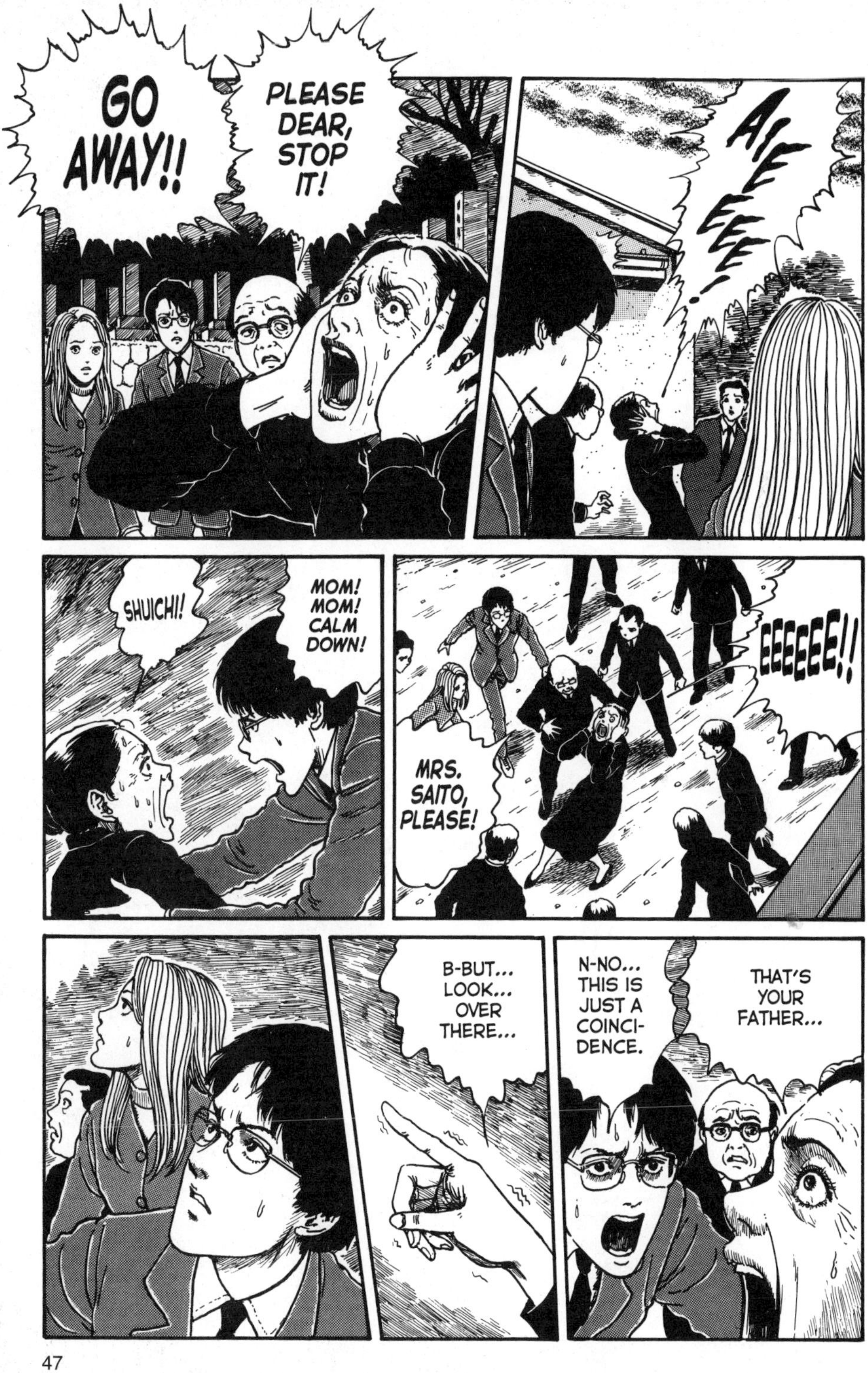
AIEEEE!
PLEASE DEAR, STOP IT!
GO AWAY!!
EEEEEE!!
MRS. SAITO, PLEASE!
MOM! MOM! CALM DOWN!
SHUICHI!
THAT'S YOUR FATHER...
N-NO... THIS IS JUST A COINCIDENCE.
B-BUT... LOOK... OVER THERE...

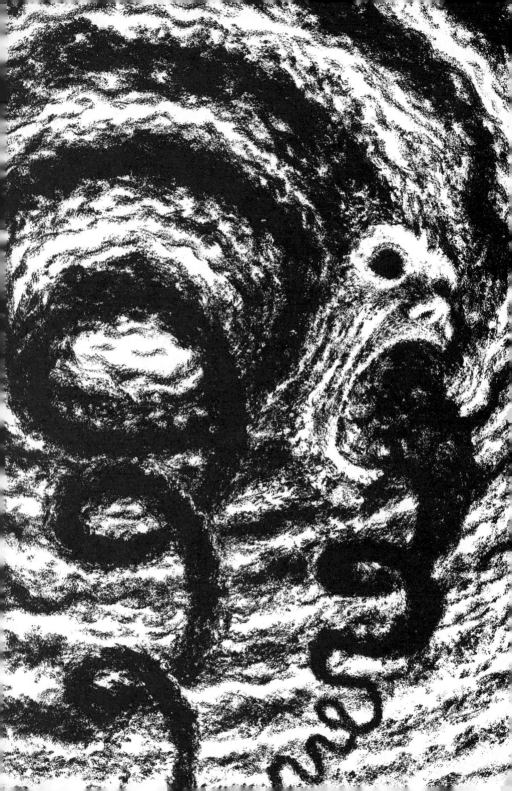

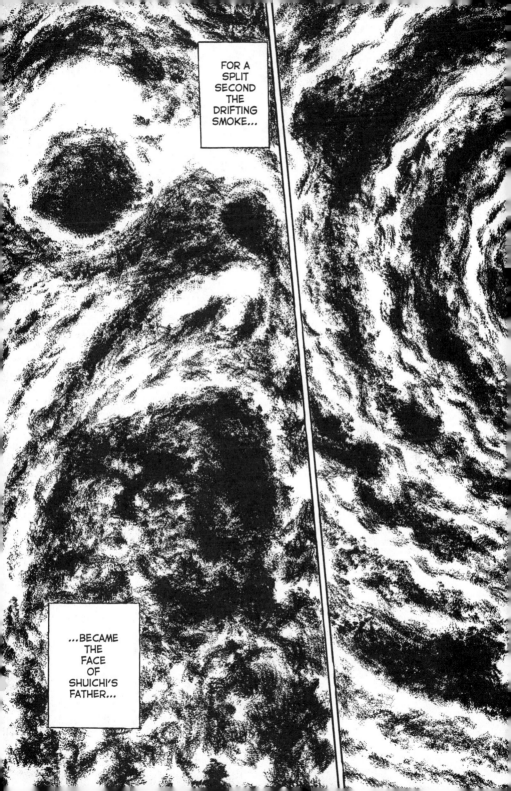

FOR A SPLIT SECOND THE DRIFTING SMOKE...

...BECAME THE FACE OF SHUICHI'S FATHER...

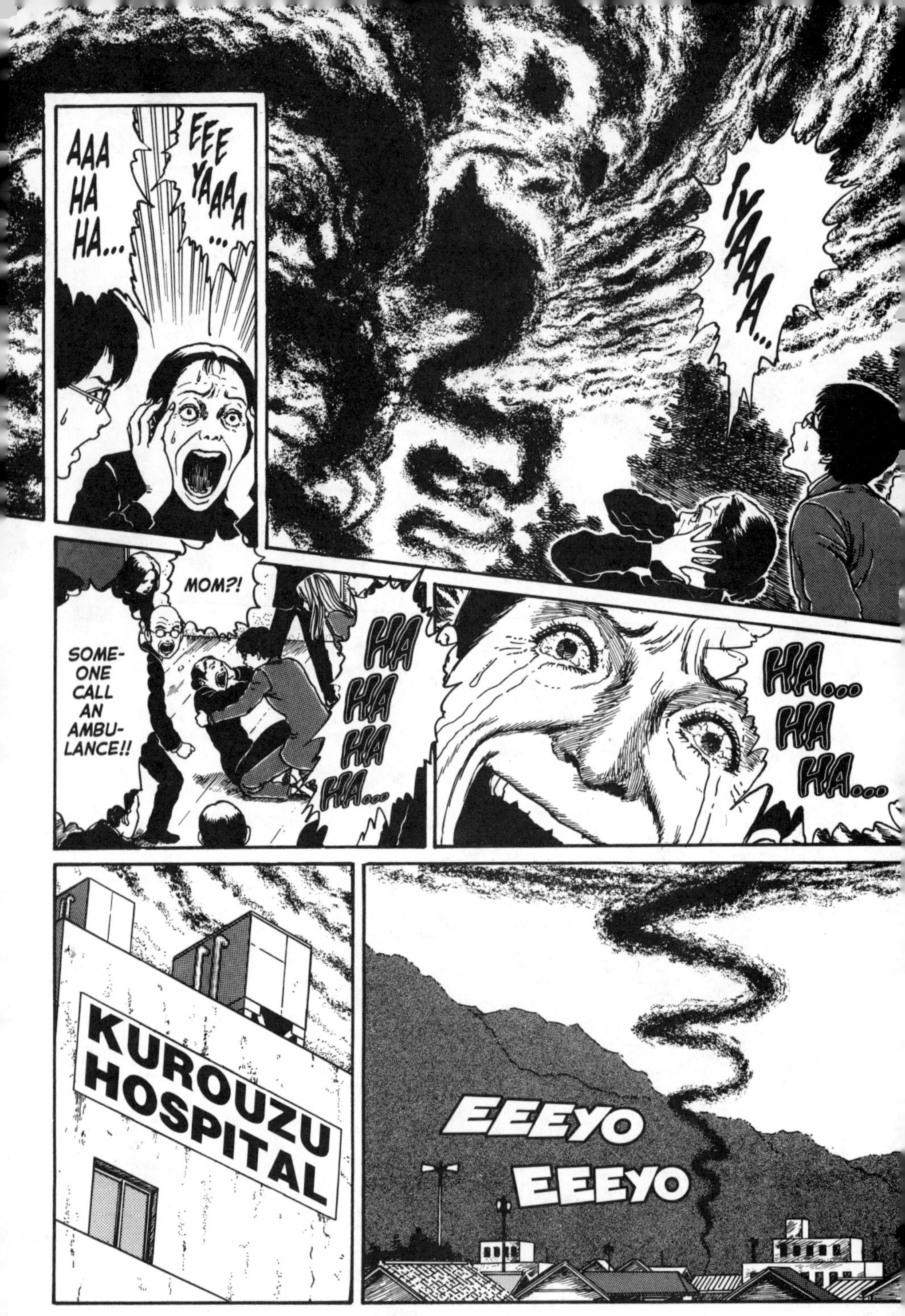
IYAAAA...
EEE YAAAA...
AAA HA HA...
HA... HA HA...
HA HA HA HA HA...
MOM?!
SOME-ONE CALL AN AMBU-LANCE!!
EEEyo
EEEyo
KUROUZU HOSPITAL

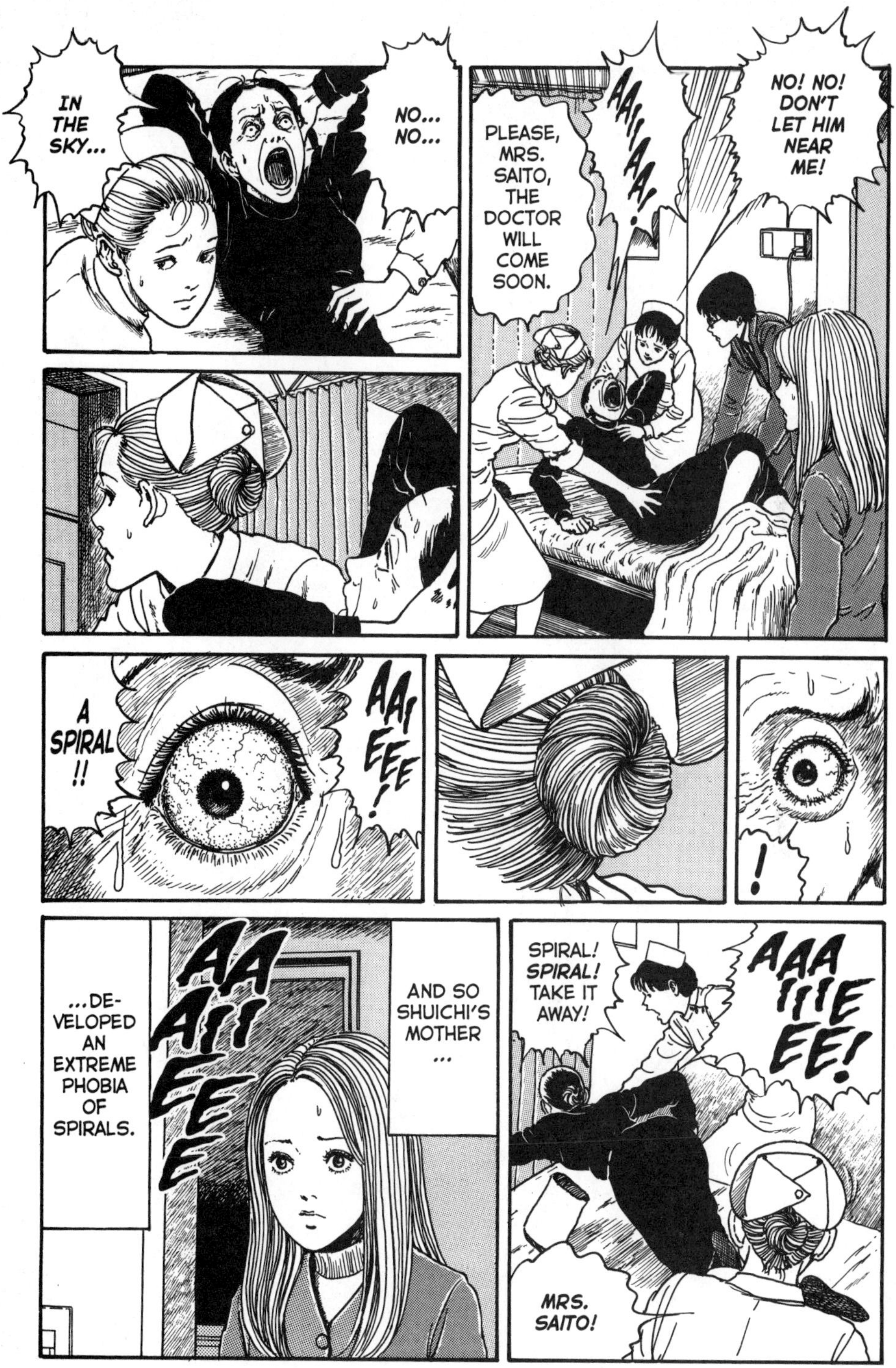

NO! NO! DON'T LET HIM NEAR ME!
AAIIIAAA!
PLEASE, MRS. SAITO, THE DOCTOR WILL COME SOON.
NO... NO...
IN THE SKY...
!
AAIEEE!
A SPIRAL !!
AAAIIIEEEE!
SPIRAL! SPIRAL! TAKE IT AWAY!
MRS. SAITO!
AND SO SHUICHI'S MOTHER ...
AAAIIEEEE
...DEVELOPED AN EXTREME PHOBIA OF SPIRALS.

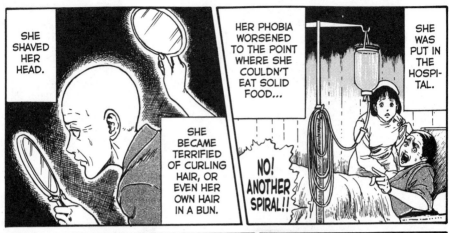

SHE WAS PUT IN THE HOSPITAL.
HER PHOBIA WORSENED TO THE POINT WHERE SHE COULDN'T EAT SOLID FOOD...
NO! ANOTHER SPIRAL!!
SHE SHAVED HER HEAD.
SHE BECAME TERRIFIED OF CURLING HAIR, OR EVEN HER OWN HAIR IN A BUN.
AND THEN...
NO!
...AS SOON AS SHE SAW HER FINGER-PRINTS HAD SPIRALS...
SNPP
...SHE CUT THE SKIN FROM HER FINGERS AND TOES!

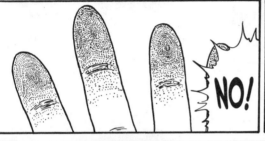

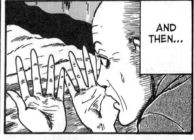

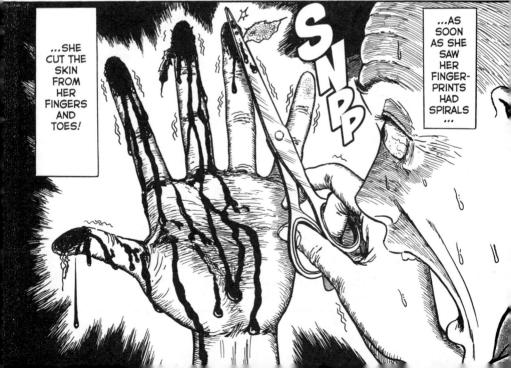

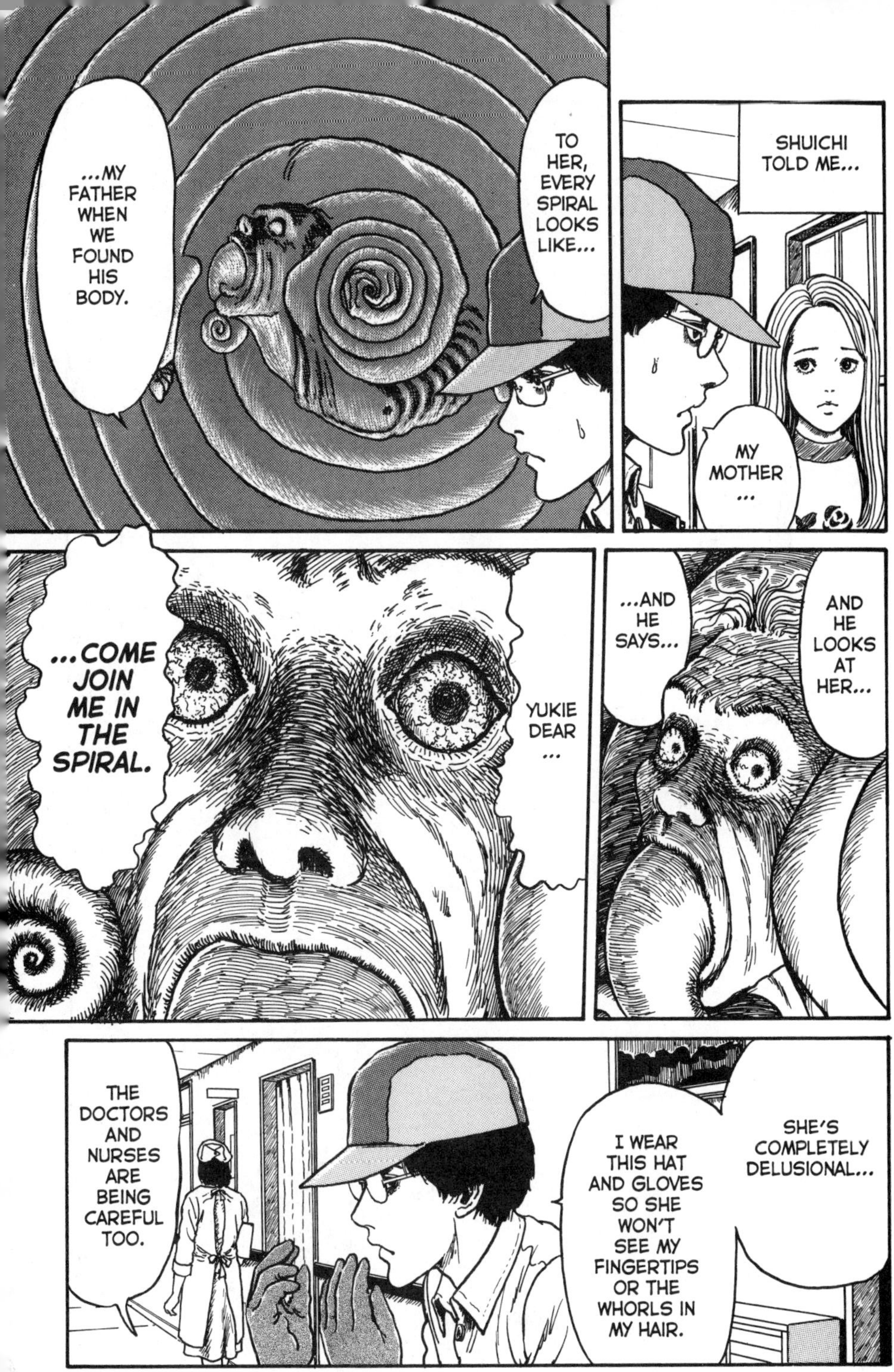
SHUICHI TOLD ME...
MY MOTHER ...
TO HER, EVERY SPIRAL LOOKS LIKE...
...MY FATHER WHEN WE FOUND HIS BODY.
AND HE LOOKS AT HER...
...AND HE SAYS...
YUKIE DEAR ...
...COME JOIN ME IN THE SPIRAL.
SHE'S COMPLETELY DELUSIONAL...
I WEAR THIS HAT AND GLOVES SO SHE WON'T SEE MY FINGERTIPS OR THE WHORLS IN MY HAIR.
THE DOCTORS AND NURSES ARE BEING CAREFUL TOO.

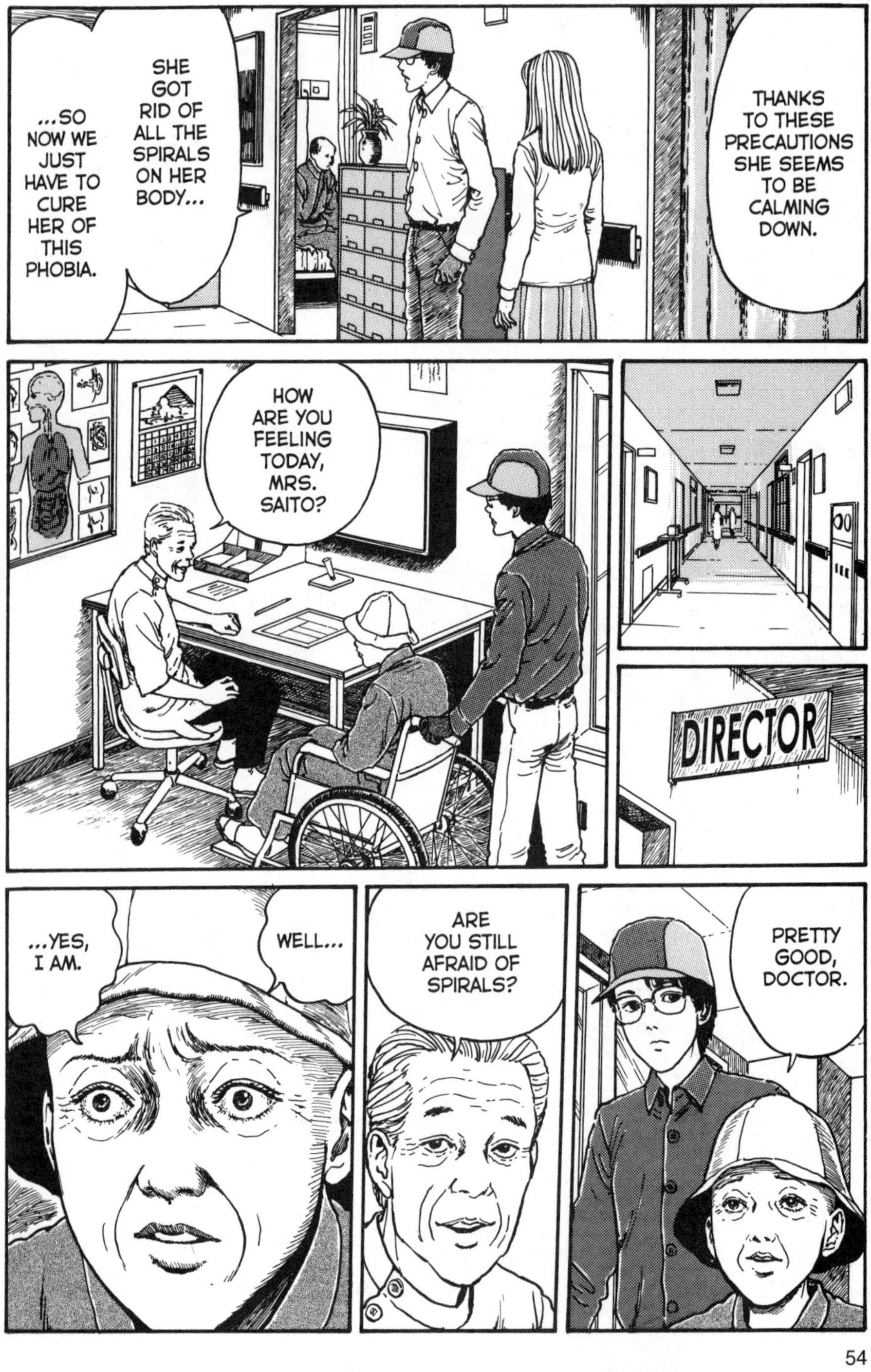
THANKS TO THESE PRECAUTIONS SHE SEEMS TO BE CALMING DOWN.
SHE GOT RID OF ALL THE SPIRALS ON HER BODY...
...SO NOW WE JUST HAVE TO CURE HER OF THIS PHOBIA.
DIRECTOR
HOW ARE YOU FEELING TODAY, MRS. SAITO?
PRETTY GOOD, DOCTOR.
ARE YOU STILL AFRAID OF SPIRALS?
WELL...
...YES, I AM.

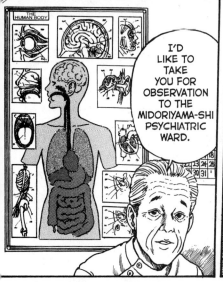

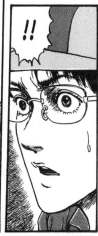

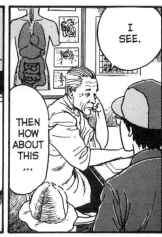

I SEE.
THEN HOW ABOUT THIS ...
!!
THE HUMAN BODY
I'D LIKE TO TAKE YOU FOR OBSERVATION TO THE MIDORIYAMA-SHI PSYCHIATRIC WARD.
I-I DON'T KNOW ABOUT THAT...
SHUICHI ...?
IS SOMETHING WRONG? I HIGHLY RECOMMEND THEM.
YOU SHOULDN'T BE AFRAID OF THE STIGMA OF STAYING AT A PSYCHIATRIC WARD.
THERE'S ABSOLUTELY NOTHING TO FEAR.
CRANIAL NERVES
SEMICIRCULAR CANALS
OSSICLES
COCHLEA
MIDDLE EAR CAVITY
EARDRUM

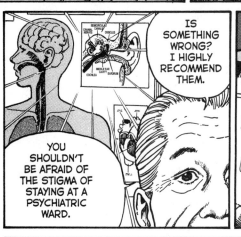

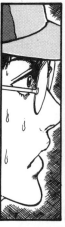

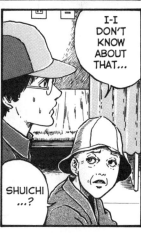

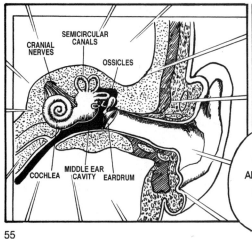

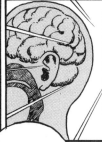

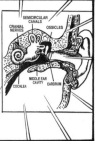

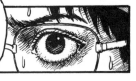

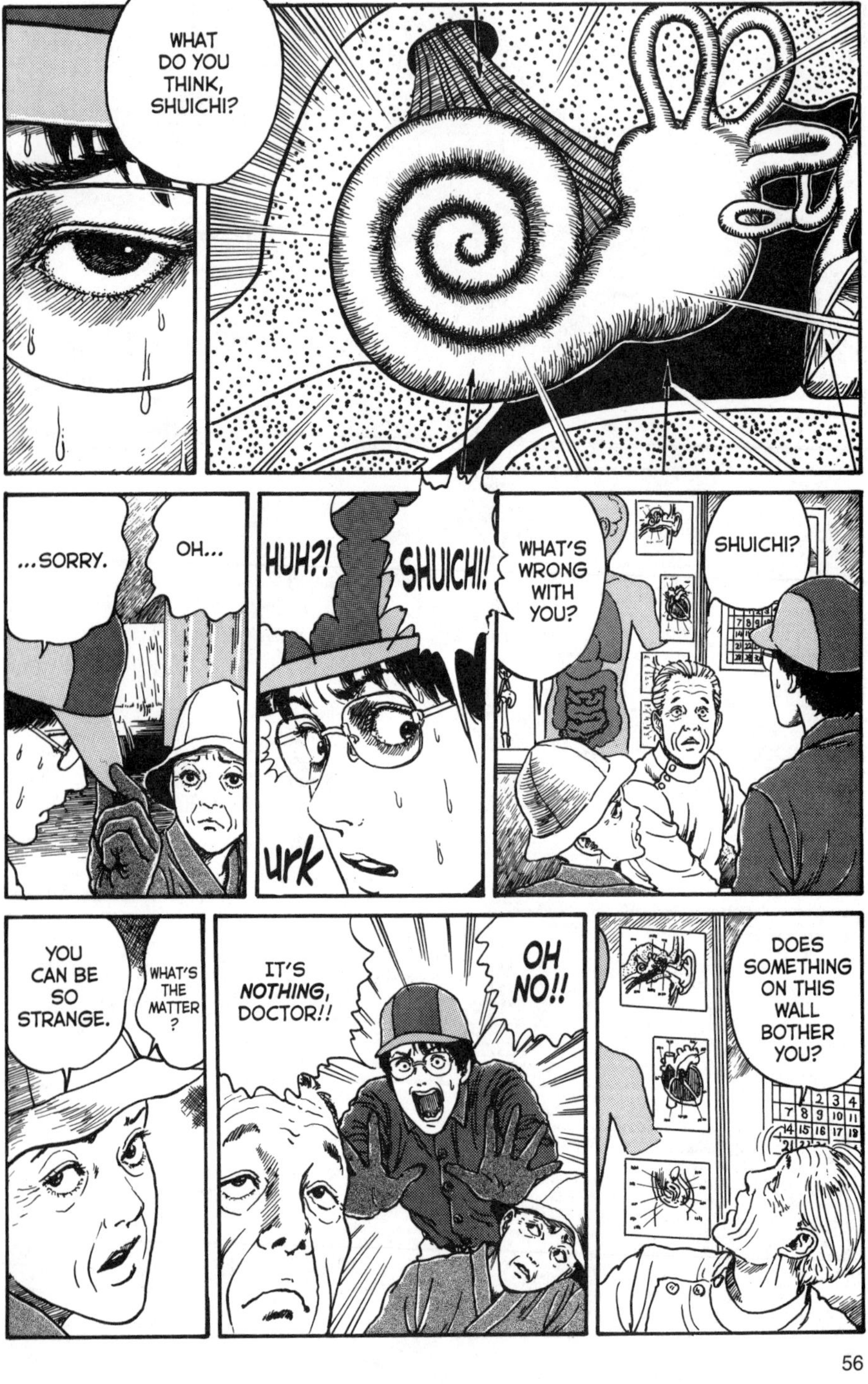
WHAT DO YOU THINK, SHUICHI?
SHUICHI?
WHAT'S WRONG WITH YOU?
SHUICHI!
HUH?!
urk
OH...
...SORRY.
DOES SOMETHING ON THIS WALL BOTHER YOU?
OH NO!!
IT'S *NOTHING*, DOCTOR!!
WHAT'S THE MATTER?
YOU CAN BE SO STRANGE.

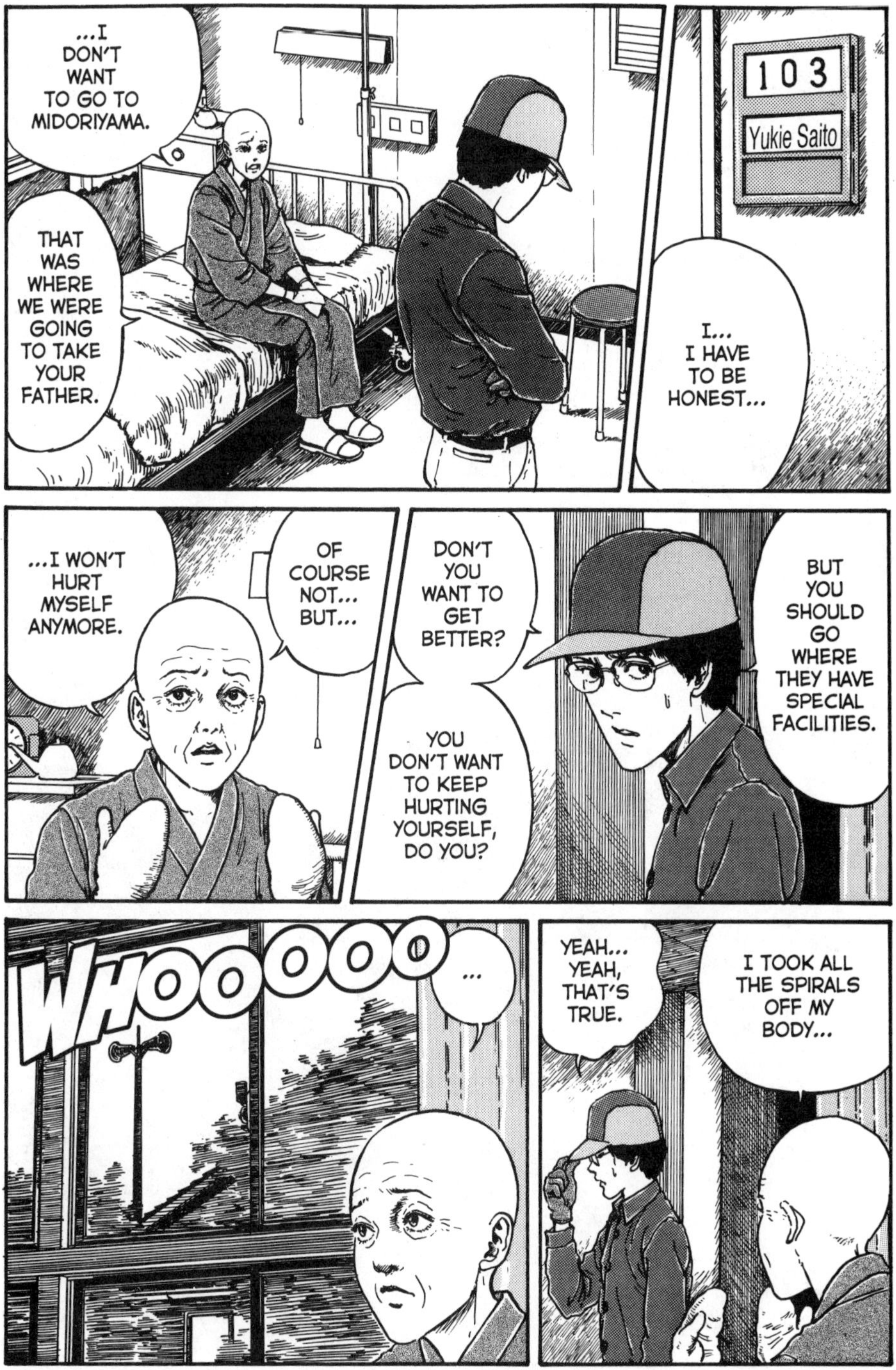
103
Yukie Saito
I... I HAVE TO BE HONEST...
...I DON'T WANT TO GO TO MIDORIYAMA.
THAT WAS WHERE WE WERE GOING TO TAKE YOUR FATHER.
BUT YOU SHOULD GO WHERE THEY HAVE SPECIAL FACILITIES.
DON'T YOU WANT TO GET BETTER?
YOU DON'T WANT TO KEEP HURTING YOURSELF, DO YOU?
OF COURSE NOT... BUT...
...I WON'T HURT MYSELF ANYMORE.
I TOOK ALL THE SPIRALS OFF MY BODY...
YEAH... YEAH, THAT'S TRUE.
WHOOOOOO
...

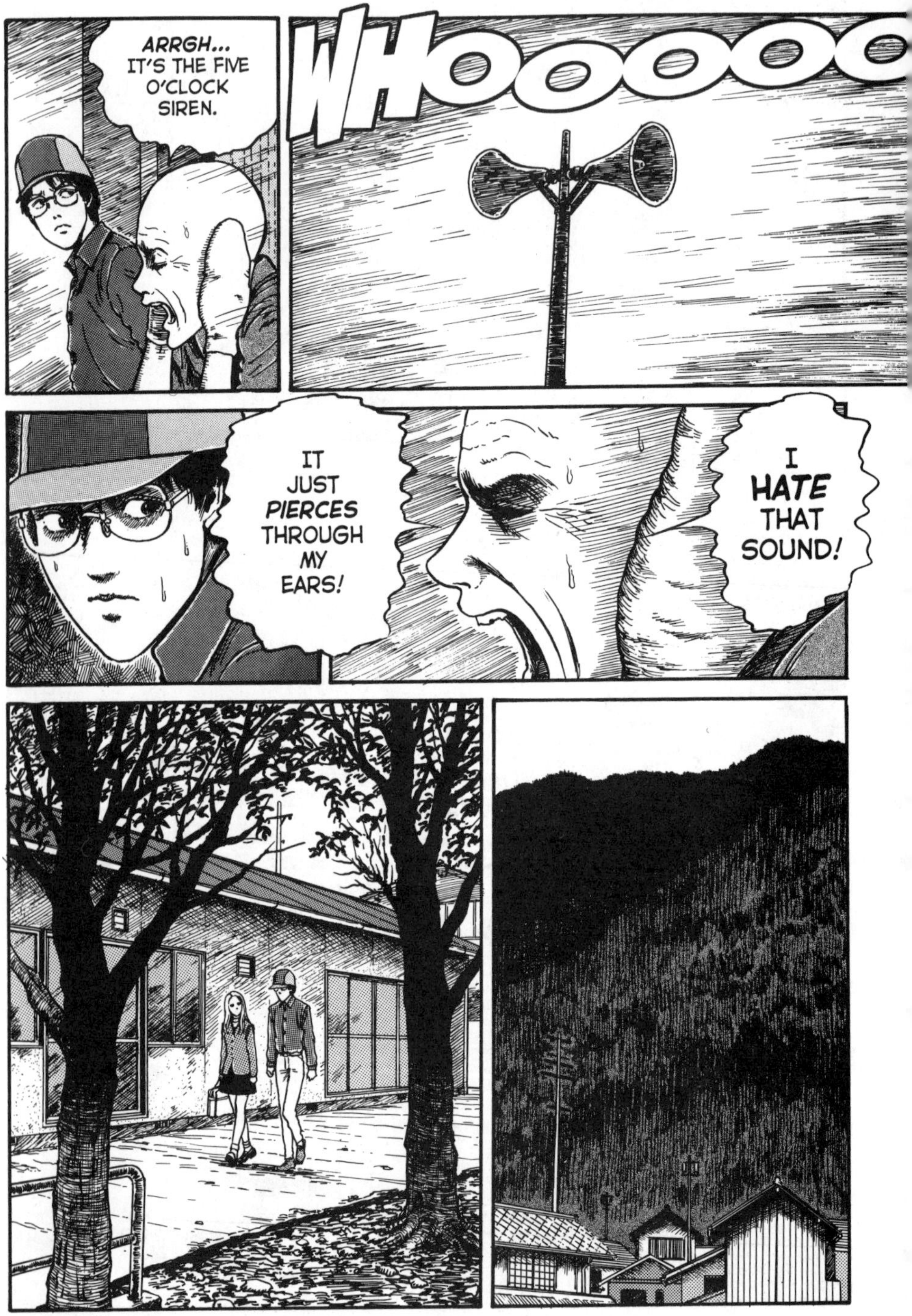
WHOOOOOO
ARRGH... IT'S THE FIVE O'CLOCK SIREN.
I HATE THAT SOUND!
IT JUST PIERCES THROUGH MY EARS!

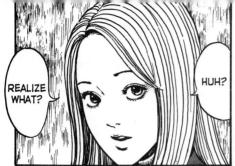

KIRIE...
...MY MOTHER DOESN'T REALIZE...
...AND HOPEFULLY SHE NEVER WILL.
HUH?
REALIZE WHAT?
I THOUGHT THAT THE HAIR AND THE FINGERPRINTS WERE THE ONLY SPIRALS ON THE HUMAN BODY...
BUT THERE'S MORE.
THERE'S THE SENSOR FOR SOUND, THE COCHLEA IN THE INNER EAR.
I SAW IT ON THE ANATOMICAL CHART IN THE DIRECTOR'S OFFICE.
SAAAA
IT'S PROBABLY THE MOST OBVIOUS SPIRAL IN THE HUMAN BODY.
WHAT WILL SHE DO IF SHE FINDS OUT THERE'S A SPIRAL *INSIDE* HER?
NO ONE CAN TELL... BUT SHE CUT OFF THE TIPS OF HER FINGERS...
...

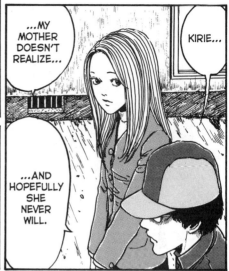

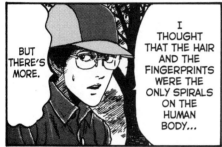

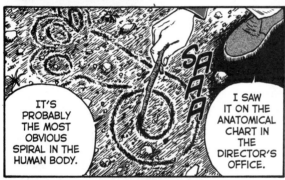

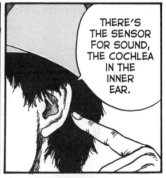

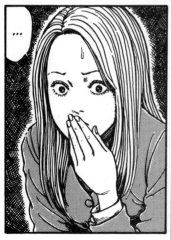

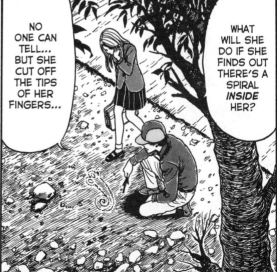

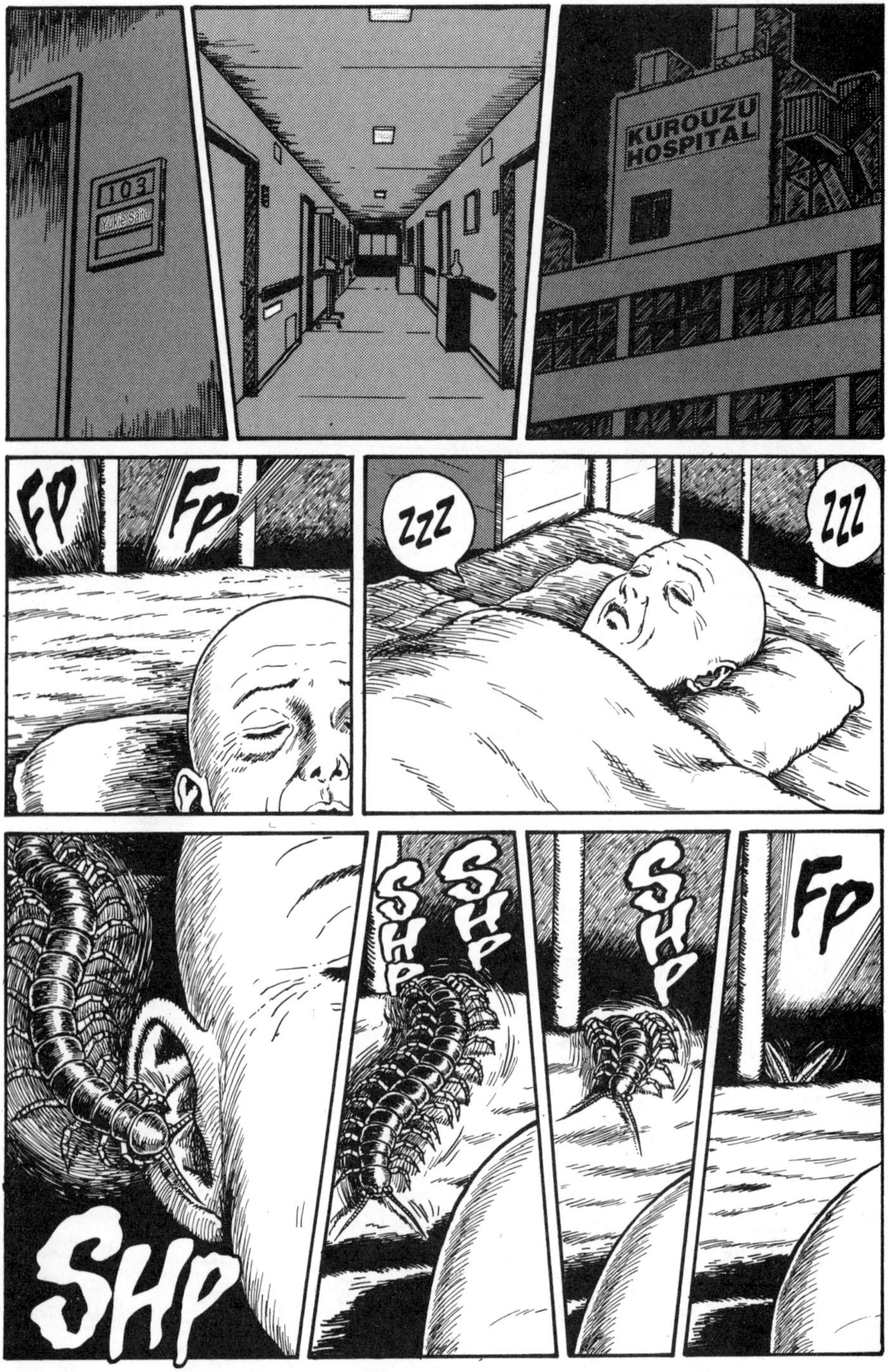
KUROUZU HOSPITAL
103
Yukie Saito
ZZZ
ZZZ
Fp
Fp
Fp
SHP
SHP
SHP
SHP

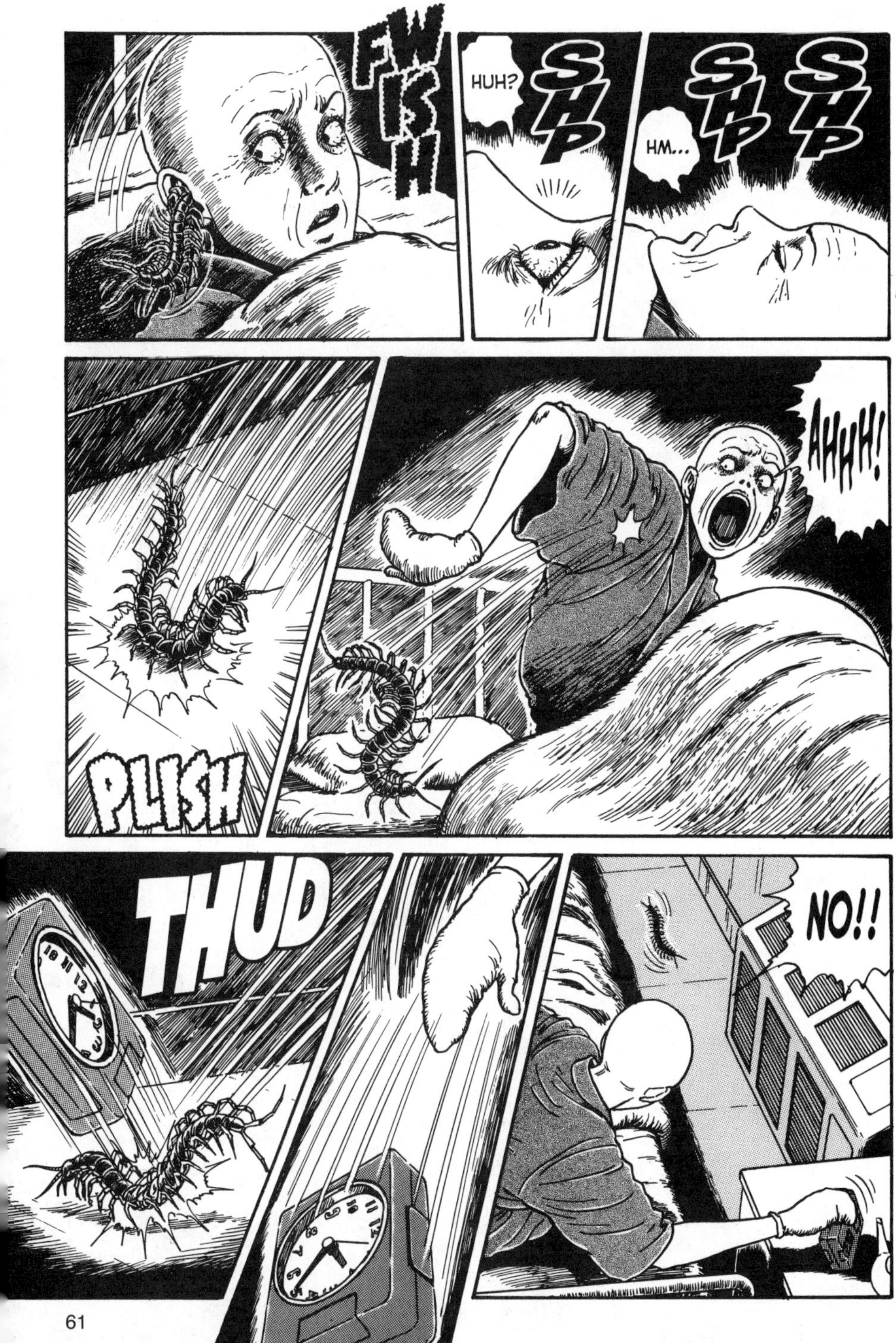
SHP
SHP
HM...
SHP
HUH?
FWISH
AHHH!
PLISH
NO!!
THUD

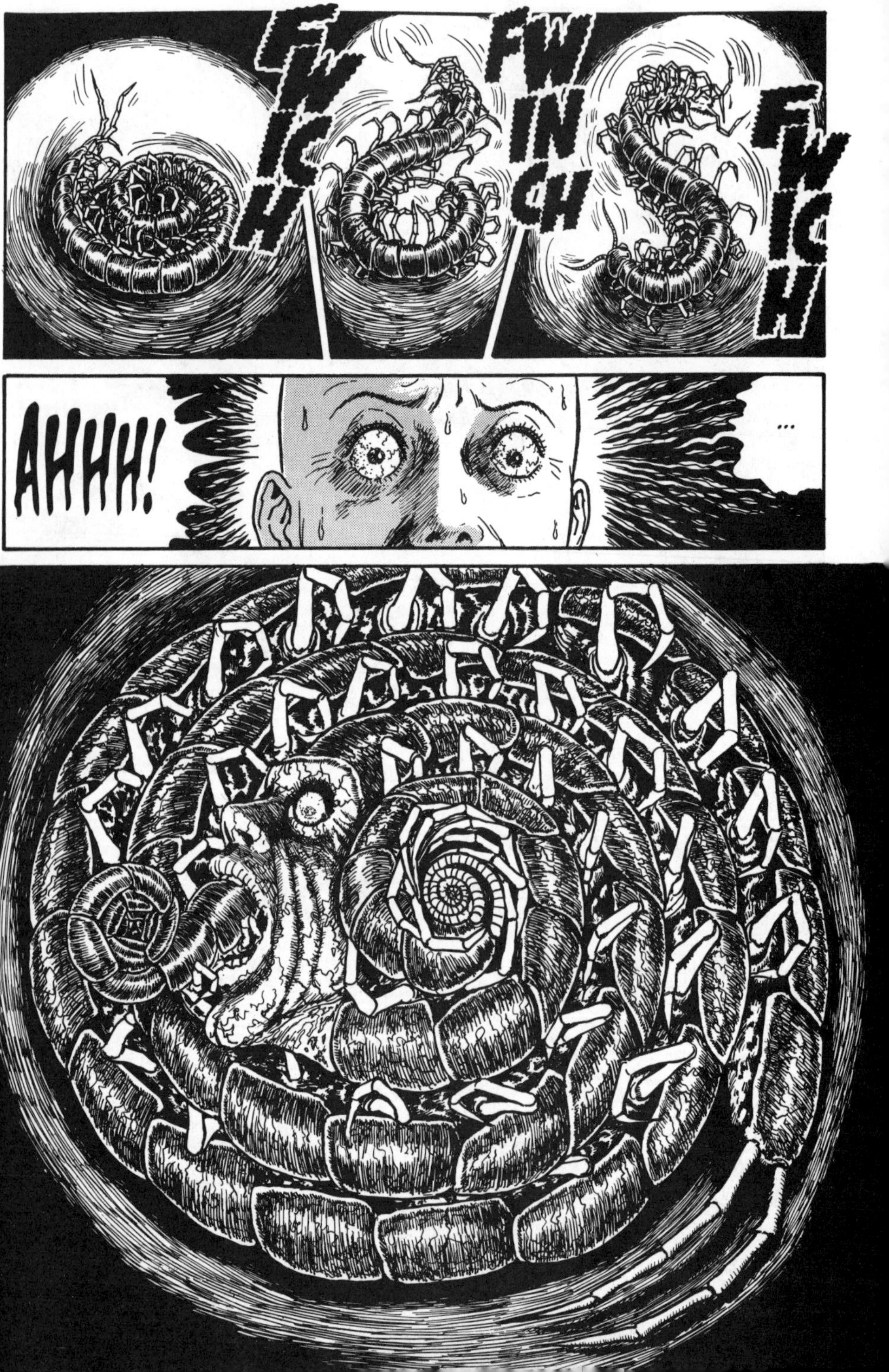
FWICH
FWINCH
FWICH
...
AHHH!

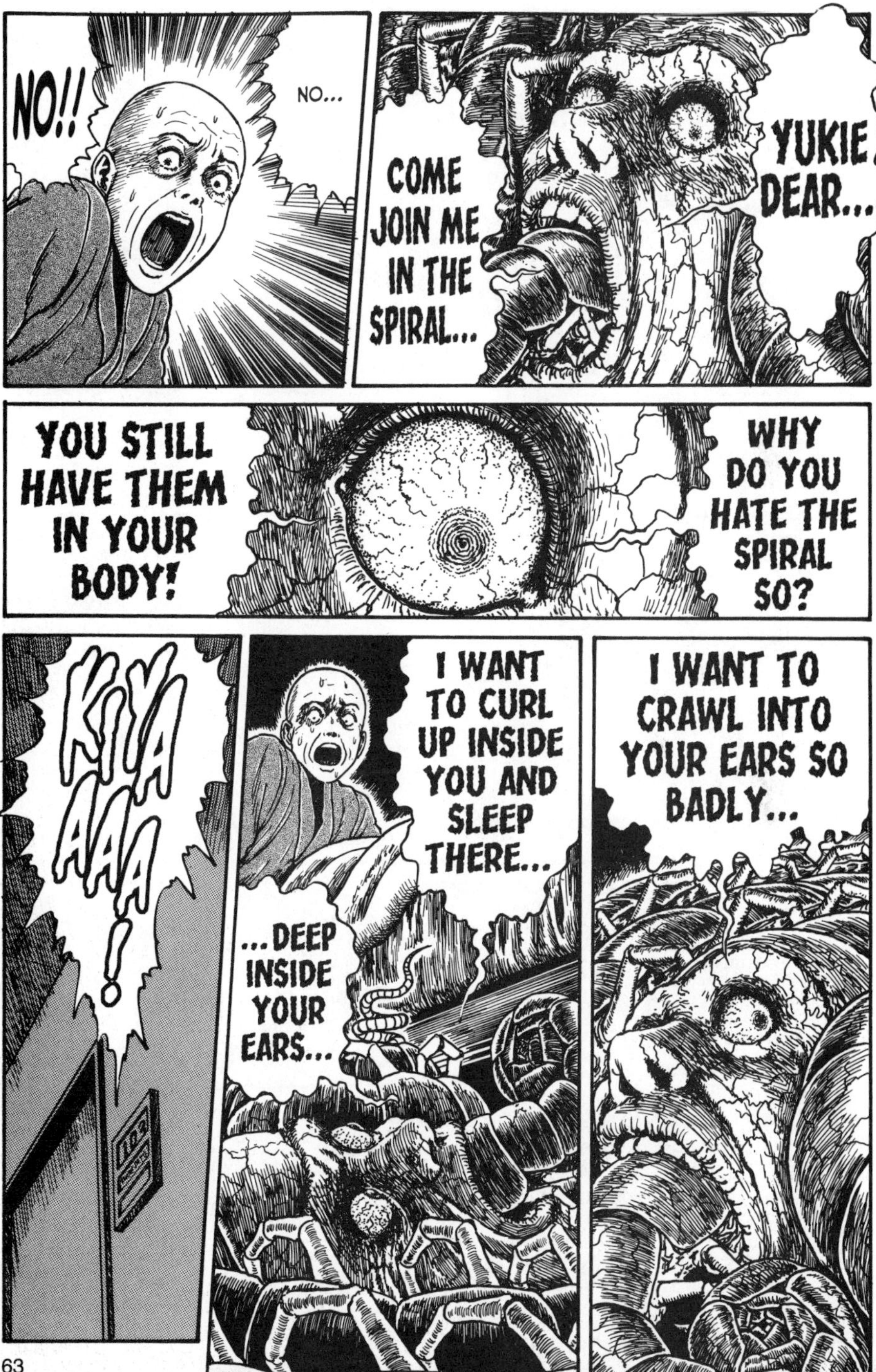
YUKIE DEAR...
COME JOIN ME IN THE SPIRAL...
NO!!
NO...
WHY DO YOU HATE THE SPIRAL SO?
YOU STILL HAVE THEM IN YOUR BODY!
I WANT TO CRAWL INTO YOUR EARS SO BADLY...
I WANT TO CURL UP INSIDE YOU AND SLEEP THERE...
...DEEP INSIDE YOUR EARS...
KIYAAAA!

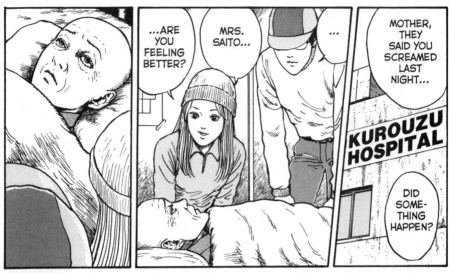

MOTHER, THEY SAID YOU SCREAMED LAST NIGHT...
KUROUZU HOSPITAL
DID SOME-THING HAPPEN?
...
MRS. SAITO...
...ARE YOU FEELING BETTER?
MRS. SAITO, IT'S TIME TO TAKE YOUR TEMPERA-TURE.
HOW ARE YOU FEELING?
I WAS WONDERING...
YES?
WHAT'S INSIDE...
...THE HUMAN EAR?
WHAT? THE EAR?
YES...

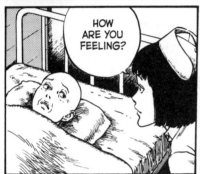

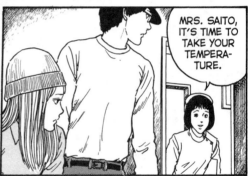

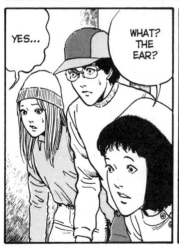

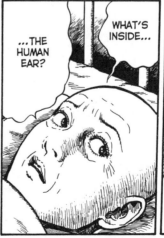

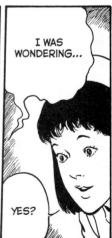

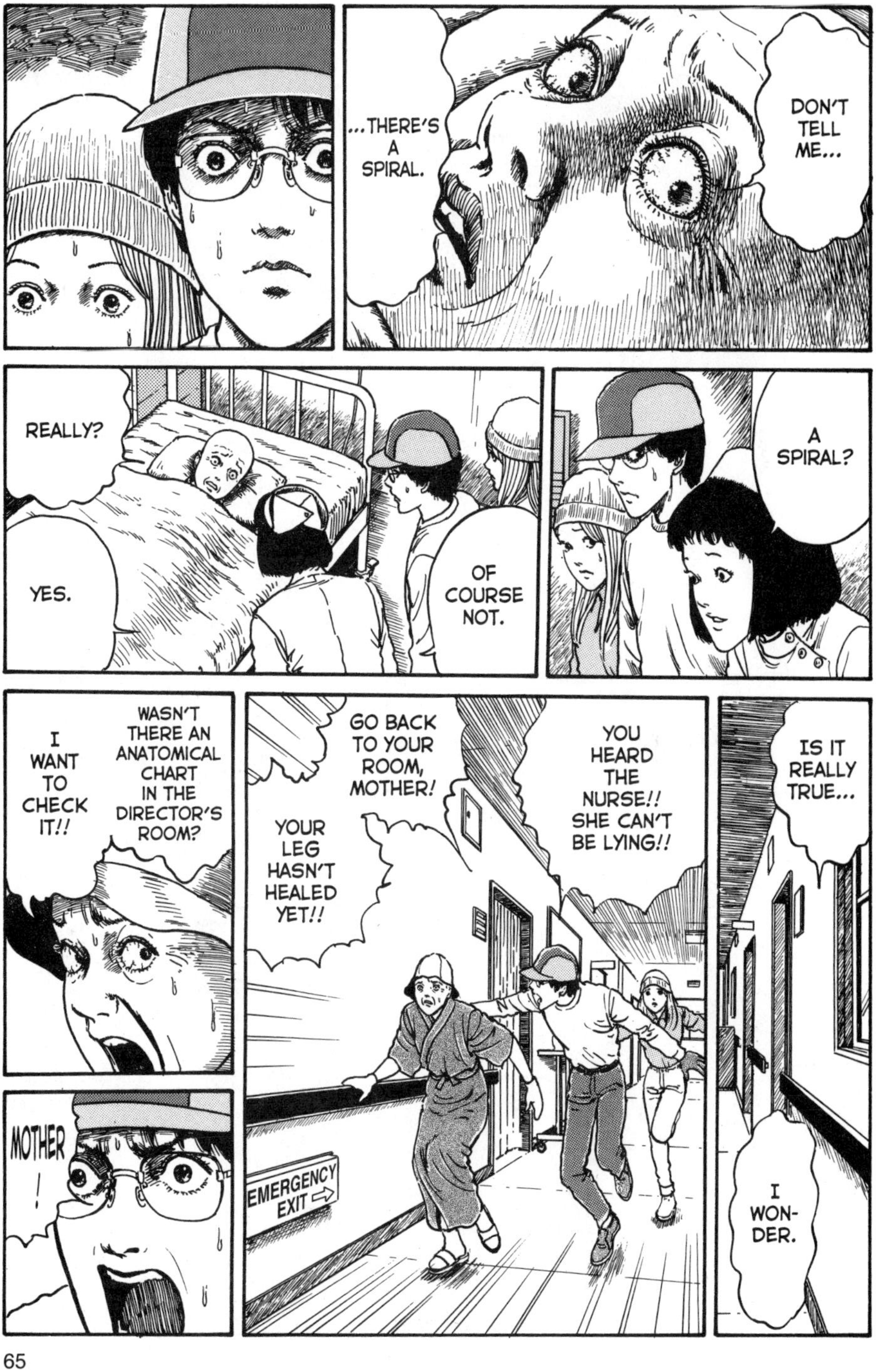
DON'T TELL ME...
...THERE'S A SPIRAL.
A SPIRAL?
REALLY?
YES.
OF COURSE NOT.
IS IT REALLY TRUE...
I WONDER.
YOU HEARD THE NURSE!! SHE CAN'T BE LYING!!
GO BACK TO YOUR ROOM, MOTHER!
YOUR LEG HASN'T HEALED YET!!
EMERGENCY EXIT
WASN'T THERE AN ANATOMICAL CHART IN THE DIRECTOR'S ROOM?
I WANT TO CHECK IT!!
MOTHER!

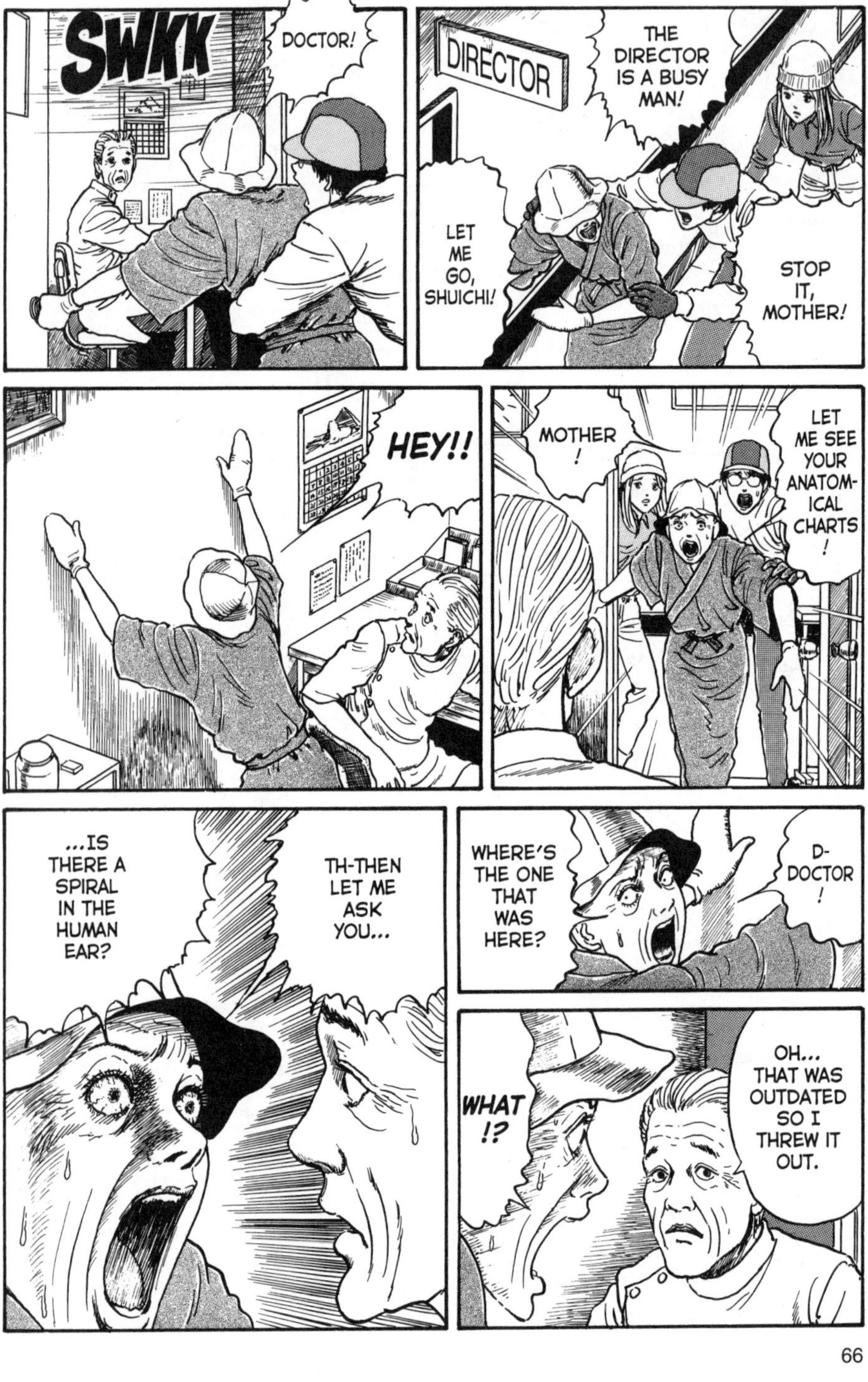
DIRECTOR
THE DIRECTOR IS A BUSY MAN!
STOP IT, MOTHER!
LET ME GO, SHUICHI!
DOCTOR!
SWKK
LET ME SEE YOUR ANATOM-ICAL CHARTS!
MOTHER!
HEY!!
D-DOCTOR!
WHERE'S THE ONE THAT WAS HERE?
OH... THAT WAS OUTDATED SO I THREW IT OUT.
WHAT!?
TH-THEN LET ME ASK YOU...
...IS THERE A SPIRAL IN THE HUMAN EAR?

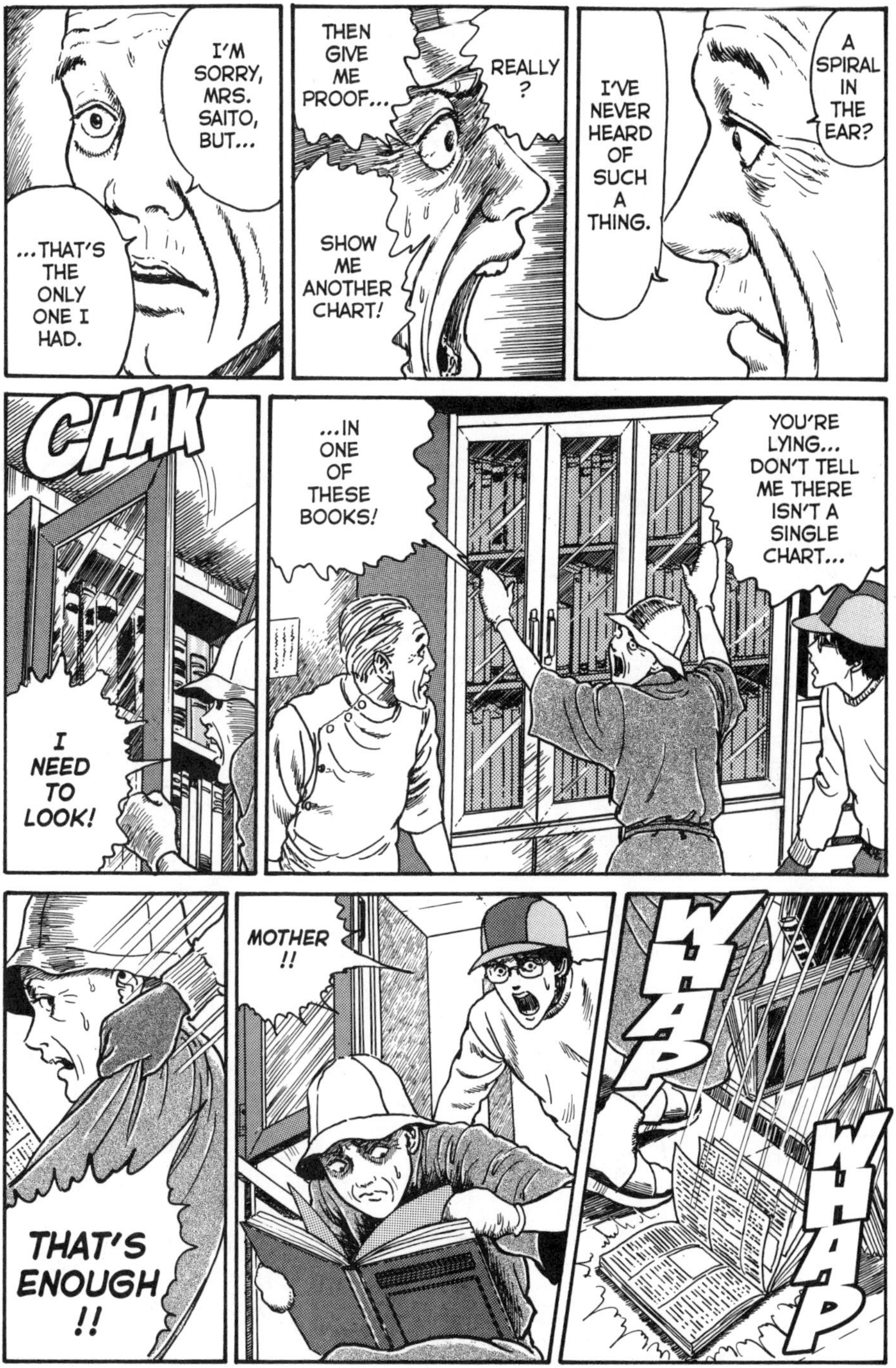
A SPIRAL IN THE EAR?
I'VE NEVER HEARD OF SUCH A THING.
REALLY?
THEN GIVE ME PROOF...
SHOW ME ANOTHER CHART!
I'M SORRY, MRS. SAITO, BUT...
...THAT'S THE ONLY ONE I HAD.
YOU'RE LYING... DON'T TELL ME THERE ISN'T A SINGLE CHART...
...IN ONE OF THESE BOOKS!
CHAK
I NEED TO LOOK!
WHAP
WHAP
MOTHER!!
THAT'S ENOUGH!!

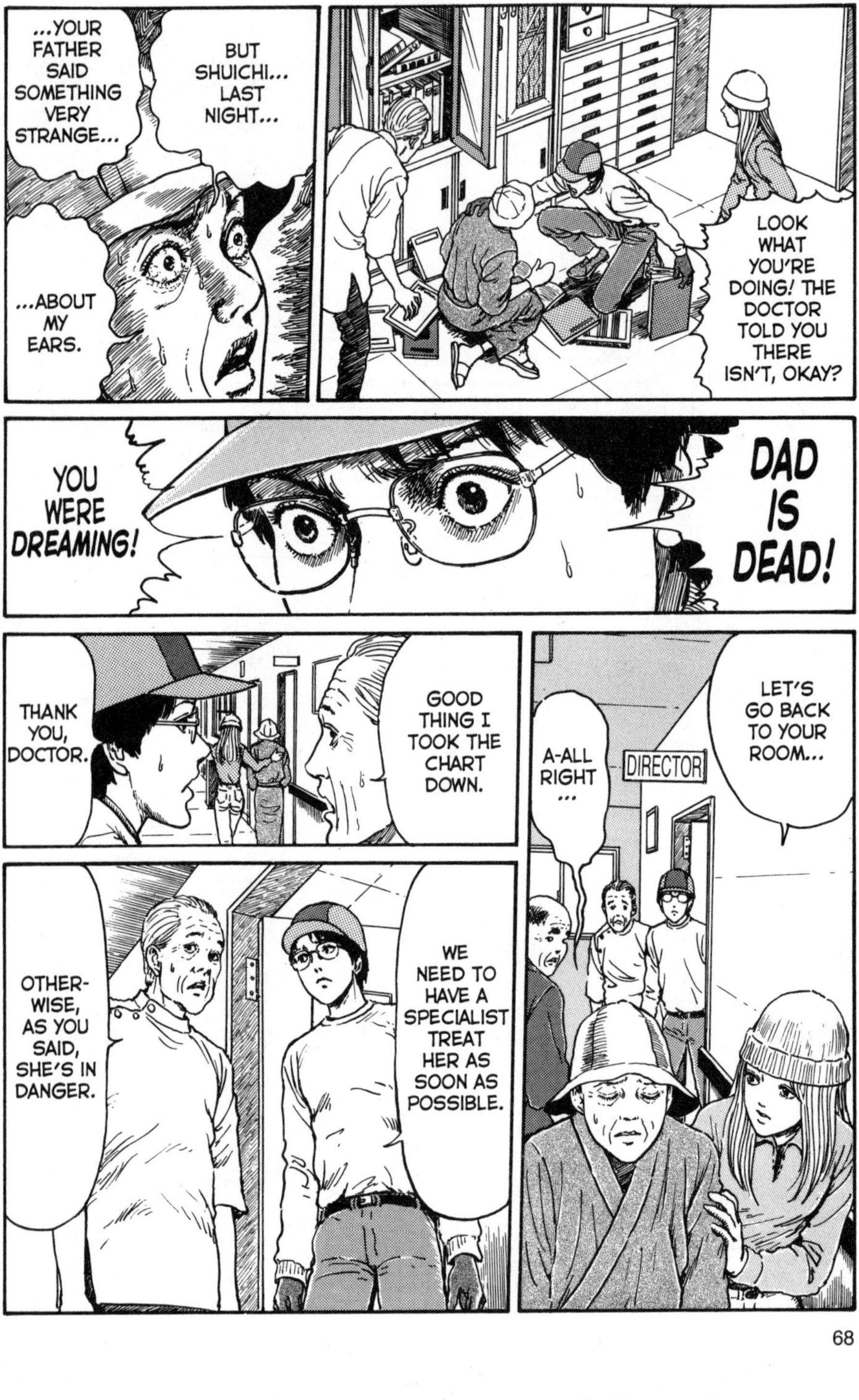
LOOK WHAT YOU'RE DOING! THE DOCTOR TOLD YOU THERE ISN'T, OKAY?
BUT SHUICHI... LAST NIGHT...
...YOUR FATHER SAID SOMETHING VERY STRANGE...
...ABOUT MY EARS.
DAD IS DEAD!
YOU WERE DREAMING!
LET'S GO BACK TO YOUR ROOM...
DIRECTOR
A-ALL RIGHT ...
GOOD THING I TOOK THE CHART DOWN.
THANK YOU, DOCTOR.
WE NEED TO HAVE A SPECIALIST TREAT HER AS SOON AS POSSIBLE.
OTHER-WISE, AS YOU SAID, SHE'S IN DANGER.

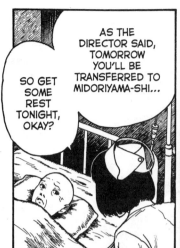

KUROUZU HOSPITAL
MRS. SAITO, THIS IS YOUR LAST NIGHT ON IV...
AS THE DIRECTOR SAID, TOMORROW YOU'LL BE TRANSFERRED TO MIDORIYAMA-SHI...
SO GET SOME REST TONIGHT, OKAY?
GOOD NIGHT.
THANK YOU... GOOD NIGHT.
CHUD
27

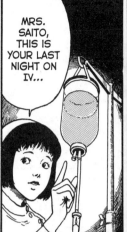

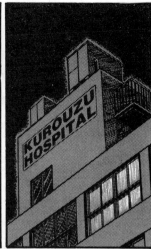

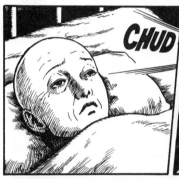

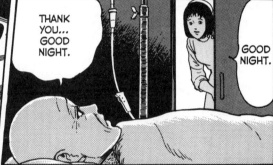

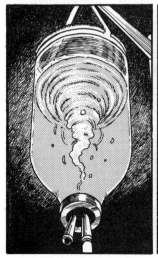

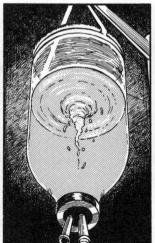

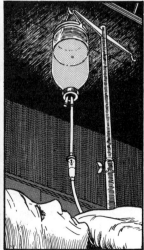

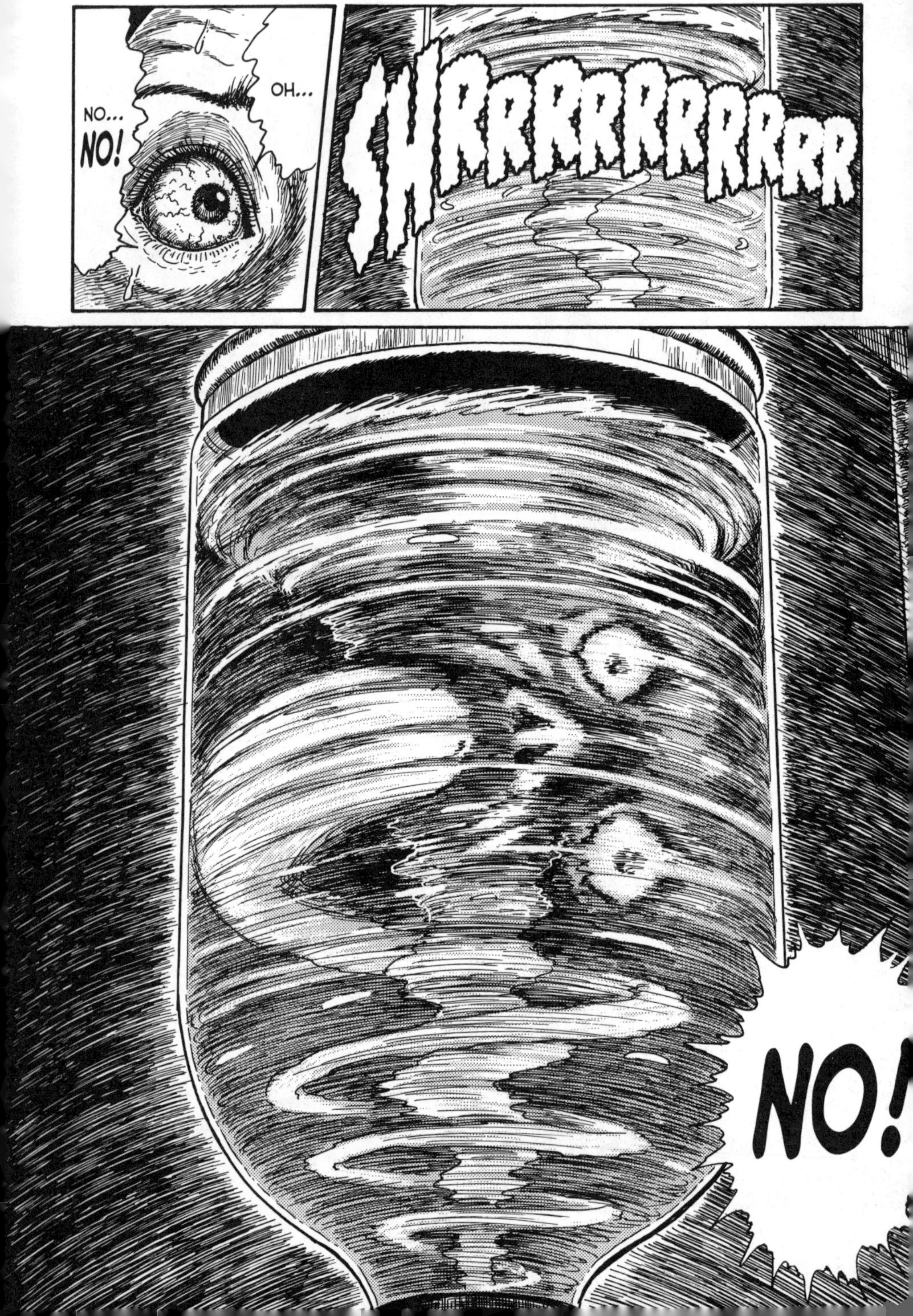
CHRRRRRRRRRR
OH...
NO...
NO!
NO!

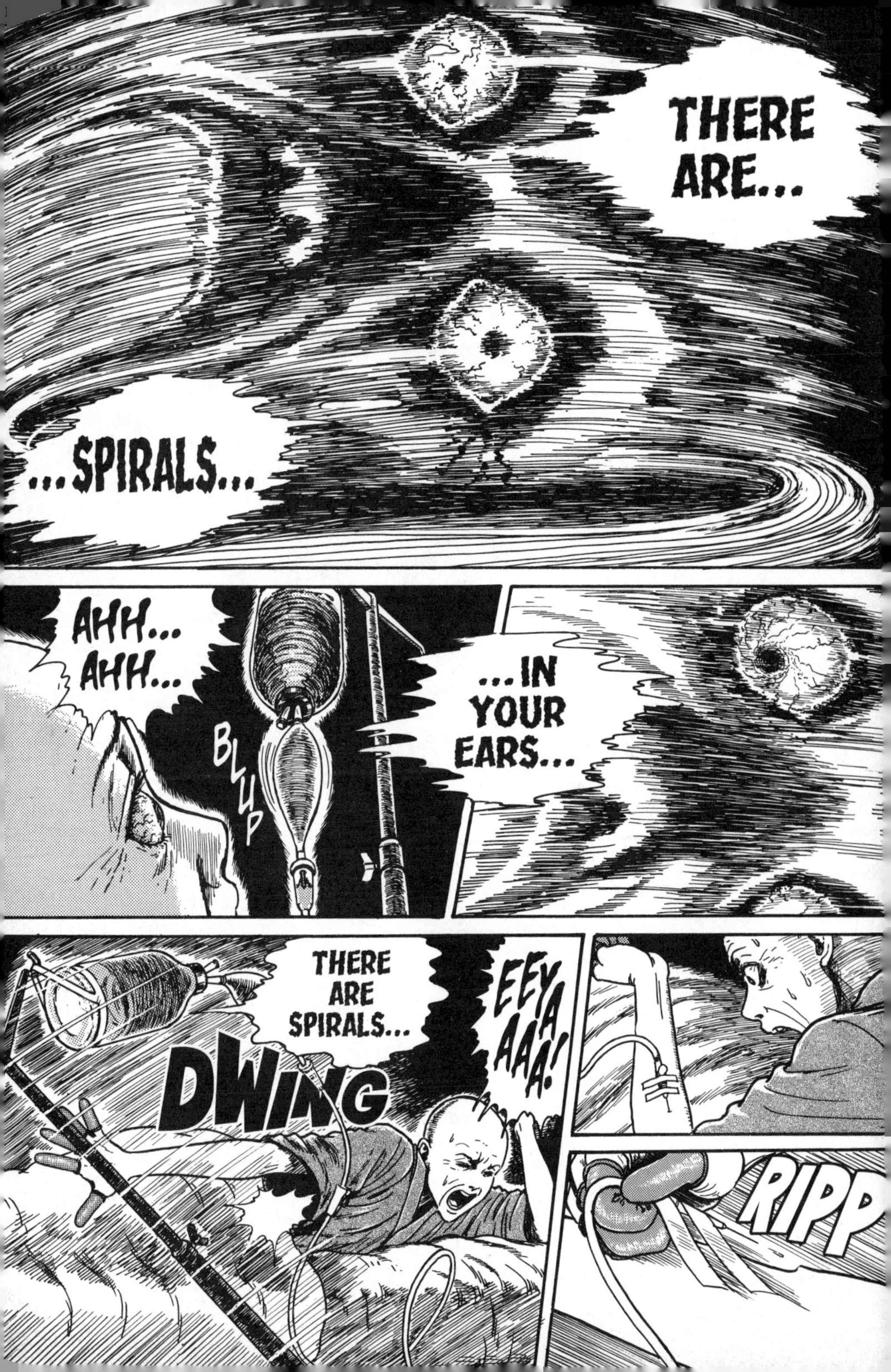
THERE ARE...
...SPIRALS...
...IN YOUR EARS...
AHH... AHH...
BLUP
RIPP
EEYAAAA!
THERE ARE SPIRALS...
DWING

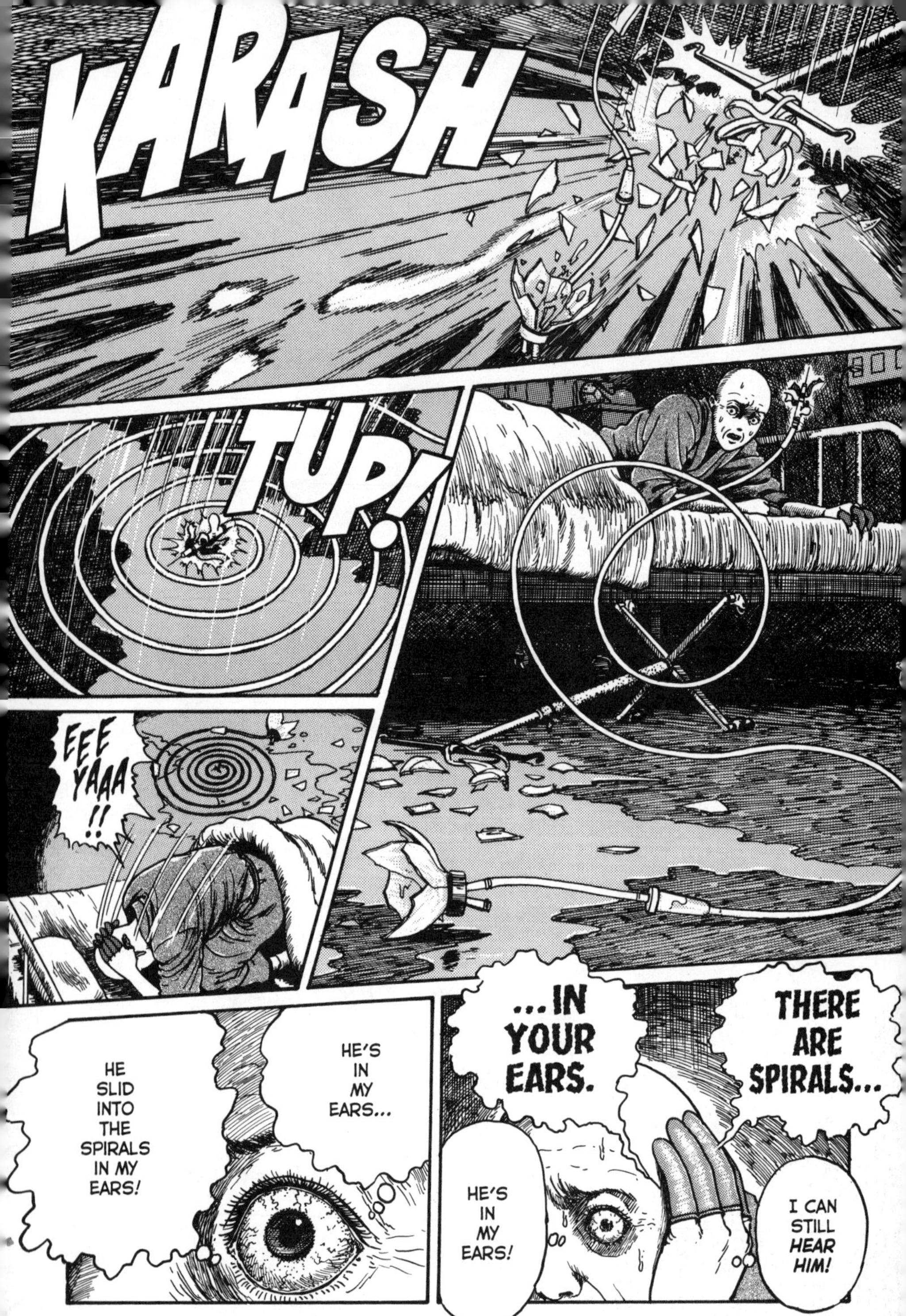
KARASH
TUP!
EEE YAAA!!
THERE ARE SPIRALS...
...IN YOUR EARS.
I CAN STILL HEAR HIM!
HE'S IN MY EARS!
HE'S IN MY EARS...
HE SLID INTO THE SPIRALS IN MY EARS!

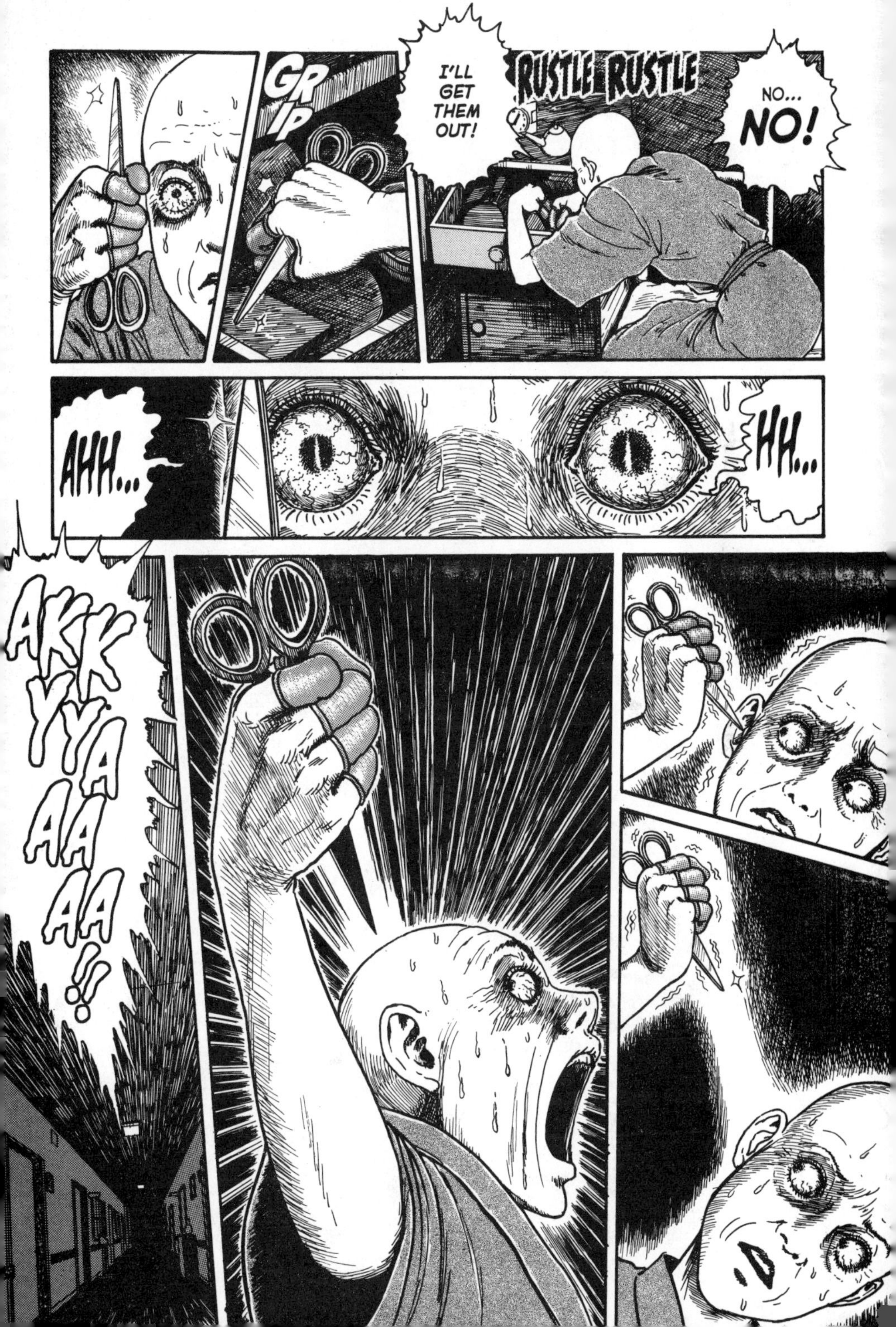
NO... NO!
RUSTLE RUSTLE
I'LL GET THEM OUT!
GRIP
HH...
AHH...
AKKYYAAAAAA!!!

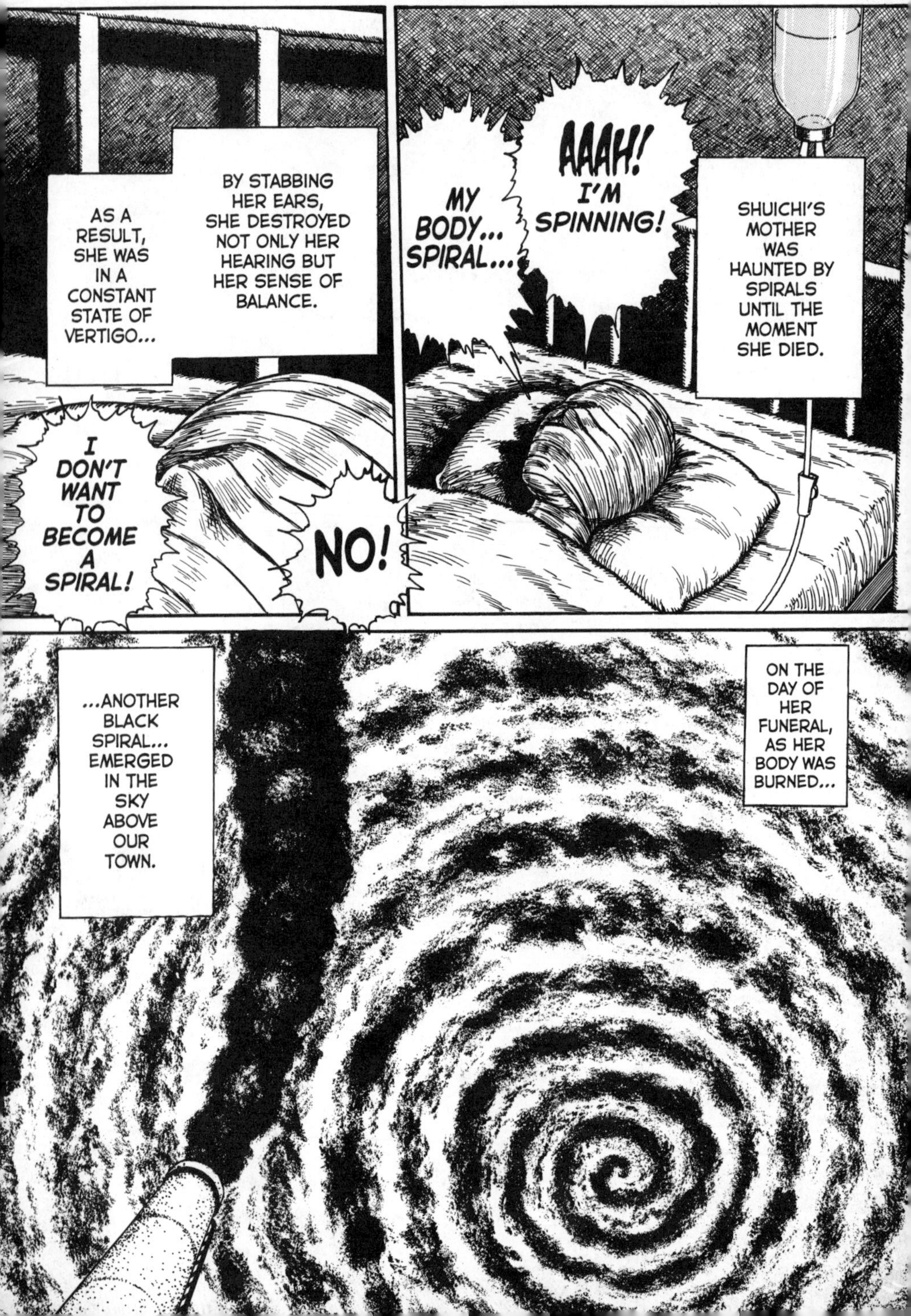

SHUICHI'S MOTHER WAS HAUNTED BY SPIRALS UNTIL THE MOMENT SHE DIED.
AAAH! I'M SPINNING!
MY BODY... SPIRAL...
BY STABBING HER EARS, SHE DESTROYED NOT ONLY HER HEARING BUT HER SENSE OF BALANCE.
AS A RESULT, SHE WAS IN A CONSTANT STATE OF VERTIGO...
NO!
I DON'T WANT TO BECOME A SPIRAL!
ON THE DAY OF HER FUNERAL, AS HER BODY WAS BURNED...
...ANOTHER BLACK SPIRAL... EMERGED IN THE SKY ABOVE OUR TOWN.

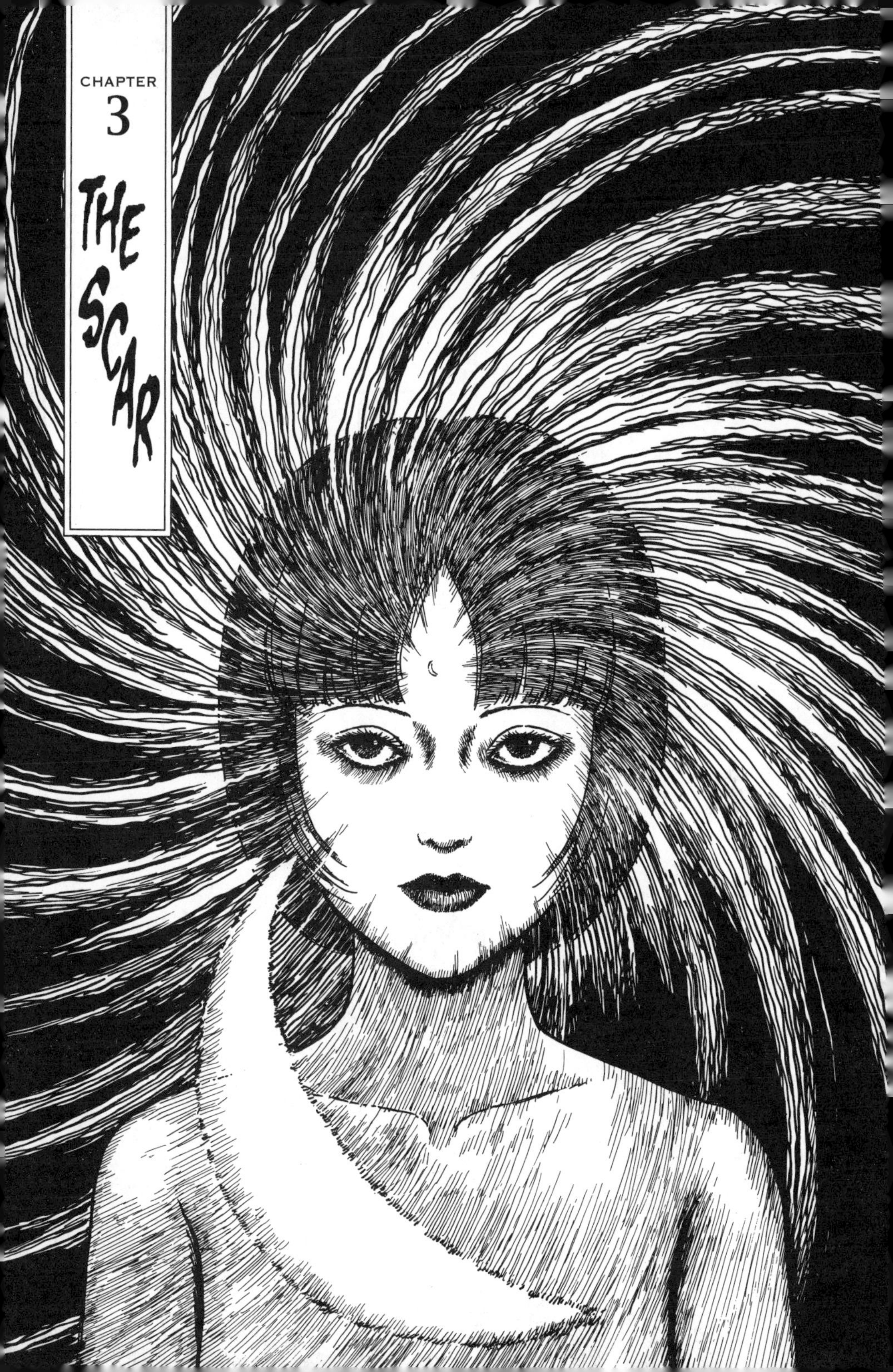
CHAPTER
3
THE SCAR

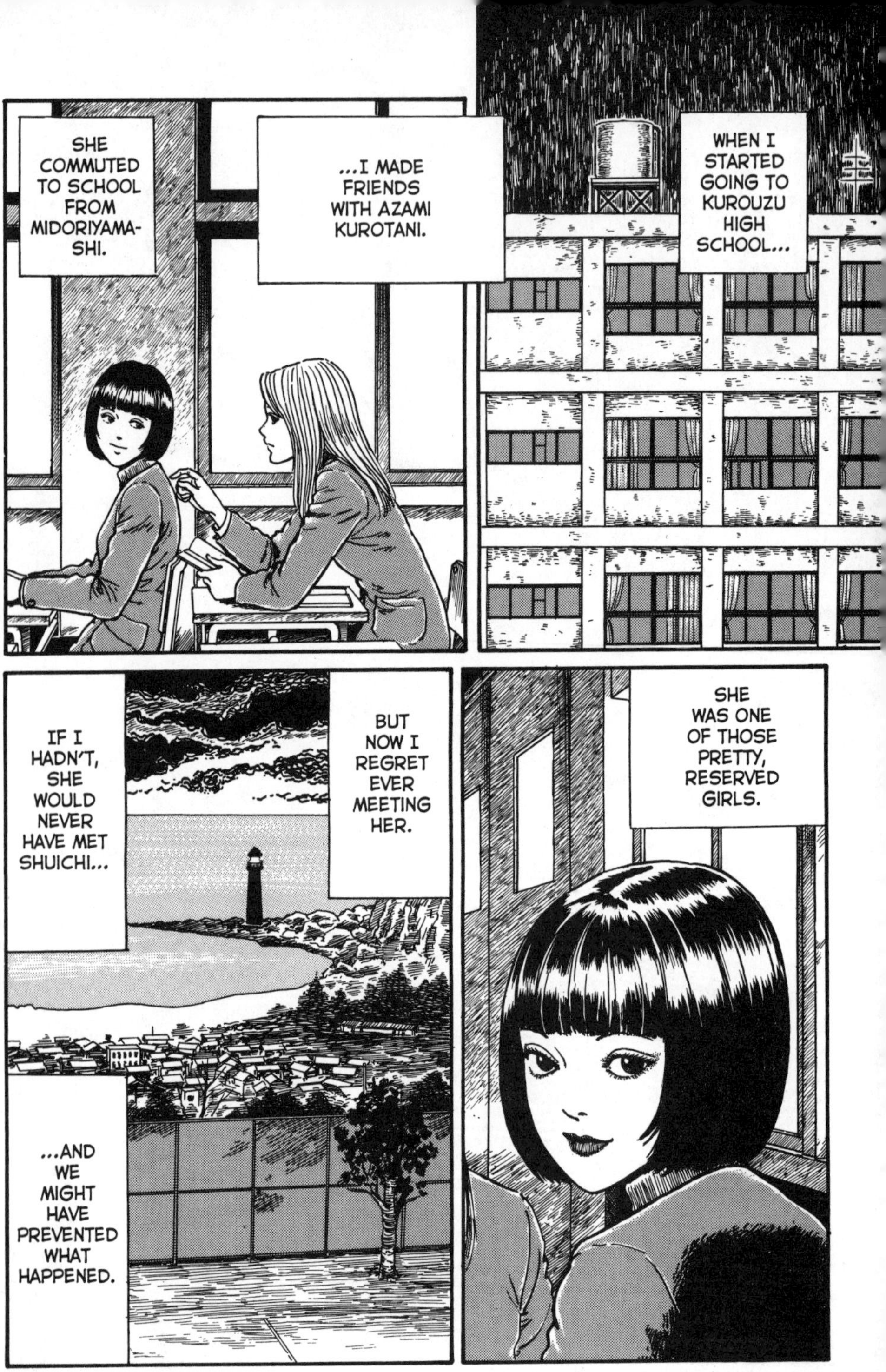
WHEN I STARTED GOING TO KUROUZU HIGH SCHOOL...
...I MADE FRIENDS WITH AZAMI KUROTANI.
SHE COMMUTED TO SCHOOL FROM MIDORIYAMA-SHI.
SHE WAS ONE OF THOSE PRETTY, RESERVED GIRLS.
BUT NOW I REGRET EVER MEETING HER.
IF I HADN'T, SHE WOULD NEVER HAVE MET SHUICHI...
...AND WE MIGHT HAVE PREVENTED WHAT HAPPENED.

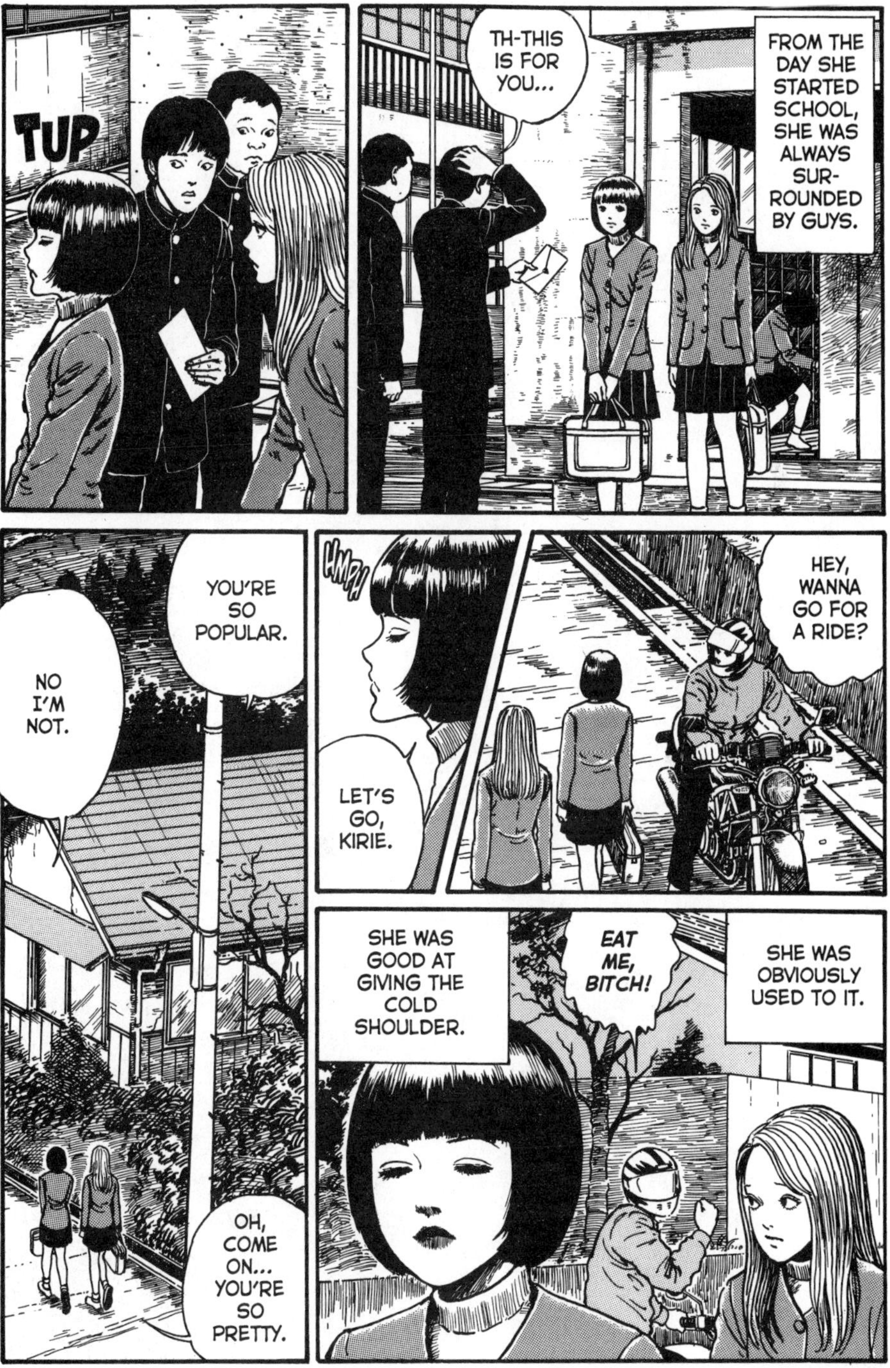
FROM THE DAY SHE STARTED SCHOOL, SHE WAS ALWAYS SUR-ROUNDED BY GUYS.
TH-THIS IS FOR YOU...
TUP
HEY, WANNA GO FOR A RIDE?
HMPH
LET'S GO, KIRIE.
SHE WAS OBVIOUSLY USED TO IT.
EAT ME, BITCH!
SHE WAS GOOD AT GIVING THE COLD SHOULDER.
YOU'RE SO POPULAR.
NO I'M NOT.
OH, COME ON... YOU'RE SO PRETTY.

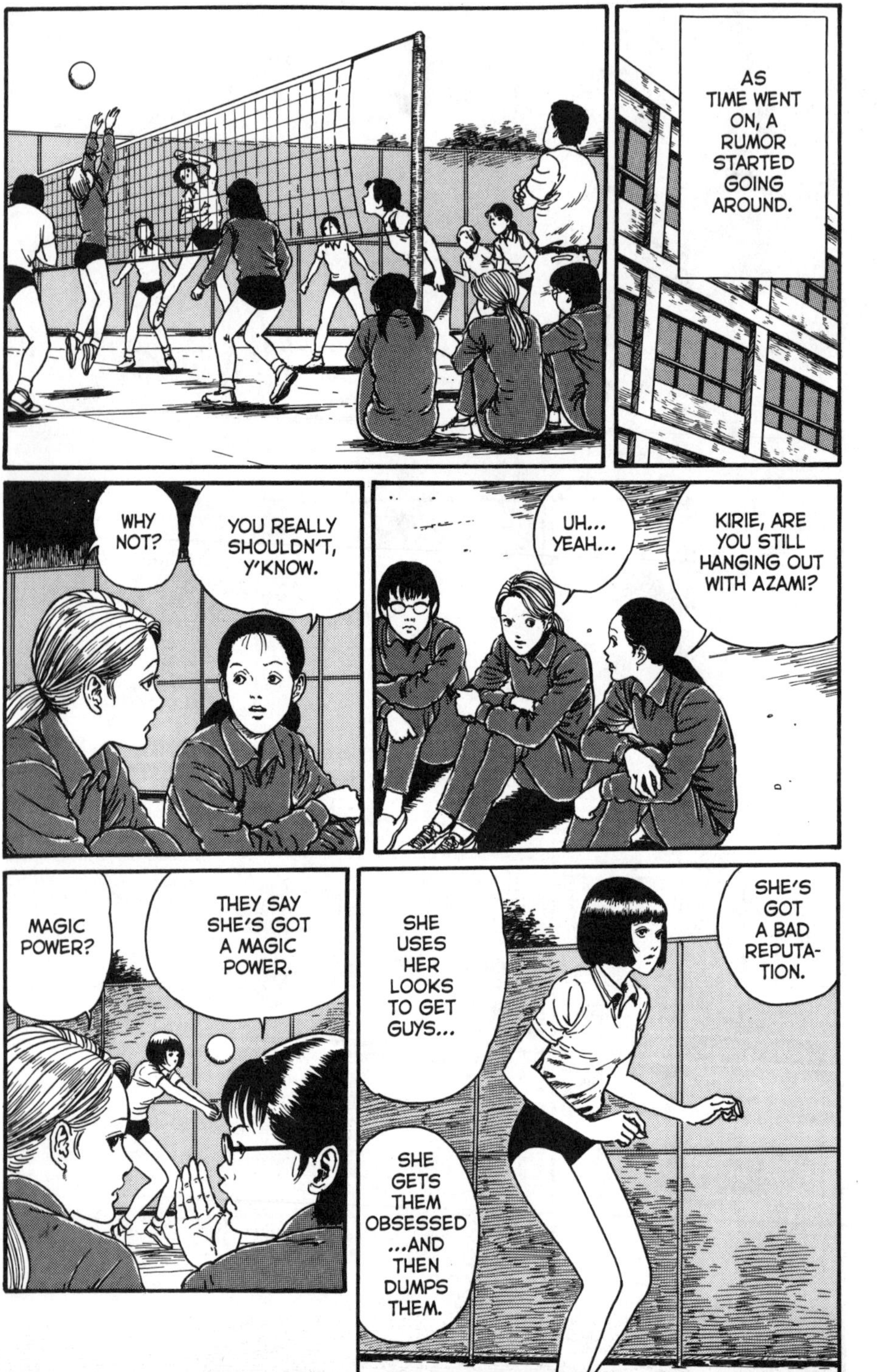
AS TIME WENT ON, A RUMOR STARTED GOING AROUND.
KIRIE, ARE YOU STILL HANGING OUT WITH AZAMI?
UH... YEAH...
YOU REALLY SHOULDN'T, Y'KNOW.
WHY NOT?
SHE'S GOT A BAD REPUTA-TION.
SHE USES HER LOOKS TO GET GUYS...
SHE GETS THEM OBSESSED ...AND THEN DUMPS THEM.
THEY SAY SHE'S GOT A MAGIC POWER.
MAGIC POWER?

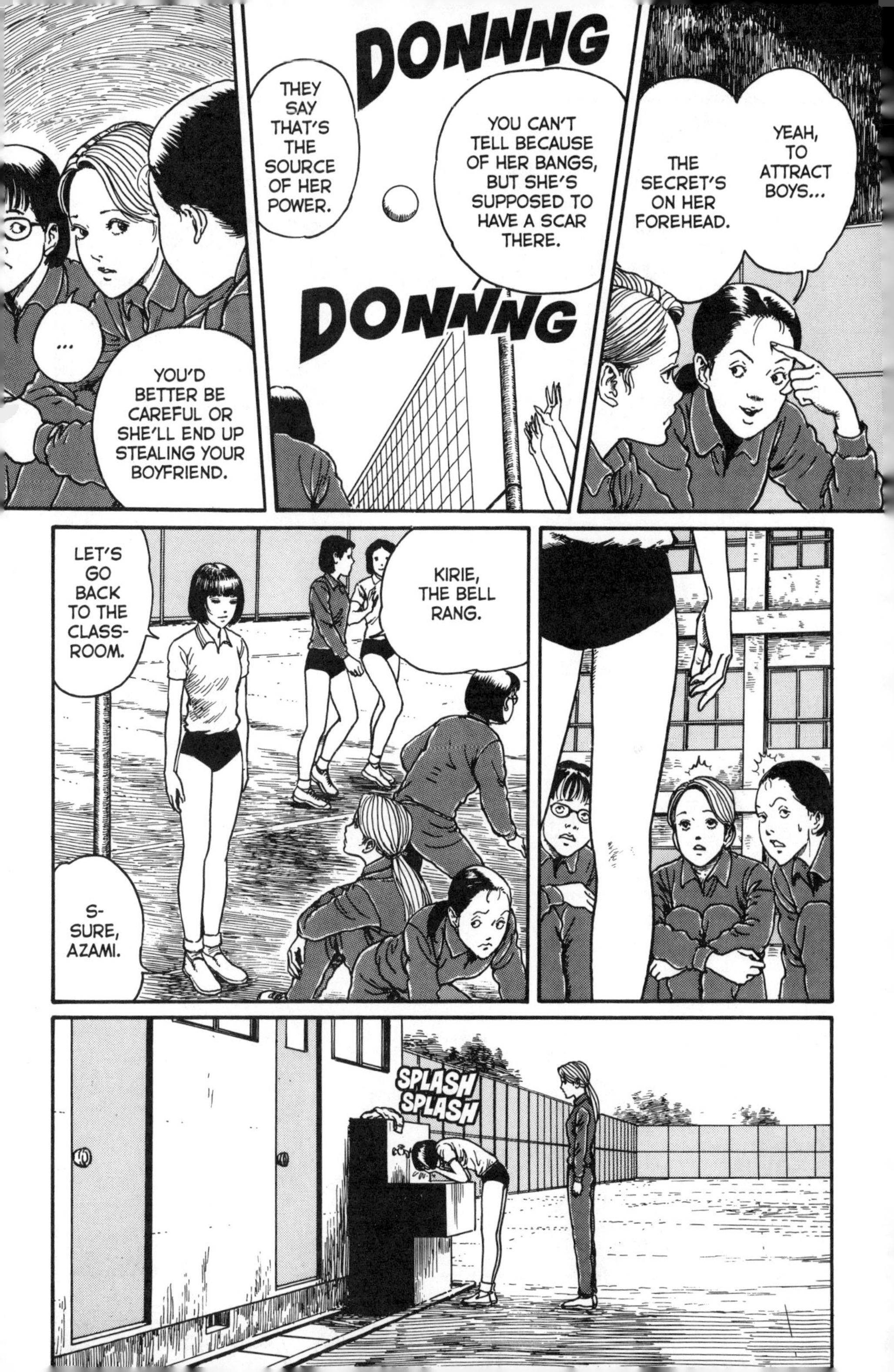
YEAH, TO ATTRACT BOYS...
THE SECRET'S ON HER FOREHEAD.
DONNNG
YOU CAN'T TELL BECAUSE OF HER BANGS, BUT SHE'S SUPPOSED TO HAVE A SCAR THERE.
THEY SAY THAT'S THE SOURCE OF HER POWER.
DONNNG
YOU'D BETTER BE CAREFUL OR SHE'LL END UP STEALING YOUR BOYFRIEND.
...
KIRIE, THE BELL RANG.
LET'S GO BACK TO THE CLASS-ROOM.
S-SURE, AZAMI.
SPLASH SPLASH

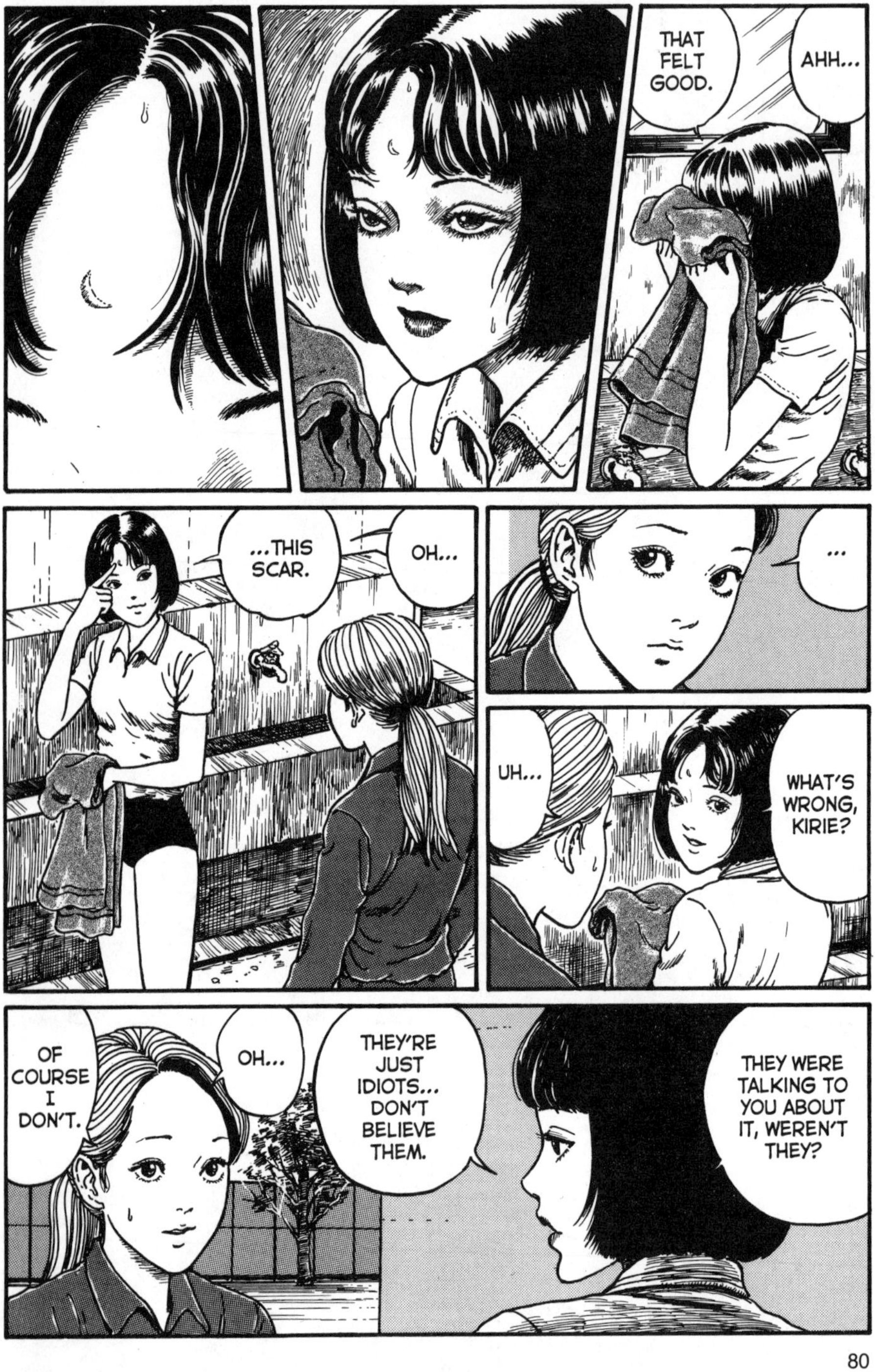
AHH...
THAT FELT GOOD.
...
WHAT'S WRONG, KIRIE?
UH...
OH...
...THIS SCAR.
THEY WERE TALKING TO YOU ABOUT IT, WEREN'T THEY?
THEY'RE JUST IDIOTS... DON'T BELIEVE THEM.
OH...
OF COURSE I DON'T.

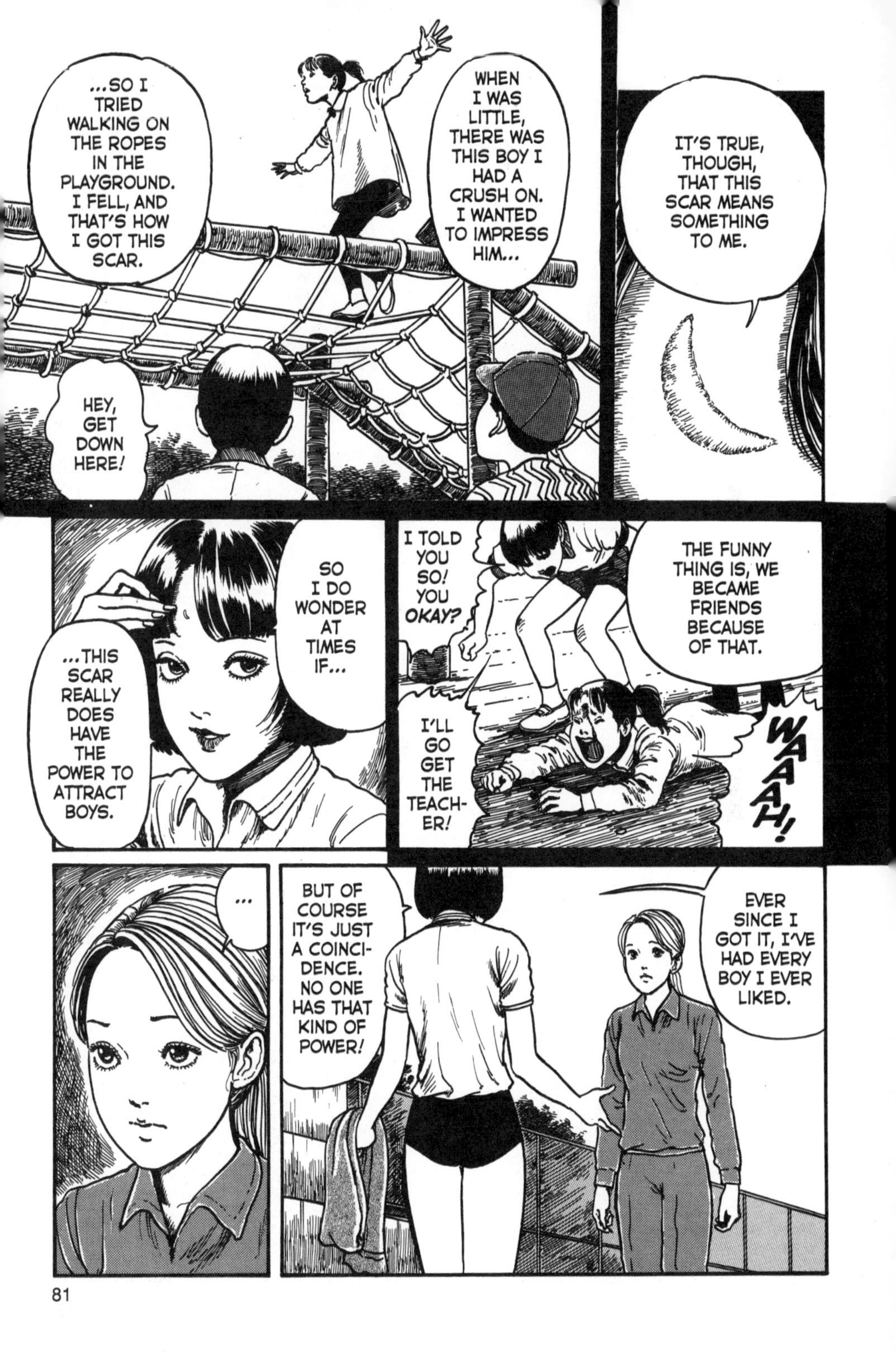
IT'S TRUE, THOUGH, THAT THIS SCAR MEANS SOMETHING TO ME.
WHEN I WAS LITTLE, THERE WAS THIS BOY I HAD A CRUSH ON. I WANTED TO IMPRESS HIM...
...SO I TRIED WALKING ON THE ROPES IN THE PLAYGROUND. I FELL, AND THAT'S HOW I GOT THIS SCAR.
HEY, GET DOWN HERE!
THE FUNNY THING IS, WE BECAME FRIENDS BECAUSE OF THAT.
WAAAH!
I TOLD YOU SO! YOU *OKAY?*
I'LL GO GET THE TEACH-ER!
SO I DO WONDER AT TIMES IF...
...THIS SCAR REALLY DOES HAVE THE POWER TO ATTRACT BOYS.
EVER SINCE I GOT IT, I'VE HAD EVERY BOY I EVER LIKED.
BUT OF COURSE IT'S JUST A COINCI-DENCE. NO ONE HAS THAT KIND OF POWER!
...

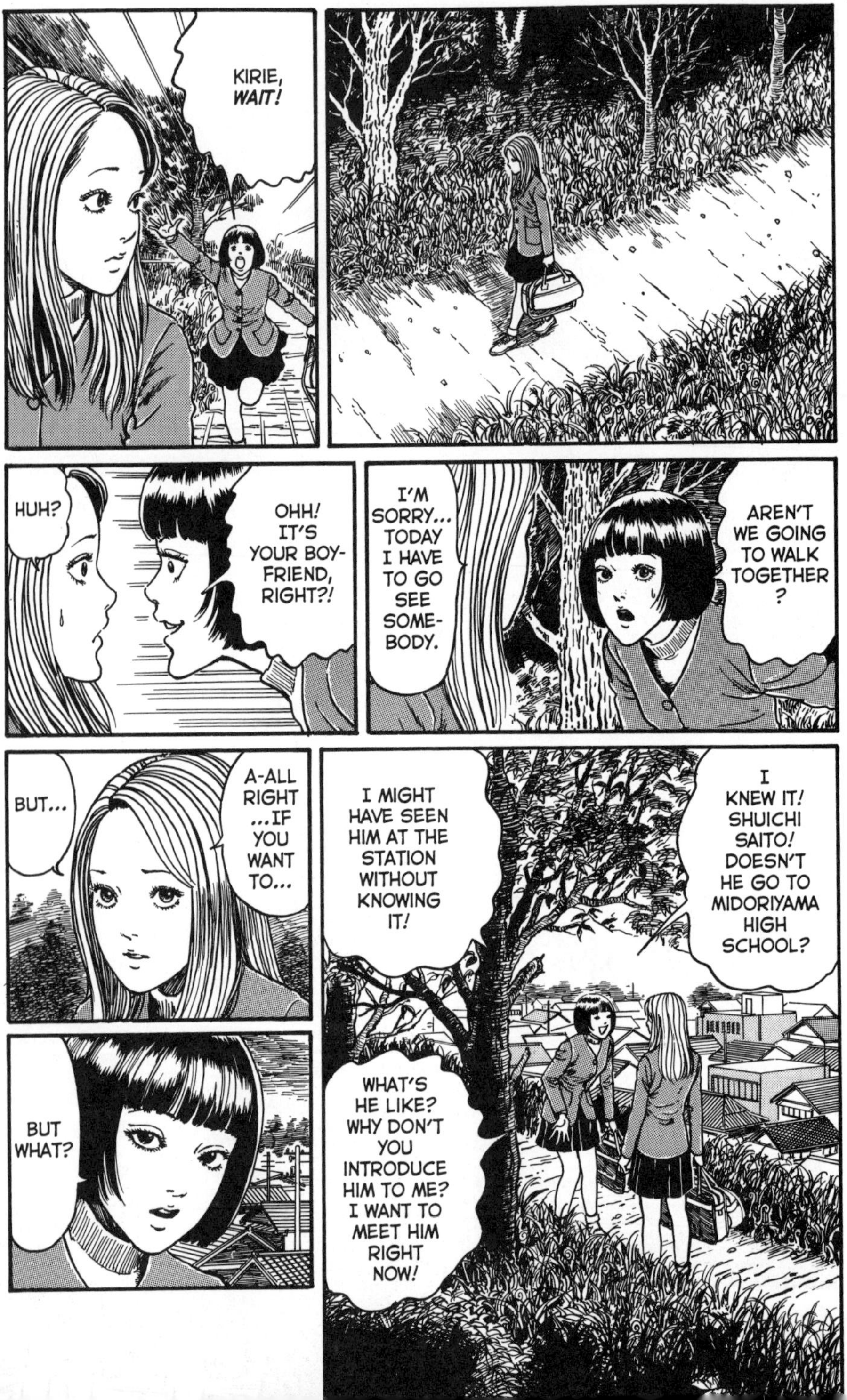
KIRIE, *WAIT!*
AREN'T WE GOING TO WALK TOGETHER?
I'M SORRY... TODAY I HAVE TO GO SEE SOMEBODY.
OHH! IT'S YOUR BOY-FRIEND, RIGHT?!
HUH?
I KNEW IT! SHUICHI SAITO! DOESN'T HE GO TO MIDORIYAMA HIGH SCHOOL?
I MIGHT HAVE SEEN HIM AT THE STATION WITHOUT KNOWING IT!
WHAT'S HE LIKE? WHY DON'T YOU INTRODUCE HIM TO ME? I WANT TO MEET HIM RIGHT NOW!
A-ALL RIGHT ...IF YOU WANT TO...
BUT...
BUT WHAT?

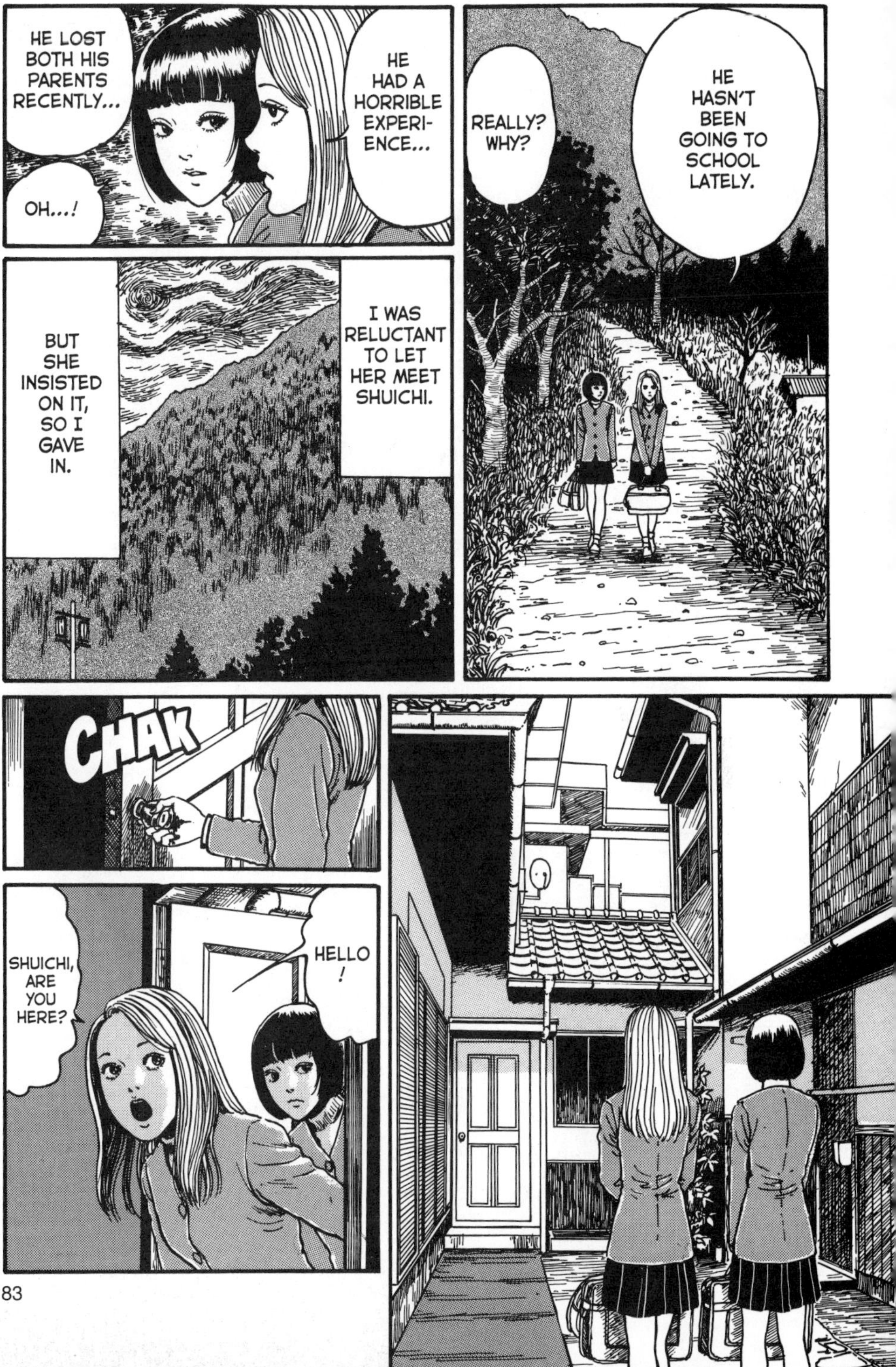
HE HASN'T BEEN GOING TO SCHOOL LATELY.
REALLY? WHY?
HE HAD A HORRIBLE EXPERI-ENCE...
HE LOST BOTH HIS PARENTS RECENTLY...
OH...!
I WAS RELUCTANT TO LET HER MEET SHUICHI.
BUT SHE INSISTED ON IT, SO I GAVE IN.
CHAK
HELLO!
SHUICHI, ARE YOU HERE?

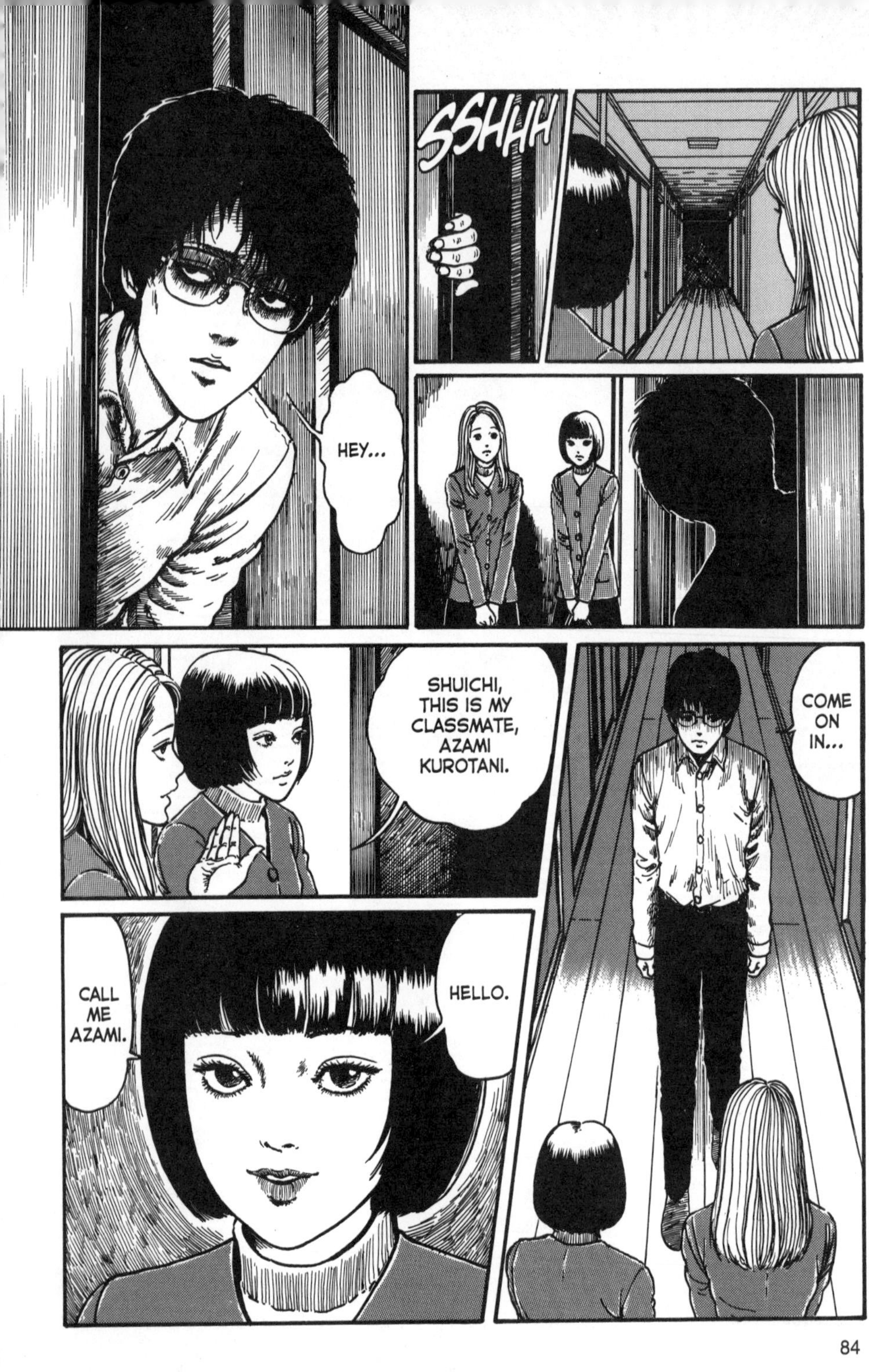
SSHHH
HEY...
COME ON IN...
SHUICHI, THIS IS MY CLASSMATE, AZAMI KUROTANI.
HELLO.
CALL ME AZAMI.

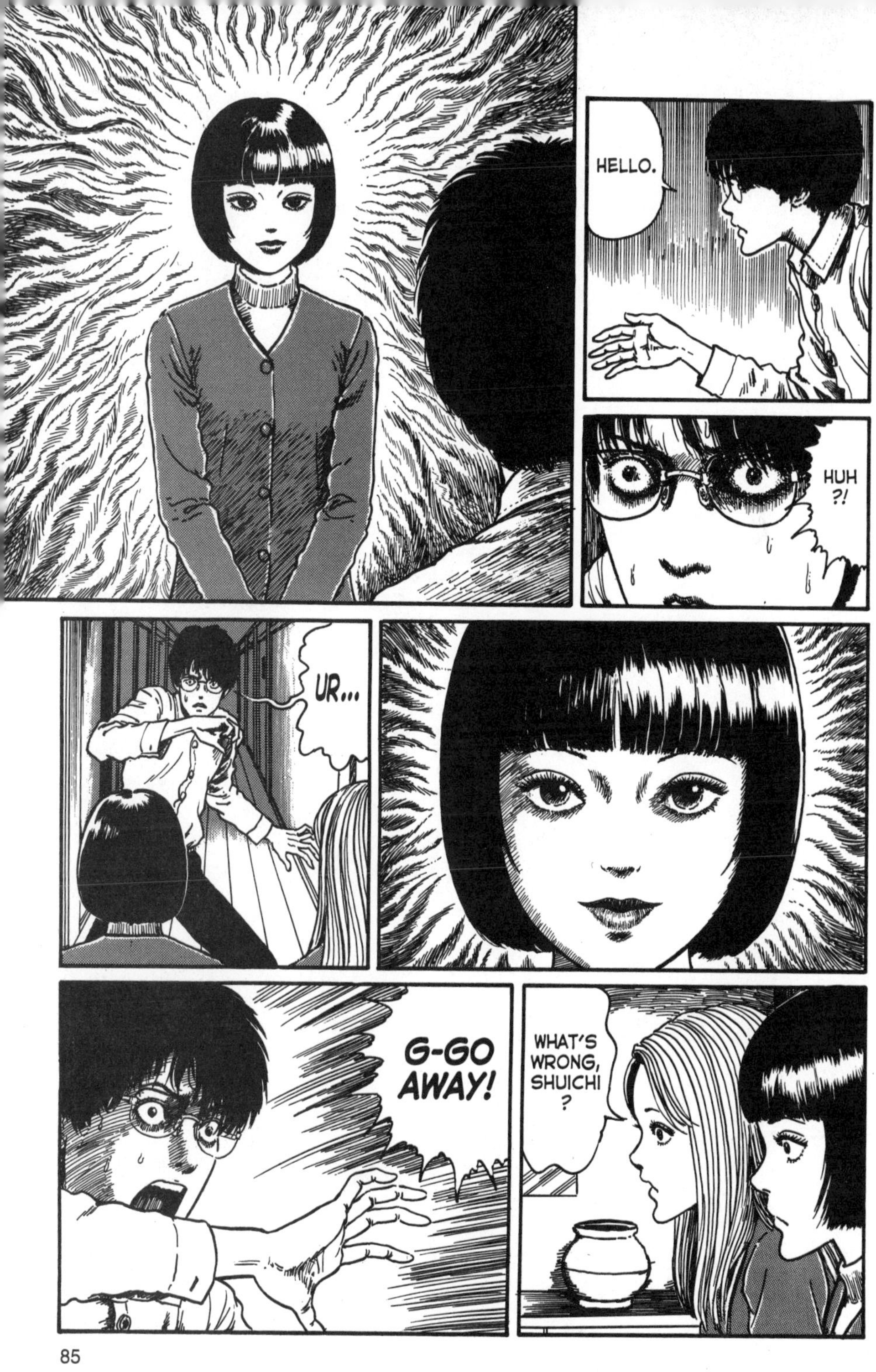
HELLO.
HUH ?!
UR...
WHAT'S WRONG, SHUICHI ?
G-GO AWAY!

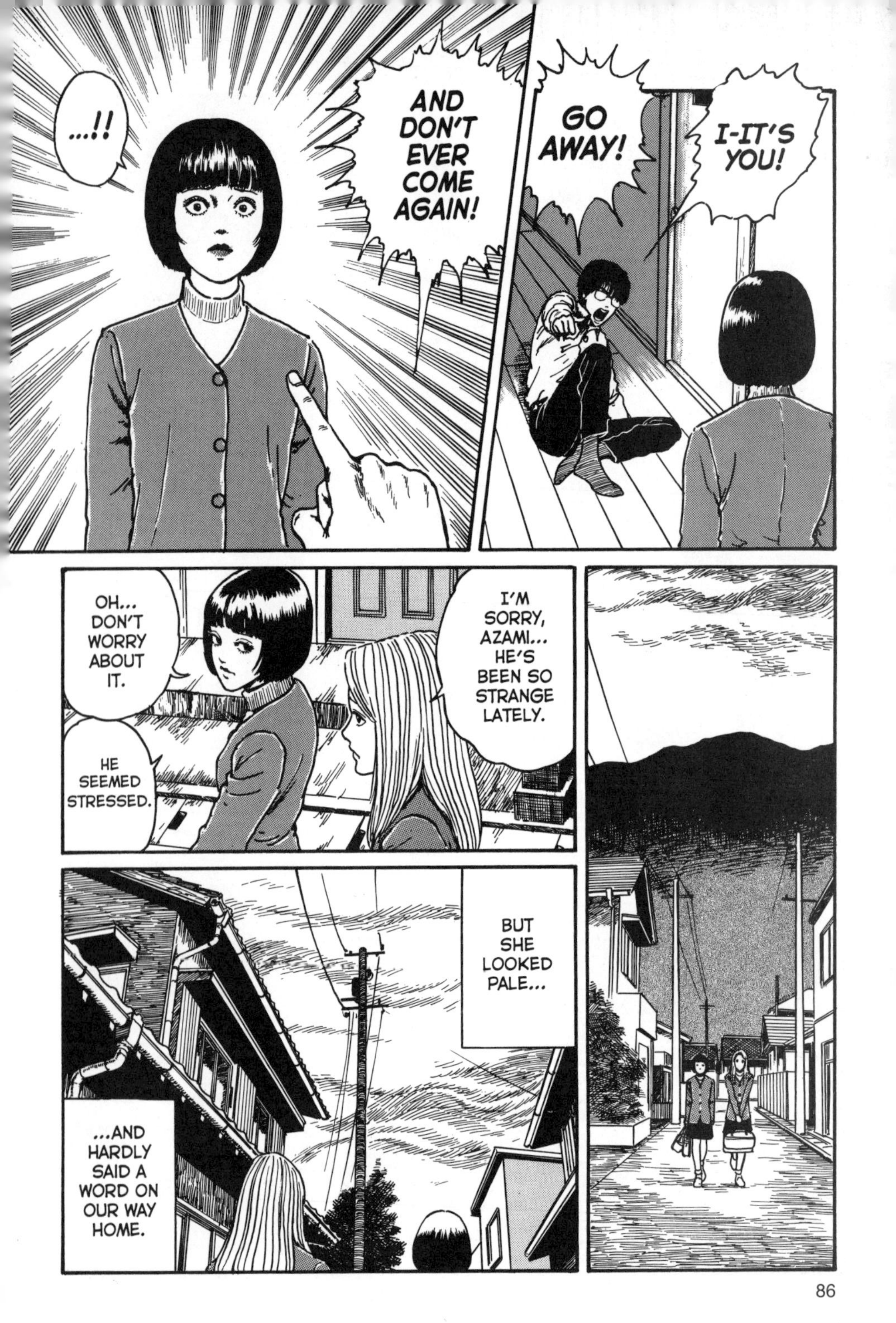
I-IT'S YOU!
GO AWAY!
AND DON'T EVER COME AGAIN!
...!!
I'M SORRY, AZAMI... HE'S BEEN SO STRANGE LATELY.
OH... DON'T WORRY ABOUT IT.
HE SEEMED STRESSED.
BUT SHE LOOKED PALE...
...AND HARDLY SAID A WORD ON OUR WAY HOME.

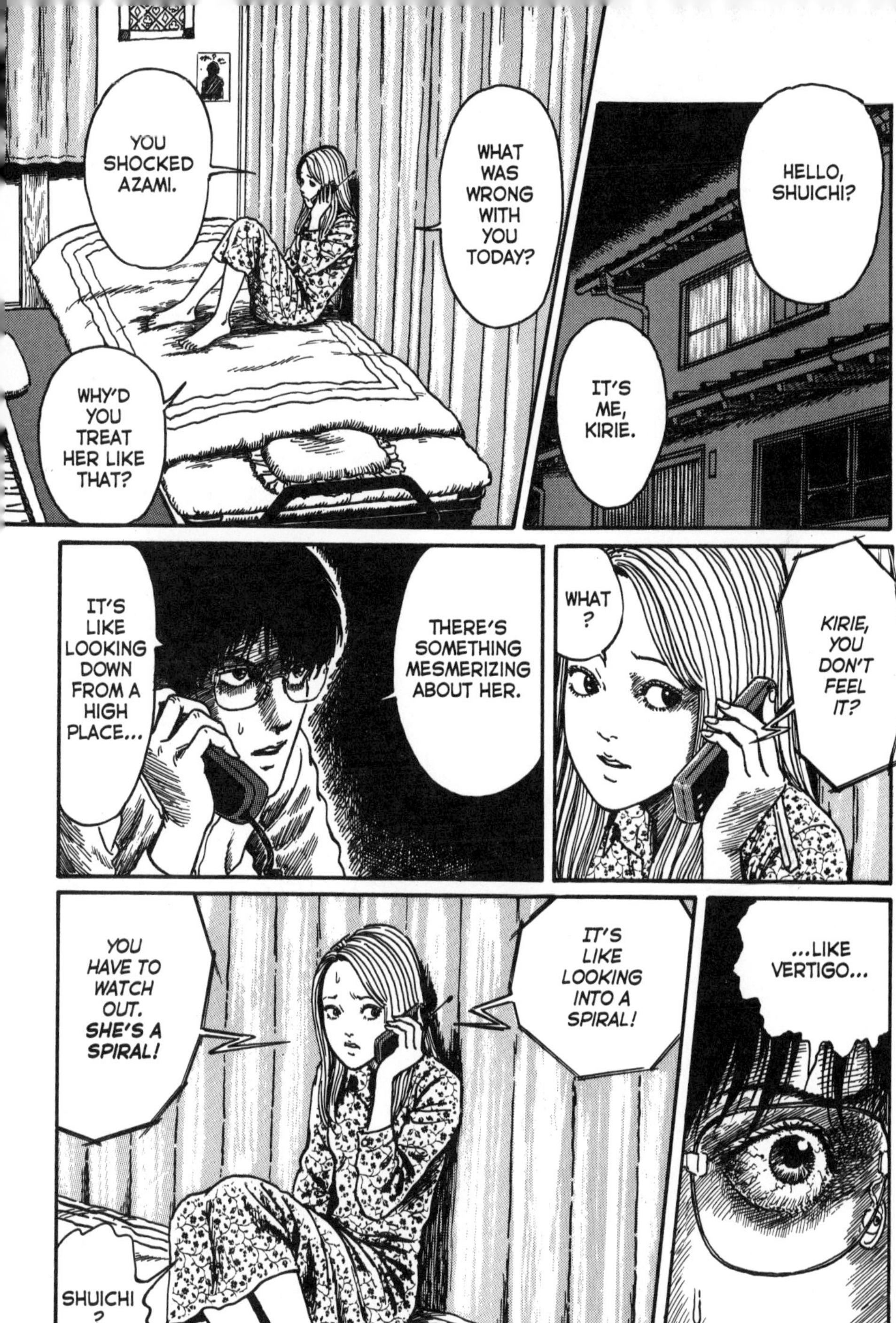
HELLO, SHUICHI?
IT'S ME, KIRIE.
WHAT WAS WRONG WITH YOU TODAY?
YOU SHOCKED AZAMI.
WHY'D YOU TREAT HER LIKE THAT?
KIRIE, YOU DON'T FEEL IT?
WHAT?
THERE'S SOMETHING MESMERIZING ABOUT HER.
IT'S LIKE LOOKING DOWN FROM A HIGH PLACE...
...LIKE VERTIGO...
IT'S LIKE LOOKING INTO A SPIRAL!
YOU HAVE TO WATCH OUT. SHE'S A SPIRAL!
SHUICHI?

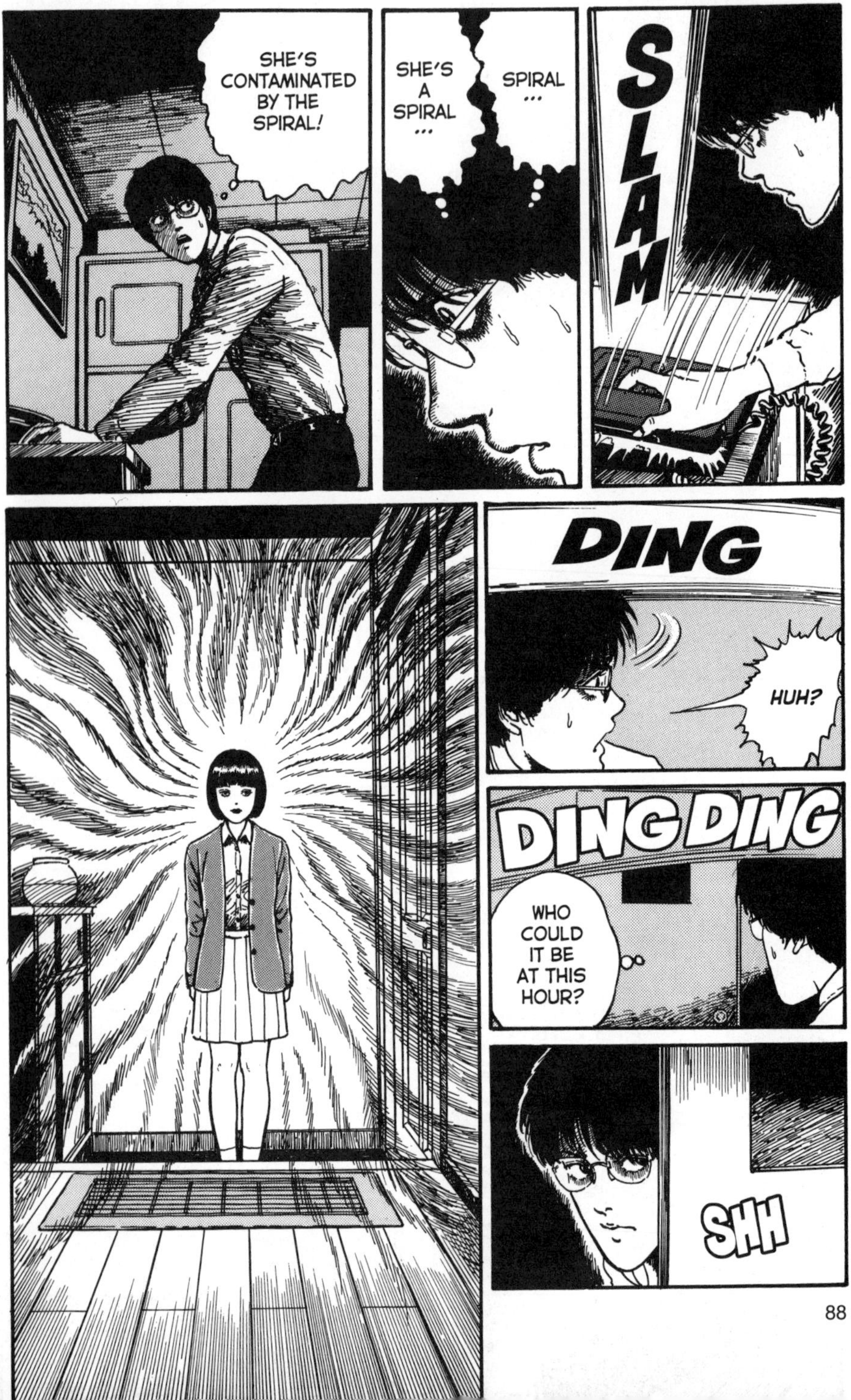
SLAM
SPIRAL ...
SHE'S A SPIRAL ...
SHE'S CONTAMINATED BY THE SPIRAL!
DING
HUH?
DING DING
WHO COULD IT BE AT THIS HOUR?
SHH

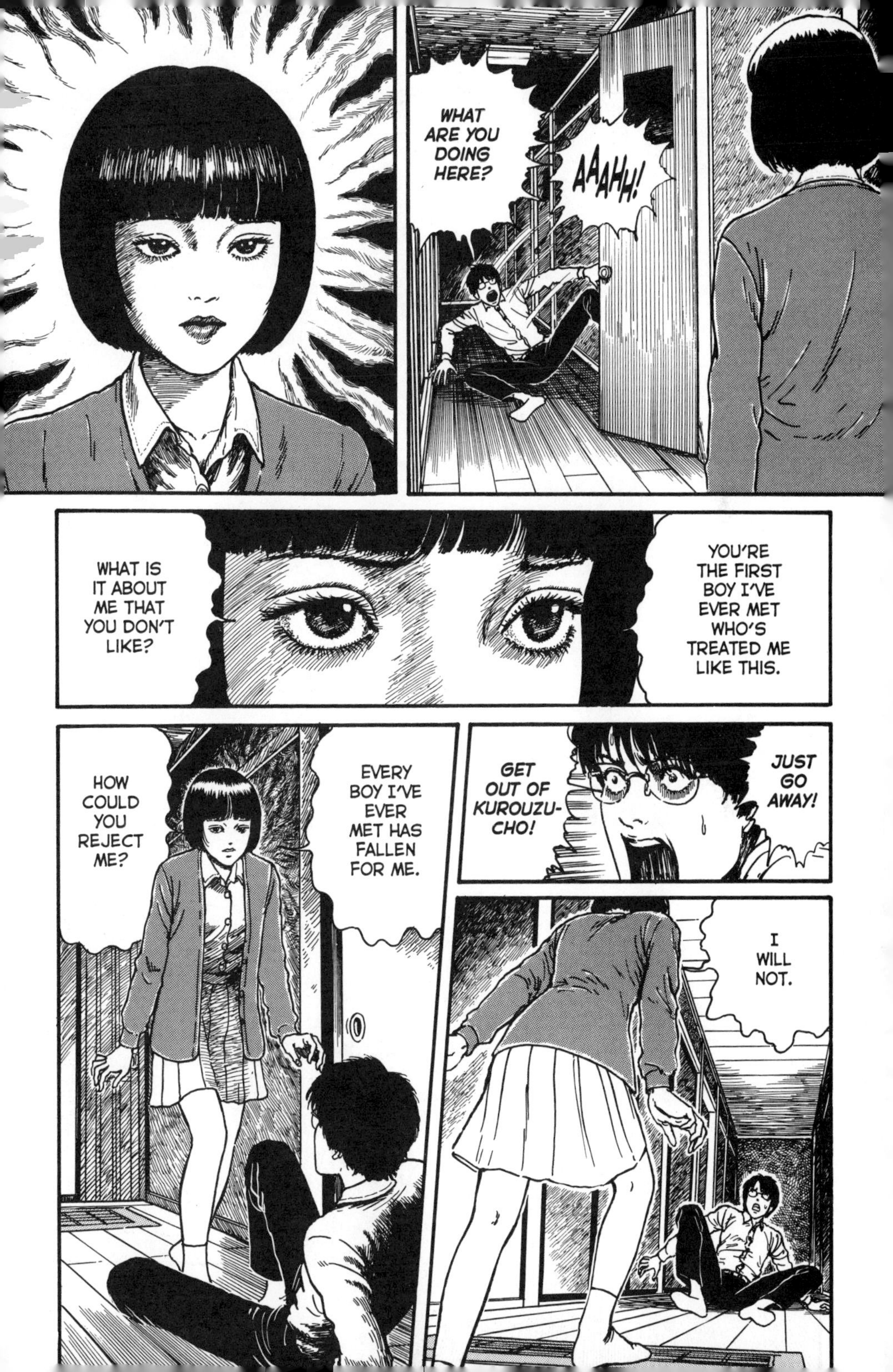
AAAHH!
WHAT ARE YOU DOING HERE?
YOU'RE THE FIRST BOY I'VE EVER MET WHO'S TREATED ME LIKE THIS.
WHAT IS IT ABOUT ME THAT YOU DON'T LIKE?
JUST GO AWAY!
GET OUT OF KUROUZU-CHO!
I WILL NOT.
EVERY BOY I'VE EVER MET HAS FALLEN FOR ME.
HOW COULD YOU REJECT ME?

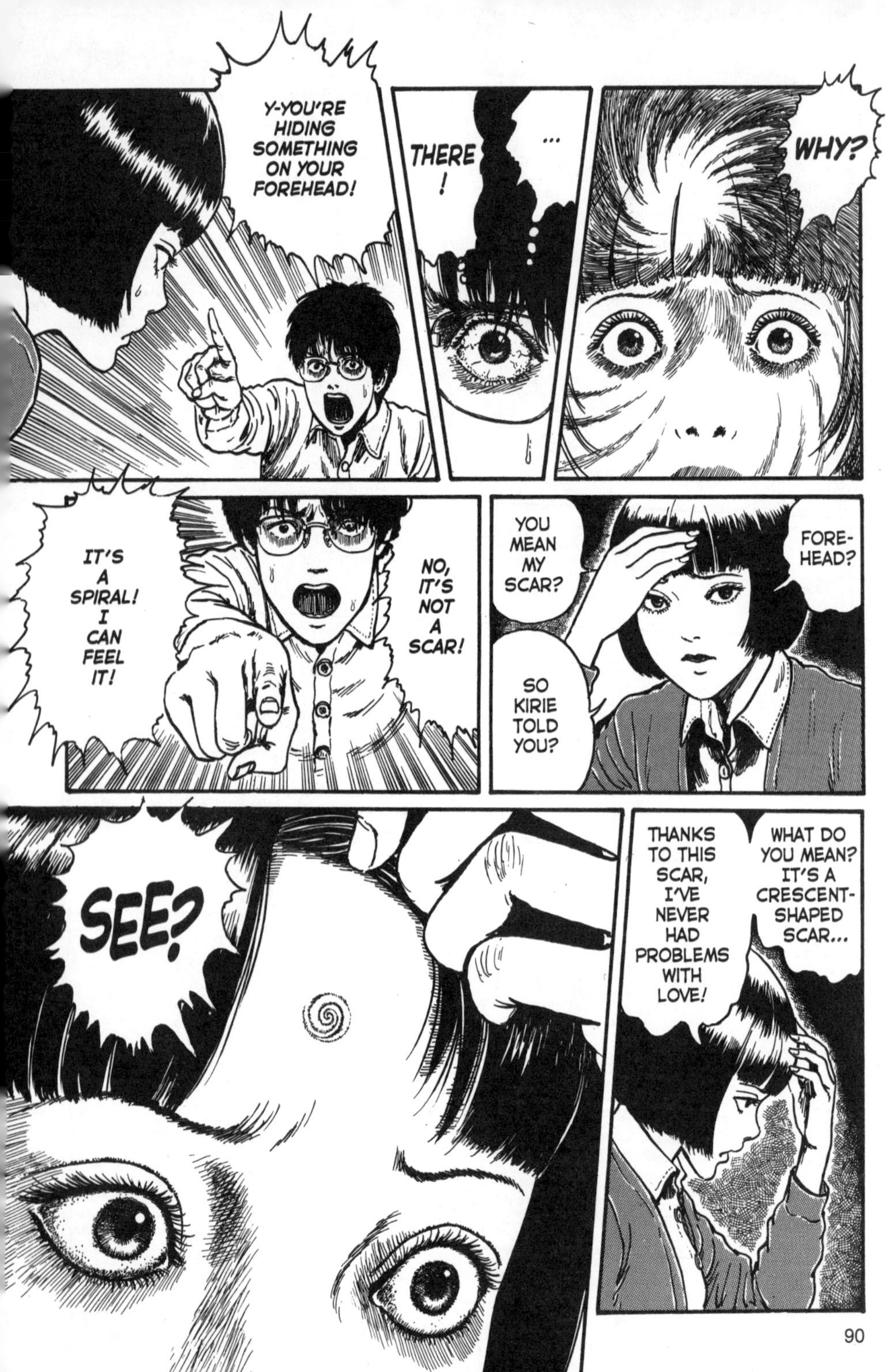
WHY?
...
THERE!
Y-YOU'RE HIDING SOMETHING ON YOUR FOREHEAD!
FORE-HEAD?
YOU MEAN MY SCAR?
SO KIRIE TOLD YOU?
NO, IT'S NOT A SCAR!
IT'S A SPIRAL! I CAN FEEL IT!
WHAT DO YOU MEAN? IT'S A CRESCENT-SHAPED SCAR...
THANKS TO THIS SCAR, I'VE NEVER HAD PROBLEMS WITH LOVE!
SEE?

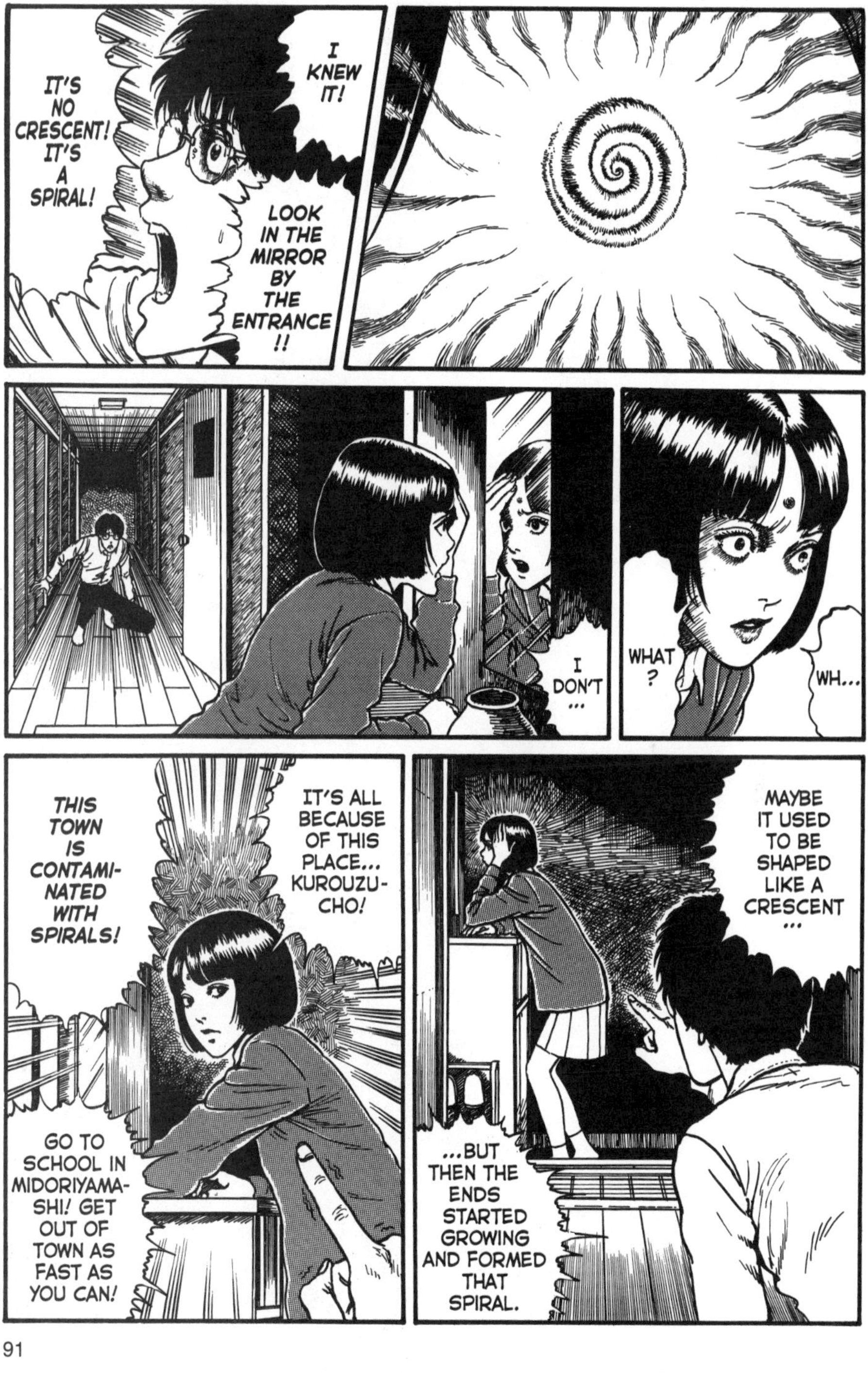
I KNEW IT!
IT'S NO CRESCENT! IT'S A SPIRAL!
LOOK IN THE MIRROR BY THE ENTRANCE!!
WH...
WHAT?
I DON'T...
MAYBE IT USED TO BE SHAPED LIKE A CRESCENT...
...BUT THEN THE ENDS STARTED GROWING AND FORMED THAT SPIRAL.
IT'S ALL BECAUSE OF THIS PLACE... KUROUZU-CHO!
THIS TOWN IS CONTAMINATED WITH SPIRALS!
GO TO SCHOOL IN MIDORIYAMA-SHI! GET OUT OF TOWN AS FAST AS YOU CAN!

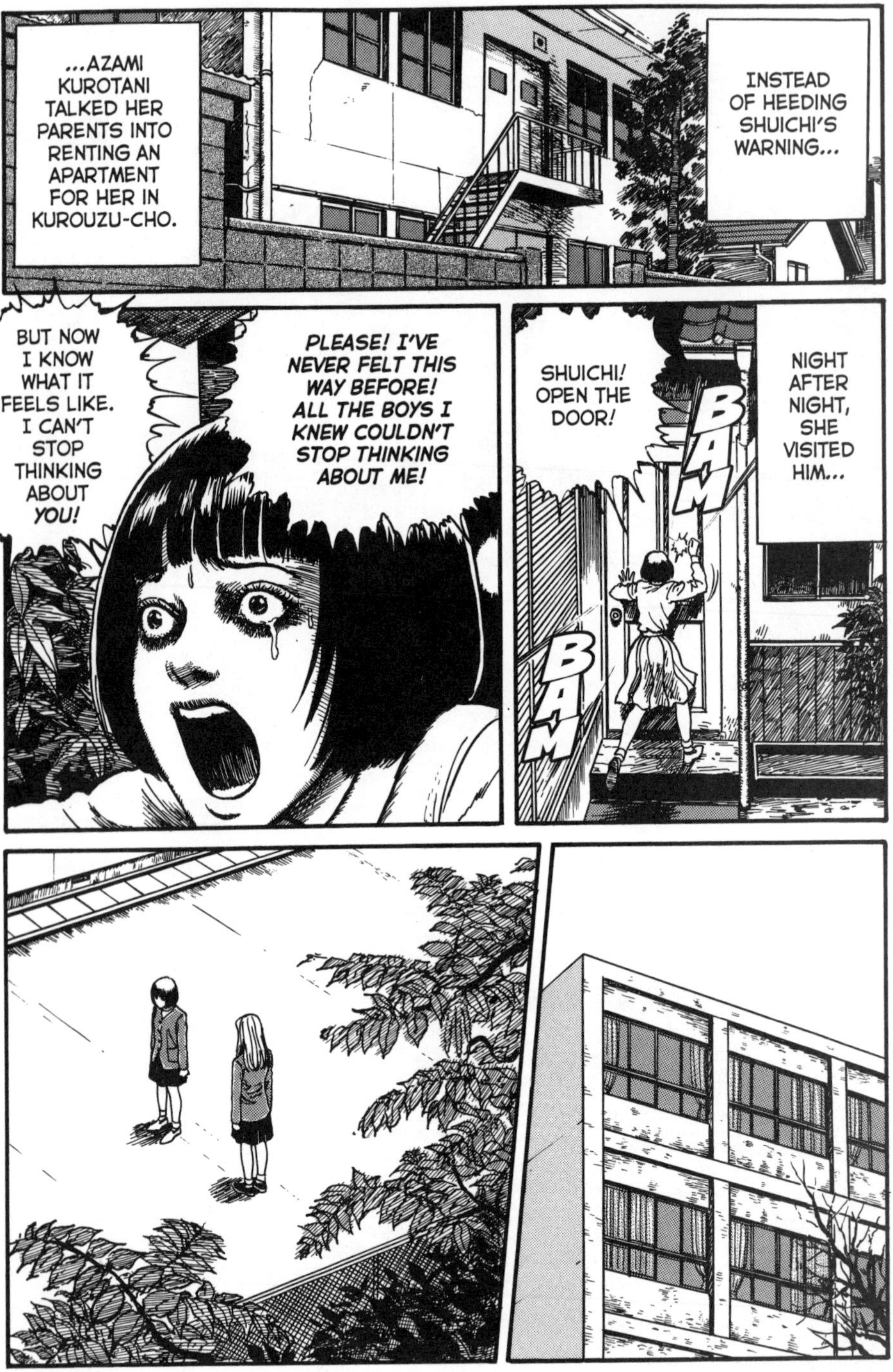
INSTEAD OF HEEDING SHUICHI'S WARNING...
...AZAMI KUROTANI TALKED HER PARENTS INTO RENTING AN APARTMENT FOR HER IN KUROUZU-CHO.
NIGHT AFTER NIGHT, SHE VISITED HIM...
SHUICHI! OPEN THE DOOR!
BAM
BAM
PLEASE! I'VE NEVER FELT THIS WAY BEFORE! ALL THE BOYS I KNEW COULDN'T STOP THINKING ABOUT ME!
BUT NOW I KNOW WHAT IT FEELS LIKE. I CAN'T STOP THINKING ABOUT YOU!

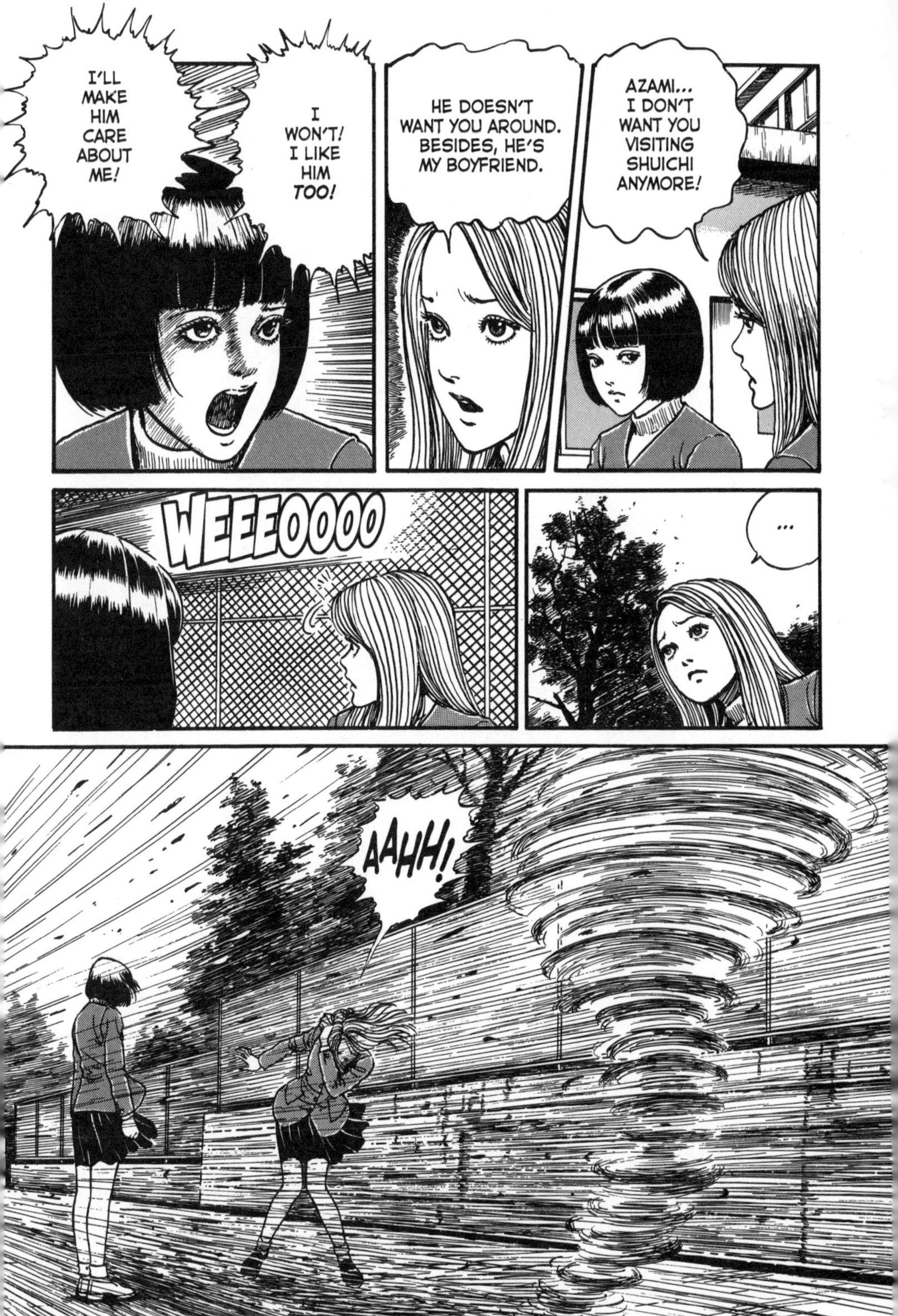
AZAMI... I DON'T WANT YOU VISITING SHUICHI ANYMORE!
HE DOESN'T WANT YOU AROUND. BESIDES, HE'S MY BOYFRIEND.
I WON'T! I LIKE HIM *TOO!*
I'LL MAKE HIM CARE ABOUT ME!
...
WEEEOOOO
AAHH!

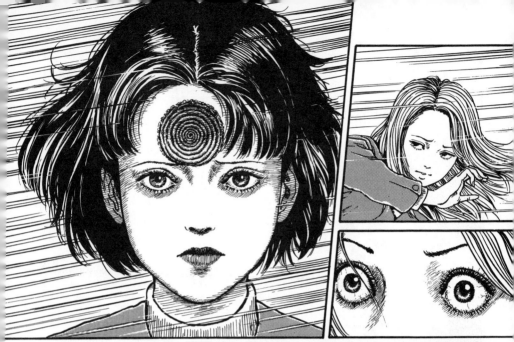

YOUR
FORE-
HEAD
...

A-
A...

AZAMI...

STOP!!

AZAMI!

FSH

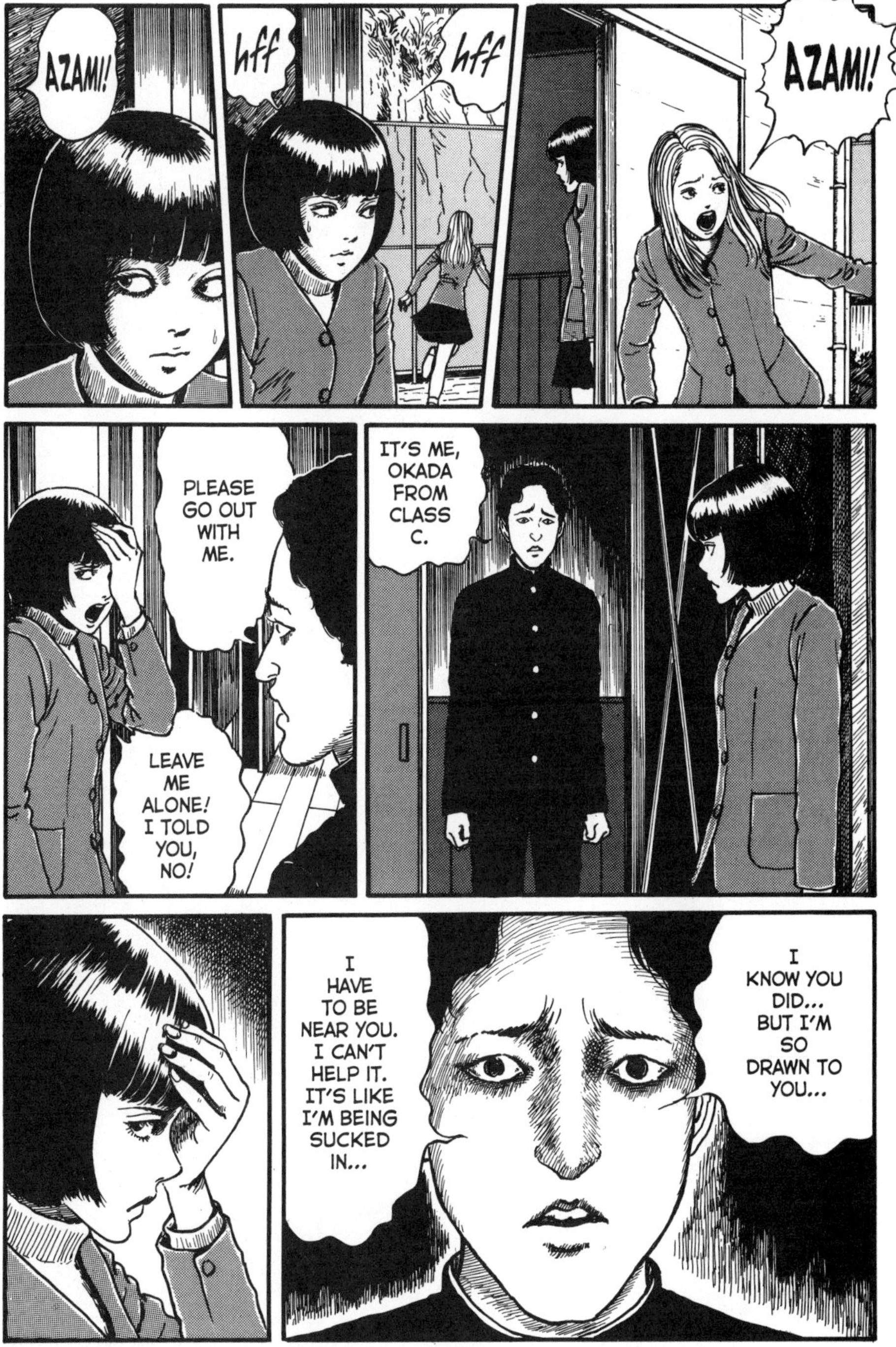
AZAMI!
hff
hff
AZAMI!
IT'S ME, OKADA FROM CLASS C.
PLEASE GO OUT WITH ME.
LEAVE ME ALONE! I TOLD YOU, NO!
I KNOW YOU DID... BUT I'M SO DRAWN TO YOU...
I HAVE TO BE NEAR YOU. I CAN'T HELP IT. IT'S LIKE I'M BEING SUCKED IN...

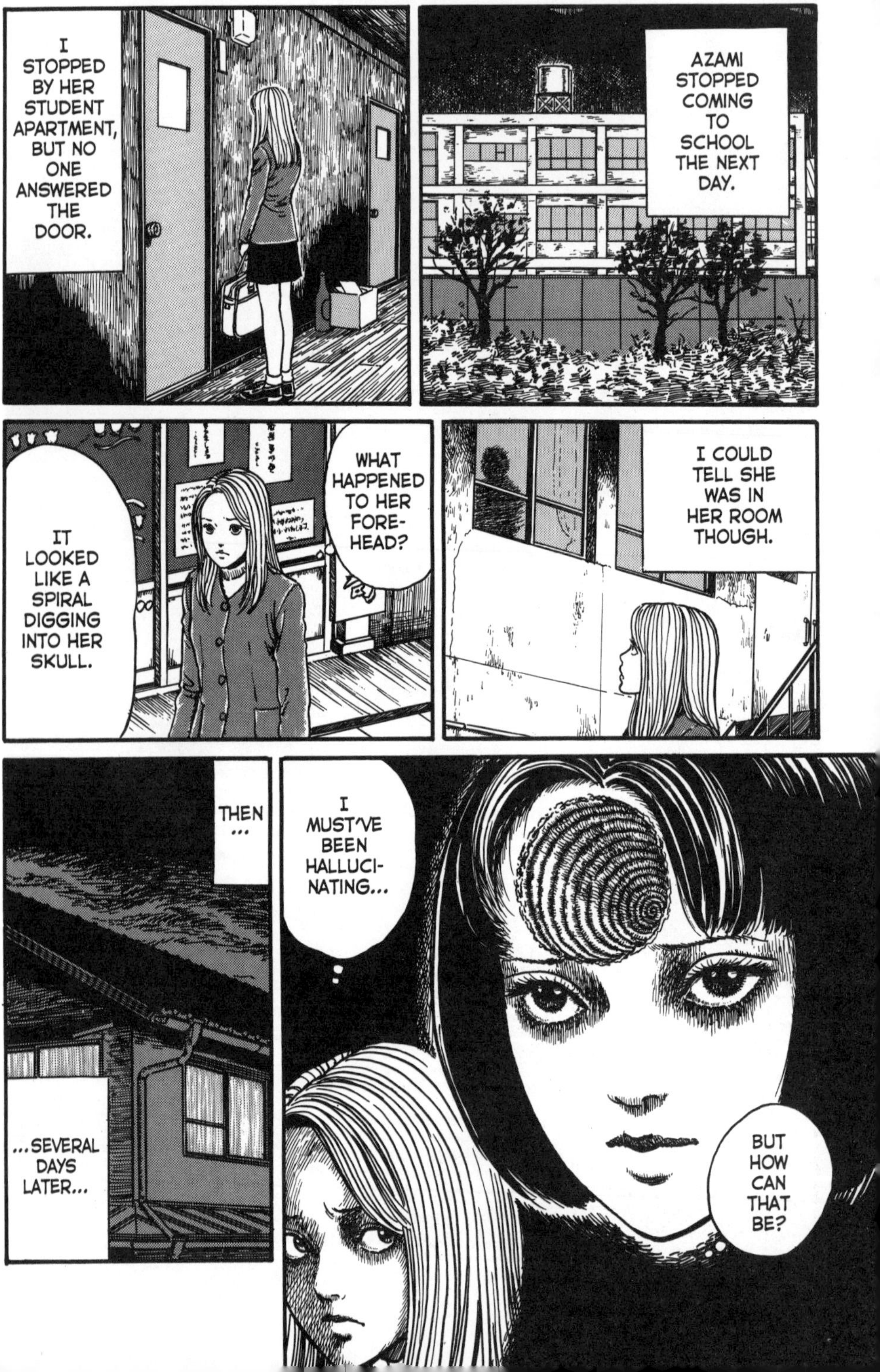
AZAMI STOPPED COMING TO SCHOOL THE NEXT DAY.
I STOPPED BY HER STUDENT APARTMENT, BUT NO ONE ANSWERED THE DOOR.
I COULD TELL SHE WAS IN HER ROOM THOUGH.
WHAT HAPPENED TO HER FORE-HEAD?
IT LOOKED LIKE A SPIRAL DIGGING INTO HER SKULL.
I MUST'VE BEEN HALLUCI-NATING...
BUT HOW CAN THAT BE?
THEN...
...SEVERAL DAYS LATER...

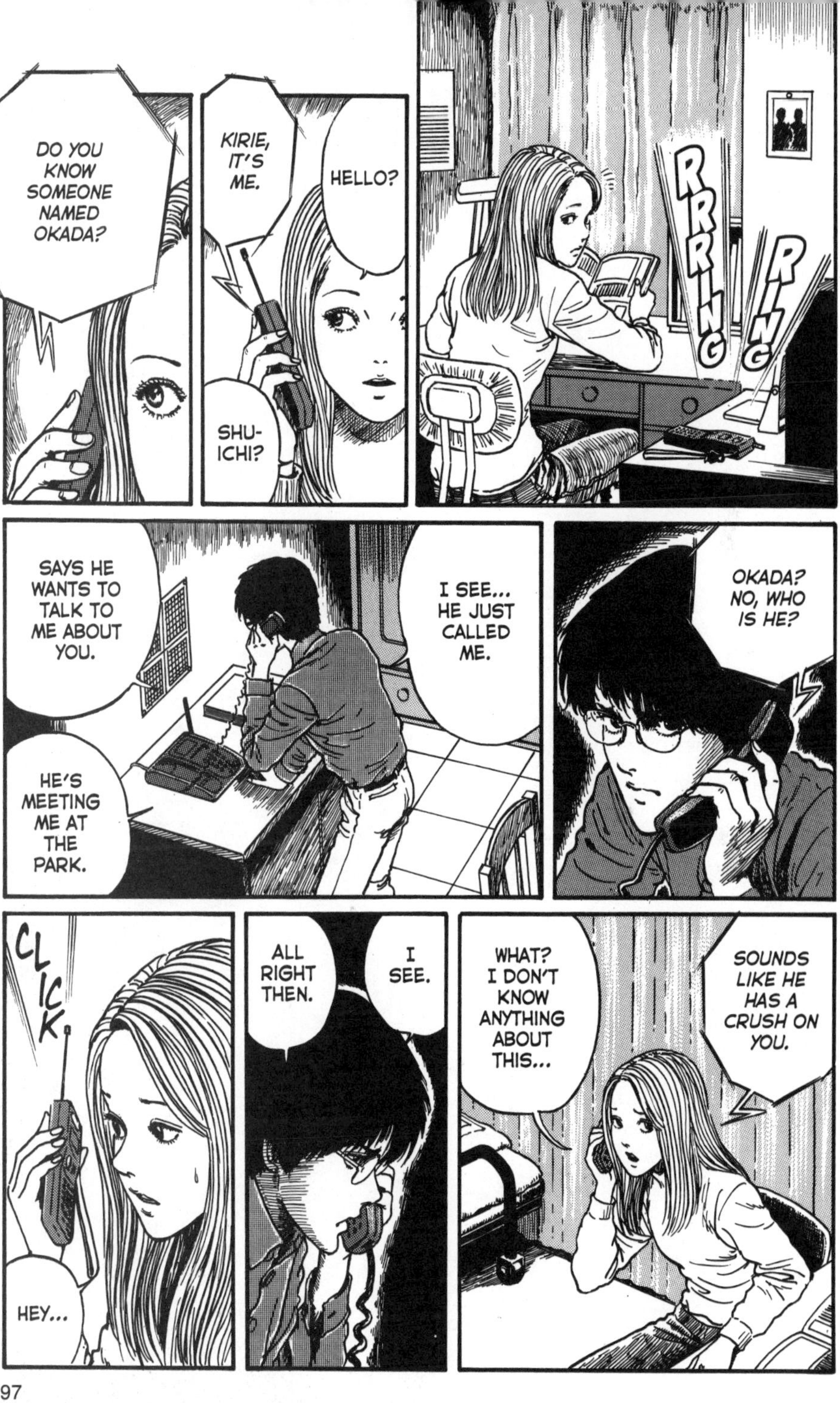
RRRING
RING
HELLO?
KIRIE, IT'S ME.
SHU-ICHI?
DO YOU KNOW SOMEONE NAMED OKADA?
OKADA? NO, WHO IS HE?
I SEE... HE JUST CALLED ME.
SAYS HE WANTS TO TALK TO ME ABOUT YOU.
HE'S MEETING ME AT THE PARK.
SOUNDS LIKE HE HAS A CRUSH ON YOU.
WHAT? I DON'T KNOW ANYTHING ABOUT THIS...
I SEE.
ALL RIGHT THEN.
CLICK
HEY...

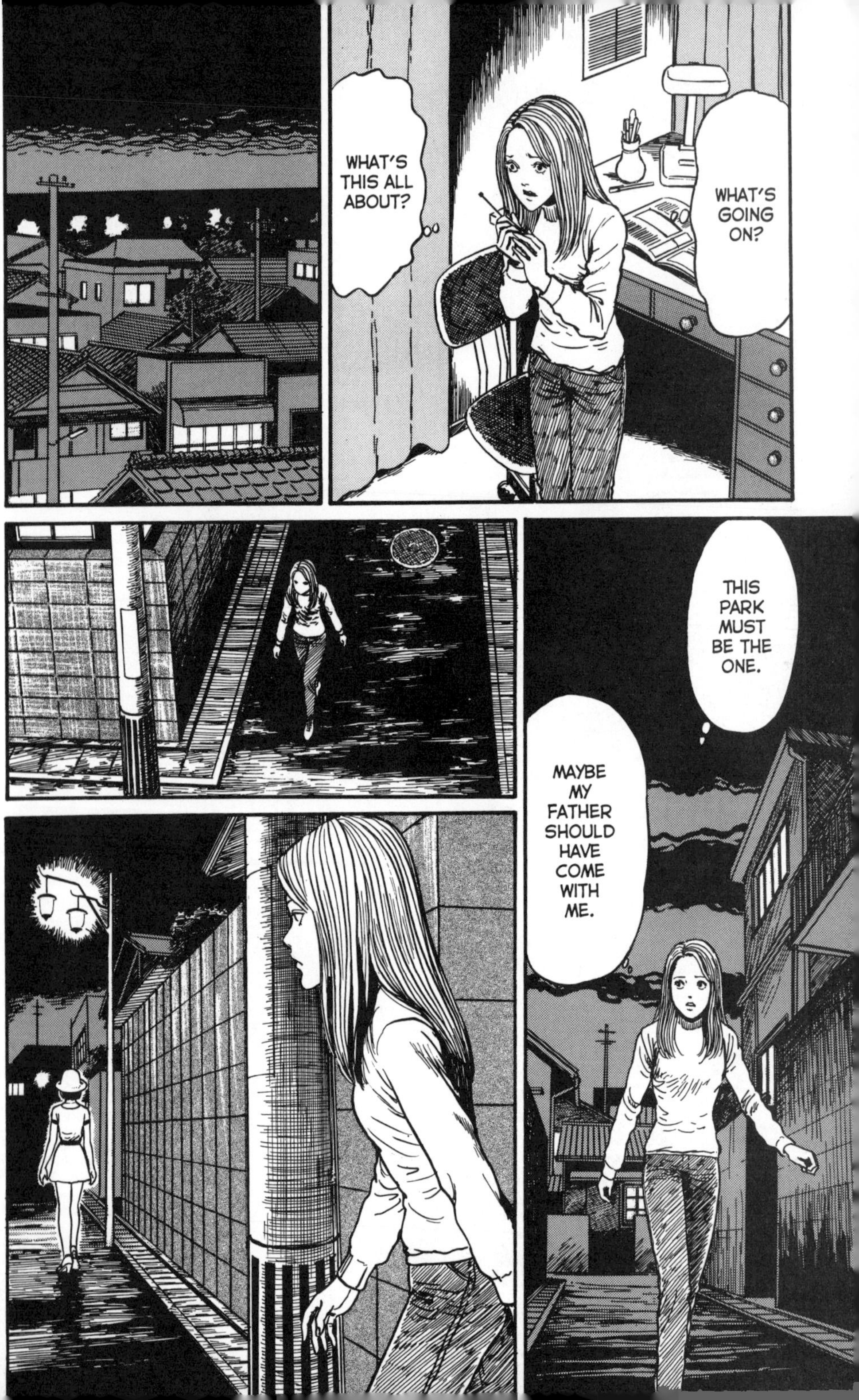
WHAT'S GOING ON?
WHAT'S THIS ALL ABOUT?
THIS PARK MUST BE THE ONE.
MAYBE MY FATHER SHOULD HAVE COME WITH ME.

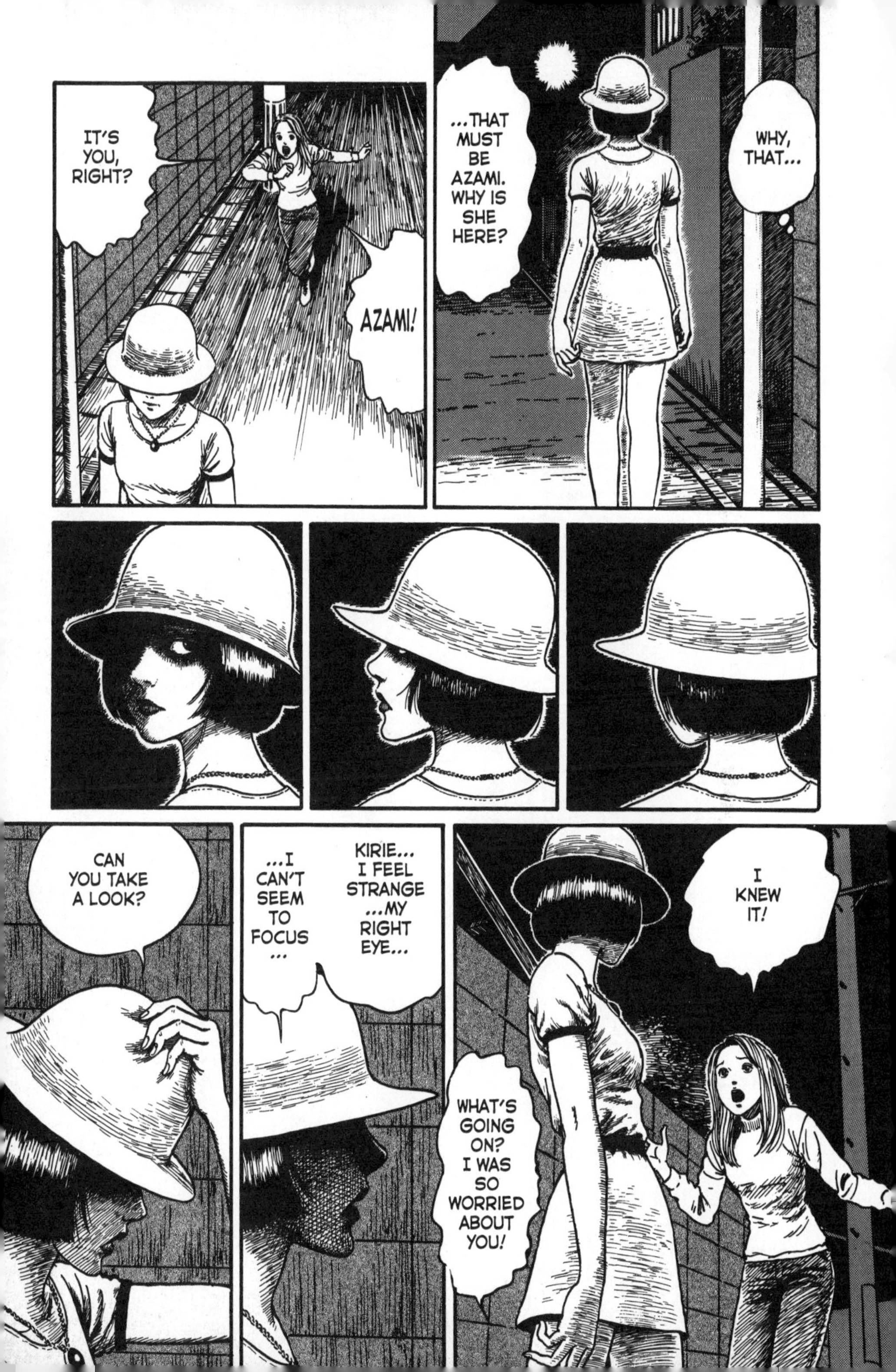
WHY, THAT...
...THAT MUST BE AZAMI. WHY IS SHE HERE?
AZAMI!
IT'S YOU, RIGHT?
I KNEW IT!
WHAT'S GOING ON? I WAS SO WORRIED ABOUT YOU!
KIRIE... I FEEL STRANGE ...MY RIGHT EYE...
...I CAN'T SEEM TO FOCUS ...
CAN YOU TAKE A LOOK?

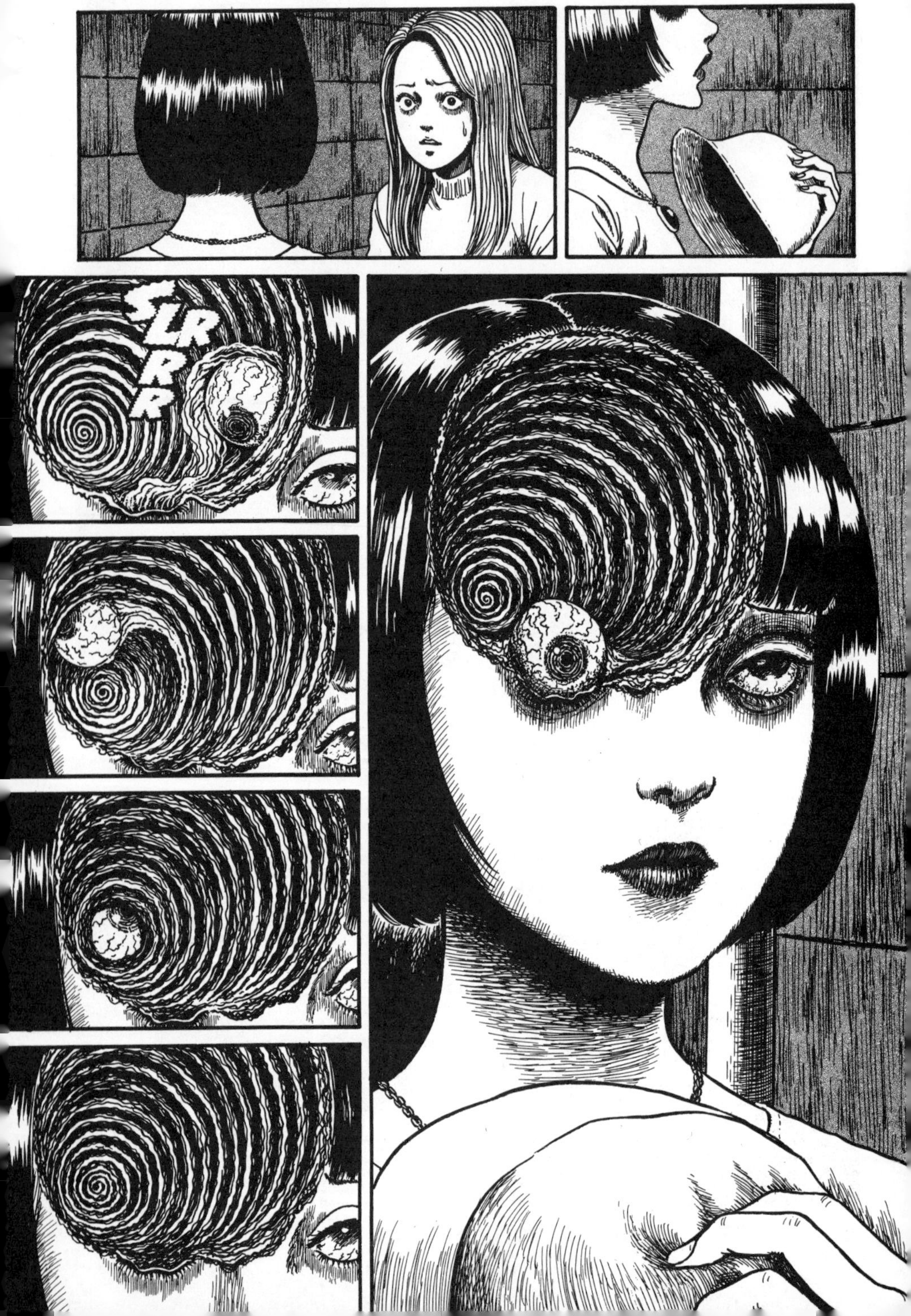
SLRRR

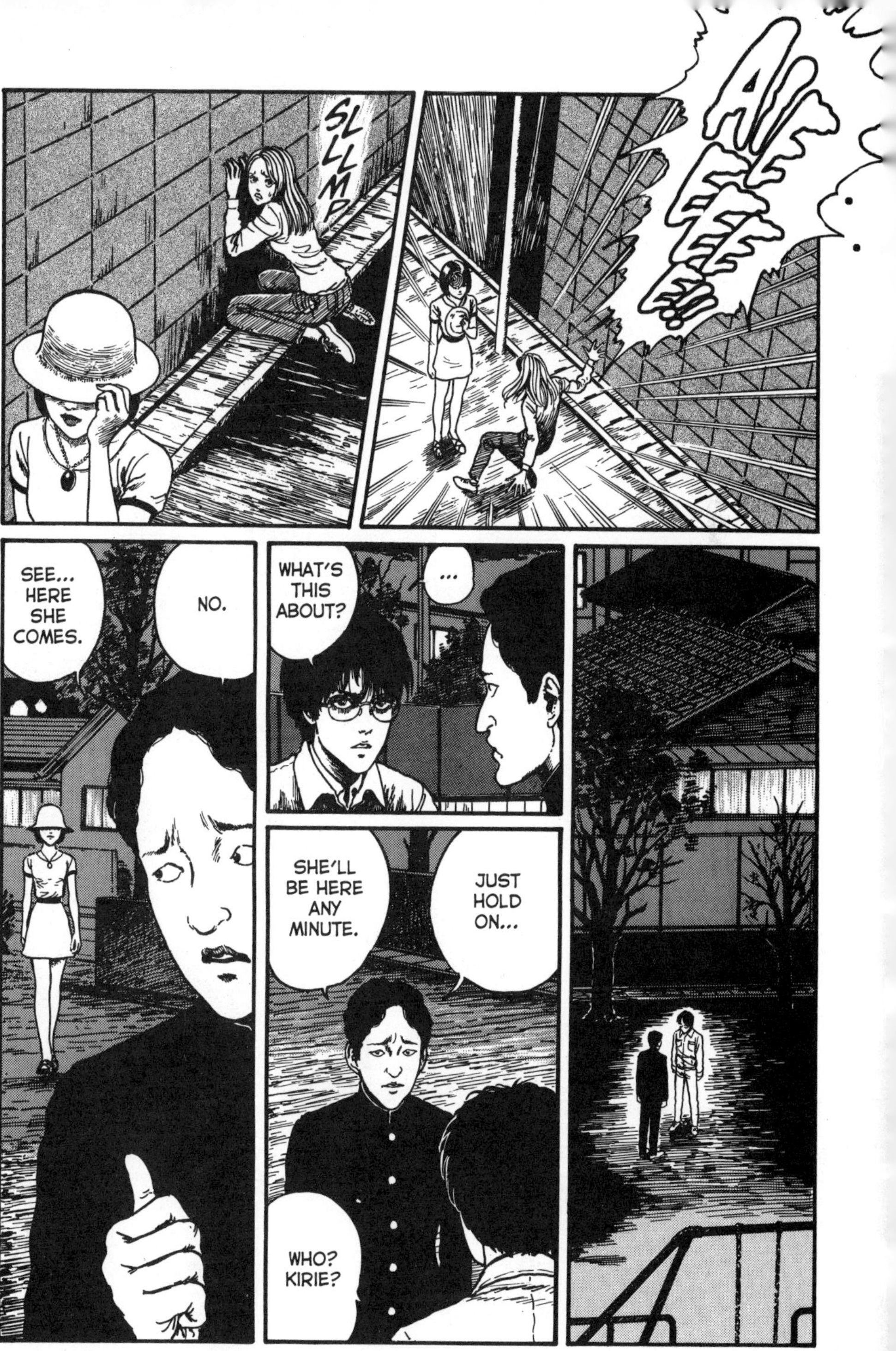
AIEEEE!!
SLLMP
...
WHAT'S THIS ABOUT?
JUST HOLD ON...
SHE'LL BE HERE ANY MINUTE.
WHO? KIRIE?
NO.
SEE... HERE SHE COMES.

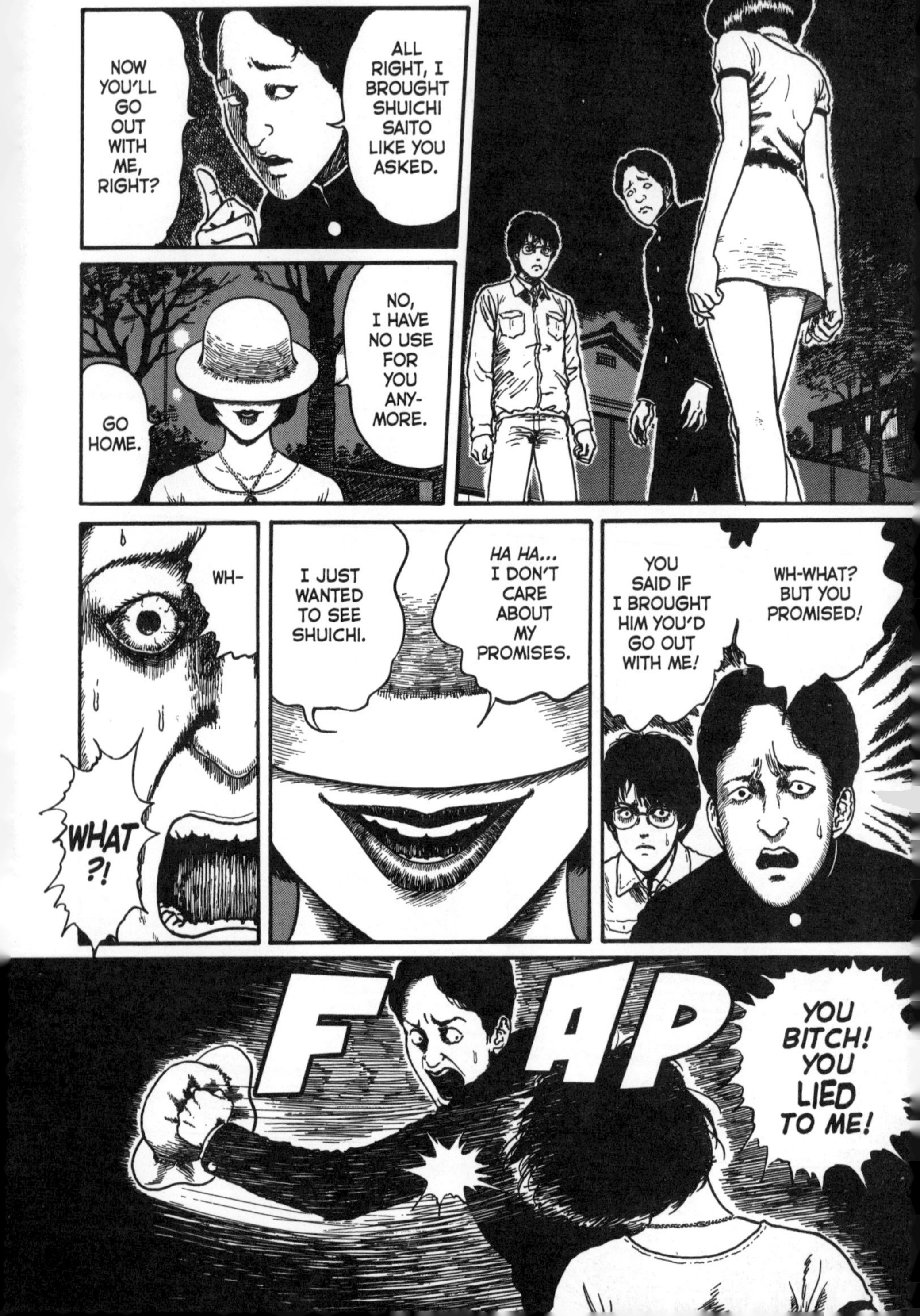
ALL RIGHT, I BROUGHT SHUICHI SAITO LIKE YOU ASKED.
NOW YOU'LL GO OUT WITH ME, RIGHT?
NO, I HAVE NO USE FOR YOU ANY-MORE.
GO HOME.
WH-WHAT? BUT YOU PROMISED!
YOU SAID IF I BROUGHT HIM YOU'D GO OUT WITH ME!
HA HA... I DON'T CARE ABOUT MY PROMISES.
I JUST WANTED TO SEE SHUICHI.
WH-
WHAT?!
YOU BITCH! YOU LIED TO ME!
F AP

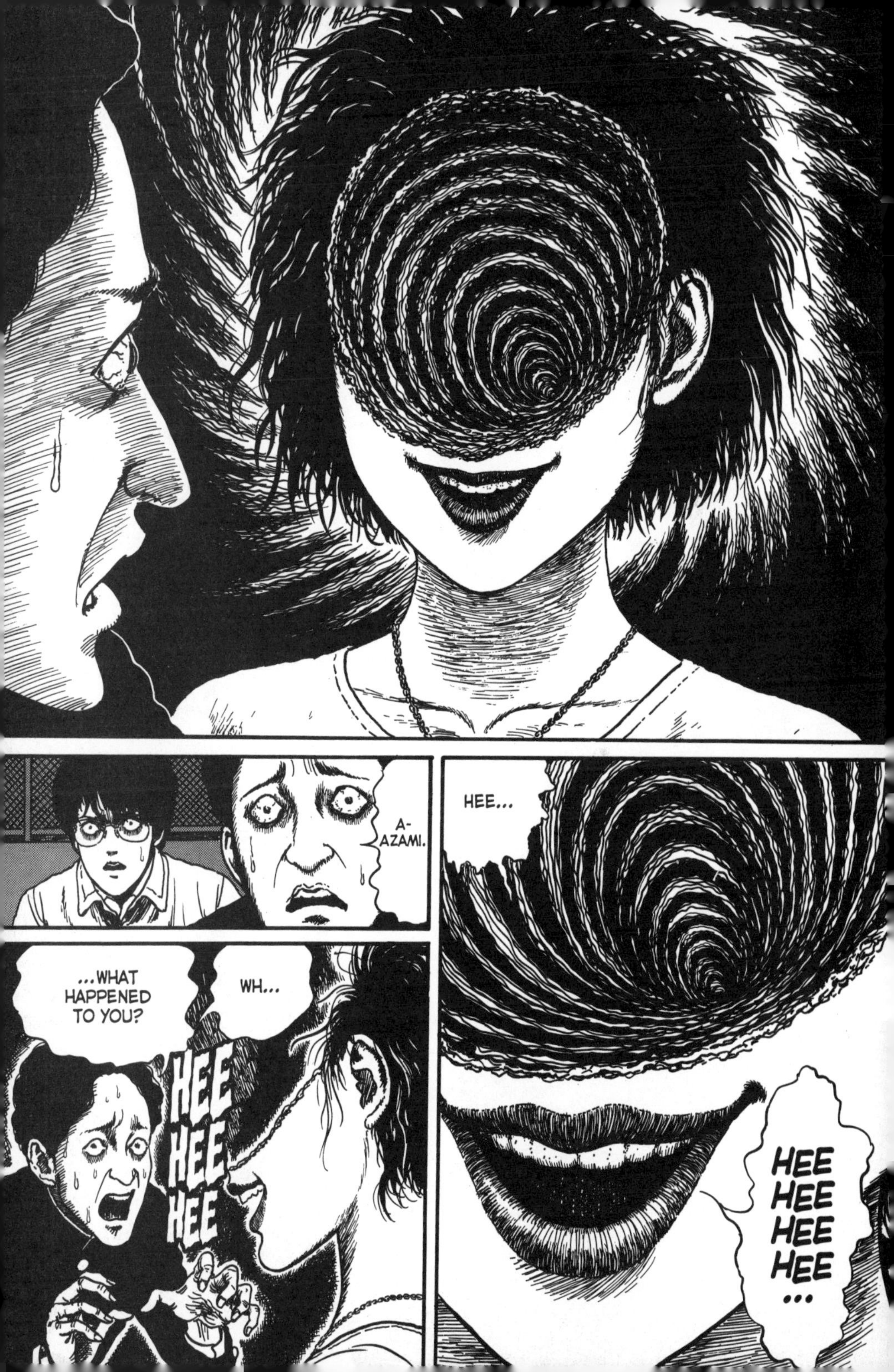
HEE...
HEE HEE HEE HEE ...
A-AZAMI.
WH...
...WHAT HAPPENED TO YOU?
HEE HEE HEE

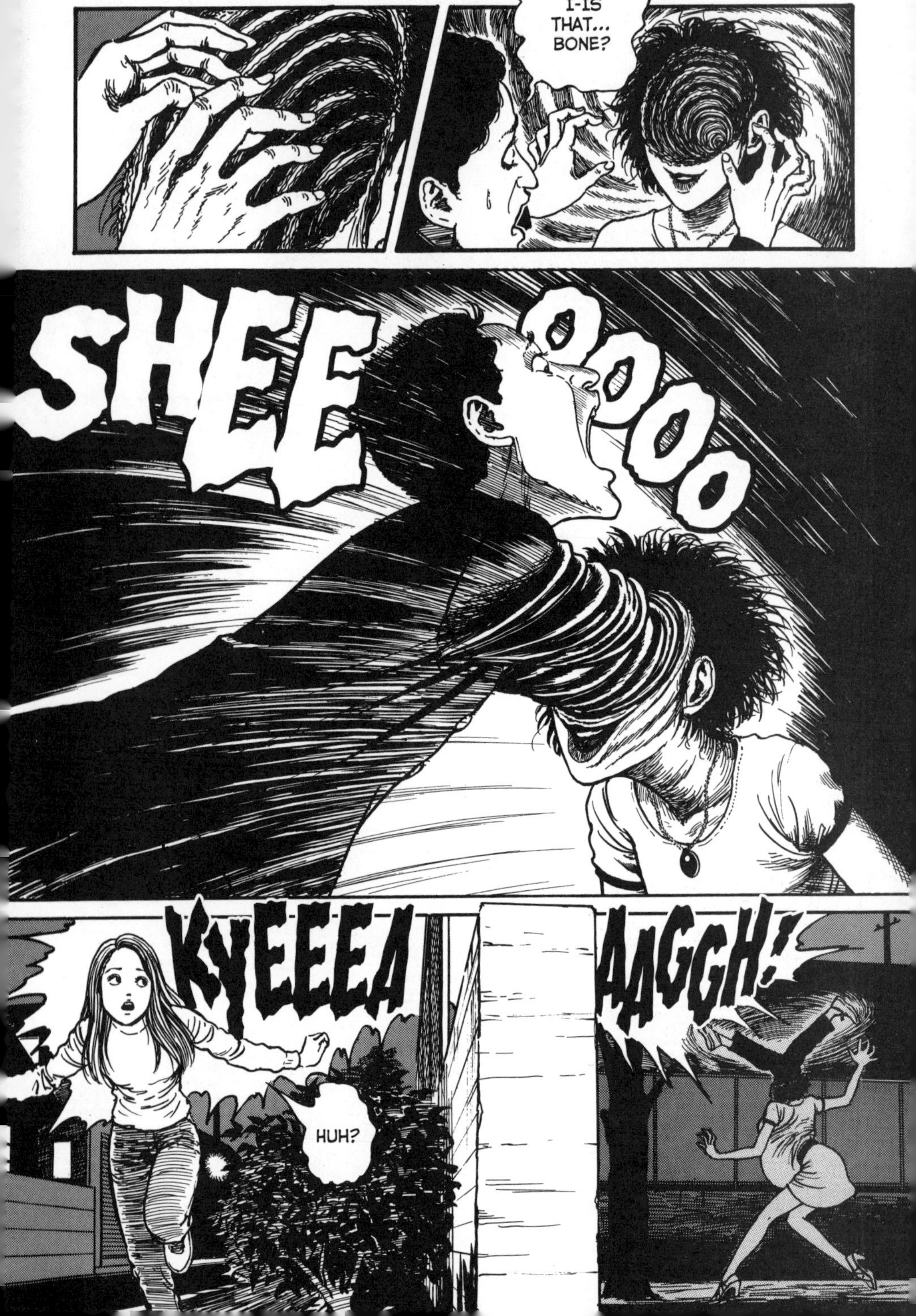
I-IS THAT... BONE?
SHEEOOOO
KYEEEAAAGGH!
HUH?

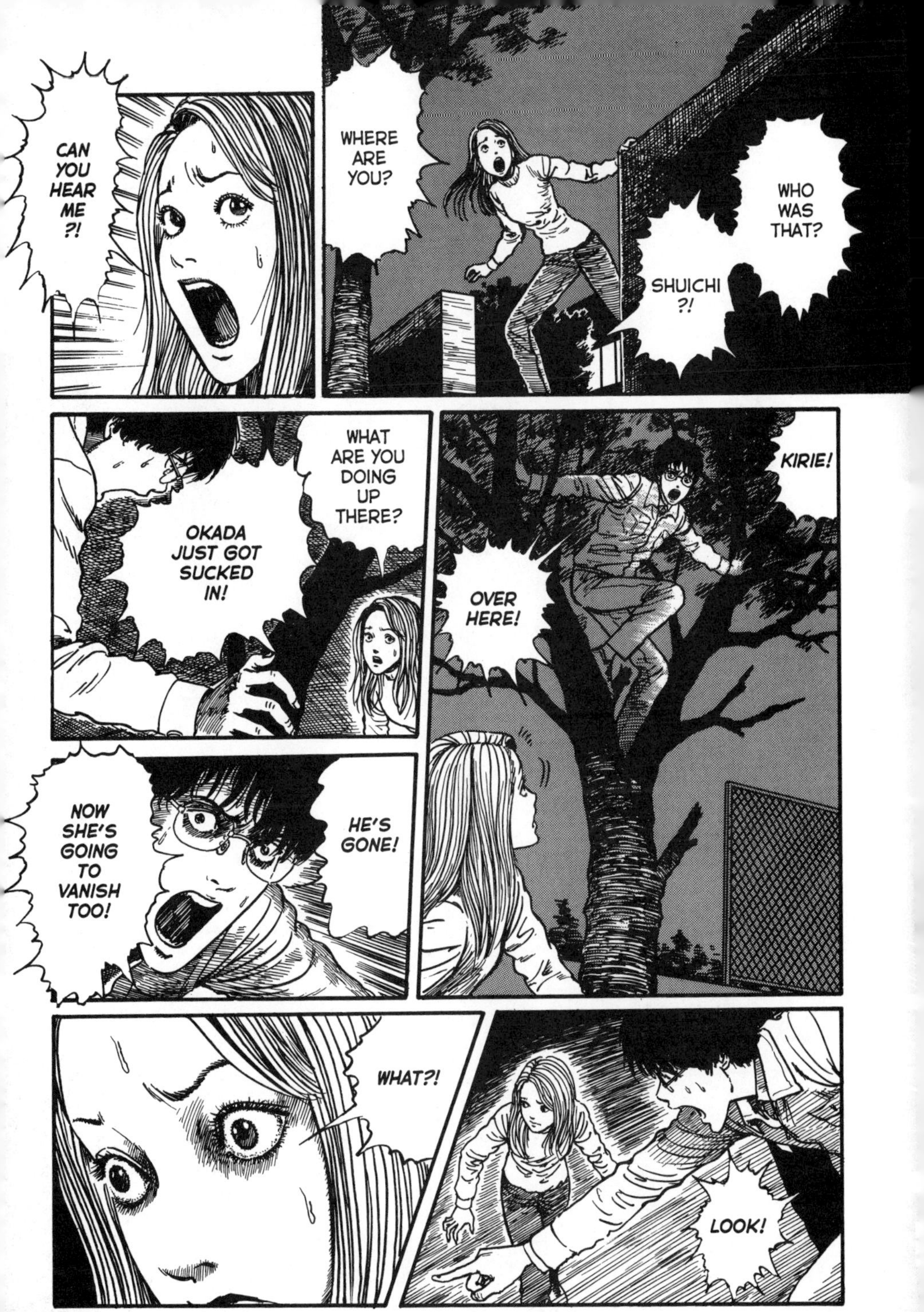
WHO WAS THAT?
SHUICHI?!
WHERE ARE YOU?
CAN YOU HEAR ME?!
KIRIE!
OVER HERE!
WHAT ARE YOU DOING UP THERE?
OKADA JUST GOT SUCKED IN!
HE'S GONE!
NOW SHE'S GOING TO VANISH TOO!
LOOK!
WHAT?!

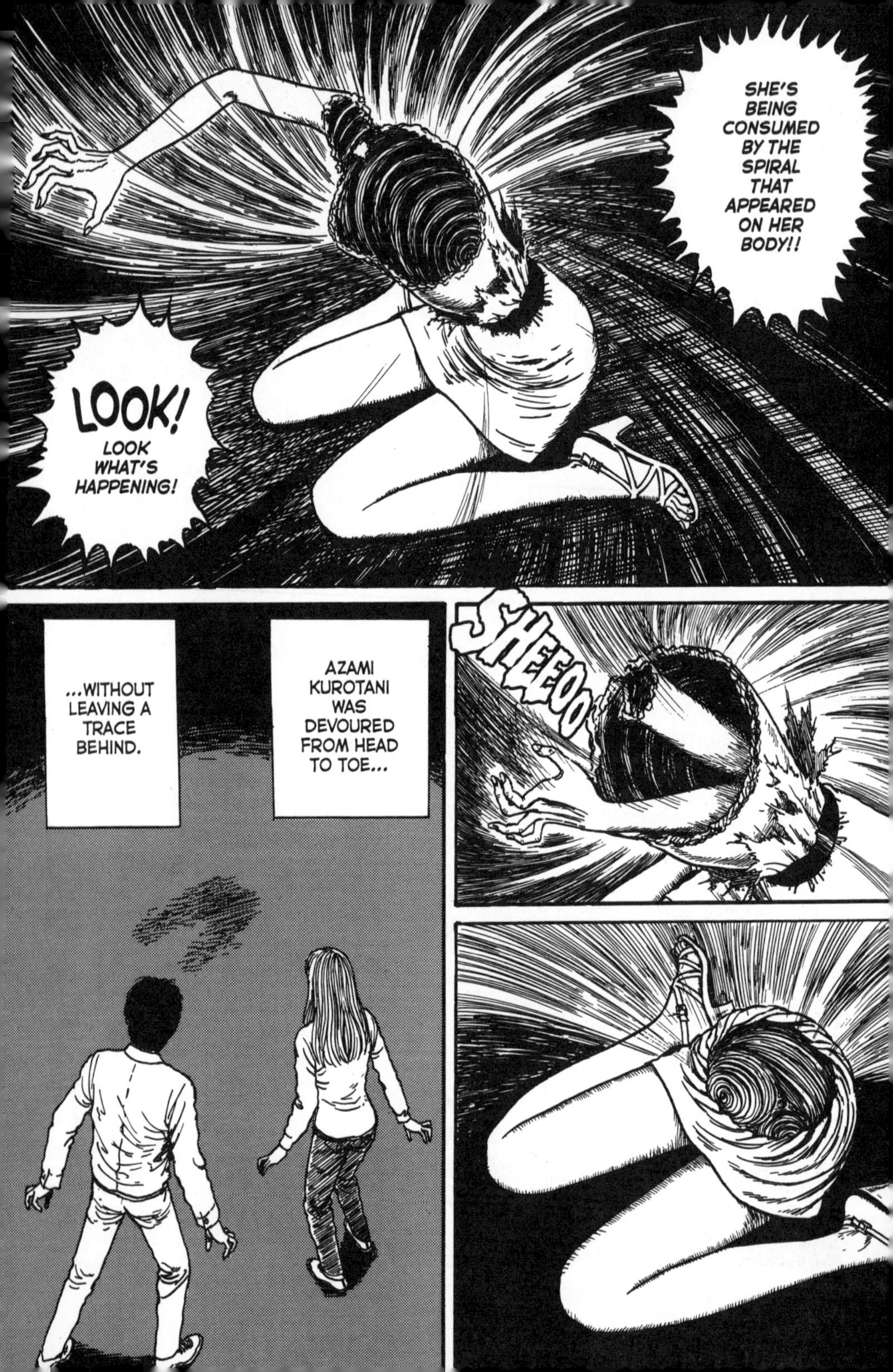
SHE'S BEING CONSUMED BY THE SPIRAL THAT APPEARED ON HER BODY!!
LOOK! LOOK WHAT'S HAPPENING!
SHEEOO
AZAMI KUROTANI WAS DEVOURED FROM HEAD TO TOE...
...WITHOUT LEAVING A TRACE BEHIND.

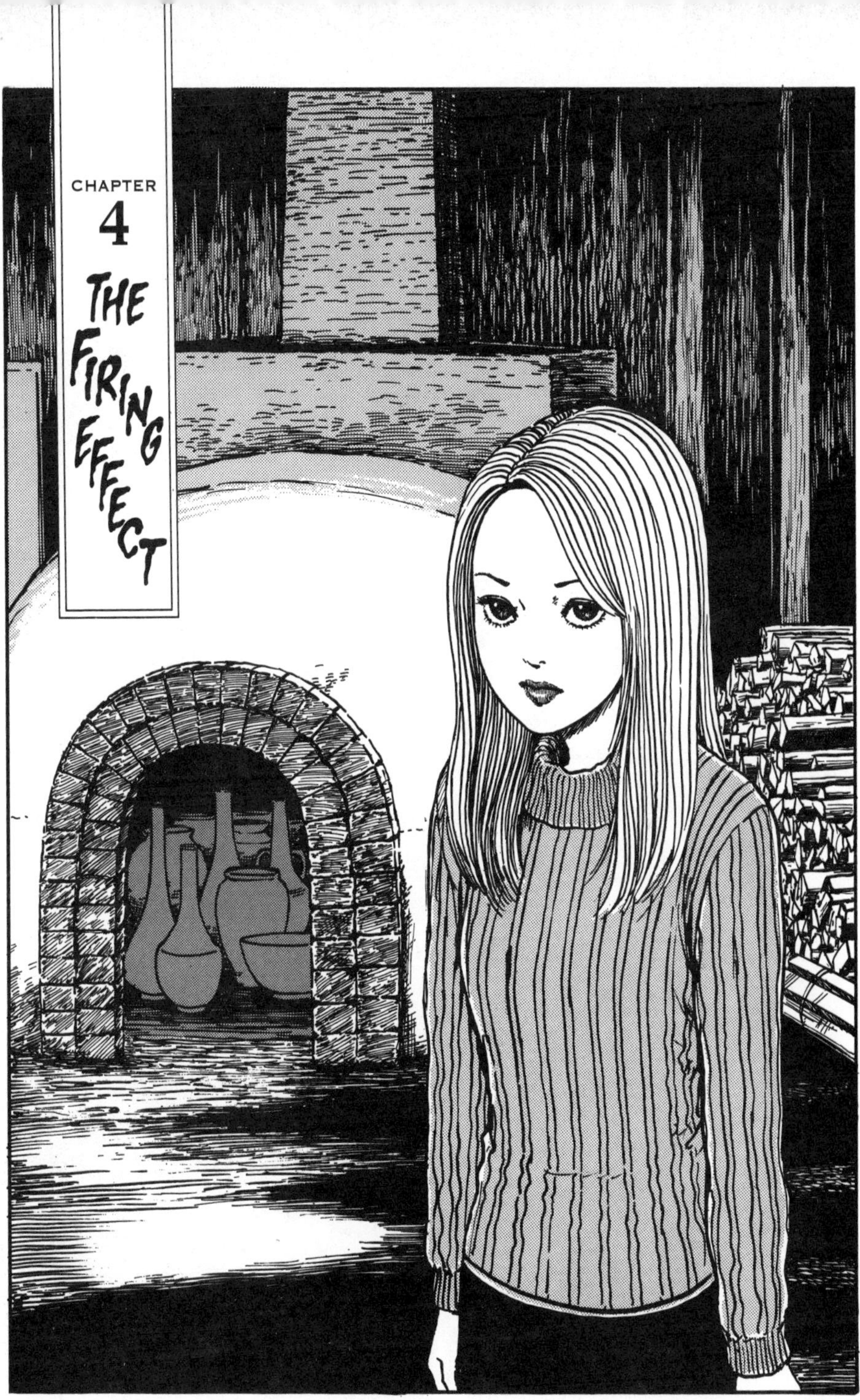
CHAPTER 4
THE FIRING EFFECT

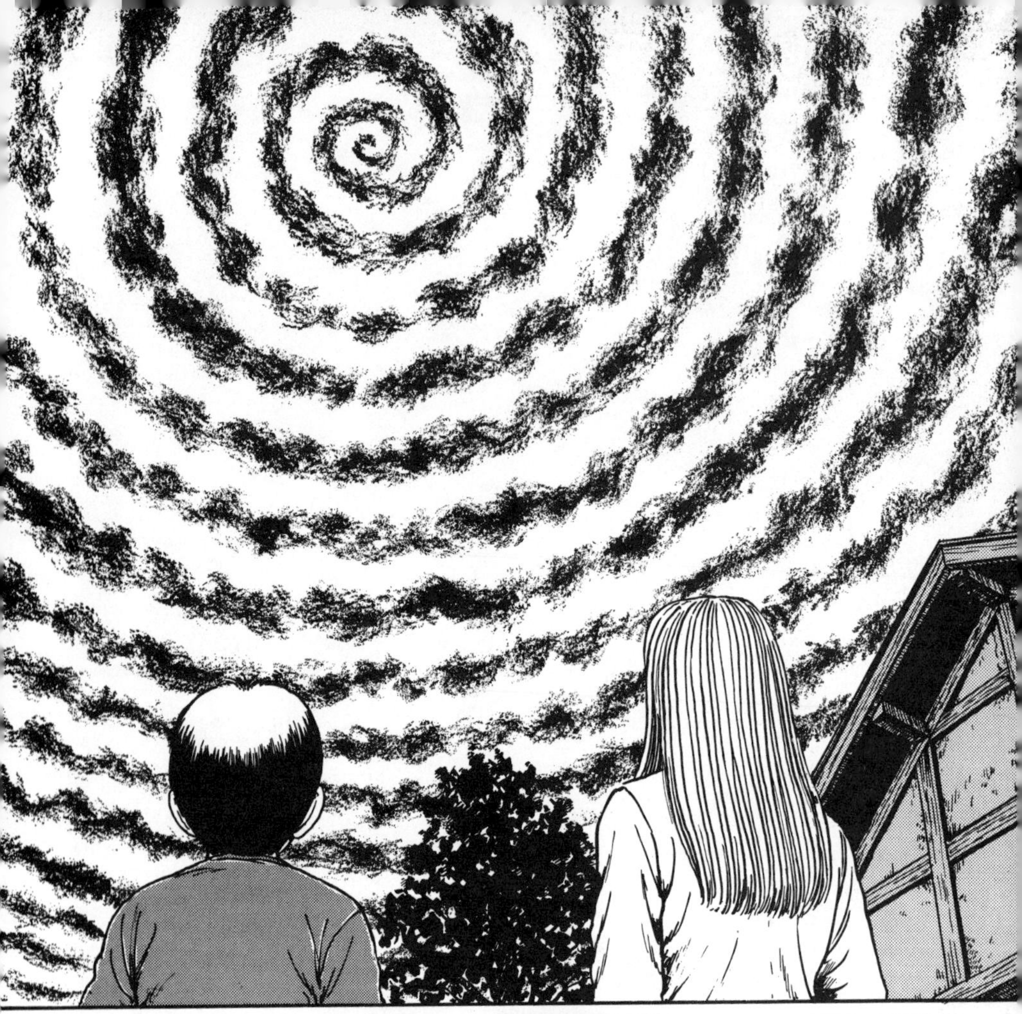

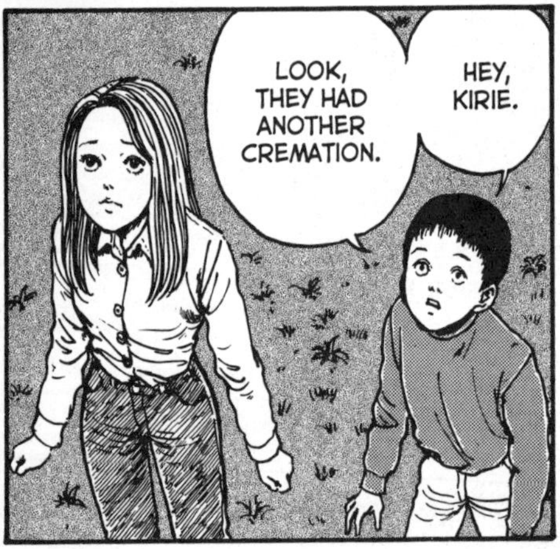
HEY, KIRIE.
LOOK, THEY HAD ANOTHER CREMATION.

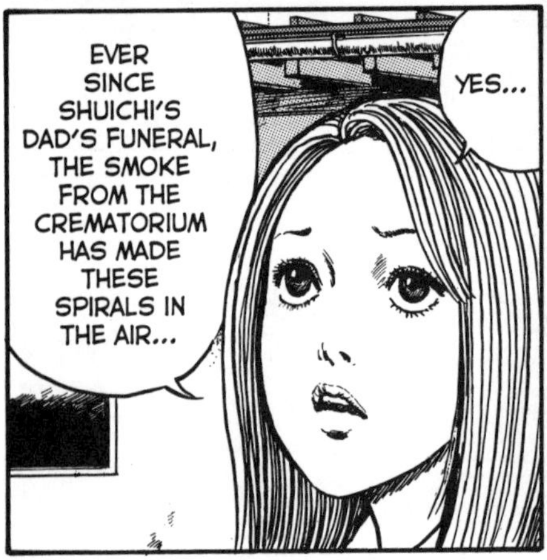
YES...
EVER SINCE SHUICHI'S DAD'S FUNERAL, THE SMOKE FROM THE CREMATORIUM HAS MADE THESE SPIRALS IN THE AIR...

SOON IT'LL FALL INTO DRAGONFLY POND.

LOOK, MITSUO...

SEE?

IT'S FALLING SLOWLY...

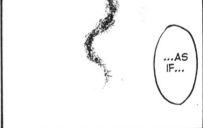

...AS IF...

...THE POND IS SUCKING IT IN...

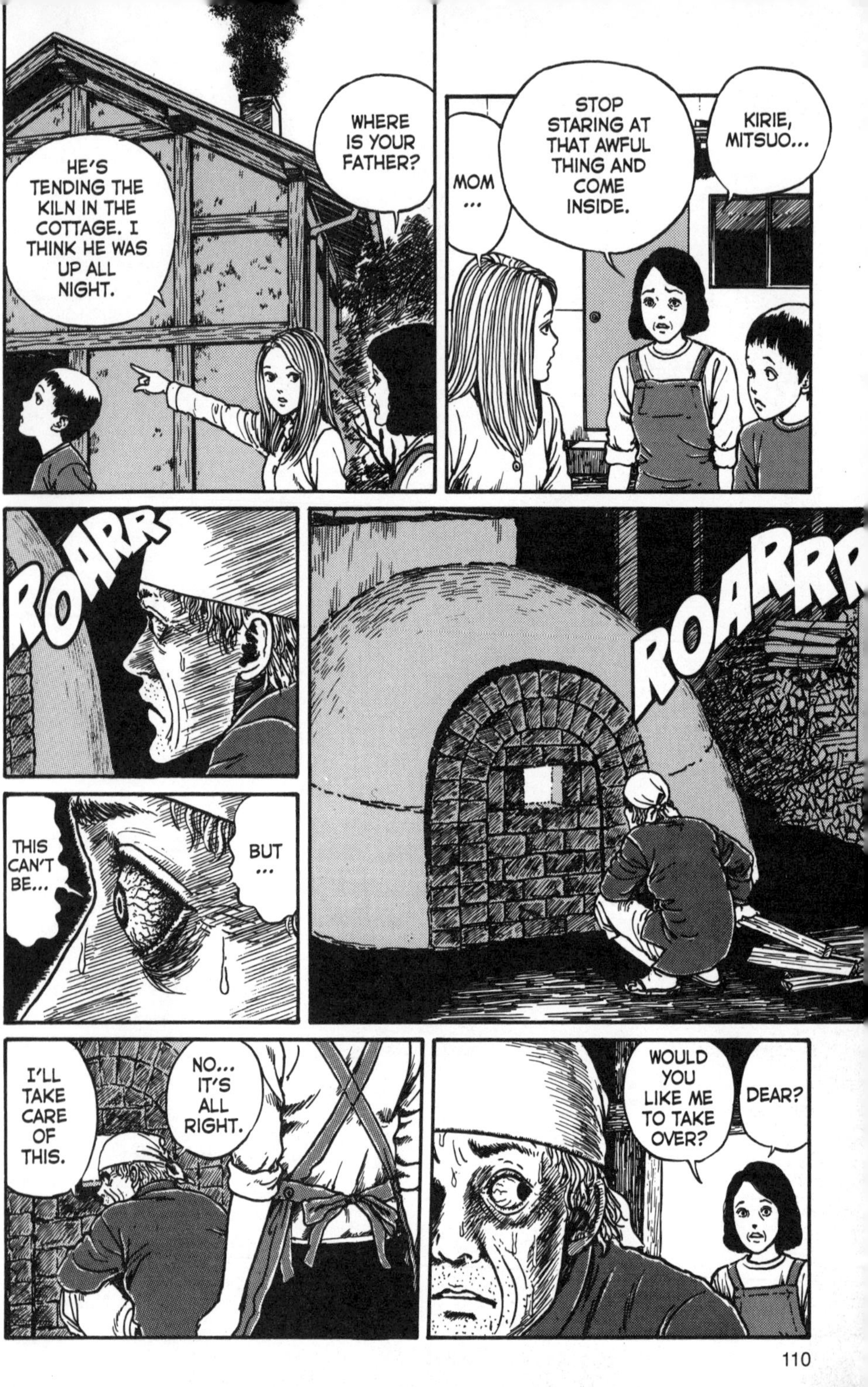
KIRIE, MITSUO...
STOP STARING AT THAT AWFUL THING AND COME INSIDE.
MOM...
WHERE IS YOUR FATHER?
HE'S TENDING THE KILN IN THE COTTAGE. I THINK HE WAS UP ALL NIGHT.
ROARRR
ROARR
THIS CAN'T BE...
BUT...
DEAR?
WOULD YOU LIKE ME TO TAKE OVER?
NO... IT'S ALL RIGHT.
I'LL TAKE CARE OF THIS.

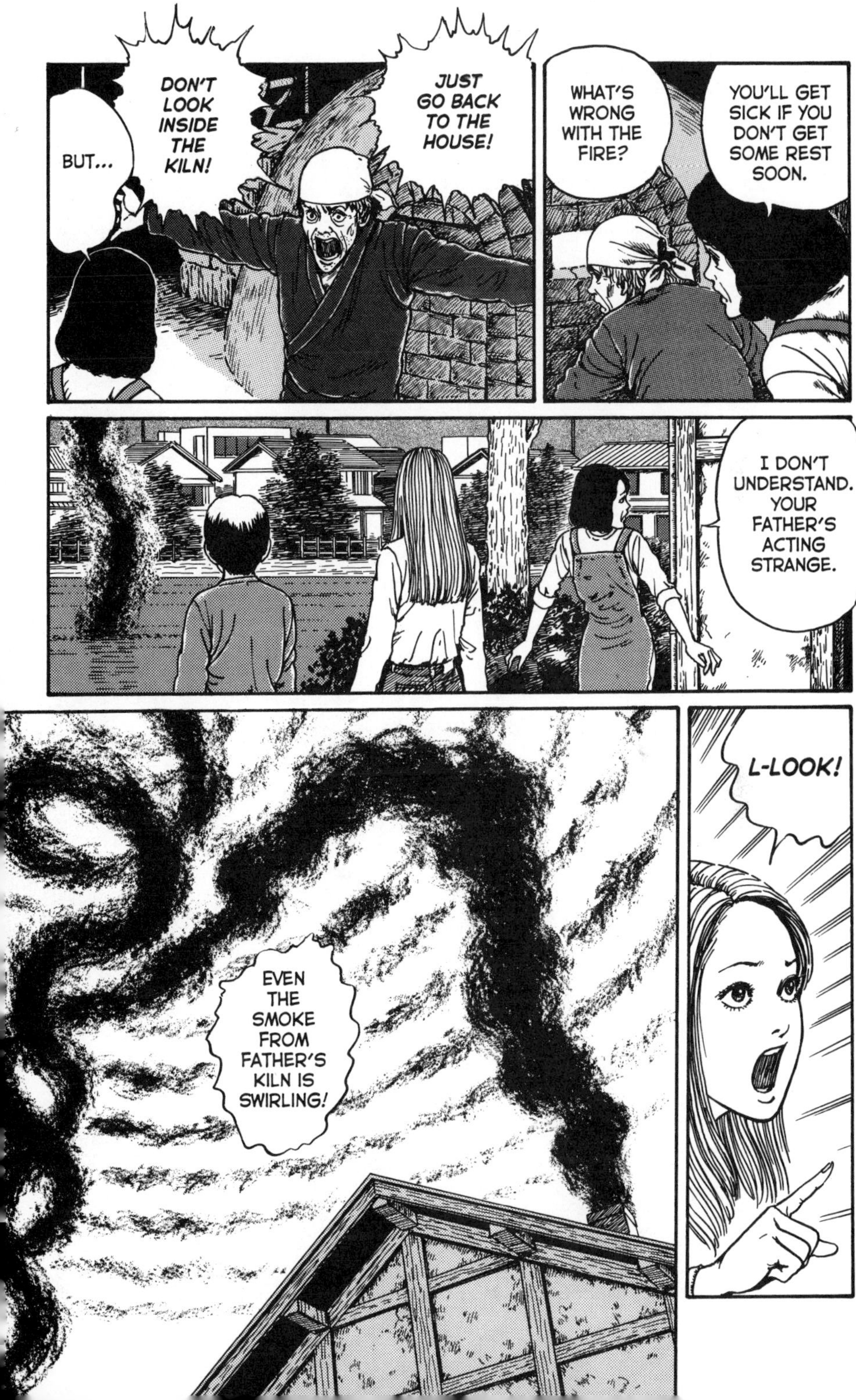
YOU'LL GET SICK IF YOU DON'T GET SOME REST SOON.
WHAT'S WRONG WITH THE FIRE?
JUST GO BACK TO THE HOUSE!
DON'T LOOK INSIDE THE KILN!
BUT...
I DON'T UNDERSTAND. YOUR FATHER'S ACTING STRANGE.
L-LOOK!
EVEN THE SMOKE FROM FATHER'S KILN IS SWIRLING!

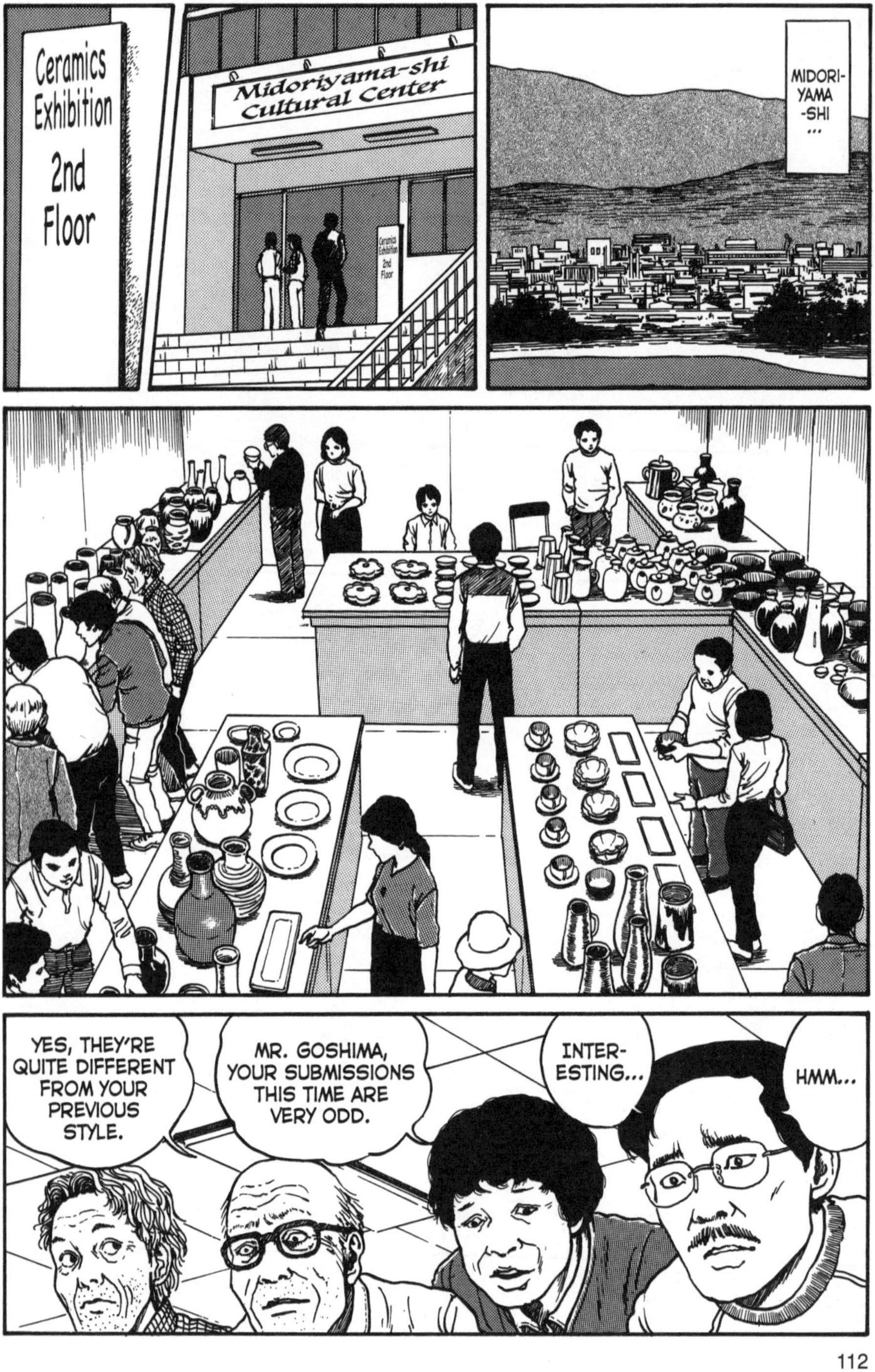
MIDORI-YAMA-SHI ...
Midoriyama-shi Cultural Center
Ceramics Exhibition 2nd Floor
Ceramics Exhibition 2nd Floor
HMM...
INTER-ESTING...
MR. GOSHIMA, YOUR SUBMISSIONS THIS TIME ARE VERY ODD.
YES, THEY'RE QUITE DIFFERENT FROM YOUR PREVIOUS STYLE.

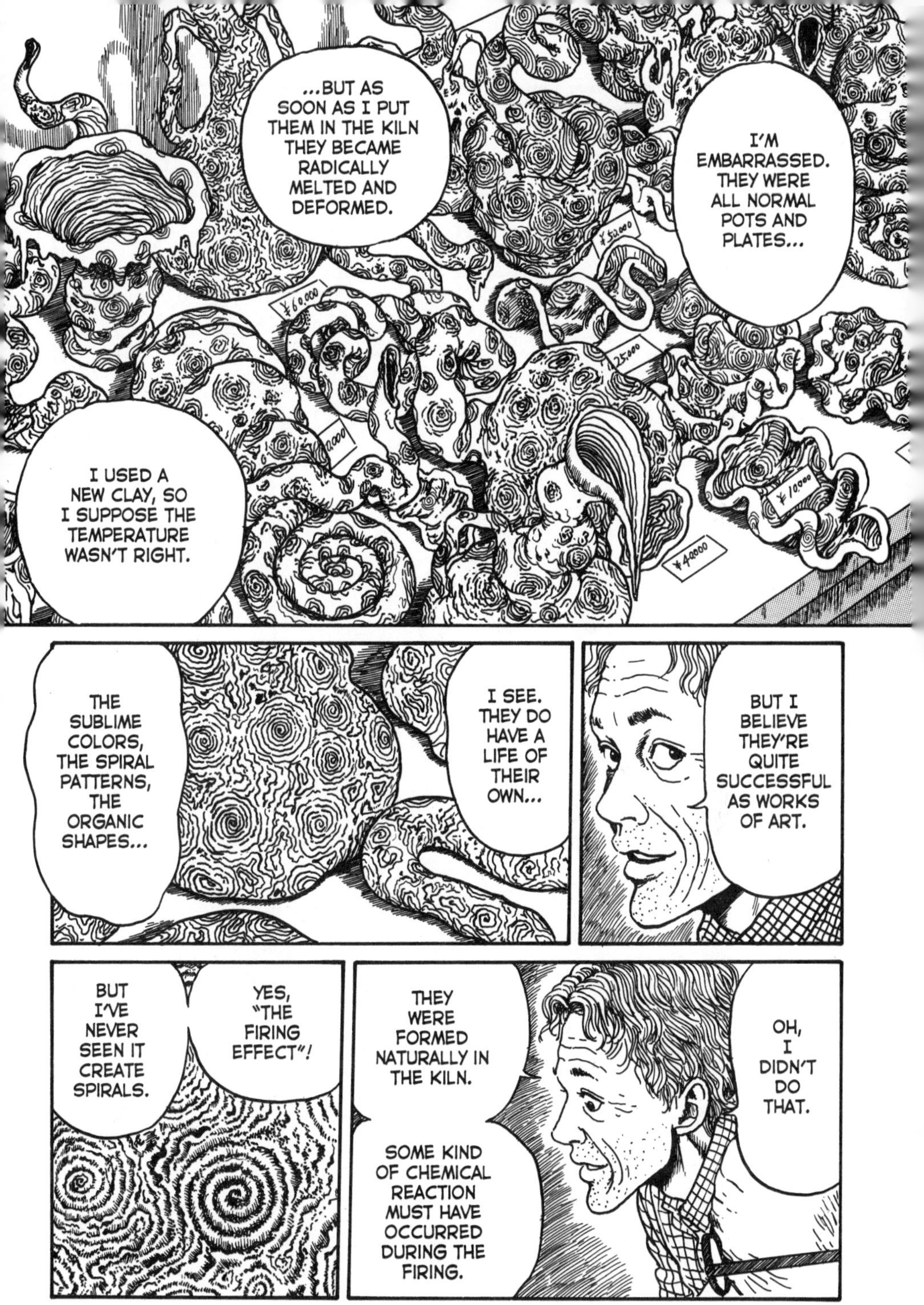
I'M EMBARRASSED. THEY WERE ALL NORMAL POTS AND PLATES...
...BUT AS SOON AS I PUT THEM IN THE KILN THEY BECAME RADICALLY MELTED AND DEFORMED.
I USED A NEW CLAY, SO I SUPPOSE THE TEMPERATURE WASN'T RIGHT.
BUT I BELIEVE THEY'RE QUITE SUCCESSFUL AS WORKS OF ART.
I SEE. THEY DO HAVE A LIFE OF THEIR OWN...
THE SUBLIME COLORS, THE SPIRAL PATTERNS, THE ORGANIC SHAPES...
OH, I DIDN'T DO THAT.
THEY WERE FORMED NATURALLY IN THE KILN.
SOME KIND OF CHEMICAL REACTION MUST HAVE OCCURRED DURING THE FIRING.
YES, "THE FIRING EFFECT"!
BUT I'VE NEVER SEEN IT CREATE SPIRALS.

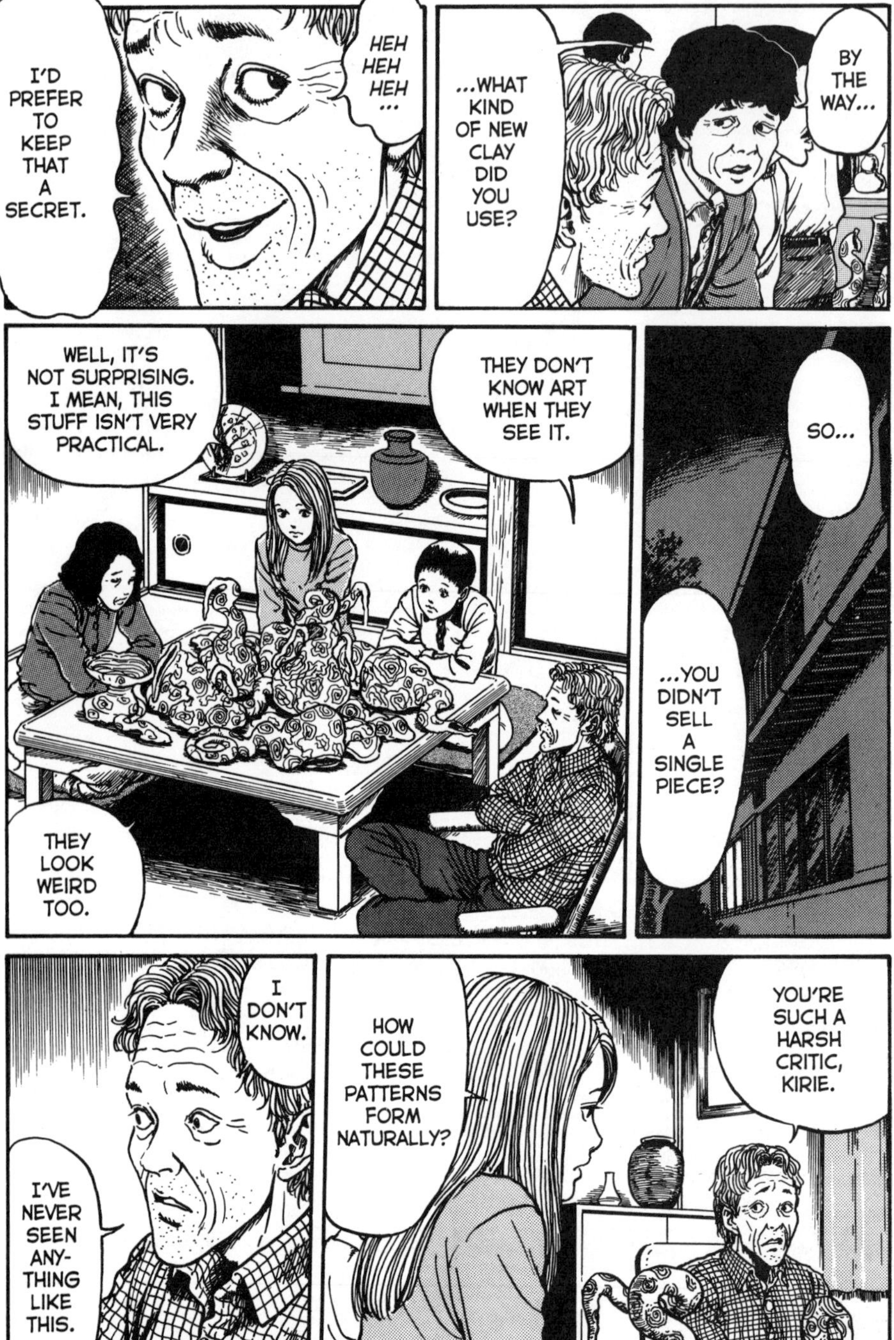
BY THE WAY...
...WHAT KIND OF NEW CLAY DID YOU USE?
HEH HEH HEH...
I'D PREFER TO KEEP THAT A SECRET.
SO...
...YOU DIDN'T SELL A SINGLE PIECE?
THEY DON'T KNOW ART WHEN THEY SEE IT.
WELL, IT'S NOT SURPRISING. I MEAN, THIS STUFF ISN'T VERY PRACTICAL.
THEY LOOK WEIRD TOO.
YOU'RE SUCH A HARSH CRITIC, KIRIE.
HOW COULD THESE PATTERNS FORM NATURALLY?
I DON'T KNOW.
I'VE NEVER SEEN ANY-THING LIKE THIS.

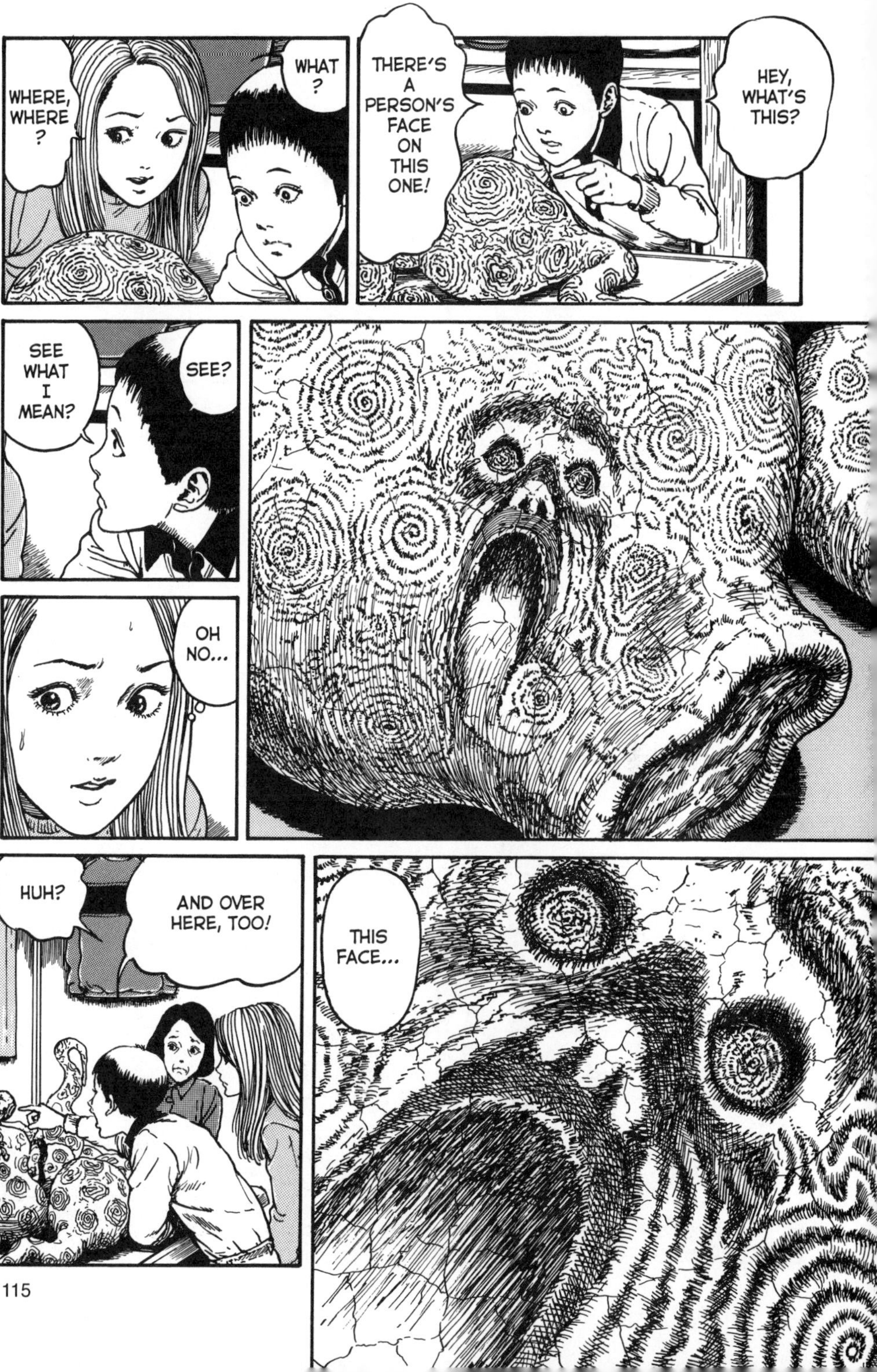
HEY, WHAT'S THIS?
THERE'S A PERSON'S FACE ON THIS ONE!
WHAT?
WHERE, WHERE?
SEE?
SEE WHAT I MEAN?
OH NO...
THIS FACE...
AND OVER HERE, TOO!
HUH?

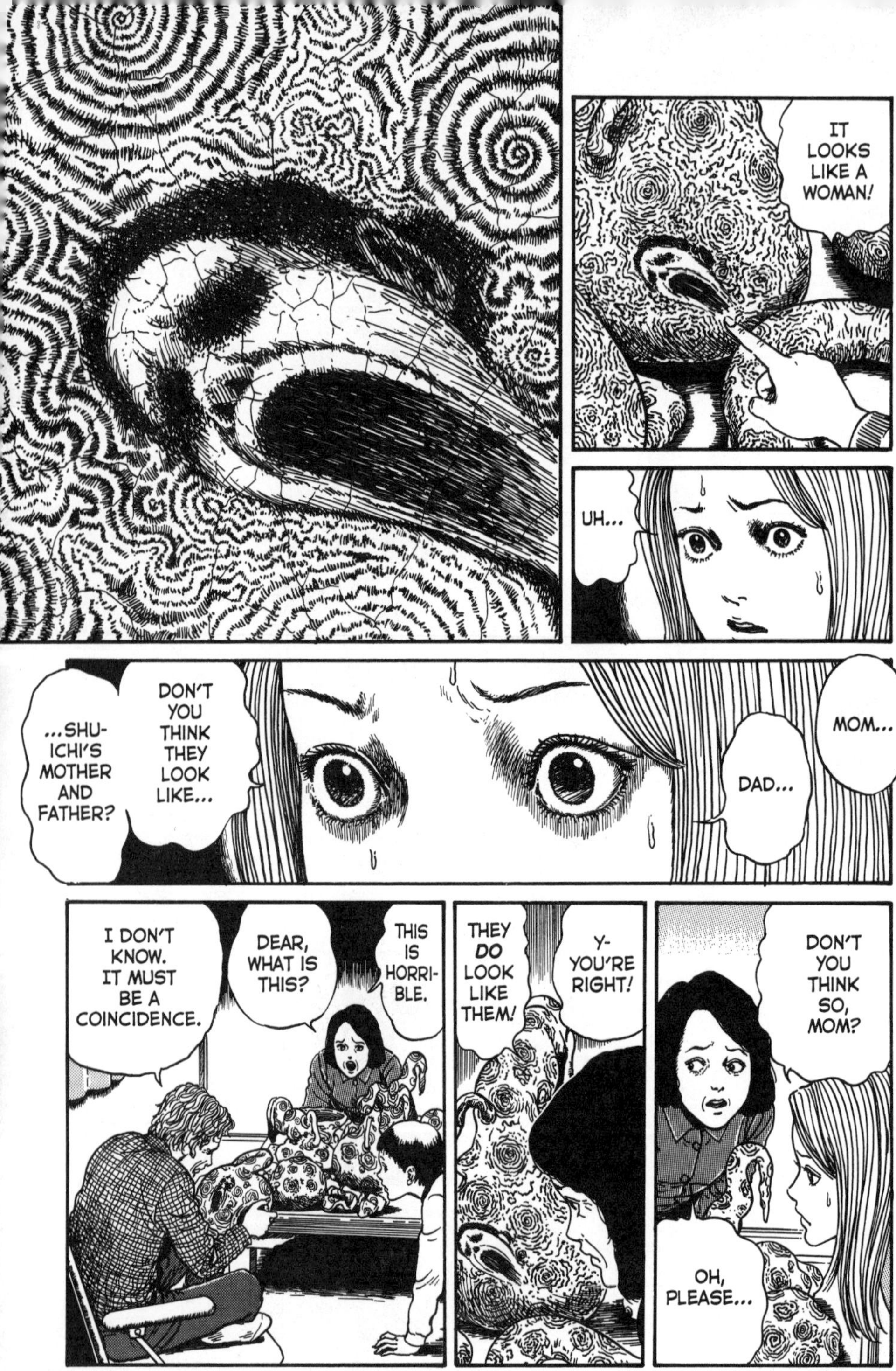
IT LOOKS LIKE A WOMAN!
UH...
MOM...
DAD...
DON'T YOU THINK THEY LOOK LIKE...
...SHUICHI'S MOTHER AND FATHER?
DON'T YOU THINK SO, MOM?
OH, PLEASE...
Y-YOU'RE RIGHT!
THEY *DO* LOOK LIKE THEM!
THIS IS HORRIBLE.
DEAR, WHAT IS THIS?
I DON'T KNOW. IT MUST BE A COINCIDENCE.

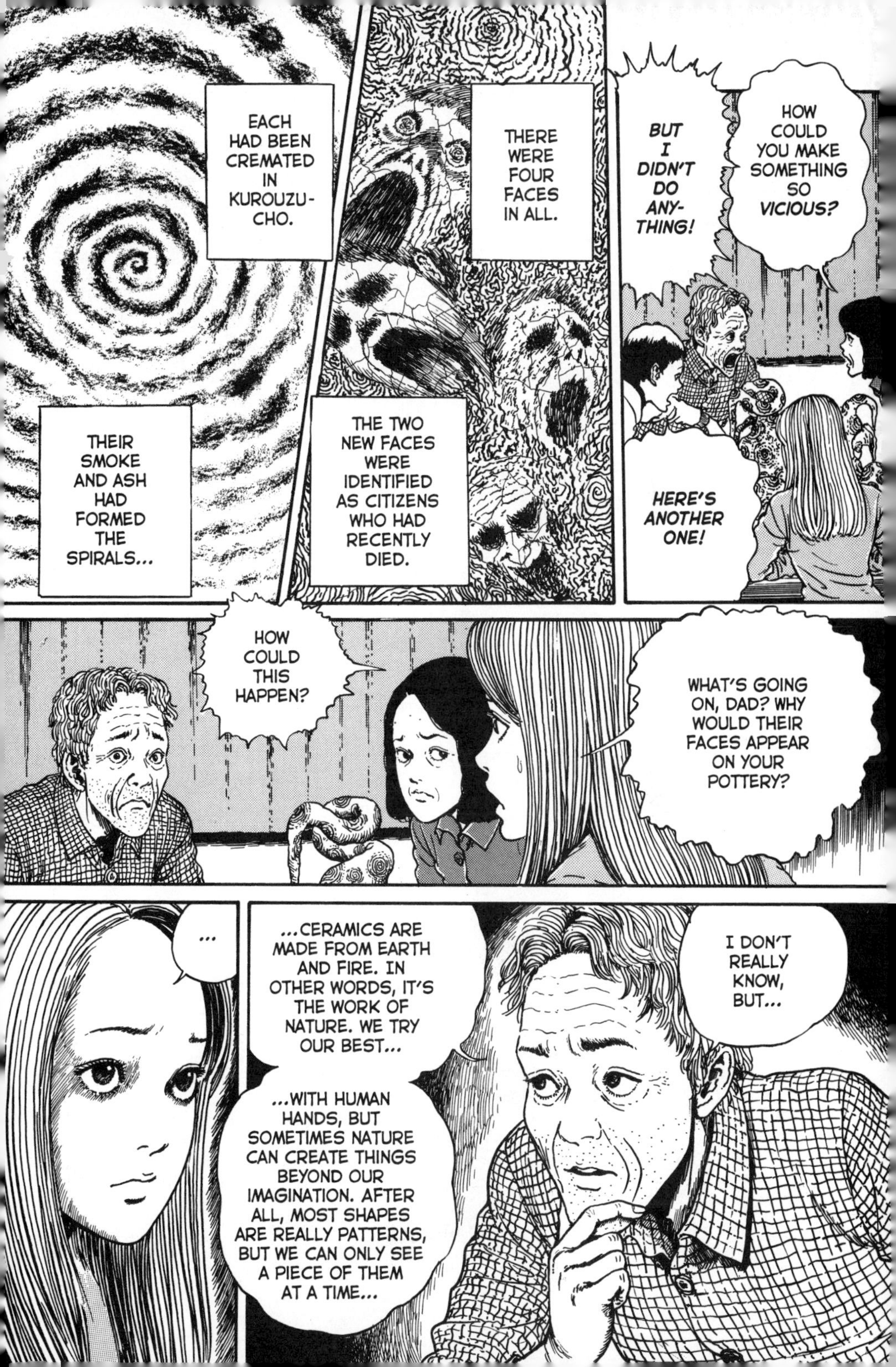

HOW COULD YOU MAKE SOMETHING SO *VICIOUS?*
BUT I DIDN'T DO ANY-THING!
HERE'S ANOTHER ONE!
THERE WERE FOUR FACES IN ALL.
THE TWO NEW FACES WERE IDENTIFIED AS CITIZENS WHO HAD RECENTLY DIED.
EACH HAD BEEN CREMATED IN KUROUZU-CHO.
THEIR SMOKE AND ASH HAD FORMED THE SPIRALS...
WHAT'S GOING ON, DAD? WHY WOULD THEIR FACES APPEAR ON YOUR POTTERY?
HOW COULD THIS HAPPEN?
I DON'T REALLY KNOW, BUT...
...CERAMICS ARE MADE FROM EARTH AND FIRE. IN OTHER WORDS, IT'S THE WORK OF NATURE. WE TRY OUR BEST...
...WITH HUMAN HANDS, BUT SOMETIMES NATURE CAN CREATE THINGS BEYOND OUR IMAGINATION. AFTER ALL, MOST SHAPES ARE REALLY PATTERNS, BUT WE CAN ONLY SEE A PIECE OF THEM AT A TIME...
...

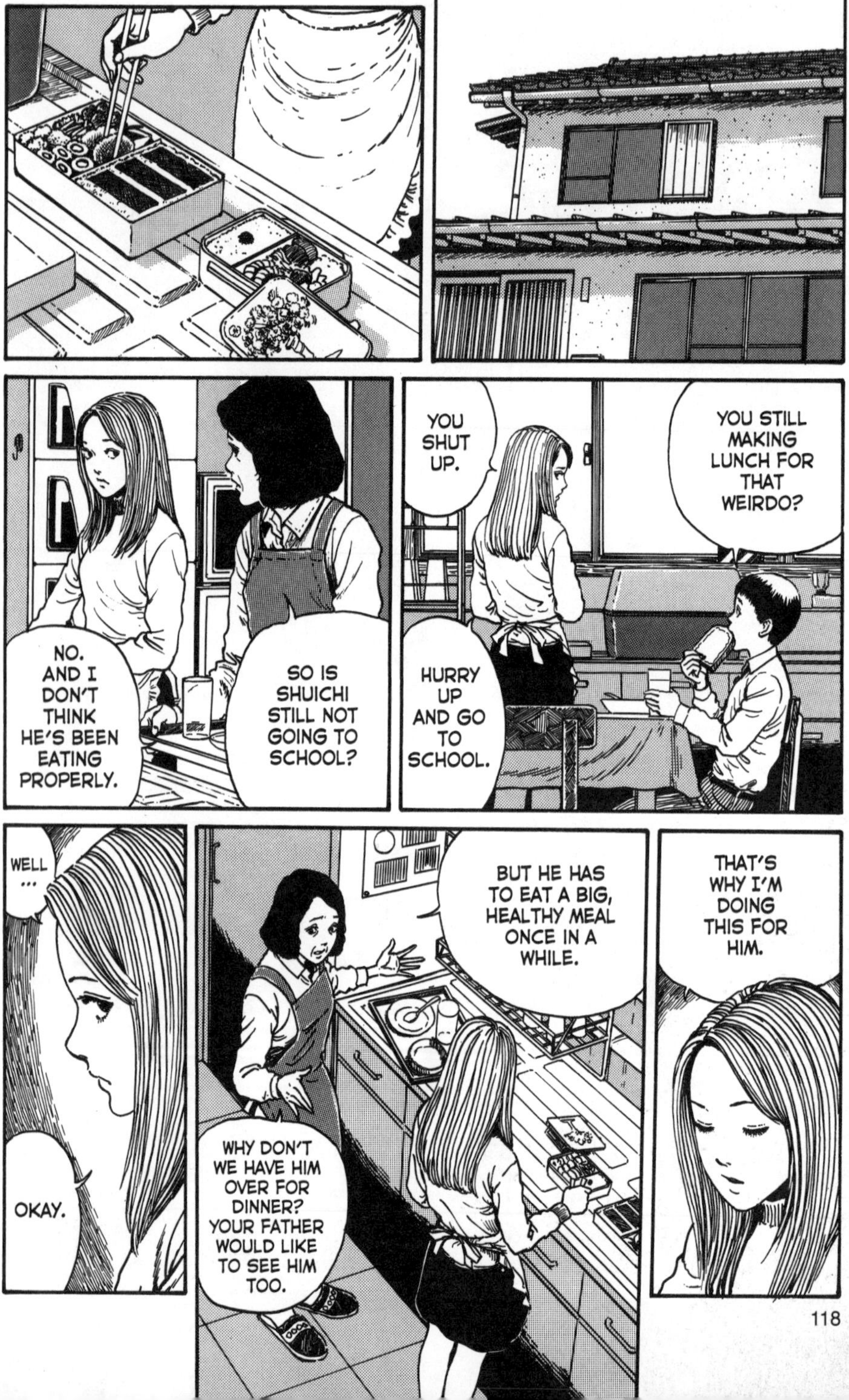
YOU STILL MAKING LUNCH FOR THAT WEIRDO?
YOU SHUT UP.
HURRY UP AND GO TO SCHOOL.
SO IS SHUICHI STILL NOT GOING TO SCHOOL?
NO. AND I DON'T THINK HE'S BEEN EATING PROPERLY.
THAT'S WHY I'M DOING THIS FOR HIM.
BUT HE HAS TO EAT A BIG, HEALTHY MEAL ONCE IN A WHILE.
WHY DON'T WE HAVE HIM OVER FOR DINNER? YOUR FATHER WOULD LIKE TO SEE HIM TOO.
WELL...
OKAY.

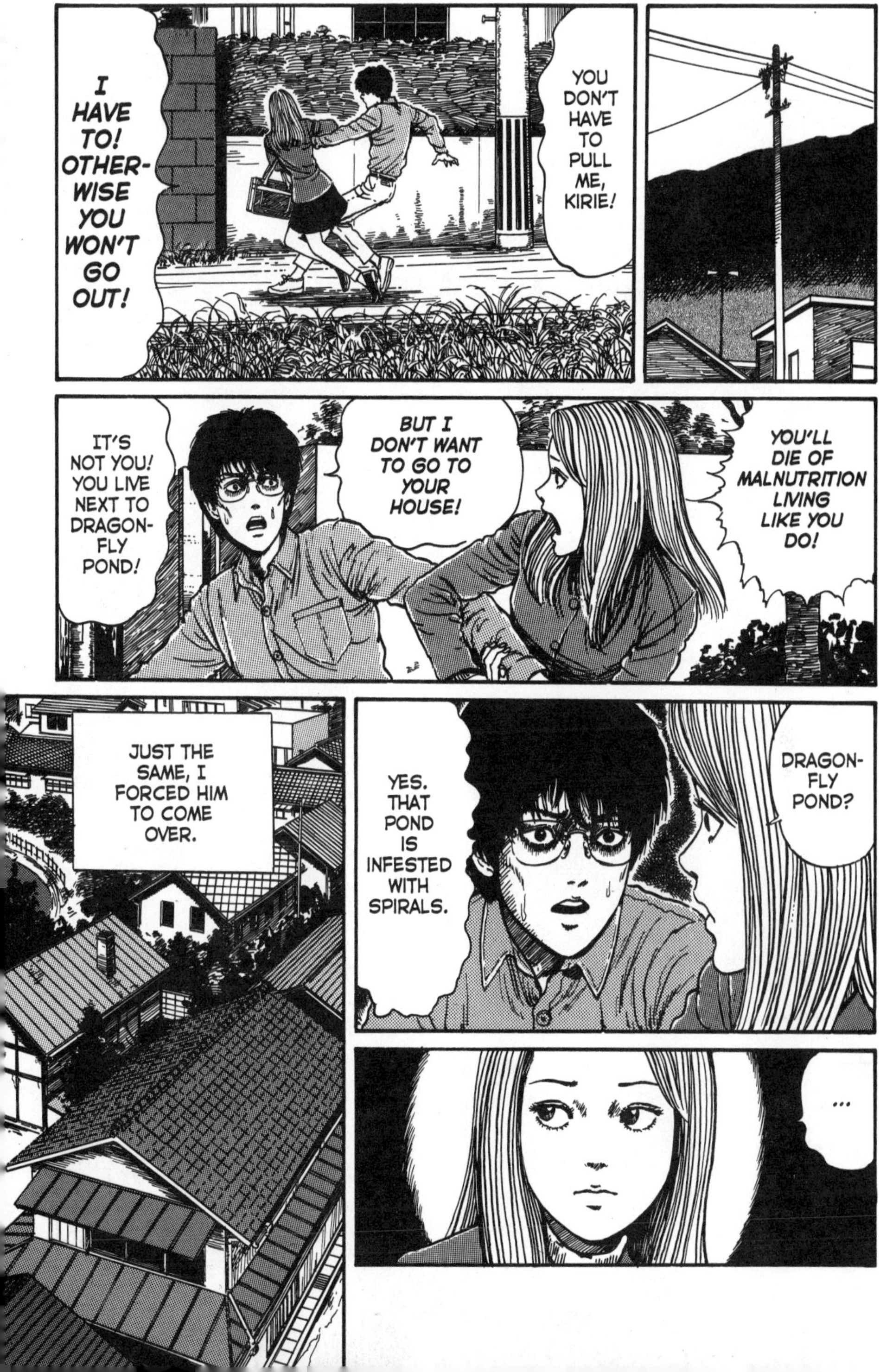
YOU DON'T HAVE TO PULL ME, KIRIE!
I HAVE TO! OTHER-WISE YOU WON'T GO OUT!
YOU'LL DIE OF MALNUTRITION LIVING LIKE YOU DO!
BUT I DON'T WANT TO GO TO YOUR HOUSE!
IT'S NOT YOU! YOU LIVE NEXT TO DRAGON-FLY POND!
DRAGON-FLY POND?
YES. THAT POND IS INFESTED WITH SPIRALS.
...
JUST THE SAME, I FORCED HIM TO COME OVER.

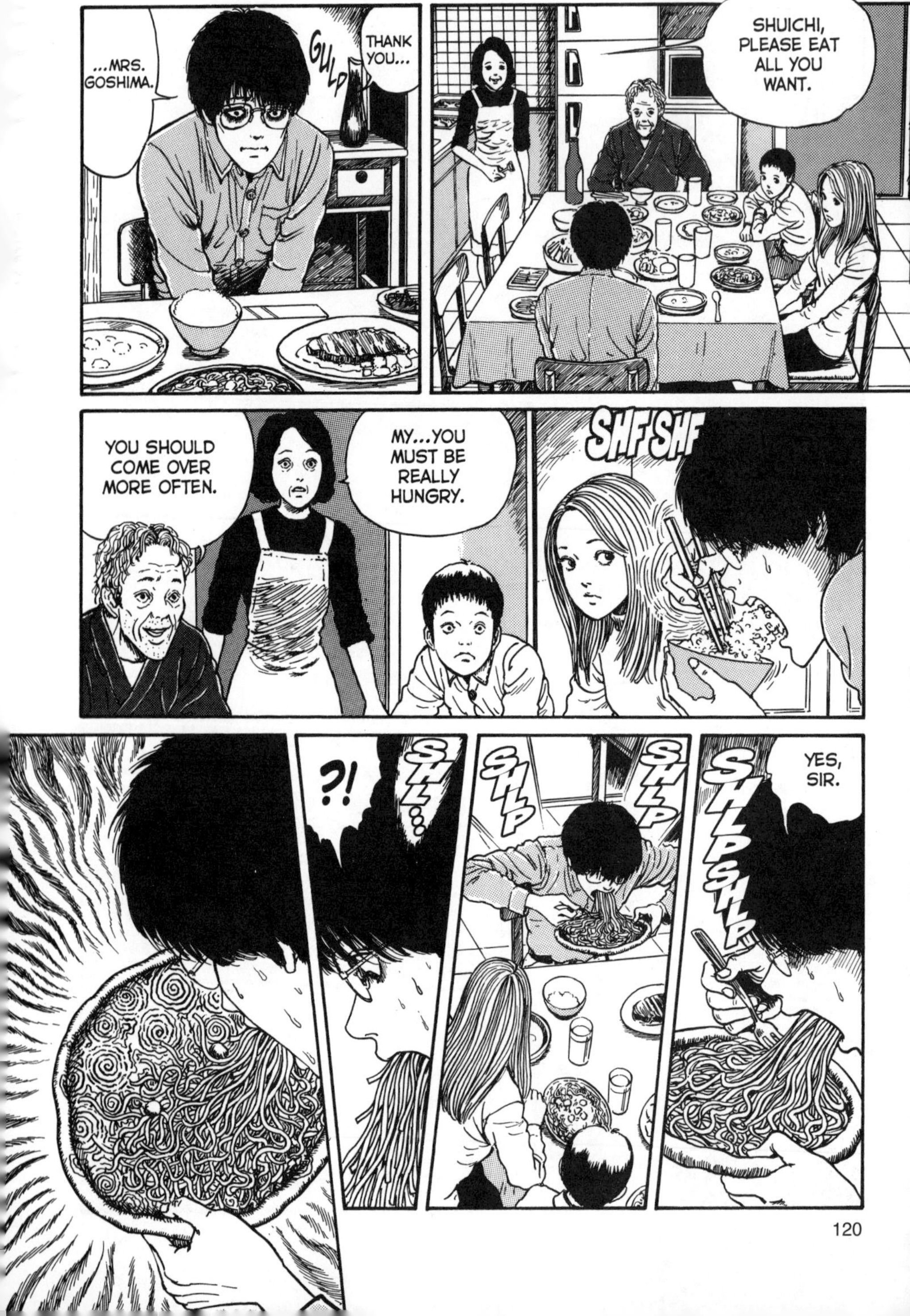
SHUICHI, PLEASE EAT ALL YOU WANT.
THANK YOU...
GULP
...MRS. GOSHIMA.
SHF SHF
MY...YOU MUST BE REALLY HUNGRY.
YOU SHOULD COME OVER MORE OFTEN.
YES, SIR.
SHLPSHLP
SHLP
SHLP
SHL...
?!

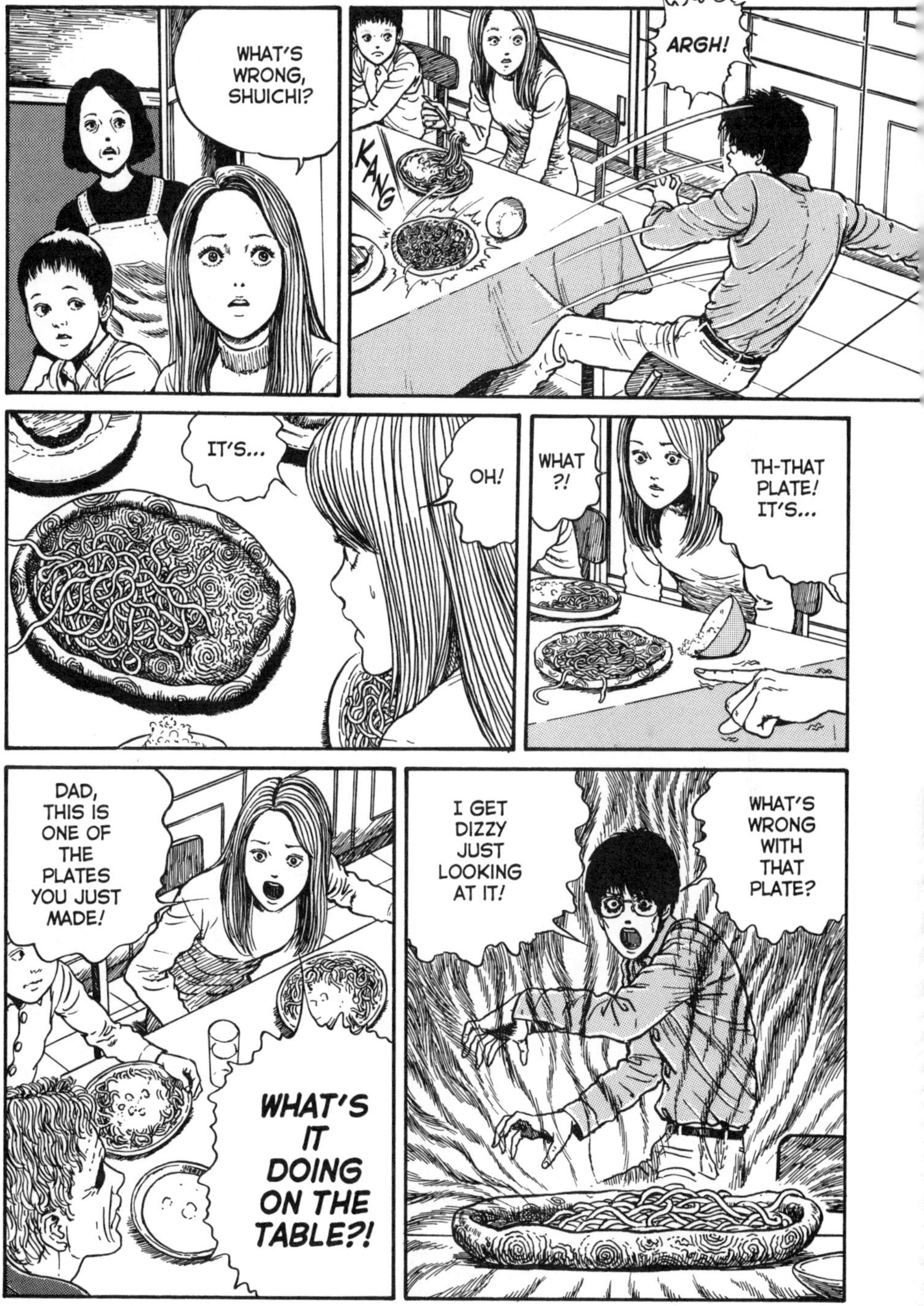
ARGH!
KANG
WHAT'S WRONG, SHUICHI?
TH-THAT PLATE! IT'S...
WHAT ?!
OH!
IT'S...
WHAT'S WRONG WITH THAT PLATE?
I GET DIZZY JUST LOOKING AT IT!
DAD, THIS IS ONE OF THE PLATES YOU JUST MADE!
WHAT'S IT DOING ON THE TABLE?!

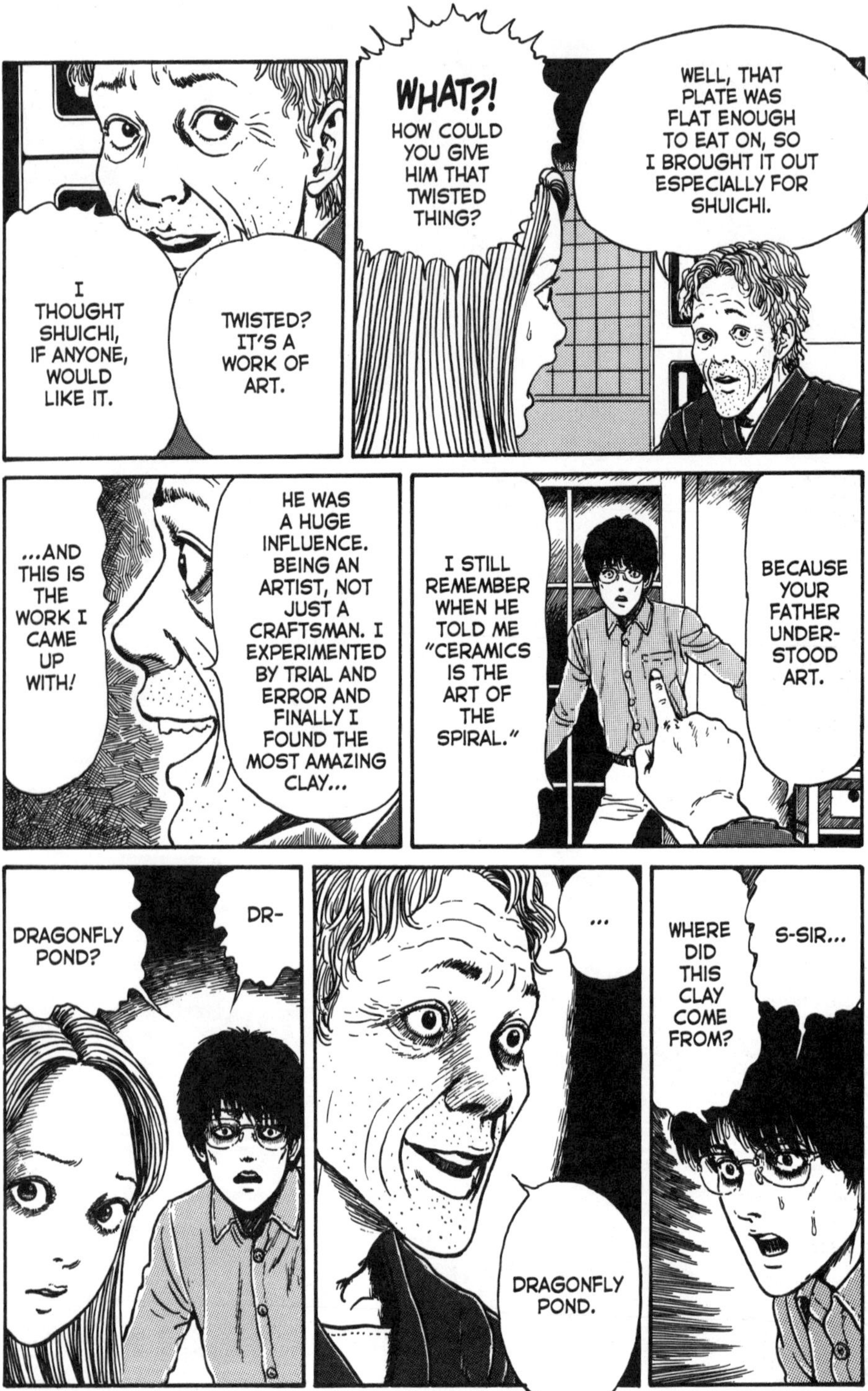
WHAT?! HOW COULD YOU GIVE HIM THAT TWISTED THING?
WELL, THAT PLATE WAS FLAT ENOUGH TO EAT ON, SO I BROUGHT IT OUT ESPECIALLY FOR SHUICHI.
TWISTED? IT'S A WORK OF ART.
I THOUGHT SHUICHI, IF ANYONE, WOULD LIKE IT.
BECAUSE YOUR FATHER UNDERSTOOD ART.
I STILL REMEMBER WHEN HE TOLD ME "CERAMICS IS THE ART OF THE SPIRAL."
HE WAS A HUGE INFLUENCE. BEING AN ARTIST, NOT JUST A CRAFTSMAN. I EXPERIMENTED BY TRIAL AND ERROR AND FINALLY I FOUND THE MOST AMAZING CLAY...
...AND THIS IS THE WORK I CAME UP WITH!
S-SIR...
WHERE DID THIS CLAY COME FROM?
...
DRAGONFLY POND.
DR-
DRAGONFLY POND?

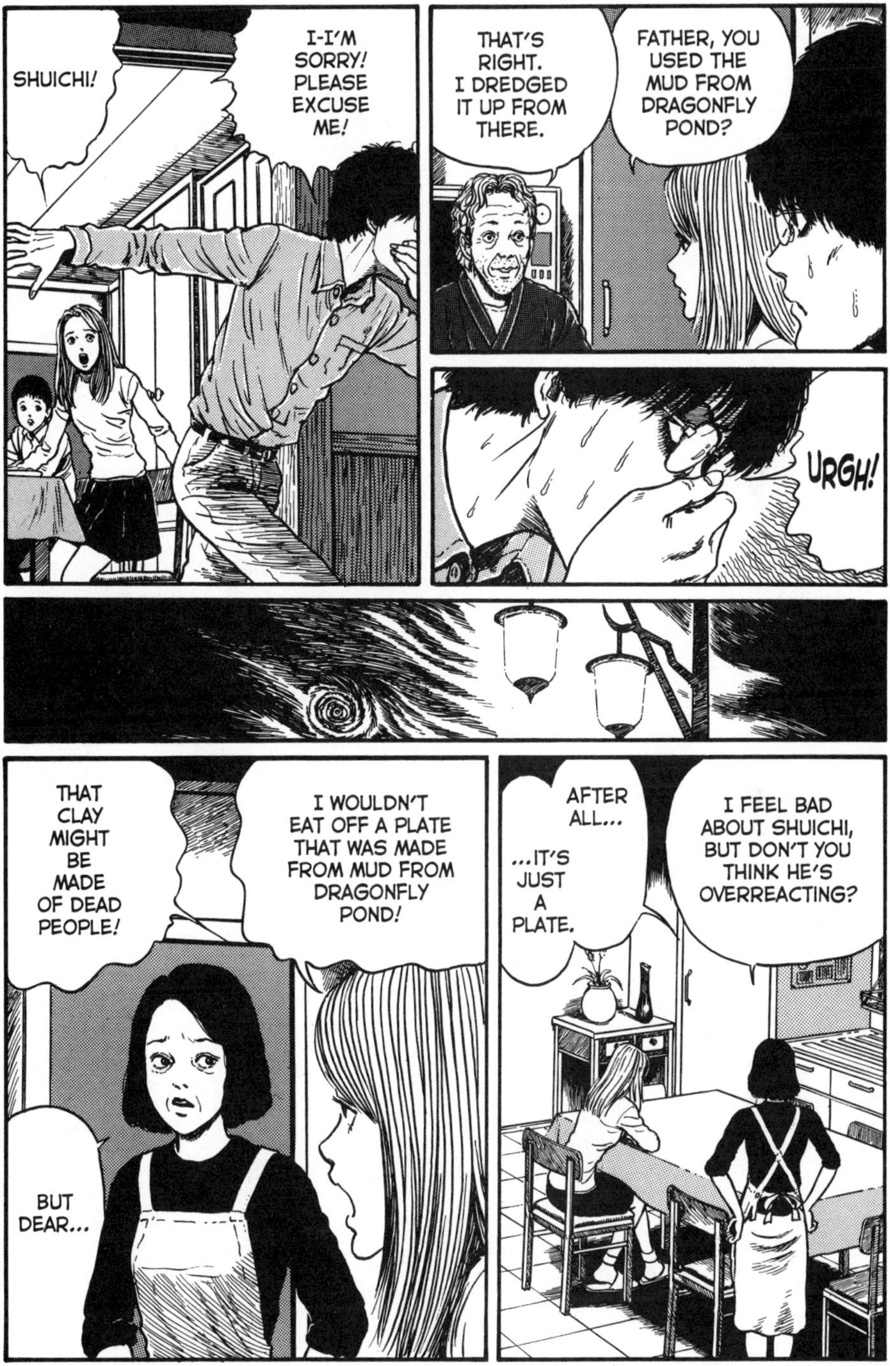
FATHER, YOU USED THE MUD FROM DRAGONFLY POND?
THAT'S RIGHT. I DREDGED IT UP FROM THERE.
URGH!
I-I'M SORRY! PLEASE EXCUSE ME!
SHUICHI!
I FEEL BAD ABOUT SHUICHI, BUT DON'T YOU THINK HE'S OVERREACTING?
AFTER ALL...
...IT'S JUST A PLATE.
I WOULDN'T EAT OFF A PLATE THAT WAS MADE FROM MUD FROM DRAGONFLY POND!
THAT CLAY MIGHT BE MADE OF DEAD PEOPLE!
BUT DEAR...

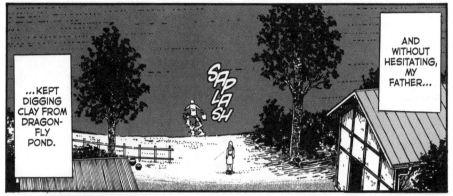

AND WITHOUT HESITATING, MY FATHER...
SAPLASH
...KEPT DIGGING CLAY FROM DRAGON-FLY POND.
GLUG GLUG
plup
SAPLASH
WHOO HA HA!
I'M SOAKING WET!
...

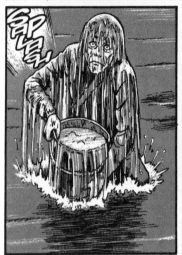

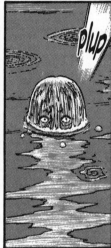

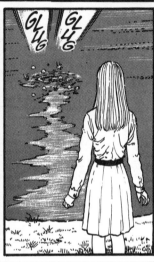

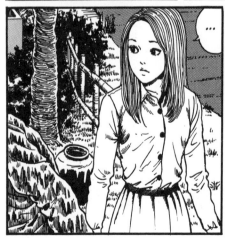

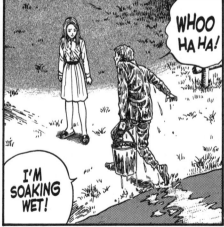

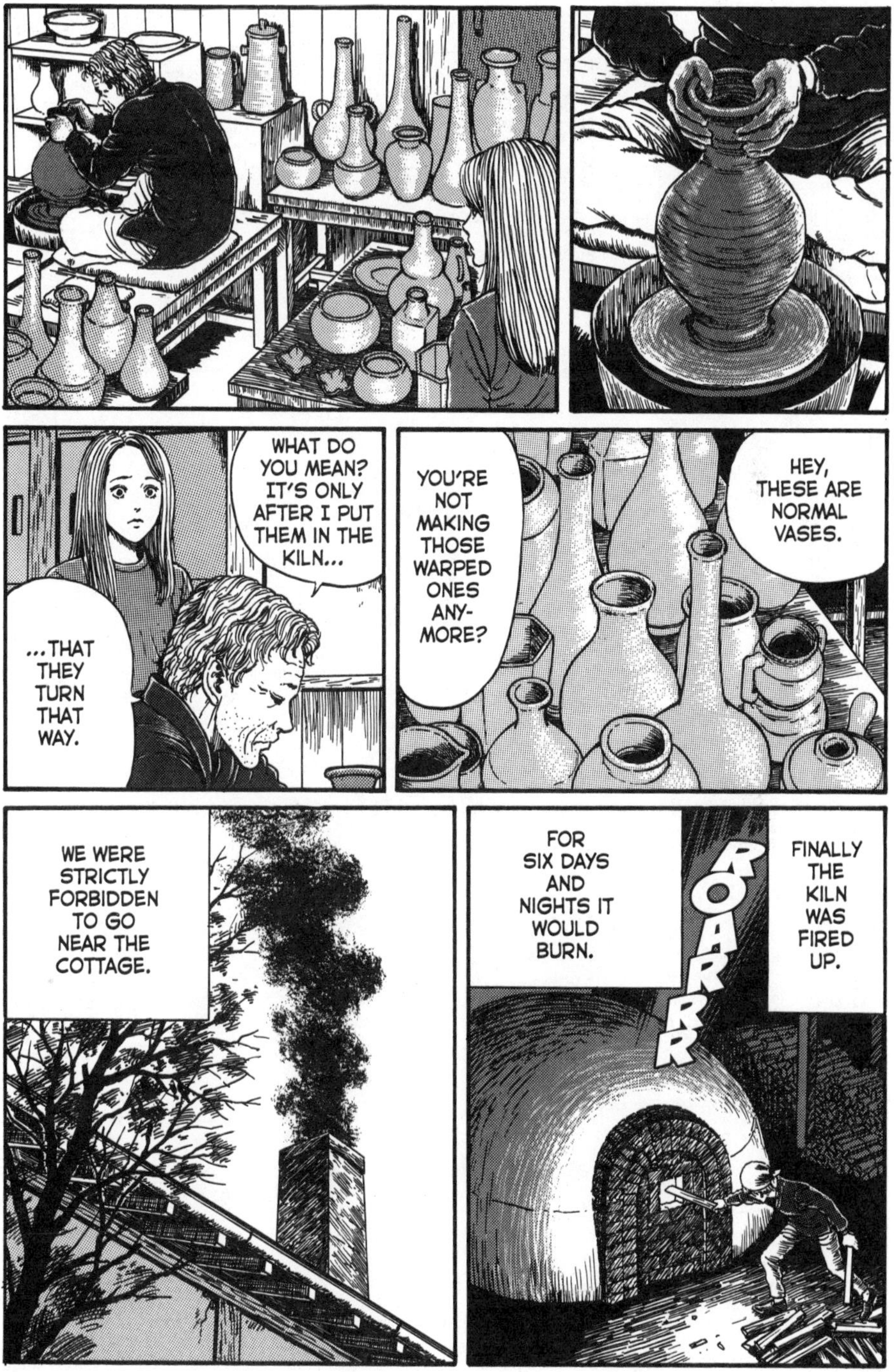
HEY, THESE ARE NORMAL VASES.
YOU'RE NOT MAKING THOSE WARPED ONES ANY-MORE?
WHAT DO YOU MEAN? IT'S ONLY AFTER I PUT THEM IN THE KILN...
...THAT THEY TURN THAT WAY.
FINALLY THE KILN WAS FIRED UP.
ROARRR
FOR SIX DAYS AND NIGHTS IT WOULD BURN.
WE WERE STRICTLY FORBIDDEN TO GO NEAR THE COTTAGE.

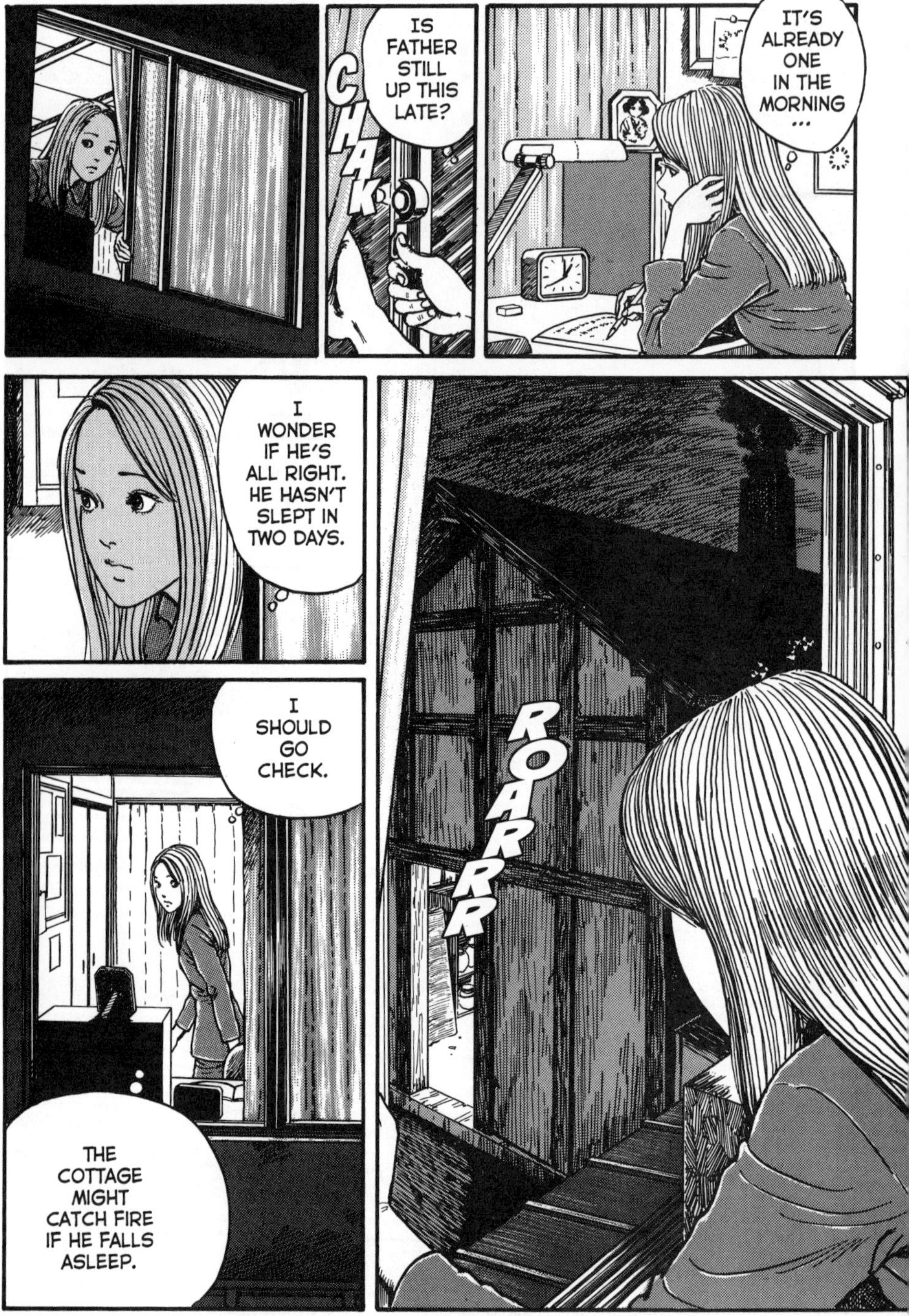
IT'S ALREADY ONE IN THE MORNING...
CHAK
IS FATHER STILL UP THIS LATE?
ROARRR
I WONDER IF HE'S ALL RIGHT. HE HASN'T SLEPT IN TWO DAYS.
I SHOULD GO CHECK.
THE COTTAGE MIGHT CATCH FIRE IF HE FALLS ASLEEP.

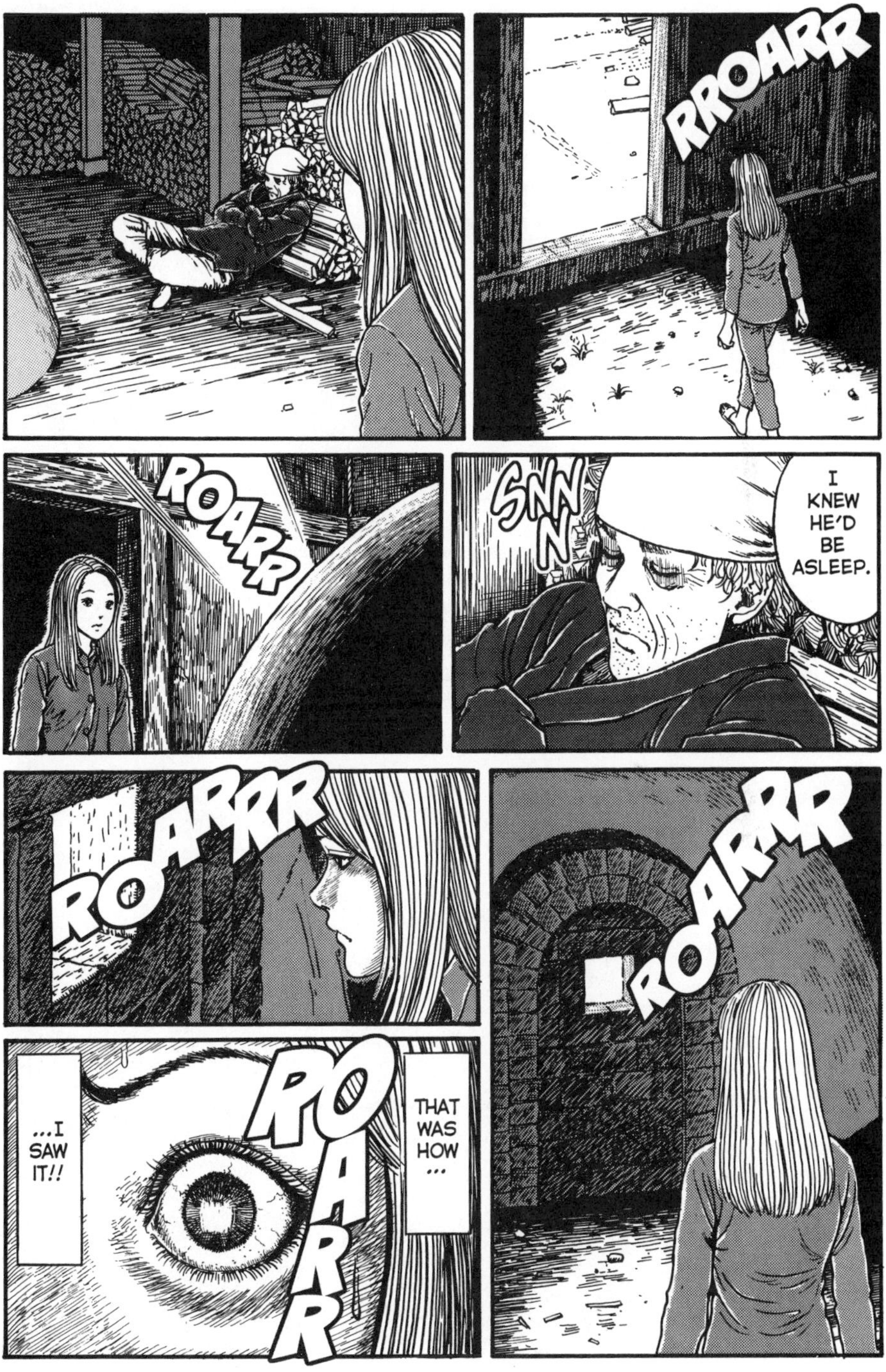
RROARR
I KNEW HE'D BE ASLEEP.
SNNN
ROARR
ROARRR
ROARRR
THAT WAS HOW ...
...I SAW IT!!
ROARR

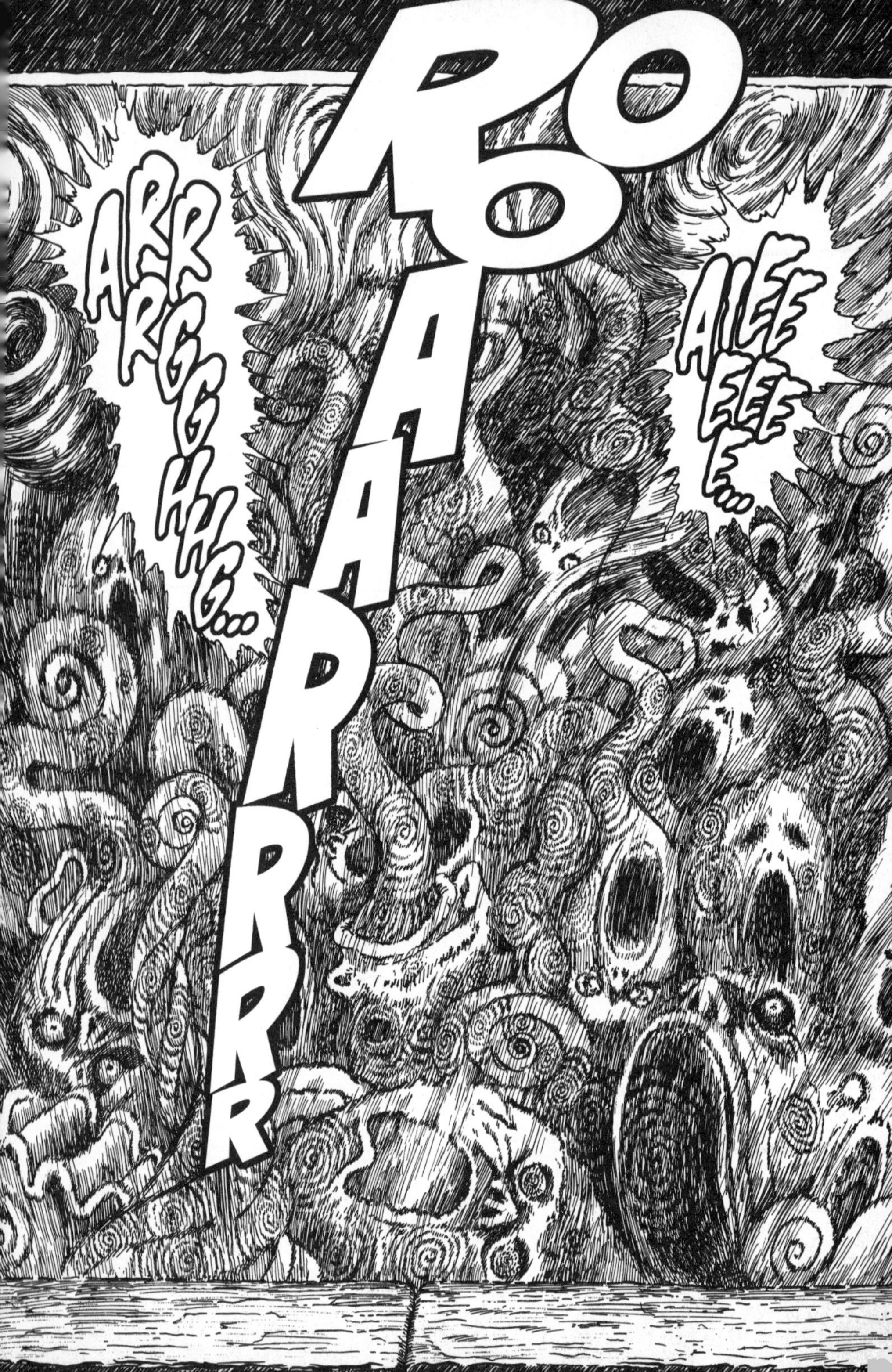
AIEEEEEE...
ROOAAARRRRRR
ARRRGGHHG...

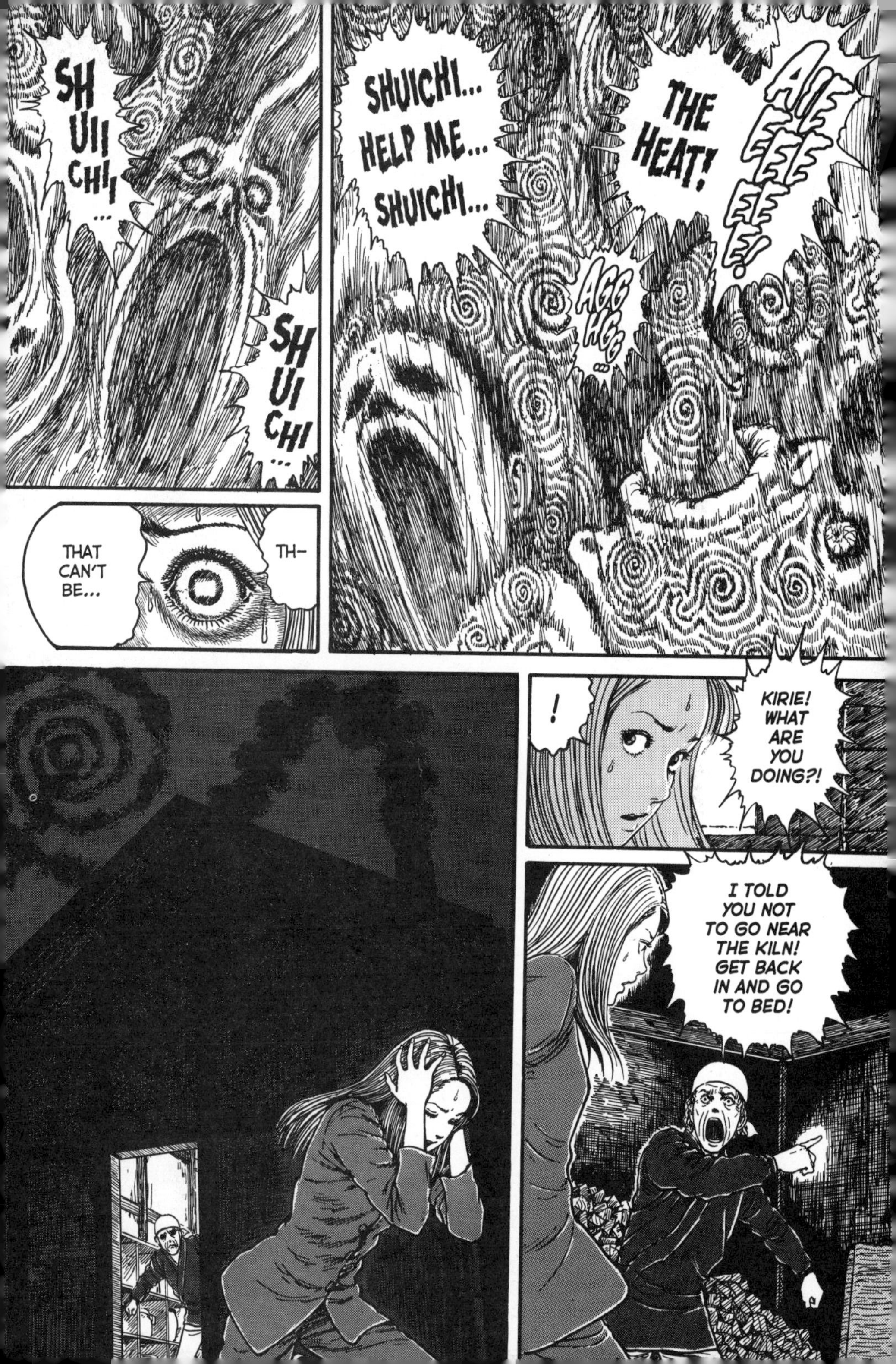
AIEEEEEE!
THE HEAT!
SHUICHI... HELP ME... SHUICHI...
AGGHGG...
SHUIICHI...
SHUICHI...
TH—
THAT CAN'T BE...
!
KIRIE! WHAT ARE YOU DOING?!
I TOLD YOU NOT TO GO NEAR THE KILN! GET BACK IN AND GO TO BED!

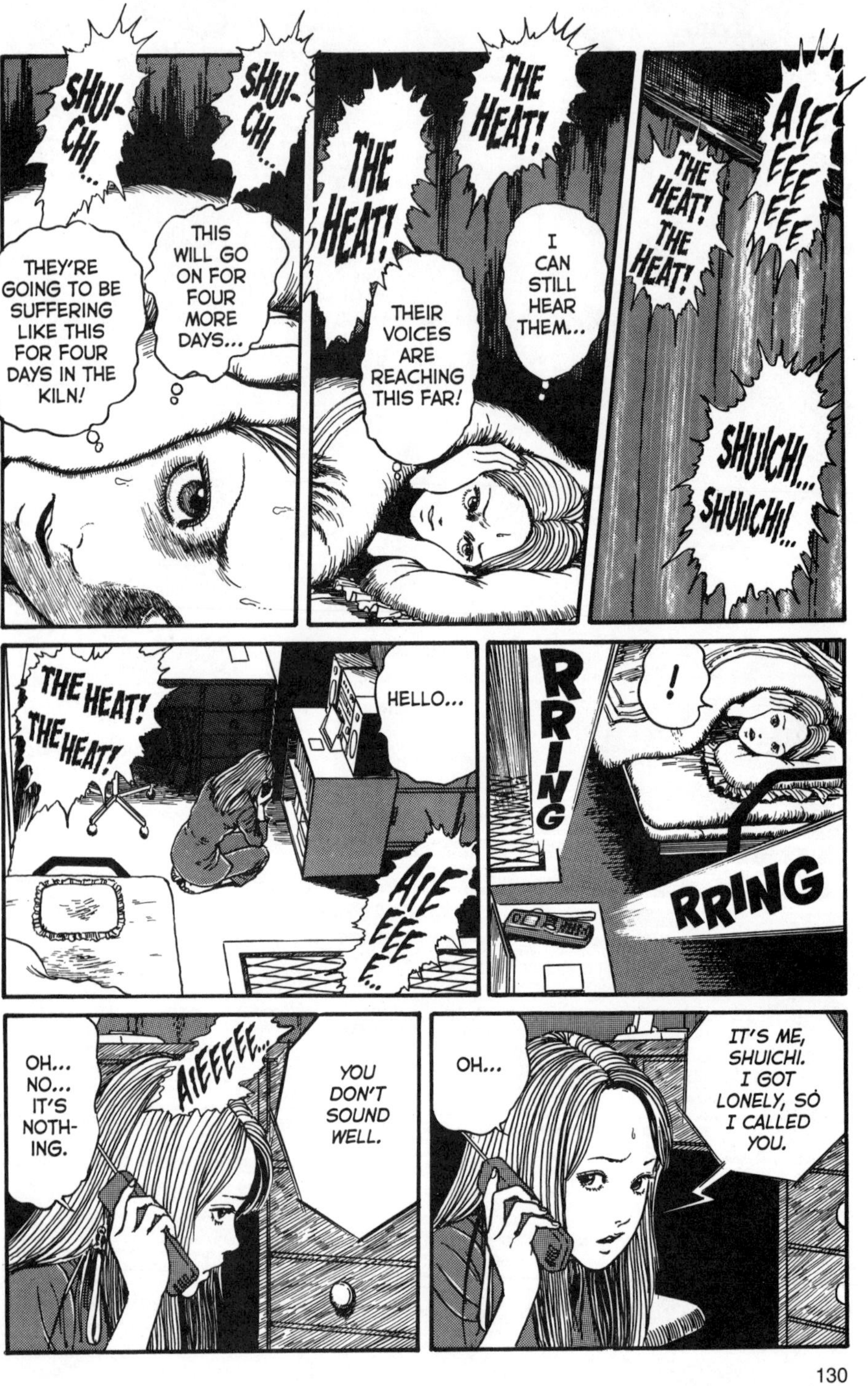
AIEEEEEEE
THE HEAT! THE HEAT!
SHUICHI... SHUICHI!...
THE HEAT!
THE HEAT!
I CAN STILL HEAR THEM...
THEIR VOICES ARE REACHING THIS FAR!
SHUI-CHI...
SHUI-CHI...
THIS WILL GO ON FOR FOUR MORE DAYS...
THEY'RE GOING TO BE SUFFERING LIKE THIS FOR FOUR DAYS IN THE KILN!
!
RRING
RRING
HELLO...
THE HEAT! THE HEAT!
AIEEEEE...
IT'S ME, SHUICHI. I GOT LONELY, SO I CALLED YOU.
OH...
YOU DON'T SOUND WELL.
AIEEEEE...
OH... NO... IT'S NOTHING.

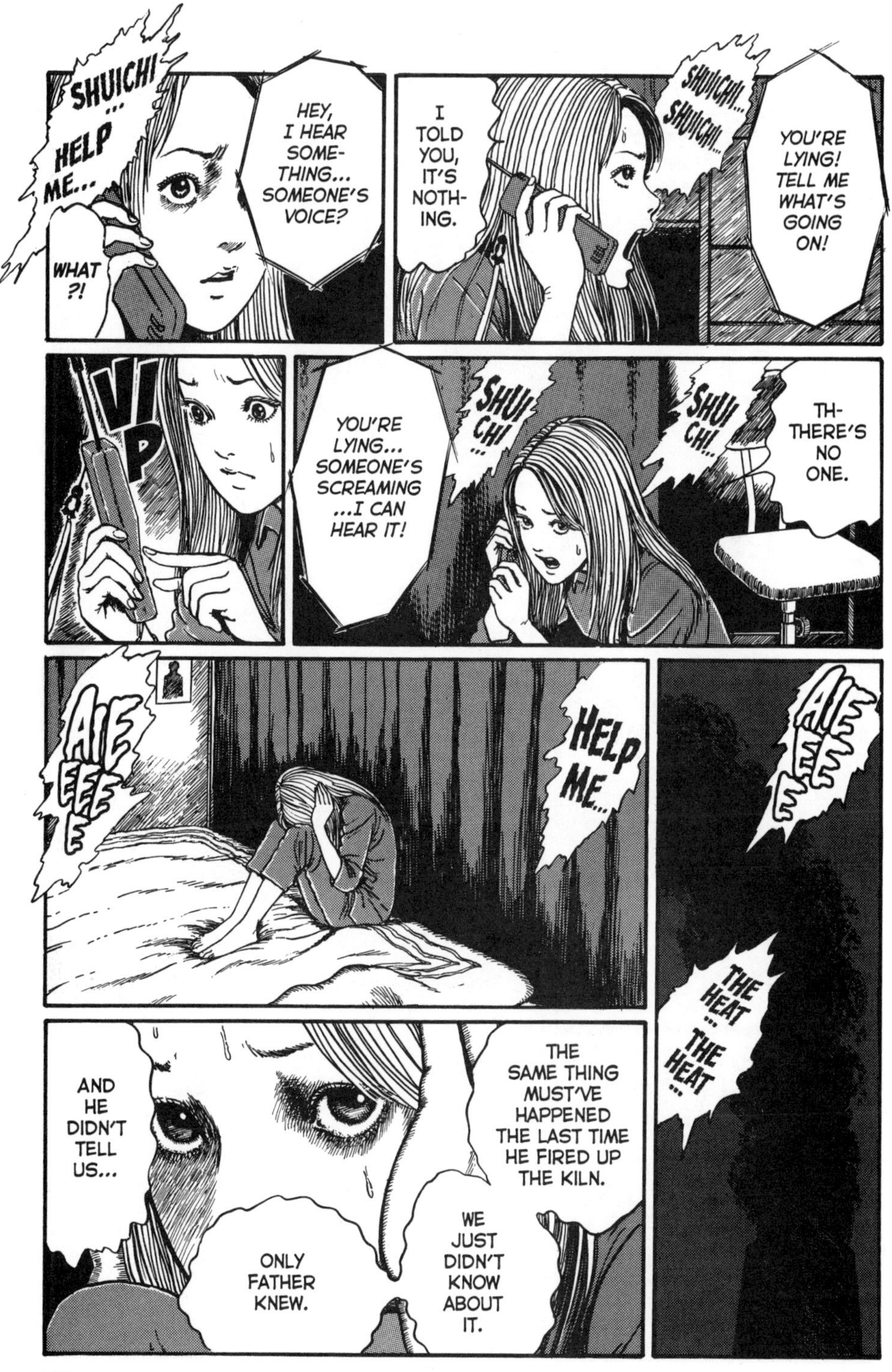
SHUICHI... SHUICHI...
YOU'RE LYING! TELL ME WHAT'S GOING ON!
I TOLD YOU, IT'S NOTHING.
HEY, I HEAR SOMETHING... SOMEONE'S VOICE?
SHUICHI... HELP ME...
WHAT?!
SHUICHI...
SHUICHI...
TH-THERE'S NO ONE.
YOU'RE LYING... SOMEONE'S SCREAMING ...I CAN HEAR IT!
VIP
AIEEEE
THE HEAT... THE HEAT...
HELP ME...
AIEEEE
THE SAME THING MUST'VE HAPPENED THE LAST TIME HE FIRED UP THE KILN.
AND HE DIDN'T TELL US...
WE JUST DIDN'T KNOW ABOUT IT.
ONLY FATHER KNEW.

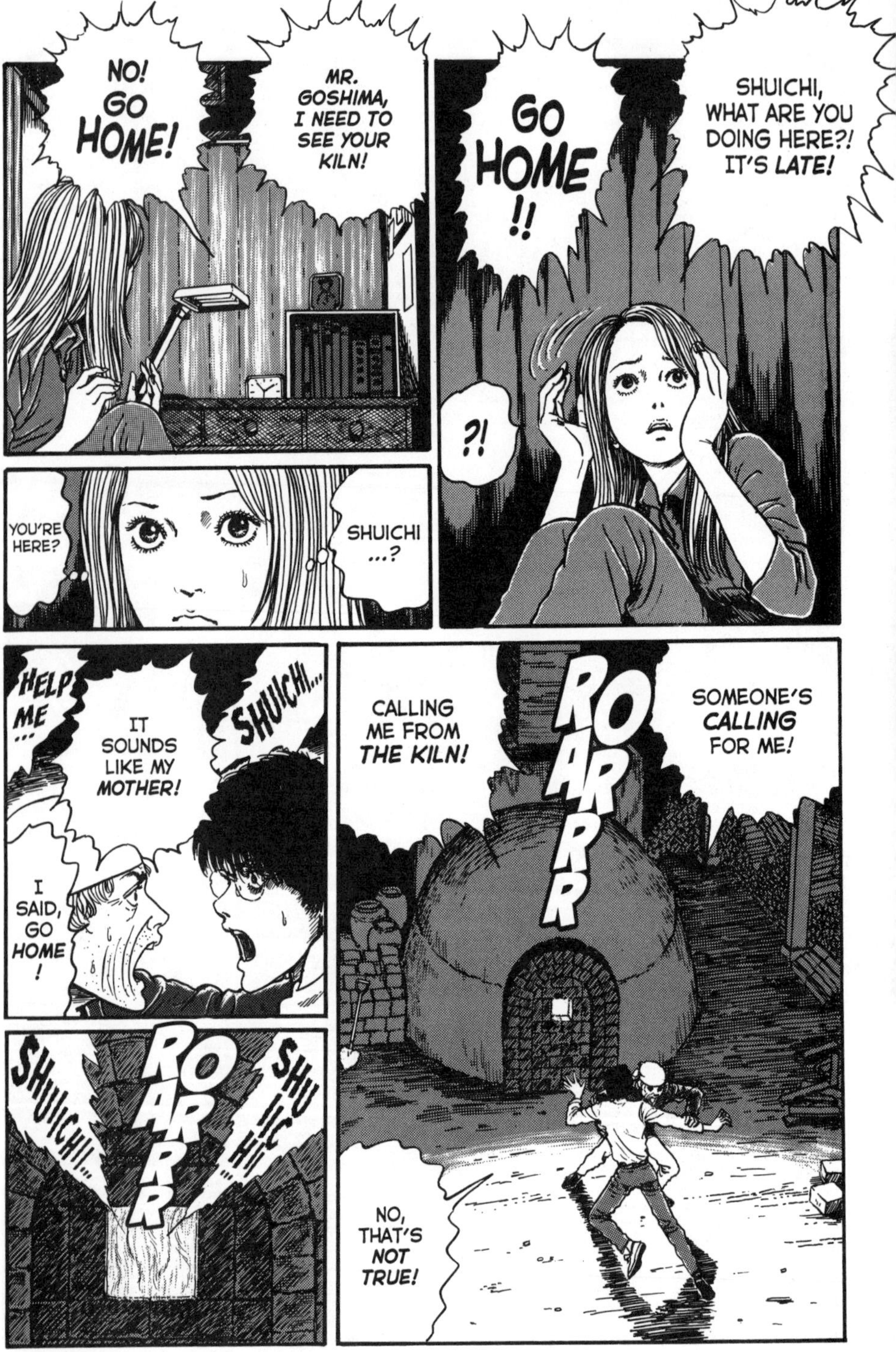
SHUICHI, WHAT ARE YOU DOING HERE?! IT'S LATE!
GO HOME!!
?!
MR. GOSHIMA, I NEED TO SEE YOUR KILN!
NO! GO HOME!
SHUICHI ...?
YOU'RE HERE?
SOMEONE'S CALLING FOR ME!
ROARRR
CALLING ME FROM THE KILN!
NO, THAT'S NOT TRUE!
SHUICHI...
IT SOUNDS LIKE MY MOTHER!
HELP ME ...
I SAID, GO HOME!
SHUICHI!!
ROARRR
SHUICHI...

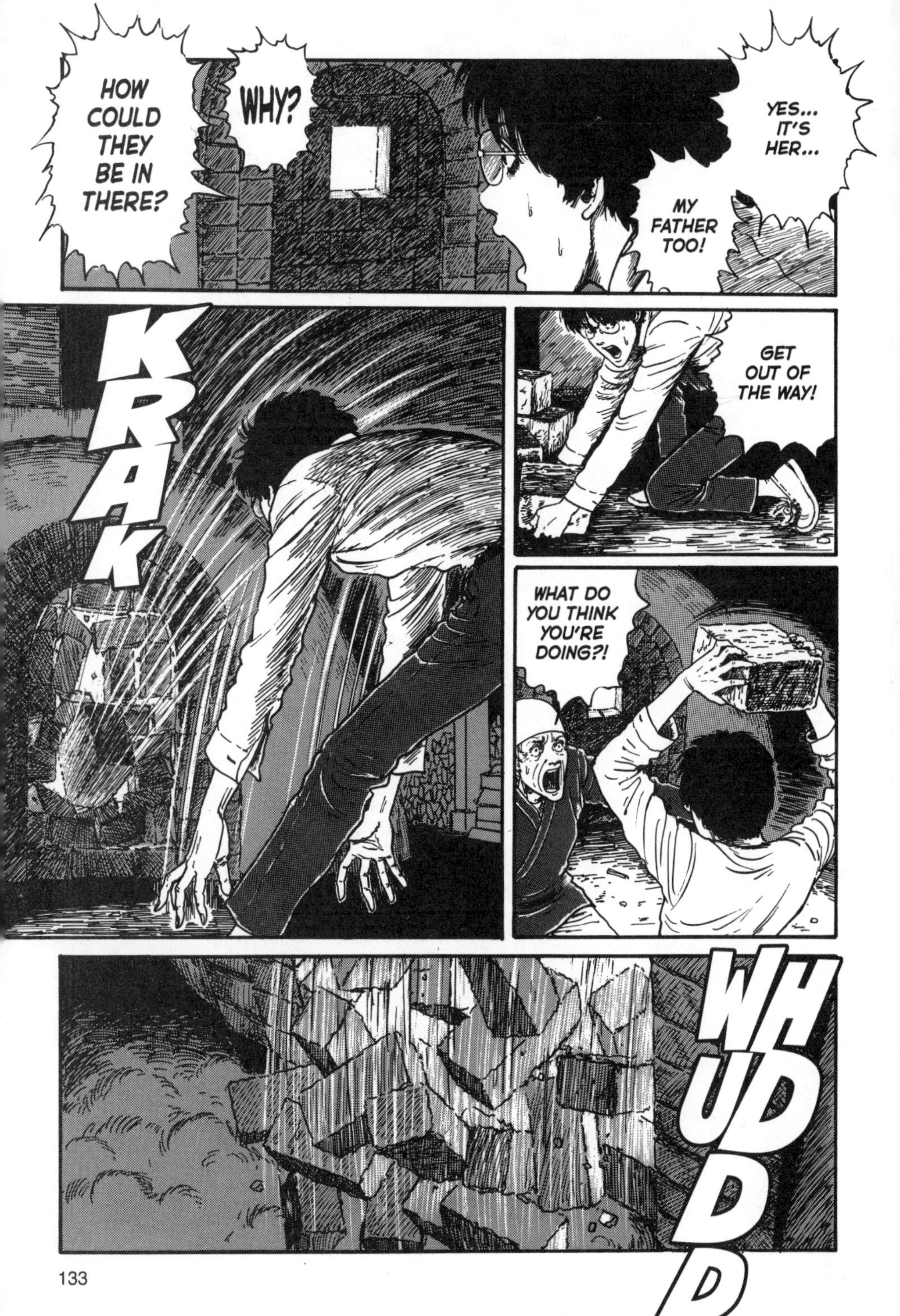
YES... IT'S HER...
MY FATHER TOO!
WHY?
HOW COULD THEY BE IN THERE?
GET OUT OF THE WAY!
WHAT DO YOU THINK YOU'RE DOING?!
KRAK
WHUDDD

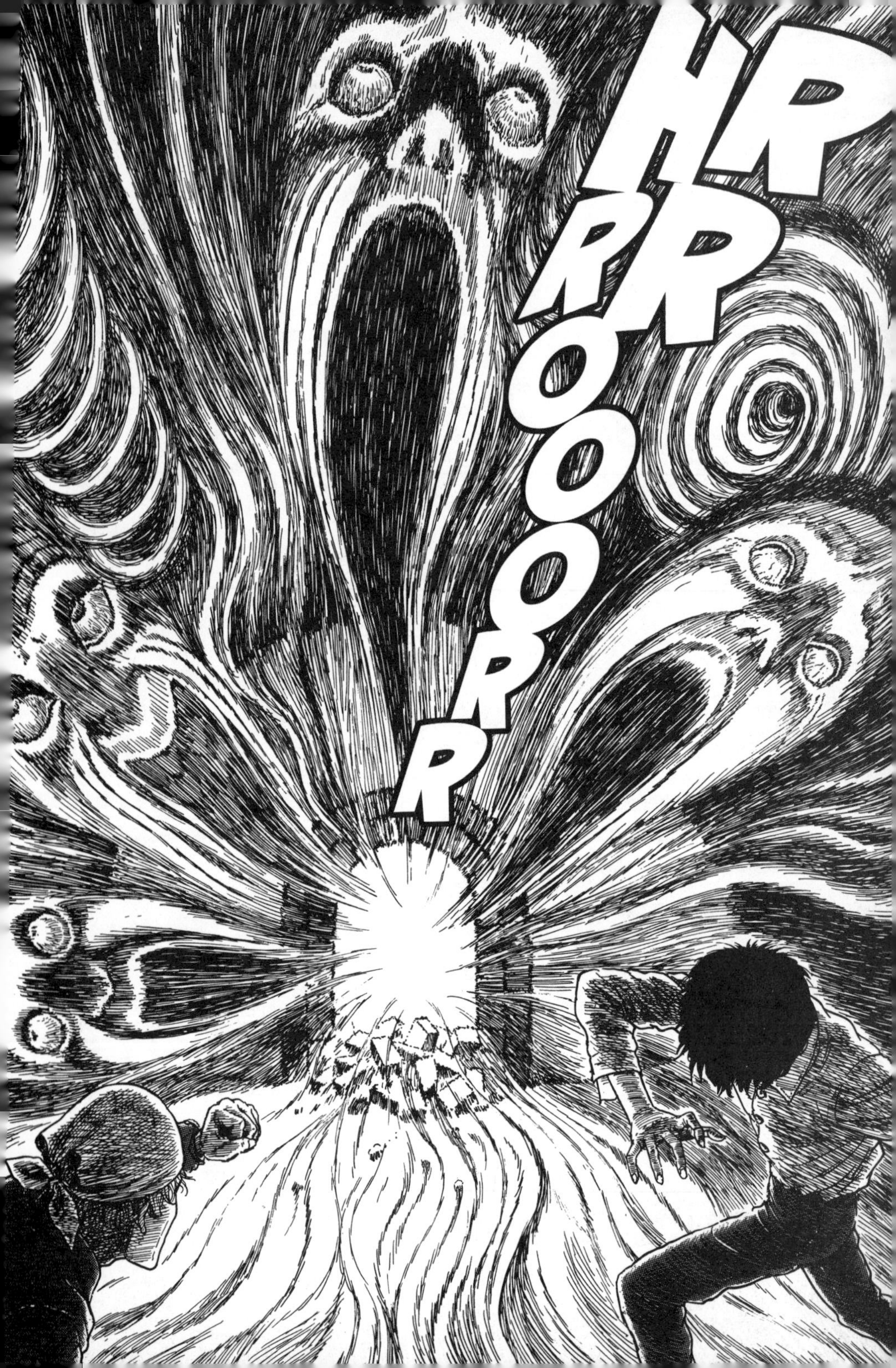
HRRROOOORRR

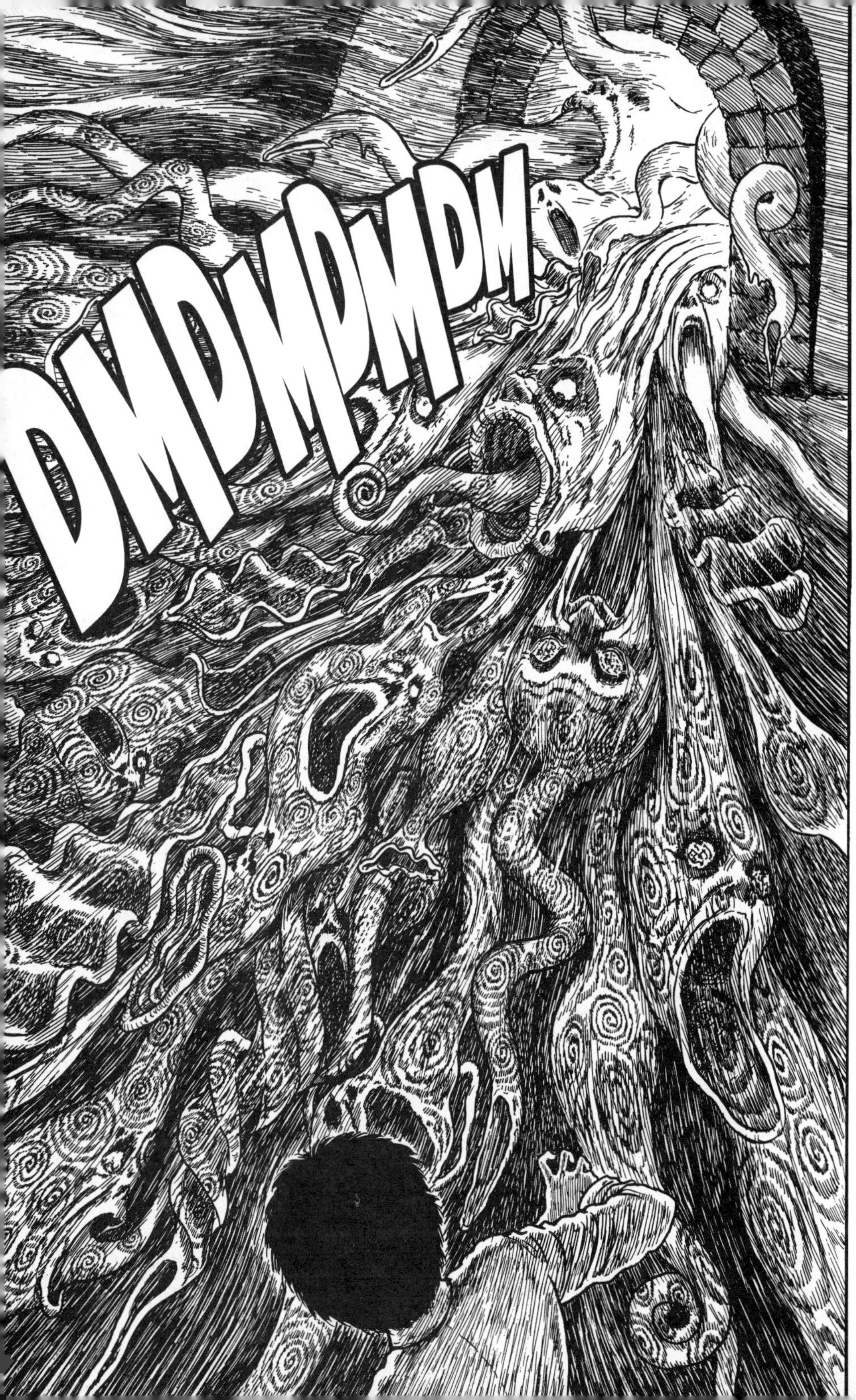
DMDMDMDMDM

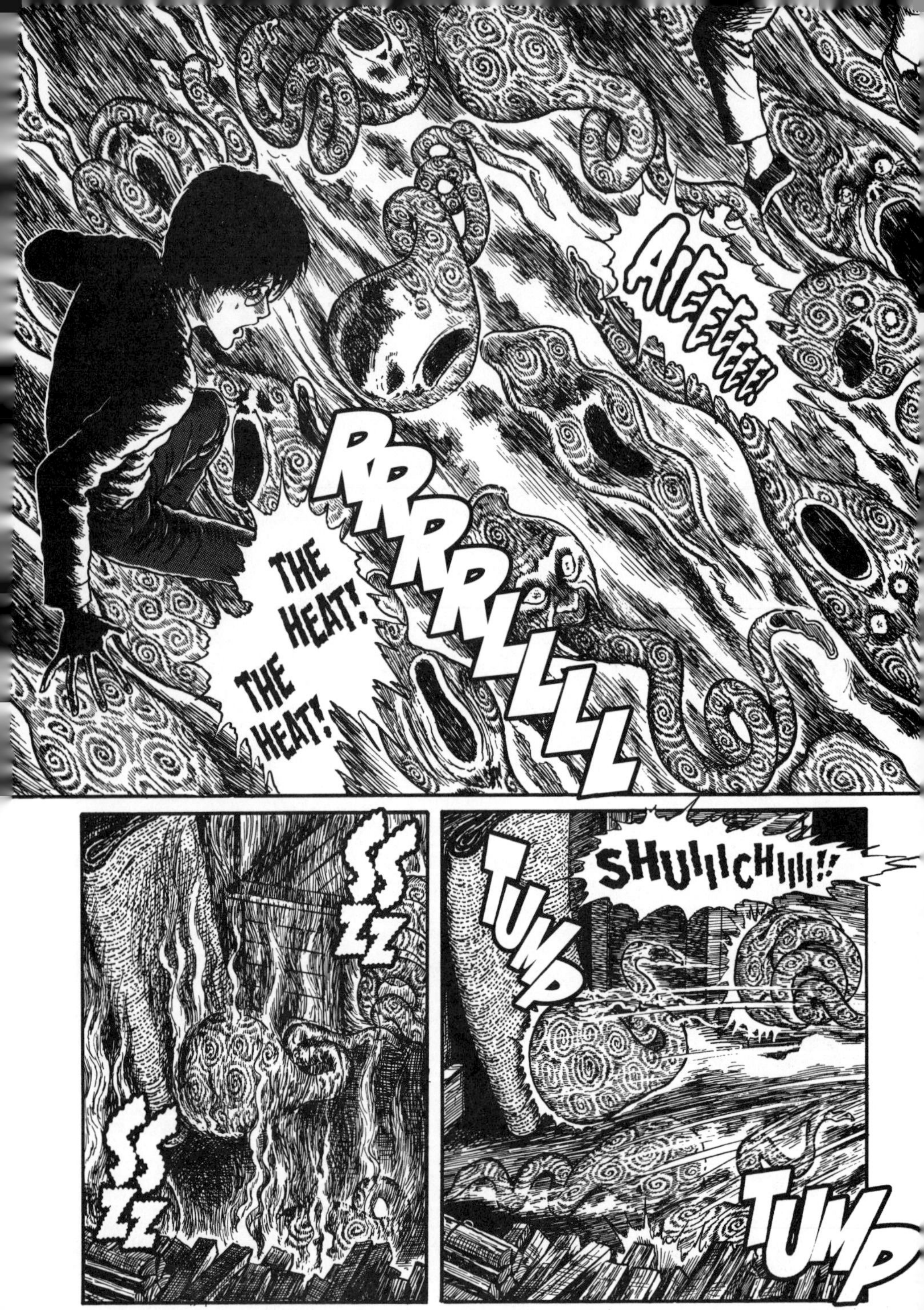
AIEEEEEE!
RRRRRLLLLLL
THE HEAT! THE HEAT!
SHUIIICHIIII!!
TUMP
TUMP
SSZZ
SSZZ

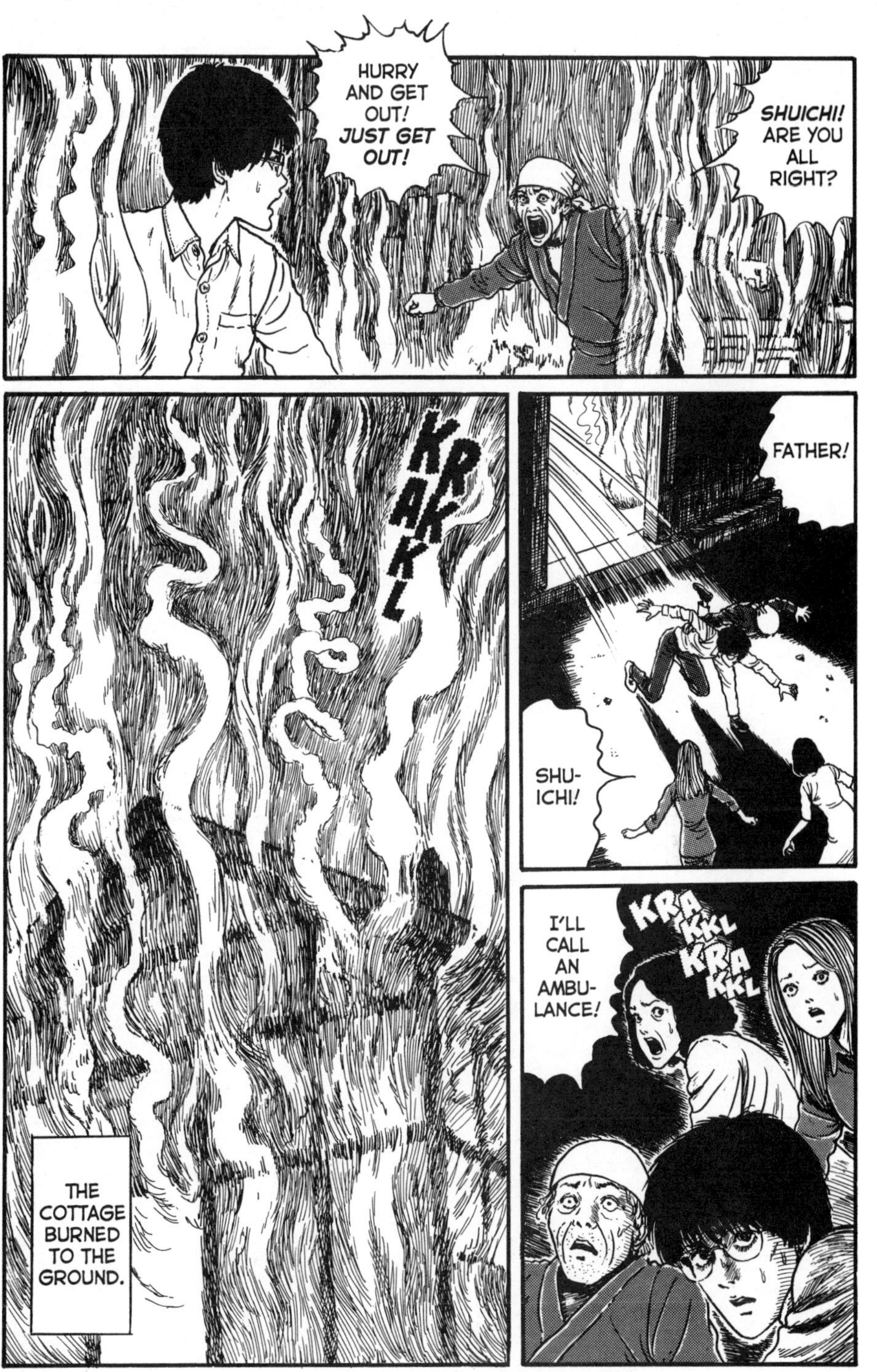
SHUICHI! ARE YOU ALL RIGHT?
HURRY AND GET OUT! JUST GET OUT!
FATHER!
SHU-ICHI!
KRAKKL KRAKKL
I'LL CALL AN AMBU-LANCE!
KRAKKL
THE COTTAGE BURNED TO THE GROUND.

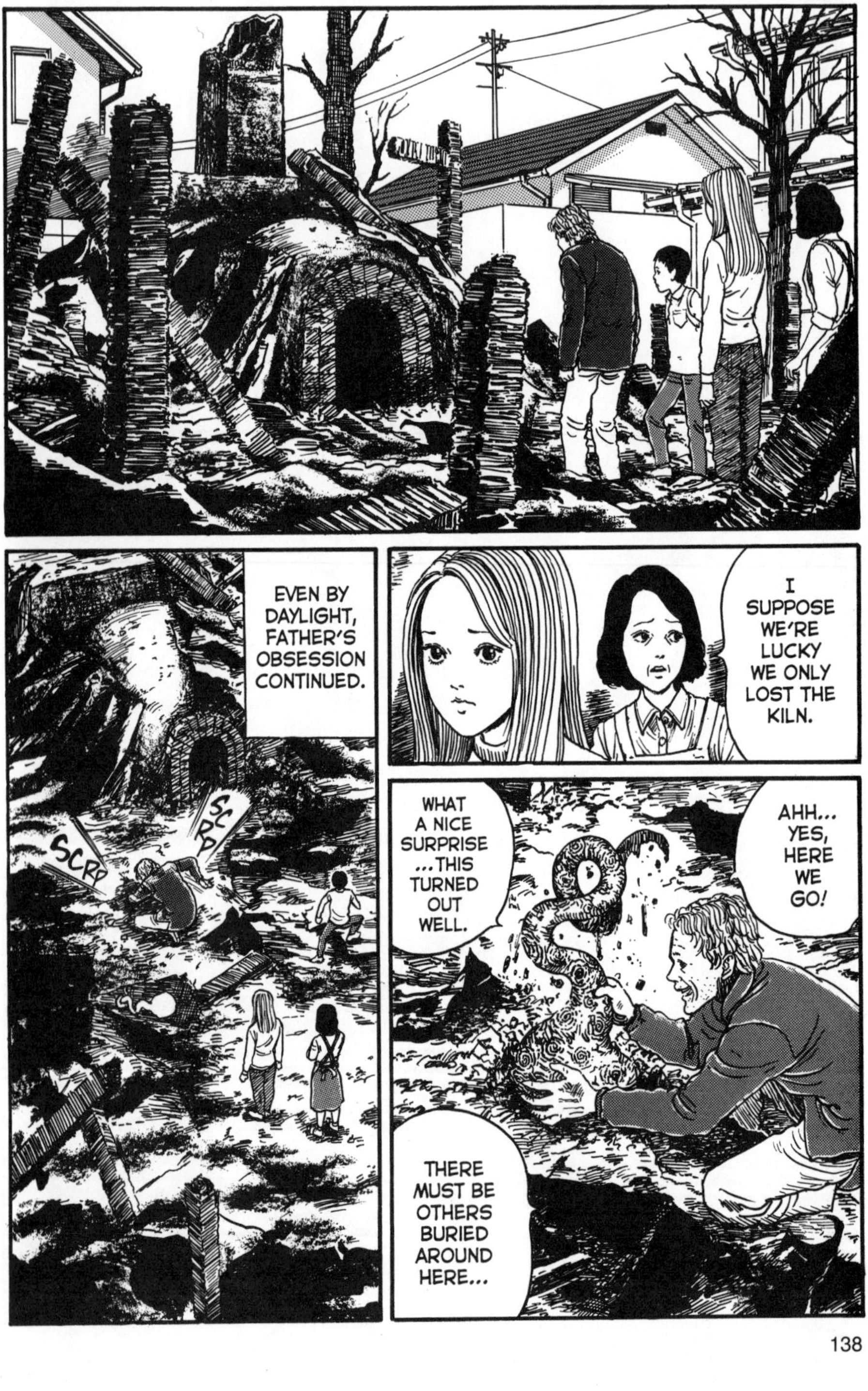
I SUPPOSE WE'RE LUCKY WE ONLY LOST THE KILN.
AHH... YES, HERE WE GO!
WHAT A NICE SURPRISE ...THIS TURNED OUT WELL.
THERE MUST BE OTHERS BURIED AROUND HERE...
EVEN BY DAYLIGHT, FATHER'S OBSESSION CONTINUED.
SCRP
SCRP

CHAPTER 5

TWISTED SOULS

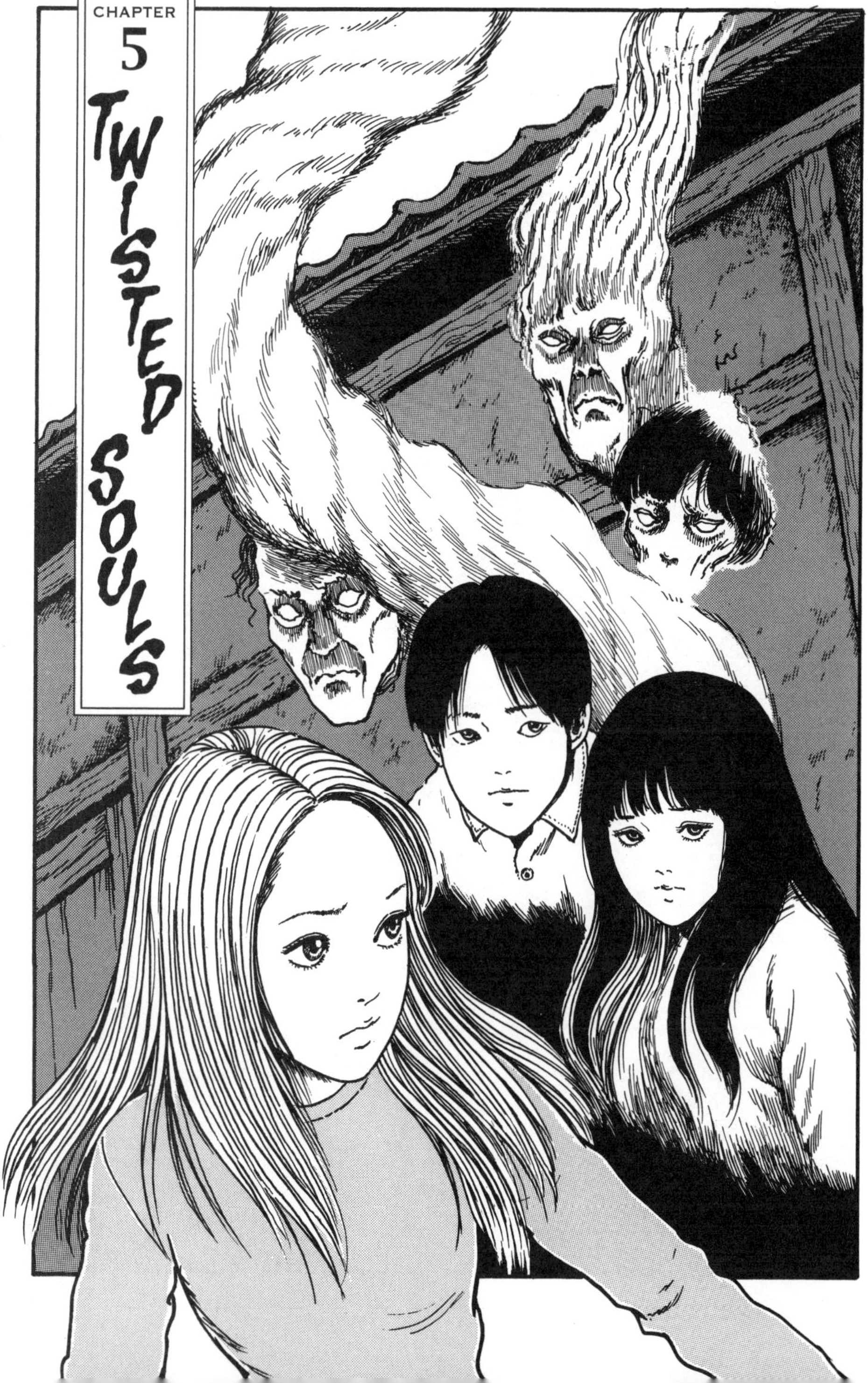

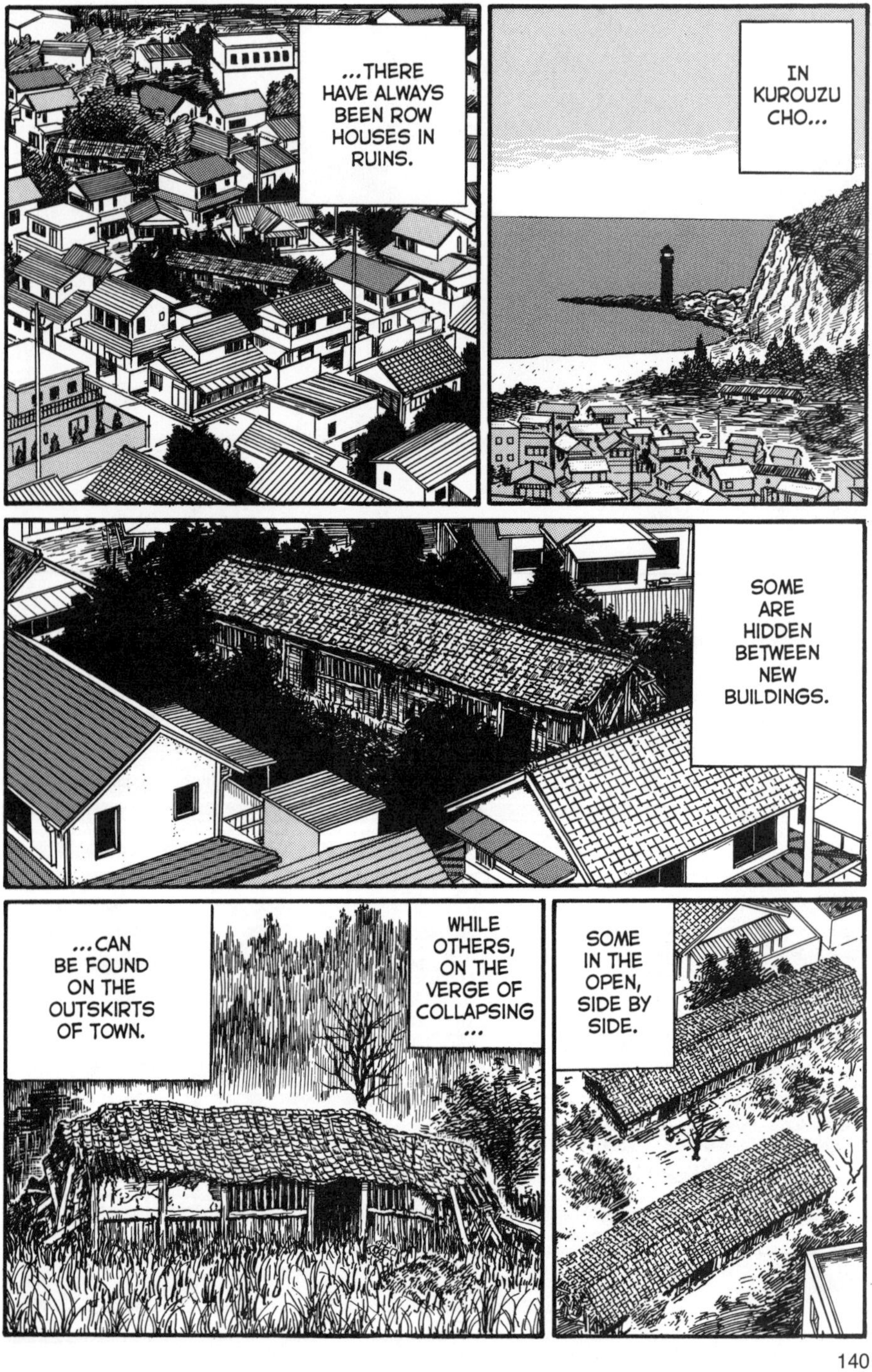
IN KUROUZU CHO...
...THERE HAVE ALWAYS BEEN ROW HOUSES IN RUINS.
SOME ARE HIDDEN BETWEEN NEW BUILDINGS.
SOME IN THE OPEN, SIDE BY SIDE.
WHILE OTHERS, ON THE VERGE OF COLLAPSING...
...CAN BE FOUND ON THE OUTSKIRTS OF TOWN.

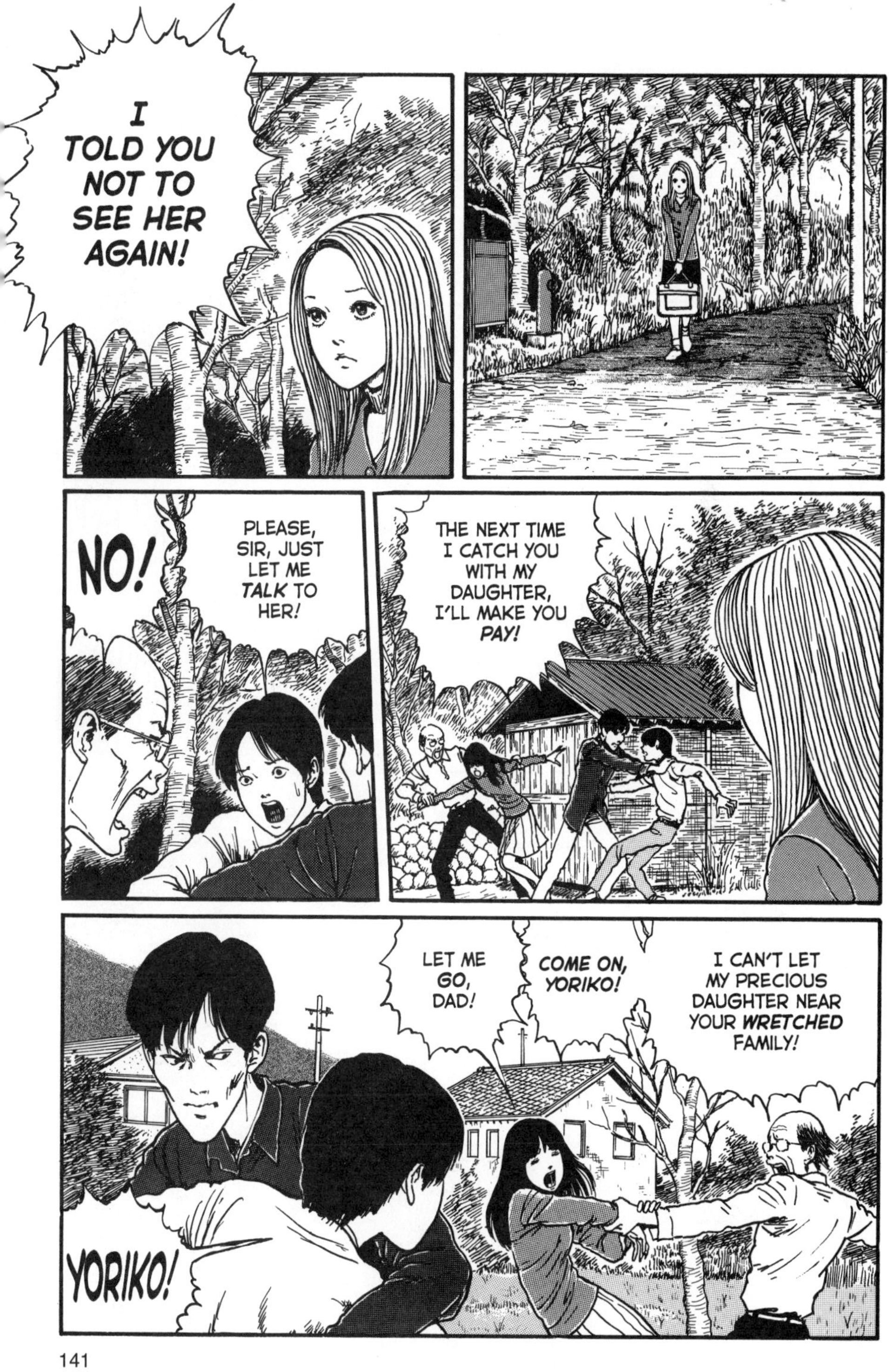
I TOLD YOU NOT TO SEE HER AGAIN!
THE NEXT TIME I CATCH YOU WITH MY DAUGHTER, I'LL MAKE YOU PAY!
PLEASE, SIR, JUST LET ME TALK TO HER!
NO!
I CAN'T LET MY PRECIOUS DAUGHTER NEAR YOUR WRETCHED FAMILY!
COME ON, YORIKO!
LET ME GO, DAD!
YORIKO!

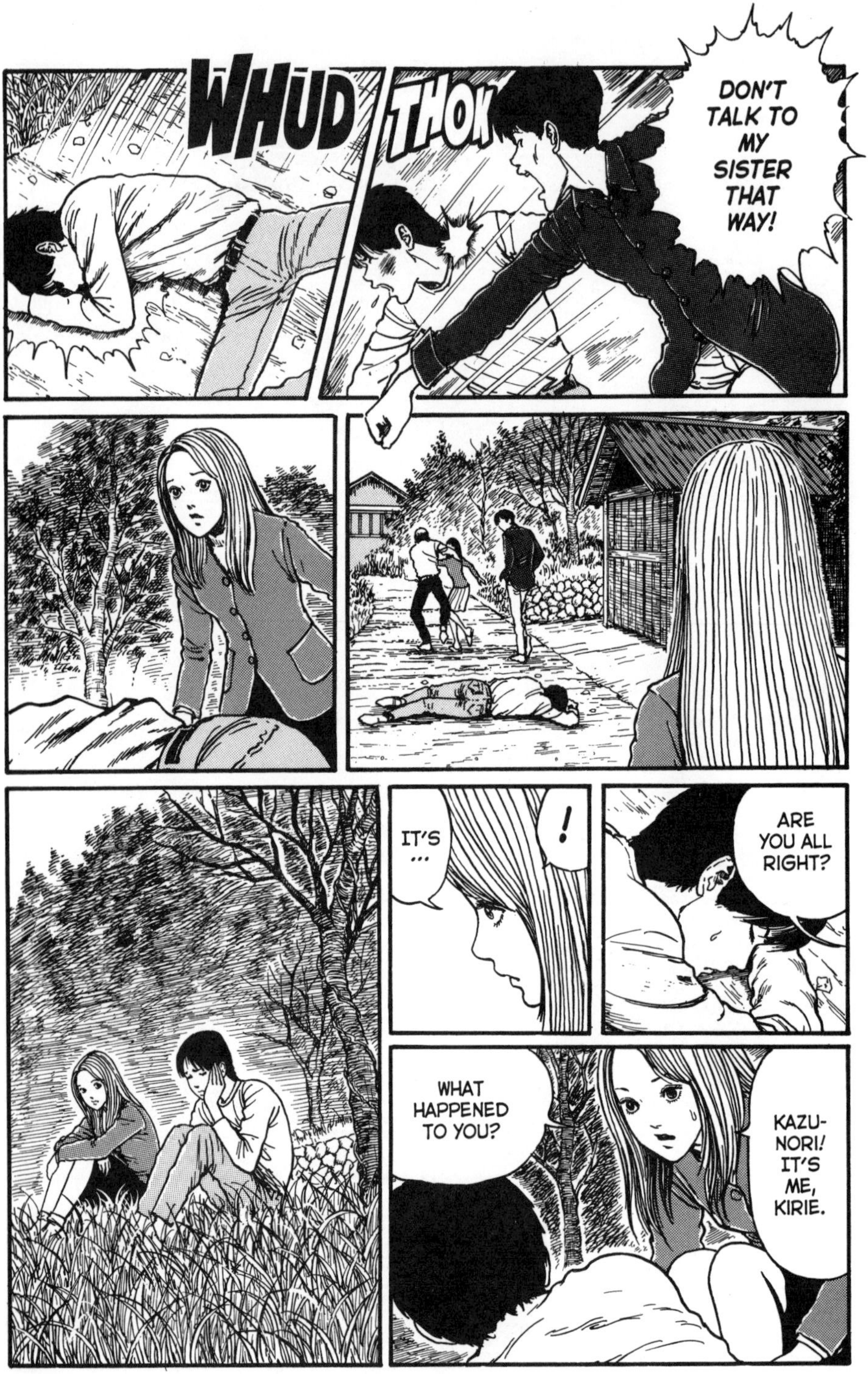
THOK
DON'T TALK TO MY SISTER THAT WAY!
WHUD
ARE YOU ALL RIGHT?
!
IT'S ...
KAZU-NORI! IT'S ME, KIRIE.
WHAT HAPPENED TO YOU?

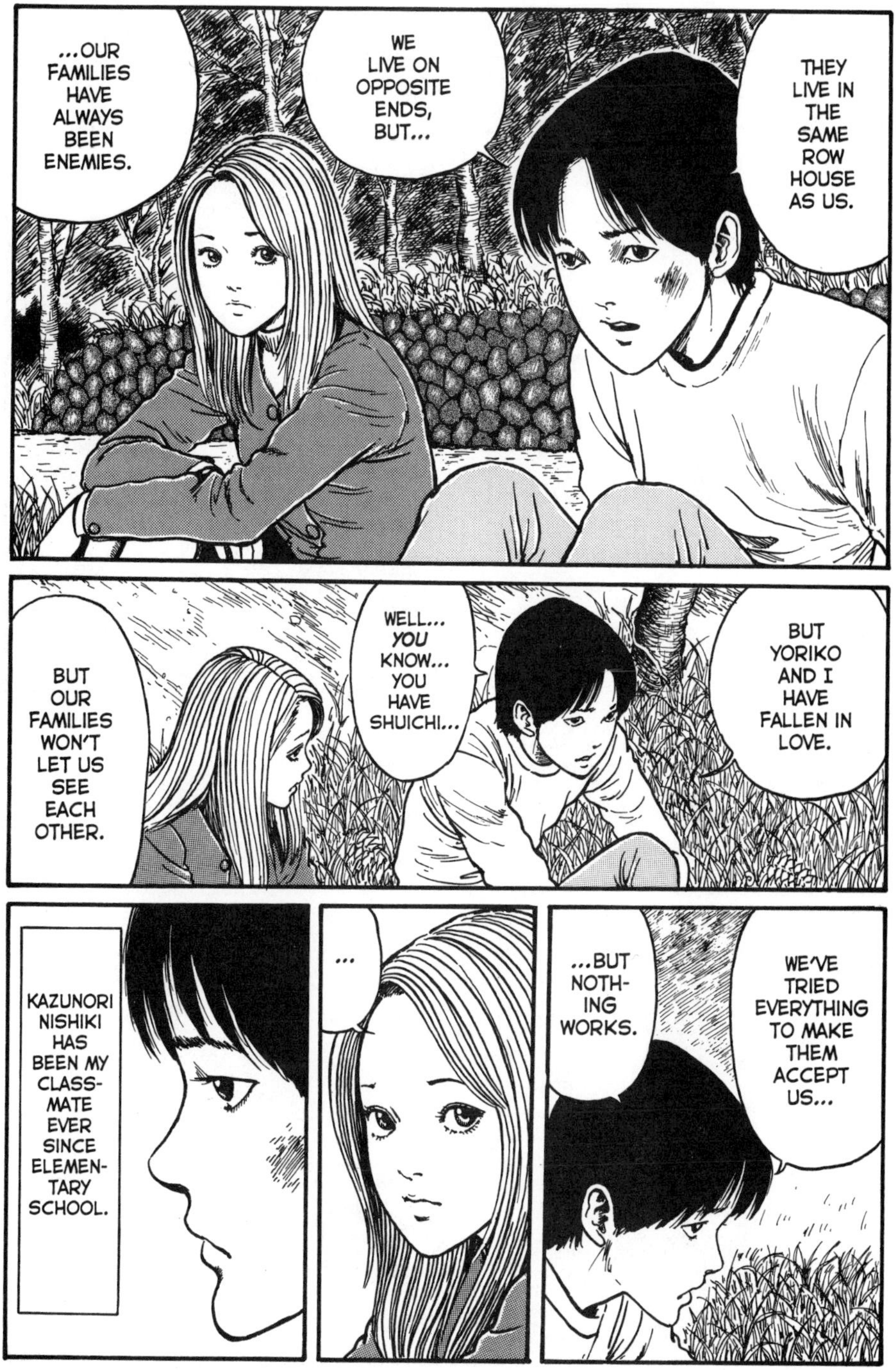
THEY LIVE IN THE SAME ROW HOUSE AS US.
WE LIVE ON OPPOSITE ENDS, BUT...
...OUR FAMILIES HAVE ALWAYS BEEN ENEMIES.
BUT YORIKO AND I HAVE FALLEN IN LOVE.
WELL... *YOU* KNOW... YOU HAVE SHUICHI...
BUT OUR FAMILIES WON'T LET US SEE EACH OTHER.
WE'VE TRIED EVERYTHING TO MAKE THEM ACCEPT US...
...BUT NOTHING WORKS.
...
KAZUNORI NISHIKI HAS BEEN MY CLASSMATE EVER SINCE ELEMENTARY SCHOOL.

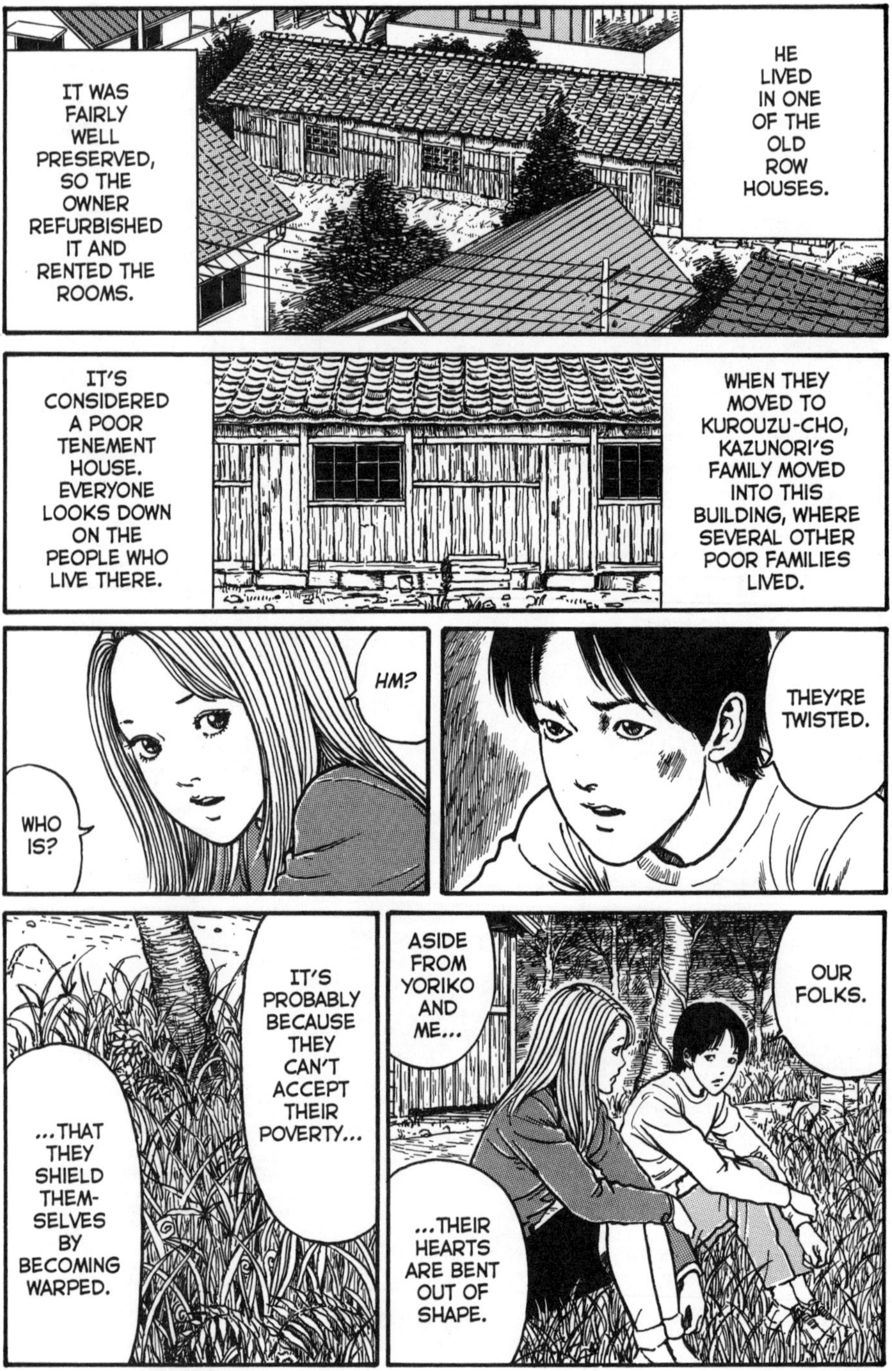
HE LIVED IN ONE OF THE OLD ROW HOUSES.
IT WAS FAIRLY WELL PRESERVED, SO THE OWNER REFURBISHED IT AND RENTED THE ROOMS.
WHEN THEY MOVED TO KUROUZU-CHO, KAZUNORI'S FAMILY MOVED INTO THIS BUILDING, WHERE SEVERAL OTHER POOR FAMILIES LIVED.
IT'S CONSIDERED A POOR TENEMENT HOUSE. EVERYONE LOOKS DOWN ON THE PEOPLE WHO LIVE THERE.
THEY'RE TWISTED.
HM?
WHO IS?
OUR FOLKS.
ASIDE FROM YORIKO AND ME...
...THEIR HEARTS ARE BENT OUT OF SHAPE.
IT'S PROBABLY BECAUSE THEY CAN'T ACCEPT THEIR POVERTY...
...THAT THEY SHIELD THEM-SELVES BY BECOMING WARPED.

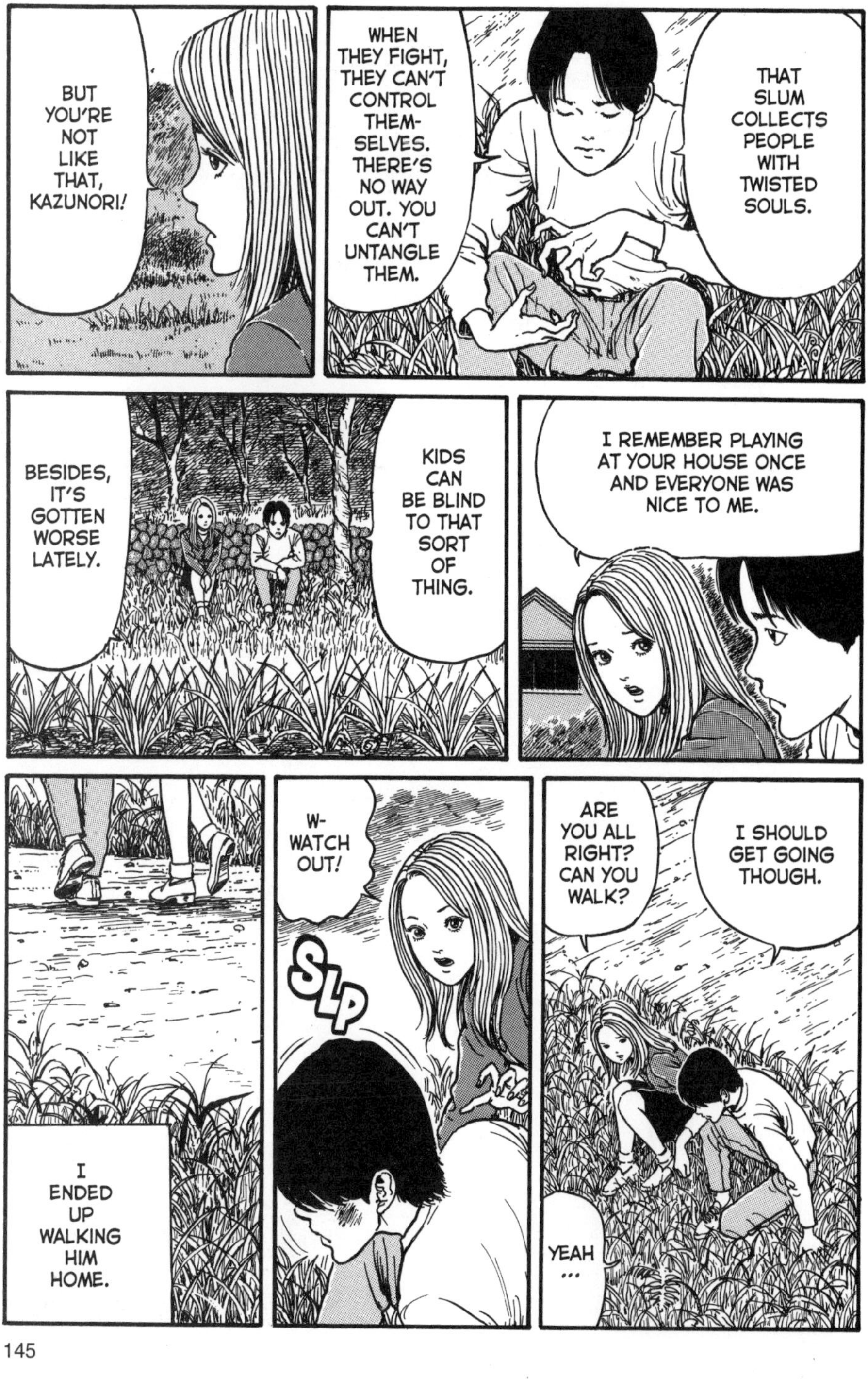
THAT SLUM COLLECTS PEOPLE WITH TWISTED SOULS.
WHEN THEY FIGHT, THEY CAN'T CONTROL THEM-SELVES. THERE'S NO WAY OUT. YOU CAN'T UNTANGLE THEM.
BUT YOU'RE NOT LIKE THAT, KAZUNORI!
I REMEMBER PLAYING AT YOUR HOUSE ONCE AND EVERYONE WAS NICE TO ME.
KIDS CAN BE BLIND TO THAT SORT OF THING.
BESIDES, IT'S GOTTEN WORSE LATELY.
I SHOULD GET GOING THOUGH.
ARE YOU ALL RIGHT? CAN YOU WALK?
YEAH...
W-WATCH OUT!
SLP
I ENDED UP WALKING HIM HOME.

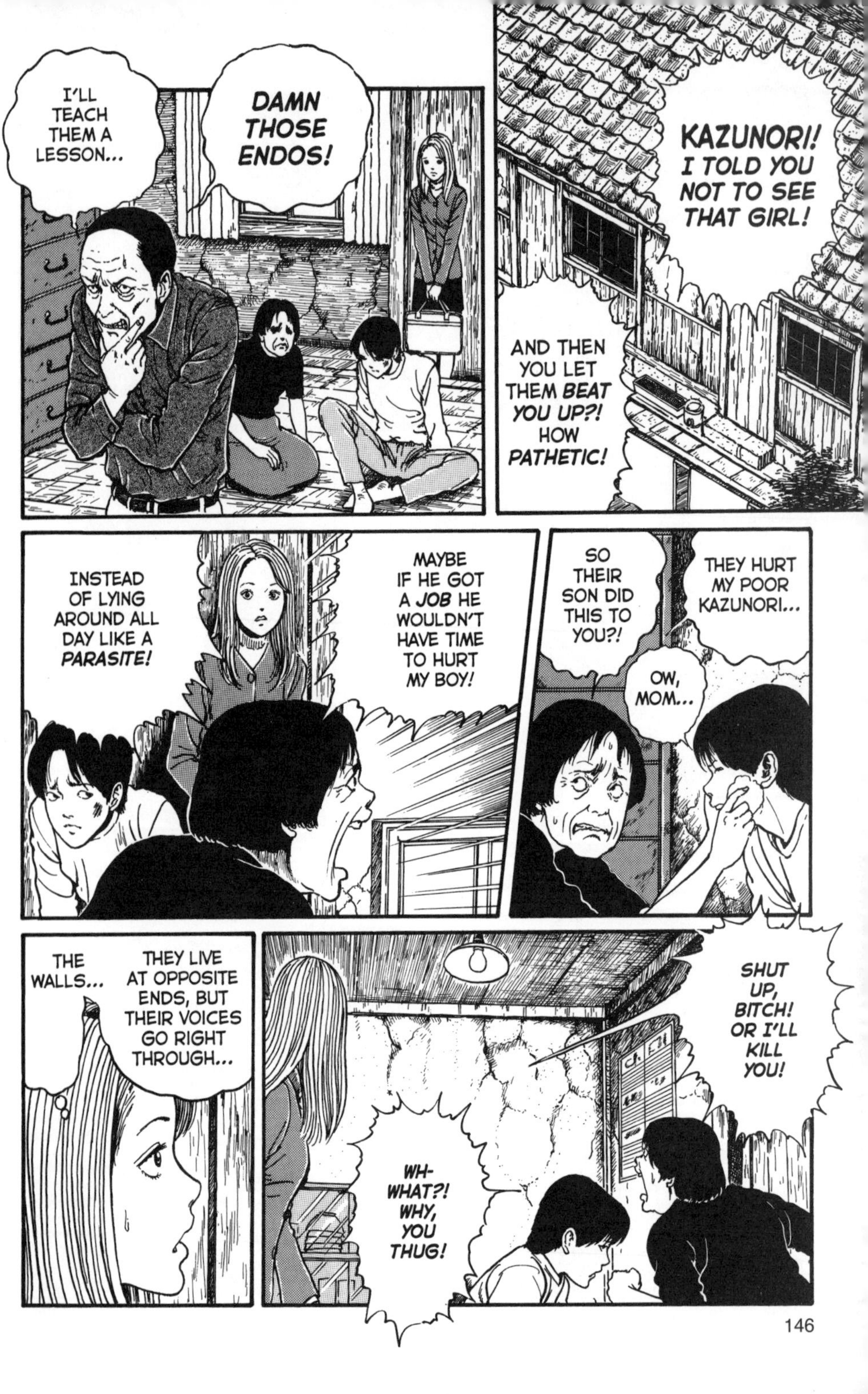
KAZUNORI!! I TOLD YOU NOT TO SEE THAT GIRL!
AND THEN YOU LET THEM *BEAT YOU UP?!* HOW *PATHETIC!*
DAMN THOSE ENDOS!
I'LL TEACH THEM A LESSON...
THEY HURT MY POOR KAZUNORI...
SO THEIR SON DID THIS TO YOU?!
OW, MOM...
MAYBE IF HE GOT A *JOB* HE WOULDN'T HAVE TIME TO HURT MY BOY!
INSTEAD OF LYING AROUND ALL DAY LIKE A *PARASITE!*
SHUT UP, BITCH! OR I'LL KILL YOU!
WH- WHAT?! WHY, YOU THUG!
THEY LIVE AT OPPOSITE ENDS, BUT THEIR VOICES GO RIGHT THROUGH...
THE WALLS...

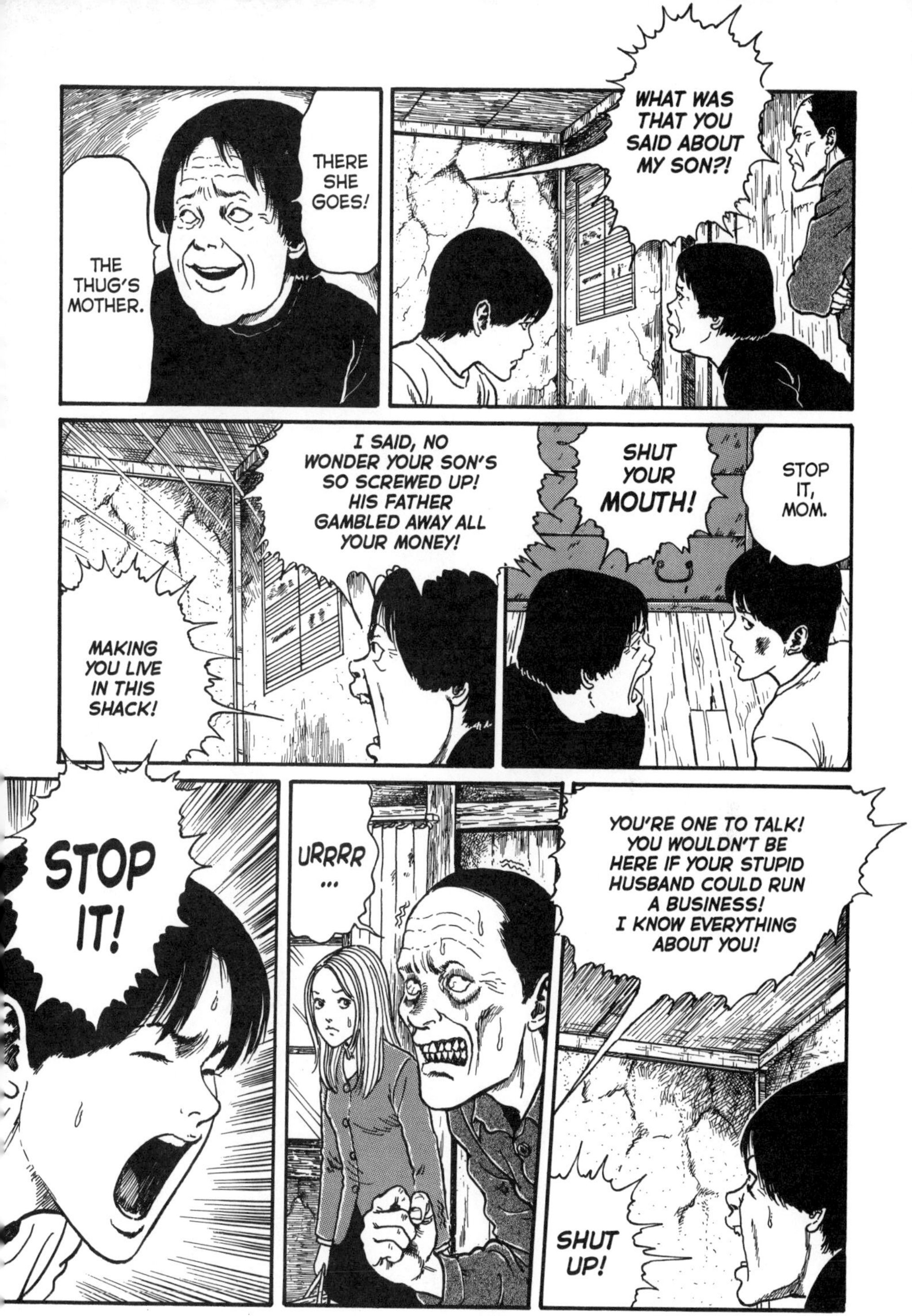
WHAT WAS THAT YOU SAID ABOUT MY SON?!
THERE SHE GOES!
THE THUG'S MOTHER.
STOP IT, MOM.
SHUT YOUR MOUTH!
I SAID, NO WONDER YOUR SON'S SO SCREWED UP! HIS FATHER GAMBLED AWAY ALL YOUR MONEY!
MAKING YOU LIVE IN THIS SHACK!
YOU'RE ONE TO TALK! YOU WOULDN'T BE HERE IF YOUR STUPID HUSBAND COULD RUN A BUSINESS! I KNOW EVERYTHING ABOUT YOU!
SHUT UP!
URRRR ...
STOP IT!

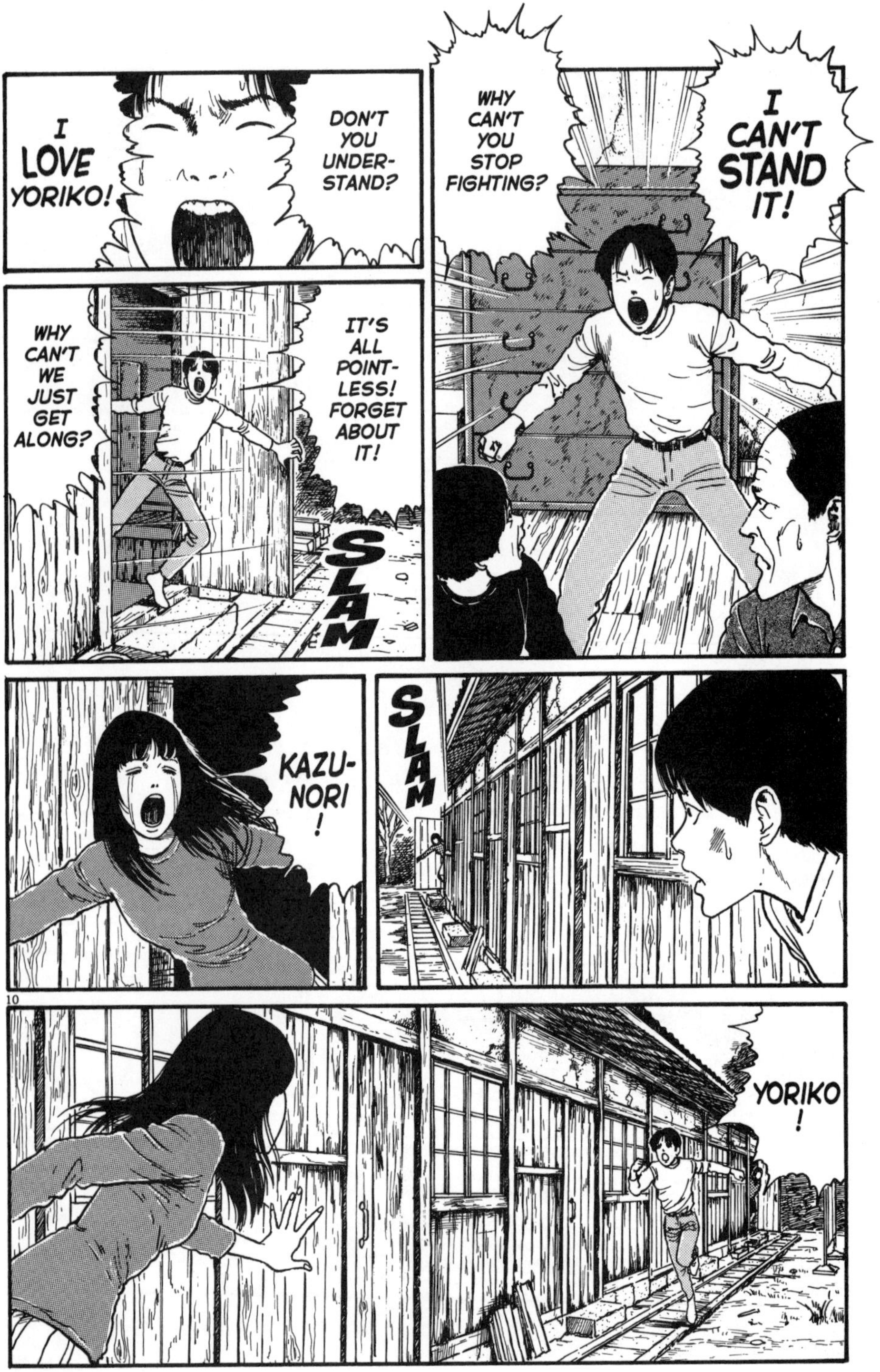
I CAN'T STAND IT!
WHY CAN'T YOU STOP FIGHTING?
DON'T YOU UNDERSTAND?
I LOVE YORIKO!
IT'S ALL POINTLESS! FORGET ABOUT IT!
WHY CAN'T WE JUST GET ALONG?
SLAM
SLAM
KAZUNORI!
YORIKO!

10

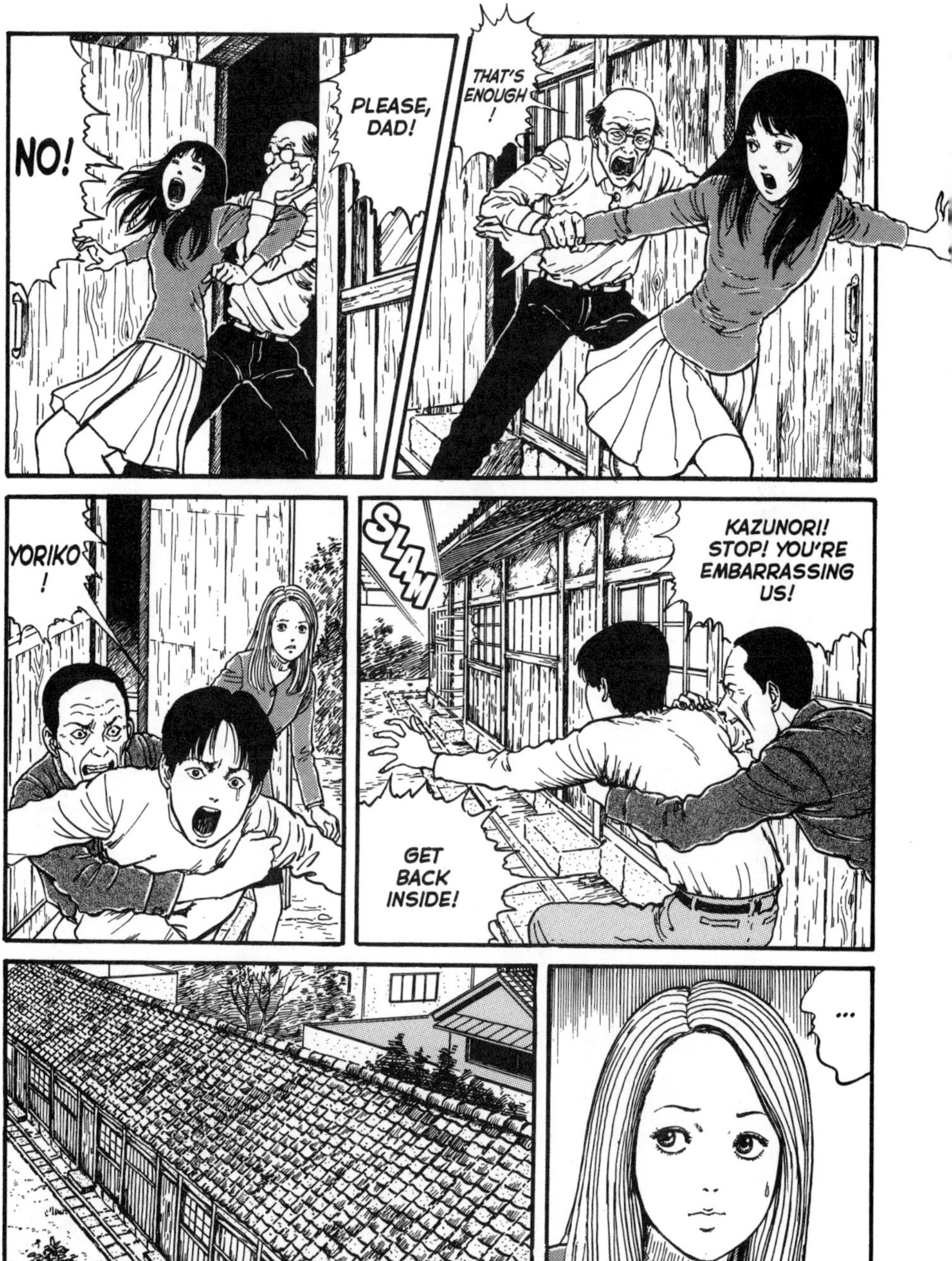
THAT'S ENOUGH!
PLEASE, DAD!
NO!
KAZUNORI! STOP! YOU'RE EMBARRASSING US!
SLAM
GET BACK INSIDE!
YORIKO!
...

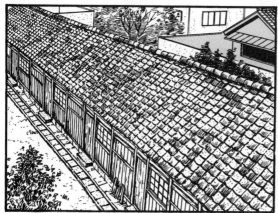

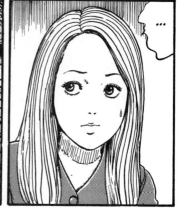

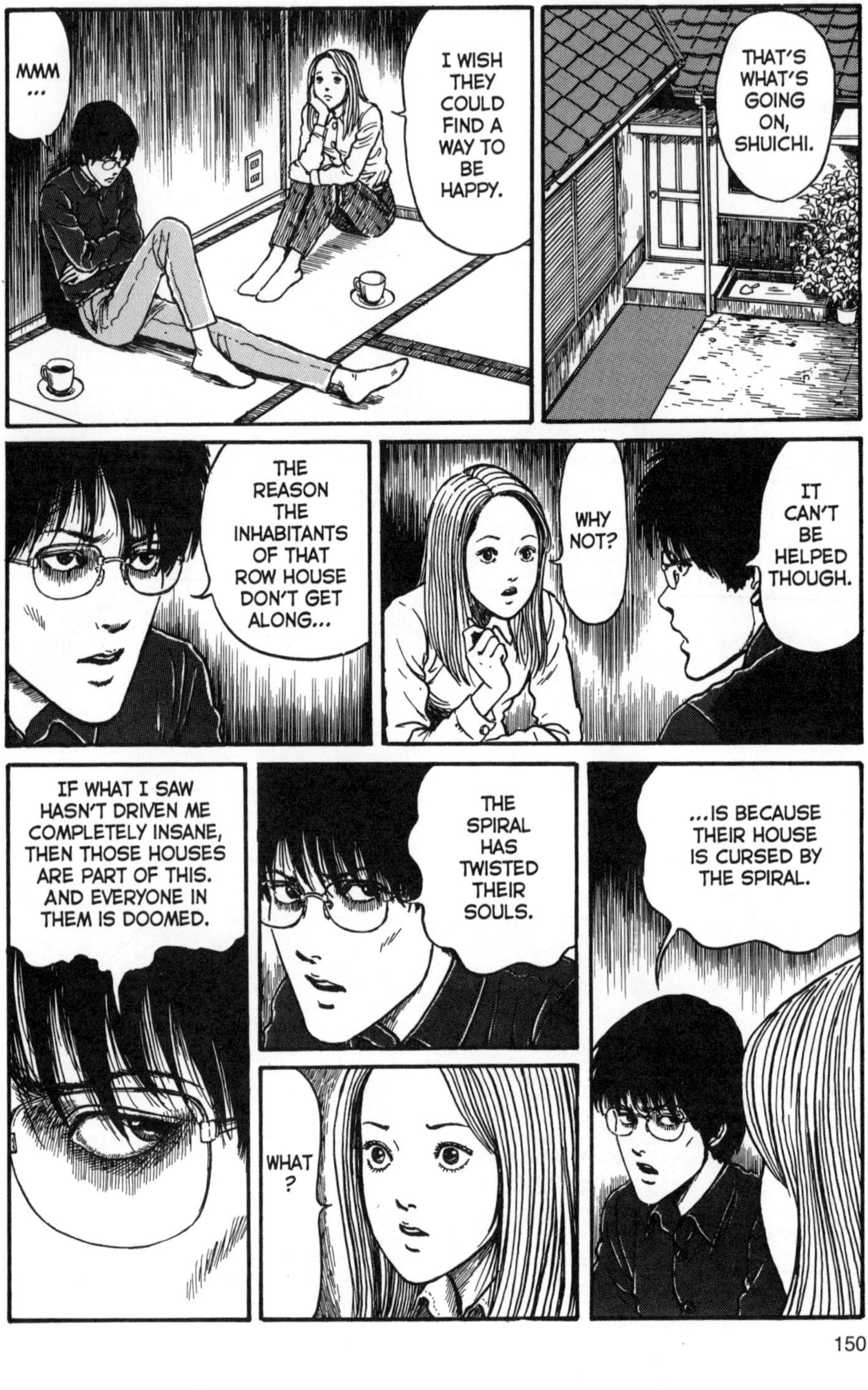
THAT'S WHAT'S GOING ON, SHUICHI.
I WISH THEY COULD FIND A WAY TO BE HAPPY.
MMM ...
IT CAN'T BE HELPED THOUGH.
WHY NOT?
THE REASON THE INHABITANTS OF THAT ROW HOUSE DON'T GET ALONG...
...IS BECAUSE THEIR HOUSE IS CURSED BY THE SPIRAL.
THE SPIRAL HAS TWISTED THEIR SOULS.
WHAT ?
IF WHAT I SAW HASN'T DRIVEN ME COMPLETELY INSANE, THEN THOSE HOUSES ARE PART OF THIS. AND EVERYONE IN THEM IS DOOMED.

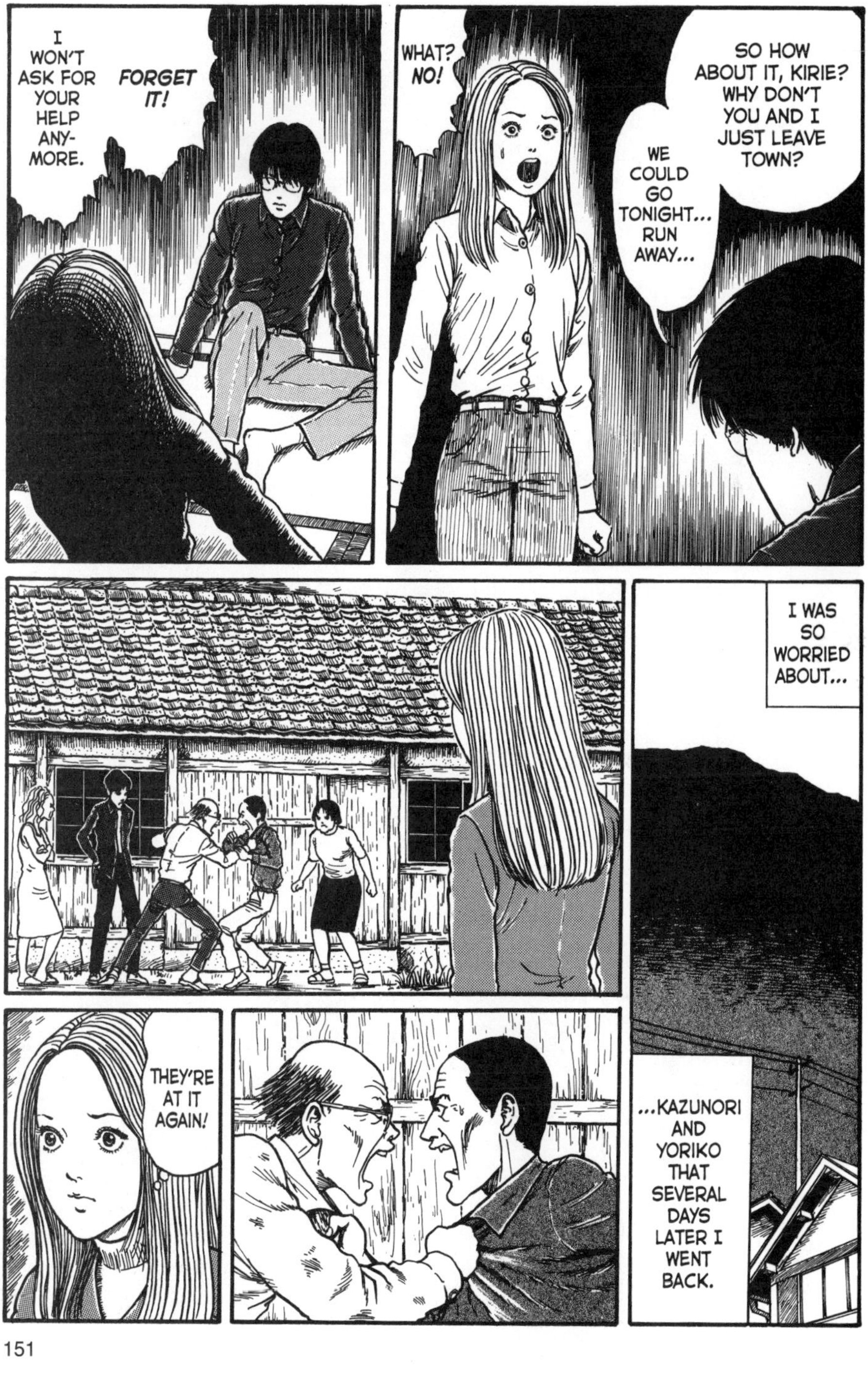
SO HOW ABOUT IT, KIRIE? WHY DON'T YOU AND I JUST LEAVE TOWN?
WE COULD GO TONIGHT... RUN AWAY...
WHAT? *NO!*
FORGET IT!
I WON'T ASK FOR YOUR HELP ANYMORE.
I WAS SO WORRIED ABOUT...
...KAZUNORI AND YORIKO THAT SEVERAL DAYS LATER I WENT BACK.
THEY'RE AT IT AGAIN!

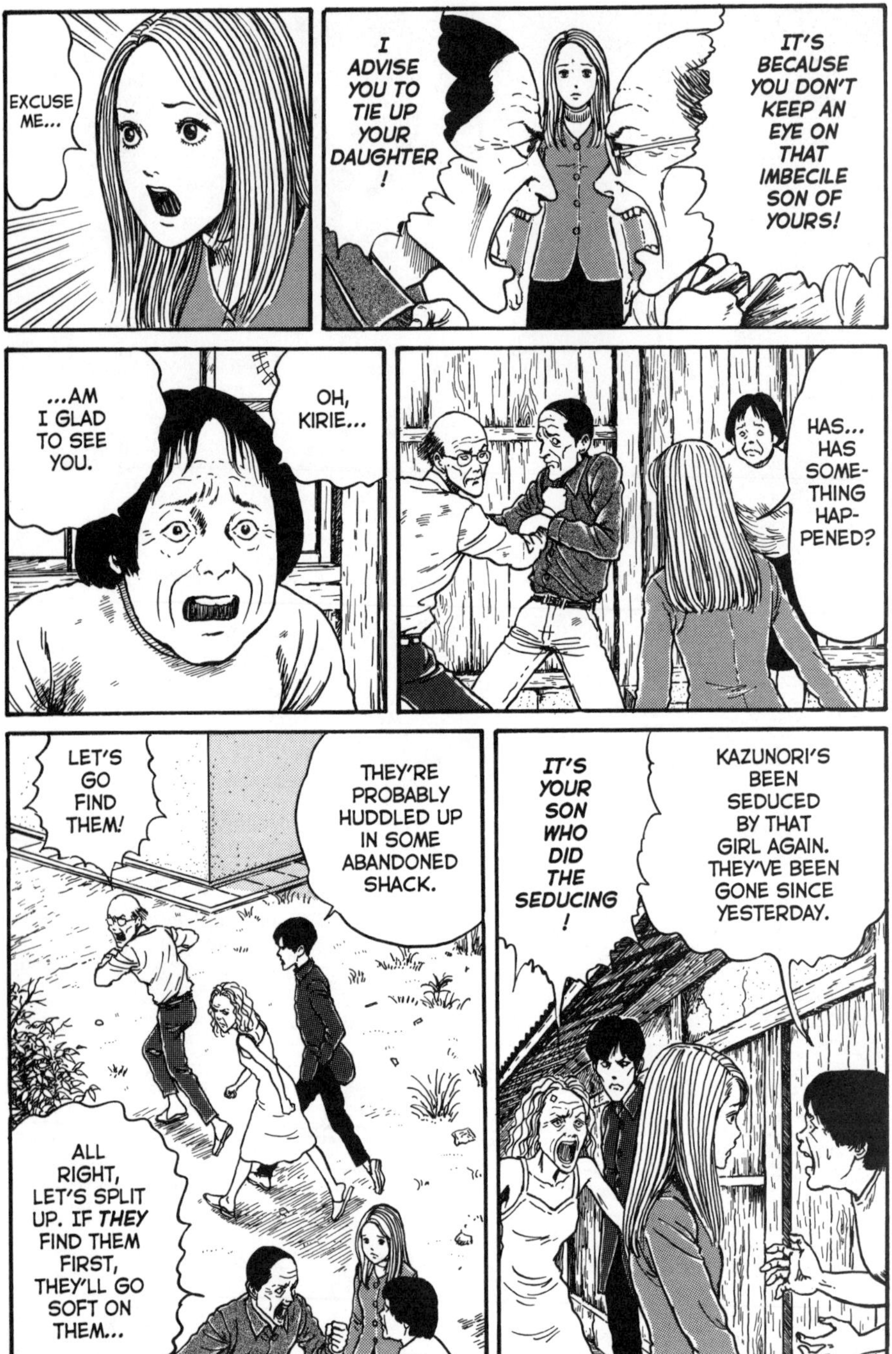
IT'S BECAUSE YOU DON'T KEEP AN EYE ON THAT IMBECILE SON OF YOURS!
I ADVISE YOU TO TIE UP YOUR DAUGHTER!
EXCUSE ME...
HAS... HAS SOMETHING HAPPENED?
OH, KIRIE...
...AM I GLAD TO SEE YOU.
KAZUNORI'S BEEN SEDUCED BY THAT GIRL AGAIN. THEY'VE BEEN GONE SINCE YESTERDAY.
IT'S YOUR SON WHO DID THE SEDUCING!
THEY'RE PROBABLY HUDDLED UP IN SOME ABANDONED SHACK.
LET'S GO FIND THEM!
ALL RIGHT, LET'S SPLIT UP. IF THEY FIND THEM FIRST, THEY'LL GO SOFT ON THEM...

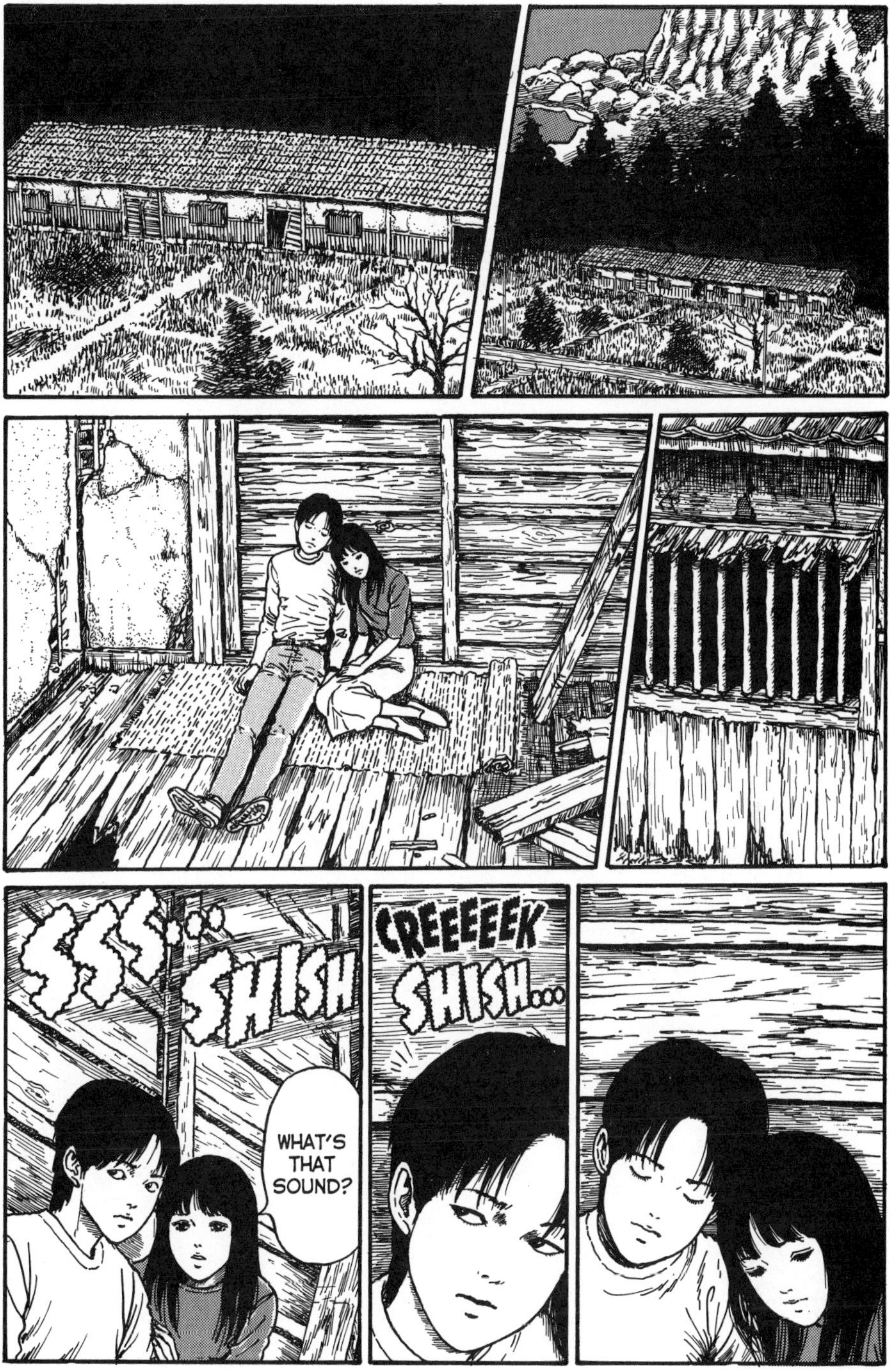
CREEEEEK
SHISH...
SSS...
SHISH
WHAT'S THAT SOUND?

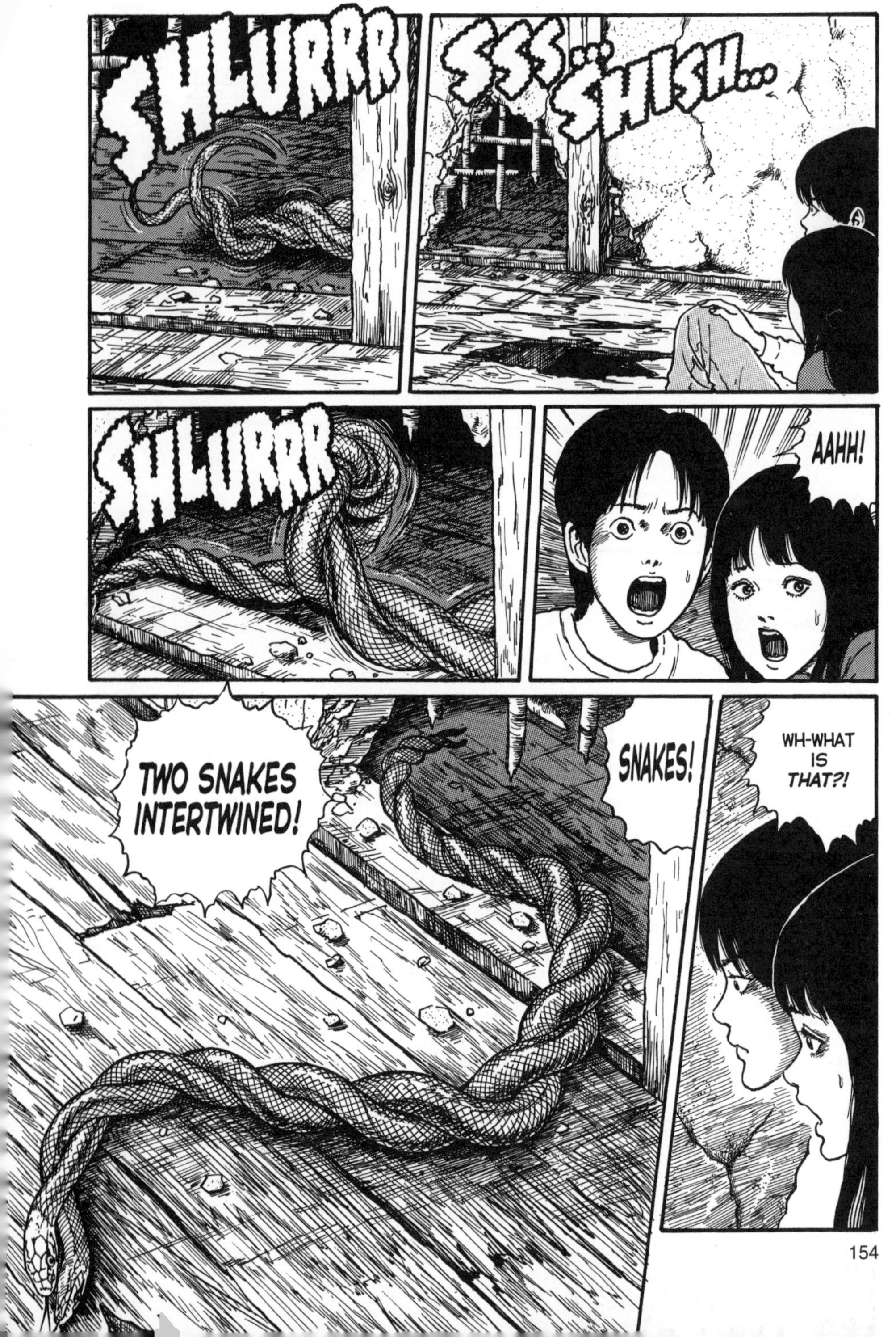
SSS... SHISH...
SHLURRR
AAHH!
SHLURRR
WH-WHAT IS THAT?!
SNAKES!
TWO SNAKES INTERTWINED!

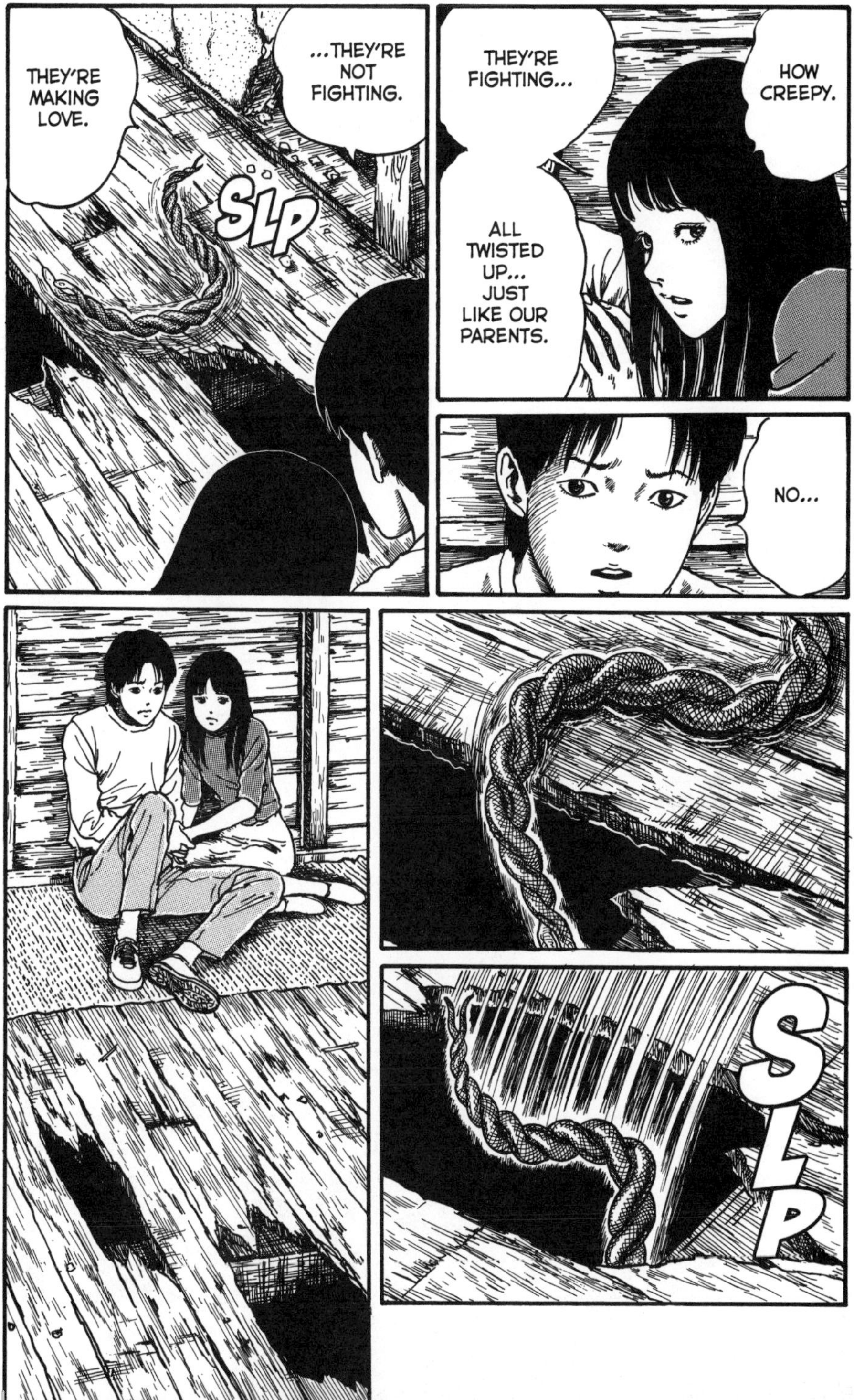
HOW CREEPY.
THEY'RE FIGHTING...
ALL TWISTED UP... JUST LIKE OUR PARENTS.
NO...
...THEY'RE NOT FIGHTING.
THEY'RE MAKING LOVE.
SLP
SLP

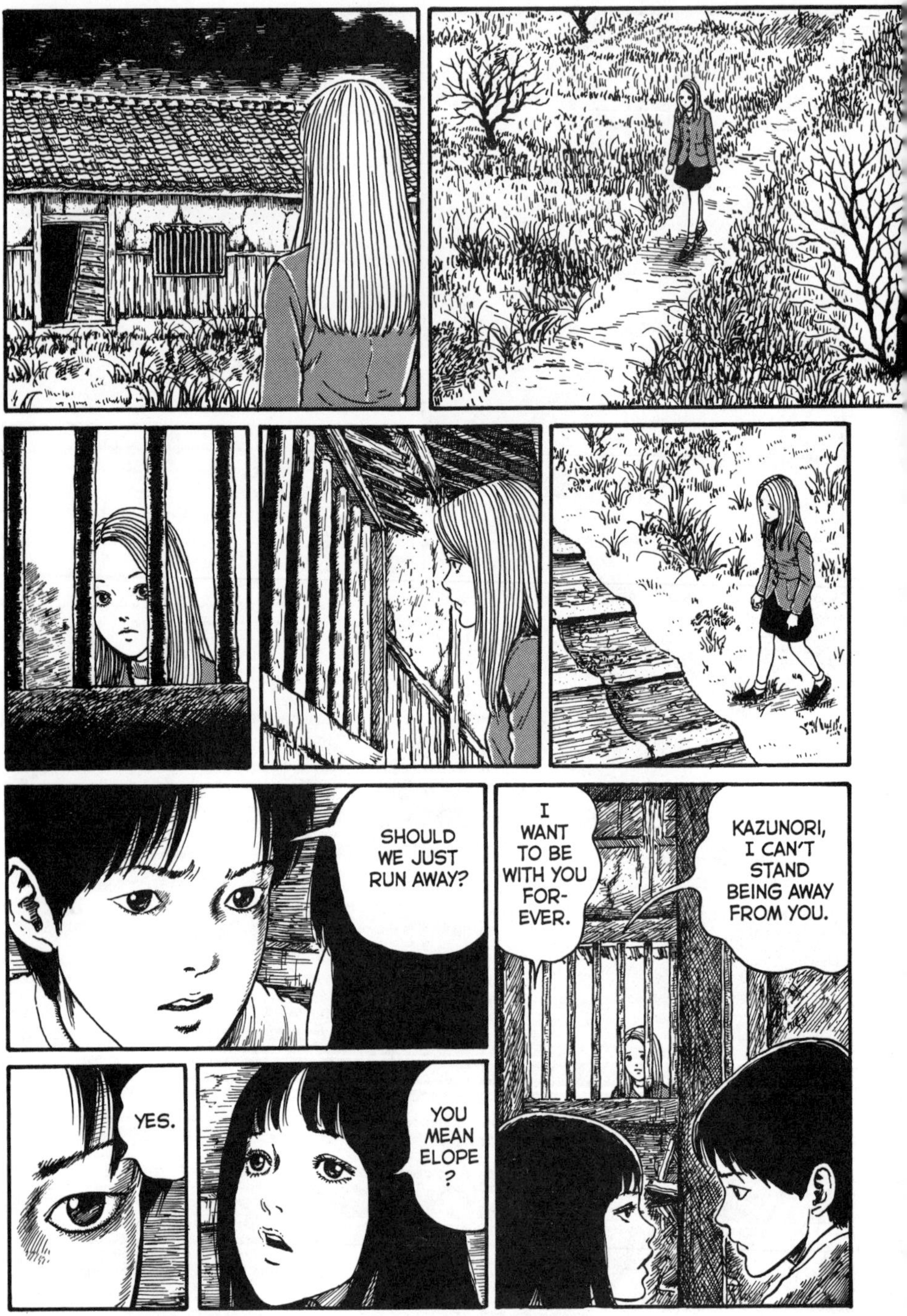
KAZUNORI, I CAN'T STAND BEING AWAY FROM YOU.
I WANT TO BE WITH YOU FOR-EVER.
SHOULD WE JUST RUN AWAY?
YOU MEAN ELOPE ?
YES.

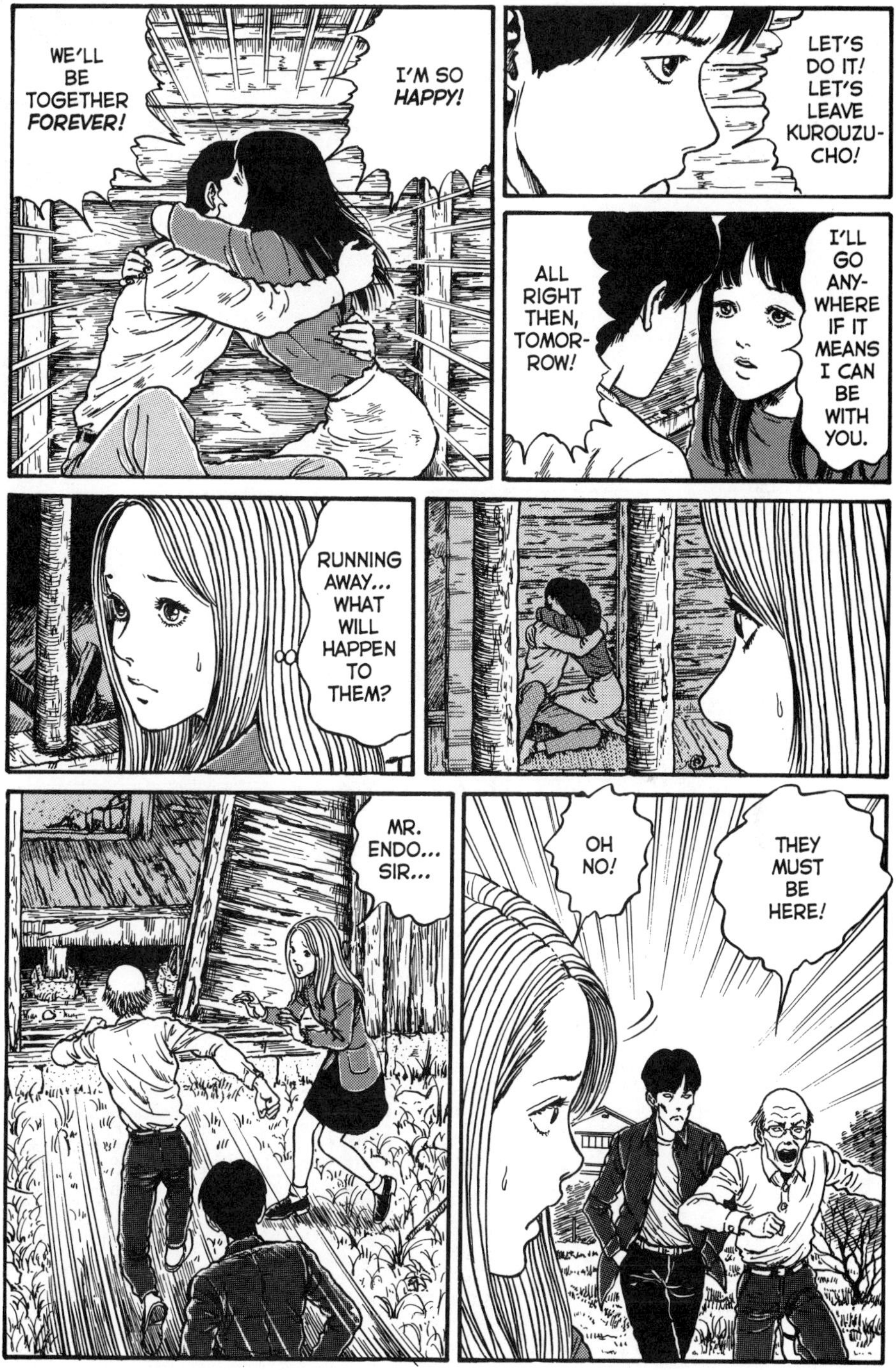
LET'S DO IT! LET'S LEAVE KUROUZU-CHO!
I'LL GO ANYWHERE IF IT MEANS I CAN BE WITH YOU.
ALL RIGHT THEN, TOMORROW!
I'M SO *HAPPY!*
WE'LL BE TOGETHER *FOREVER!*
RUNNING AWAY... WHAT WILL HAPPEN TO THEM?
THEY MUST BE HERE!
OH NO!
MR. ENDO... SIR...

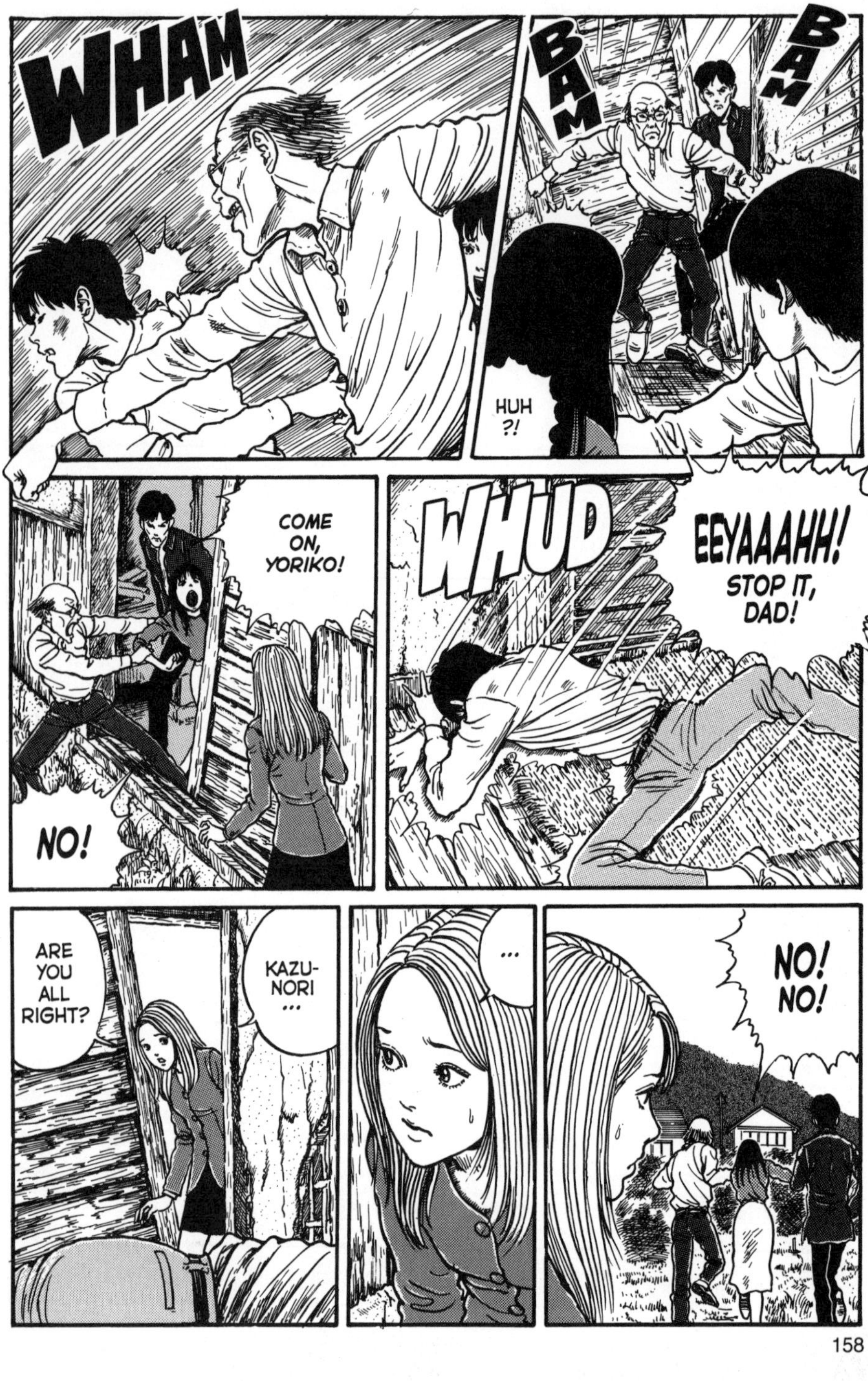
BAM
BAM
HUH ?!
WHAM
WHUD
EEYAAAHH!
STOP IT, DAD!
COME ON, YORIKO!
NO!
NO! NO!
...
KAZUNORI ...
ARE YOU ALL RIGHT?

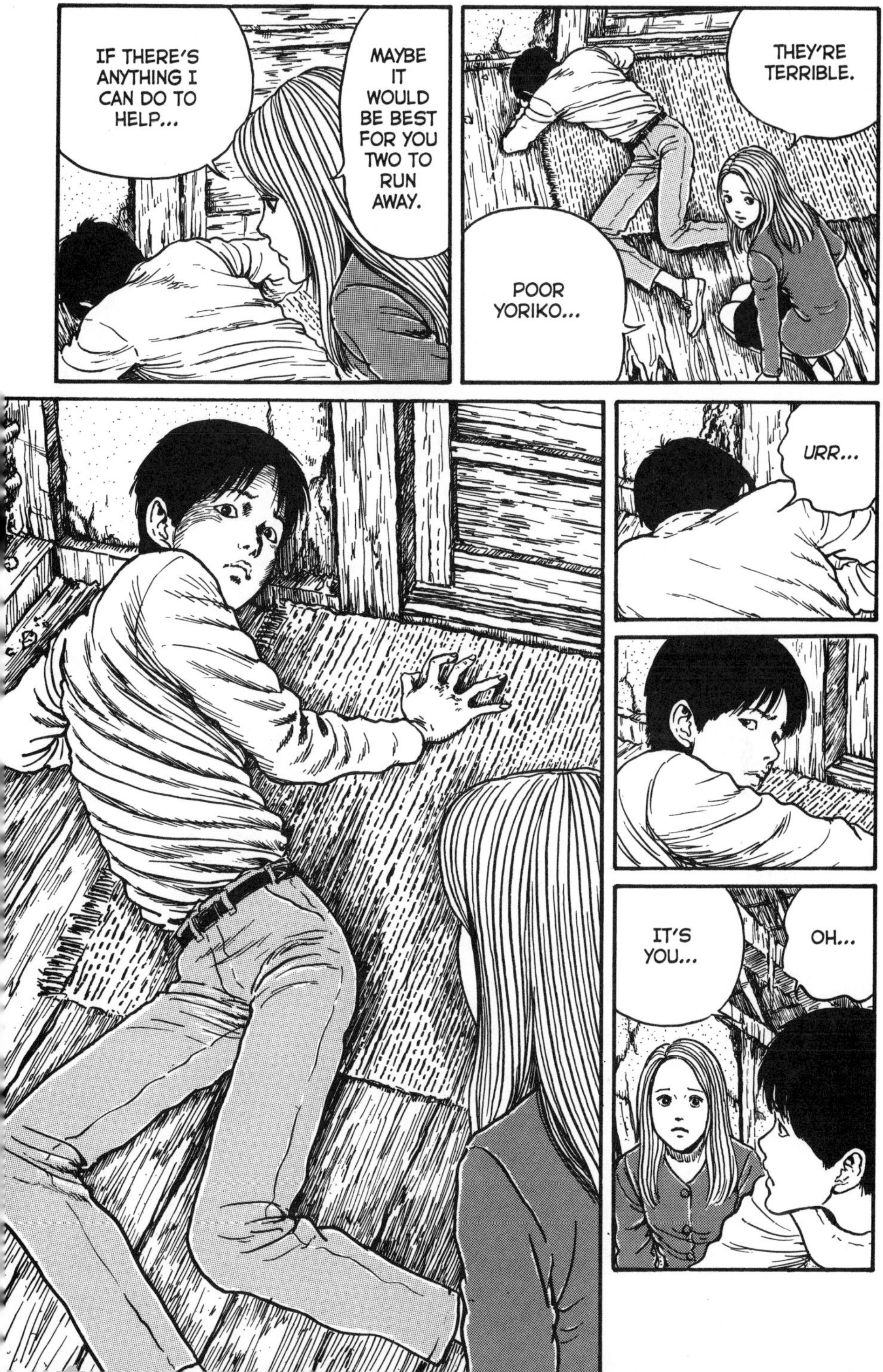
THEY'RE TERRIBLE.
POOR YORIKO...
MAYBE IT WOULD BE BEST FOR YOU TWO TO RUN AWAY.
IF THERE'S ANYTHING I CAN DO TO HELP...
URR...
OH...
IT'S YOU...

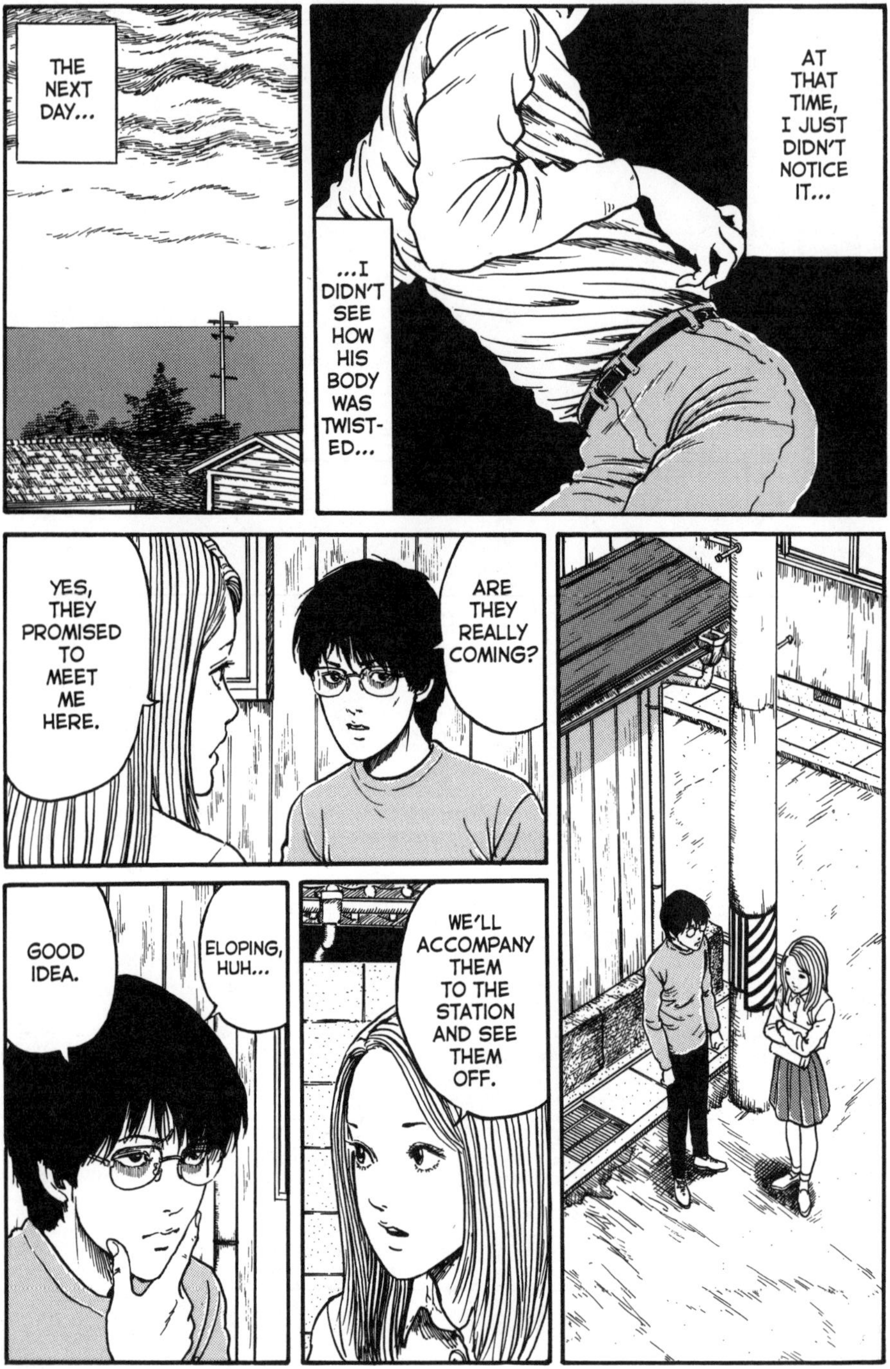
AT THAT TIME, I JUST DIDN'T NOTICE IT...
...I DIDN'T SEE HOW HIS BODY WAS TWIST-ED...
THE NEXT DAY...
ARE THEY REALLY COMING?
YES, THEY PROMISED TO MEET ME HERE.
WE'LL ACCOMPANY THEM TO THE STATION AND SEE THEM OFF.
ELOPING, HUH...
GOOD IDEA.

HERE THEY COME!
Huff Huff
Huff Huff
WHAT HAPPENED? WHAT'S THE RUSH?
OUR PARENTS SAW US LEAVING!
THEY HAVE SOMEONE WAITING AT THE STATION!
OUR FATHERS ARE AFTER US NOW!
WHAT SHOULD WE DO THEN?
WE'LL CIRCLE AROUND TO THE ROAD OUT OF TOWN!
AND HEAD TO THE BEACH!
YES! LET'S GO!

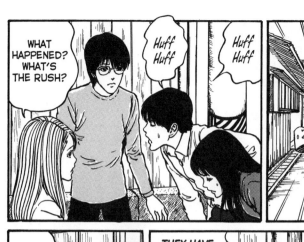

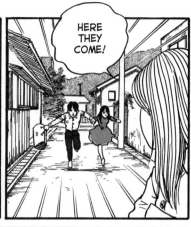

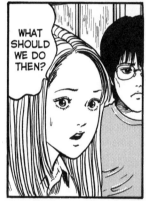

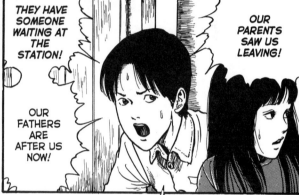

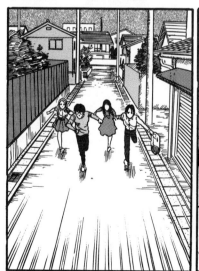

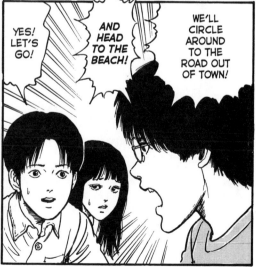

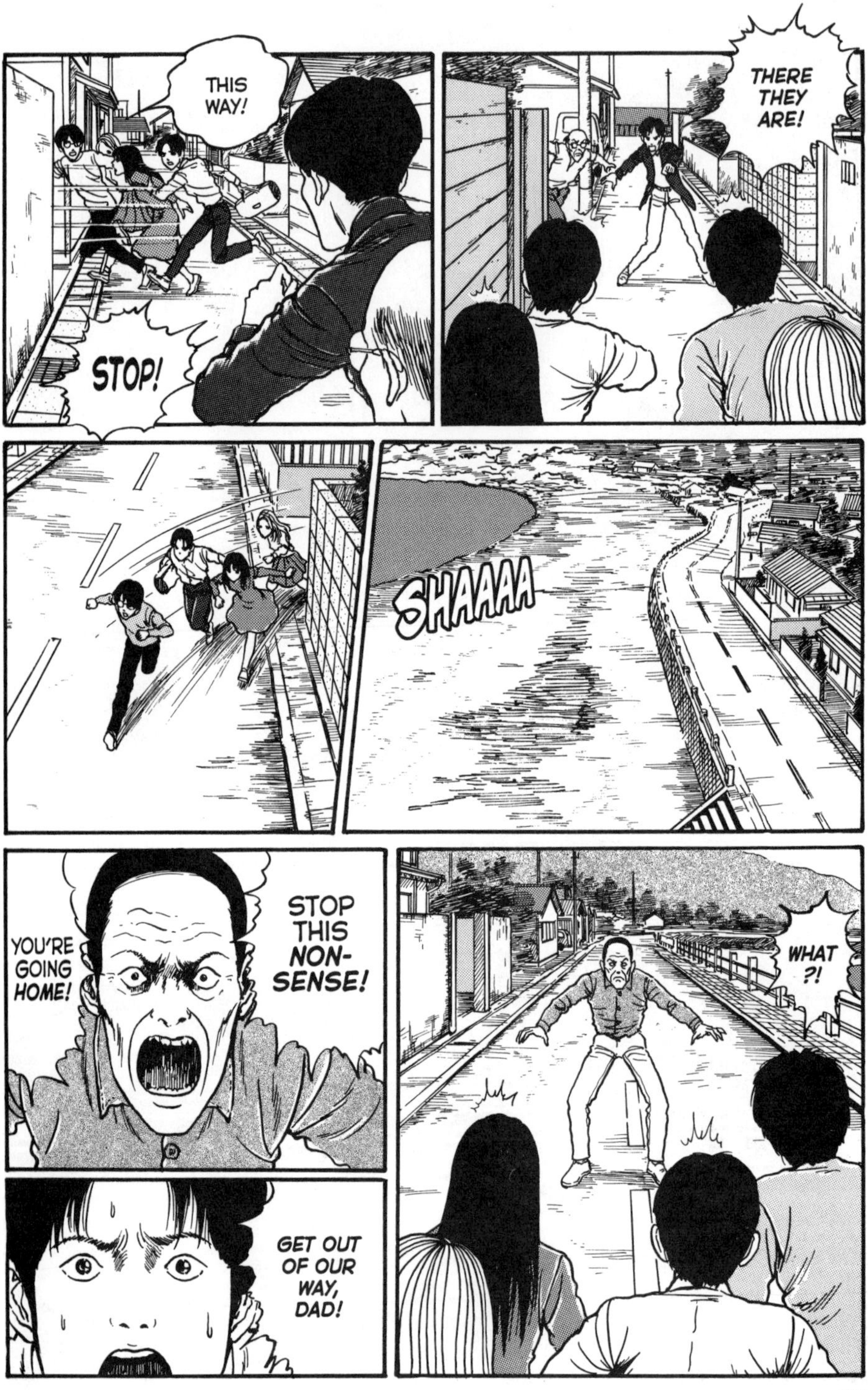
THERE THEY ARE!
THIS WAY!
STOP!
SHAAAA
WHAT?!
STOP THIS NON-SENSE!
YOU'RE GOING HOME!
GET OUT OF OUR WAY, DAD!

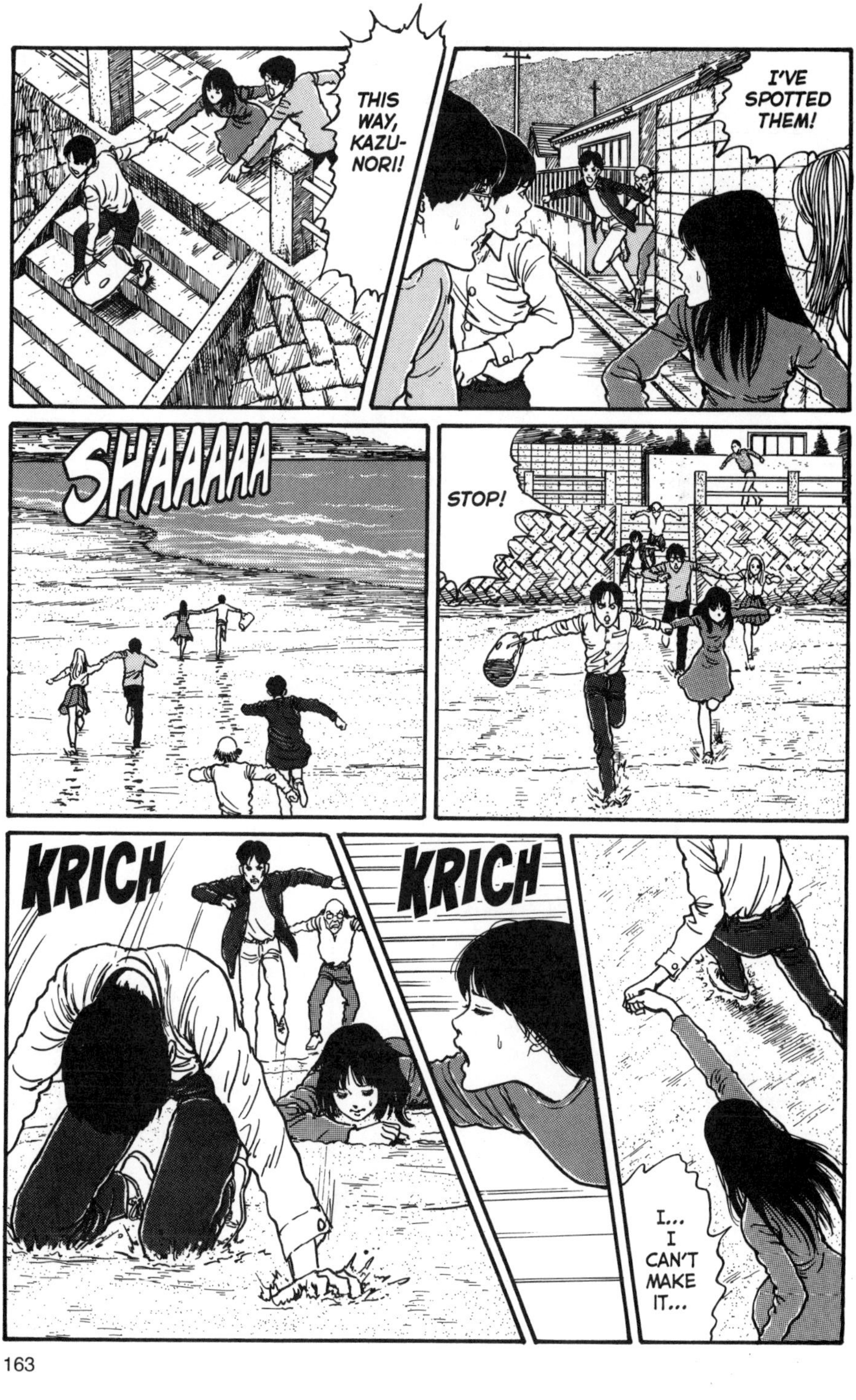

I'VE SPOTTED THEM!
THIS WAY, KAZUNORI!
STOP!
SHAAAAA
I... I CAN'T MAKE IT...
KRICH
KRICH

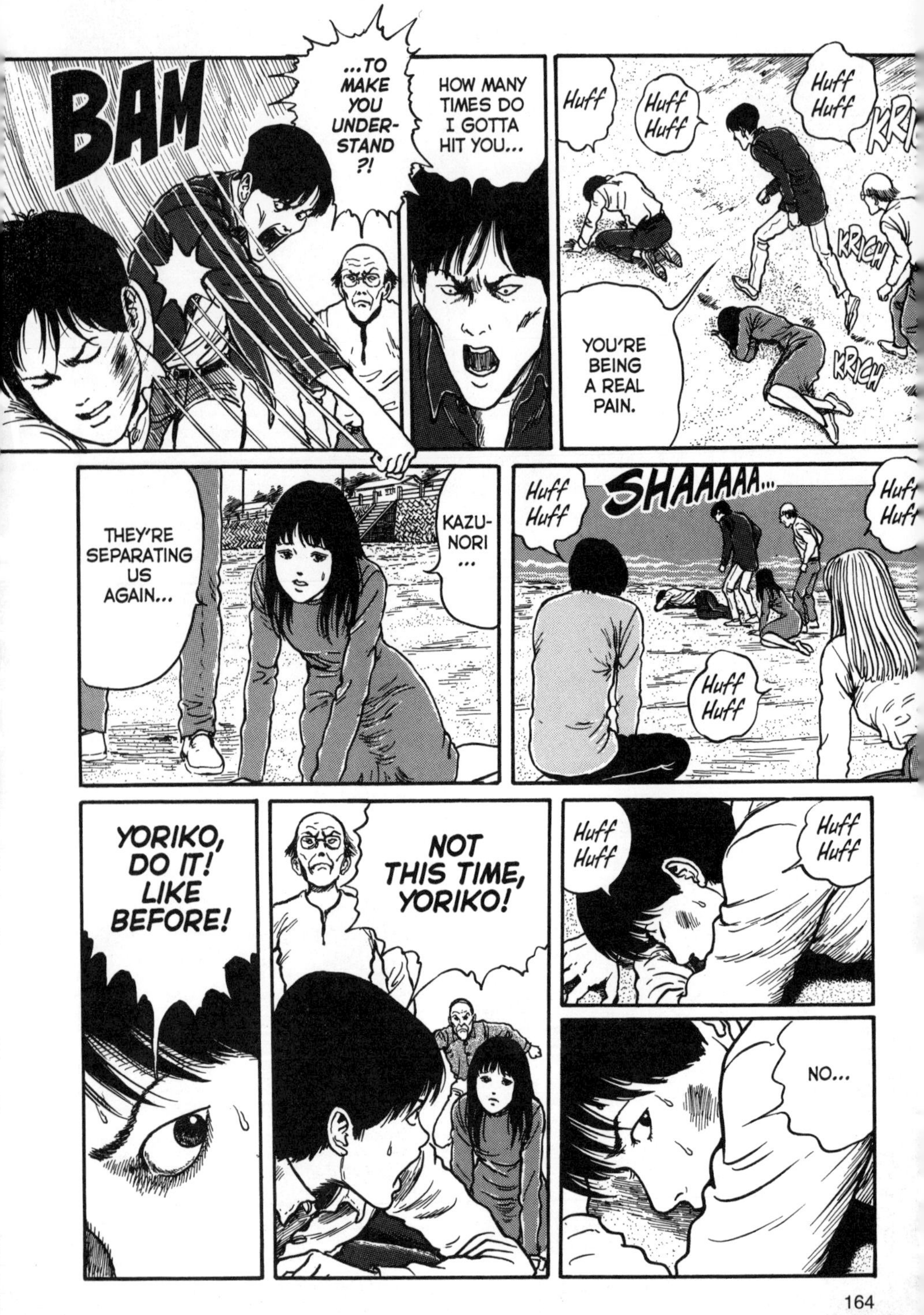
Huff Huff
Huff Huff
Huff
KRICH
YOU'RE BEING A REAL PAIN.
KRICH
HOW MANY TIMES DO I GOTTA HIT YOU...
...TO MAKE YOU UNDER-STAND ?!
BAM
Huff Huff
SHAAAAA...
Huff Huff
Huff Huff
KAZU-NORI ...
THEY'RE SEPARATING US AGAIN...
Huff Huff
Huff Huff
NO...
NOT THIS TIME, YORIKO!
YORIKO, DO IT! LIKE BEFORE!

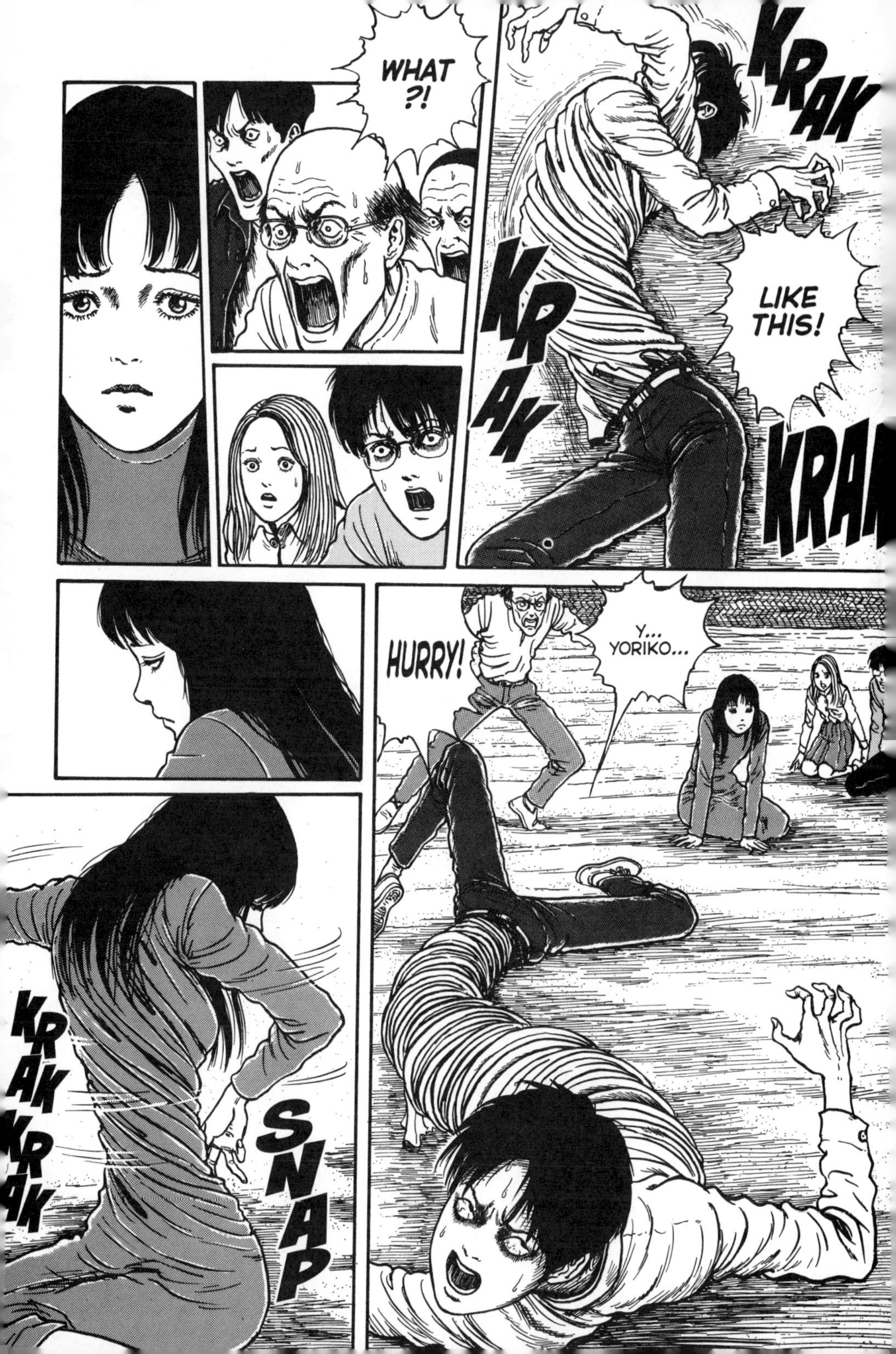
KRAK
LIKE THIS!
KRAK
KRAK
WHAT ?!
Y... YORIKO...
HURRY!
SNAP
KRAK KRAK KRAK

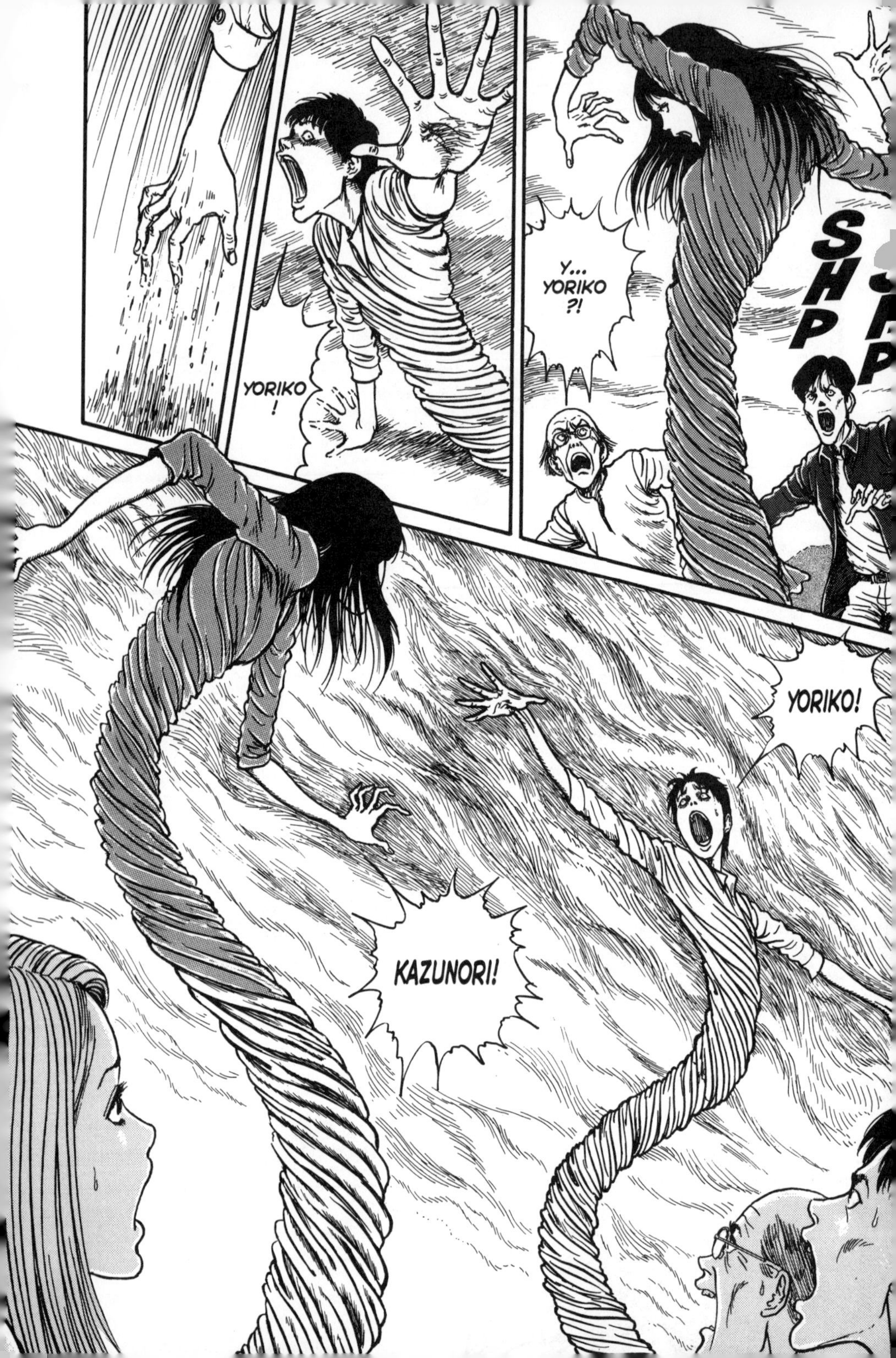
SHP
Y... YORIKO ?!
YORIKO !
YORIKO!
KAZUNORI!

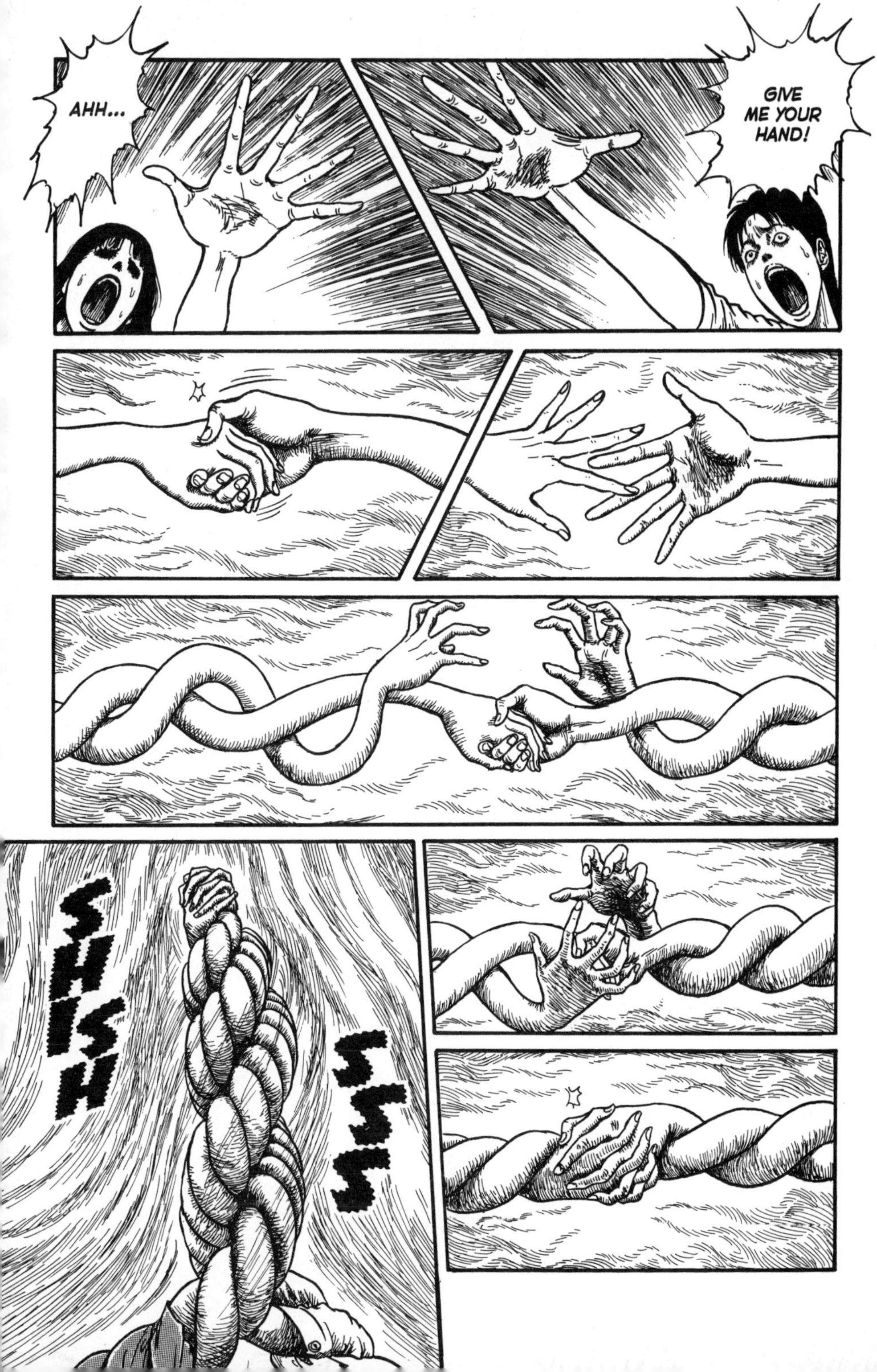
GIVE ME YOUR HAND!
AHH...
SHISH
SSS

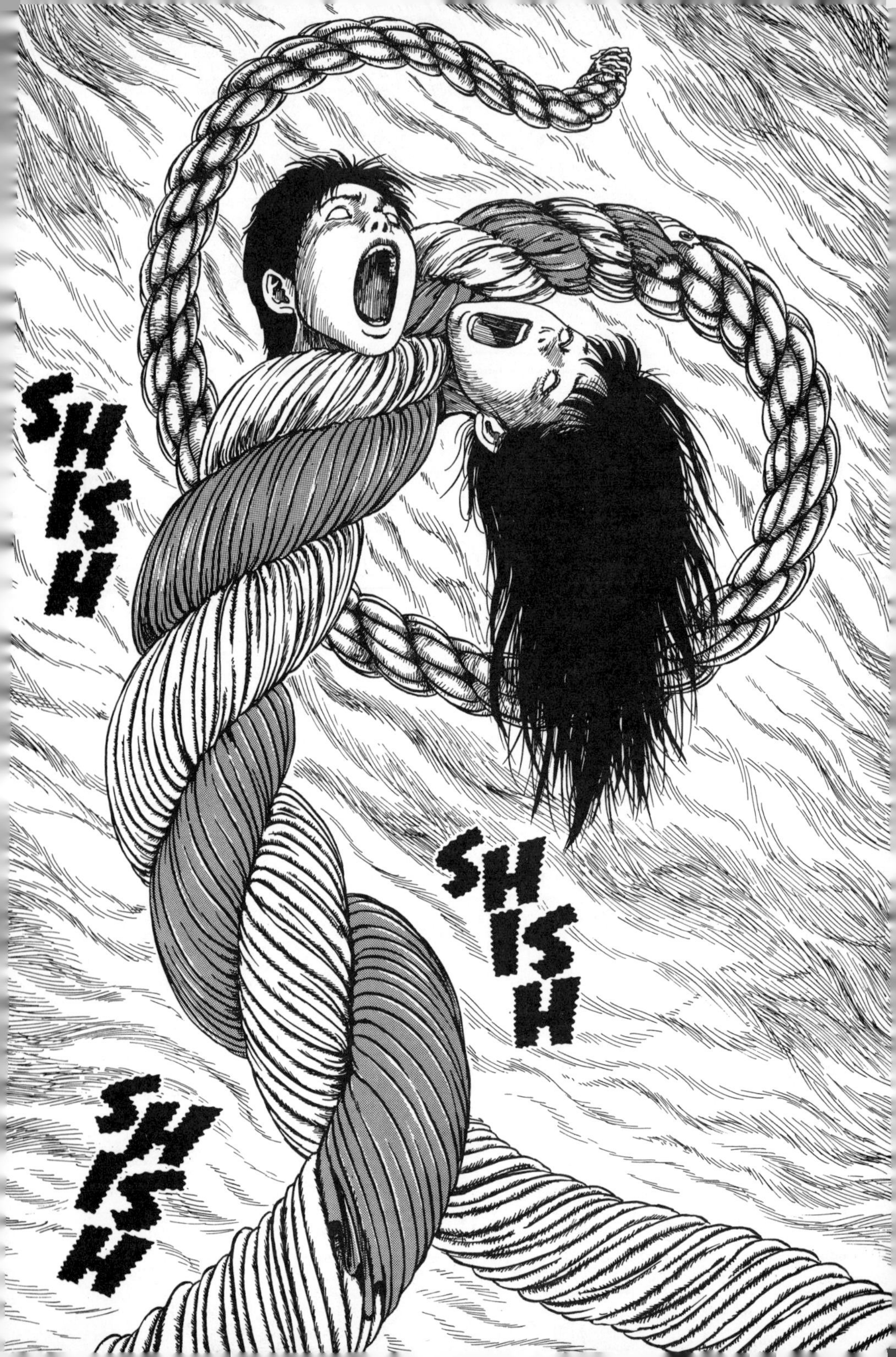
SHISH
SHISH
SHISH

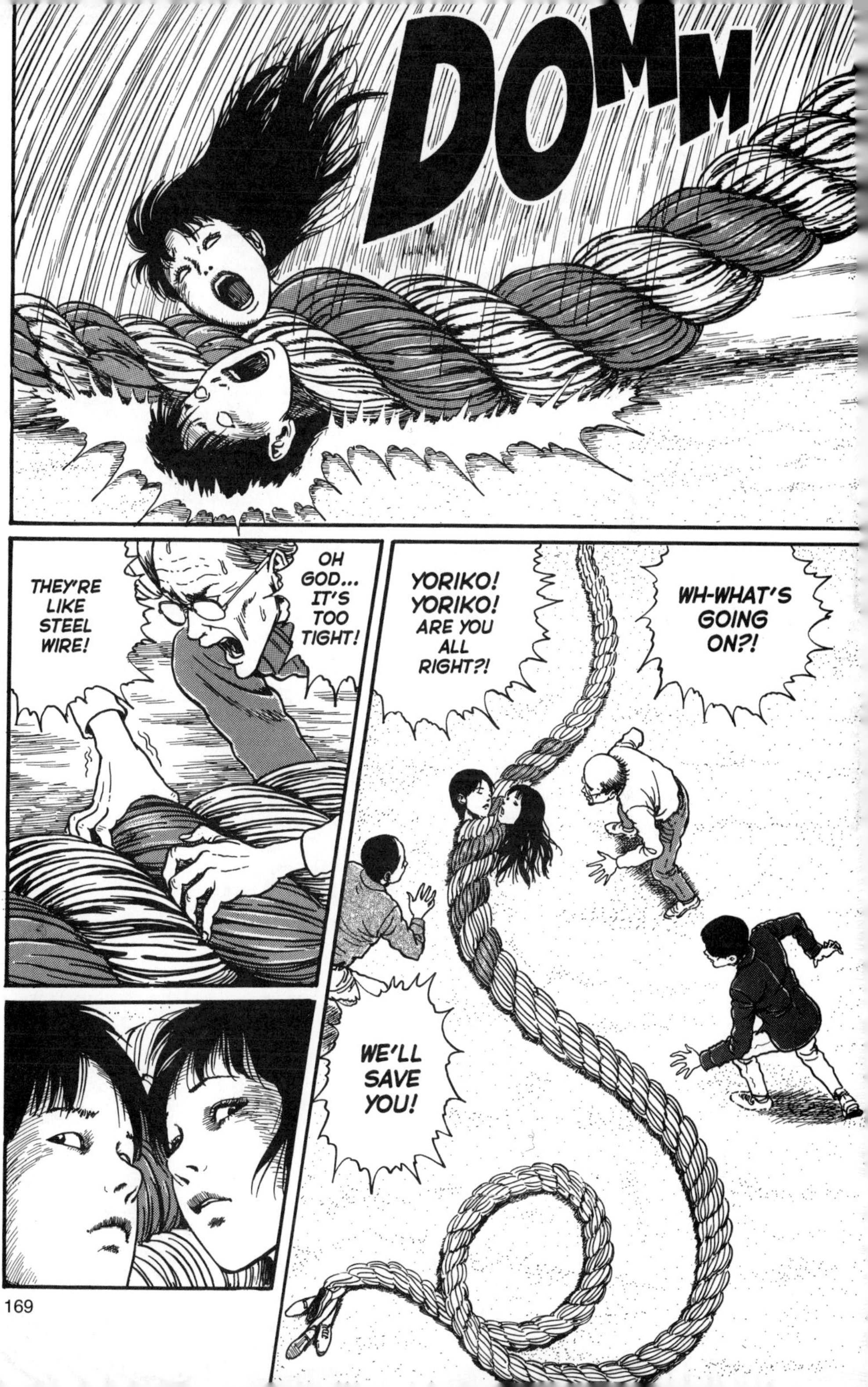
DOMM
WH-WHAT'S GOING ON?!
YORIKO! YORIKO! ARE YOU ALL RIGHT?!
WE'LL SAVE YOU!
OH GOD... IT'S TOO TIGHT!
THEY'RE LIKE STEEL WIRE!

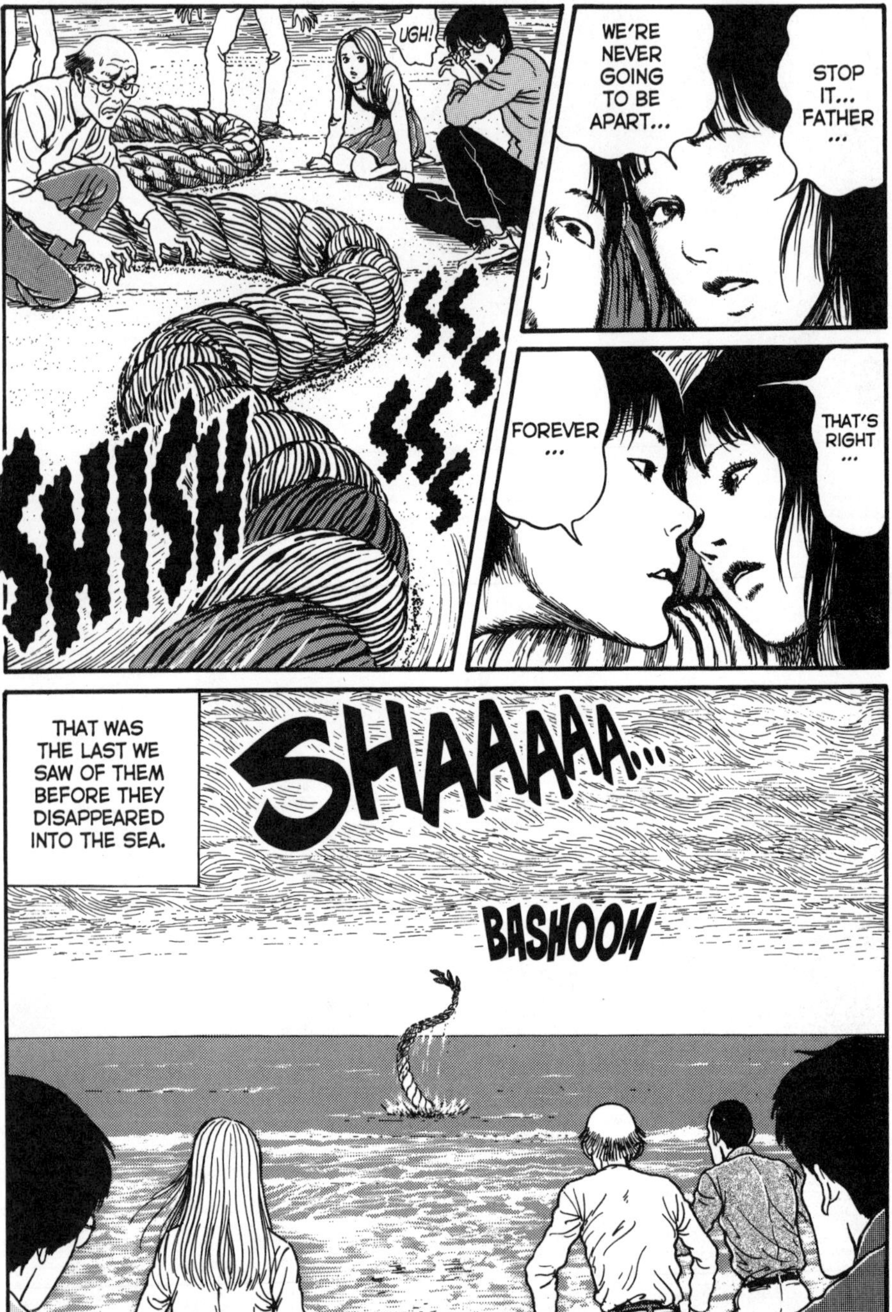
STOP IT... FATHER...
WE'RE NEVER GOING TO BE APART...
THAT'S RIGHT...
FOREVER...
UGH!
SSSS
SSSS
SHISH
THAT WAS THE LAST WE SAW OF THEM BEFORE THEY DISAPPEARED INTO THE SEA.
SHAAAAA...
BASHOOM

CHAPTER
6
MEDUSA

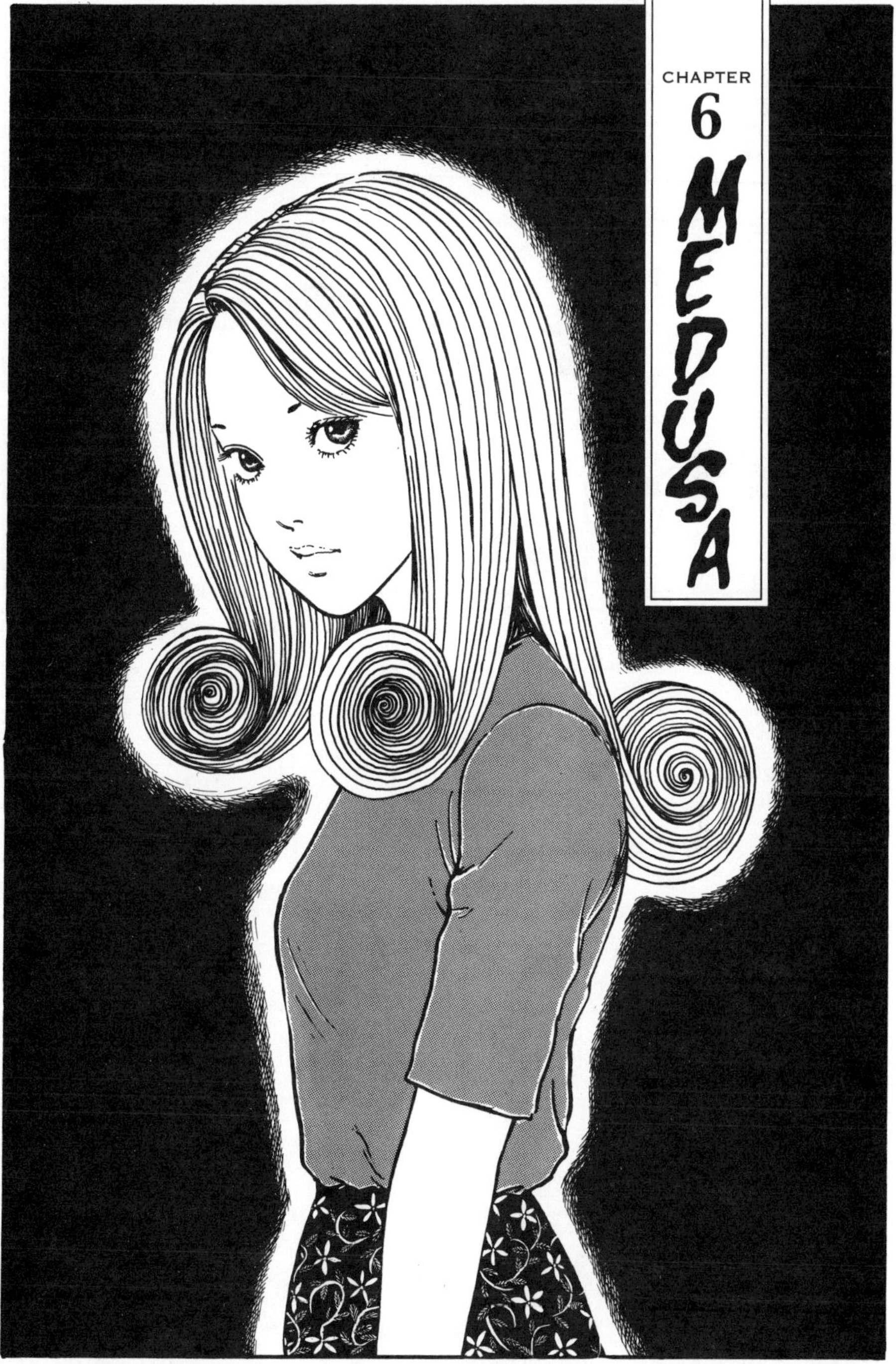

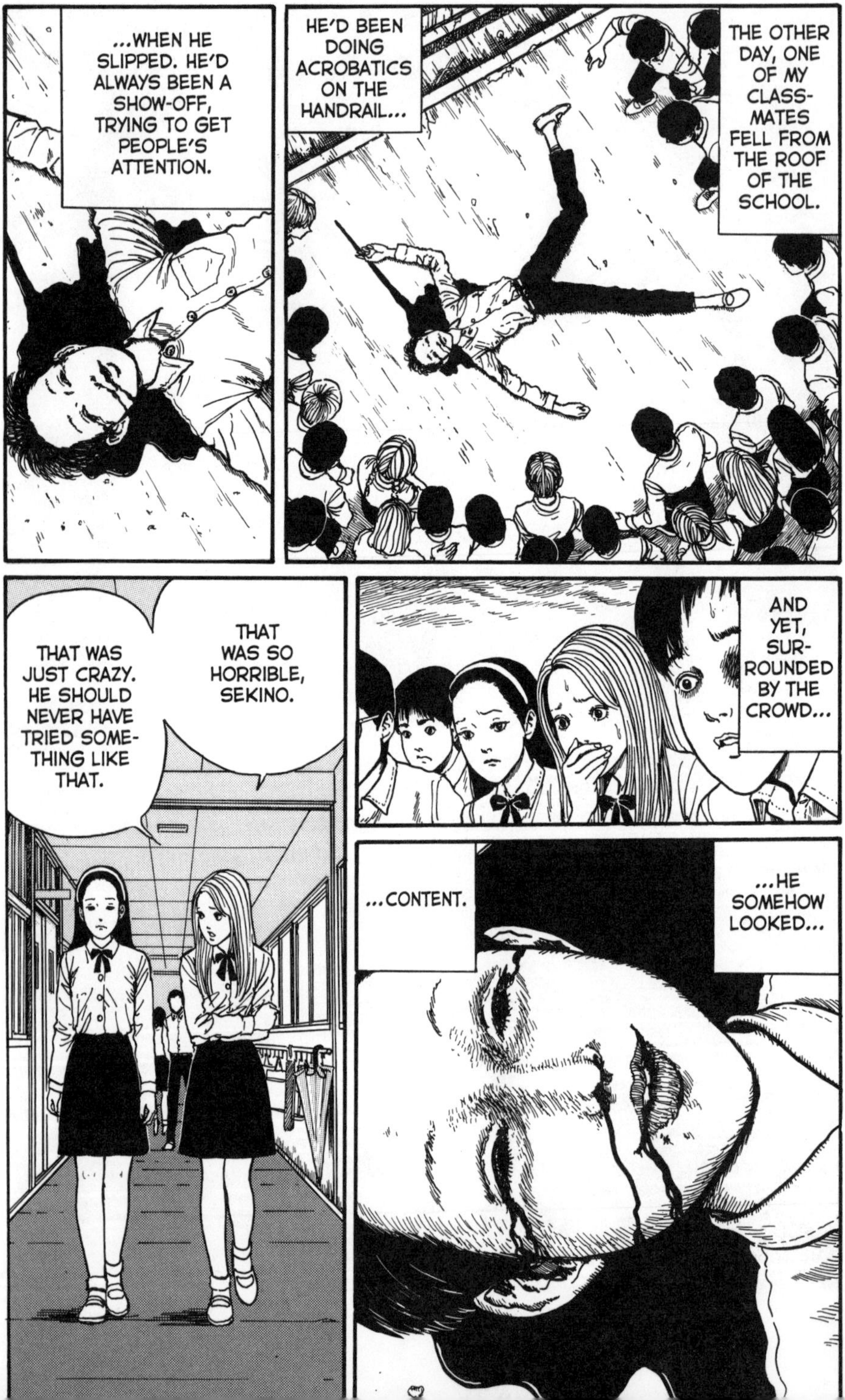
THE OTHER DAY, ONE OF MY CLASSMATES FELL FROM THE ROOF OF THE SCHOOL.
HE'D BEEN DOING ACROBATICS ON THE HANDRAIL...
...WHEN HE SLIPPED. HE'D ALWAYS BEEN A SHOW-OFF, TRYING TO GET PEOPLE'S ATTENTION.
AND YET, SURROUNDED BY THE CROWD...
...HE SOMEHOW LOOKED...
...CONTENT.
THAT WAS SO HORRIBLE, SEKINO.
THAT WAS JUST CRAZY. HE SHOULD NEVER HAVE TRIED SOMETHING LIKE THAT.

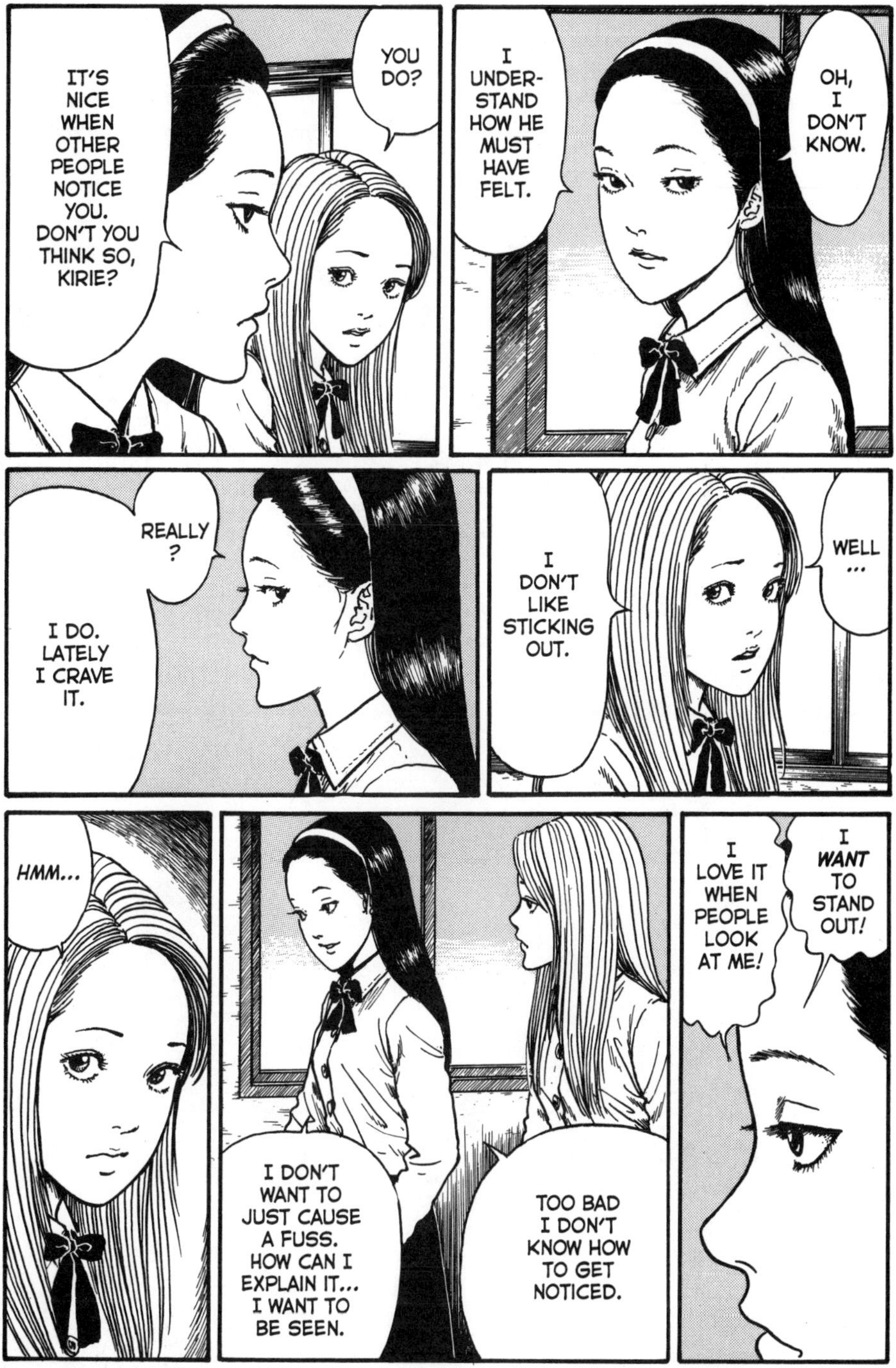
OH, I DON'T KNOW.
I UNDER-STAND HOW HE MUST HAVE FELT.
YOU DO?
IT'S NICE WHEN OTHER PEOPLE NOTICE YOU. DON'T YOU THINK SO, KIRIE?
WELL...
I DON'T LIKE STICKING OUT.
REALLY?
I DO. LATELY I CRAVE IT.
I *WANT* TO STAND OUT!
I LOVE IT WHEN PEOPLE LOOK AT ME!
TOO BAD I DON'T KNOW HOW TO GET NOTICED.
I DON'T WANT TO JUST CAUSE A FUSS. HOW CAN I EXPLAIN IT... I WANT TO BE SEEN.
HMM...

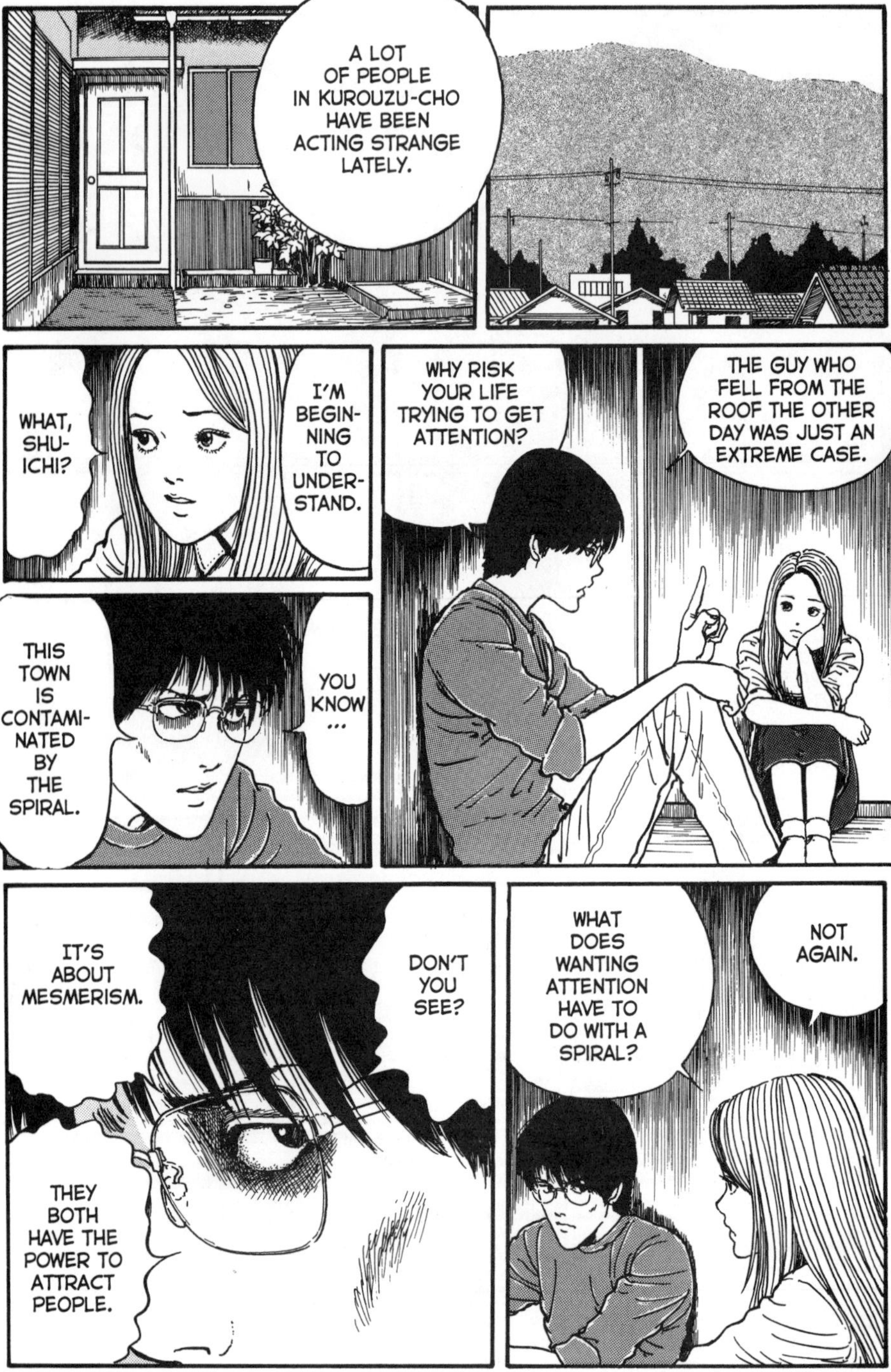
A LOT OF PEOPLE IN KUROUZU-CHO HAVE BEEN ACTING STRANGE LATELY.
THE GUY WHO FELL FROM THE ROOF THE OTHER DAY WAS JUST AN EXTREME CASE.
WHY RISK YOUR LIFE TRYING TO GET ATTENTION?
I'M BEGIN-NING TO UNDER-STAND.
WHAT, SHU-ICHI?
YOU KNOW...
THIS TOWN IS CONTAMI-NATED BY THE SPIRAL.
NOT AGAIN.
WHAT DOES WANTING ATTENTION HAVE TO DO WITH A SPIRAL?
DON'T YOU SEE?
IT'S ABOUT MESMERISM.
THEY BOTH HAVE THE POWER TO ATTRACT PEOPLE.

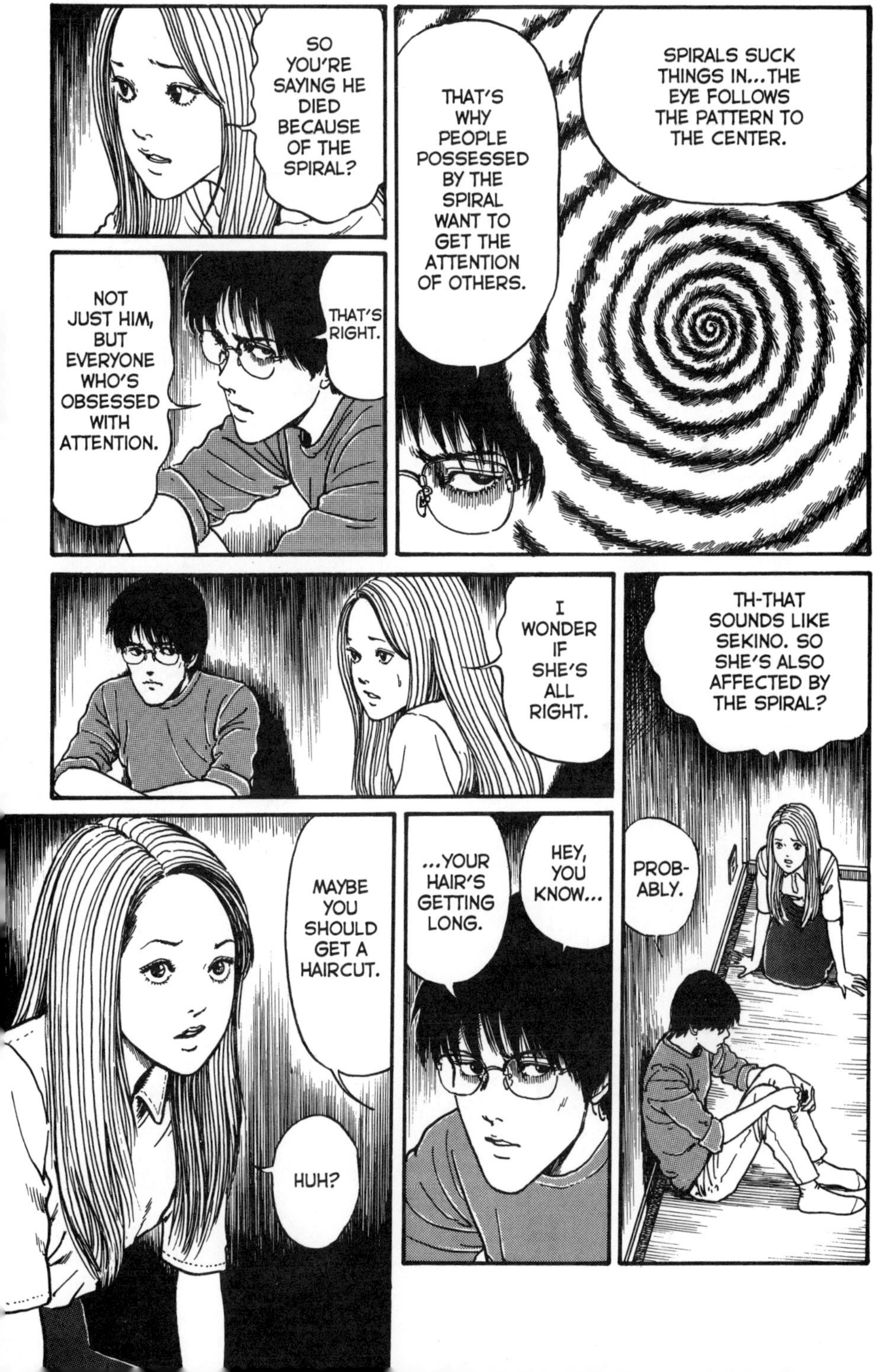
SO YOU'RE SAYING HE DIED BECAUSE OF THE SPIRAL?
THAT'S RIGHT.
NOT JUST HIM, BUT EVERYONE WHO'S OBSESSED WITH ATTENTION.
SPIRALS SUCK THINGS IN...THE EYE FOLLOWS THE PATTERN TO THE CENTER.
THAT'S WHY PEOPLE POSSESSED BY THE SPIRAL WANT TO GET THE ATTENTION OF OTHERS.
I WONDER IF SHE'S ALL RIGHT.
TH-THAT SOUNDS LIKE SEKINO. SO SHE'S ALSO AFFECTED BY THE SPIRAL?
PROB-ABLY.
HEY, YOU KNOW...
...YOUR HAIR'S GETTING LONG.
MAYBE YOU SHOULD GET A HAIRCUT.
HUH?

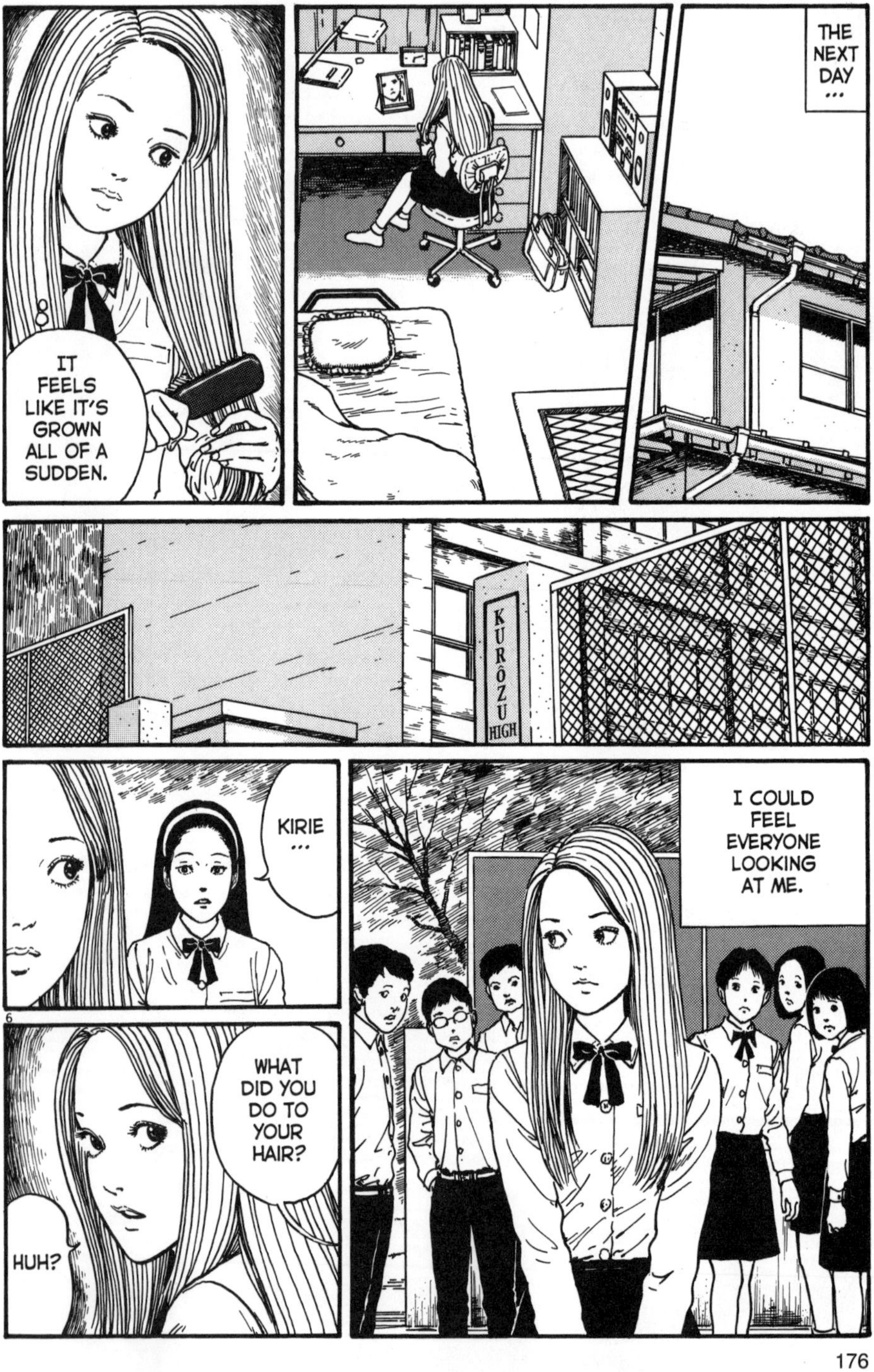
THE NEXT DAY ...
IT FEELS LIKE IT'S GROWN ALL OF A SUDDEN.
KURÔZU HIGH
I COULD FEEL EVERYONE LOOKING AT ME.
KIRIE ...
WHAT DID YOU DO TO YOUR HAIR?
HUH?

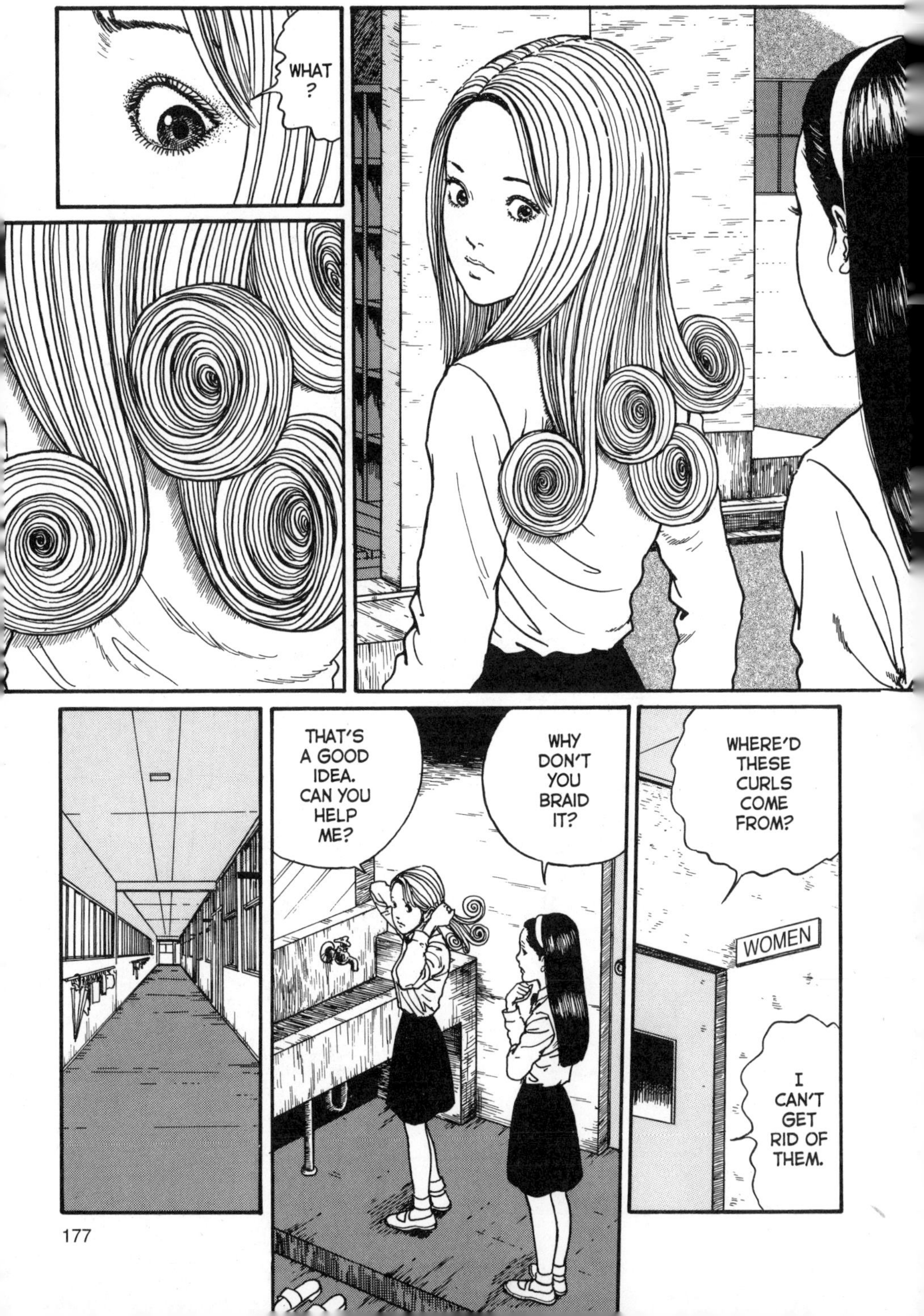
WHAT ?
WHERE'D THESE CURLS COME FROM?
WOMEN
I CAN'T GET RID OF THEM.
WHY DON'T YOU BRAID IT?
THAT'S A GOOD IDEA. CAN YOU HELP ME?

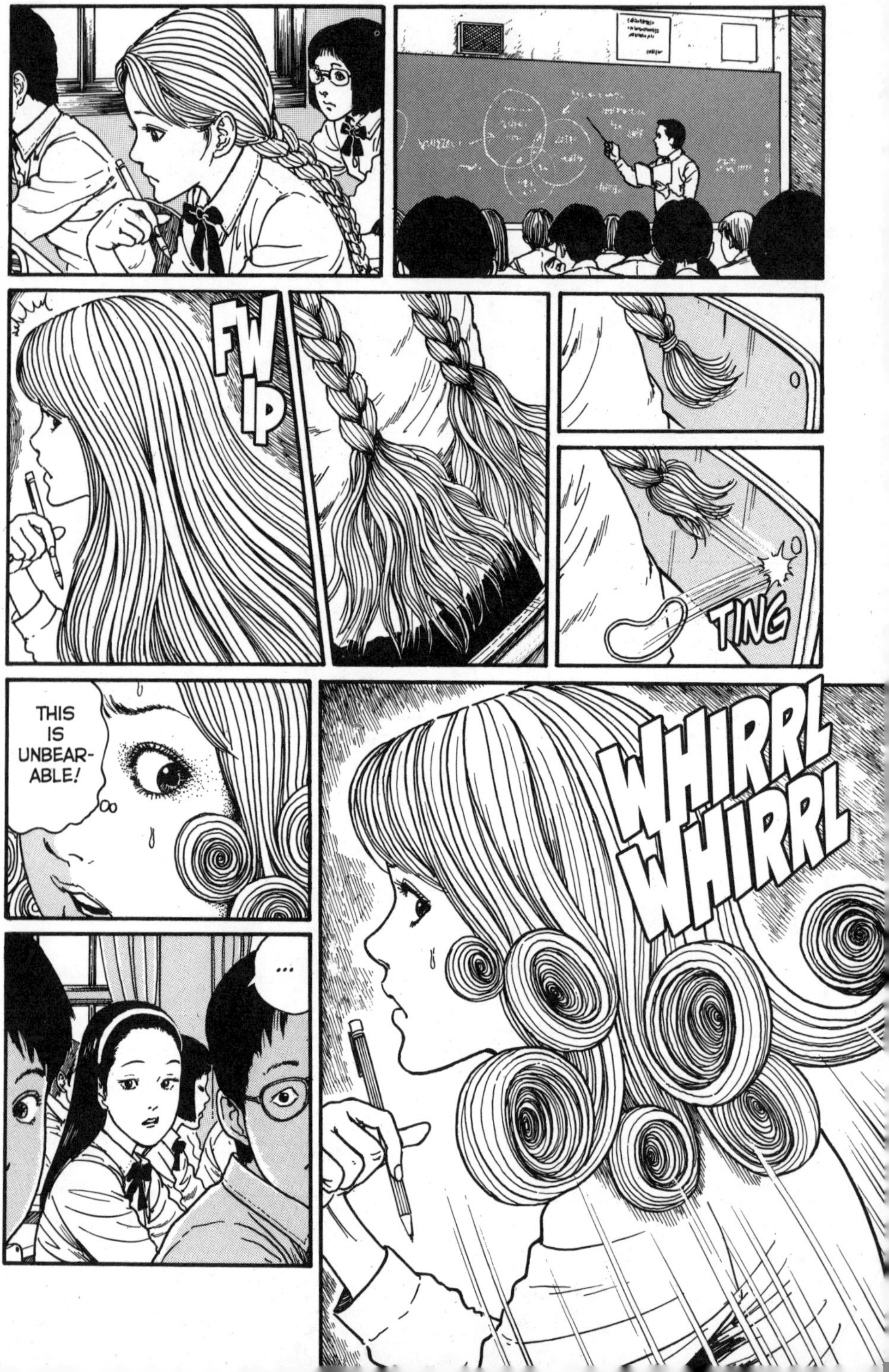
TING
FWIP
WHIRRL WHIRRL
THIS IS UNBEARABLE!
...

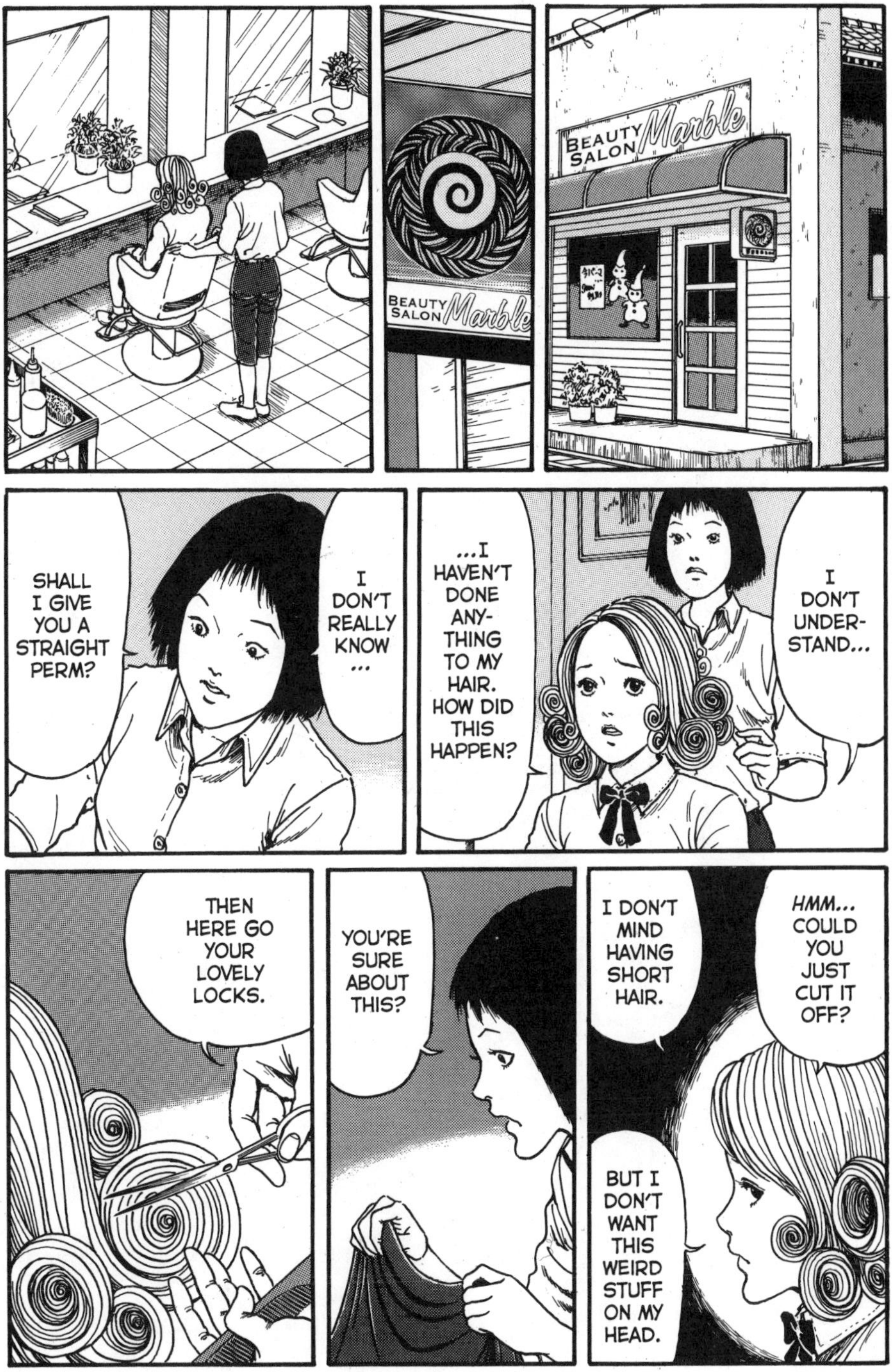
BEAUTY SALON Marble
BEAUTY SALON Marble
I DON'T UNDERSTAND...
...I HAVEN'T DONE ANYTHING TO MY HAIR. HOW DID THIS HAPPEN?
I DON'T REALLY KNOW...
SHALL I GIVE YOU A STRAIGHT PERM?
HMM... COULD YOU JUST CUT IT OFF?
I DON'T MIND HAVING SHORT HAIR.
BUT I DON'T WANT THIS WEIRD STUFF ON MY HEAD.
YOU'RE SURE ABOUT THIS?
THEN HERE GO YOUR LOVELY LOCKS.

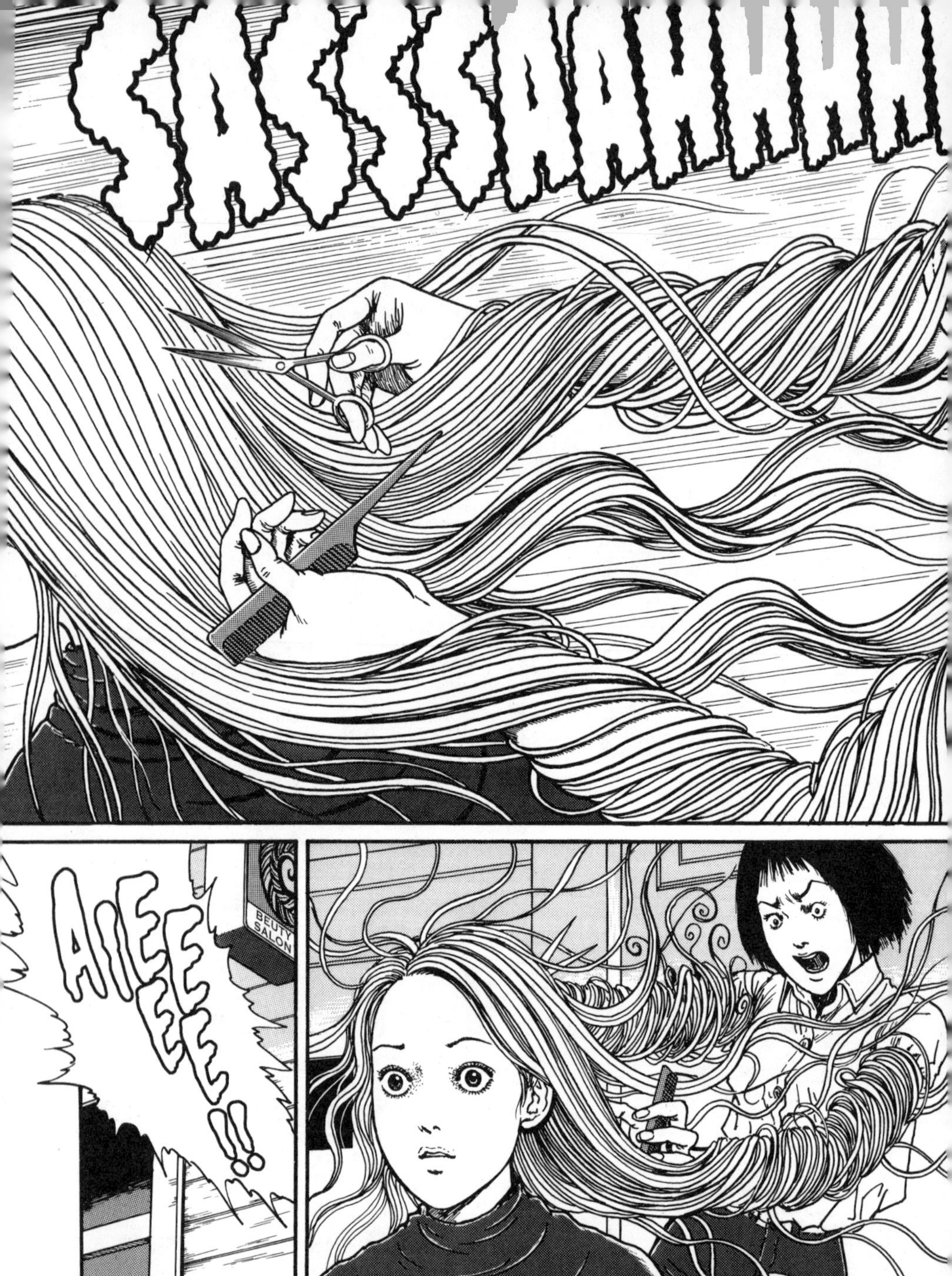
SASSSAAHHHH
BEUTY SALON
AIEEEE!!

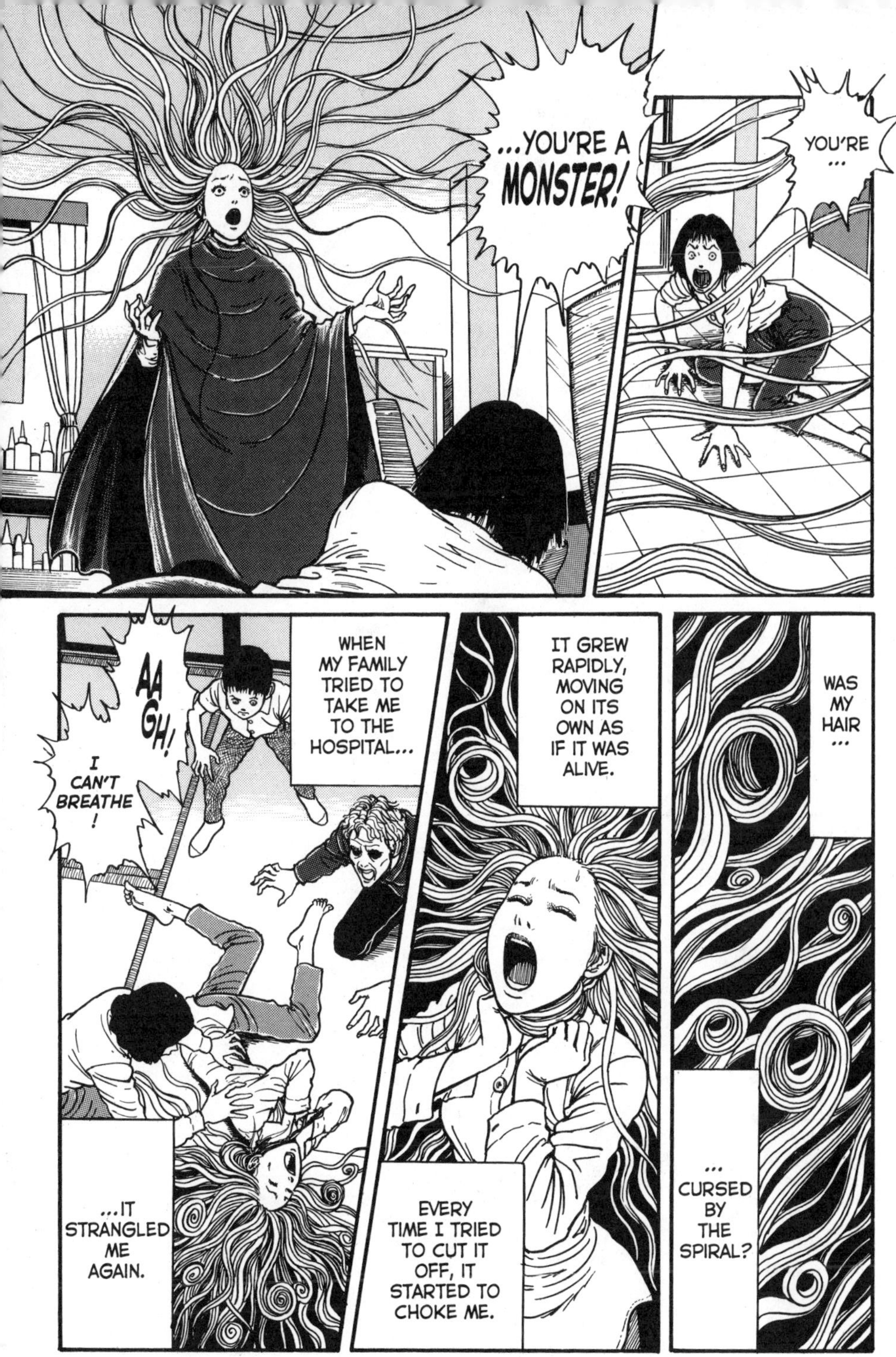
YOU'RE ...
...YOU'RE A MONSTER!
WAS MY HAIR ...
... CURSED BY THE SPIRAL?
IT GREW RAPIDLY, MOVING ON ITS OWN AS IF IT WAS ALIVE.
EVERY TIME I TRIED TO CUT IT OFF, IT STARTED TO CHOKE ME.
WHEN MY FAMILY TRIED TO TAKE ME TO THE HOSPITAL...
AAGH!
I CAN'T BREATHE!
...IT STRANGLED ME AGAIN.

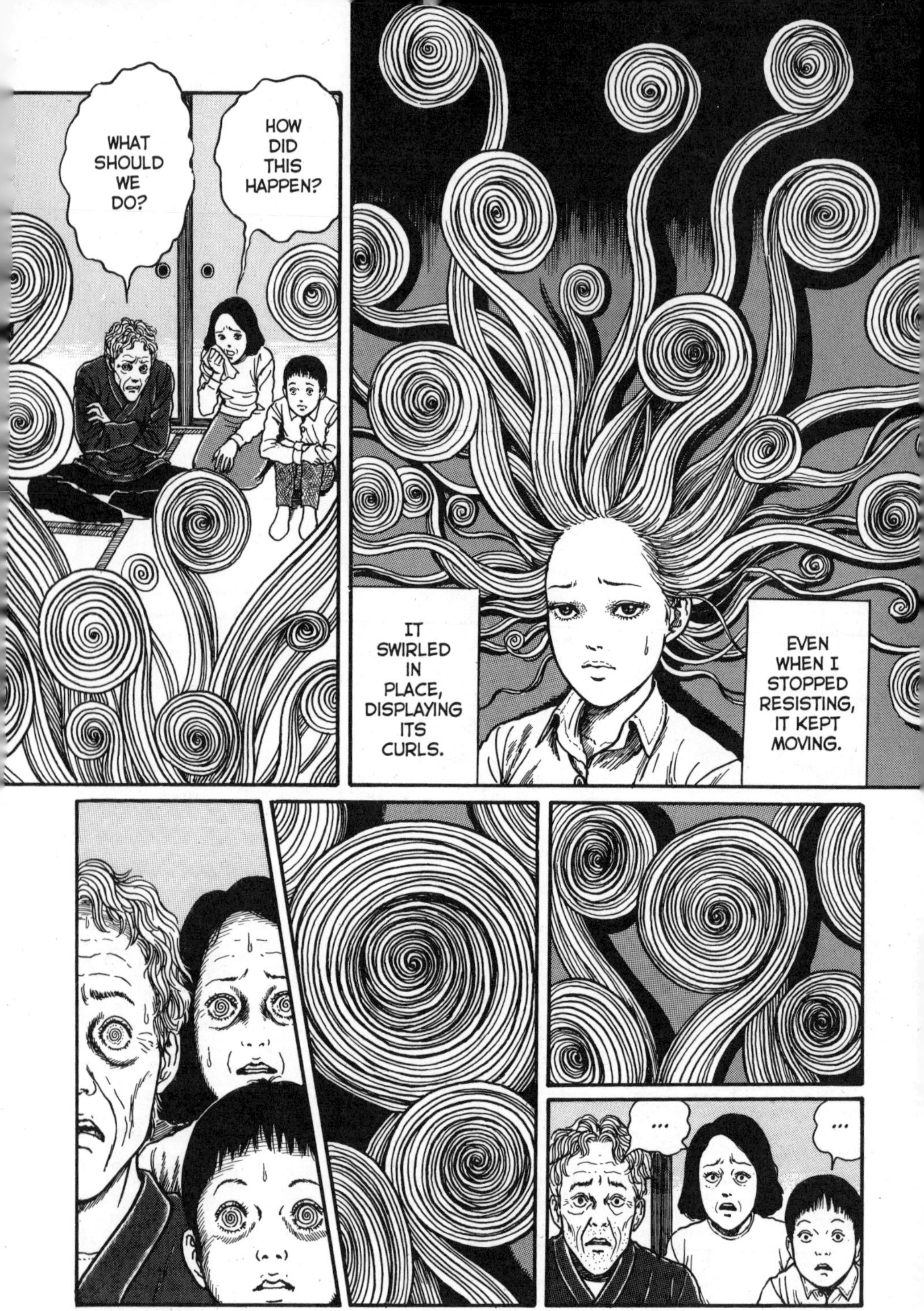
EVEN WHEN I STOPPED RESISTING, IT KEPT MOVING.
IT SWIRLED IN PLACE, DISPLAYING ITS CURLS.
HOW DID THIS HAPPEN?
WHAT SHOULD WE DO?
...
...

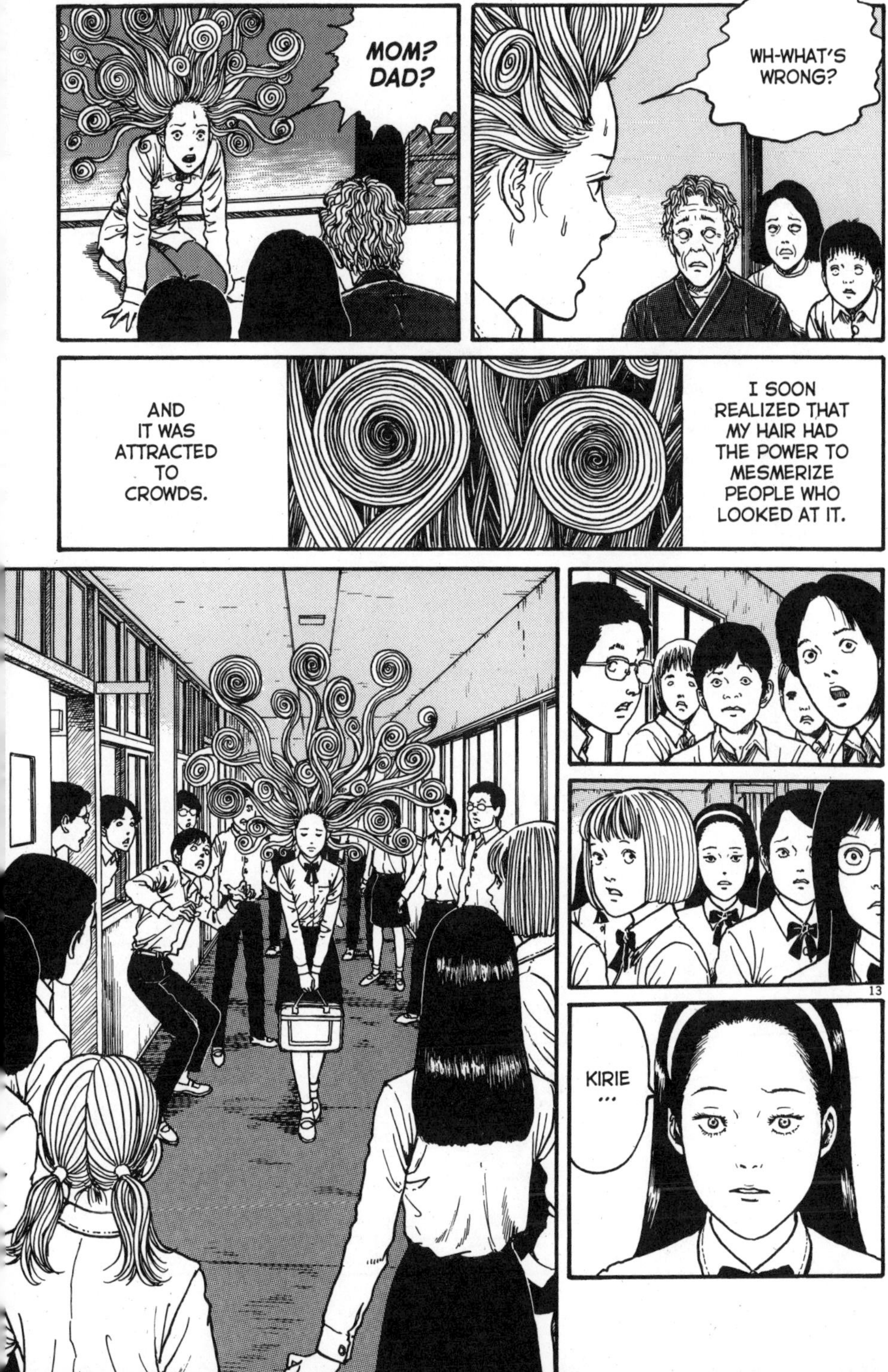
WH-WHAT'S WRONG?
MOM? DAD?
I SOON REALIZED THAT MY HAIR HAD THE POWER TO MESMERIZE PEOPLE WHO LOOKED AT IT.
AND IT WAS ATTRACTED TO CROWDS.
KIRIE ...

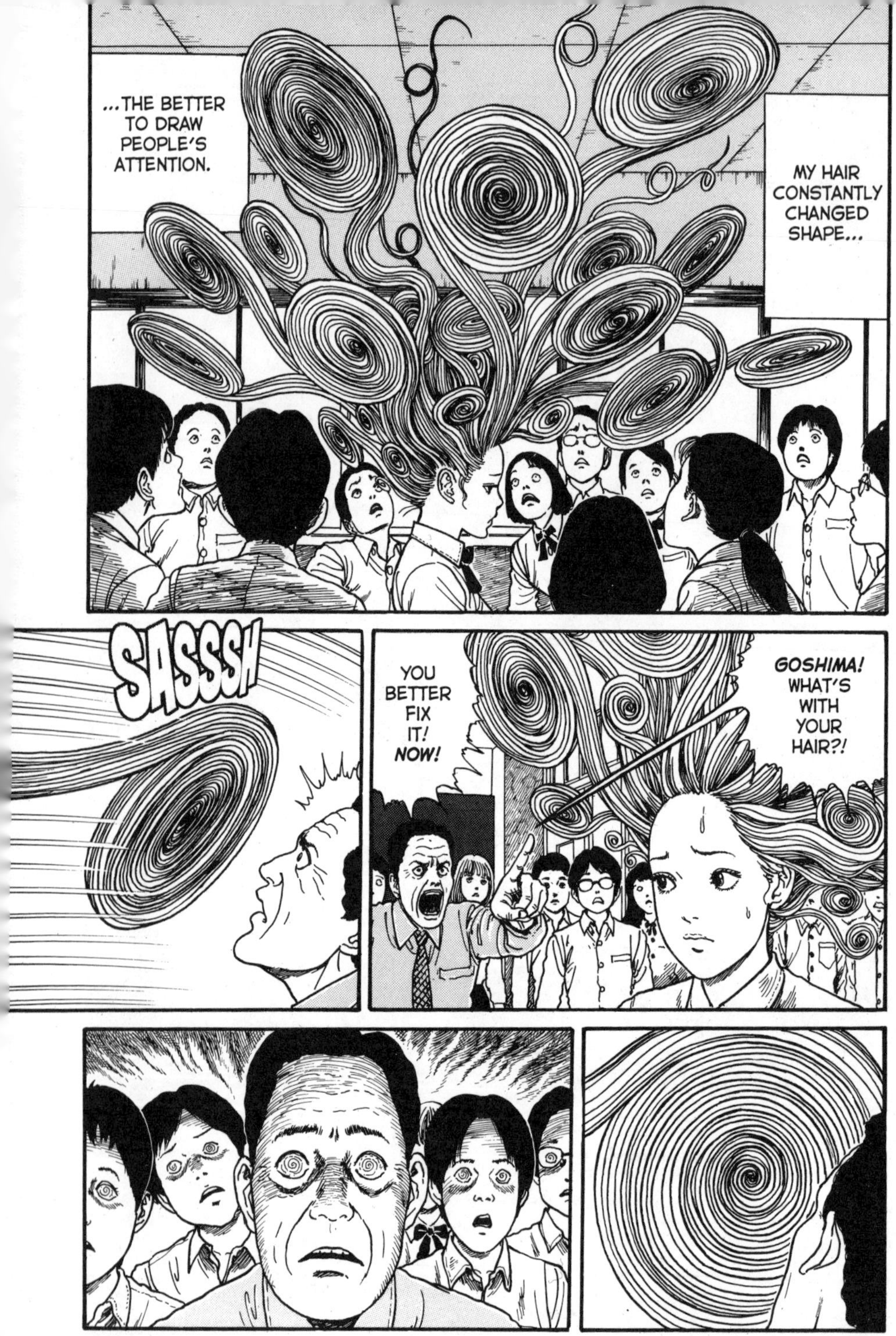
MY HAIR CONSTANTLY CHANGED SHAPE...
...THE BETTER TO DRAW PEOPLE'S ATTENTION.
GOSHIMA! WHAT'S WITH YOUR HAIR?!
YOU BETTER FIX IT! NOW!
SASSSH

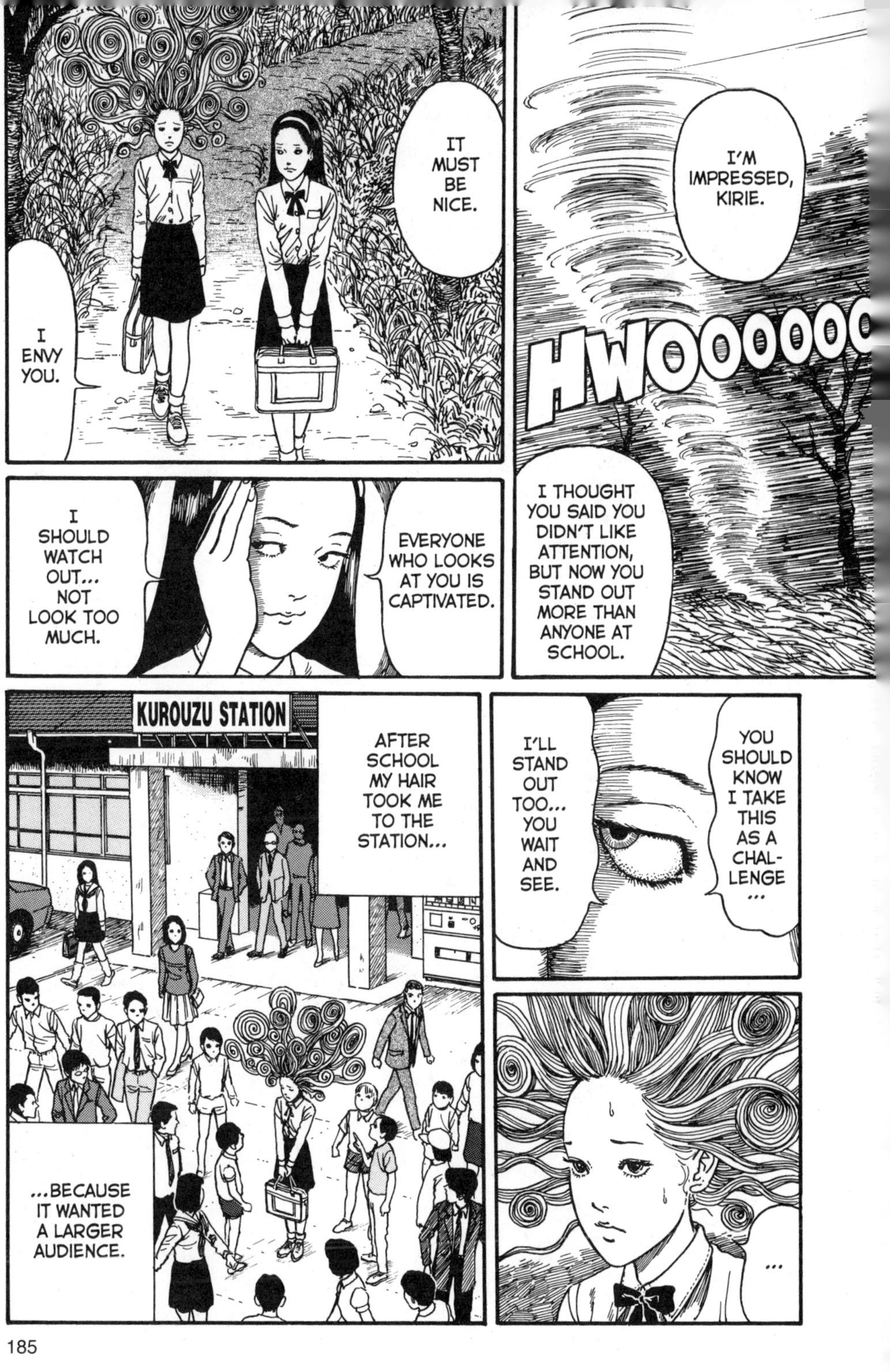

I'M IMPRESSED, KIRIE.
HWOOOOOO
I THOUGHT YOU SAID YOU DIDN'T LIKE ATTENTION, BUT NOW YOU STAND OUT MORE THAN ANYONE AT SCHOOL.
IT MUST BE NICE.
I ENVY YOU.
EVERYONE WHO LOOKS AT YOU IS CAPTIVATED.
I SHOULD WATCH OUT... NOT LOOK TOO MUCH.
YOU SHOULD KNOW I TAKE THIS AS A CHAL-LENGE...
I'LL STAND OUT TOO... YOU WAIT AND SEE.
...
AFTER SCHOOL MY HAIR TOOK ME TO THE STATION...
KUROUZU STATION
...BECAUSE IT WANTED A LARGER AUDIENCE.

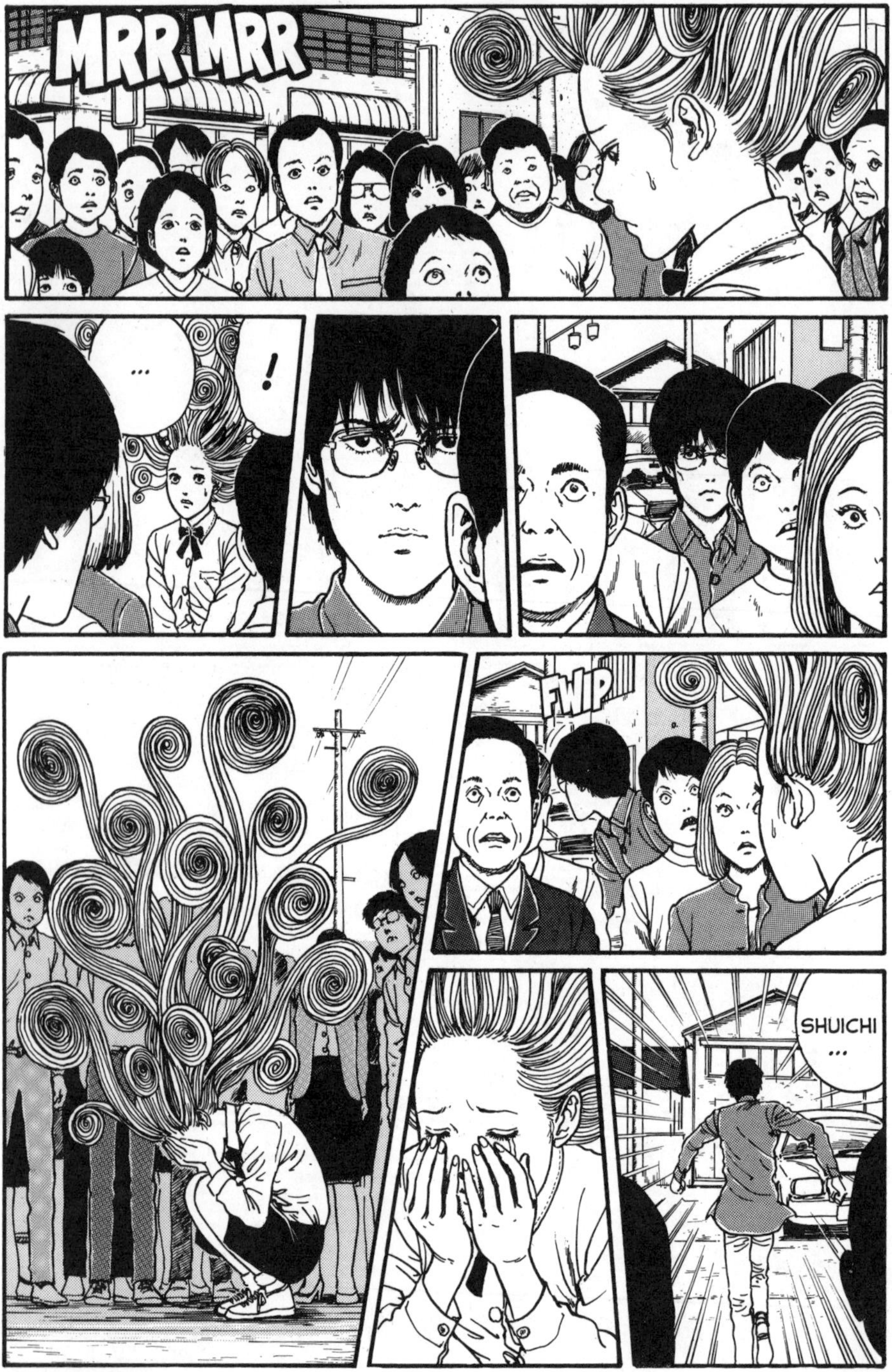
MRR MRR
!
...
FWIP
SHUICHI ...

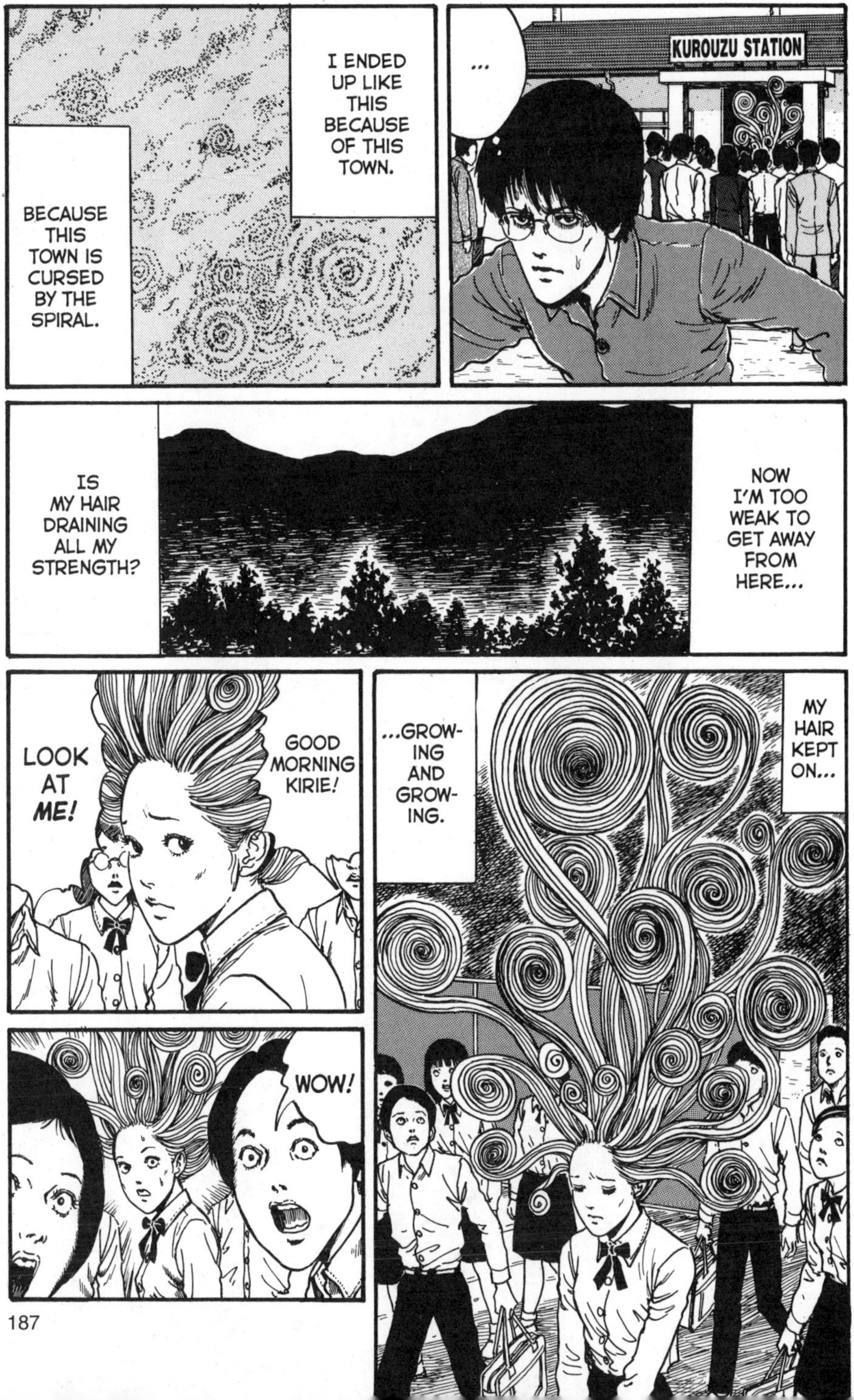
...
KUROUZU STATION
I ENDED UP LIKE THIS BECAUSE OF THIS TOWN.
BECAUSE THIS TOWN IS CURSED BY THE SPIRAL.
NOW I'M TOO WEAK TO GET AWAY FROM HERE...
IS MY HAIR DRAINING ALL MY STRENGTH?
MY HAIR KEPT ON...
...GROWING AND GROWING.
GOOD MORNING KIRIE!
LOOK AT *ME!*
WOW!

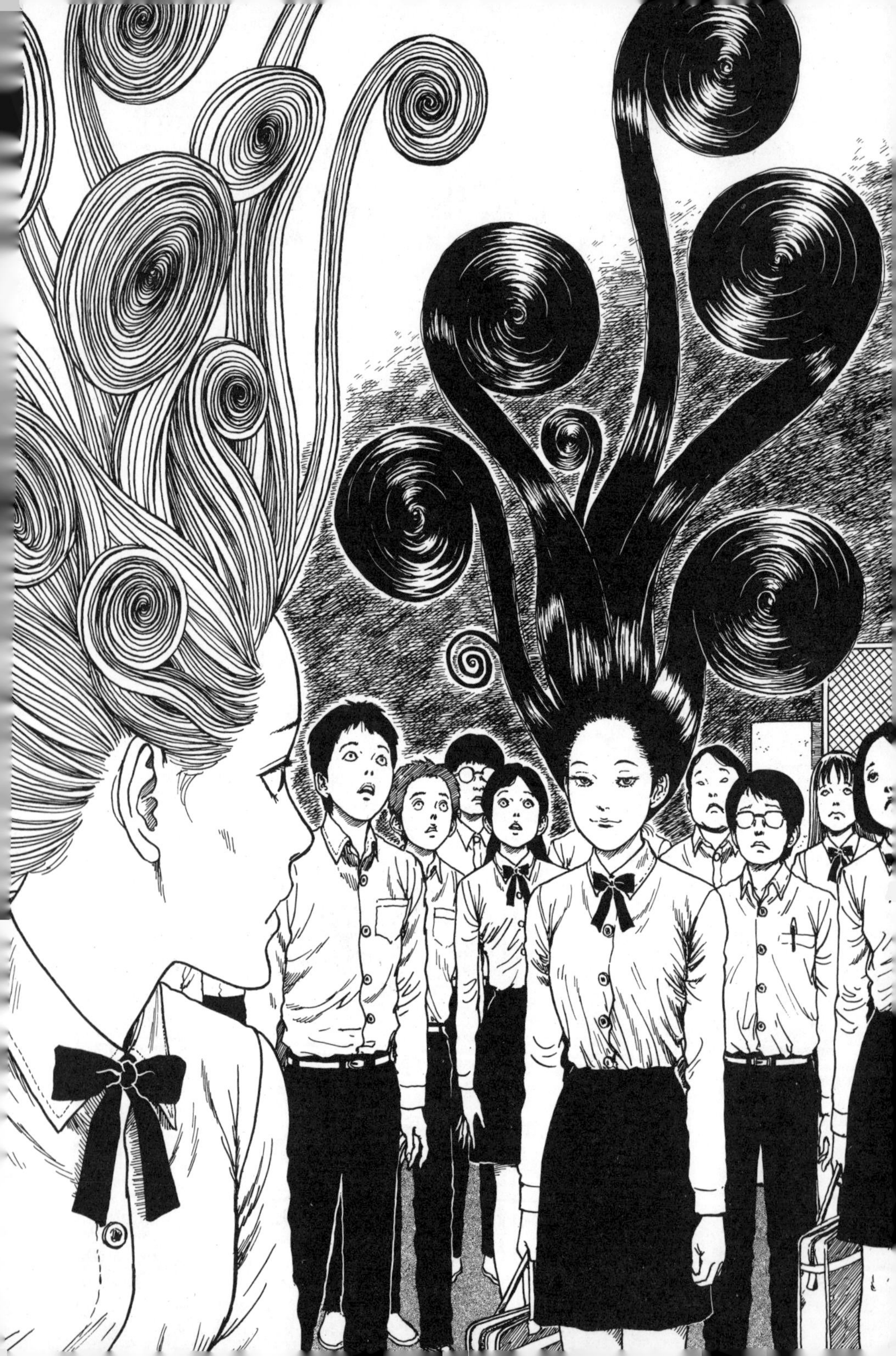

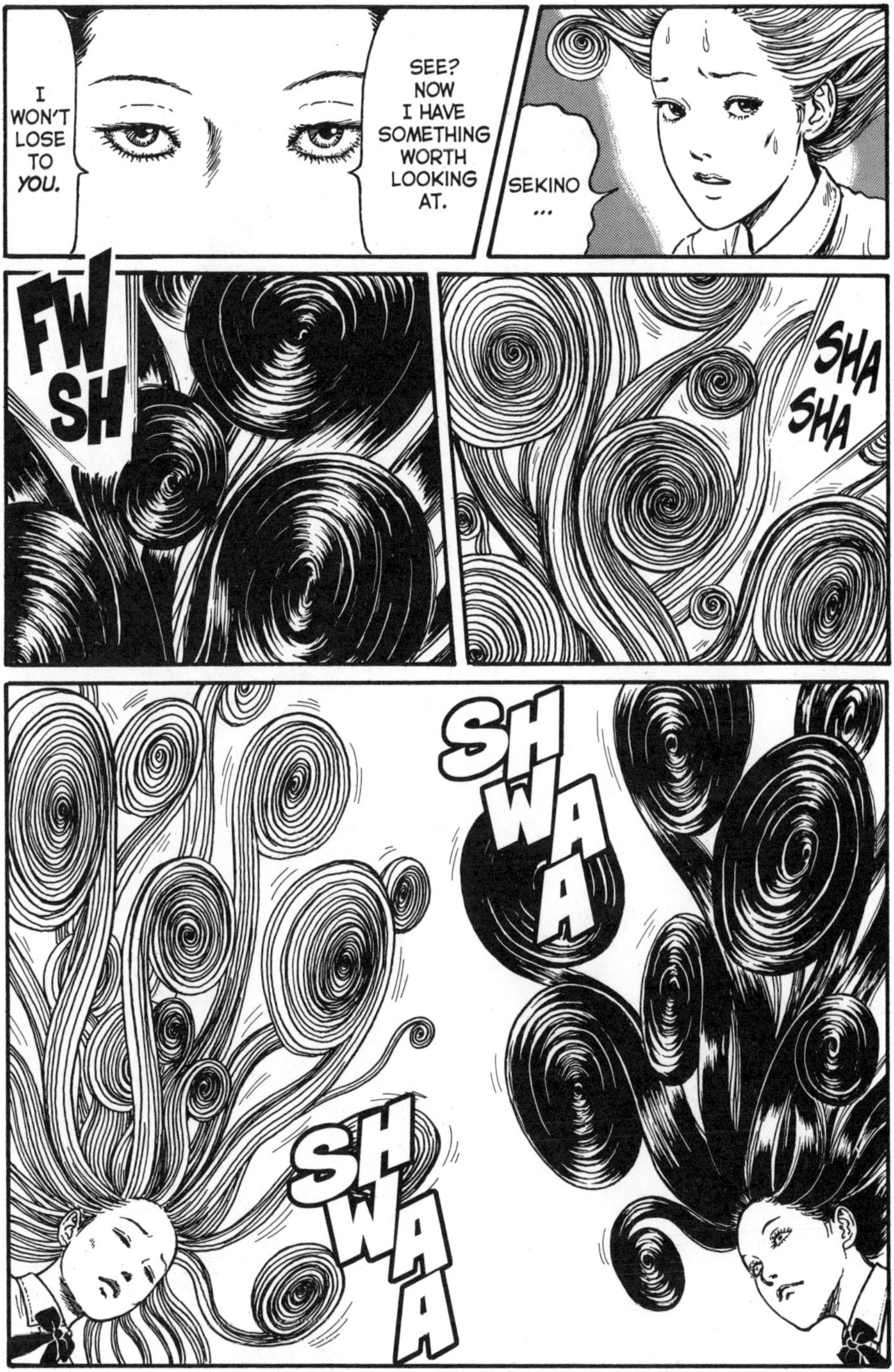
SEKINO ...
SEE? NOW I HAVE SOMETHING WORTH LOOKING AT.
I WON'T LOSE TO *YOU.*
SHA SHA
FWISH
SHWAAA
SHWAAA

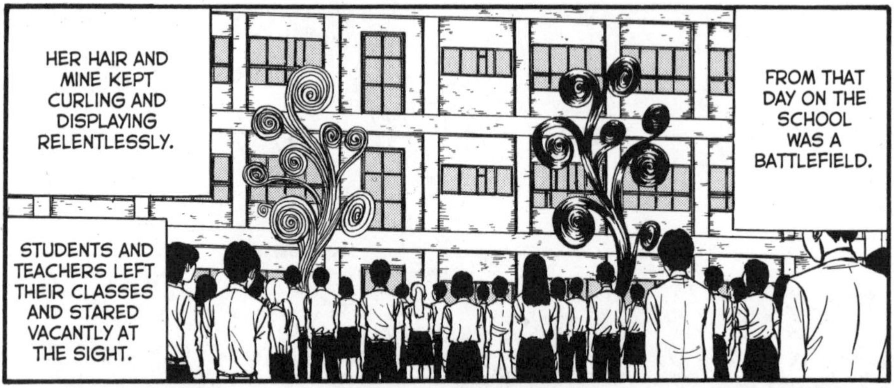
FROM THAT DAY ON THE SCHOOL WAS A BATTLEFIELD.
HER HAIR AND MINE KEPT CURLING AND DISPLAYING RELENTLESSLY.
STUDENTS AND TEACHERS LEFT THEIR CLASSES AND STARED VACANTLY AT THE SIGHT.
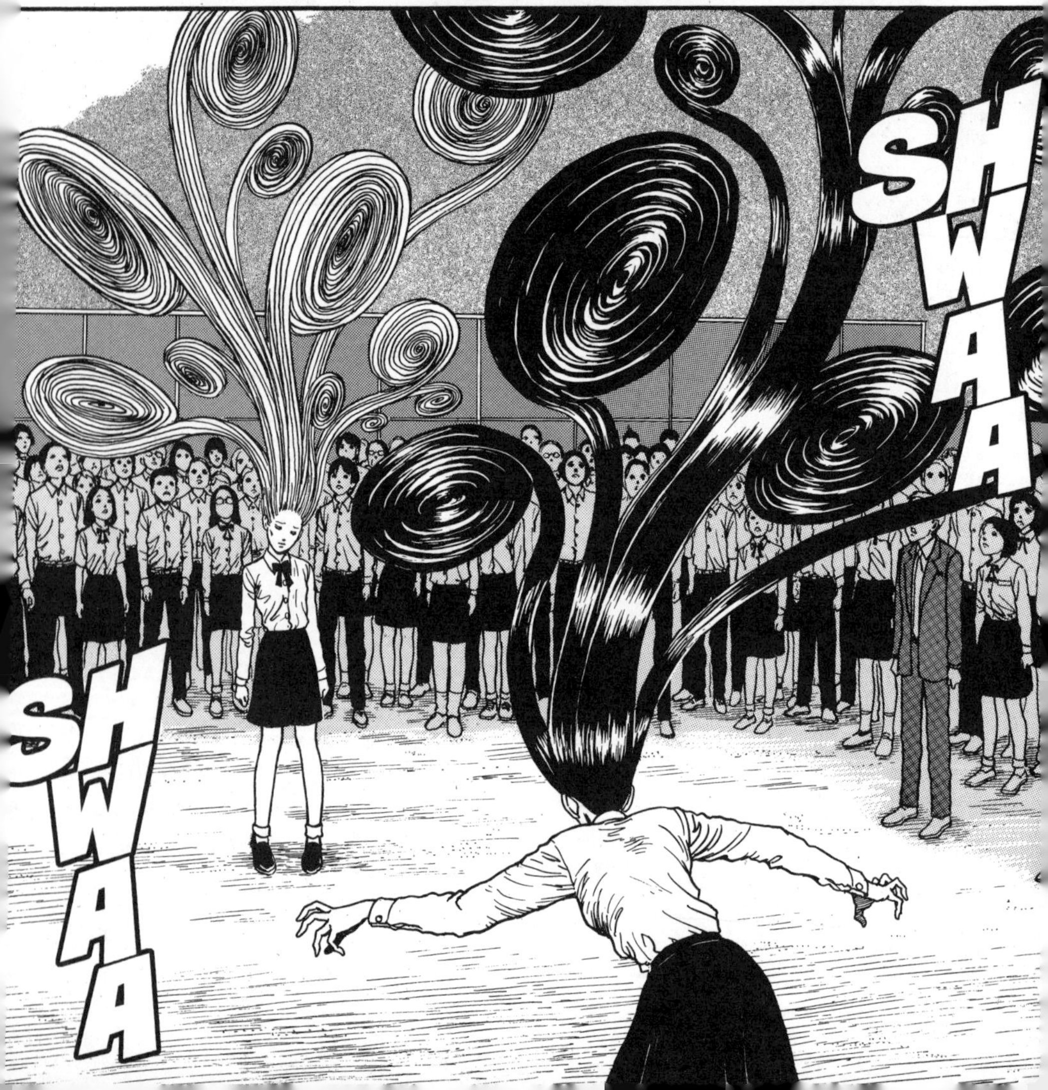
SHWAA
SHWAAA

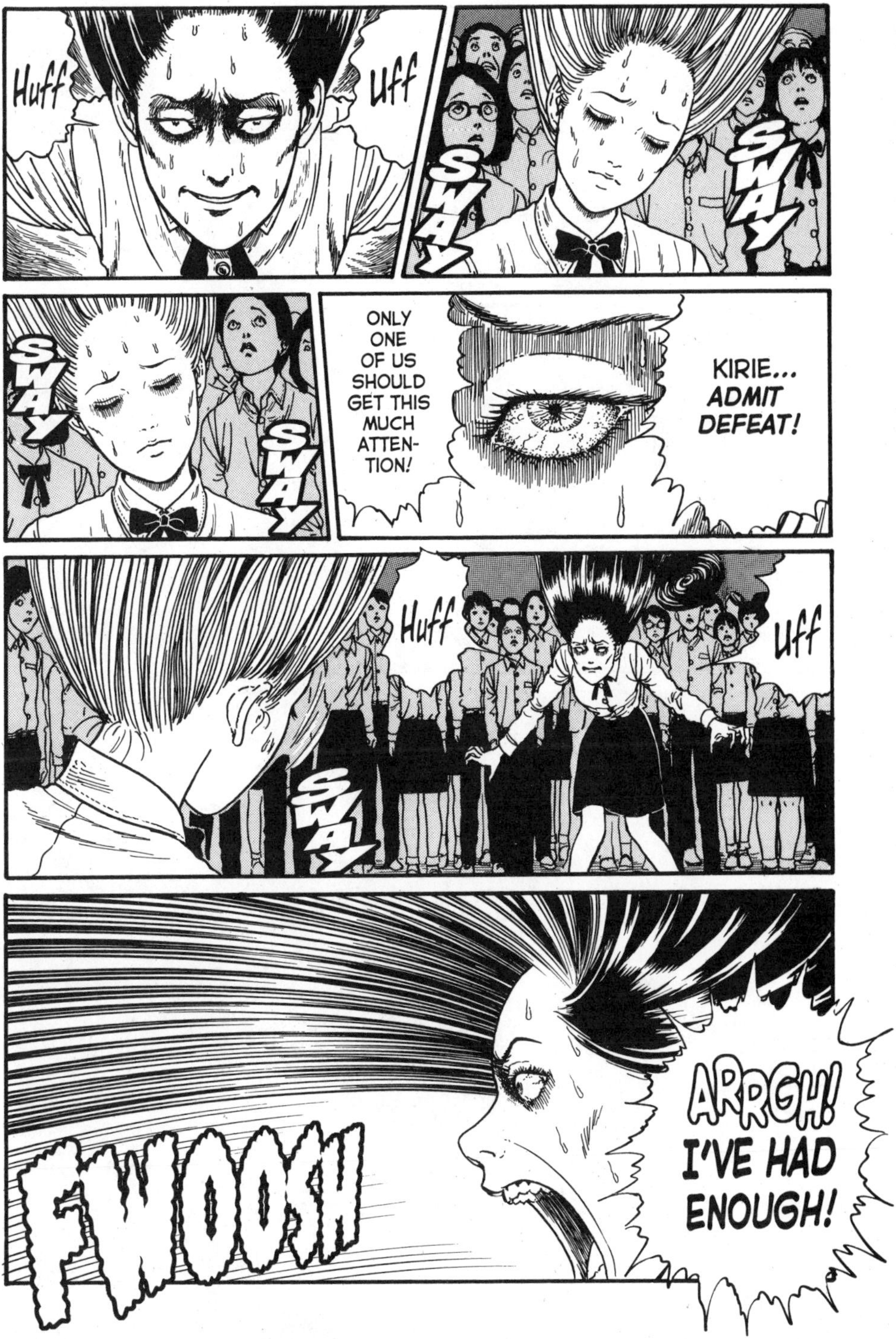
SWAY
SWAY
Uff
Huff
KIRIE... ADMIT DEFEAT!
ONLY ONE OF US SHOULD GET THIS MUCH ATTENTION!
SWAY
SWAY
Uff
Huff
SWAY
ARRGH! I'VE HAD ENOUGH!
FWOOSH

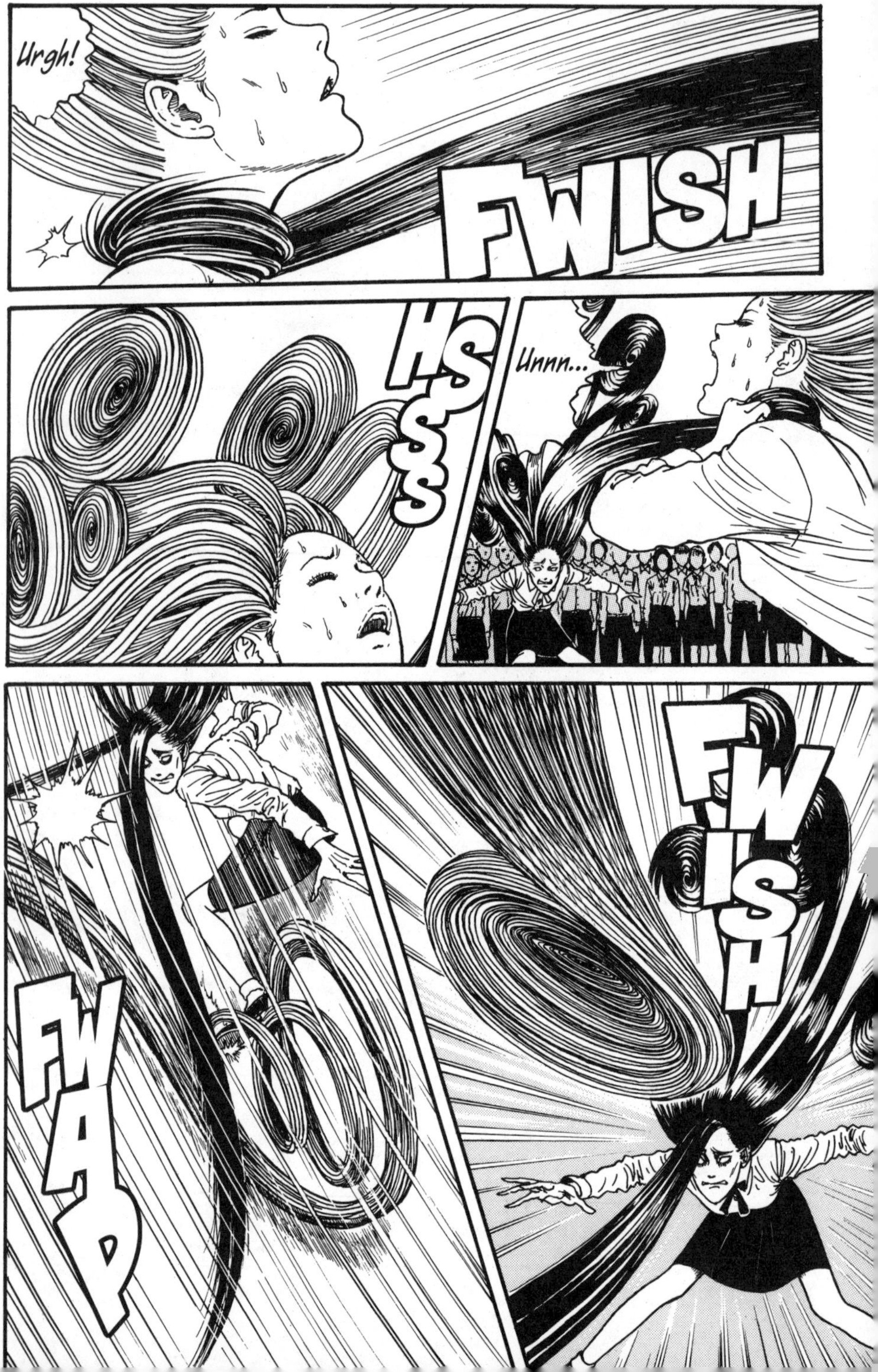
Urgh!
FWISH
Unnn...
HSSS
FWISH
FWAP

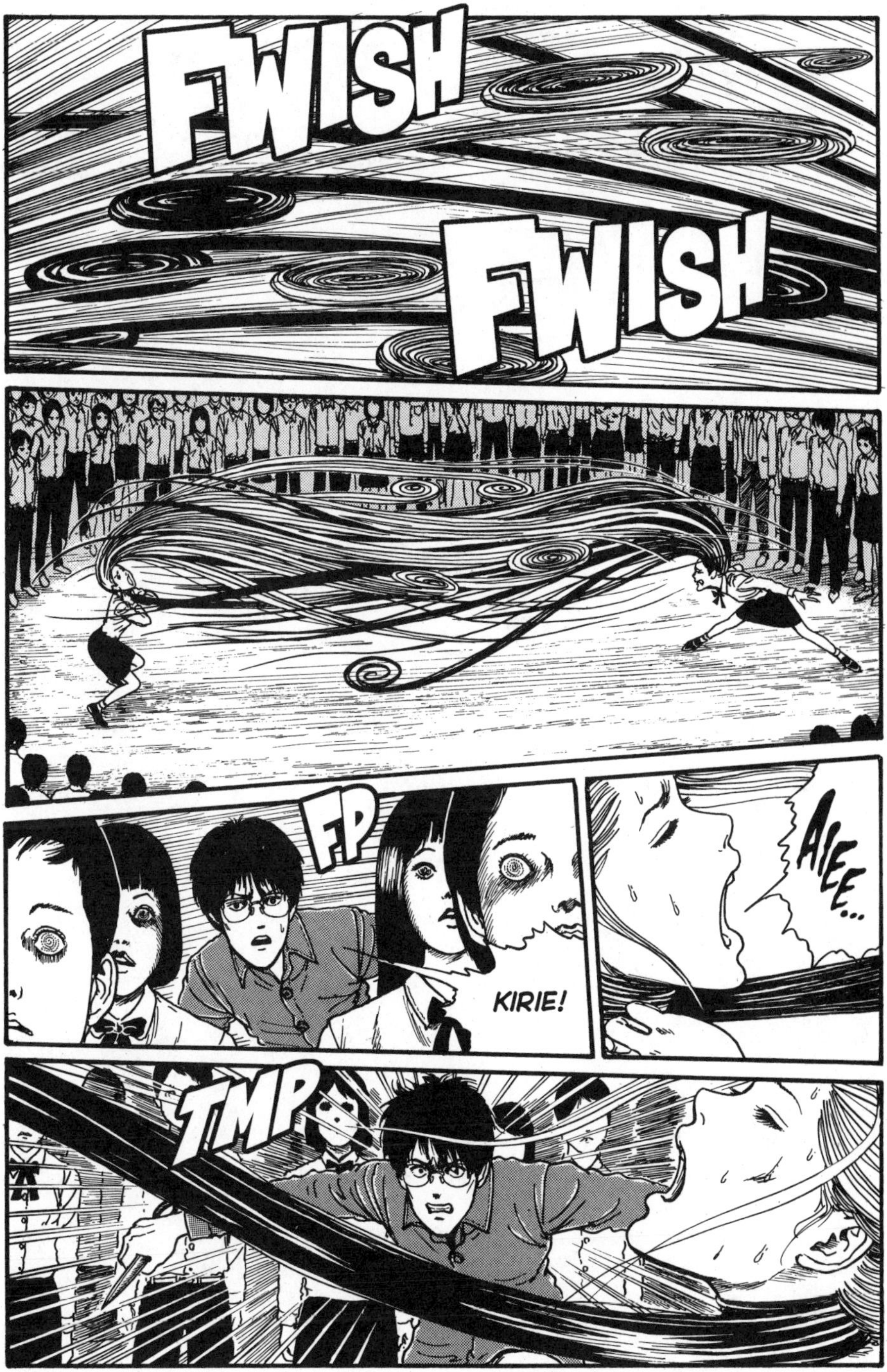
FWISH
FWISH
AIEE...
FP
KIRIE!
TMP

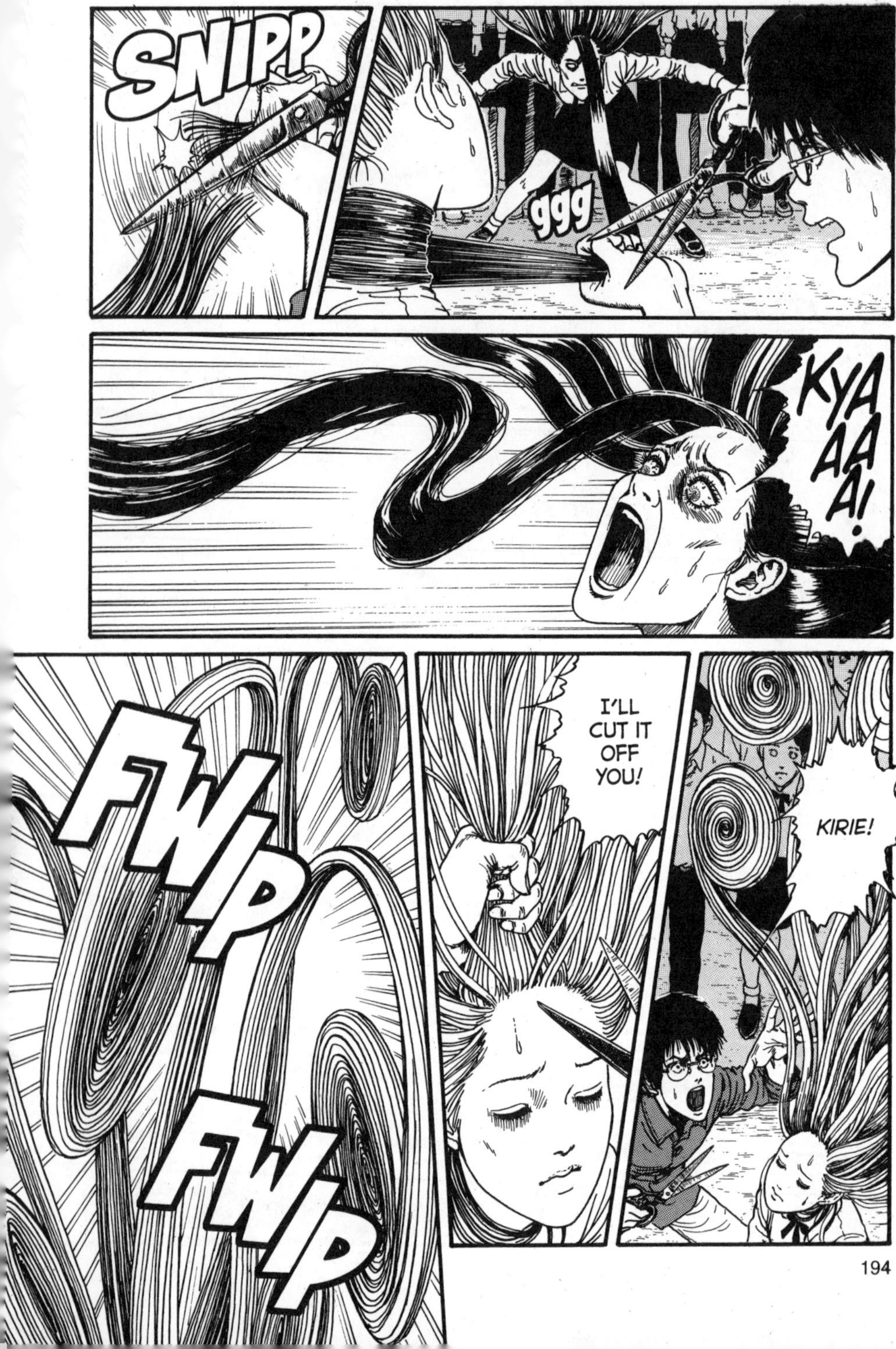
ggg
SNIPP
KYAAAAA!
KIRIE!
I'LL CUT IT OFF YOU!
FWIP FWIP

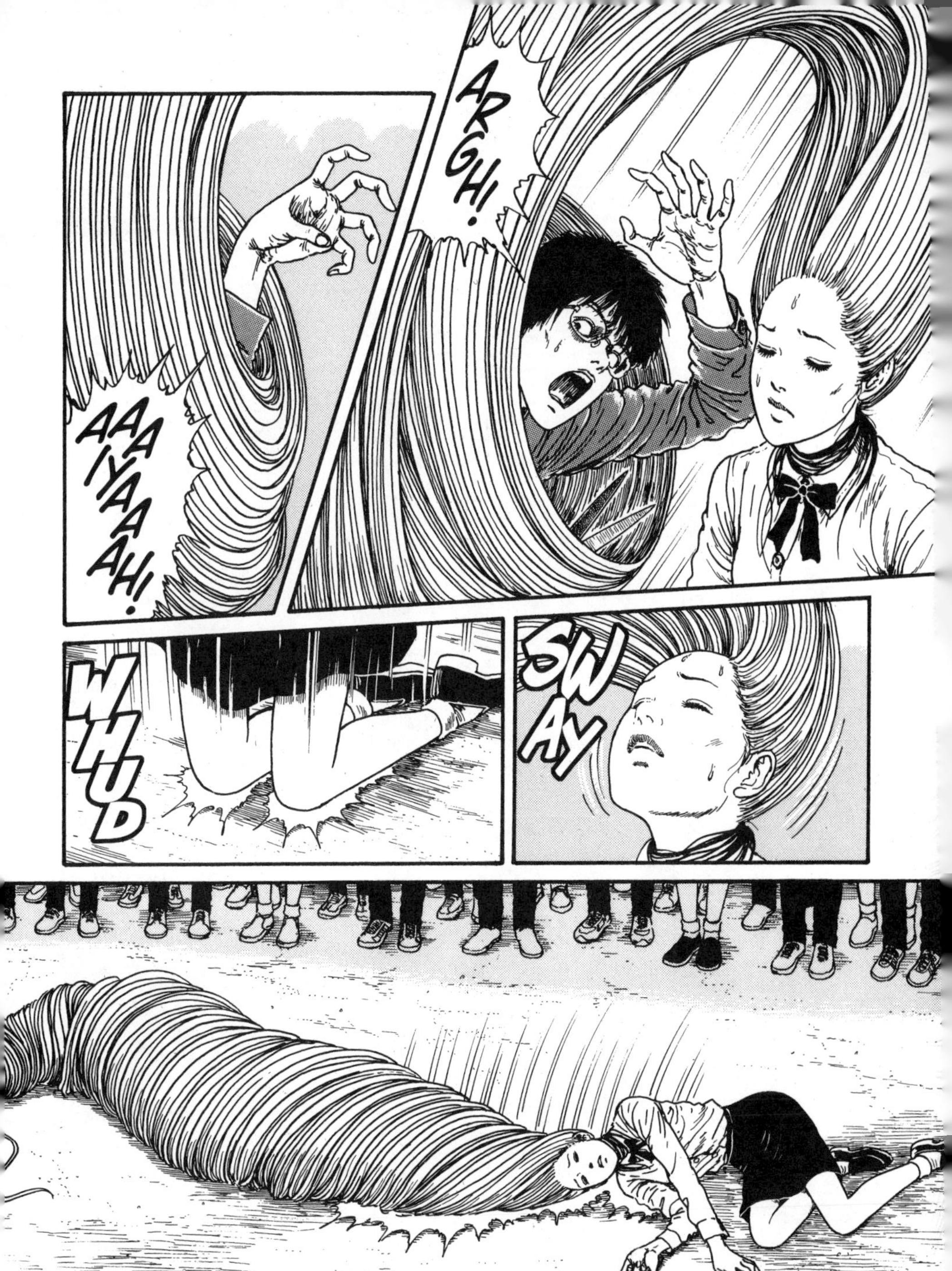
ARGH!
AAAIYAAAAH!
SWAY
WHUD

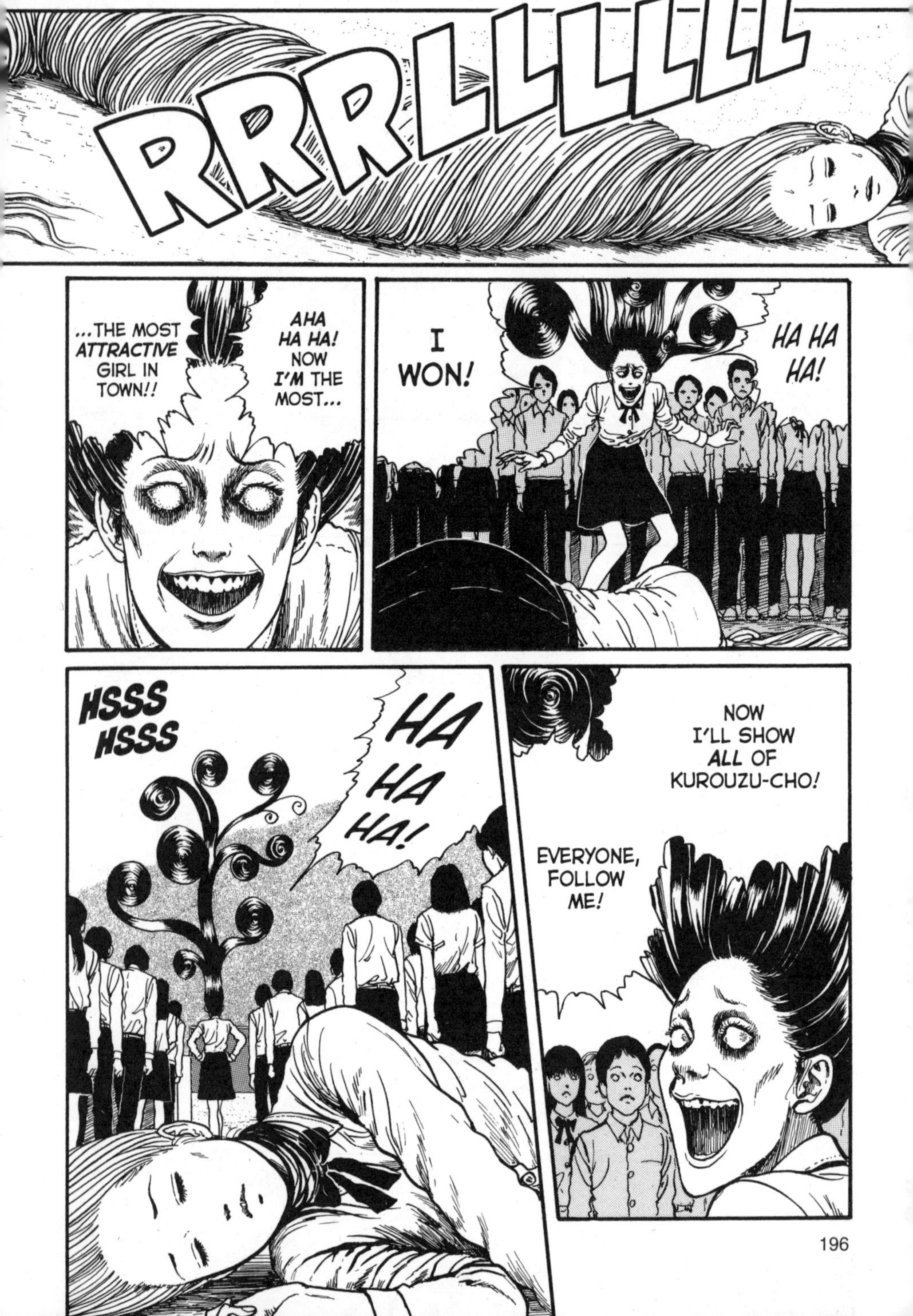
RRRLLLLLL
HA HA HA!
I WON!
AHA HA HA! NOW I'M THE MOST...
...THE MOST ATTRACTIVE GIRL IN TOWN!!
NOW I'LL SHOW ALL OF KUROUZU-CHO!
EVERYONE, FOLLOW ME!
HA HA HA HA!
HSSS HSSS

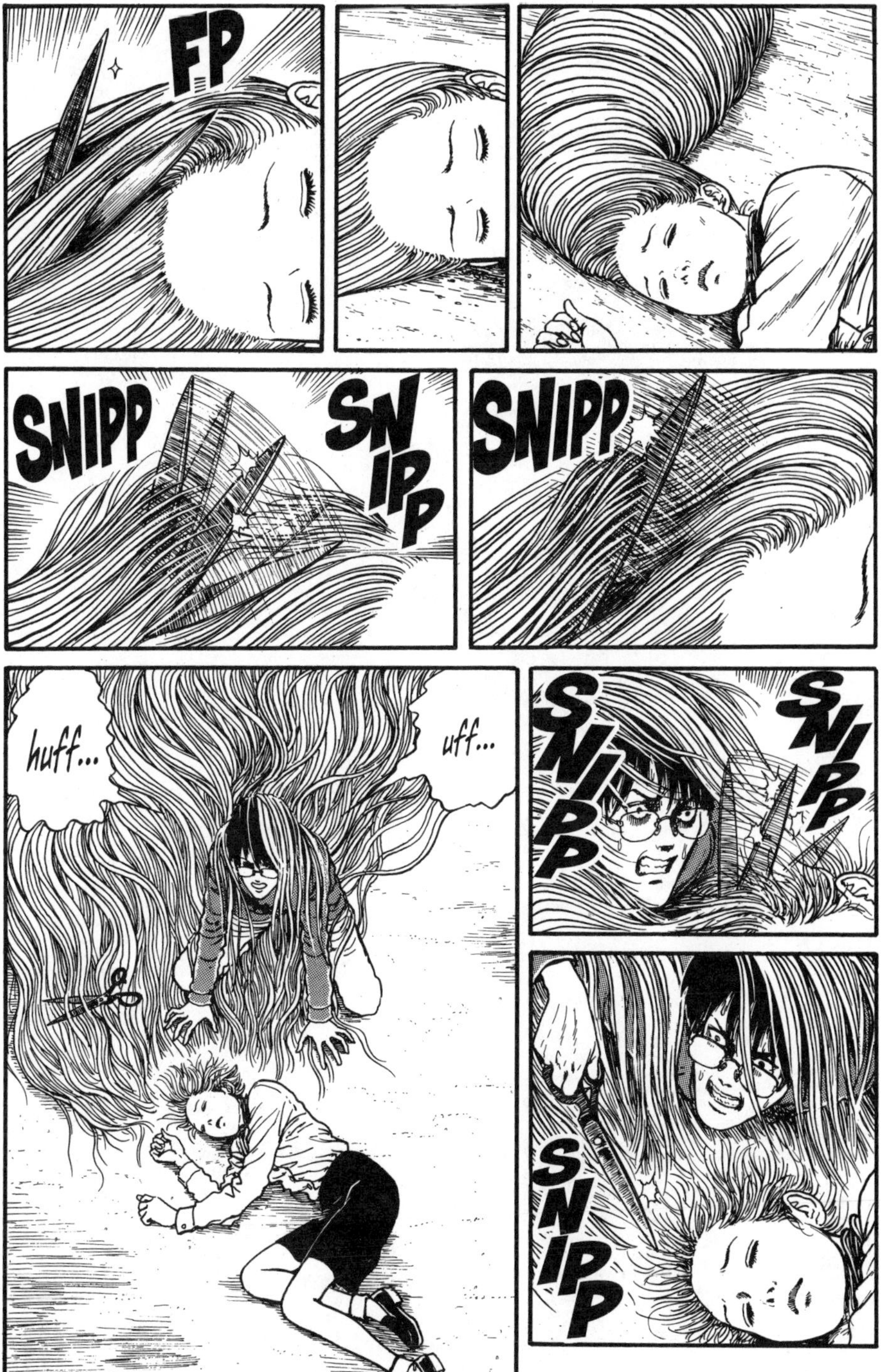
FP
SNIPP
SNIPP
SNIPP
SNIPP
SNIPP
SNIPP
uff...
huff...

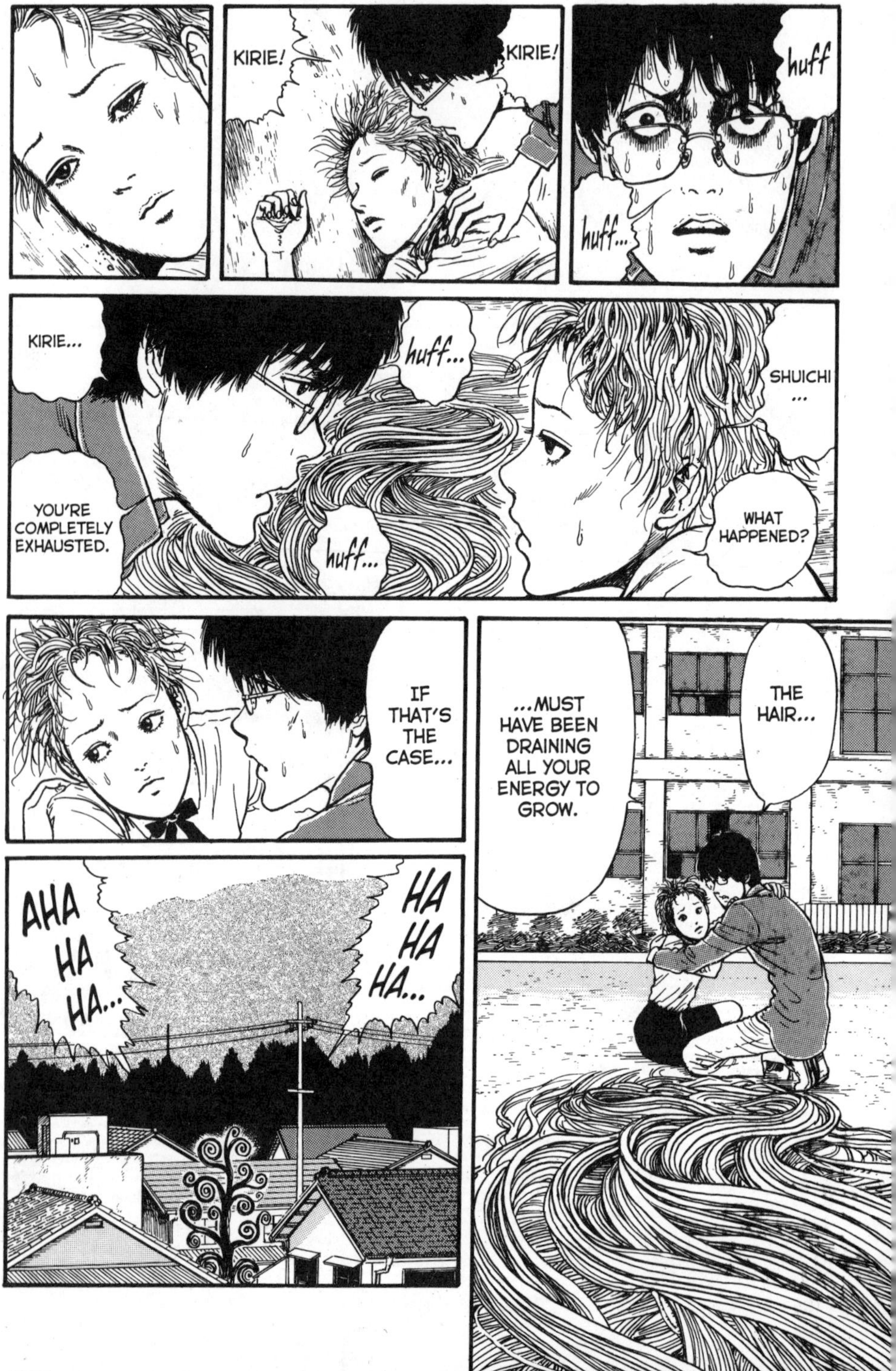
huff
huff...
KIRIE!
KIRIE!
SHUICHI ...
WHAT HAPPENED?
huff...
huff...
KIRIE...
YOU'RE COMPLETELY EXHAUSTED.
THE HAIR...
...MUST HAVE BEEN DRAINING ALL YOUR ENERGY TO GROW.
IF THAT'S THE CASE...
HA HA HA...
AHA HA HA...

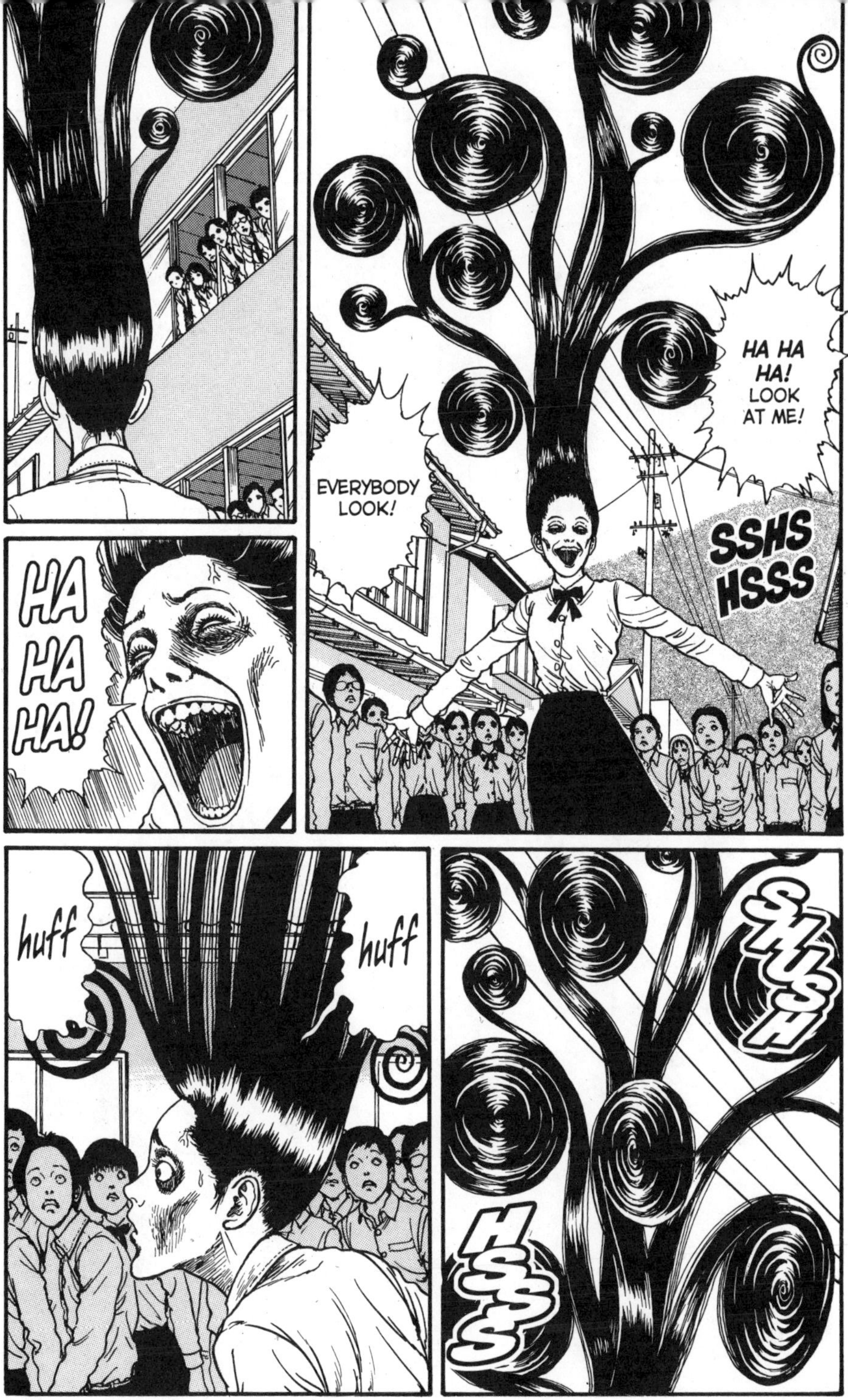

HA HA HA! LOOK AT ME!
EVERYBODY LOOK!
SSHS HSSS
HA HA HA!
SHUSH
HSSS
huff
huff

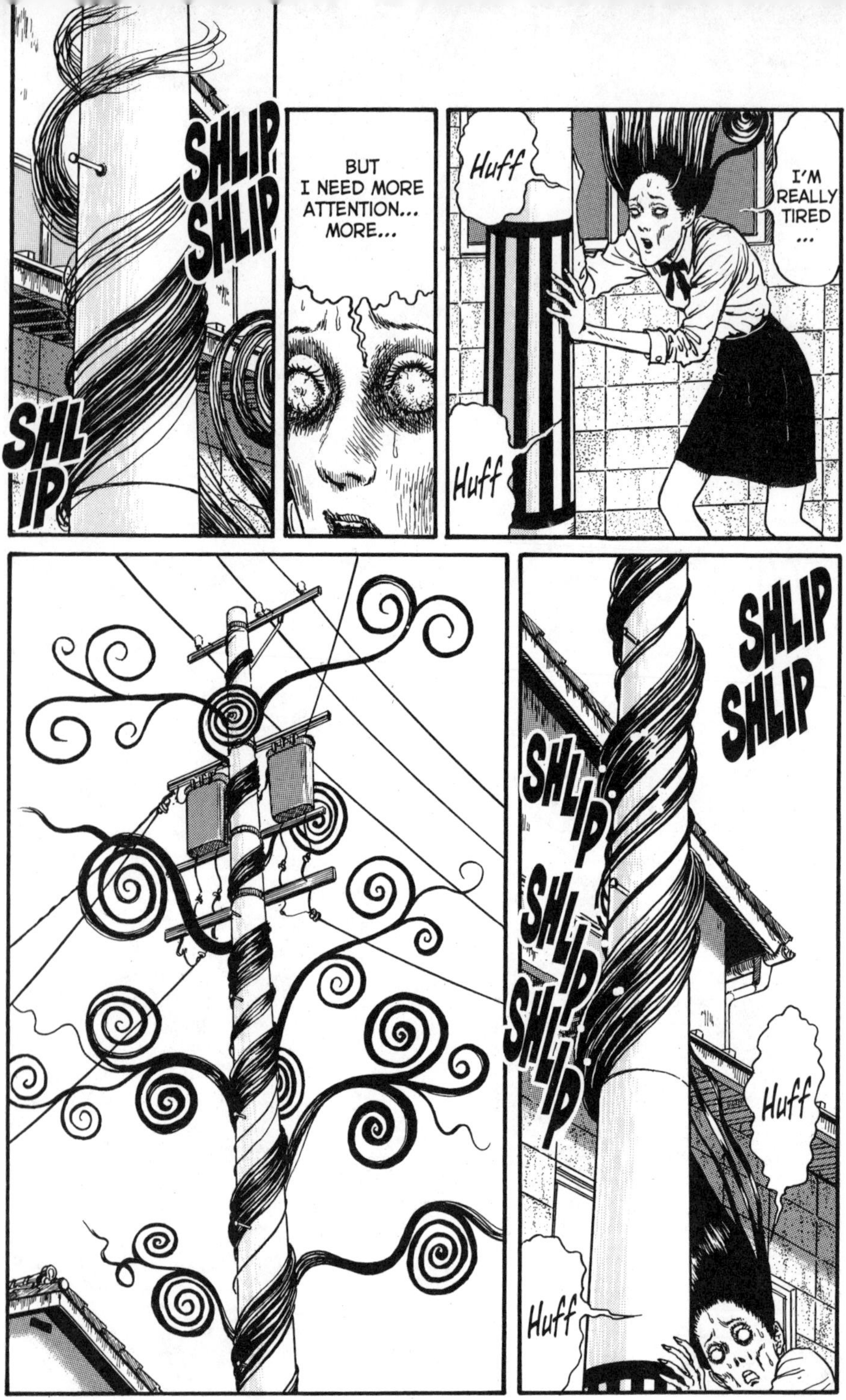
I'M REALLY TIRED ...
Huff
Huff
BUT I NEED MORE ATTENTION... MORE...
SHLIP SHLIP
SHLIP
SHLIP SHLIP
SHLIP SHLIP SHLIP
Huff
Huff

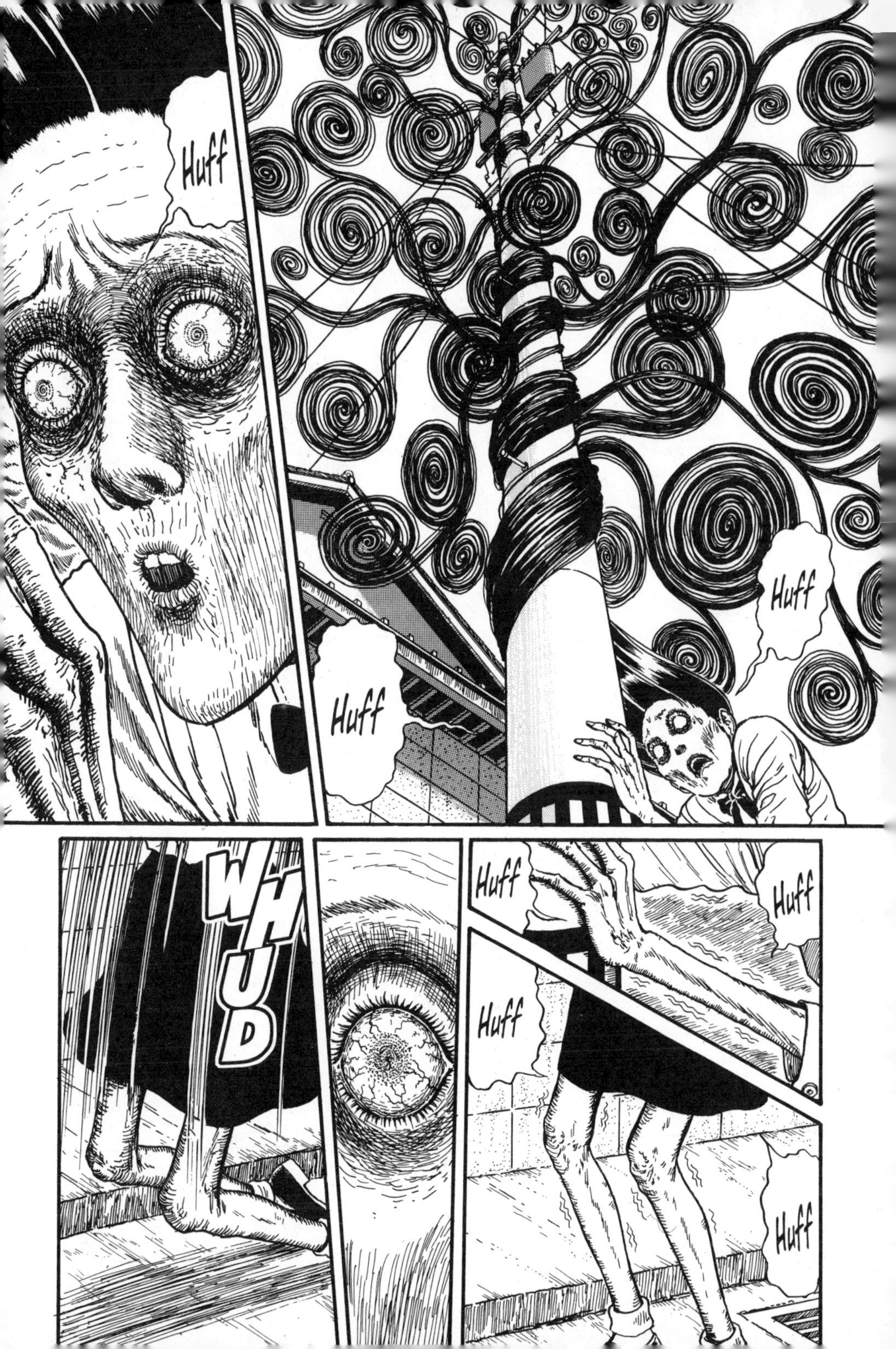
Huff
Huff
Huff
Huff
Huff
Huff
Huff
WHUD

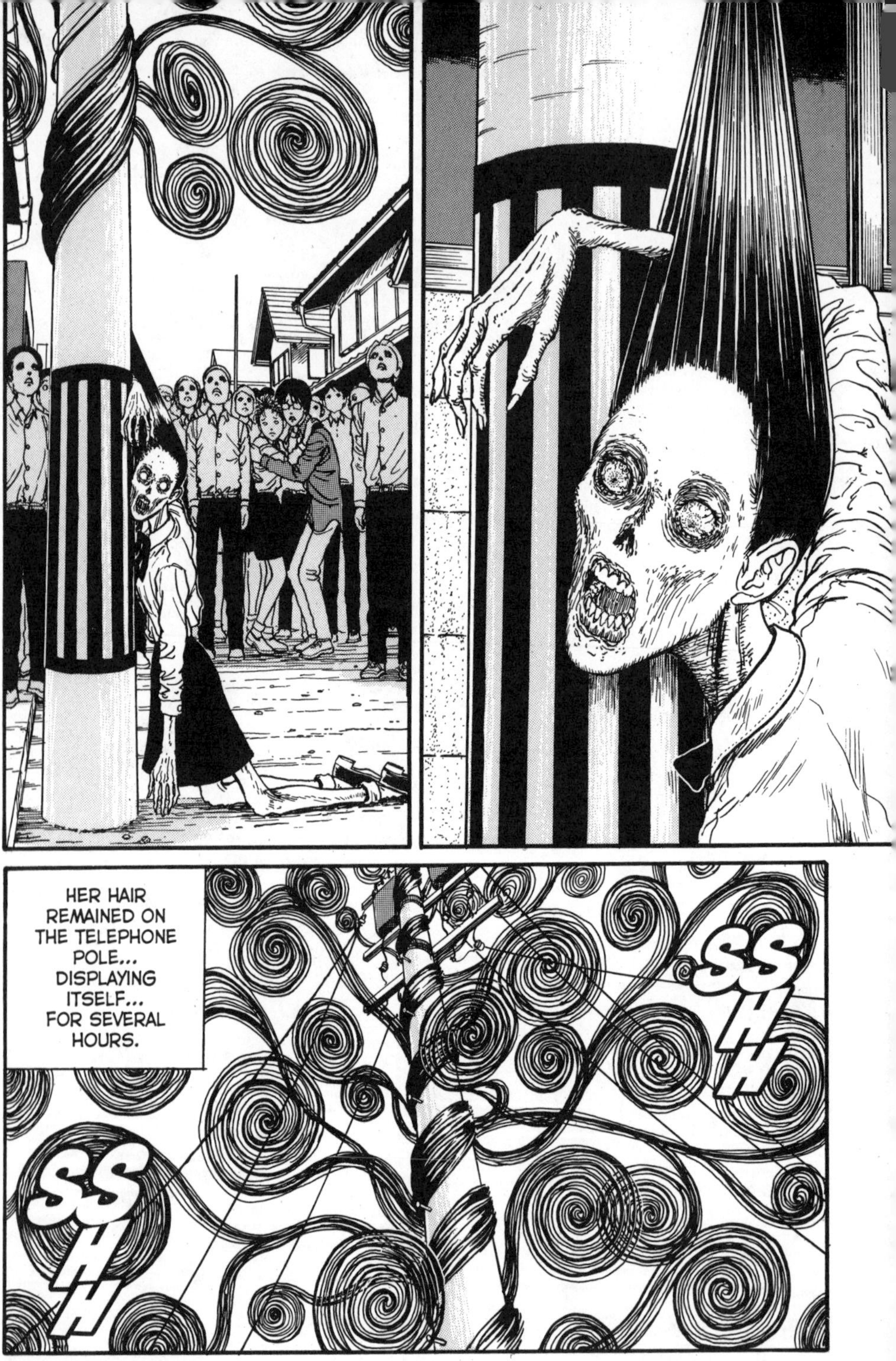
HER HAIR REMAINED ON THE TELEPHONE POLE... DISPLAYING ITSELF... FOR SEVERAL HOURS.
SSHH
SSHH

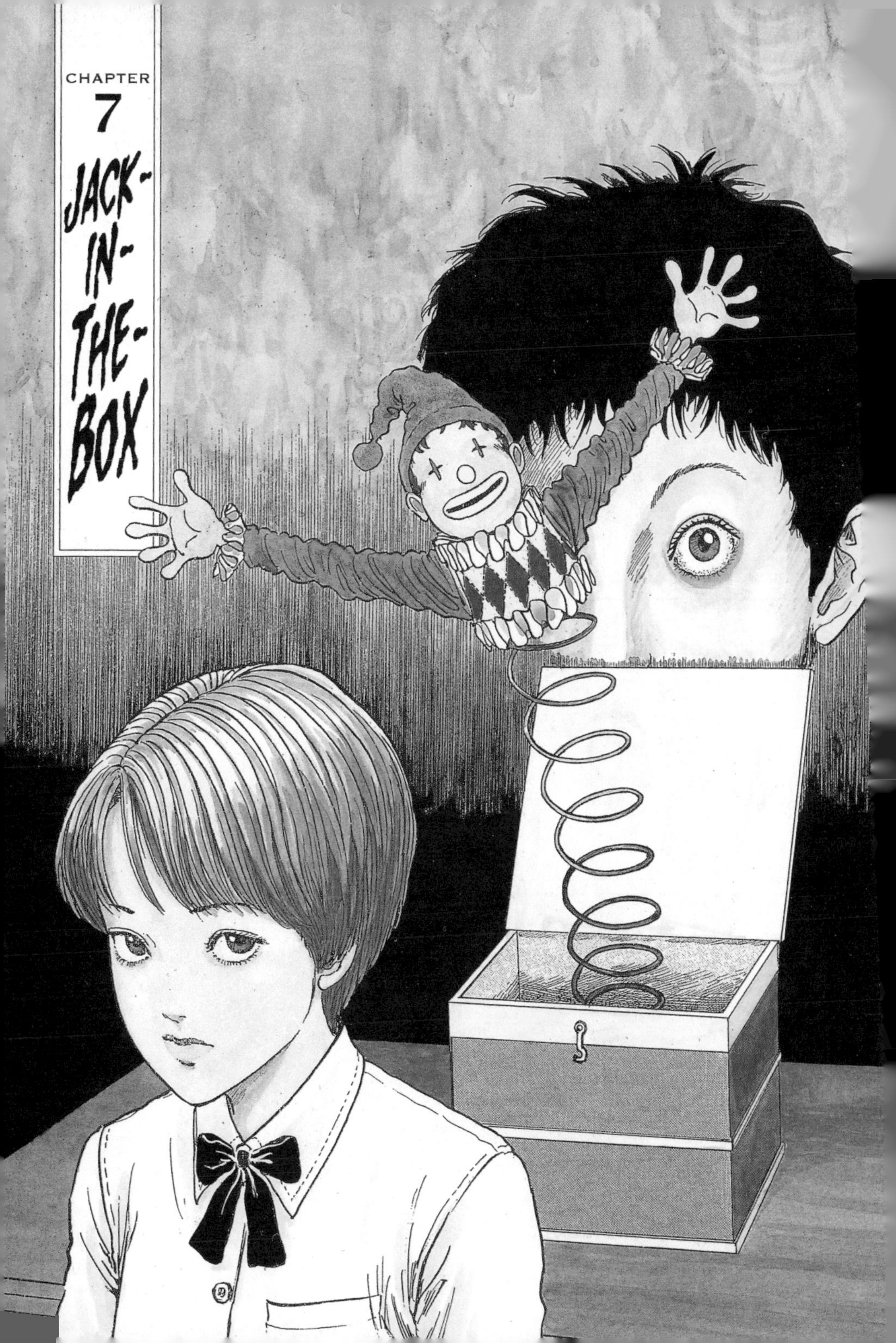
CHAPTER
7
JACK-IN-THE-BOX

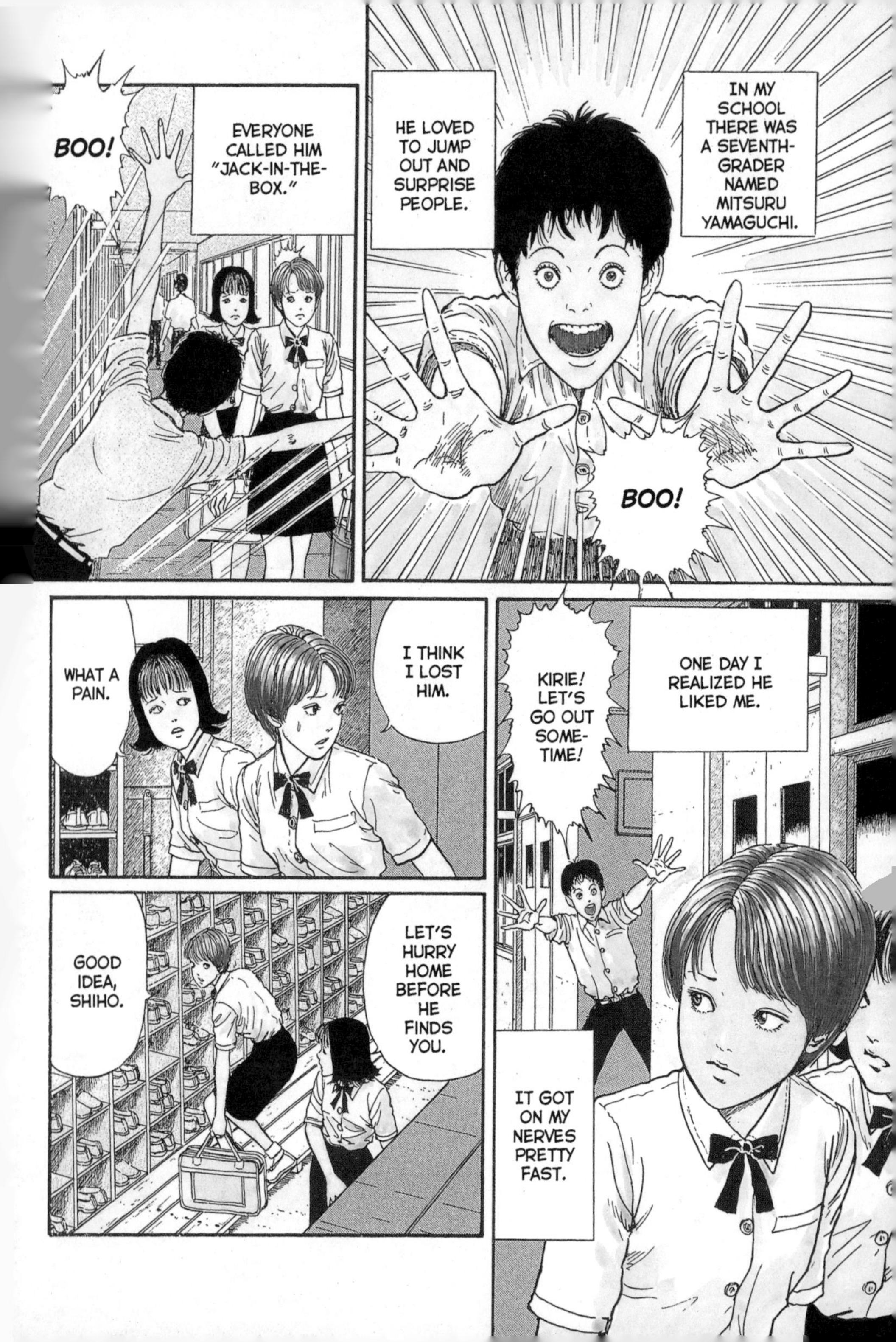
IN MY SCHOOL THERE WAS A SEVENTH-GRADER NAMED MITSURU YAMAGUCHI.
HE LOVED TO JUMP OUT AND SURPRISE PEOPLE.
BOO!
EVERYONE CALLED HIM "JACK-IN-THE-BOX."
BOO!
ONE DAY I REALIZED HE LIKED ME.
KIRIE! LET'S GO OUT SOME-TIME!
IT GOT ON MY NERVES PRETTY FAST.
I THINK I LOST HIM.
WHAT A PAIN.
LET'S HURRY HOME BEFORE HE FINDS YOU.
GOOD IDEA, SHIHO.

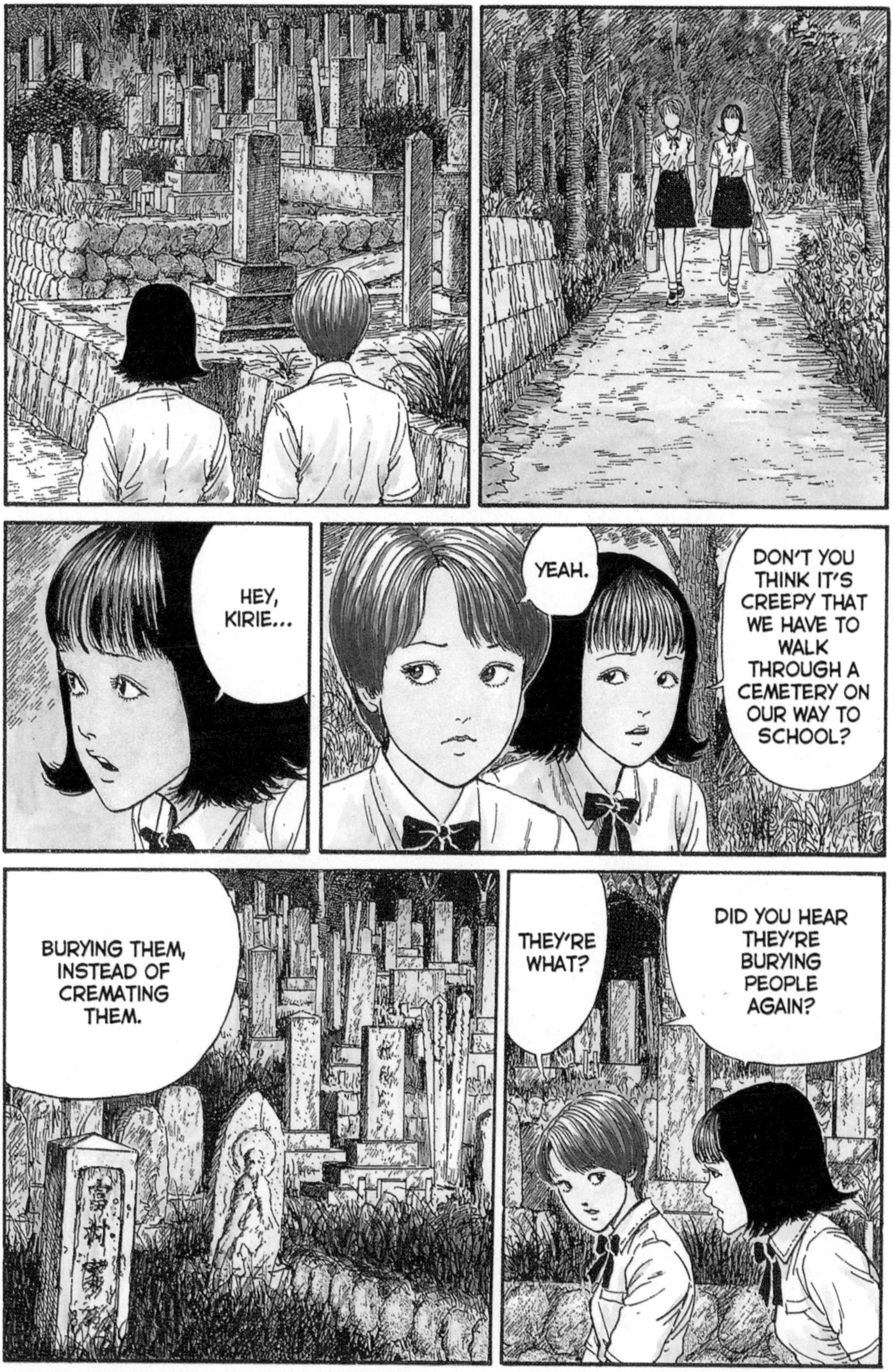
DON'T YOU THINK IT'S CREEPY THAT WE HAVE TO WALK THROUGH A CEMETERY ON OUR WAY TO SCHOOL?
YEAH.
HEY, KIRIE...
DID YOU HEAR THEY'RE BURYING PEOPLE AGAIN?
THEY'RE WHAT?
BURYING THEM, INSTEAD OF CREMATING THEM.

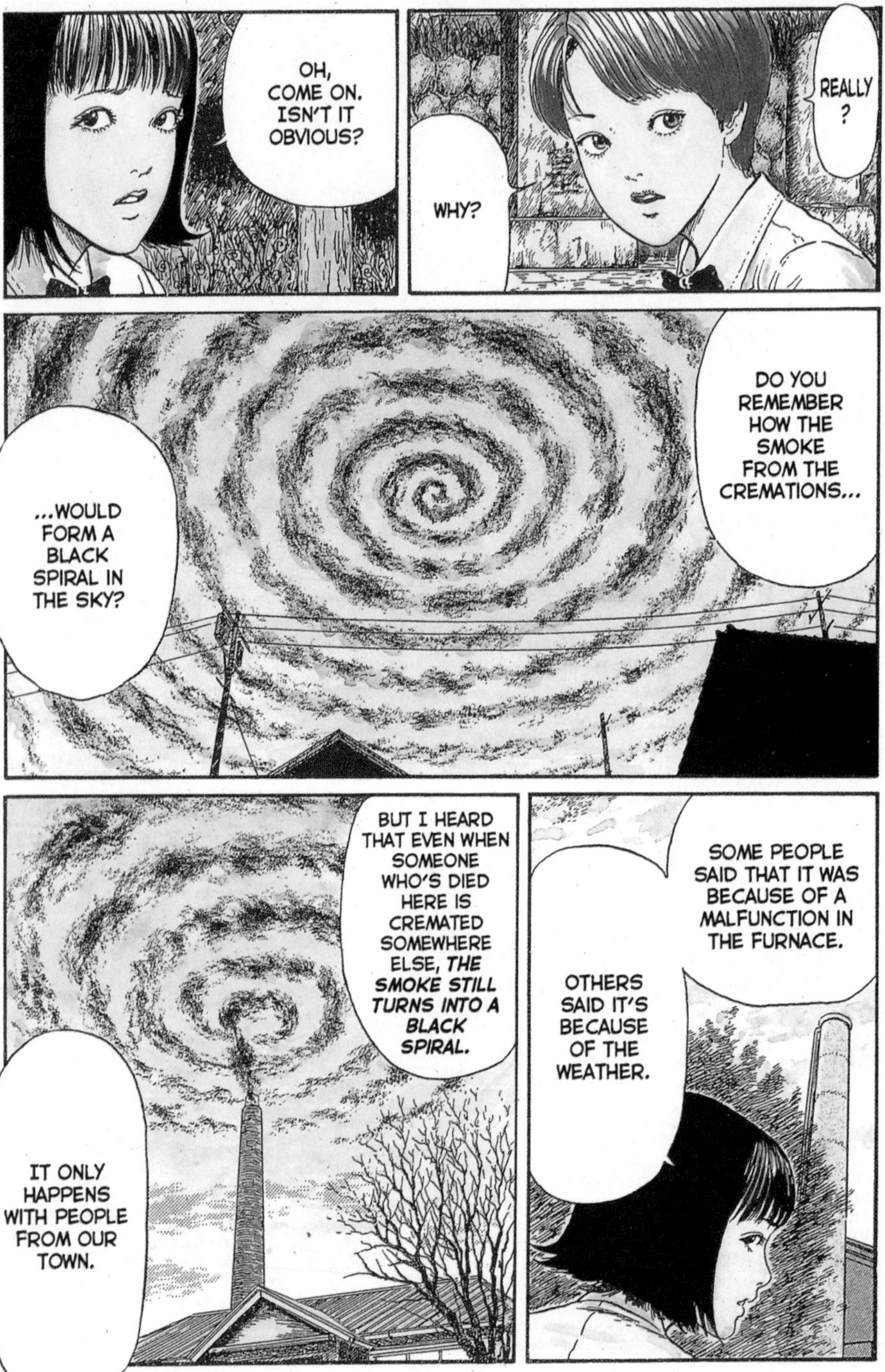
REALLY?
WHY?
OH, COME ON. ISN'T IT OBVIOUS?
DO YOU REMEMBER HOW THE SMOKE FROM THE CREMATIONS...
...WOULD FORM A BLACK SPIRAL IN THE SKY?
SOME PEOPLE SAID THAT IT WAS BECAUSE OF A MALFUNCTION IN THE FURNACE.
OTHERS SAID IT'S BECAUSE OF THE WEATHER.
BUT I HEARD THAT EVEN WHEN SOMEONE WHO'S DIED HERE IS CREMATED SOMEWHERE ELSE, *THE SMOKE STILL TURNS INTO A BLACK SPIRAL.*
IT ONLY HAPPENS WITH PEOPLE FROM OUR TOWN.

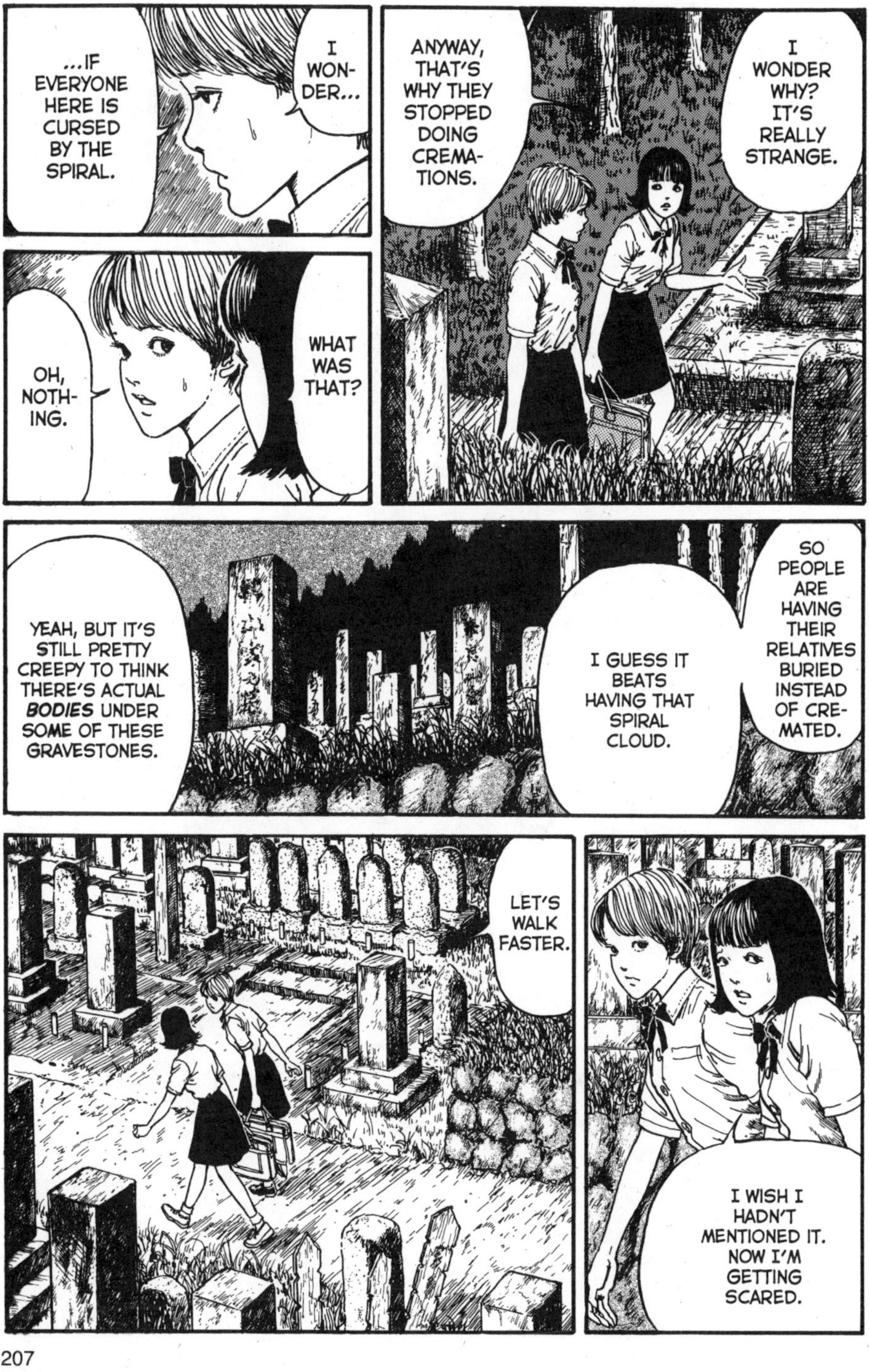
I WONDER WHY? IT'S REALLY STRANGE.
ANYWAY, THAT'S WHY THEY STOPPED DOING CREMATIONS.
I WONDER...
...IF EVERYONE HERE IS CURSED BY THE SPIRAL.
WHAT WAS THAT?
OH, NOTHING.
SO PEOPLE ARE HAVING THEIR RELATIVES BURIED INSTEAD OF CREMATED.
I GUESS IT BEATS HAVING THAT SPIRAL CLOUD.
YEAH, BUT IT'S STILL PRETTY CREEPY TO THINK THERE'S ACTUAL *BODIES* UNDER SOME OF THESE GRAVESTONES.
I WISH I HADN'T MENTIONED IT. NOW I'M GETTING SCARED.
LET'S WALK FASTER.

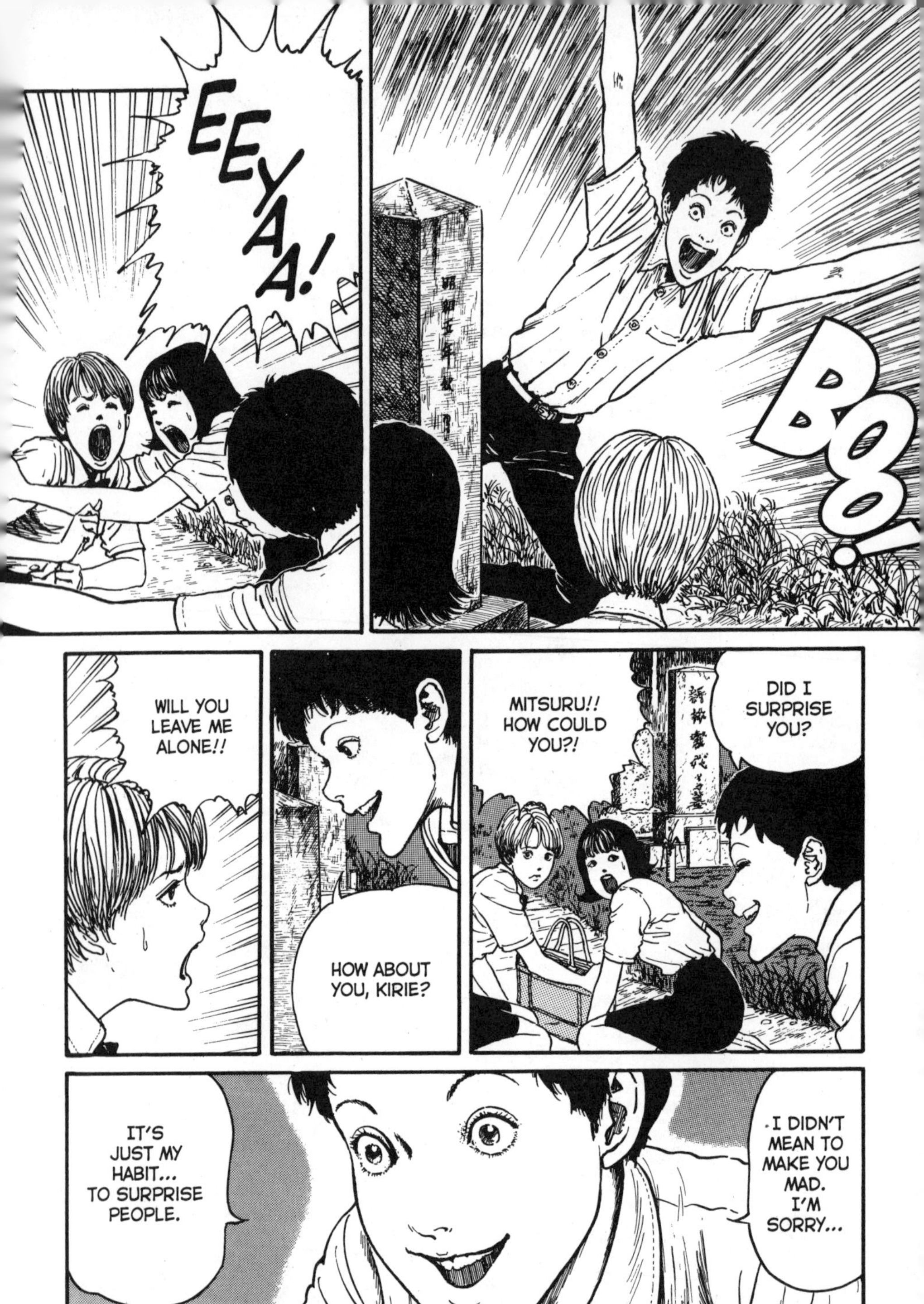
BOO!
EEYAA!
DID I SURPRISE YOU?
MITSURU!! HOW COULD YOU?!
HOW ABOUT YOU, KIRIE?
WILL YOU LEAVE ME ALONE!!
I DIDN'T MEAN TO MAKE YOU MAD. I'M SORRY...
IT'S JUST MY HABIT... TO SURPRISE PEOPLE.

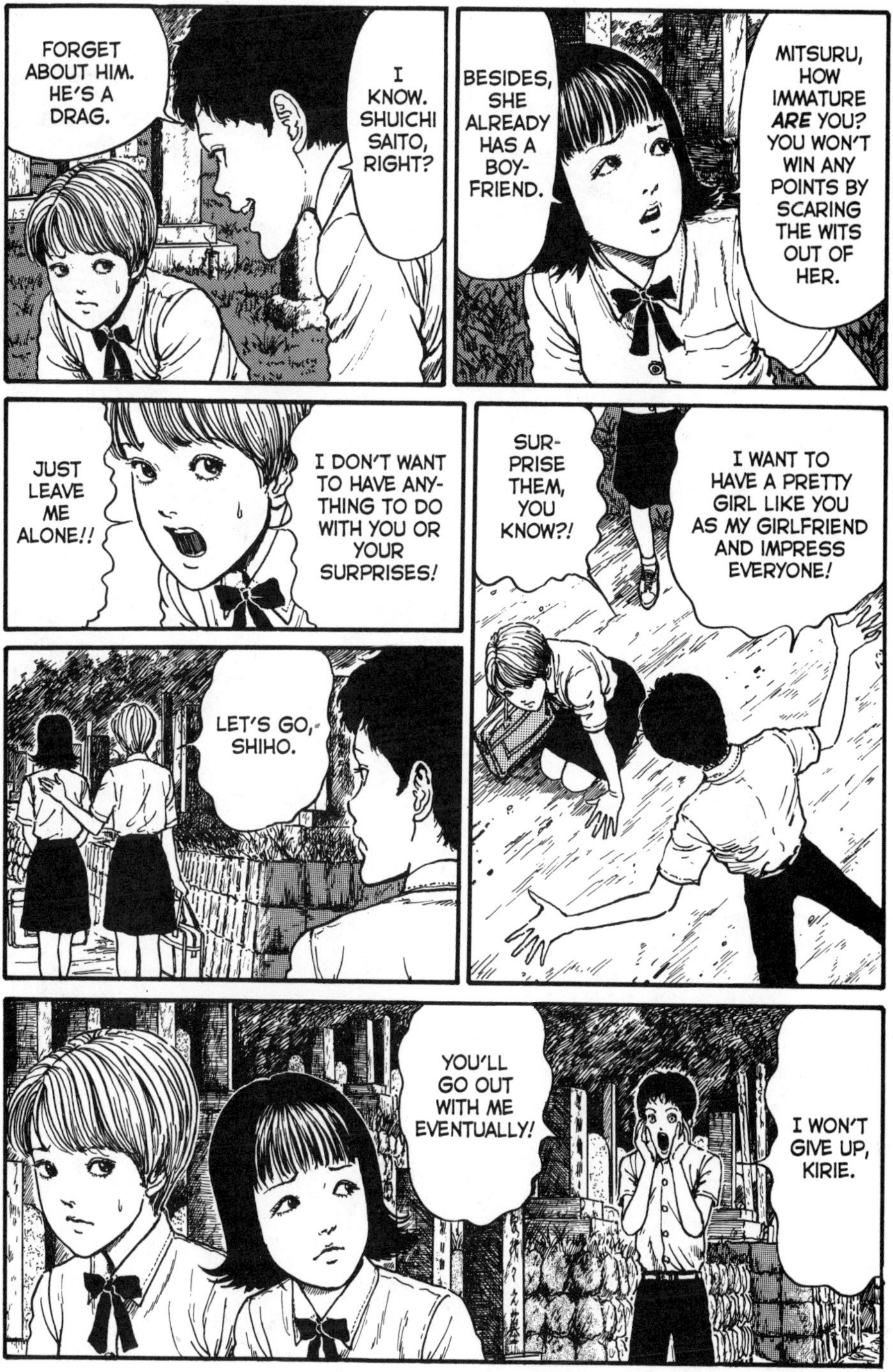
MITSURU, HOW IMMATURE ARE YOU? YOU WON'T WIN ANY POINTS BY SCARING THE WITS OUT OF HER.
BESIDES, SHE ALREADY HAS A BOY-FRIEND.
I KNOW. SHUICHI SAITO, RIGHT?
FORGET ABOUT HIM. HE'S A DRAG.
I WANT TO HAVE A PRETTY GIRL LIKE YOU AS MY GIRLFRIEND AND IMPRESS EVERYONE!
SUR-PRISE THEM, YOU KNOW?!
I DON'T WANT TO HAVE ANY-THING TO DO WITH YOU OR YOUR SURPRISES!
JUST LEAVE ME ALONE!!
LET'S GO, SHIHO.
I WON'T GIVE UP, KIRIE.
YOU'LL GO OUT WITH ME EVENTUALLY!

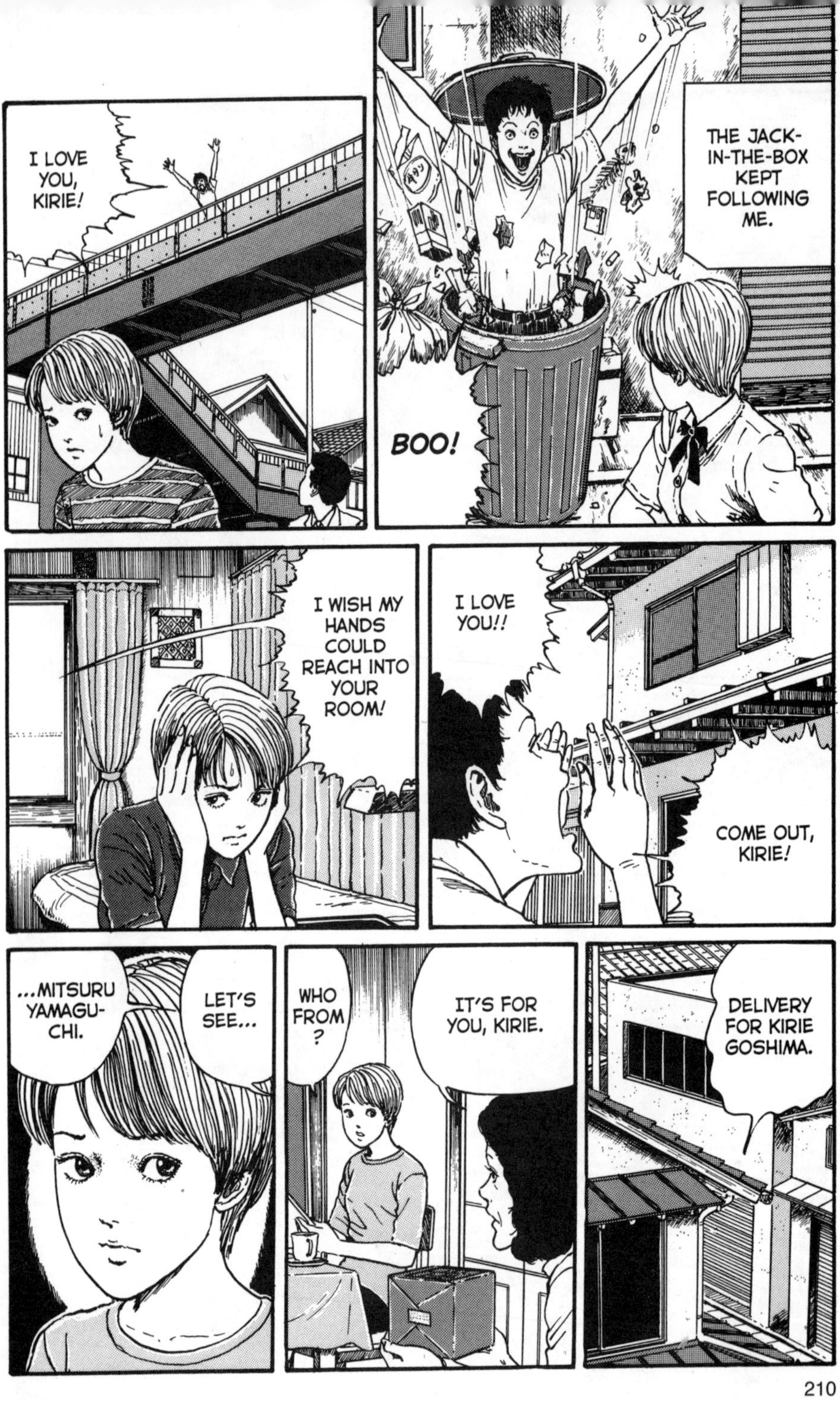
THE JACK-IN-THE-BOX KEPT FOLLOWING ME.
BOO!
I LOVE YOU, KIRIE!
I LOVE YOU!!
COME OUT, KIRIE!
I WISH MY HANDS COULD REACH INTO YOUR ROOM!
DELIVERY FOR KIRIE GOSHIMA.
IT'S FOR YOU, KIRIE.
WHO FROM?
LET'S SEE...
...MITSURU YAMAGUCHI.

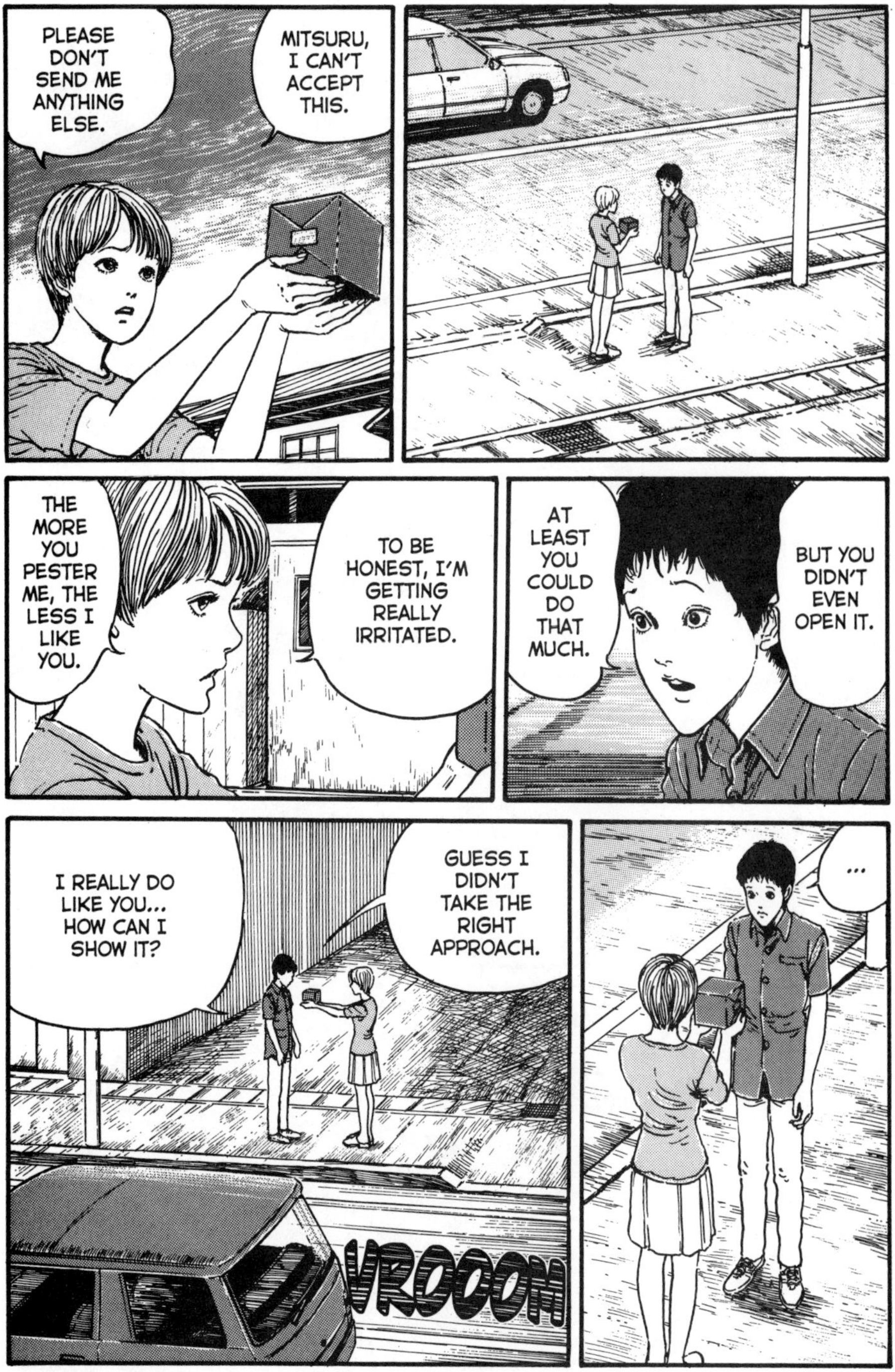
MITSURU, I CAN'T ACCEPT THIS.
PLEASE DON'T SEND ME ANYTHING ELSE.
BUT YOU DIDN'T EVEN OPEN IT.
AT LEAST YOU COULD DO THAT MUCH.
TO BE HONEST, I'M GETTING REALLY IRRITATED.
THE MORE YOU PESTER ME, THE LESS I LIKE YOU.
...
GUESS I DIDN'T TAKE THE RIGHT APPROACH.
I REALLY DO LIKE YOU... HOW CAN I SHOW IT?
VROOOM

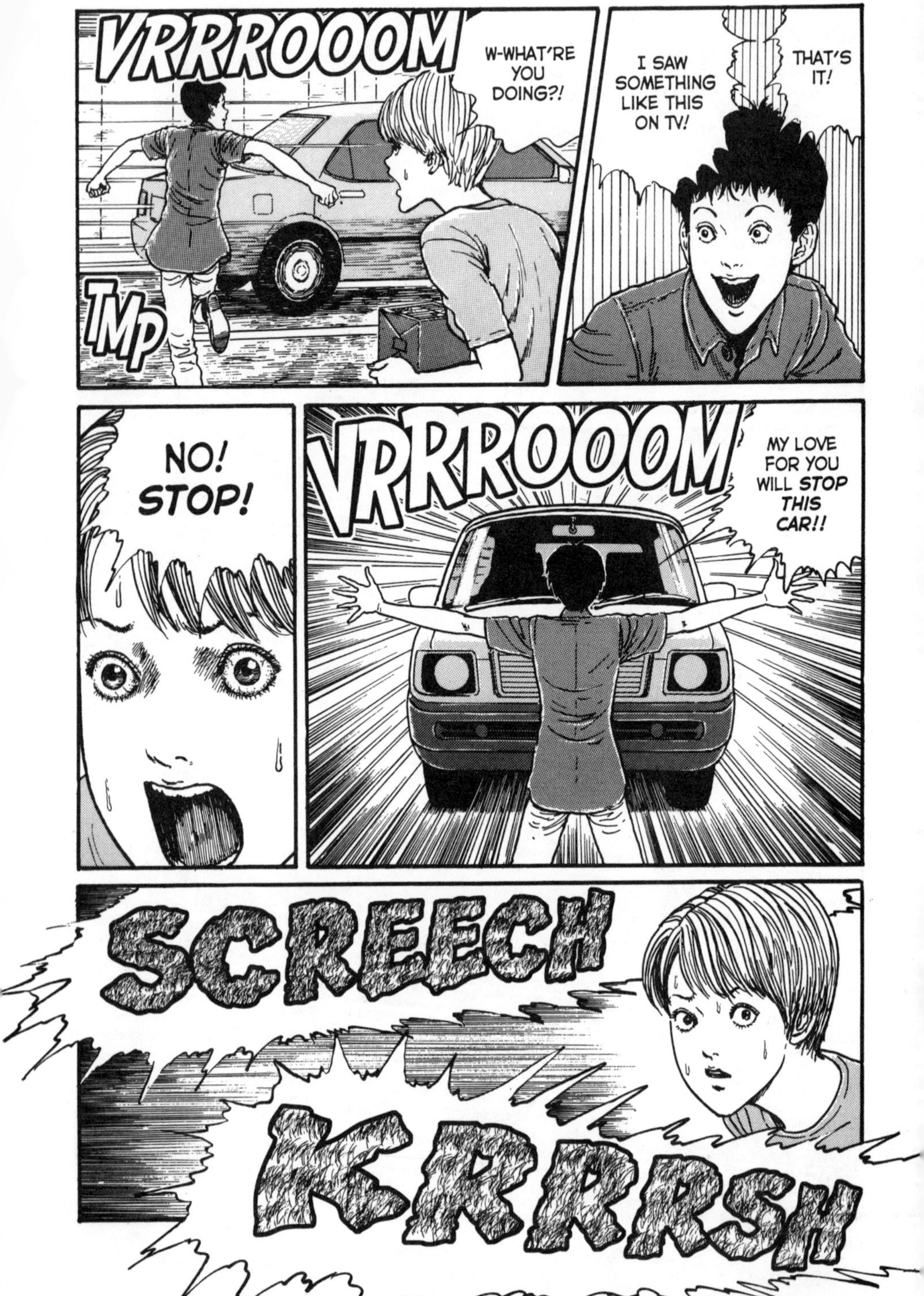
THAT'S IT!
I SAW SOMETHING LIKE THIS ON TV!
W-WHAT'RE YOU DOING?!
VRRROOOM
TMP
MY LOVE FOR YOU WILL STOP THIS CAR!!
VRRROOOM
NO! STOP!
SCREECH
KRRRSH

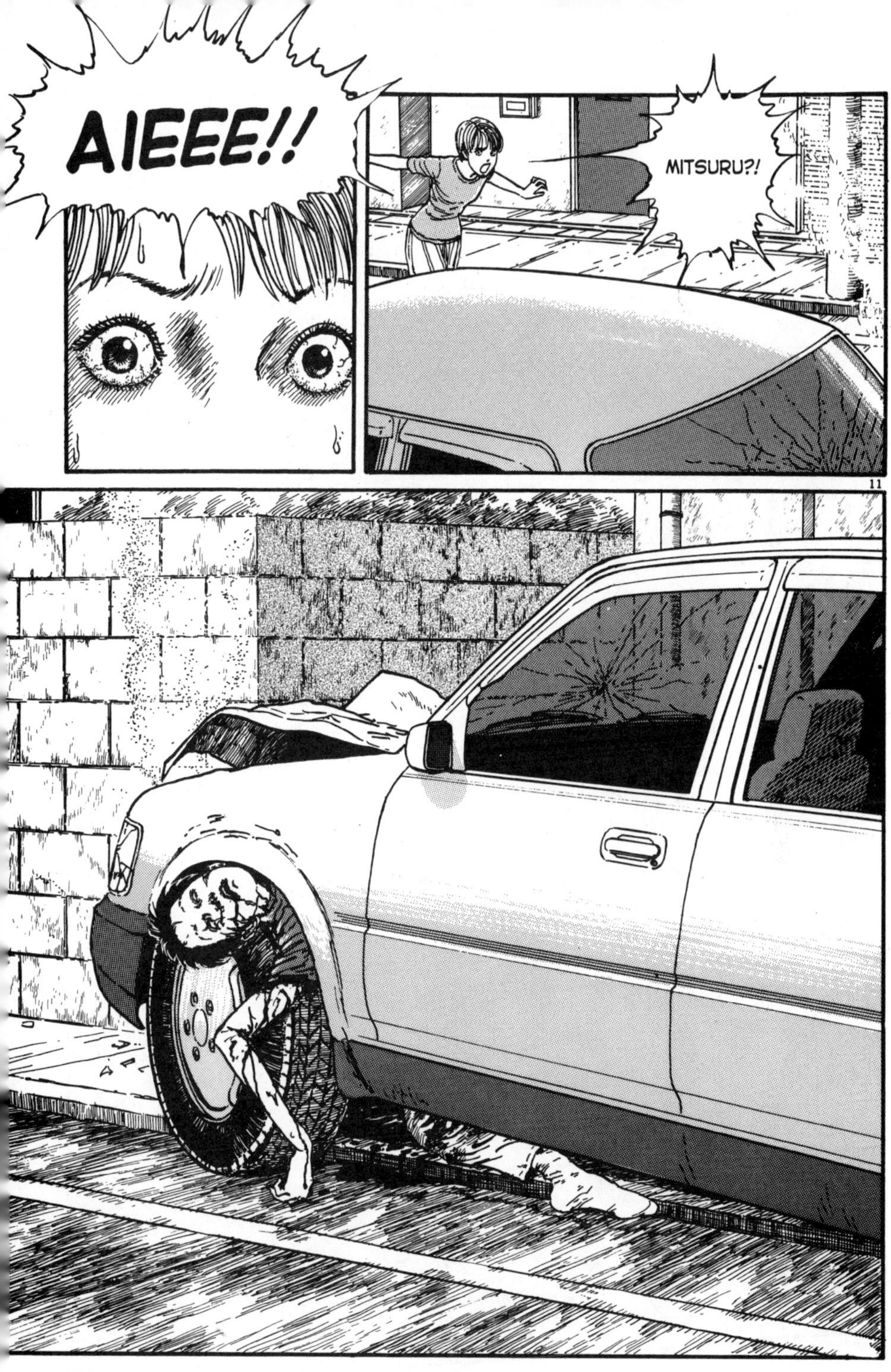
MITSURU?!
AIEEE!!
11

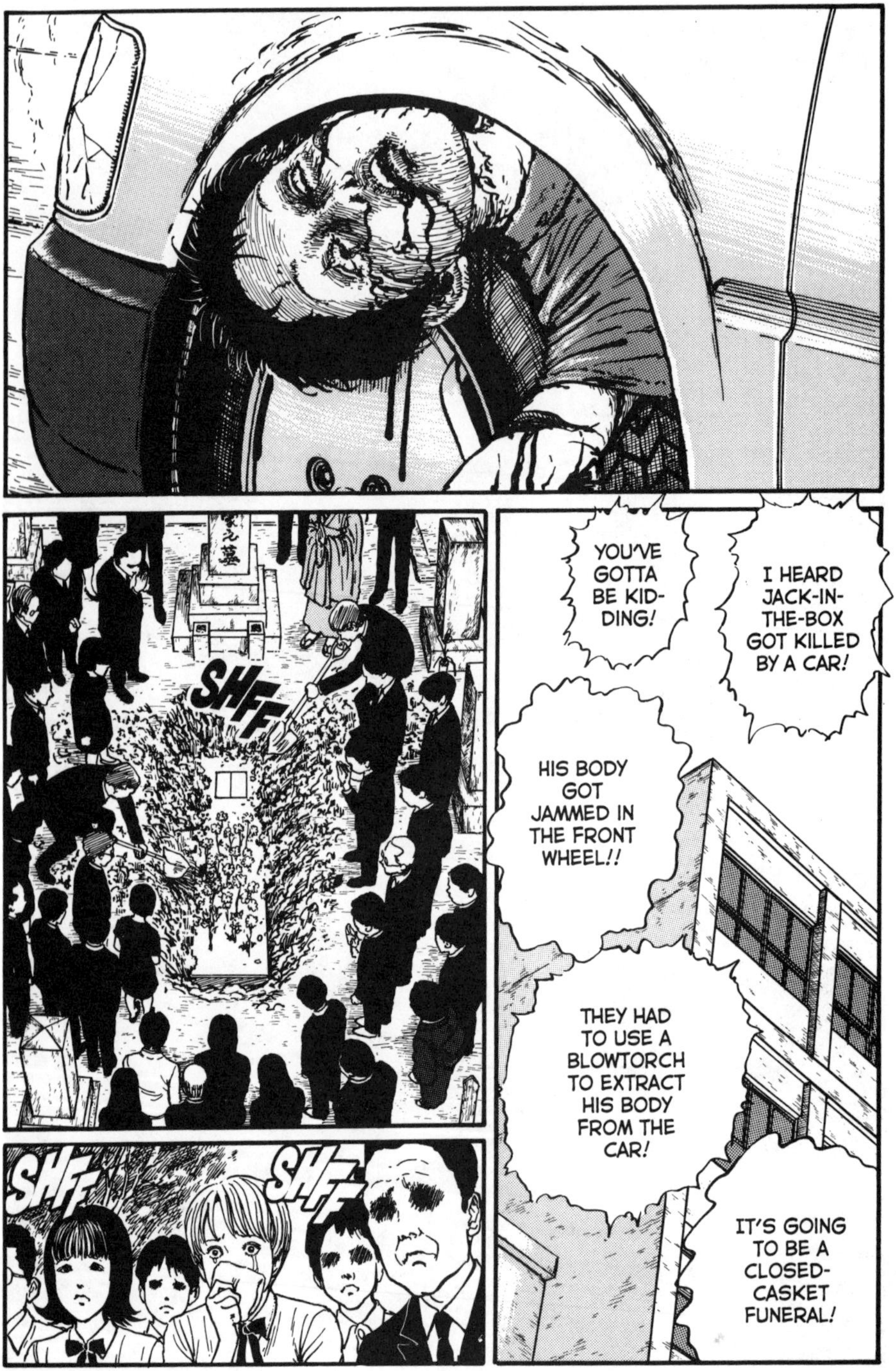
I HEARD JACK-IN-THE-BOX GOT KILLED BY A CAR!
YOU'VE GOTTA BE KID-DING!
HIS BODY GOT JAMMED IN THE FRONT WHEEL!!
THEY HAD TO USE A BLOWTORCH TO EXTRACT HIS BODY FROM THE CAR!
IT'S GOING TO BE A CLOSED-CASKET FUNERAL!
SHFF
SHFF
SHFF

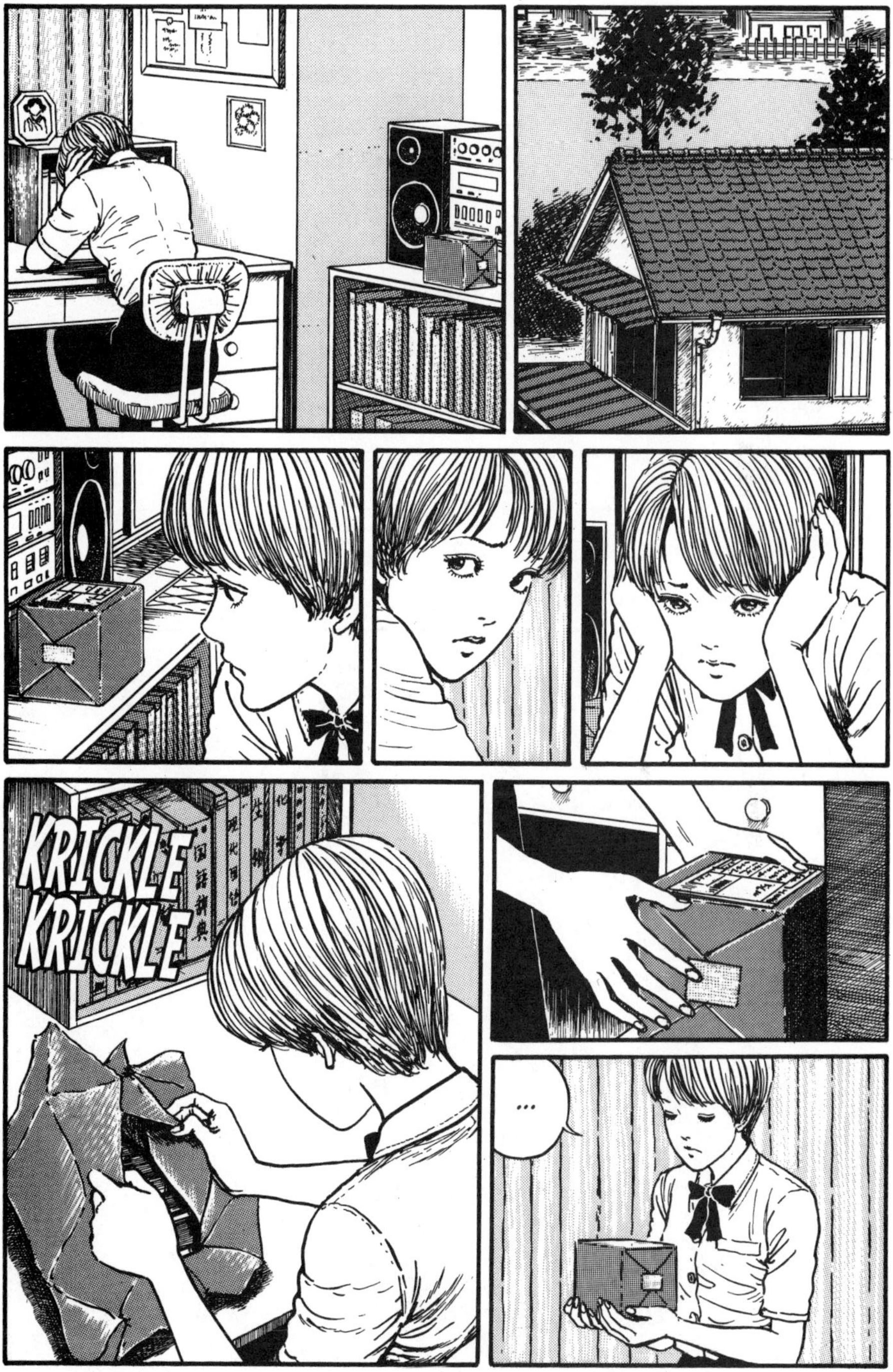
KRICKLE KRICKLE
...

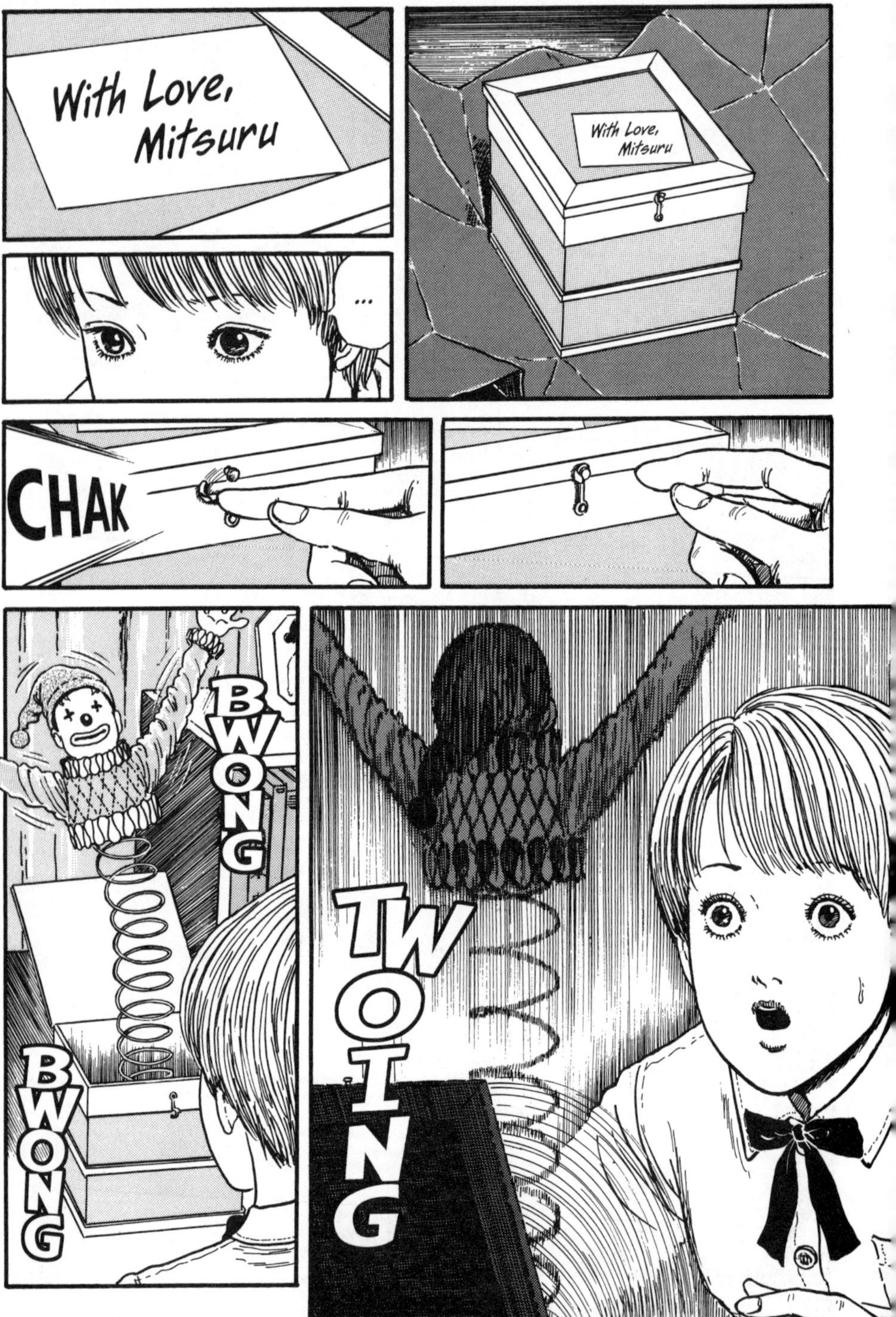

With Love,
Mitsuru
With Love,
Mitsuru
...
CHAK
TWOING
BWONG
BWONG

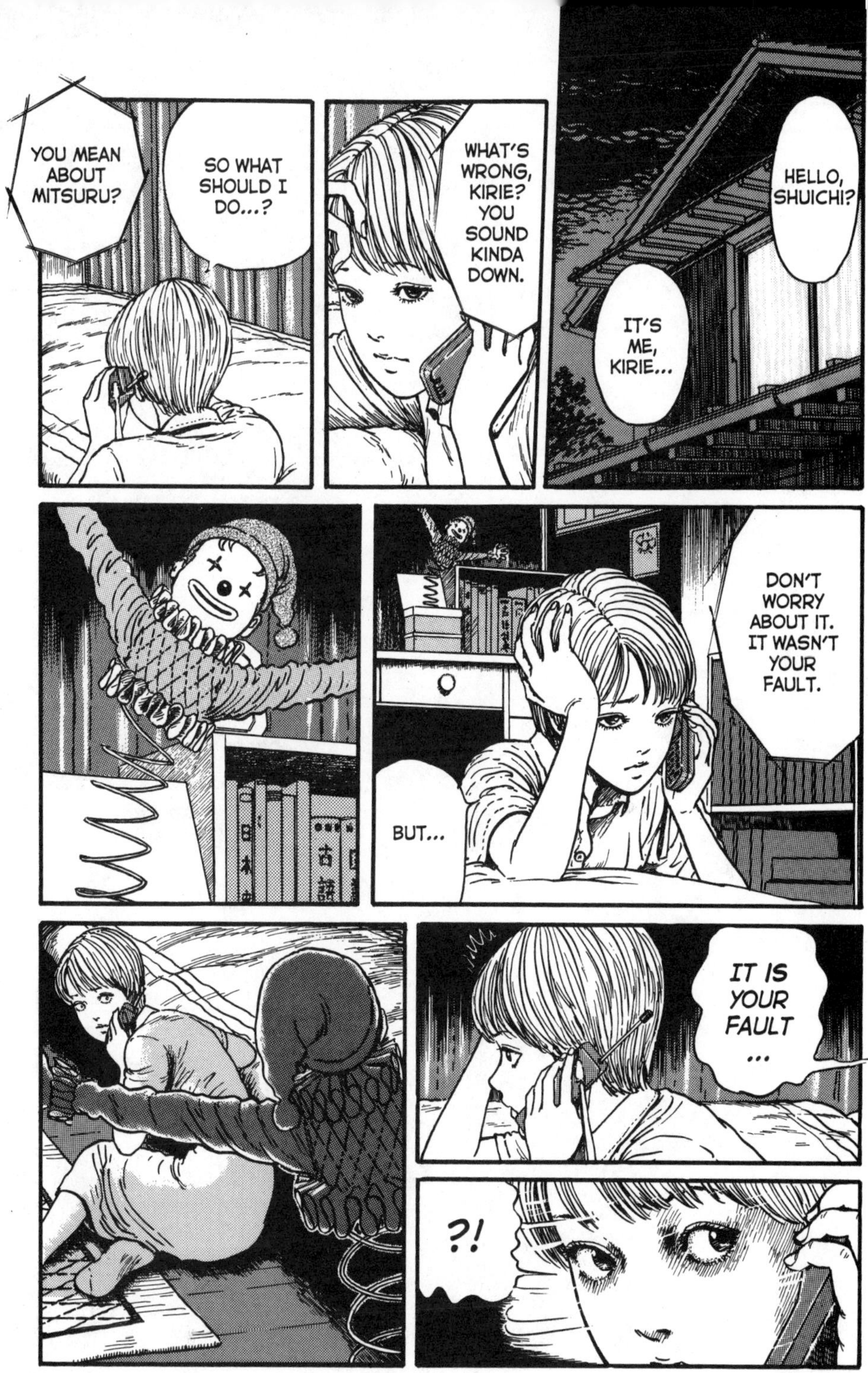
HELLO, SHUICHI?
IT'S ME, KIRIE...
WHAT'S WRONG, KIRIE? YOU SOUND KINDA DOWN.
SO WHAT SHOULD I DO...?
YOU MEAN ABOUT MITSURU?
DON'T WORRY ABOUT IT. IT WASN'T YOUR FAULT.
BUT...
IT IS YOUR FAULT ...
?!

HE DIED FOR YOU, DIDN'T HE?

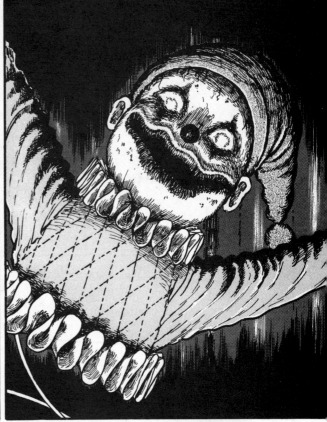

AIEEE!!

AND NOW...

...HE'LL COME BACK FOR YOU...

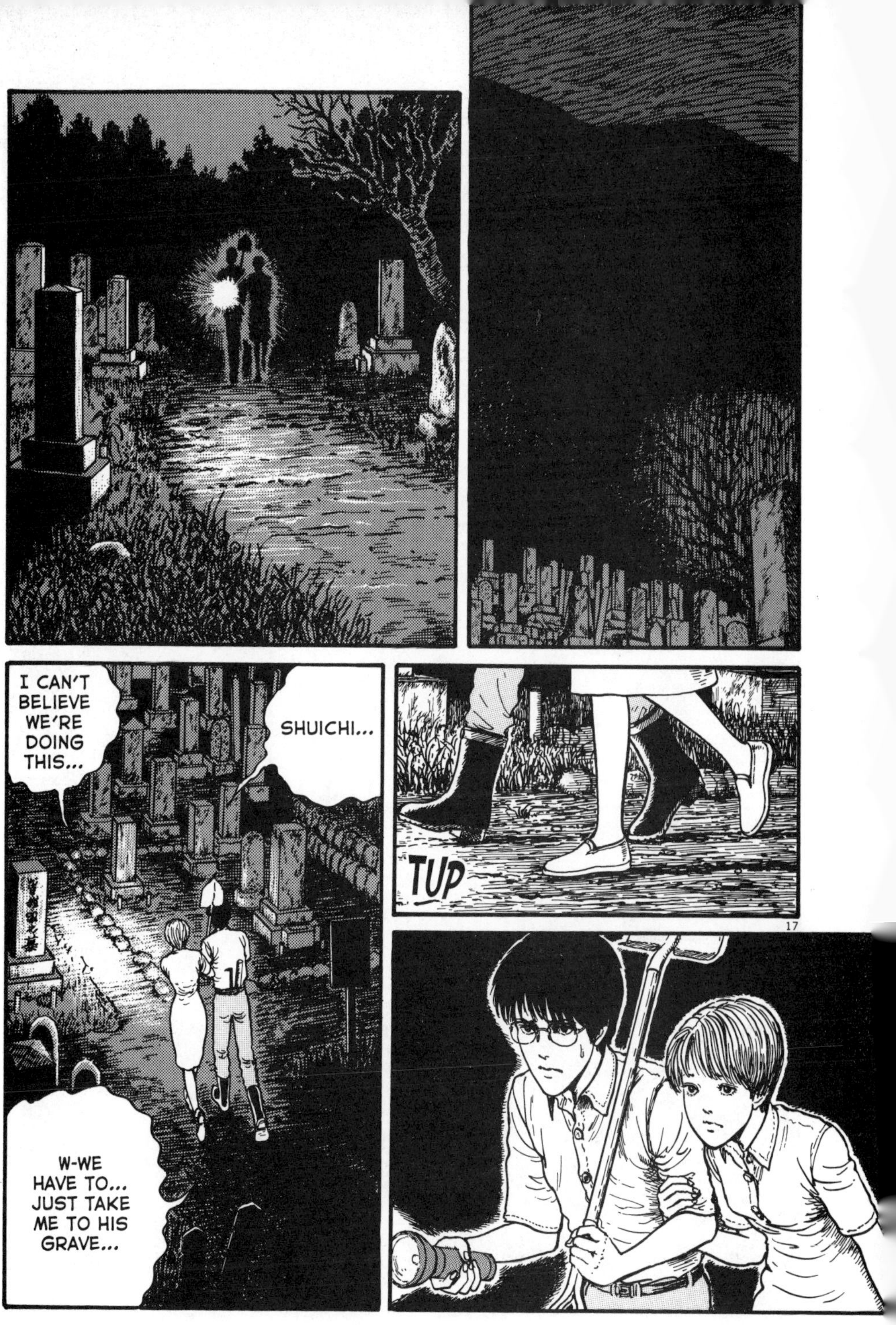
TUP
SHUICHI...
I CAN'T BELIEVE WE'RE DOING THIS...
W-WE HAVE TO... JUST TAKE ME TO HIS GRAVE...
17

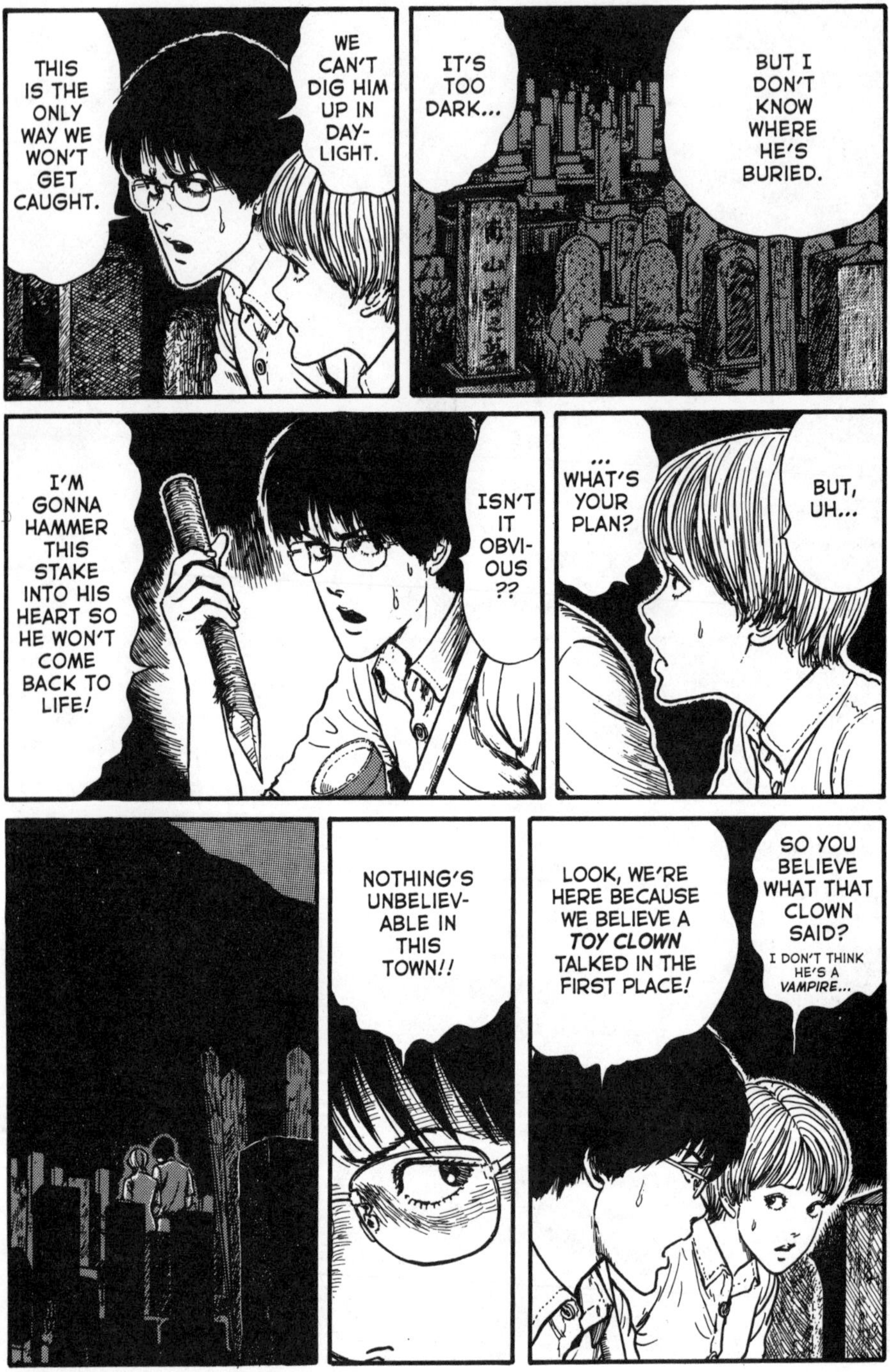
BUT I DON'T KNOW WHERE HE'S BURIED.
IT'S TOO DARK...
WE CAN'T DIG HIM UP IN DAY-LIGHT.
THIS IS THE ONLY WAY WE WON'T GET CAUGHT.
BUT, UH...
...WHAT'S YOUR PLAN?
ISN'T IT OBVIOUS??
I'M GONNA HAMMER THIS STAKE INTO HIS HEART SO HE WON'T COME BACK TO LIFE!
SO YOU BELIEVE WHAT THAT CLOWN SAID?
I DON'T THINK HE'S A *VAMPIRE*...
LOOK, WE'RE HERE BECAUSE WE BELIEVE A ***TOY CLOWN*** TALKED IN THE FIRST PLACE!
NOTHING'S UNBELIEV-ABLE IN THIS TOWN!!

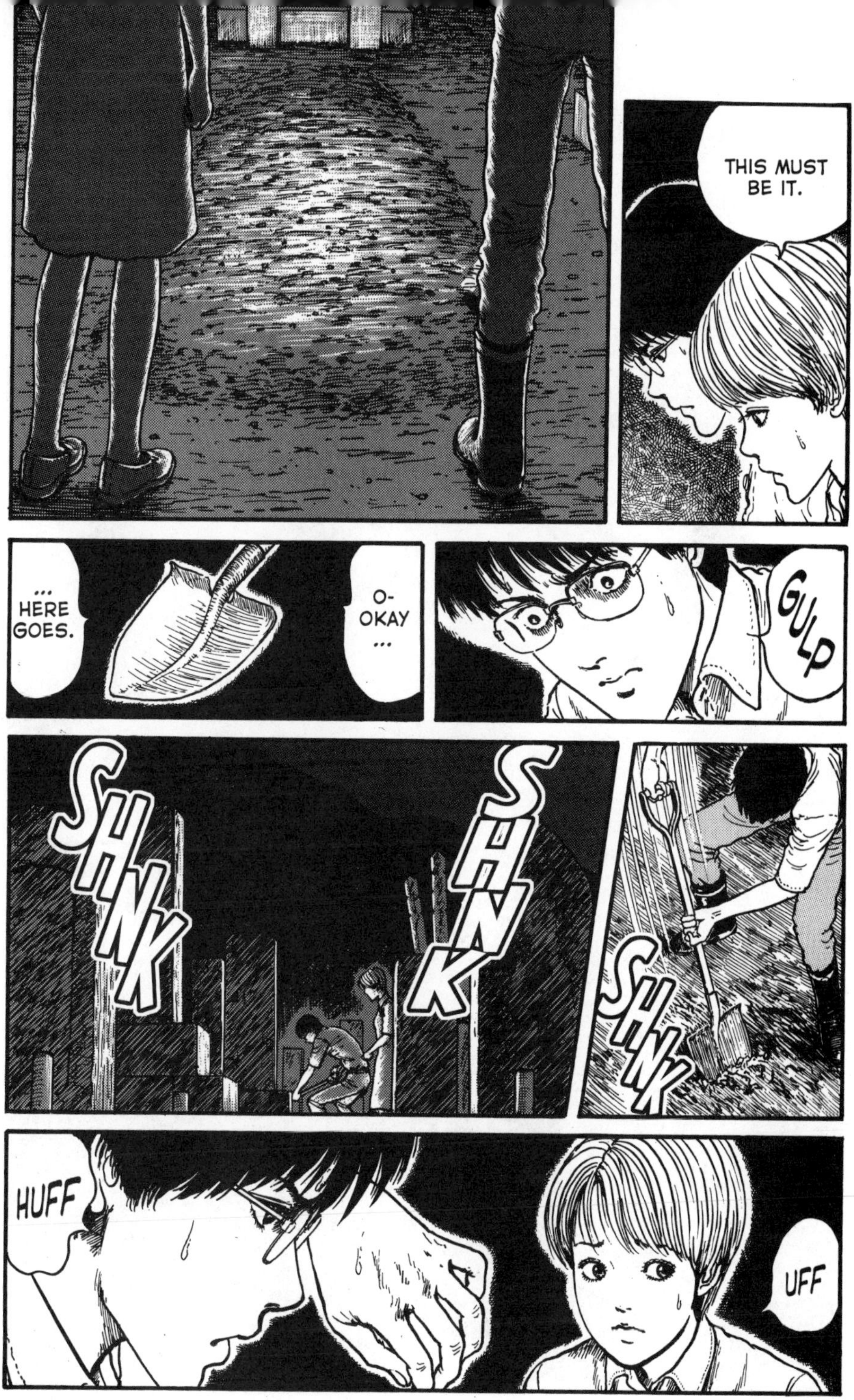
THIS MUST BE IT.
GULP
O-OKAY ...
... HERE GOES.
SHNK
SHNK
SHNK
UFF
HUFF

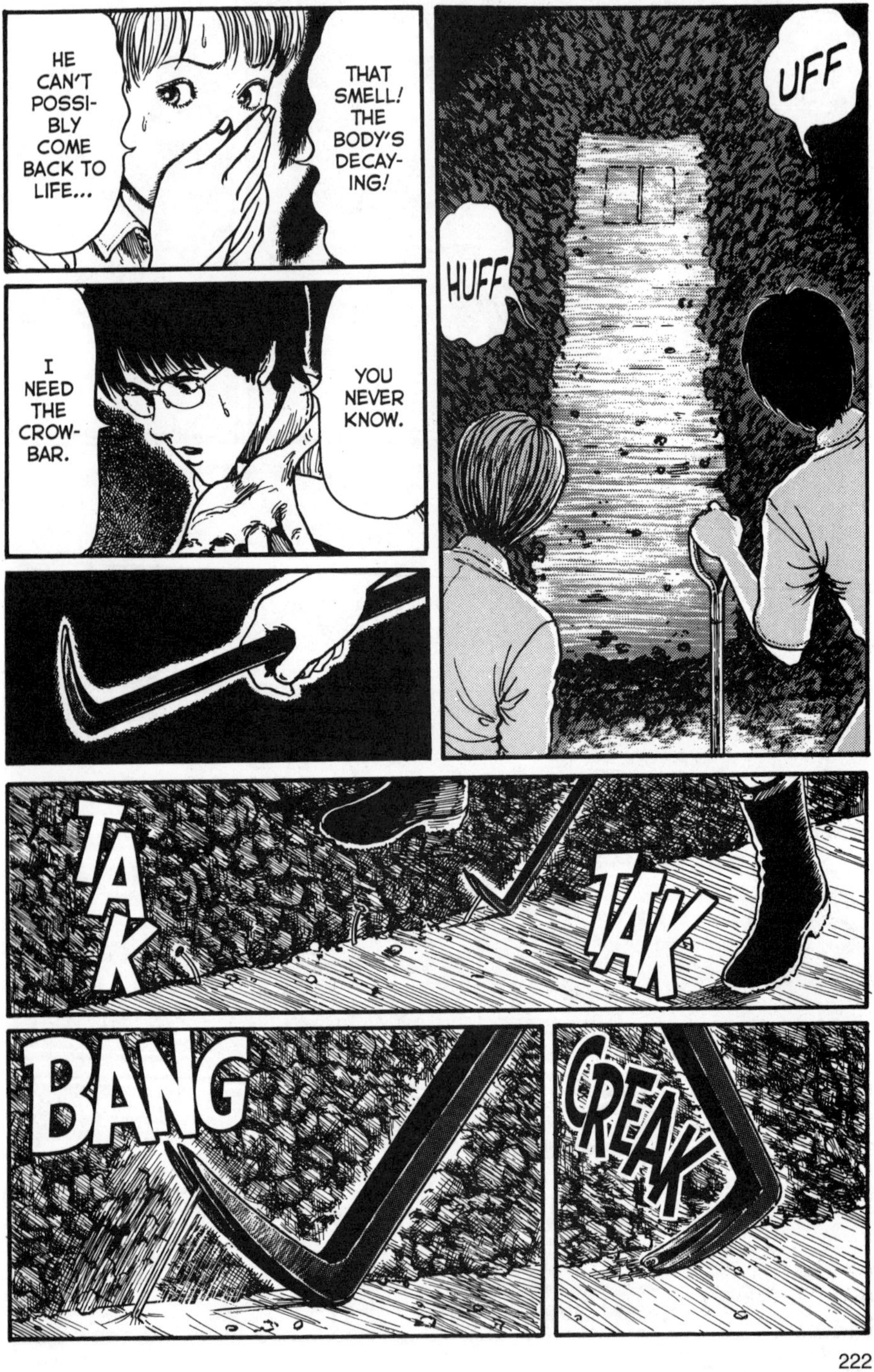
UFF
HUFF
THAT SMELL! THE BODY'S DECAYING!
HE CAN'T POSSIBLY COME BACK TO LIFE...
YOU NEVER KNOW.
I NEED THE CROWBAR.
TAK
TAK
CREAK
BANG

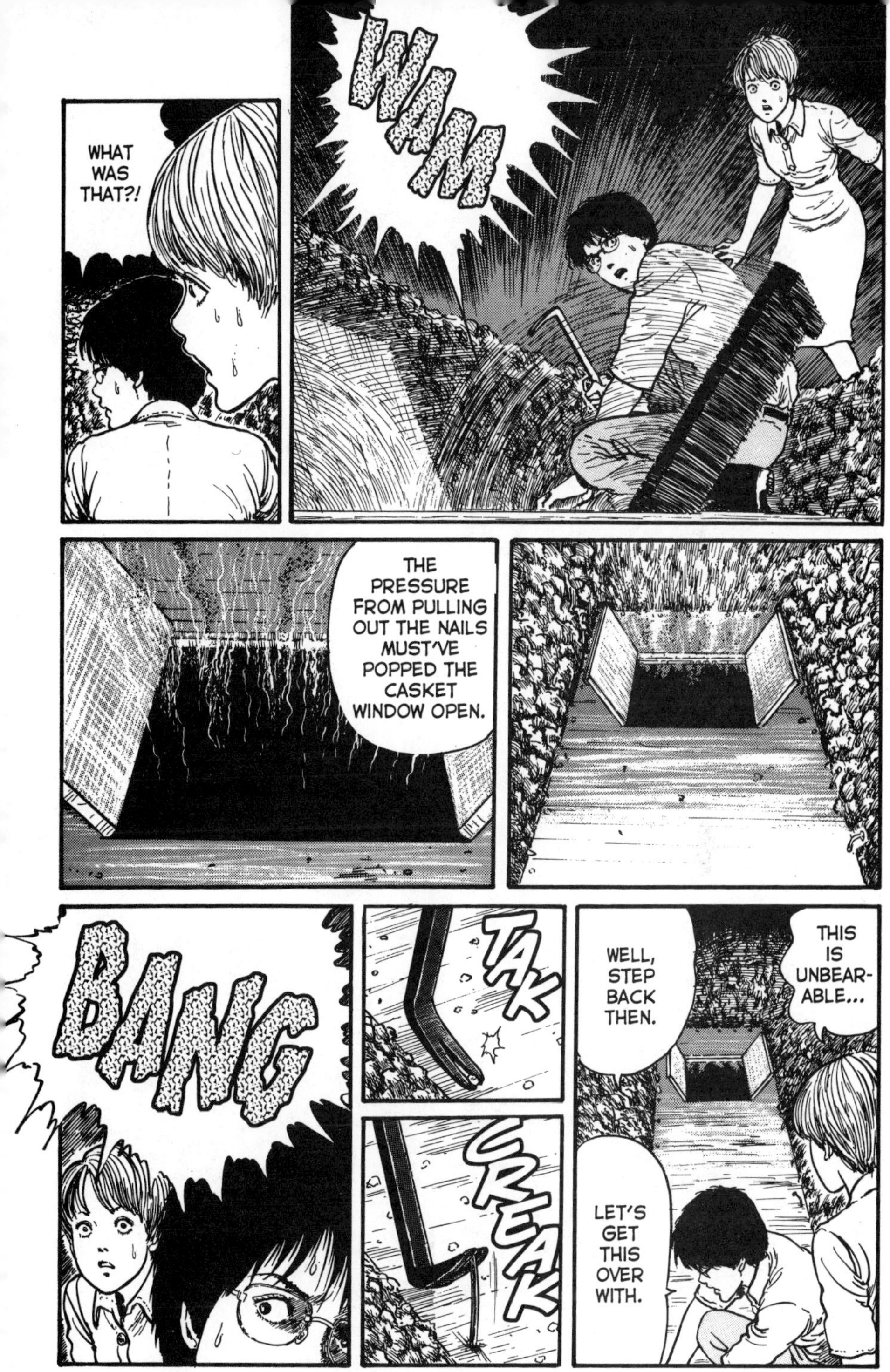
WAM
WHAT WAS THAT?!
THE PRESSURE FROM PULLING OUT THE NAILS MUST'VE POPPED THE CASKET WINDOW OPEN.
THIS IS UNBEARABLE...
WELL, STEP BACK THEN.
LET'S GET THIS OVER WITH.
TAK
CREAK
BANG

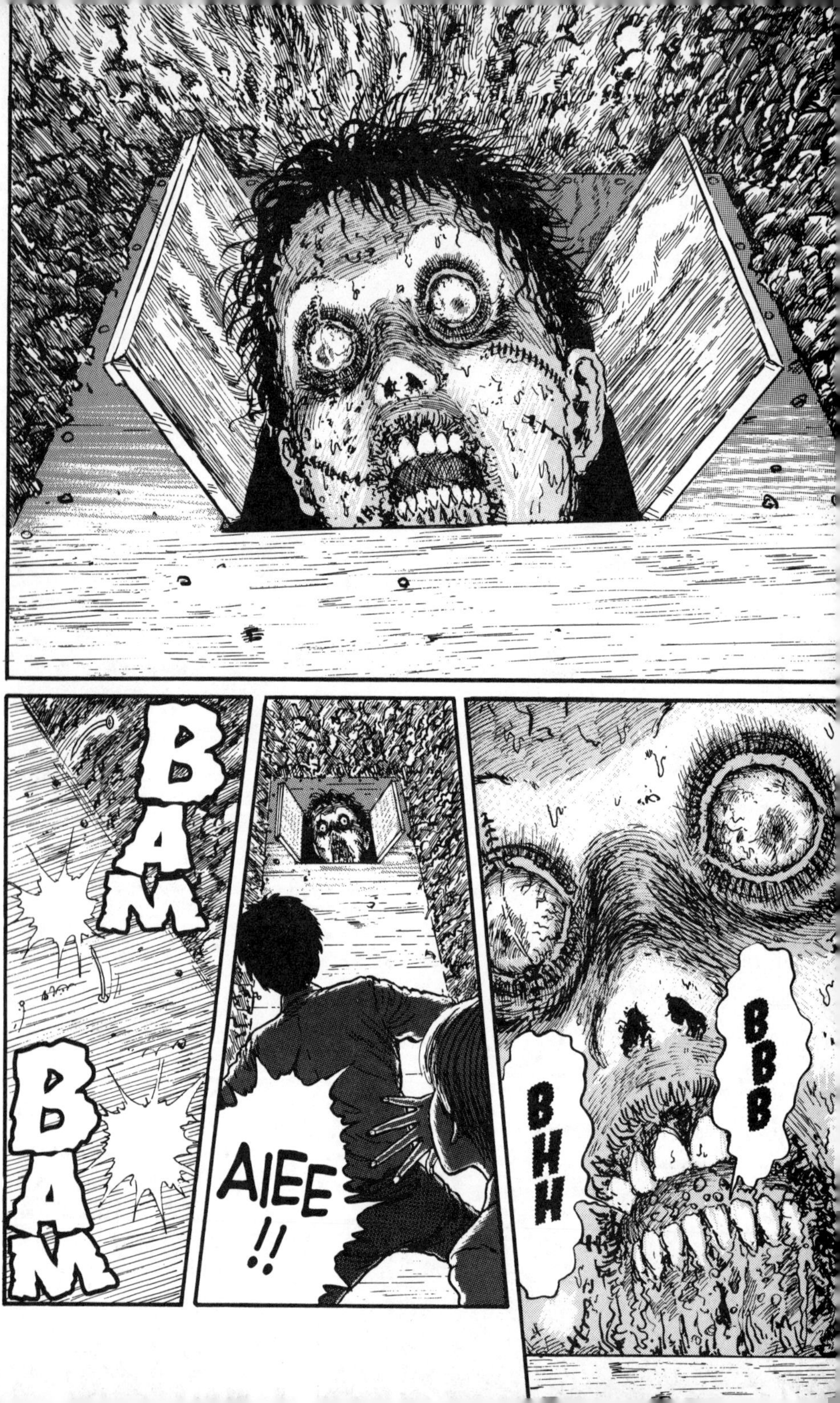
BBB
BHH
AIEE !!
BAM
BAM

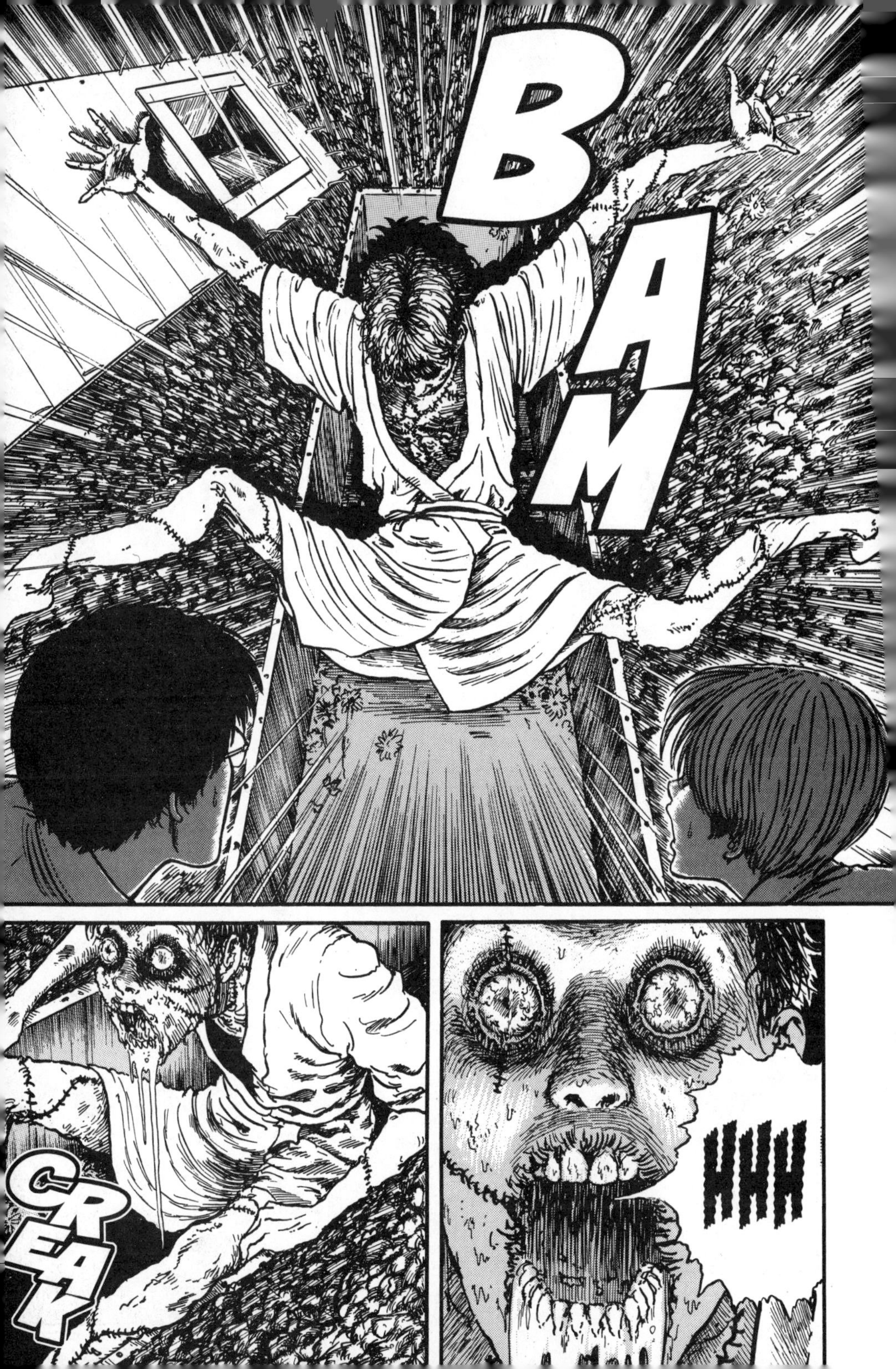
BAM
HHH
CREAK

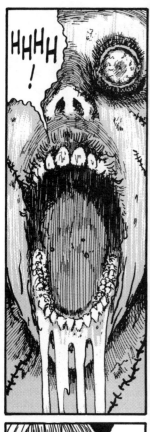

HHHH!

KIRIE...

...RUN!

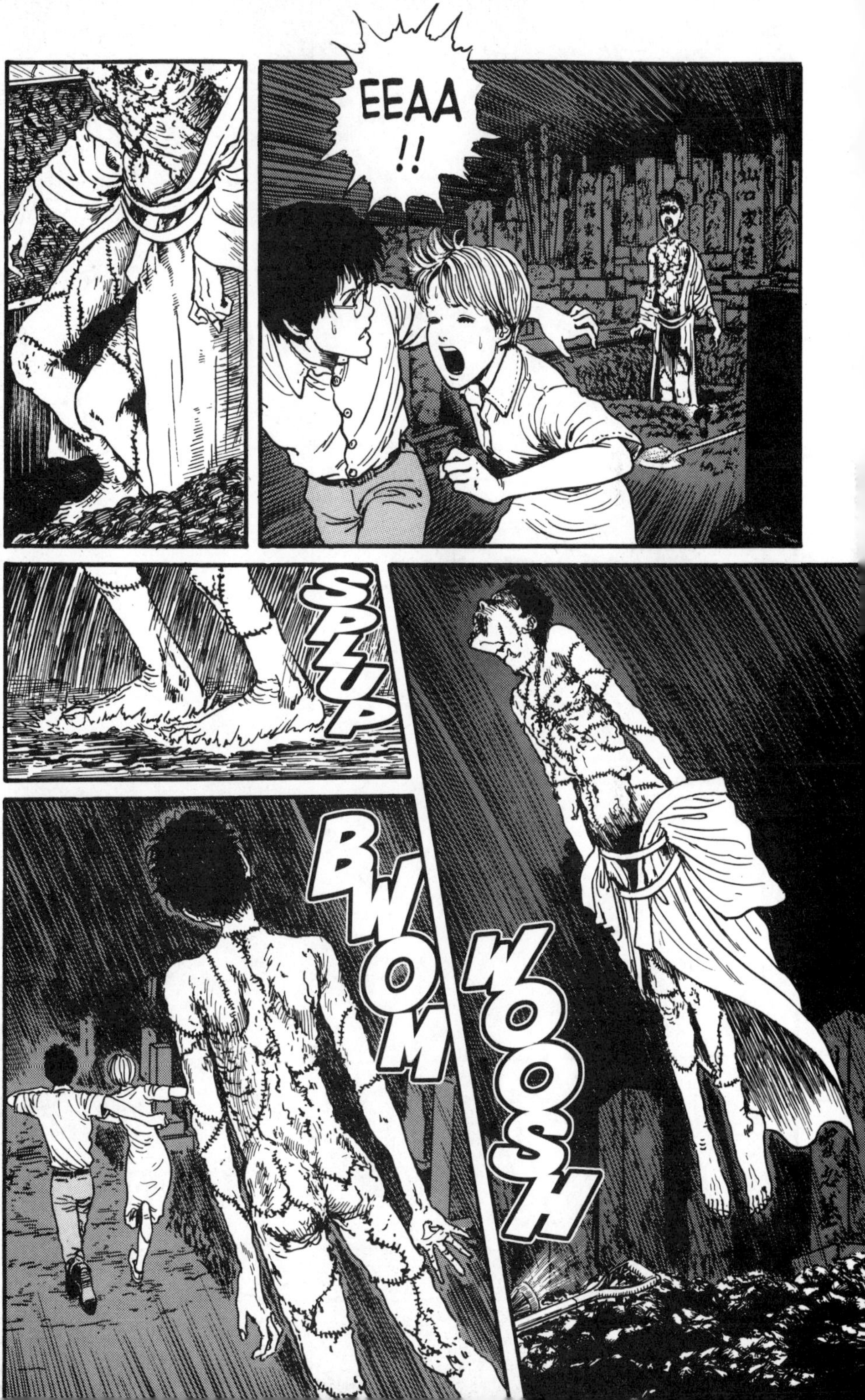
EEAA !!
WOOSH
SPLUP
BWOM

HUFF HUFF
NO!
BWOM
BWOM
HOW CAN HE JUMP AROUND LIKE THAT?!
I...I DON'T KNOW!!
PLAP
WOOSH
SHLUP
26

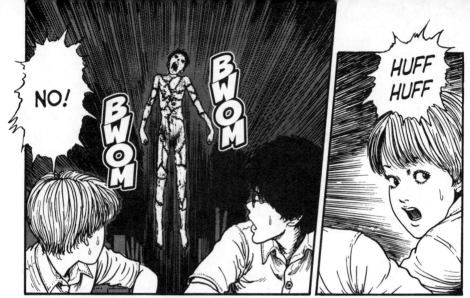

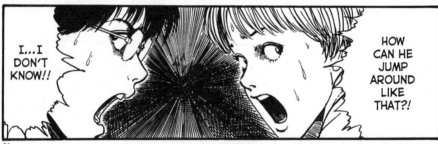

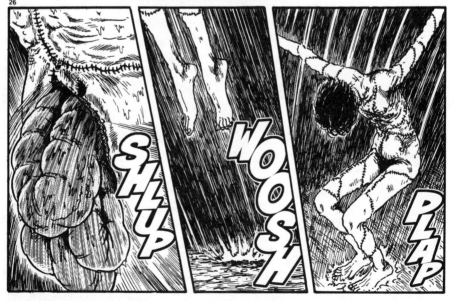

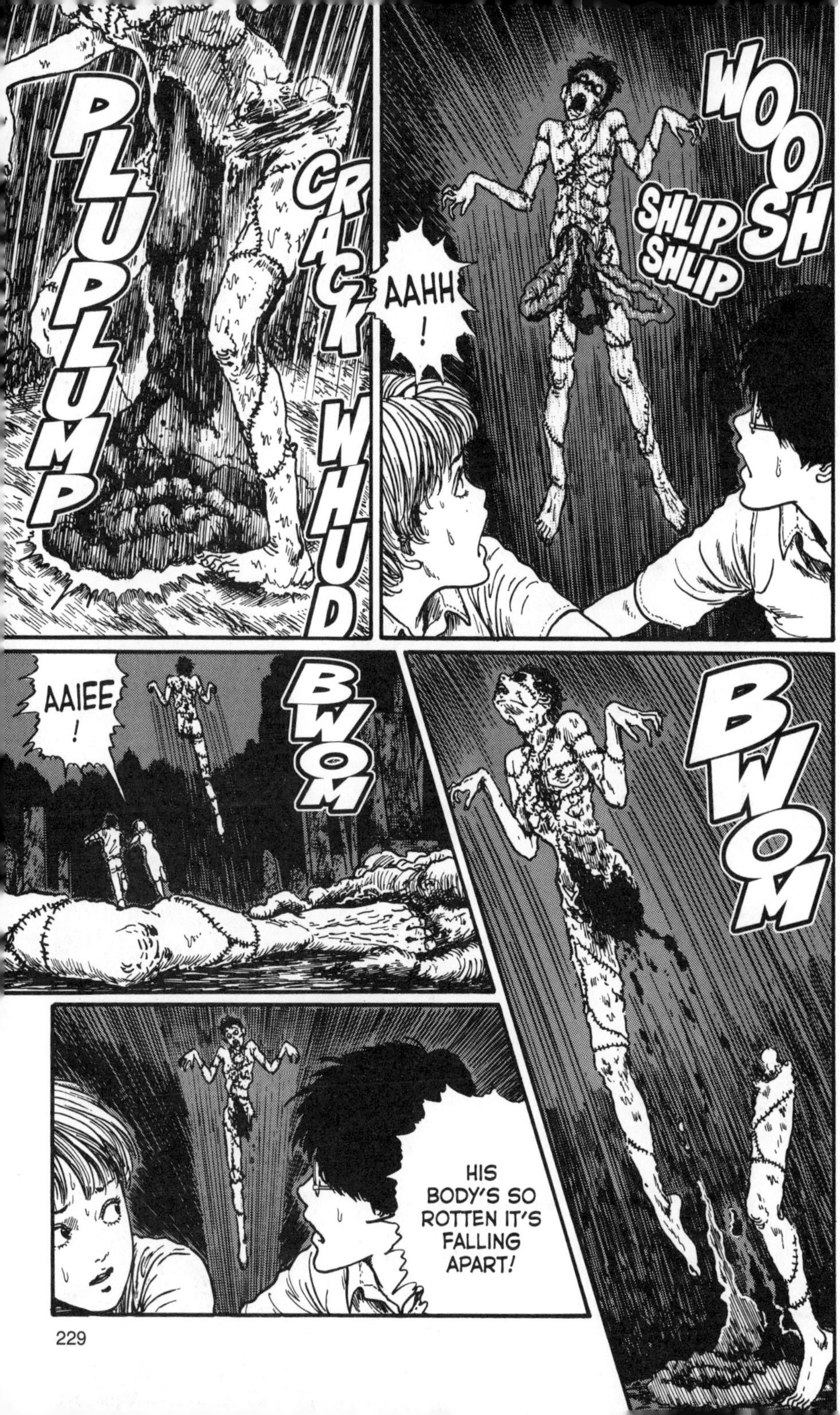
WOOSH
SHLIP SHLIP
AAHH!
CRACK
PLUPLUMP
WHUD
BWOM
AAIEE!
BWOM
HIS BODY'S SO ROTTEN IT'S FALLING APART!

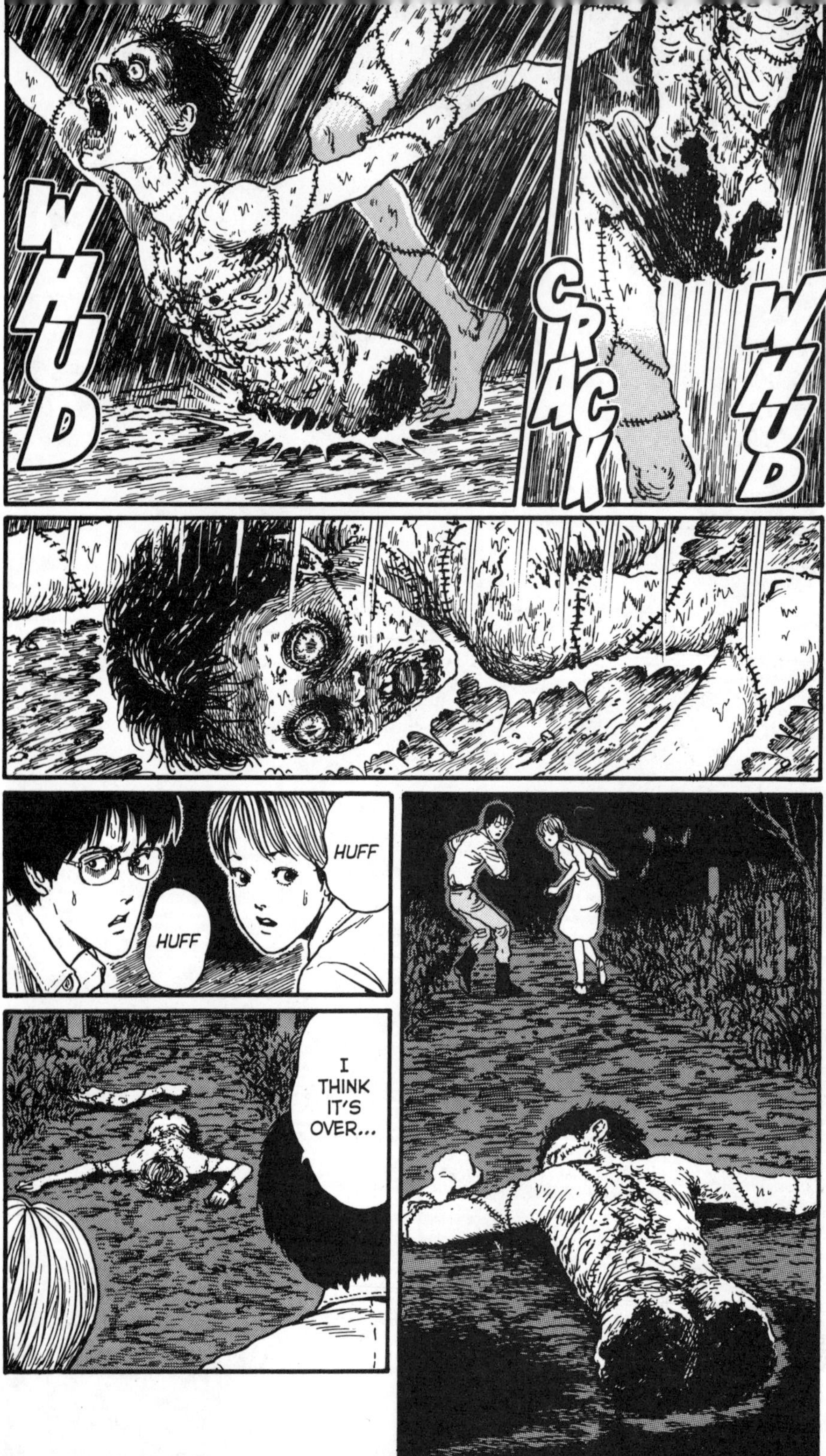
WHUD
CRACK
WHUD
HUFF
HUFF
I THINK IT'S OVER...

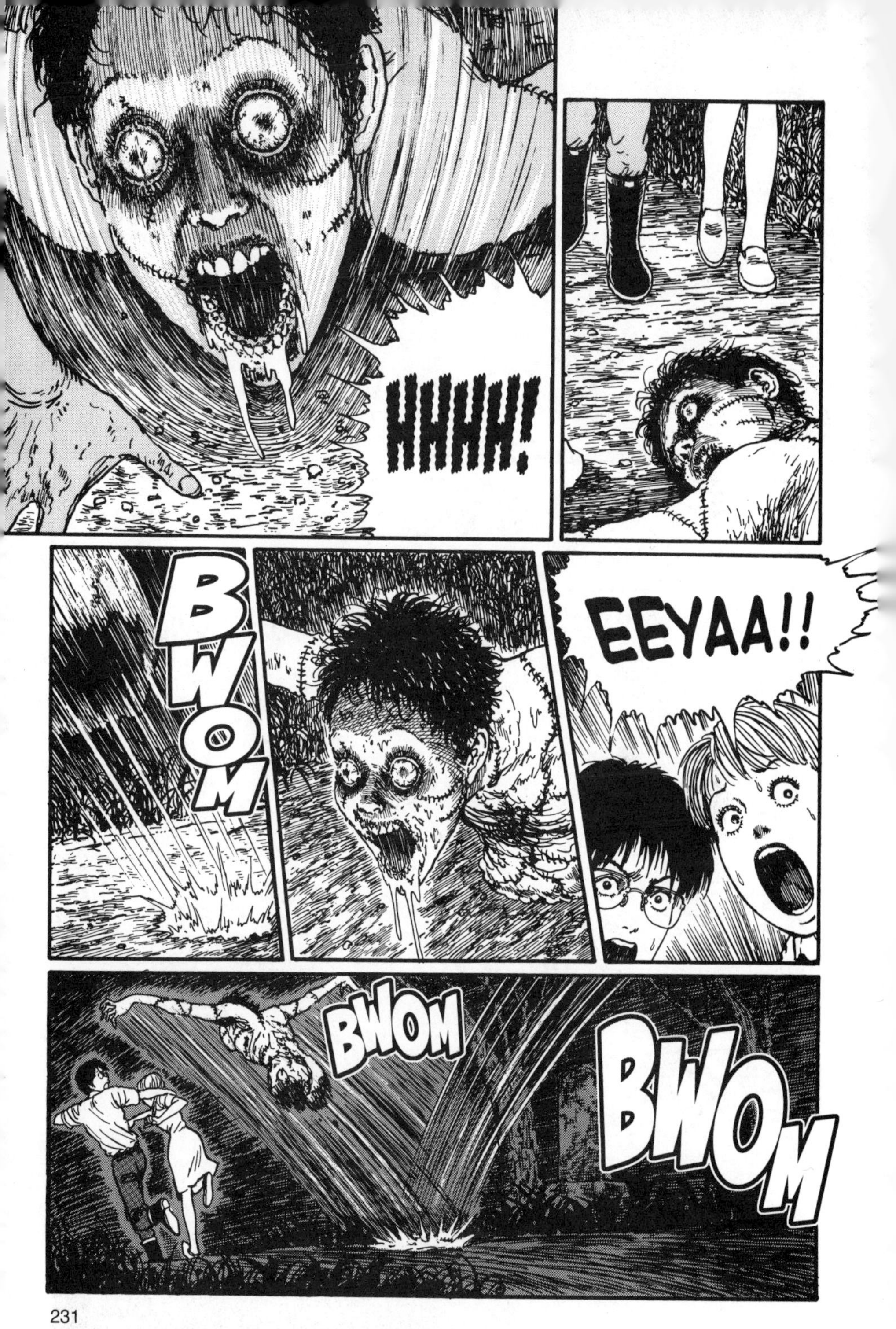
HHHH!
EEYAA!!
BWOM
BWOM
BWOM

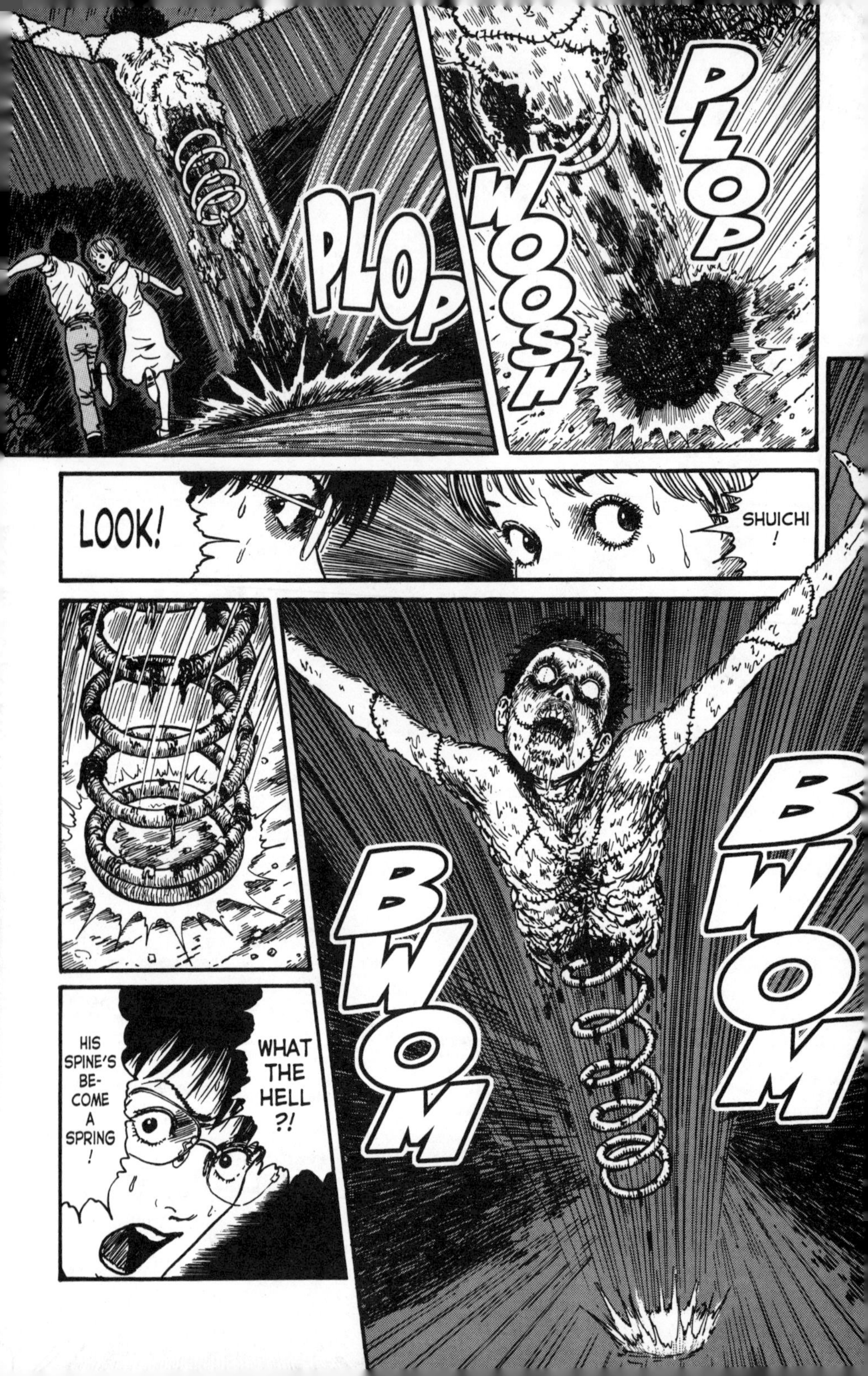
PLOP
WOOSH
PLOP
SHUICHI!
LOOK!
BWOM
BWOM
WHAT THE HELL?!
HIS SPINE'S BECOME A SPRING!

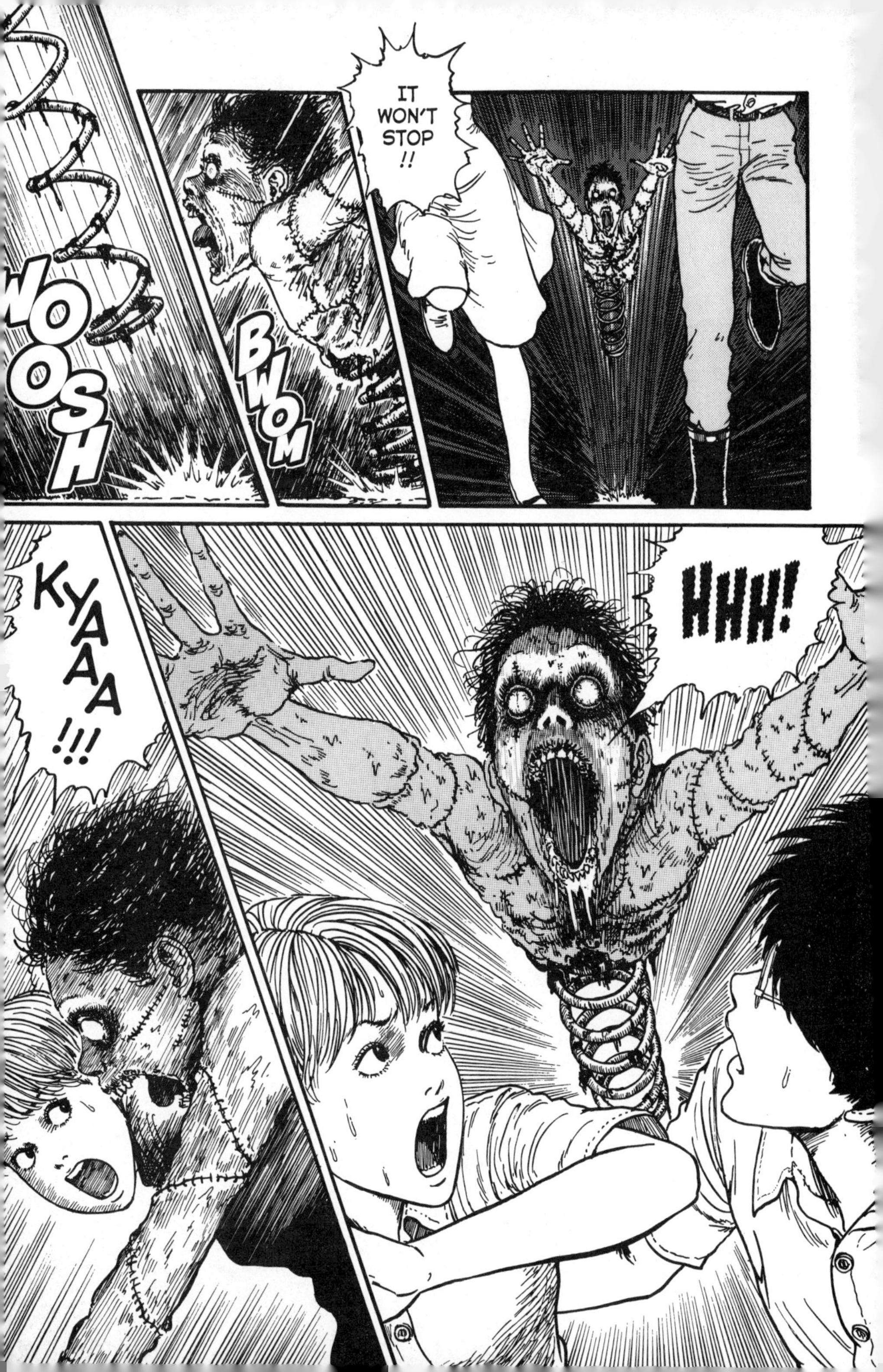
IT WON'T STOP !!
BWOM
WOOSH
HHH!
KYAAA !!!

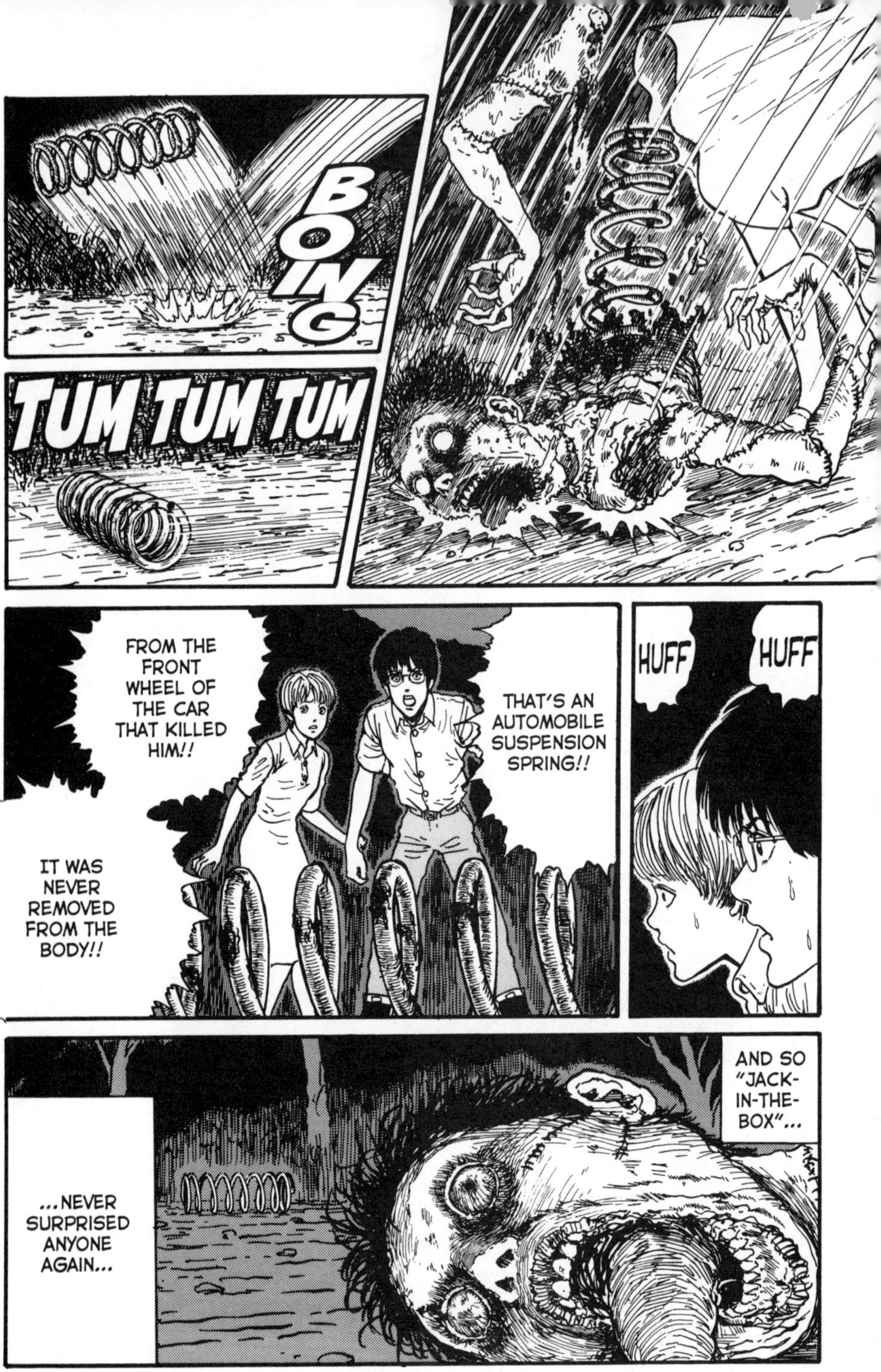
BOING
TUM TUM TUM
HUFF
HUFF
THAT'S AN AUTOMOBILE SUSPENSION SPRING!!
FROM THE FRONT WHEEL OF THE CAR THAT KILLED HIM!!
IT WAS NEVER REMOVED FROM THE BODY!!
AND SO "JACK-IN-THE-BOX"...
...NEVER SURPRISED ANYONE AGAIN...

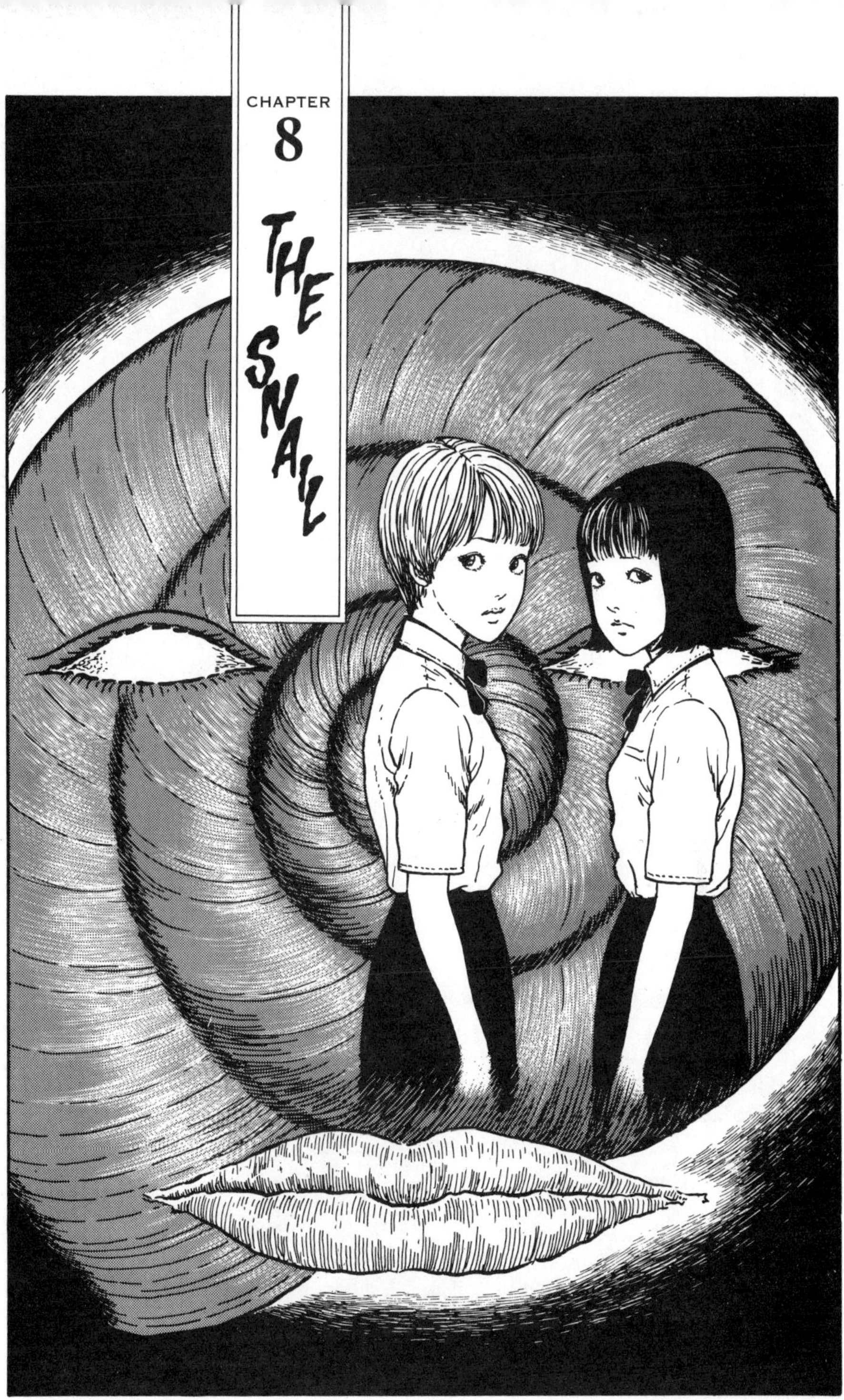
CHAPTER
8
THE SNAIL

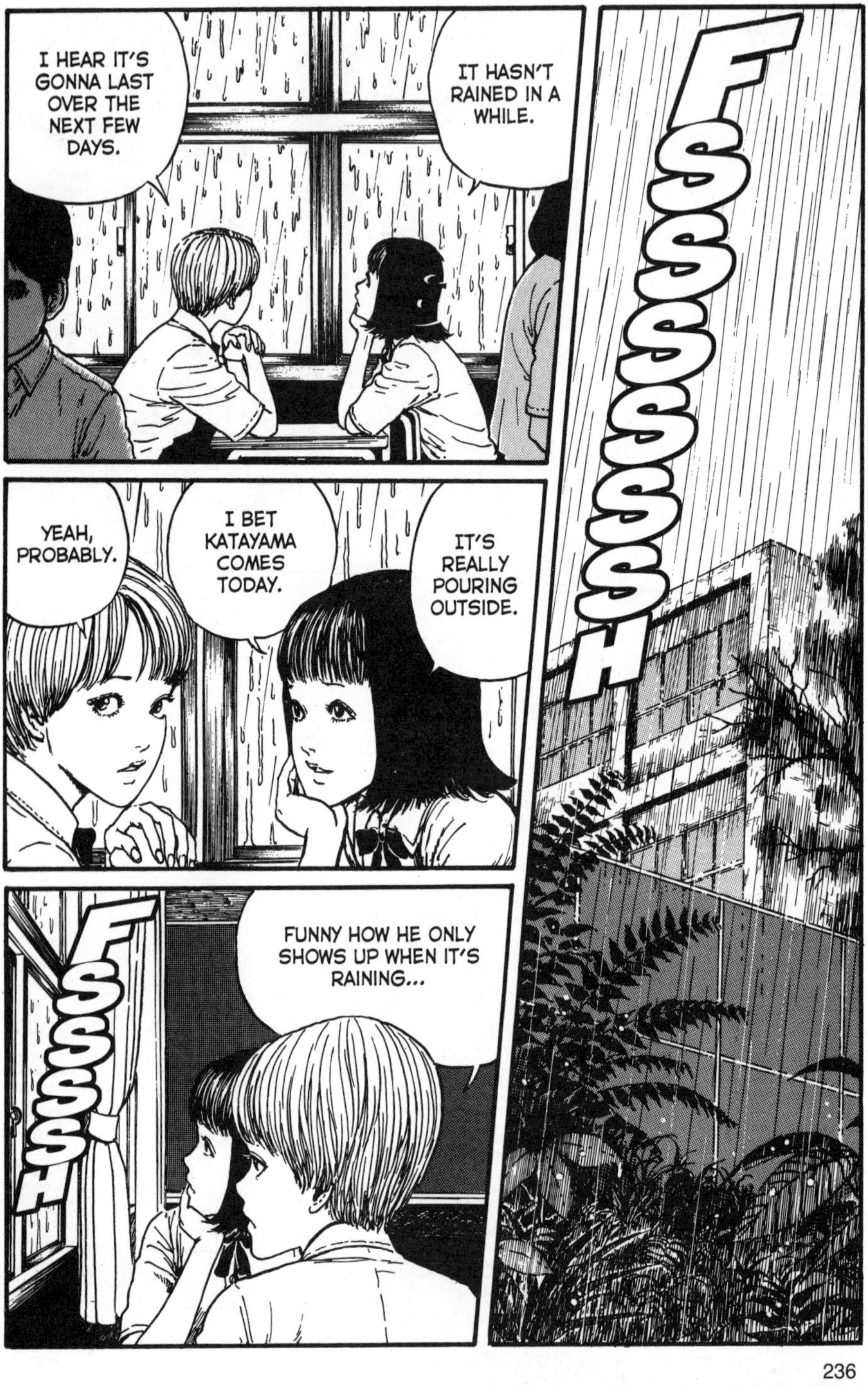

FSSSSSSSSH
IT HASN'T RAINED IN A WHILE.
I HEAR IT'S GONNA LAST OVER THE NEXT FEW DAYS.
IT'S REALLY POURING OUTSIDE.
I BET KATAYAMA COMES TODAY.
YEAH, PROBABLY.
FUNNY HOW HE ONLY SHOWS UP WHEN IT'S RAINING...
FSSSSH

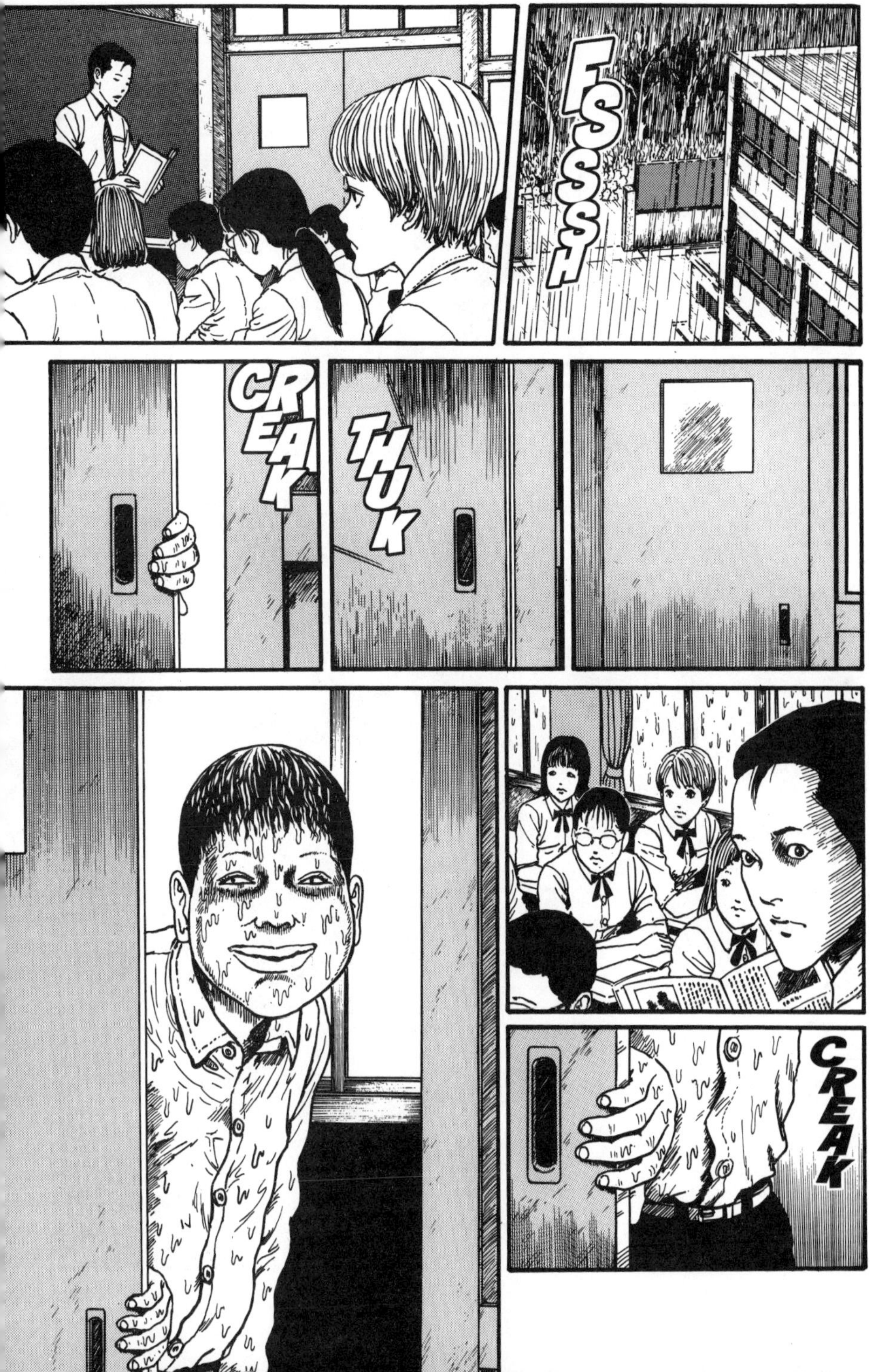
FSSSH
THUK
CREAK
CREAK

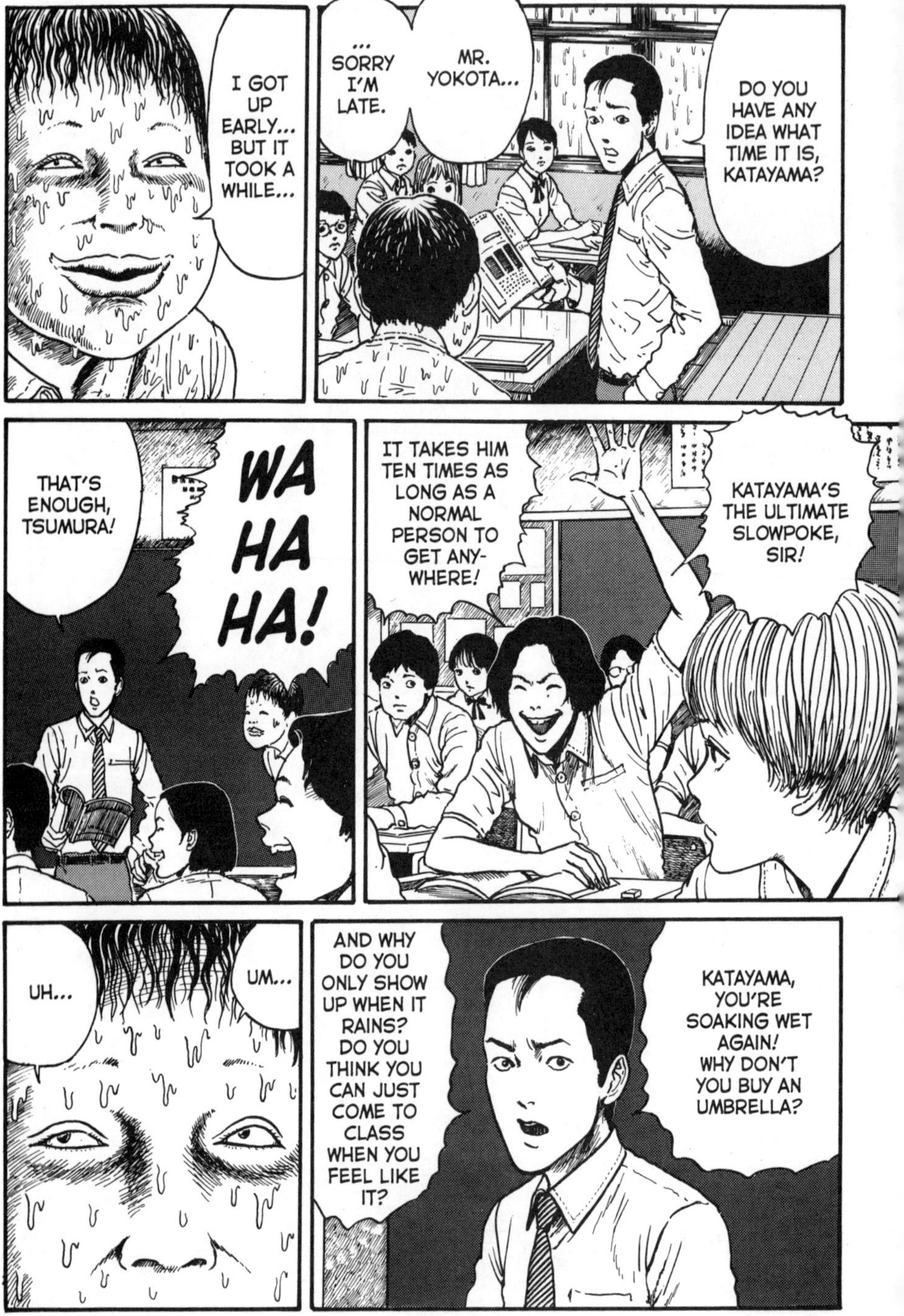
DO YOU HAVE ANY IDEA WHAT TIME IT IS, KATAYAMA?
MR. YOKOTA...
... SORRY I'M LATE.
I GOT UP EARLY... BUT IT TOOK A WHILE...
KATAYAMA'S THE ULTIMATE SLOWPOKE, SIR!
IT TAKES HIM TEN TIMES AS LONG AS A NORMAL PERSON TO GET ANY-WHERE!
WA HA HA HA!
THAT'S ENOUGH, TSUMURA!
KATAYAMA, YOU'RE SOAKING WET AGAIN! WHY DON'T YOU BUY AN UMBRELLA?
AND WHY DO YOU ONLY SHOW UP WHEN IT RAINS? DO YOU THINK YOU CAN JUST COME TO CLASS WHEN YOU FEEL LIKE IT?
UM...
UH...

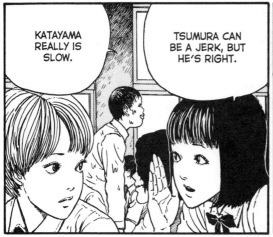

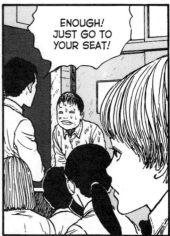

ENOUGH! JUST GO TO YOUR SEAT!
TSUMURA CAN BE A JERK, BUT HE'S RIGHT.
KATAYAMA REALLY IS SLOW.
FSSSSH
DING
DONG
HEY! FOURTH PERIOD GYM!
WE'RE PLAYING VOLLEY-BALL!
RIGHT ON!
SWAK

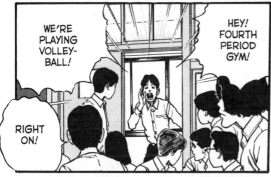

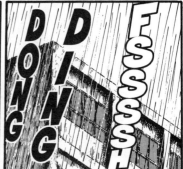

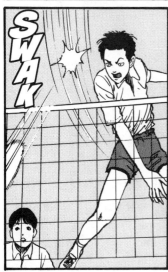

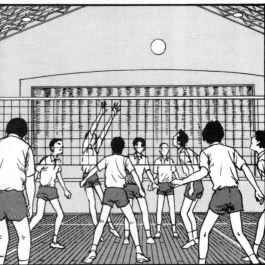

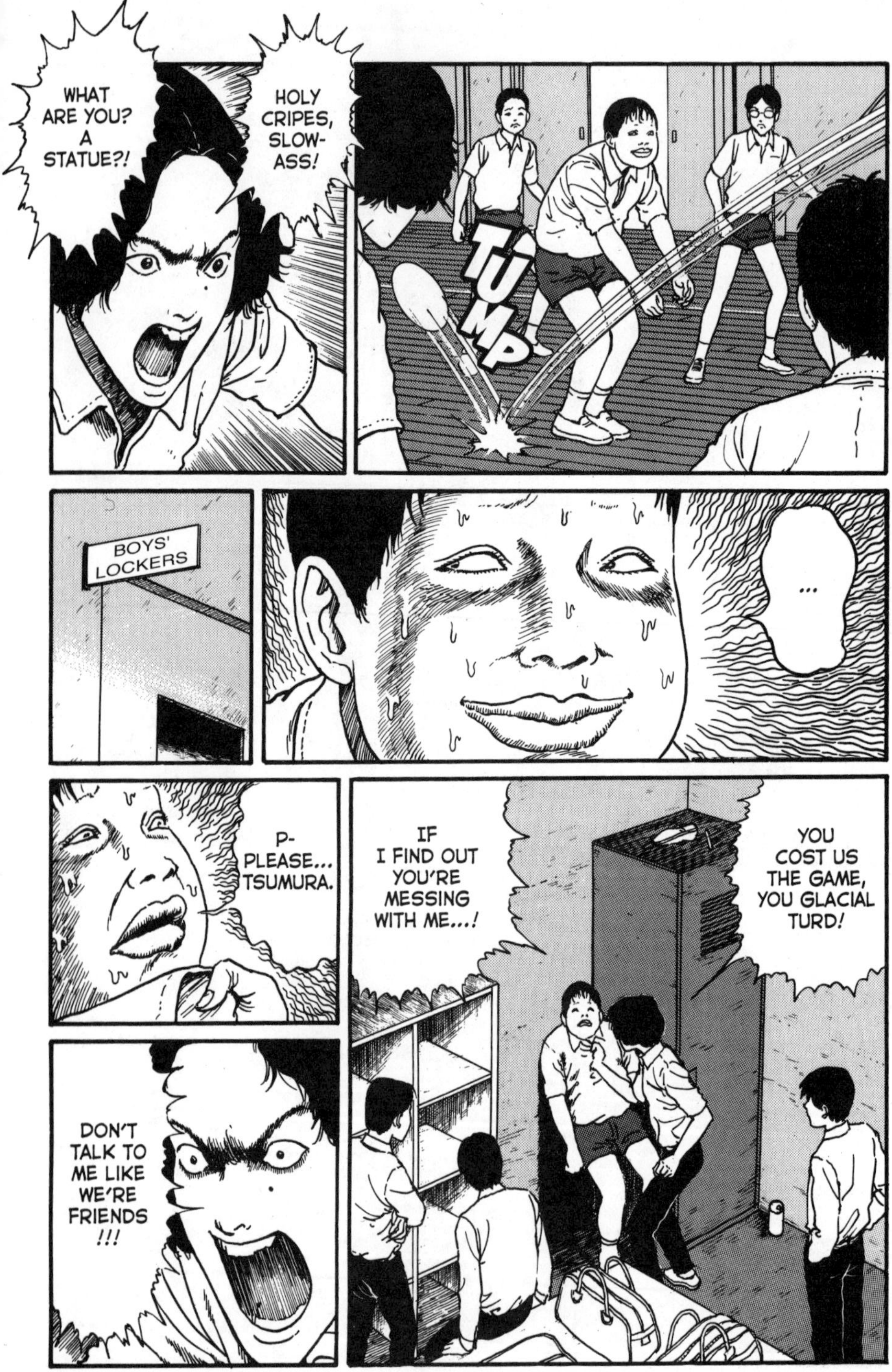
HOLY CRIPES, SLOW-ASS!
TUMP
WHAT ARE YOU? A STATUE?!
...
BOYS' LOCKERS
YOU COST US THE GAME, YOU GLACIAL TURD!
IF I FIND OUT YOU'RE MESSING WITH ME...!
P-PLEASE... TSUMURA.
DON'T TALK TO ME LIKE WE'RE FRIENDS!!!

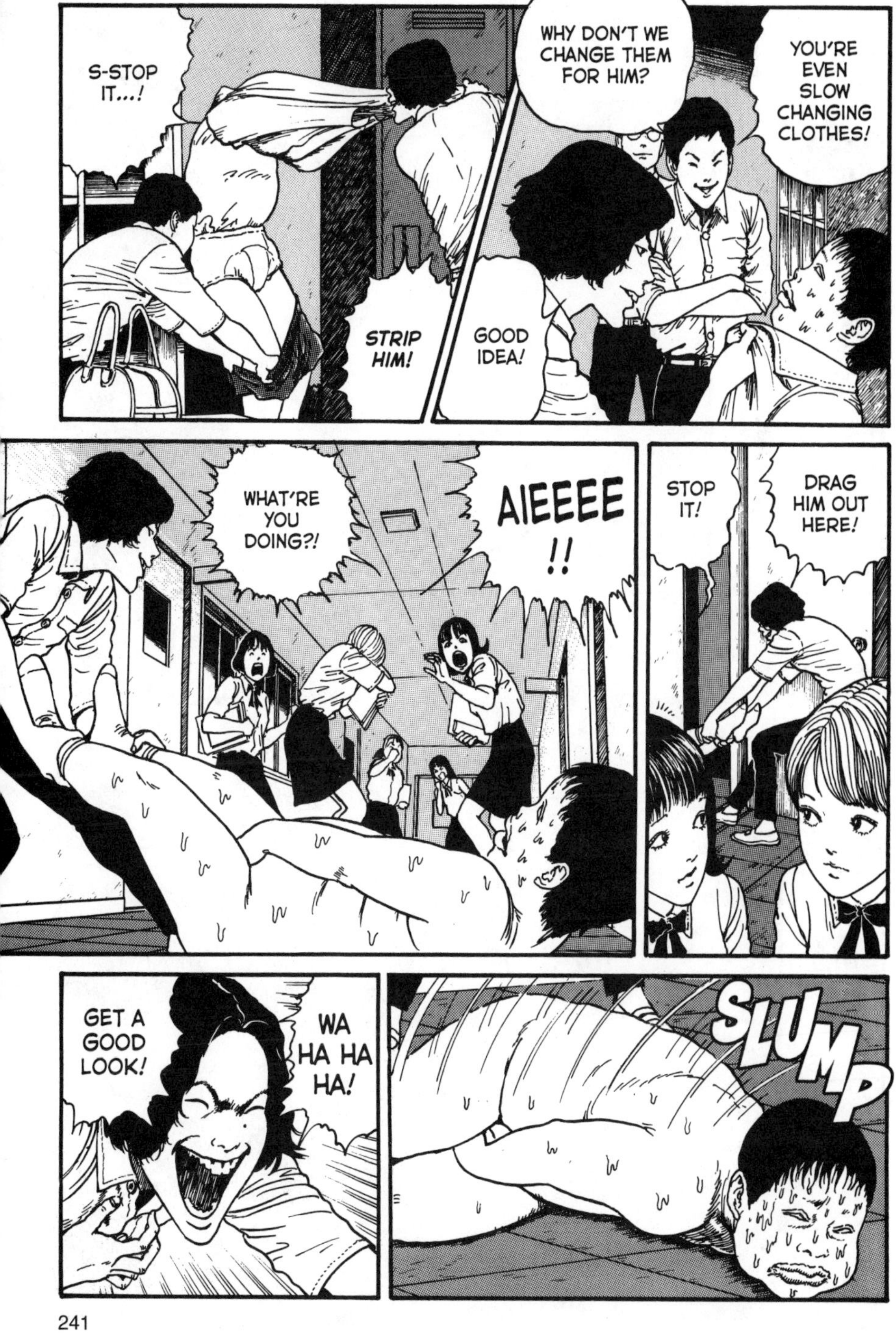
YOU'RE EVEN SLOW CHANGING CLOTHES!
WHY DON'T WE CHANGE THEM FOR HIM?
GOOD IDEA!
STRIP HIM!
S-STOP IT...!
DRAG HIM OUT HERE!
STOP IT!
AIEEEE !!
WHAT'RE YOU DOING?!
SLUMP
WA HA HA HA!
GET A GOOD LOOK!

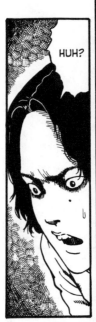

HUH?
AN OMI-NOUS SPIRAL ...
... SHINED ON KATA-YAMA'S BACK.
SLUFF
SLUFF
SLUFF

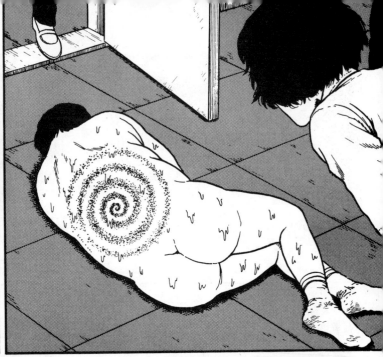

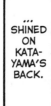

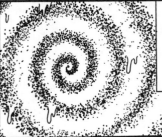

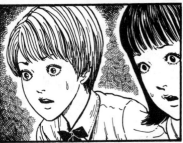

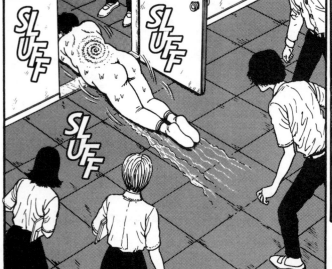

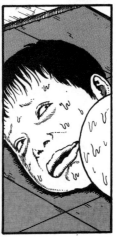

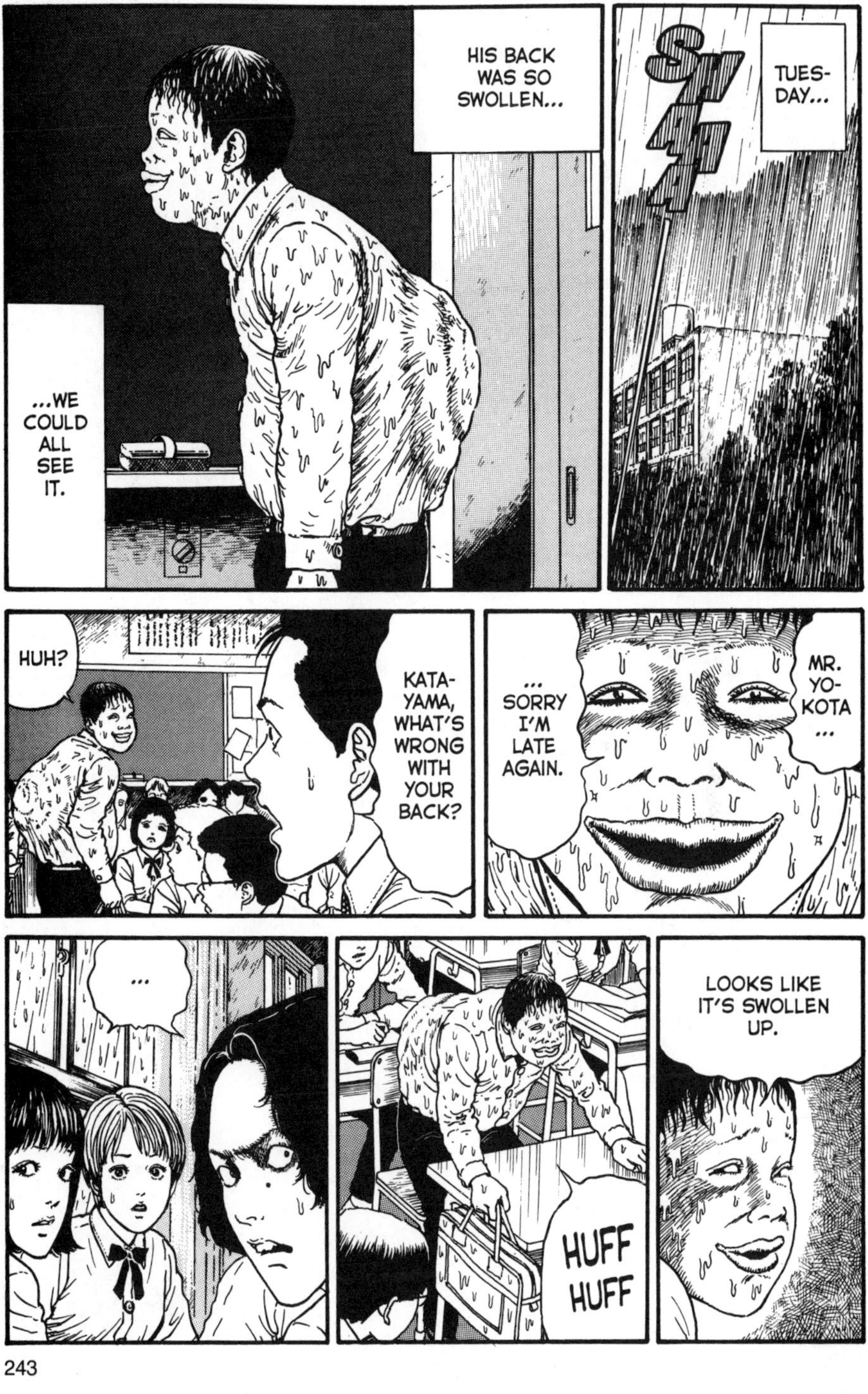
TUES-DAY...
HIS BACK WAS SO SWOLLEN...
...WE COULD ALL SEE IT.
MR. YO-KOTA ...
... SORRY I'M LATE AGAIN.
KATA-YAMA, WHAT'S WRONG WITH YOUR BACK?
HUH?
LOOKS LIKE IT'S SWOLLEN UP.
HUFF HUFF
...

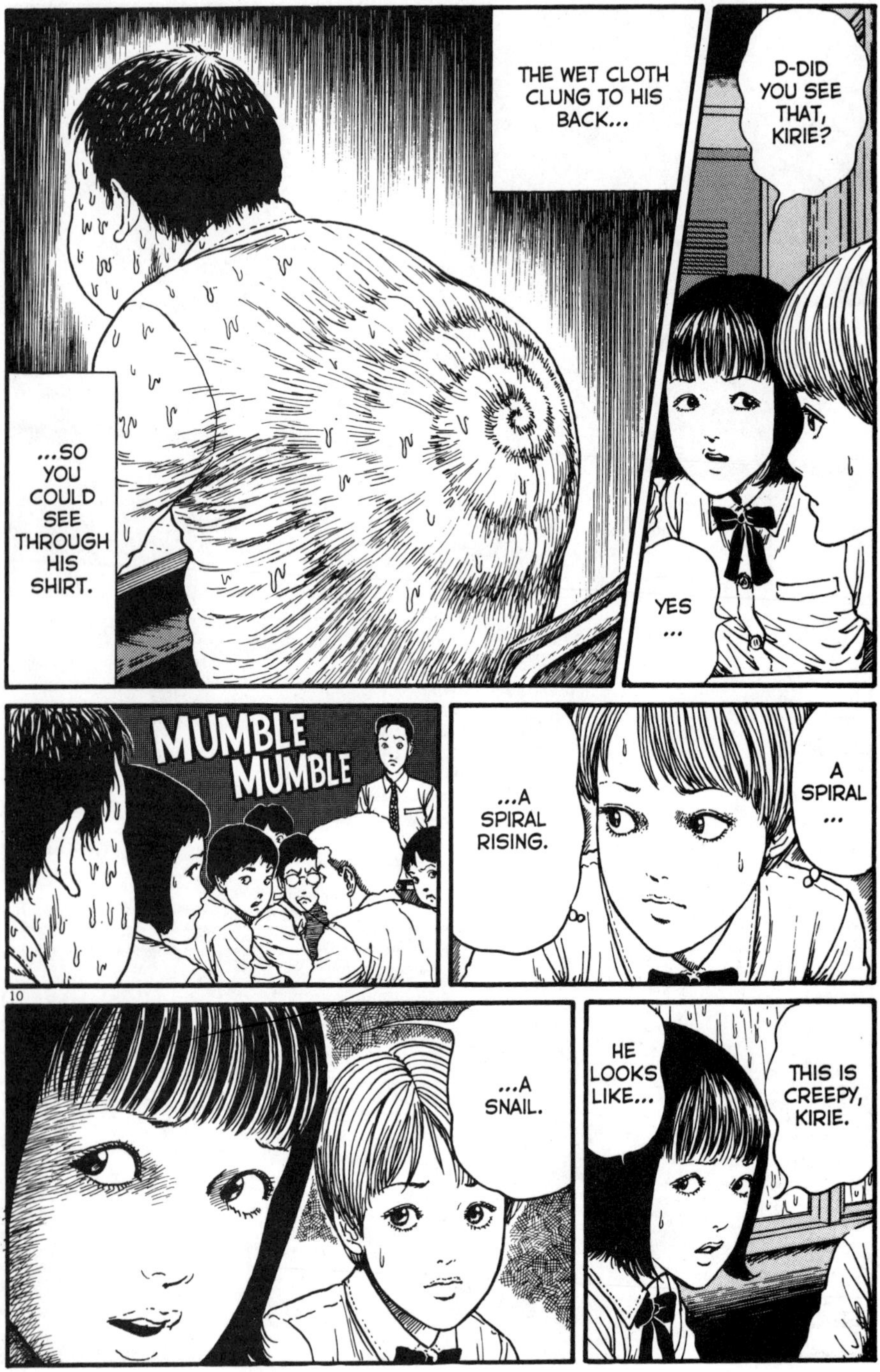
D-DID YOU SEE THAT, KIRIE?
YES ...
THE WET CLOTH CLUNG TO HIS BACK...
...SO YOU COULD SEE THROUGH HIS SHIRT.
A SPIRAL ...
...A SPIRAL RISING.
MUMBLE MUMBLE
THIS IS CREEPY, KIRIE.
HE LOOKS LIKE...
...A SNAIL.

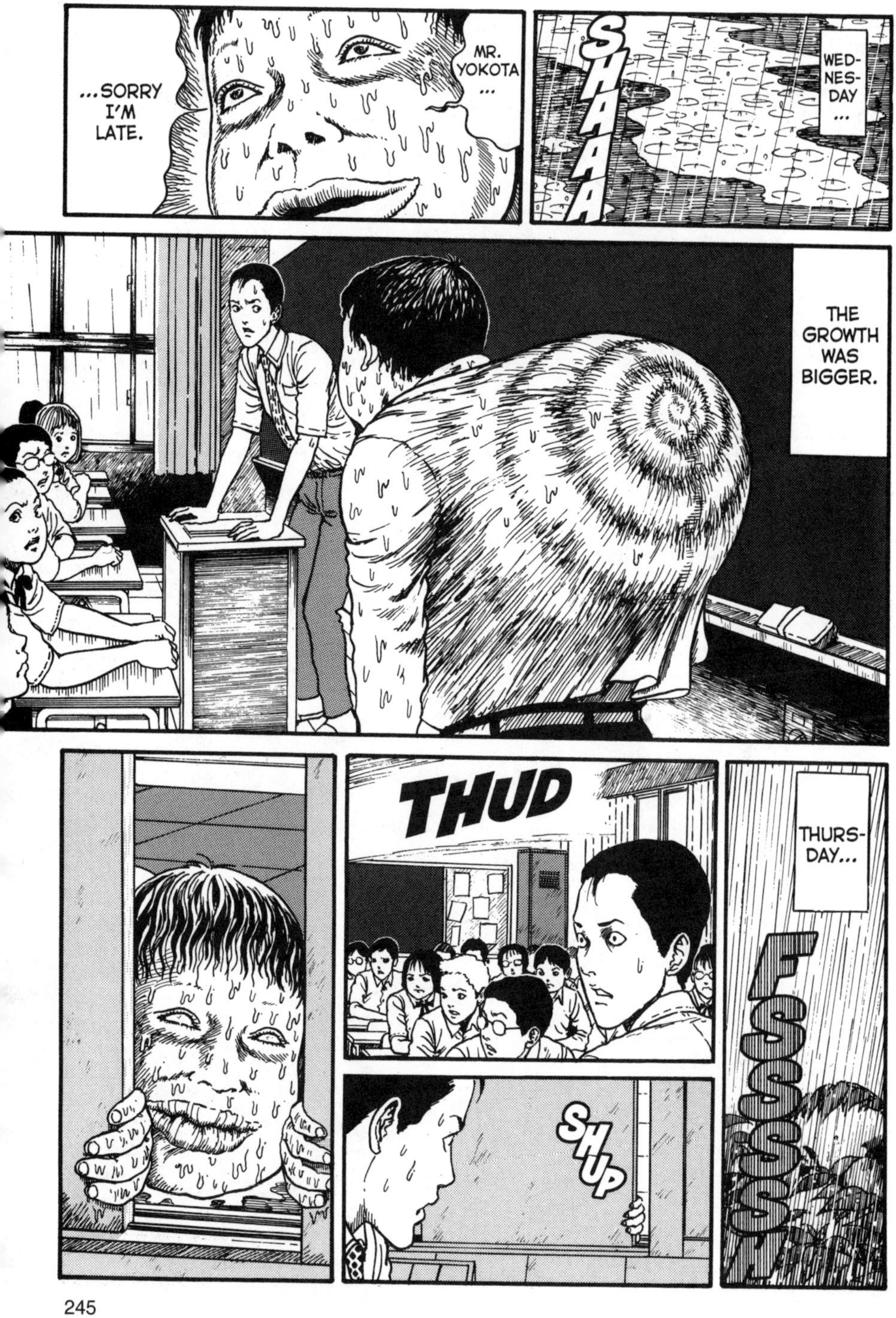
WEDNESDAY...
SHAAAA
MR. YOKOTA...
...SORRY I'M LATE.
THE GROWTH WAS BIGGER.
THURSDAY...
FSSSSS
THUD
SHUP

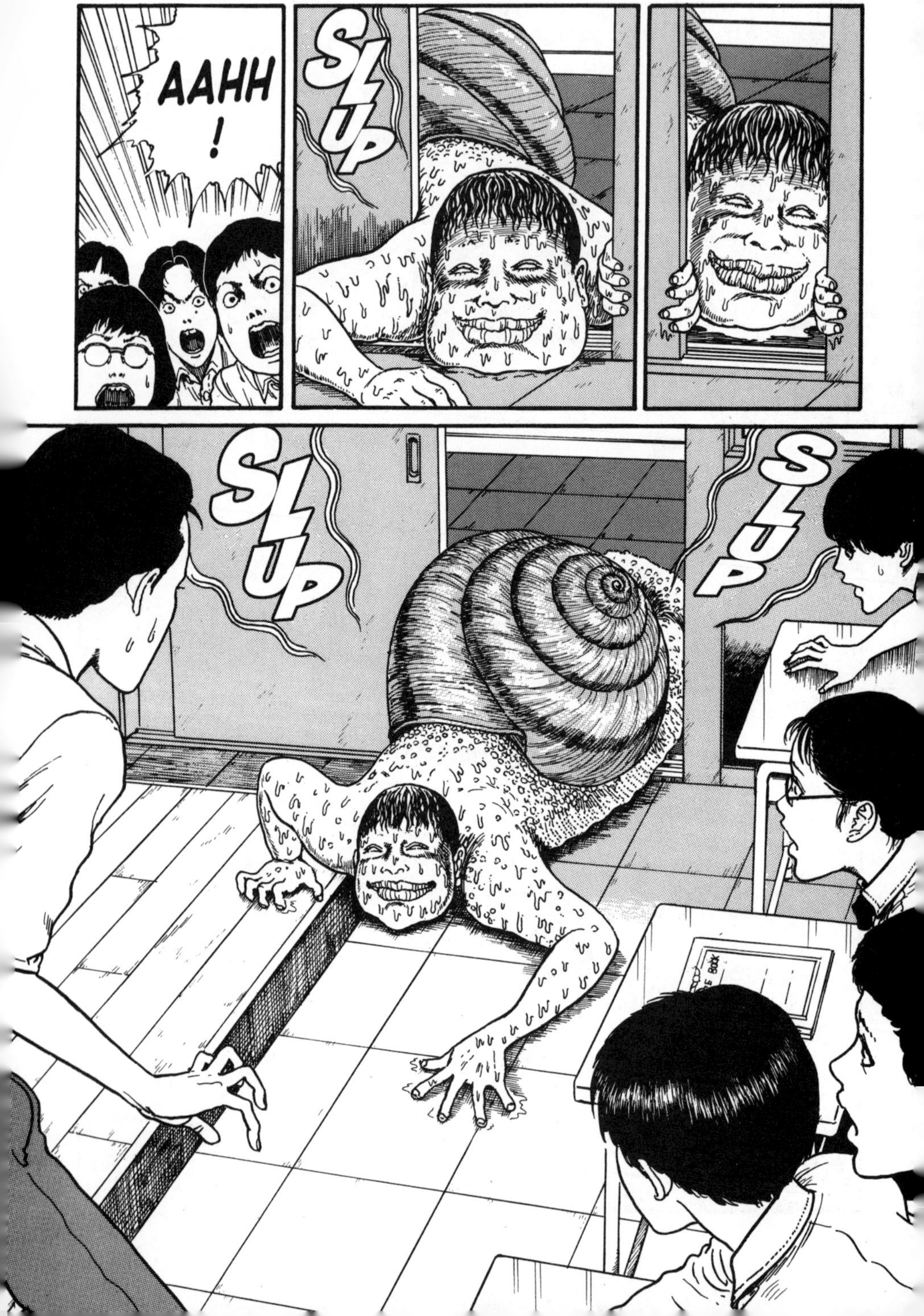
SLUP
AAHH!
SLUP
SLUP

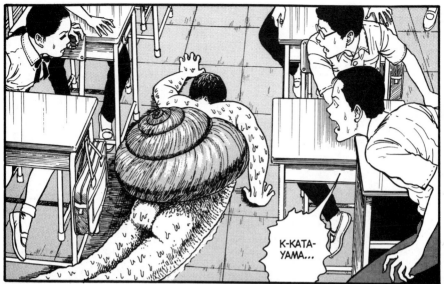

K-KATA-YAMA...

AIEE!!

ARGH!!

SLUP

SLUP

SLUP

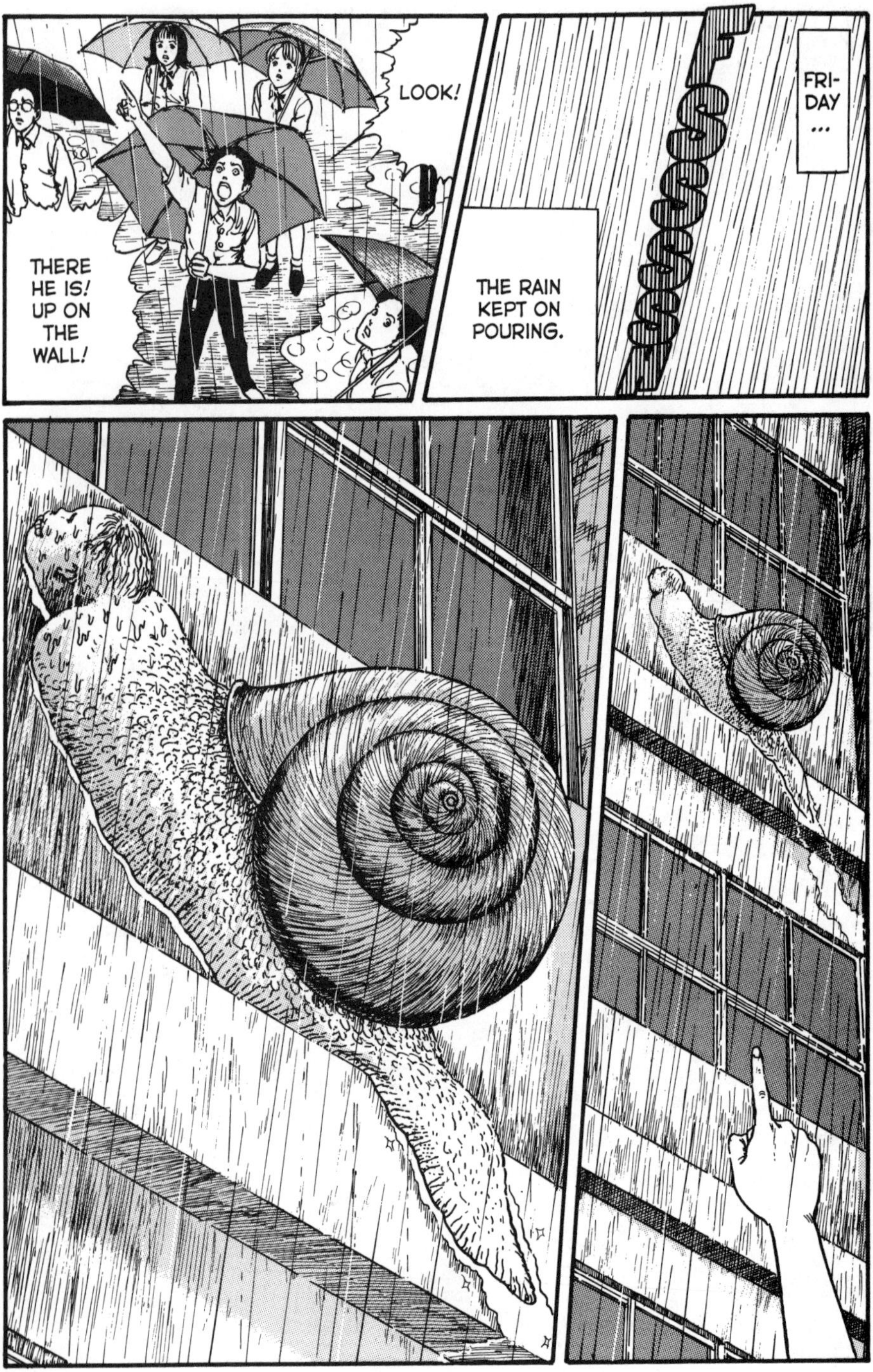

FRI-DAY...
THE RAIN KEPT ON POURING.
LOOK!
THERE HE IS! UP ON THE WALL!

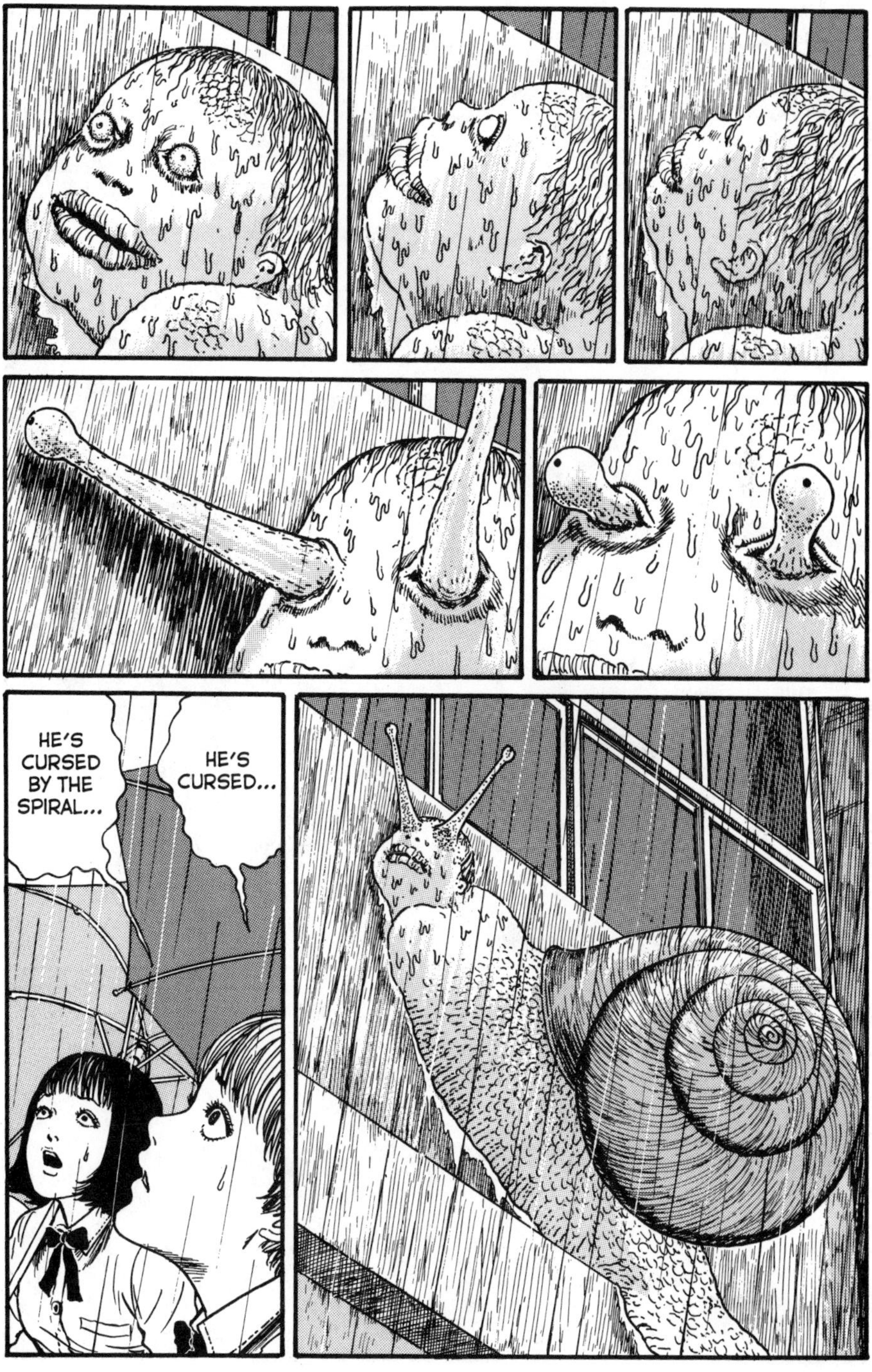
HE'S CURSED...
HE'S CURSED BY THE SPIRAL...

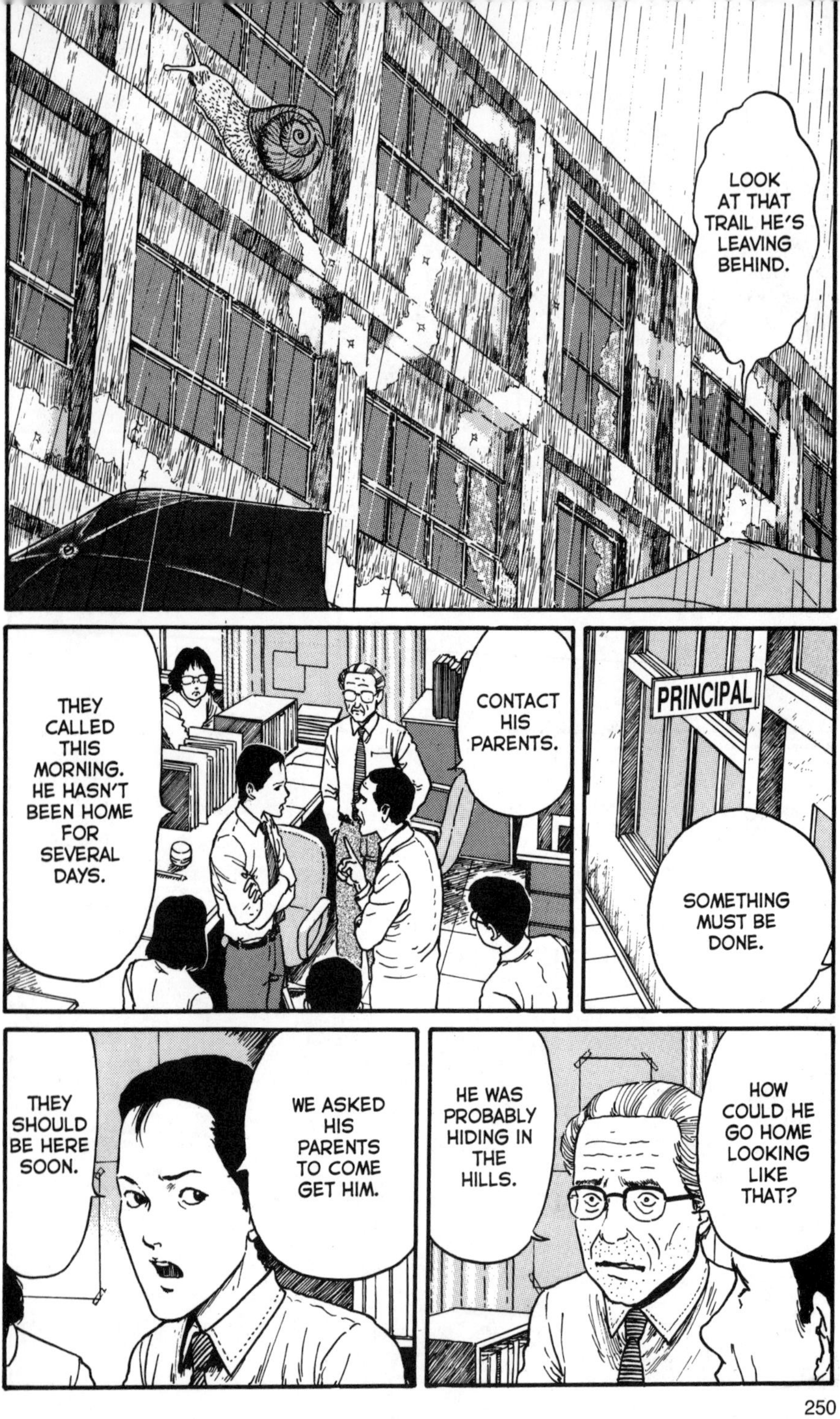
LOOK AT THAT TRAIL HE'S LEAVING BEHIND.
PRINCIPAL
SOMETHING MUST BE DONE.
CONTACT HIS PARENTS.
THEY CALLED THIS MORNING. HE HASN'T BEEN HOME FOR SEVERAL DAYS.
HOW COULD HE GO HOME LOOKING LIKE THAT?
HE WAS PROBABLY HIDING IN THE HILLS.
WE ASKED HIS PARENTS TO COME GET HIM.
THEY SHOULD BE HERE SOON.

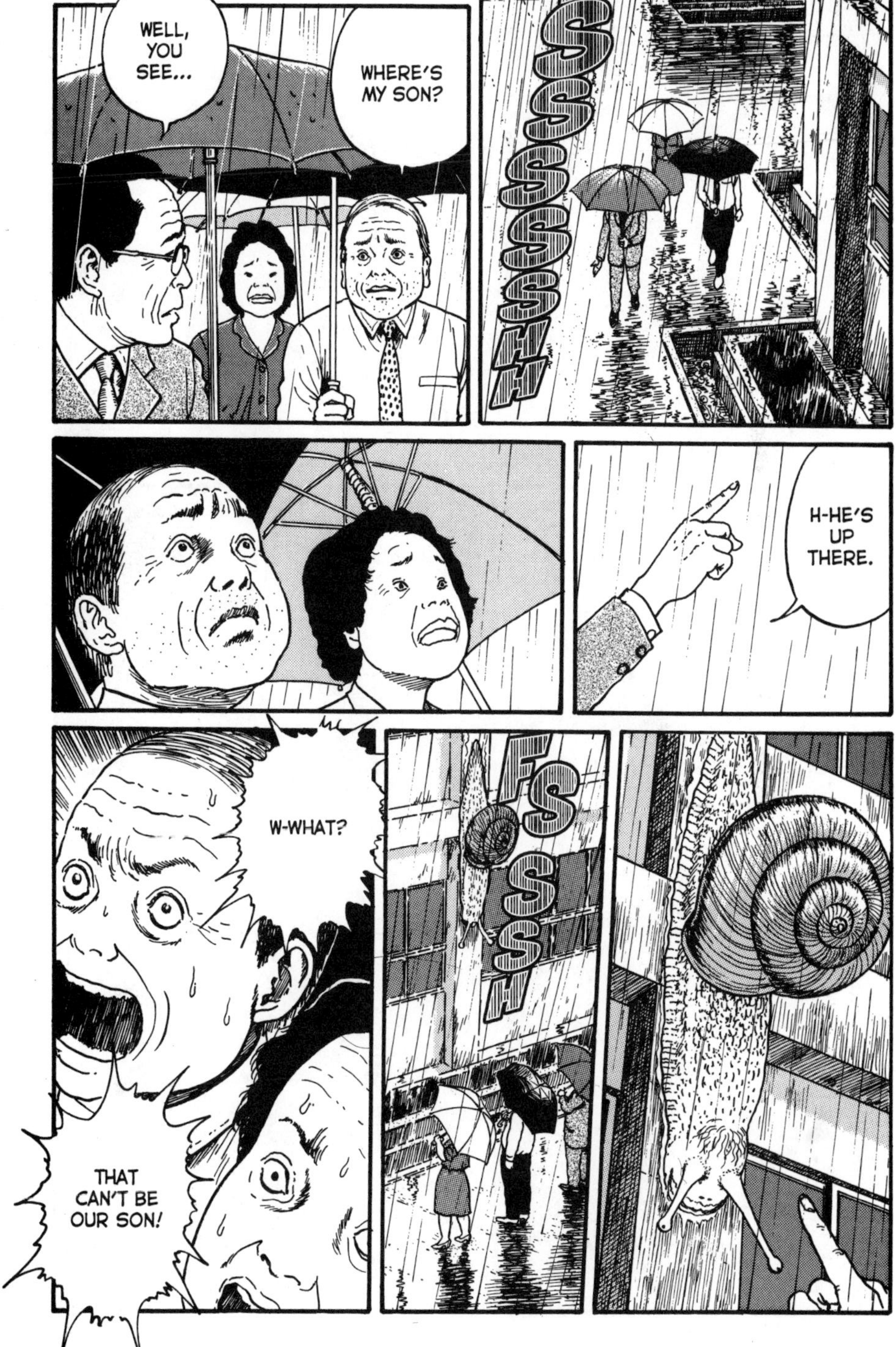
FSSSSSHH
WHERE'S MY SON?
WELL, YOU SEE...
H-HE'S UP THERE.
FSSSH
W-WHAT?
THAT CAN'T BE OUR SON!

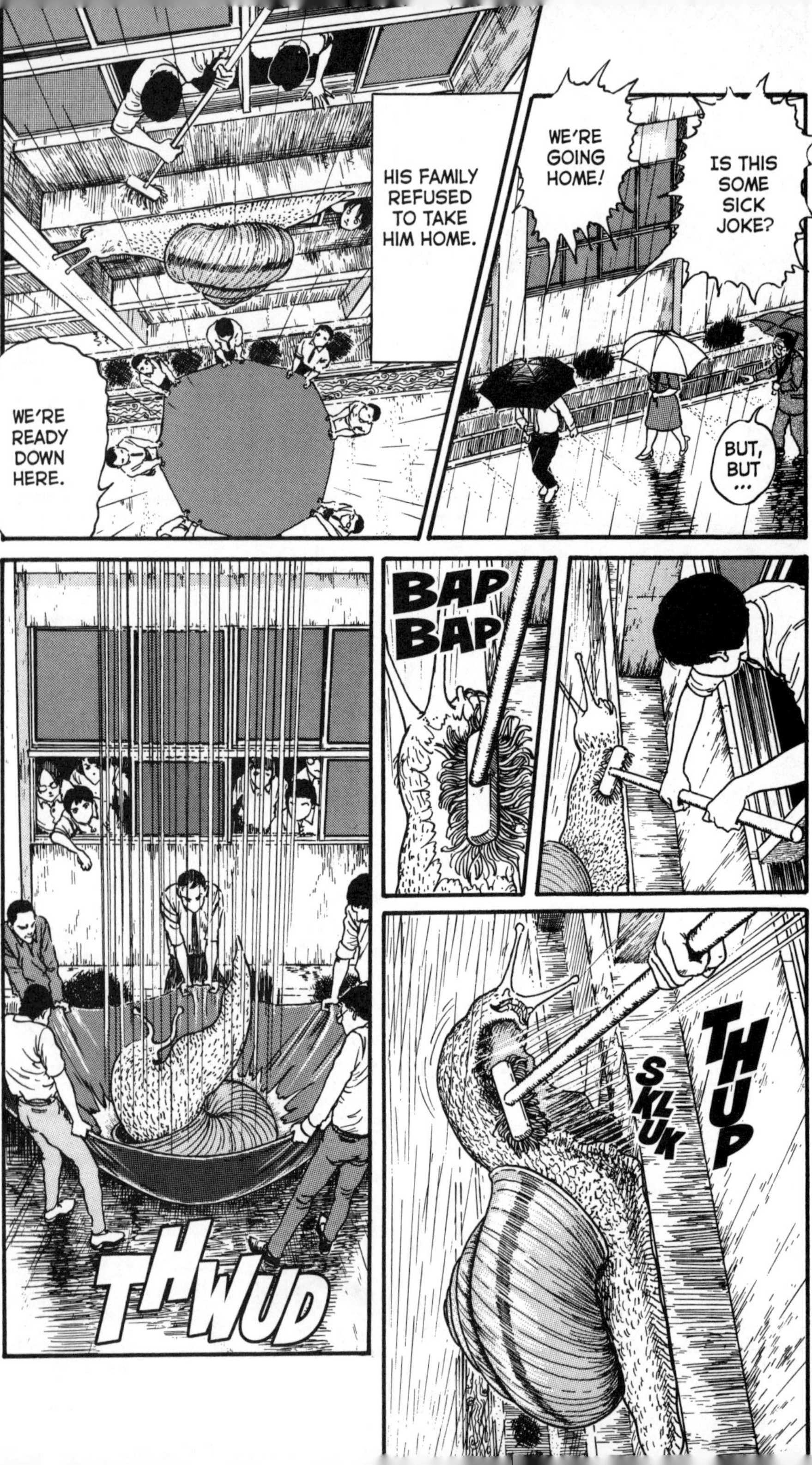
WE'RE GOING HOME!
IS THIS SOME SICK JOKE?
BUT, BUT ...
HIS FAMILY REFUSED TO TAKE HIM HOME.
WE'RE READY DOWN HERE.
BAP BAP
THUP
SKLUK
THWUD

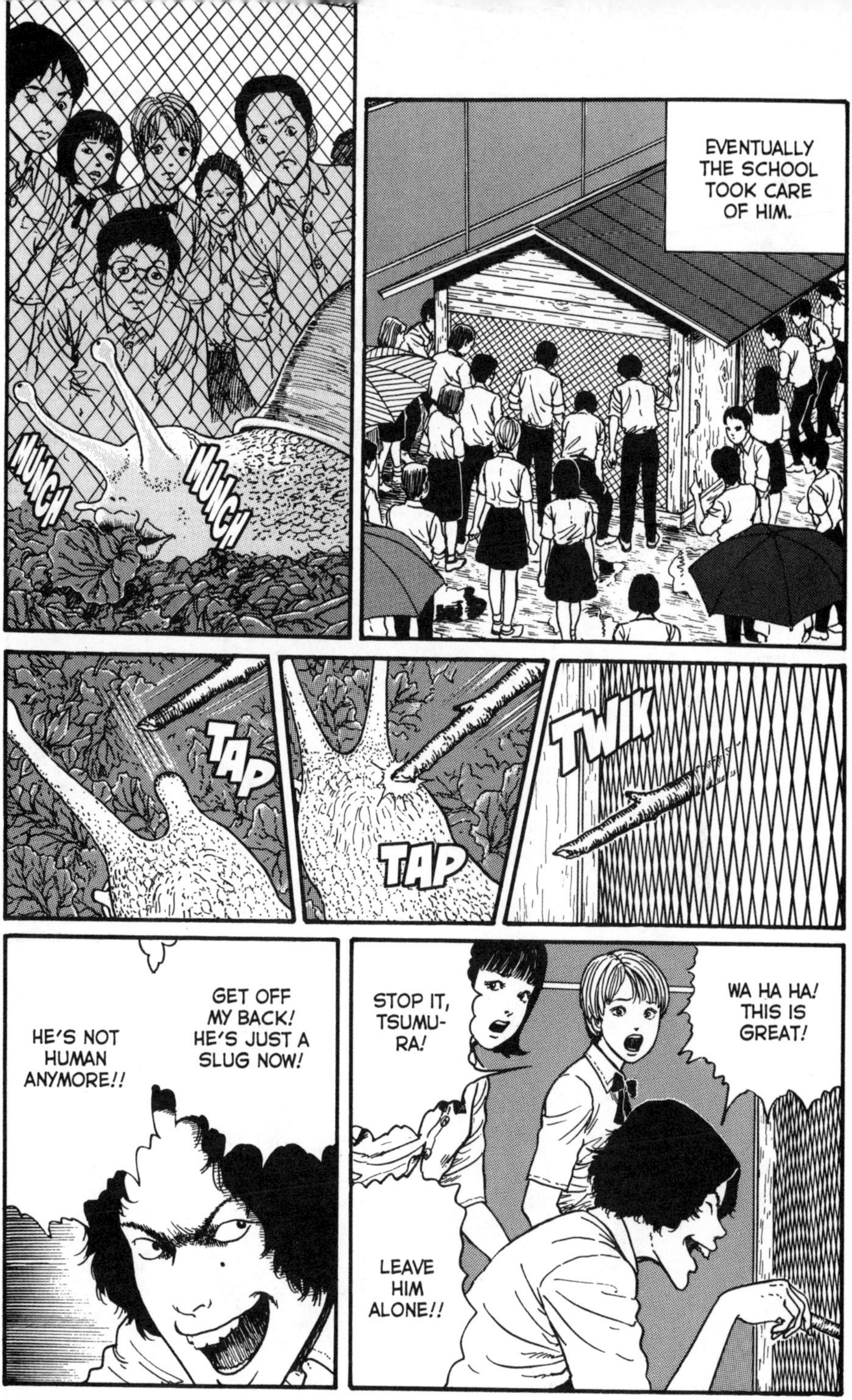
EVENTUALLY THE SCHOOL TOOK CARE OF HIM.
MUNCH
MUNCH
TWIK
TAP
TAP
WA HA HA! THIS IS GREAT!
STOP IT, TSUMU-RA!
LEAVE HIM ALONE!!
GET OFF MY BACK! HE'S JUST A SLUG NOW!
HE'S NOT HUMAN ANYMORE!!

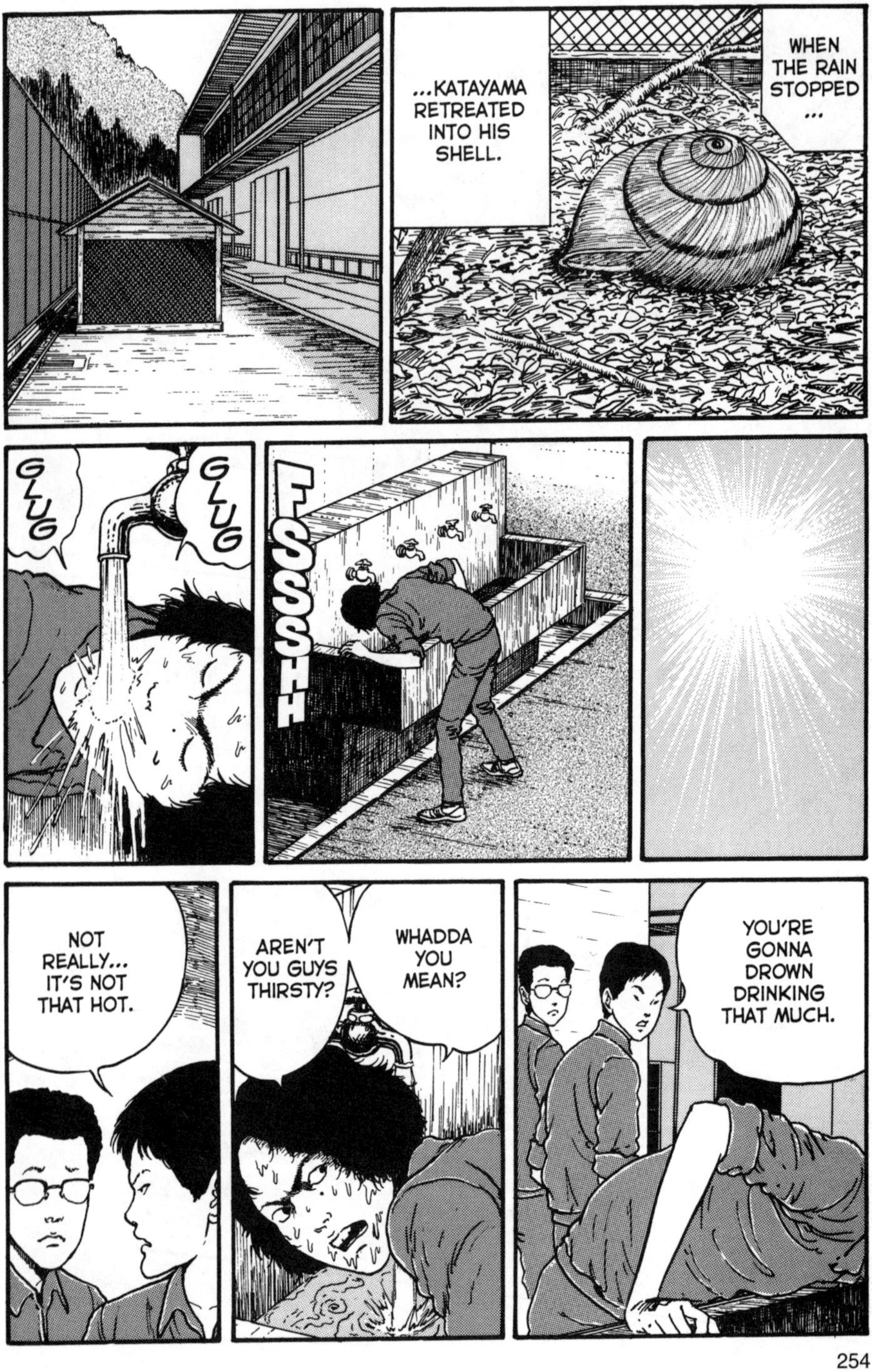
WHEN THE RAIN STOPPED ...
...KATAYAMA RETREATED INTO HIS SHELL.
FSSSHH
GLUG
GLUG
YOU'RE GONNA DROWN DRINKING THAT MUCH.
WHADDA YOU MEAN?
AREN'T YOU GUYS THIRSTY?
NOT REALLY... IT'S NOT THAT HOT.

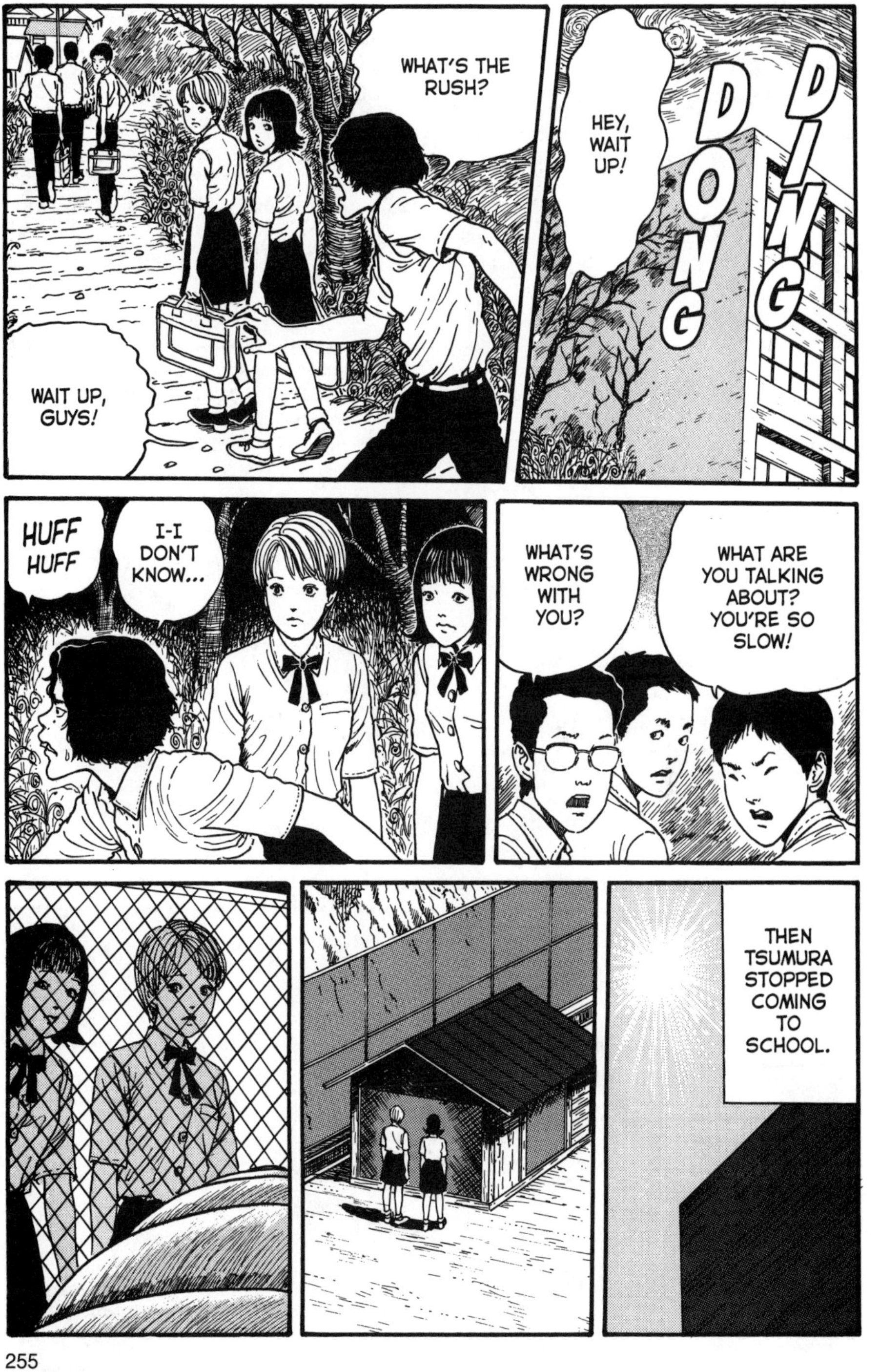
HEY, WAIT UP!
DING
DONG
WHAT'S THE RUSH?
WAIT UP, GUYS!
WHAT ARE YOU TALKING ABOUT? YOU'RE SO SLOW!
WHAT'S WRONG WITH YOU?
I-I DON'T KNOW...
HUFF HUFF
THEN TSUMURA STOPPED COMING TO SCHOOL.

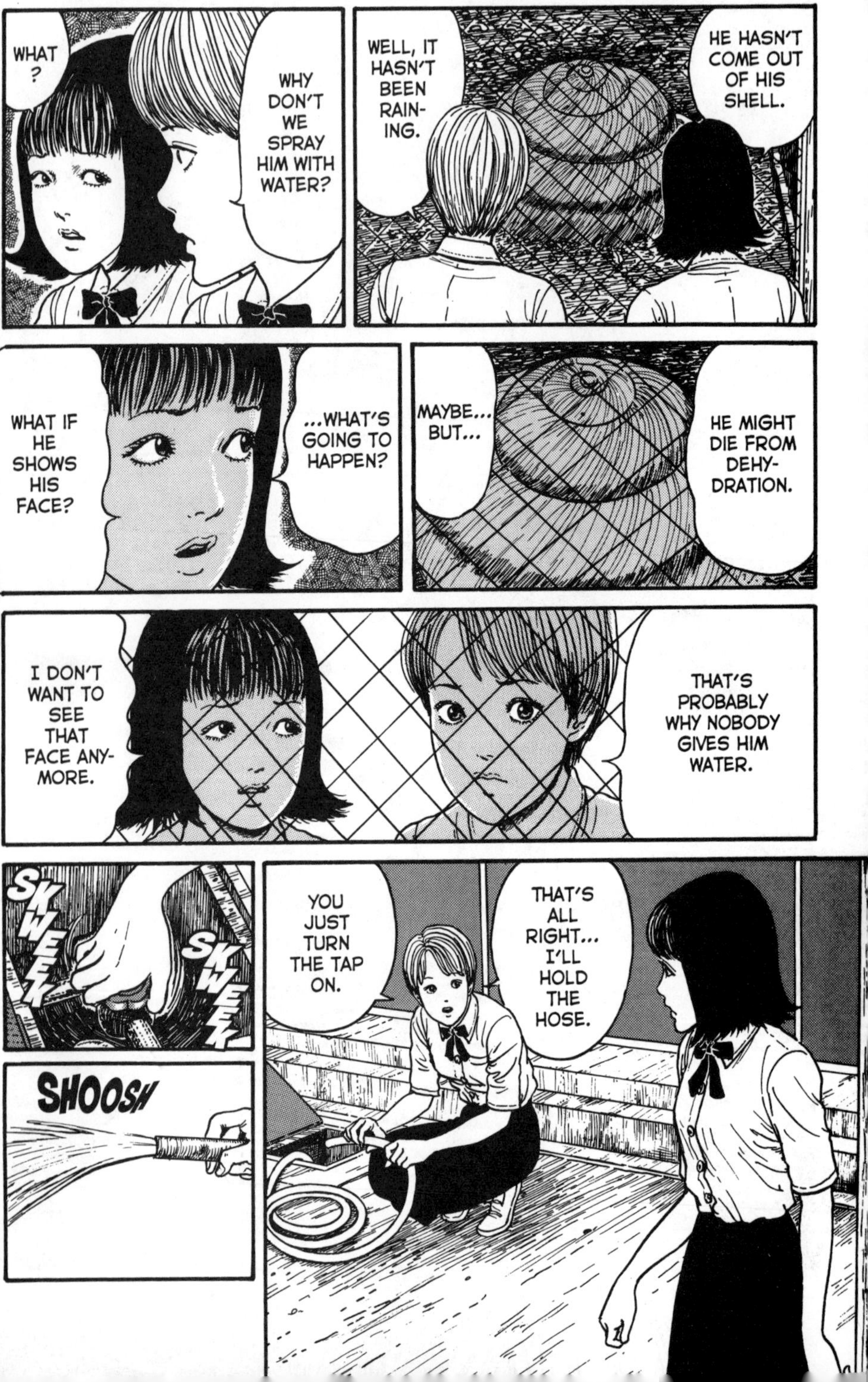
HE HASN'T COME OUT OF HIS SHELL.
WELL, IT HASN'T BEEN RAIN-ING.
WHY DON'T WE SPRAY HIM WITH WATER?
WHAT ?
HE MIGHT DIE FROM DEHY-DRATION.
MAYBE... BUT...
...WHAT'S GOING TO HAPPEN?
WHAT IF HE SHOWS HIS FACE?
THAT'S PROBABLY WHY NOBODY GIVES HIM WATER.
I DON'T WANT TO SEE THAT FACE ANY-MORE.
THAT'S ALL RIGHT... I'LL HOLD THE HOSE.
YOU JUST TURN THE TAP ON.
SKWEEK
SKWEEK
SHOOSH

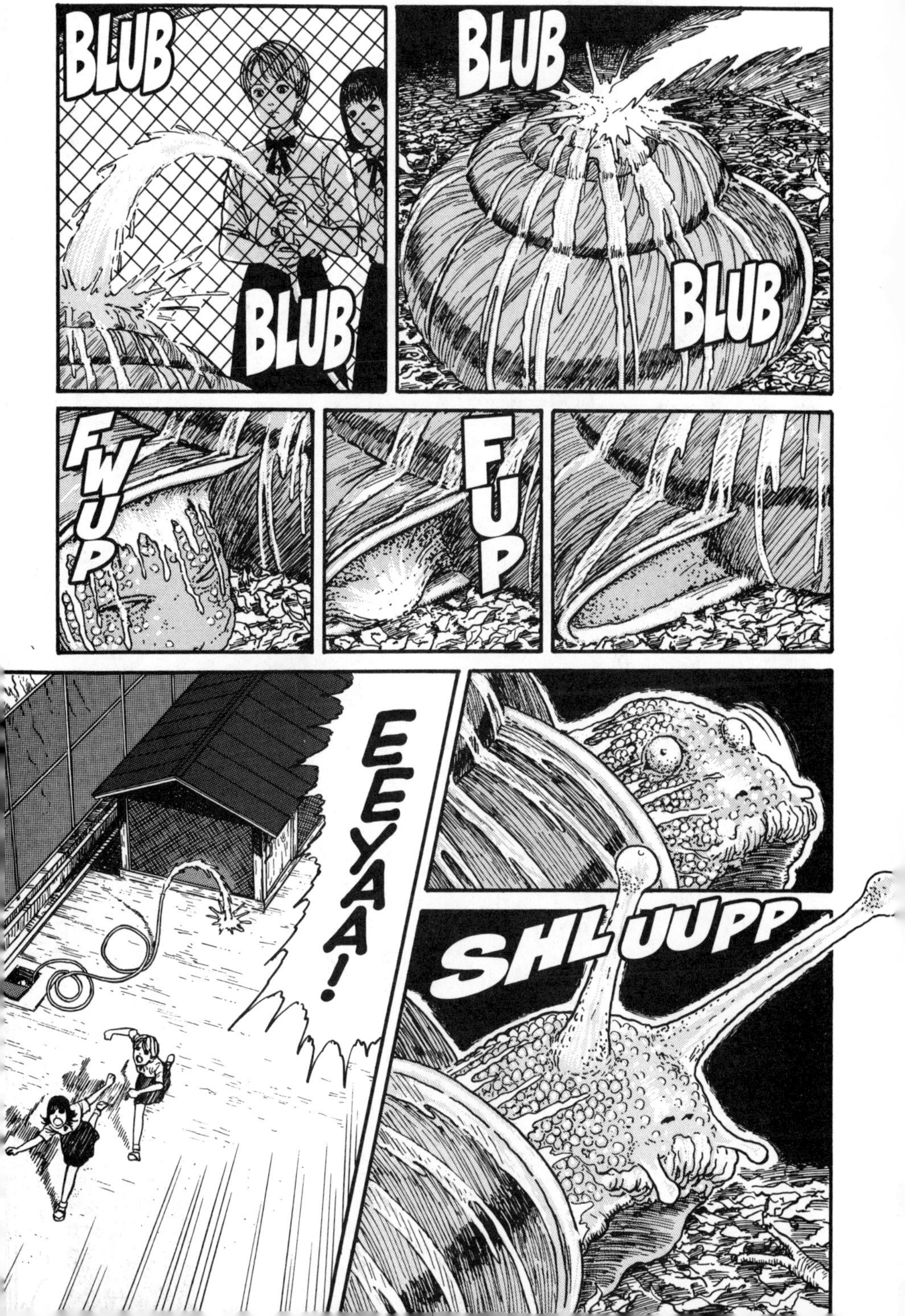
BLUB
BLUB
BLUB
BLUB
FUP
FWUP
SHLUUPP
EEYAA!

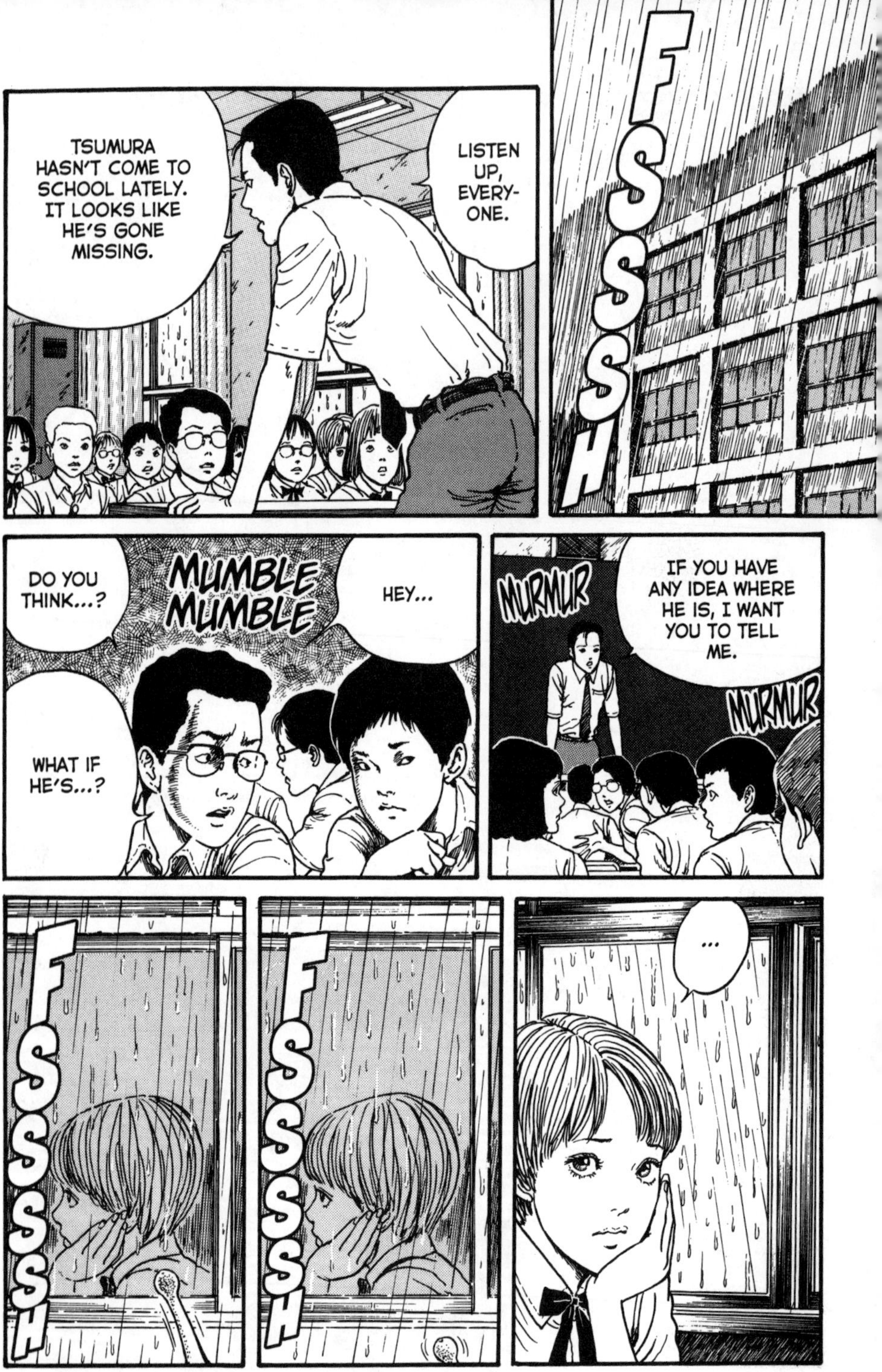
FSSSH
LISTEN UP, EVERY-ONE.
TSUMURA HASN'T COME TO SCHOOL LATELY. IT LOOKS LIKE HE'S GONE MISSING.
MURMUR
IF YOU HAVE ANY IDEA WHERE HE IS, I WANT YOU TO TELL ME.
MURMUR
HEY...
MUMBLE MUMBLE
DO YOU THINK...?
WHAT IF HE'S...?
...
FSSSSH
FSSSSH

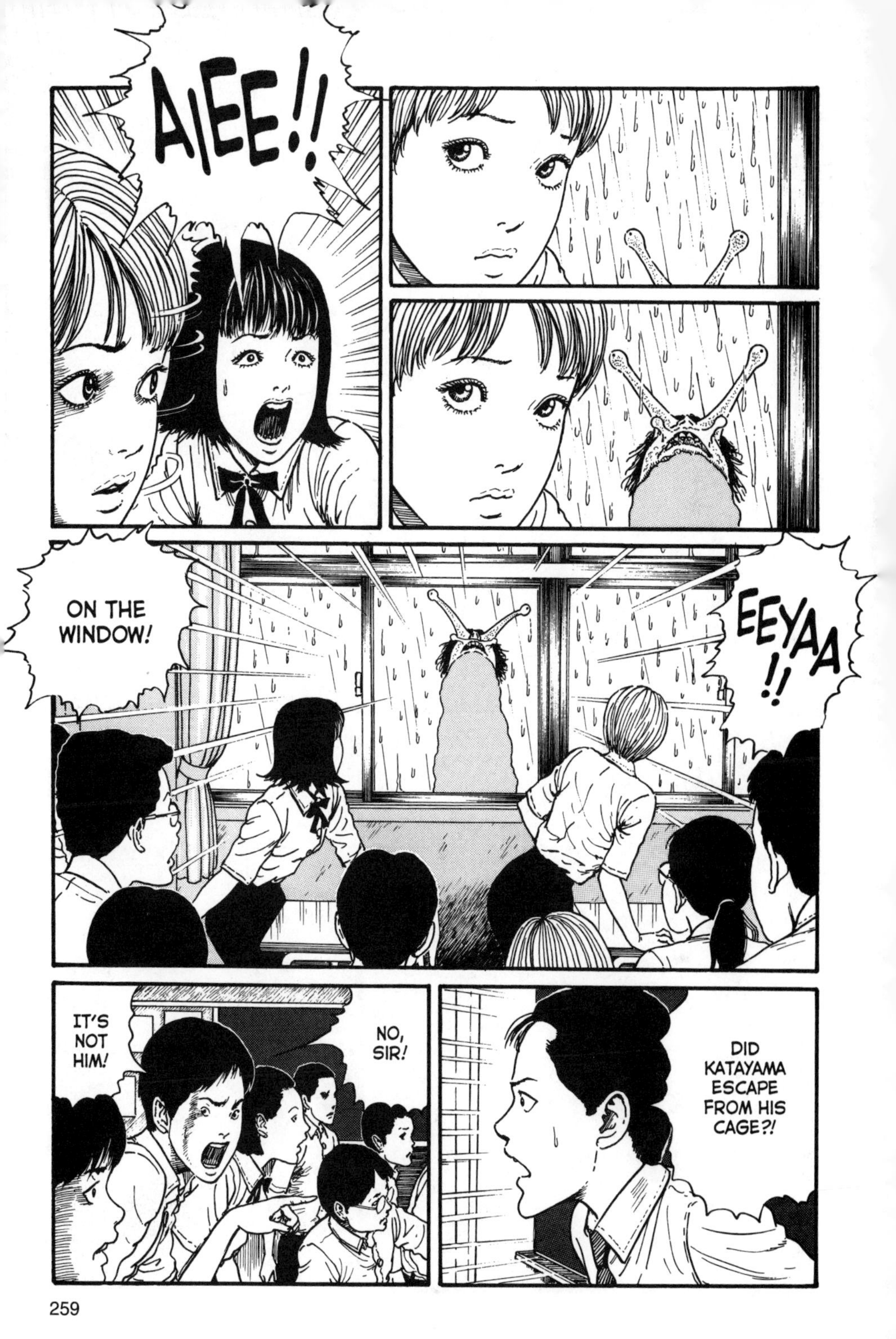
AIEE!!
EEYAA!!
ON THE WINDOW!
DID KATAYAMA ESCAPE FROM HIS CAGE?!
NO, SIR!
IT'S NOT HIM!

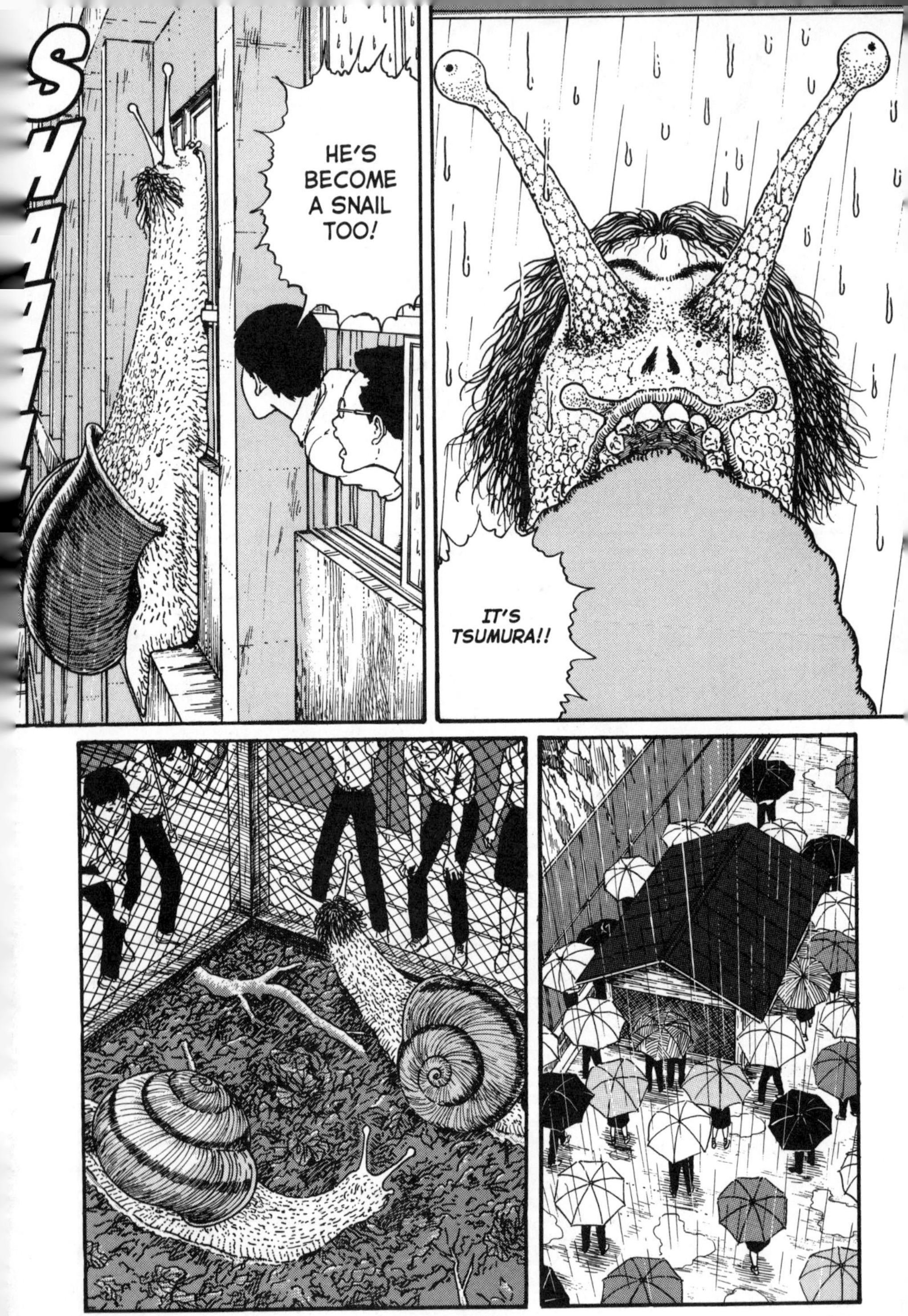
IT'S TSUMURA!!
HE'S BECOME A SNAIL TOO!

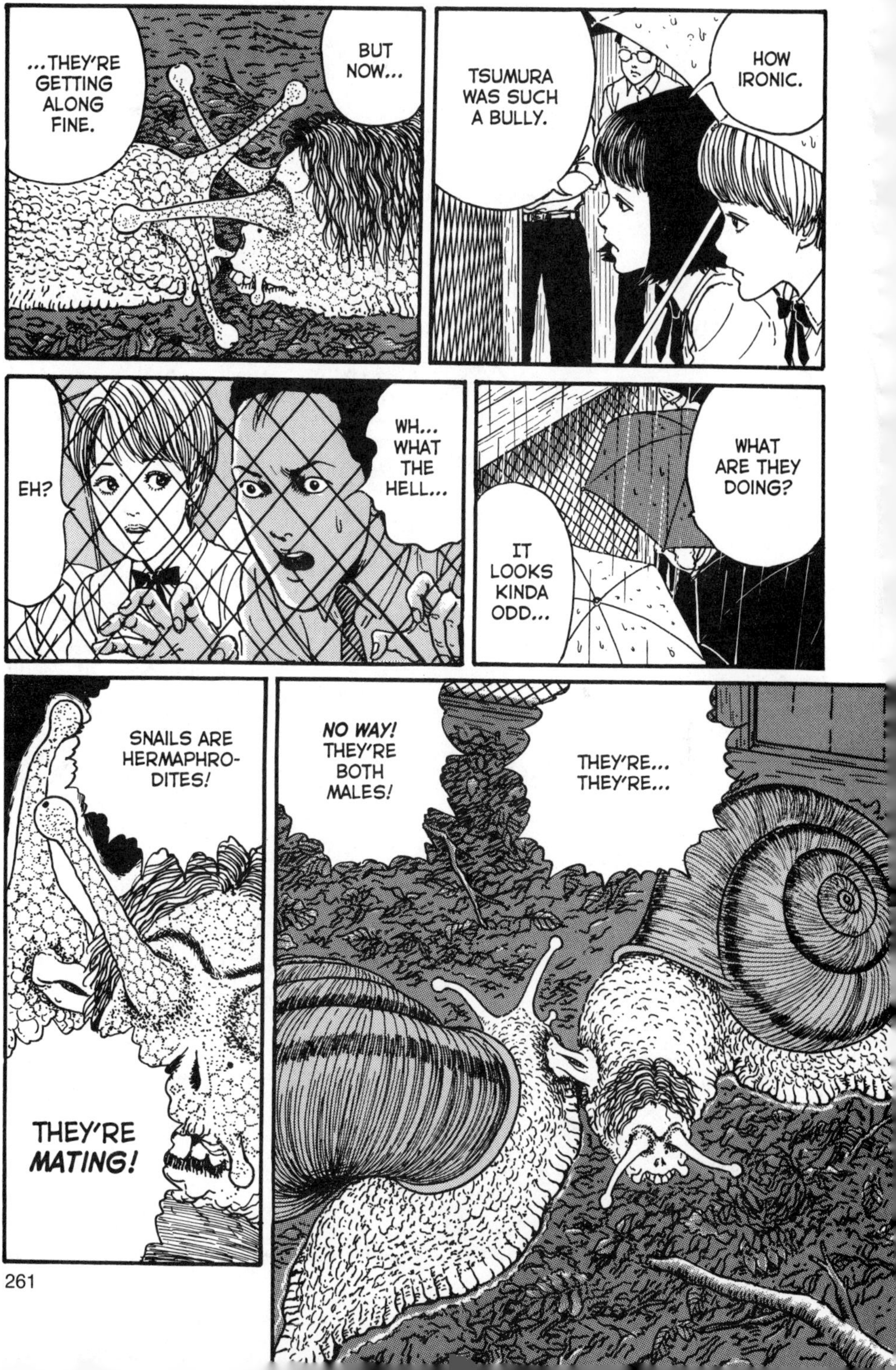

HOW IRONIC.
TSUMURA WAS SUCH A BULLY.
BUT NOW...
...THEY'RE GETTING ALONG FINE.
WHAT ARE THEY DOING?
IT LOOKS KINDA ODD...
WH... WHAT THE HELL...
EH?
THEY'RE... THEY'RE...
NO WAY! THEY'RE BOTH MALES!
SNAILS ARE HERMAPHRODITES!
THEY'RE *MATING!*

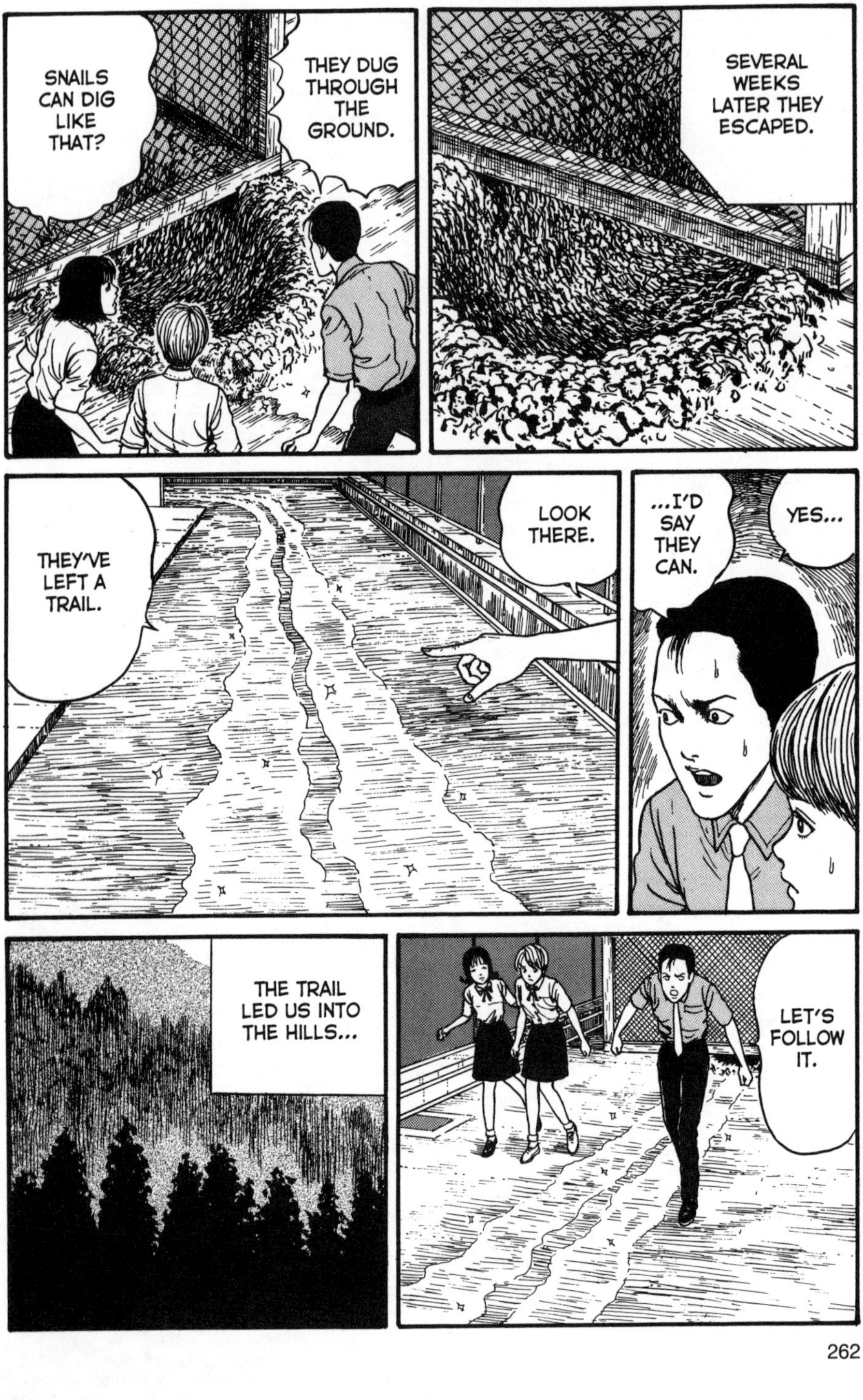
SEVERAL WEEKS LATER THEY ESCAPED.
THEY DUG THROUGH THE GROUND.
SNAILS CAN DIG LIKE THAT?
YES...
...I'D SAY THEY CAN.
LOOK THERE.
THEY'VE LEFT A TRAIL.
LET'S FOLLOW IT.
THE TRAIL LED US INTO THE HILLS...

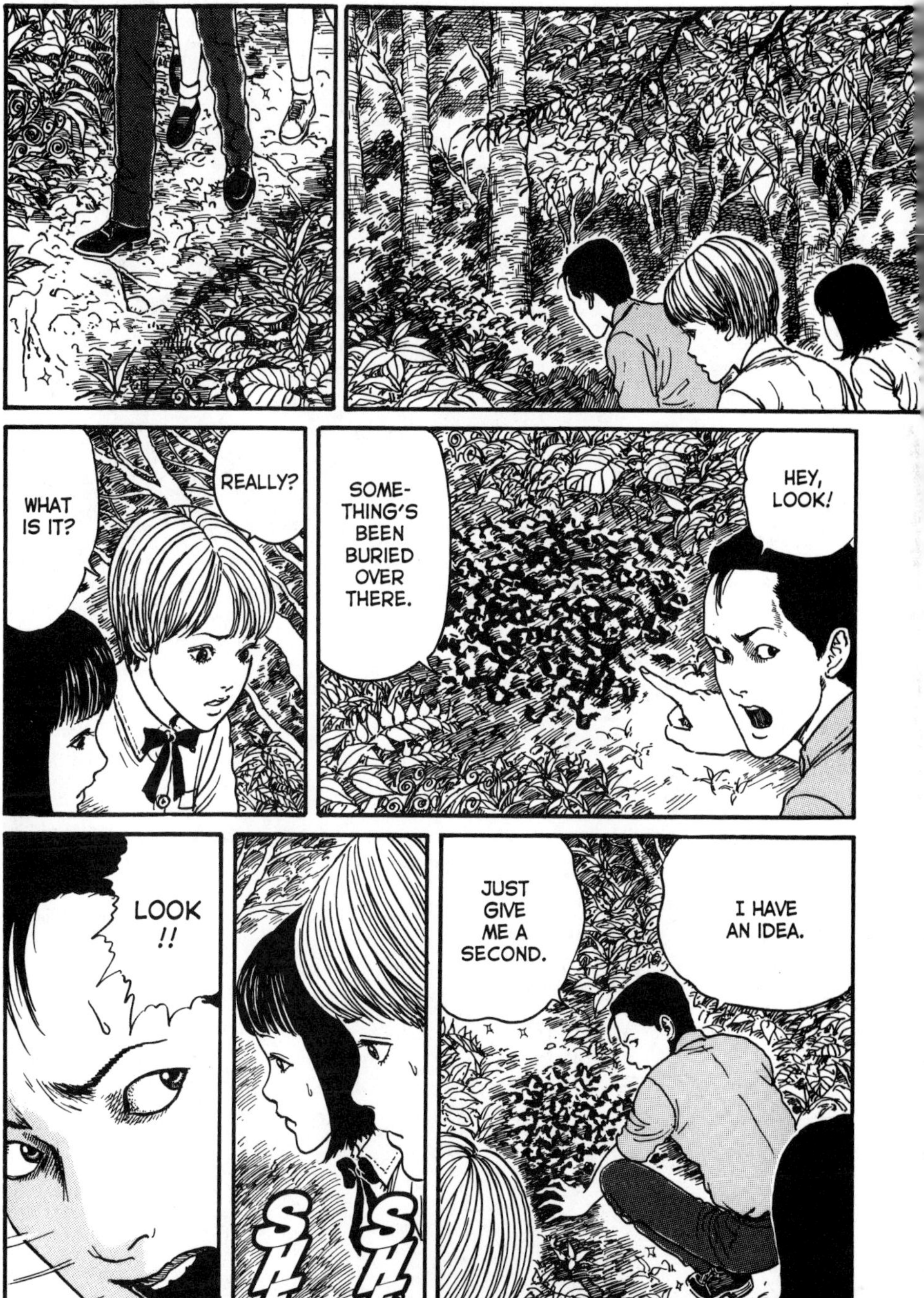
HEY, LOOK!
SOME-THING'S BEEN BURIED OVER THERE.
REALLY?
WHAT IS IT?
I HAVE AN IDEA.
JUST GIVE ME A SECOND.
SHF
SHF
LOOK !!

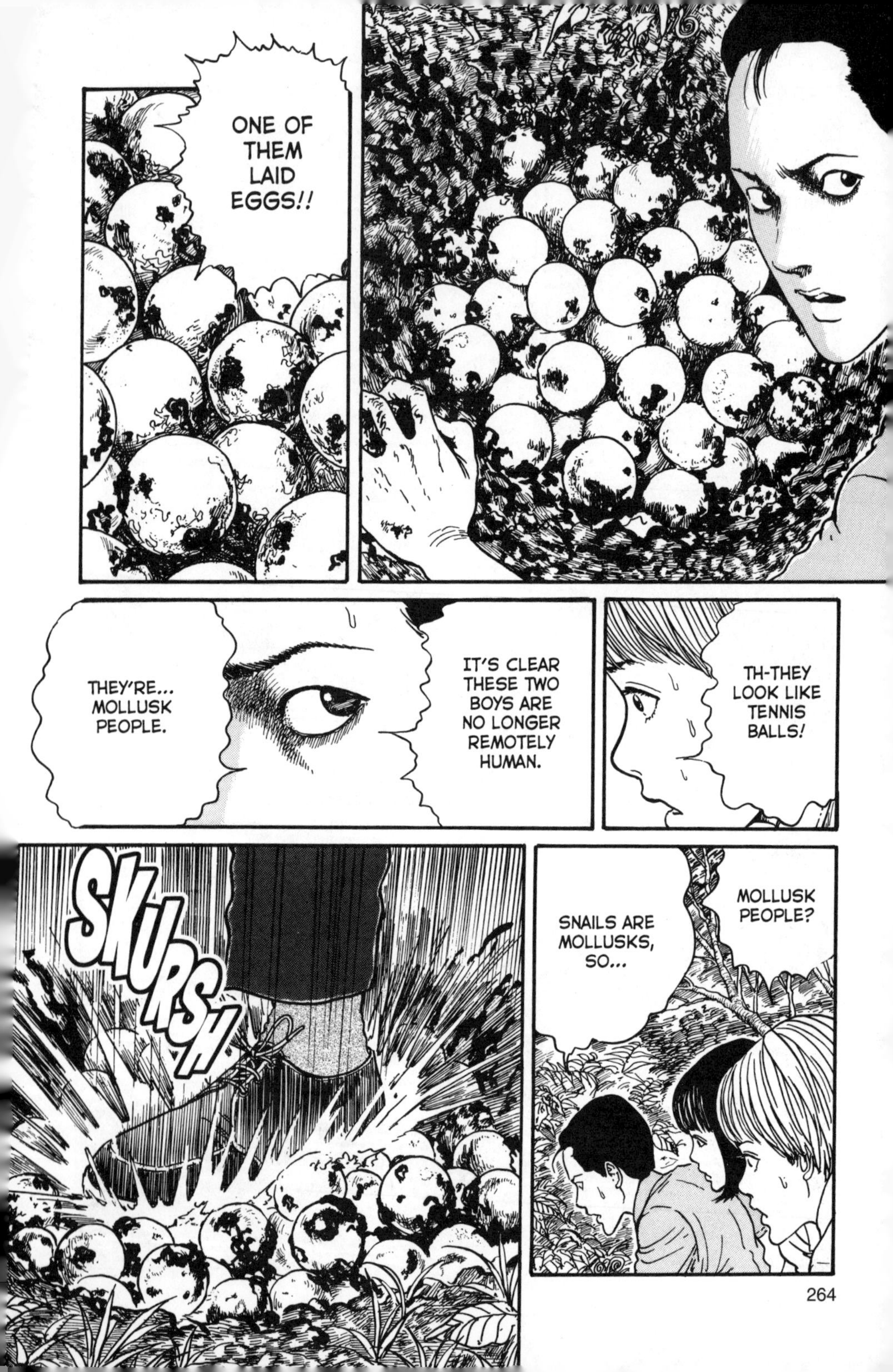
ONE OF THEM LAID EGGS!!
TH-THEY LOOK LIKE TENNIS BALLS!
IT'S CLEAR THESE TWO BOYS ARE NO LONGER REMOTELY HUMAN.
THEY'RE... MOLLUSK PEOPLE.
MOLLUSK PEOPLE?
SNAILS ARE MOLLUSKS, SO...
SKURSH

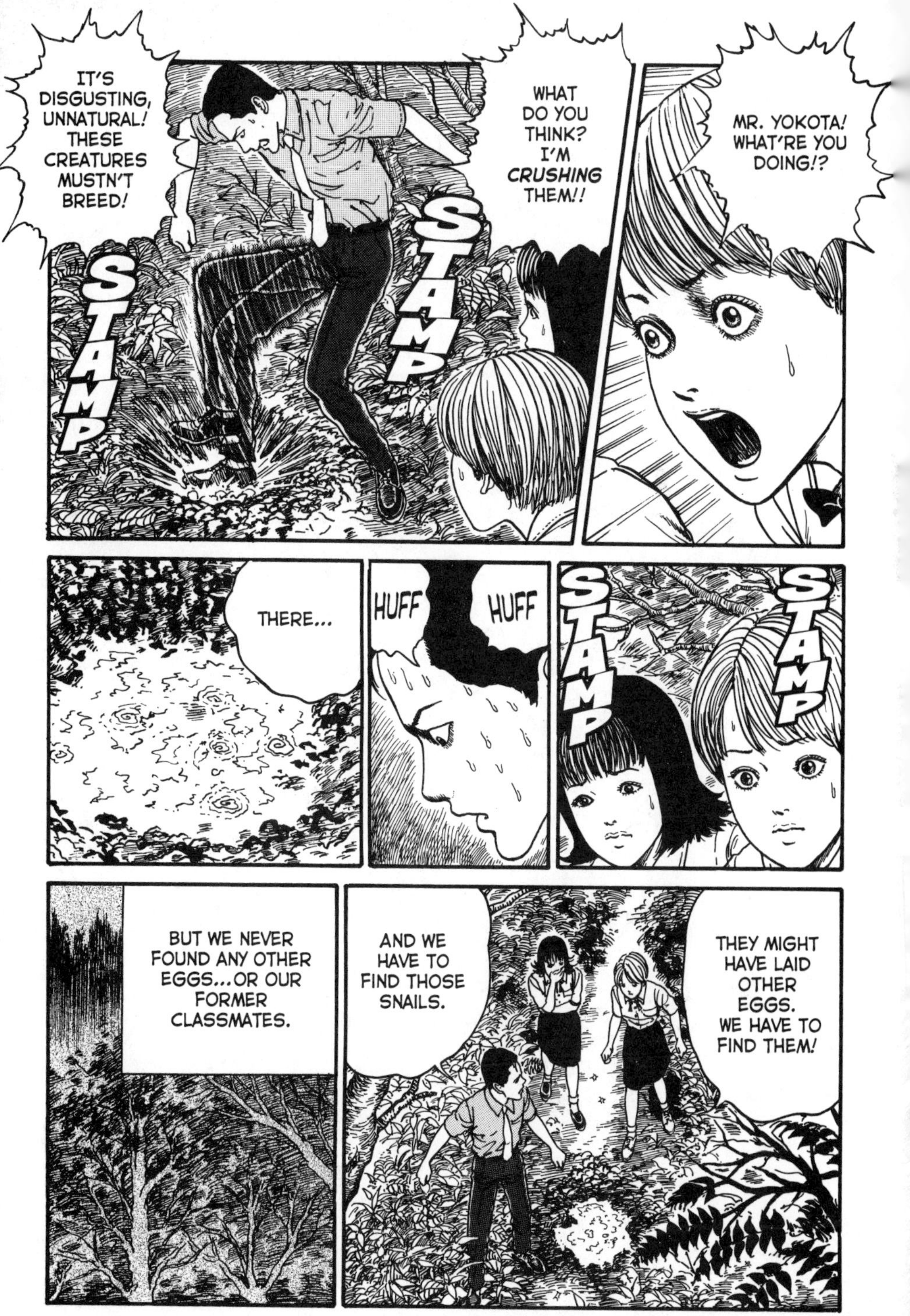
MR. YOKOTA! WHAT'RE YOU DOING!?
WHAT DO YOU THINK? I'M *CRUSHING* THEM!!
STAMP
IT'S DISGUSTING, UNNATURAL! THESE CREATURES MUSTN'T BREED!
STAMP
STAMP
STAMP
HUFF
HUFF
THERE...
THEY MIGHT HAVE LAID OTHER EGGS. WE HAVE TO FIND THEM!
AND WE HAVE TO FIND THOSE SNAILS.
BUT WE NEVER FOUND ANY OTHER EGGS...OR OUR FORMER CLASSMATES.

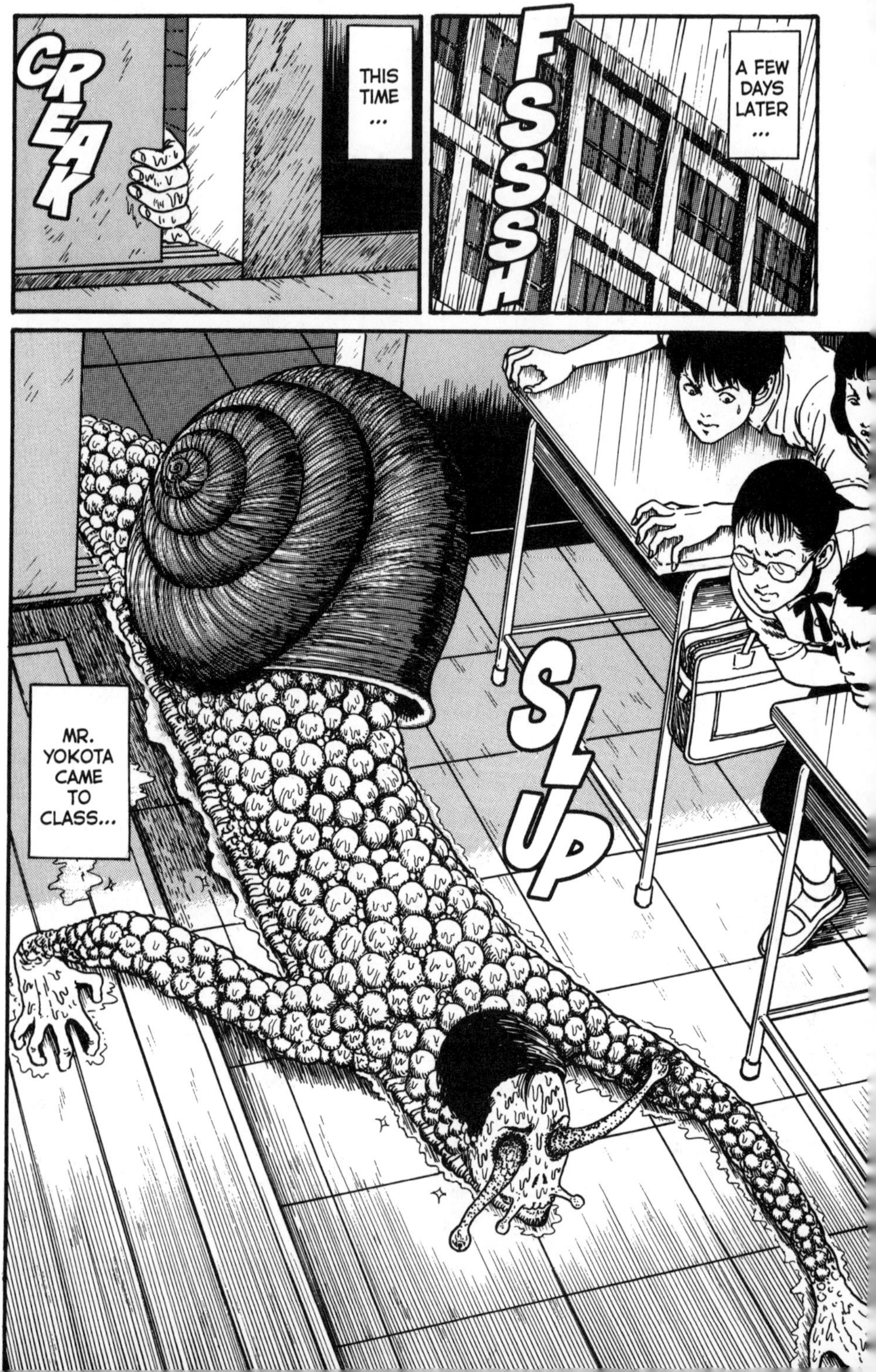
A FEW DAYS LATER ...
FSSSH
THIS TIME ...
CREAK
SLUP
MR. YOKOTA CAME TO CLASS...

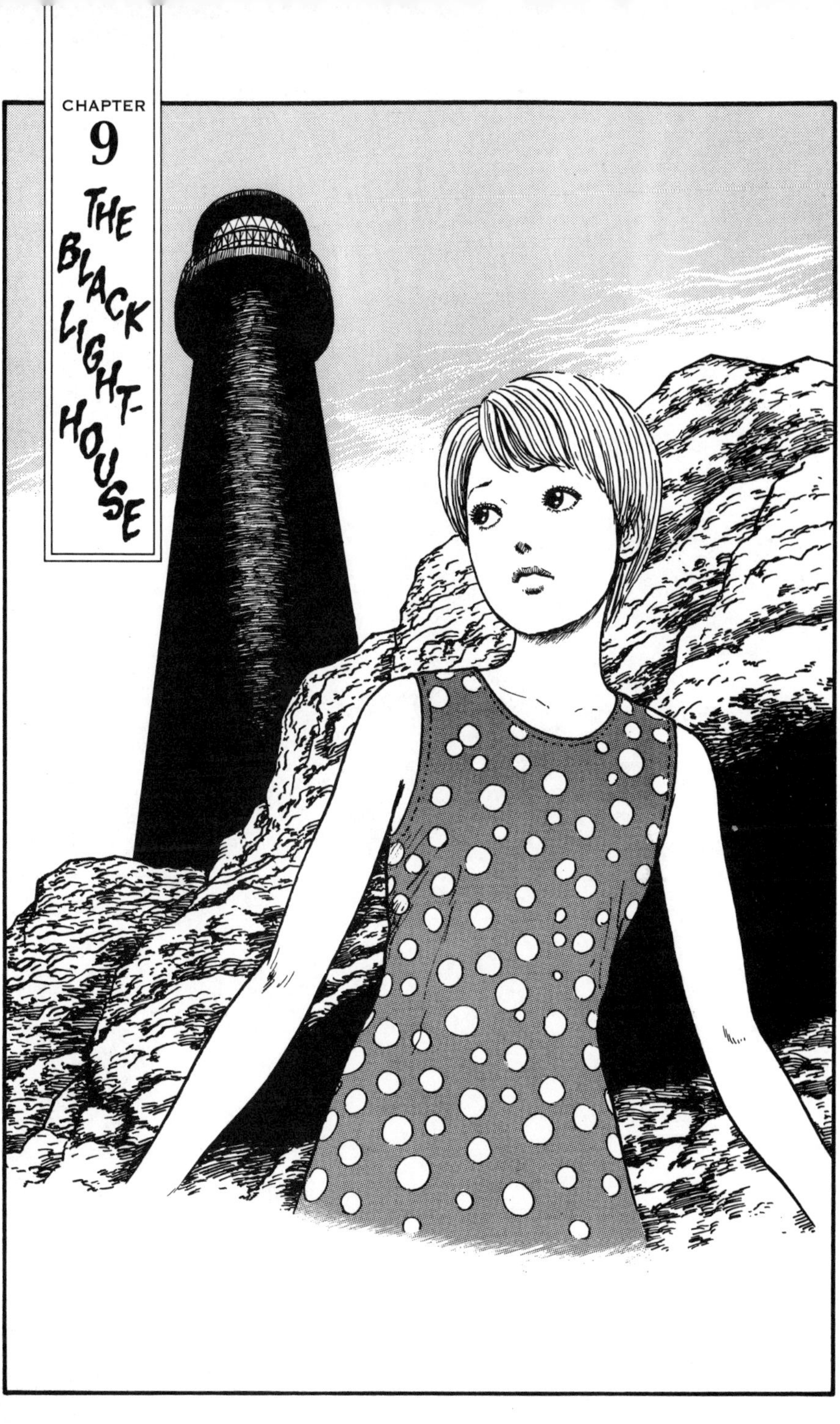
CHAPTER
9
THE BLACK LIGHT-HOUSE

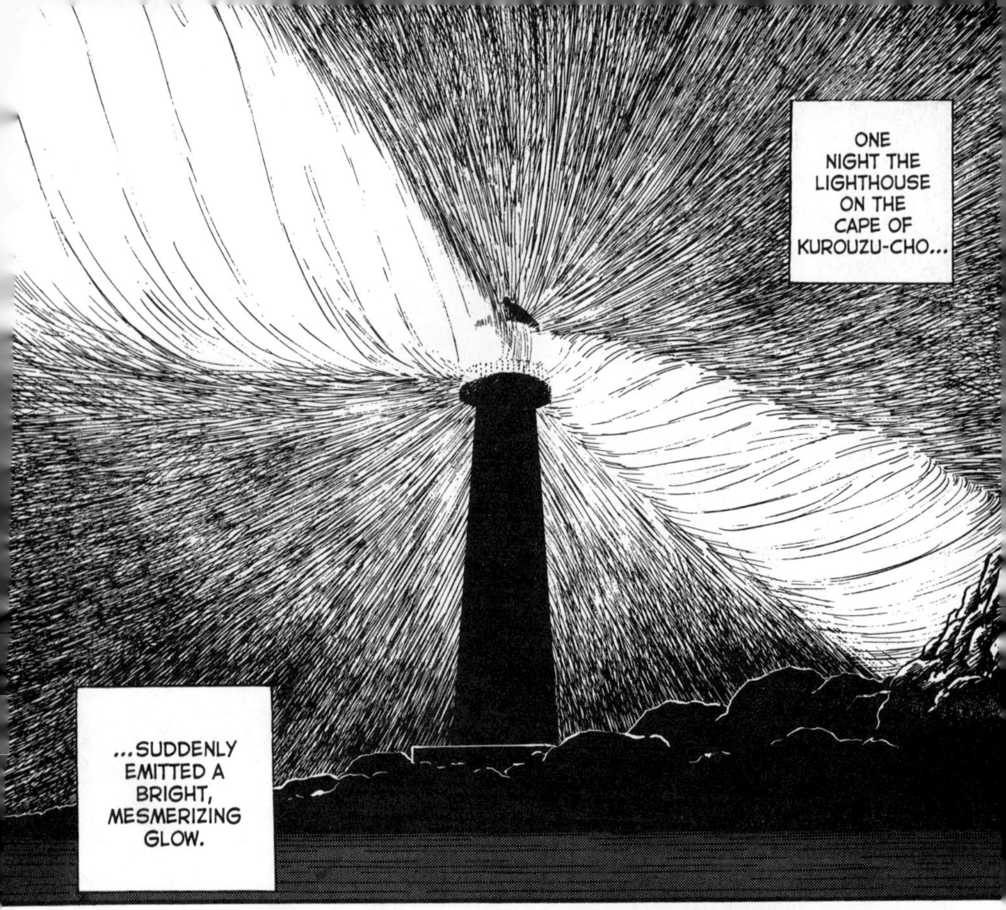
ONE NIGHT THE LIGHTHOUSE ON THE CAPE OF KUROUZU-CHO...
...SUDDENLY EMITTED A BRIGHT, MESMERIZING GLOW.

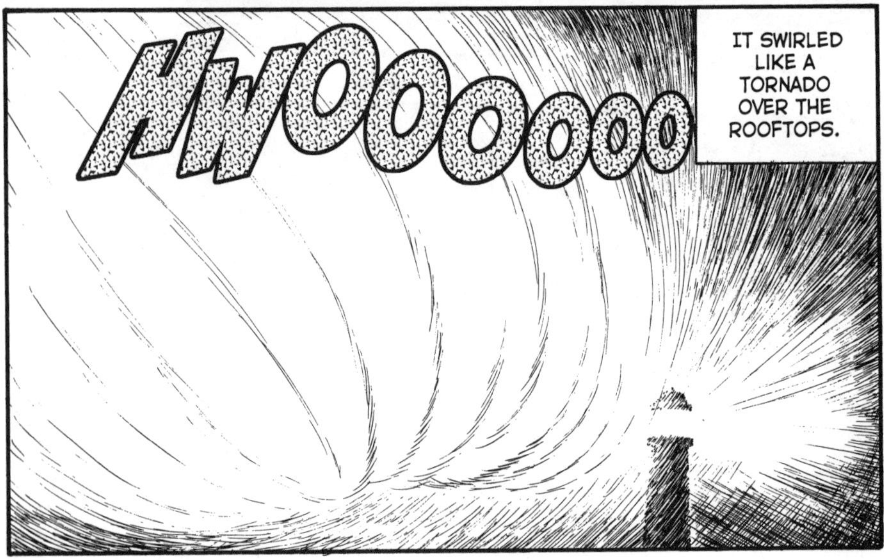
IT SWIRLED LIKE A TORNADO OVER THE ROOFTOPS.
HWOOOOOOO

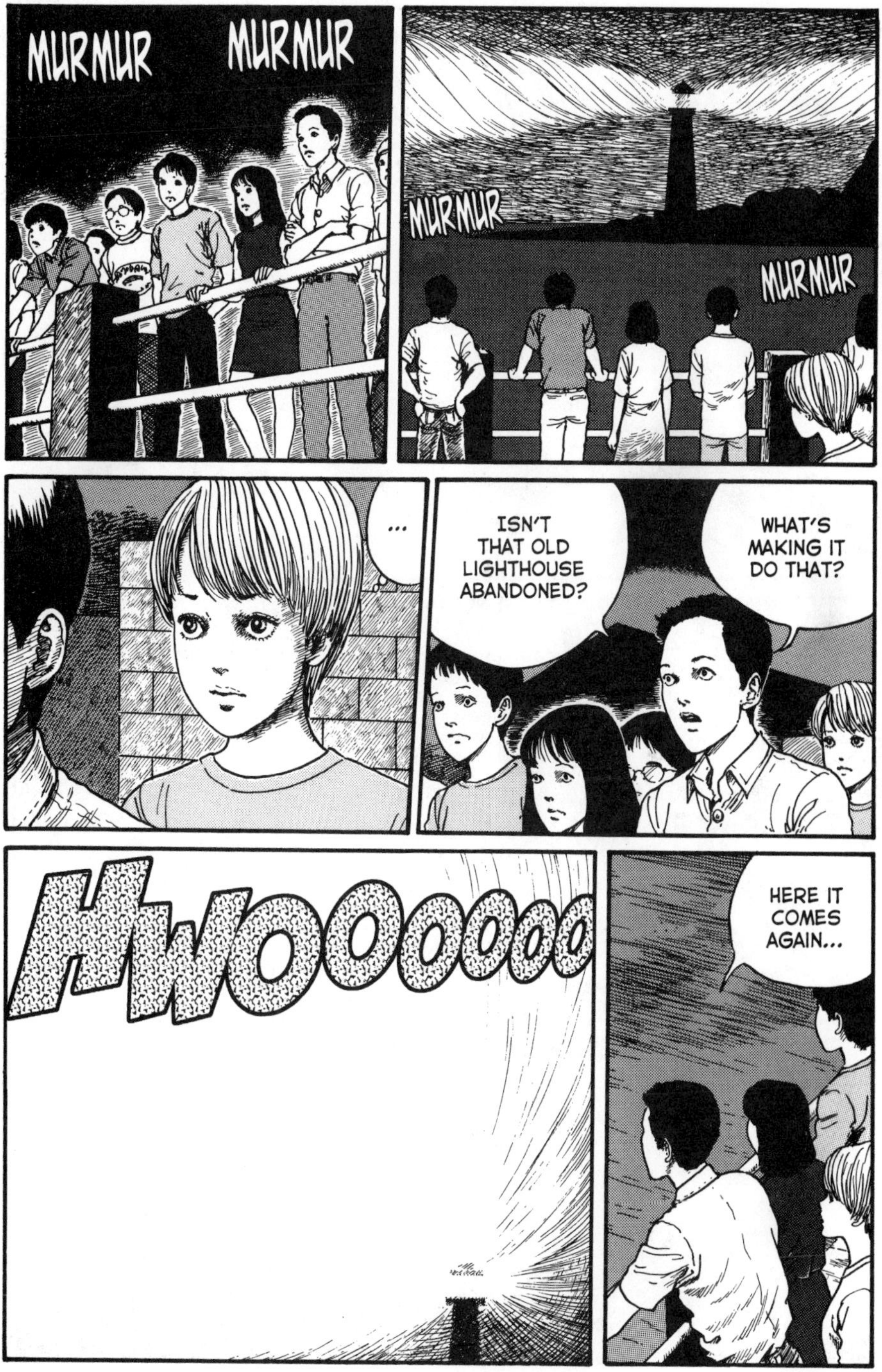
MURMUR
MURMUR
MURMUR
MURMUR
WHAT'S MAKING IT DO THAT?
ISN'T THAT OLD LIGHTHOUSE ABANDONED?
...
HERE IT COMES AGAIN...
HWOOOOOO

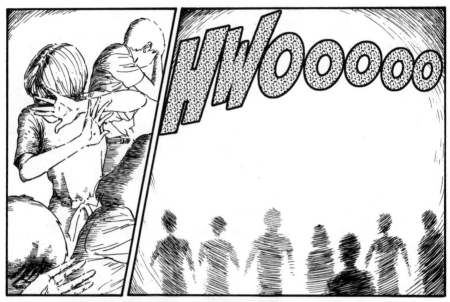

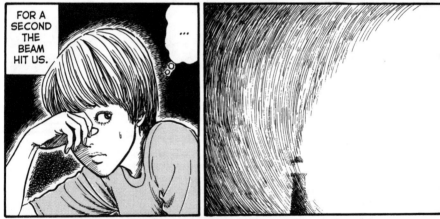

HWOOOOOO
...
FOR A SECOND THE BEAM HIT US.
EVERY NIGHT AFTER THAT THE LIGHT...
...BURST FORTH FROM THE LIGHT-HOUSE.
EVERY NIGHT AT DUSK...

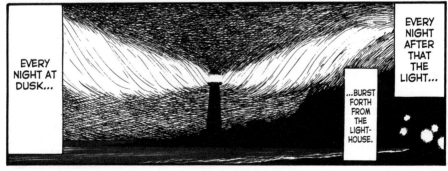

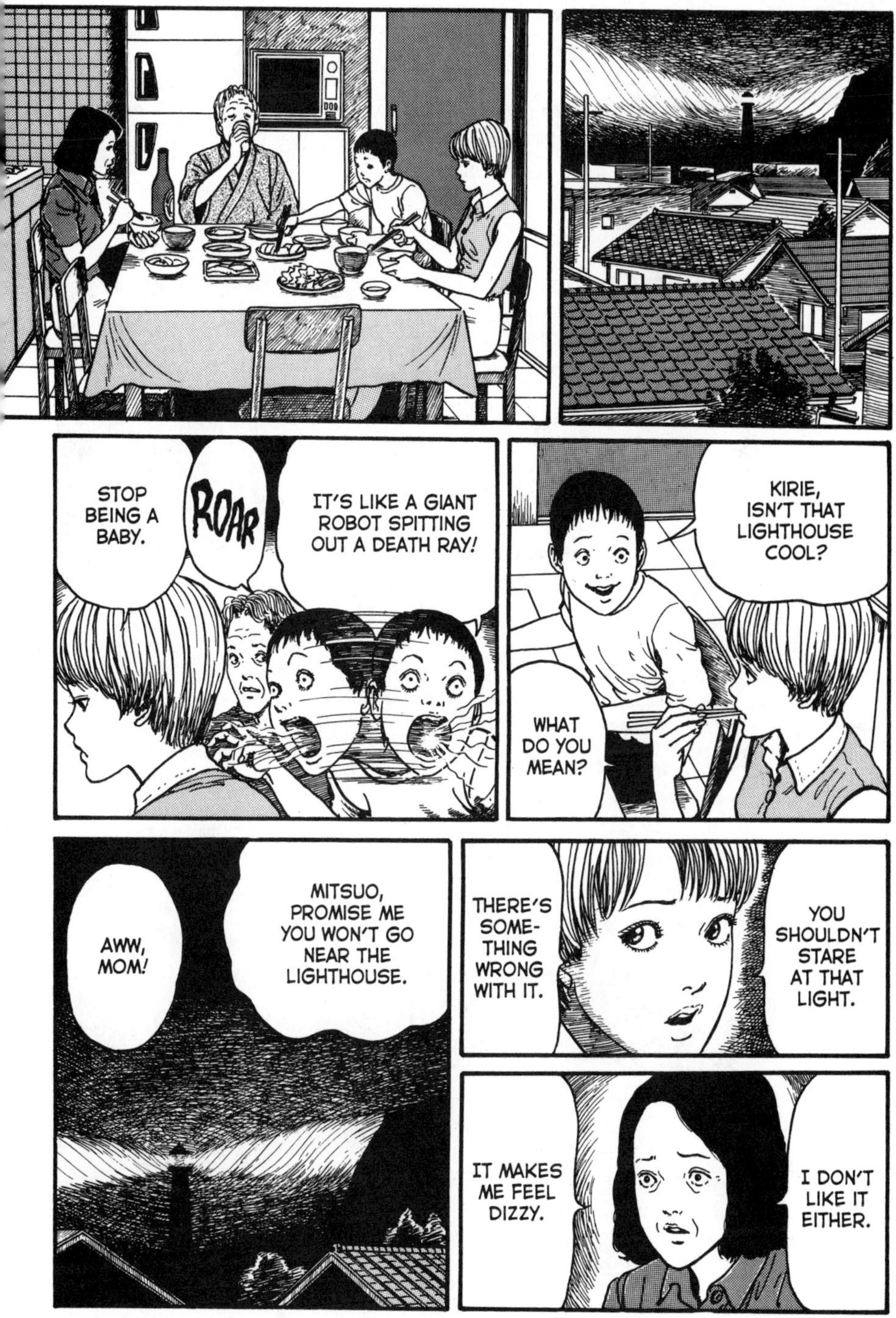
KIRIE, ISN'T THAT LIGHTHOUSE COOL?
WHAT DO YOU MEAN?
IT'S LIKE A GIANT ROBOT SPITTING OUT A DEATH RAY!
ROAR
STOP BEING A BABY.
YOU SHOULDN'T STARE AT THAT LIGHT.
THERE'S SOME-THING WRONG WITH IT.
I DON'T LIKE IT EITHER.
IT MAKES ME FEEL DIZZY.
MITSUO, PROMISE ME YOU WON'T GO NEAR THE LIGHTHOUSE.
AWW, MOM!

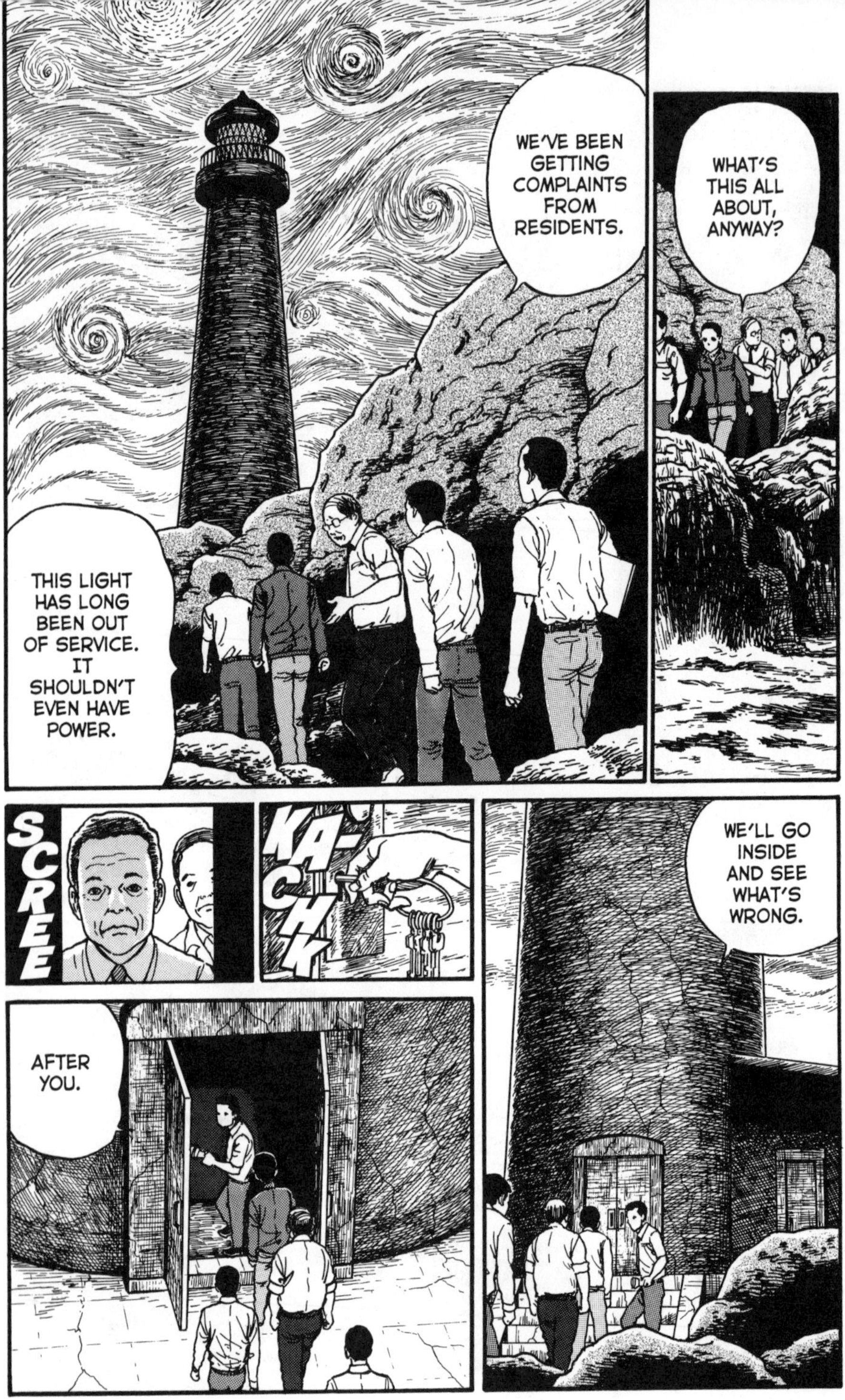
WHAT'S THIS ALL ABOUT, ANYWAY?
WE'VE BEEN GETTING COMPLAINTS FROM RESIDENTS.
THIS LIGHT HAS LONG BEEN OUT OF SERVICE. IT SHOULDN'T EVEN HAVE POWER.
WE'LL GO INSIDE AND SEE WHAT'S WRONG.
KA-CHK
SCREE
AFTER YOU.

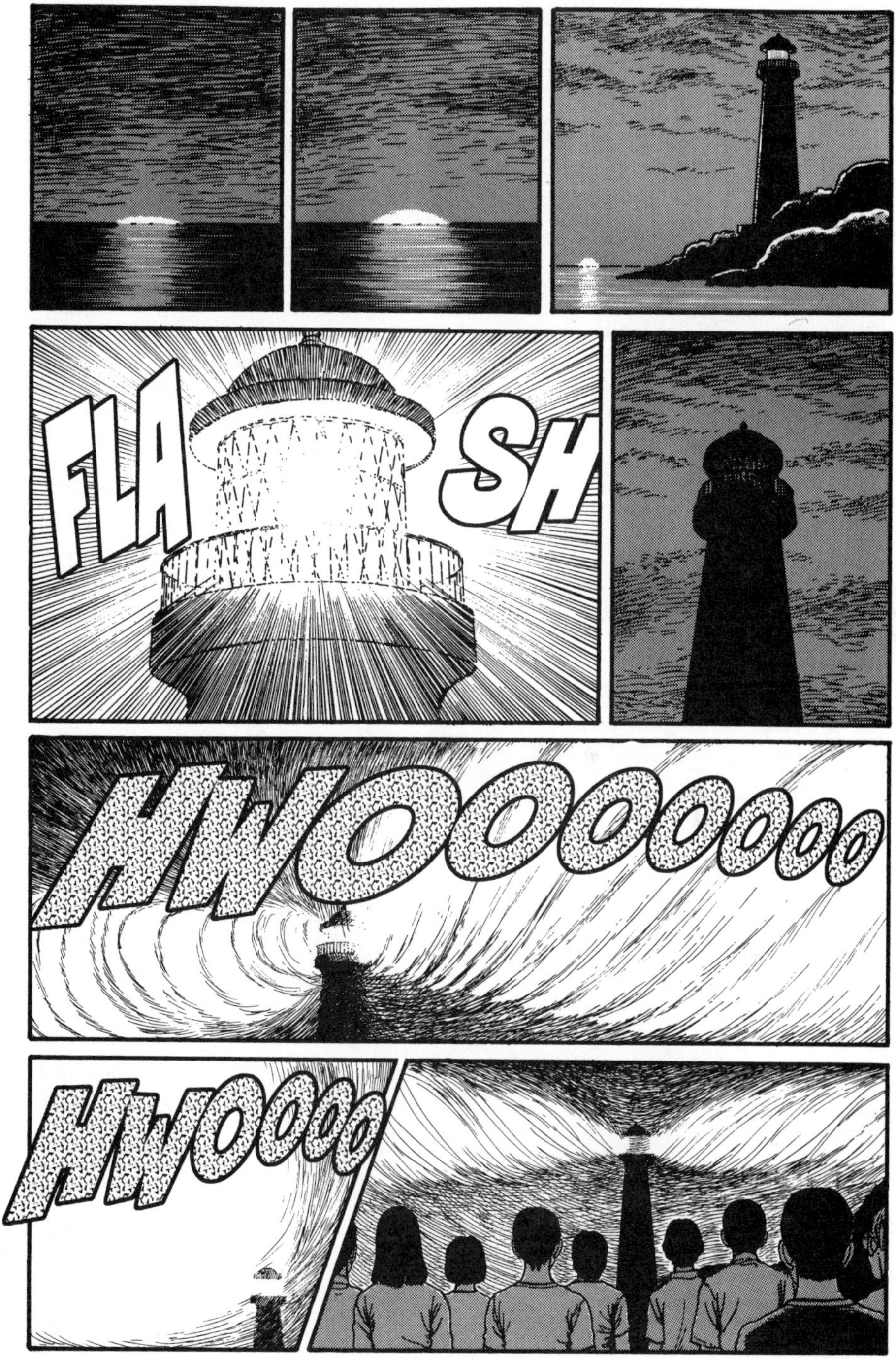
FLASH
HWOOOOOOOO
HWOOOO

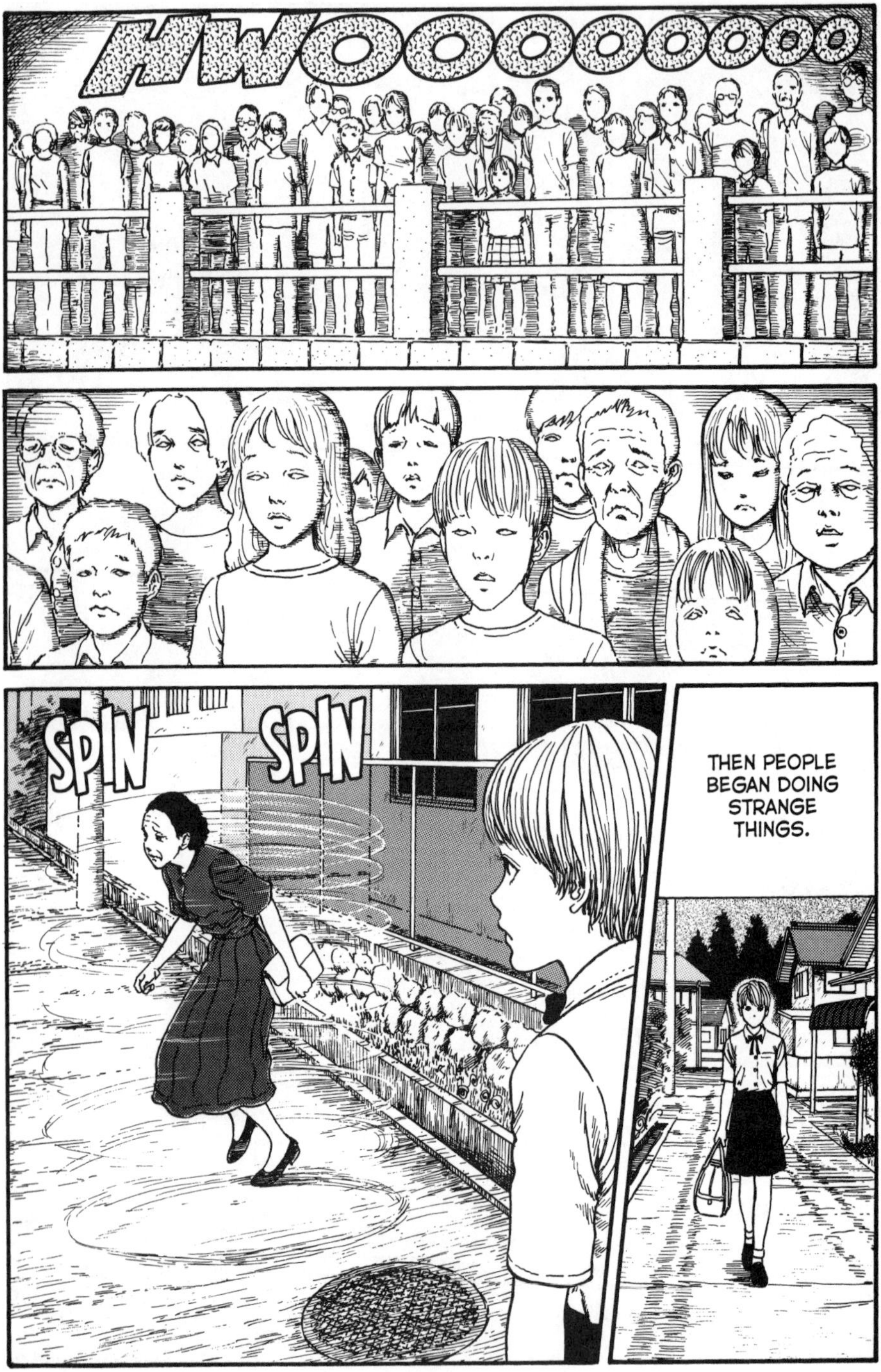
HWOOOOOOOO
THEN PEOPLE BEGAN DOING STRANGE THINGS.
SPIN
SPIN

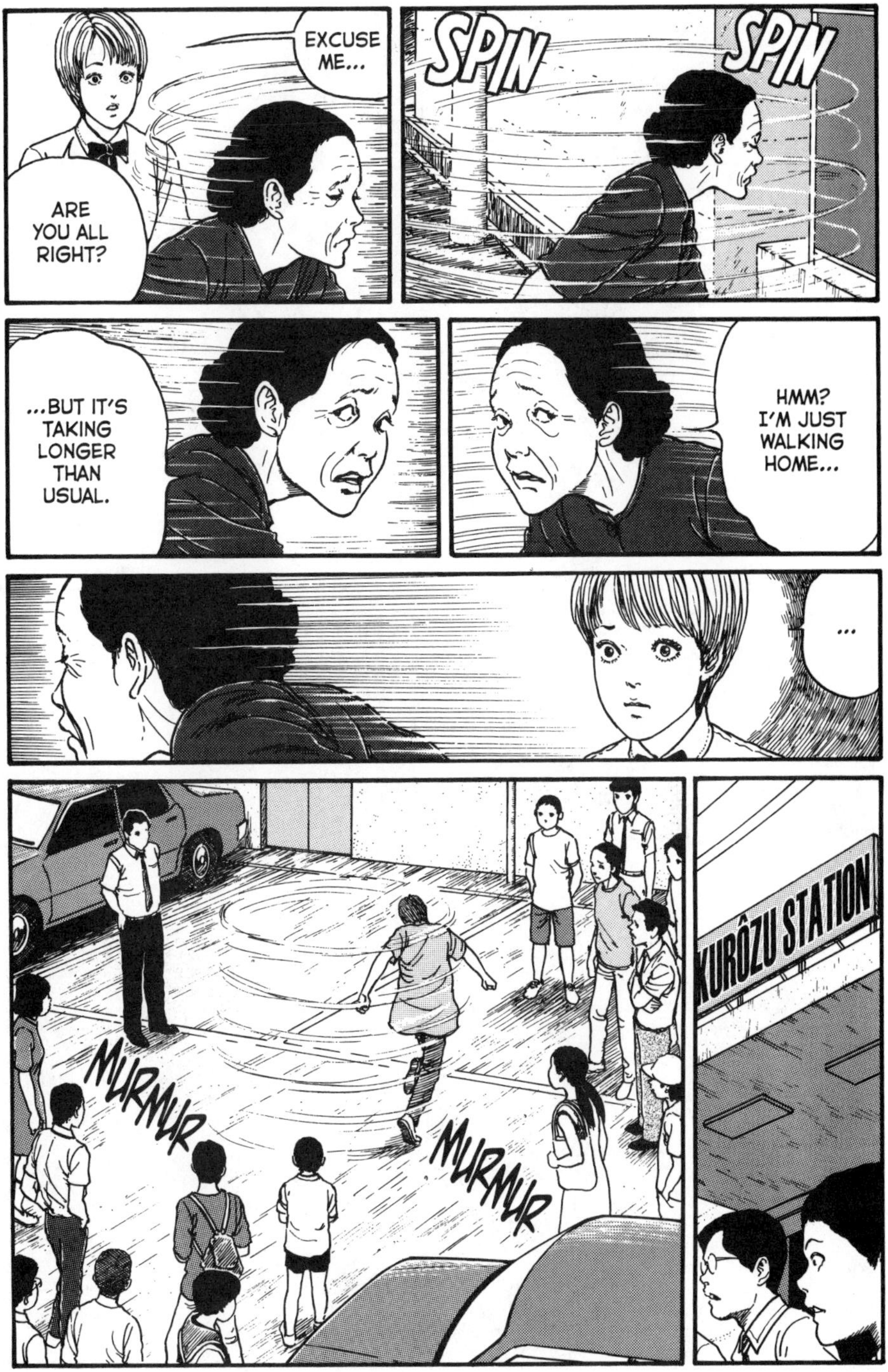
SPIN
SPIN
EXCUSE ME...
ARE YOU ALL RIGHT?
HMM? I'M JUST WALKING HOME...
...BUT IT'S TAKING LONGER THAN USUAL.
...
KURÔZU STATION
MURMUR
MURMUR

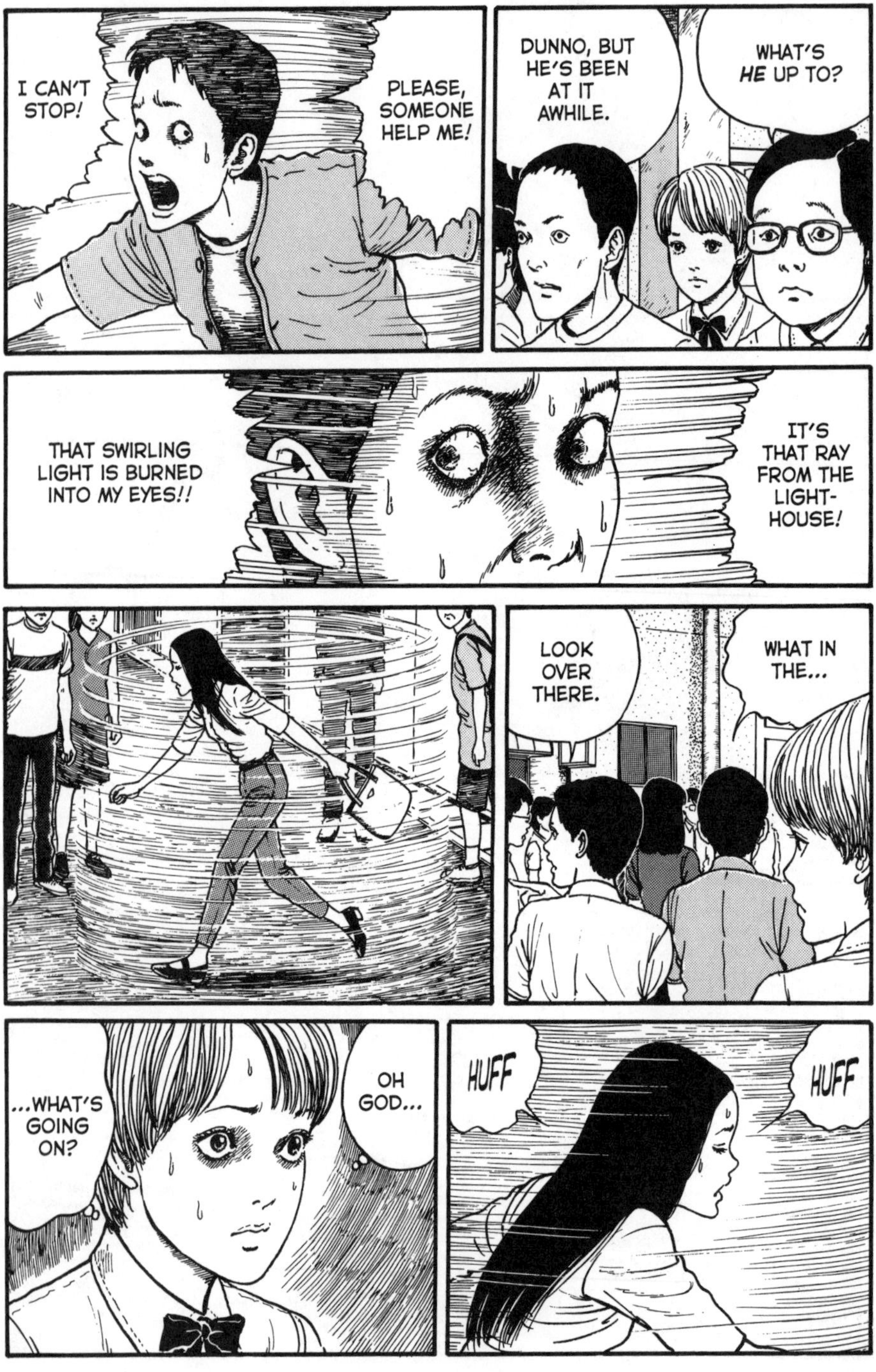
WHAT'S *HE* UP TO?
DUNNO, BUT HE'S BEEN AT IT AWHILE.
PLEASE, SOMEONE HELP ME!
I CAN'T STOP!
IT'S THAT RAY FROM THE LIGHT-HOUSE!
THAT SWIRLING LIGHT IS BURNED INTO *MY* EYES!!
WHAT IN THE...
LOOK OVER THERE.
HUFF
HUFF
OH GOD...
...WHAT'S GOING ON?

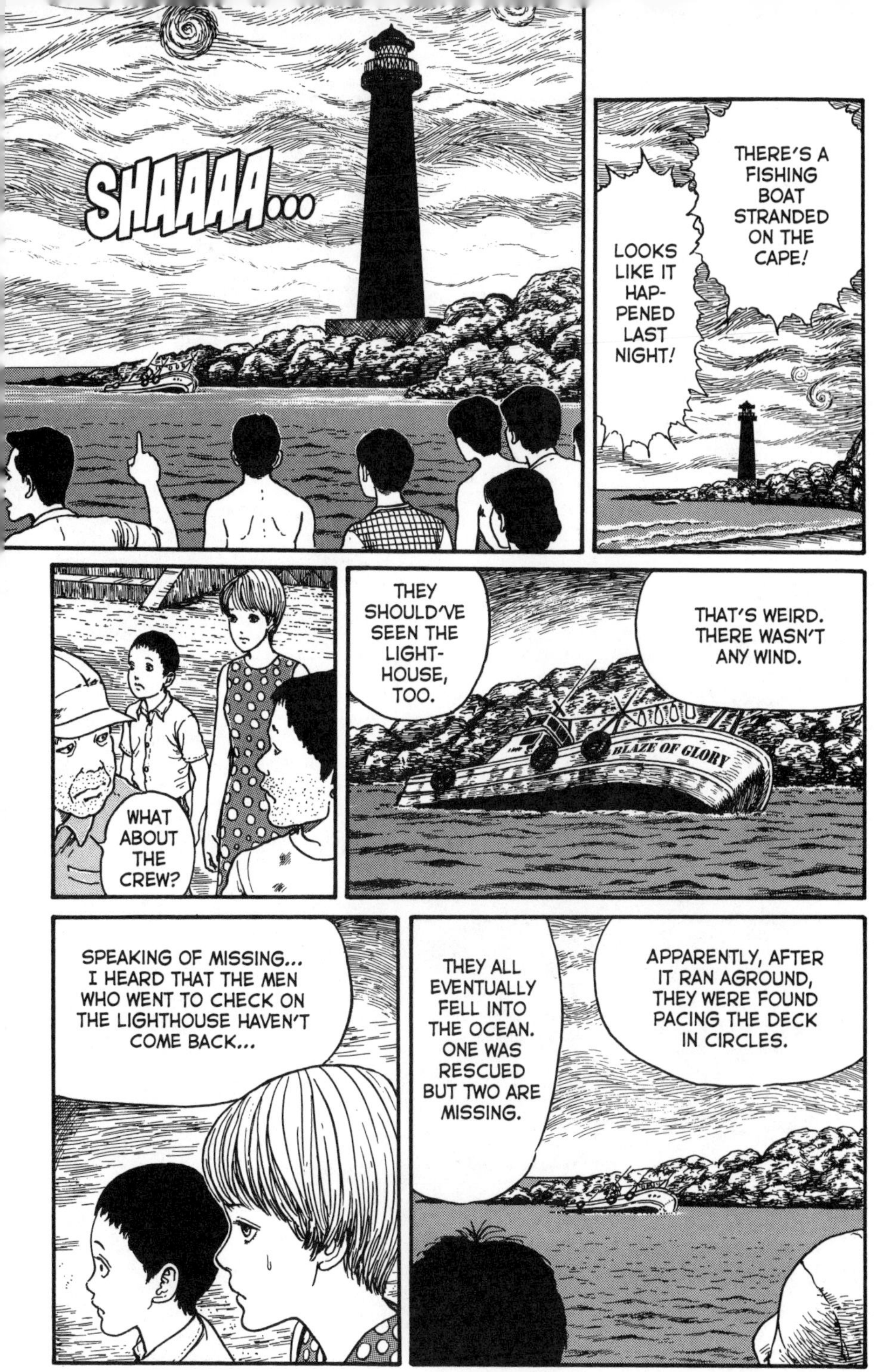
THERE'S A FISHING BOAT STRANDED ON THE CAPE!
LOOKS LIKE IT HAP-PENED LAST NIGHT!
SHAAAA...
THAT'S WEIRD. THERE WASN'T ANY WIND.
THEY SHOULD'VE SEEN THE LIGHT-HOUSE, TOO.
BLAZE OF GLORY
WHAT ABOUT THE CREW?
APPARENTLY, AFTER IT RAN AGROUND, THEY WERE FOUND PACING THE DECK IN CIRCLES.
THEY ALL EVENTUALLY FELL INTO THE OCEAN. ONE WAS RESCUED BUT TWO ARE MISSING.
SPEAKING OF MISSING... I HEARD THAT THE MEN WHO WENT TO CHECK ON THE LIGHTHOUSE HAVEN'T COME BACK...

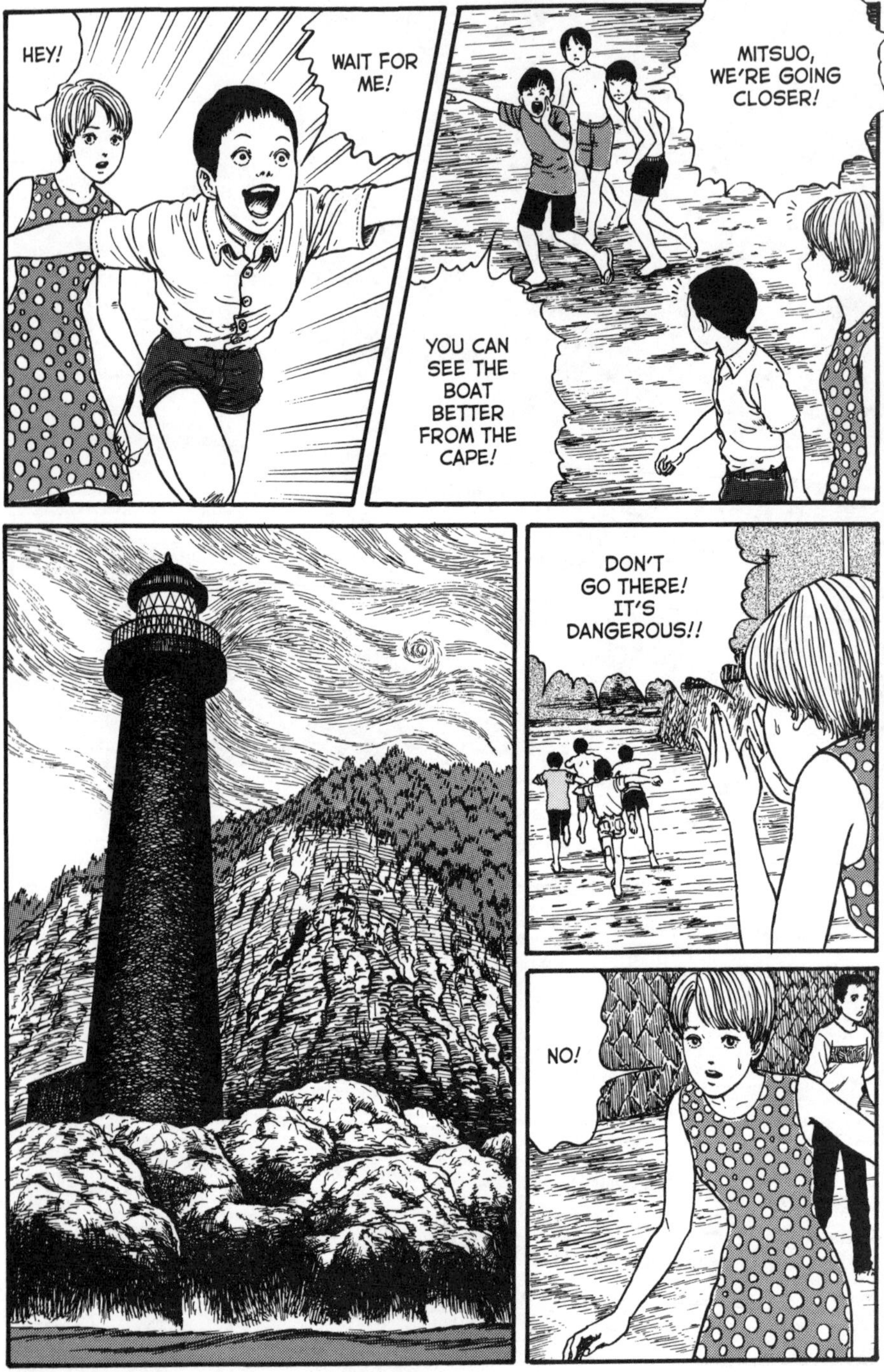
MITSUO, WE'RE GOING CLOSER!
YOU CAN SEE THE BOAT BETTER FROM THE CAPE!
WAIT FOR ME!
HEY!
DON'T GO THERE! IT'S DANGEROUS!!
NO!

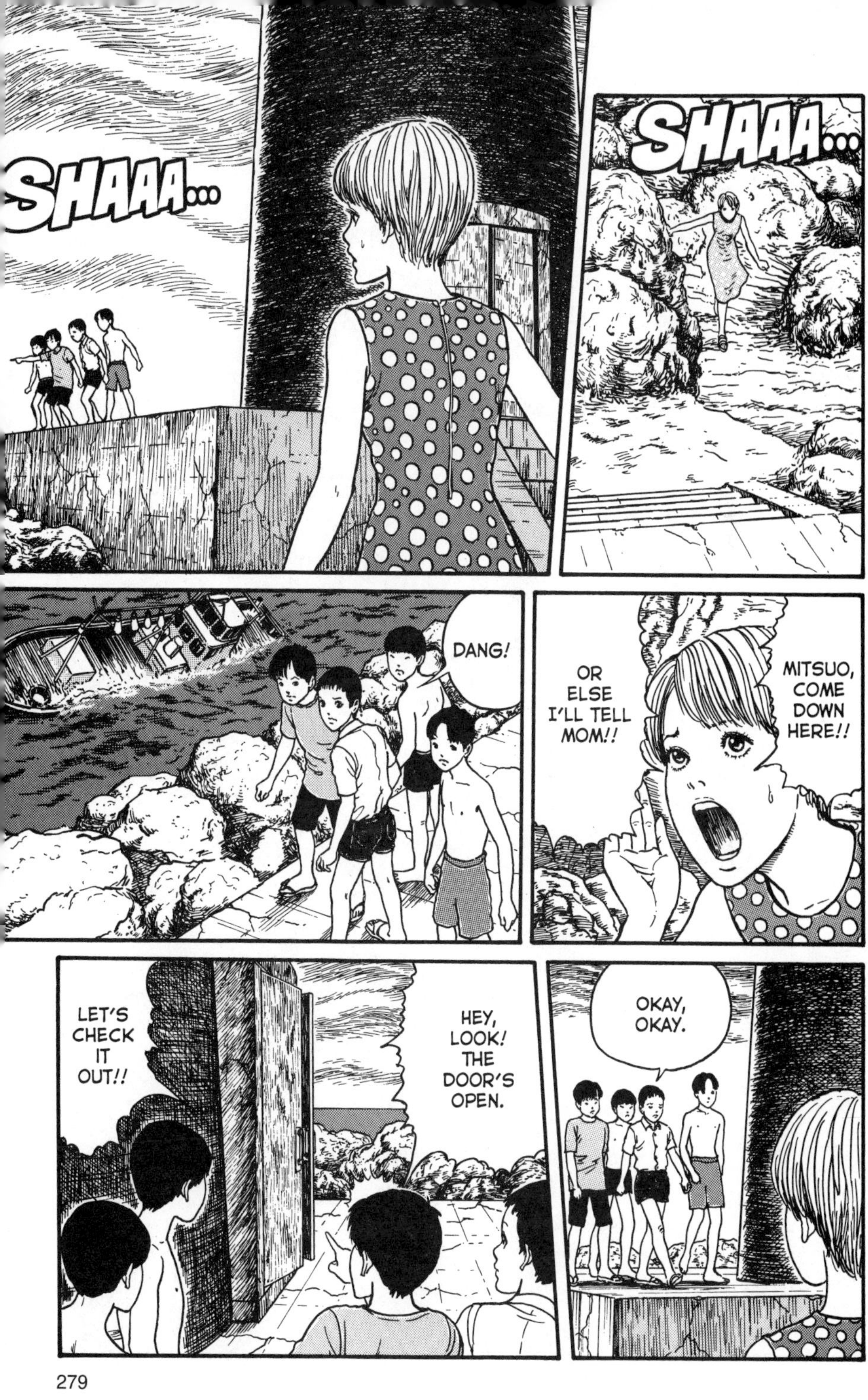
SHAAA...
SHAAA...
MITSUO, COME DOWN HERE!!
OR ELSE I'LL TELL MOM!!
DANG!
OKAY, OKAY.
HEY, LOOK! THE DOOR'S OPEN.
LET'S CHECK IT OUT!!

MITSUO!

YEAH!

STOP!

COME BACK!

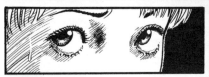

...

MITSUO!

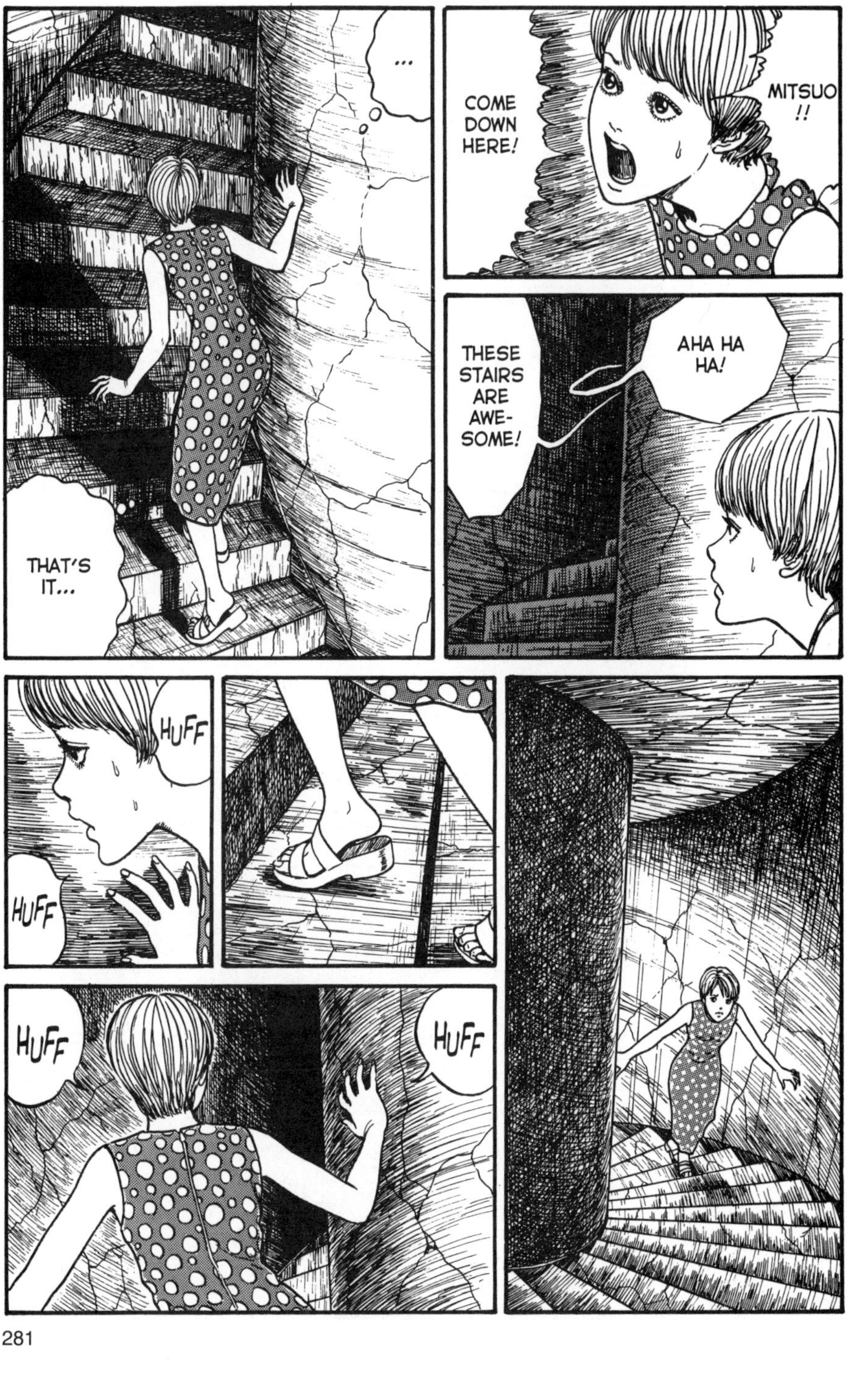
MITSUO!!
COME DOWN HERE!
AHA HA HA!
THESE STAIRS ARE AWE-SOME!
...
THAT'S IT...
HUFF
HUFF
HUFF
HUFF

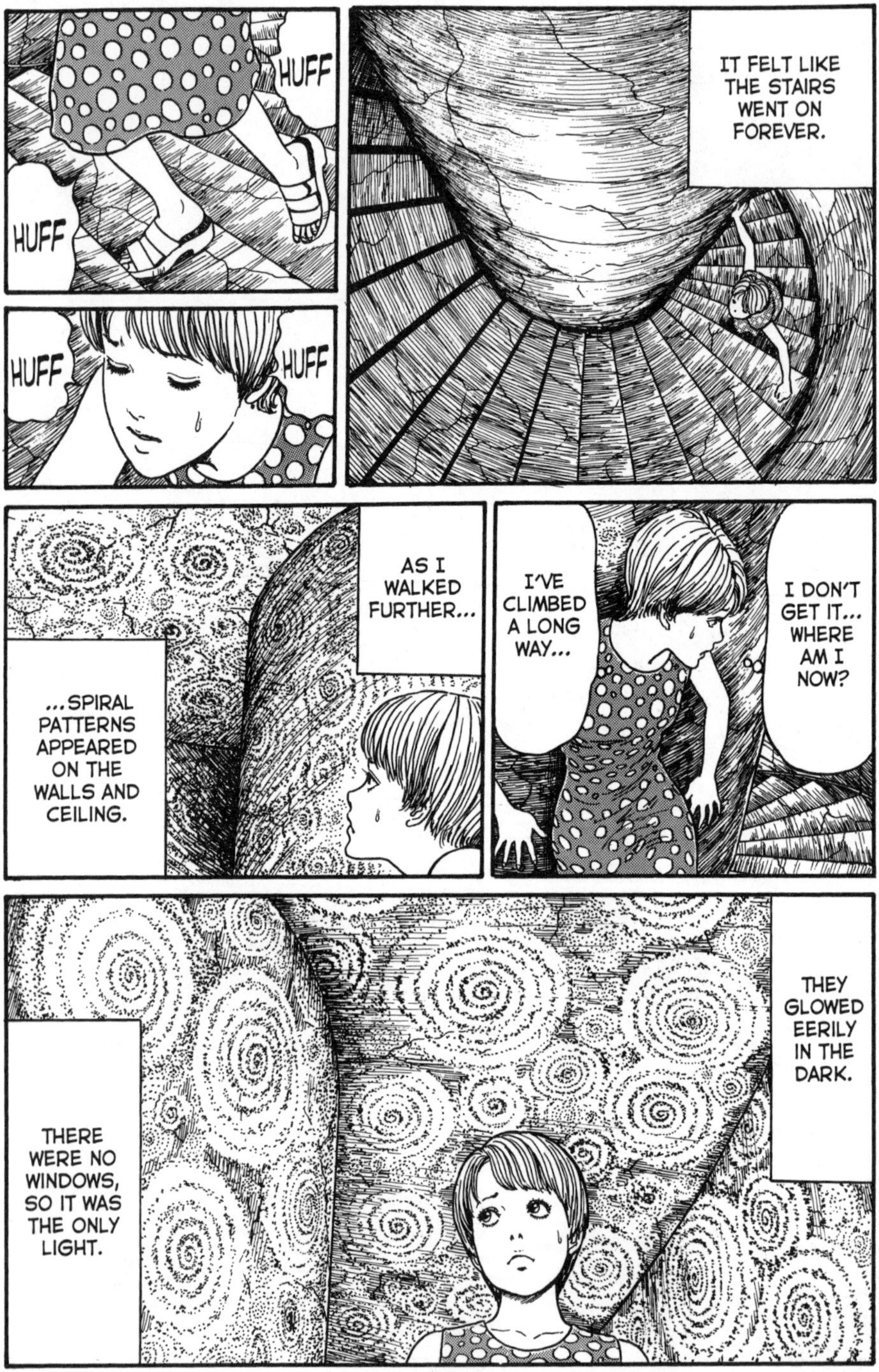
IT FELT LIKE THE STAIRS WENT ON FOREVER.
HUFF
HUFF
HUFF
HUFF
I DON'T GET IT... WHERE AM I NOW?
I'VE CLIMBED A LONG WAY...
AS I WALKED FURTHER...
...SPIRAL PATTERNS APPEARED ON THE WALLS AND CEILING.
THEY GLOWED EERILY IN THE DARK.
THERE WERE NO WINDOWS, SO IT WAS THE ONLY LIGHT.

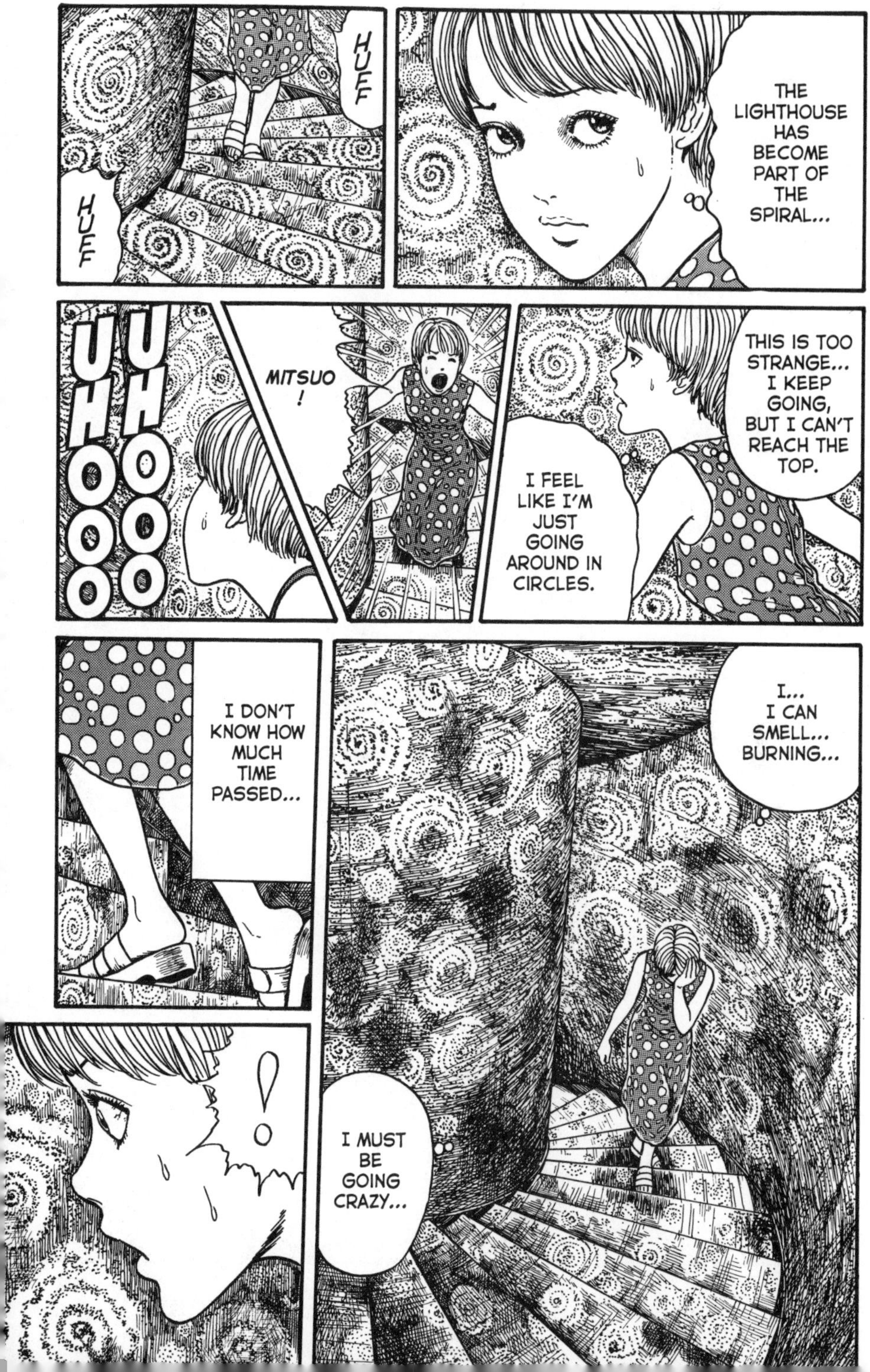
THE LIGHTHOUSE HAS BECOME PART OF THE SPIRAL...
HUFF
HUFF
THIS IS TOO STRANGE... I KEEP GOING, BUT I CAN'T REACH THE TOP.
I FEEL LIKE I'M JUST GOING AROUND IN CIRCLES.
MITSUO!
UHOOOO
UHOOOO
I... I CAN SMELL... BURNING...
I MUST BE GOING CRAZY...
I DON'T KNOW HOW MUCH TIME PASSED...
!

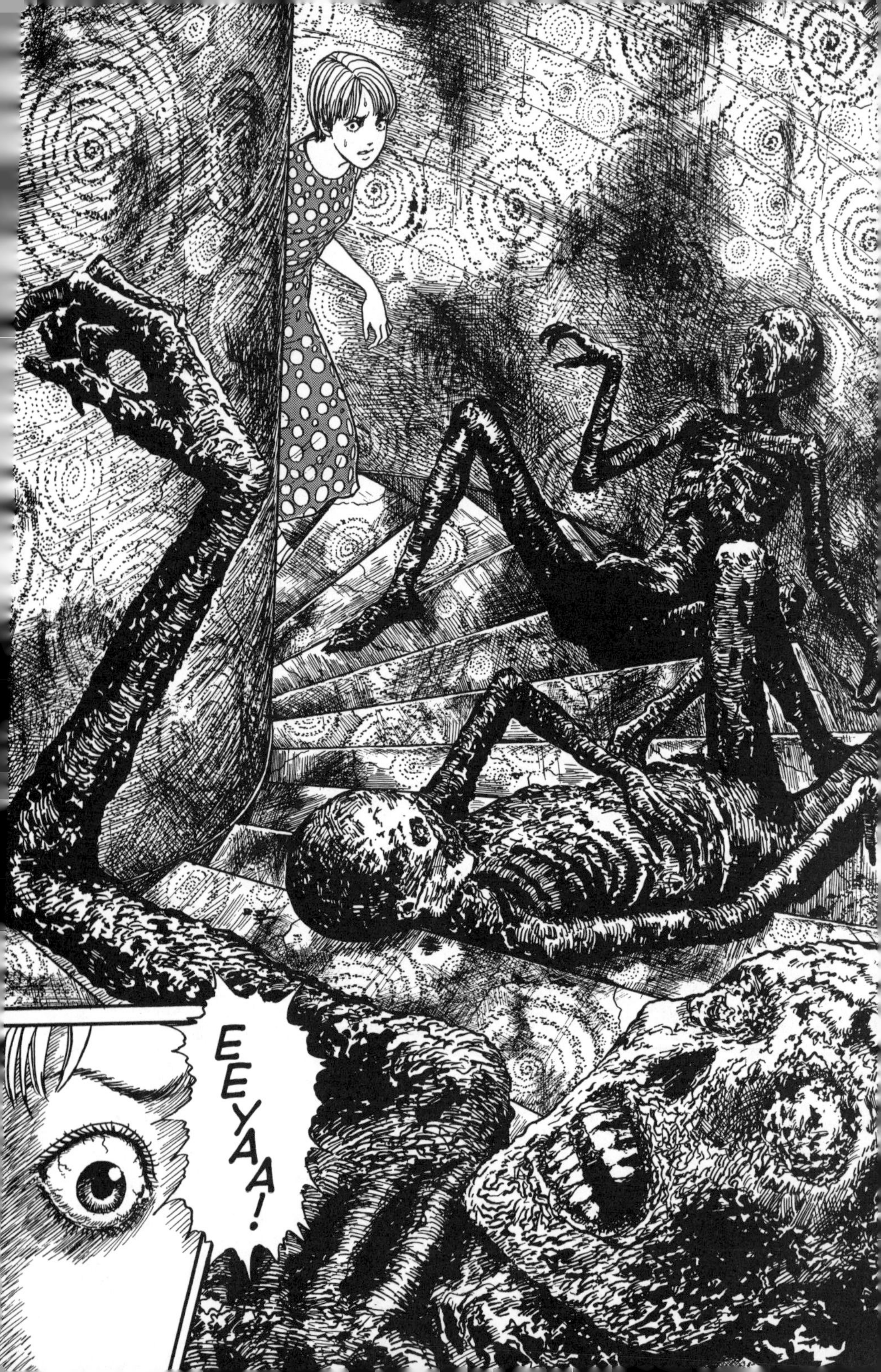
EEYAA!

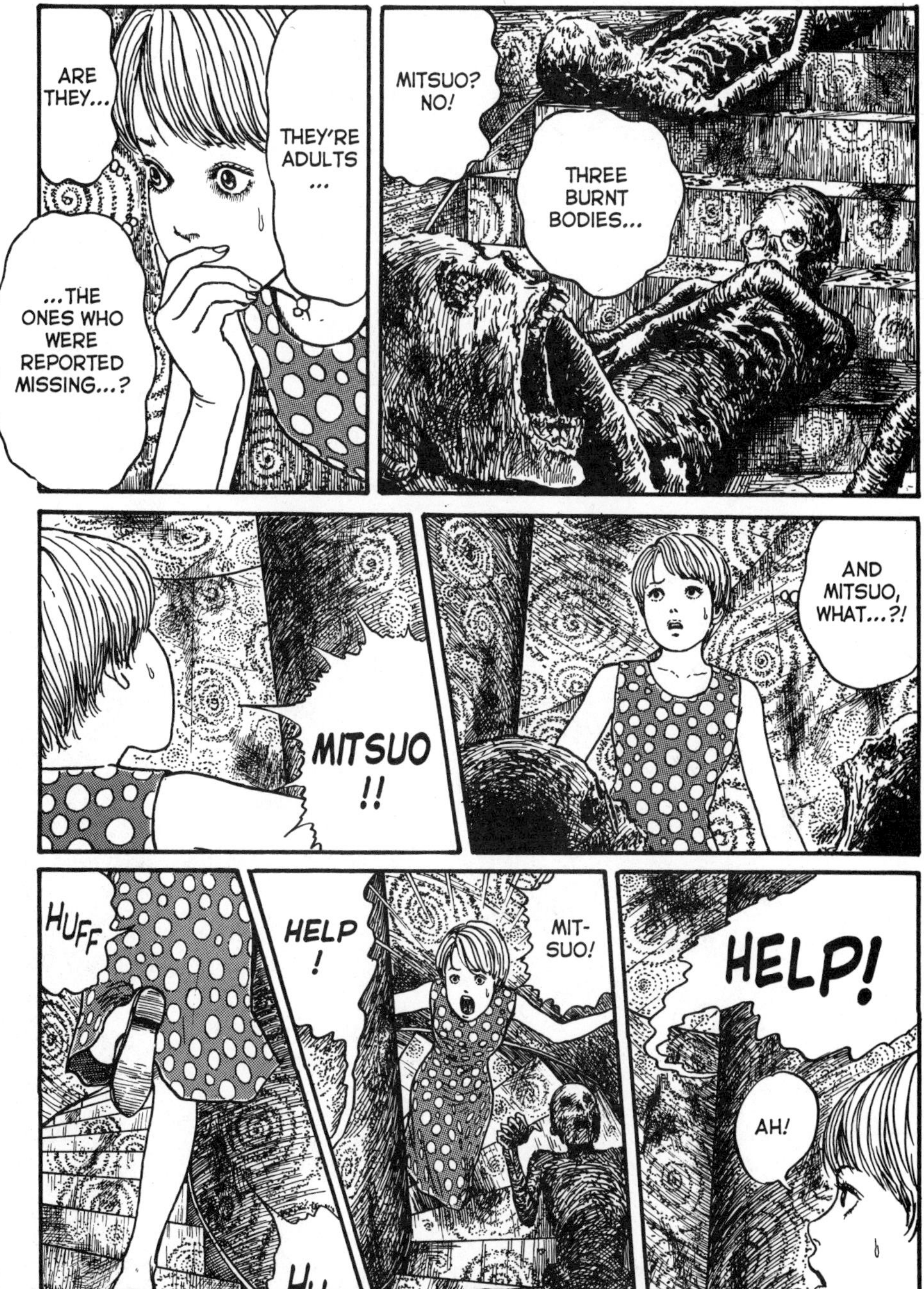
MITSUO? NO!
THREE BURNT BODIES...
THEY'RE ADULTS ...
ARE THEY...
...THE ONES WHO WERE REPORTED MISSING...?
AND MITSUO, WHAT...?!
MITSUO !!
HELP!
AH!
MIT-SUO!
HELP !
HUFF
HUFF

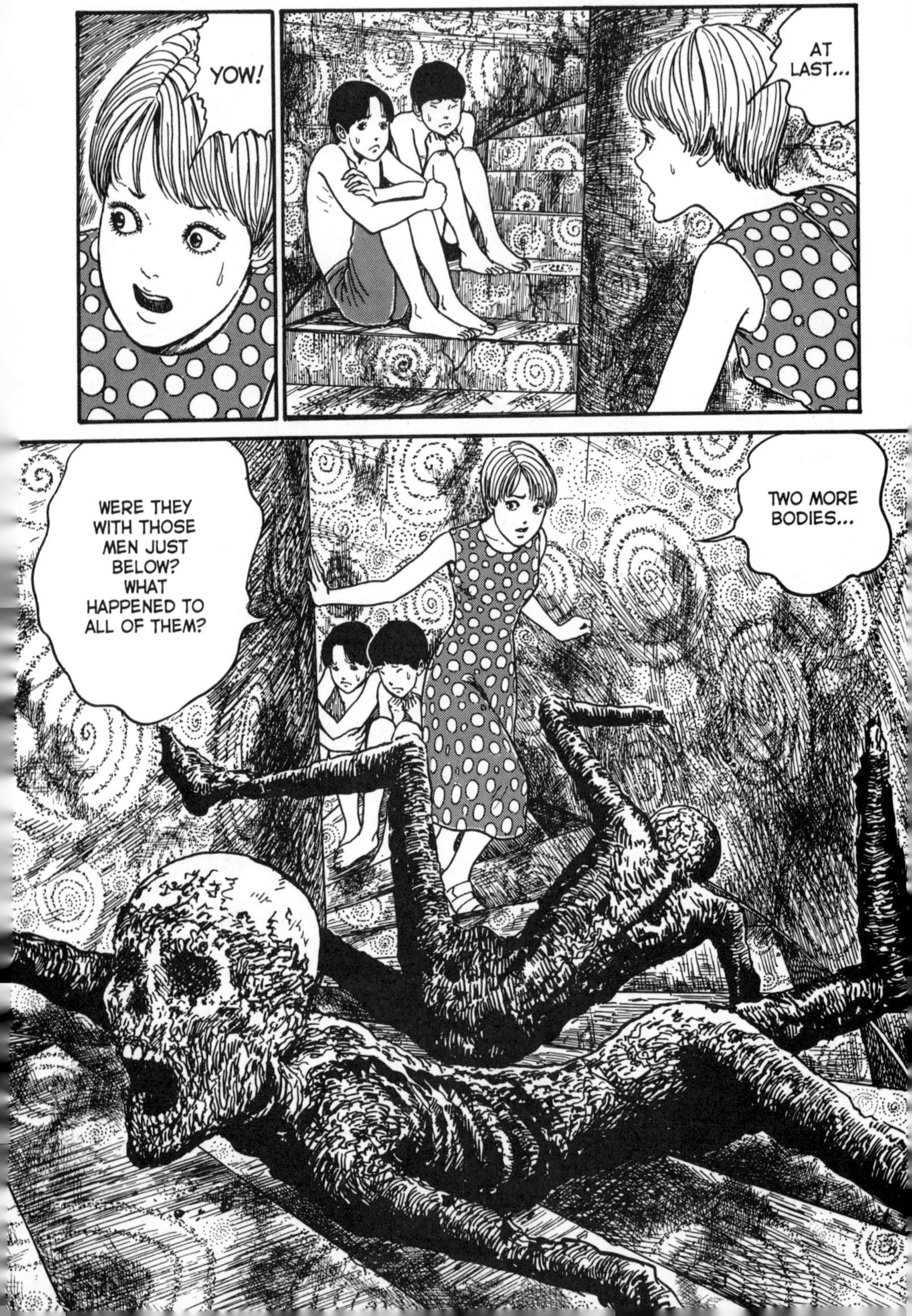
AT LAST...
YOW!
TWO MORE BODIES...
WERE THEY WITH THOSE MEN JUST BELOW? WHAT HAPPENED TO ALL OF THEM?

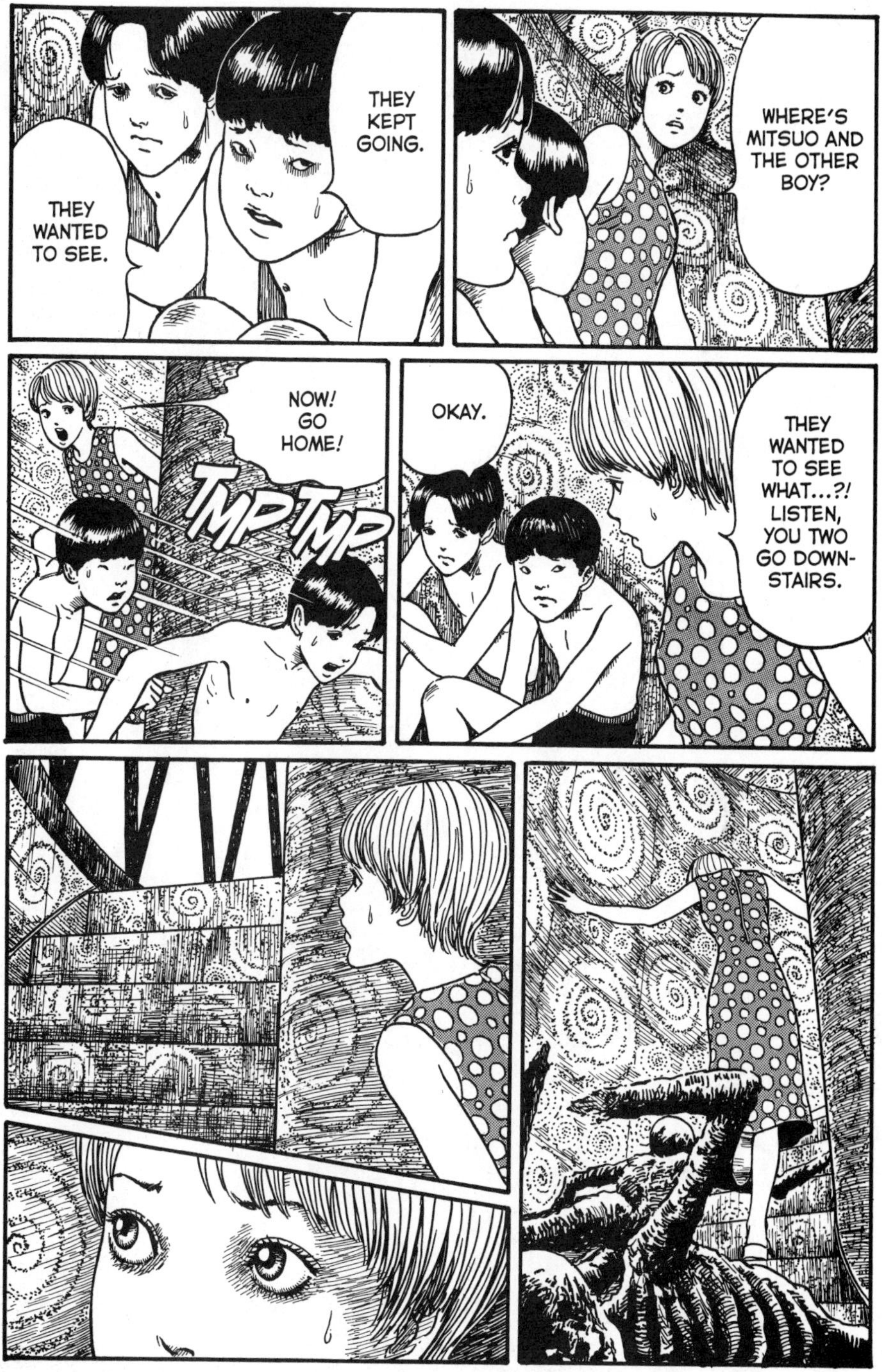
WHERE'S MITSUO AND THE OTHER BOY?
THEY KEPT GOING.
THEY WANTED TO SEE.
THEY WANTED TO SEE WHAT...?! LISTEN, YOU TWO GO DOWN-STAIRS.
OKAY.
NOW! GO HOME!
TMPTMP

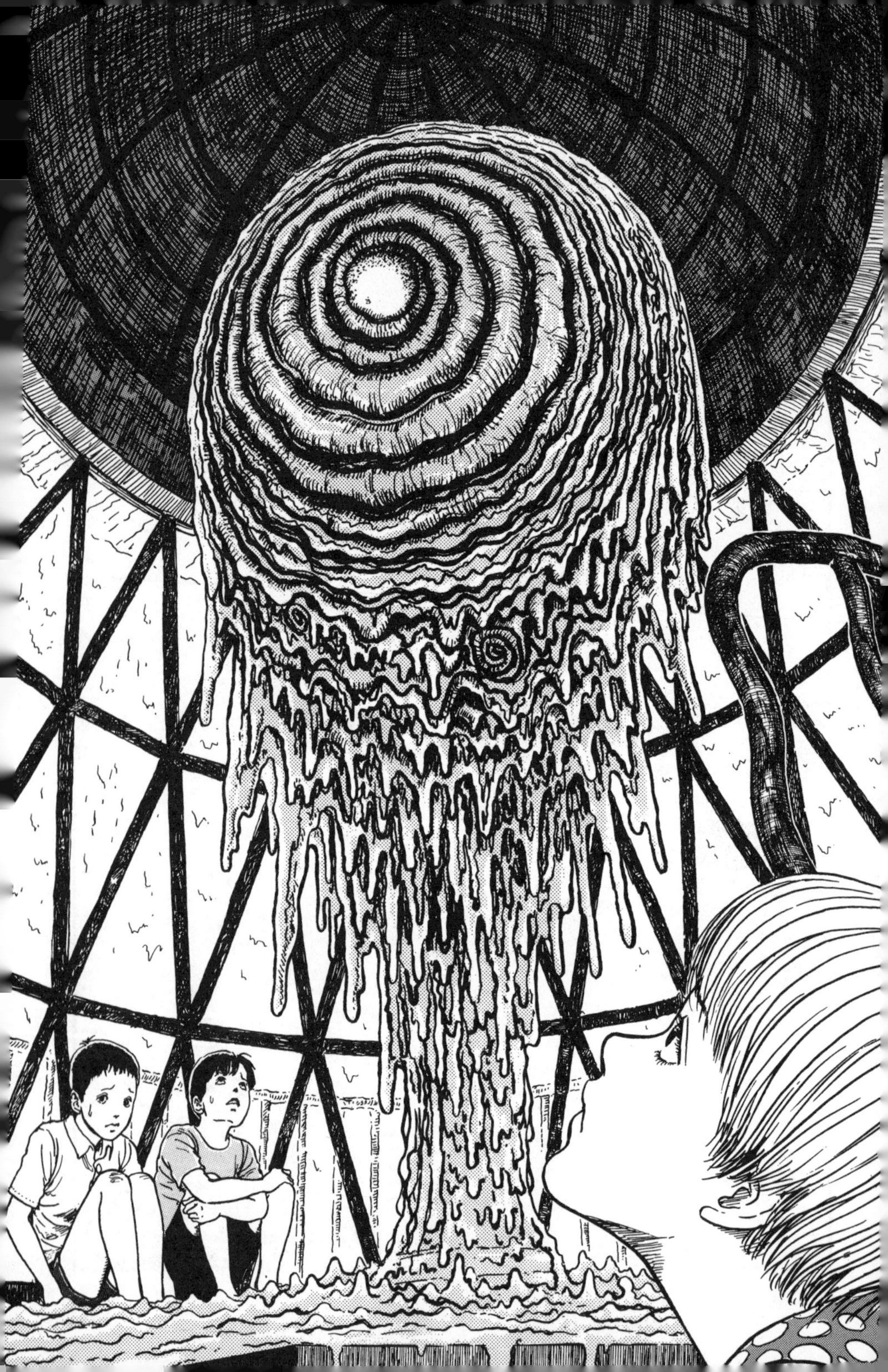

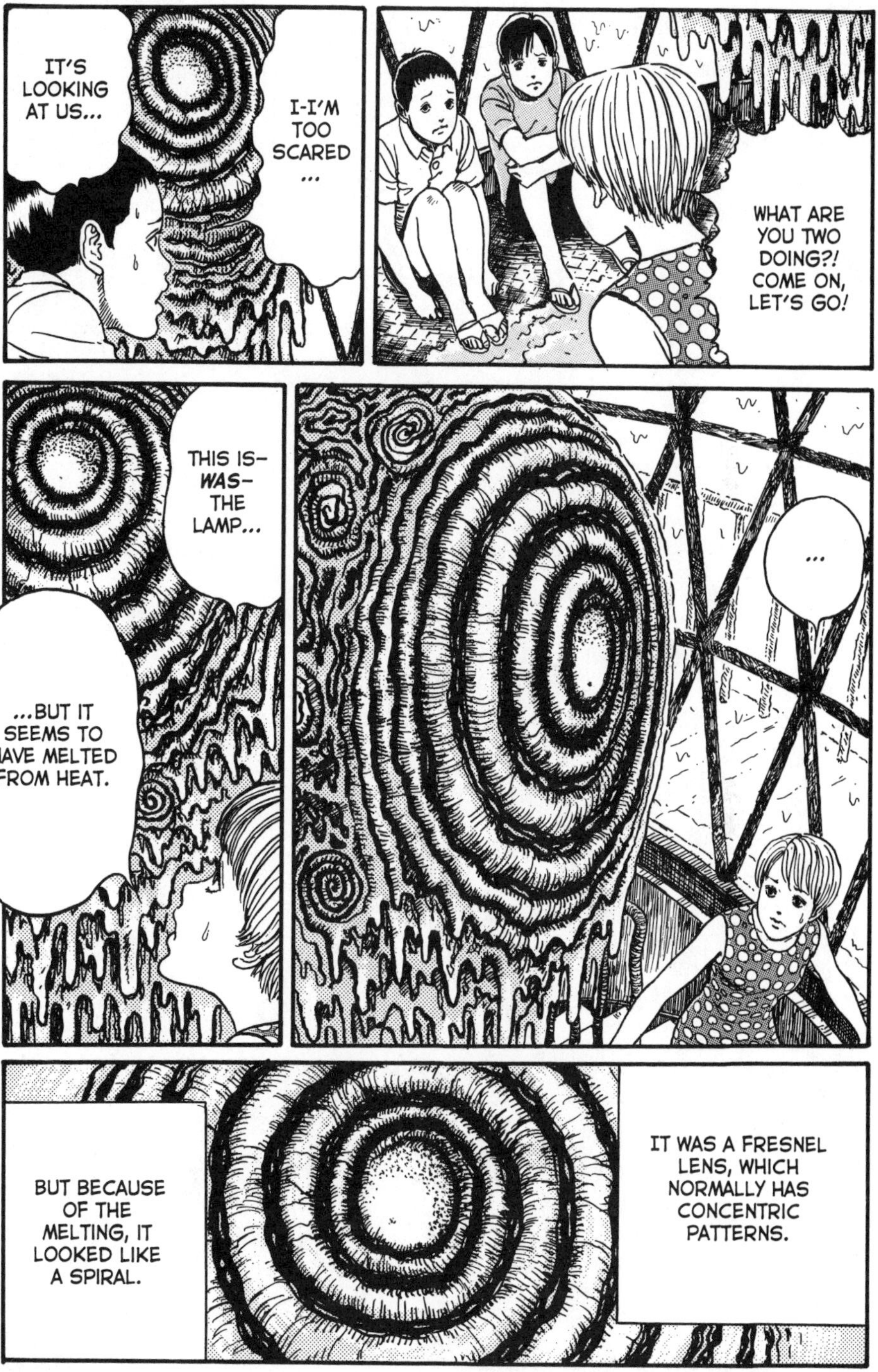
WHAT ARE YOU TWO DOING?! COME ON, LET'S GO!
I-I'M TOO SCARED ...
IT'S LOOKING AT US...
...
THIS IS—*WAS*—THE LAMP...
...BUT IT SEEMS TO HAVE MELTED FROM HEAT.
IT WAS A FRESNEL LENS, WHICH NORMALLY HAS CONCENTRIC PATTERNS.
BUT BECAUSE OF THE MELTING, IT LOOKED LIKE A SPIRAL.

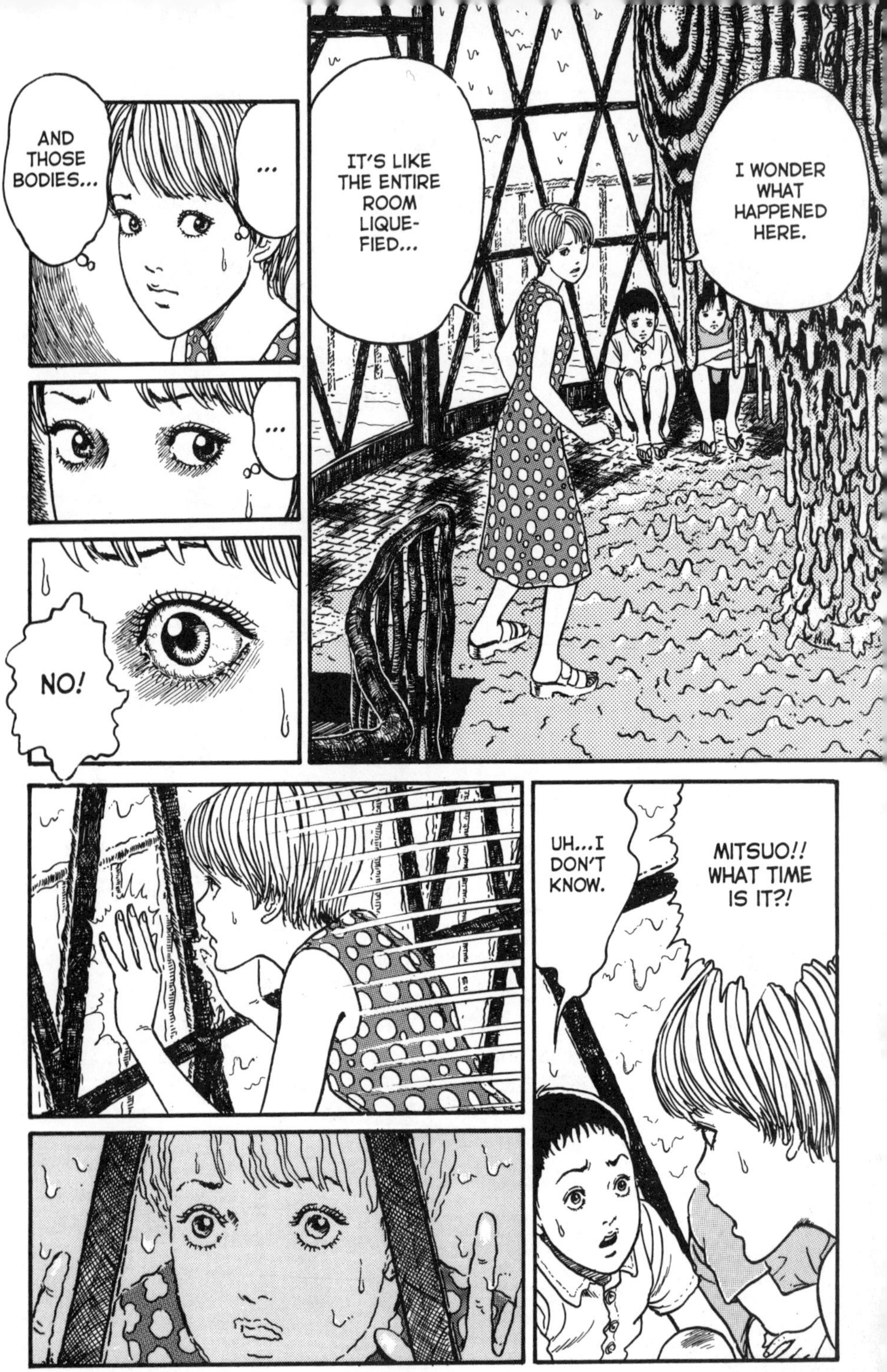
I WONDER WHAT HAPPENED HERE.
IT'S LIKE THE ENTIRE ROOM LIQUE-FIED...
AND THOSE BODIES...
...
...
NO!
MITSUO!! WHAT TIME IS IT?!
UH...I DON'T KNOW.

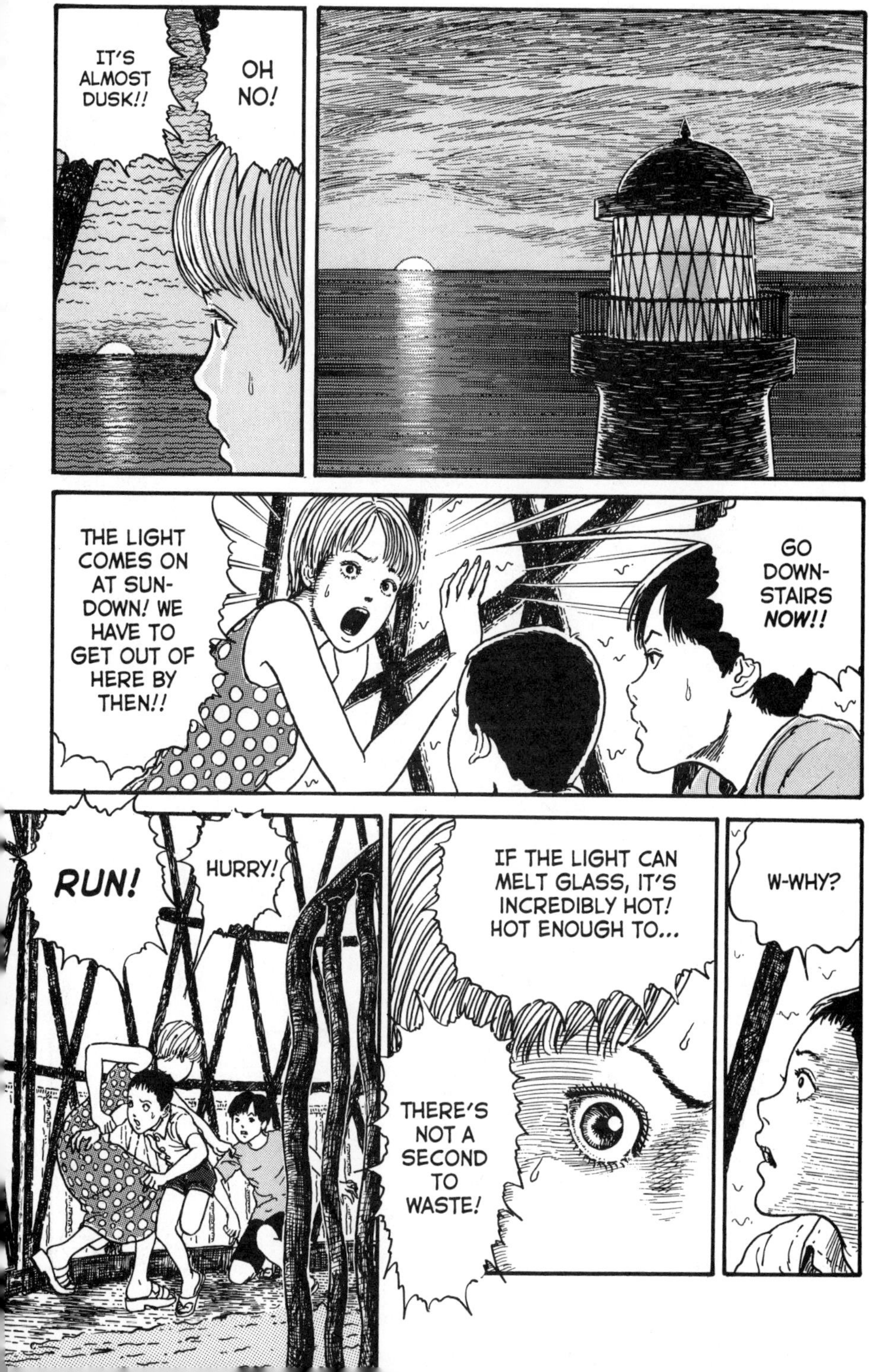
OH NO!
IT'S ALMOST DUSK!!
GO DOWN-STAIRS NOW!!
THE LIGHT COMES ON AT SUN-DOWN! WE HAVE TO GET OUT OF HERE BY THEN!!
W-WHY?
IF THE LIGHT CAN MELT GLASS, IT'S INCREDIBLY HOT! HOT ENOUGH TO...
THERE'S NOT A SECOND TO WASTE!
HURRY!
RUN!

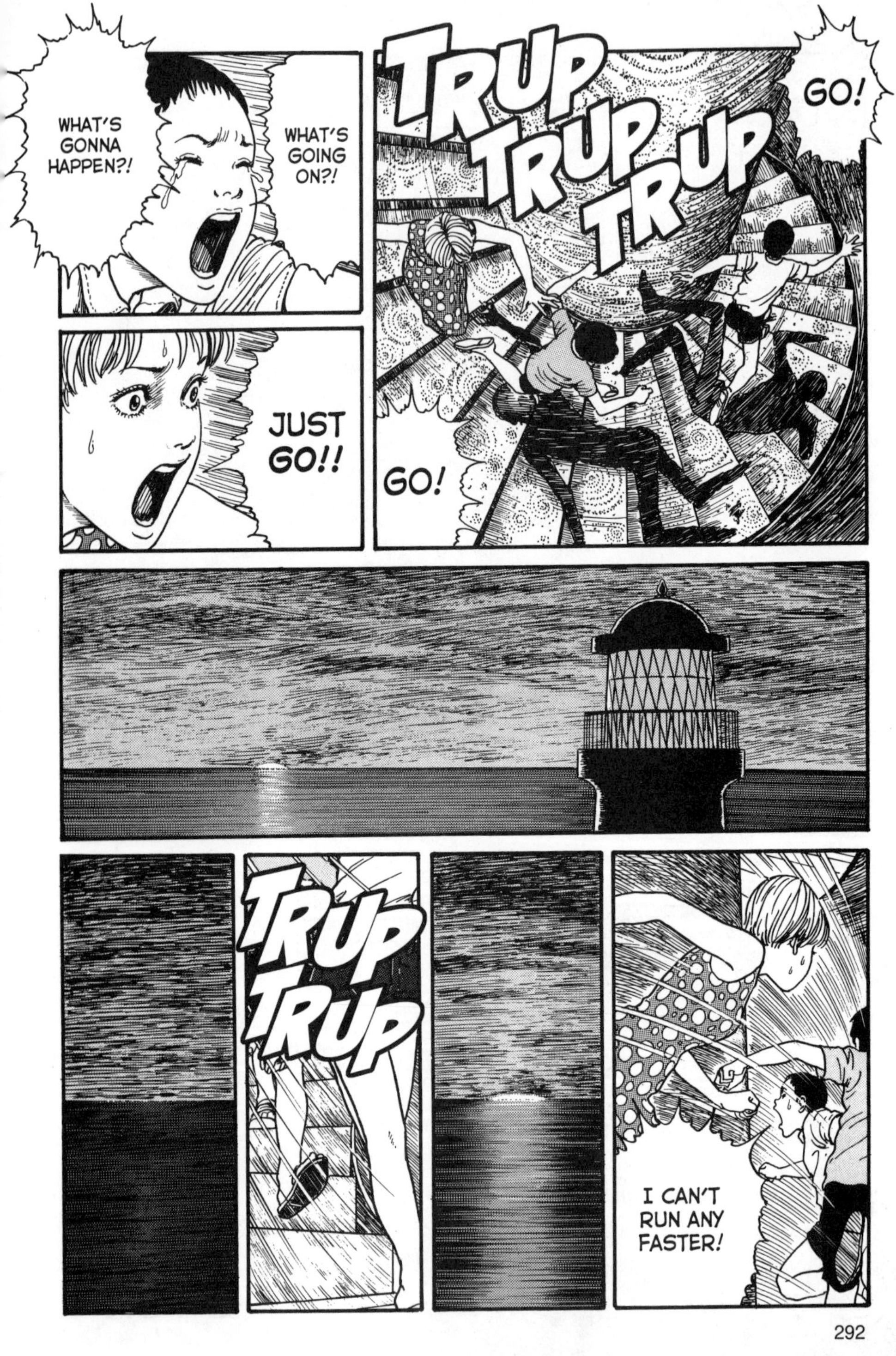
GO!
TRUP TRUP TRUP
GO!
WHAT'S GOING ON?!
WHAT'S GONNA HAPPEN?!
JUST GO!!
I CAN'T RUN ANY FASTER!
TRUP TRUP

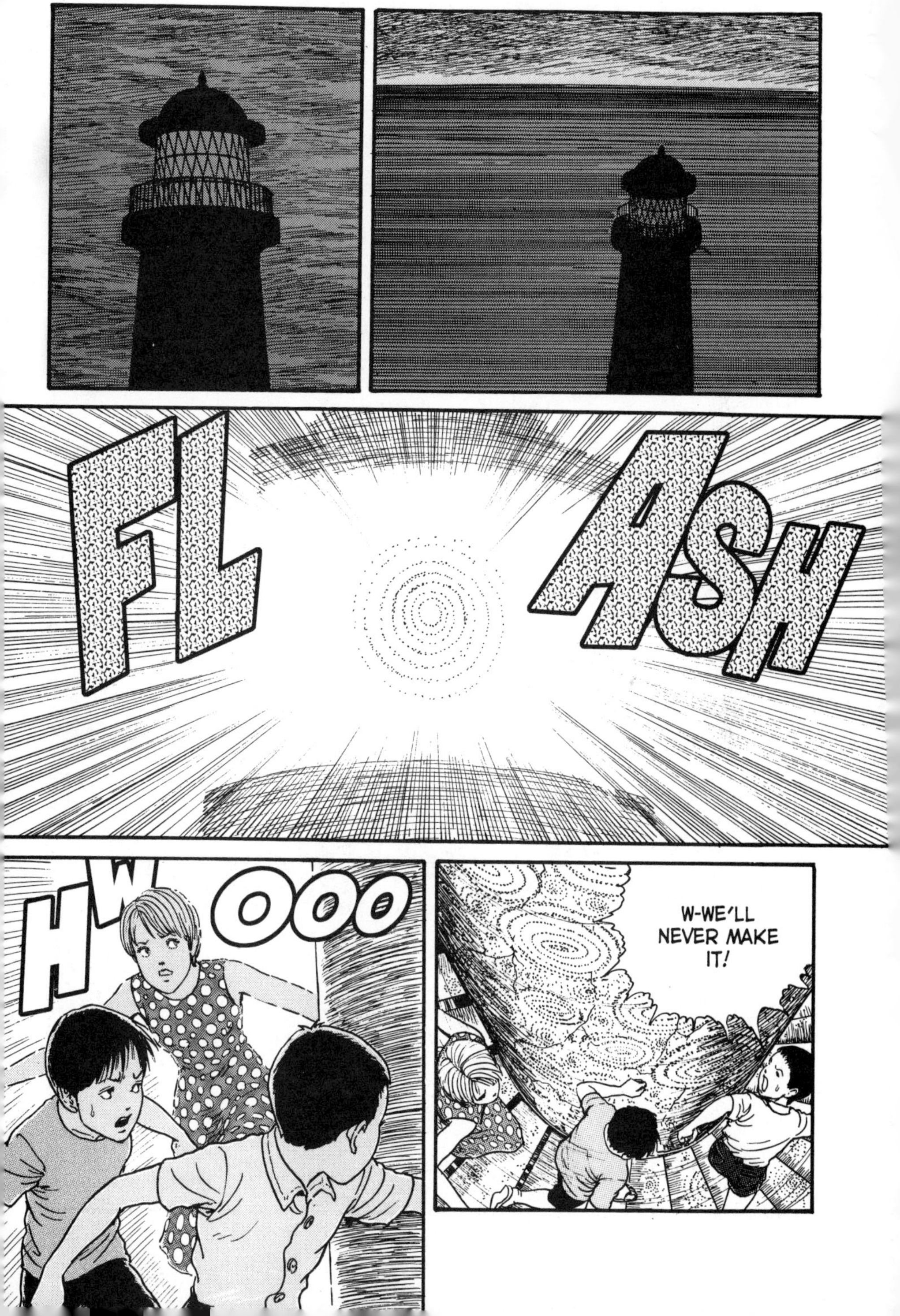
FLASH
W-WE'LL NEVER MAKE IT!
HWOOO

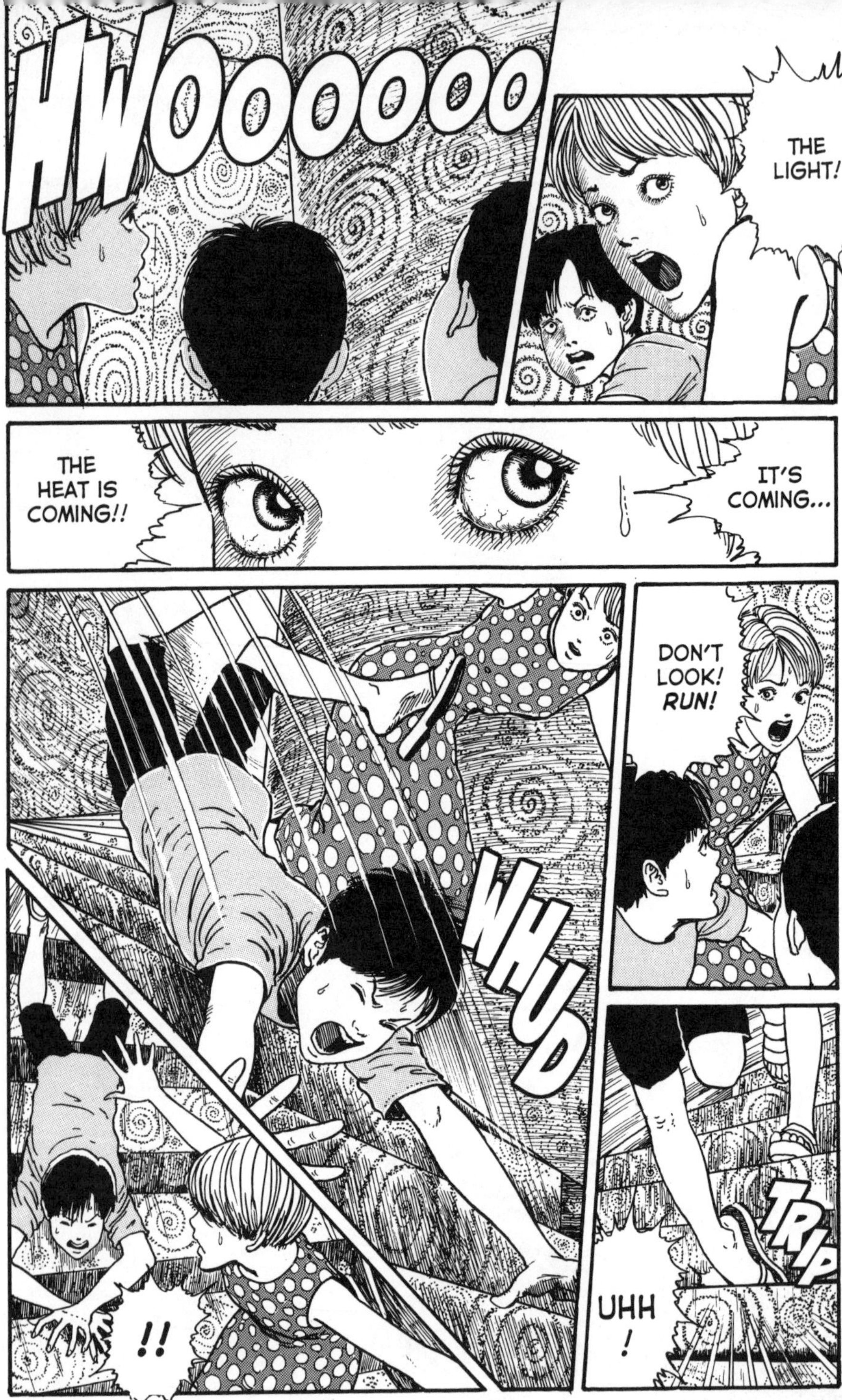
THE LIGHT!
HWOOOOOO
IT'S COMING...
THE HEAT IS COMING!!
DON'T LOOK! RUN!
TRIP
UHH !
WHUD
!!

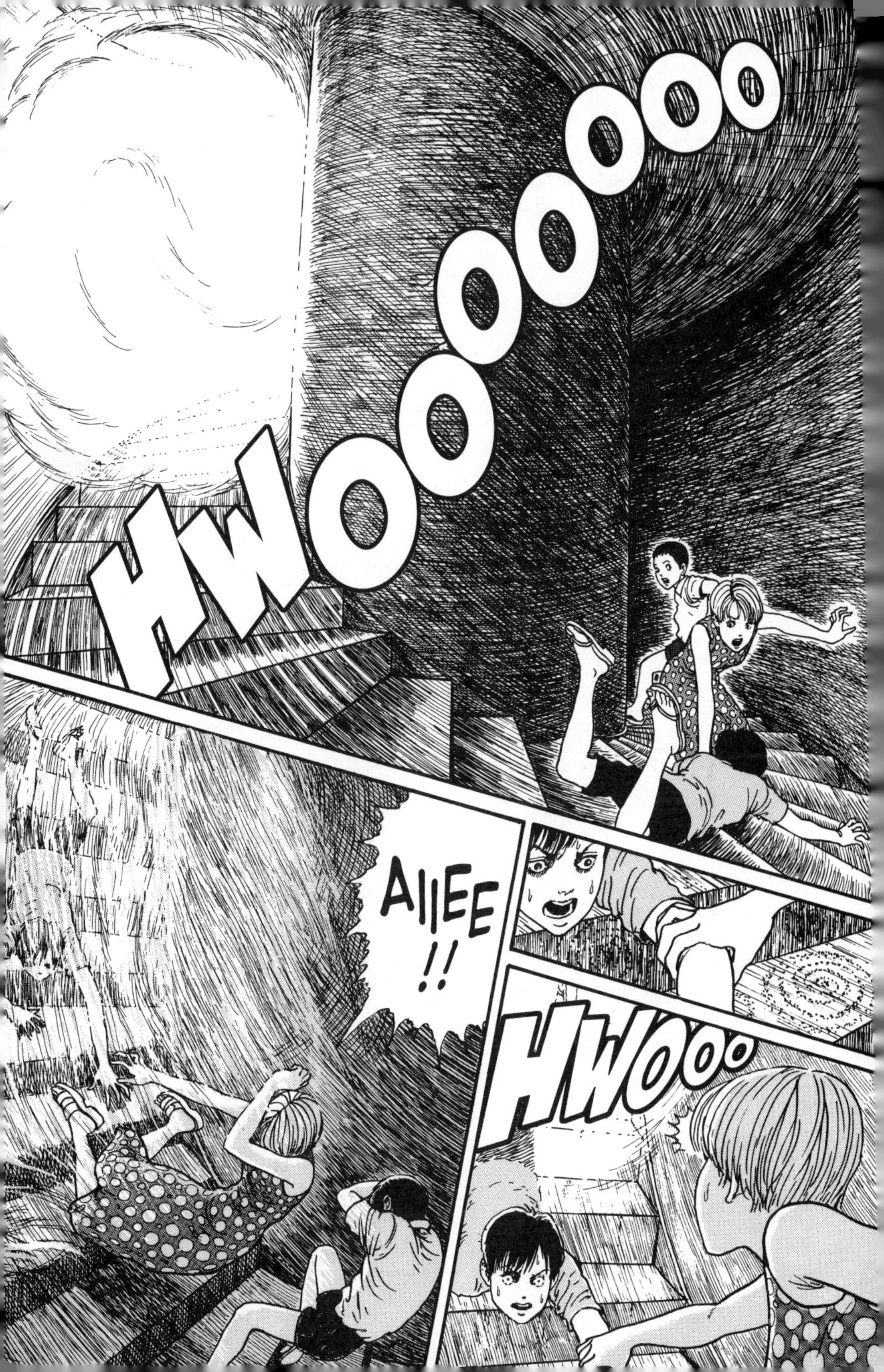
HWOOOOOOO
HWOOO
AIIEE !!

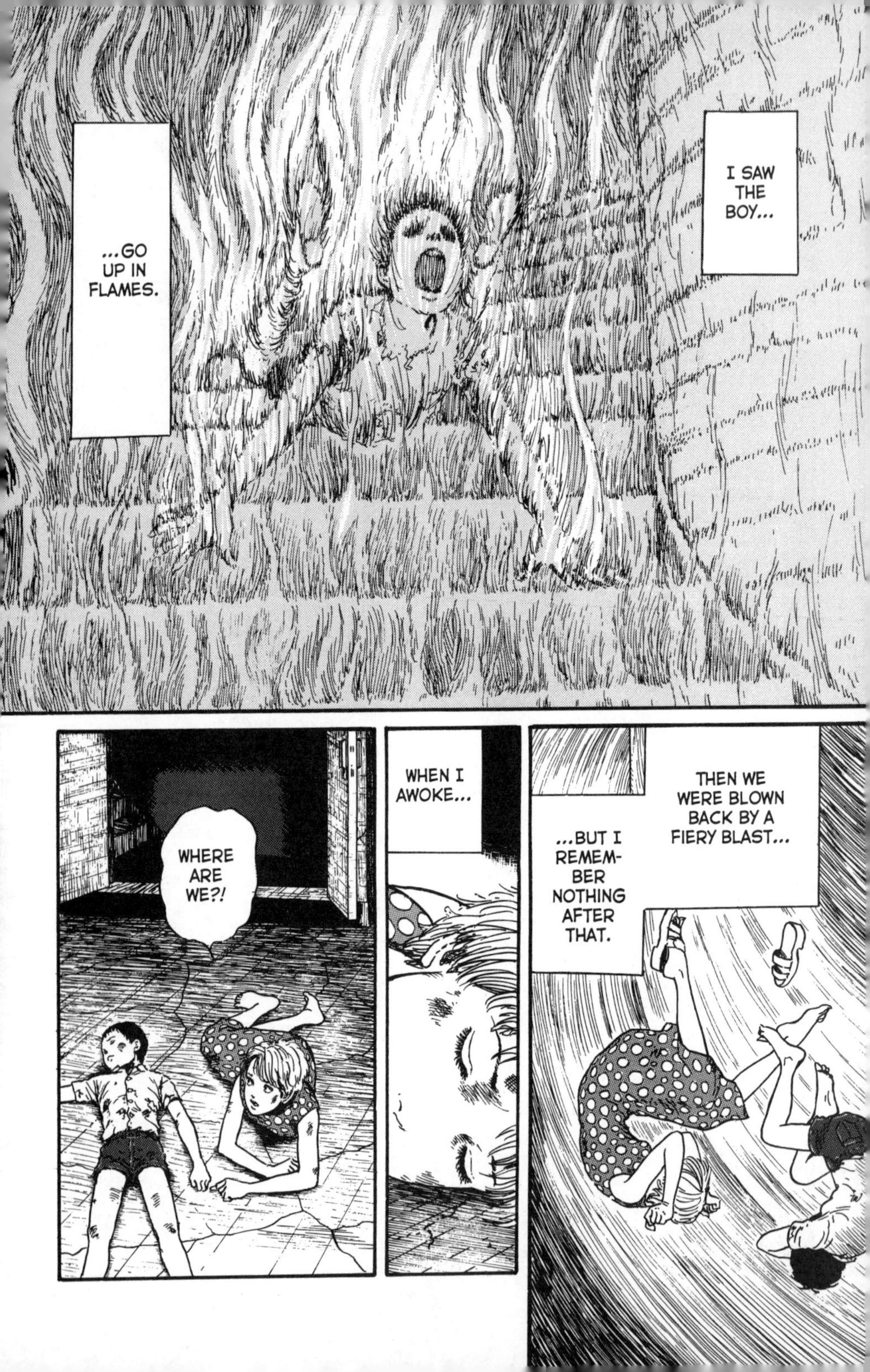
I SAW THE BOY...
...GO UP IN FLAMES.
THEN WE WERE BLOWN BACK BY A FIERY BLAST...
...BUT I REMEMBER NOTHING AFTER THAT.
WHEN I AWOKE...
WHERE ARE WE?!

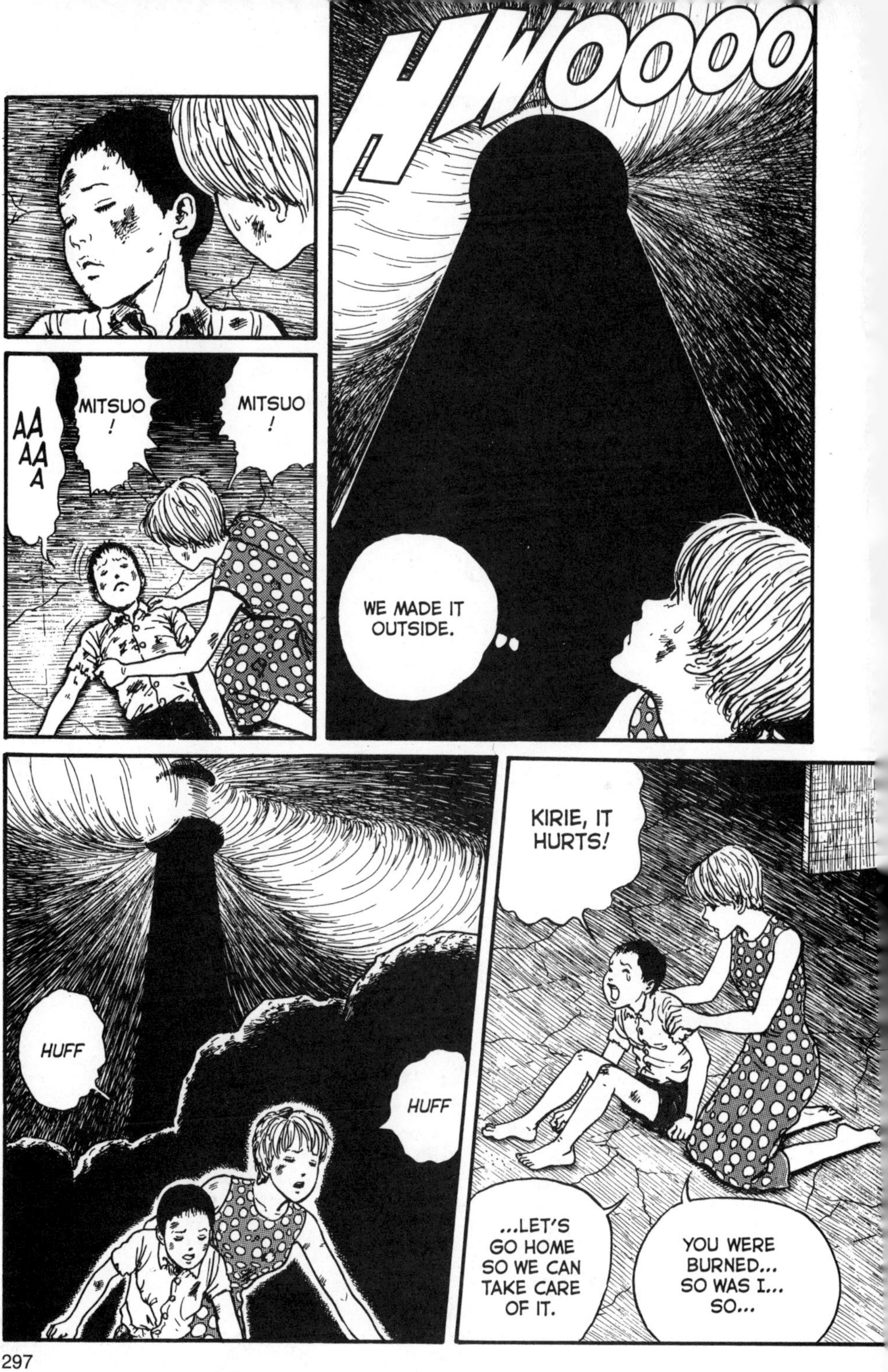
HWOOOO
WE MADE IT OUTSIDE.
MITSUO!
MITSUO!
AAAAA
KIRIE, IT HURTS!
YOU WERE BURNED... SO WAS I... SO...
...LET'S GO HOME SO WE CAN TAKE CARE OF IT.
HUFF
HUFF

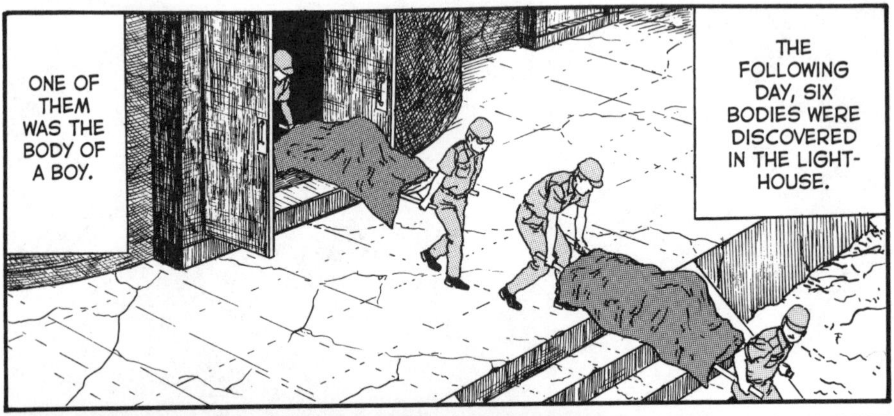
THE FOLLOWING DAY, SIX BODIES WERE DISCOVERED IN THE LIGHT-HOUSE.
ONE OF THEM WAS THE BODY OF A BOY.

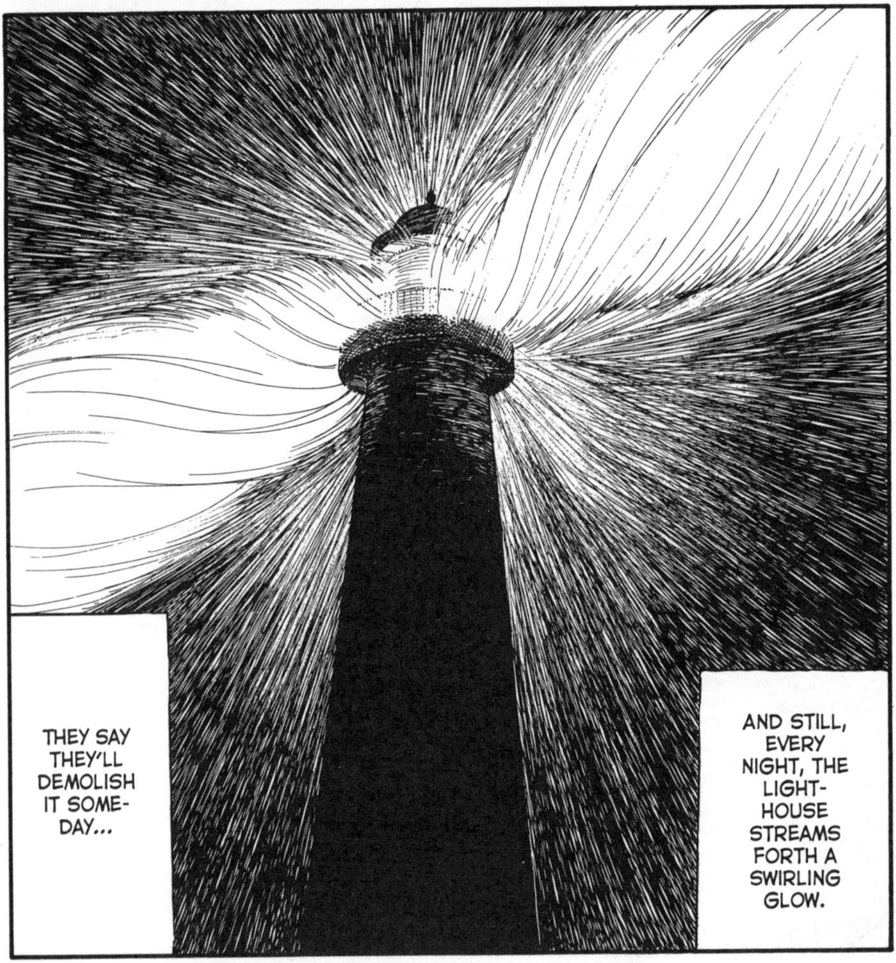
AND STILL, EVERY NIGHT, THE LIGHT-HOUSE STREAMS FORTH A SWIRLING GLOW.
THEY SAY THEY'LL DEMOLISH IT SOME-DAY...

CHAPTER 10 MOSQUITOES

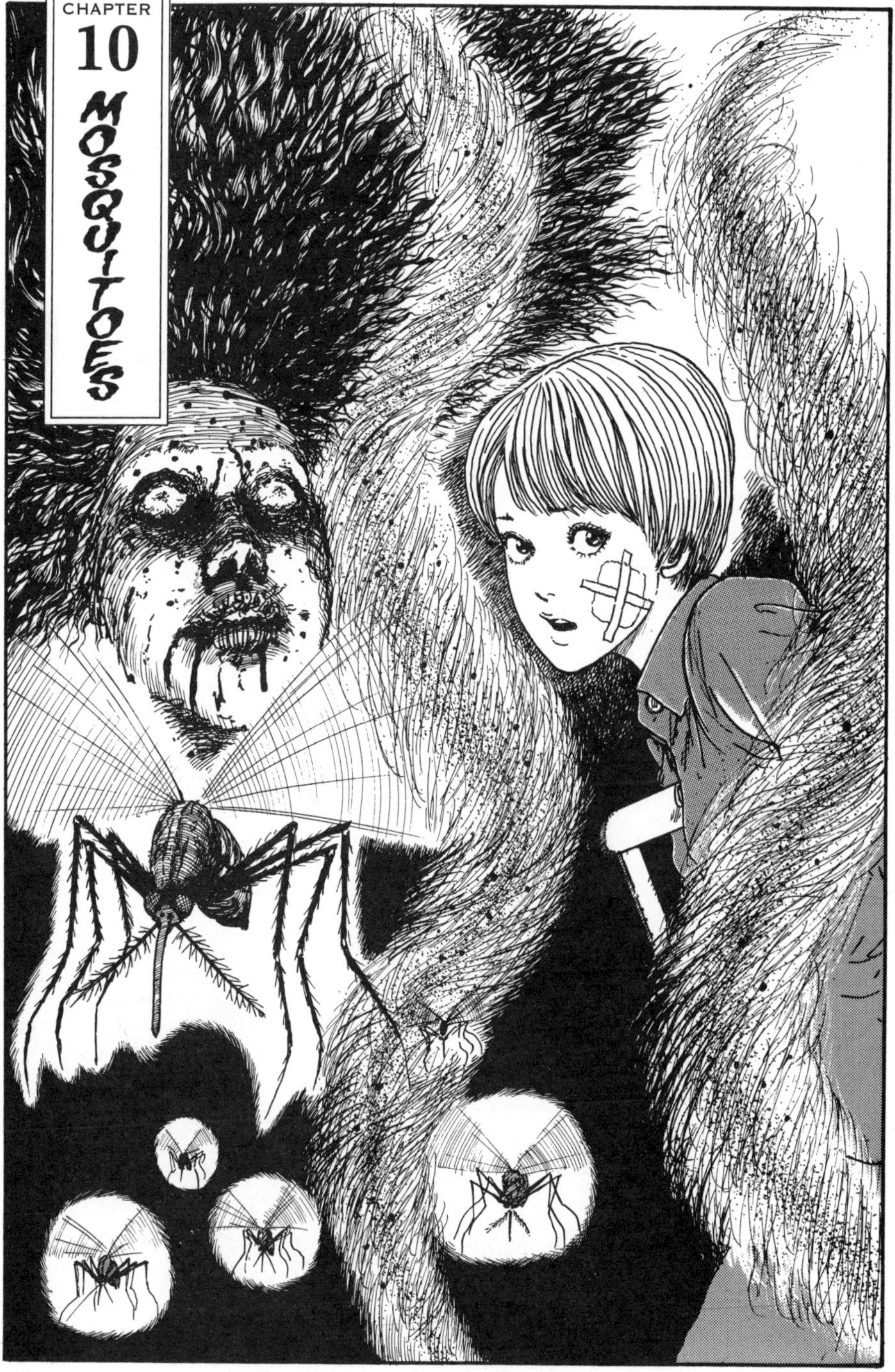

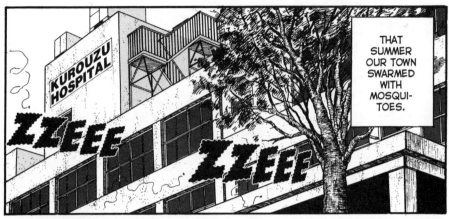

KUROUZU HOSPITAL
ZZEEE
ZZEEE
THAT SUMMER OUR TOWN SWARMED WITH MOSQUITOES.
205
Kirie Goshima
AS FOR ME, I HAD TO SPEND HALF THE SUMMER IN THE HOSPITAL.
THE BURNS AND BRUISES I RECEIVED IN THE LIGHTHOUSE WERE UNEXPECTEDLY SEVERE.
BIG COMIC
ZZEEE
MY BROTHER MITSUO WASN'T HURT AS BAD, SO HE WAS RELEASED AHEAD OF ME.

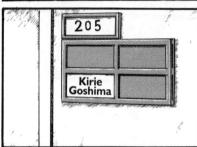

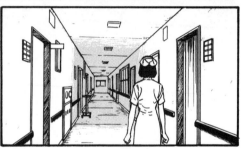

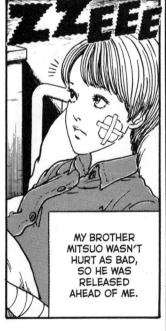

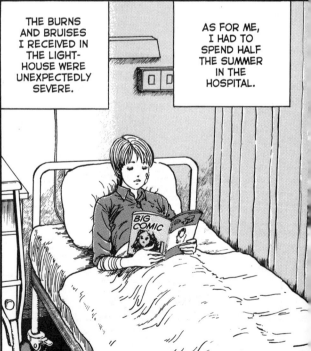

NOT AGAIN.
GEEZ, THESE MOSQUI- TOES...
ZZEEE
ZZEEEEE
WHUFF
WHUFF
ZZEEE
ZZEEE
...
THAT YEAR THE LITTLE PESTS ACTED ODDLY.
THEY WOULD FLY IN DROWSY SPIRALS.
JUST WATCHING THEM MADE YOU SLEEPY, AND THE NEXT THING YOU KNEW, YOU'D BEEN BITTEN.
ZZEEEE

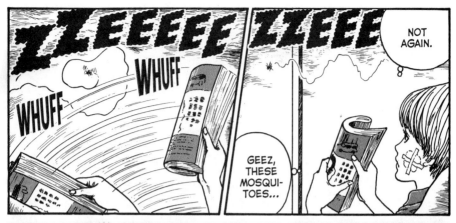

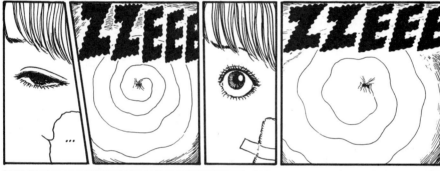

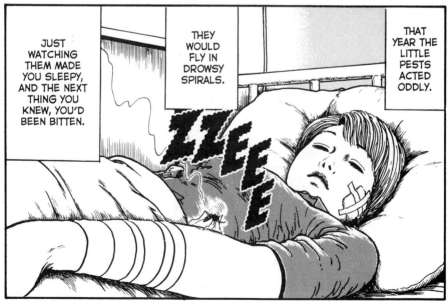

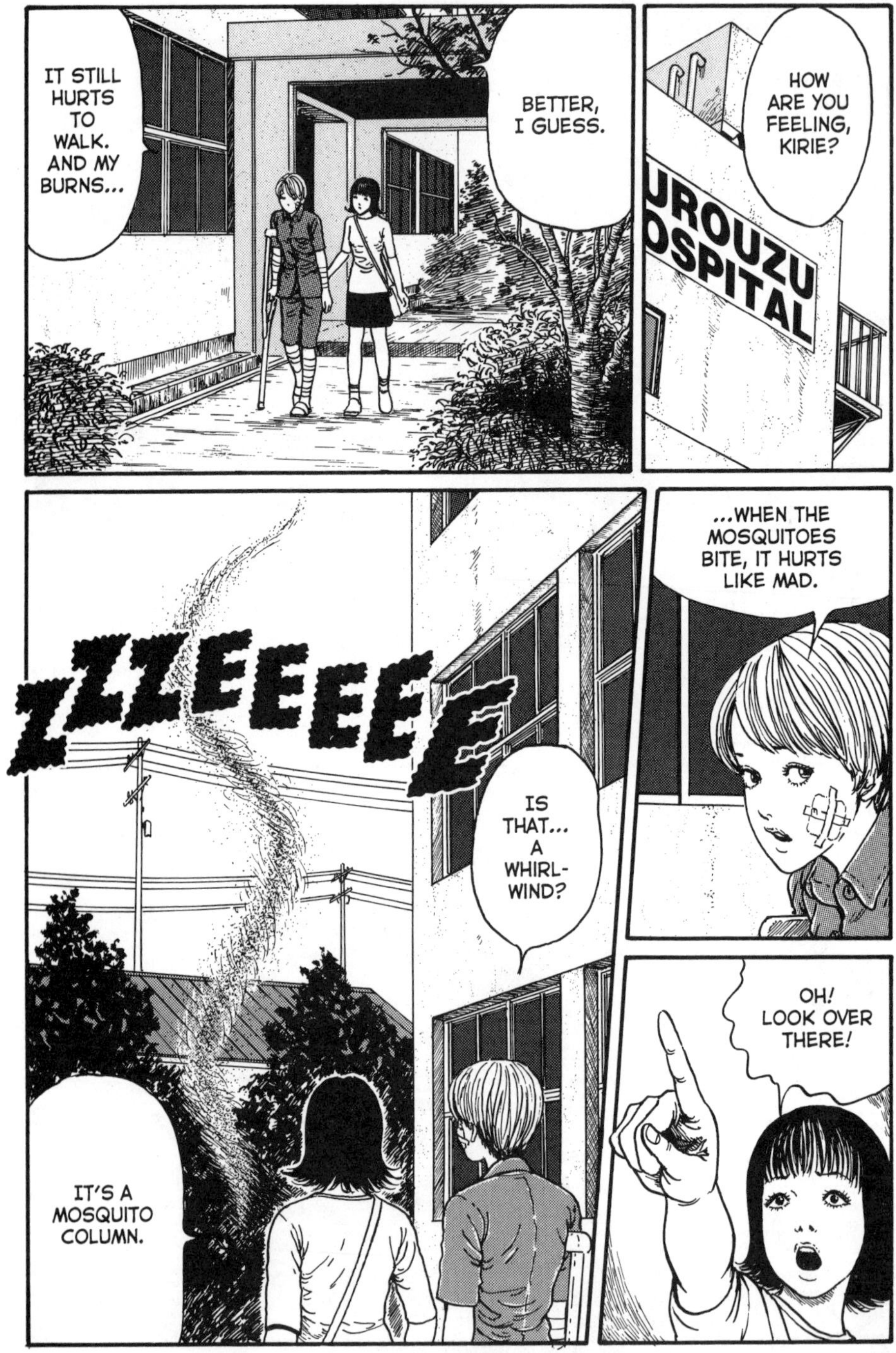
HOW ARE YOU FEELING, KIRIE?
UROUZU OSPITAL
BETTER, I GUESS.
IT STILL HURTS TO WALK. AND MY BURNS...
...WHEN THE MOSQUITOES BITE, IT HURTS LIKE MAD.
OH! LOOK OVER THERE!
ZZZEEEEE
IS THAT... A WHIRL-WIND?
IT'S A MOSQUITO COLUMN.

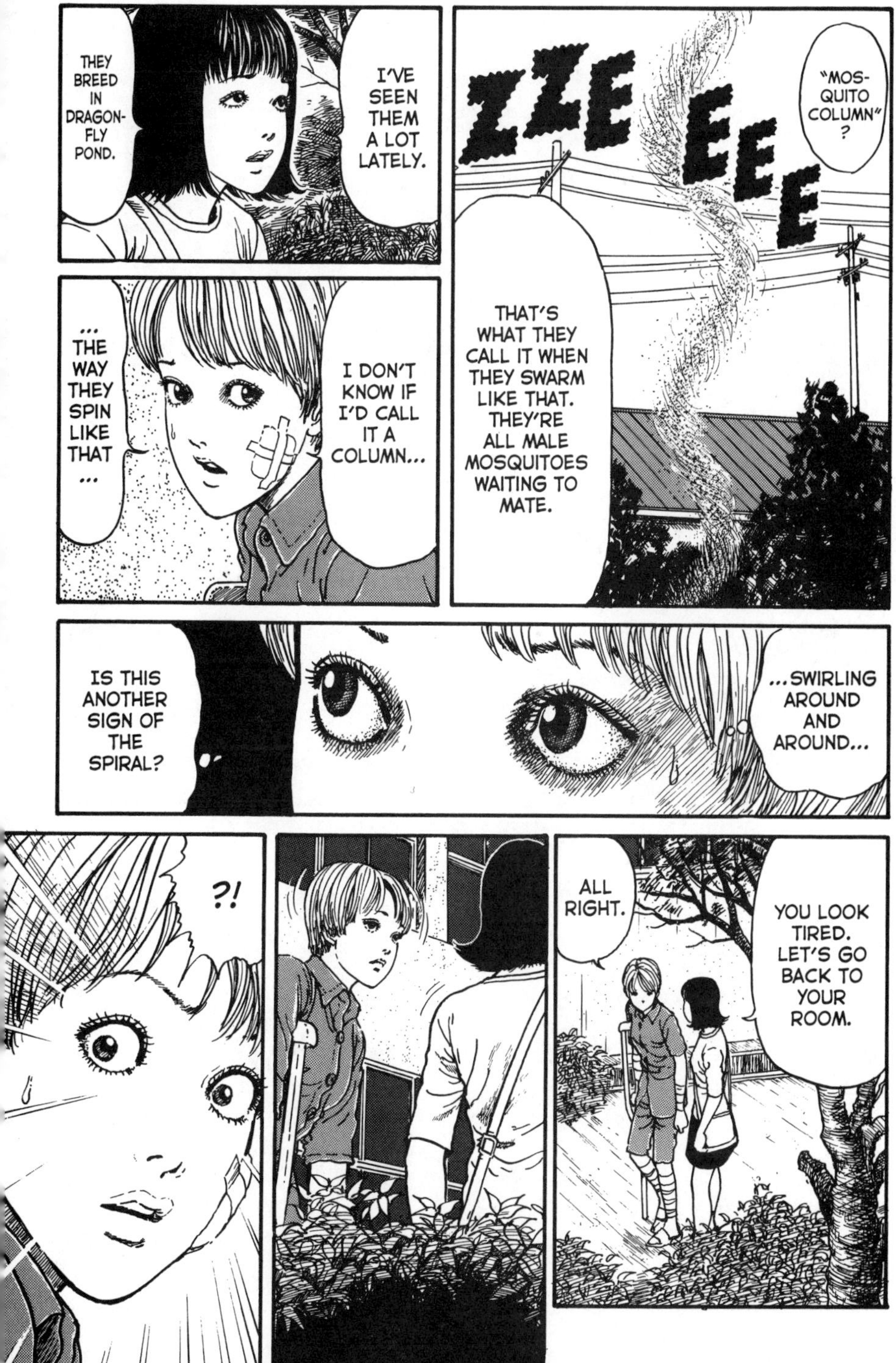
"MOSQUITO COLUMN"?
ZZEEEE
THAT'S WHAT THEY CALL IT WHEN THEY SWARM LIKE THAT. THEY'RE ALL MALE MOSQUITOES WAITING TO MATE.
I'VE SEEN THEM A LOT LATELY.
THEY BREED IN DRAGONFLY POND.
I DON'T KNOW IF I'D CALL IT A COLUMN...
...THE WAY THEY SPIN LIKE THAT...
...SWIRLING AROUND AND AROUND...
IS THIS ANOTHER SIGN OF THE SPIRAL?
YOU LOOK TIRED. LET'S GO BACK TO YOUR ROOM.
ALL RIGHT.
?!

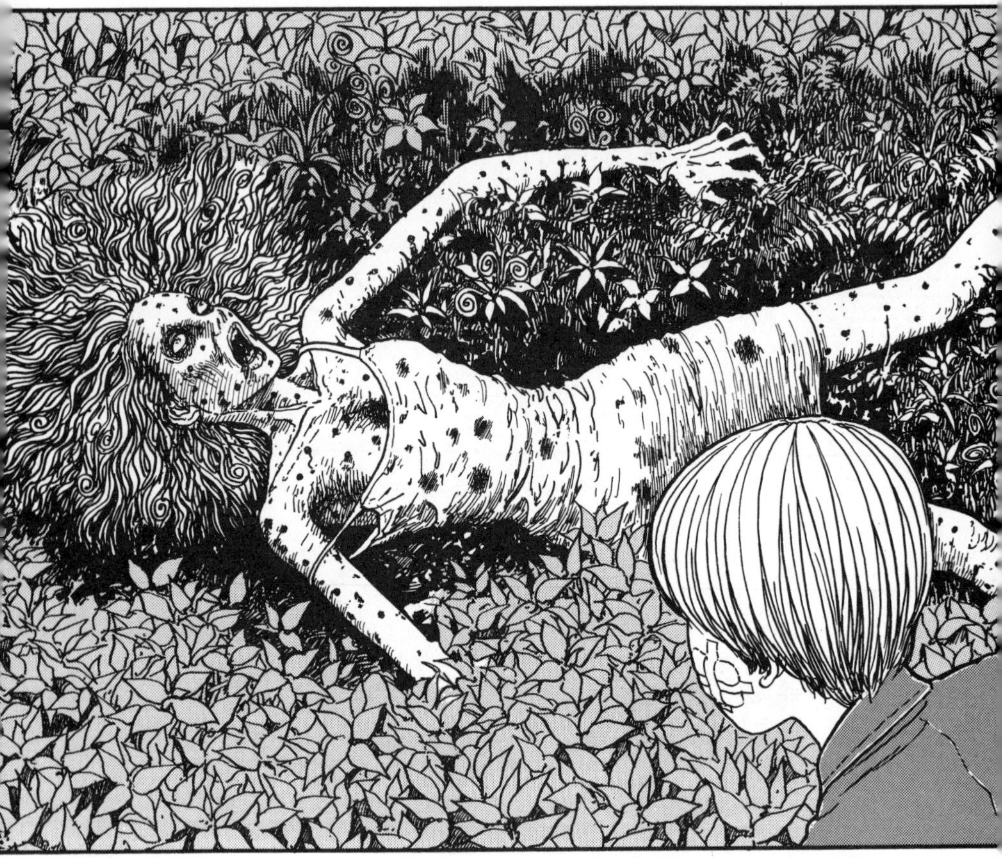

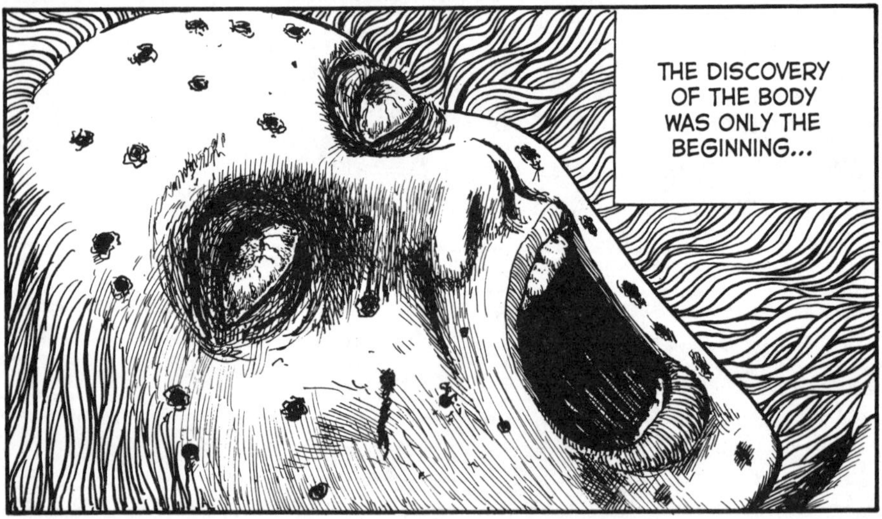
THE DISCOVERY OF THE BODY WAS ONLY THE BEGINNING...

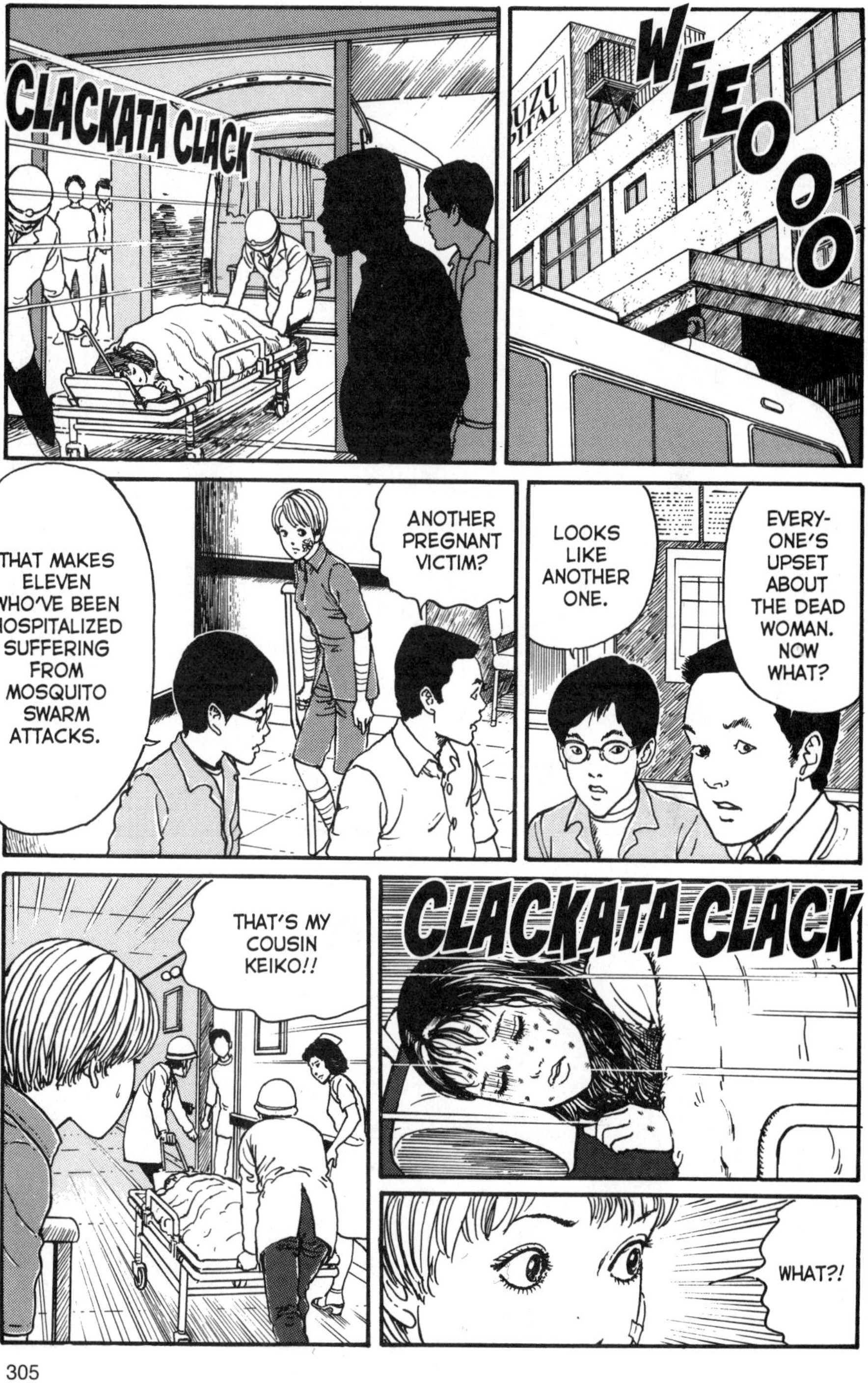
WEEOOO
CLACKATA CLACK
EVERY-ONE'S UPSET ABOUT THE DEAD WOMAN. NOW WHAT?
LOOKS LIKE ANOTHER ONE.
ANOTHER PREGNANT VICTIM?
THAT MAKES ELEVEN WHO'VE BEEN HOSPITALIZED SUFFERING FROM MOSQUITO SWARM ATTACKS.
CLACKATA CLACK
WHAT?!
THAT'S MY COUSIN KEIKO!!

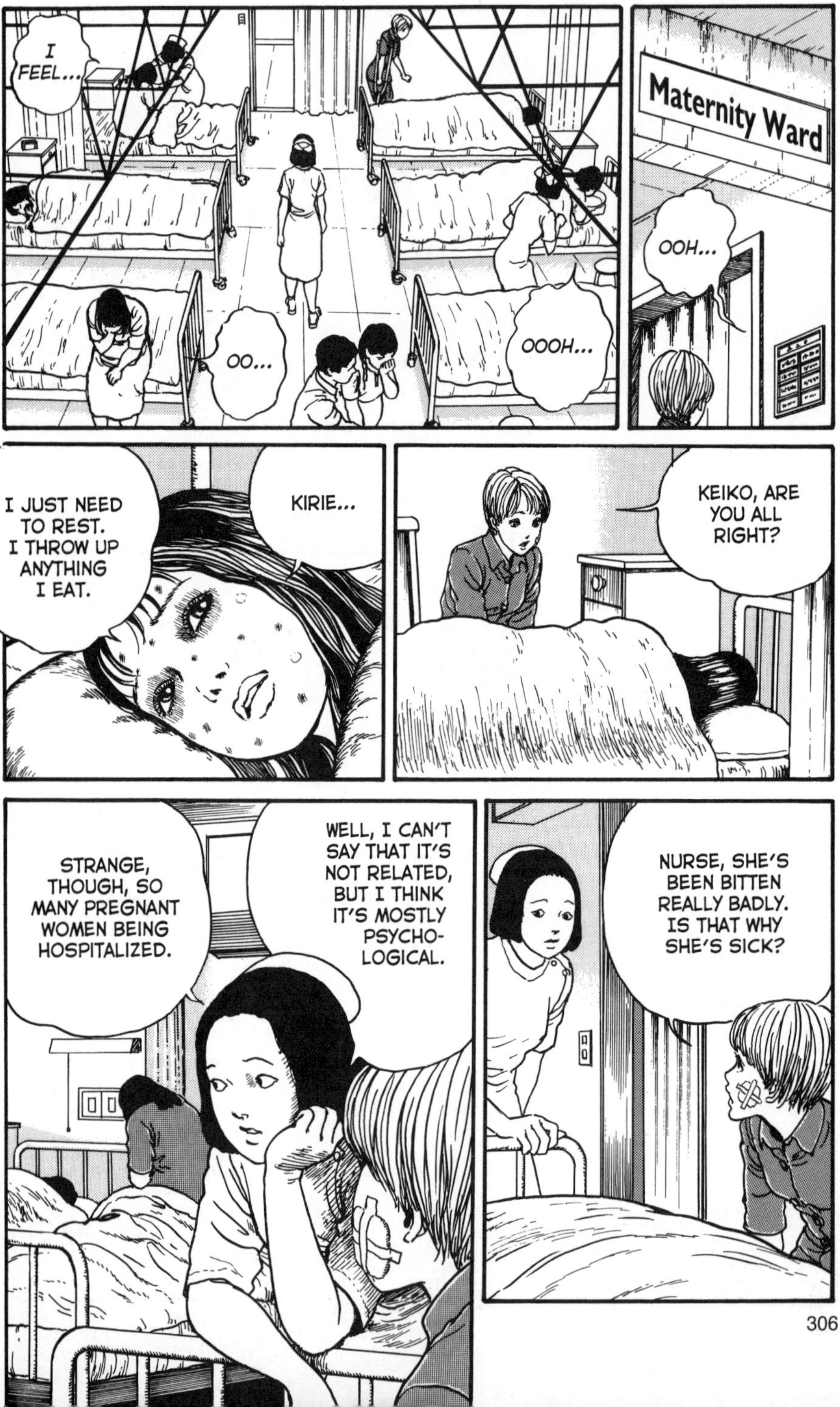
Maternity Ward
OOH...
I FEEL...
OOOH...
OO...
KEIKO, ARE YOU ALL RIGHT?
KIRIE...
I JUST NEED TO REST. I THROW UP ANYTHING I EAT.
NURSE, SHE'S BEEN BITTEN REALLY BADLY. IS THAT WHY SHE'S SICK?
WELL, I CAN'T SAY THAT IT'S NOT RELATED, BUT I THINK IT'S MOSTLY PSYCHO-LOGICAL.
STRANGE, THOUGH, SO MANY PREGNANT WOMEN BEING HOSPITALIZED.

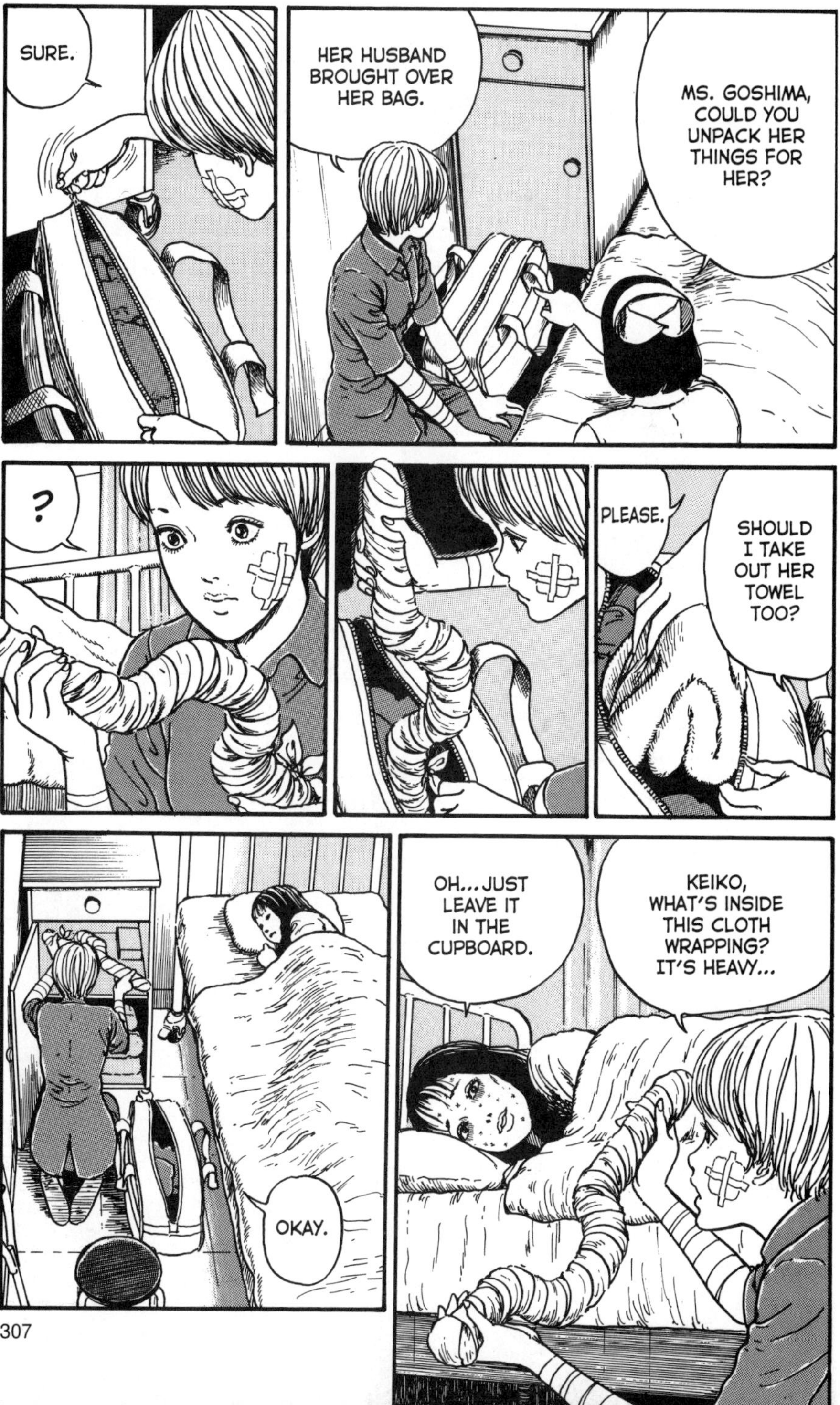
MS. GOSHIMA, COULD YOU UNPACK HER THINGS FOR HER?
HER HUSBAND BROUGHT OVER HER BAG.
SURE.
SHOULD I TAKE OUT HER TOWEL TOO?
PLEASE.
?
KEIKO, WHAT'S INSIDE THIS CLOTH WRAPPING? IT'S HEAVY...
OH...JUST LEAVE IT IN THE CUPBOARD.
OKAY.

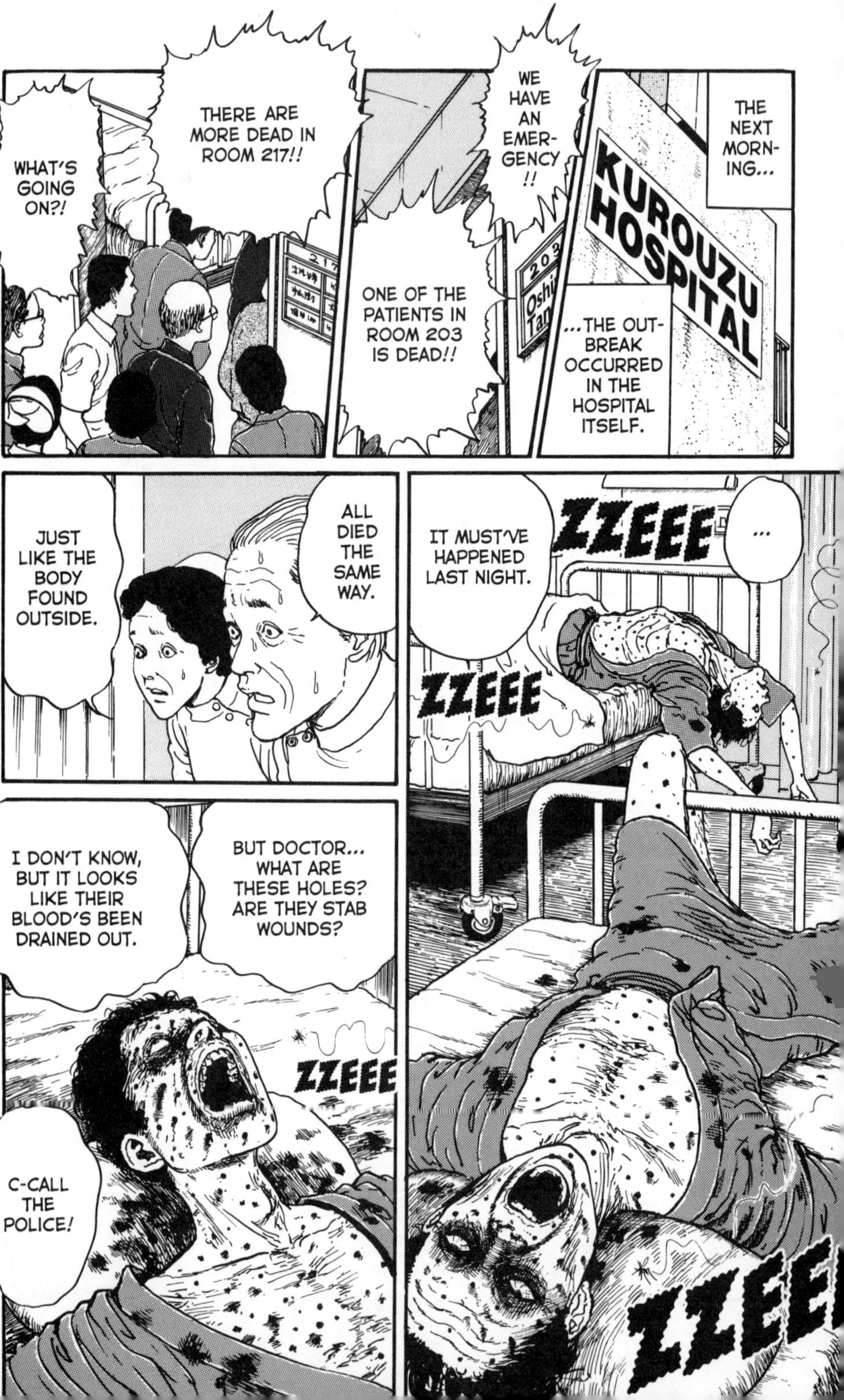
THE NEXT MORNING...
KUROUZU HOSPITAL
...THE OUTBREAK OCCURRED IN THE HOSPITAL ITSELF.
WE HAVE AN EMERGENCY!!
ONE OF THE PATIENTS IN ROOM 203 IS DEAD!!
THERE ARE MORE DEAD IN ROOM 217!!
WHAT'S GOING ON?!
...
ZZEEE
IT MUST'VE HAPPENED LAST NIGHT.
ZZEEE
ZZEE
ALL DIED THE SAME WAY.
JUST LIKE THE BODY FOUND OUTSIDE.
BUT DOCTOR... WHAT ARE THESE HOLES? ARE THEY STAB WOUNDS?
I DON'T KNOW, BUT IT LOOKS LIKE THEIR BLOOD'S BEEN DRAINED OUT.
ZZEEE
C-CALL THE POLICE!

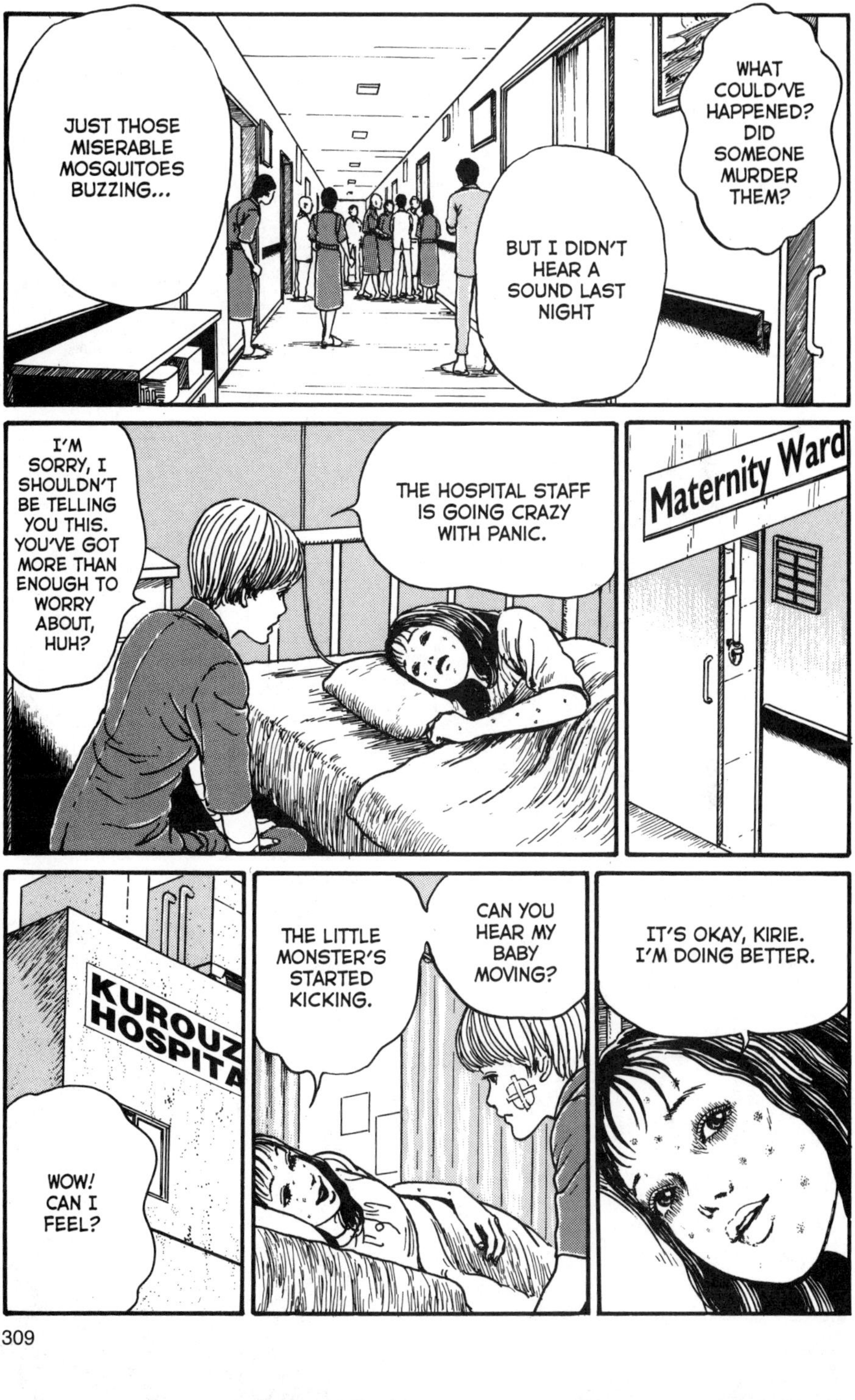
WHAT COULD'VE HAPPENED? DID SOMEONE MURDER THEM?
BUT I DIDN'T HEAR A SOUND LAST NIGHT
JUST THOSE MISERABLE MOSQUITOES BUZZING...
Maternity Ward
THE HOSPITAL STAFF IS GOING CRAZY WITH PANIC.
I'M SORRY, I SHOULDN'T BE TELLING YOU THIS. YOU'VE GOT MORE THAN ENOUGH TO WORRY ABOUT, HUH?
IT'S OKAY, KIRIE. I'M DOING BETTER.
CAN YOU HEAR MY BABY MOVING?
THE LITTLE MONSTER'S STARTED KICKING.
KUROUZ
HOSPITA
WOW! CAN I FEEL?

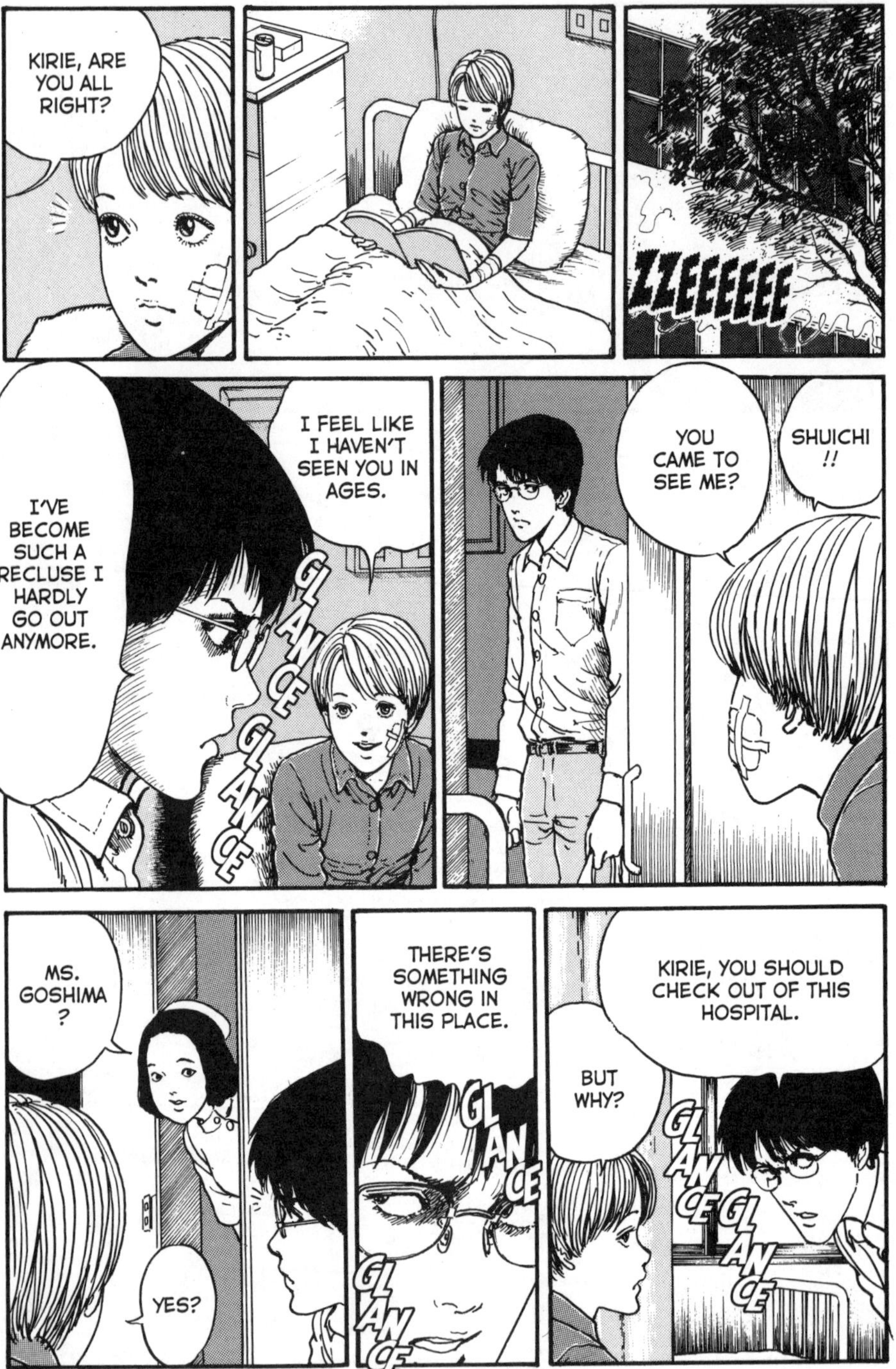
ZZEEEEEE
KIRIE, ARE YOU ALL RIGHT?
SHUICHI !!
YOU CAME TO SEE ME?
I FEEL LIKE I HAVEN'T SEEN YOU IN AGES.
GLANCE
GLANCE
I'VE BECOME SUCH A RECLUSE I HARDLY GO OUT ANYMORE.
KIRIE, YOU SHOULD CHECK OUT OF THIS HOSPITAL.
BUT WHY?
GLANCE
GLANCE
THERE'S SOMETHING WRONG IN THIS PLACE.
GLANCE
GLANCE
MS. GOSHIMA?
YES?

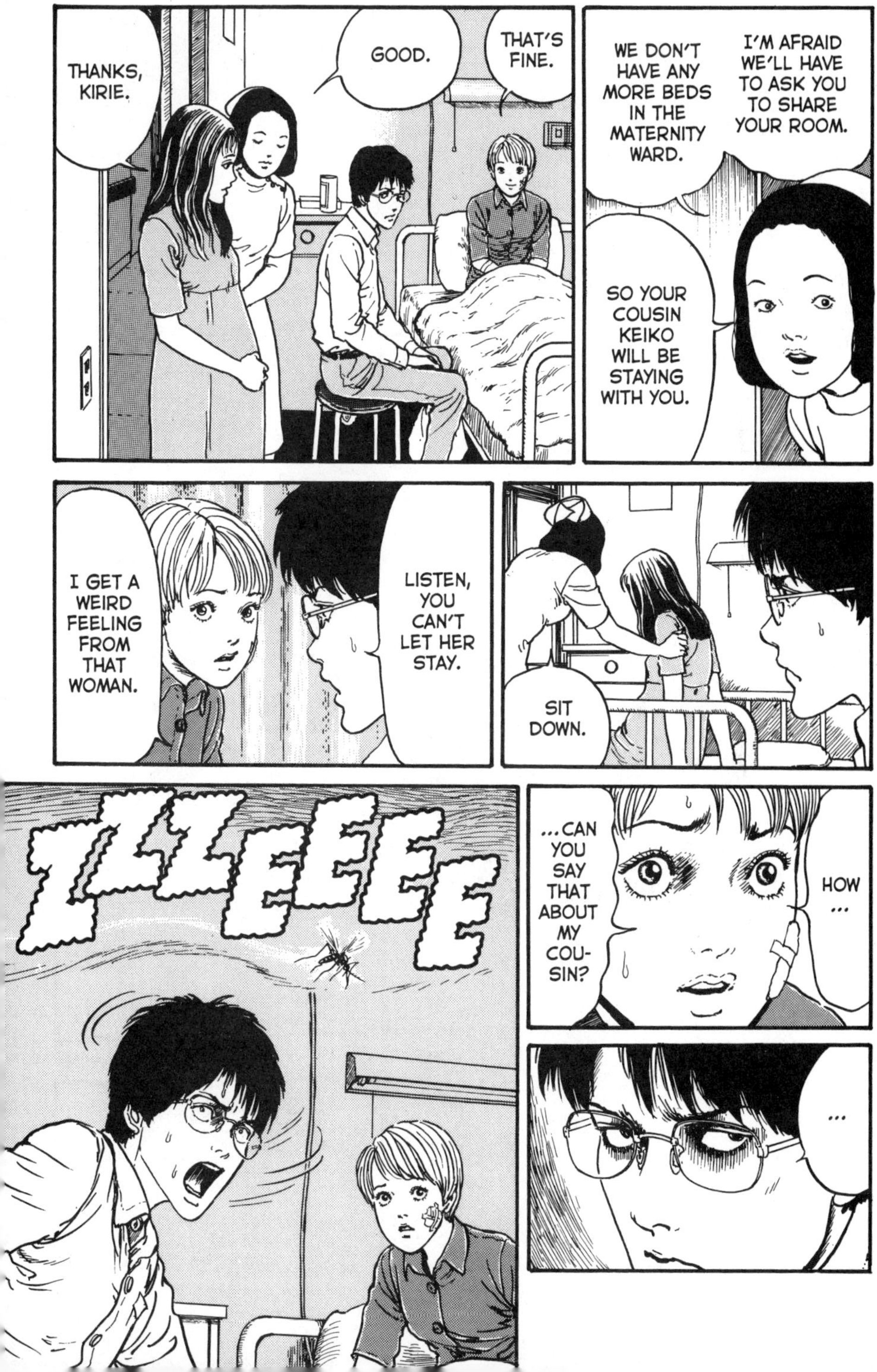
I'M AFRAID WE'LL HAVE TO ASK YOU TO SHARE YOUR ROOM.
WE DON'T HAVE ANY MORE BEDS IN THE MATERNITY WARD.
SO YOUR COUSIN KEIKO WILL BE STAYING WITH YOU.
THAT'S FINE.
GOOD.
THANKS, KIRIE.
SIT DOWN.
LISTEN, YOU CAN'T LET HER STAY.
I GET A WEIRD FEELING FROM THAT WOMAN.
HOW ...
...CAN YOU SAY THAT ABOUT MY COUSIN?
...
ZZZEEEEE

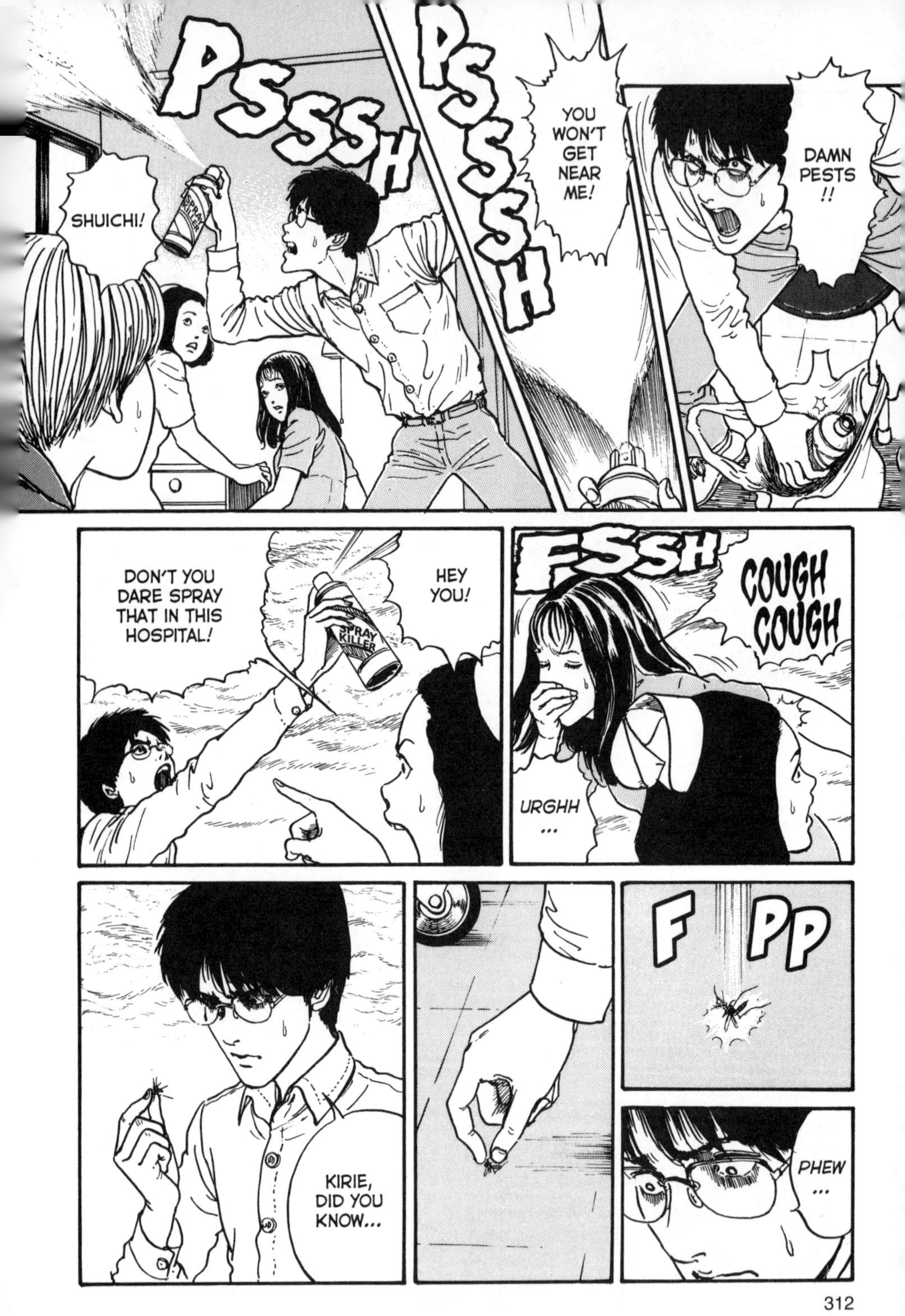
DAMN PESTS!!
PSSSH
YOU WON'T GET NEAR ME!
PSSSH
SHUICHI!
SPRAY KILLER
FSSH
COUGH COUGH
URGHH...
HEY YOU!
DON'T YOU DARE SPRAY THAT IN THIS HOSPITAL!
SPRAY KILLER
F PP
PHEW...
KIRIE, DID YOU KNOW...

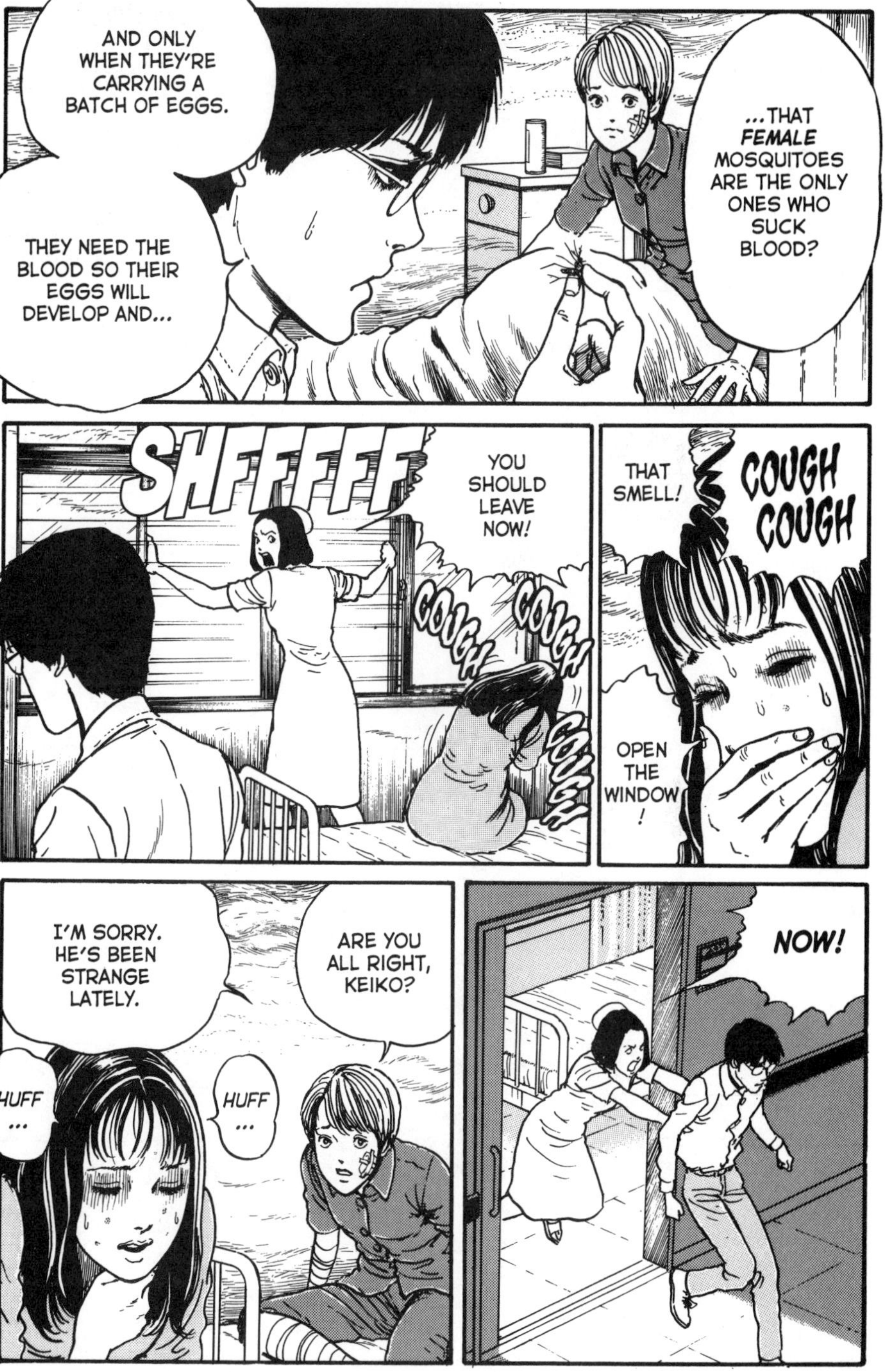
...THAT FEMALE MOSQUITOES ARE THE ONLY ONES WHO SUCK BLOOD?
AND ONLY WHEN THEY'RE CARRYING A BATCH OF EGGS.
THEY NEED THE BLOOD SO THEIR EGGS WILL DEVELOP AND...
COUGH COUGH
THAT SMELL!
OPEN THE WINDOW!
YOU SHOULD LEAVE NOW!
SHFFFFF
COUGH
COUGH
COUGH
NOW!
ARE YOU ALL RIGHT, KEIKO?
I'M SORRY. HE'S BEEN STRANGE LATELY.
HUFF...
HUFF...

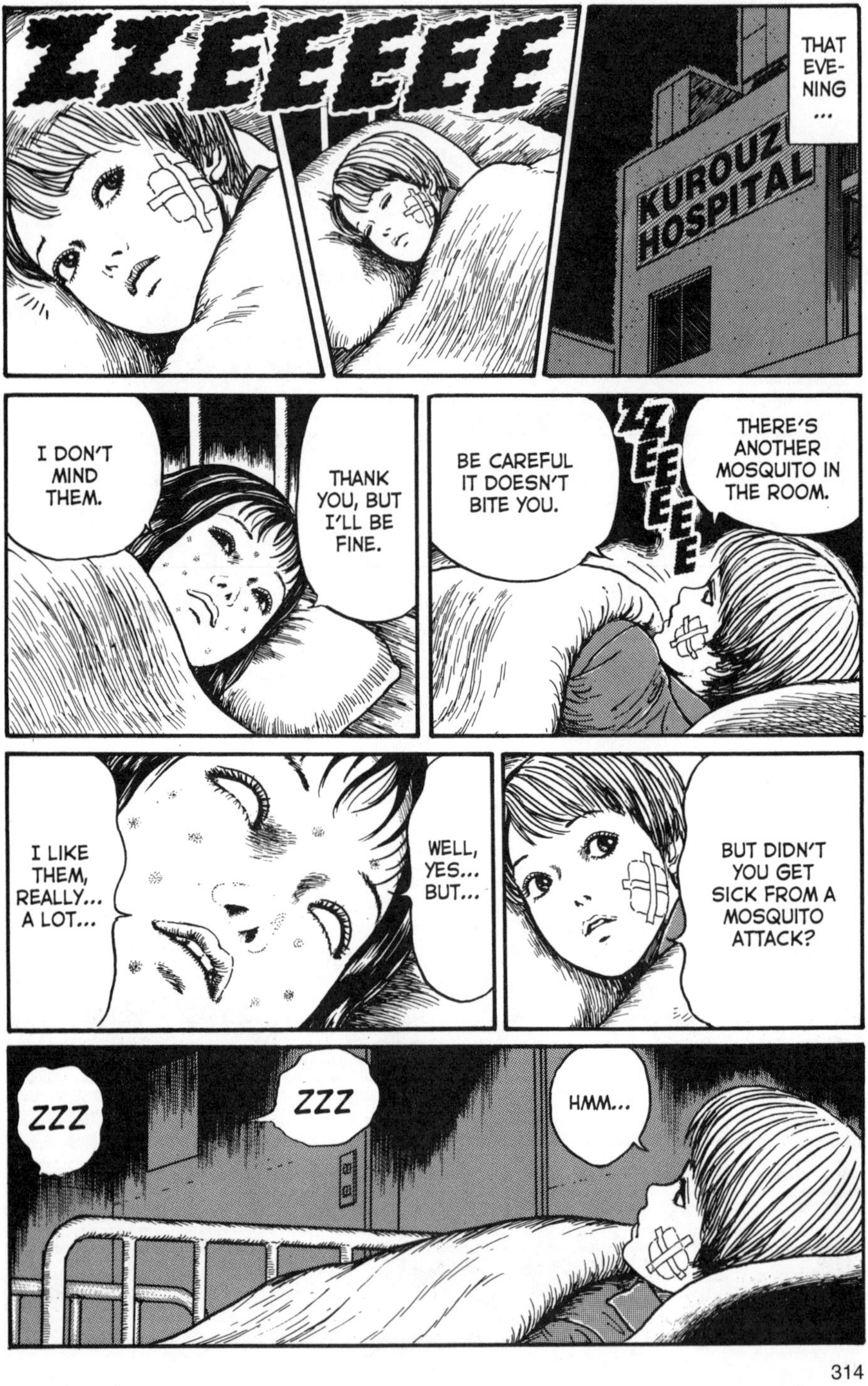
THAT EVENING...
KUROUZ HOSPITAL
ZZEEEEE
THERE'S ANOTHER MOSQUITO IN THE ROOM.
ZZEEEEE
BE CAREFUL IT DOESN'T BITE YOU.
THANK YOU, BUT I'LL BE FINE.
I DON'T MIND THEM.
BUT DIDN'T YOU GET SICK FROM A MOSQUITO ATTACK?
WELL, YES... BUT...
I LIKE THEM, REALLY... A LOT...
HMM...
ZZZ
ZZZ

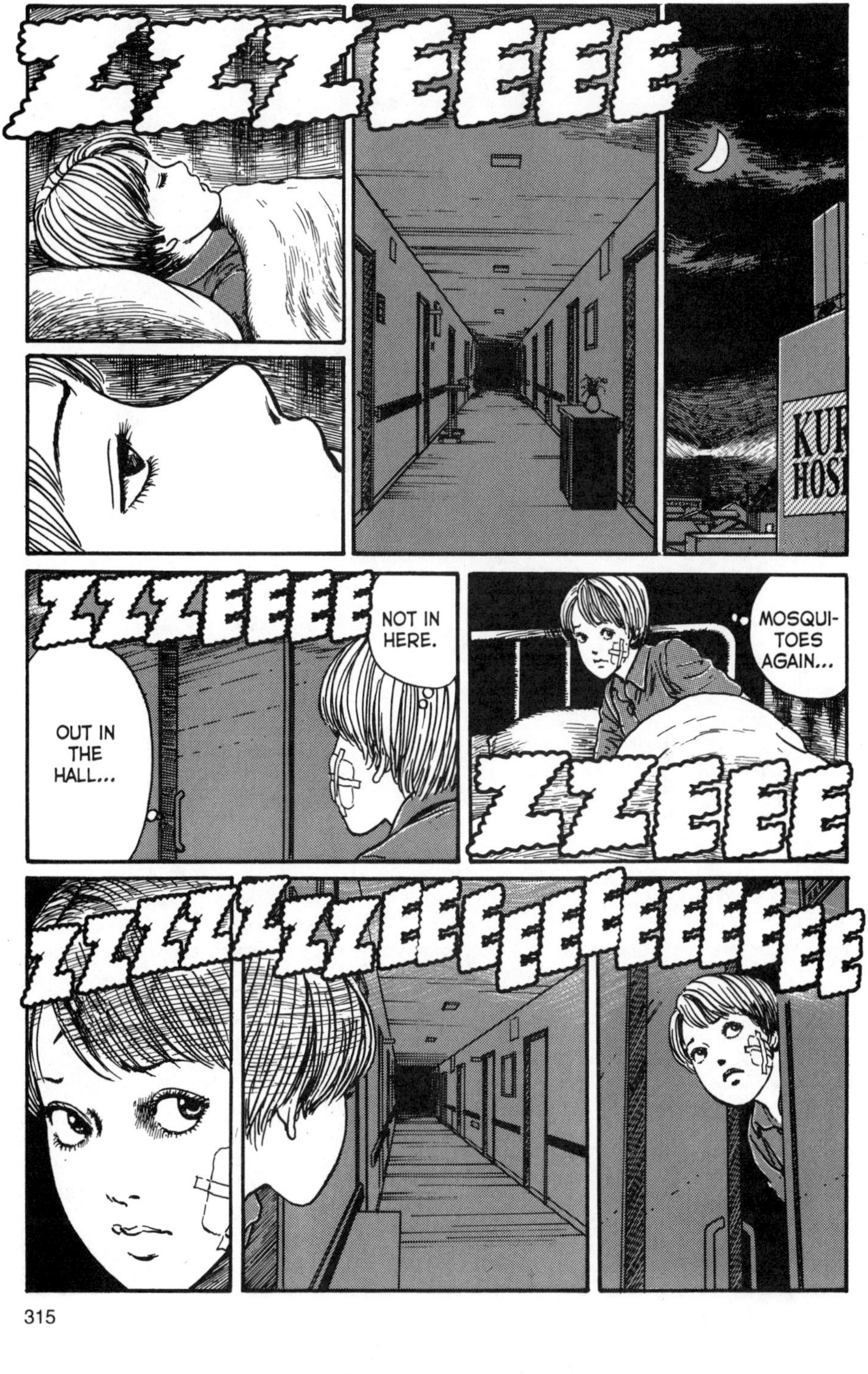
ZZZEEEE
MOSQUI-TOES AGAIN...
ZZEEE
ZZZEEEE
NOT IN HERE.
OUT IN THE HALL...
ZZZZZZEEEEEEEEEEEE

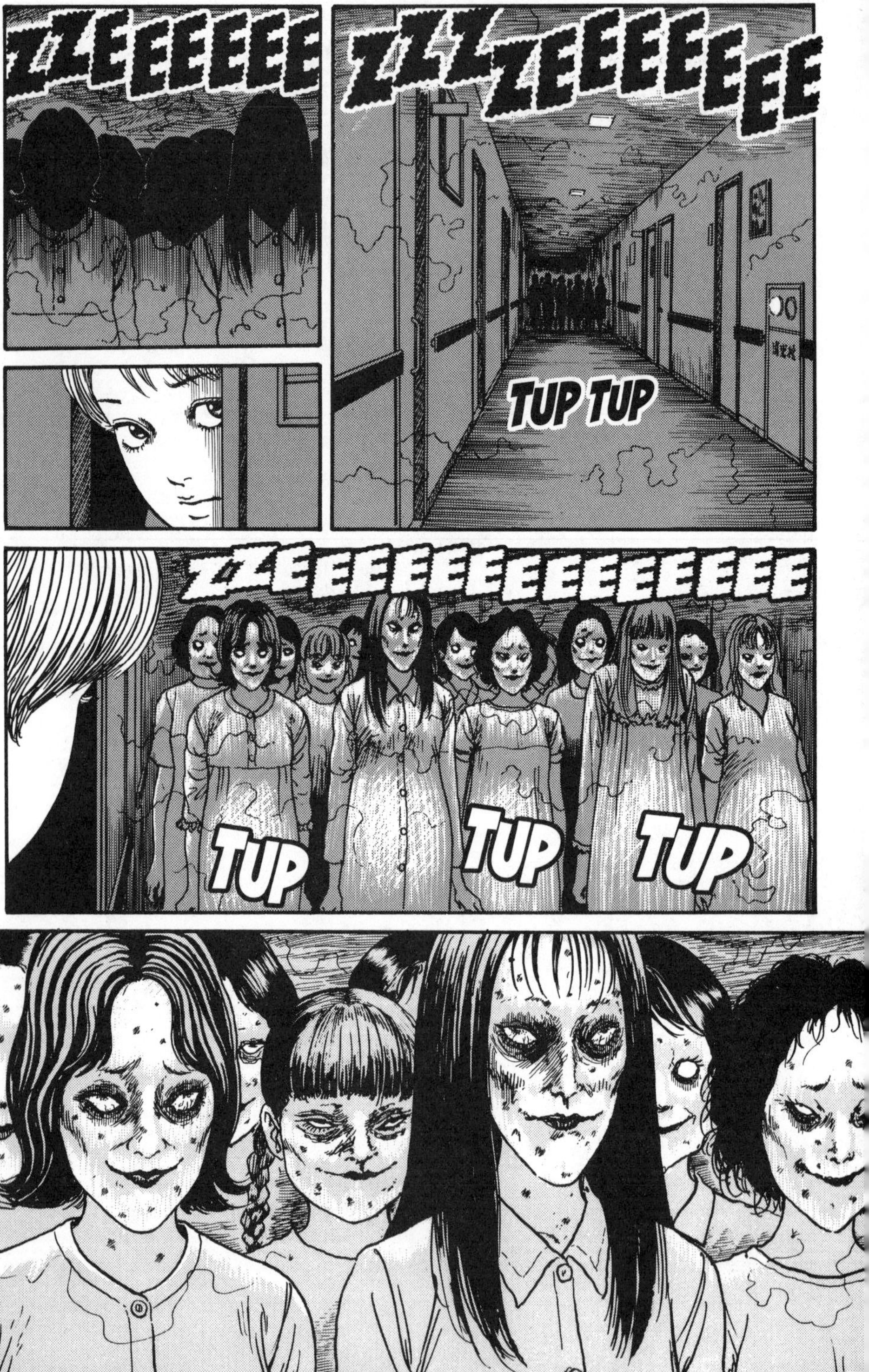
ZZZ ZEEEEEEEE
TUP TUP
ZZEEEEEE
ZZEEEEEEEEEEEEEEE
TUP
TUP
TUP

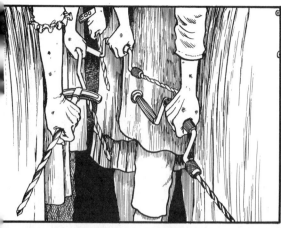

EH?!

THEY'RE ALL FROM THE MATERNITY WARD.

TUP

TUP

WHAT... ARE THEY...

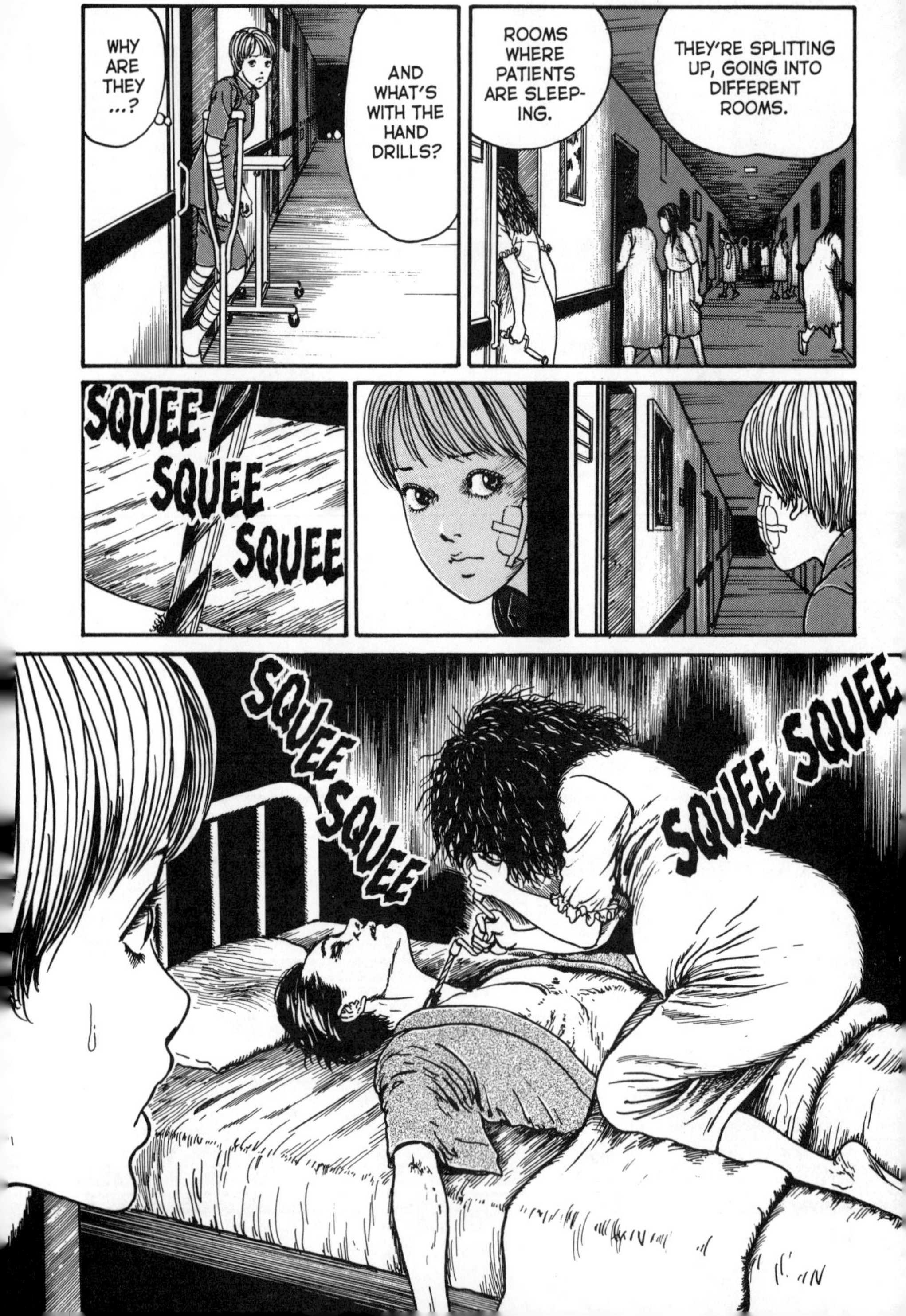

THEY'RE SPLITTING UP, GOING INTO DIFFERENT ROOMS.
ROOMS WHERE PATIENTS ARE SLEEP-ING.
WHY ARE THEY ...?
AND WHAT'S WITH THE HAND DRILLS?
SQUEE SQUEE SQUEE
SQUEE SQUEE
SQUEE SQUEE

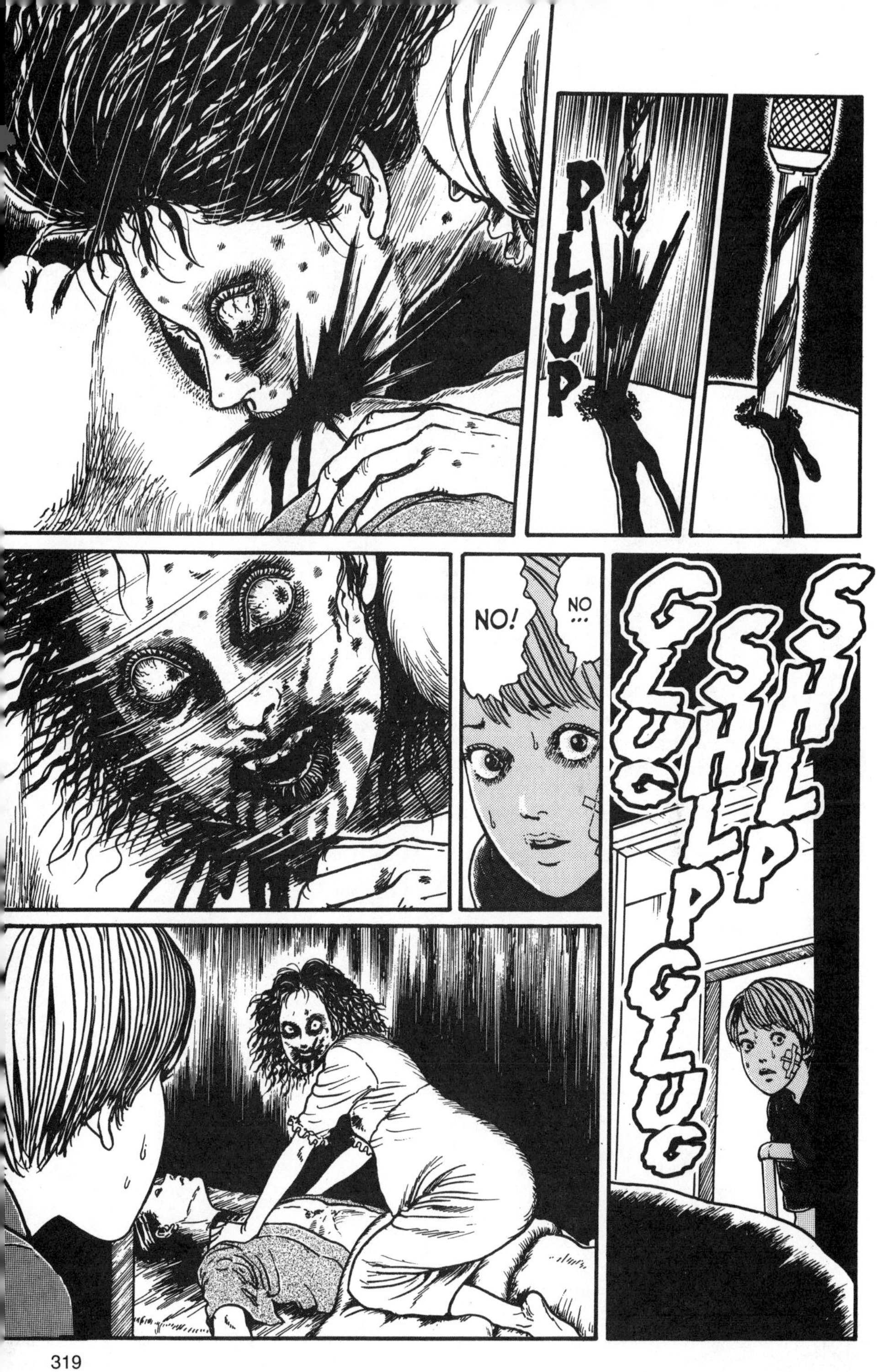
PLUP
SHLP
SHLP
GLUG
GLUG
NO...
NO!

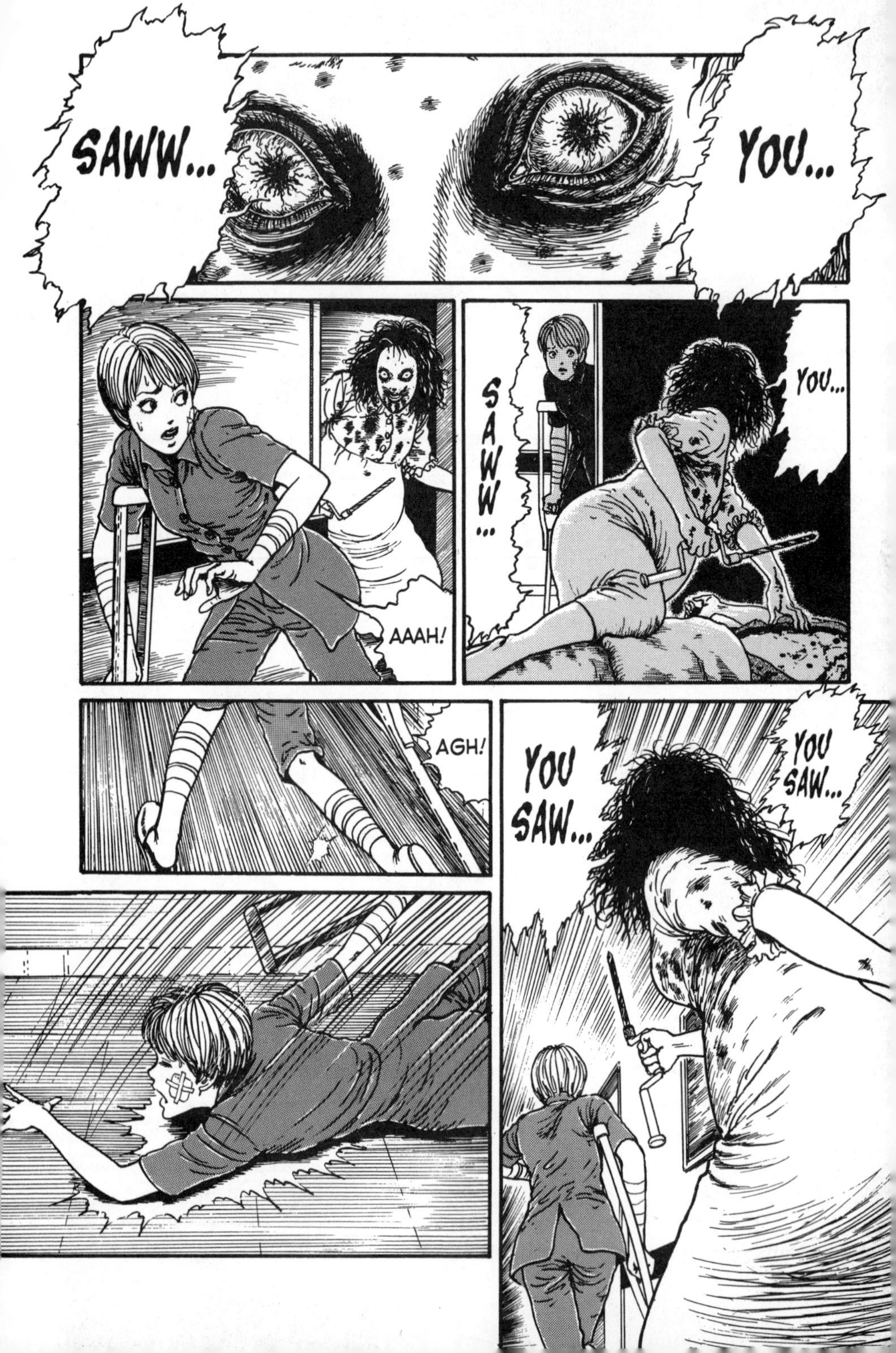

YOU...
SAWW...
YOU...
SAWW...
AAAH!
YOU SAW...
YOU SAW...
AGH!

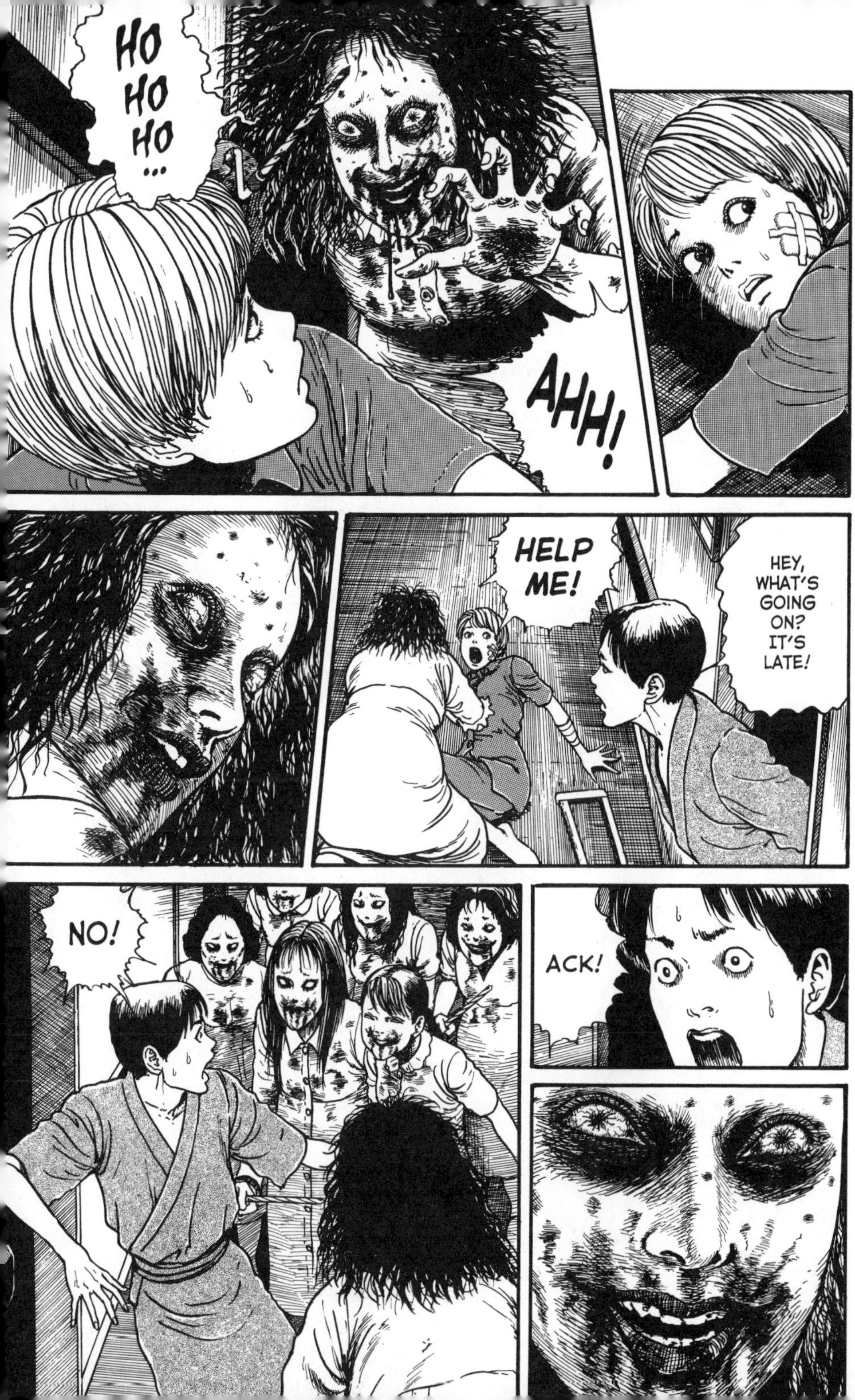
HO HO HO ...
AHH!
HEY, WHAT'S GOING ON? IT'S LATE!
HELP ME!
ACK!
NO!

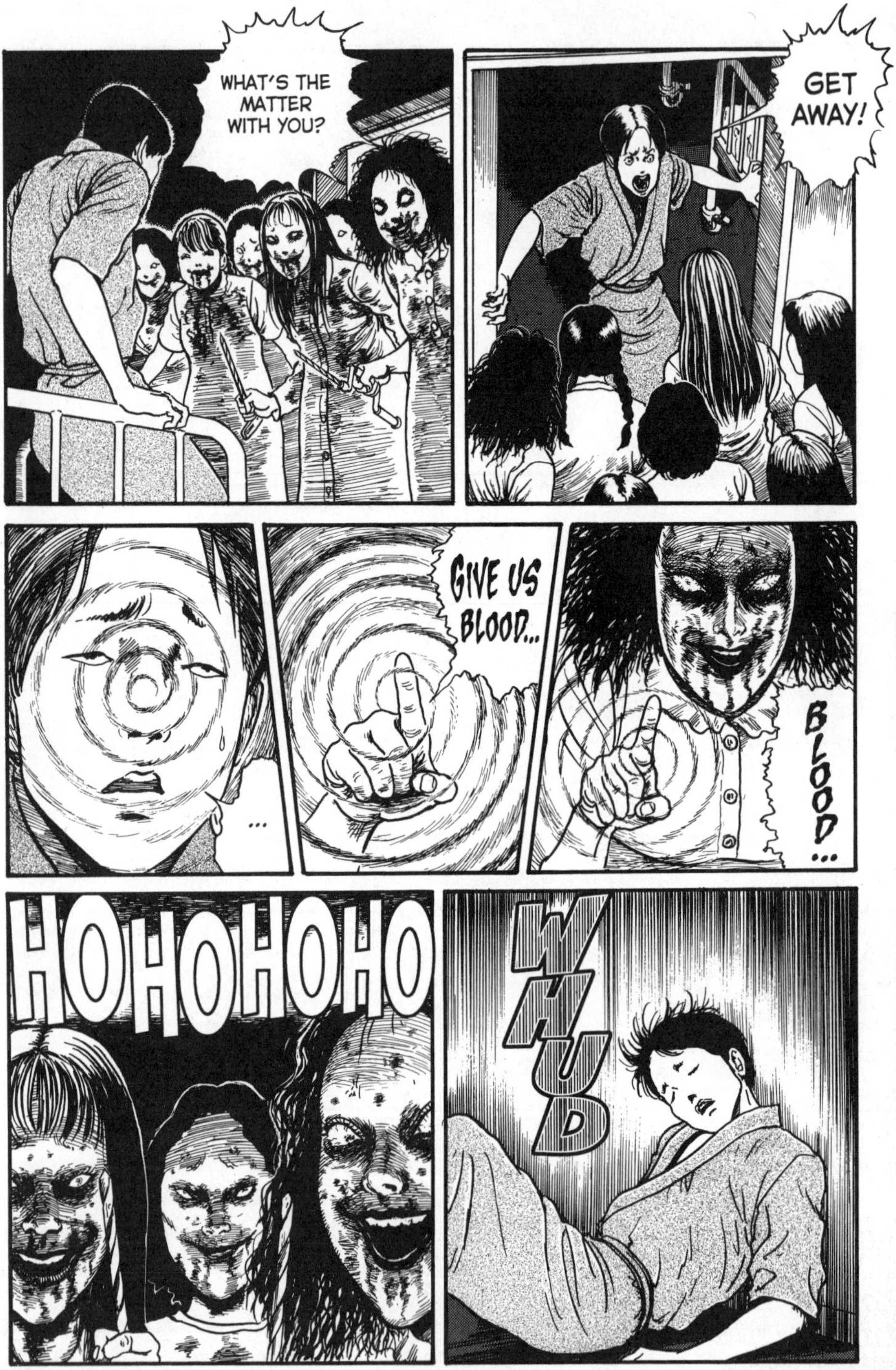
GET AWAY!
WHAT'S THE MATTER WITH YOU?
BLOOD...
GIVE US BLOOD...
...
WHUD
HOHOHOHO

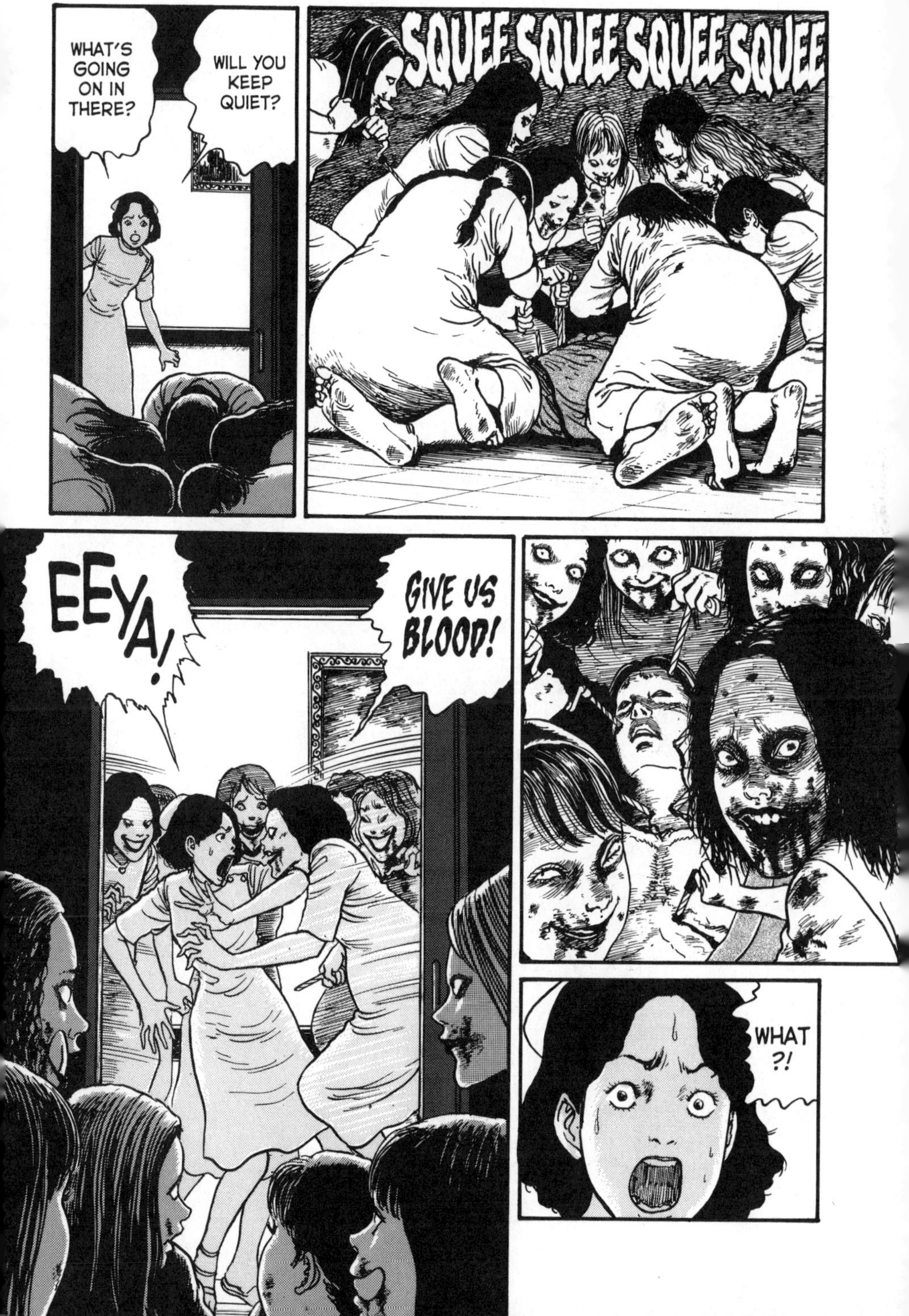
SQUEE SQUEE SQUEE SQUEE
WILL YOU KEEP QUIET?
WHAT'S GOING ON IN THERE?
WHAT ?!
GIVE US BLOOD!
EEYA!

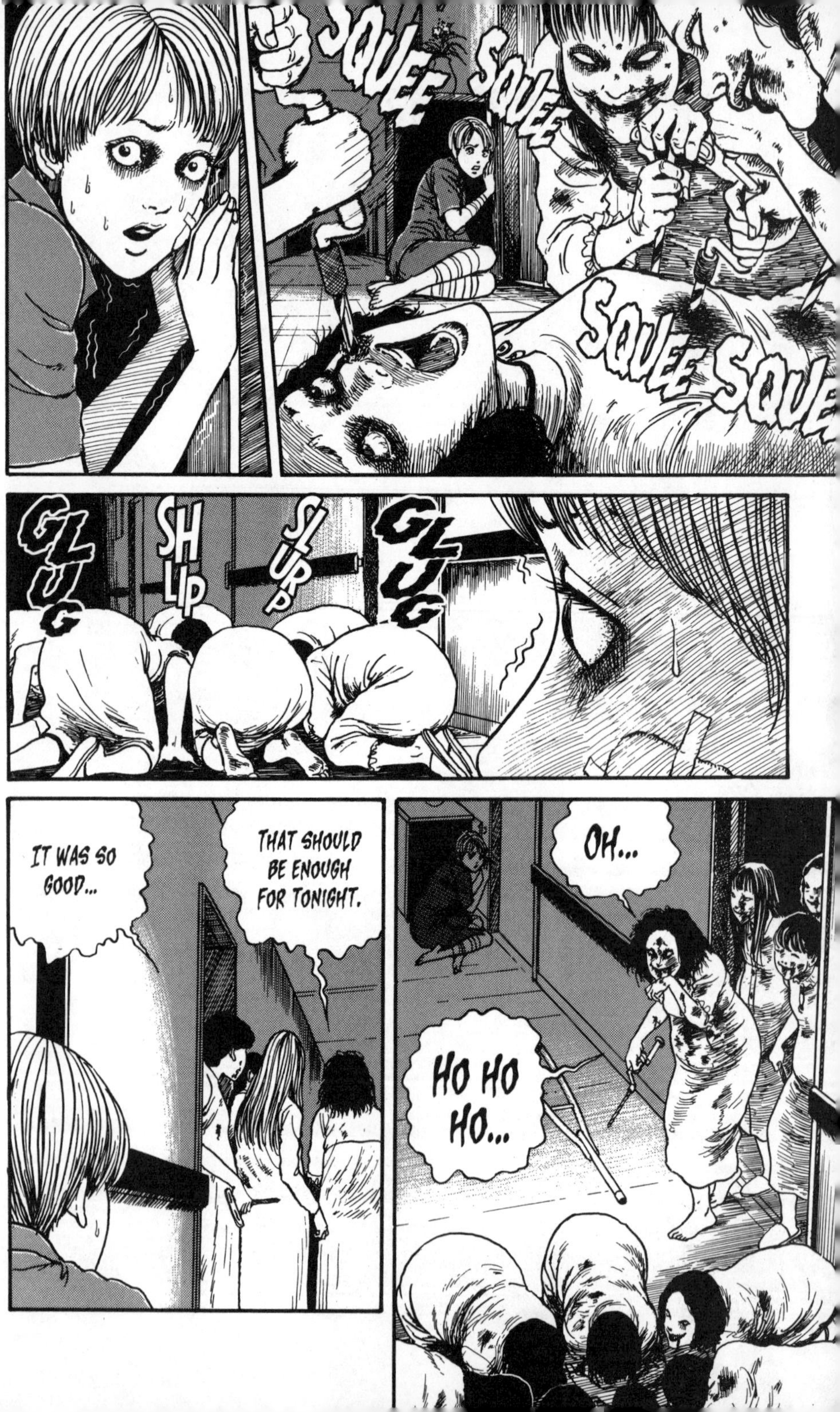
SQUEE SQUEE
SQUEE SQUE
GLUG
SLURP
SHLIP
GLUG
OH...
HO HO HO...
THAT SHOULD BE ENOUGH FOR TONIGHT.
IT WAS SO GOOD...

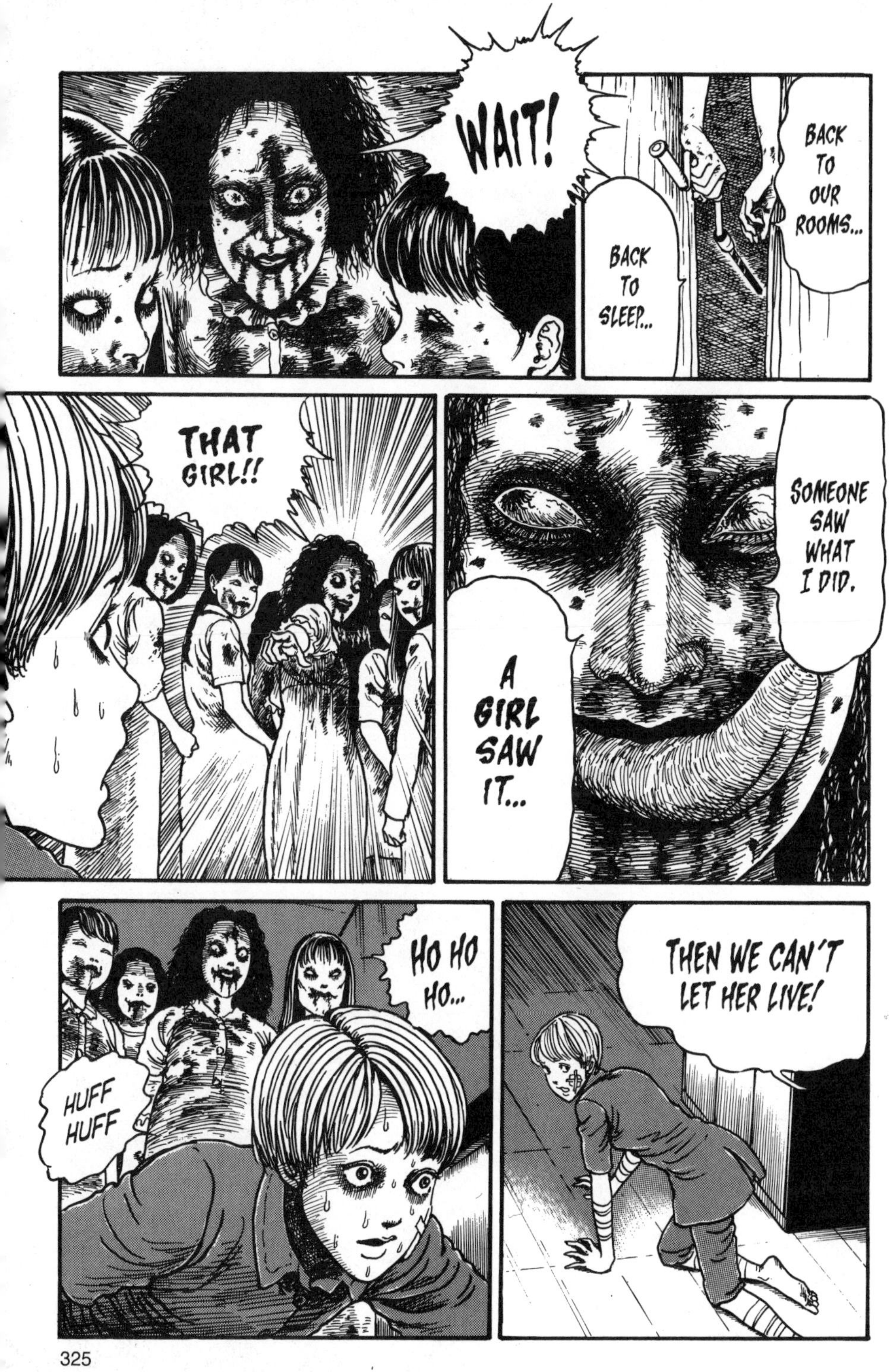
BACK TO OUR ROOMS...
BACK TO SLEEP...
WAIT!
SOMEONE SAW WHAT I DID.
A GIRL SAW IT...
THAT GIRL!!
THEN WE CAN'T LET HER LIVE!
HO HO HO...
HUFF HUFF

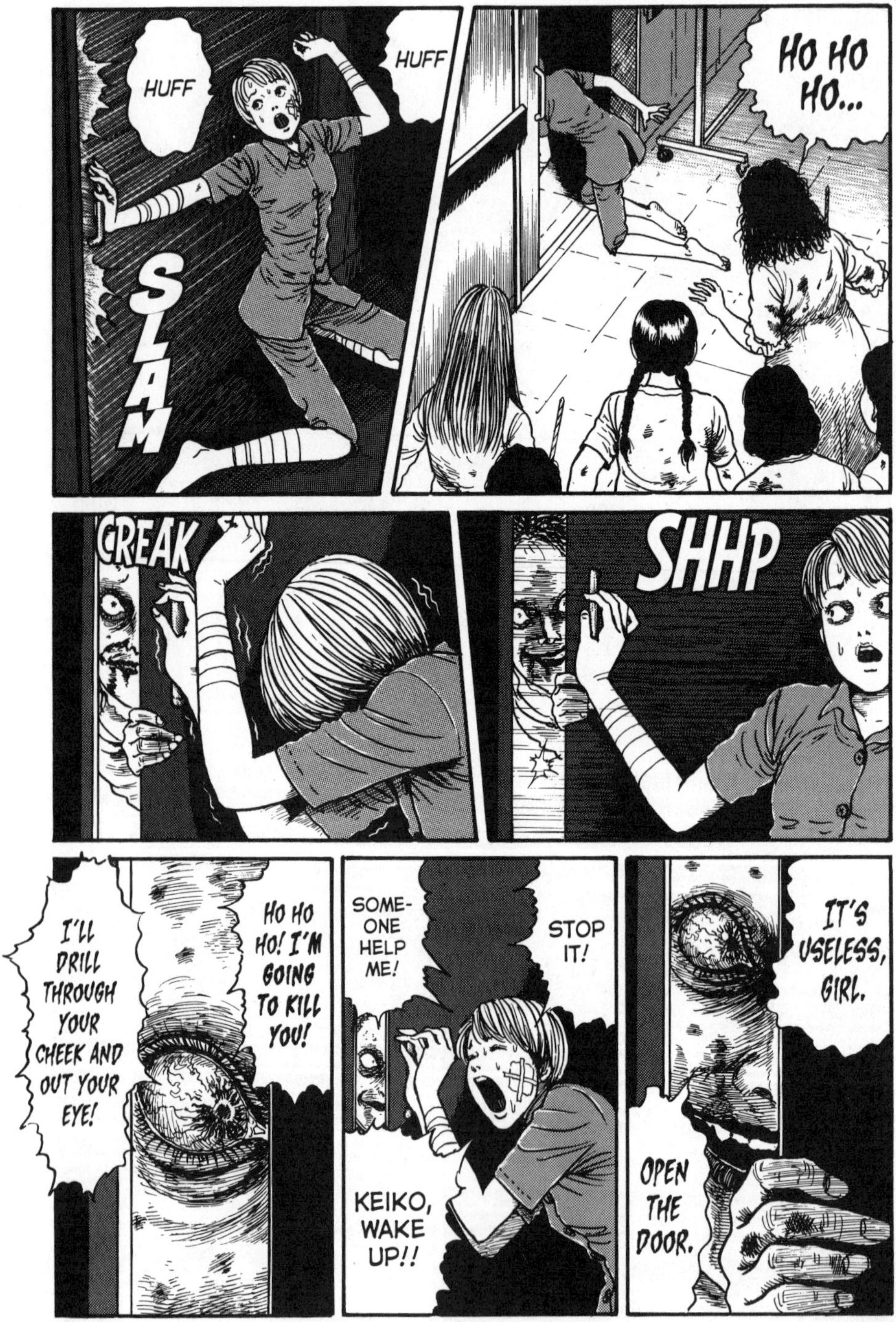
HO HO HO...
HUFF
HUFF
SLAM
SHHP
CREAK
IT'S USELESS, GIRL.
OPEN THE DOOR.
STOP IT!
SOME-ONE HELP ME!
KEIKO, WAKE UP!!
HO HO HO! I'M GOING TO KILL YOU!
I'LL DRILL THROUGH YOUR CHEEK AND OUT YOUR EYE!

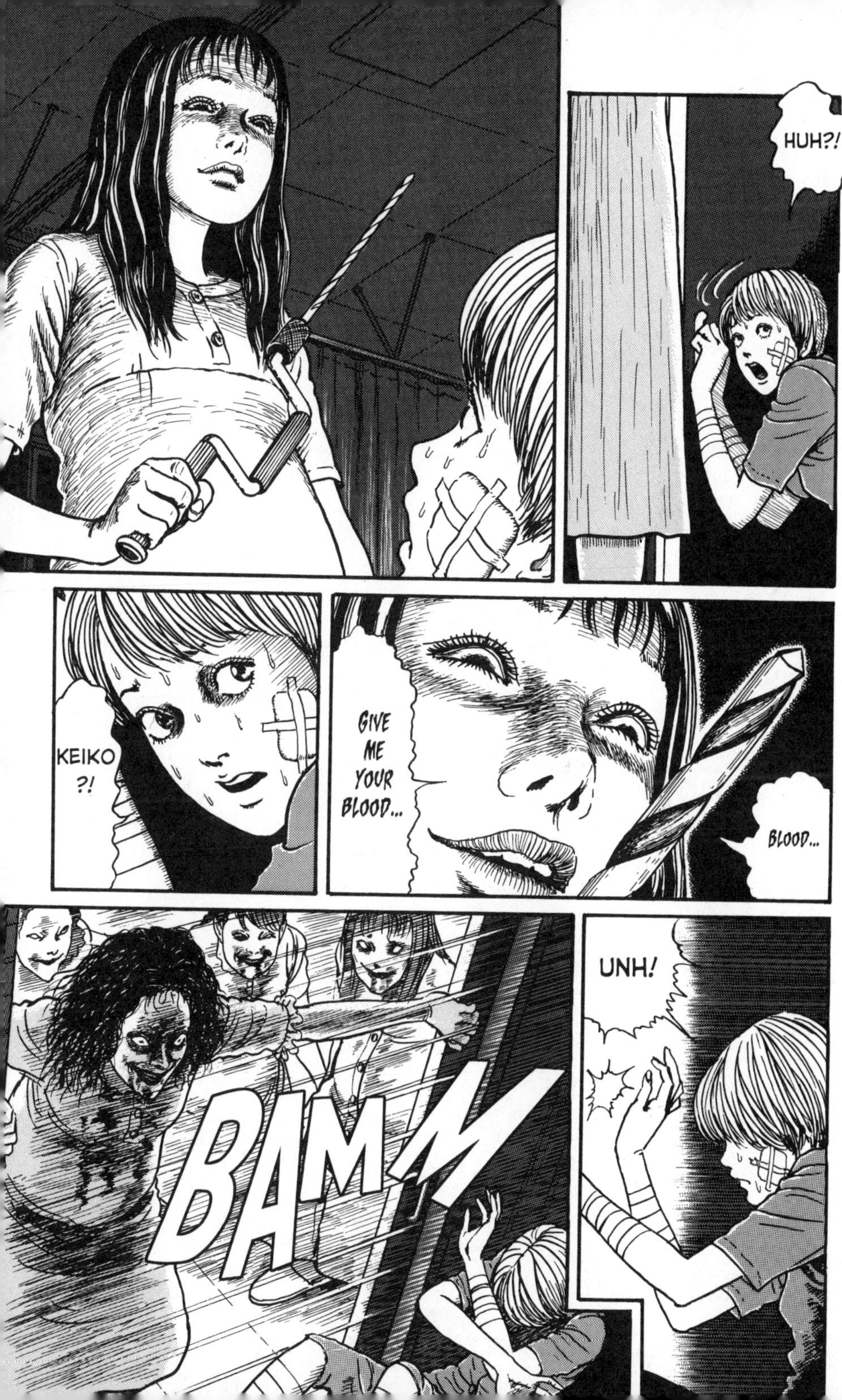
HUH?!
GIVE ME YOUR BLOOD...
BLOOD...
KEIKO ?!
UNH!
BAMM

STOP IT!

AHAHAHA

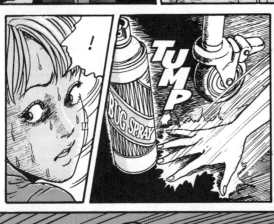

!

BUG SPRAY

TUMP

DIE!!

PSSSSSSSSH

BUG SPRAY

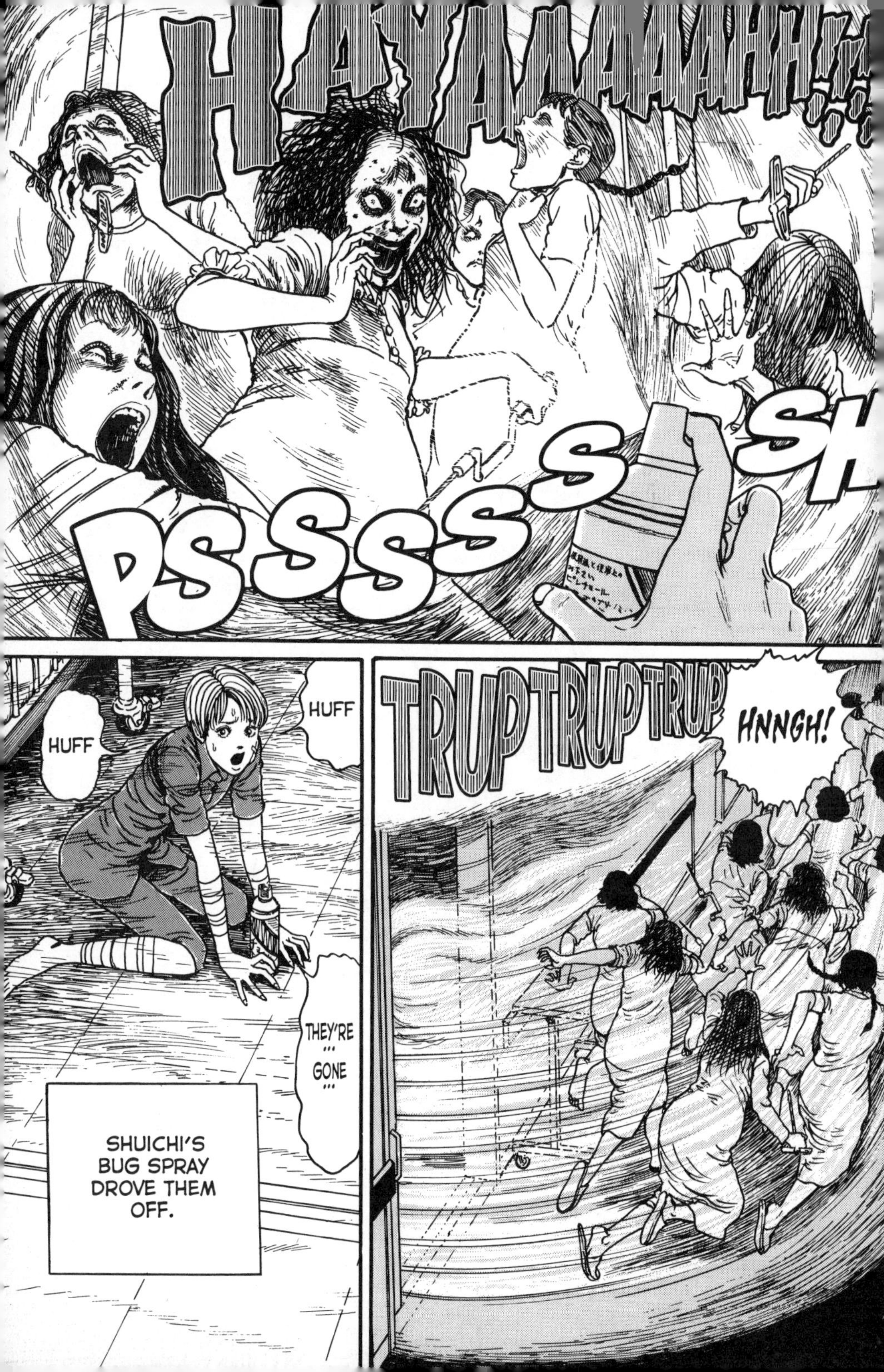
HAYAAAAH!!
PSSSSSSH
TRUP TRUP TRUP
HNNGH!
HUFF
HUFF
THEY'RE... GONE...
SHUICHI'S BUG SPRAY DROVE THEM OFF.

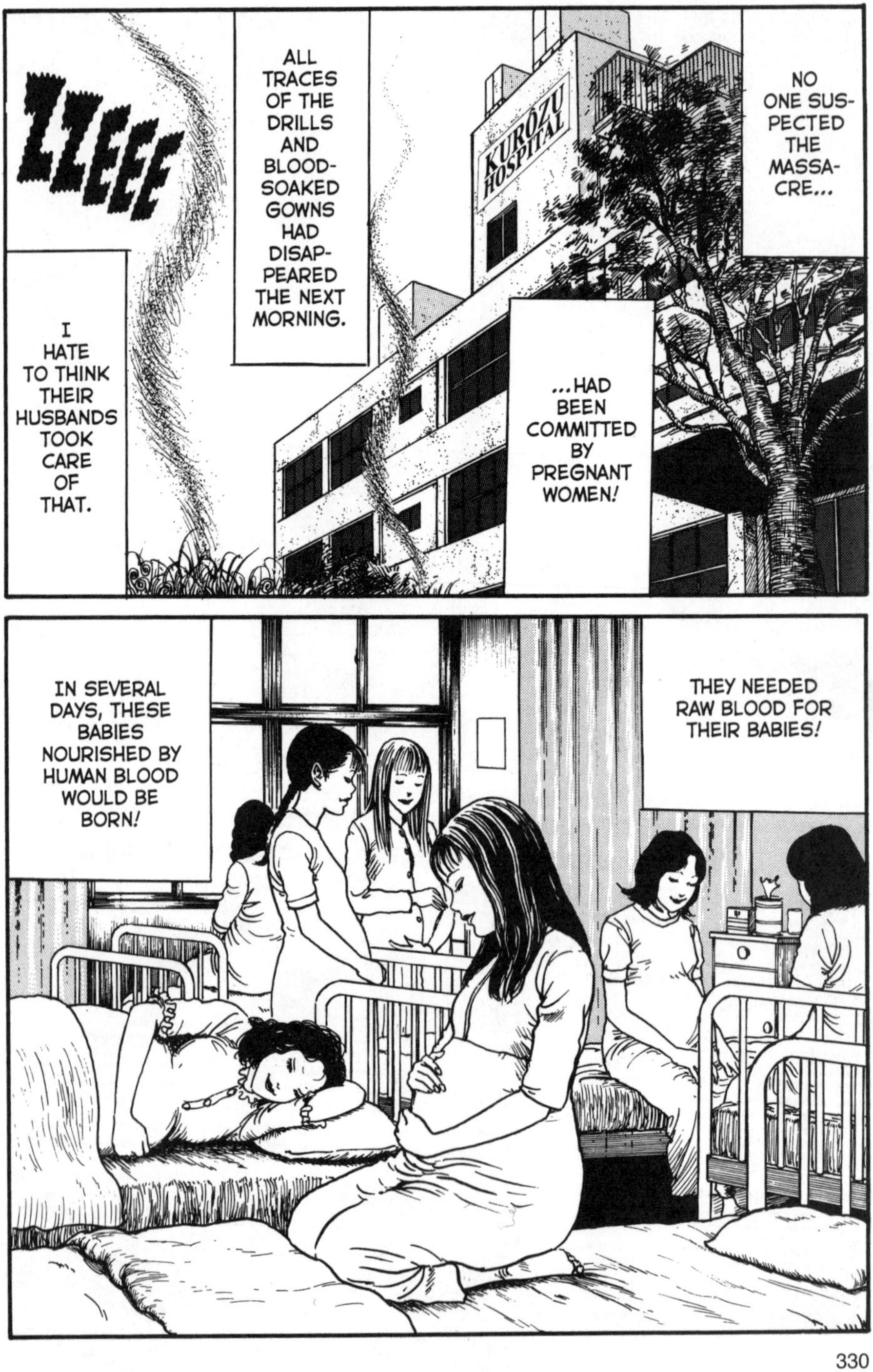
NO ONE SUSPECTED THE MASSACRE...
...HAD BEEN COMMITTED BY PREGNANT WOMEN!
ALL TRACES OF THE DRILLS AND BLOOD-SOAKED GOWNS HAD DISAPPEARED THE NEXT MORNING.
ZZEEE
I HATE TO THINK THEIR HUSBANDS TOOK CARE OF THAT.
KUROZU HOSPITAL
THEY NEEDED RAW BLOOD FOR THEIR BABIES!
IN SEVERAL DAYS, THESE BABIES NOURISHED BY HUMAN BLOOD WOULD BE BORN!

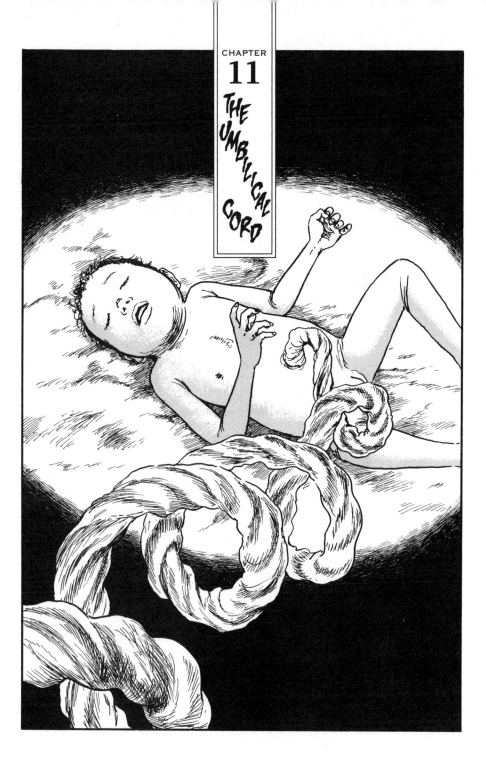

CHAPTER

11

THE UMBILICAL CORD

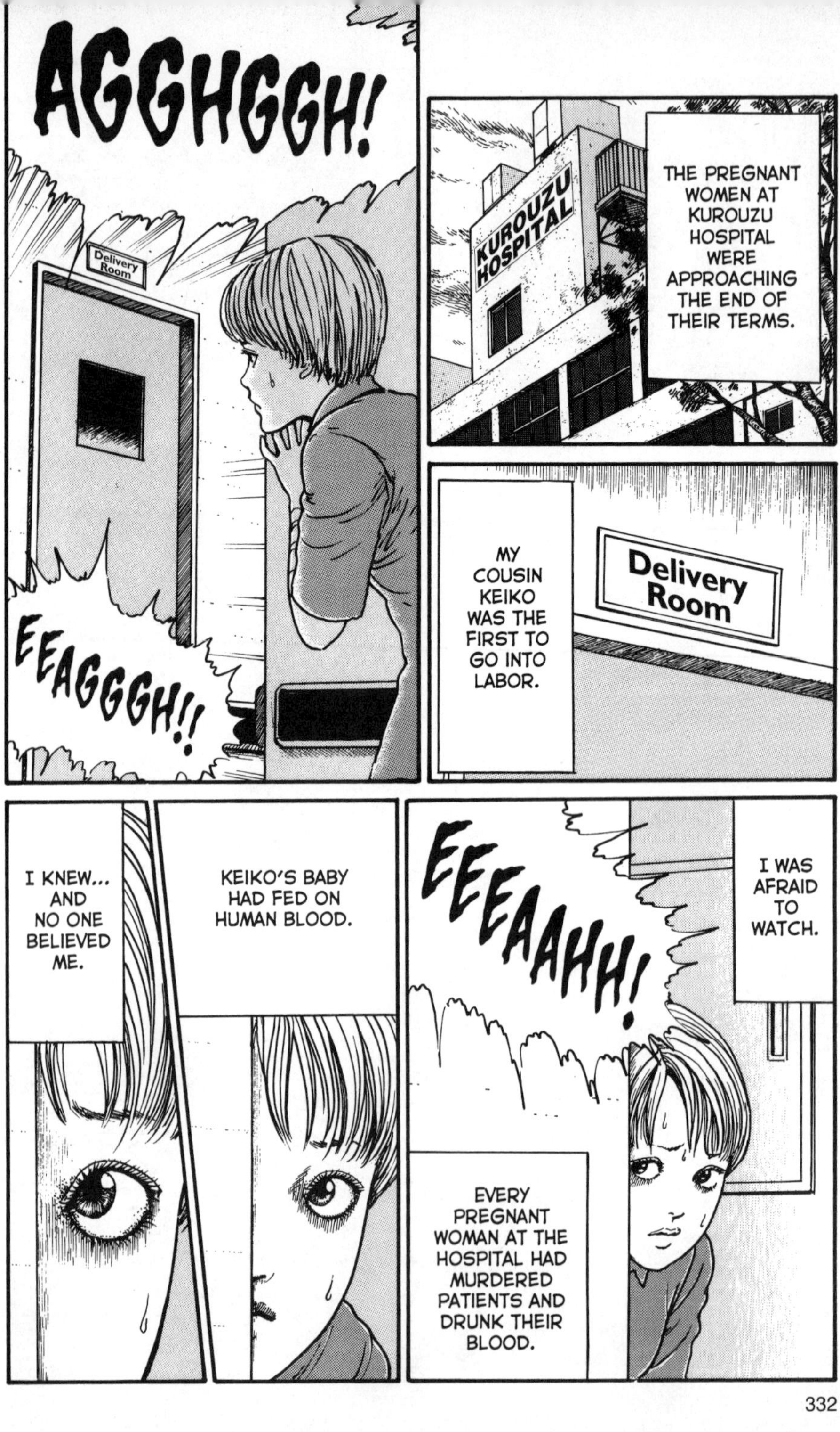
KUROUZU HOSPITAL
THE PREGNANT WOMEN AT KUROUZU HOSPITAL WERE APPROACHING THE END OF THEIR TERMS.
Delivery Room
MY COUSIN KEIKO WAS THE FIRST TO GO INTO LABOR.
AGGHGGH!
Delivery Room
EEAGGGH!!
I WAS AFRAID TO WATCH.
EEEAAHH!
EVERY PREGNANT WOMAN AT THE HOSPITAL HAD MURDERED PATIENTS AND DRUNK THEIR BLOOD.
KEIKO'S BABY HAD FED ON HUMAN BLOOD.
I KNEW... AND NO ONE BELIEVED ME.

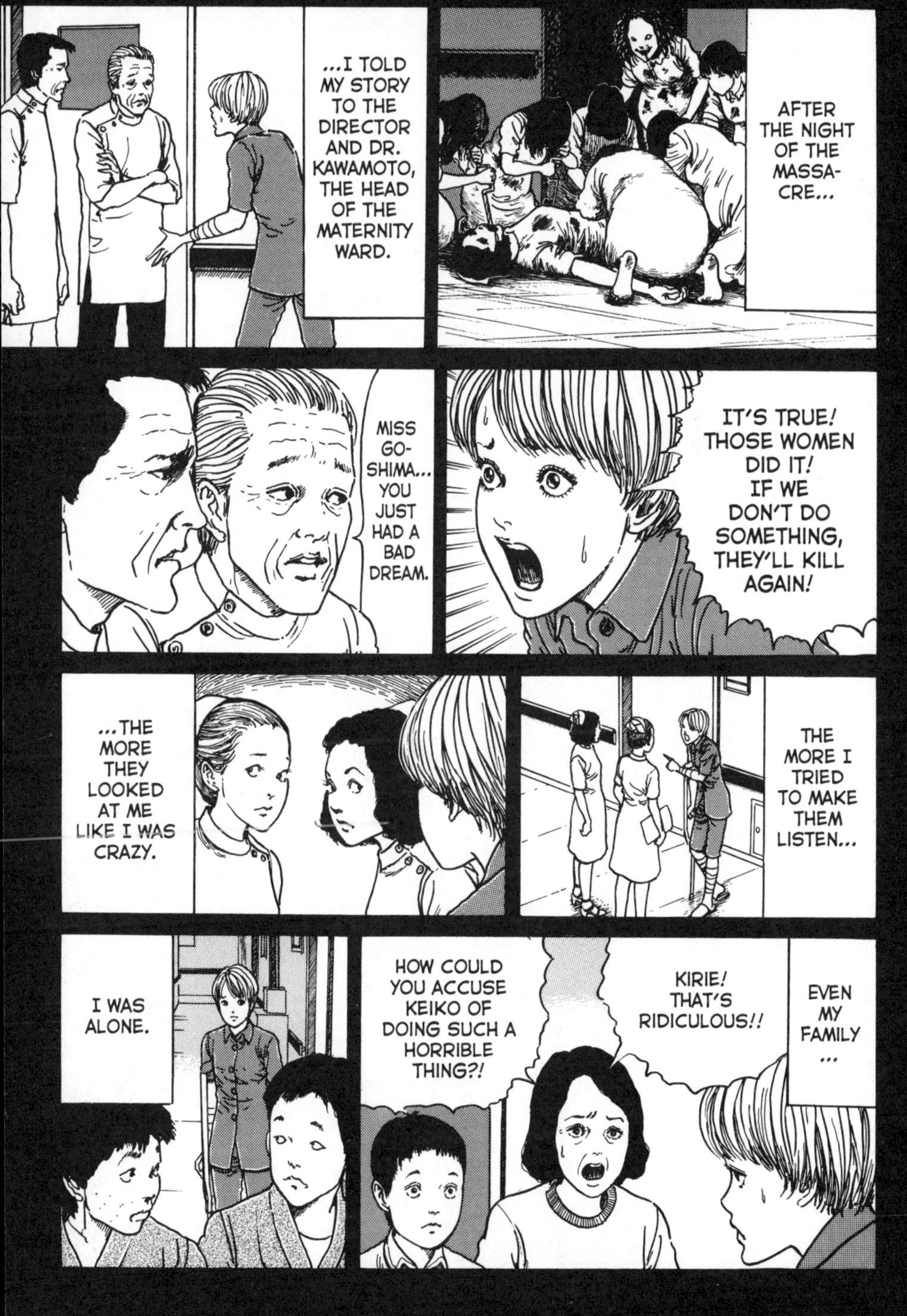
AFTER THE NIGHT OF THE MASSA-CRE...
...I TOLD MY STORY TO THE DIRECTOR AND DR. KAWAMOTO, THE HEAD OF THE MATERNITY WARD.
IT'S TRUE! THOSE WOMEN DID IT! IF WE DON'T DO SOMETHING, THEY'LL KILL AGAIN!
MISS GO-SHIMA... YOU JUST HAD A BAD DREAM.
THE MORE I TRIED TO MAKE THEM LISTEN...
...THE MORE THEY LOOKED AT ME LIKE I WAS CRAZY.
EVEN MY FAMILY ...
KIRIE! THAT'S RIDICULOUS!!
HOW COULD YOU ACCUSE KEIKO OF DOING SUCH A HORRIBLE THING?!
I WAS ALONE.

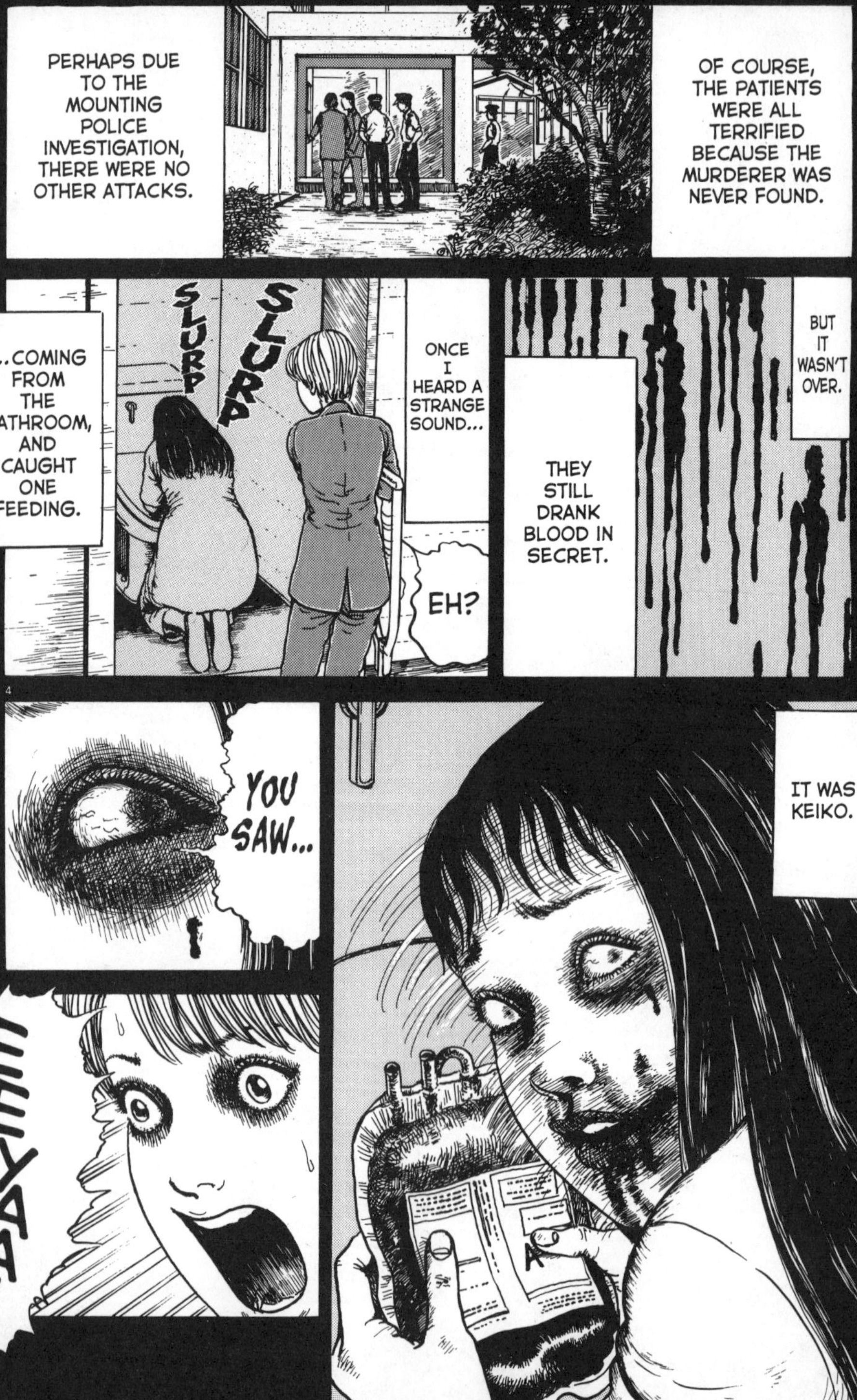
OF COURSE, THE PATIENTS WERE ALL TERRIFIED BECAUSE THE MURDERER WAS NEVER FOUND.
PERHAPS DUE TO THE MOUNTING POLICE INVESTIGATION, THERE WERE NO OTHER ATTACKS.
BUT IT WASN'T OVER.
THEY STILL DRANK BLOOD IN SECRET.
ONCE I HEARD A STRANGE SOUND...
SLURP
SLURP
EH?
...COMING FROM THE BATHROOM, AND CAUGHT ONE FEEDING.
IT WAS KEIKO.
A
YOU SAW...
EEYAA!

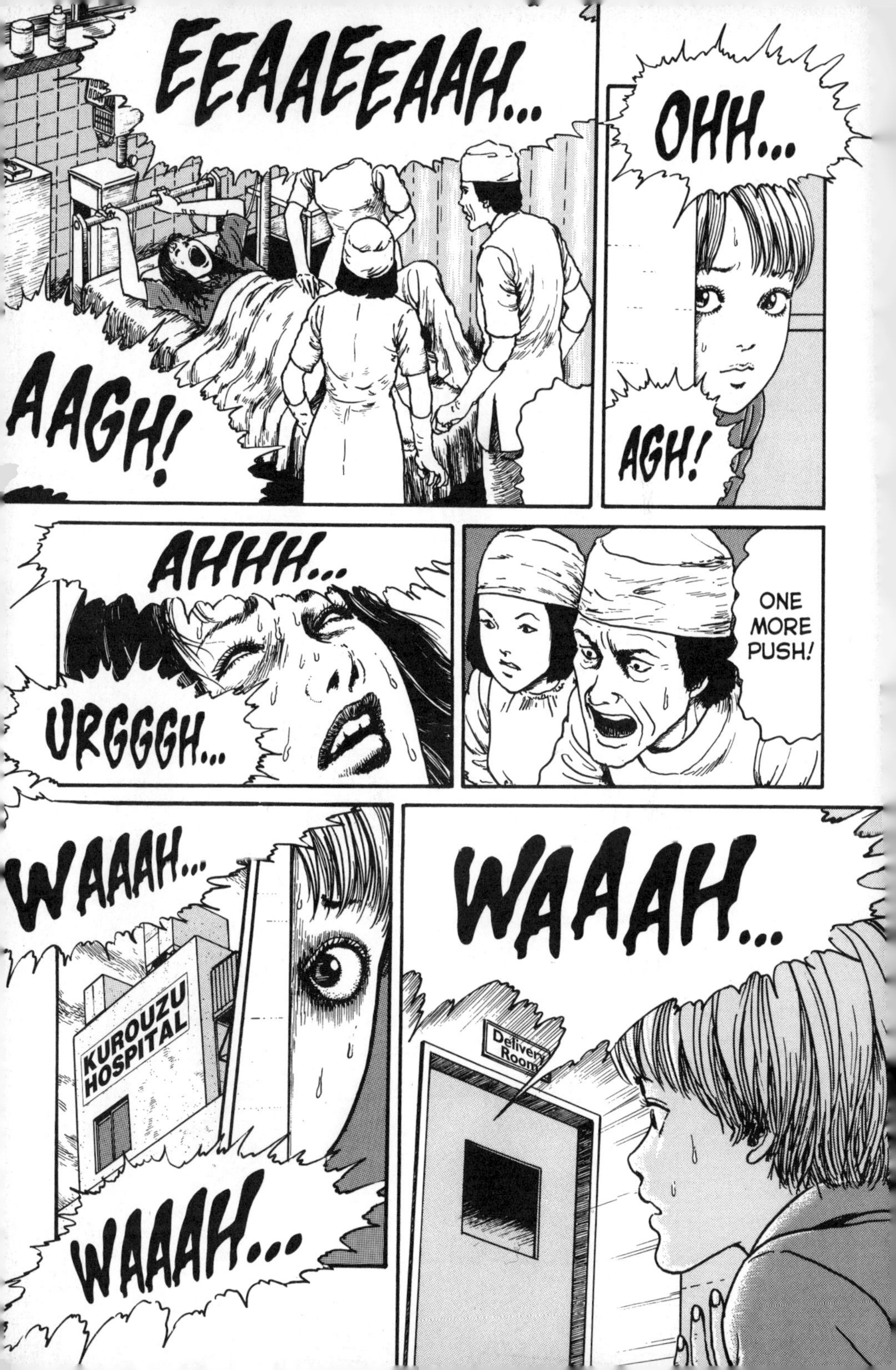

OHH...
AGH!
EEAAEEAAH...
AAGH!
ONE MORE PUSH!
AHHH...
URGGGH...
WAAAH...
Delivery Room
WAAAH...
KUROUZU HOSPITAL
WAAAH...

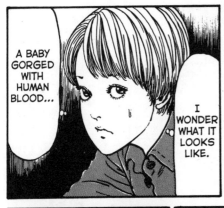

SO IT'S BEEN BORN.
A BABY GORGED WITH HUMAN BLOOD...
I WONDER WHAT IT LOOKS LIKE.
Nursery
Keiko Nakayama
IT WAS THE SWEETEST BABY I HAD EVER SEEN.

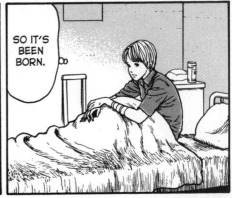

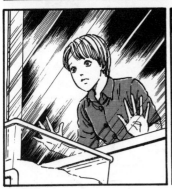

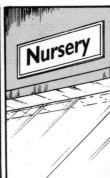

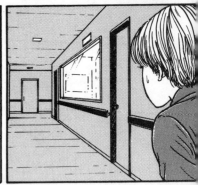

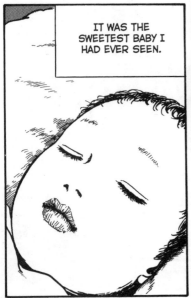

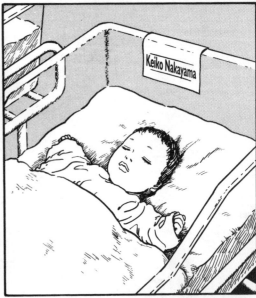

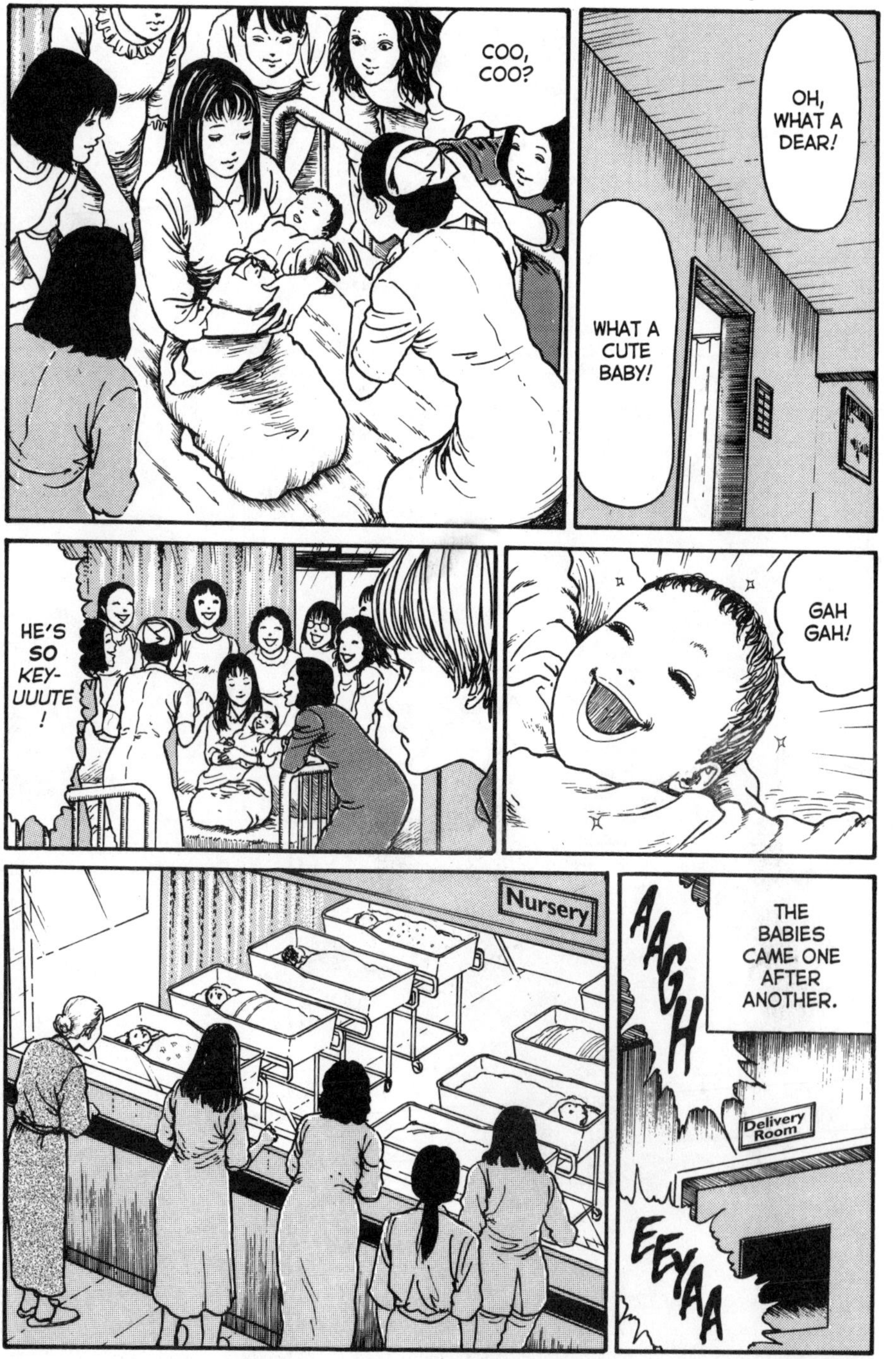
OH, WHAT A DEAR!
WHAT A CUTE BABY!
COO, COO?
GAH GAH!
HE'S SO KEY-UUUTE!
THE BABIES CAME ONE AFTER ANOTHER.
AAGH
Delivery Room
EEYAA
Nursery

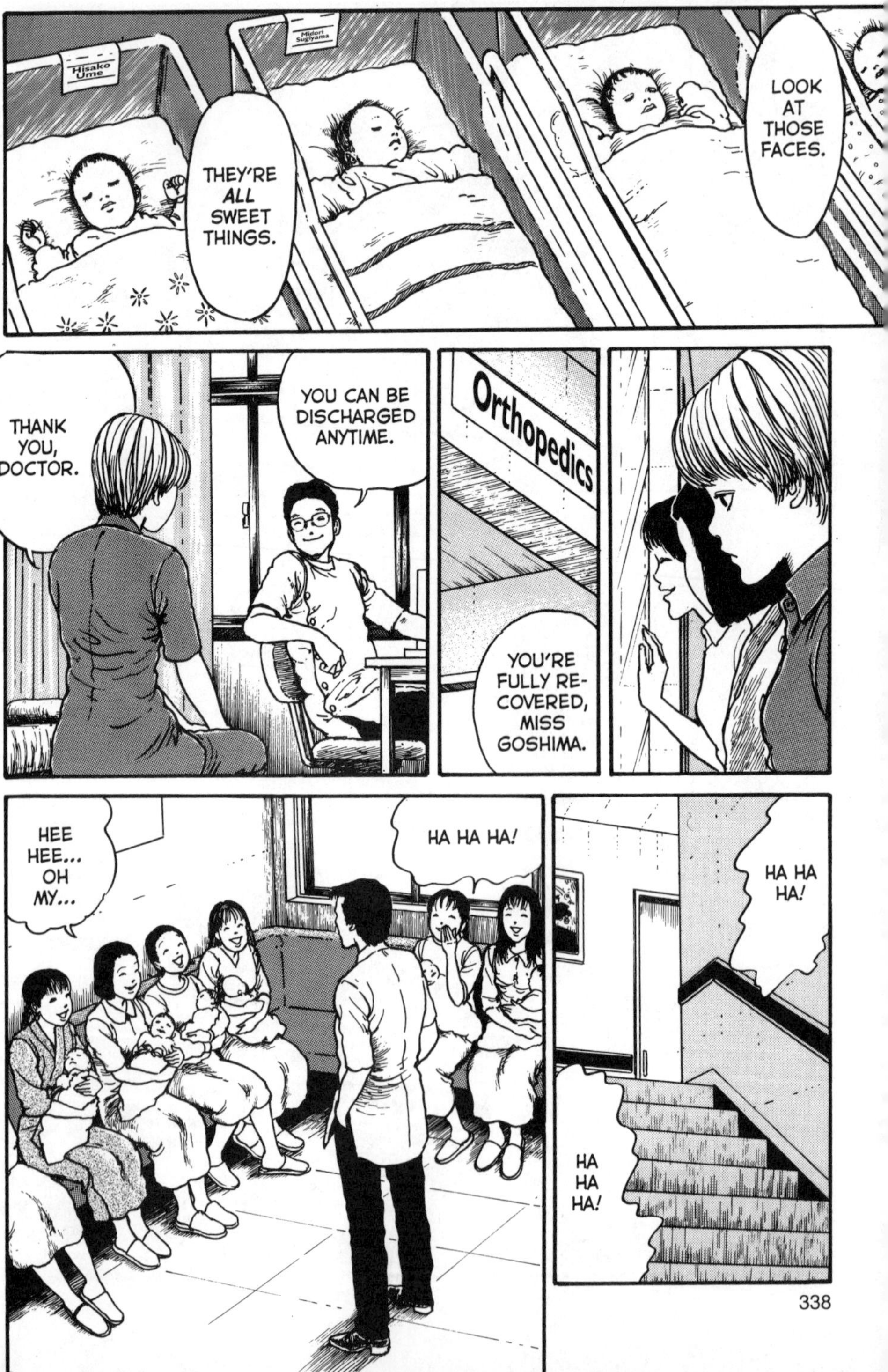
LOOK AT THOSE FACES.
Hisako Ume
Midori Sugiyama
THEY'RE *ALL* SWEET THINGS.
Orthopedics
YOU'RE FULLY RE-COVERED, MISS GOSHIMA.
YOU CAN BE DISCHARGED ANYTIME.
THANK YOU, DOCTOR.
HA HA HA!
HA HA HA!
HA HA HA!
HEE HEE... OH MY...

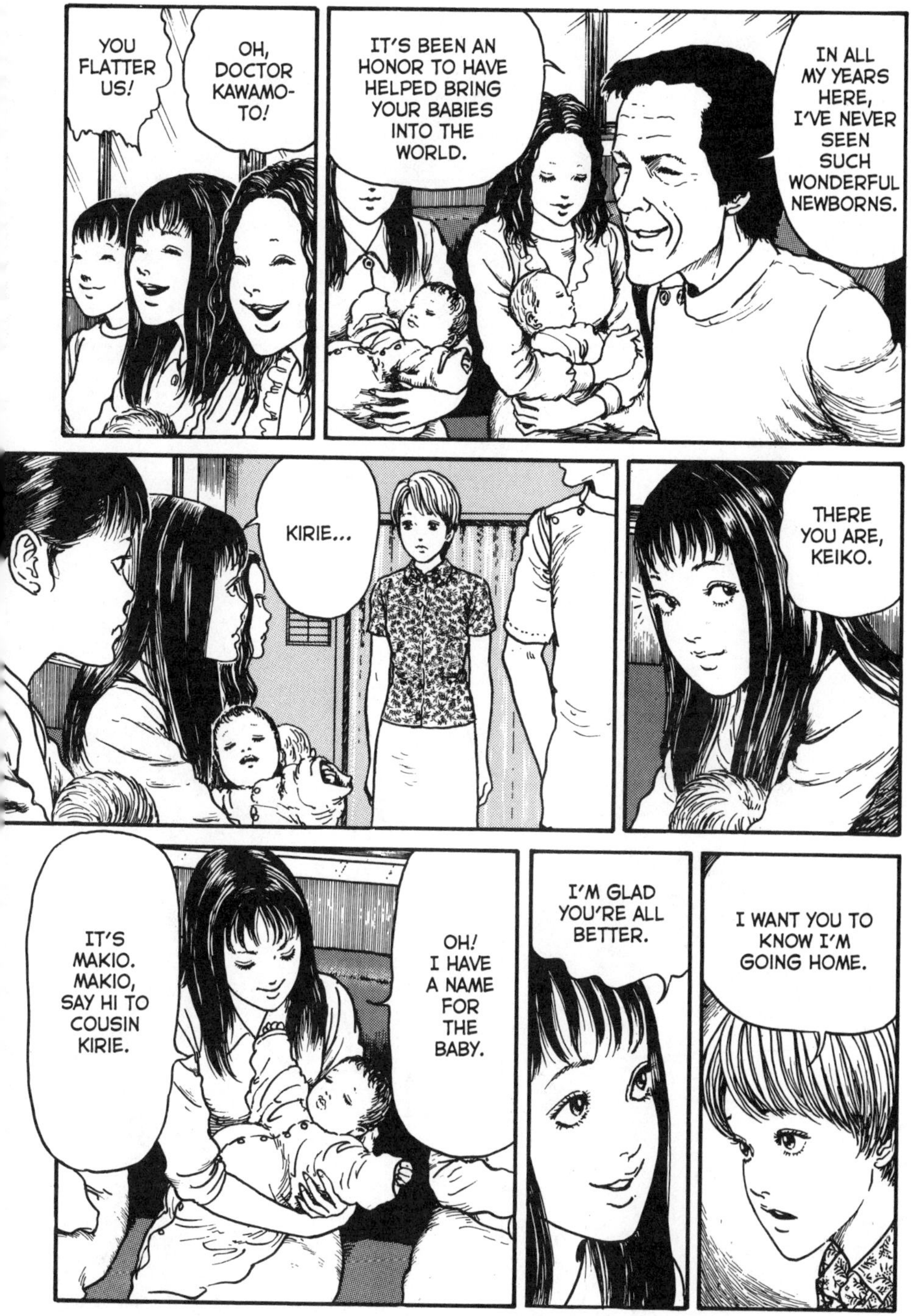
IN ALL MY YEARS HERE, I'VE NEVER SEEN SUCH WONDERFUL NEWBORNS.
IT'S BEEN AN HONOR TO HAVE HELPED BRING YOUR BABIES INTO THE WORLD.
OH, DOCTOR KAWAMOTO!
YOU FLATTER US!
THERE YOU ARE, KEIKO.
KIRIE...
I WANT YOU TO KNOW I'M GOING HOME.
I'M GLAD YOU'RE ALL BETTER.
OH! I HAVE A NAME FOR THE BABY.
IT'S MAKIO. MAKIO, SAY HI TO COUSIN KIRIE.

HM?

HE'S SO CUTE.

...

GOO GOO...

IS SOMETHING WRONG WITH MAKIO?

UMM... KEIKO?

HIS TUMMY'S PUFFED UP.

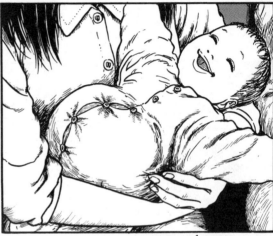

...

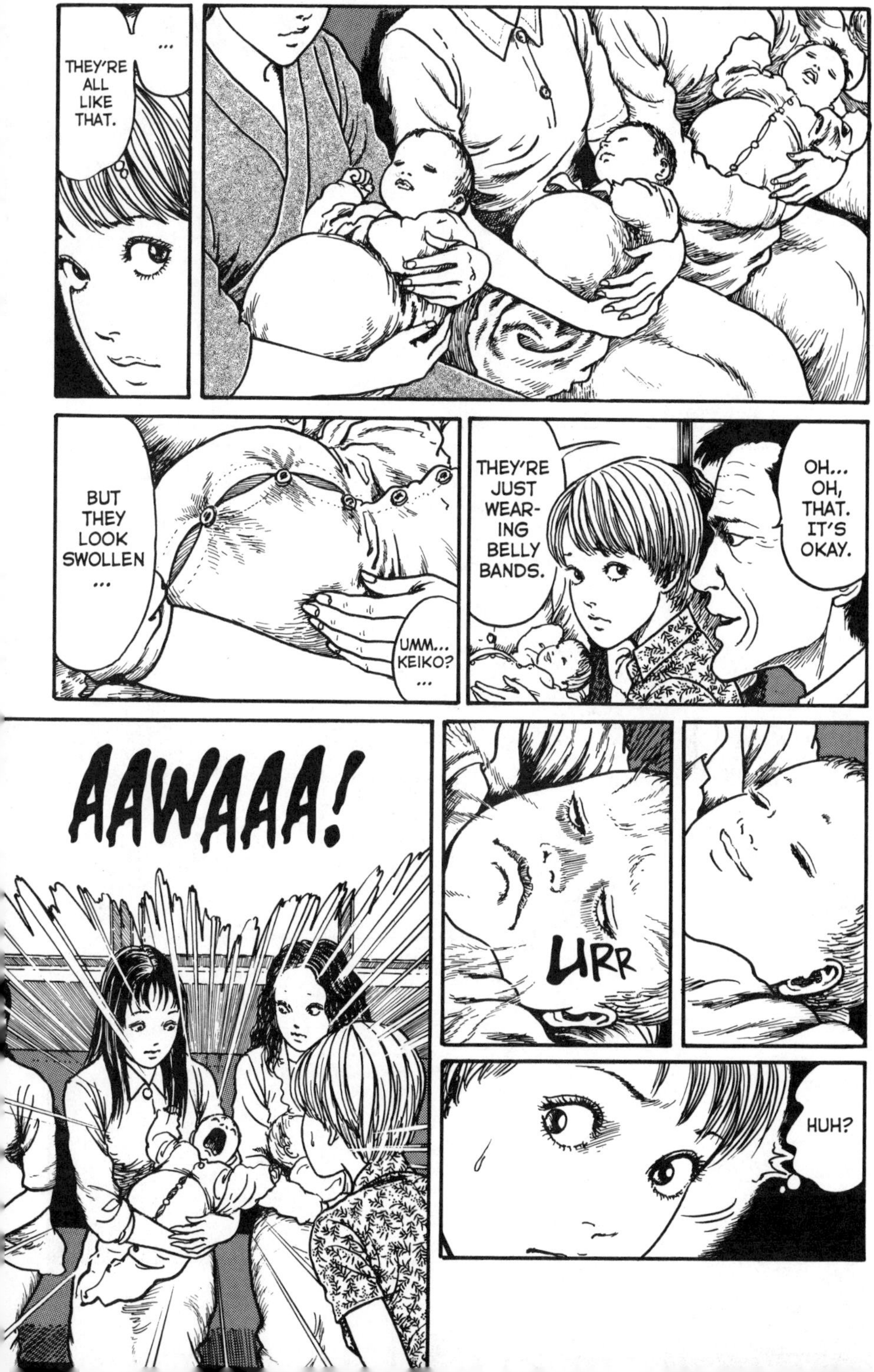

...
THEY'RE ALL LIKE THAT.
OH... OH, THAT. IT'S OKAY.
THEY'RE JUST WEAR-ING BELLY BANDS.
BUT THEY LOOK SWOLLEN ...
UMM... KEIKO? ...
URR
HUH?
AAWAAA!

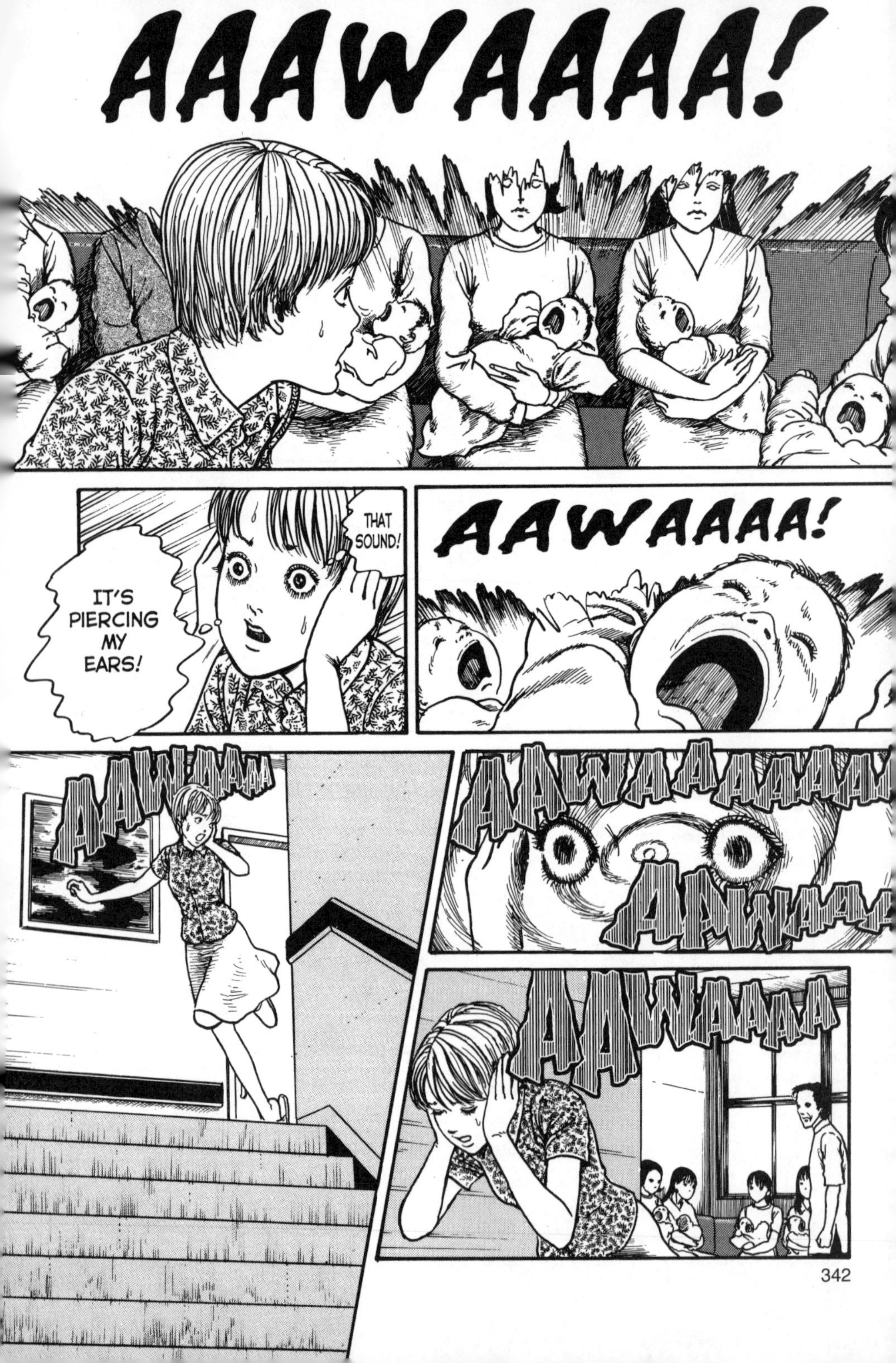
AAAWAAAA!
AAWAAAA!
THAT SOUND!
IT'S PIERCING MY EARS!
AAWAAAA

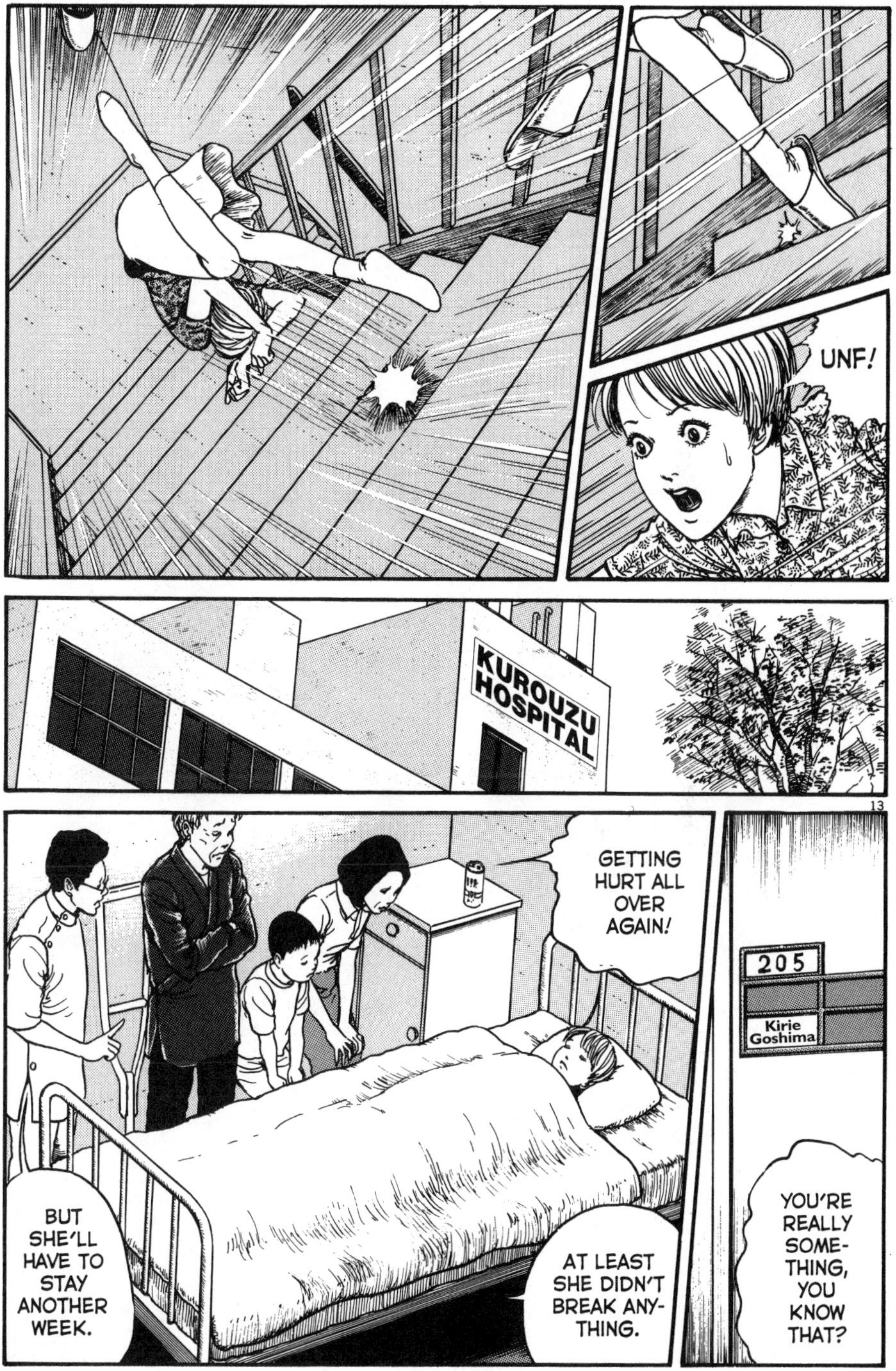
UNF!
KUROUZU HOSPITAL
205
Kirie Goshima
YOU'RE REALLY SOMETHING, YOU KNOW THAT?
GETTING HURT ALL OVER AGAIN!
AT LEAST SHE DIDN'T BREAK ANYTHING.
BUT SHE'LL HAVE TO STAY ANOTHER WEEK.

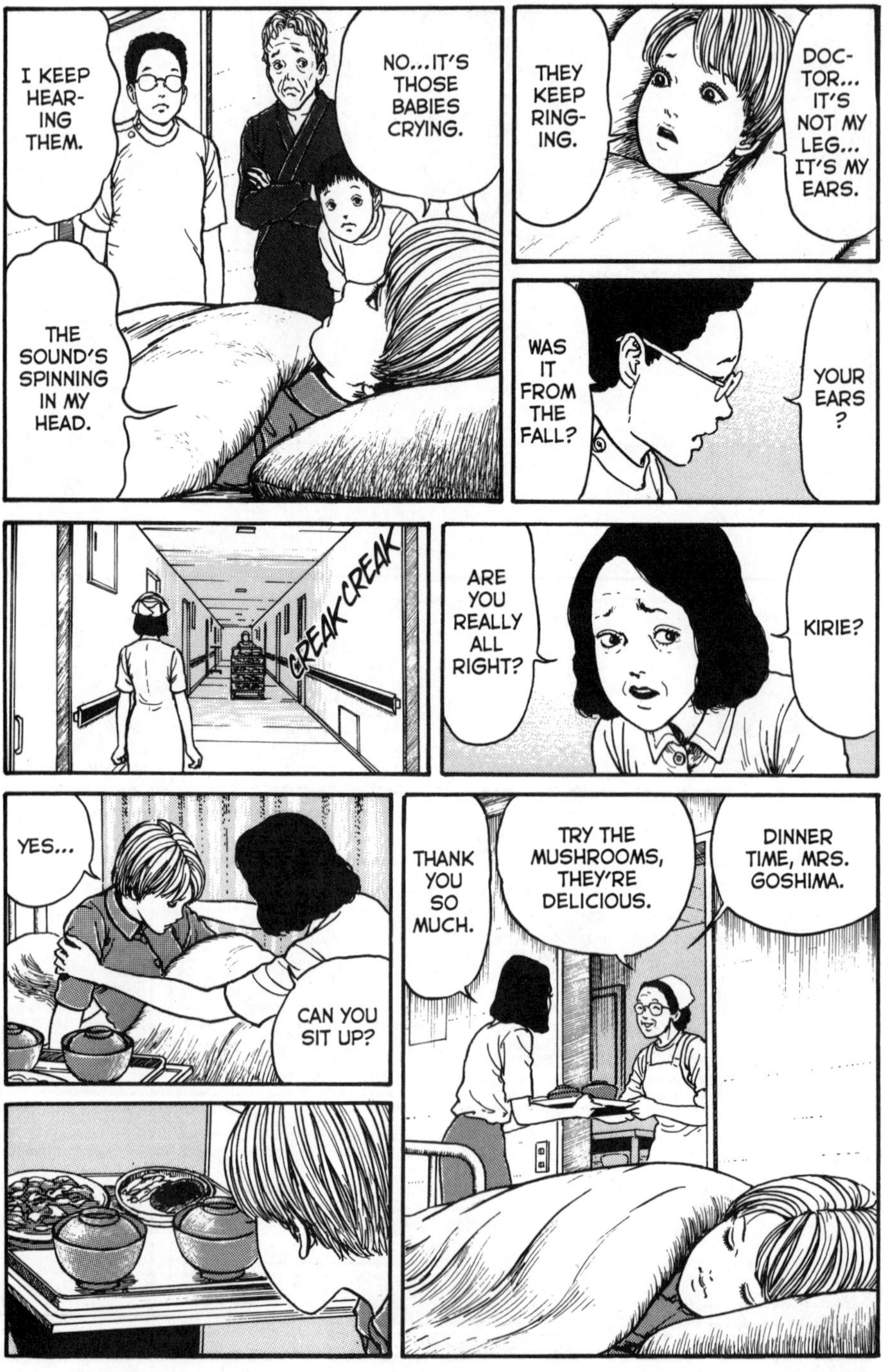
DOC-
TOR...
IT'S
NOT MY
LEG...
IT'S MY
EARS.
THEY KEEP RING-ING.
YOUR EARS?
WAS IT FROM THE FALL?
NO...IT'S THOSE BABIES CRYING.
I KEEP HEAR-ING THEM.
THE SOUND'S SPINNING IN MY HEAD.
KIRIE?
ARE YOU REALLY ALL RIGHT?
CREAK CREAK
DINNER TIME, MRS. GOSHIMA.
TRY THE MUSHROOMS, THEY'RE DELICIOUS.
THANK YOU SO MUCH.
CAN YOU SIT UP?
YES...

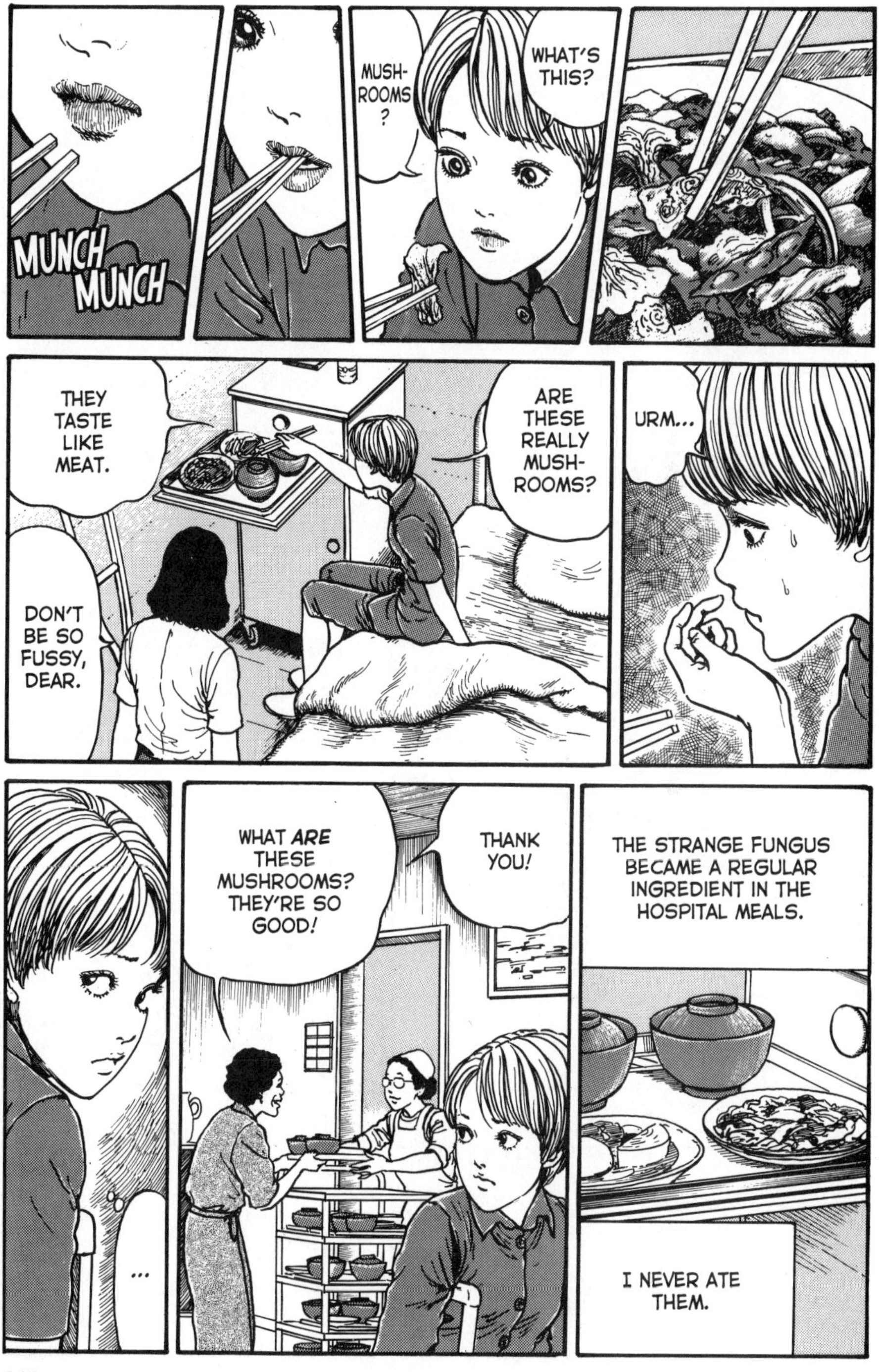
WHAT'S THIS?
MUSH-ROOMS?
MUNCH MUNCH
URM...
ARE THESE REALLY MUSH-ROOMS?
THEY TASTE LIKE MEAT.
DON'T BE SO FUSSY, DEAR.
THE STRANGE FUNGUS BECAME A REGULAR INGREDIENT IN THE HOSPITAL MEALS.
I NEVER ATE THEM.
THANK YOU!
WHAT ARE THESE MUSHROOMS? THEY'RE SO GOOD!
...

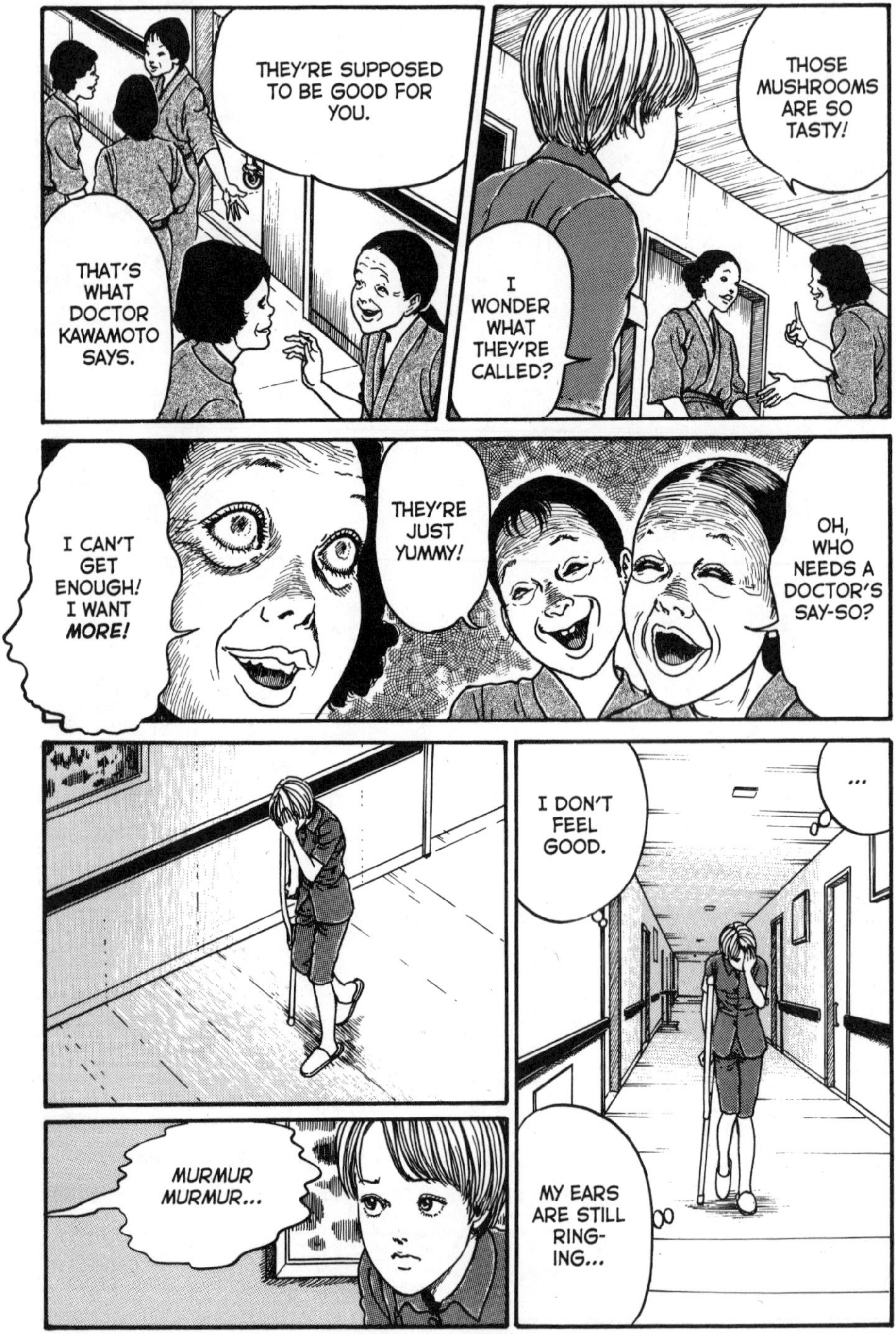
THOSE MUSHROOMS ARE SO TASTY!
I WONDER WHAT THEY'RE CALLED?
THEY'RE SUPPOSED TO BE GOOD FOR YOU.
THAT'S WHAT DOCTOR KAWAMOTO SAYS.
OH, WHO NEEDS A DOCTOR'S SAY-SO?
THEY'RE JUST YUMMY!
I CAN'T GET ENOUGH! I WANT *MORE!*
...
I DON'T FEEL GOOD.
MY EARS ARE STILL RING-ING...
MURMUR MURMUR...

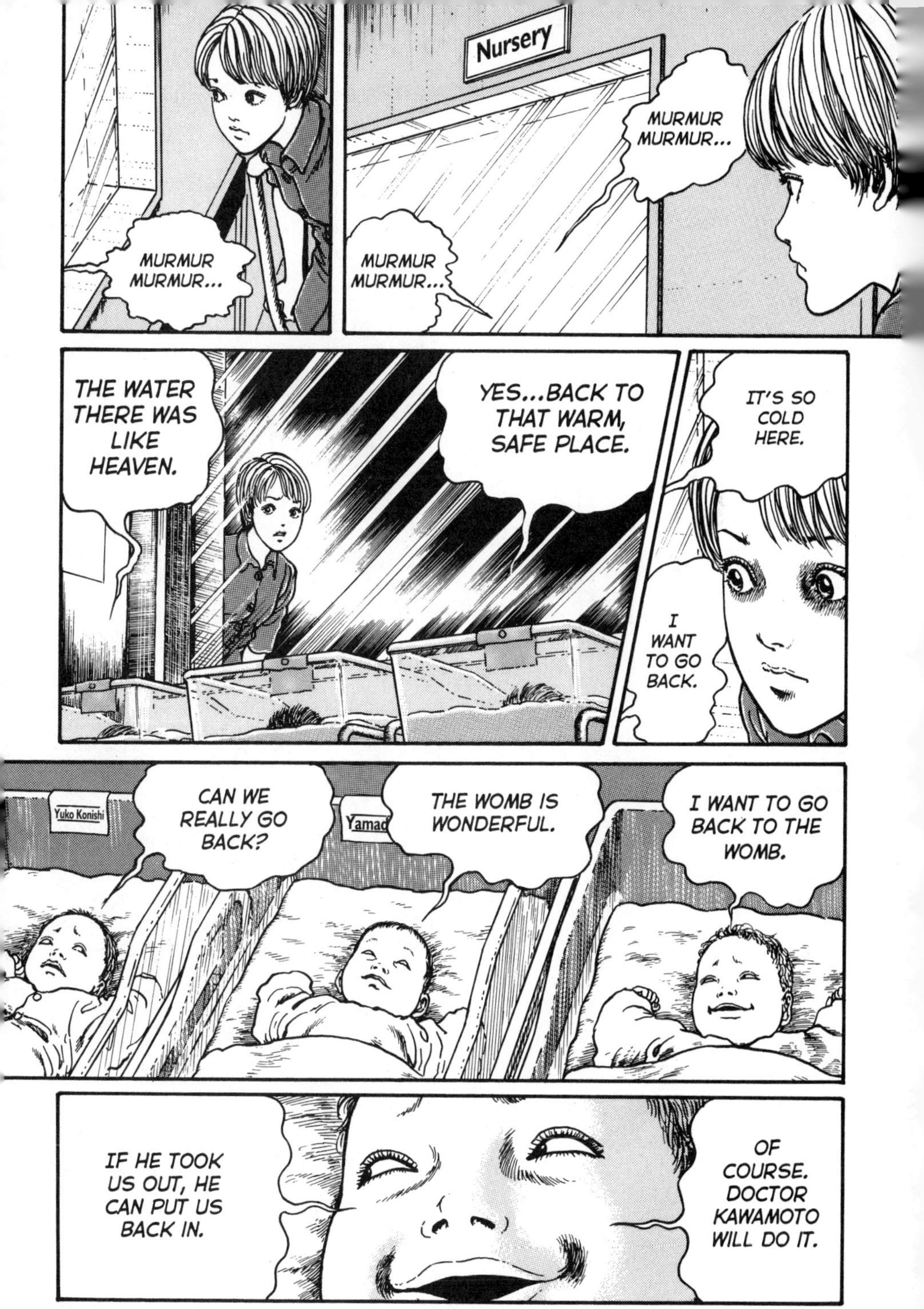
Nursery
MURMUR MURMUR...
MURMUR MURMUR...
MURMUR MURMUR...
IT'S SO COLD HERE.
I WANT TO GO BACK.
YES...BACK TO THAT WARM, SAFE PLACE.
THE WATER THERE WAS LIKE HEAVEN.
I WANT TO GO BACK TO THE WOMB.
Yamad
THE WOMB IS WONDERFUL.
Yuko Konishi
CAN WE REALLY GO BACK?
OF COURSE. DOCTOR KAWAMOTO WILL DO IT.
IF HE TOOK US OUT, HE CAN PUT US BACK IN.

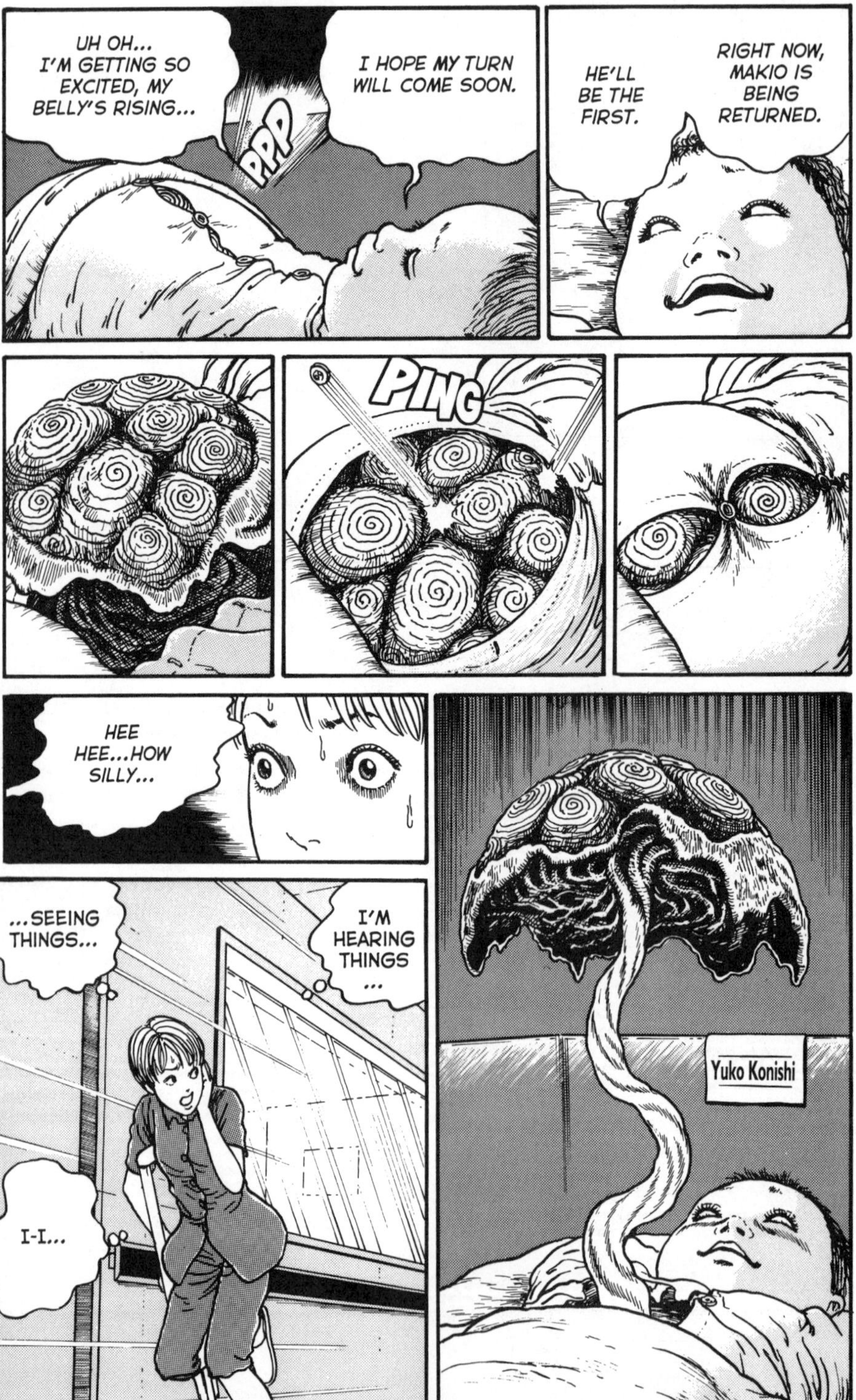
RIGHT NOW, MAKIO IS BEING RETURNED.
HE'LL BE THE FIRST.
I HOPE MY TURN WILL COME SOON.
UH OH... I'M GETTING SO EXCITED, MY BELLY'S RISING...
PPP
PING
Yuko Konishi
HEE HEE...HOW SILLY...
I'M HEARING THINGS ...
...SEEING THINGS...
I-I...

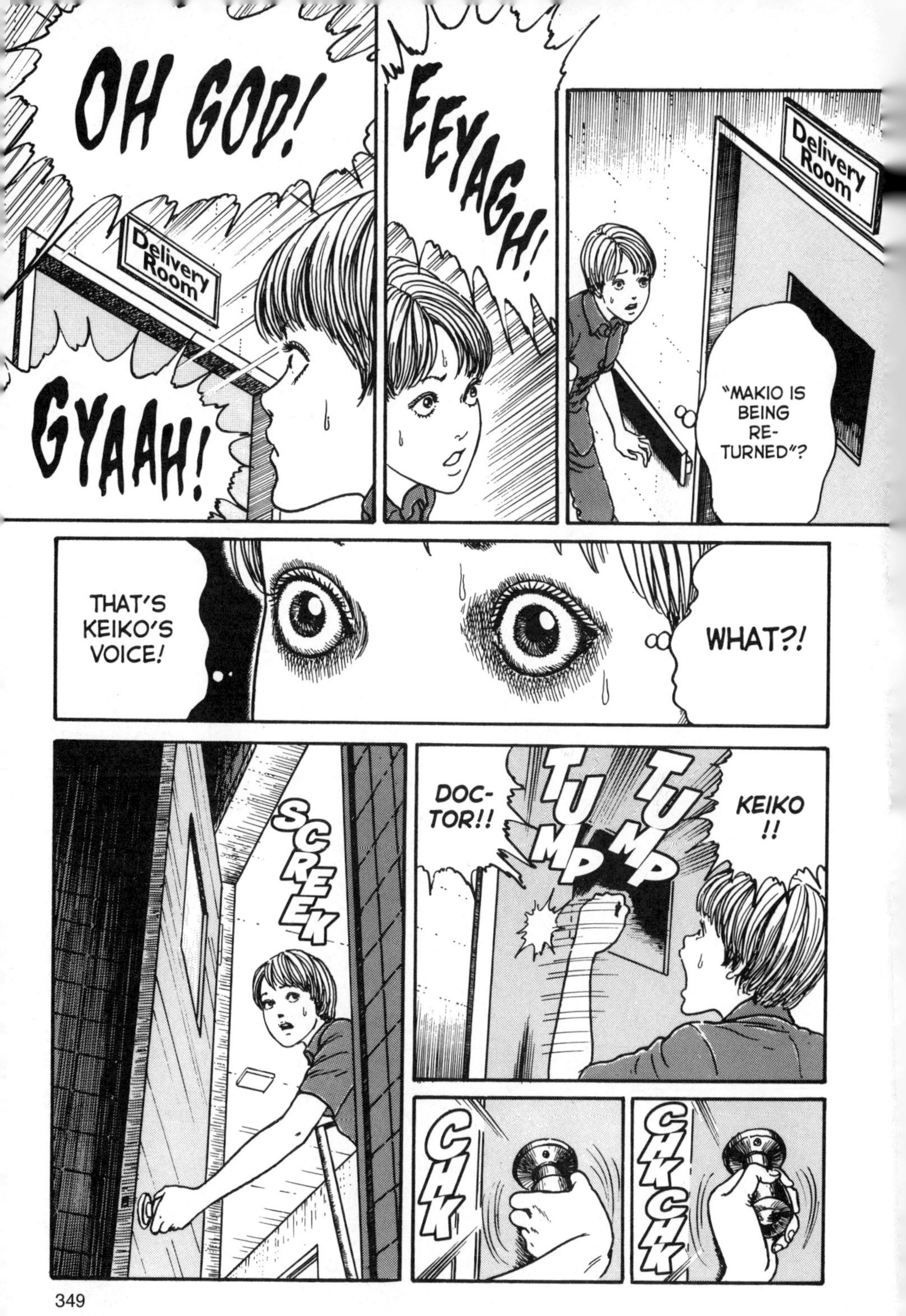
Delivery Room
"MAKIO IS BEING RE-TURNED"?
EEYAGH!
OH GOD!
Delivery Room
GYAAH!
WHAT?!
THAT'S KEIKO'S VOICE!
KEIKO !!
TUMP
TUMP
DOC-TOR!!
CHKCHK
CHK
SCREEK

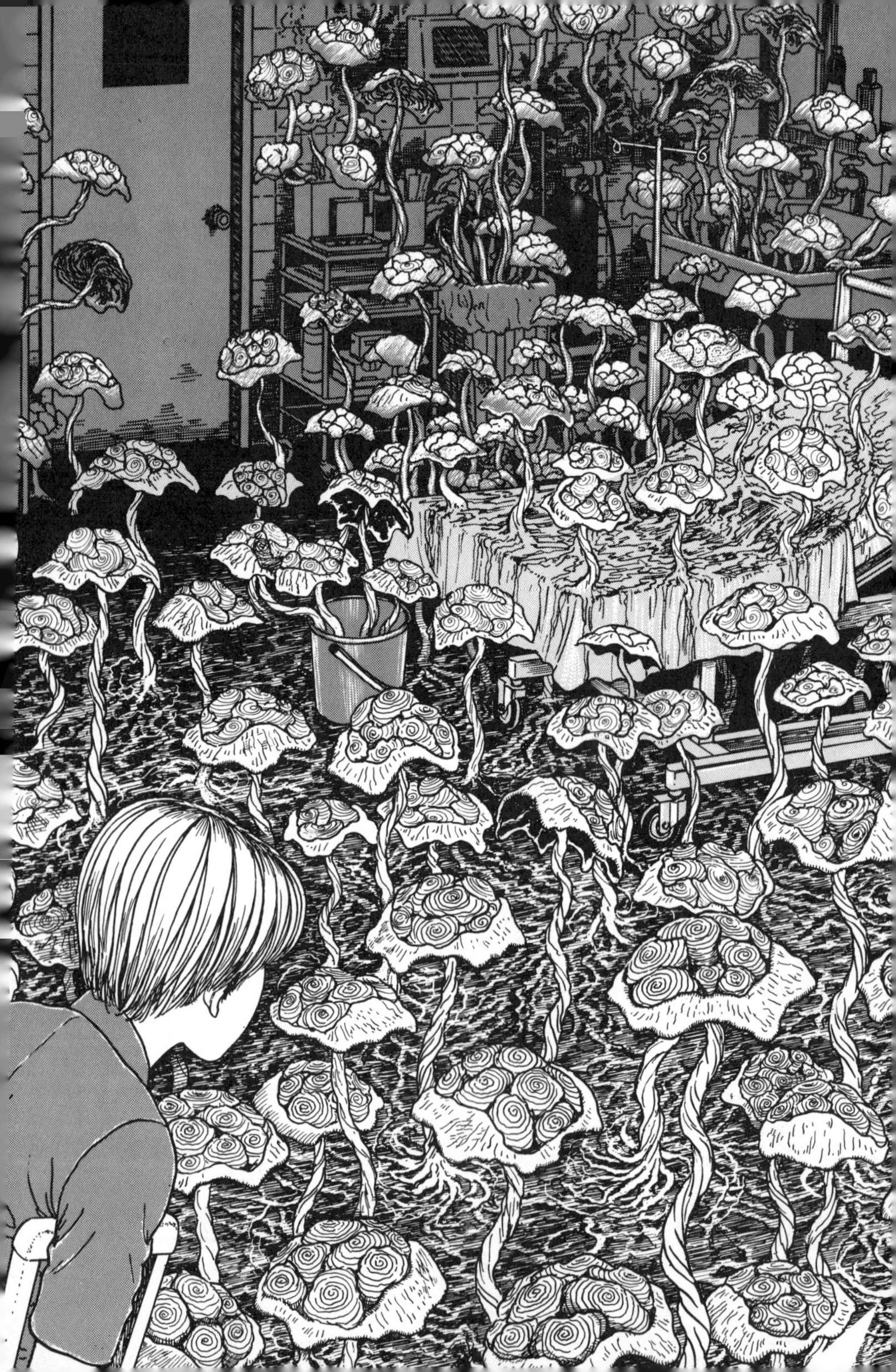

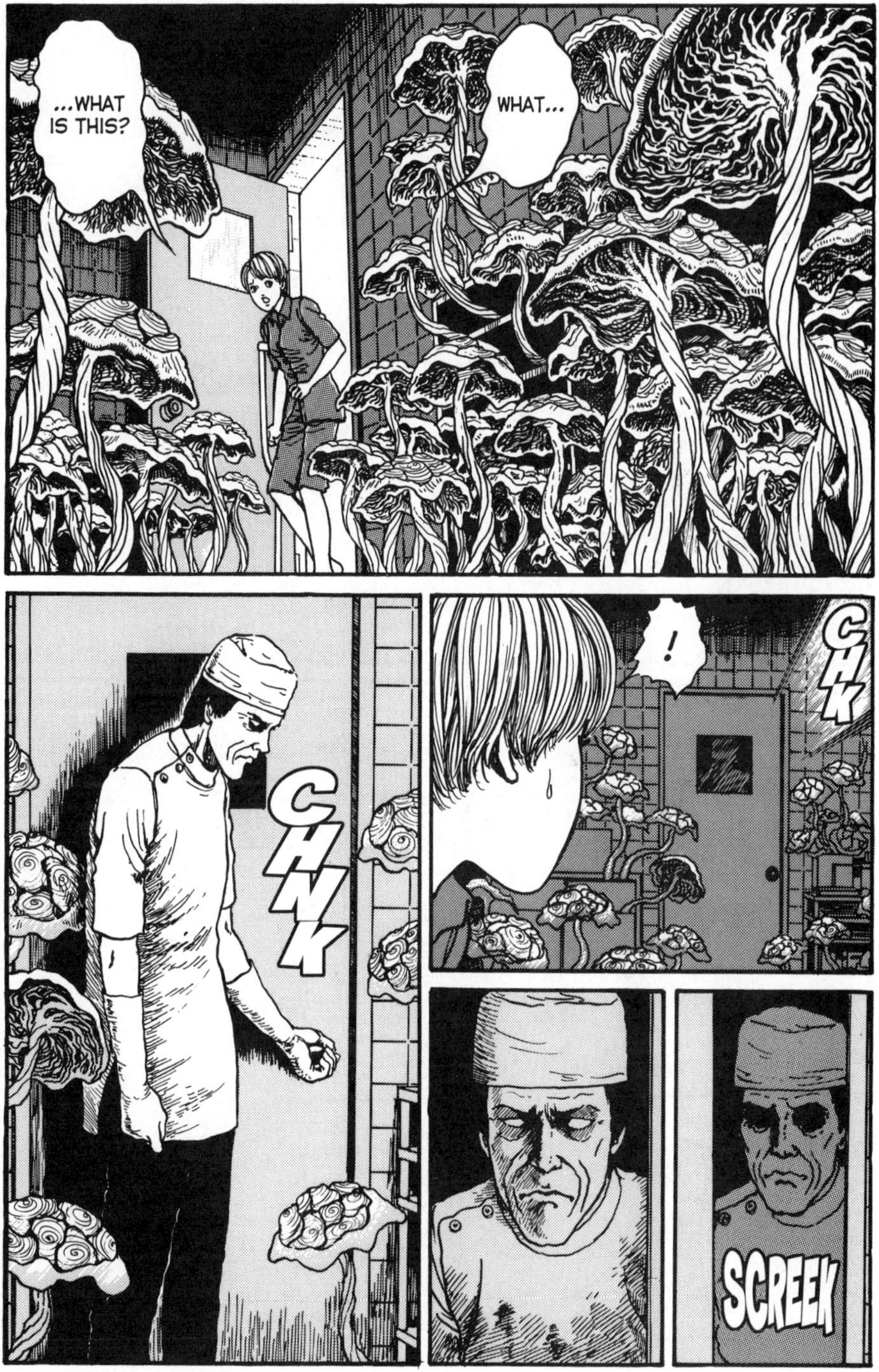
WHAT...
...WHAT IS THIS?
!
CHK
SCREEK
CHNK

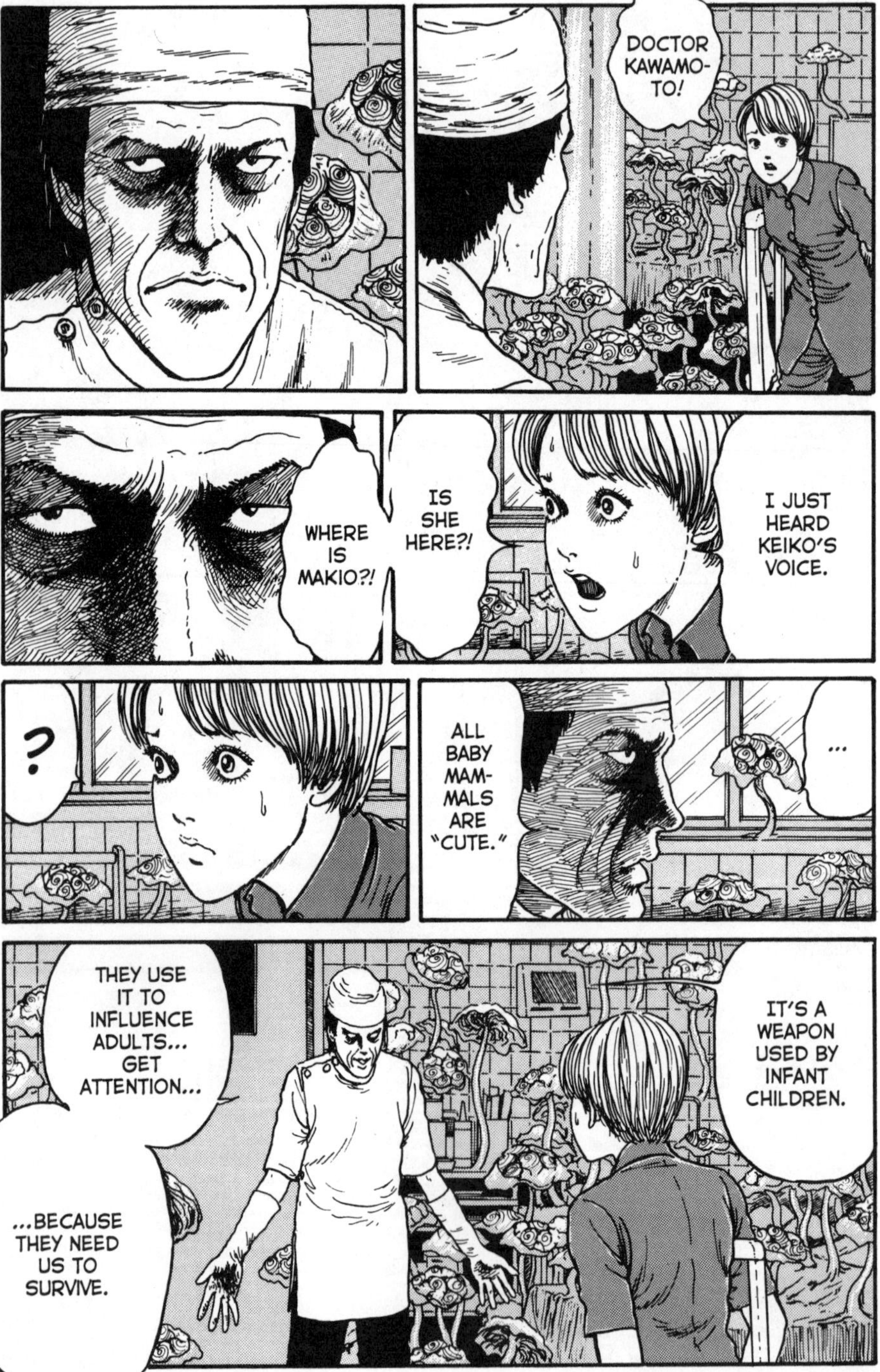
DOCTOR KAWAMO-TO!
I JUST HEARD KEIKO'S VOICE.
IS SHE HERE?!
WHERE IS MAKIO?!
...
ALL BABY MAM-MALS ARE "CUTE."
?
IT'S A WEAPON USED BY INFANT CHILDREN.
THEY USE IT TO INFLUENCE ADULTS... GET ATTENTION...
...BECAUSE THEY NEED US TO SURVIVE.

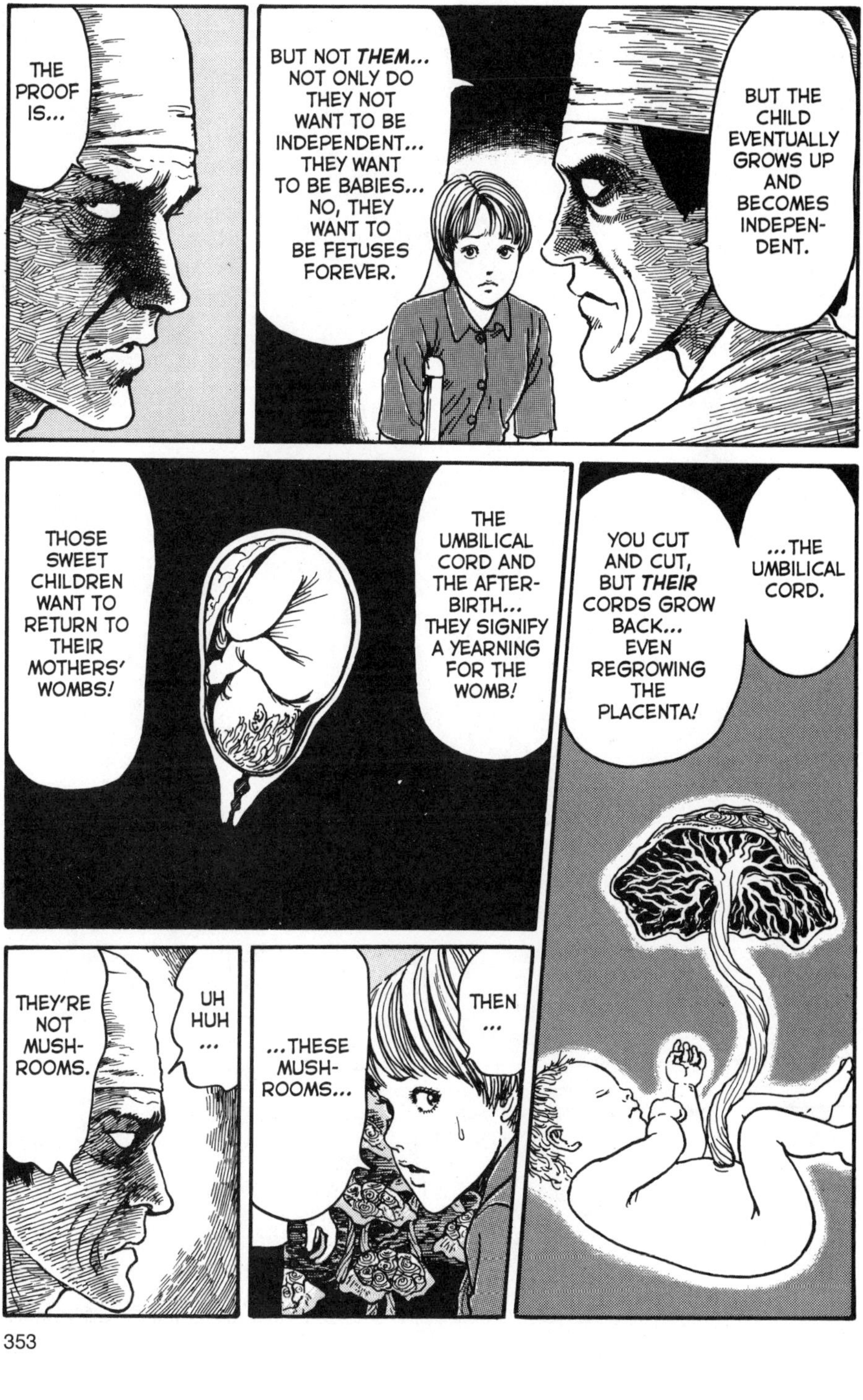

BUT THE CHILD EVENTUALLY GROWS UP AND BECOMES INDEPENDENT.
BUT NOT *THEM*... NOT ONLY DO THEY NOT WANT TO BE INDEPENDENT... THEY WANT TO BE BABIES... NO, THEY WANT TO BE FETUSES FOREVER.
THE PROOF IS...
...THE UMBILICAL CORD.
YOU CUT AND CUT, BUT *THEIR* CORDS GROW BACK... EVEN REGROWING THE PLACENTA!
THE UMBILICAL CORD AND THE AFTERBIRTH... THEY SIGNIFY A YEARNING FOR THE WOMB!
THOSE SWEET CHILDREN WANT TO RETURN TO THEIR MOTHERS' WOMBS!
THEN...
...THESE MUSHROOMS...
UH HUH...
THEY'RE NOT MUSHROOMS.

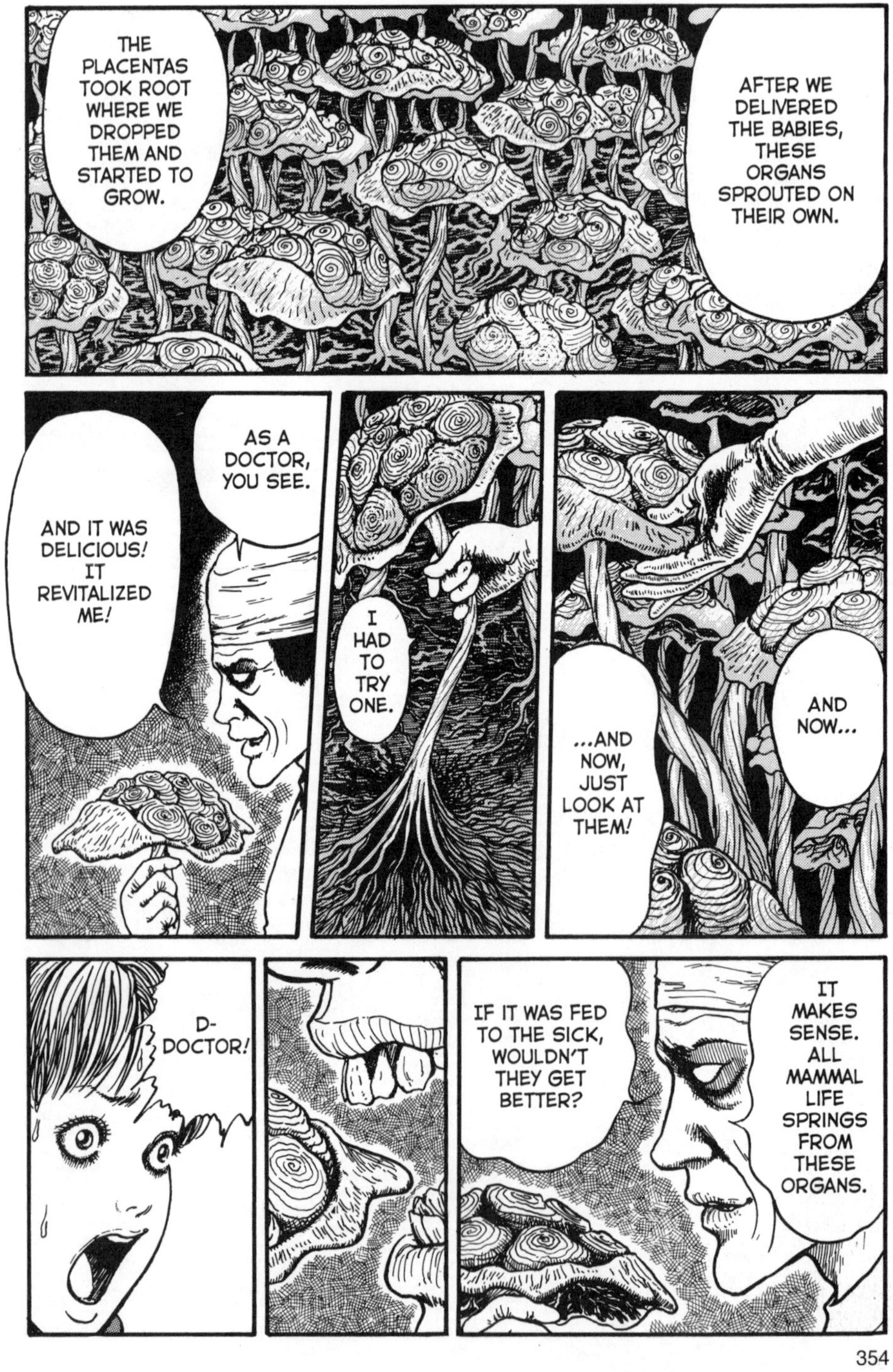
AFTER WE DELIVERED THE BABIES, THESE ORGANS SPROUTED ON THEIR OWN.
THE PLACENTAS TOOK ROOT WHERE WE DROPPED THEM AND STARTED TO GROW.
AND NOW...
...AND NOW, JUST LOOK AT THEM!
I HAD TO TRY ONE.
AS A DOCTOR, YOU SEE.
AND IT WAS DELICIOUS! IT REVITALIZED ME!
IT MAKES SENSE. ALL MAMMAL LIFE SPRINGS FROM THESE ORGANS.
IF IT WAS FED TO THE SICK, WOULDN'T THEY GET BETTER?
D-DOCTOR!

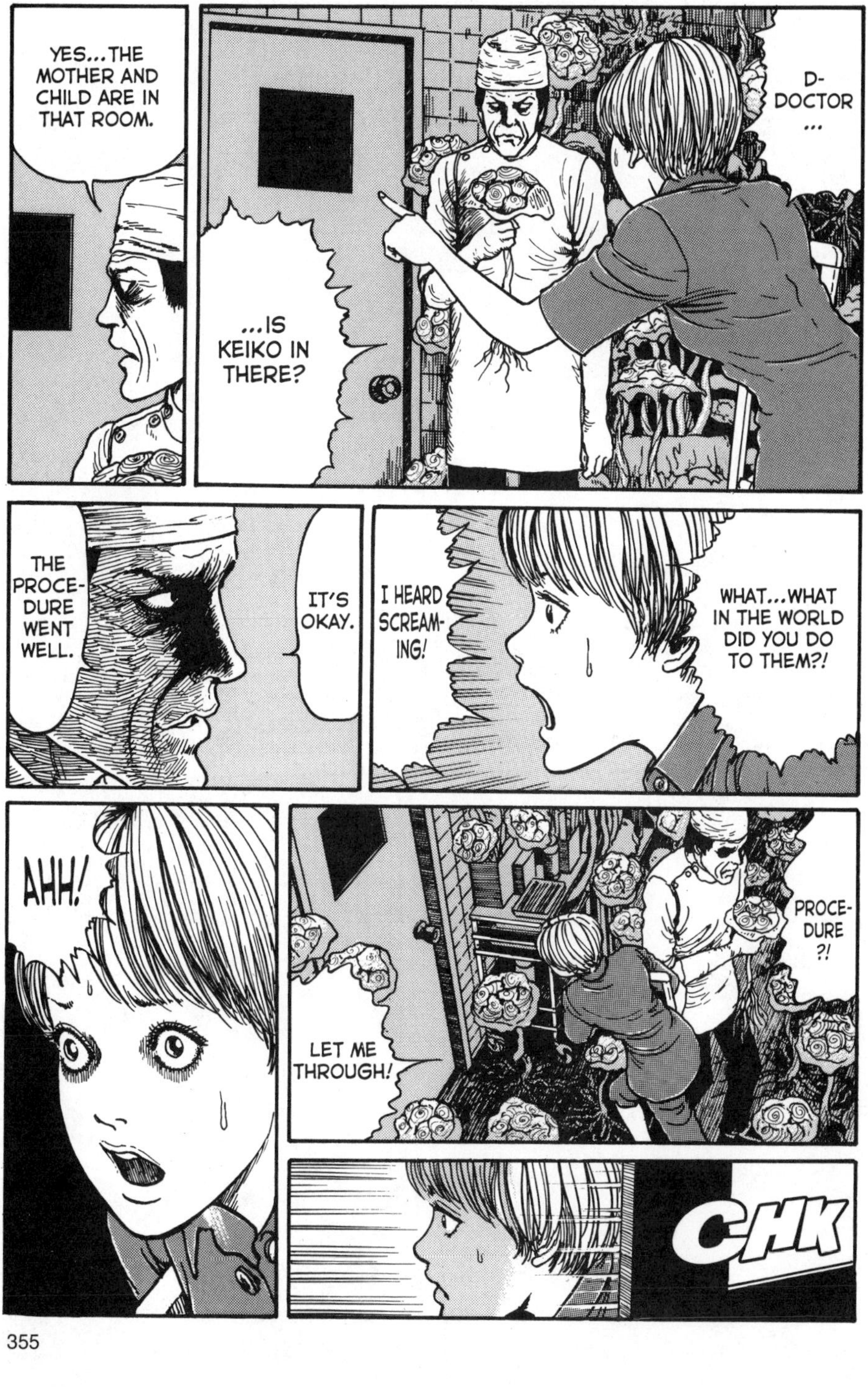
D-DOCTOR ...
...IS KEIKO IN THERE?
YES...THE MOTHER AND CHILD ARE IN THAT ROOM.
WHAT...WHAT IN THE WORLD DID YOU DO TO THEM?!
I HEARD SCREAMING!
IT'S OKAY.
THE PROCEDURE WENT WELL.
PROCEDURE?!
LET ME THROUGH!
CHK
AHH!

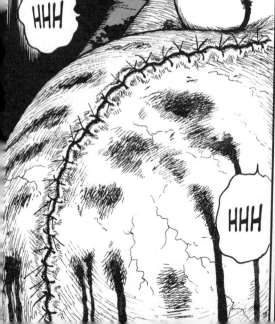

HHH

HHH

HHH

HHH

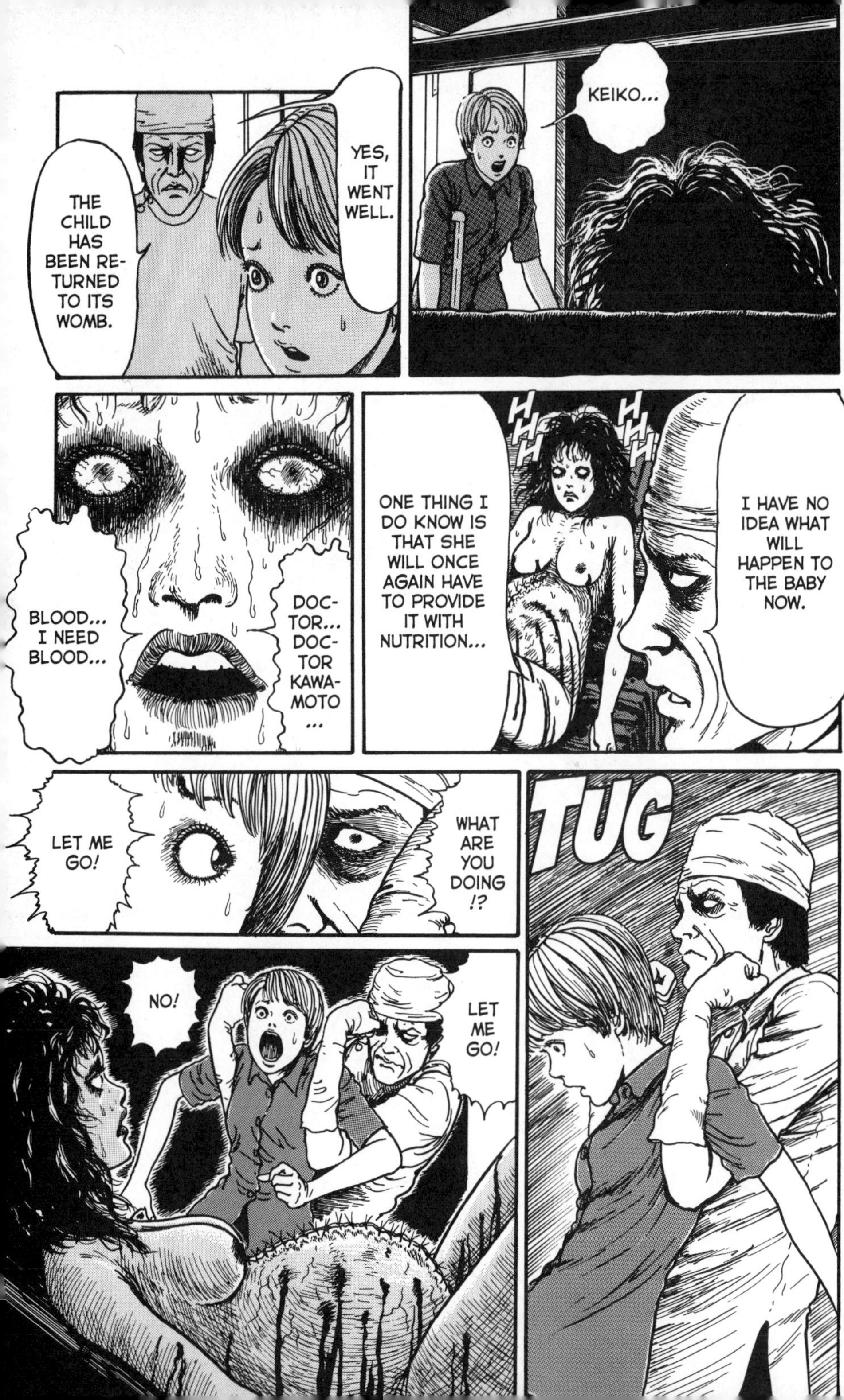
KEIKO...
YES, IT WENT WELL.
THE CHILD HAS BEEN RE-TURNED TO ITS WOMB.
I HAVE NO IDEA WHAT WILL HAPPEN TO THE BABY NOW.
ONE THING I DO KNOW IS THAT SHE WILL ONCE AGAIN HAVE TO PROVIDE IT WITH NUTRITION...
DOC-TOR... DOC-TOR KAWA-MOTO...
BLOOD... I NEED BLOOD...
TUG
WHAT ARE YOU DOING!?
LET ME GO!
LET ME GO!
NO!

KEIKO!

HERE... HERE!

HURRY... GIVE ME...

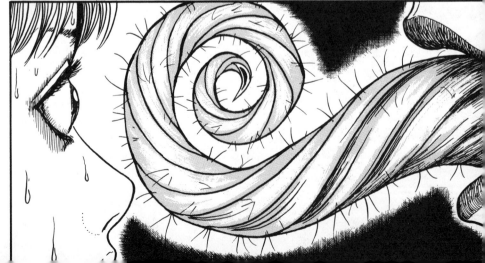

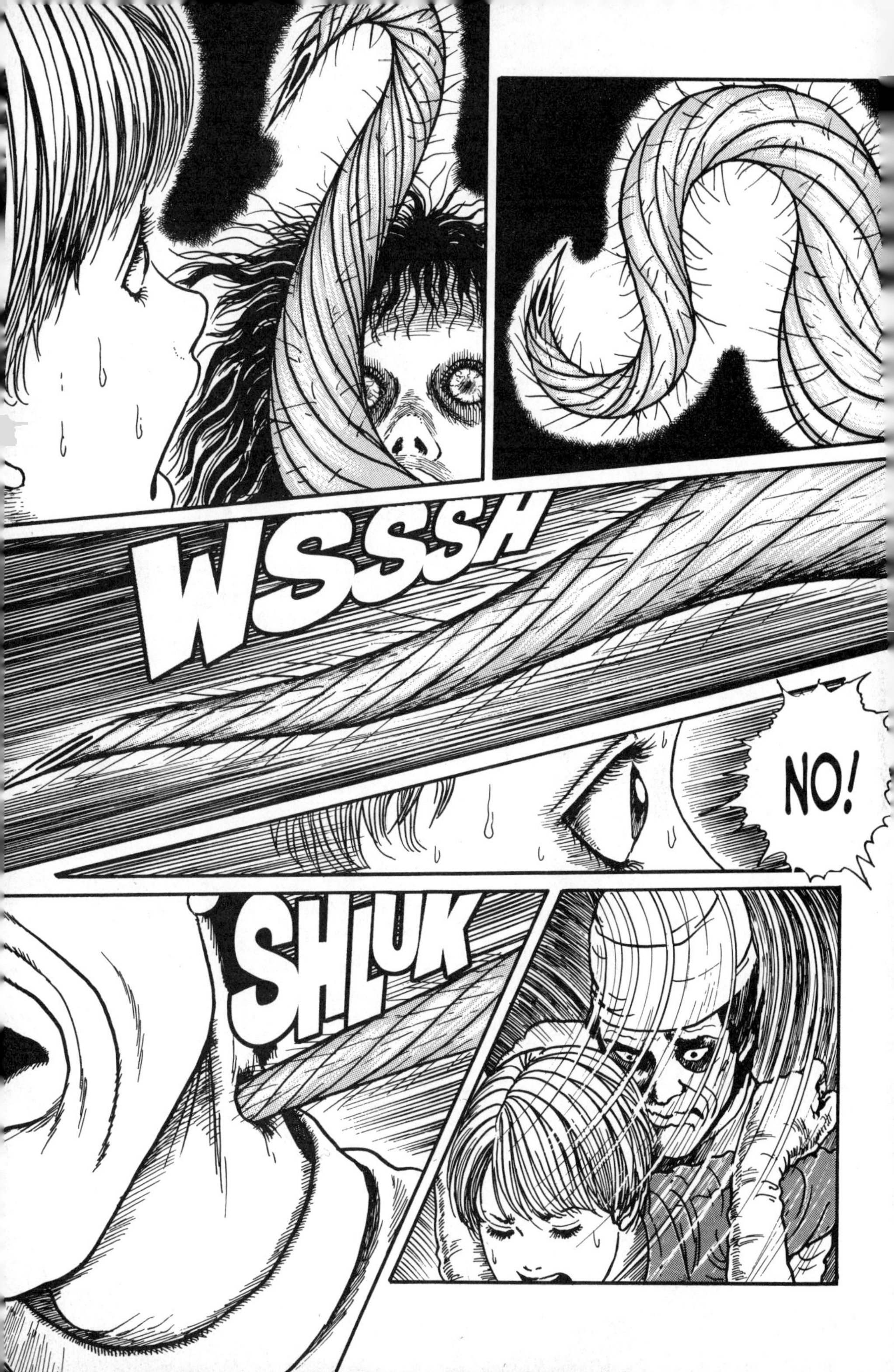
WSSSH
NO!
SHLUK

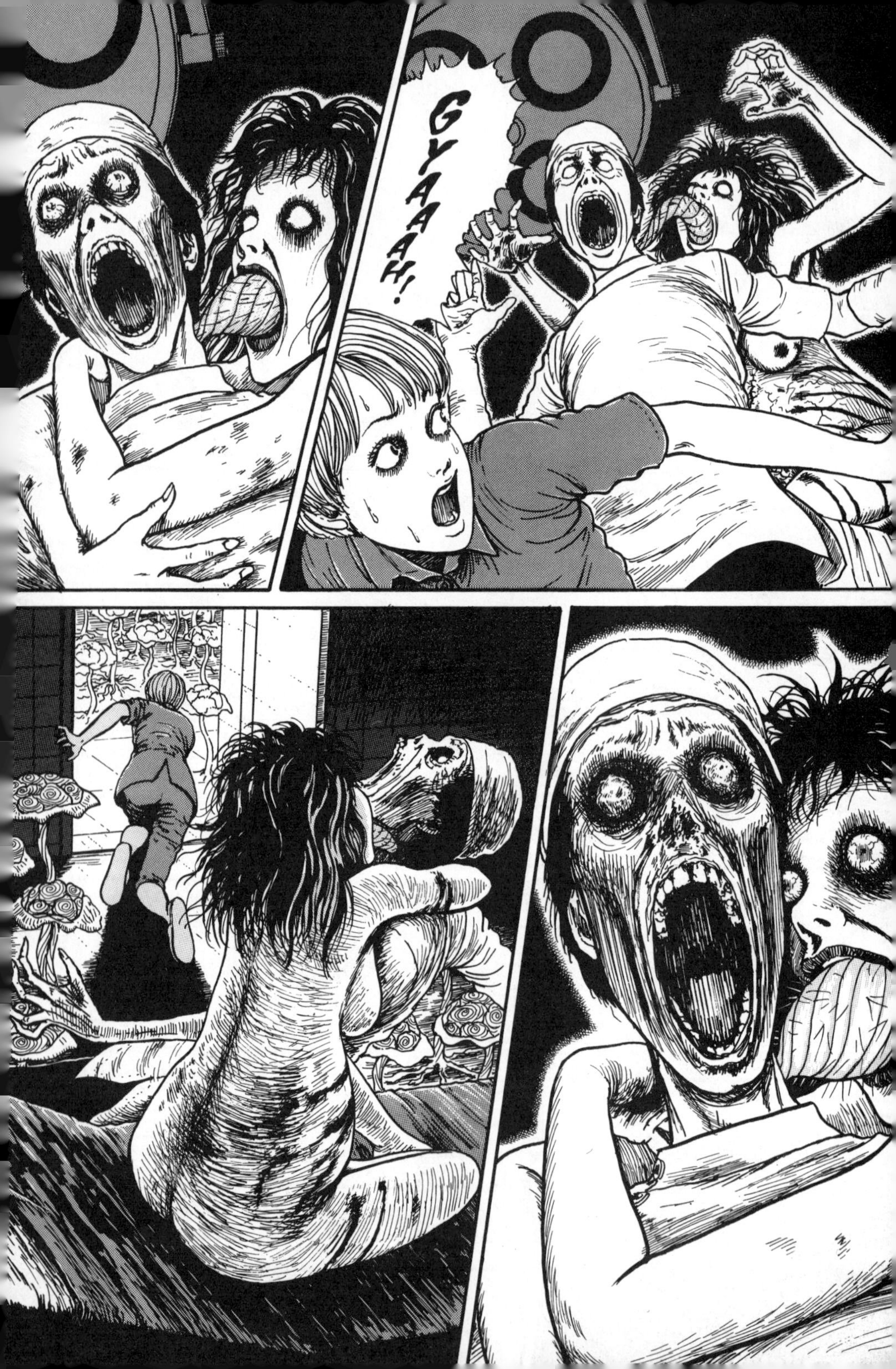
GYAAAAH!

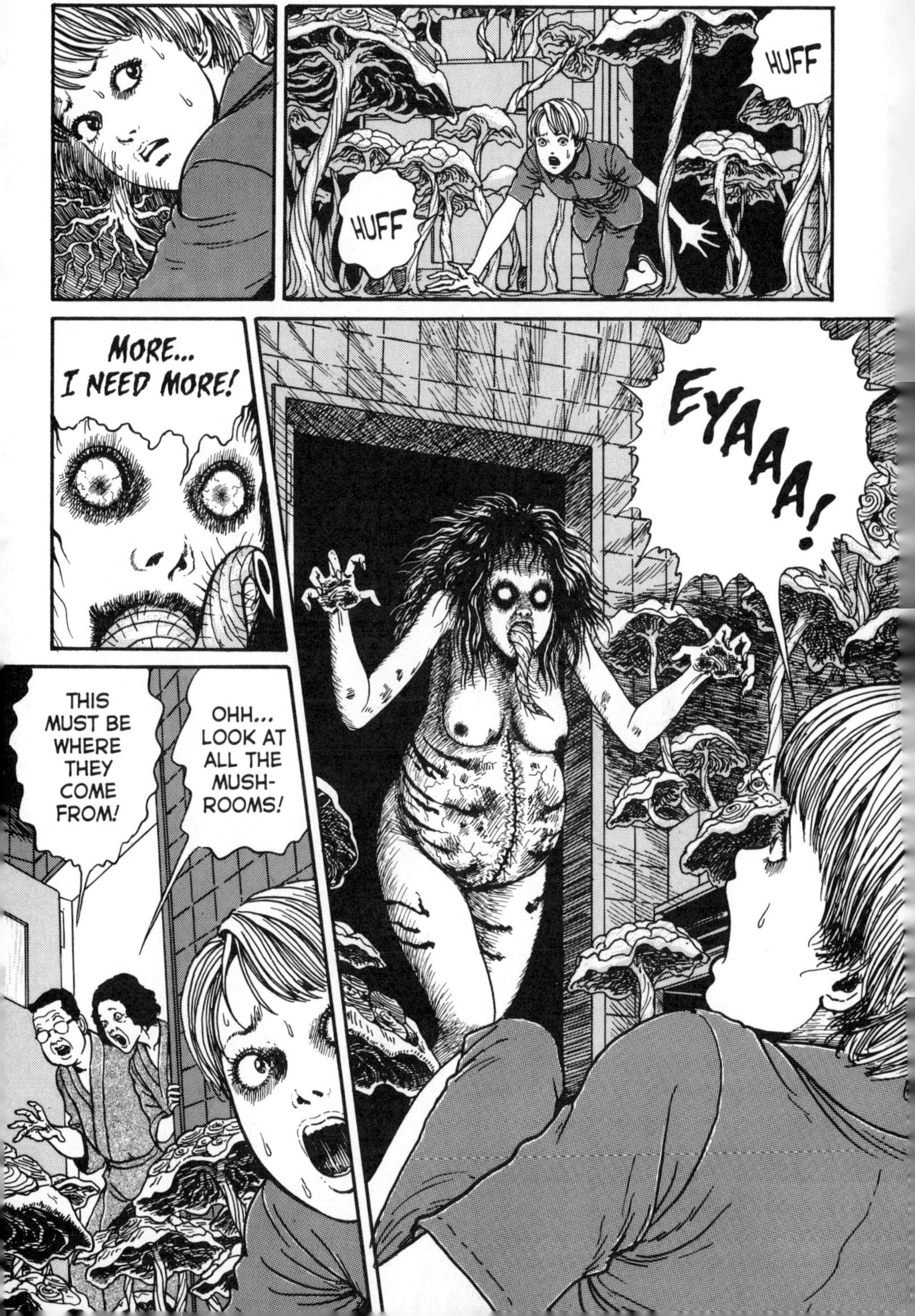
HUFF
HUFF
EYAAAA!
MORE... I NEED MORE!
OHH... LOOK AT ALL THE MUSH-ROOMS!
THIS MUST BE WHERE THEY COME FROM!

CHOMP

LET'S EAT!

PLEASE HELP ME!

LOOK HOW MANY THERE ARE!

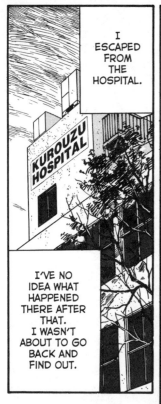

I ESCAPED FROM THE HOSPITAL.

KUROUZU HOSPITAL

I'VE NO IDEA WHAT HAPPENED THERE AFTER THAT. I WASN'T ABOUT TO GO BACK AND FIND OUT.

EEYAA!

SHHUK

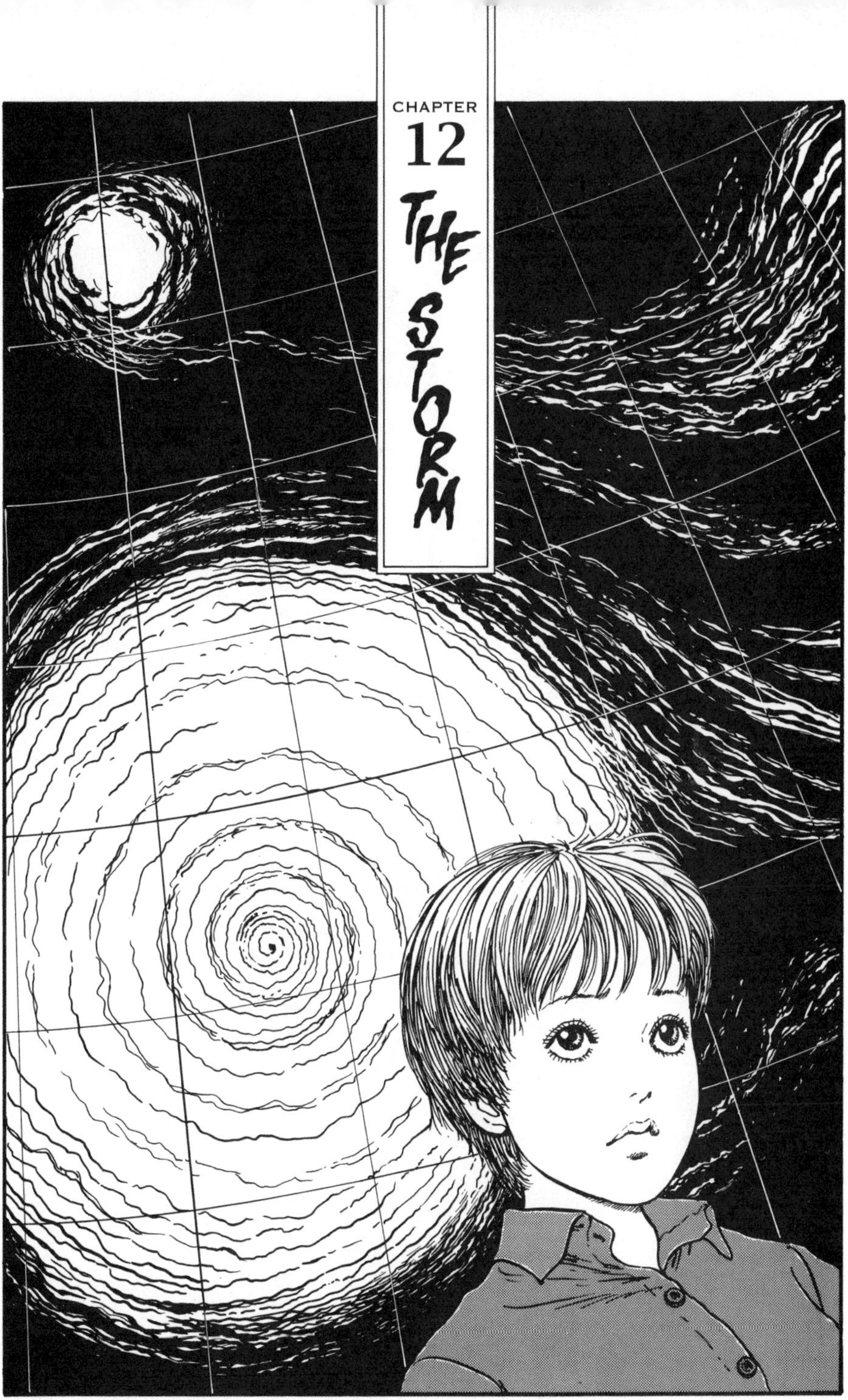
CHAPTER
12
THE STORM

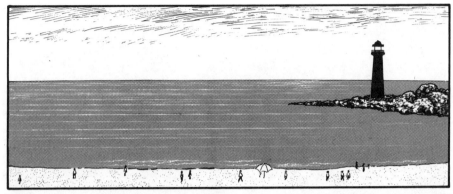

SHAAAAAAA

SHAAAAA

SHAAAAAAA

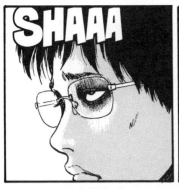

Y'KNOW, SHUICHI...
...IF IT WEREN'T FOR YOU I'D HAVE DIED A LONG TIME AGO...
SHAAA
HWOOOOO
HWOOOOo
SHAAA
HHWWOOOOOOOO
HWOOOOO
WHAT'S THAT NOISE?
HWOOOOO...

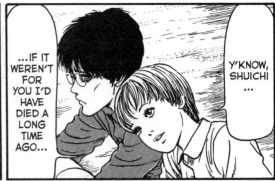

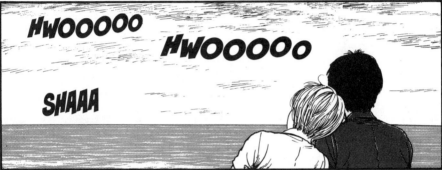

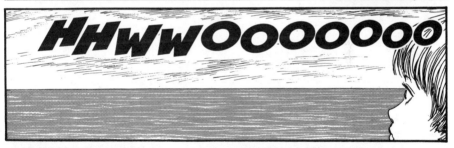

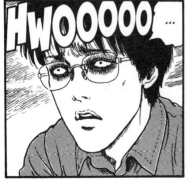

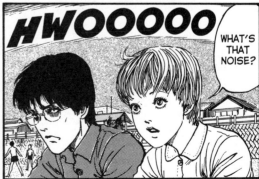

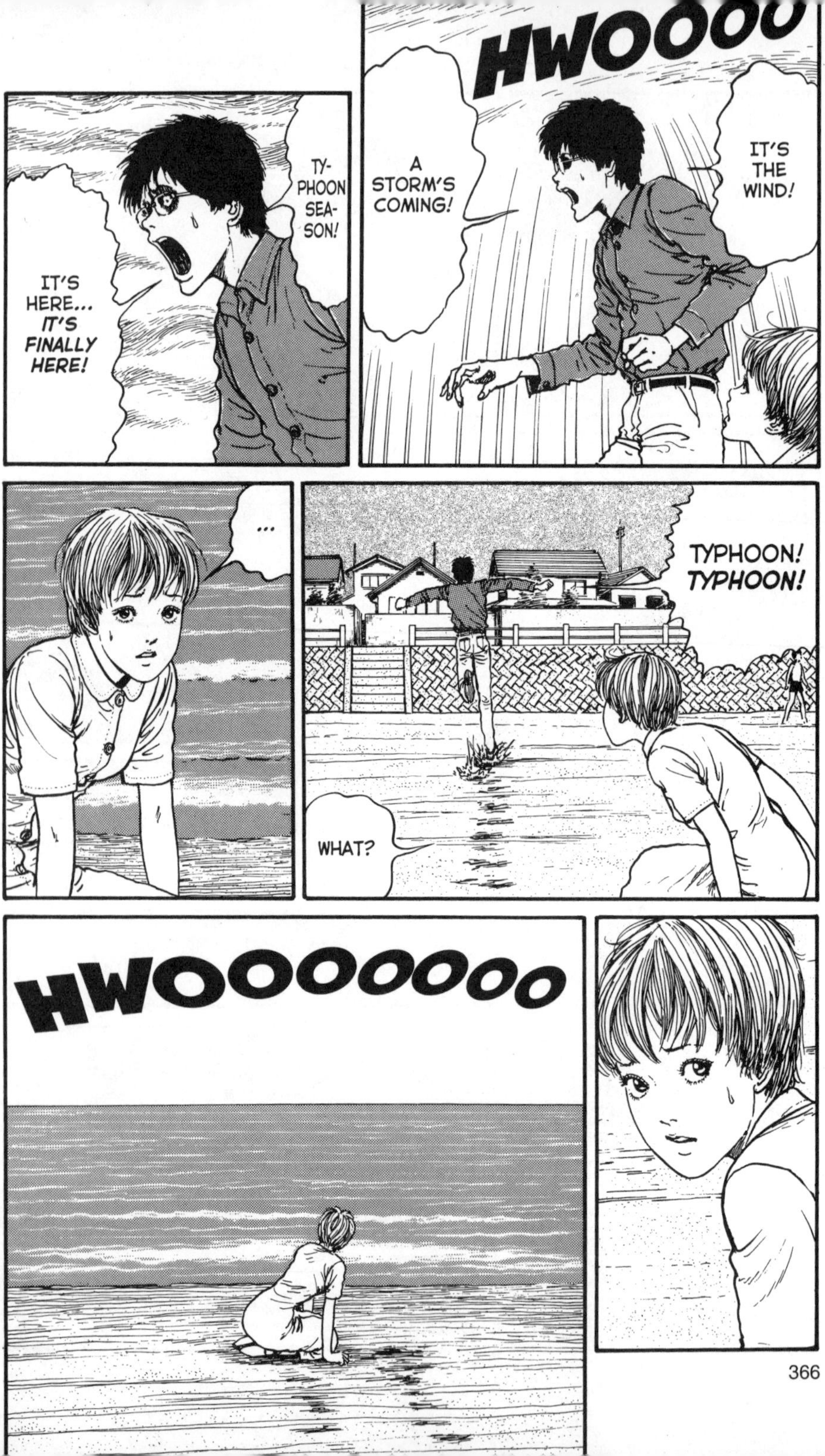
HWOOOO
IT'S THE WIND!
A STORM'S COMING!
TY-PHOON SEA-SON!
IT'S HERE... IT'S FINALLY HERE!
TYPHOON! TYPHOON!
WHAT?
...
HWOOOOOOO

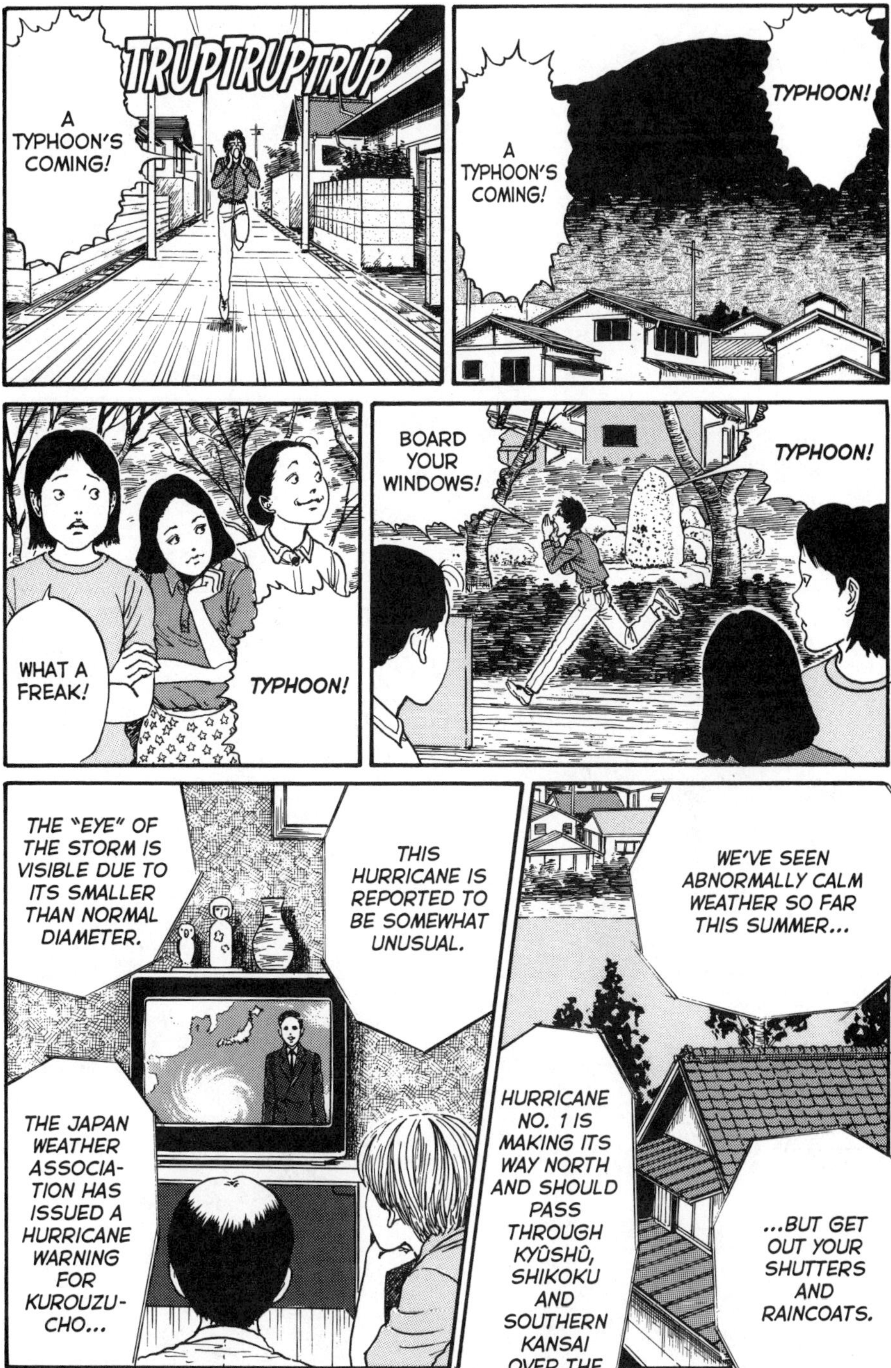
TYPHOON!
A TYPHOON'S COMING!
TRUPTRUPTRUP
A TYPHOON'S COMING!
TYPHOON!
BOARD YOUR WINDOWS!
TYPHOON!
WHAT A FREAK!
WE'VE SEEN ABNORMALLY CALM WEATHER SO FAR THIS SUMMER...
...BUT GET OUT YOUR SHUTTERS AND RAINCOATS.
HURRICANE NO. 1 IS MAKING ITS WAY NORTH AND SHOULD PASS THROUGH KYÛSHÛ, SHIKOKU AND SOUTHERN KANSAI OVER THE WEEKEND.
THIS HURRICANE IS REPORTED TO BE SOMEWHAT UNUSUAL.
THE "EYE" OF THE STORM IS VISIBLE DUE TO ITS SMALLER THAN NORMAL DIAMETER.
THE JAPAN WEATHER ASSOCIATION HAS ISSUED A HURRICANE WARNING FOR KUROUZU-CHO...

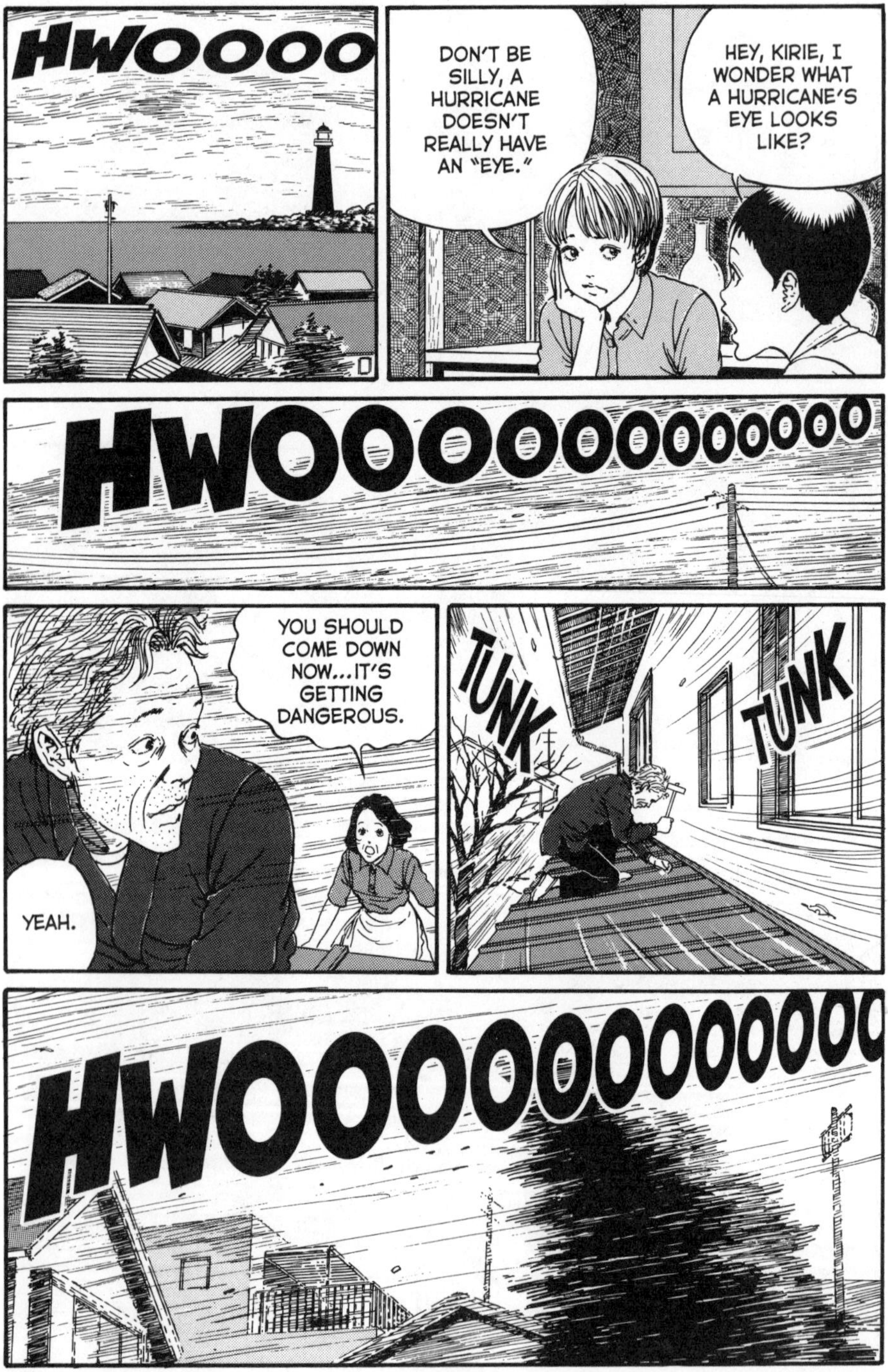
HEY, KIRIE, I WONDER WHAT A HURRICANE'S EYE LOOKS LIKE?
DON'T BE SILLY, A HURRICANE DOESN'T REALLY HAVE AN "EYE."
HWOOOO
HWOOOOOOOOOOOO
TUNK
TUNK
YOU SHOULD COME DOWN NOW...IT'S GETTING DANGEROUS.
YEAH.
HWOOOOOOOOOOOO

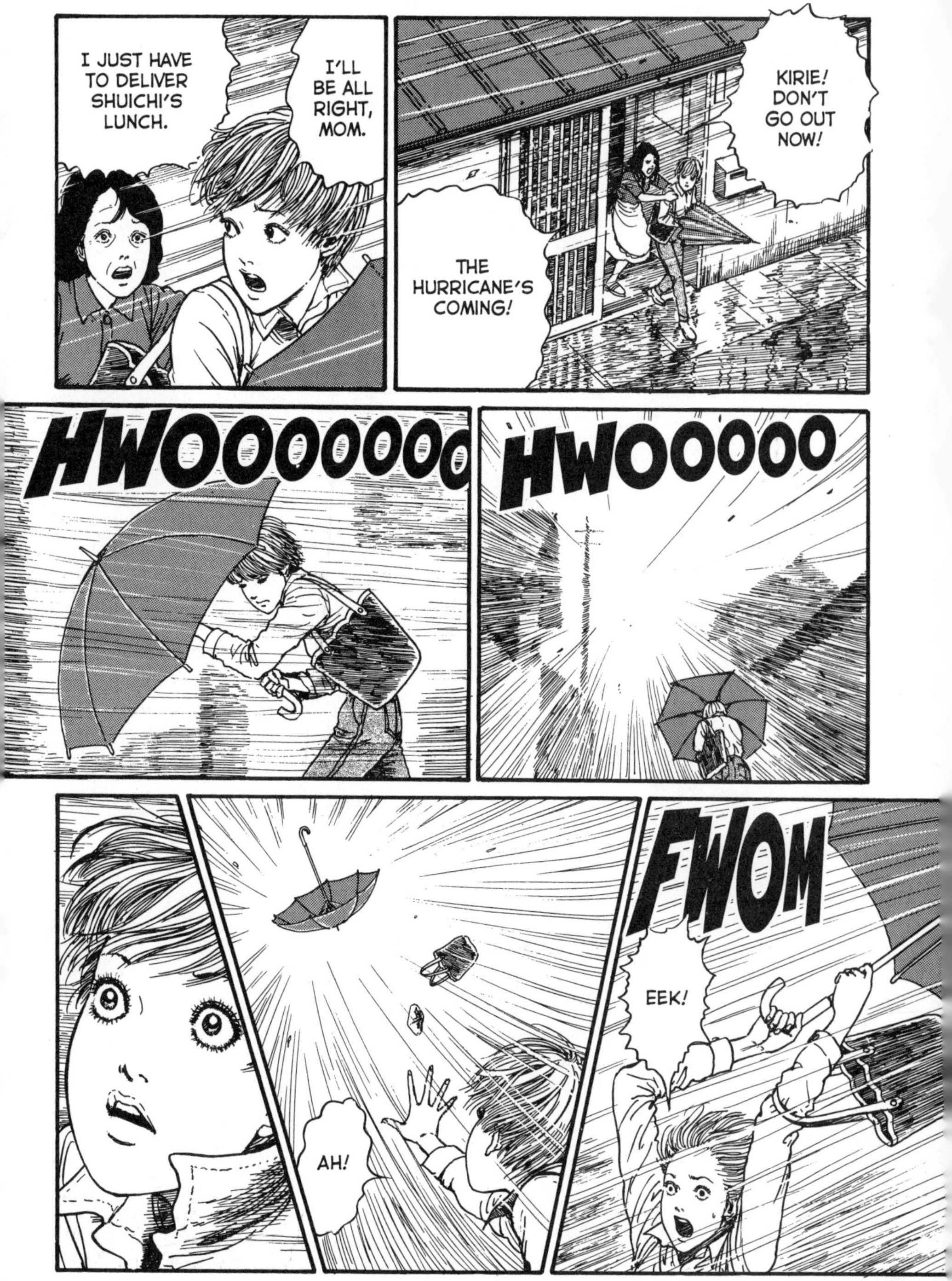
KIRIE! DON'T GO OUT NOW!
THE HURRICANE'S COMING!
I'LL BE ALL RIGHT, MOM.
I JUST HAVE TO DELIVER SHUICHI'S LUNCH.
HWOOOOO
HWOOOOOOO
FWOM
EEK!
AH!

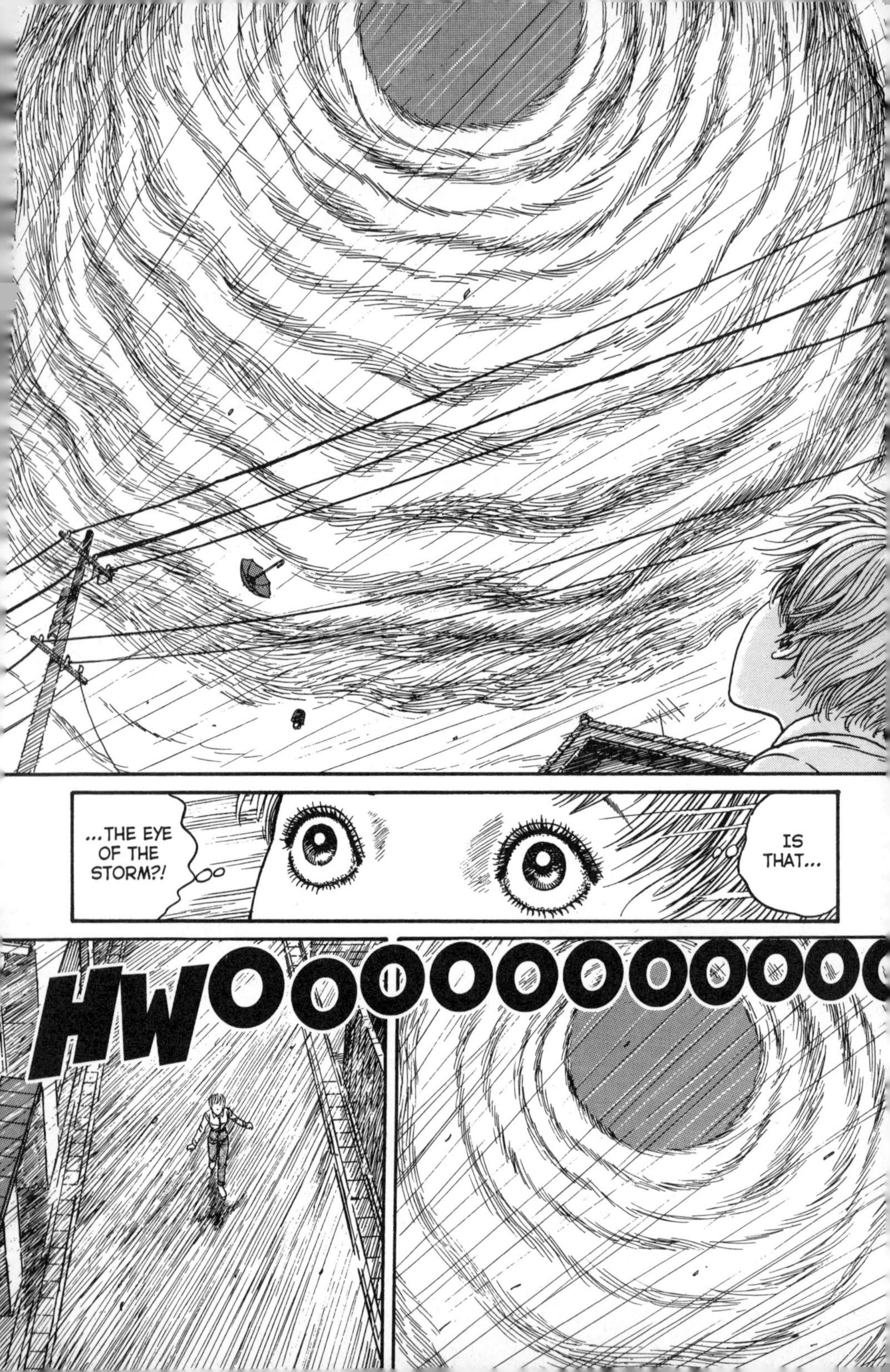
IS THAT...
...THE EYE OF THE STORM?!
HWOOOOOOOOOOO

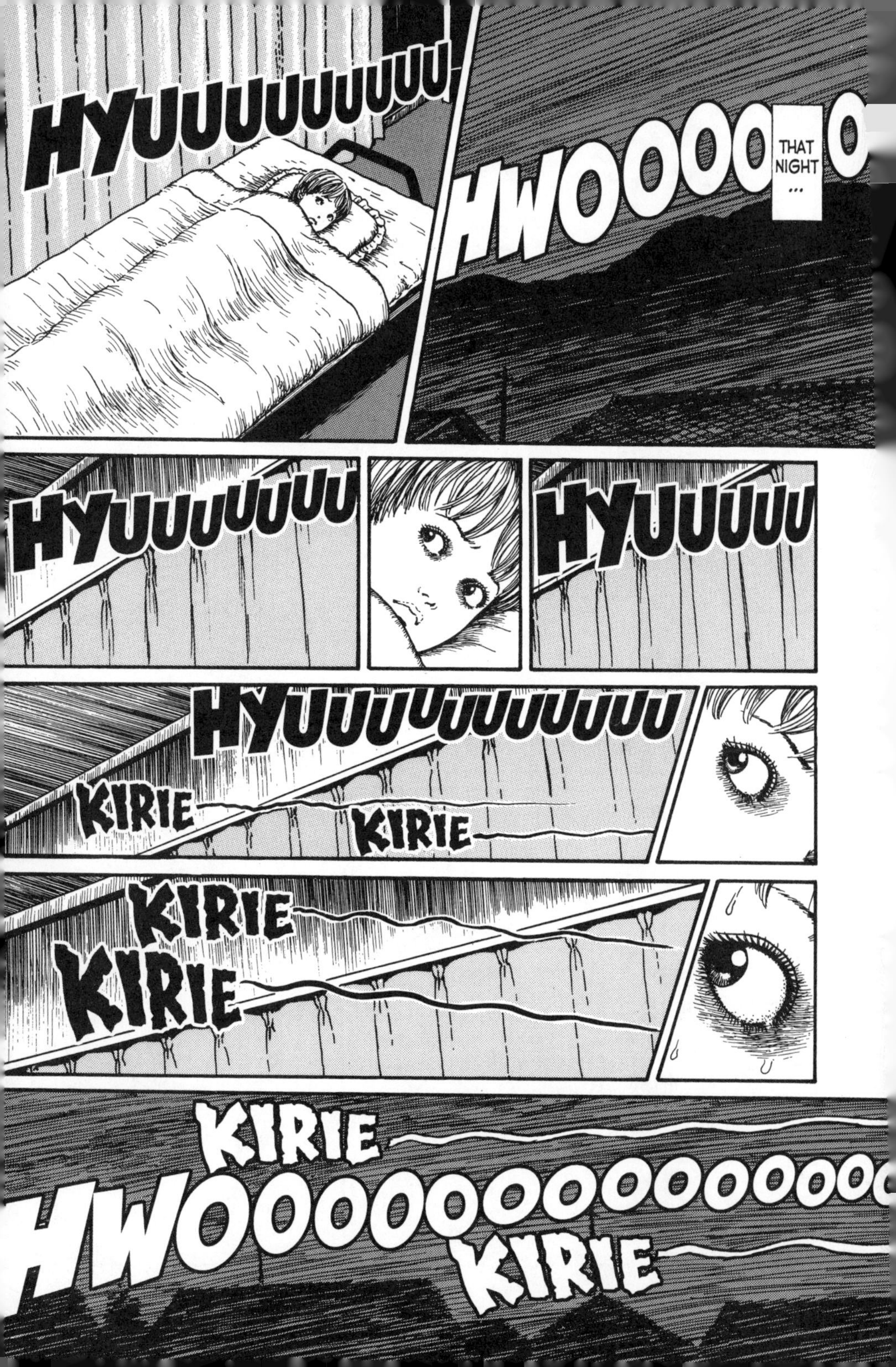
THAT NIGHT ...
HWOOOOOO
HYUUUUUUUUUU
HYUUUUUU
HYUUUUUUUU
HYUUUUUUUUUUUUU
KIRIE
KIRIE
KIRIE
KIRIE
KIRIE
HWOOOOOOOOOOOOOOOO
KIRIE

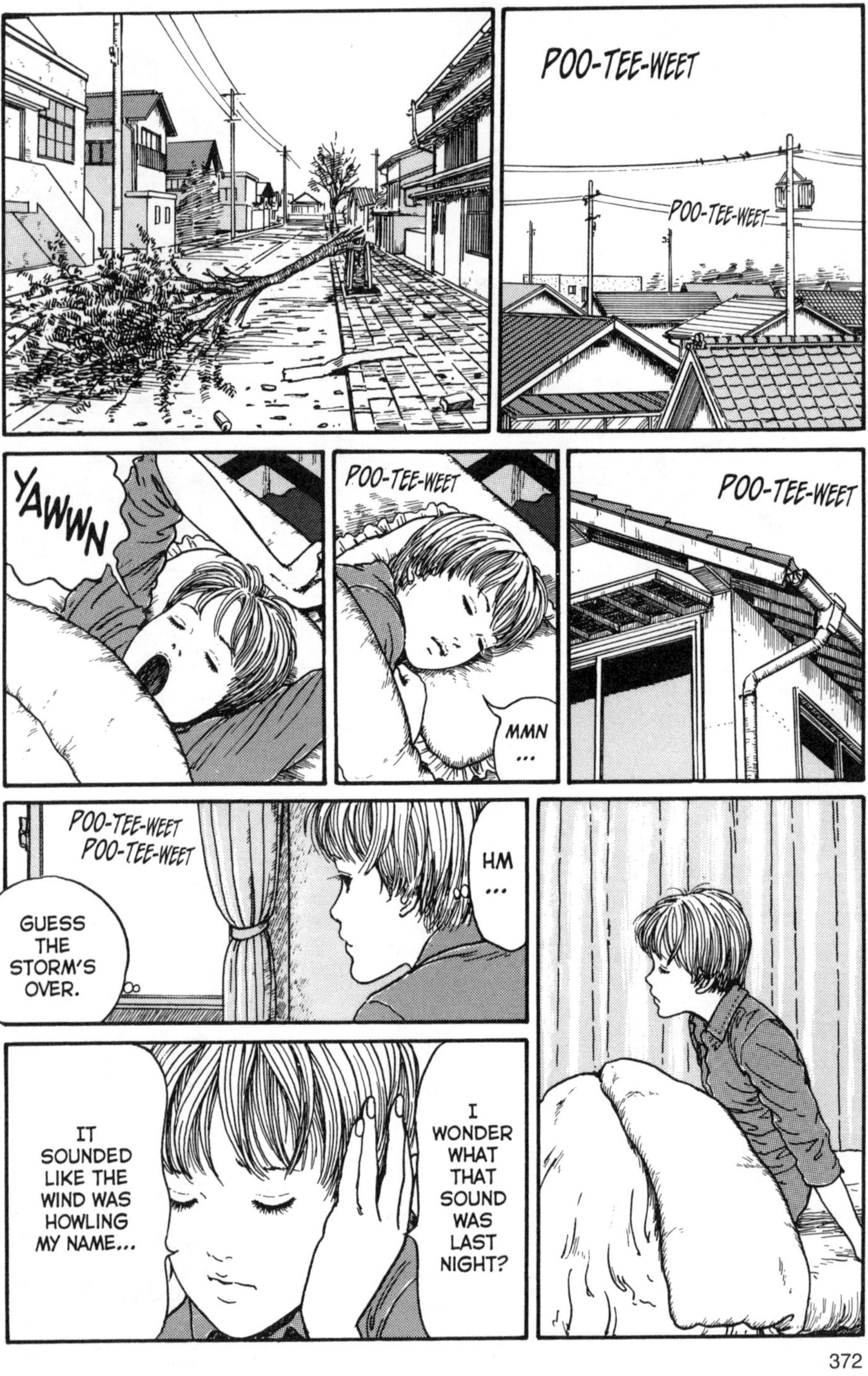
POO-TEE-WEET
POO-TEE-WEET
POO-TEE-WEET
POO-TEE-WEET
MMN ...
YAWWN
POO-TEE-WEET
POO-TEE-WEET
HM ...
GUESS THE STORM'S OVER.
I WONDER WHAT THAT SOUND WAS LAST NIGHT?
IT SOUNDED LIKE THE WIND WAS HOWLING MY NAME...

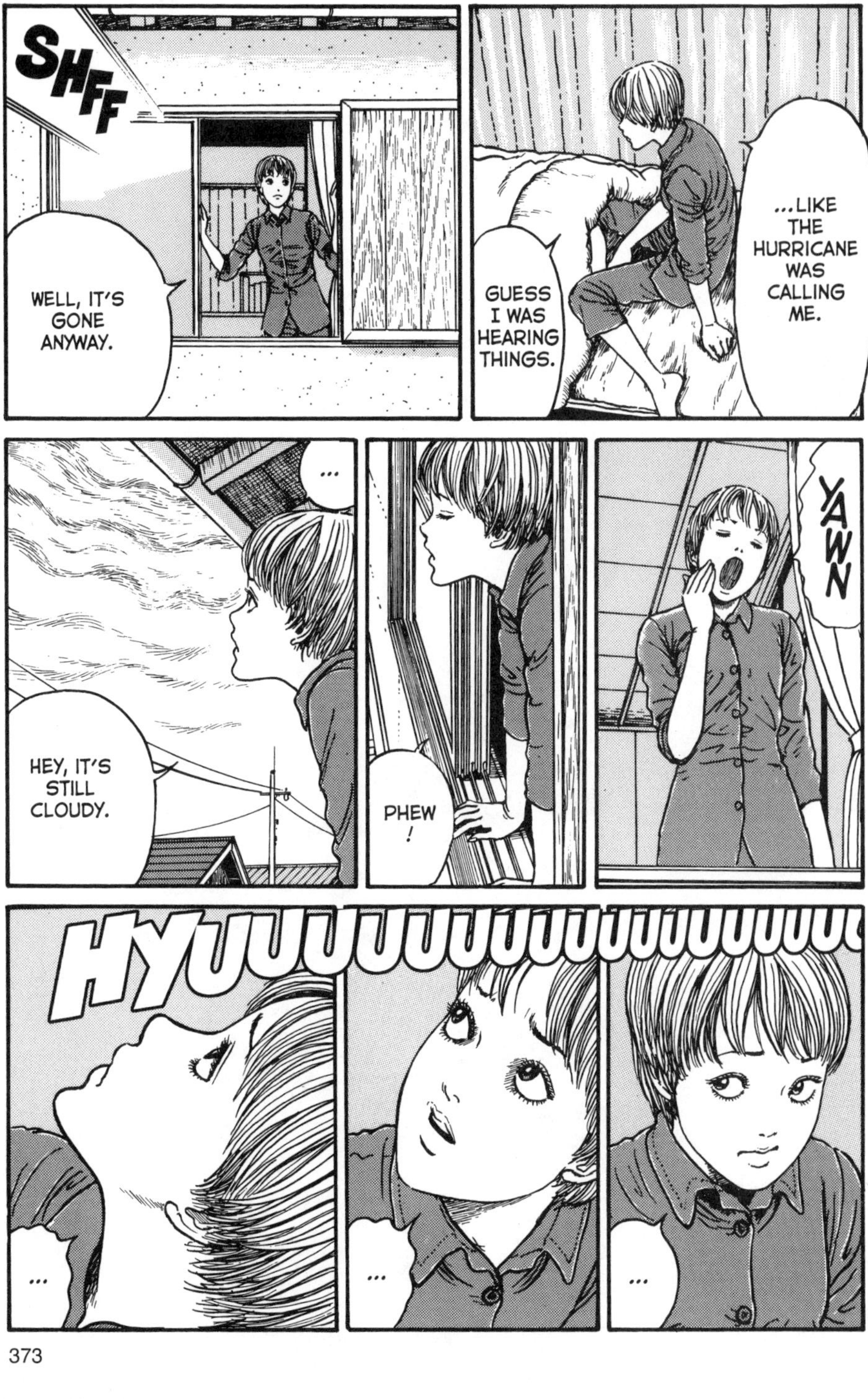

...LIKE THE HURRICANE WAS CALLING ME.
GUESS I WAS HEARING THINGS.
SHFF
WELL, IT'S GONE ANYWAY.
YAWN
PHEW!
...
HEY, IT'S STILL CLOUDY.
HYUUUUUUUUUUUUUUUUUU
...
...
...

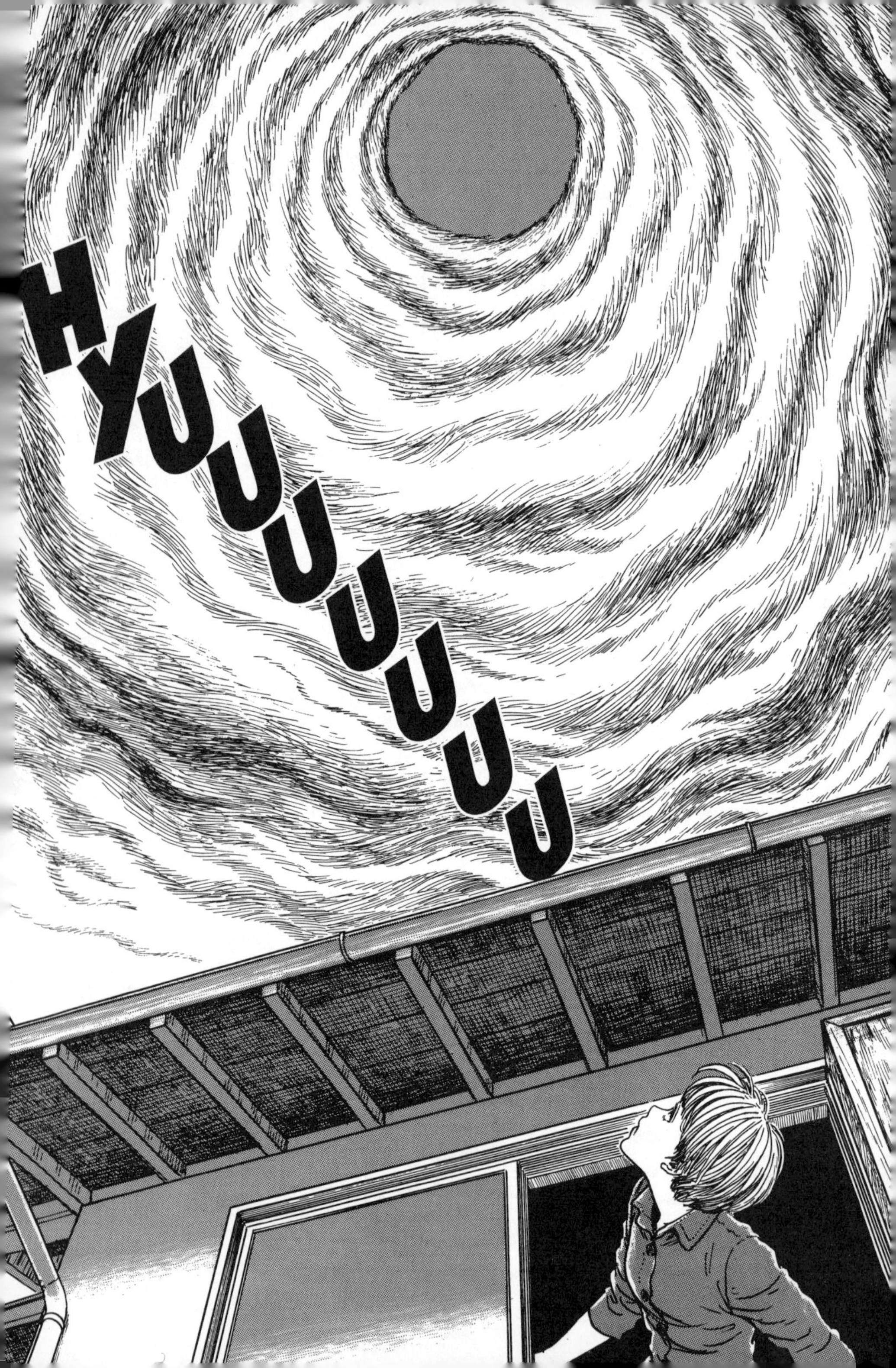
HYUUUUUUU

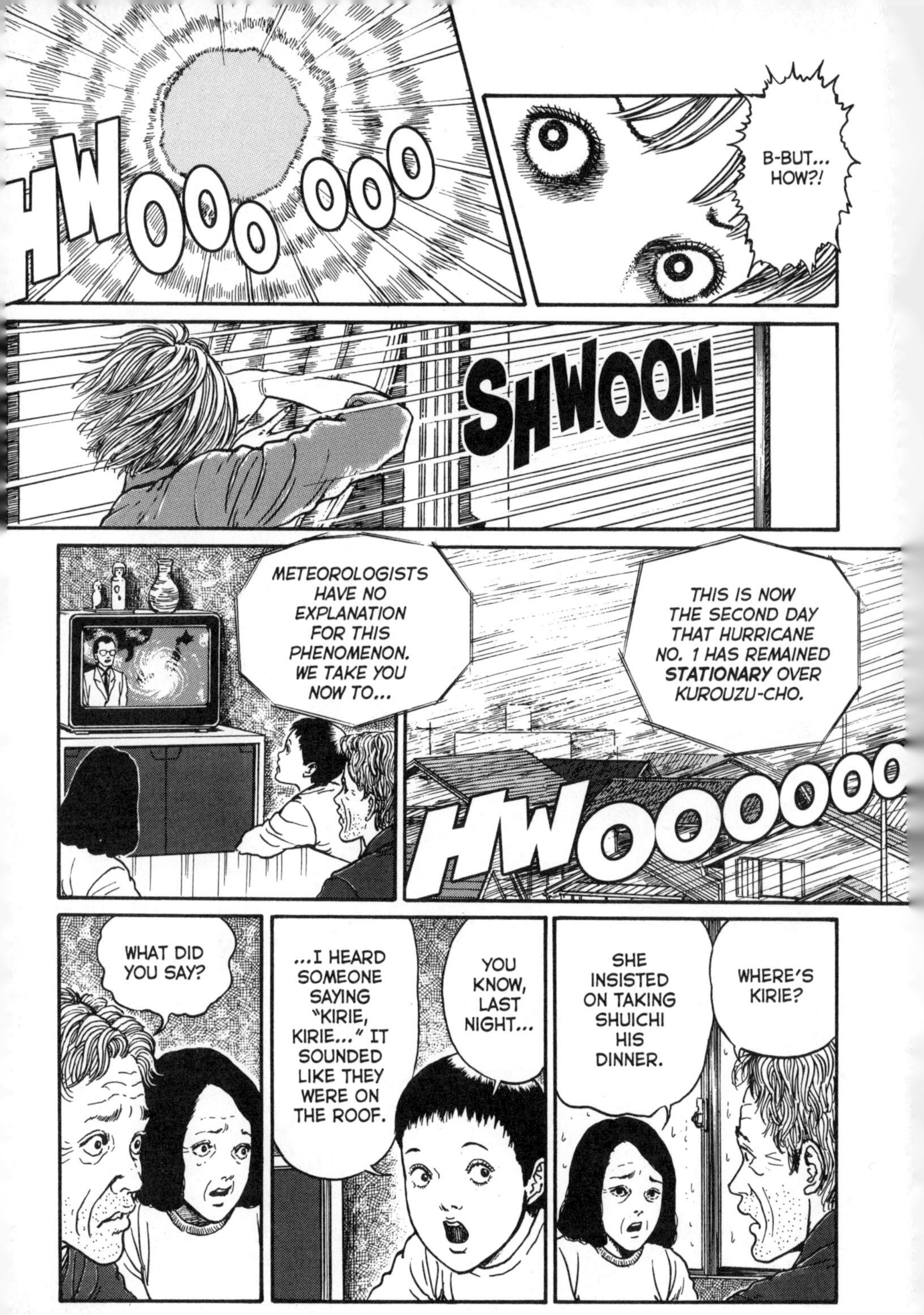
B-BUT... HOW?!
HWOOOOOO
SHWOOM
THIS IS NOW THE SECOND DAY THAT HURRICANE NO. 1 HAS REMAINED **STATIONARY** OVER KUROUZU-CHO.
HWOOOOOO
METEOROLOGISTS HAVE NO EXPLANATION FOR THIS PHENOMENON. WE TAKE YOU NOW TO...
WHERE'S KIRIE?
SHE INSISTED ON TAKING SHUICHI HIS DINNER.
YOU KNOW, LAST NIGHT...
...I HEARD SOMEONE SAYING "KIRIE, KIRIE..." IT SOUNDED LIKE THEY WERE ON THE ROOF.
WHAT DID YOU SAY?

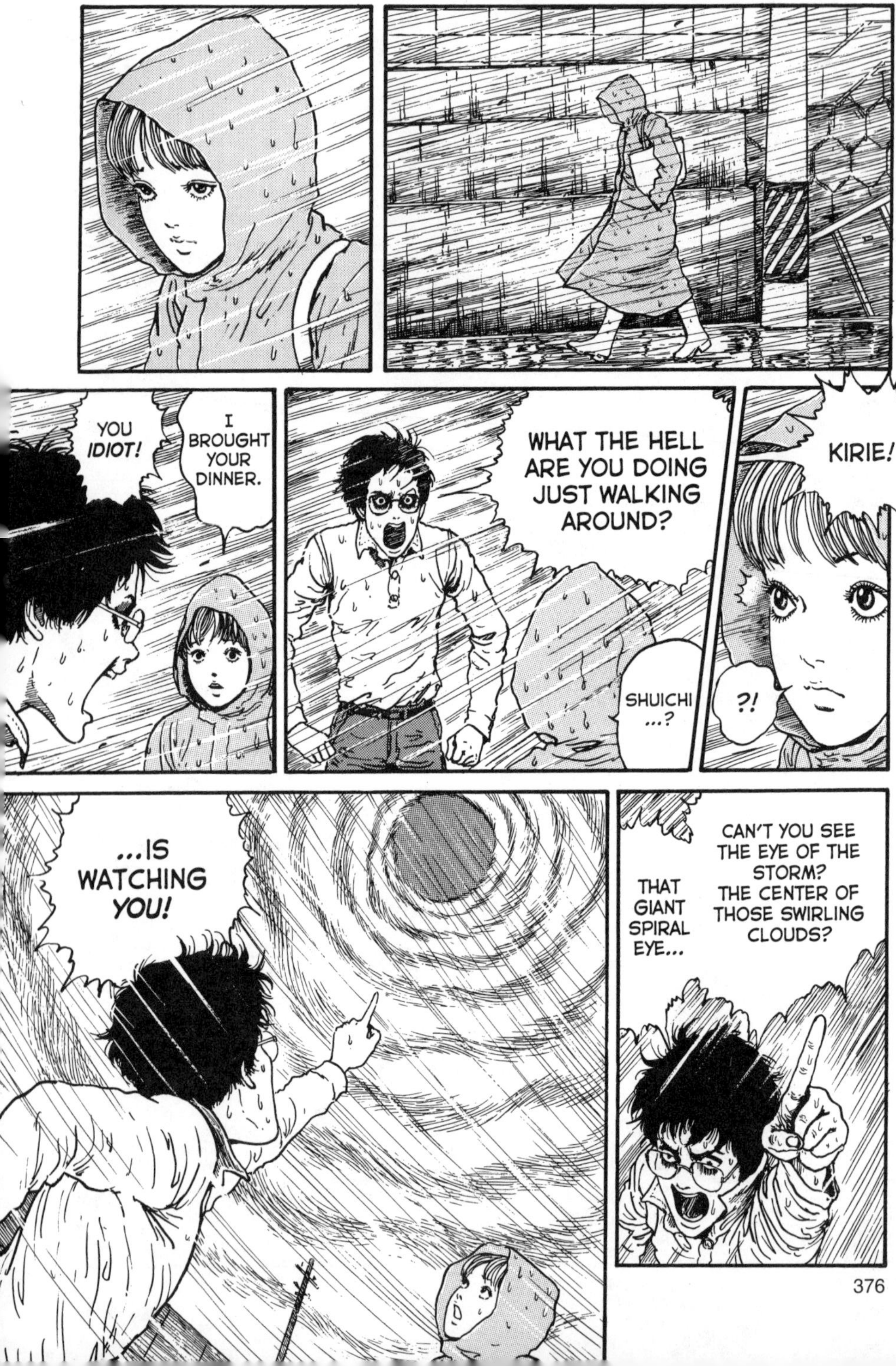
KIRIE!
?!
SHUICHI ...?
WHAT THE HELL ARE YOU DOING JUST WALKING AROUND?
I BROUGHT YOUR DINNER.
YOU *IDIOT!*
CAN'T YOU SEE THE EYE OF THE STORM? THE CENTER OF THOSE SWIRLING CLOUDS?
THAT GIANT SPIRAL EYE...
...IS WATCHING *YOU!*

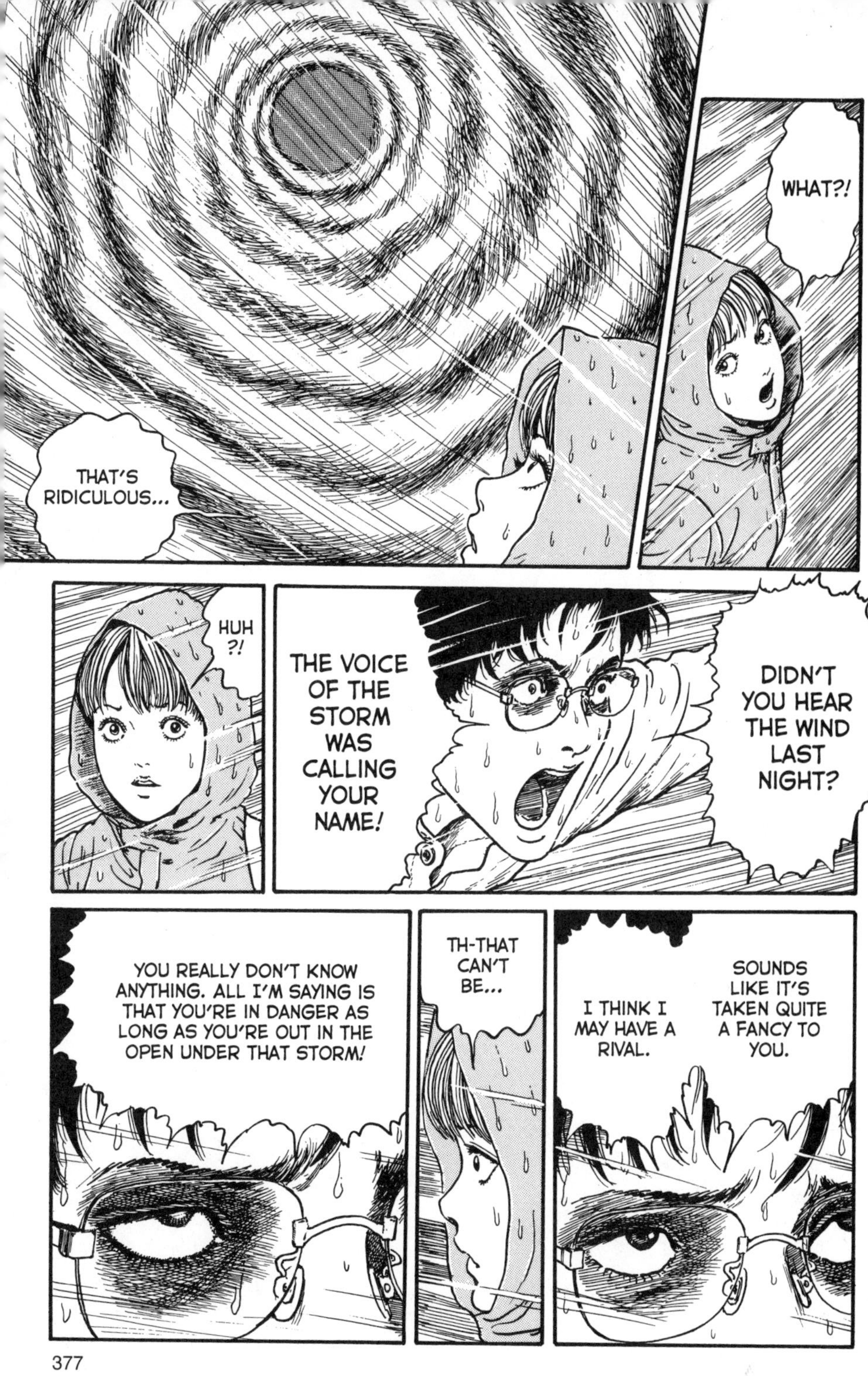
WHAT?!
THAT'S RIDICULOUS...
DIDN'T YOU HEAR THE WIND LAST NIGHT?
THE VOICE OF THE STORM WAS CALLING YOUR NAME!
HUH ?!
SOUNDS LIKE IT'S TAKEN QUITE A FANCY TO YOU.
I THINK I MAY HAVE A RIVAL.
TH-THAT CAN'T BE...
YOU REALLY DON'T KNOW ANYTHING. ALL I'M SAYING IS THAT YOU'RE IN DANGER AS LONG AS YOU'RE OUT IN THE OPEN UNDER THAT STORM!

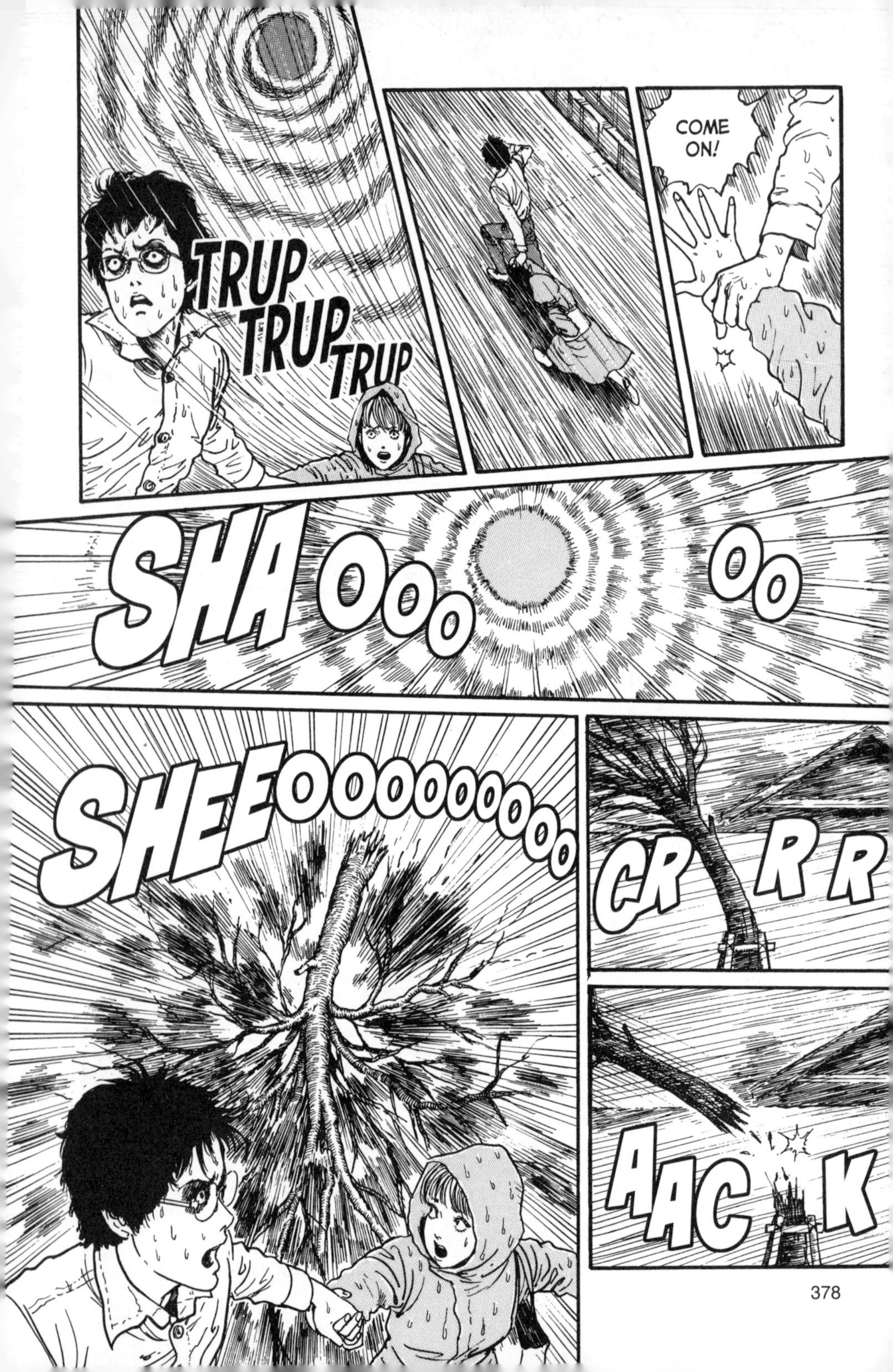
COME ON!
TRUP TRUP TRUP
SHA OOO OO
CR R R
AAC K
SHEEOOOOOOOOO

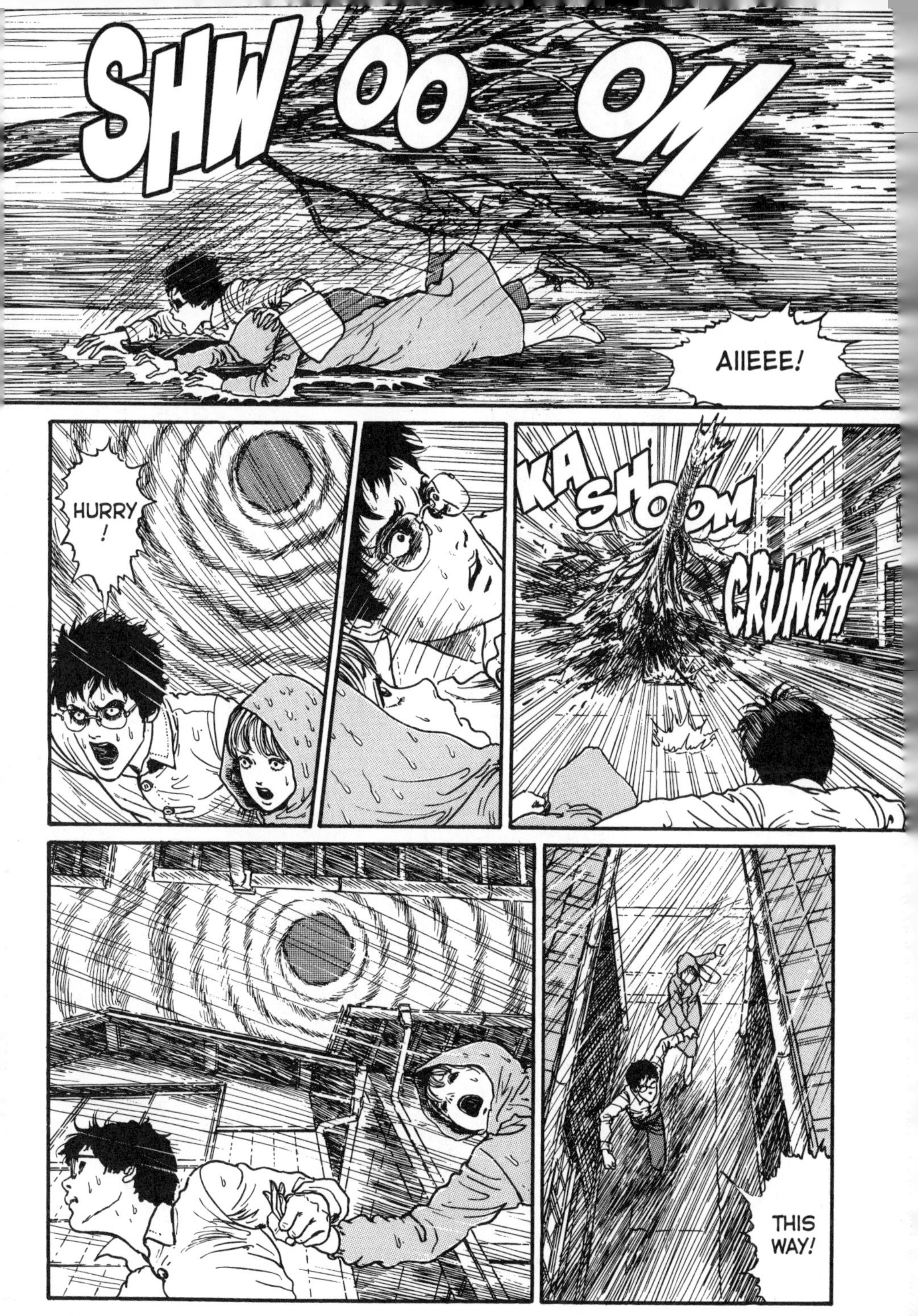
SHWOOOM
AIIEEE!
KA SHOOOM
CRUNCH
HURRY!
THIS WAY!

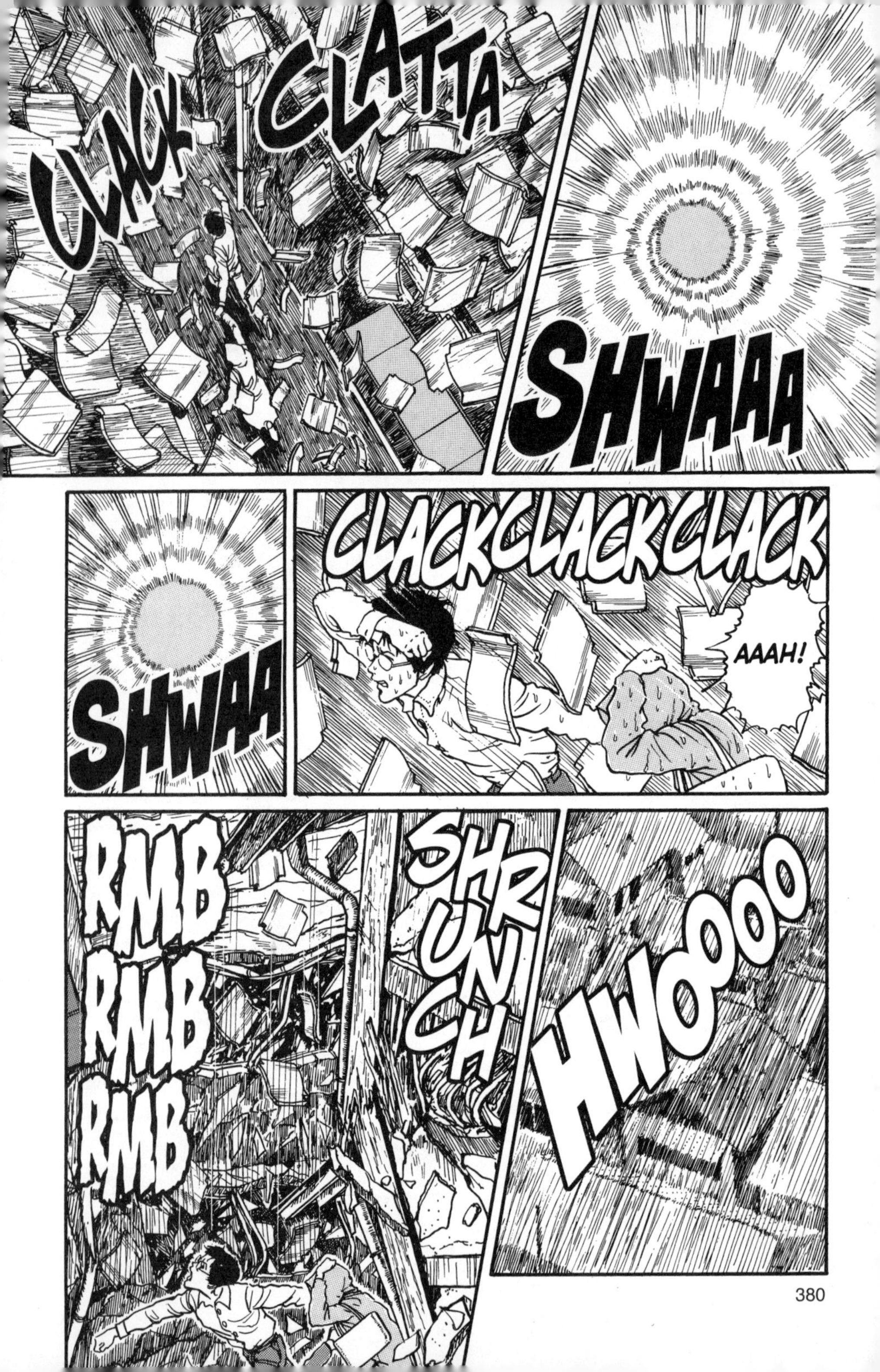
SHWAAA
CLATTA
CLACK
CLACKCLACKCLACK
AAAH!
SHWAA
HWOOOOO
SHRUNCH
RMB
RMB
RMB

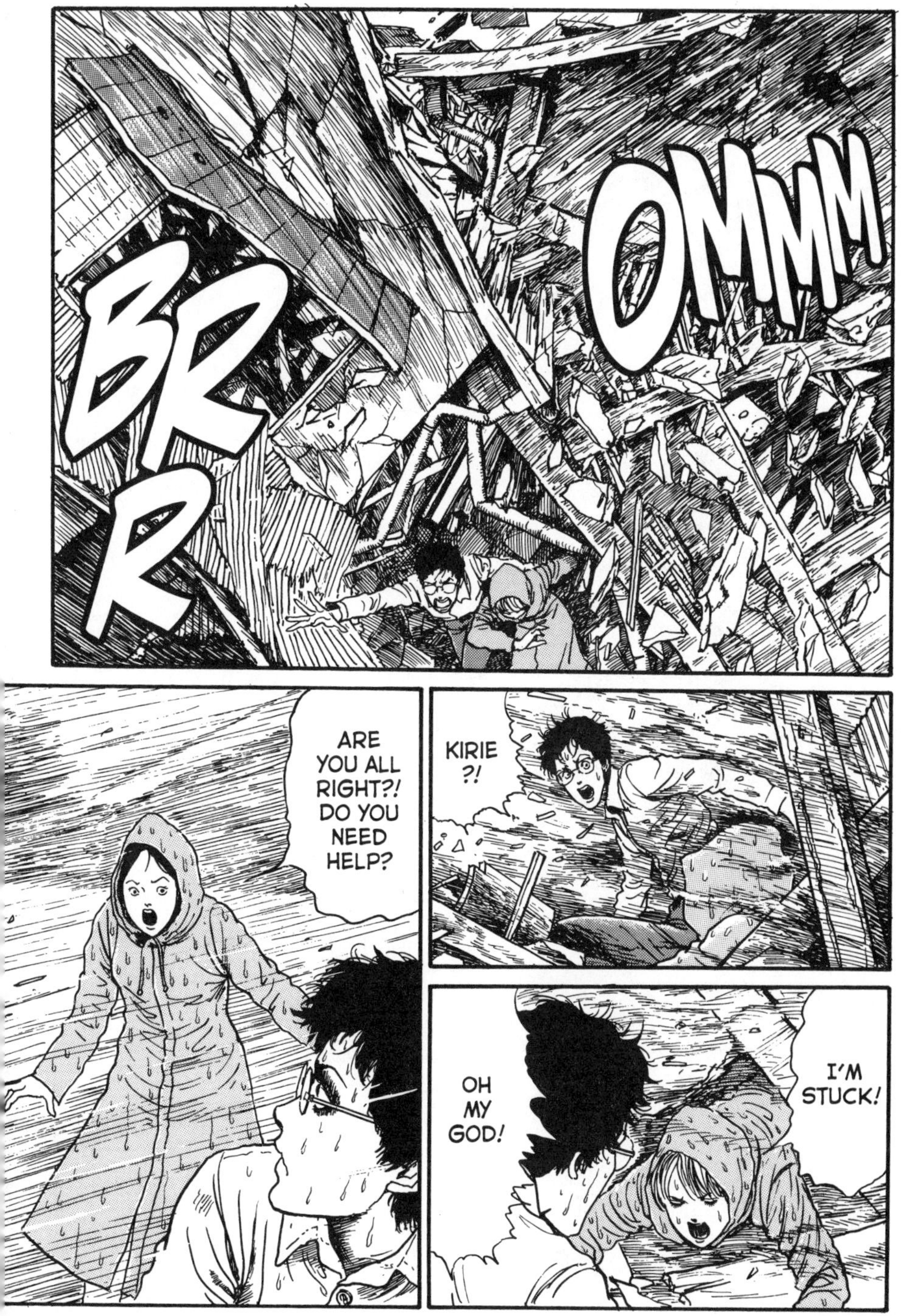
BRR
OMMMM
KIRIE ?!
I'M STUCK!
OH MY GOD!
ARE YOU ALL RIGHT?! DO YOU NEED HELP?

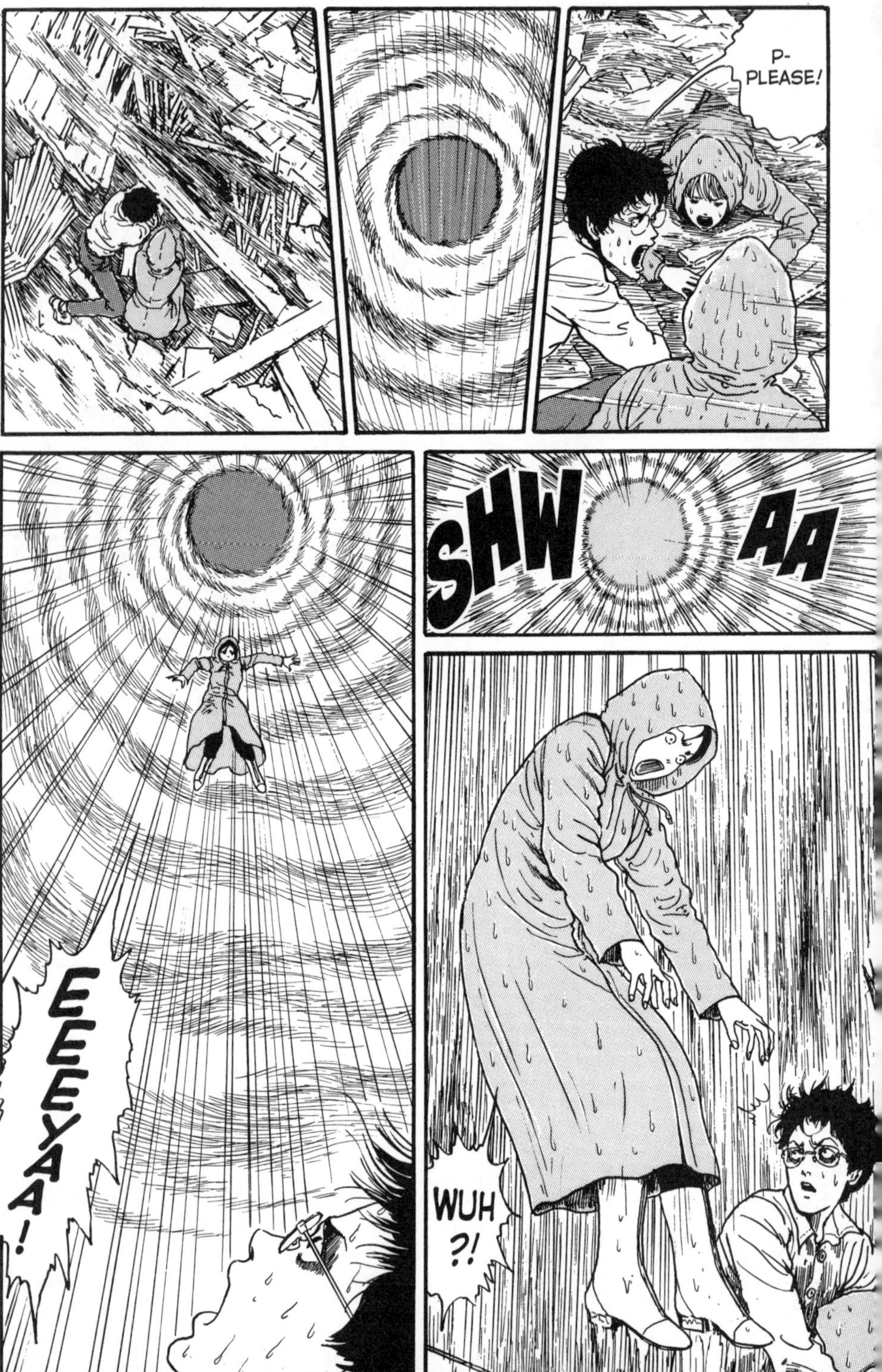
P-
PLEASE!
SHW AA
WUH
?!
EEEEYAA!

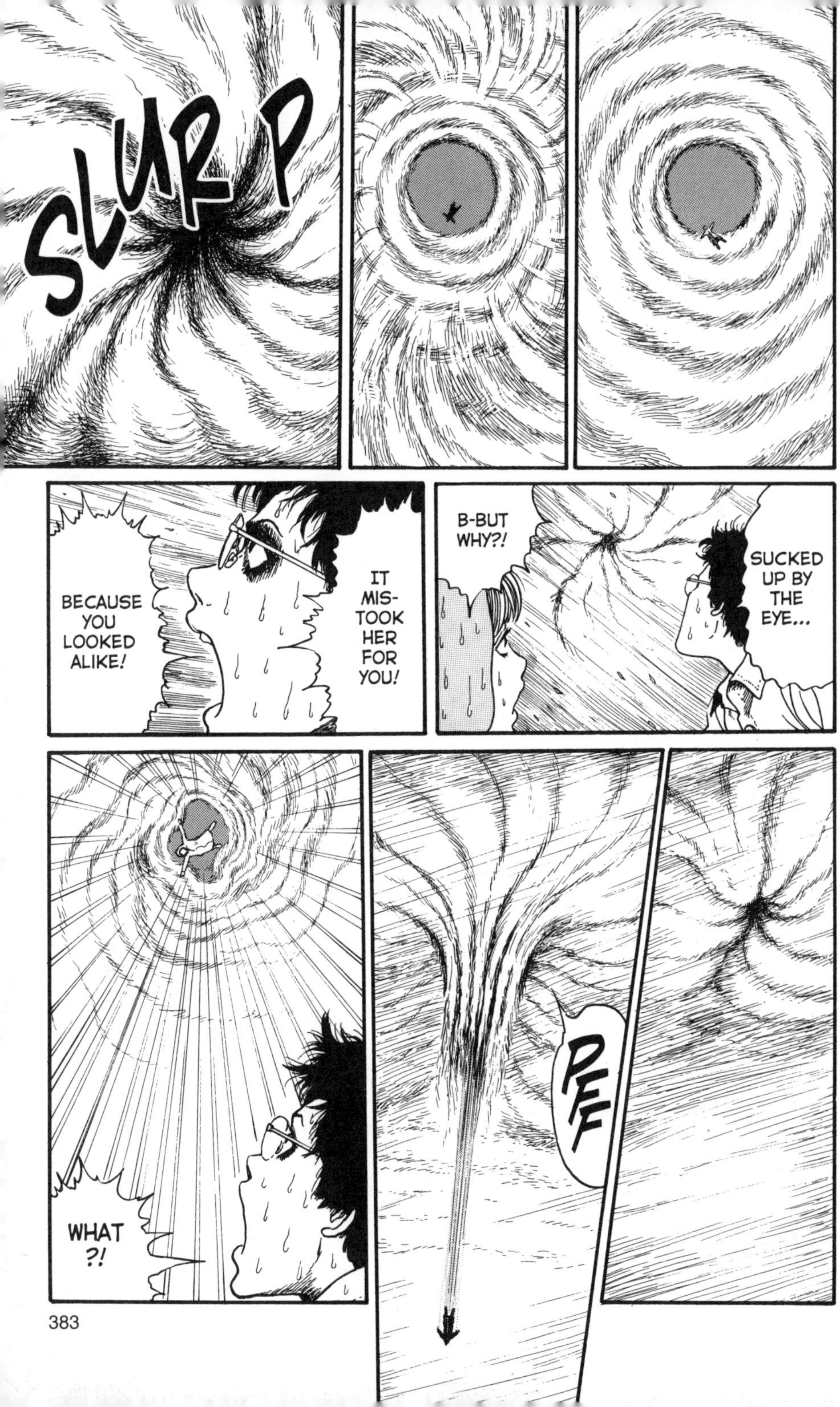
SLURP
SUCKED UP BY THE EYE...
B-BUT WHY?!
IT MIS-TOOK HER FOR YOU!
BECAUSE YOU LOOKED ALIKE!
PFF
WHAT?!

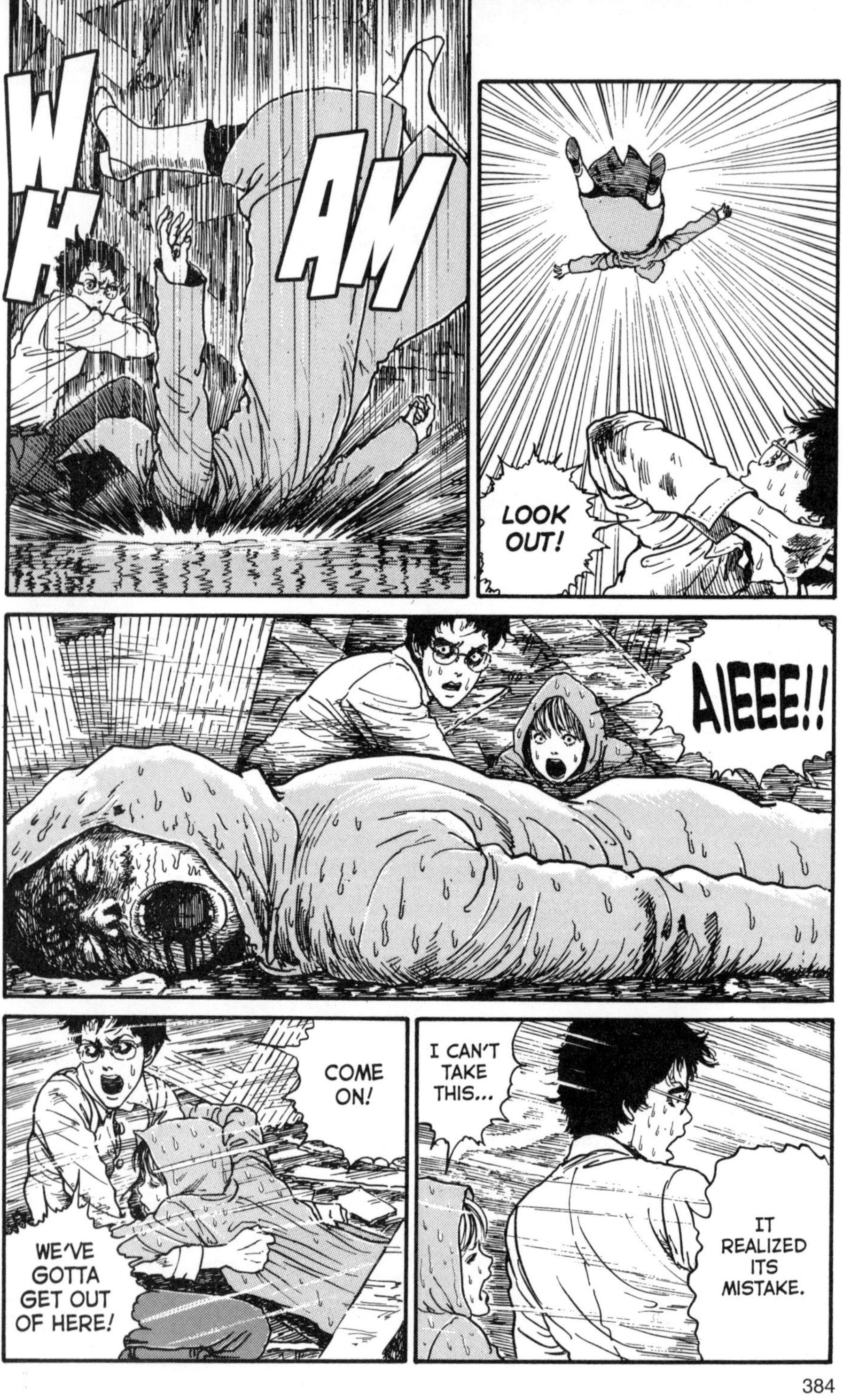
LOOK OUT!
WHAM
AIEEE!!
I CAN'T TAKE THIS...
IT REALIZED ITS MISTAKE.
COME ON!
WE'VE GOTTA GET OUT OF HERE!

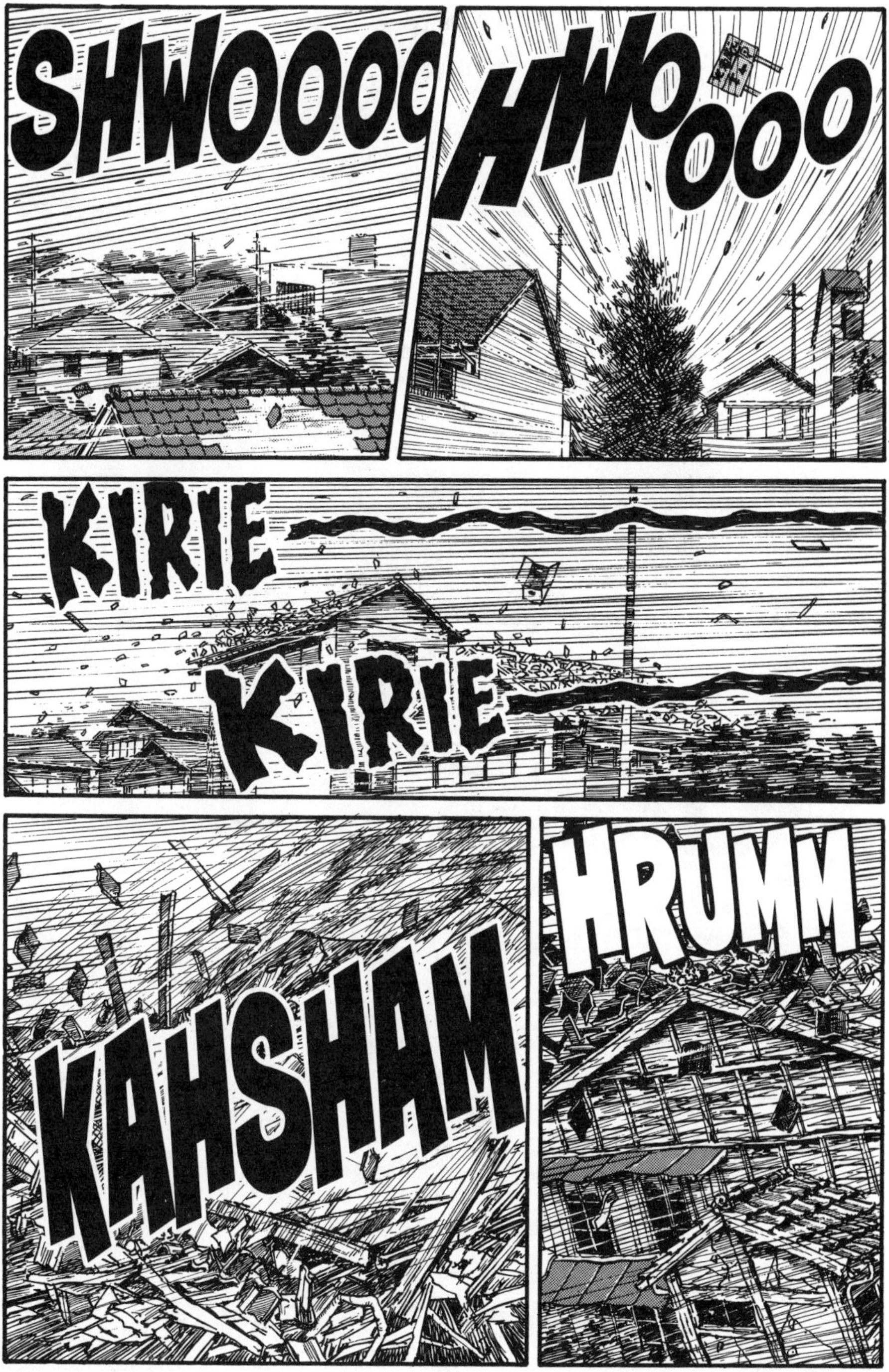
HWOOOOO
SHWOOOO
KIRIE
KIRIE
HRUMM
KAHSHAM

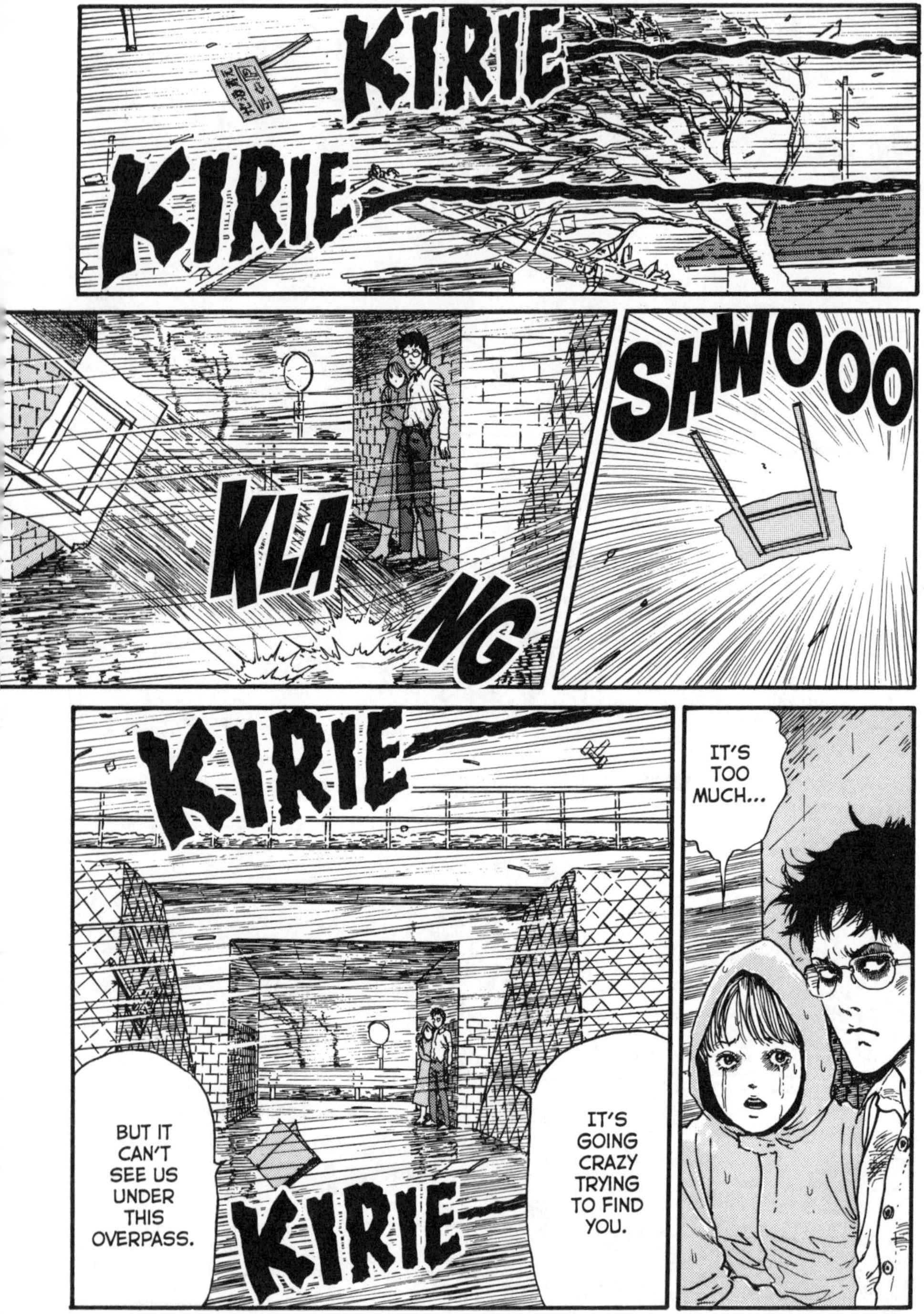

KIRIE
KIRIE
SHWOOO
KLANG
IT'S TOO MUCH...
KIRIE
IT'S GOING CRAZY TRYING TO FIND YOU.
BUT IT CAN'T SEE US UNDER THIS OVERPASS.
KIRIE

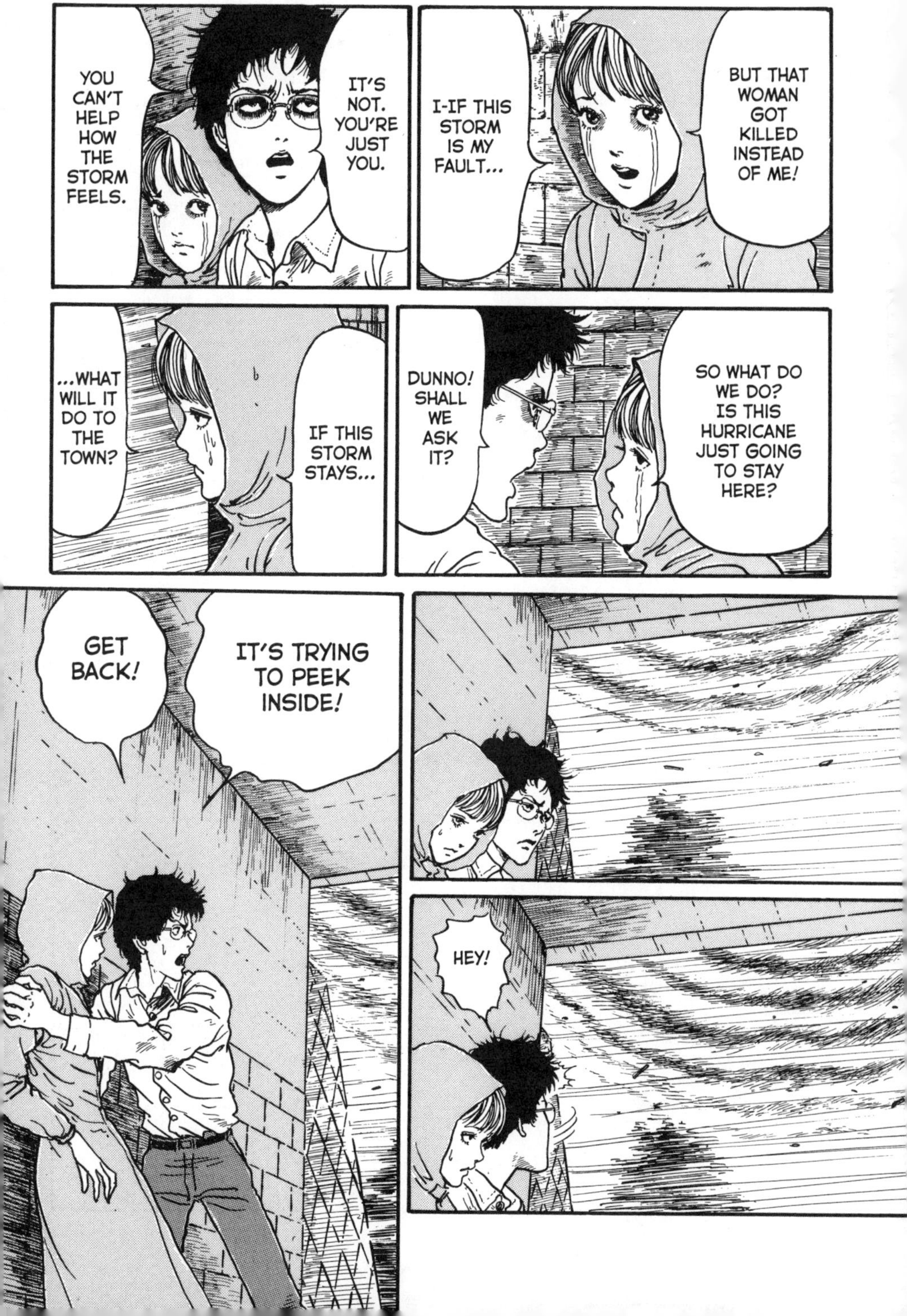
BUT THAT WOMAN GOT KILLED INSTEAD OF ME!
I-IF THIS STORM IS MY FAULT...
IT'S NOT. YOU'RE JUST YOU.
YOU CAN'T HELP HOW THE STORM FEELS.
SO WHAT DO WE DO? IS THIS HURRICANE JUST GOING TO STAY HERE?
DUNNO! SHALL WE ASK IT?
IF THIS STORM STAYS...
...WHAT WILL IT DO TO THE TOWN?
HEY!
IT'S TRYING TO PEEK INSIDE!
GET BACK!

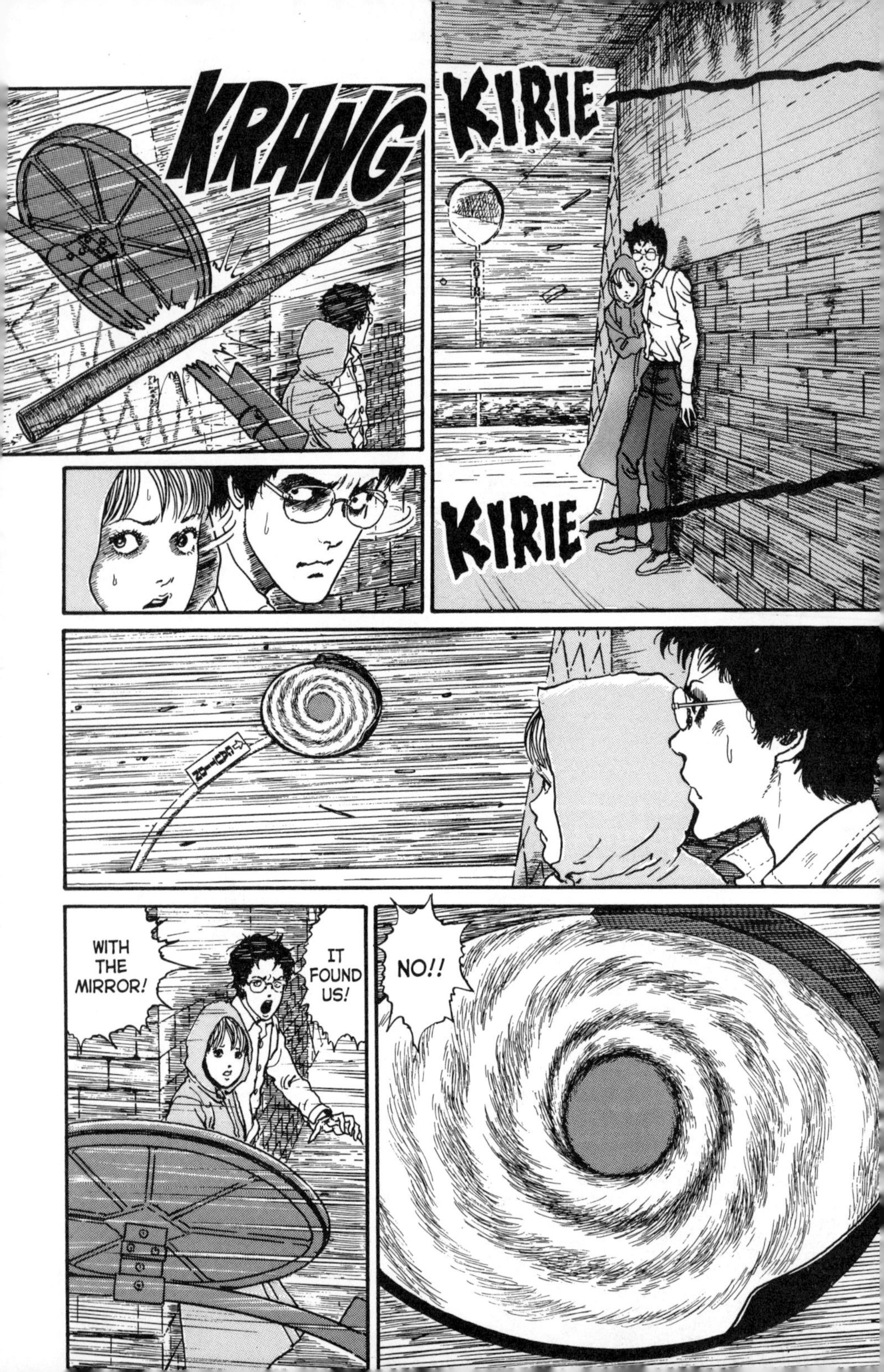
KIRIE
KIRIE
KRANG
NO!!
IT FOUND US!
WITH THE MIRROR!

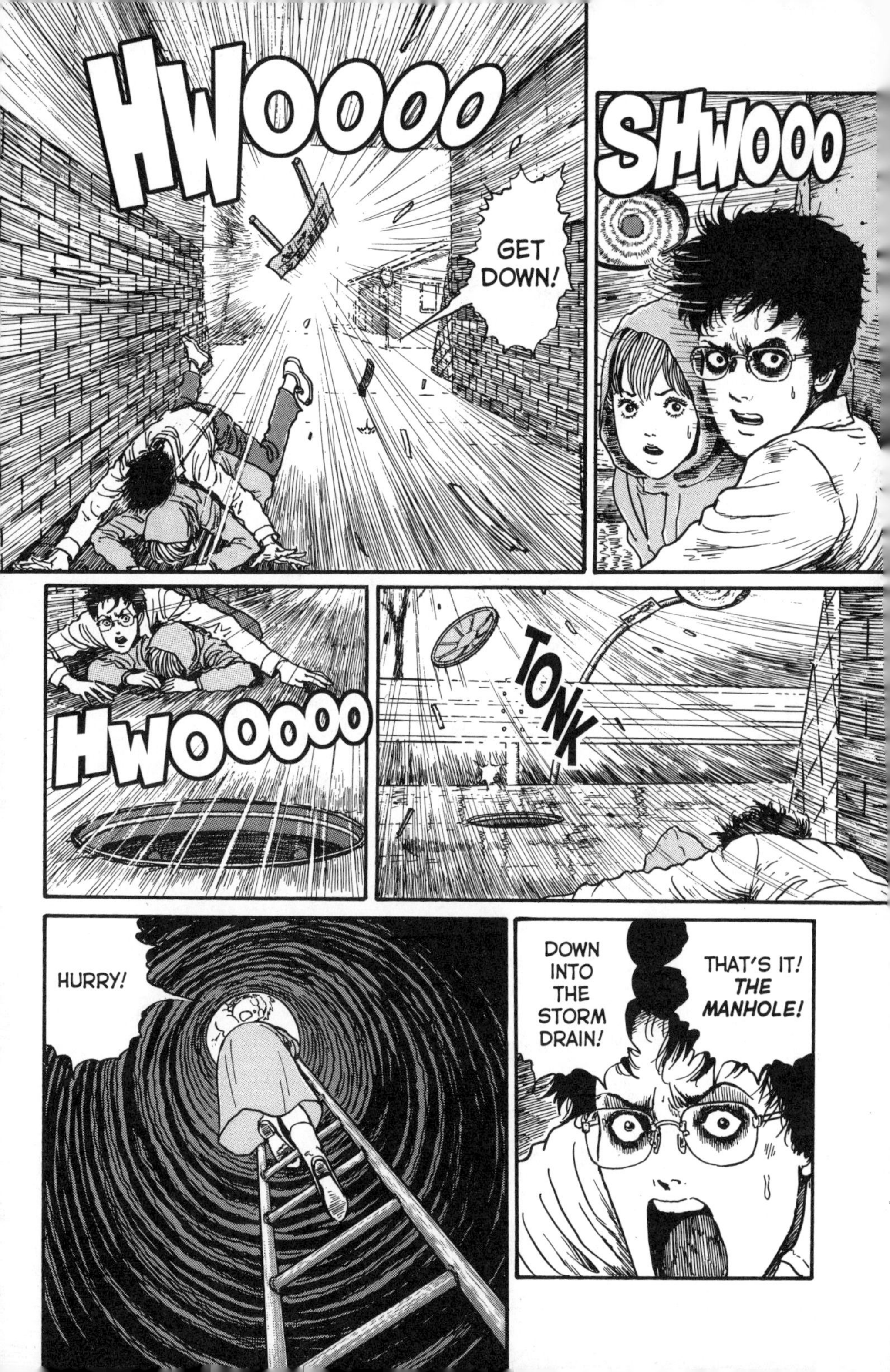
SHWOOO
HWOOOO
GET DOWN!
TONK
HWOOOOO
THAT'S IT! *THE MANHOLE!*
DOWN INTO THE STORM DRAIN!
HURRY!

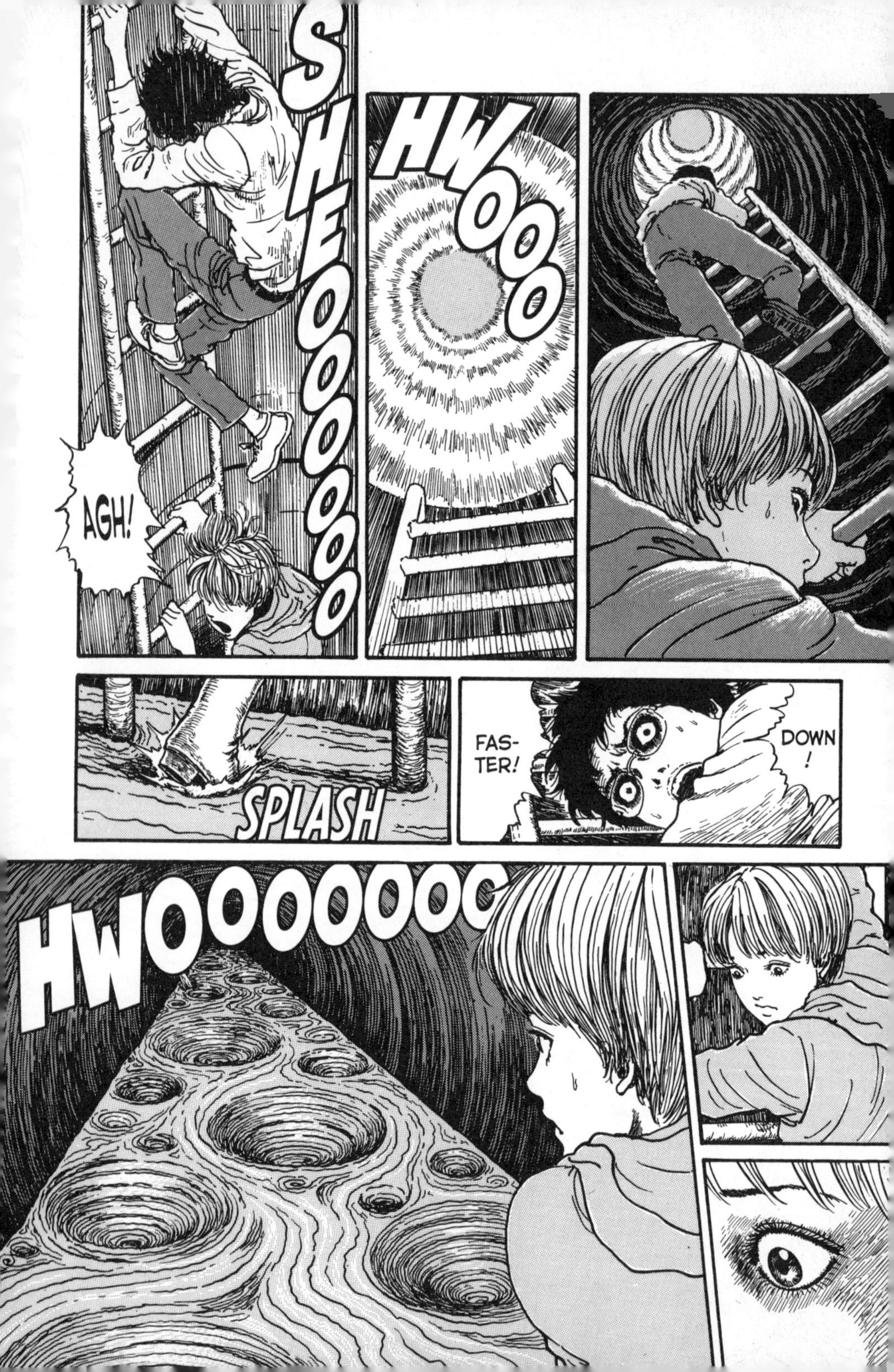
HWOOO
SHEOOOOOOOOO
AGH!
DOWN!
FASTER!
SPLASH
HWOOOOOOO

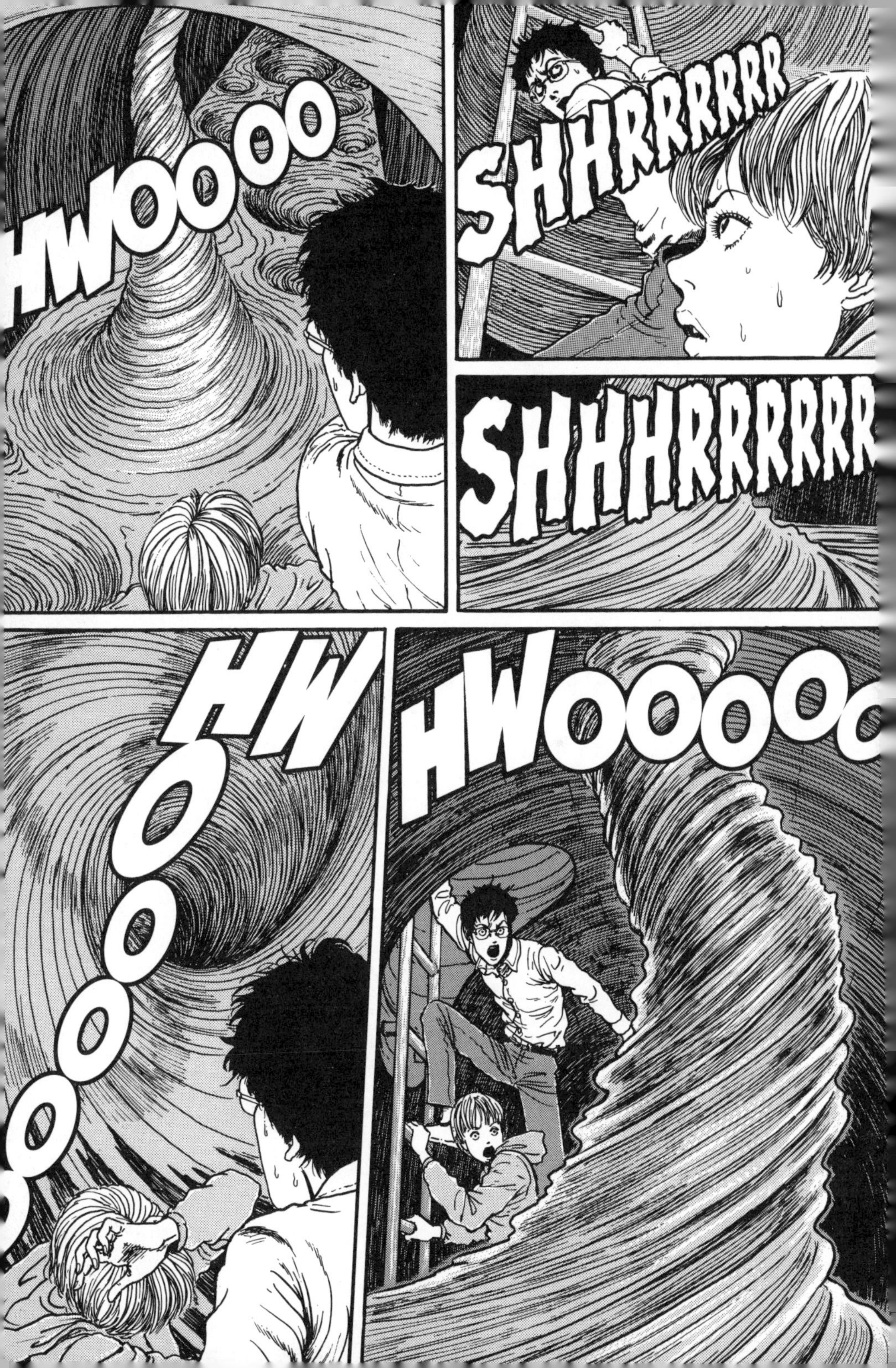
SHHRRRRRR
SHHHRRRRRR
HWOOOOO
HWOOOOOO
HWOOOOOO

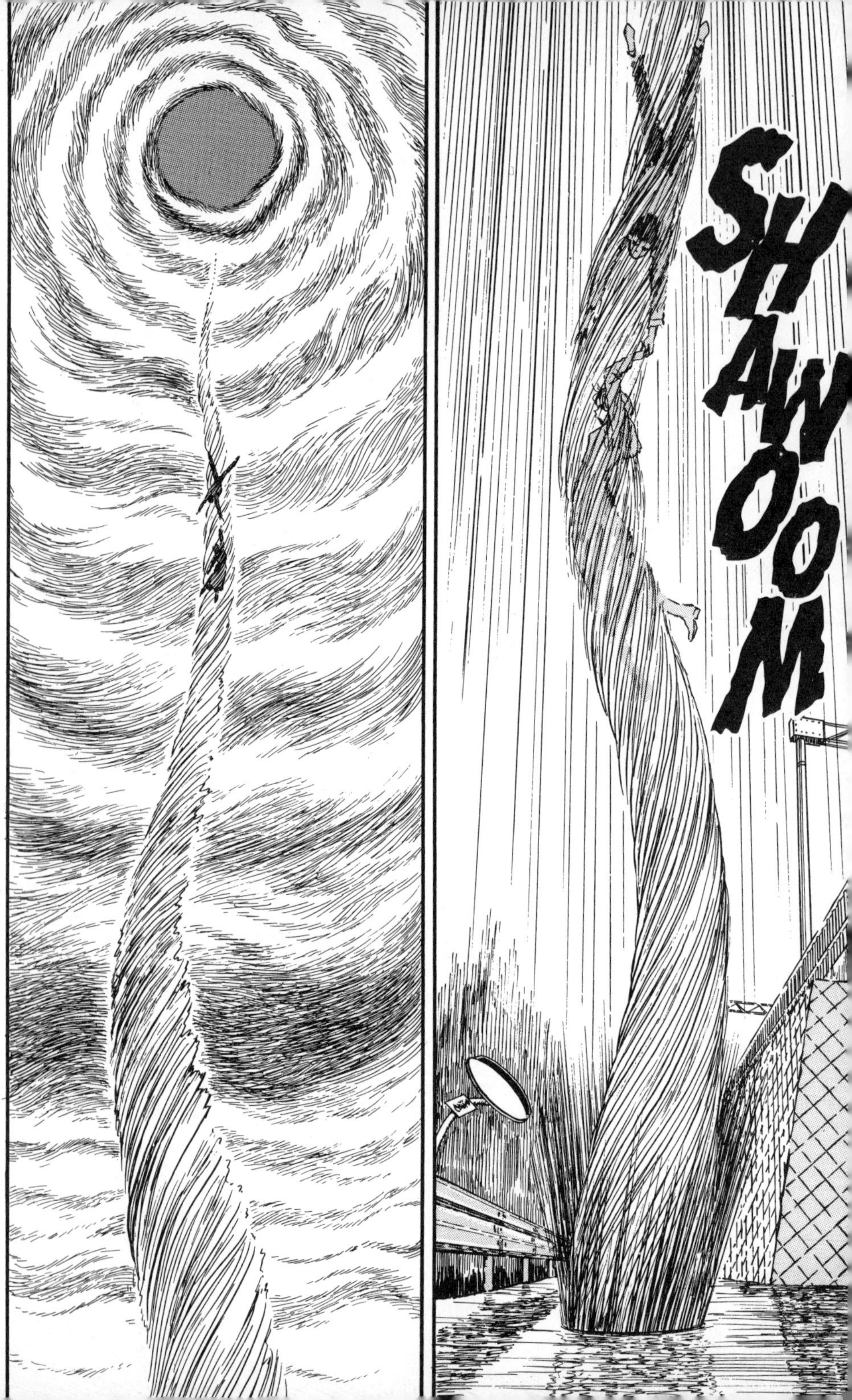
SHAWOOM

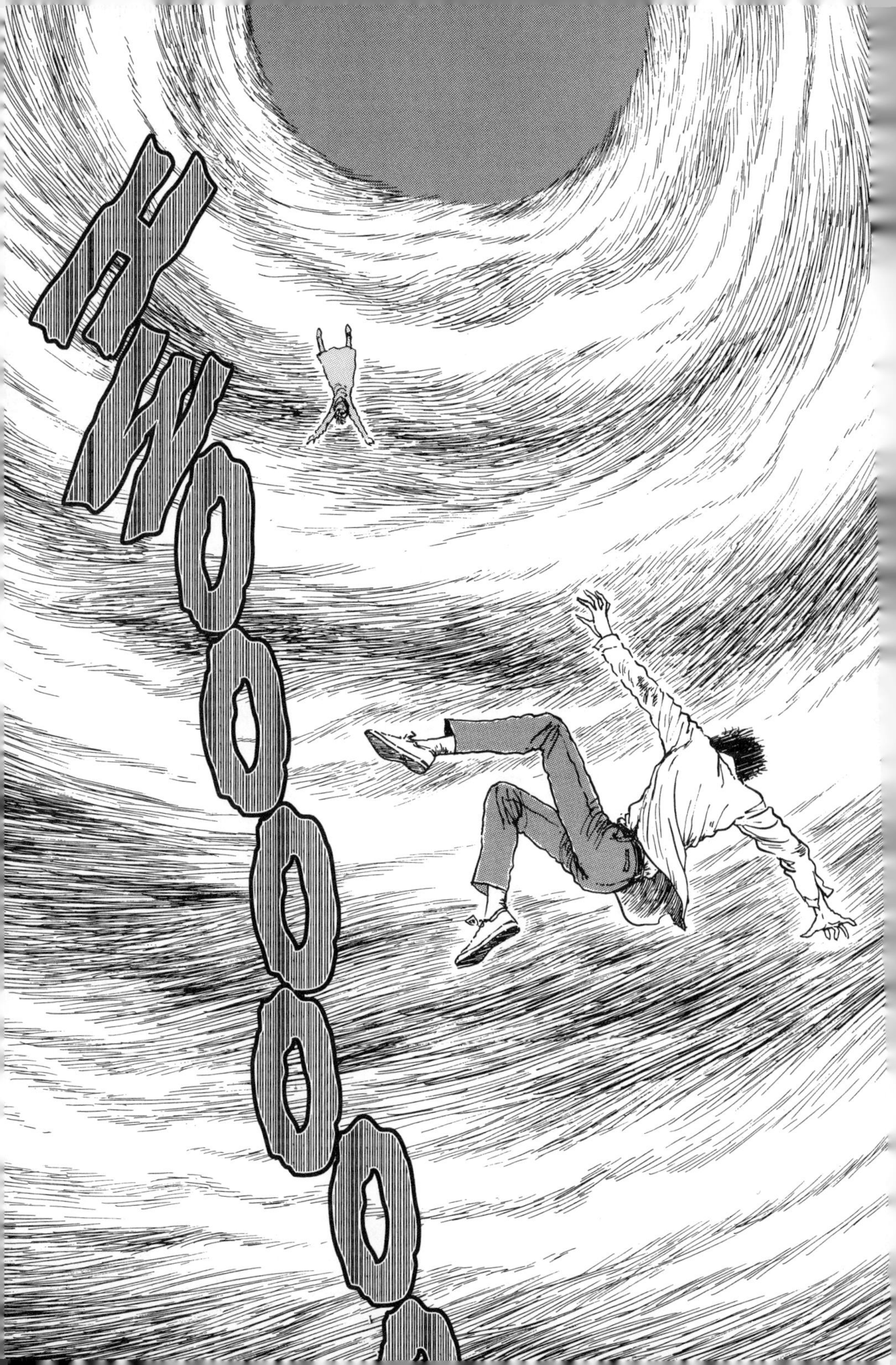
SWOOOOOO

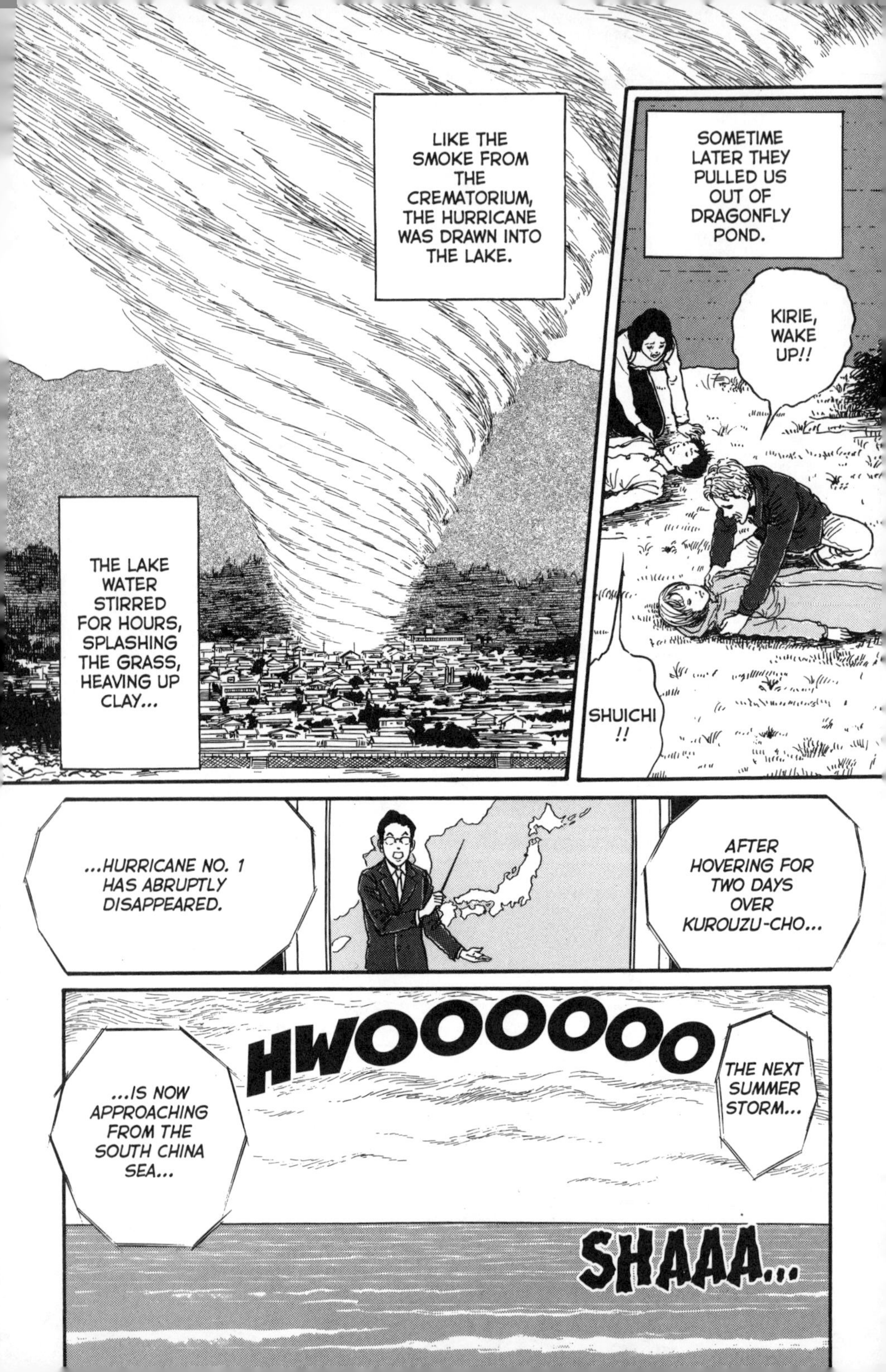
LIKE THE SMOKE FROM THE CREMATORIUM, THE HURRICANE WAS DRAWN INTO THE LAKE.
THE LAKE WATER STIRRED FOR HOURS, SPLASHING THE GRASS, HEAVING UP CLAY...
SOMETIME LATER THEY PULLED US OUT OF DRAGONFLY POND.
KIRIE, WAKE UP!!
SHUICHI!!
AFTER HOVERING FOR TWO DAYS OVER KUROUZU-CHO...
...HURRICANE NO. 1 HAS ABRUPTLY DISAPPEARED.
THE NEXT SUMMER STORM...
HWOOOOOOO
...IS NOW APPROACHING FROM THE SOUTH CHINA SEA...
SHAAA...

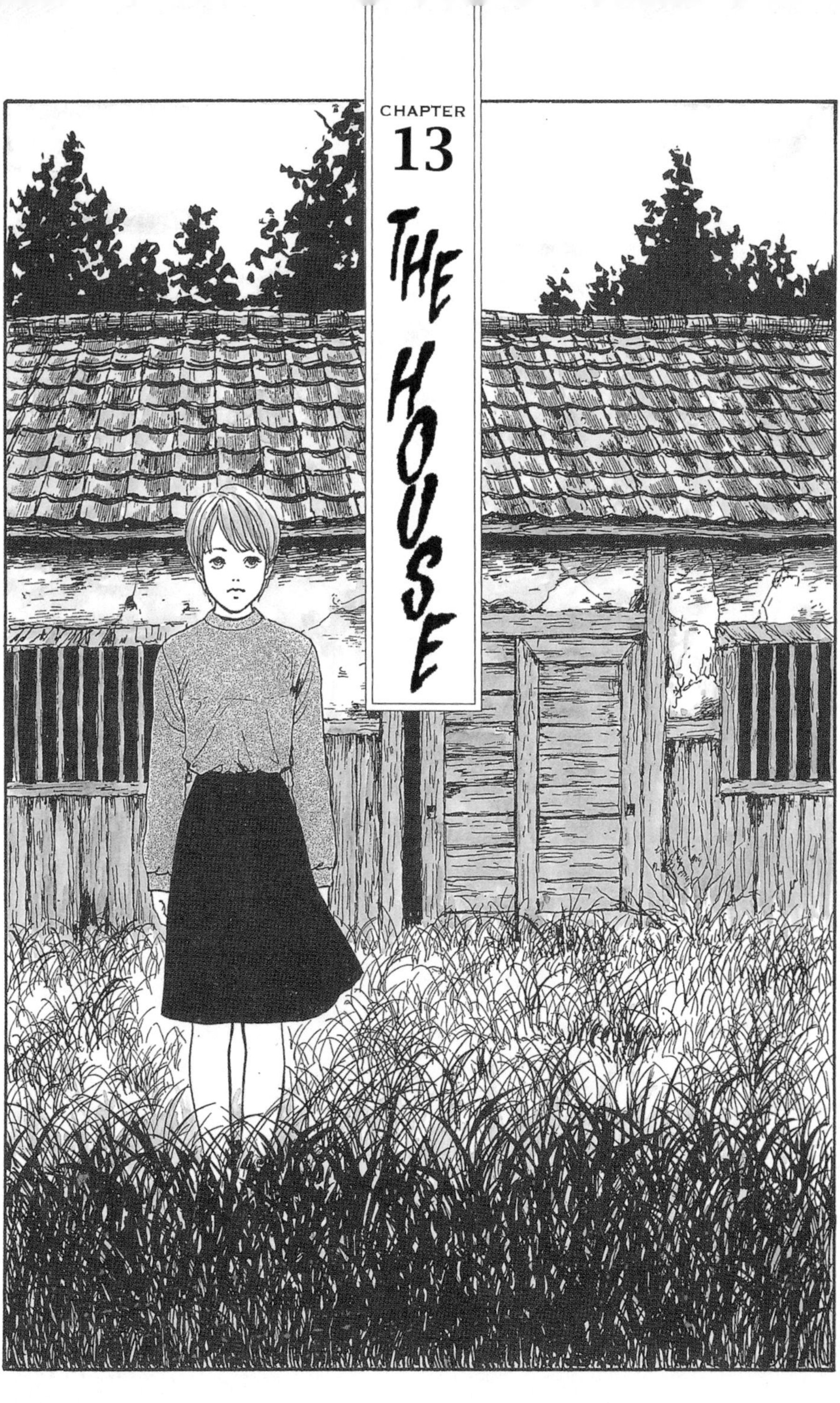
CHAPTER
13
THE HOUSE

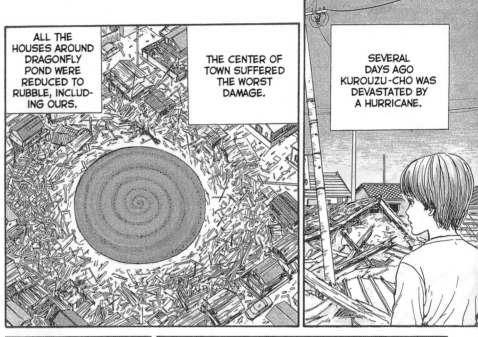

SEVERAL DAYS AGO KUROUZU-CHO WAS DEVASTATED BY A HURRICANE.
THE CENTER OF TOWN SUFFERED THE WORST DAMAGE.
ALL THE HOUSES AROUND DRAGONFLY POND WERE REDUCED TO RUBBLE, INCLUDING OURS.
THE HURRICANE WAS SUCKED INTO THE POND, AS IF BY SOME MAGNETIC ATTRACTION.
THE HOUSES NEARBY WERE DESTROYED.
BY A MIRACLE, MY FAMILY SURVIVED...
...BUT WE HAD TO FIND ANOTHER PLACE TO LIVE.

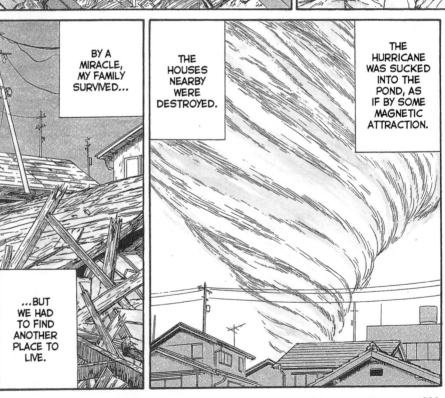

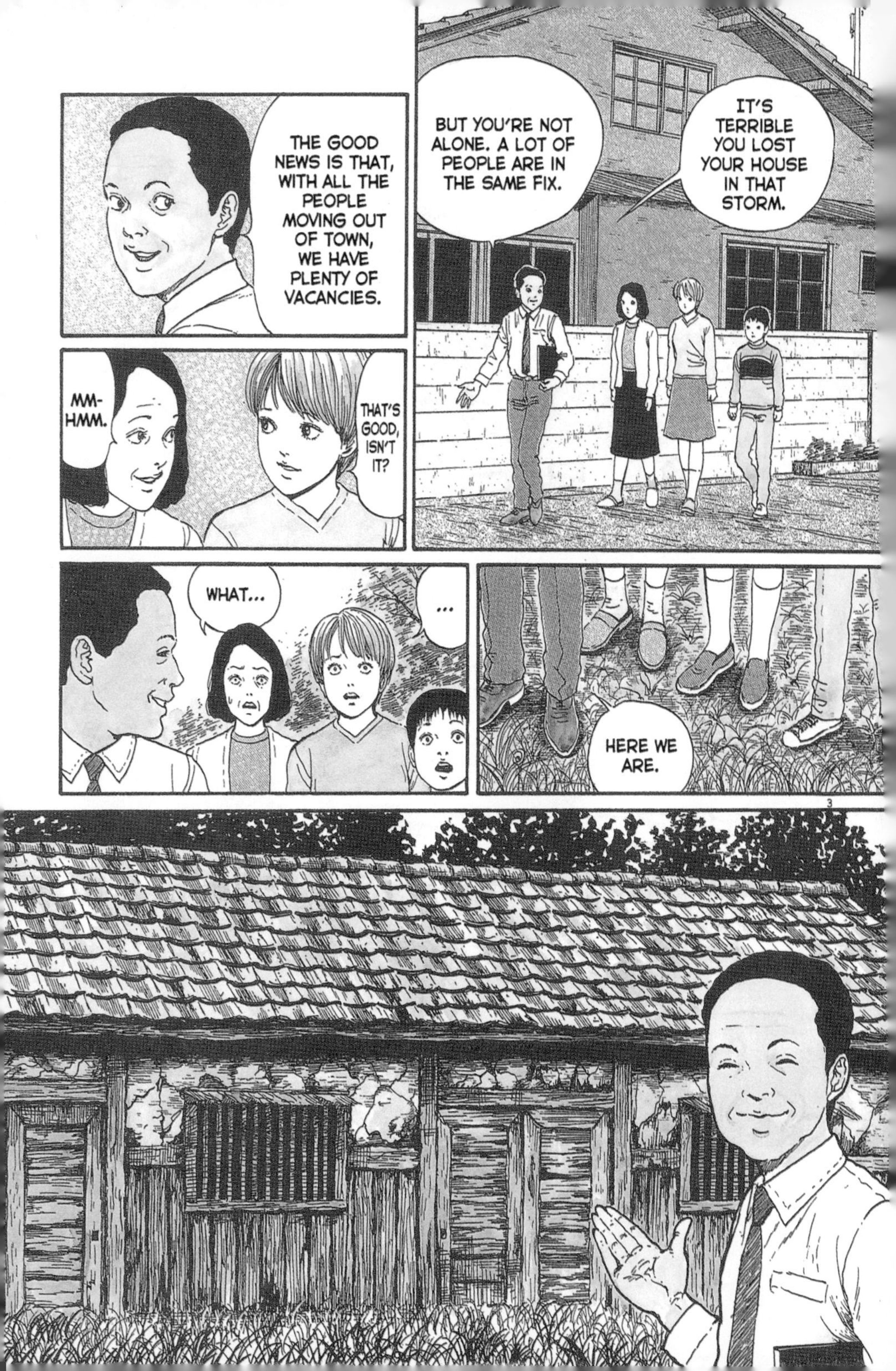
IT'S TERRIBLE YOU LOST YOUR HOUSE IN THAT STORM.
BUT YOU'RE NOT ALONE. A LOT OF PEOPLE ARE IN THE SAME FIX.
THE GOOD NEWS IS THAT, WITH ALL THE PEOPLE MOVING OUT OF TOWN, WE HAVE PLENTY OF VACANCIES.
THAT'S GOOD, ISN'T IT?
MM-HMM.
HERE WE ARE.
...
WHAT...

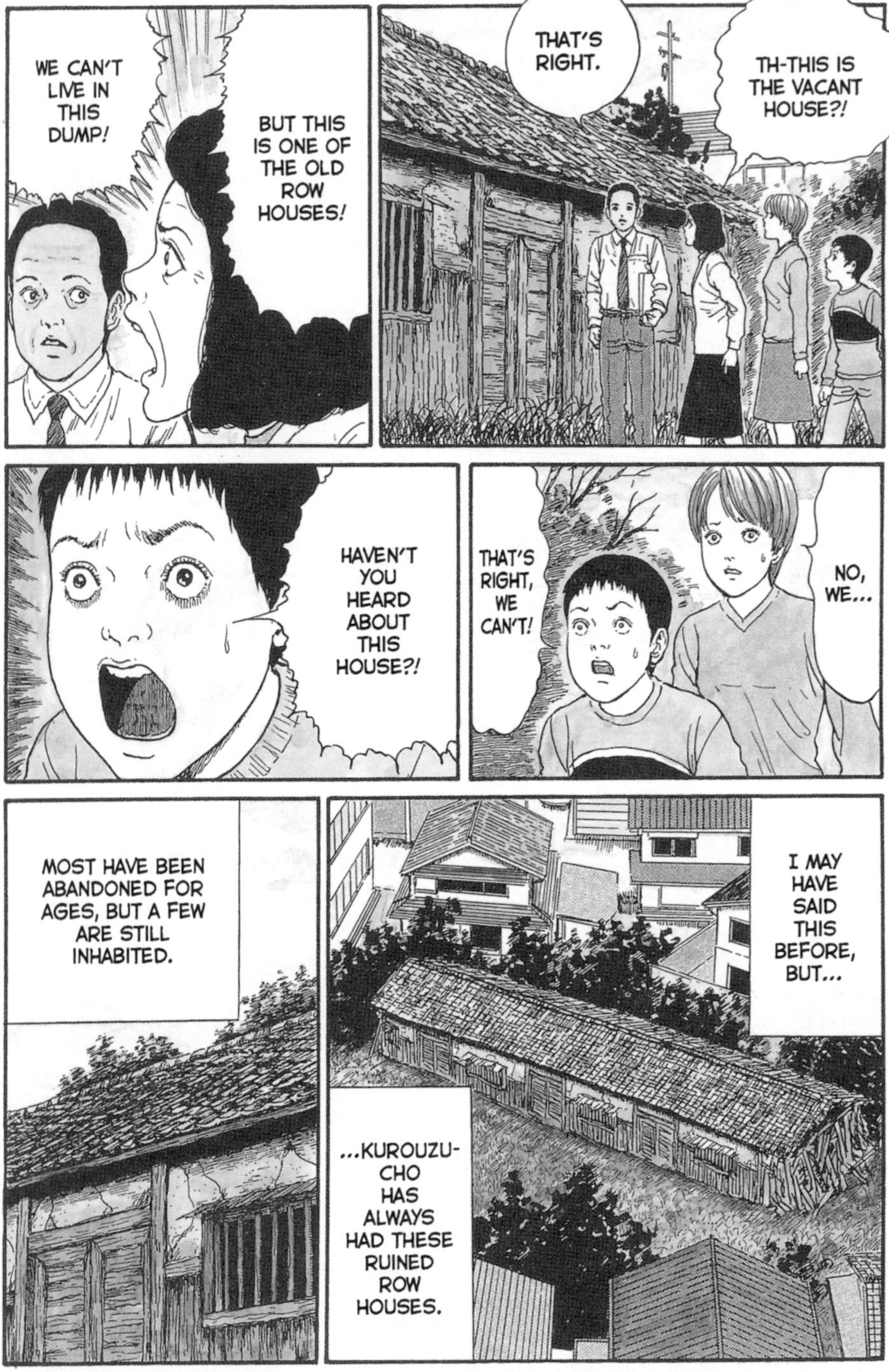
TH-THIS IS THE VACANT HOUSE?!
THAT'S RIGHT.
BUT THIS IS ONE OF THE OLD ROW HOUSES!
WE CAN'T LIVE IN THIS DUMP!
NO, WE...
THAT'S RIGHT, WE CAN'T!
HAVEN'T YOU HEARD ABOUT THIS HOUSE?!
I MAY HAVE SAID THIS BEFORE, BUT...
...KUROUZU-CHO HAS ALWAYS HAD THESE RUINED ROW HOUSES.
MOST HAVE BEEN ABANDONED FOR AGES, BUT A FEW ARE STILL INHABITED.

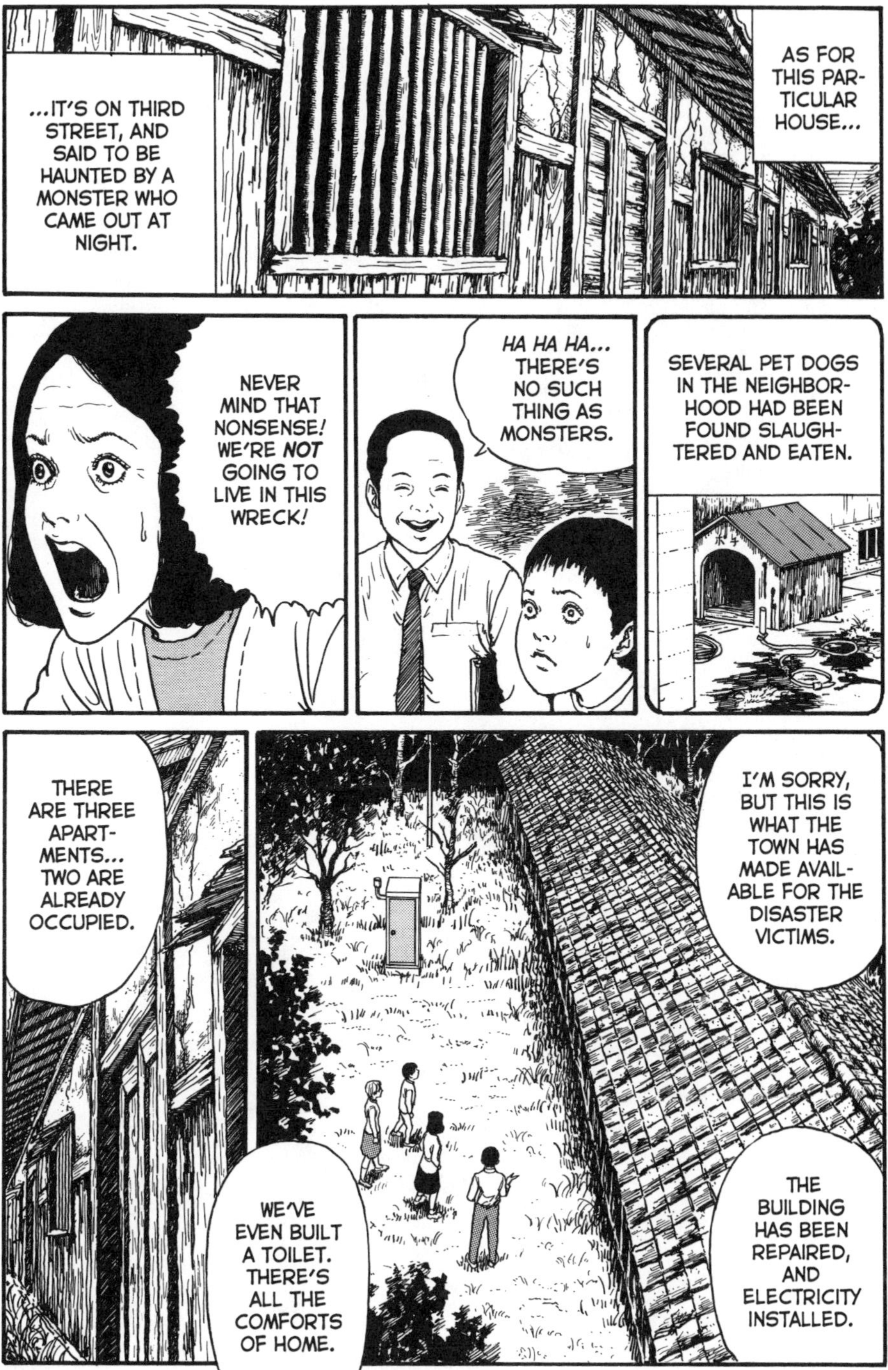
AS FOR THIS PARTICULAR HOUSE...
...IT'S ON THIRD STREET, AND SAID TO BE HAUNTED BY A MONSTER WHO CAME OUT AT NIGHT.
SEVERAL PET DOGS IN THE NEIGHBORHOOD HAD BEEN FOUND SLAUGHTERED AND EATEN.
HA HA HA... THERE'S NO SUCH THING AS MONSTERS.
NEVER MIND THAT NONSENSE! WE'RE ***NOT*** GOING TO LIVE IN THIS WRECK!
I'M SORRY, BUT THIS IS WHAT THE TOWN HAS MADE AVAILABLE FOR THE DISASTER VICTIMS.
THE BUILDING HAS BEEN REPAIRED, AND ELECTRICITY INSTALLED.
WE'VE EVEN BUILT A TOILET. THERE'S ALL THE COMFORTS OF HOME.
THERE ARE THREE APARTMENTS... TWO ARE ALREADY OCCUPIED.

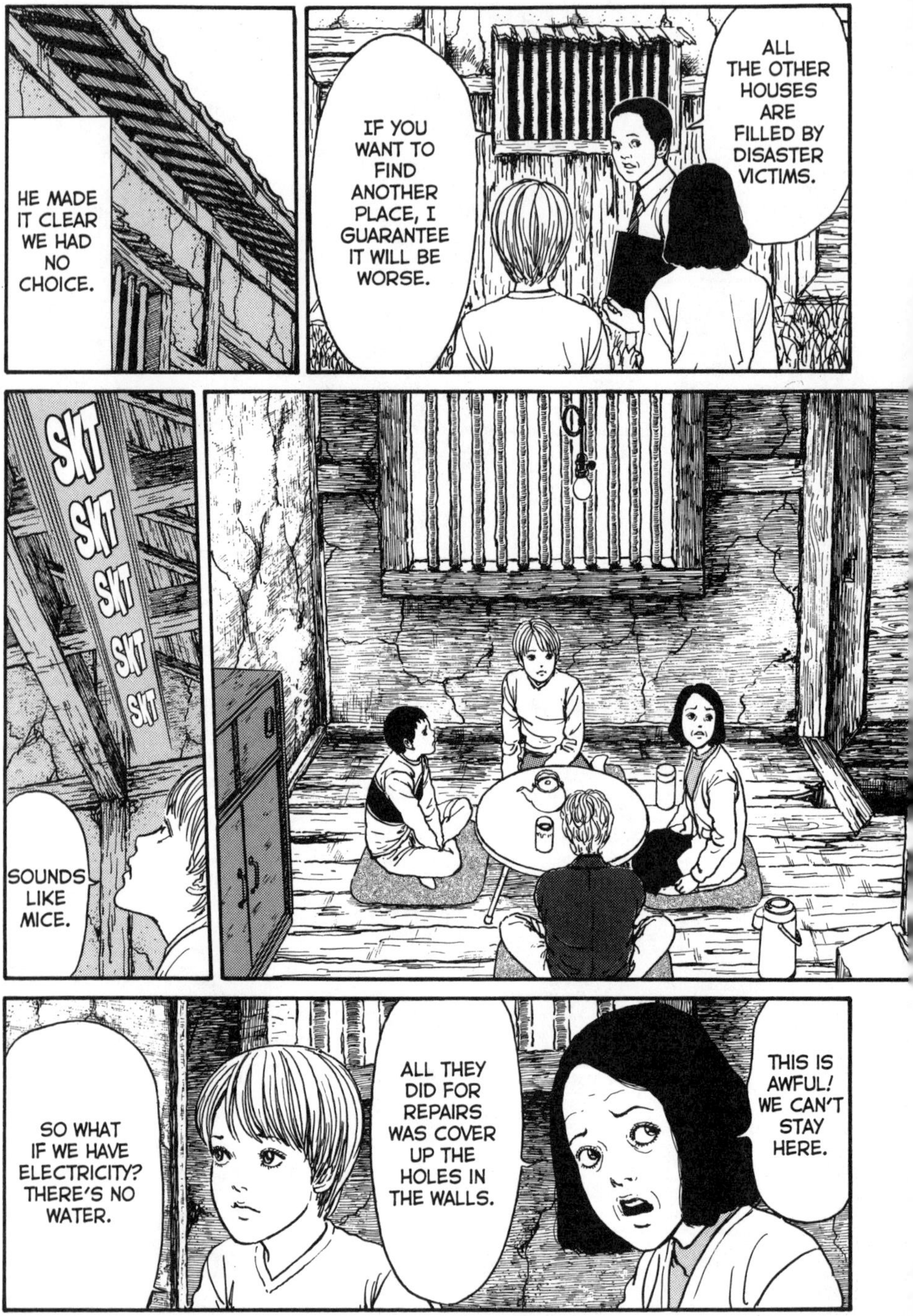
ALL THE OTHER HOUSES ARE FILLED BY DISASTER VICTIMS.
IF YOU WANT TO FIND ANOTHER PLACE, I GUARANTEE IT WILL BE WORSE.
HE MADE IT CLEAR WE HAD NO CHOICE.
SKT SKT SKT SKT SKT
SOUNDS LIKE MICE.
THIS IS AWFUL! WE CAN'T STAY HERE.
ALL THEY DID FOR REPAIRS WAS COVER UP THE HOLES IN THE WALLS.
SO WHAT IF WE HAVE ELECTRICITY? THERE'S NO WATER.

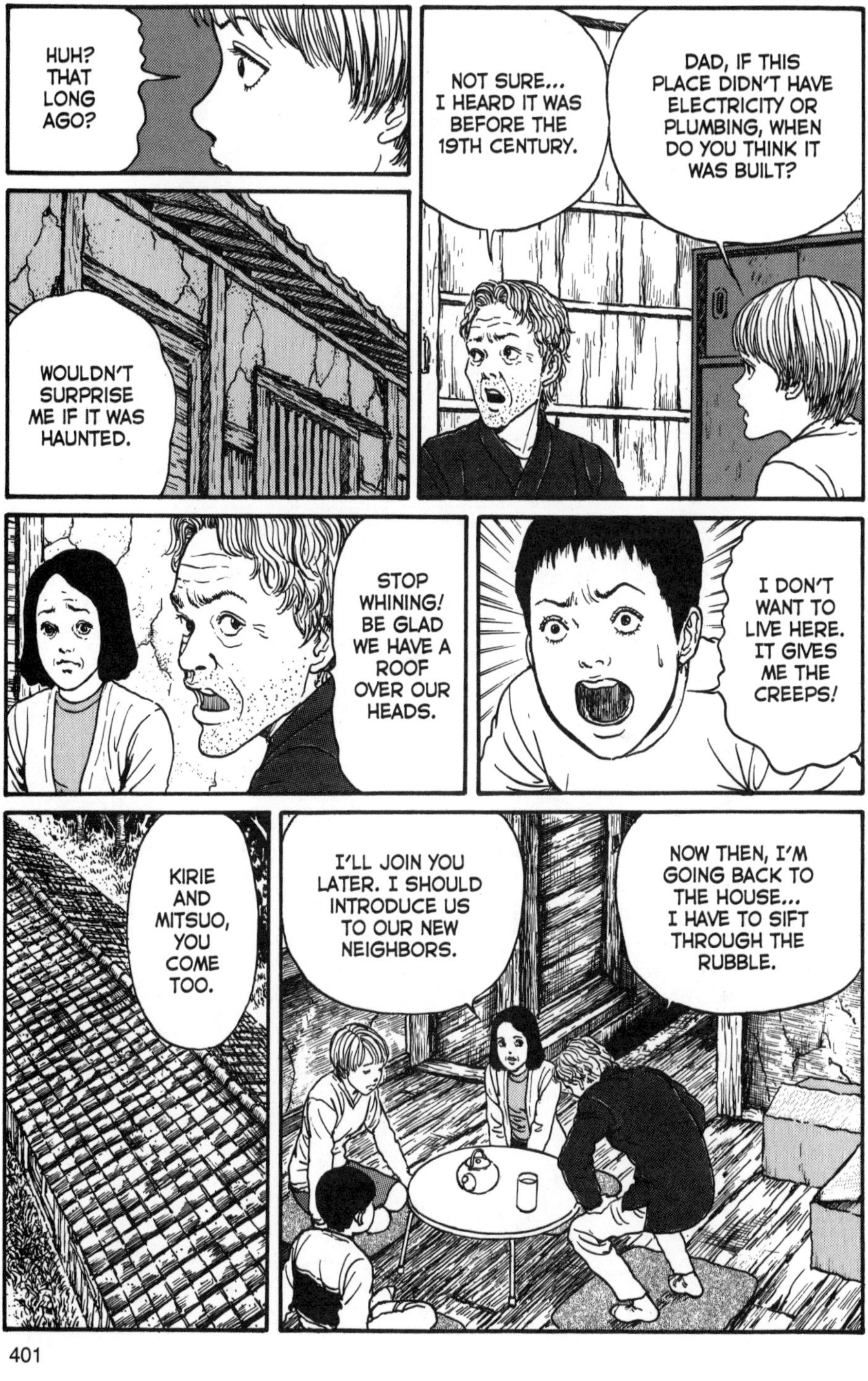
DAD, IF THIS PLACE DIDN'T HAVE ELECTRICITY OR PLUMBING, WHEN DO YOU THINK IT WAS BUILT?
NOT SURE... I HEARD IT WAS BEFORE THE 19TH CENTURY.
HUH? THAT LONG AGO?
WOULDN'T SURPRISE ME IF IT WAS HAUNTED.
I DON'T WANT TO LIVE HERE. IT GIVES ME THE CREEPS!
STOP WHINING! BE GLAD WE HAVE A ROOF OVER OUR HEADS.
NOW THEN, I'M GOING BACK TO THE HOUSE... I HAVE TO SIFT THROUGH THE RUBBLE.
I'LL JOIN YOU LATER. I SHOULD INTRODUCE US TO OUR NEW NEIGHBORS.
KIRIE AND MITSUO, YOU COME TOO.

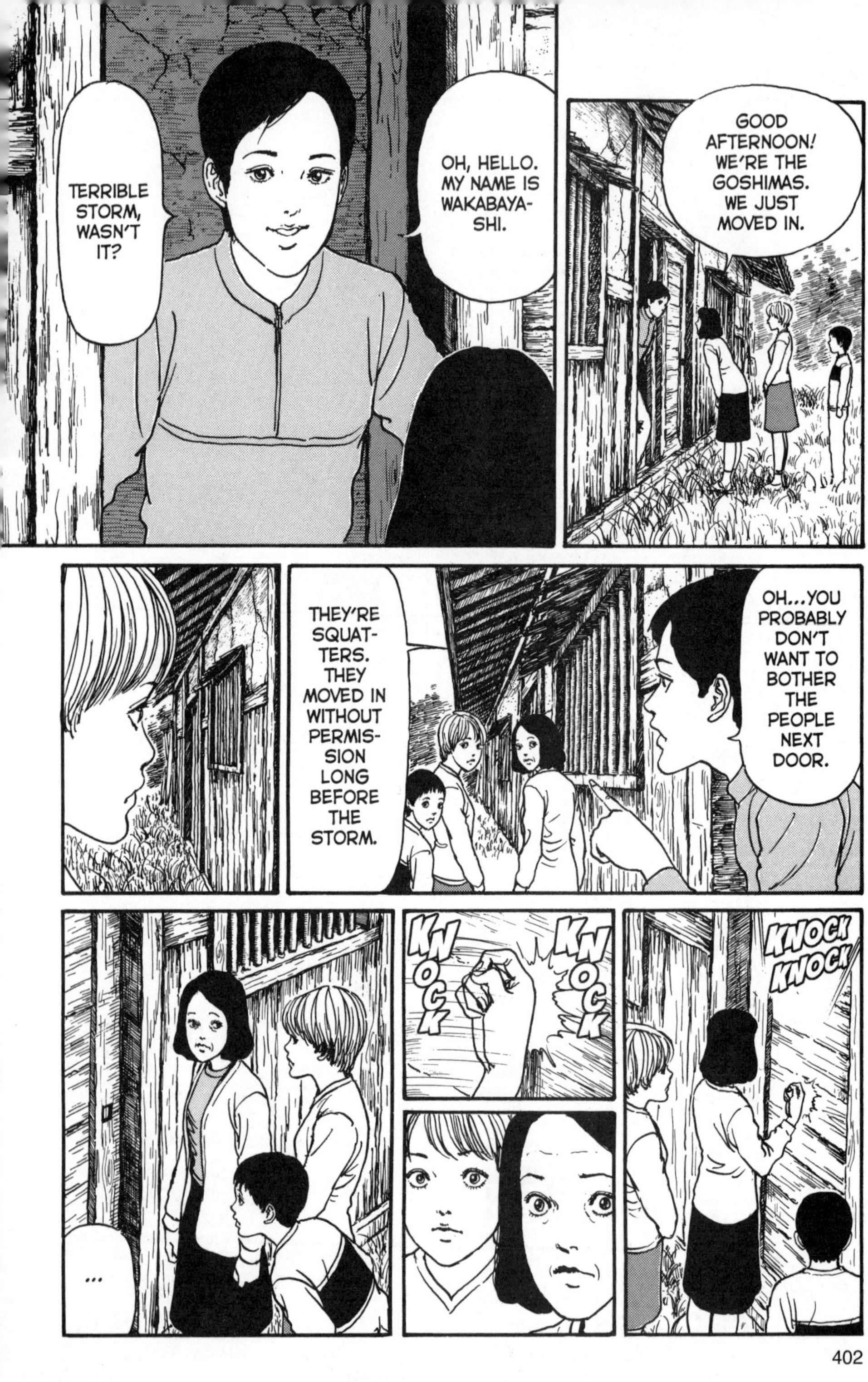
GOOD AFTERNOON! WE'RE THE GOSHIMAS. WE JUST MOVED IN.
OH, HELLO. MY NAME IS WAKABAYA-SHI.
TERRIBLE STORM, WASN'T IT?
OH...YOU PROBABLY DON'T WANT TO BOTHER THE PEOPLE NEXT DOOR.
THEY'RE SQUAT-TERS. THEY MOVED IN WITHOUT PERMIS-SION LONG BEFORE THE STORM.
KNOCK KNOCK
KNOCK
KNOCK
...

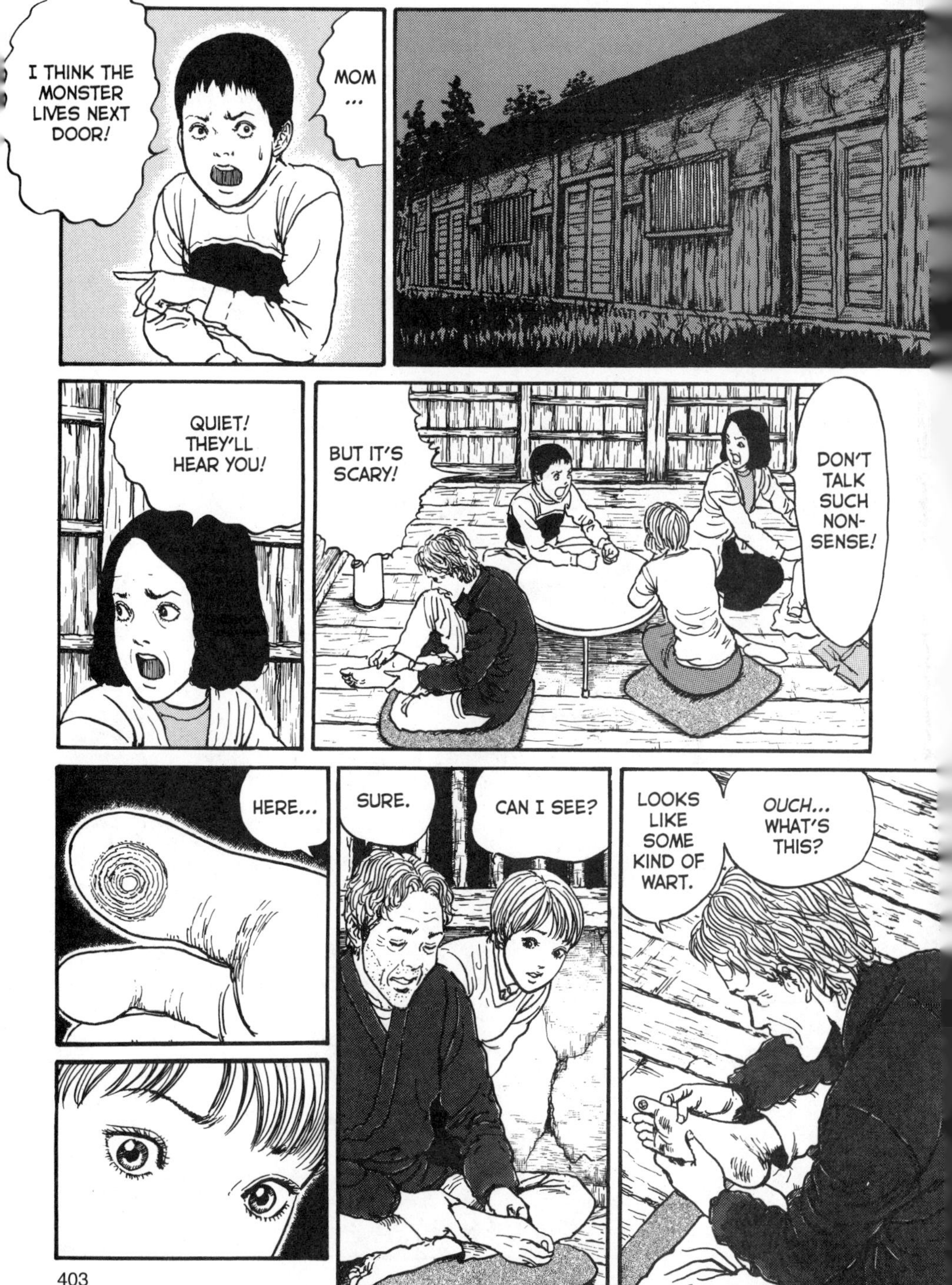
MOM ...
I THINK THE MONSTER LIVES NEXT DOOR!
DON'T TALK SUCH NON-SENSE!
BUT IT'S SCARY!
QUIET! THEY'LL HEAR YOU!
OUCH... WHAT'S THIS?
LOOKS LIKE SOME KIND OF WART.
CAN I SEE?
SURE.
HERE...

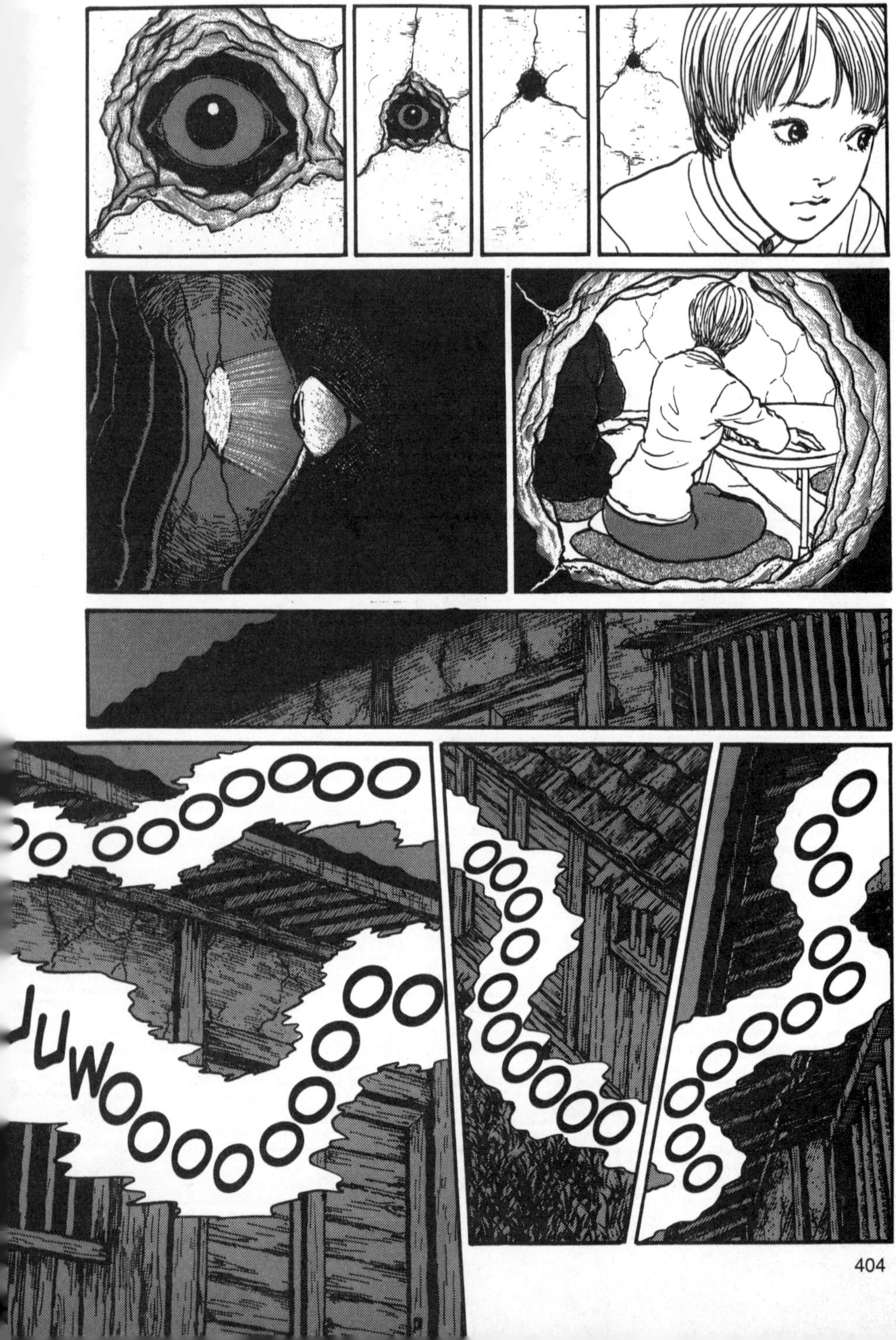
OOOOOOOOOOOOOO
OOOOOOOOOOOOOOO
UUWOOOOOOOOOOOOOOOOOOOOO

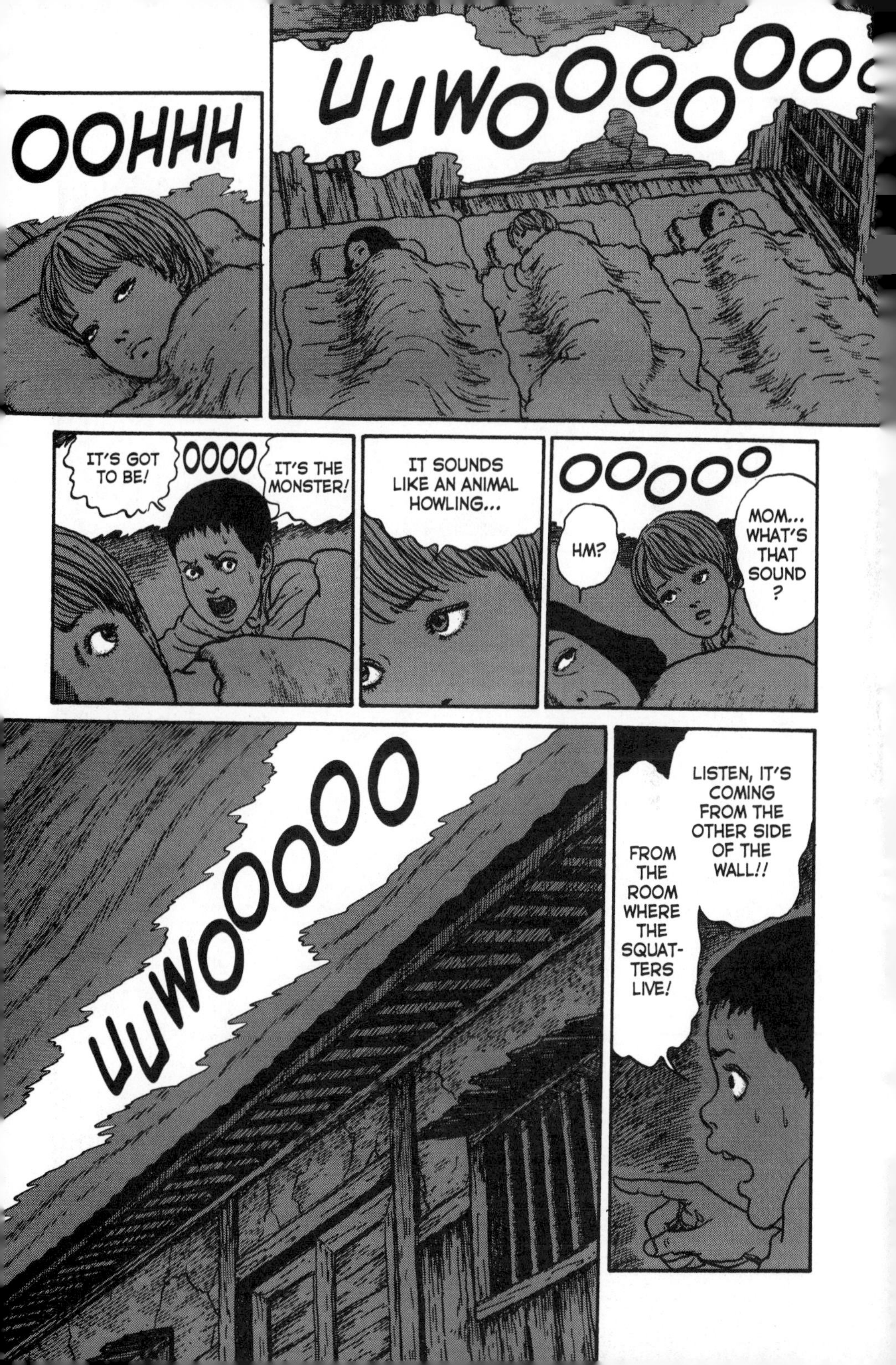
UUWOOOOOOO
OOHHH
OOOOOO
MOM... WHAT'S THAT SOUND?
HM?
IT SOUNDS LIKE AN ANIMAL HOWLING...
IT'S THE MONSTER!
OOOO
IT'S GOT TO BE!
LISTEN, IT'S COMING FROM THE OTHER SIDE OF THE WALL!!
FROM THE ROOM WHERE THE SQUAT-TERS LIVE!
UUWOOOOOO

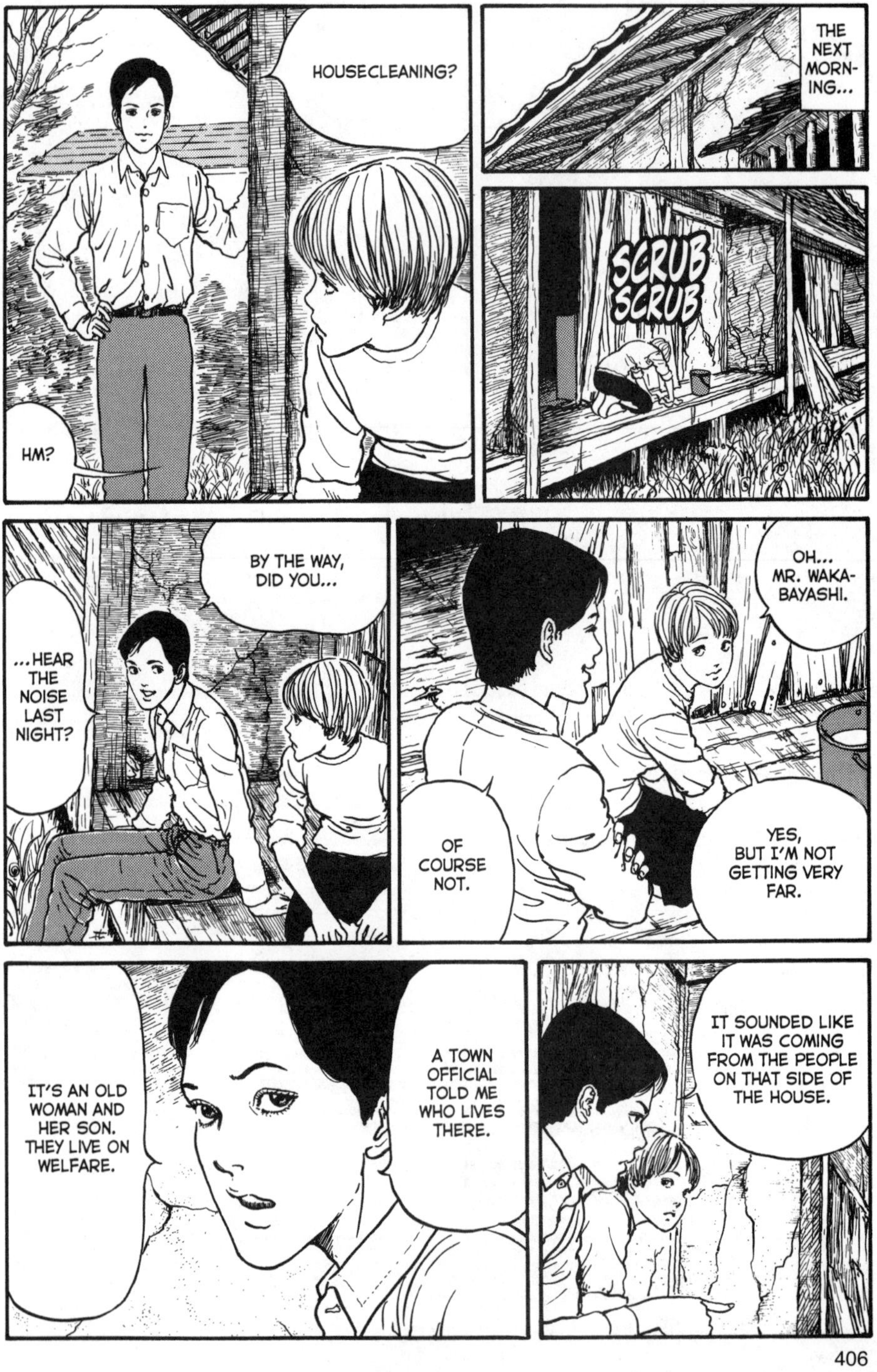
THE NEXT MORNING...
SCRUB SCRUB
HOUSECLEANING?
HM?
OH... MR. WAKABAYASHI.
YES, BUT I'M NOT GETTING VERY FAR.
OF COURSE NOT.
BY THE WAY, DID YOU...
...HEAR THE NOISE LAST NIGHT?
IT SOUNDED LIKE IT WAS COMING FROM THE PEOPLE ON THAT SIDE OF THE HOUSE.
A TOWN OFFICIAL TOLD ME WHO LIVES THERE.
IT'S AN OLD WOMAN AND HER SON. THEY LIVE ON WELFARE.

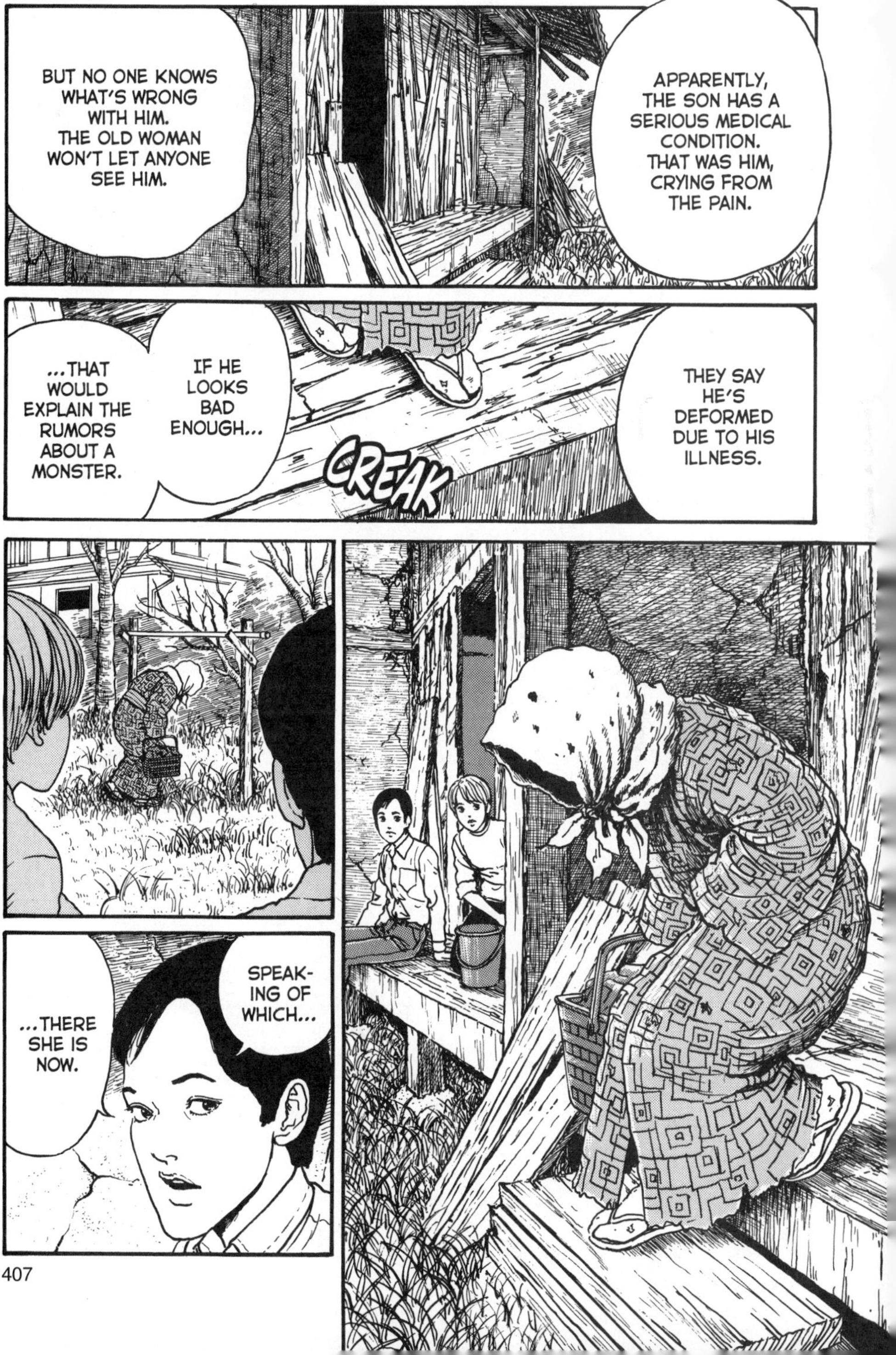
APPARENTLY, THE SON HAS A SERIOUS MEDICAL CONDITION. THAT WAS HIM, CRYING FROM THE PAIN.
BUT NO ONE KNOWS WHAT'S WRONG WITH HIM. THE OLD WOMAN WON'T LET ANYONE SEE HIM.
THEY SAY HE'S DEFORMED DUE TO HIS ILLNESS.
CREAK
IF HE LOOKS BAD ENOUGH...
...THAT WOULD EXPLAIN THE RUMORS ABOUT A MONSTER.
SPEAK-ING OF WHICH...
...THERE SHE IS NOW.

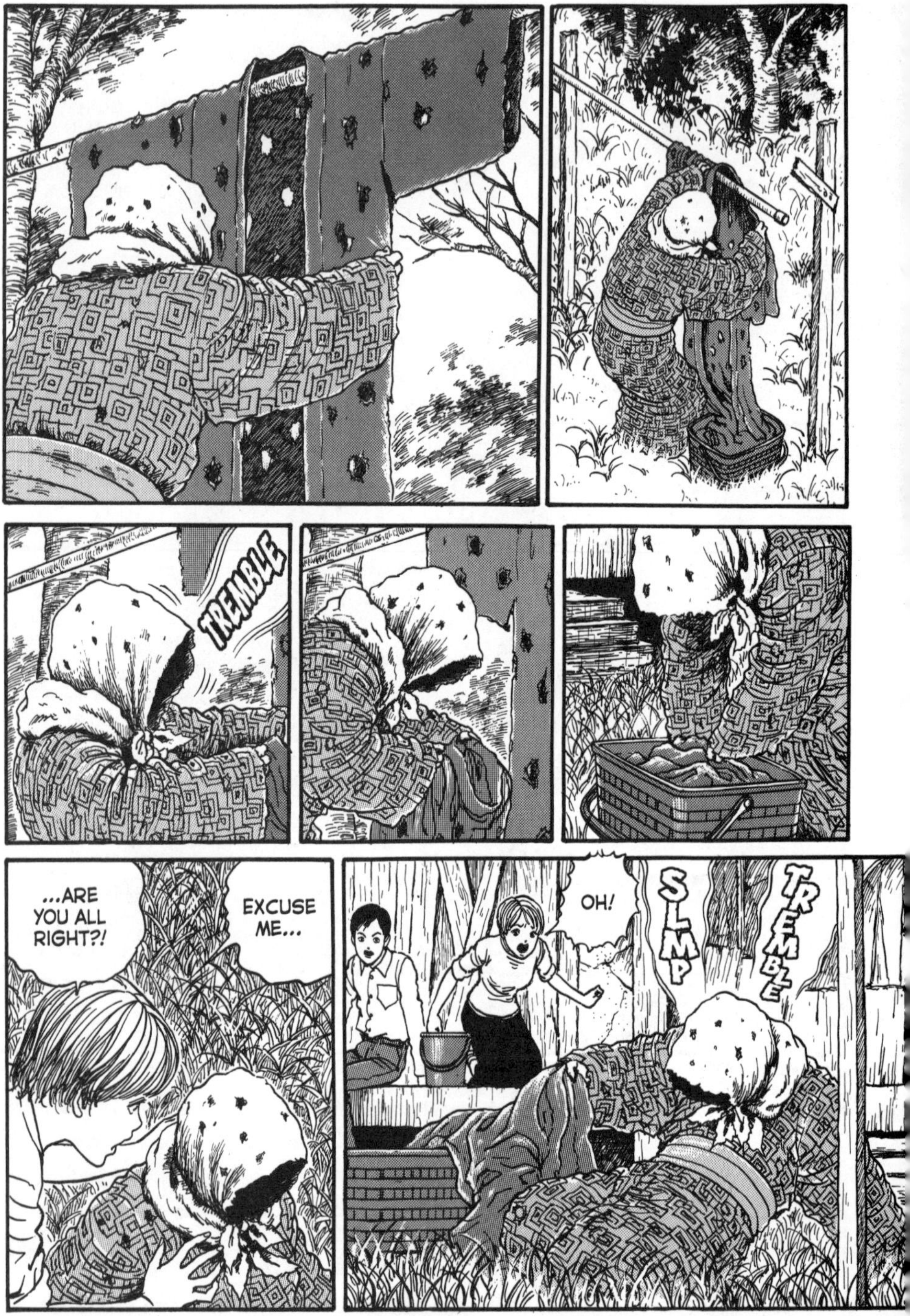
TREMBLE
TREMBLE
SLMP
OH!
EXCUSE ME...
...ARE YOU ALL RIGHT?!

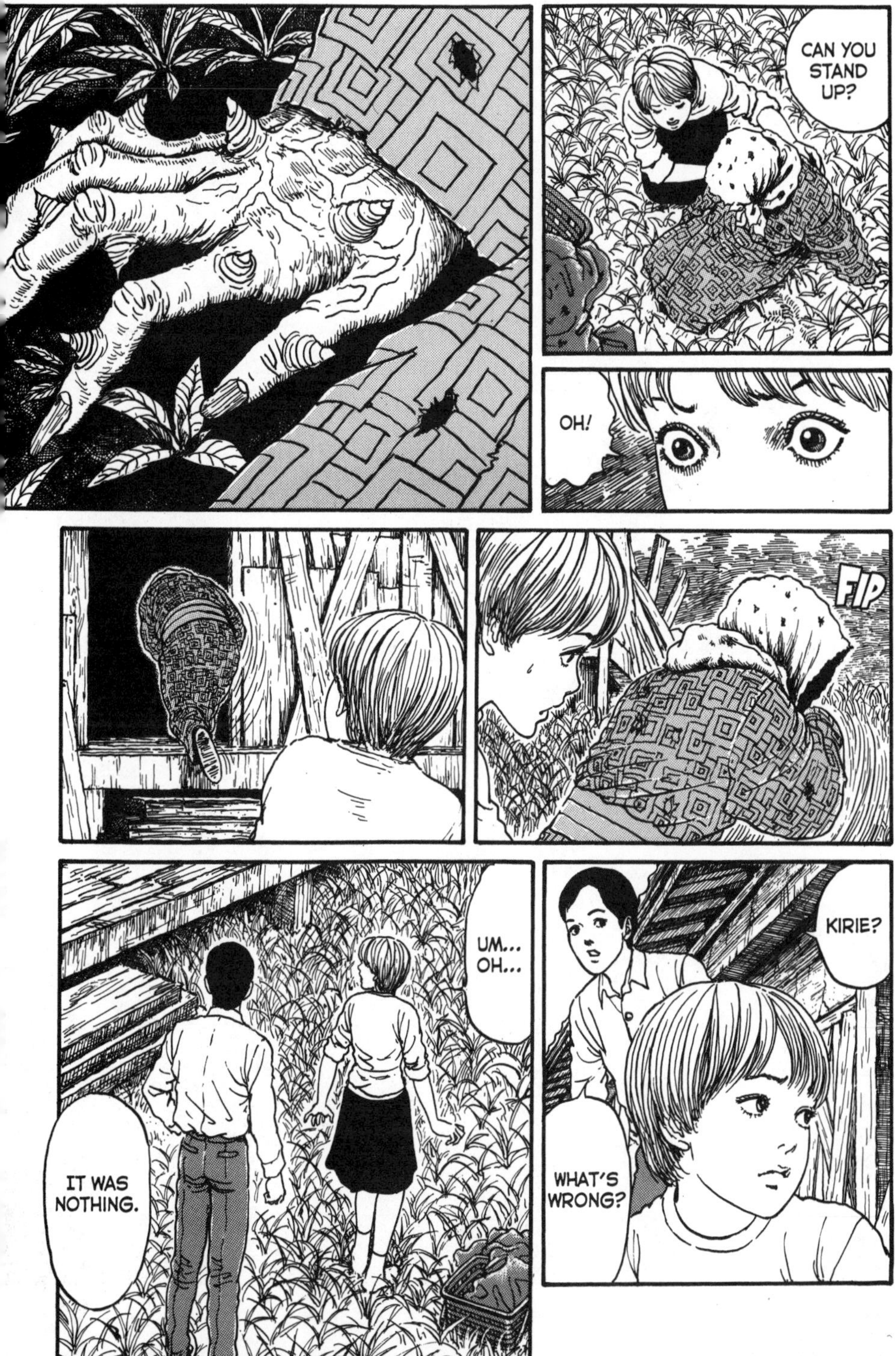
CAN YOU STAND UP?
OH!
FIP
KIRIE?
WHAT'S WRONG?
UM... OH...
IT WAS NOTHING.

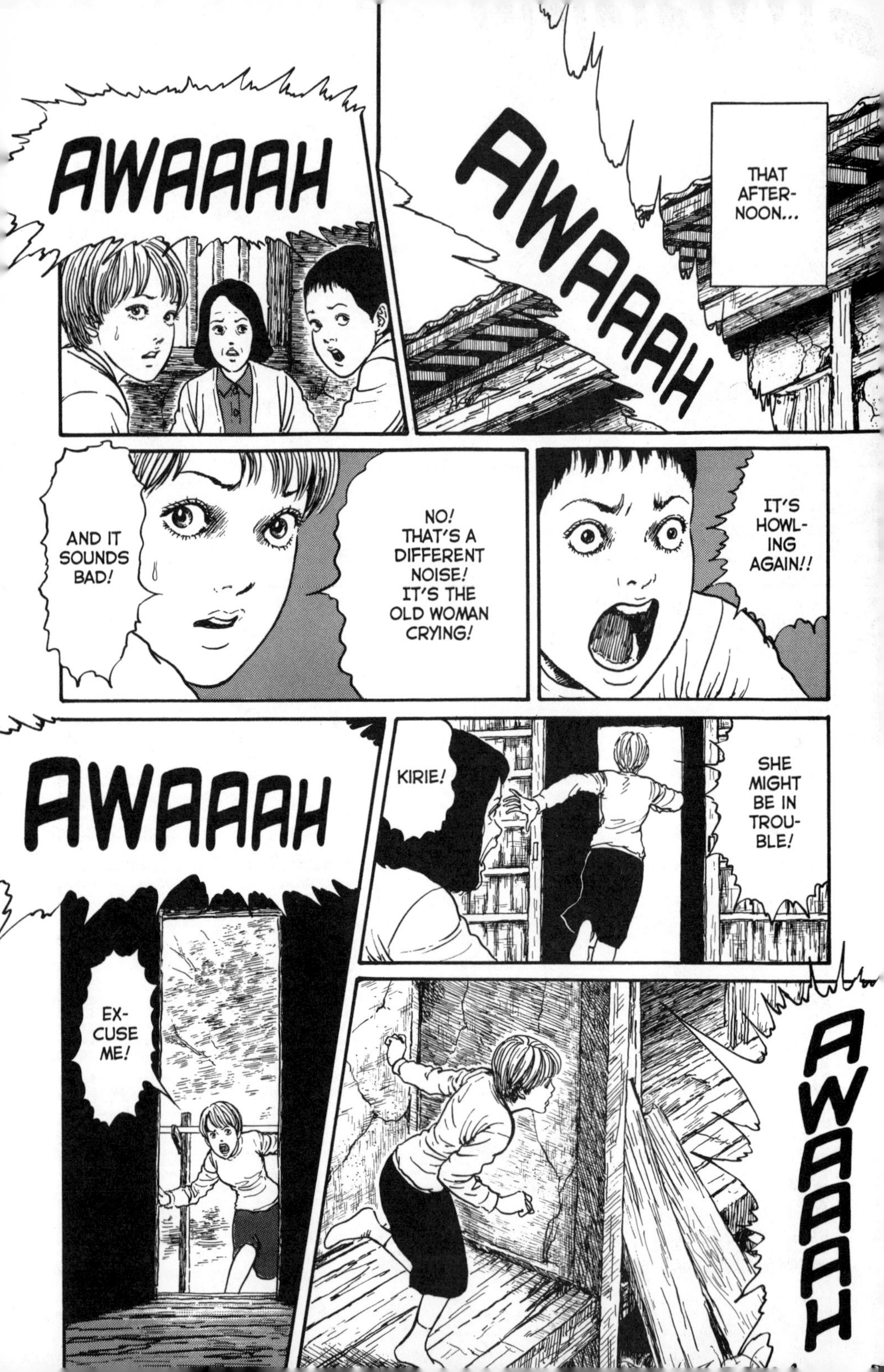
THAT AFTERNOON...
AWAAAH
AWAAAH
IT'S HOWLING AGAIN!!
NO! THAT'S A DIFFERENT NOISE! IT'S THE OLD WOMAN CRYING!
AND IT SOUNDS BAD!
SHE MIGHT BE IN TROUBLE!
KIRIE!
AWAAAH
AWAAAH
EXCUSE ME!

AWAAHH

ARE
YOU
ALL
RIGHT
?!

AWAAAH

MY SON...
MY SON...

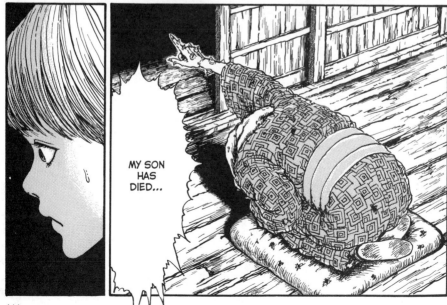

MY SON
HAS
DIED...

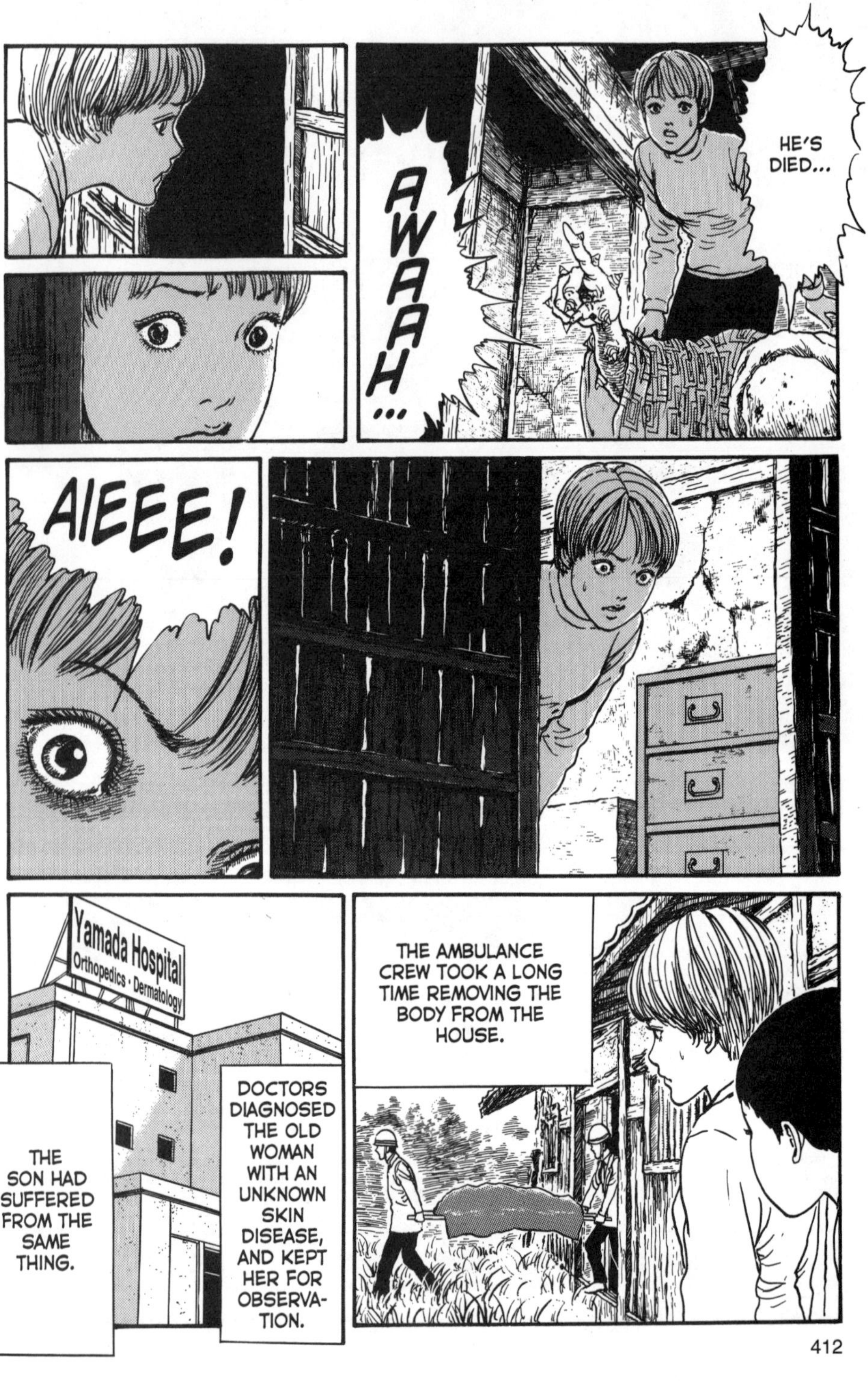
HE'S DIED...
AWAAAH...
AIEEE!
THE AMBULANCE CREW TOOK A LONG TIME REMOVING THE BODY FROM THE HOUSE.
Yamada Hospital
Orthopedics • Dermatology
DOCTORS DIAGNOSED THE OLD WOMAN WITH AN UNKNOWN SKIN DISEASE, AND KEPT HER FOR OBSERVATION.
THE SON HAD SUFFERED FROM THE SAME THING.

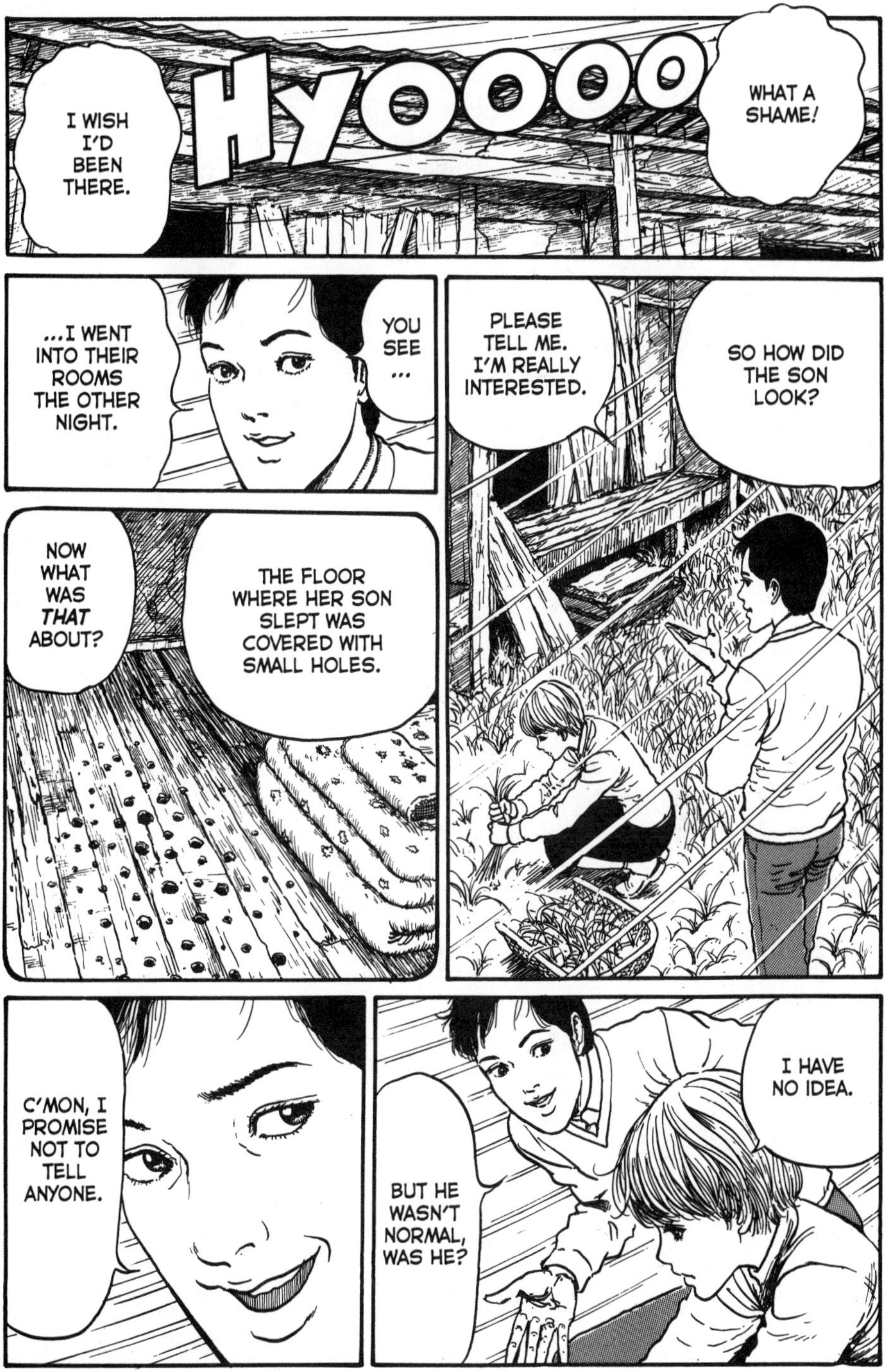
WHAT A SHAME!
HYOOOO
I WISH I'D BEEN THERE.
SO HOW DID THE SON LOOK?
PLEASE TELL ME. I'M REALLY INTERESTED.
YOU SEE ...
...I WENT INTO THEIR ROOMS THE OTHER NIGHT.
THE FLOOR WHERE HER SON SLEPT WAS COVERED WITH SMALL HOLES.
NOW WHAT WAS *THAT* ABOUT?
I HAVE NO IDEA.
BUT HE WASN'T NORMAL, WAS HE?
C'MON, I PROMISE NOT TO TELL ANYONE.

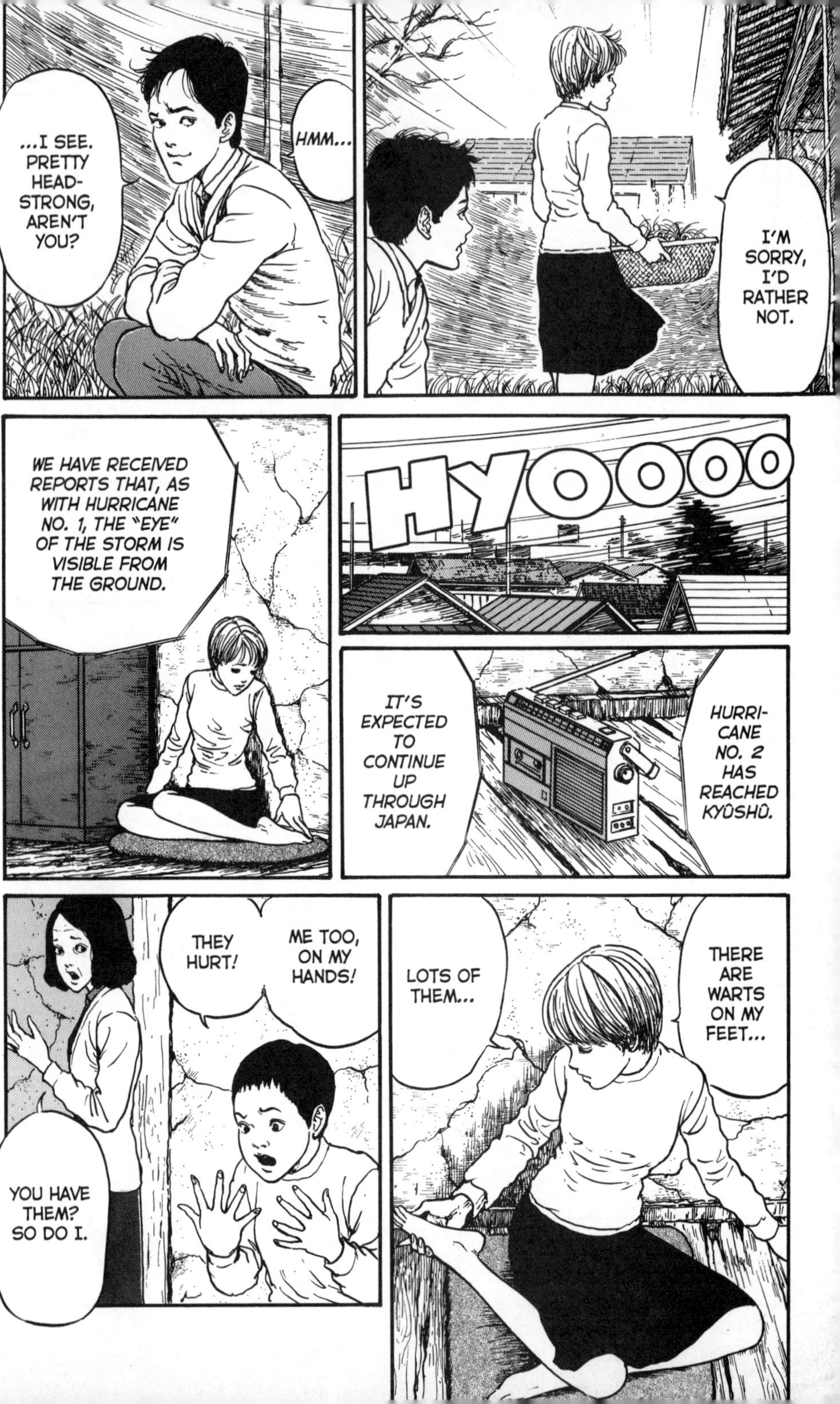
I'M SORRY, I'D RATHER NOT.
HMM...
...I SEE. PRETTY HEAD-STRONG, AREN'T YOU?
HYOOOO
HURRI-CANE NO. 2 HAS REACHED KYŪSHŪ.
IT'S EXPECTED TO CONTINUE UP THROUGH JAPAN.
WE HAVE RECEIVED REPORTS THAT, AS WITH HURRICANE NO. 1, THE "EYE" OF THE STORM IS VISIBLE FROM THE GROUND.
THERE ARE WARTS ON MY FEET...
LOTS OF THEM...
ME TOO, ON MY HANDS!
THEY HURT!
YOU HAVE THEM? SO DO I.

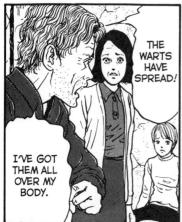

I'M HOME!
HYOOOOOO
CREAK
OOW... MY FEET!
THE WARTS HAVE SPREAD!
I'VE GOT THEM ALL OVER MY BODY.
OH NO...
HEH HEH...
YOU DON'T KNOW I'VE BEEN WATCHING YOU EVER SINCE YOU MOVED IN HERE.
KIRIE, YOU'RE SO BEAUTIFUL AND WILLFUL...I CAN'T KEEP MY EYES OFF YOU.
BUT I CAN ONLY SEE SO MUCH THROUGH THIS HOLE. I'LL HAVE TO MAKE A NEW ONE SOON.

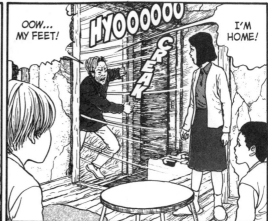

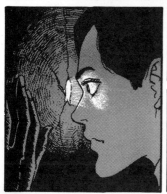

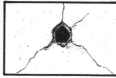

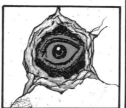

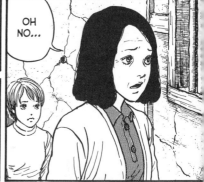

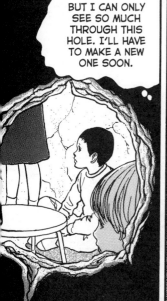

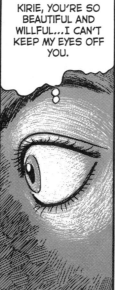

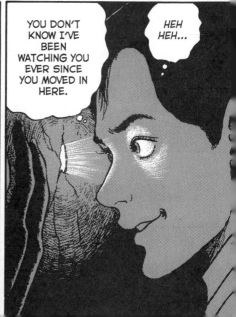

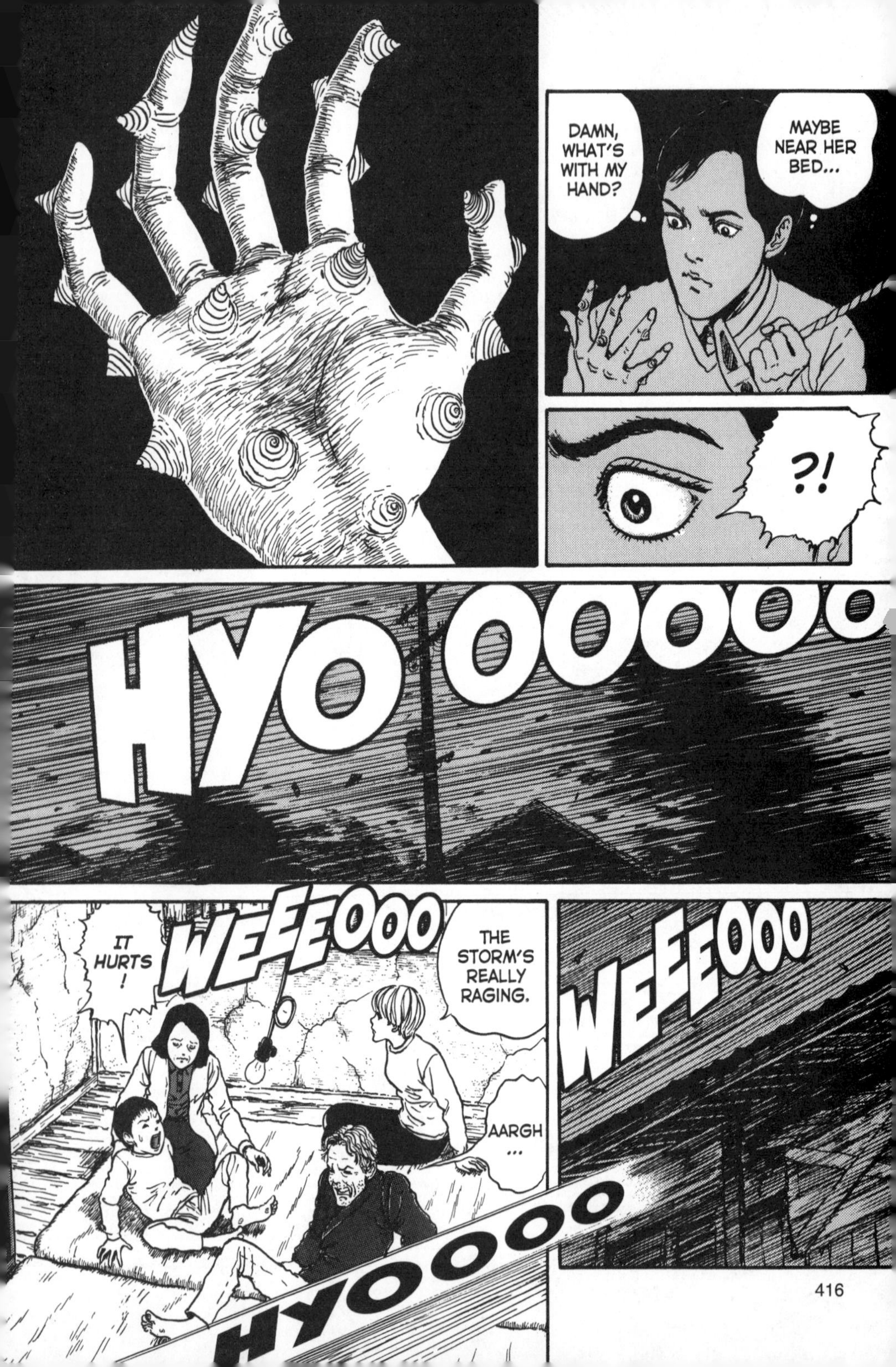
MAYBE NEAR HER BED...
DAMN, WHAT'S WITH MY HAND?
?!
HYOOOOOOO
WEEEOOO
THE STORM'S REALLY RAGING.
WEEEOOO
IT HURTS!
AARGH...
HYOOOOO

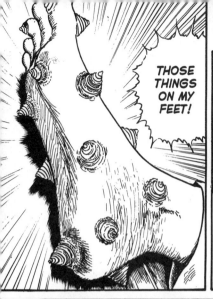

IT HURTS! IT HURTS!
W-WE CAN'T GO TO THE HOSPITAL IN THIS STORM...
AHH! WHAT'S THIS?!
THOSE THINGS ON MY FEET!
WEEEOOOOOOOO
CRRRAC
CRASH
THEY'RE ...
...THE SAME THINGS I SAW ON THAT OLD WOMAN AND HER SON!!
HYOOO
THESE AREN'T WARTS!

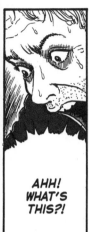

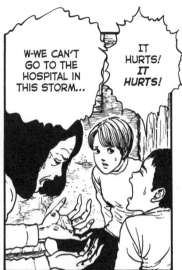

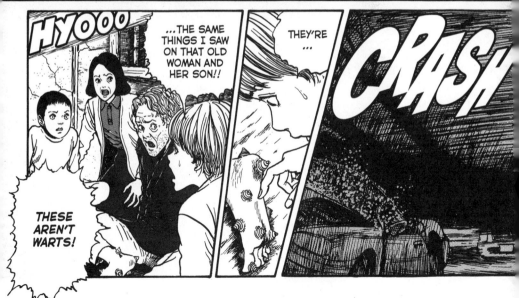

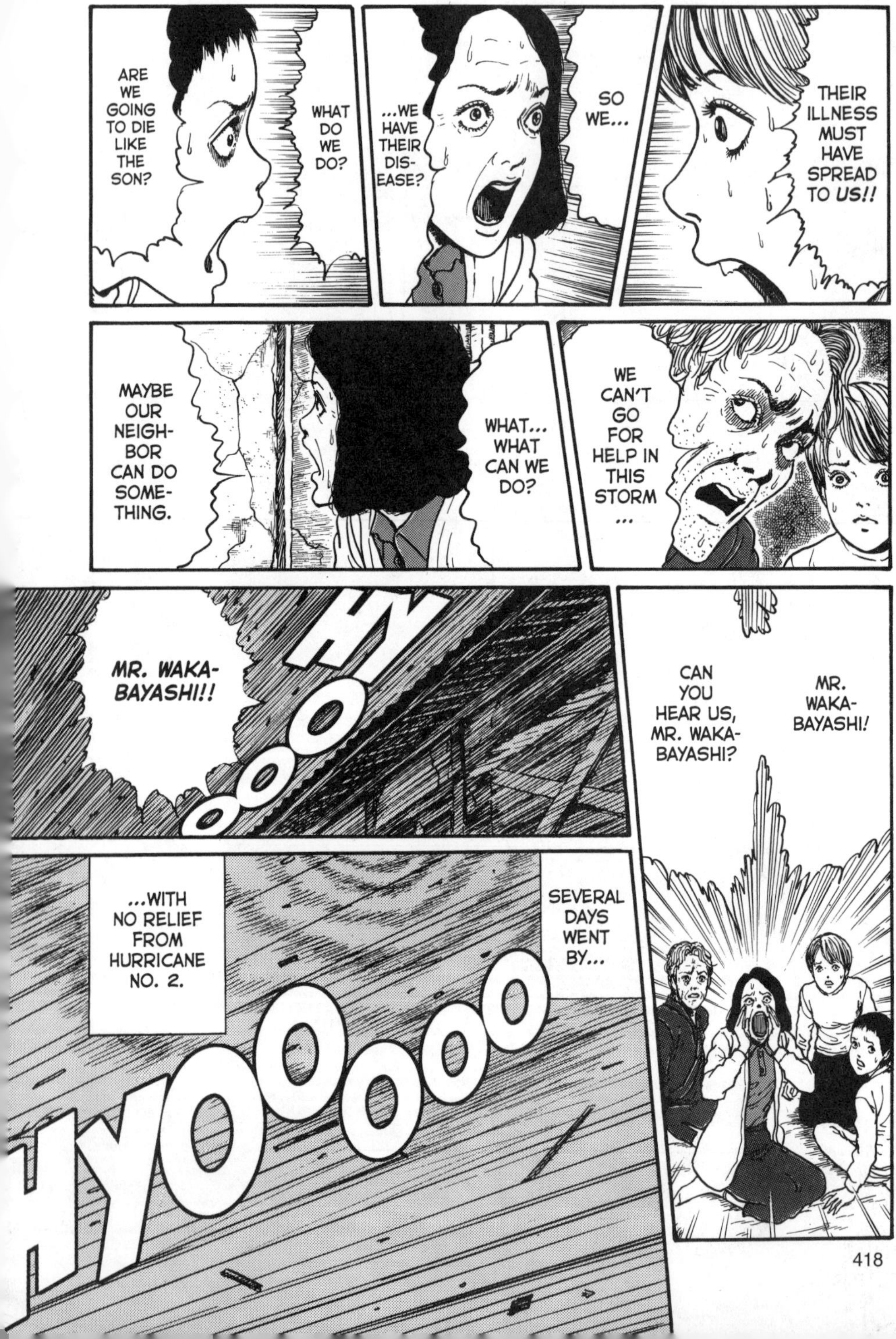
THEIR ILLNESS MUST HAVE SPREAD TO *US!!*
SO WE...
...WE HAVE THEIR DIS-EASE?
WHAT DO WE DO?
ARE WE GOING TO DIE LIKE THE SON?
WE CAN'T GO FOR HELP IN THIS STORM ...
WHAT... WHAT CAN WE DO?
MAYBE OUR NEIGH-BOR CAN DO SOME-THING.
MR. WAKA-BAYASHI!
CAN YOU HEAR US, MR. WAKA-BAYASHI?
HYOOOO
MR. WAKA-BAYASHI!!
SEVERAL DAYS WENT BY...
...WITH NO RELIEF FROM HURRICANE NO. 2.
HYOOOOOOO

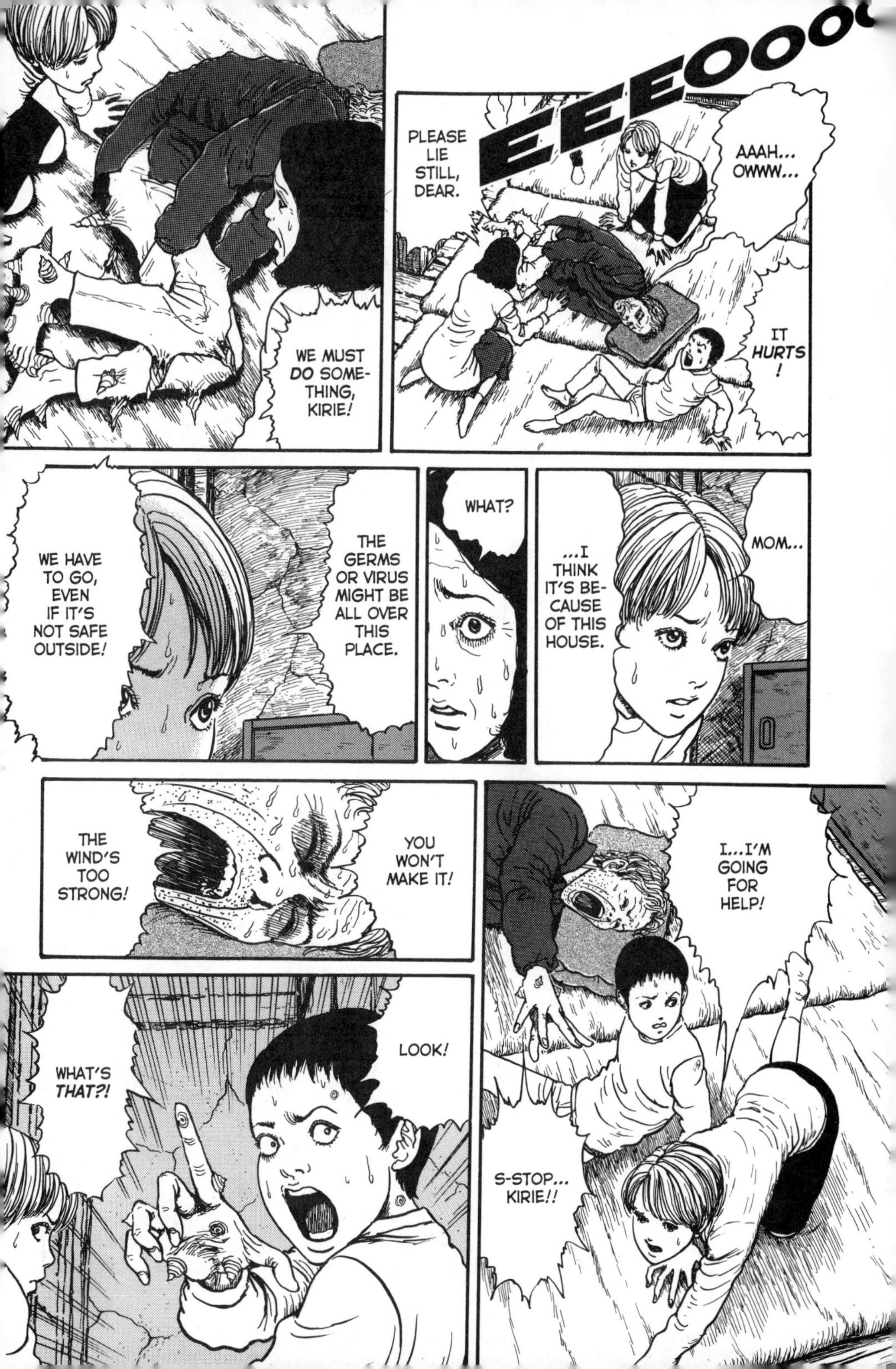
EEEOOOO
AAAH... OWWW...
PLEASE LIE STILL, DEAR.
IT *HURTS*!
WE MUST *DO* SOMETHING, KIRIE!
MOM...
...I THINK IT'S BECAUSE OF THIS HOUSE.
WHAT?
THE GERMS OR VIRUS MIGHT BE ALL OVER THIS PLACE.
WE HAVE TO GO, EVEN IF IT'S NOT SAFE OUTSIDE!
I...I'M GOING FOR HELP!
S-STOP... KIRIE!!
YOU WON'T MAKE IT!
THE WIND'S TOO STRONG!
LOOK!
WHAT'S *THAT*?!

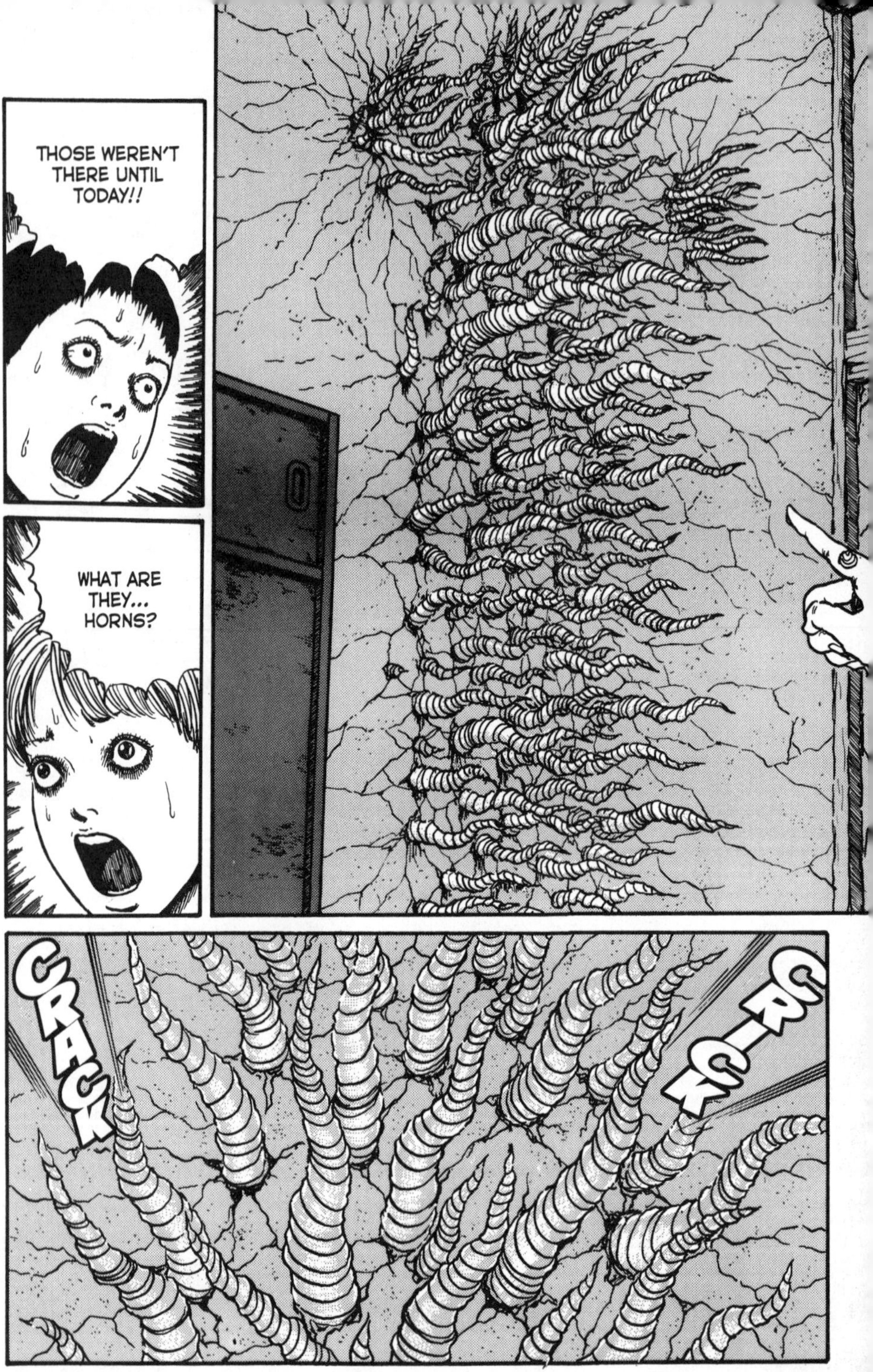
THOSE WEREN'T THERE UNTIL TODAY!!
WHAT ARE THEY... HORNS?
CRACK
CRACK

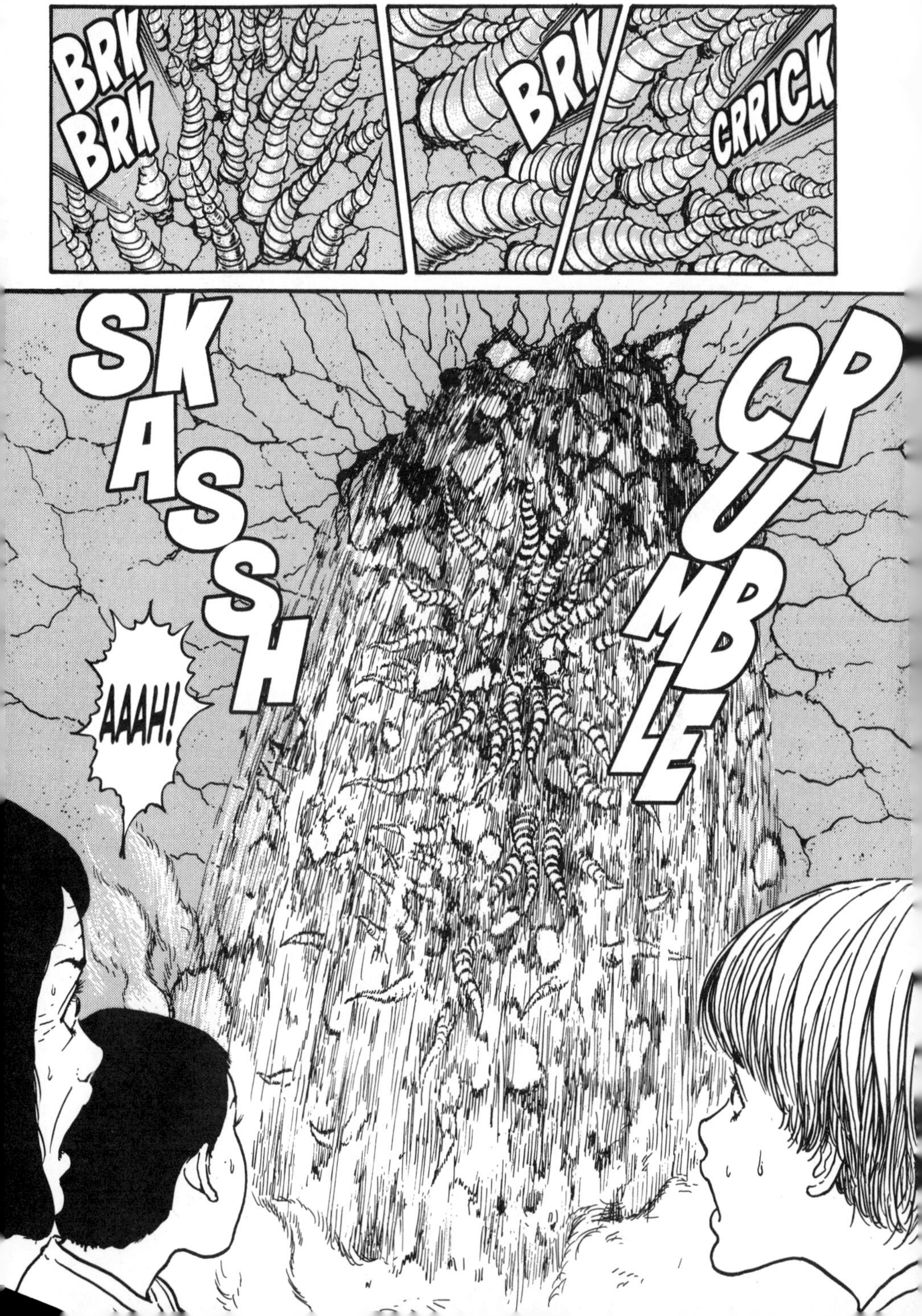
CRRICK
BRK
BRK BRK
CRUMBLE
SKASSH
AAAH!

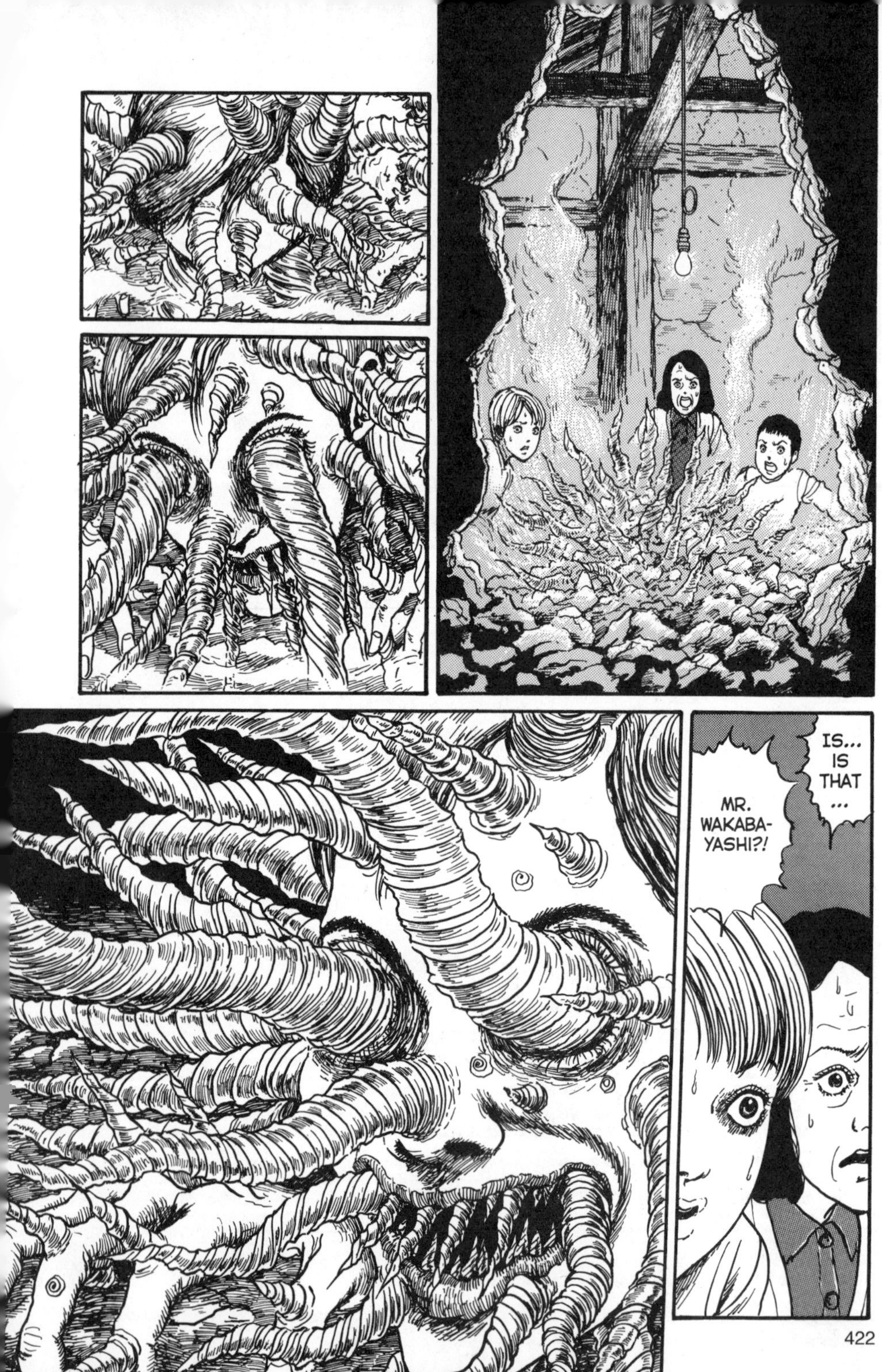
IS... IS THAT ...
MR. WAKABA-YASHI?!

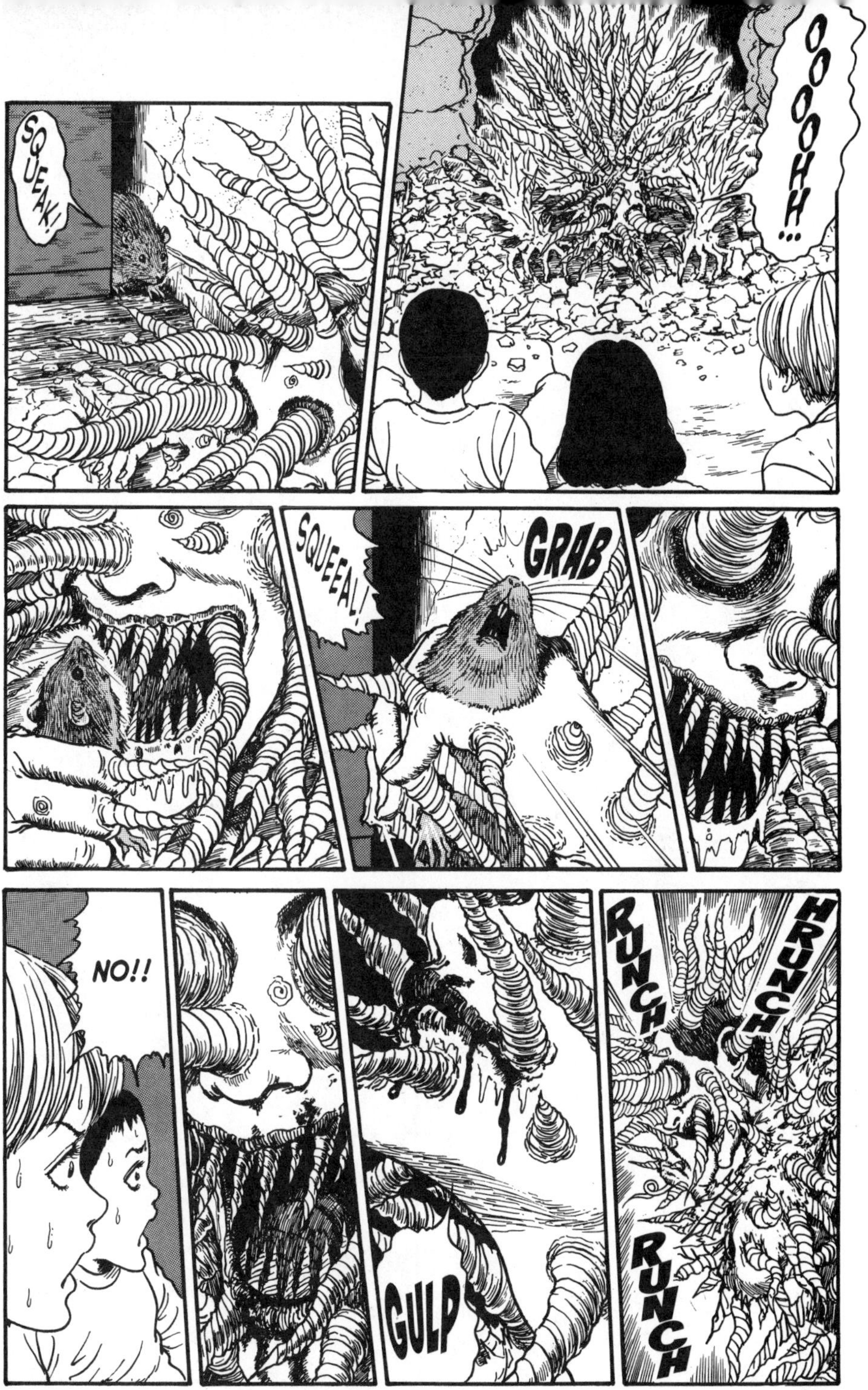
OOOOOHH!!
SQUEAK!
GRAB
SQUEEAL!
HRUNCH
RUNCH
RUNCH
GULP
NO!!

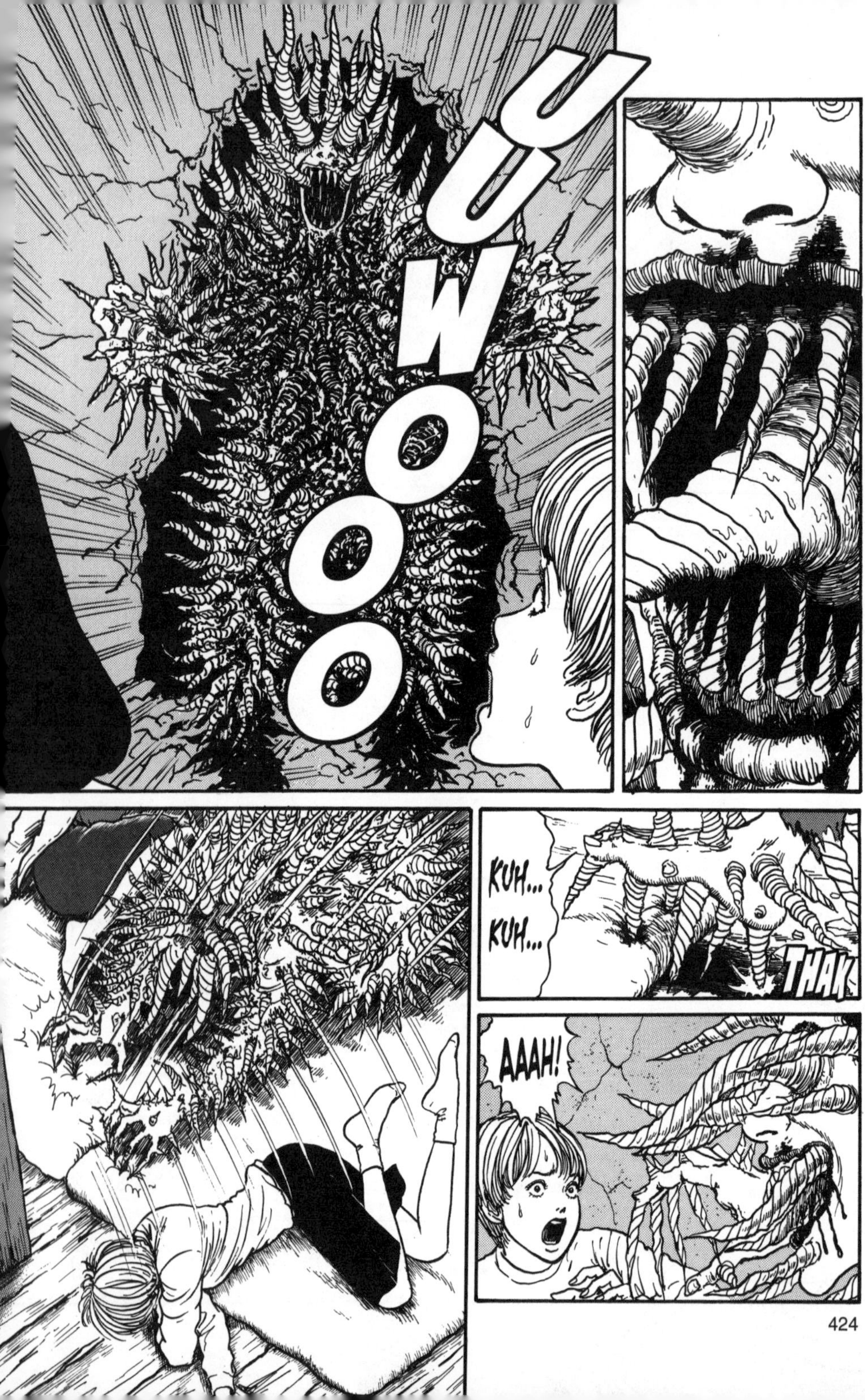
UUWOOOO
KUH...
KUH...
THAK
AAAH!

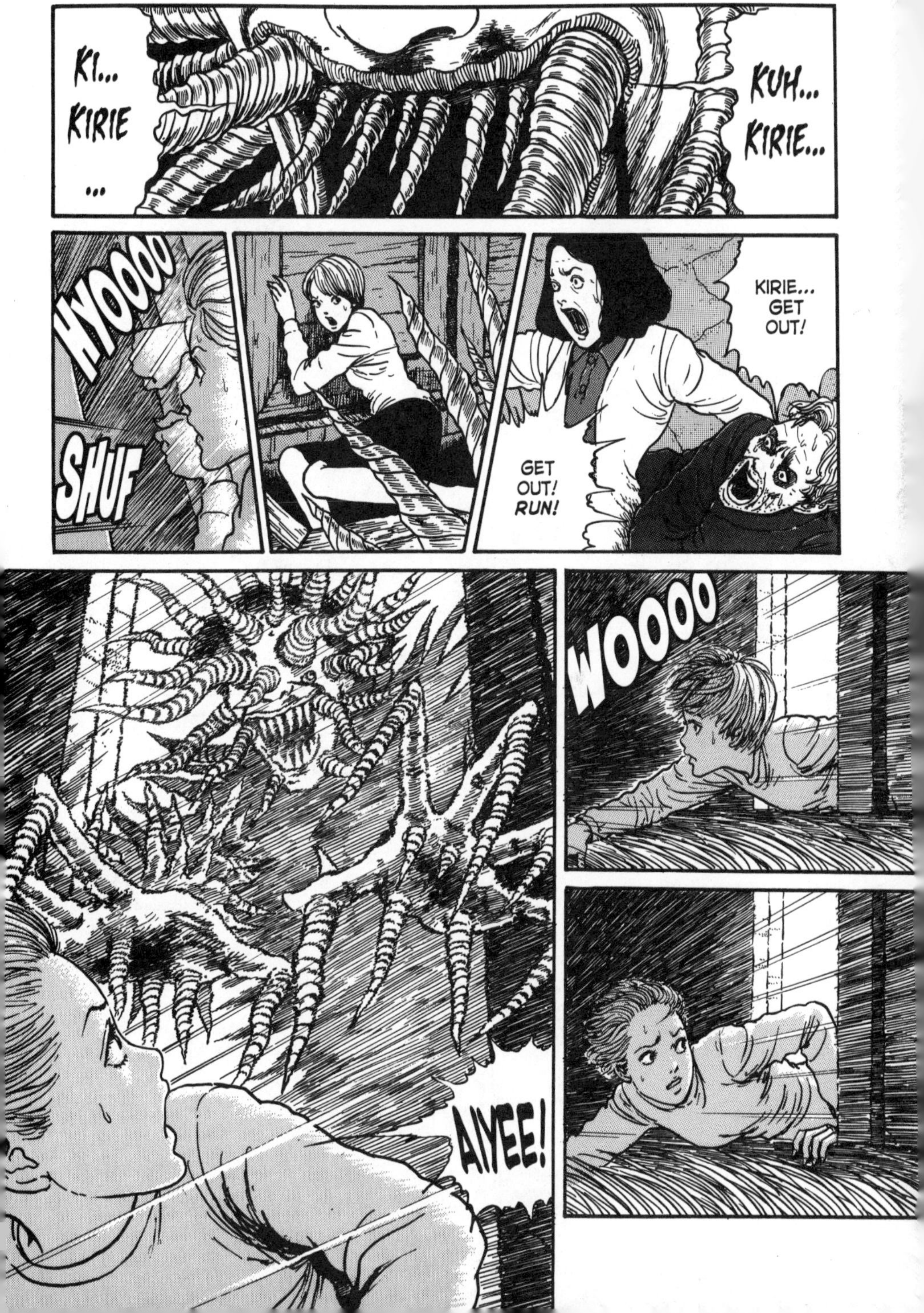
KUH... KIRIE...
KI... KIRIE ...
KIRIE... GET OUT!
GET OUT! RUN!
HYOOOO
SHUF
WOOOO
AIYEE!

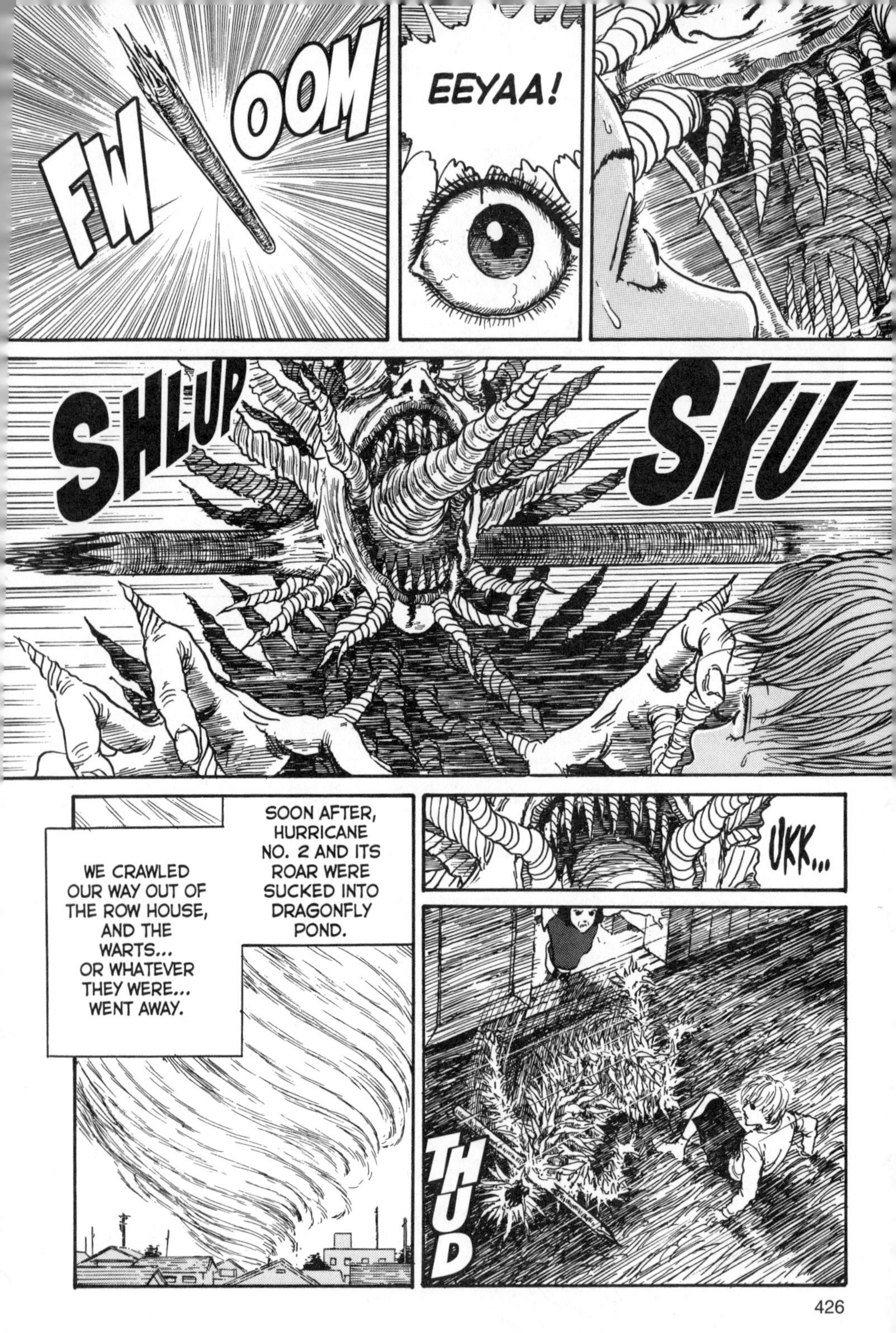
EEYAA!
FWOOM
SKU
SHLUP
UKK...
THUD
SOON AFTER, HURRICANE NO. 2 AND ITS ROAR WERE SUCKED INTO DRAGONFLY POND.
WE CRAWLED OUR WAY OUT OF THE ROW HOUSE, AND THE WARTS... OR WHATEVER THEY WERE... WENT AWAY.

CHAPTER 14
BUTTERFLIES

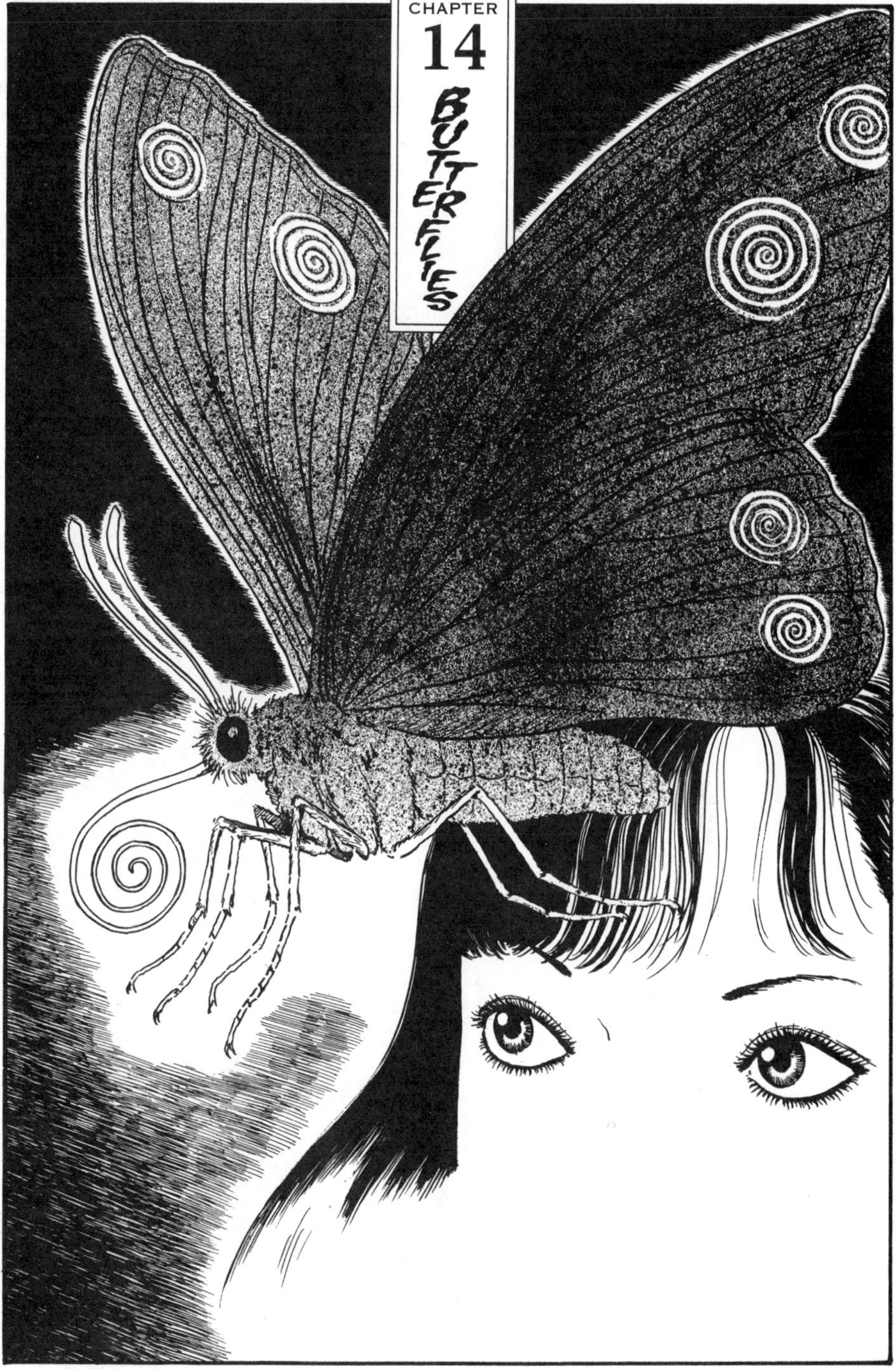

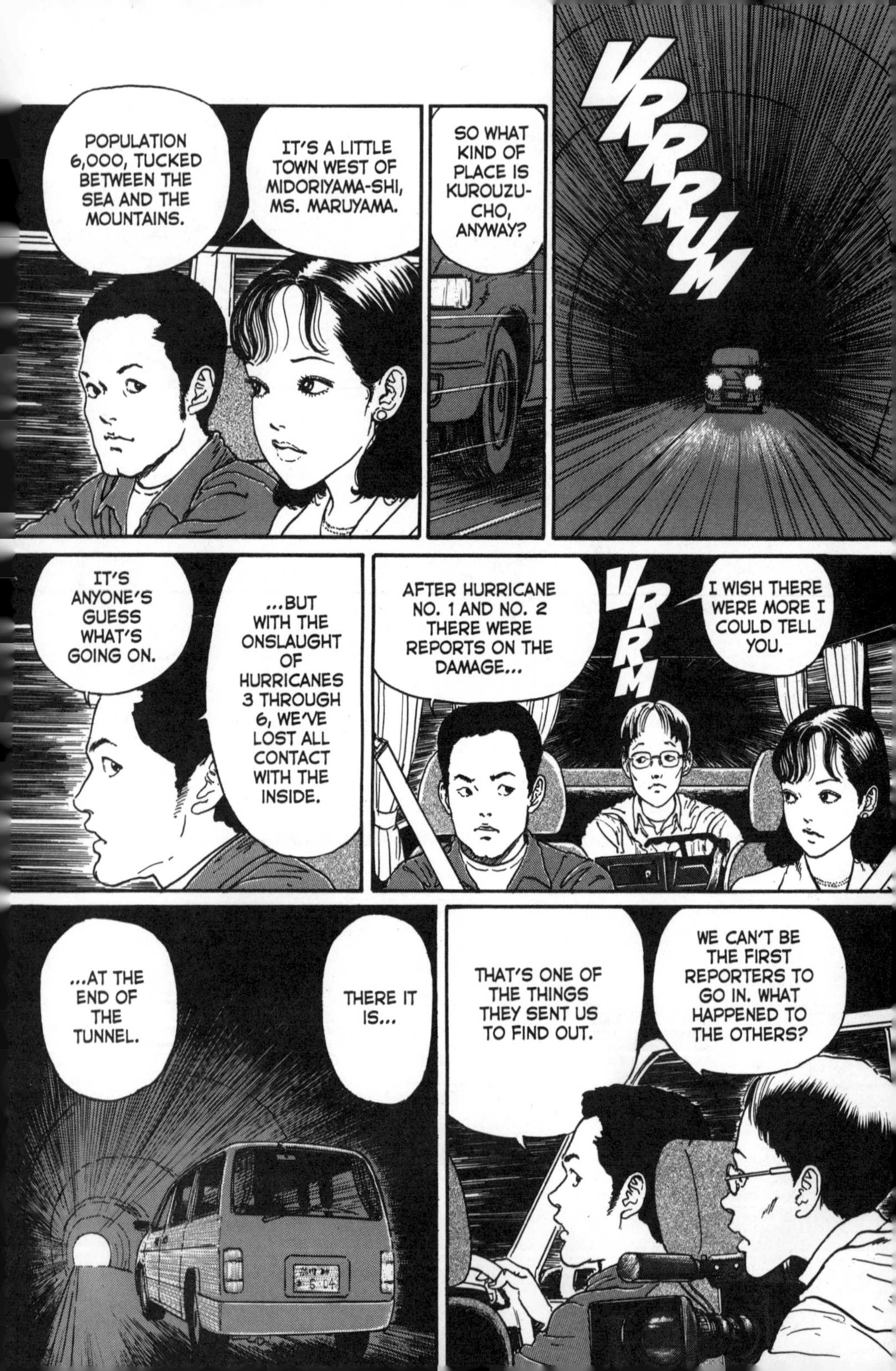
VRRRUM
SO WHAT KIND OF PLACE IS KUROUZU-CHO, ANYWAY?
IT'S A LITTLE TOWN WEST OF MIDORIYAMA-SHI, MS. MARUYAMA.
POPULATION 6,000, TUCKED BETWEEN THE SEA AND THE MOUNTAINS.
I WISH THERE WERE MORE I COULD TELL YOU.
VRRM
AFTER HURRICANE NO. 1 AND NO. 2 THERE WERE REPORTS ON THE DAMAGE...
...BUT WITH THE ONSLAUGHT OF HURRICANES 3 THROUGH 6, WE'VE LOST ALL CONTACT WITH THE INSIDE.
IT'S ANYONE'S GUESS WHAT'S GOING ON.
WE CAN'T BE THE FIRST REPORTERS TO GO IN. WHAT HAPPENED TO THE OTHERS?
THAT'S ONE OF THE THINGS THEY SENT US TO FIND OUT.
THERE IT IS...
...AT THE END OF THE TUNNEL.

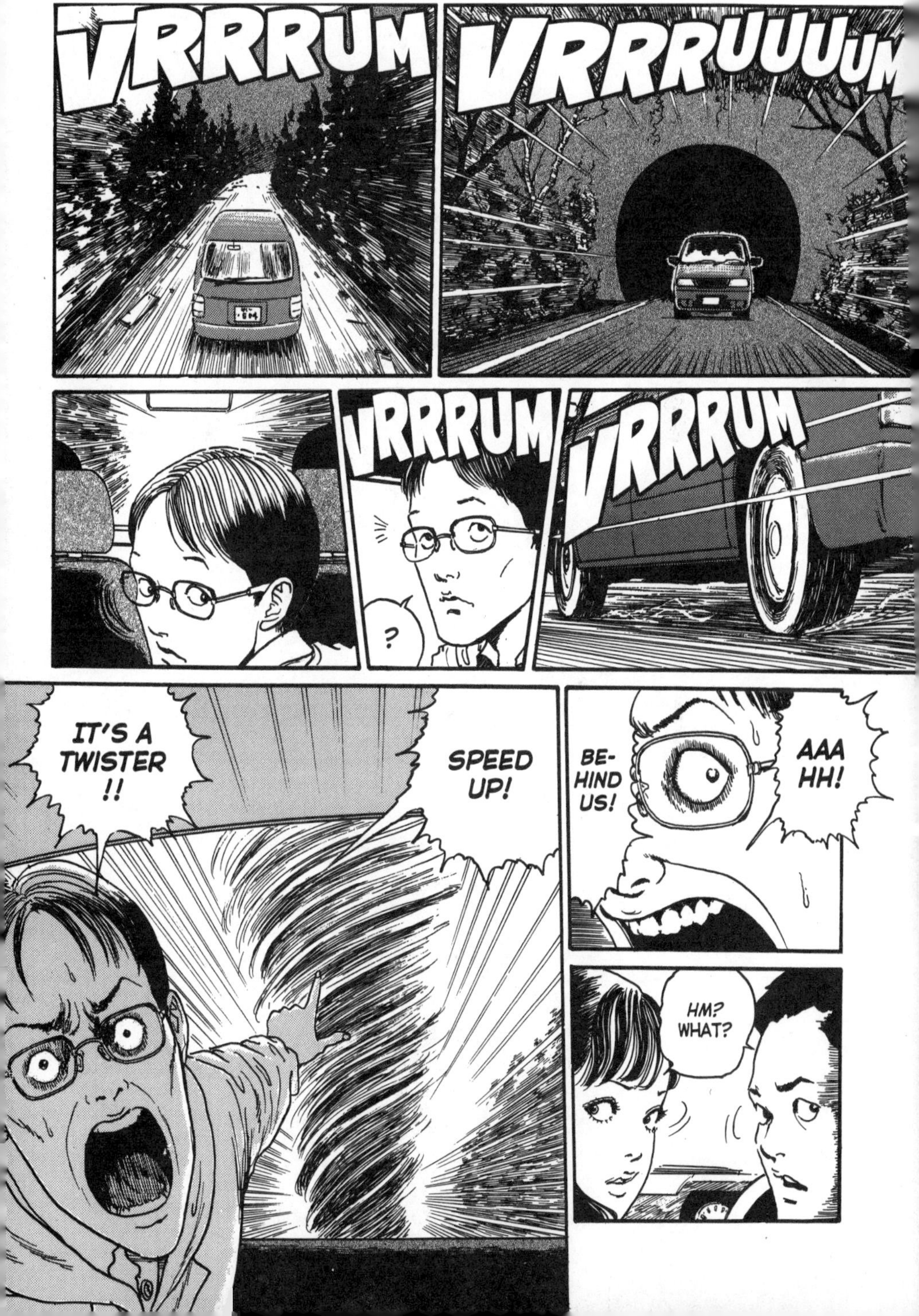
VRRRUUUUUM
VRRRUM
VRRRUM
VRRRUM
?
AAA HH!
BE-HIND US!
HM? WHAT?
SPEED UP!
IT'S A TWISTER !!

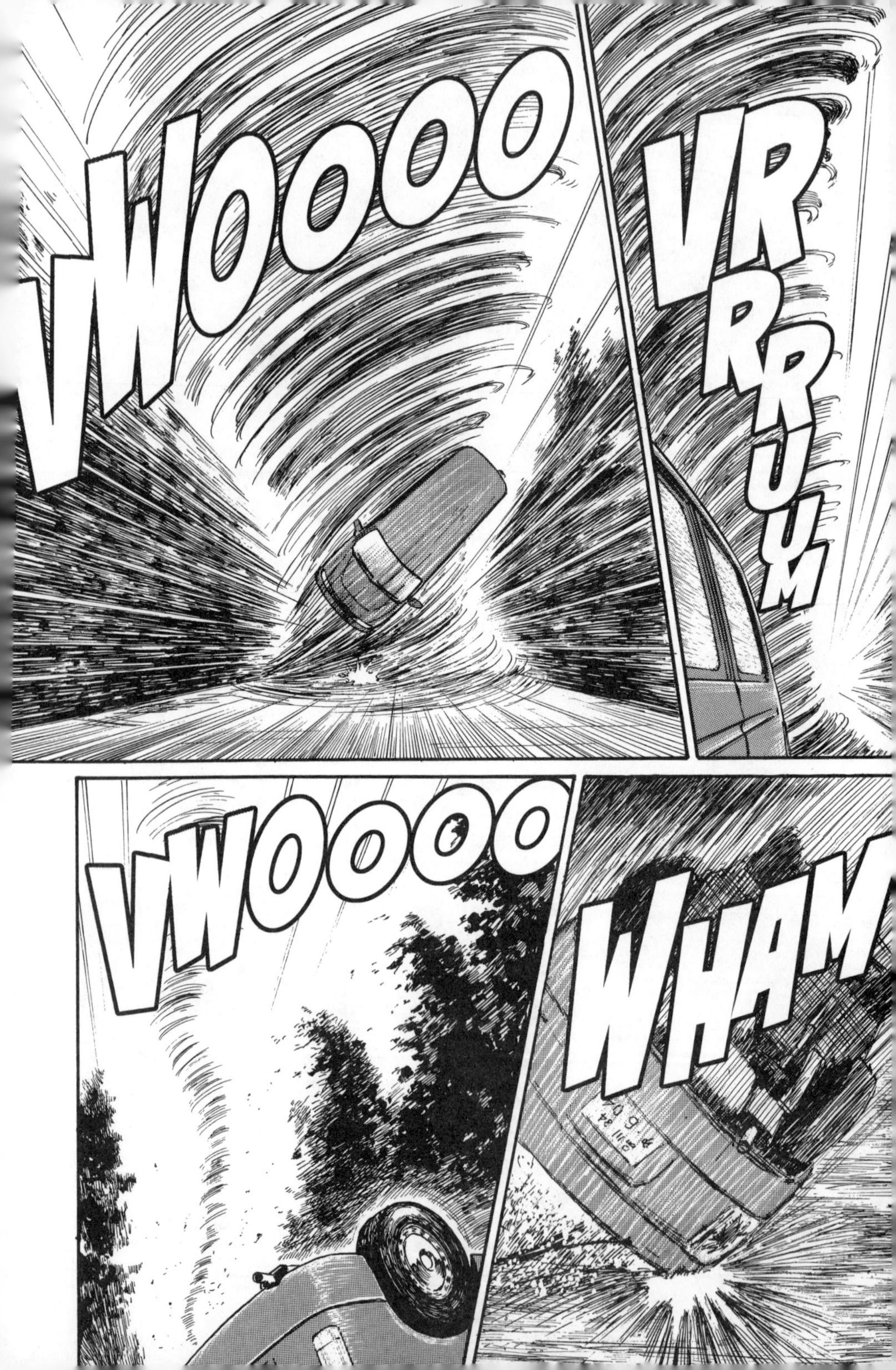
VRRRUM
VWOOOOO
WHAM
VWOOOOO

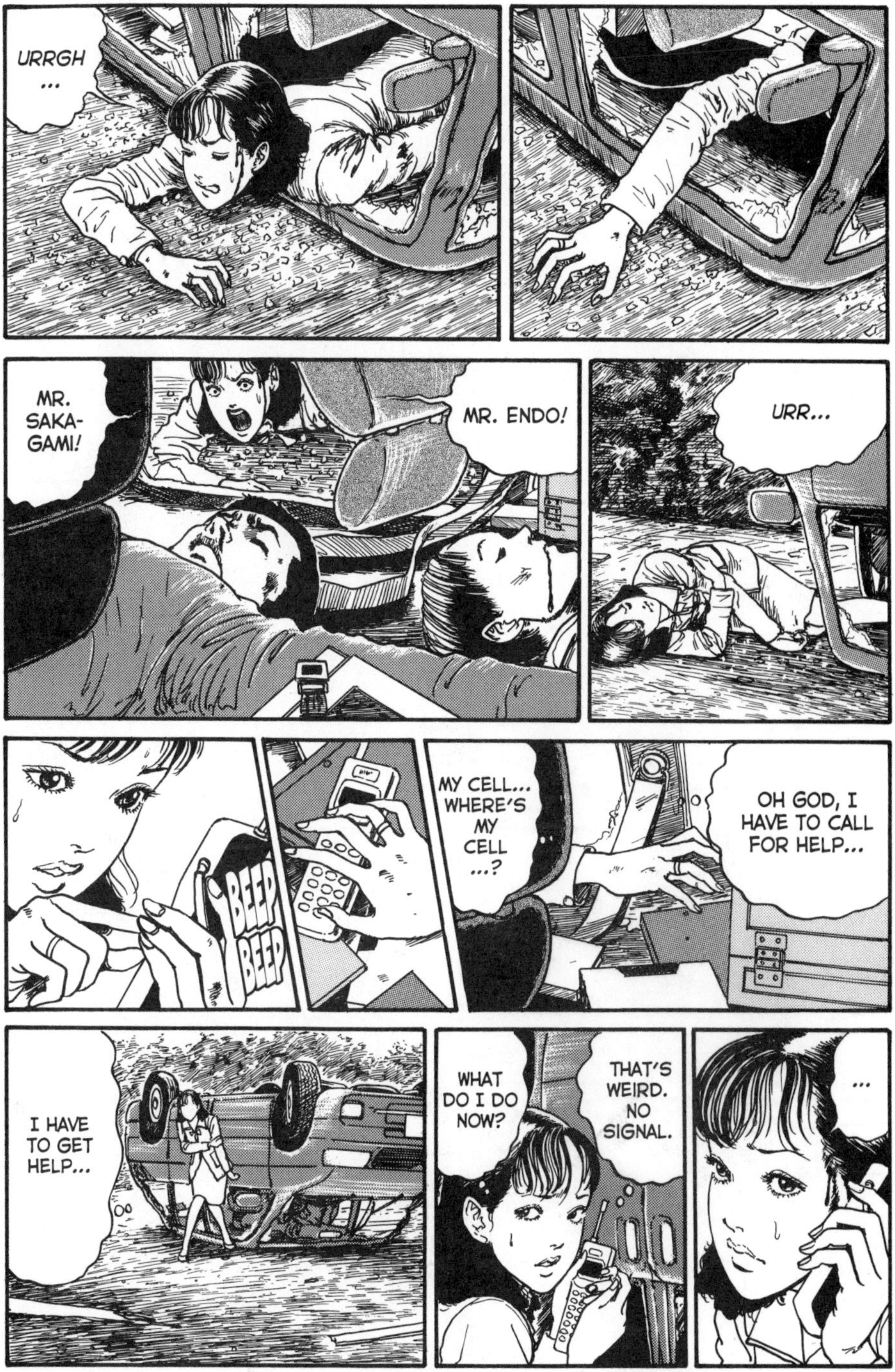
URRGH ...
URR...
MR. ENDO!
MR. SAKA-GAMI!
OH GOD, I HAVE TO CALL FOR HELP...
MY CELL... WHERE'S MY CELL ...?
BEEP BEEP
...
THAT'S WEIRD. NO SIGNAL.
WHAT DO I DO NOW?
I HAVE TO GET HELP...

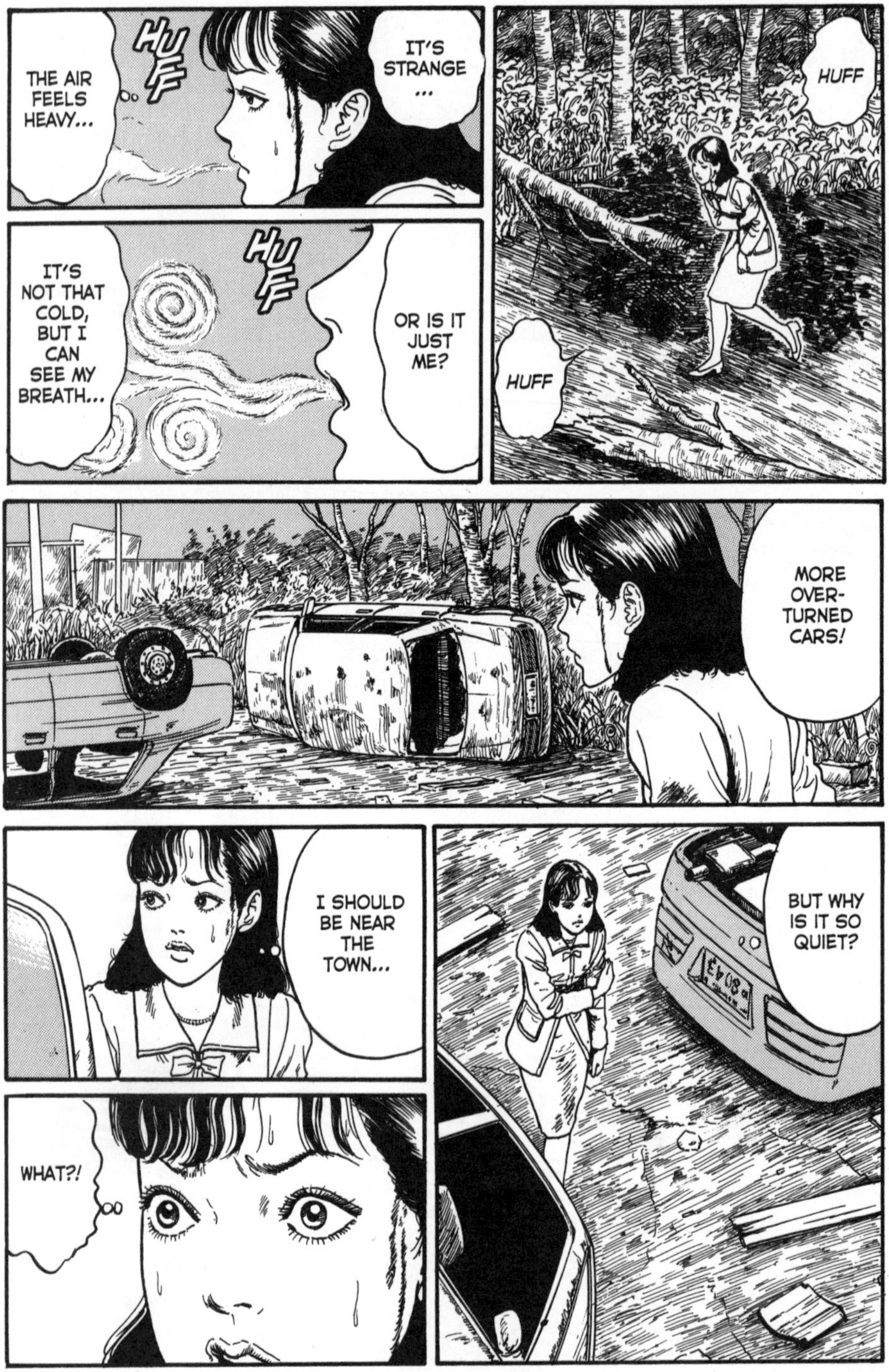
HUFF
HUFF
IT'S STRANGE ...
HUFF
THE AIR FEELS HEAVY...
OR IS IT JUST ME?
HUFF
IT'S NOT THAT COLD, BUT I CAN SEE MY BREATH...
MORE OVER-TURNED CARS!
BUT WHY IS IT SO QUIET?
I SHOULD BE NEAR THE TOWN...
WHAT?!

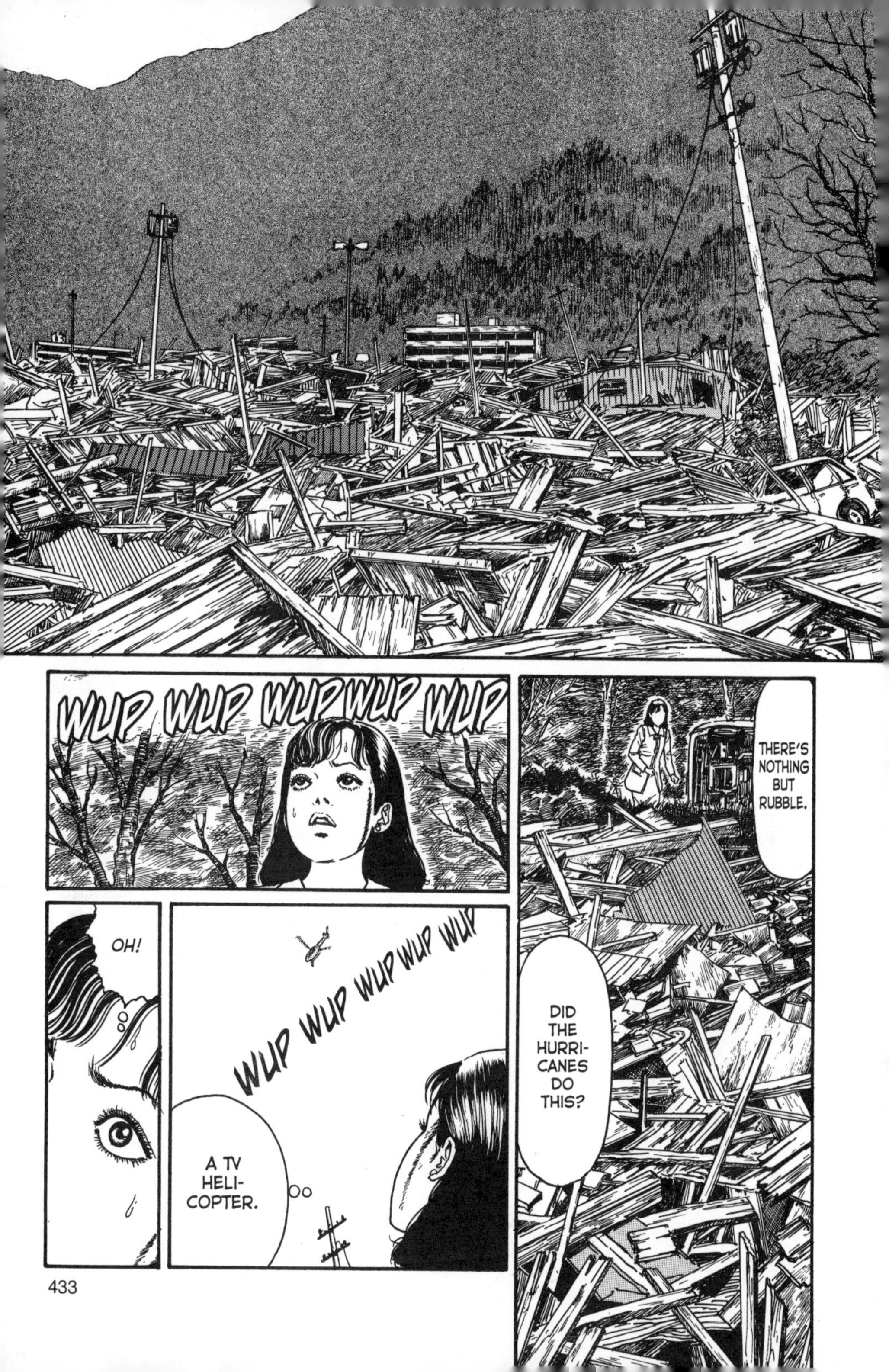
THERE'S NOTHING BUT RUBBLE.
DID THE HURRICANES DO THIS?
WUP WUP WUP WUP WUP
WUP WUP WUP WUP WUP
A TV HELICOPTER.
OH!

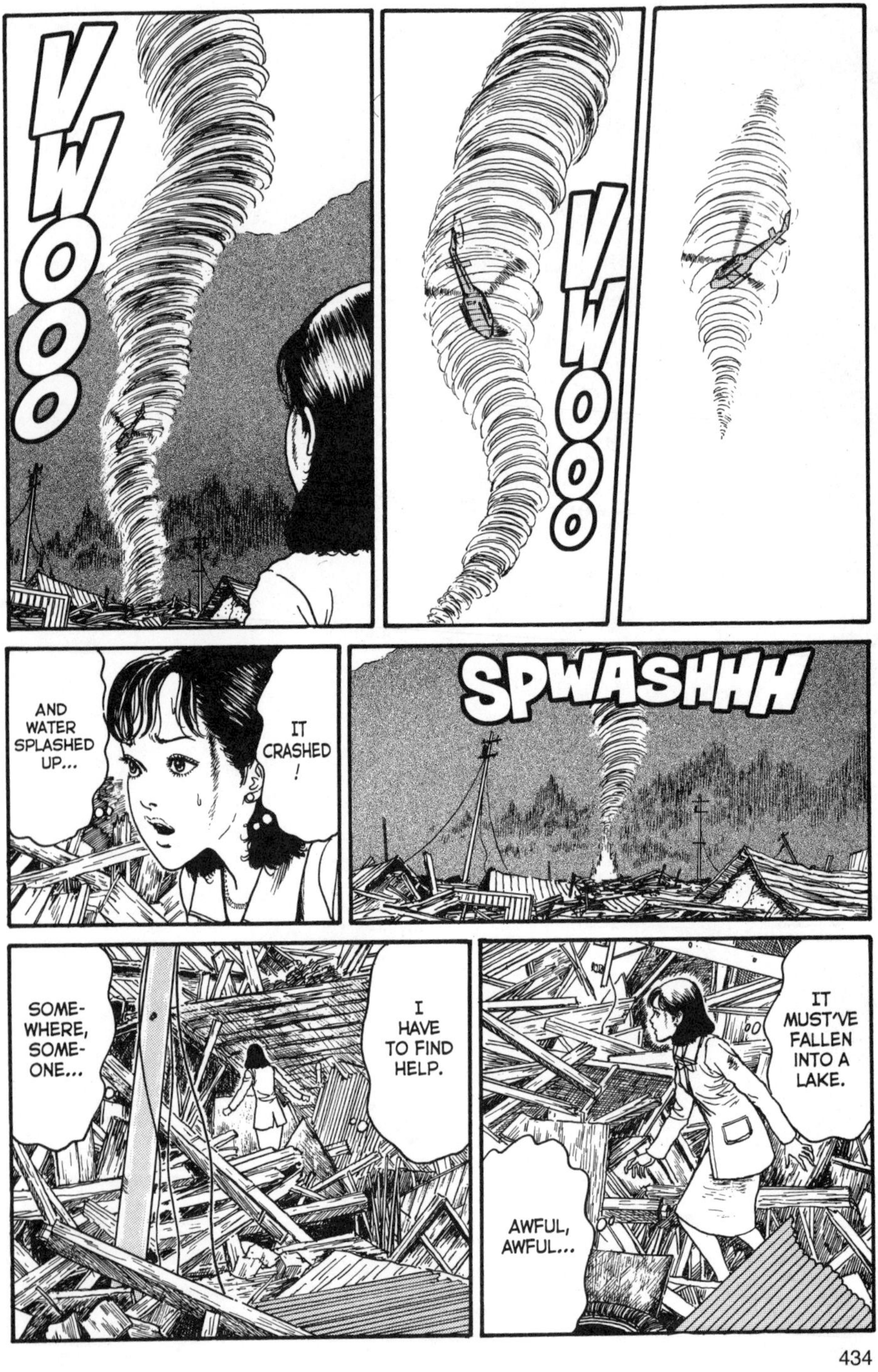
VWOOO
VWOOOO
SPWASHHH
IT CRASHED!
AND WATER SPLASHED UP...
IT MUST'VE FALLEN INTO A LAKE.
AWFUL, AWFUL...
I HAVE TO FIND HELP.
SOME-WHERE, SOME-ONE...

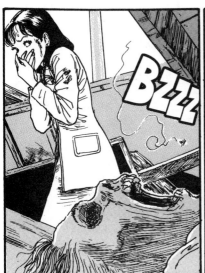

AAHH!
BZZZ
THIS IS HORRIBLE. THE RUINS ARE FULL OF CORPSES...
IS ANYONE LEFT ALIVE?
RMBRMBRMBRMB
WHAT'S THAT?
IT'S COMING FROM WHERE THE COPTER ...
RMB RMB
STP
RMB RMB

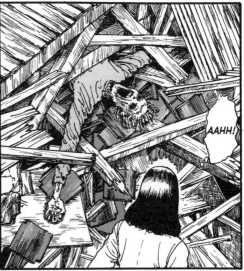

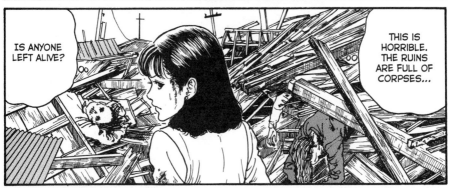

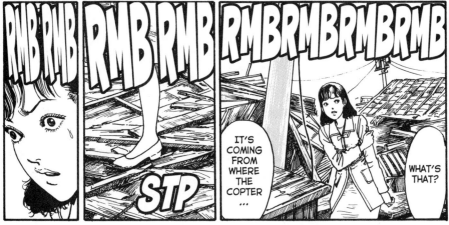

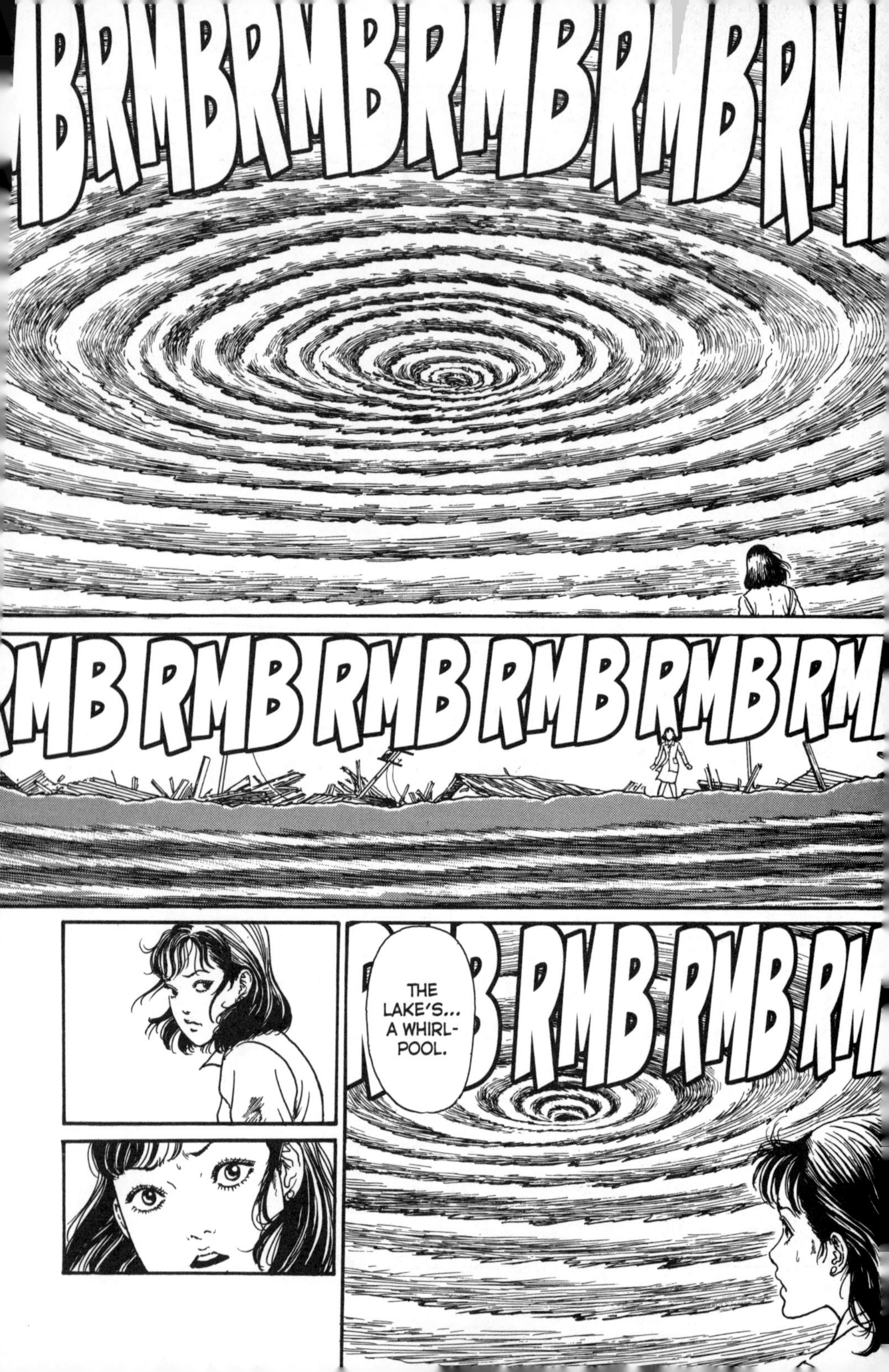
BRMBRMBRMBRMBRMBRMBRM
RMB RMB RMB RMB RMB RM
THE LAKE'S... A WHIRLPOOL.
RMB RMB RM

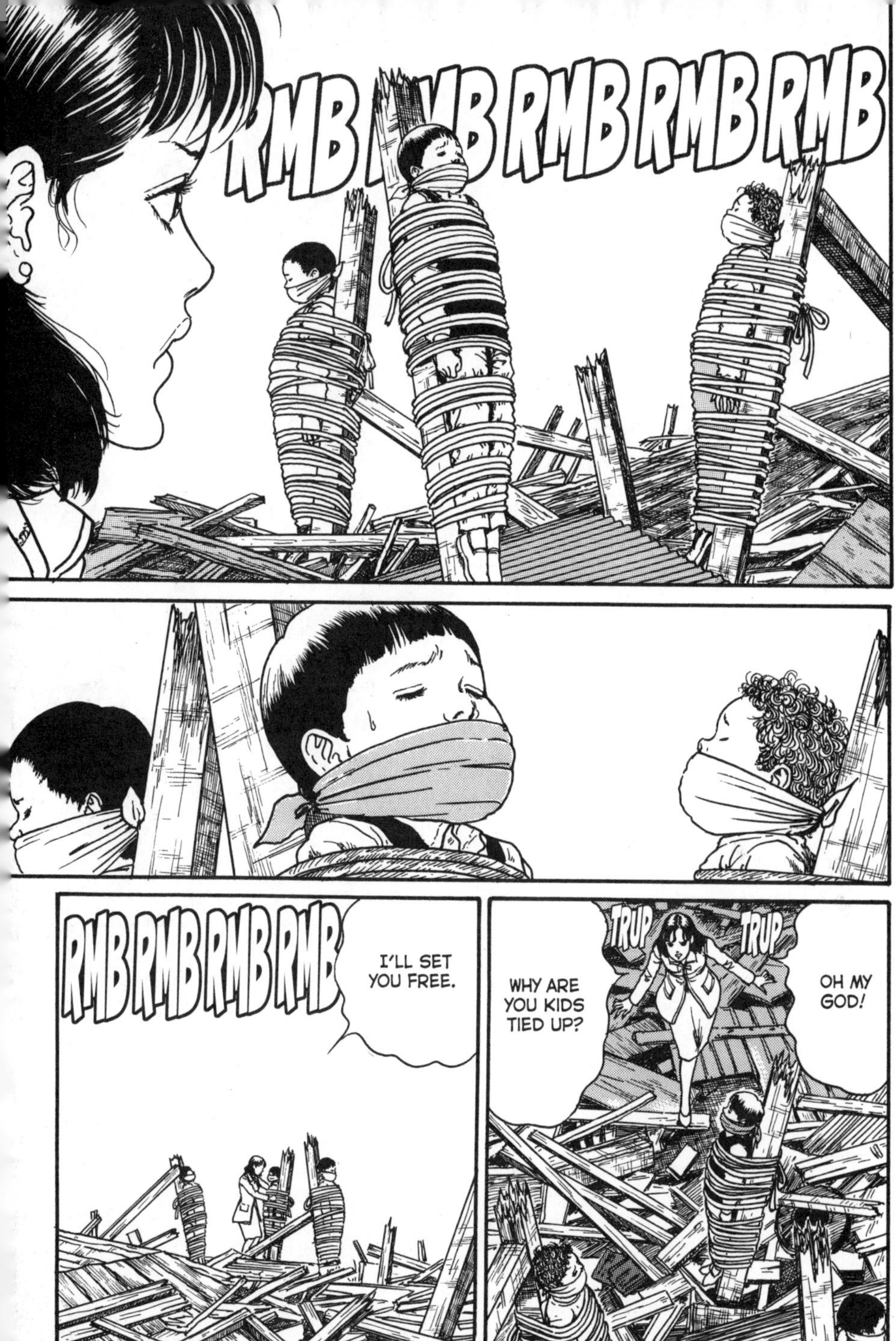
RMB RMB RMB RMB RMB
OH MY GOD!
TRUP TRUP
WHY ARE YOU KIDS TIED UP?
I'LL SET YOU FREE.
RMB RMB RMB RMB

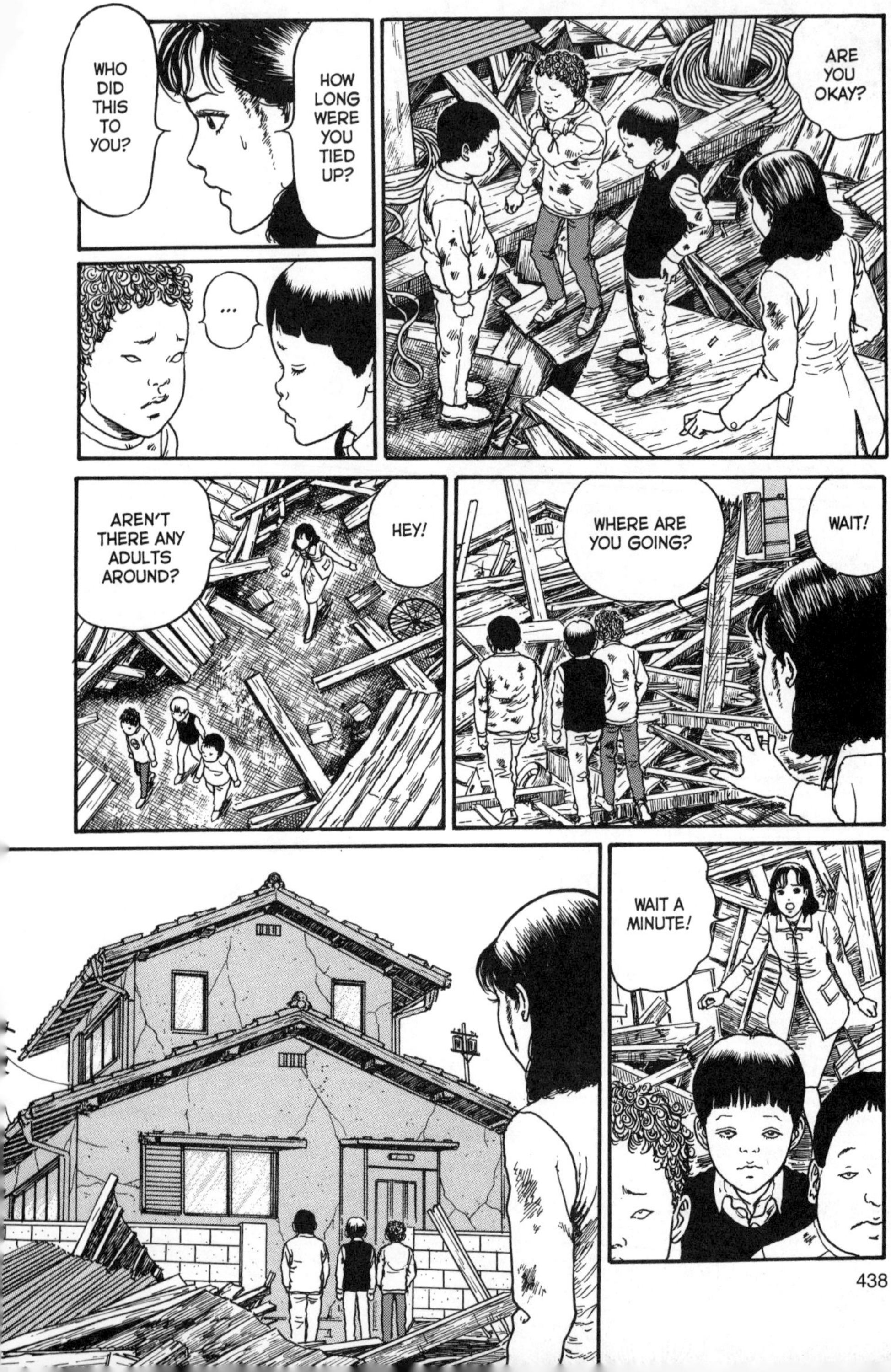
ARE YOU OKAY?
HOW LONG WERE YOU TIED UP?
WHO DID THIS TO YOU?
...
WAIT!
WHERE ARE YOU GOING?
HEY!
AREN'T THERE ANY ADULTS AROUND?
WAIT A MINUTE!

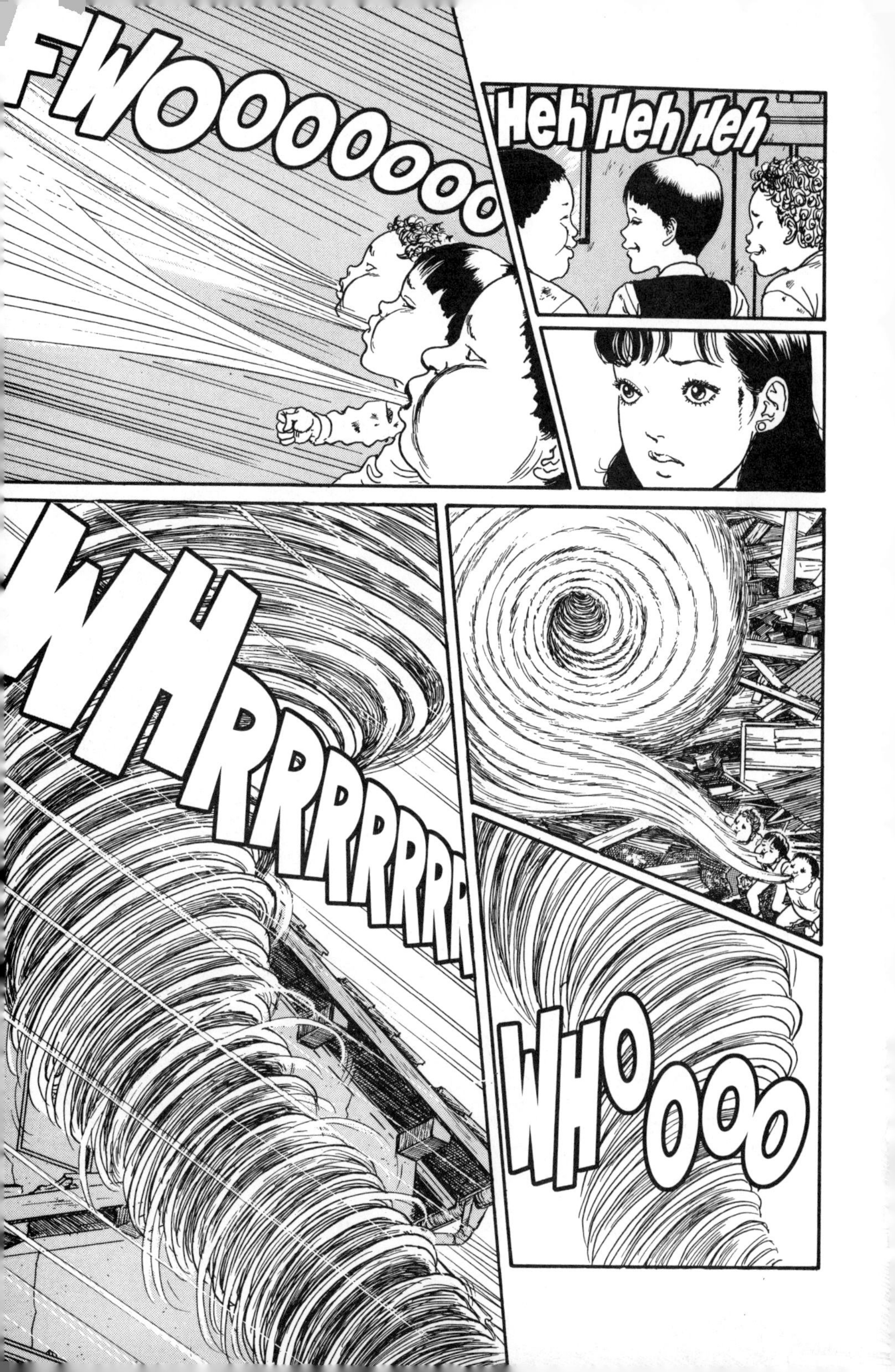
Heh Heh Heh
FWOOOOOOO
WHOOOO
WHRRRRRRRRR

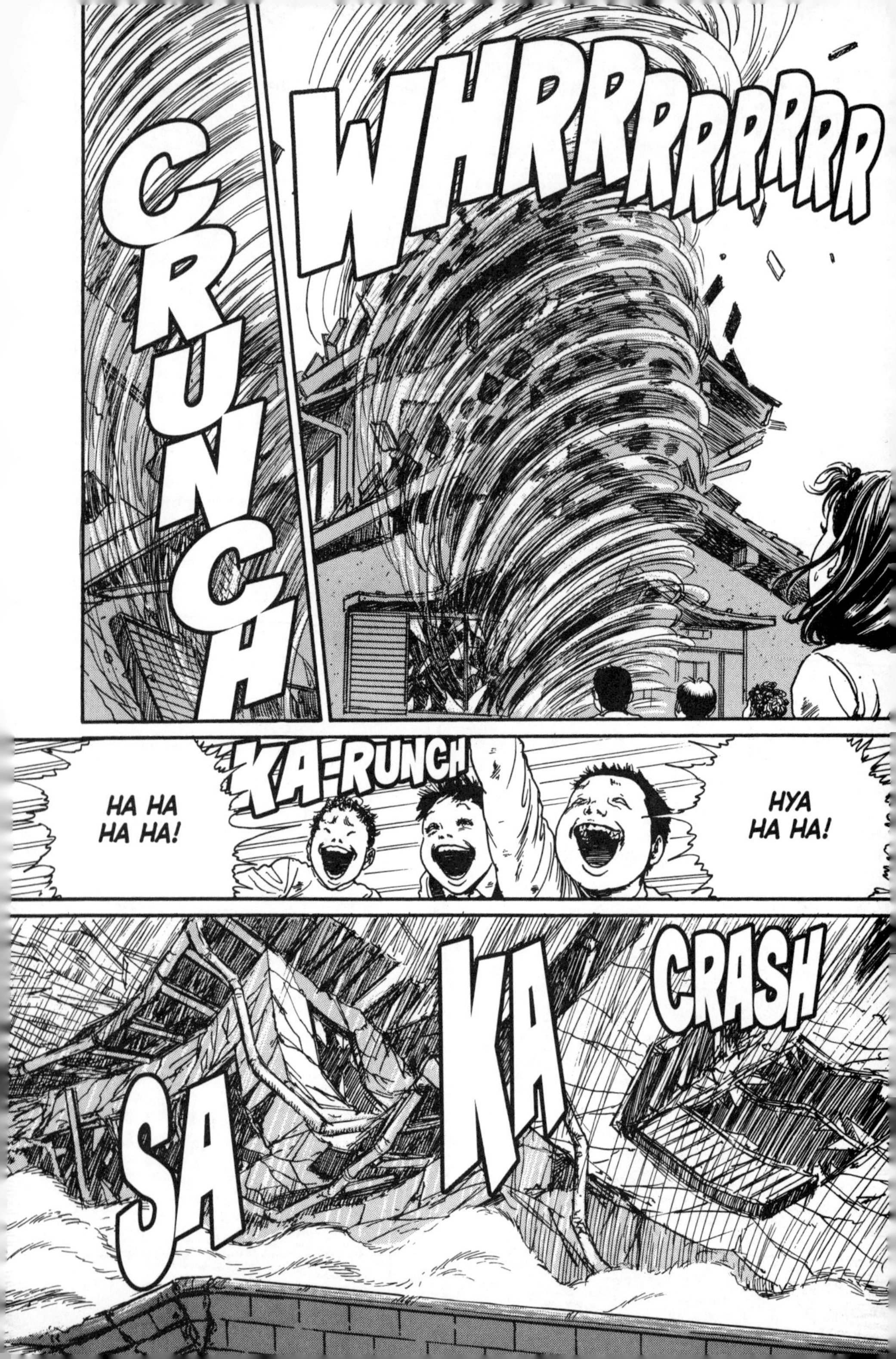
WHRRRRRRRR
CRUNCH
HYA HA HA!
KA-RUNCH
HA HA HA HA!
CRASH
SA KA

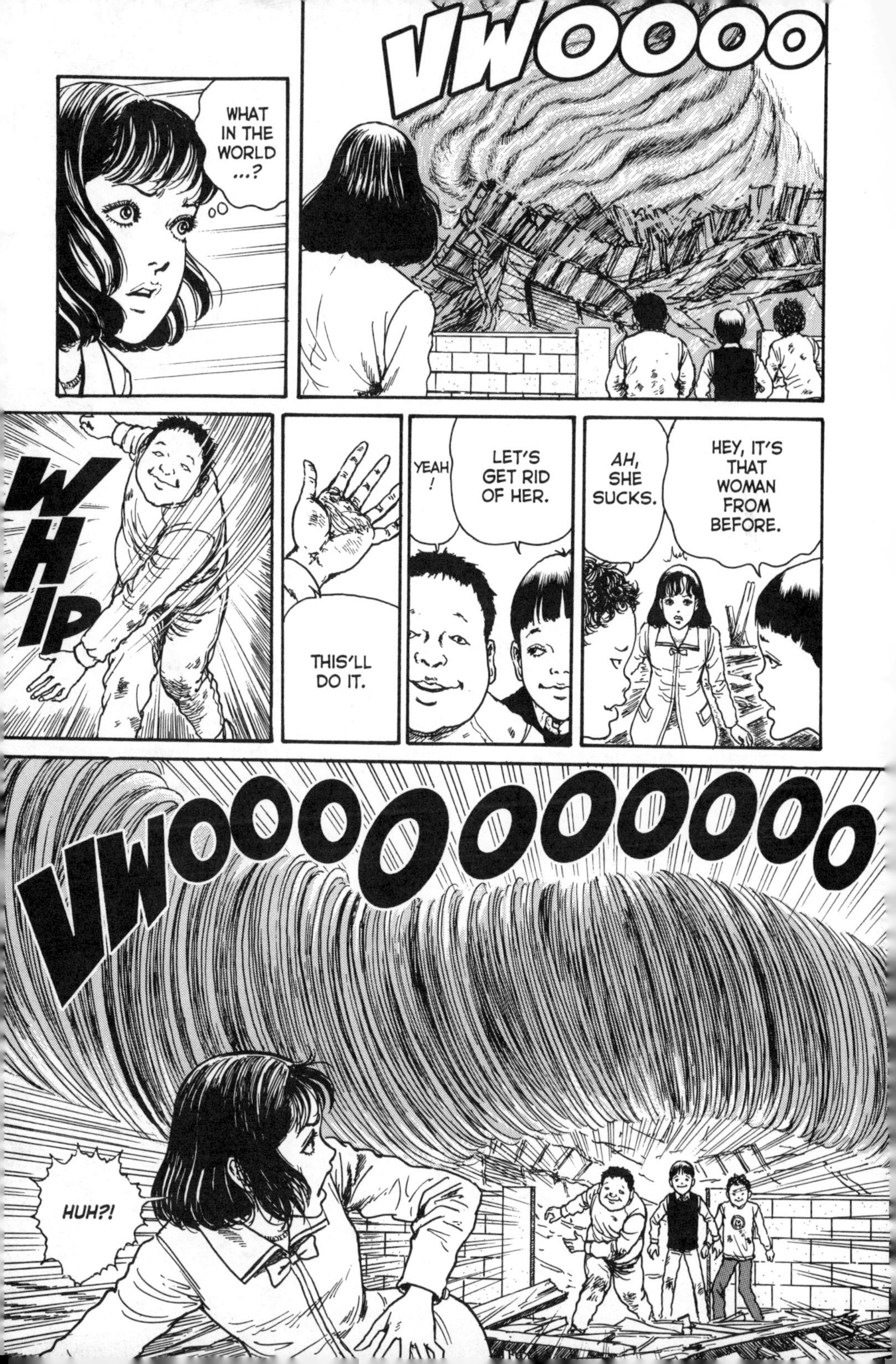
VWOOOO
WHAT IN THE WORLD ...?
HEY, IT'S THAT WOMAN FROM BEFORE.
AH, SHE SUCKS.
LET'S GET RID OF HER.
YEAH!
THIS'LL DO IT.
WHIP
VWOOOOOOOOO
HUH?!

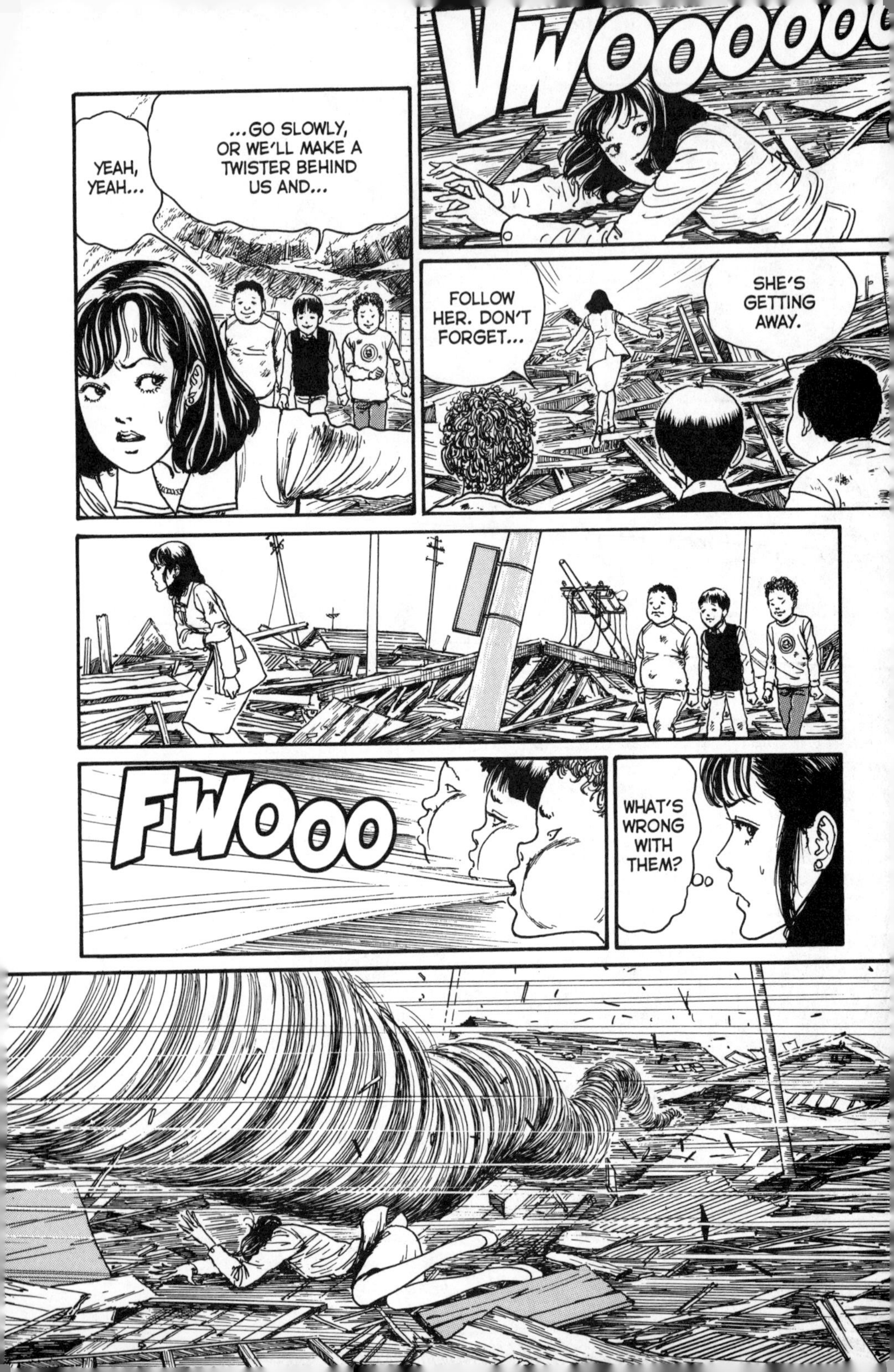
VWOOOOO
SHE'S GETTING AWAY.
FOLLOW HER. DON'T FORGET...
...GO SLOWLY, OR WE'LL MAKE A TWISTER BEHIND US AND...
YEAH, YEAH...
WHAT'S WRONG WITH THEM?
FWOOO

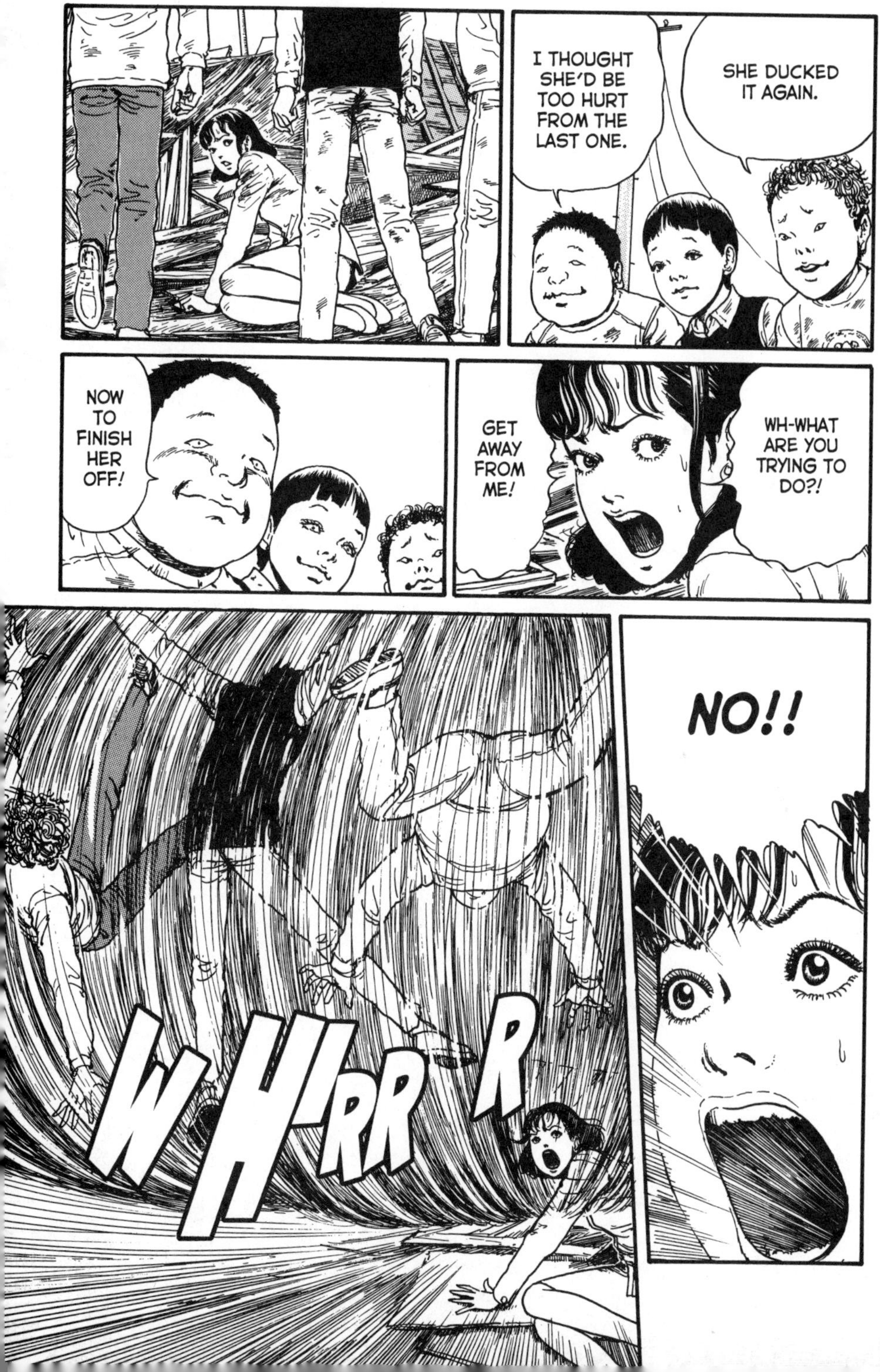
SHE DUCKED IT AGAIN.
I THOUGHT SHE'D BE TOO HURT FROM THE LAST ONE.
WH-WHAT ARE YOU TRYING TO DO?!
GET AWAY FROM ME!
NOW TO FINISH HER OFF!
NO!!
WHRRR

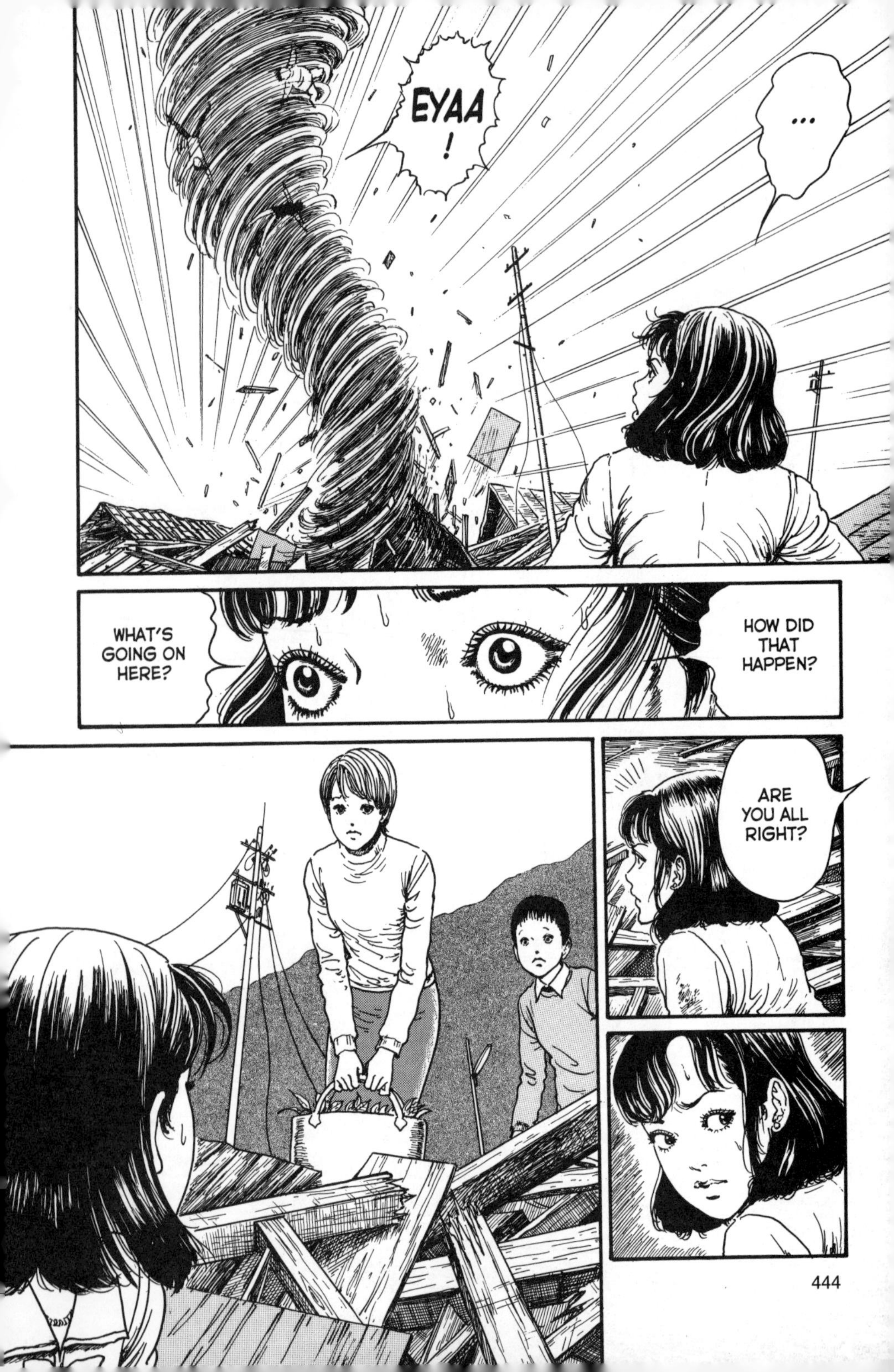
...
EYAA!
HOW DID THAT HAPPEN?
WHAT'S GOING ON HERE?
ARE YOU ALL RIGHT?

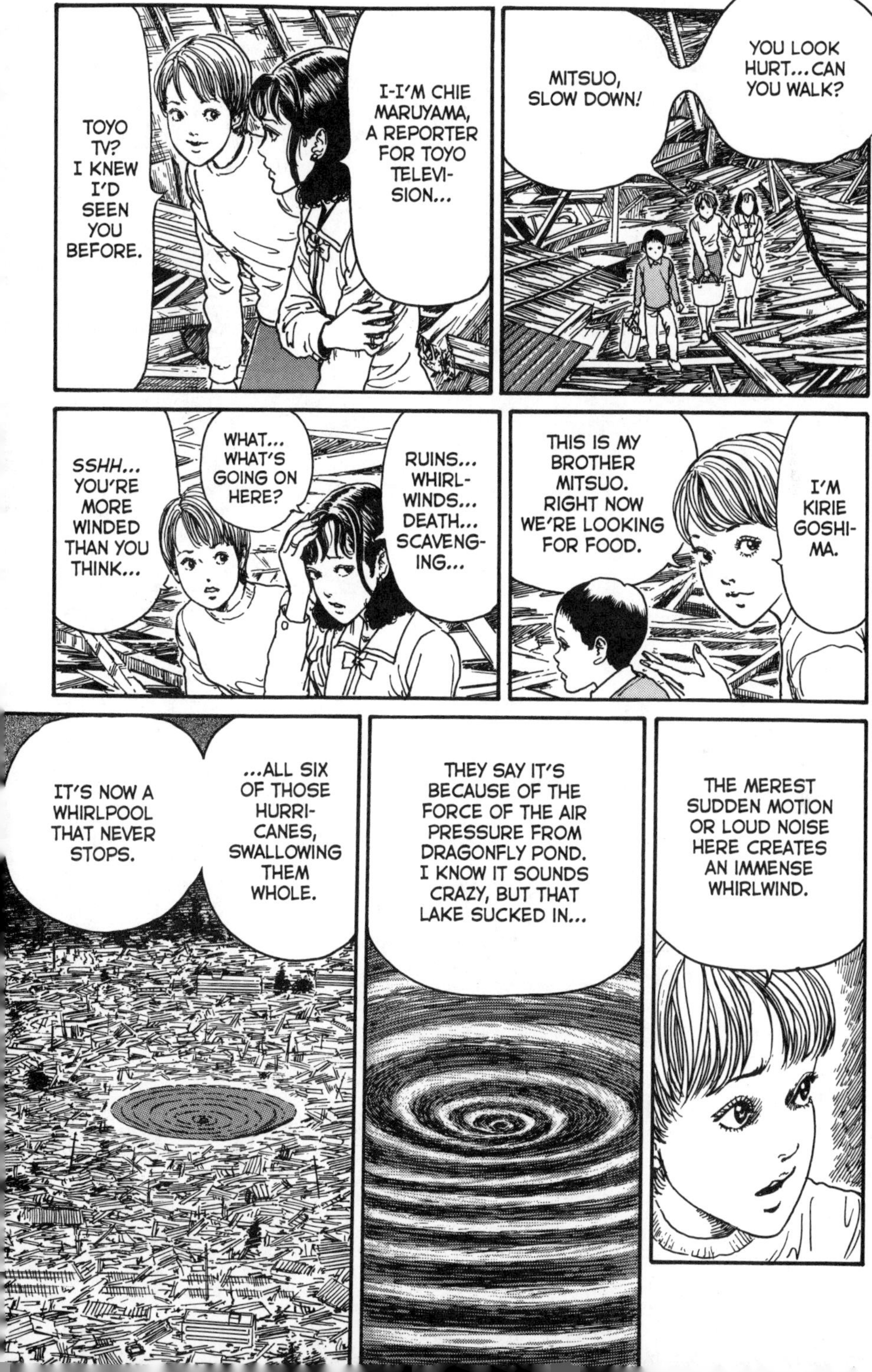
YOU LOOK HURT...CAN YOU WALK?
MITSUO, SLOW DOWN!
I-I'M CHIE MARUYAMA, A REPORTER FOR TOYO TELEVISION...
TOYO TV? I KNEW I'D SEEN YOU BEFORE.
I'M KIRIE GOSHIMA.
THIS IS MY BROTHER MITSUO. RIGHT NOW WE'RE LOOKING FOR FOOD.
RUINS... WHIRLWINDS... DEATH... SCAVENGING...
WHAT... WHAT'S GOING ON HERE?
SSHH... YOU'RE MORE WINDED THAN YOU THINK...
THE MEREST SUDDEN MOTION OR LOUD NOISE HERE CREATES AN IMMENSE WHIRLWIND.
THEY SAY IT'S BECAUSE OF THE FORCE OF THE AIR PRESSURE FROM DRAGONFLY POND. I KNOW IT SOUNDS CRAZY, BUT THAT LAKE SUCKED IN...
...ALL SIX OF THOSE HURRICANES, SWALLOWING THEM WHOLE.
IT'S NOW A WHIRLPOOL THAT NEVER STOPS.

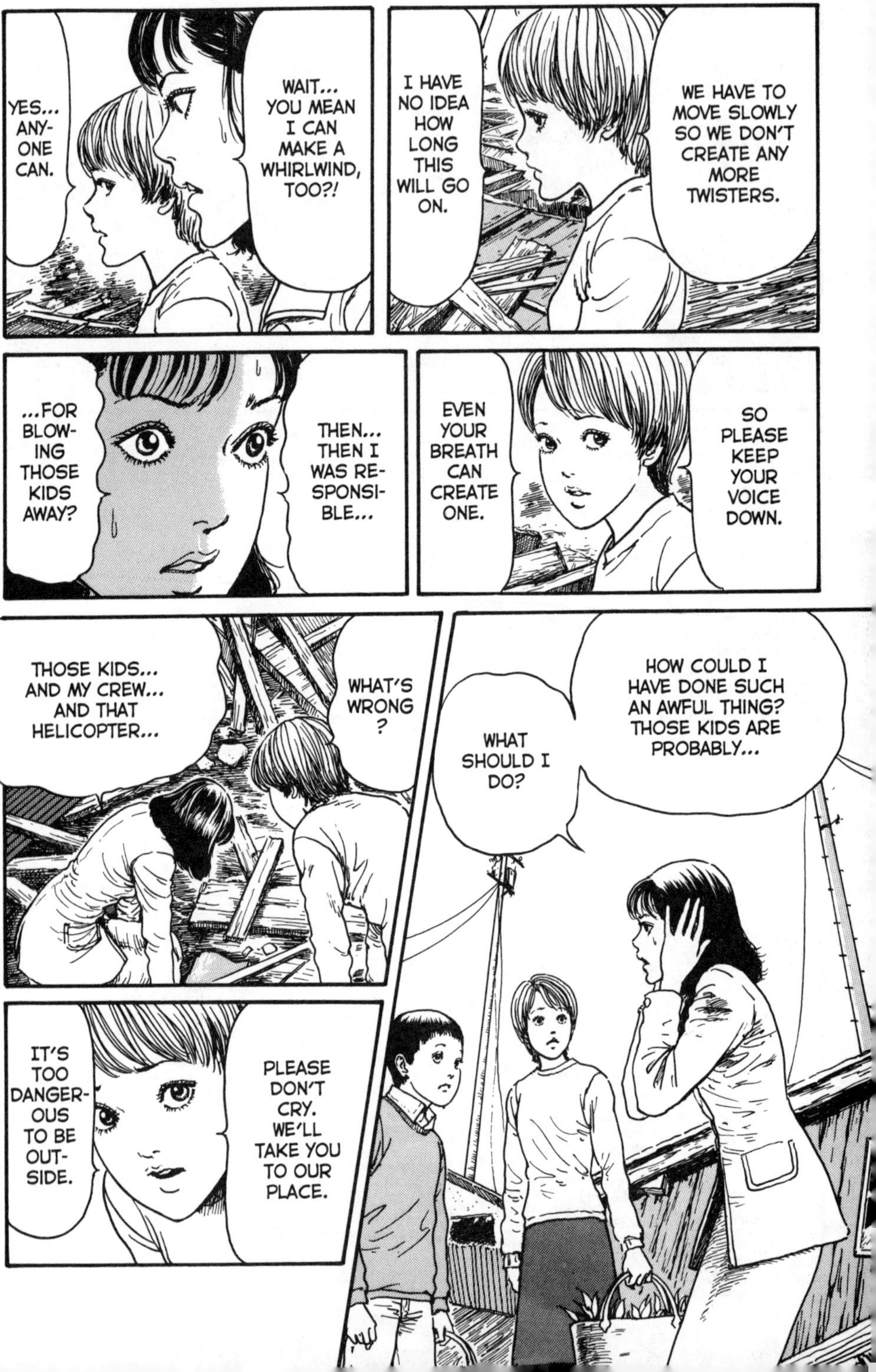
WE HAVE TO MOVE SLOWLY SO WE DON'T CREATE ANY MORE TWISTERS.
I HAVE NO IDEA HOW LONG THIS WILL GO ON.
WAIT... YOU MEAN I CAN MAKE A WHIRLWIND, TOO?!
YES... ANYONE CAN.
SO PLEASE KEEP YOUR VOICE DOWN.
EVEN YOUR BREATH CAN CREATE ONE.
THEN... THEN I WAS RESPONSIBLE...
...FOR BLOWING THOSE KIDS AWAY?
HOW COULD I HAVE DONE SUCH AN AWFUL THING? THOSE KIDS ARE PROBABLY...
WHAT SHOULD I DO?
WHAT'S WRONG?
THOSE KIDS... AND MY CREW... AND THAT HELICOPTER...
PLEASE DON'T CRY. WE'LL TAKE YOU TO OUR PLACE.
IT'S TOO DANGEROUS TO BE OUTSIDE.

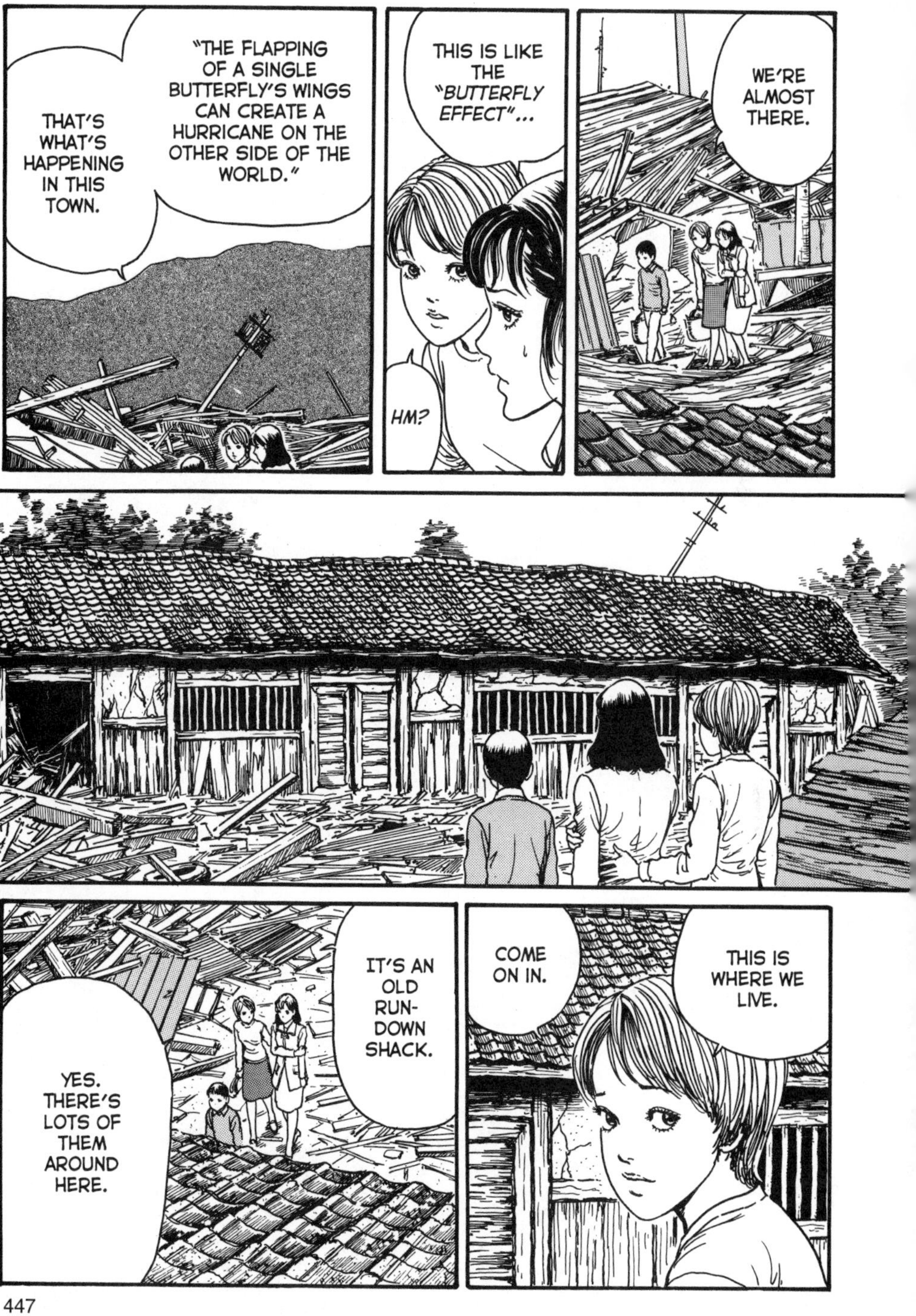
WE'RE ALMOST THERE.
THIS IS LIKE THE "BUTTERFLY EFFECT"...
HM?
"THE FLAPPING OF A SINGLE BUTTERFLY'S WINGS CAN CREATE A HURRICANE ON THE OTHER SIDE OF THE WORLD."
THAT'S WHAT'S HAPPENING IN THIS TOWN.
THIS IS WHERE WE LIVE.
COME ON IN.
IT'S AN OLD RUN-DOWN SHACK.
YES. THERE'S LOTS OF THEM AROUND HERE.

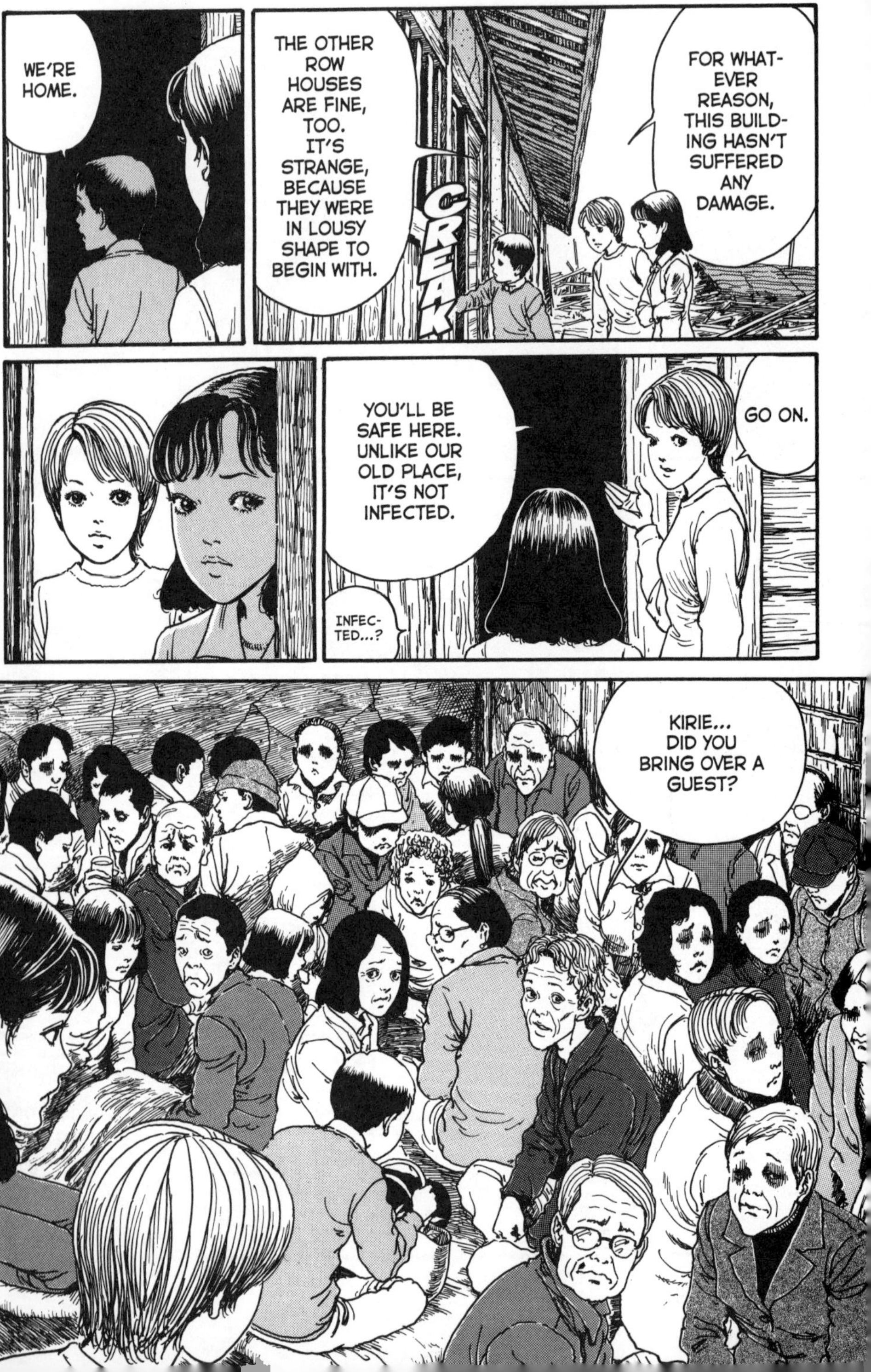
FOR WHAT-EVER REASON, THIS BUILD-ING HASN'T SUFFERED ANY DAMAGE.
THE OTHER ROW HOUSES ARE FINE, TOO. IT'S STRANGE, BECAUSE THEY WERE IN LOUSY SHAPE TO BEGIN WITH.
CREAK
WE'RE HOME.
GO ON.
YOU'LL BE SAFE HERE. UNLIKE OUR OLD PLACE, IT'S NOT INFECTED.
INFEC-TED...?
KIRIE... DID YOU BRING OVER A GUEST?

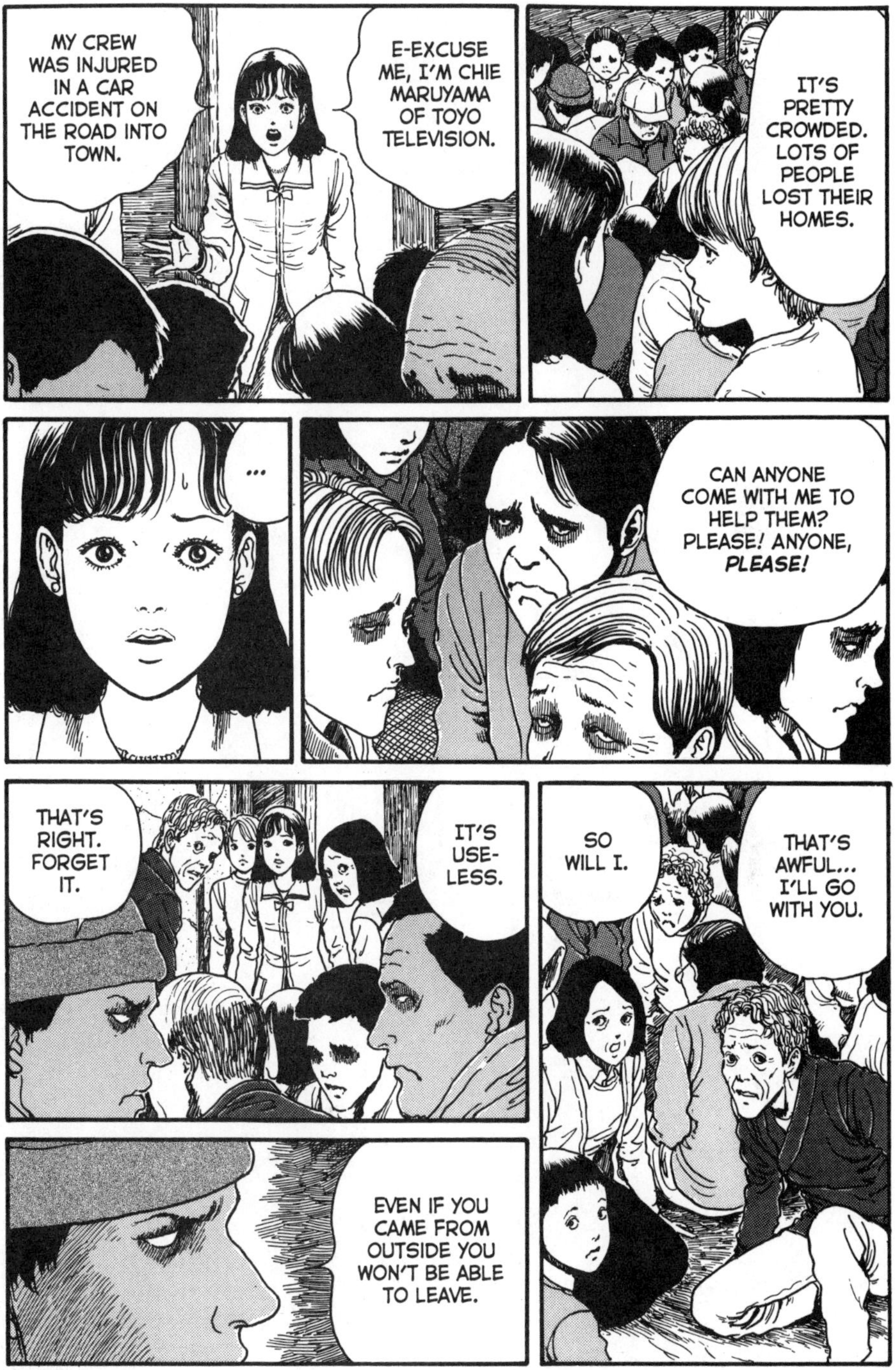
IT'S PRETTY CROWDED. LOTS OF PEOPLE LOST THEIR HOMES.
E-EXCUSE ME, I'M CHIE MARUYAMA OF TOYO TELEVISION.
MY CREW WAS INJURED IN A CAR ACCIDENT ON THE ROAD INTO TOWN.
CAN ANYONE COME WITH ME TO HELP THEM? PLEASE! ANYONE, *PLEASE!*
...
THAT'S AWFUL... I'LL GO WITH YOU.
SO WILL I.
IT'S USE- LESS.
THAT'S RIGHT. FORGET IT.
EVEN IF YOU CAME FROM OUTSIDE YOU WON'T BE ABLE TO LEAVE.

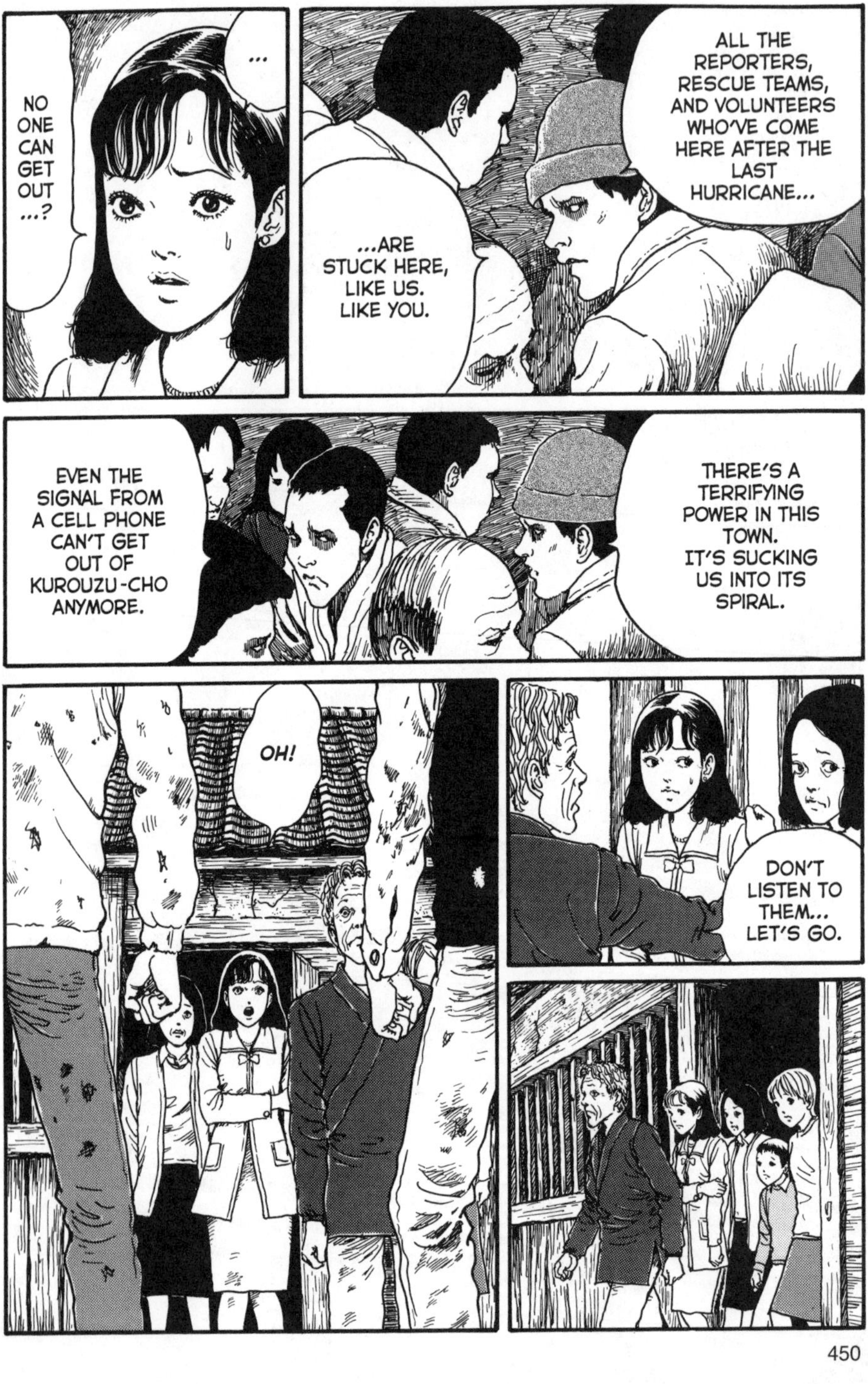
ALL THE REPORTERS, RESCUE TEAMS, AND VOLUNTEERS WHO'VE COME HERE AFTER THE LAST HURRICANE...
...ARE STUCK HERE, LIKE US. LIKE YOU.
...
NO ONE CAN GET OUT ...?
THERE'S A TERRIFYING POWER IN THIS TOWN. IT'S SUCKING US INTO ITS SPIRAL.
EVEN THE SIGNAL FROM A CELL PHONE CAN'T GET OUT OF KUROUZU-CHO ANYMORE.
DON'T LISTEN TO THEM... LET'S GO.
OH!

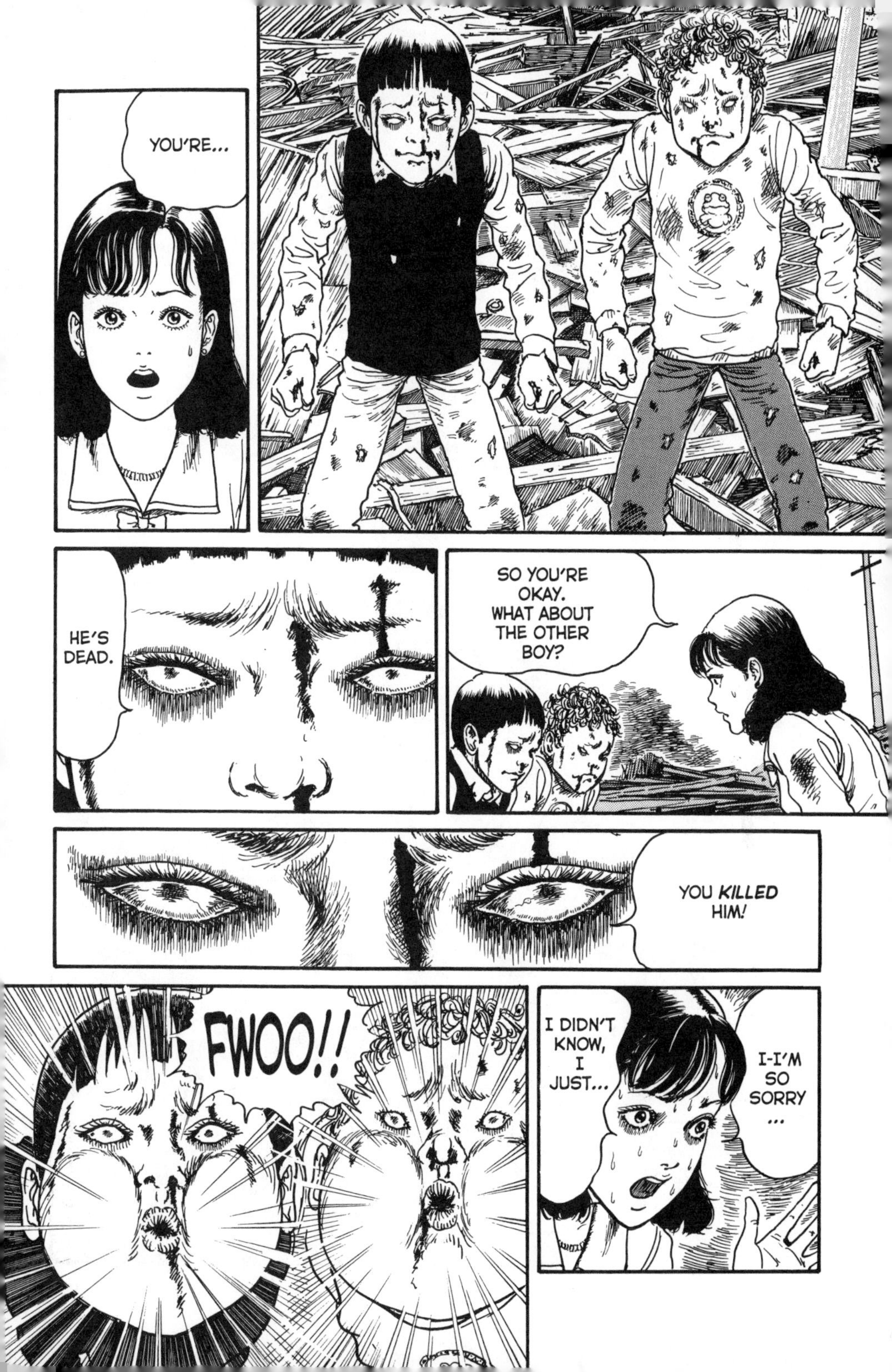
YOU'RE...
SO YOU'RE OKAY. WHAT ABOUT THE OTHER BOY?
HE'S DEAD.
YOU *KILLED* HIM!
I-I'M SO SORRY ...
I DIDN'T KNOW, I JUST...
FWOO!!

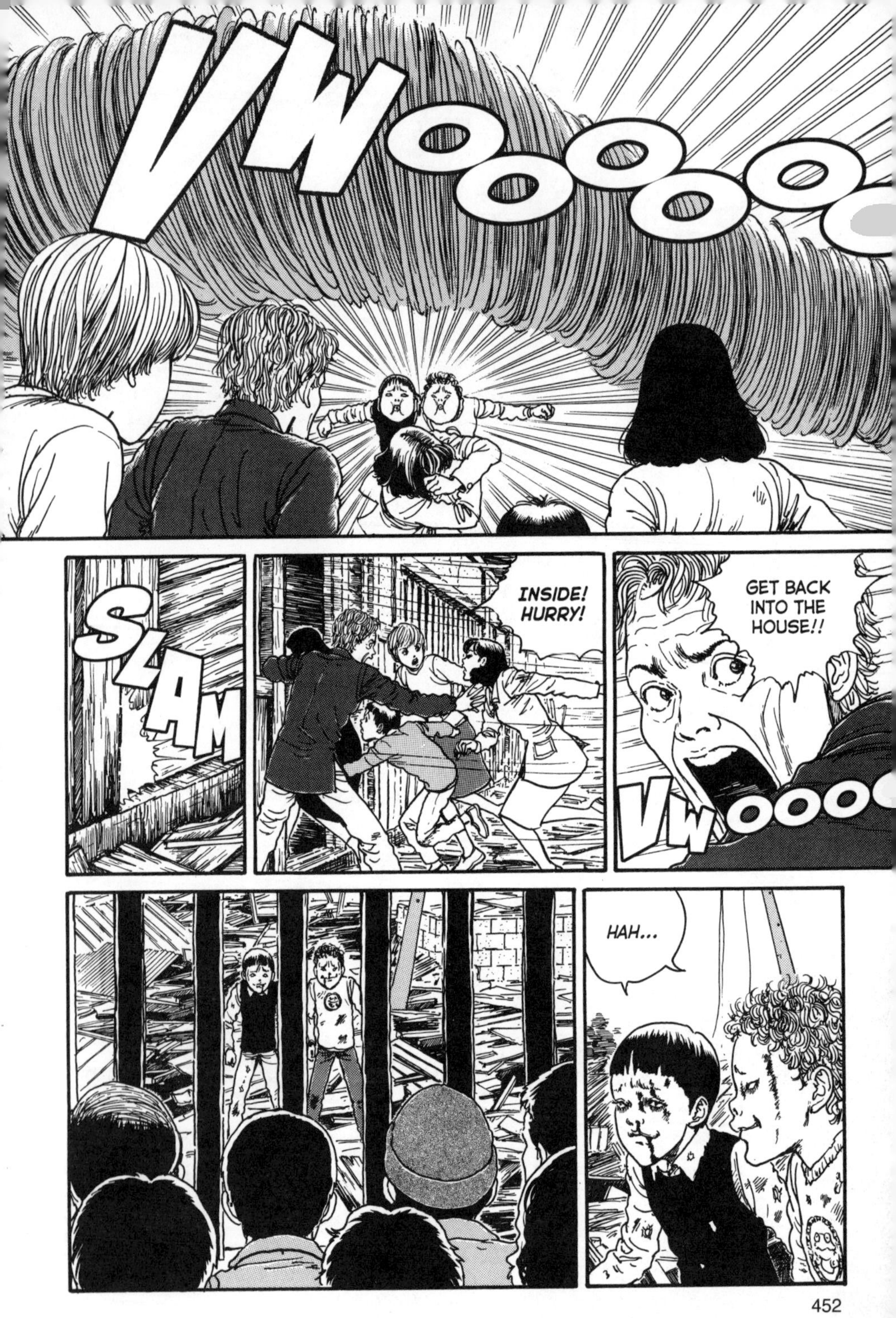
VWOOOOOO
GET BACK INTO THE HOUSE!!
VWOOOO
INSIDE! HURRY!
SLAM
HAH...

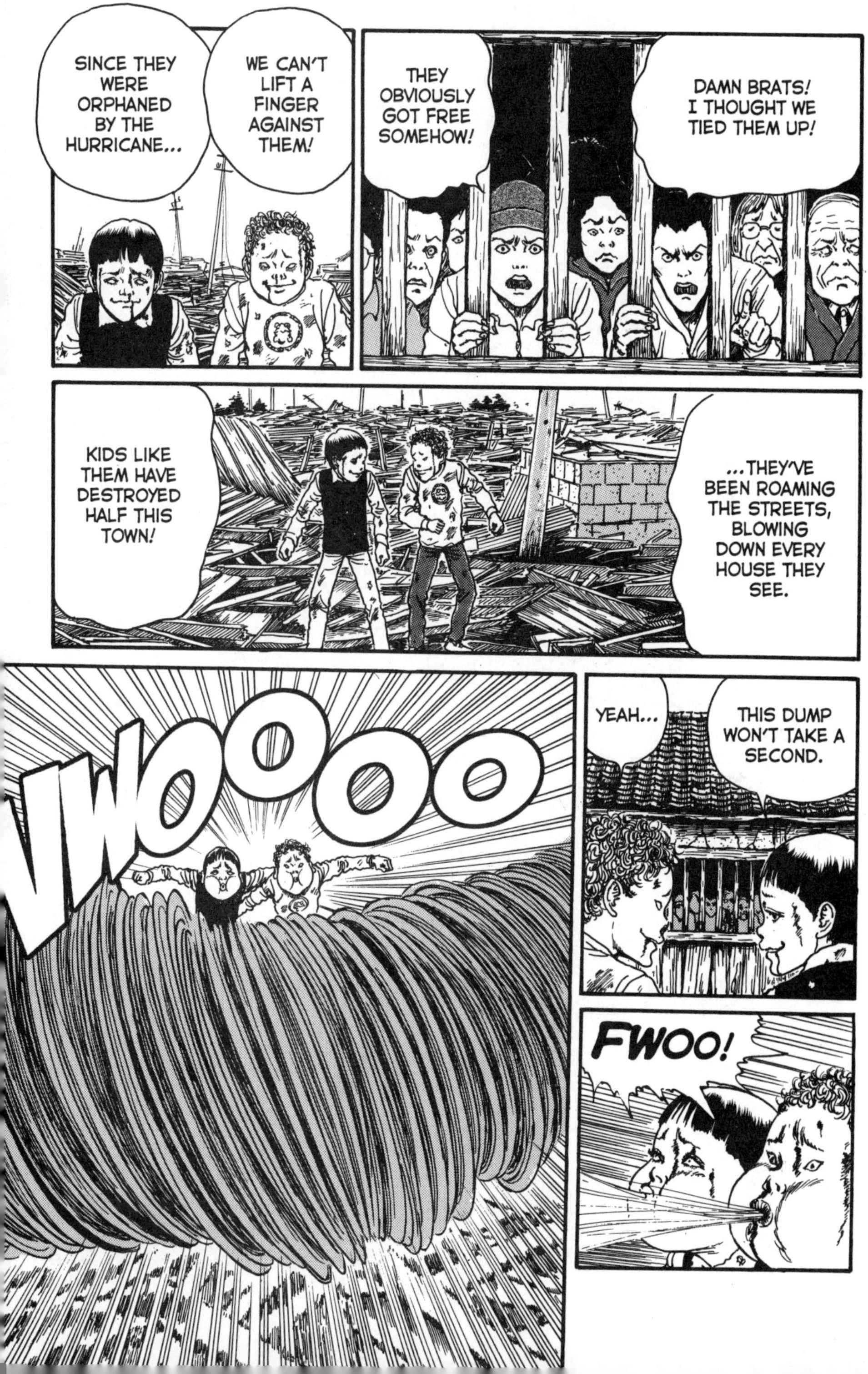
DAMN BRATS! I THOUGHT WE TIED THEM UP!
THEY OBVIOUSLY GOT FREE SOMEHOW!
WE CAN'T LIFT A FINGER AGAINST THEM!
SINCE THEY WERE ORPHANED BY THE HURRICANE...
...THEY'VE BEEN ROAMING THE STREETS, BLOWING DOWN EVERY HOUSE THEY SEE.
KIDS LIKE THEM HAVE DESTROYED HALF THIS TOWN!
THIS DUMP WON'T TAKE A SECOND.
YEAH...
FWOO!
VWOOOO

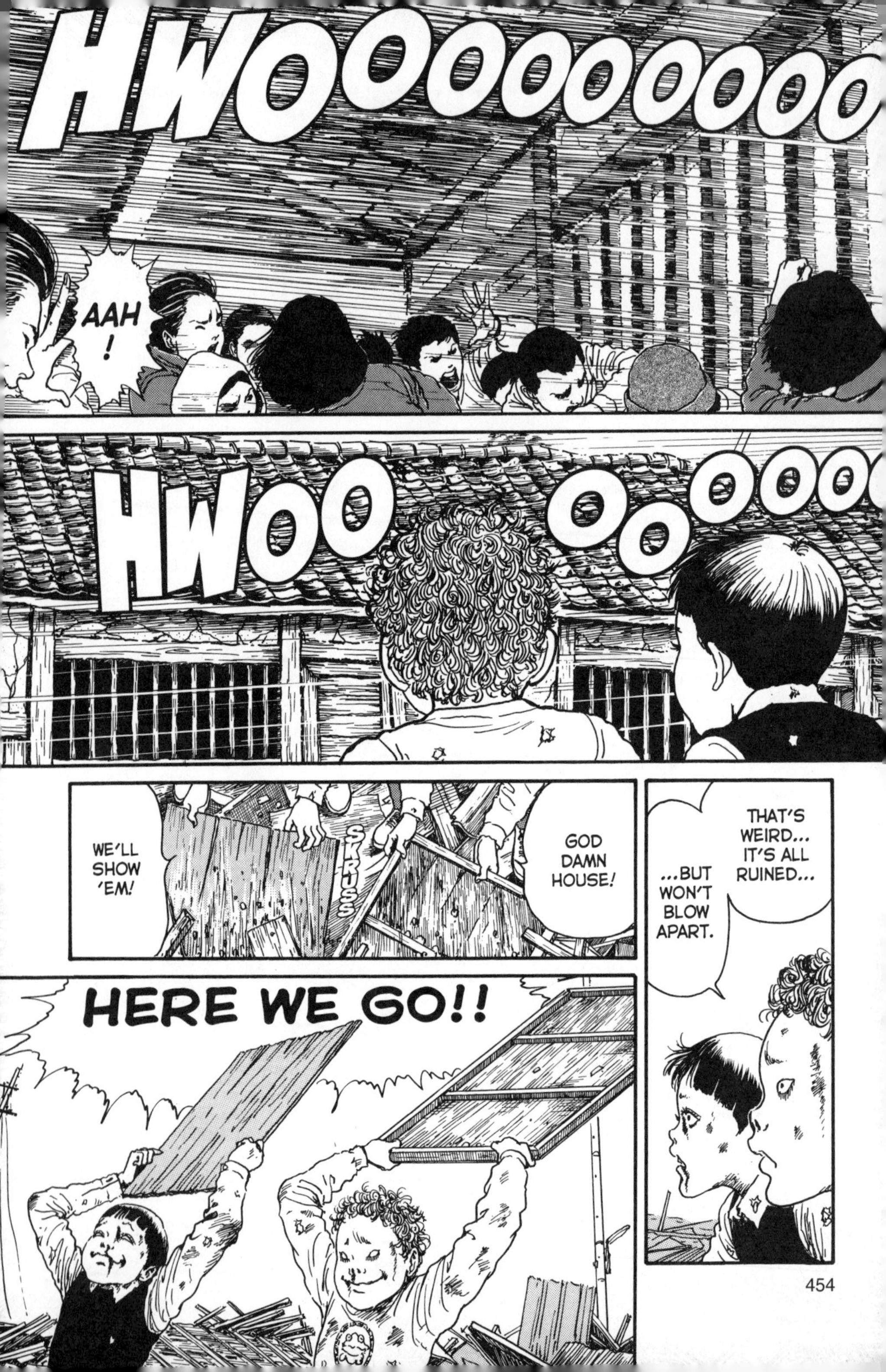
HWOOOOOOOOO
AAH!
HWOO OOOOOO
THAT'S WEIRD... IT'S ALL RUINED...
...BUT WON'T BLOW APART.
GOD DAMN HOUSE!
SKRUSS
WE'LL SHOW 'EM!
HERE WE GO!!

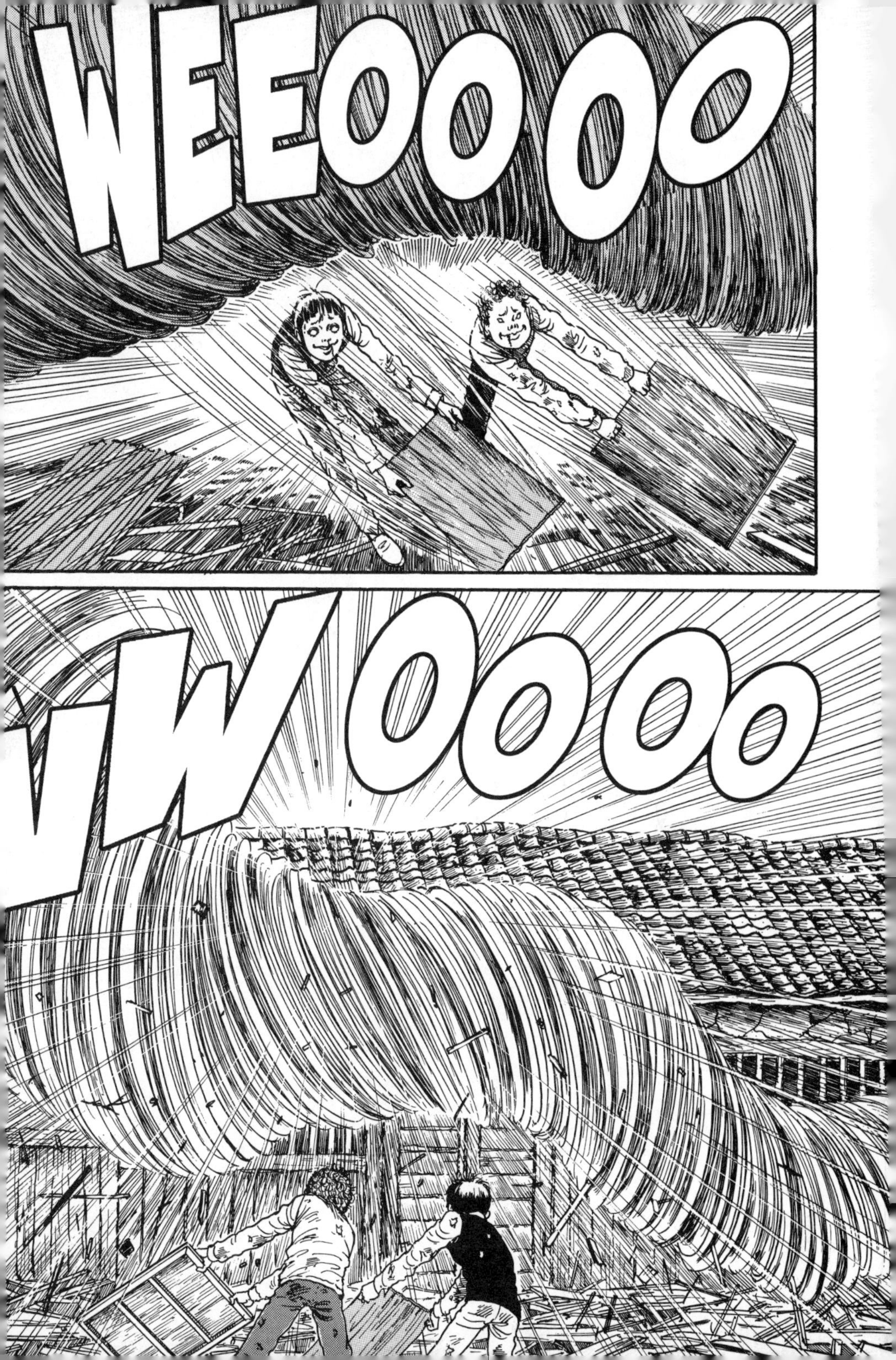
WEEOOOOO
WOOOOO

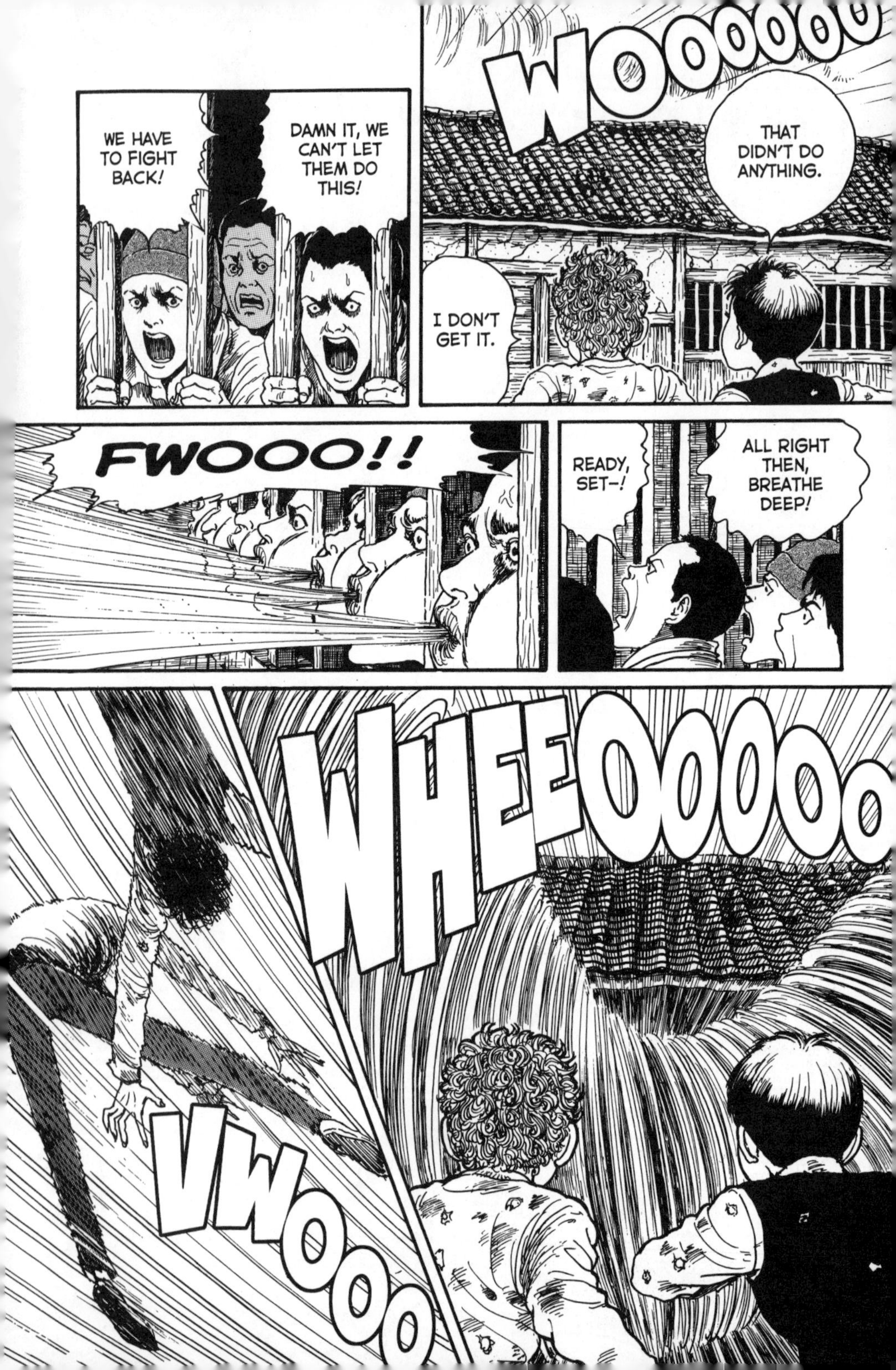
WOOOOOO
THAT DIDN'T DO ANYTHING.
I DON'T GET IT.
DAMN IT, WE CAN'T LET THEM DO THIS!
WE HAVE TO FIGHT BACK!
ALL RIGHT THEN, BREATHE DEEP!
READY, SET–!
FWOOO!!
WHEEOOOOO
VWOOOO

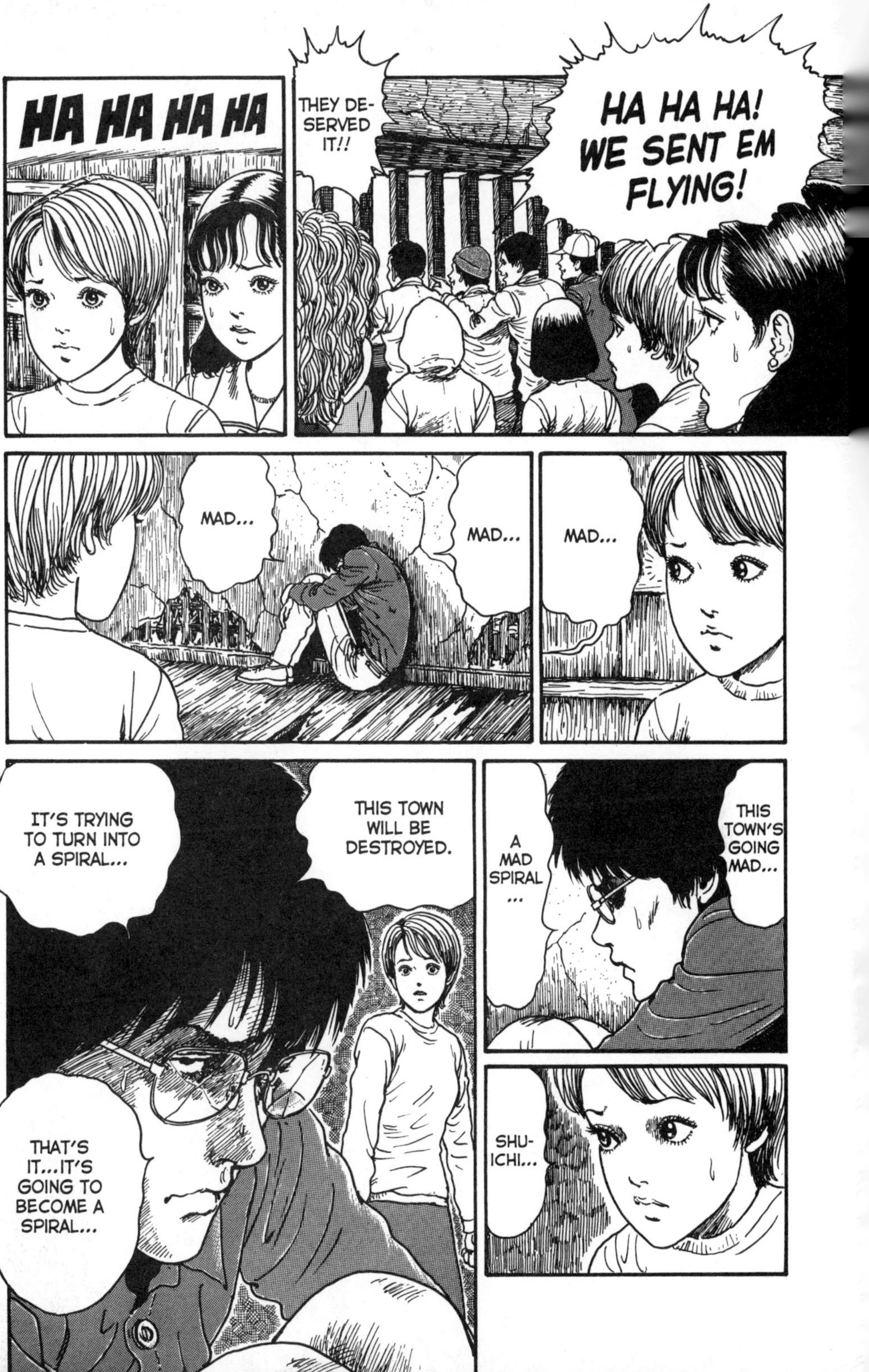
HA HA HA! WE SENT EM FLYING!
THEY DE-SERVED IT!!
HA HA HA HA
MAD...
MAD...
MAD...
THIS TOWN'S GOING MAD...
A MAD SPIRAL ...
SHU-ICHI...
THIS TOWN WILL BE DESTROYED.
IT'S TRYING TO TURN INTO A SPIRAL...
THAT'S IT...IT'S GOING TO BECOME A SPIRAL...

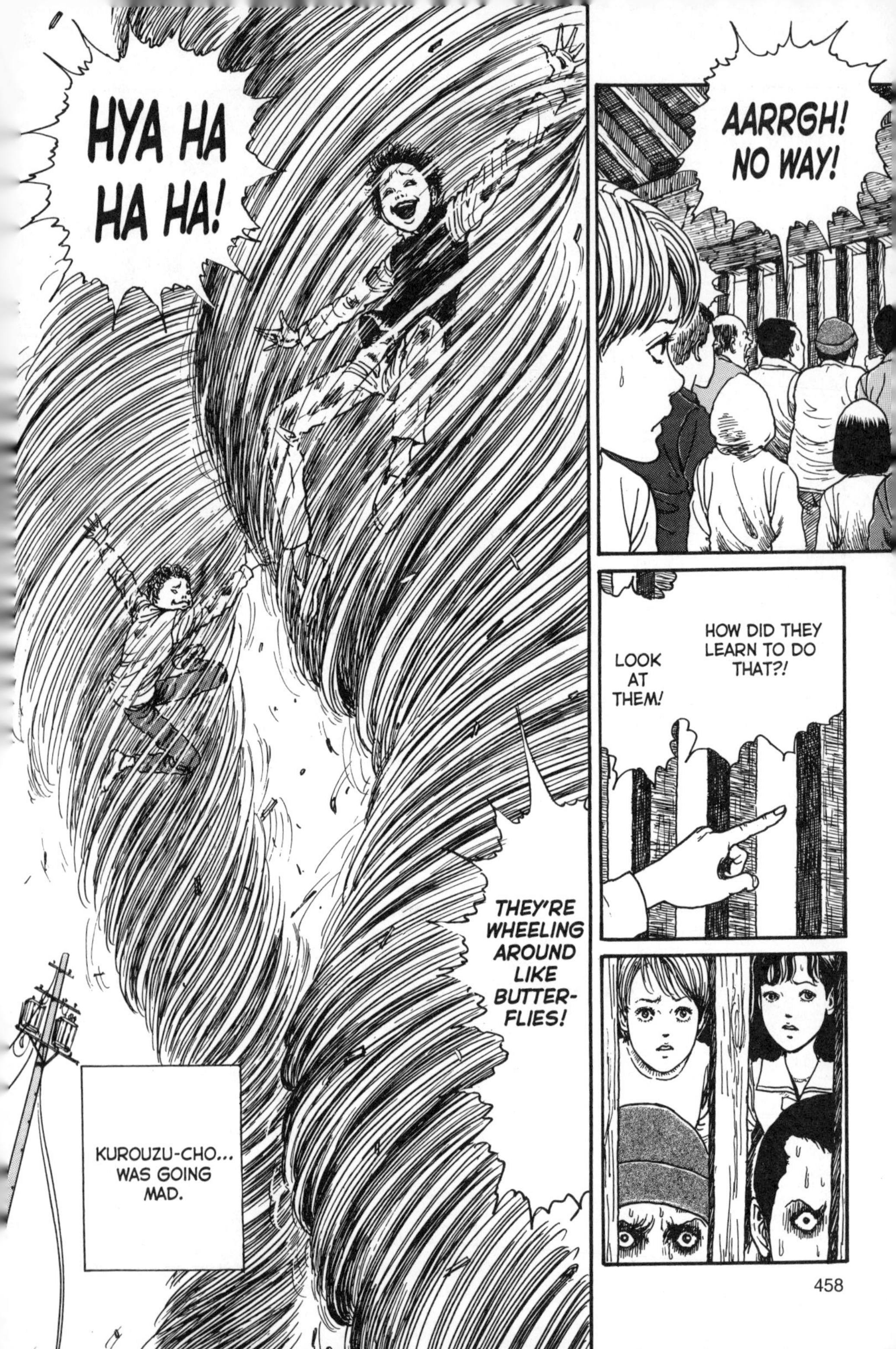
AARRGH! NO WAY!
HOW DID THEY LEARN TO DO THAT?!
LOOK AT THEM!
HYA HA HA HA!
THEY'RE WHEELING AROUND LIKE BUTTER-FLIES!
KUROUZU-CHO... WAS GOING MAD.

CHAPTER 15
CHAOS

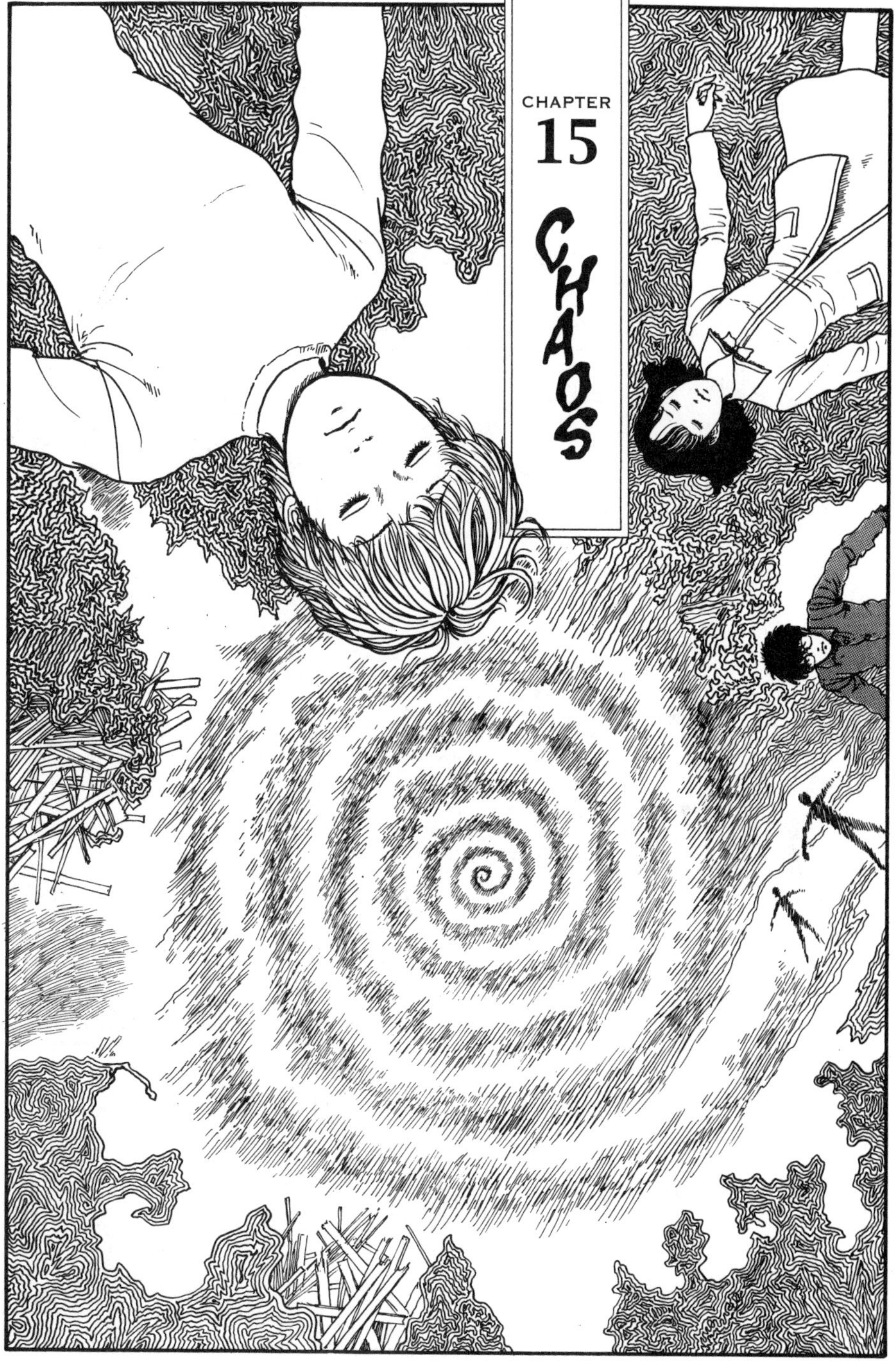

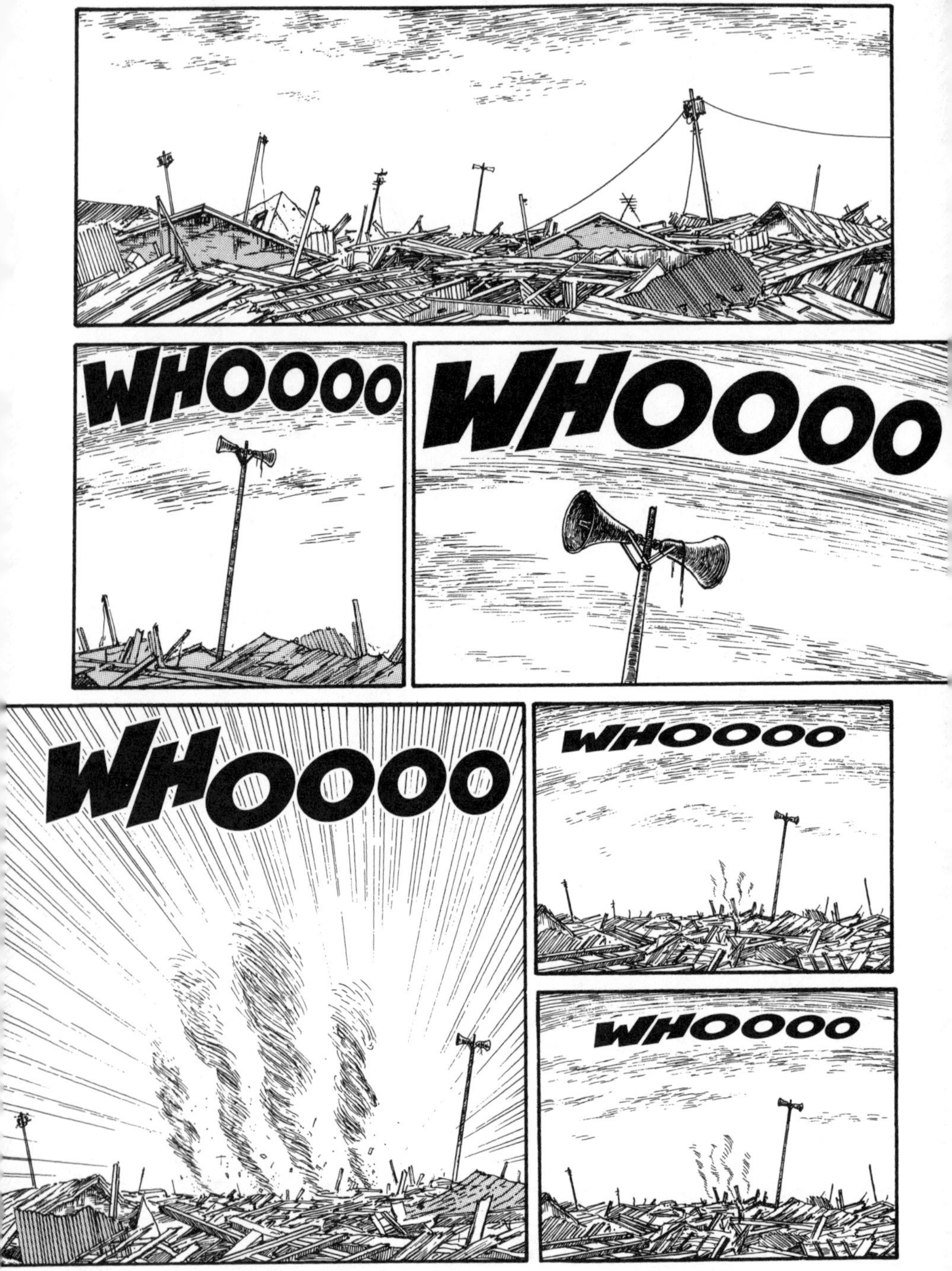
WHOOOO
WHOOOO
WHOOOO
WHOOOO
WHOOOO

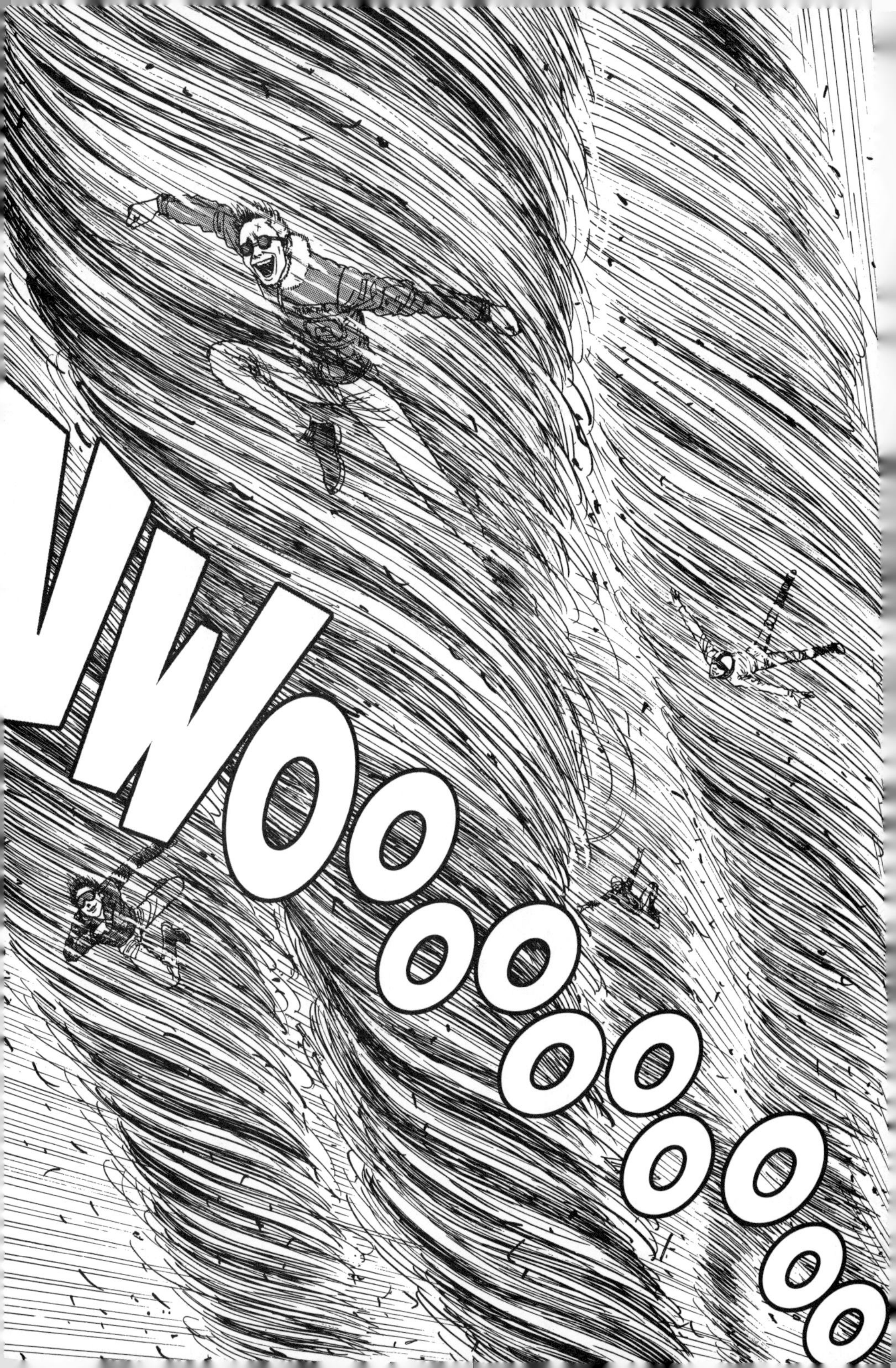
WOOOOOOOOOO

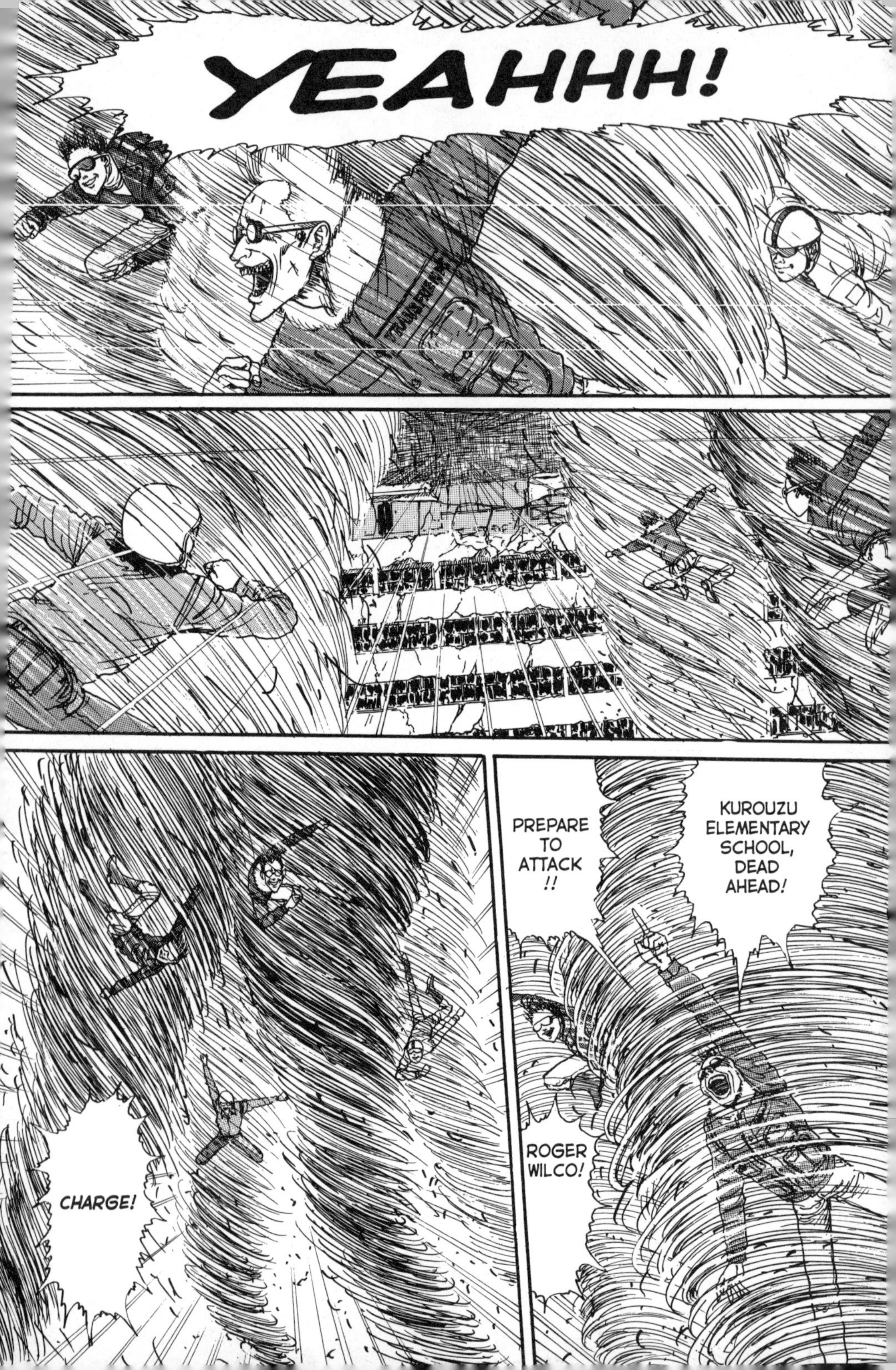
YEAHHH!
KUROUZU ELEMENTARY SCHOOL, DEAD AHEAD!
PREPARE TO ATTACK!!
ROGER WILCO!
CHARGE!

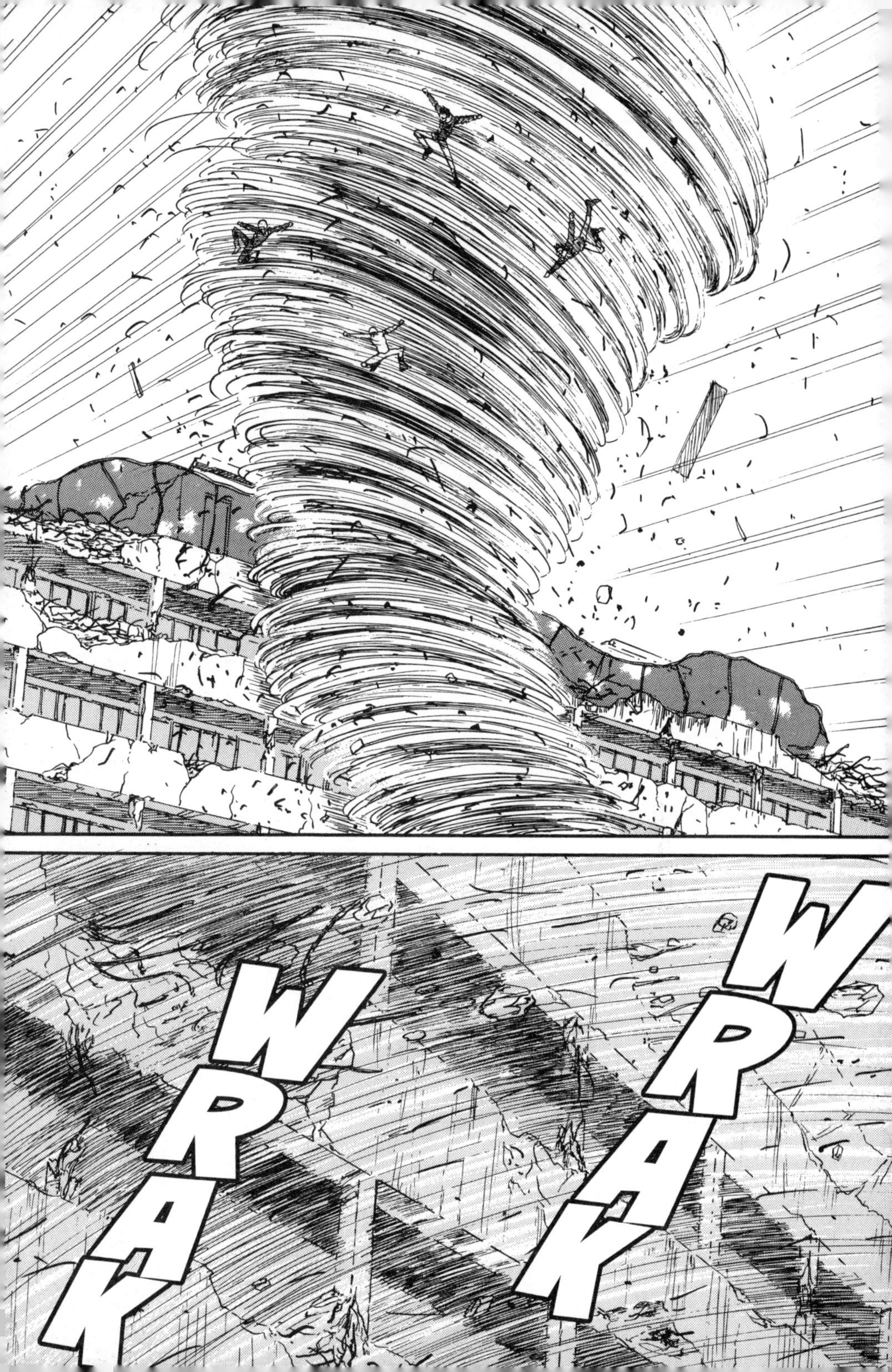
WRAK
WRAK

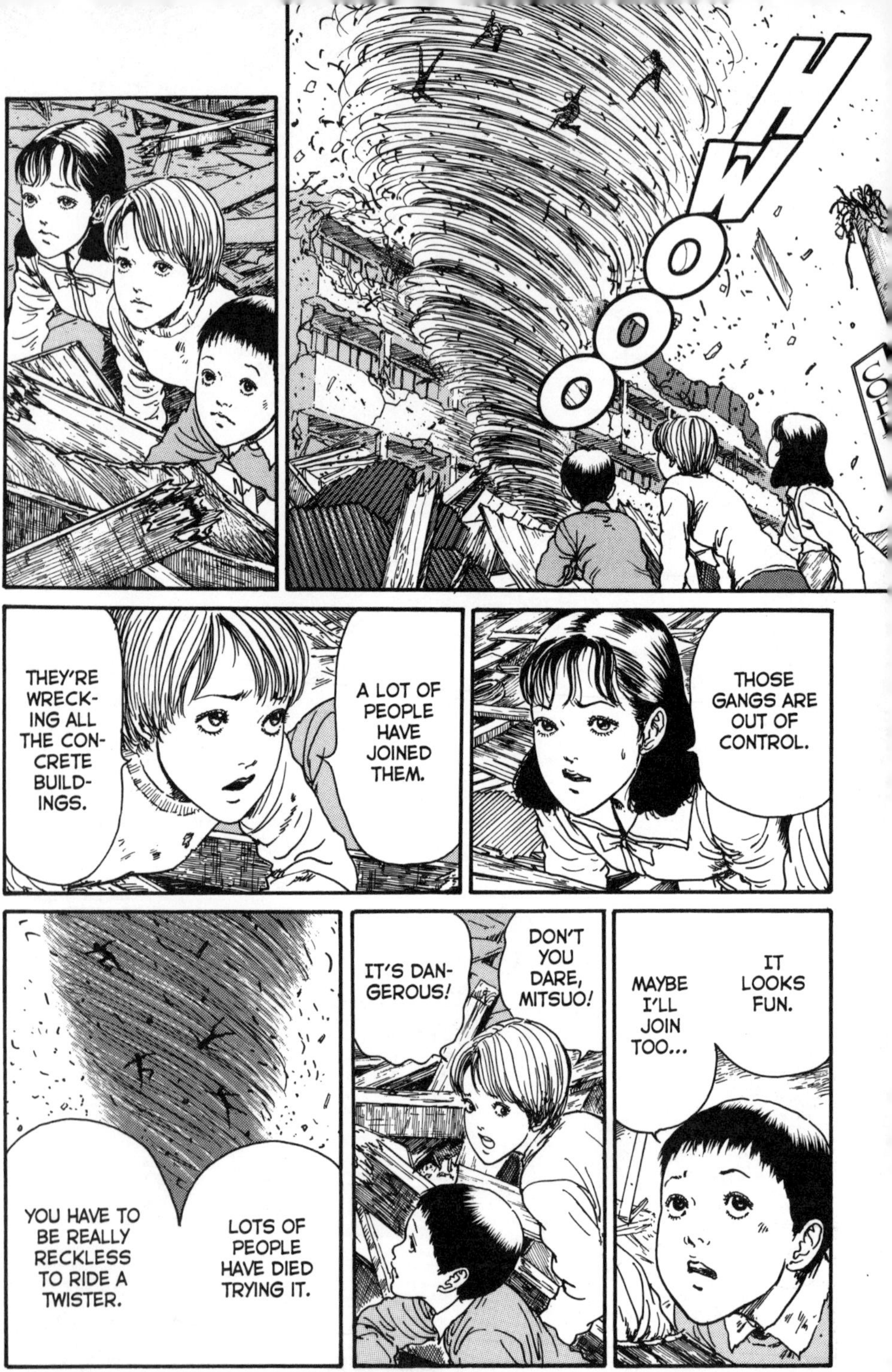

HWOOOO
THOSE GANGS ARE OUT OF CONTROL.
A LOT OF PEOPLE HAVE JOINED THEM.
THEY'RE WRECKING ALL THE CONCRETE BUILDINGS.
IT LOOKS FUN.
MAYBE I'LL JOIN TOO...
DON'T YOU DARE, MITSUO!
IT'S DANGEROUS!
LOTS OF PEOPLE HAVE DIED TRYING IT.
YOU HAVE TO BE REALLY RECKLESS TO RIDE A TWISTER.

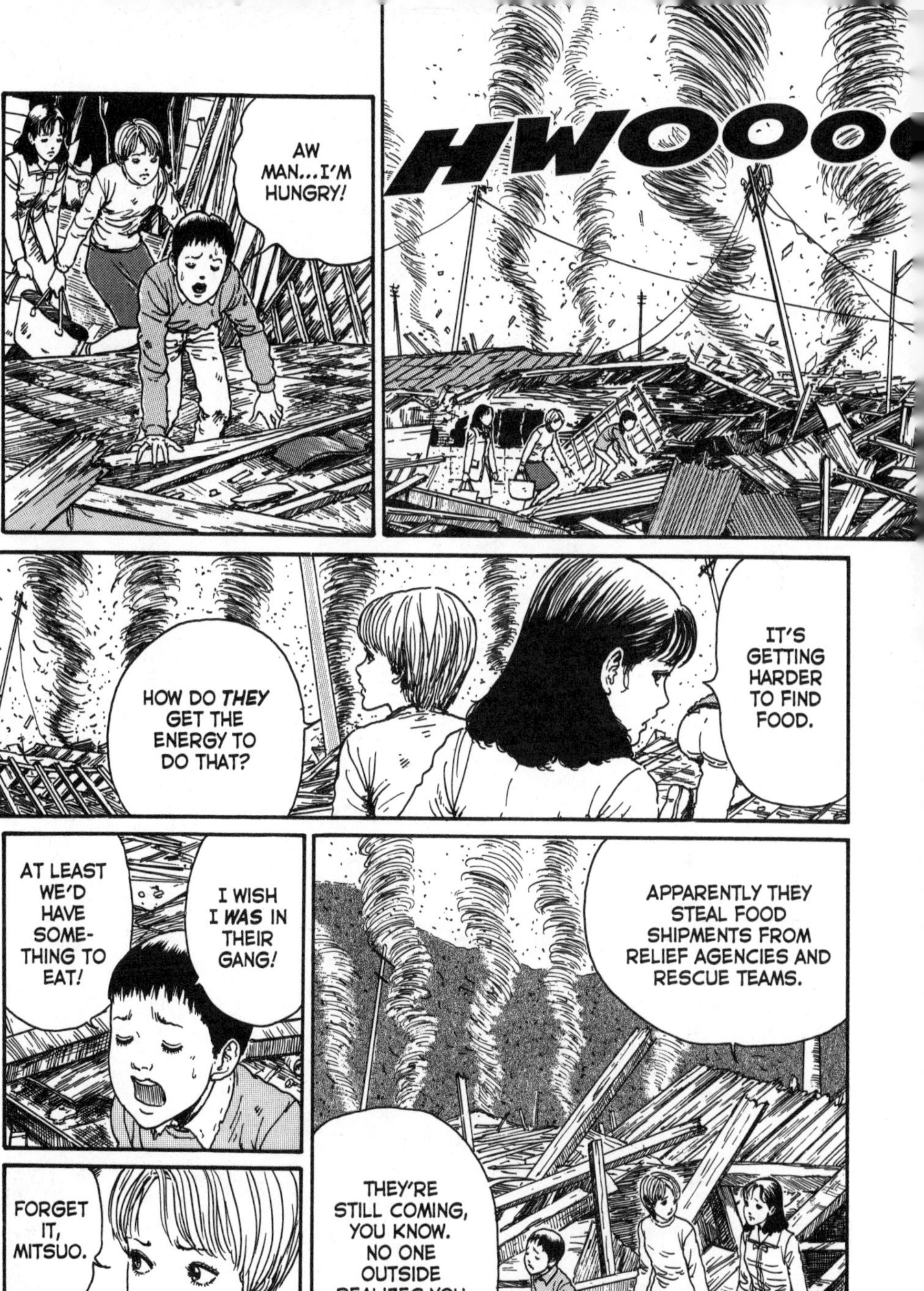
HWOOO
AW MAN...I'M HUNGRY!
IT'S GETTING HARDER TO FIND FOOD.
HOW DO *THEY* GET THE ENERGY TO DO THAT?
APPARENTLY THEY STEAL FOOD SHIPMENTS FROM RELIEF AGENCIES AND RESCUE TEAMS.
THEY'RE STILL COMING, YOU KNOW. NO ONE OUTSIDE REALIZES YOU CAN'T GET OUT...
I WISH I *WAS* IN THEIR GANG!
AT LEAST WE'D HAVE SOME-THING TO EAT!
FORGET IT, MITSUO.

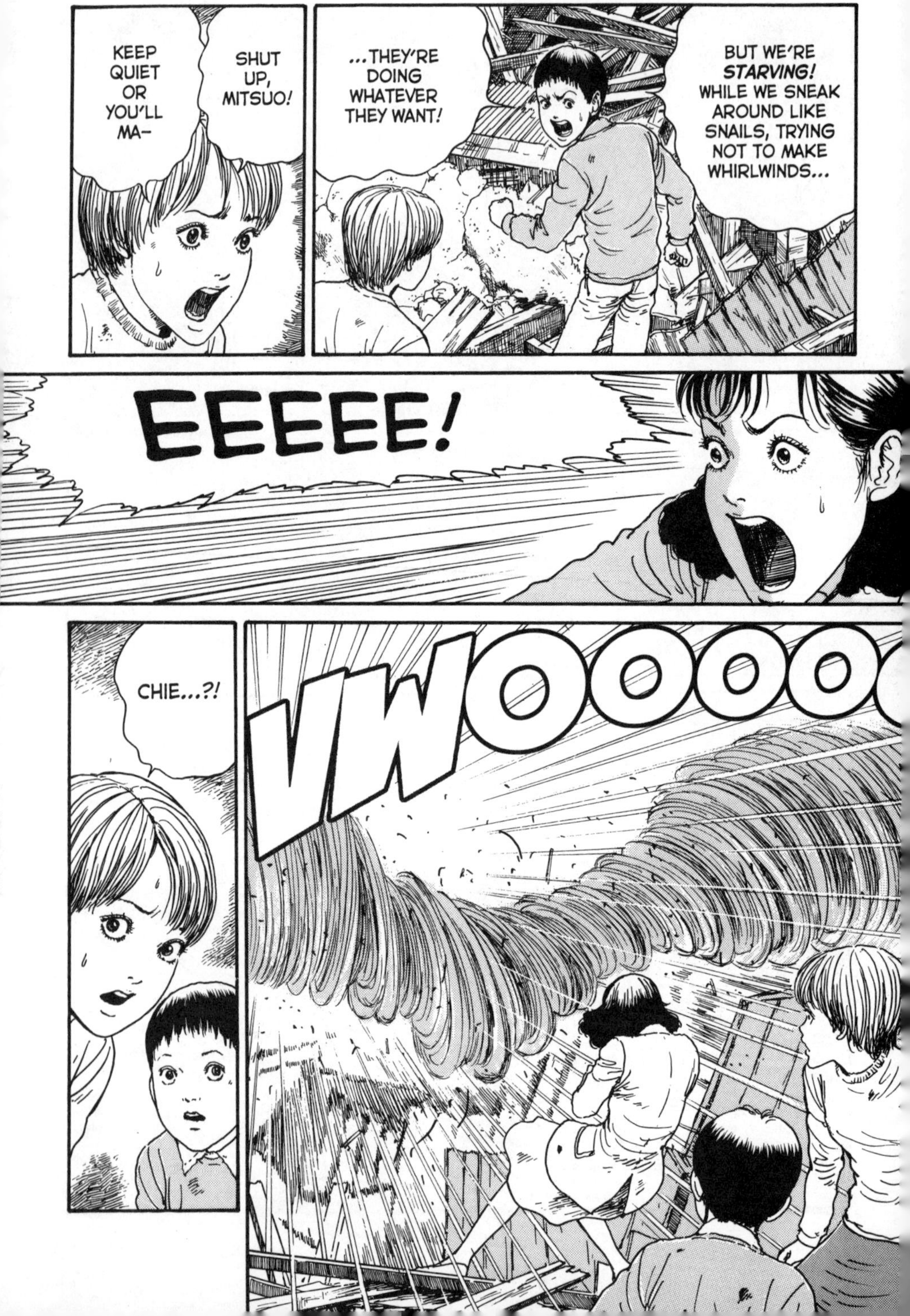
BUT WE'RE **STARVING!** WHILE WE SNEAK AROUND LIKE SNAILS, TRYING NOT TO MAKE WHIRLWINDS...
...THEY'RE DOING WHATEVER THEY WANT!
SHUT UP, MITSUO!
KEEP QUIET OR YOU'LL MA–
EEEEE!
VWOOOOO
CHIE...?!

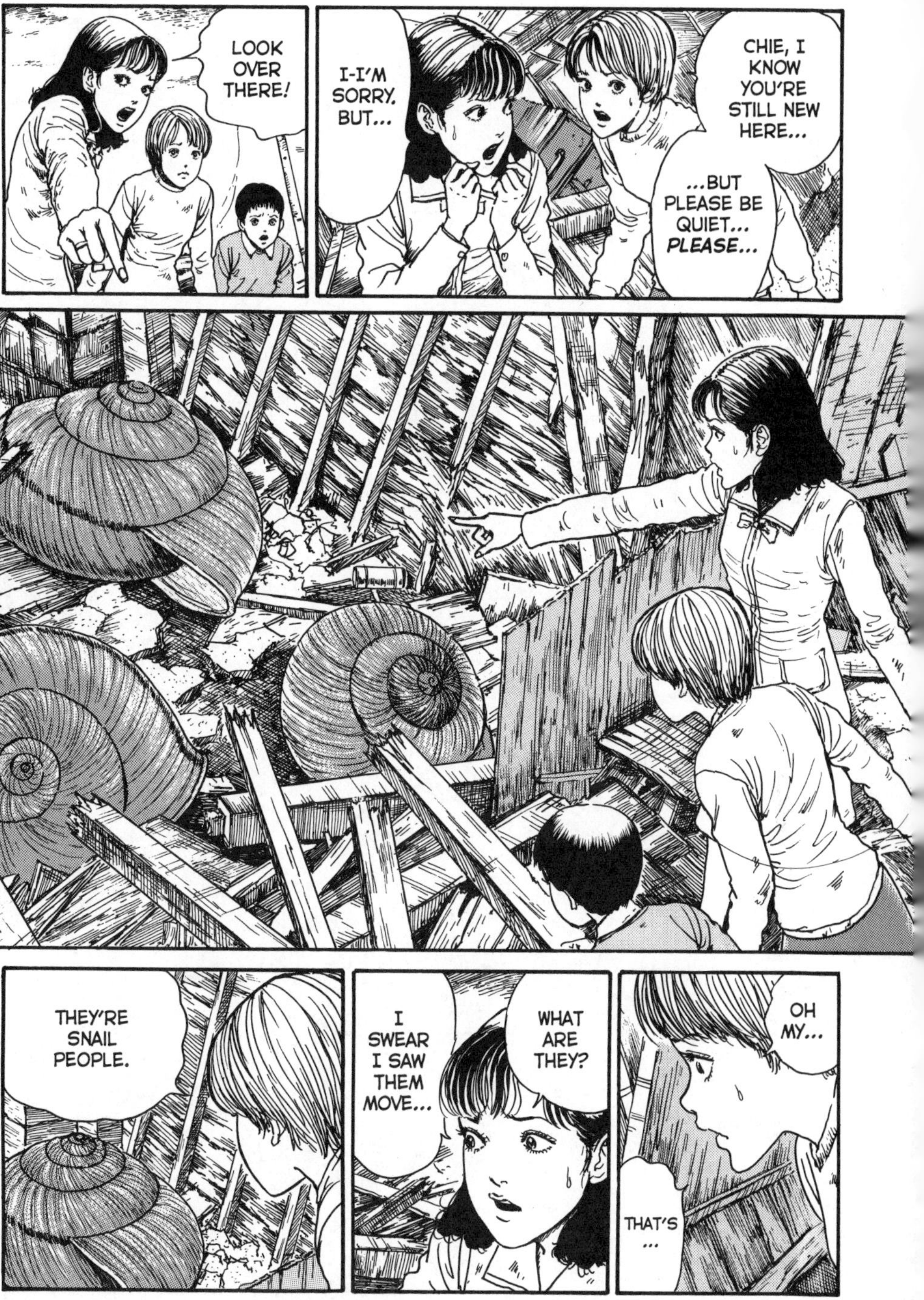
CHIE, I KNOW YOU'RE STILL NEW HERE...
...BUT PLEASE BE QUIET... *PLEASE...*
I-I'M SORRY. BUT...
LOOK OVER THERE!
OH MY...
THAT'S ...
WHAT ARE THEY?
I SWEAR I SAW THEM MOVE...
THEY'RE SNAIL PEOPLE.

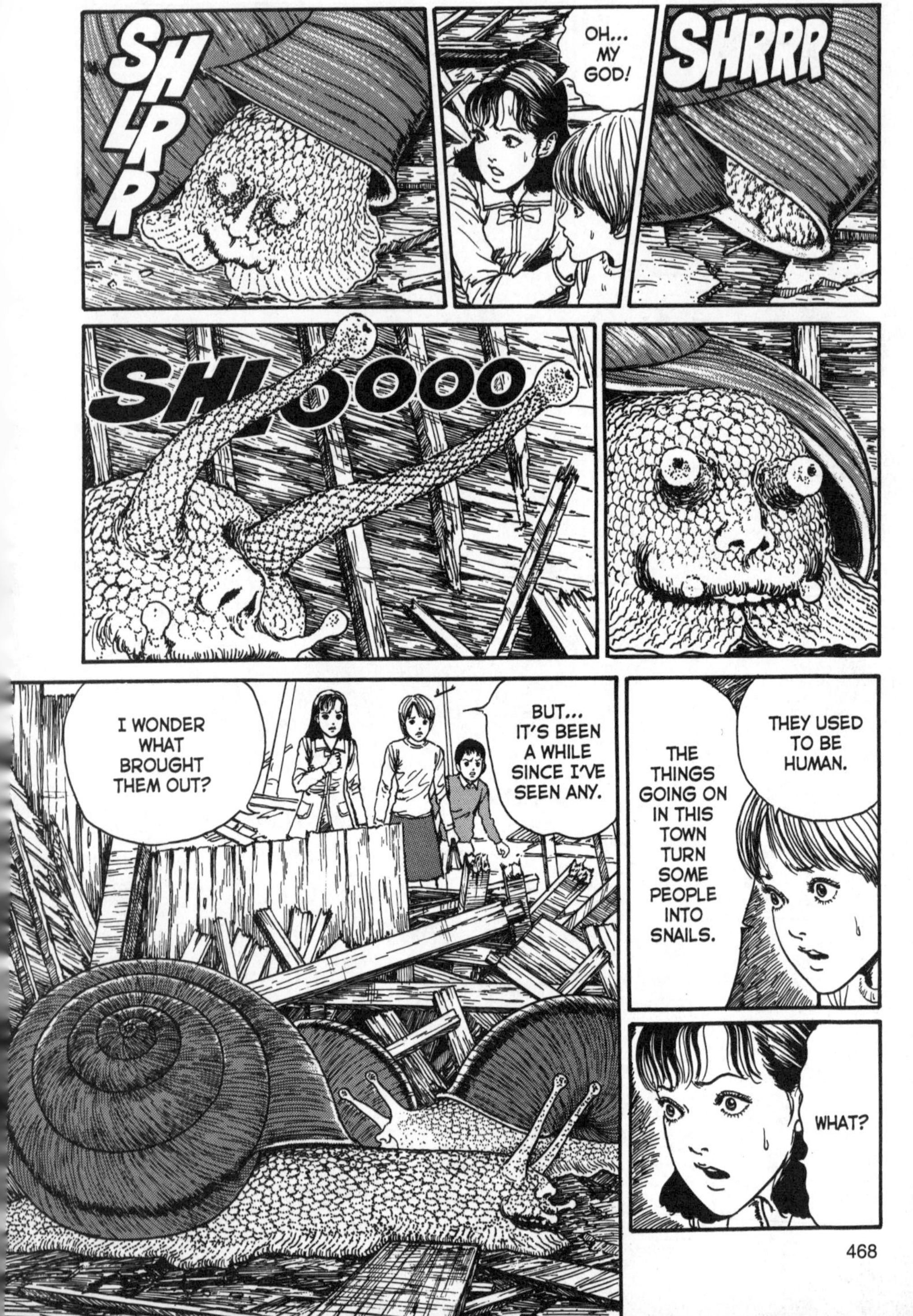
SHRRR
OH... MY GOD!
SHLRR
SHOOOO
THEY USED TO BE HUMAN.
THE THINGS GOING ON IN THIS TOWN TURN SOME PEOPLE INTO SNAILS.
WHAT?
BUT... IT'S BEEN A WHILE SINCE I'VE SEEN ANY.
I WONDER WHAT BROUGHT THEM OUT?

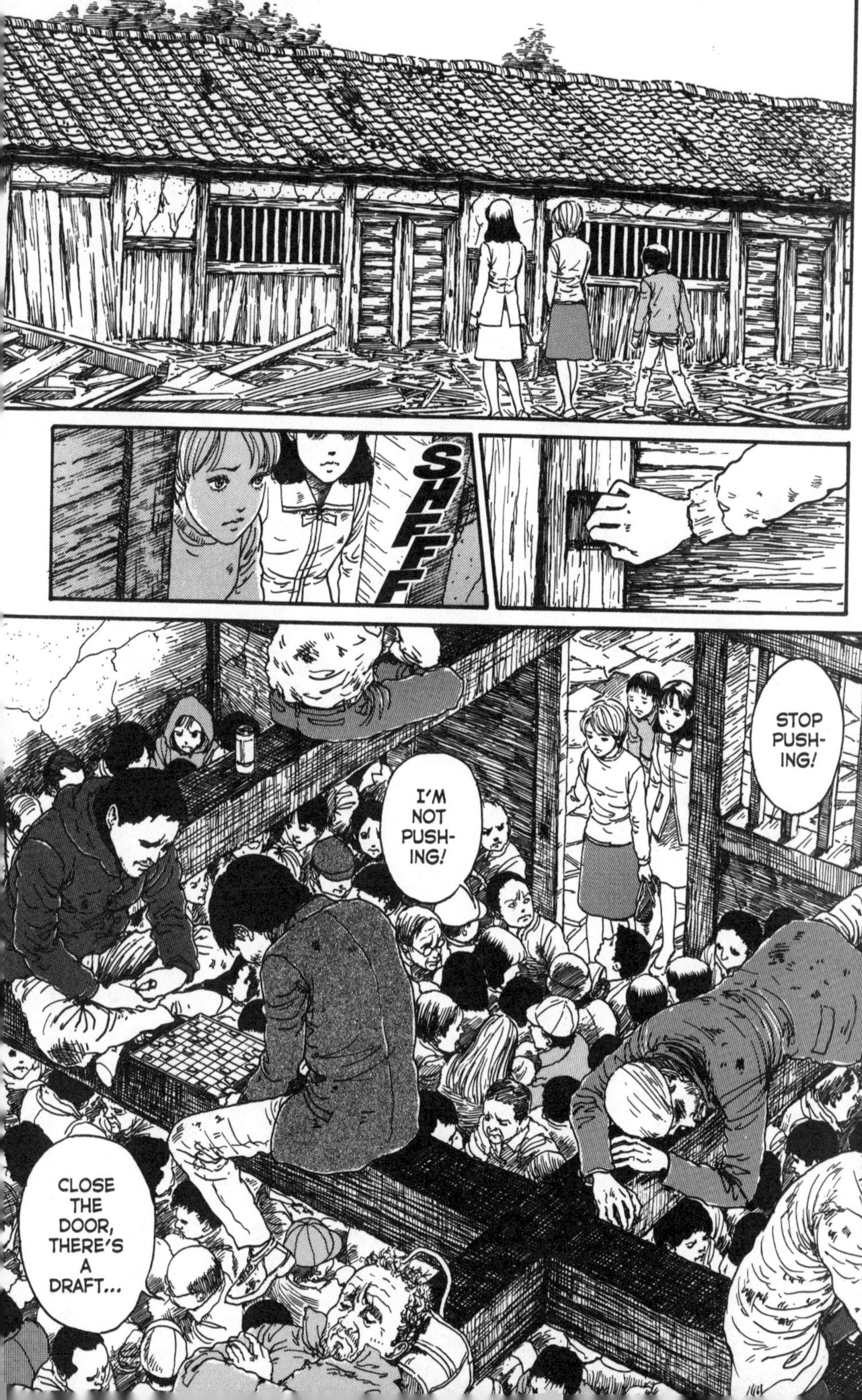
SHFFF
STOP PUSHING!
I'M NOT PUSHING!
CLOSE THE DOOR, THERE'S A DRAFT...

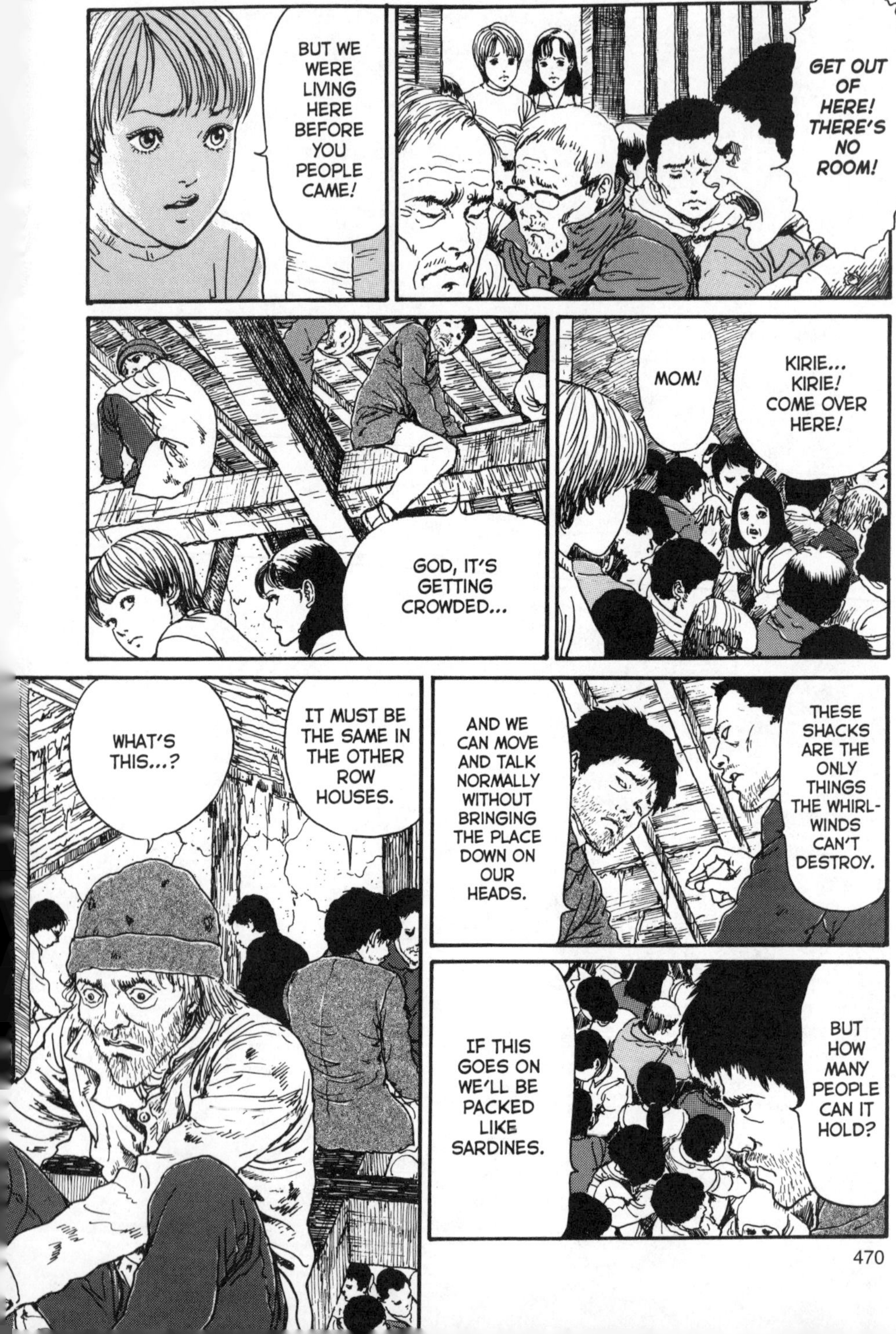
GET OUT OF HERE! THERE'S NO ROOM!
BUT WE WERE LIVING HERE BEFORE YOU PEOPLE CAME!
KIRIE... KIRIE! COME OVER HERE!
MOM!
GOD, IT'S GETTING CROWDED...
THESE SHACKS ARE THE ONLY THINGS THE WHIRLWINDS CAN'T DESTROY.
AND WE CAN MOVE AND TALK NORMALLY WITHOUT BRINGING THE PLACE DOWN ON OUR HEADS.
BUT HOW MANY PEOPLE CAN IT HOLD?
IF THIS GOES ON WE'LL BE PACKED LIKE SARDINES.
IT MUST BE THE SAME IN THE OTHER ROW HOUSES.
WHAT'S THIS...?

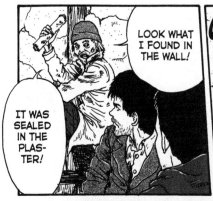

GRIP
CRACK
LOOK WHAT I FOUND IN THE WALL!
IT WAS SEALED IN THE PLAS-TER!
LOOKS LIKE A SCROLL!
IT LOOKS OLD. UNTIE IT.
YEAH ...
OOPS!
TUMP
AGH!
THAT *HURT*, YOU PRICK! GET DOWN FROM THERE!
YEAH? COME UP AND *MAKE ME!*
YOU SON OF A BITCH! I'LL KILL YOU!
YOU CAN'T TOUCH ME! SHUT UP!

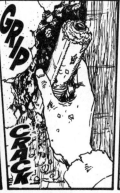

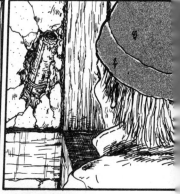

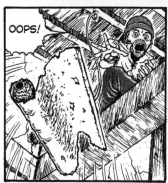

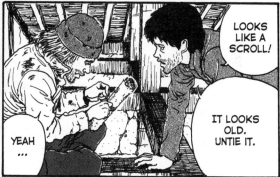

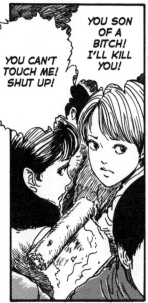

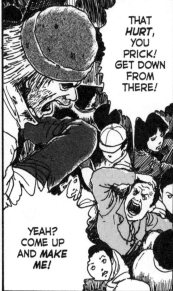

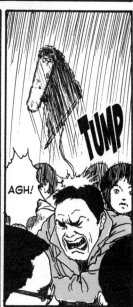

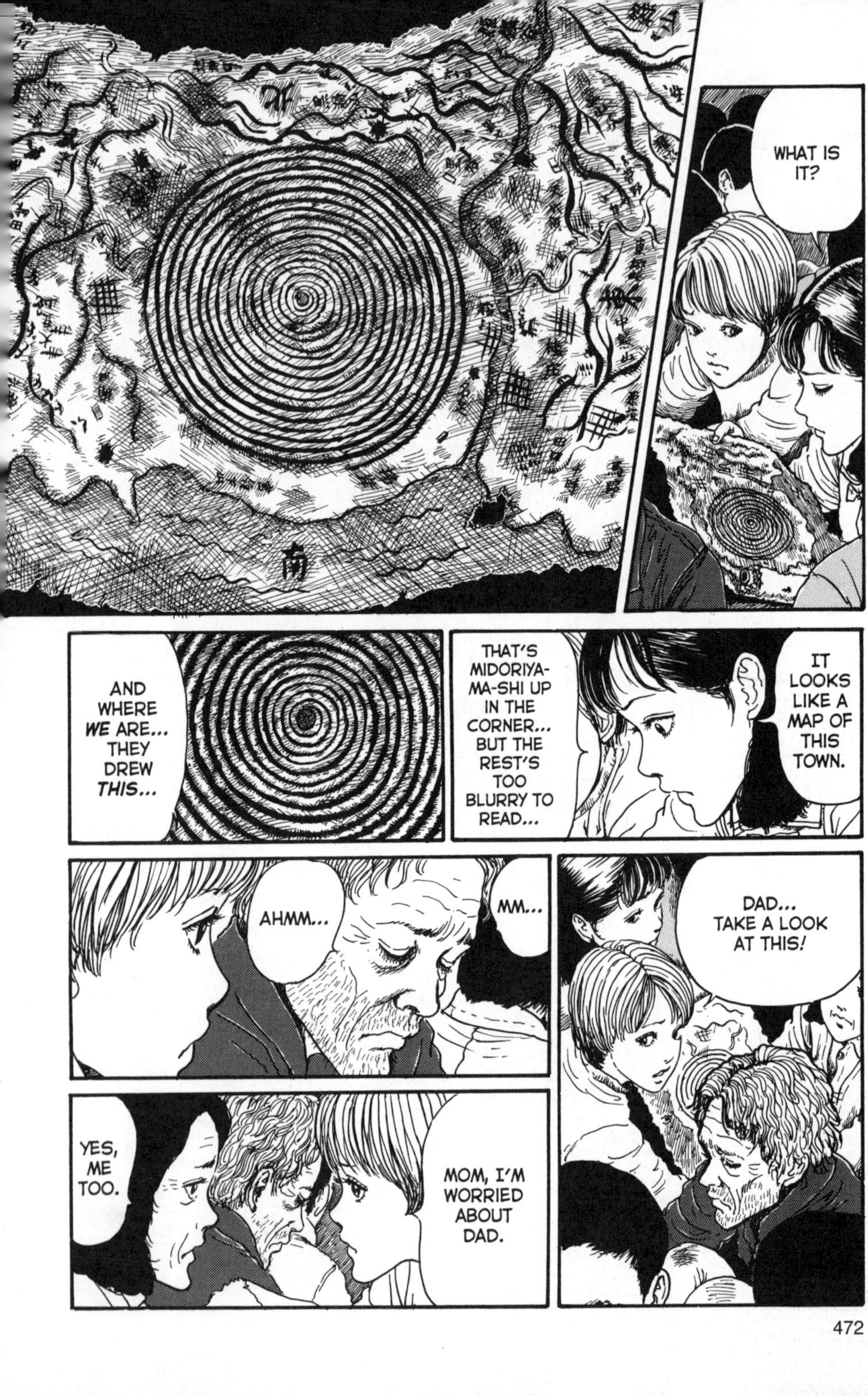
WHAT IS IT?
南
IT LOOKS LIKE A MAP OF THIS TOWN.
THAT'S MIDORIYAMA-SHI UP IN THE CORNER... BUT THE REST'S TOO BLURRY TO READ...
AND WHERE *WE* ARE... THEY DREW *THIS*...
DAD... TAKE A LOOK AT THIS!
MM...
AHMM...
MOM, I'M WORRIED ABOUT DAD.
YES, ME TOO.

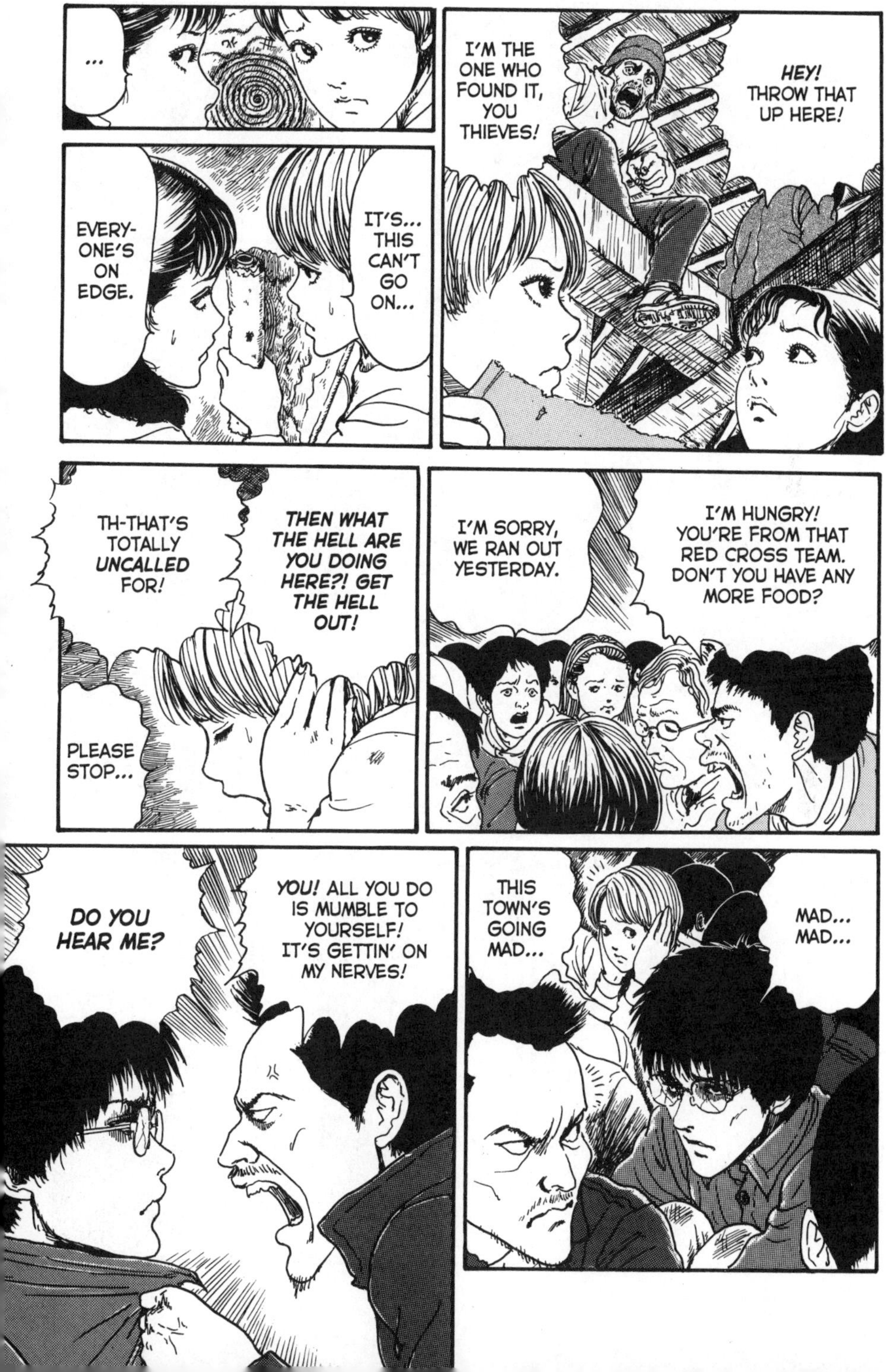
HEY! THROW THAT UP HERE!
I'M THE ONE WHO FOUND IT, YOU THIEVES!
...
IT'S... THIS CAN'T GO ON...
EVERY-ONE'S ON EDGE.
I'M HUNGRY! YOU'RE FROM THAT RED CROSS TEAM. DON'T YOU HAVE ANY MORE FOOD?
I'M SORRY, WE RAN OUT YESTERDAY.
THEN WHAT THE HELL ARE YOU DOING HERE?! GET THE HELL OUT!
TH-THAT'S TOTALLY UNCALLED FOR!
PLEASE STOP...
MAD... MAD...
THIS TOWN'S GOING MAD...
YOU! ALL YOU DO IS MUMBLE TO YOURSELF! IT'S GETTIN' ON MY NERVES!
DO YOU HEAR ME?

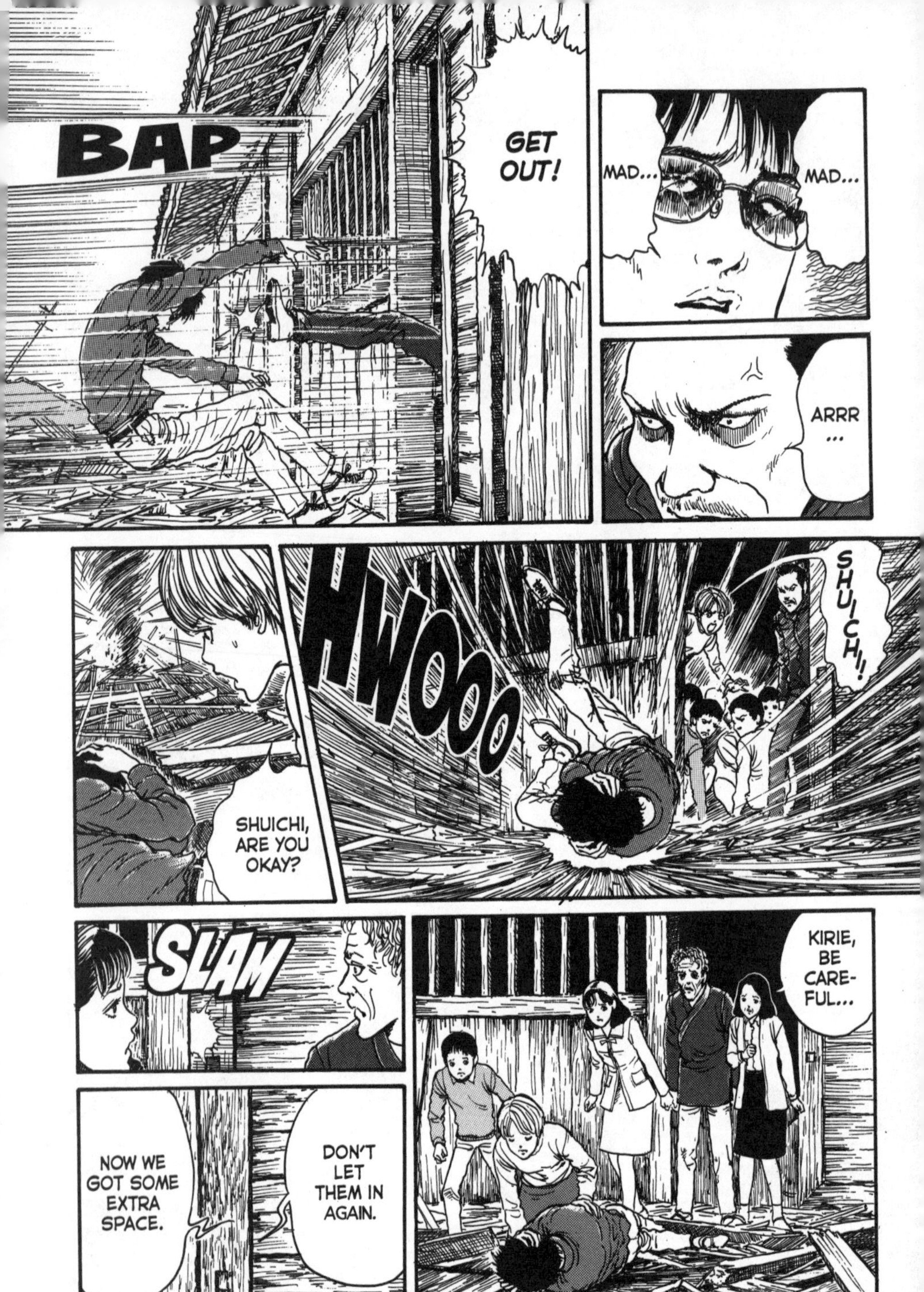
MAD...
MAD...
ARRR ...
GET OUT!
BAP
SHUICHI!!
HWOOO
SHUICHI, ARE YOU OKAY?
KIRIE, BE CARE-FUL...
SLAM
DON'T LET THEM IN AGAIN.
NOW WE GOT SOME EXTRA SPACE.

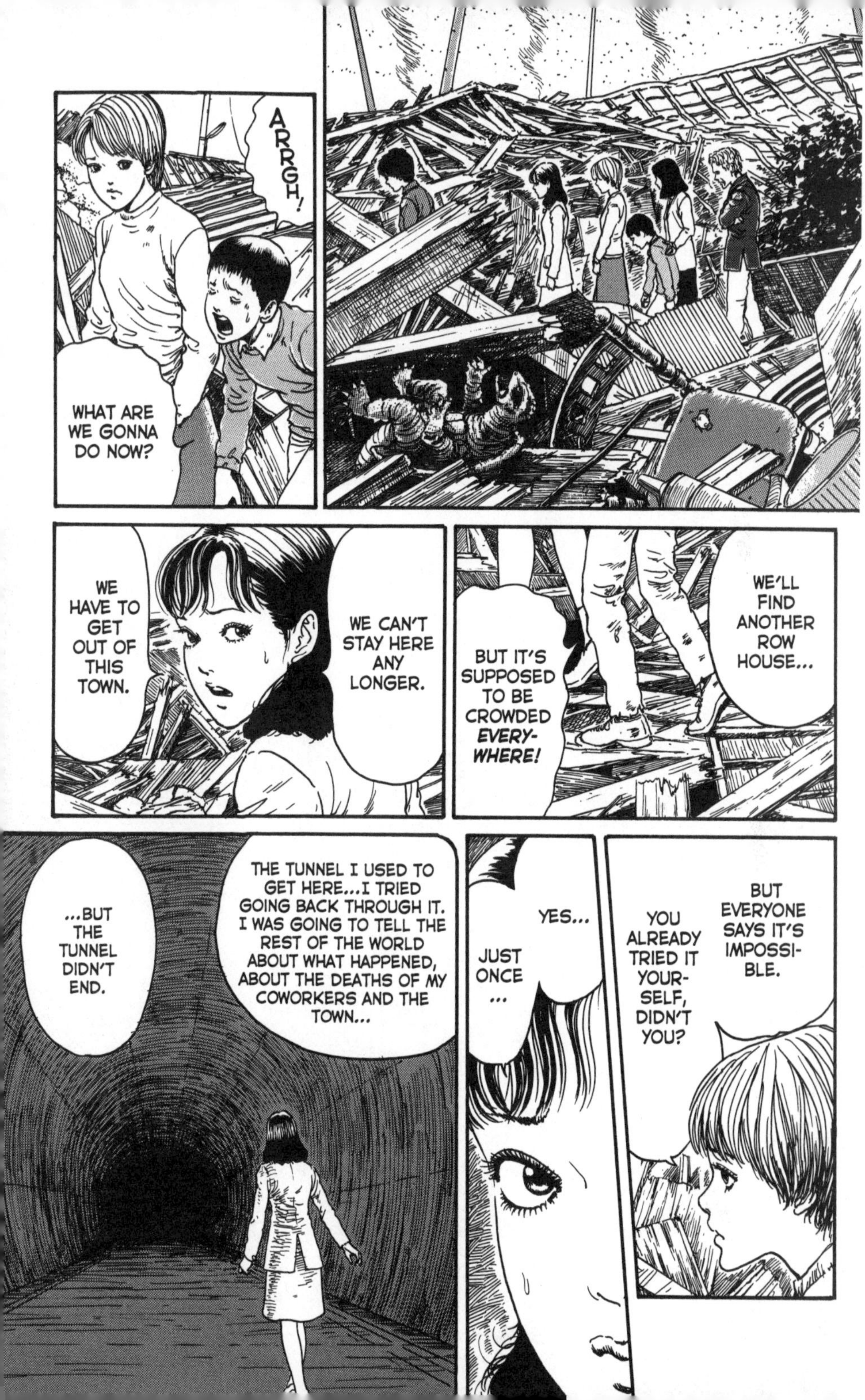
ARRGH!
WHAT ARE WE GONNA DO NOW?
WE'LL FIND ANOTHER ROW HOUSE...
BUT IT'S SUPPOSED TO BE CROWDED *EVERY-WHERE!*
WE CAN'T STAY HERE ANY LONGER.
WE HAVE TO GET OUT OF THIS TOWN.
BUT EVERYONE SAYS IT'S IMPOSSI-BLE.
YOU ALREADY TRIED IT YOUR-SELF, DIDN'T YOU?
YES...
JUST ONCE ...
THE TUNNEL I USED TO GET HERE...I TRIED GOING BACK THROUGH IT. I WAS GOING TO TELL THE REST OF THE WORLD ABOUT WHAT HAPPENED, ABOUT THE DEATHS OF MY COWORKERS AND THE TOWN...
...BUT THE TUNNEL DIDN'T END.

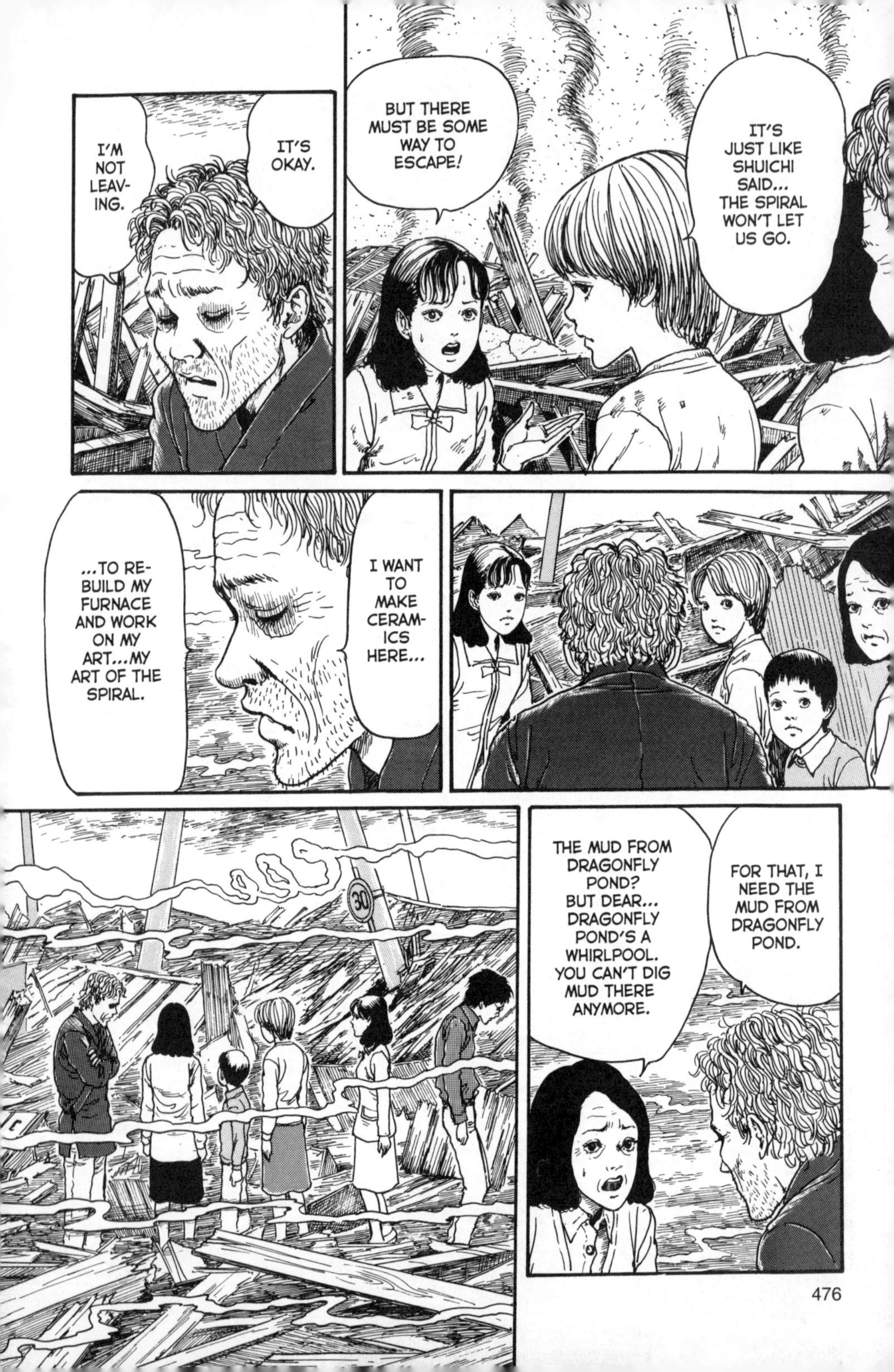
IT'S JUST LIKE SHUICHI SAID... THE SPIRAL WON'T LET US GO.
BUT THERE MUST BE SOME WAY TO ESCAPE!
IT'S OKAY.
I'M NOT LEAVING.
I WANT TO MAKE CERAMICS HERE...
...TO REBUILD MY FURNACE AND WORK ON MY ART...MY ART OF THE SPIRAL.
FOR THAT, I NEED THE MUD FROM DRAGONFLY POND.
THE MUD FROM DRAGONFLY POND? BUT DEAR... DRAGONFLY POND'S A WHIRLPOOL. YOU CAN'T DIG MUD THERE ANYMORE.
30

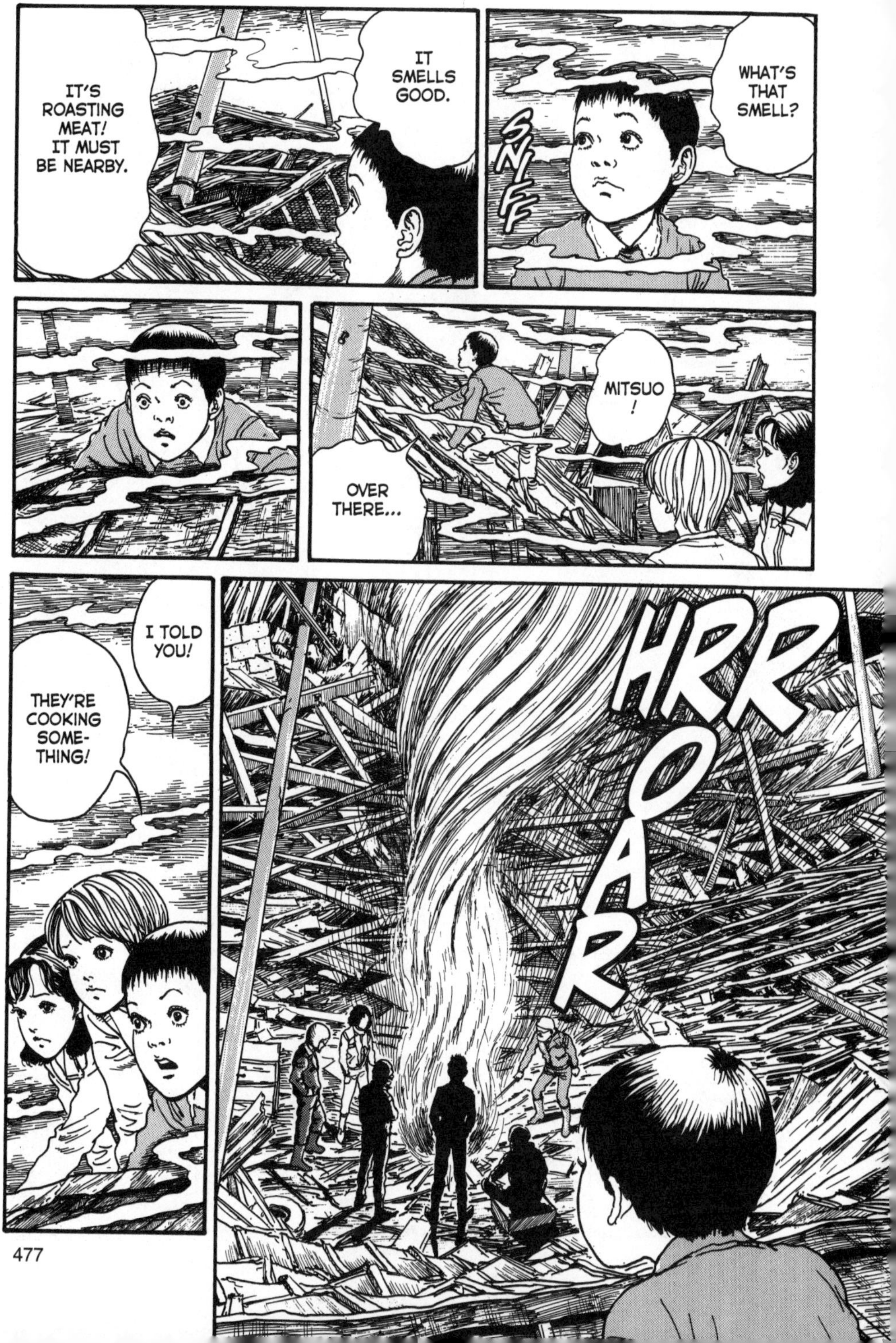
WHAT'S THAT SMELL?
SNIFF
IT SMELLS GOOD.
IT'S ROASTING MEAT! IT MUST BE NEARBY.
MITSUO!
OVER THERE...
HRROAR
I TOLD YOU!
THEY'RE COOKING SOMETHING!

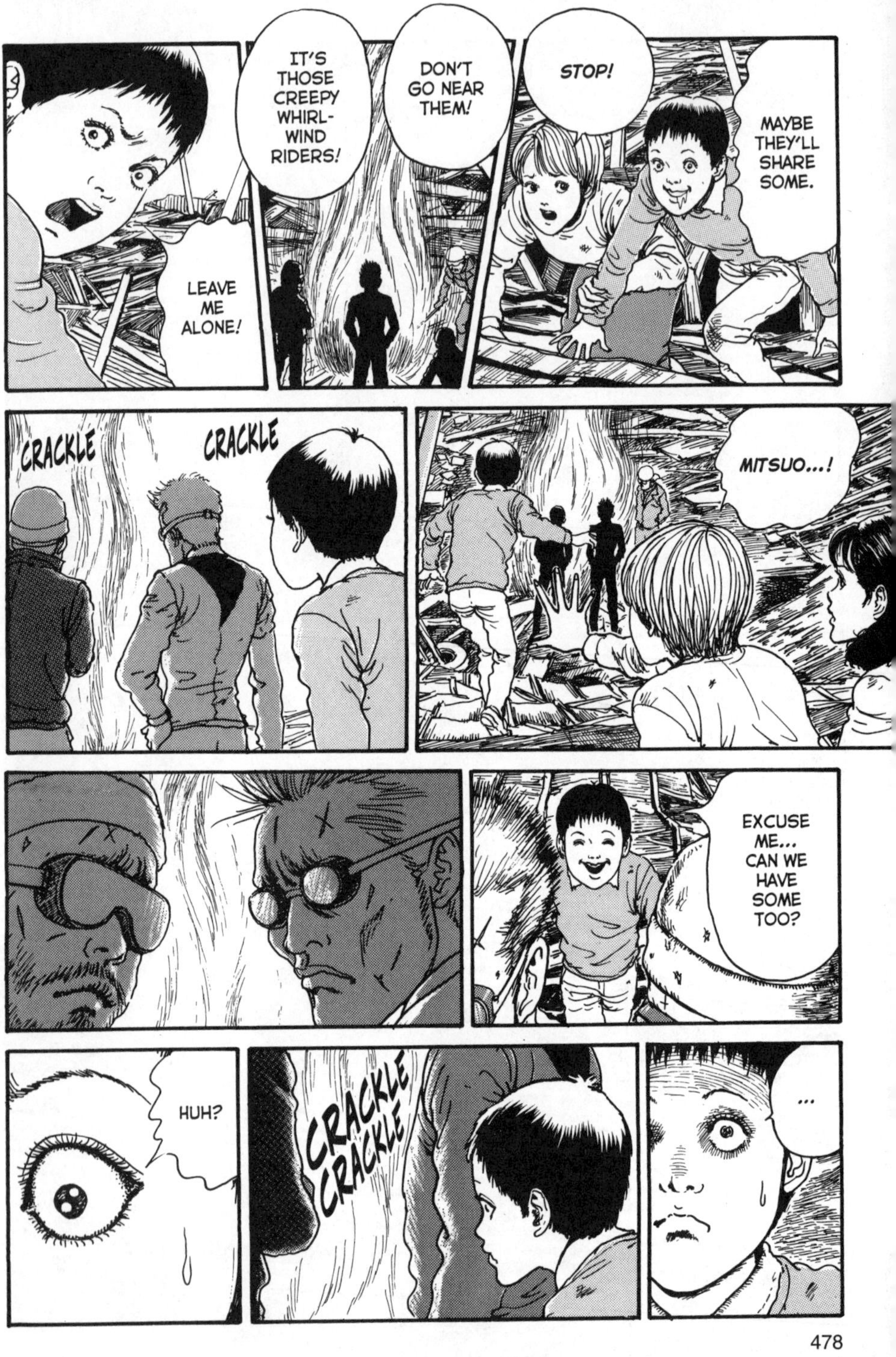
MAYBE THEY'LL SHARE SOME.
STOP!
DON'T GO NEAR THEM!
IT'S THOSE CREEPY WHIRL-WIND RIDERS!
LEAVE ME ALONE!
MITSUO...!
CRACKLE
CRACKLE
EXCUSE ME... CAN WE HAVE SOME TOO?
...
CRACKLE CRACKLE
HUH?

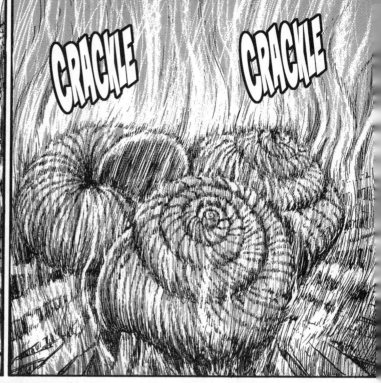

CRACKLE CRACKLE

KICH

YEAH...

I THINK THEY'RE DONE.

THWUD

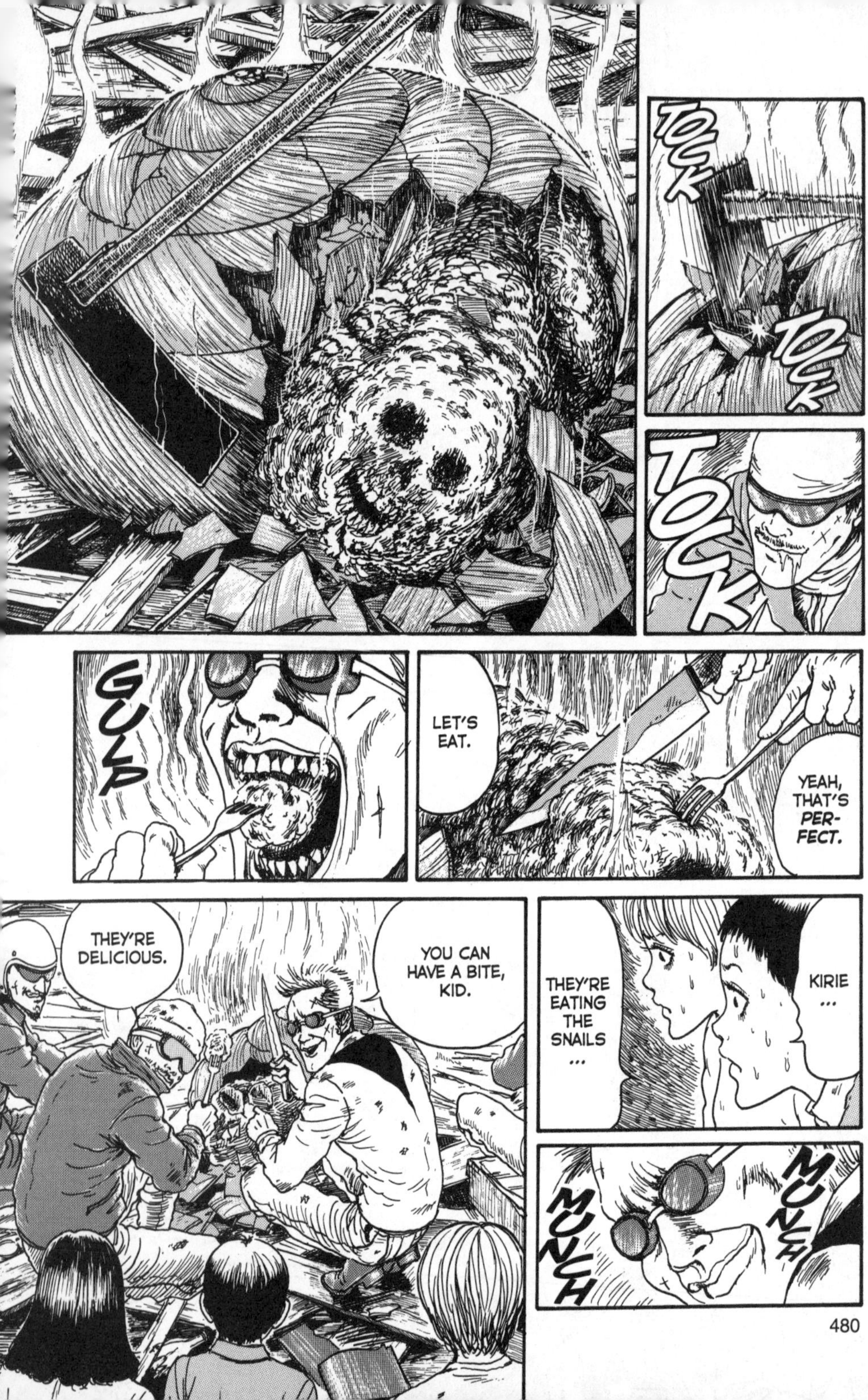
TOCK
TOCK
TOCK
YEAH, THAT'S PERFECT.
LET'S EAT.
GULP
KIRIE ...
THEY'RE EATING THE SNAILS ...
MUNCH
MUNCH
YOU CAN HAVE A BITE, KID.
THEY'RE DELICIOUS.

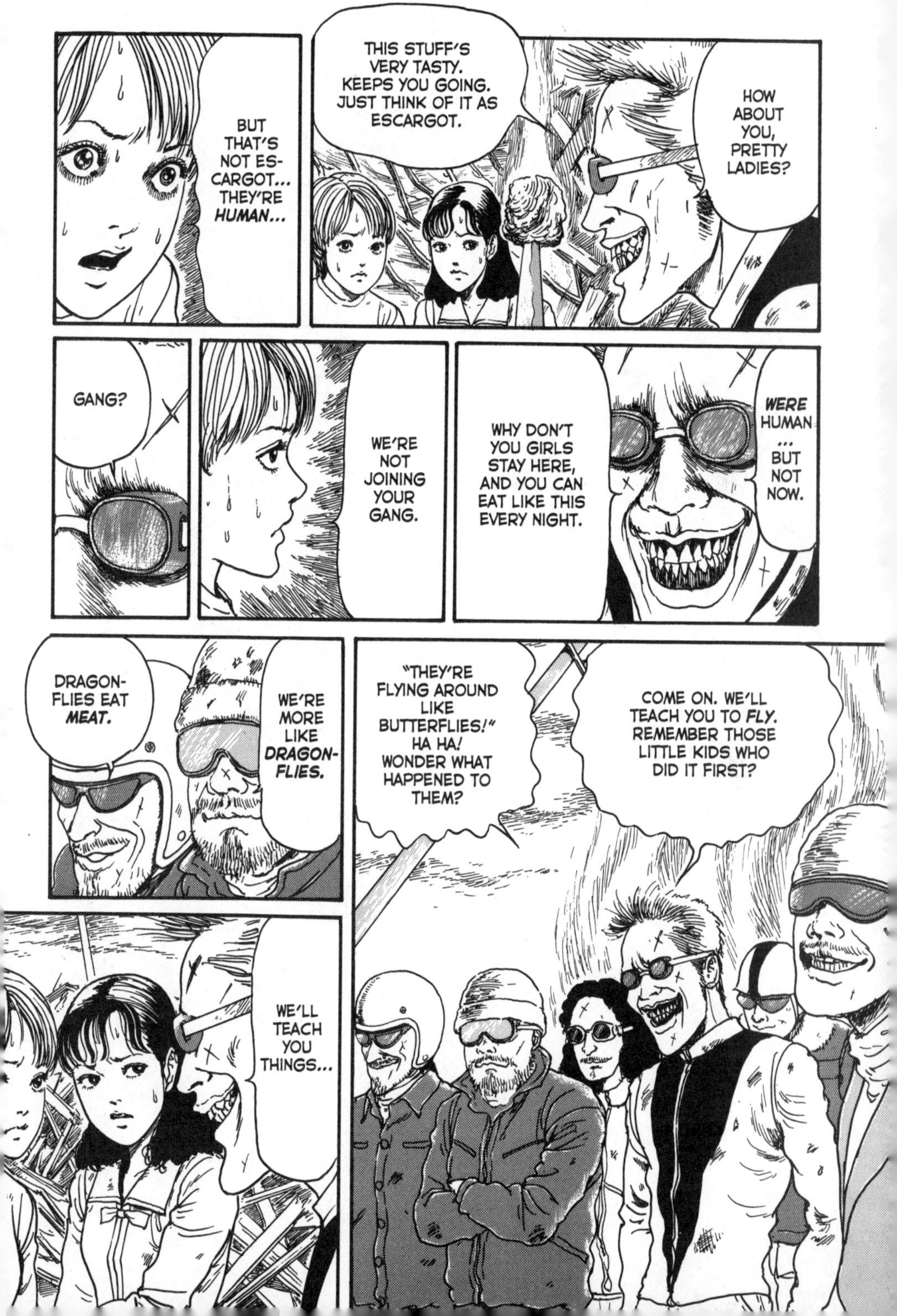
HOW ABOUT YOU, PRETTY LADIES?
THIS STUFF'S VERY TASTY. KEEPS YOU GOING. JUST THINK OF IT AS ESCARGOT.
BUT THAT'S NOT ES-CARGOT... THEY'RE *HUMAN*...
WERE HUMAN ... BUT NOT NOW.
WHY DON'T YOU GIRLS STAY HERE, AND YOU CAN EAT LIKE THIS EVERY NIGHT.
WE'RE NOT JOINING YOUR GANG.
GANG?
COME ON. WE'LL TEACH YOU TO *FLY*. REMEMBER THOSE LITTLE KIDS WHO DID IT FIRST?
"THEY'RE FLYING AROUND LIKE BUTTERFLIES!" HA HA! WONDER WHAT HAPPENED TO THEM?
WE'RE MORE LIKE *DRAGON-FLIES.*
DRAGON-FLIES EAT *MEAT.*
WE'LL TEACH YOU THINGS...

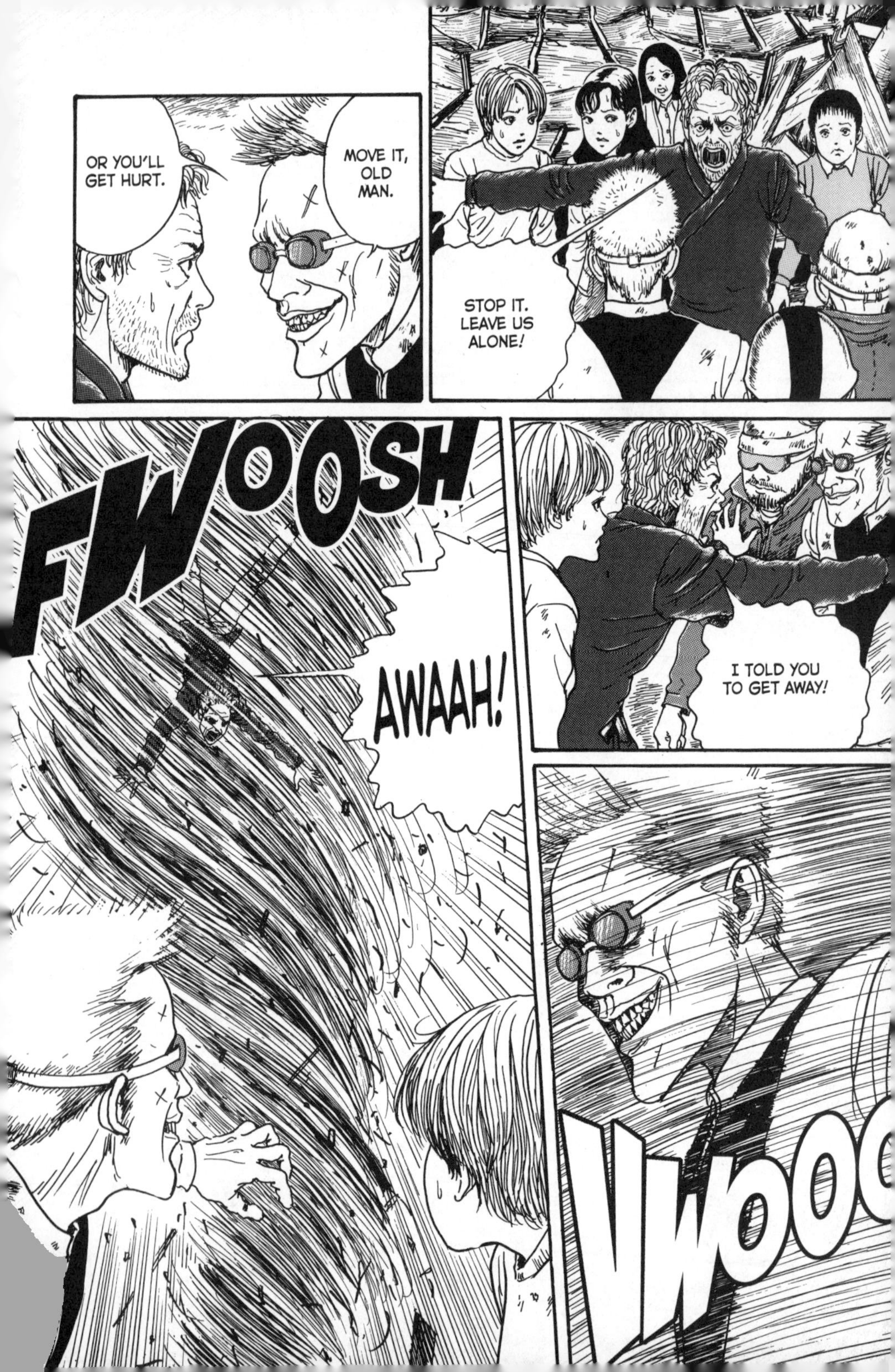
STOP IT. LEAVE US ALONE!
MOVE IT, OLD MAN.
OR YOU'LL GET HURT.
I TOLD YOU TO GET AWAY!
VWOO
FWOOSH
AWAAH!

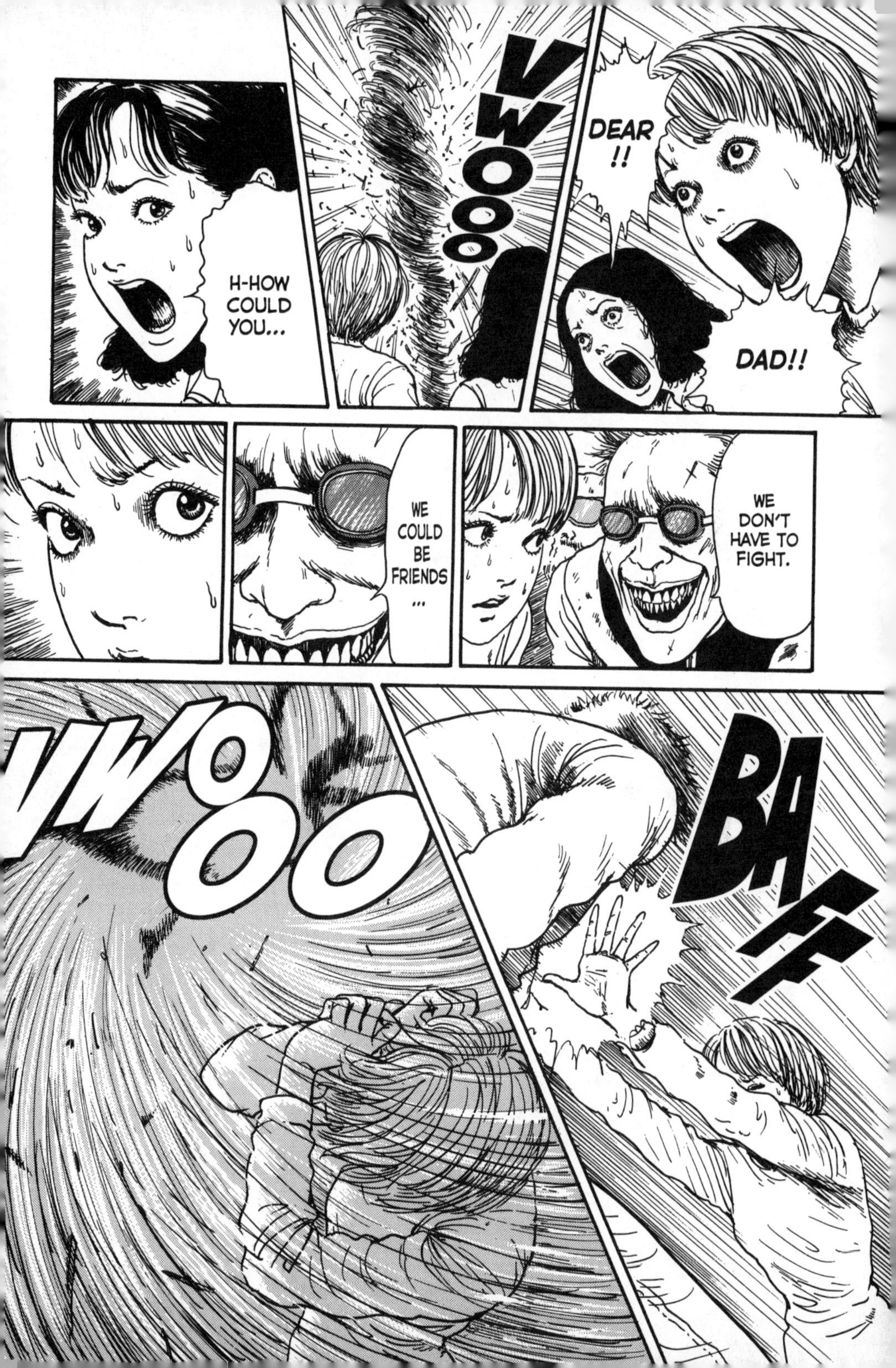
DEAR !!
DAD!!
VWOOO
H-HOW COULD YOU...
WE DON'T HAVE TO FIGHT.
WE COULD BE FRIENDS ...
BAFF
VWOOO

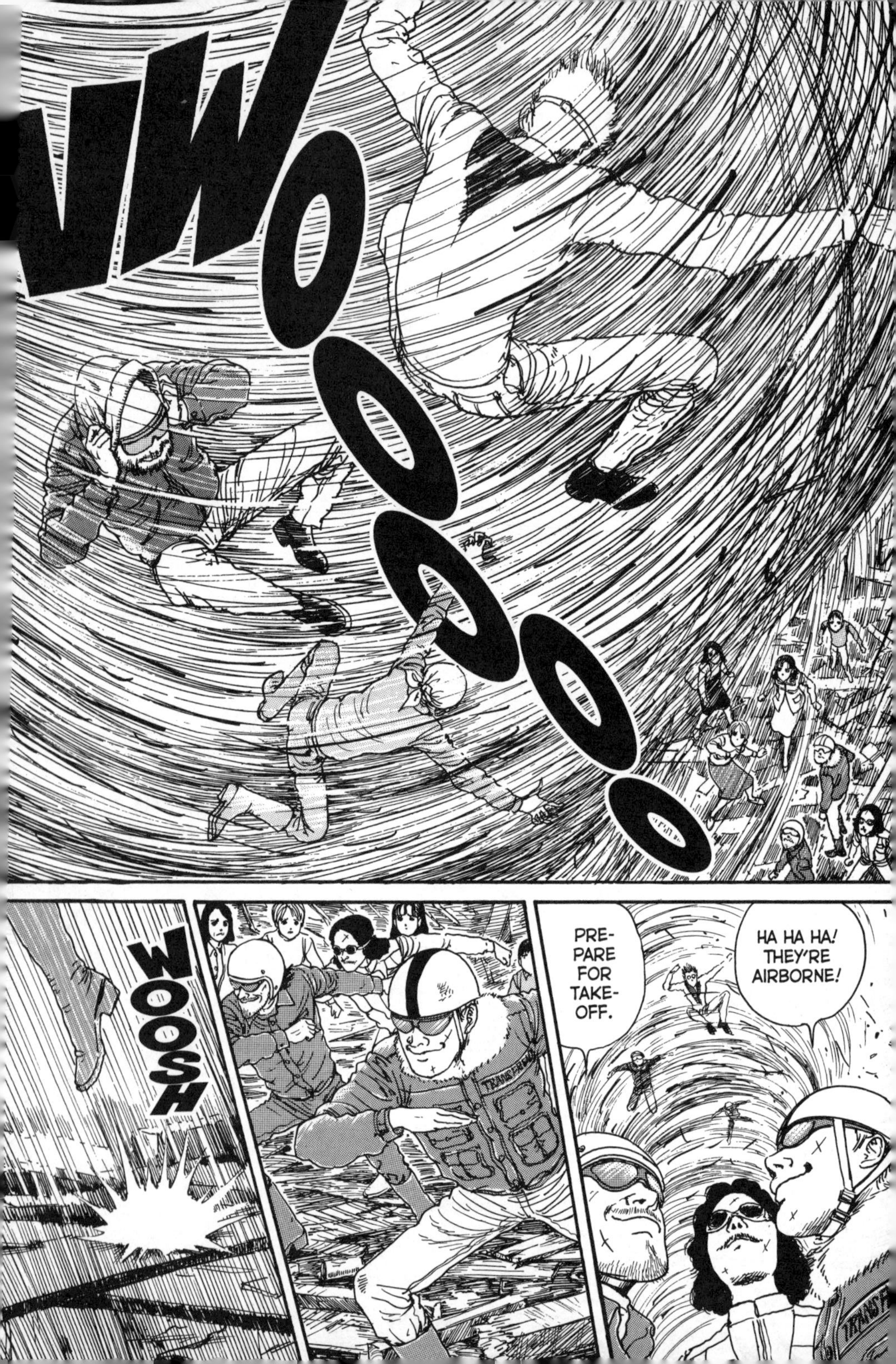
WOOOOOOOO
HA HA HA! THEY'RE AIRBORNE!
PREPARE FOR TAKE-OFF.
WOOSH

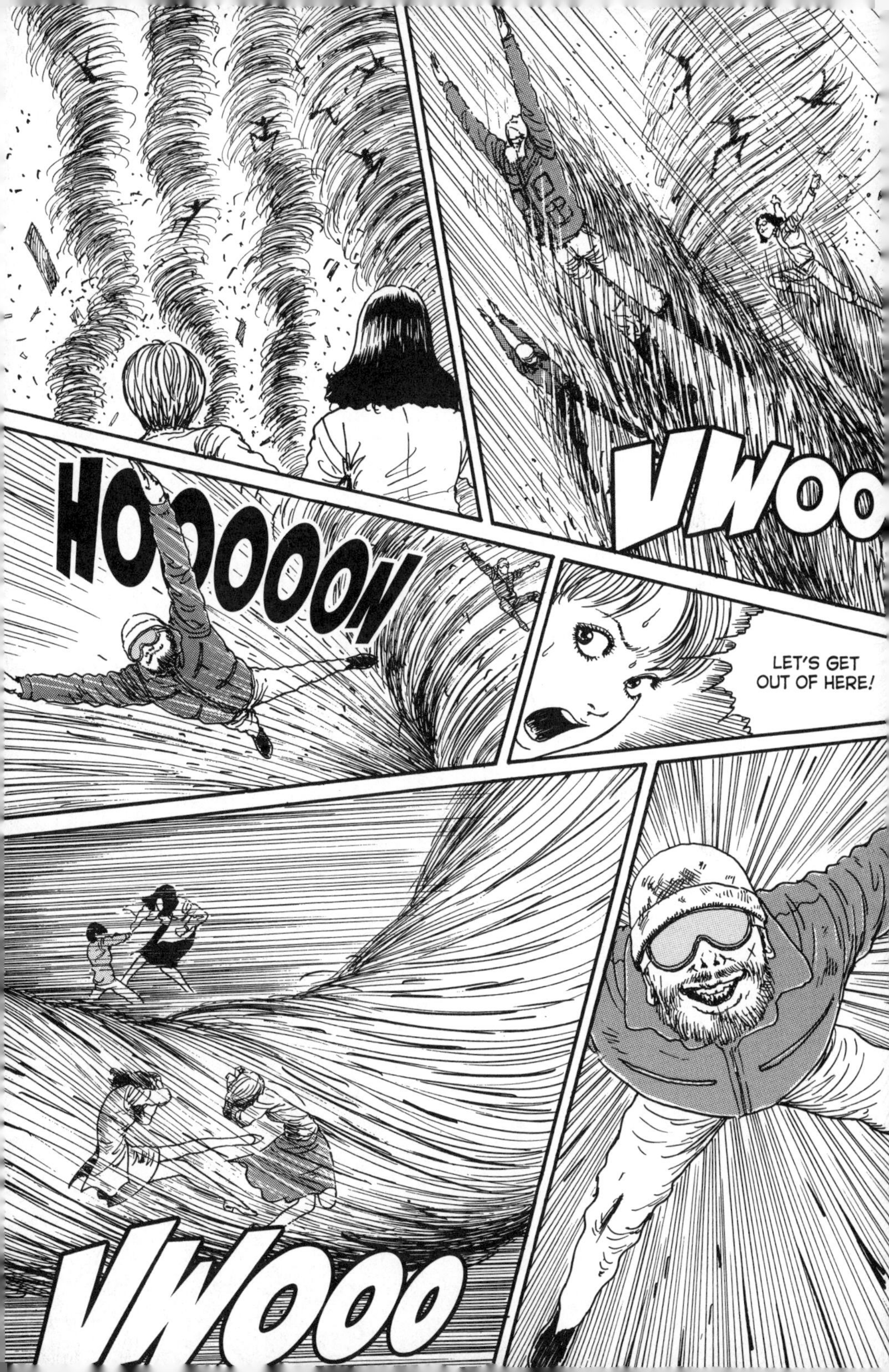
VWOO
LET'S GET OUT OF HERE!
HOOOOON
VWOOO

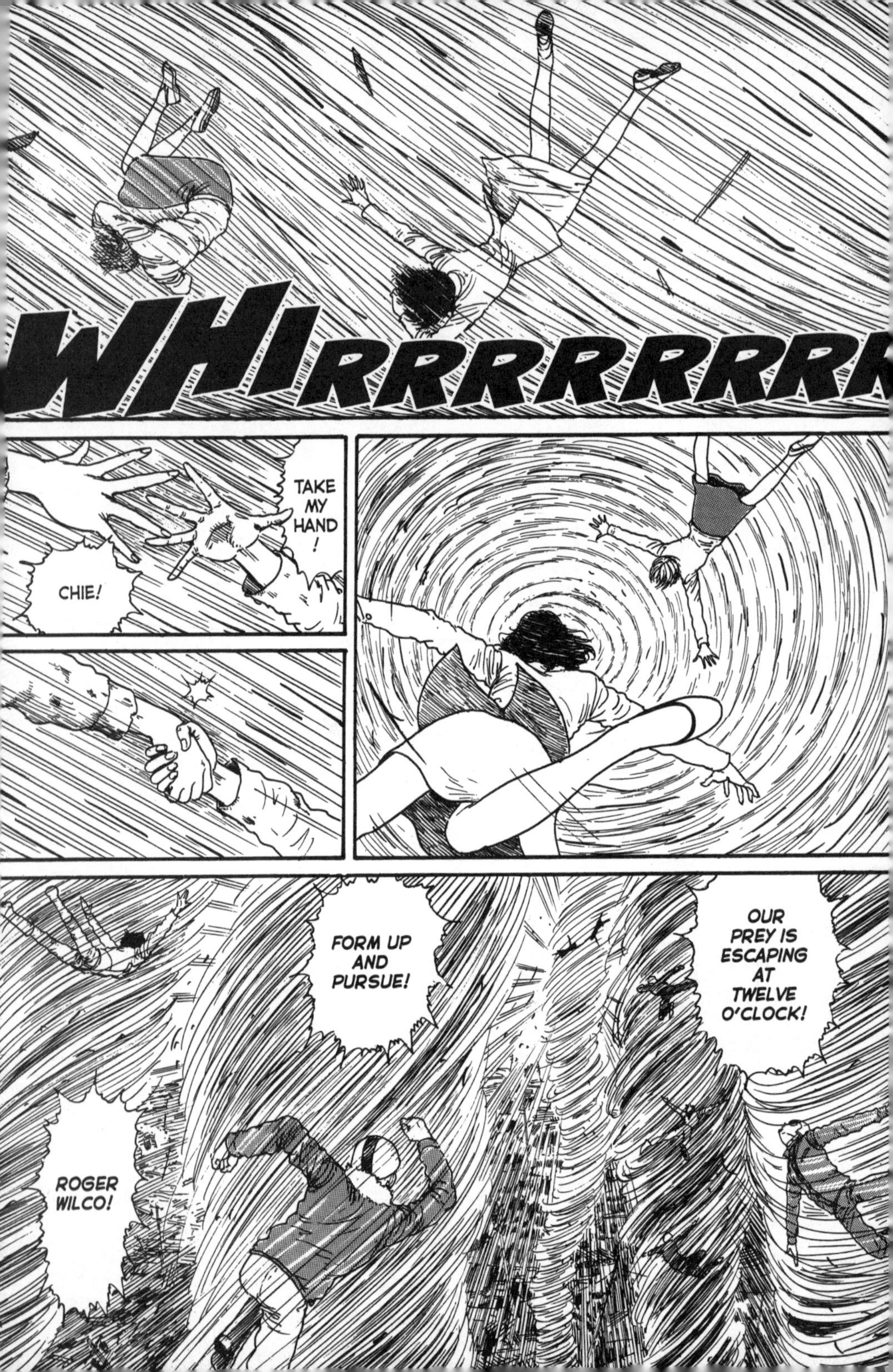
WHIRRRRRRRRR
TAKE MY HAND!
CHIE!
OUR PREY IS ESCAPING AT TWELVE O'CLOCK!
FORM UP AND PURSUE!
ROGER WILCO!

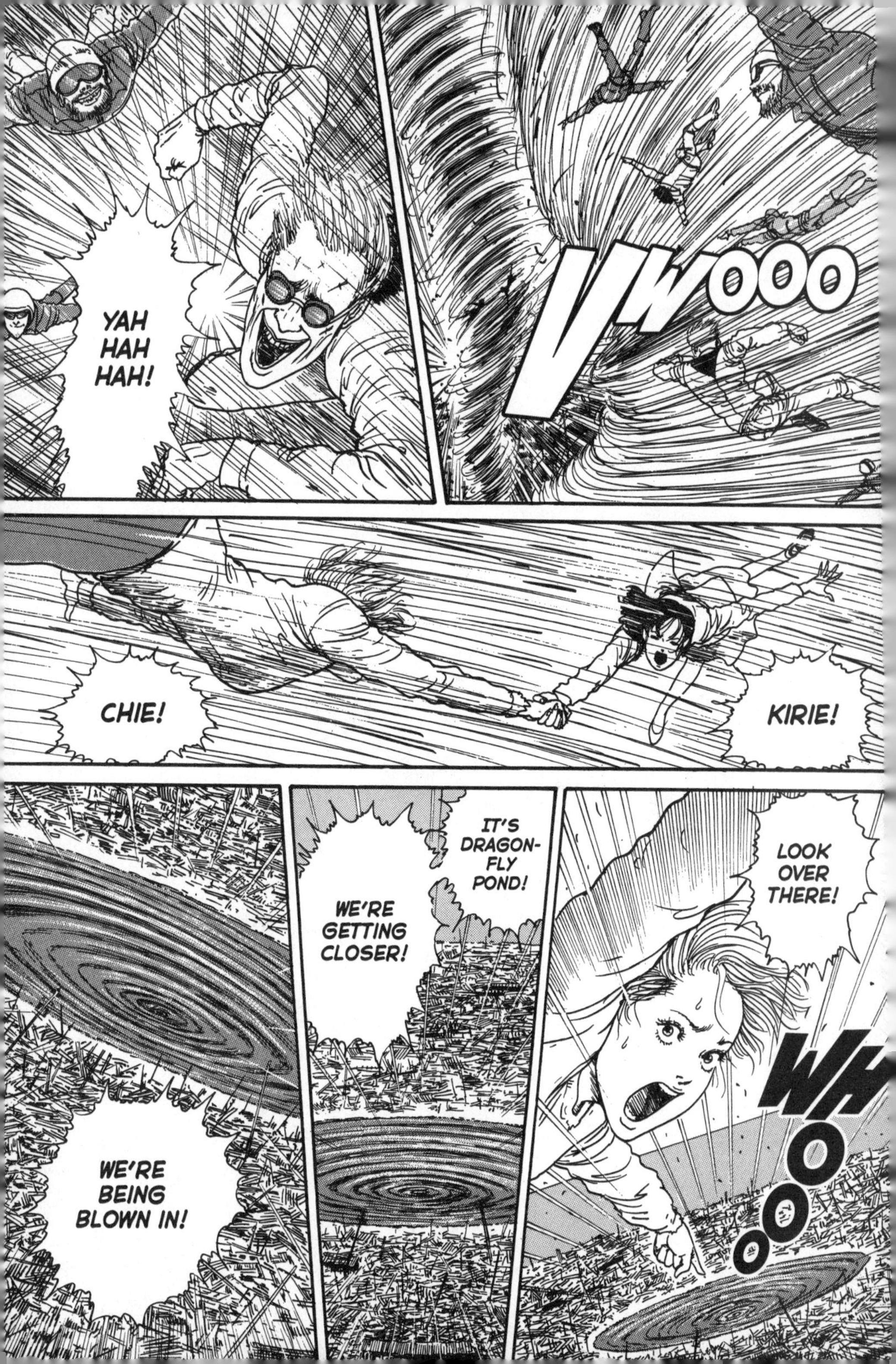
VWOOO
YAH HAH HAH!
KIRIE!
CHIE!
LOOK OVER THERE!
WHOOOO
IT'S DRAGON-FLY POND!
WE'RE GETTING CLOSER!
WE'RE BEING BLOWN IN!

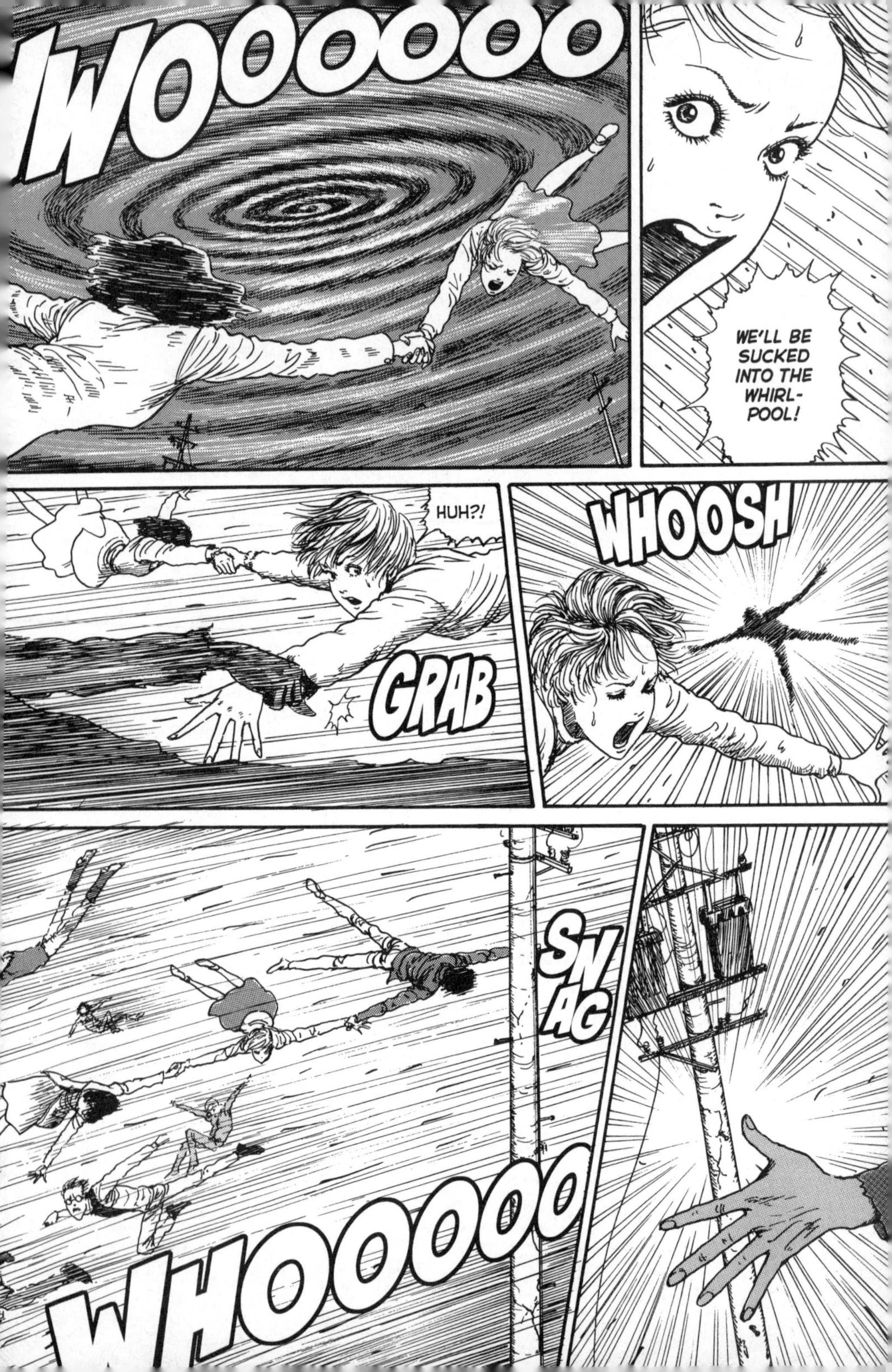
WE'LL BE SUCKED INTO THE WHIRL-POOL!
WOOOOOO
WHOOSH
HUH?!
GRAB
SNAG
WHOOOOOO

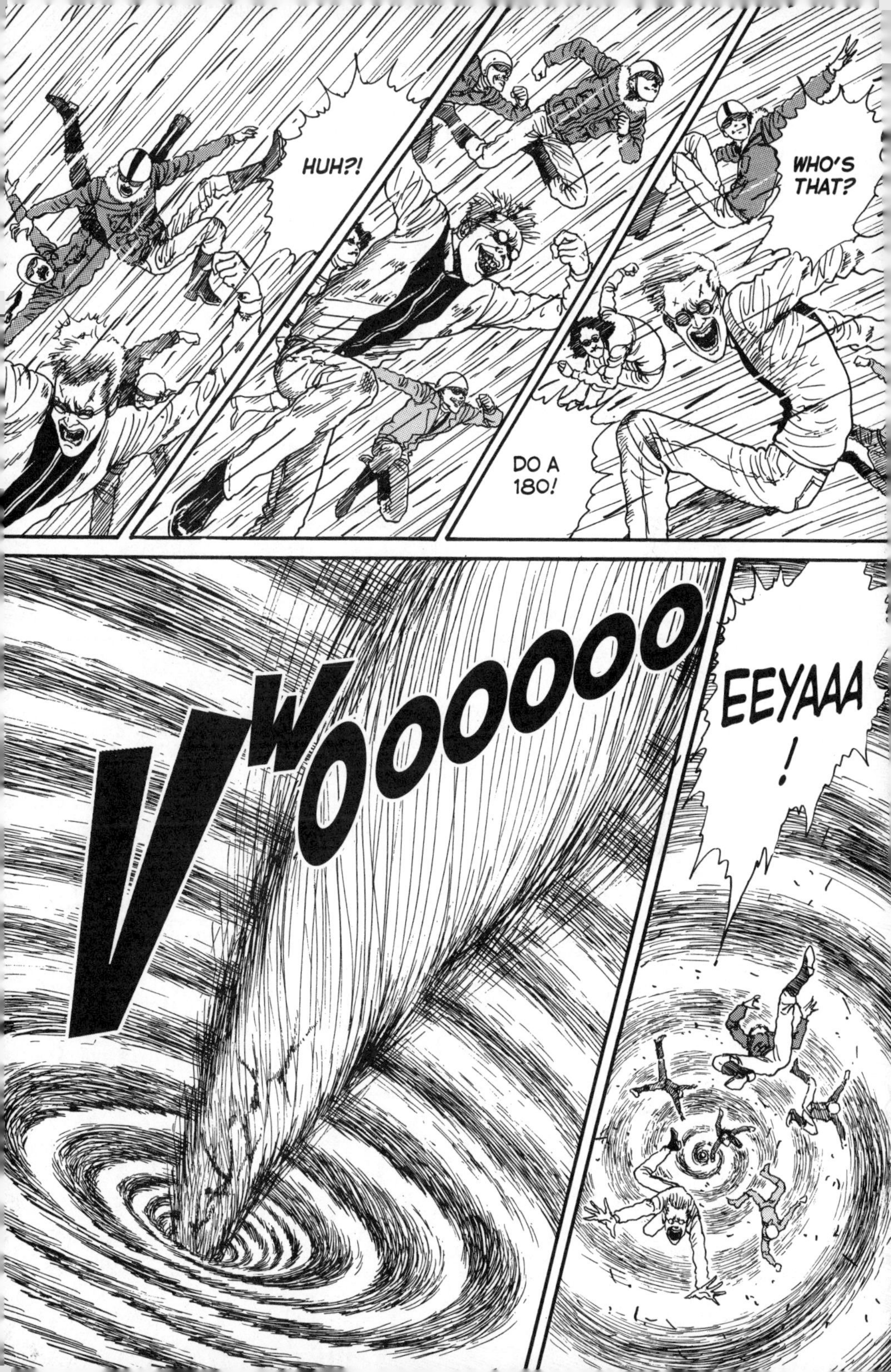
WHO'S THAT?
DO A 180!
HUH?!
EEYAAA!
VWOOOOOOO

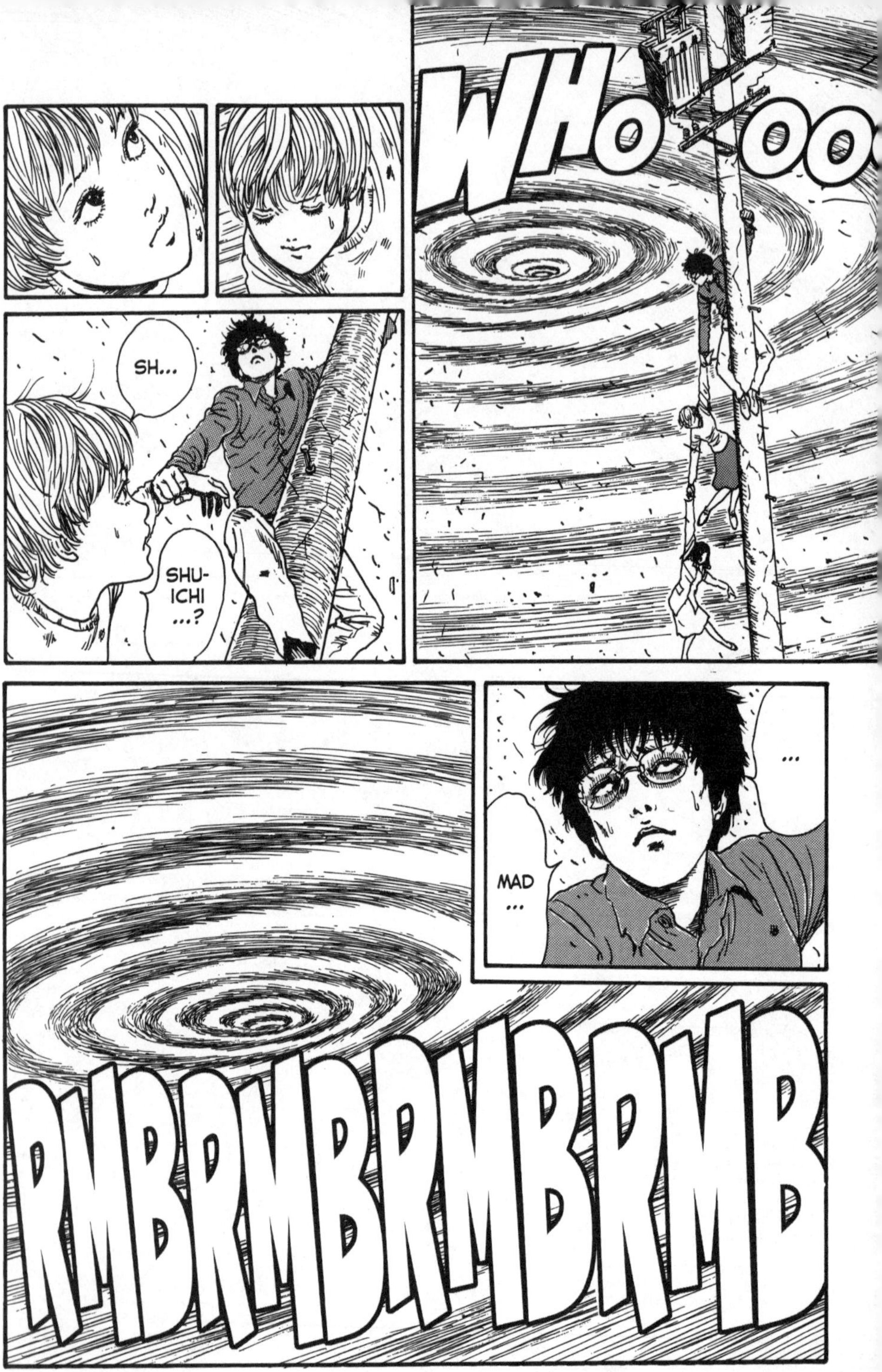
WHOOO
SH...
SHU-ICHI ...?
...
MAD ...
RMBRMBRMBRMBRMB

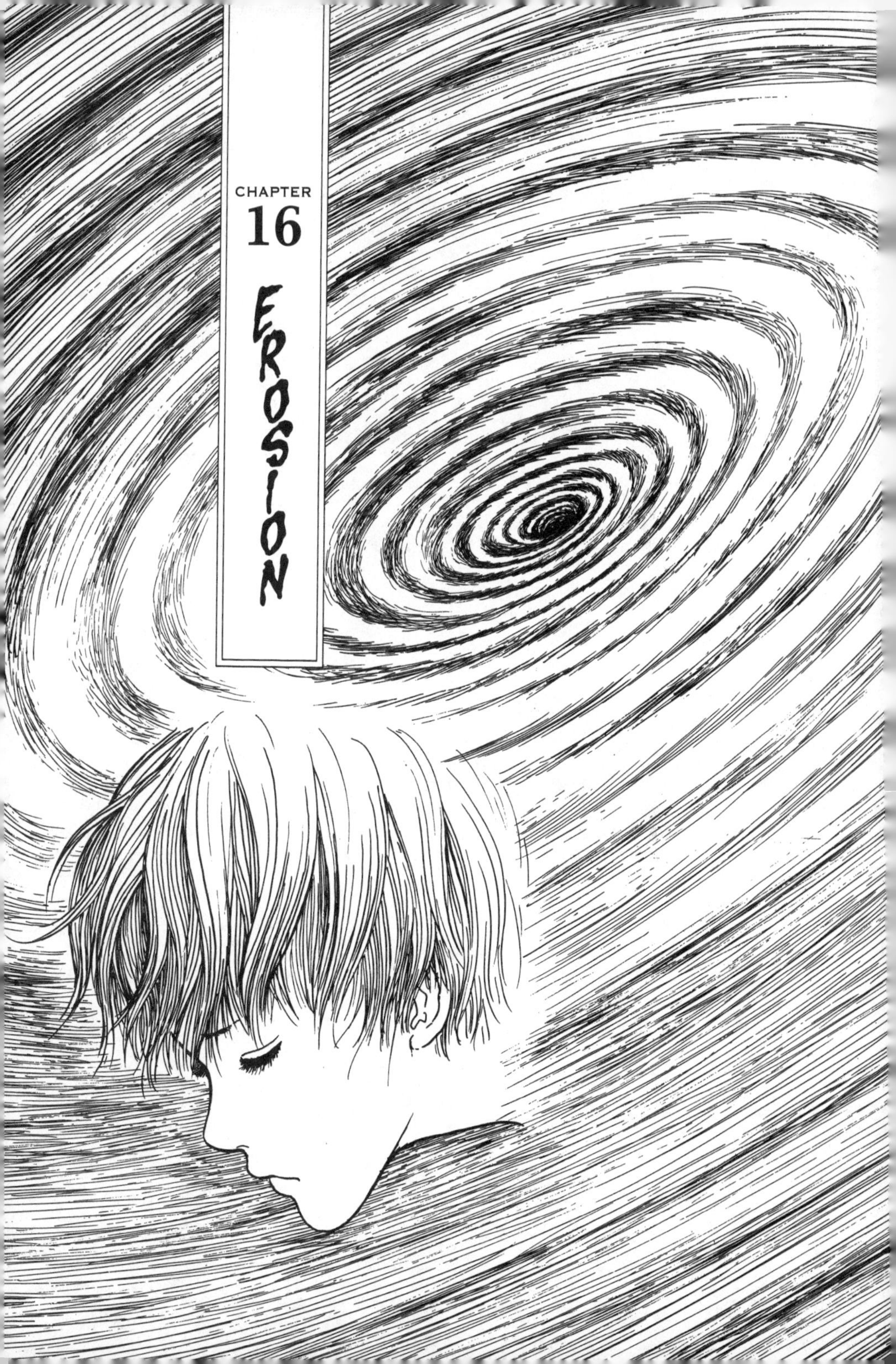
CHAPTER
16
EROSION

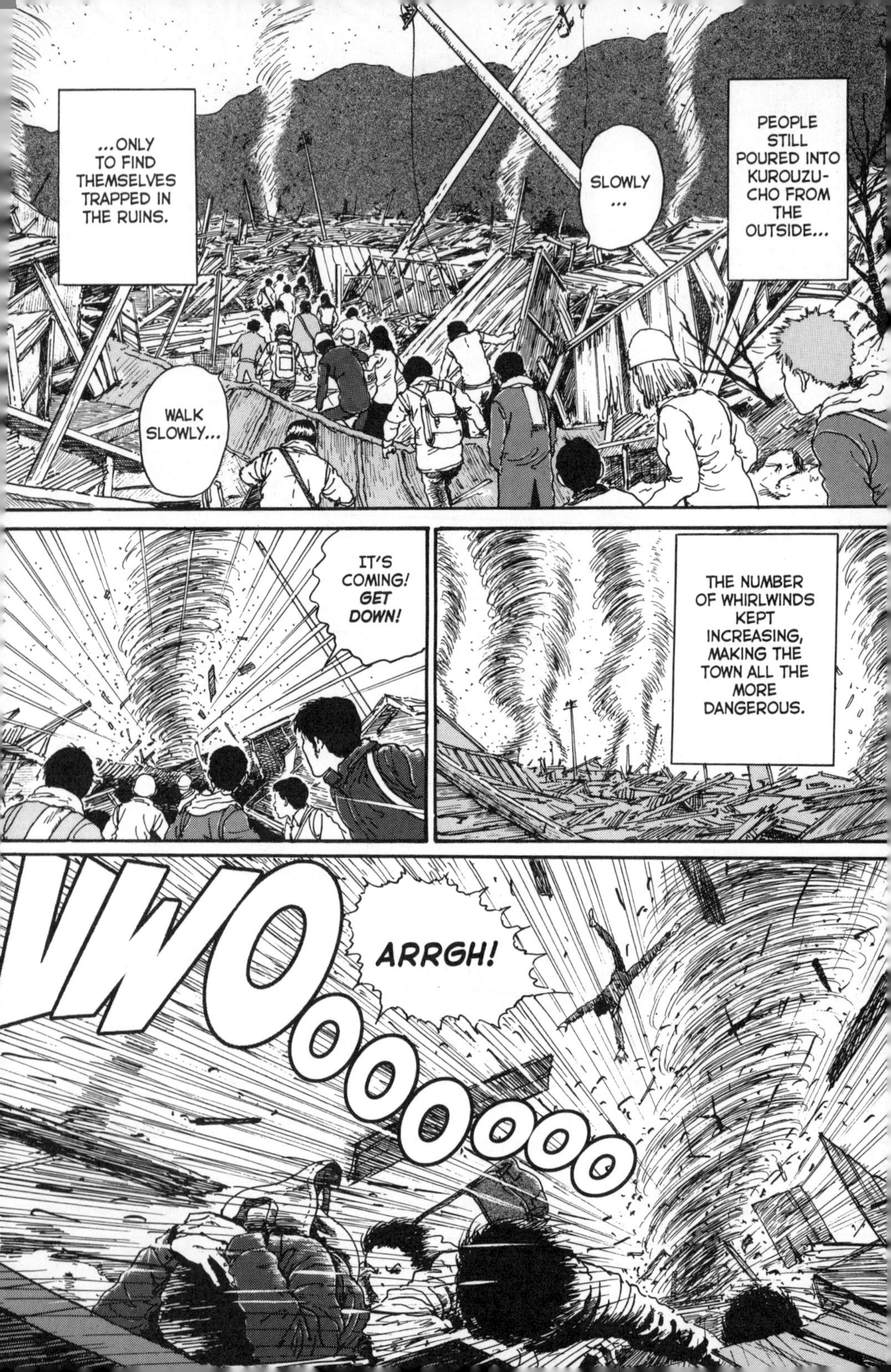
PEOPLE STILL POURED INTO KUROUZU-CHO FROM THE OUTSIDE...
SLOWLY ...
...ONLY TO FIND THEMSELVES TRAPPED IN THE RUINS.
WALK SLOWLY...
THE NUMBER OF WHIRLWINDS KEPT INCREASING, MAKING THE TOWN ALL THE MORE DANGEROUS.
IT'S COMING! GET DOWN!
ARRGH!
WOOOOOOOOO

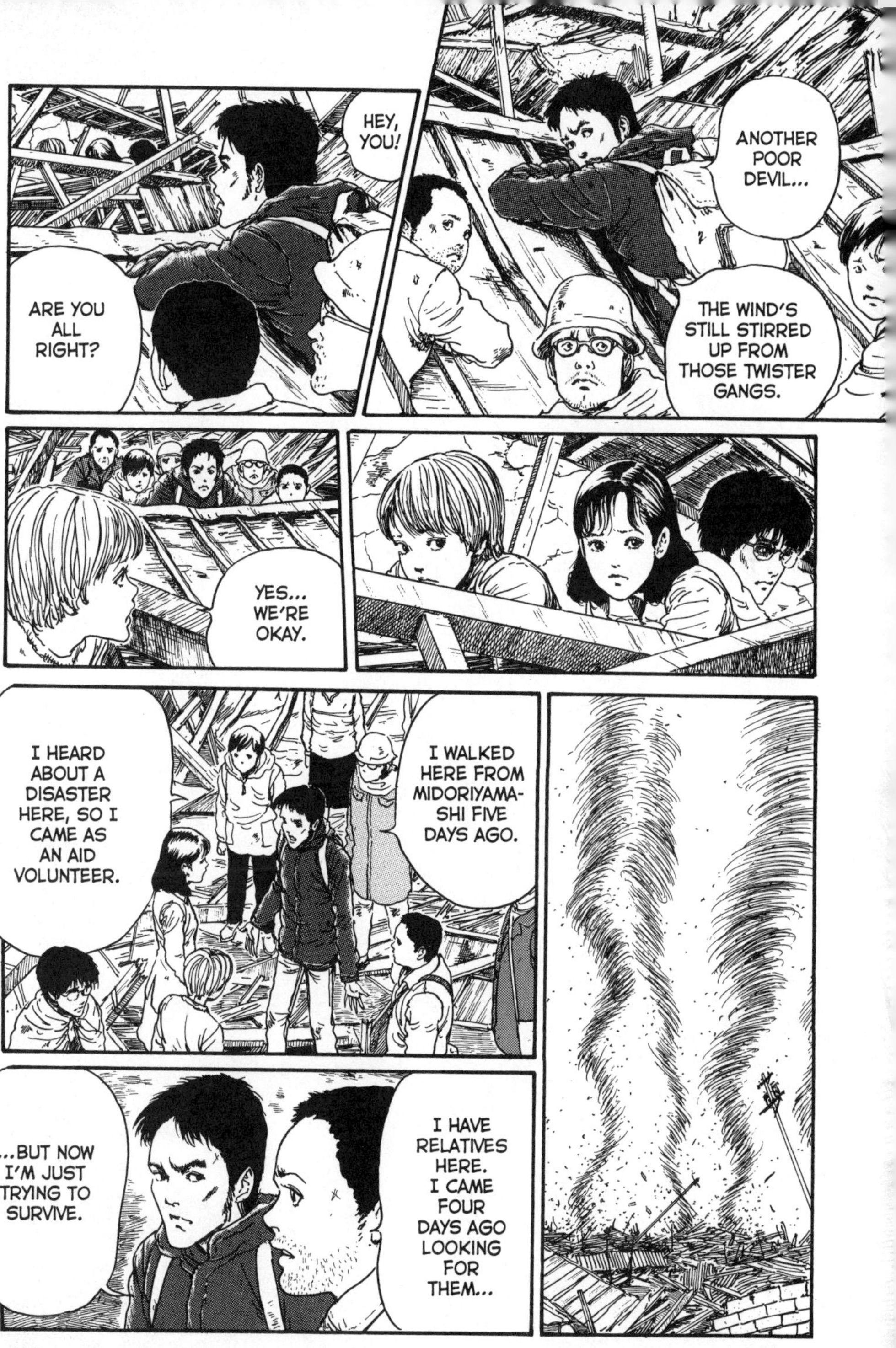
ANOTHER POOR DEVIL...
THE WIND'S STILL STIRRED UP FROM THOSE TWISTER GANGS.
HEY, YOU!
ARE YOU ALL RIGHT?
YES... WE'RE OKAY.
I WALKED HERE FROM MIDORIYAMA-SHI FIVE DAYS AGO.
I HEARD ABOUT A DISASTER HERE, SO I CAME AS AN AID VOLUNTEER.
I HAVE RELATIVES HERE. I CAME FOUR DAYS AGO LOOKING FOR THEM...
...BUT NOW I'M JUST TRYING TO SURVIVE.

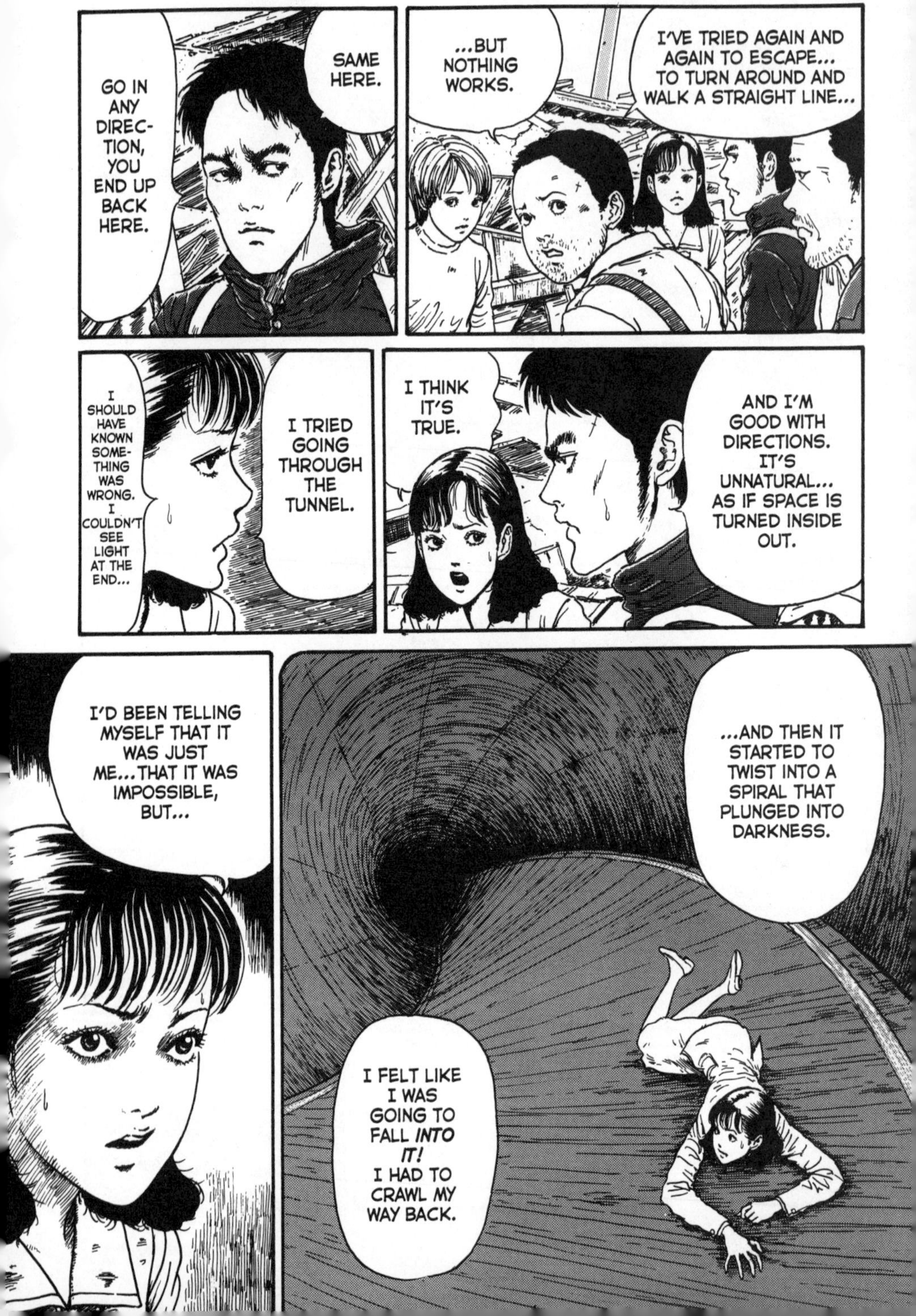

I'VE TRIED AGAIN AND AGAIN TO ESCAPE... TO TURN AROUND AND WALK A STRAIGHT LINE...
...BUT NOTHING WORKS.
SAME HERE.
GO IN ANY DIRECTION, YOU END UP BACK HERE.
AND I'M GOOD WITH DIRECTIONS. IT'S UNNATURAL... AS IF SPACE IS TURNED INSIDE OUT.
I THINK IT'S TRUE.
I TRIED GOING THROUGH THE TUNNEL.
I SHOULD HAVE KNOWN SOMETHING WAS WRONG. I COULDN'T SEE LIGHT AT THE END...
...AND THEN IT STARTED TO TWIST INTO A SPIRAL THAT PLUNGED INTO DARKNESS.
I FELT LIKE I WAS GOING TO FALL *INTO IT!* I HAD TO CRAWL MY WAY BACK.
I'D BEEN TELLING MYSELF THAT IT WAS JUST ME...THAT IT WAS IMPOSSIBLE, BUT...

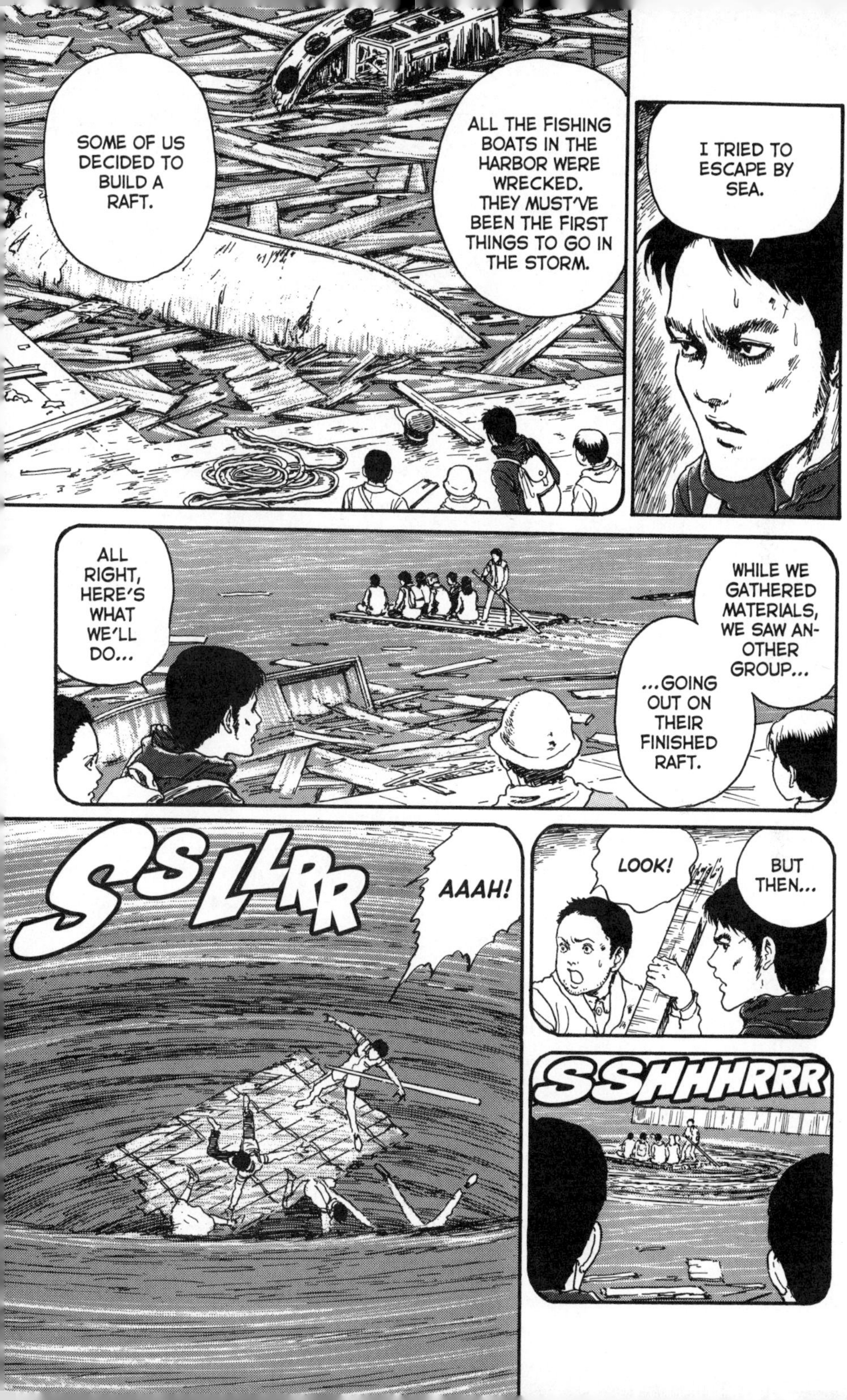
I TRIED TO ESCAPE BY SEA.
ALL THE FISHING BOATS IN THE HARBOR WERE WRECKED. THEY MUST'VE BEEN THE FIRST THINGS TO GO IN THE STORM.
SOME OF US DECIDED TO BUILD A RAFT.
WHILE WE GATHERED MATERIALS, WE SAW AN-OTHER GROUP...
...GOING OUT ON THEIR FINISHED RAFT.
ALL RIGHT, HERE'S WHAT WE'LL DO...
BUT THEN...
LOOK!
SSHHHRRR
AAAH!
SSLLRR

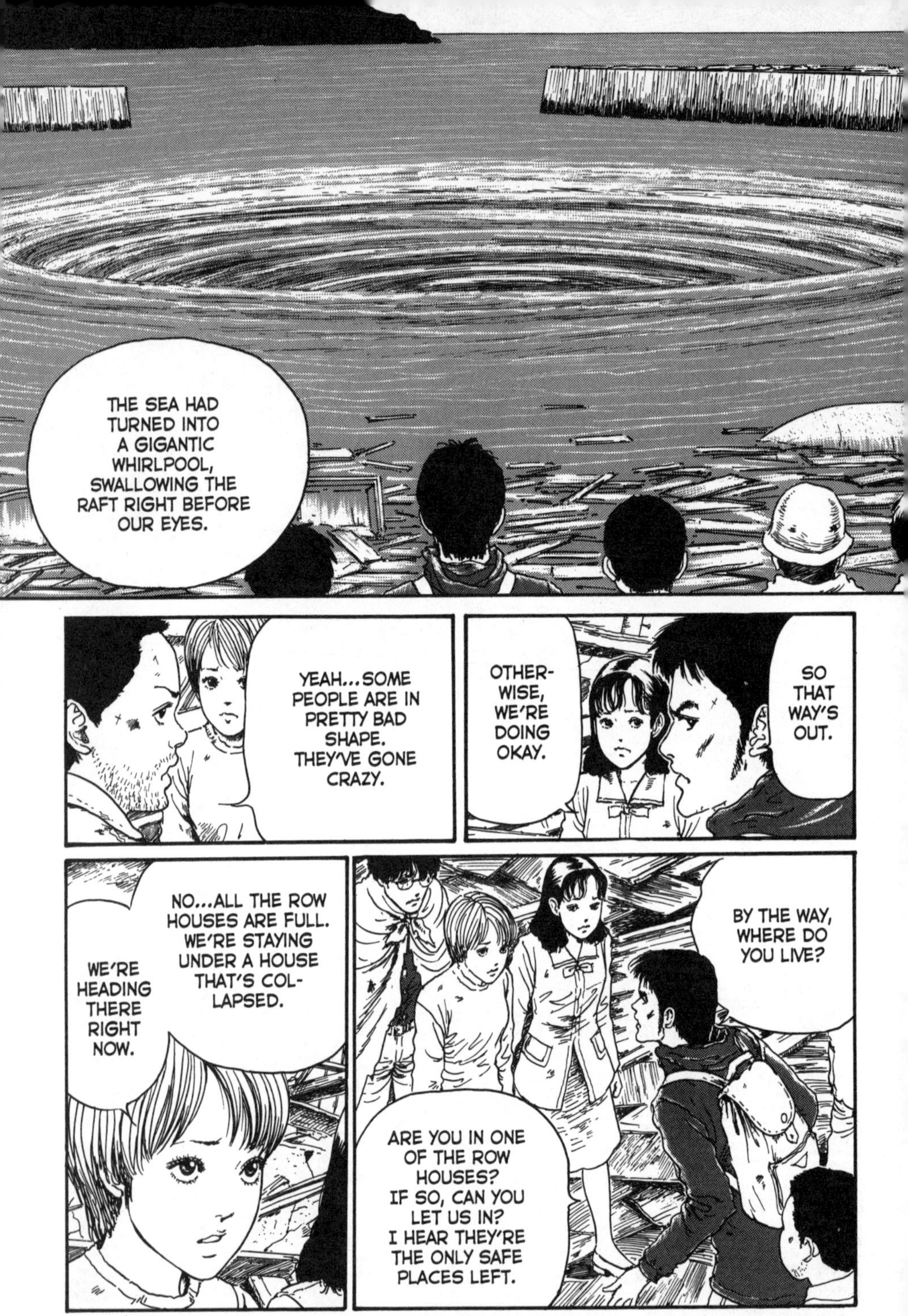
THE SEA HAD TURNED INTO A GIGANTIC WHIRLPOOL, SWALLOWING THE RAFT RIGHT BEFORE OUR EYES.
SO THAT WAY'S OUT.
OTHER-WISE, WE'RE DOING OKAY.
YEAH...SOME PEOPLE ARE IN PRETTY BAD SHAPE. THEY'VE GONE CRAZY.
BY THE WAY, WHERE DO YOU LIVE?
ARE YOU IN ONE OF THE ROW HOUSES? IF SO, CAN YOU LET US IN? I HEAR THEY'RE THE ONLY SAFE PLACES LEFT.
NO...ALL THE ROW HOUSES ARE FULL. WE'RE STAYING UNDER A HOUSE THAT'S COL-LAPSED.
WE'RE HEADING THERE RIGHT NOW.

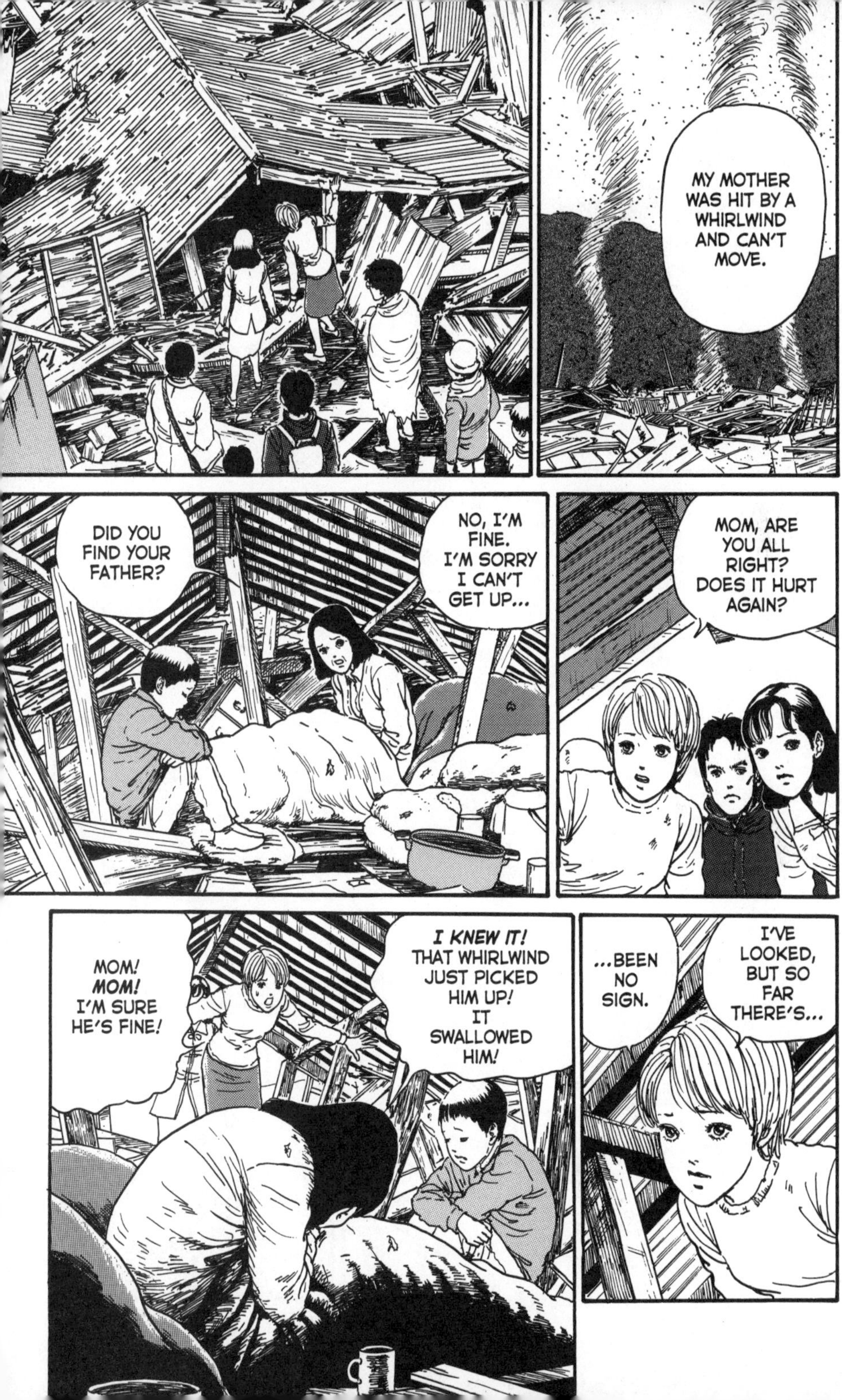
MY MOTHER WAS HIT BY A WHIRLWIND AND CAN'T MOVE.
MOM, ARE YOU ALL RIGHT? DOES IT HURT AGAIN?
NO, I'M FINE. I'M SORRY I CAN'T GET UP...
DID YOU FIND YOUR FATHER?
I'VE LOOKED, BUT SO FAR THERE'S...
...BEEN NO SIGN.
I KNEW IT! THAT WHIRLWIND JUST PICKED HIM UP! IT SWALLOWED HIM!
MOM! ***MOM!*** I'M SURE HE'S FINE!

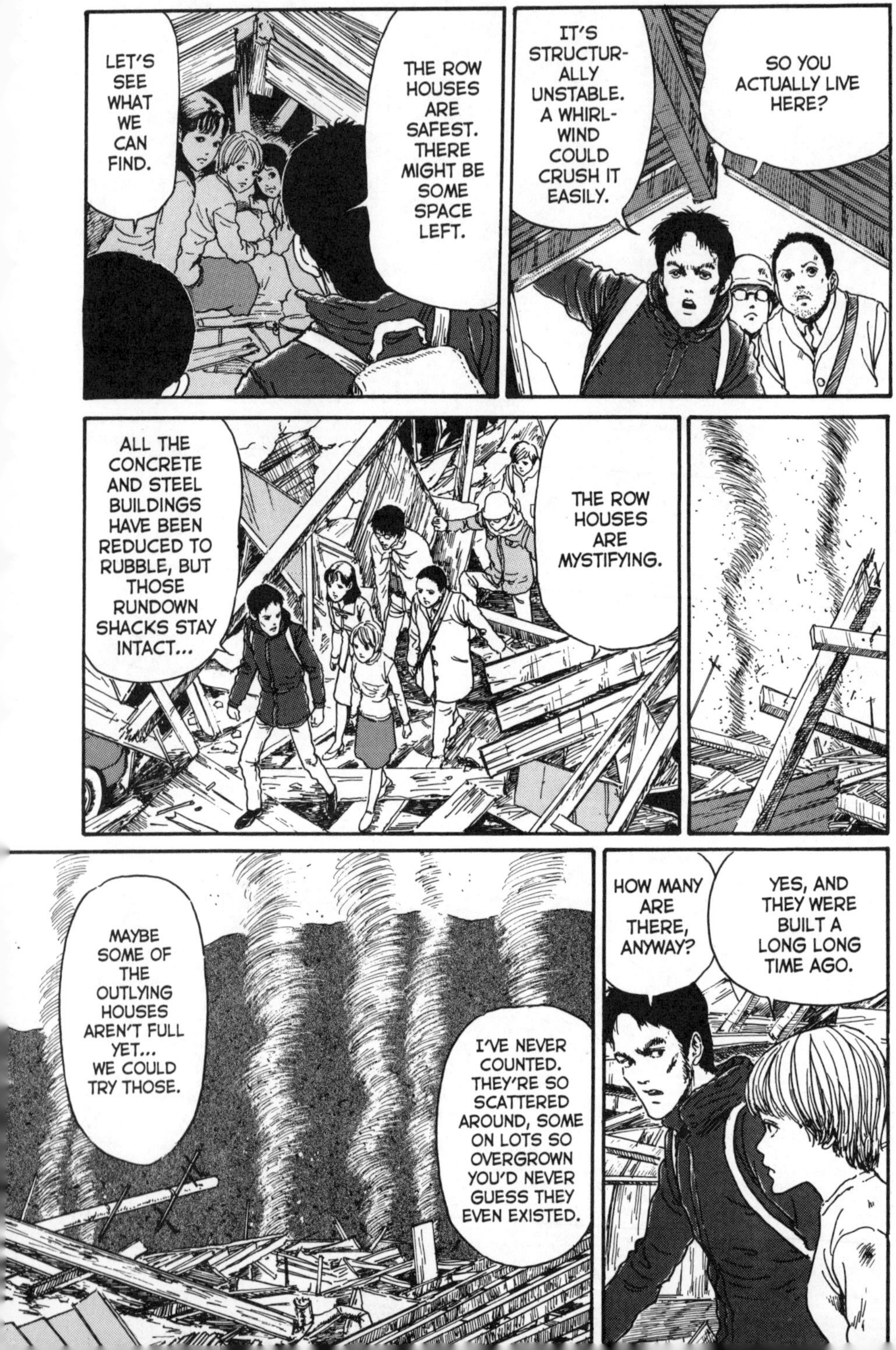
SO YOU ACTUALLY LIVE HERE?
IT'S STRUCTURALLY UNSTABLE. A WHIRLWIND COULD CRUSH IT EASILY.
THE ROW HOUSES ARE SAFEST. THERE MIGHT BE SOME SPACE LEFT.
LET'S SEE WHAT WE CAN FIND.
THE ROW HOUSES ARE MYSTIFYING.
ALL THE CONCRETE AND STEEL BUILDINGS HAVE BEEN REDUCED TO RUBBLE, BUT THOSE RUNDOWN SHACKS STAY INTACT...
YES, AND THEY WERE BUILT A LONG LONG TIME AGO.
HOW MANY ARE THERE, ANYWAY?
I'VE NEVER COUNTED. THEY'RE SO SCATTERED AROUND, SOME ON LOTS SO OVERGROWN YOU'D NEVER GUESS THEY EVEN EXISTED.
MAYBE SOME OF THE OUTLYING HOUSES AREN'T FULL YET... WE COULD TRY THOSE.

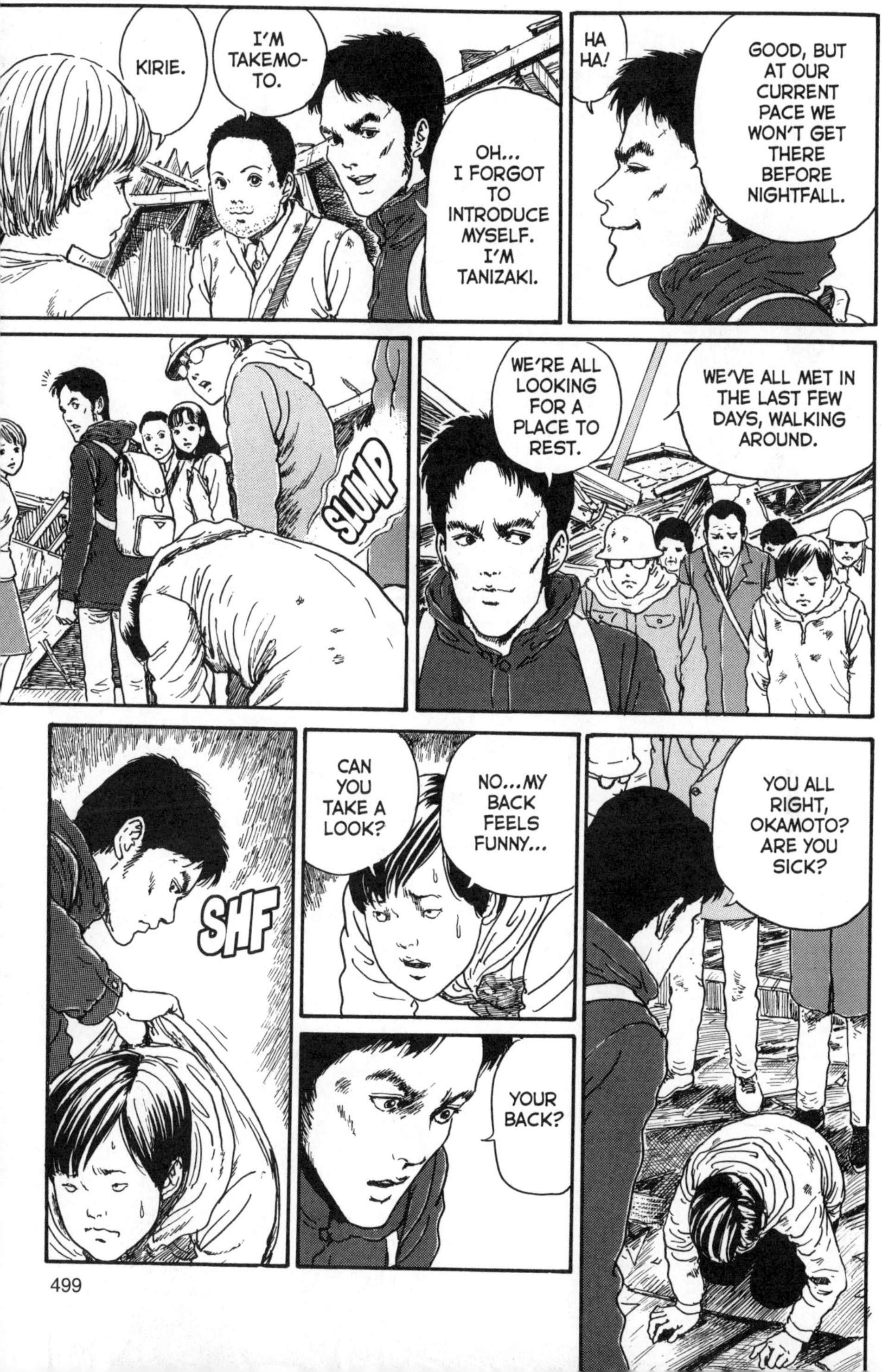
HA HA!
GOOD, BUT AT OUR CURRENT PACE WE WON'T GET THERE BEFORE NIGHTFALL.
OH... I FORGOT TO INTRODUCE MYSELF. I'M TANIZAKI.
I'M TAKEMO-TO.
KIRIE.
WE'VE ALL MET IN THE LAST FEW DAYS, WALKING AROUND.
WE'RE ALL LOOKING FOR A PLACE TO REST.
SLUMP
YOU ALL RIGHT, OKAMOTO? ARE YOU SICK?
NO...MY BACK FEELS FUNNY...
CAN YOU TAKE A LOOK?
YOUR BACK?
SHF

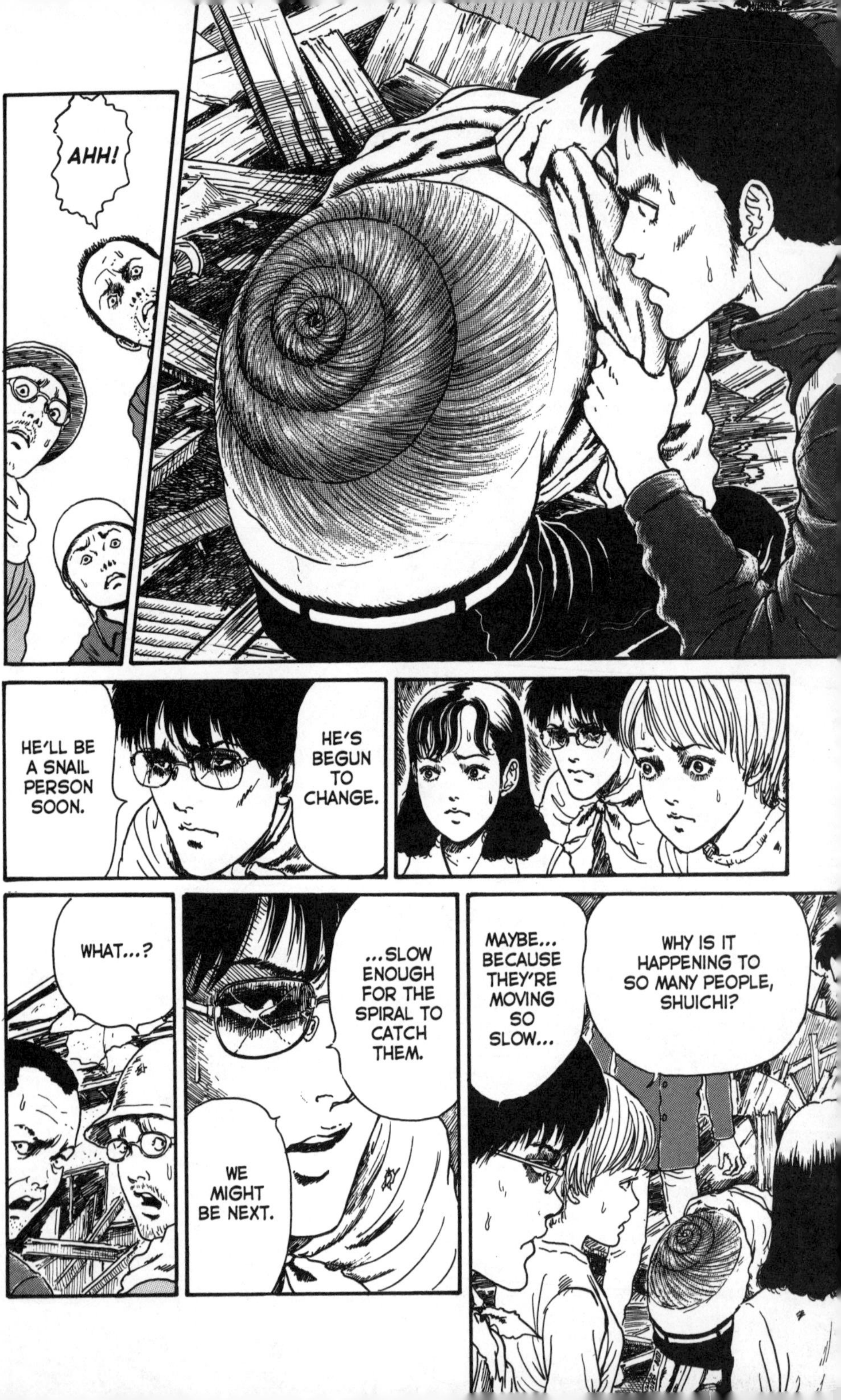
AHH!
HE'S BEGUN TO CHANGE.
HE'LL BE A SNAIL PERSON SOON.
WHY IS IT HAPPENING TO SO MANY PEOPLE, SHUICHI?
MAYBE... BECAUSE THEY'RE MOVING SO SLOW...
...SLOW ENOUGH FOR THE SPIRAL TO CATCH THEM.
WE MIGHT BE NEXT.
WHAT...?

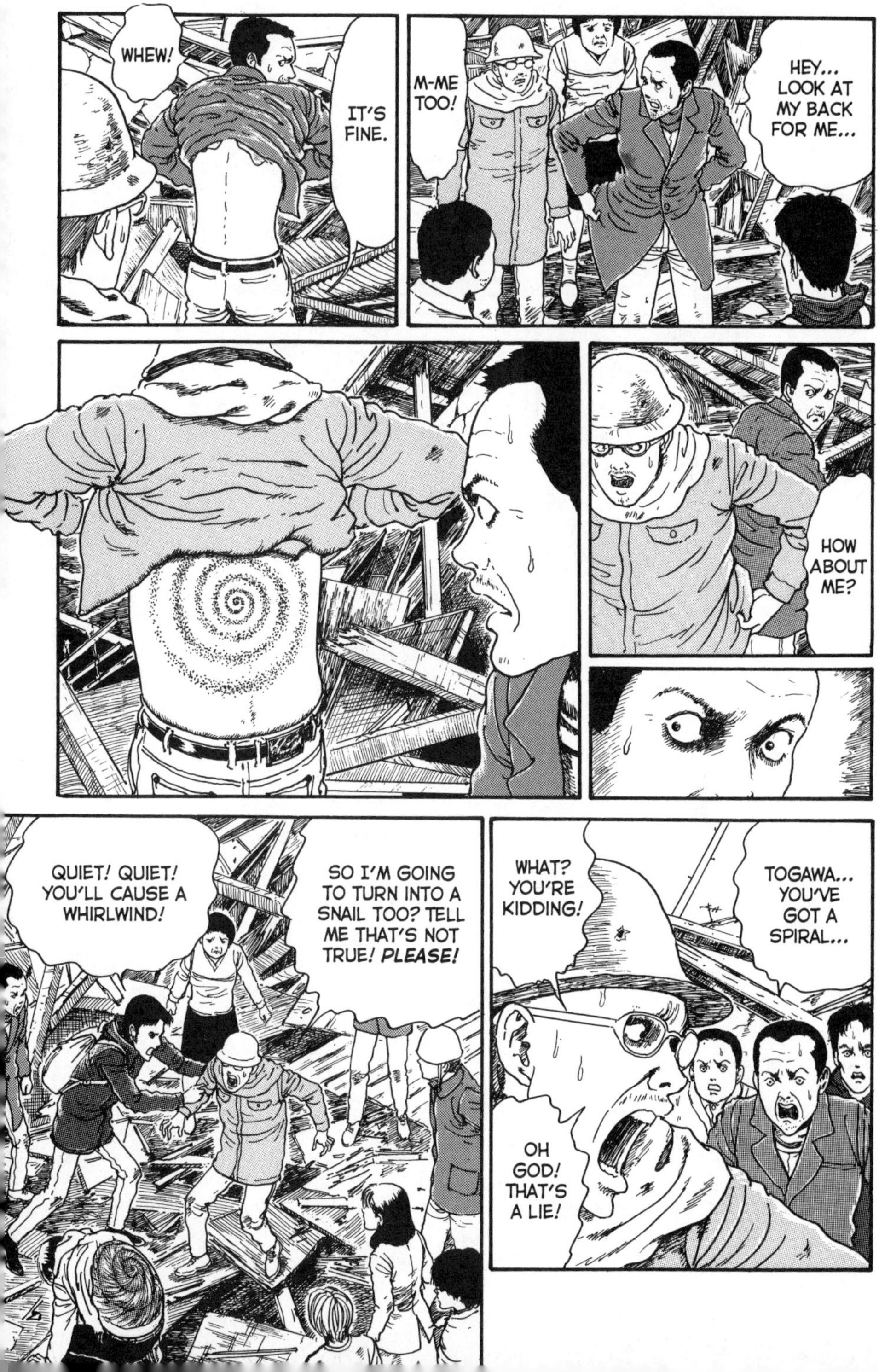
HEY... LOOK AT MY BACK FOR ME...
M-ME TOO!
IT'S FINE.
WHEW!
HOW ABOUT ME?
TOGAWA... YOU'VE GOT A SPIRAL...
WHAT? YOU'RE KIDDING!
OH GOD! THAT'S A LIE!
SO I'M GOING TO TURN INTO A SNAIL TOO? TELL ME THAT'S NOT TRUE! *PLEASE!*
QUIET! QUIET! YOU'LL CAUSE A WHIRLWIND!

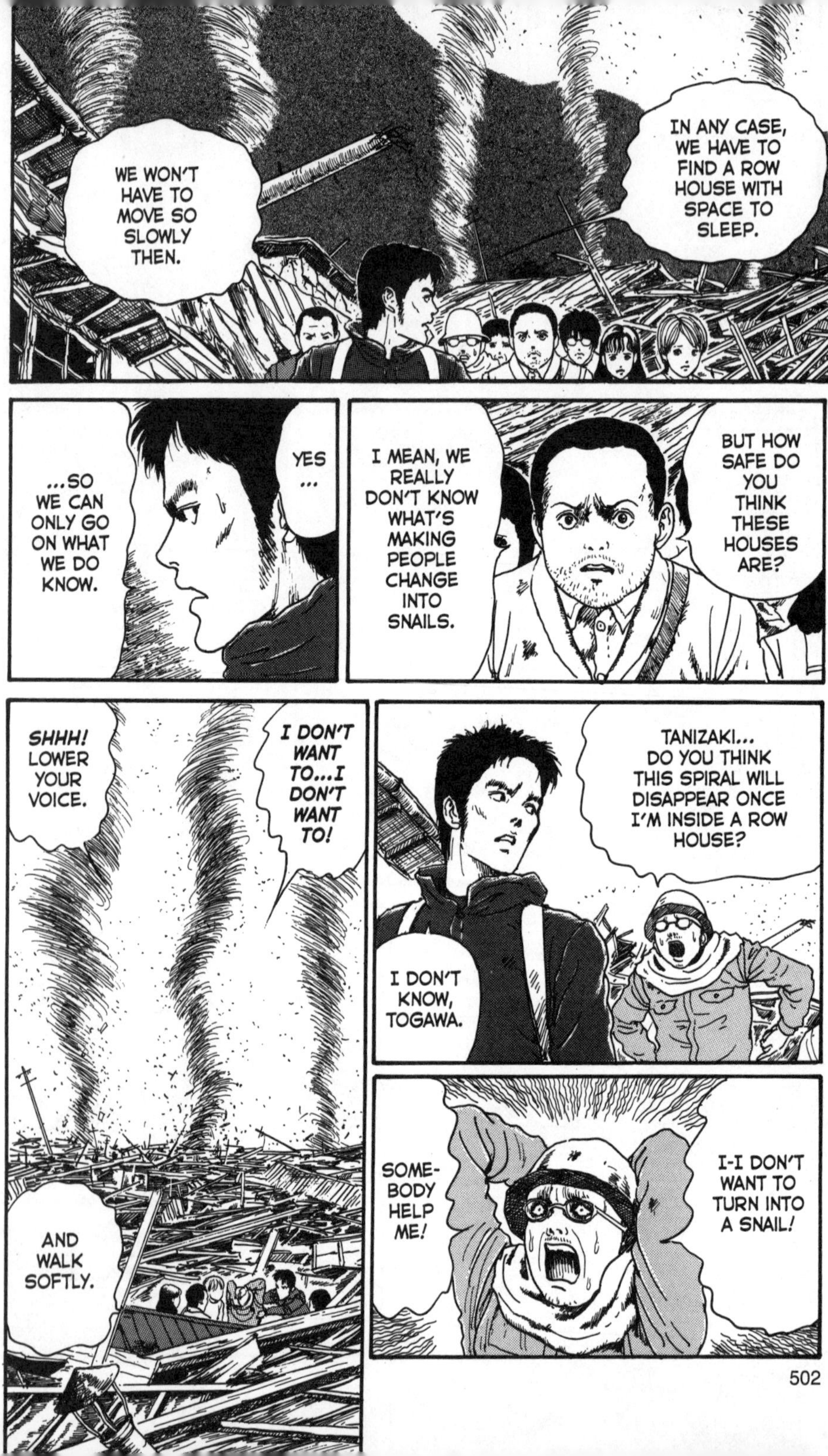
IN ANY CASE, WE HAVE TO FIND A ROW HOUSE WITH SPACE TO SLEEP.
WE WON'T HAVE TO MOVE SO SLOWLY THEN.
BUT HOW SAFE DO YOU THINK THESE HOUSES ARE?
I MEAN, WE REALLY DON'T KNOW WHAT'S MAKING PEOPLE CHANGE INTO SNAILS.
YES ...
...SO WE CAN ONLY GO ON WHAT WE DO KNOW.
TANIZAKI... DO YOU THINK THIS SPIRAL WILL DISAPPEAR ONCE I'M INSIDE A ROW HOUSE?
I DON'T KNOW, TOGAWA.
I-I DON'T WANT TO TURN INTO A SNAIL!
SOME-BODY HELP ME!
I DON'T WANT TO...I DON'T WANT TO!
SHHH! LOWER YOUR VOICE.
AND WALK SOFTLY.

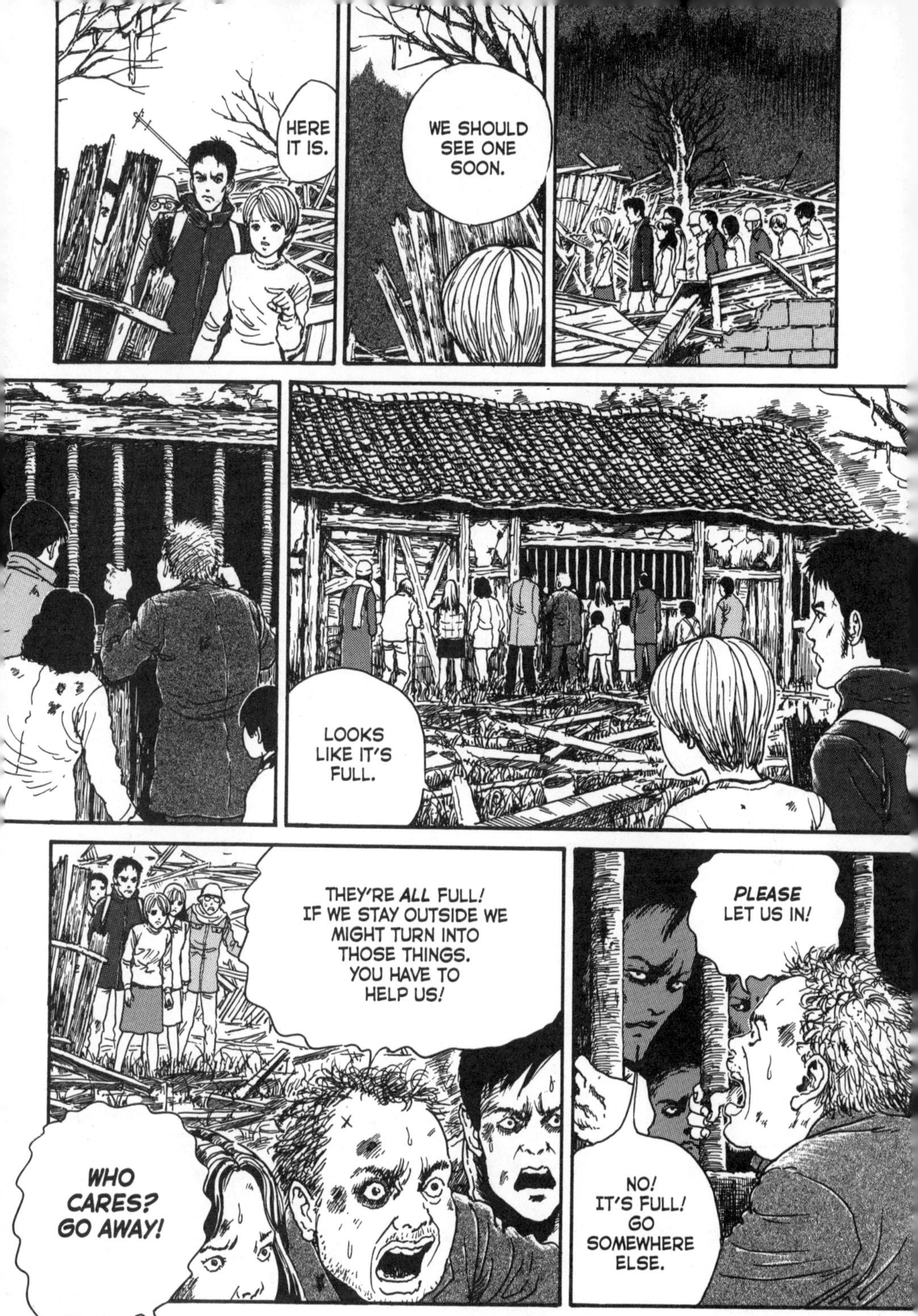
WE SHOULD SEE ONE SOON.
HERE IT IS.
LOOKS LIKE IT'S FULL.
PLEASE LET US IN!
NO! IT'S FULL! GO SOMEWHERE ELSE.
THEY'RE *ALL* FULL! IF WE STAY OUTSIDE WE MIGHT TURN INTO THOSE THINGS. YOU HAVE TO HELP US!
WHO CARES? GO AWAY!

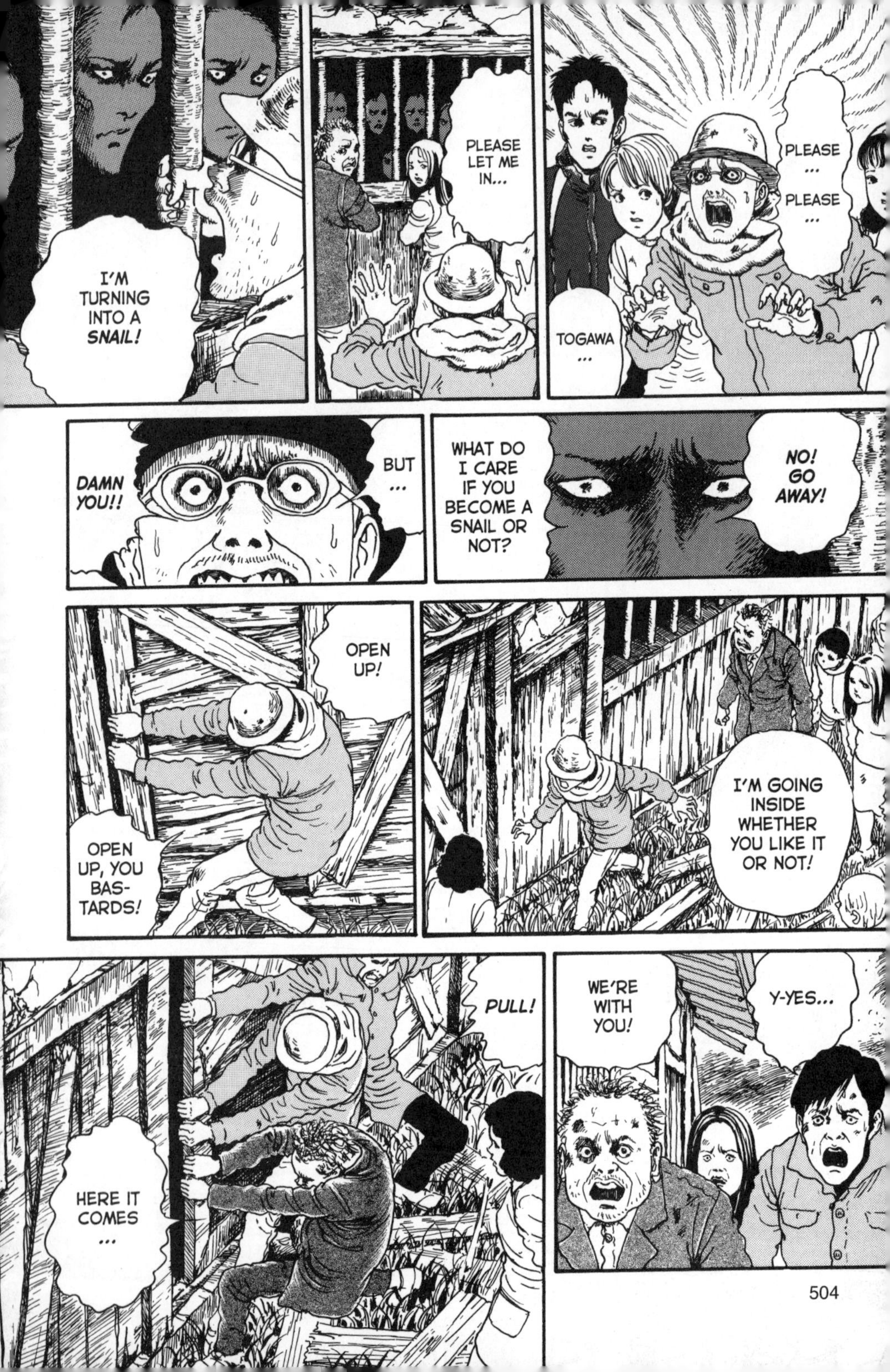
PLEASE ... PLEASE ...
TOGAWA ...
PLEASE LET ME IN...
I'M TURNING INTO A *SNAIL!*
NO! GO AWAY!
WHAT DO I CARE IF YOU BECOME A SNAIL OR NOT?
BUT ...
DAMN YOU!!
I'M GOING INSIDE WHETHER YOU LIKE IT OR NOT!
OPEN UP!
OPEN UP, YOU BAS-TARDS!
Y-YES...
WE'RE WITH YOU!
PULL!
HERE IT COMES ...

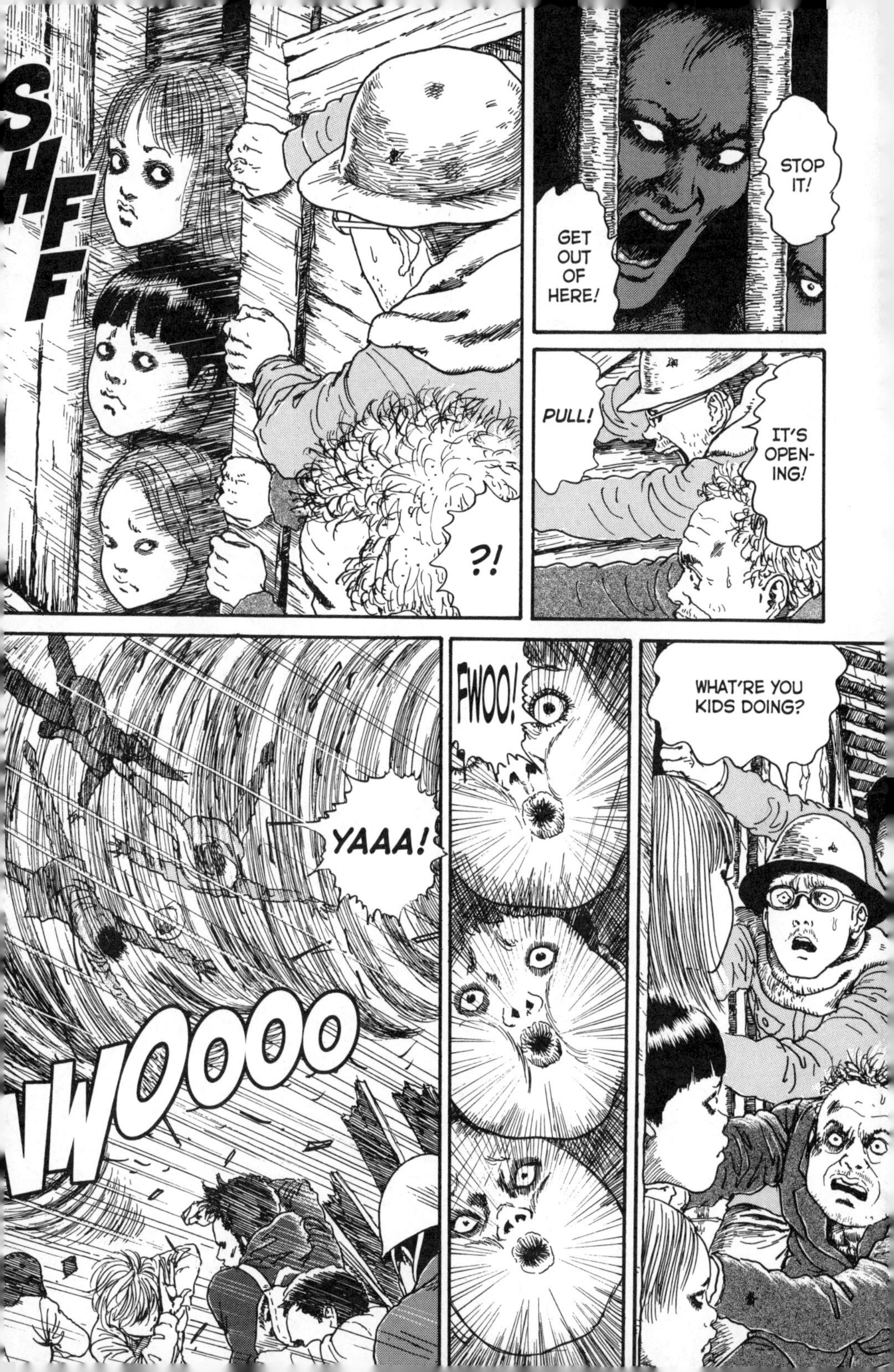
STOP IT!
GET OUT OF HERE!
IT'S OPEN-ING!
PULL!
SHFF
?!
WHAT'RE YOU KIDS DOING?
FWOO!
YAAA!
WOOOOO

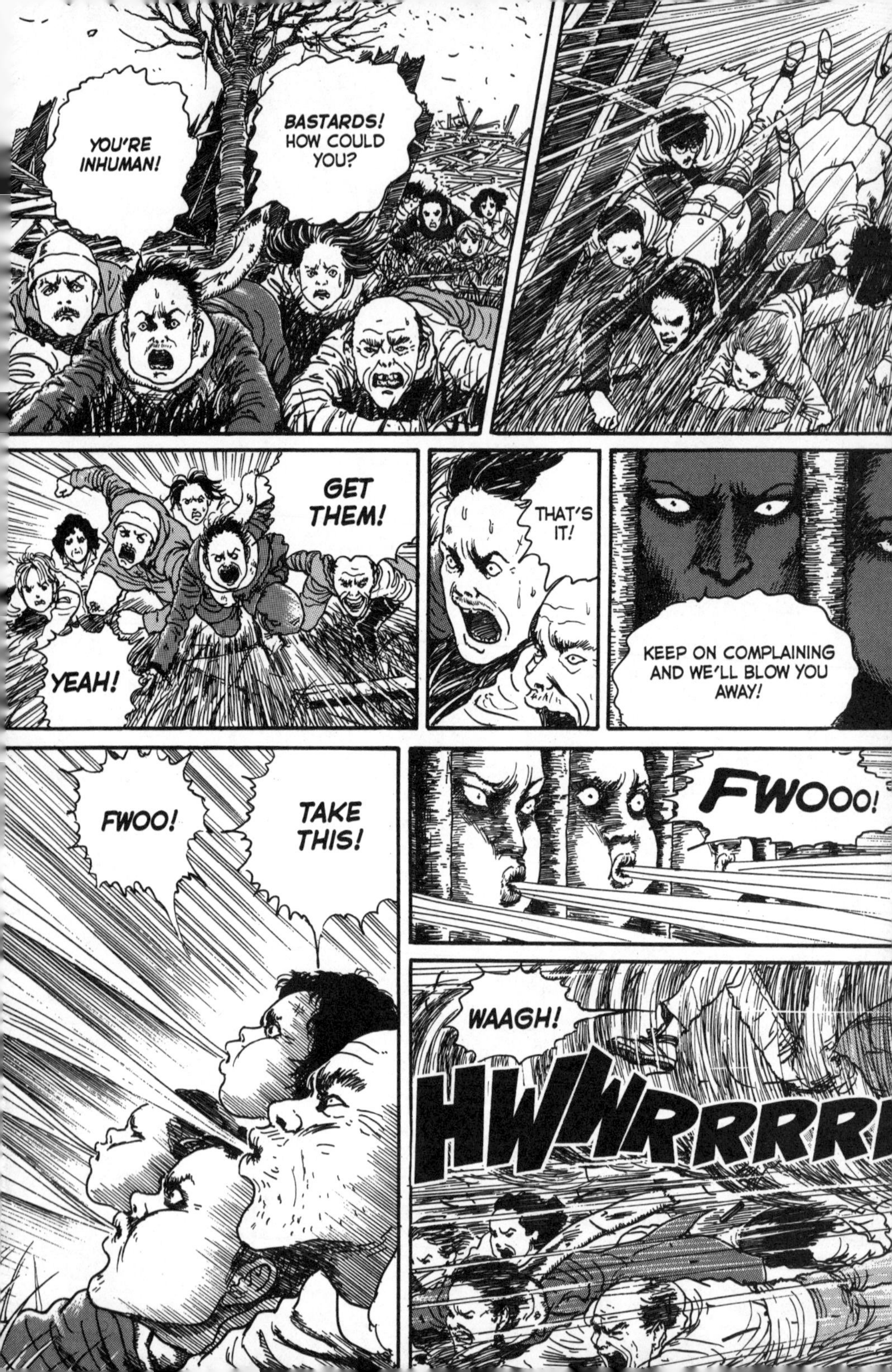
BASTARDS! HOW COULD YOU?
YOU'RE INHUMAN!
KEEP ON COMPLAINING AND WE'LL BLOW YOU AWAY!
THAT'S IT!
GET THEM!
YEAH!
FWOOO!
WAAGH!
HWWRRRRR
TAKE THIS!
FWOO!

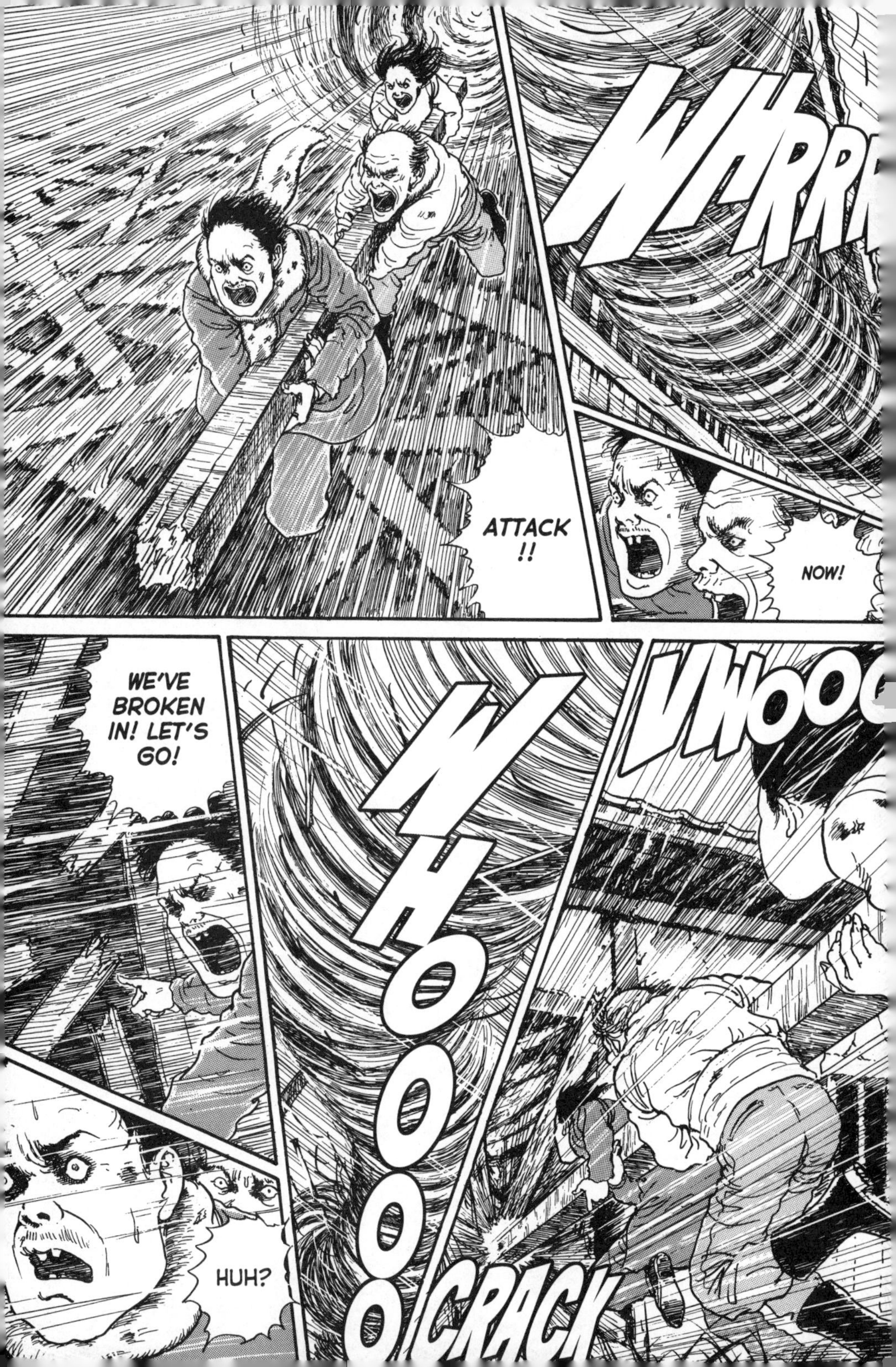
WHRRR
NOW!
ATTACK !!
VWOOO
CRACK
WHOOOOOO
WE'VE BROKEN IN! LET'S GO!
HUH?

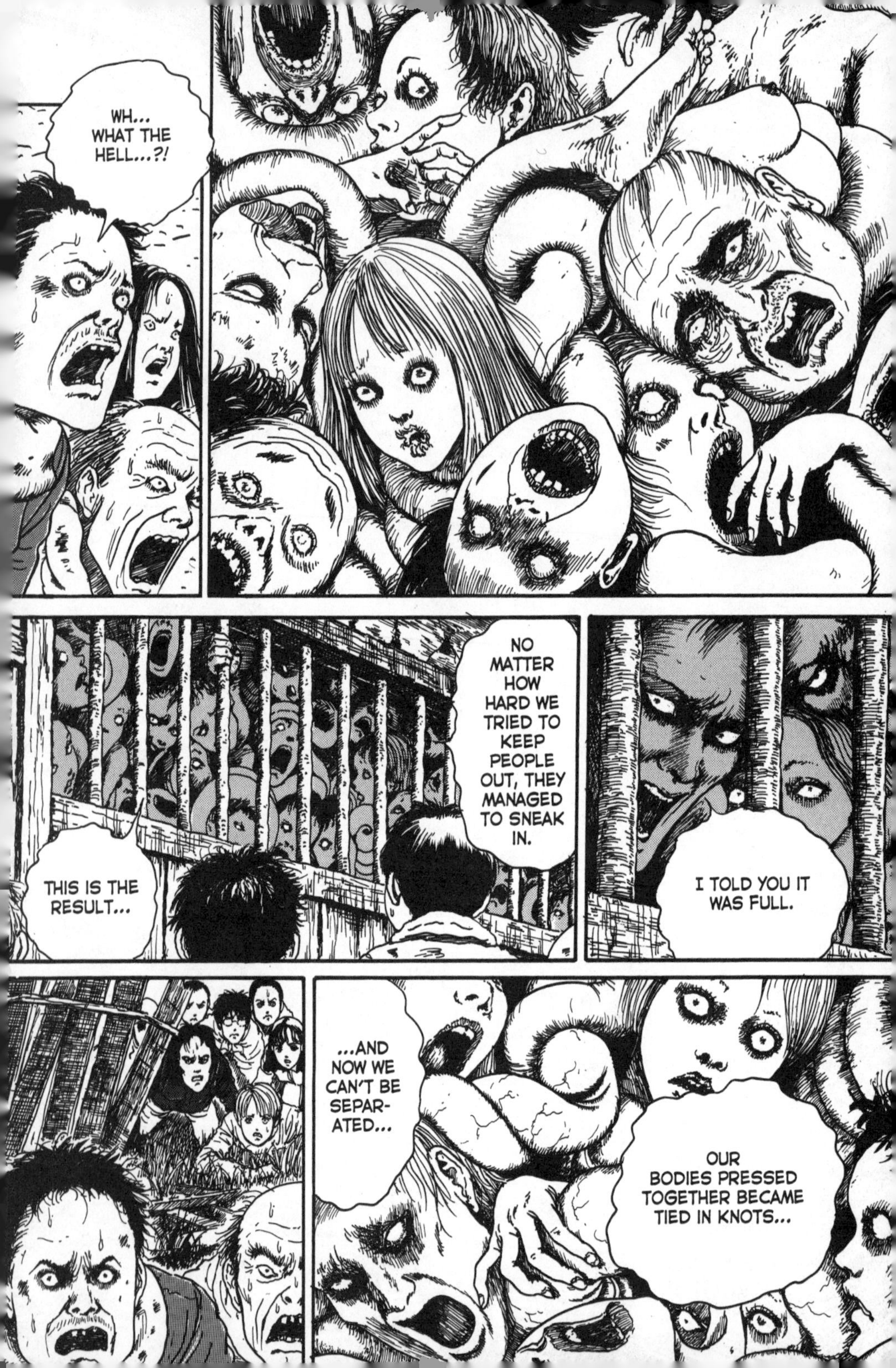
WH... WHAT THE HELL...?!
I TOLD YOU IT WAS FULL.
NO MATTER HOW HARD WE TRIED TO KEEP PEOPLE OUT, THEY MANAGED TO SNEAK IN.
THIS IS THE RESULT...
OUR BODIES PRESSED TOGETHER BECAME TIED IN KNOTS...
...AND NOW WE CAN'T BE SEPARATED...

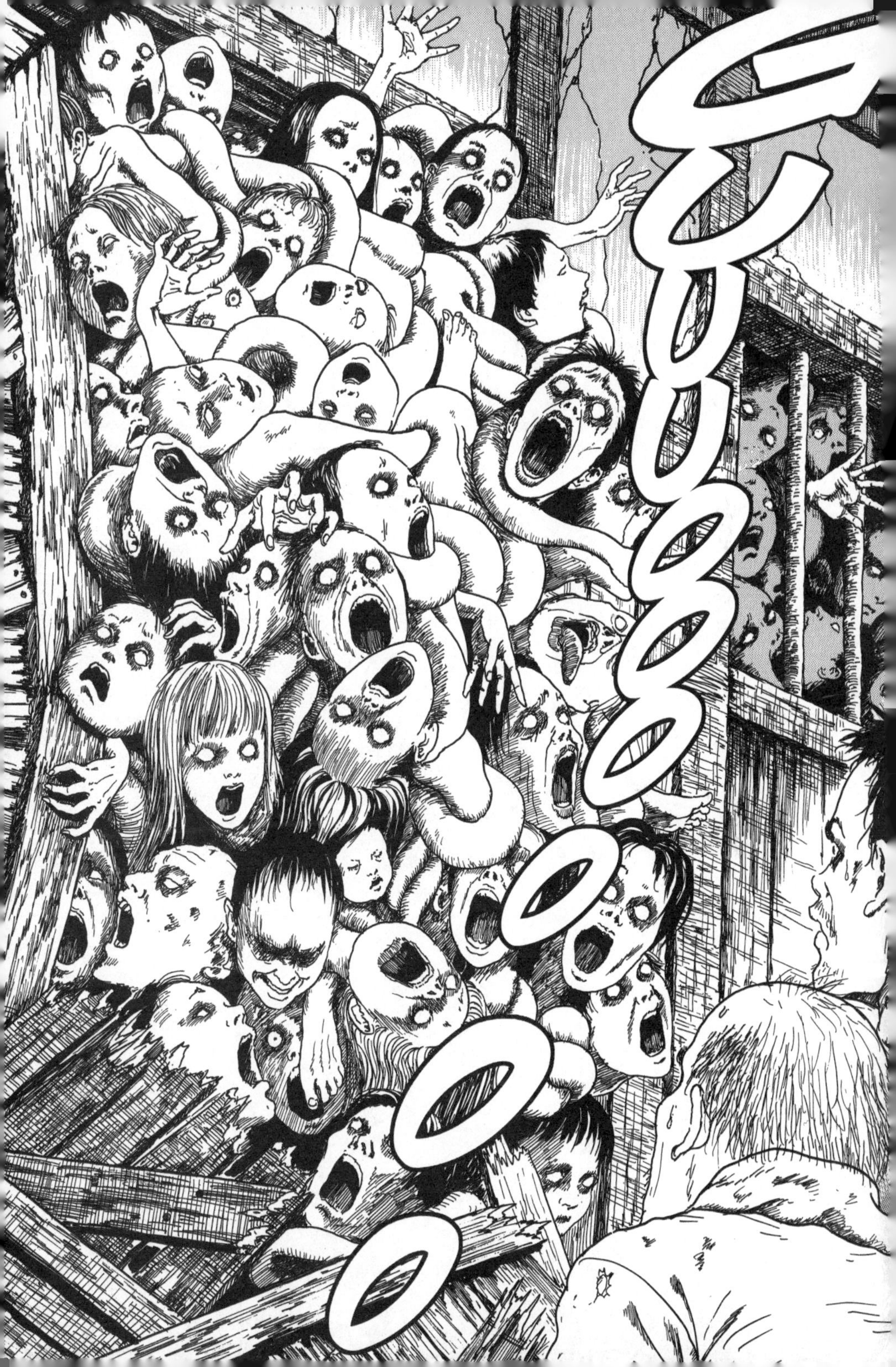

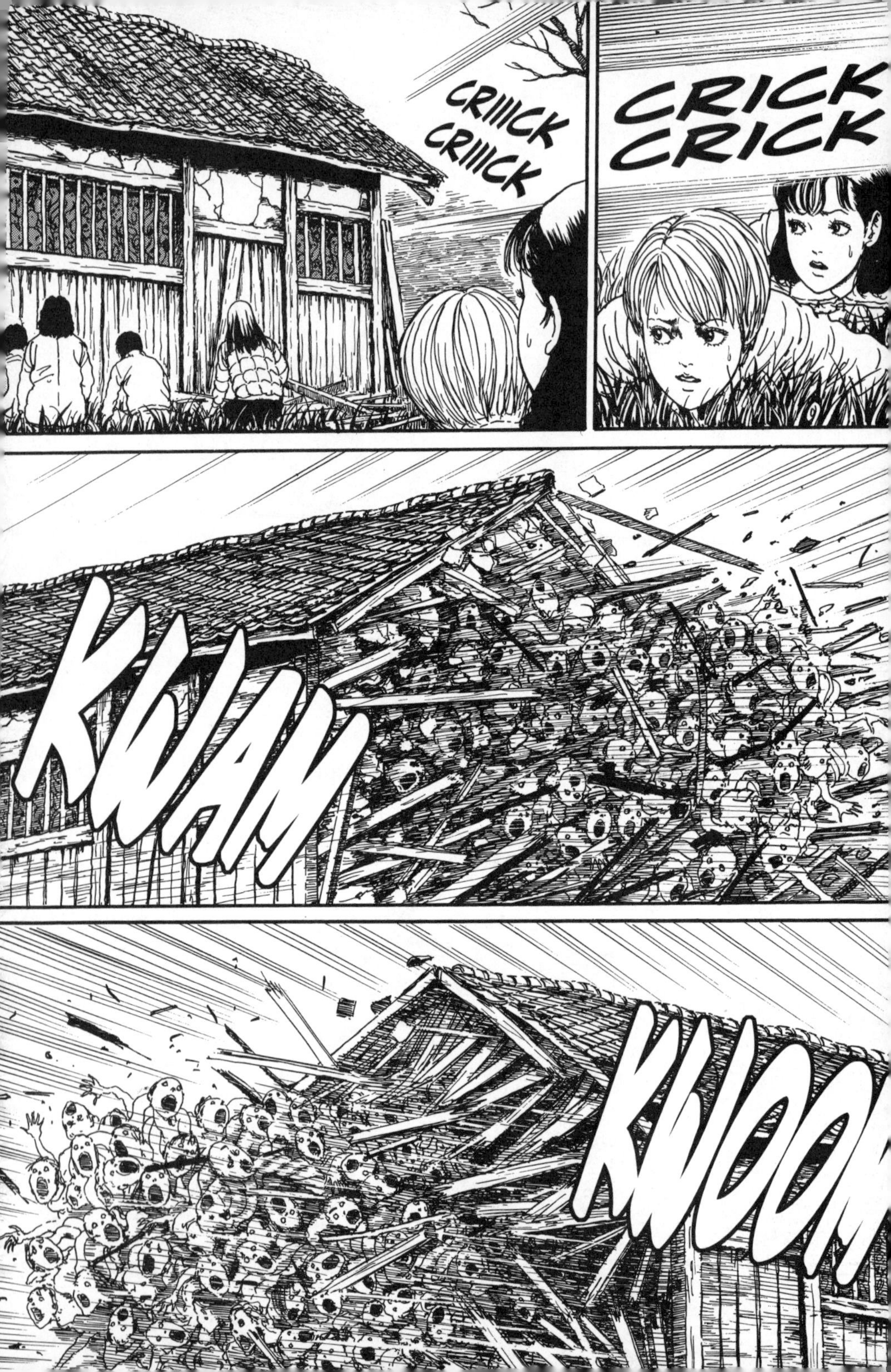
CRICK CRICK
CRIIICK CRIIICK
KWAM
KWOOM

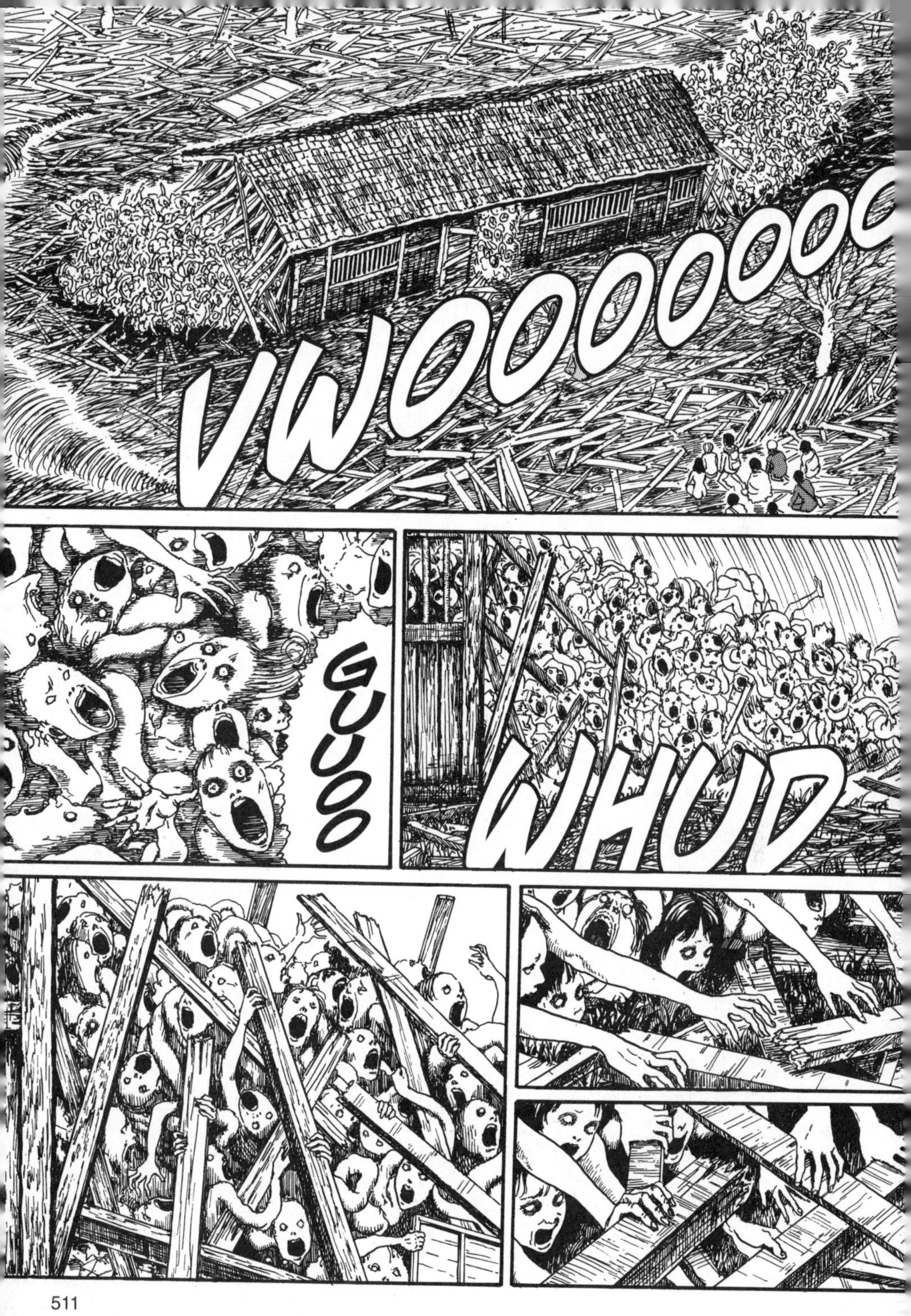
VWOOOOOOOO
WHUD
GUUOO

WHAT'RE THEY DOING?

WHEEOOOO

COVERING THEIR EXPOSED BODIES WITH THE SCRAP WOOD, I THINK.

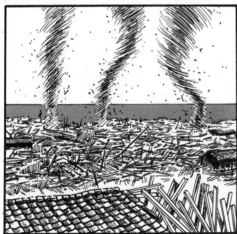

AND ADD ONTO THE HOUSE, TOO.

SO THERE'S THAT OPTION ...

HMM ...

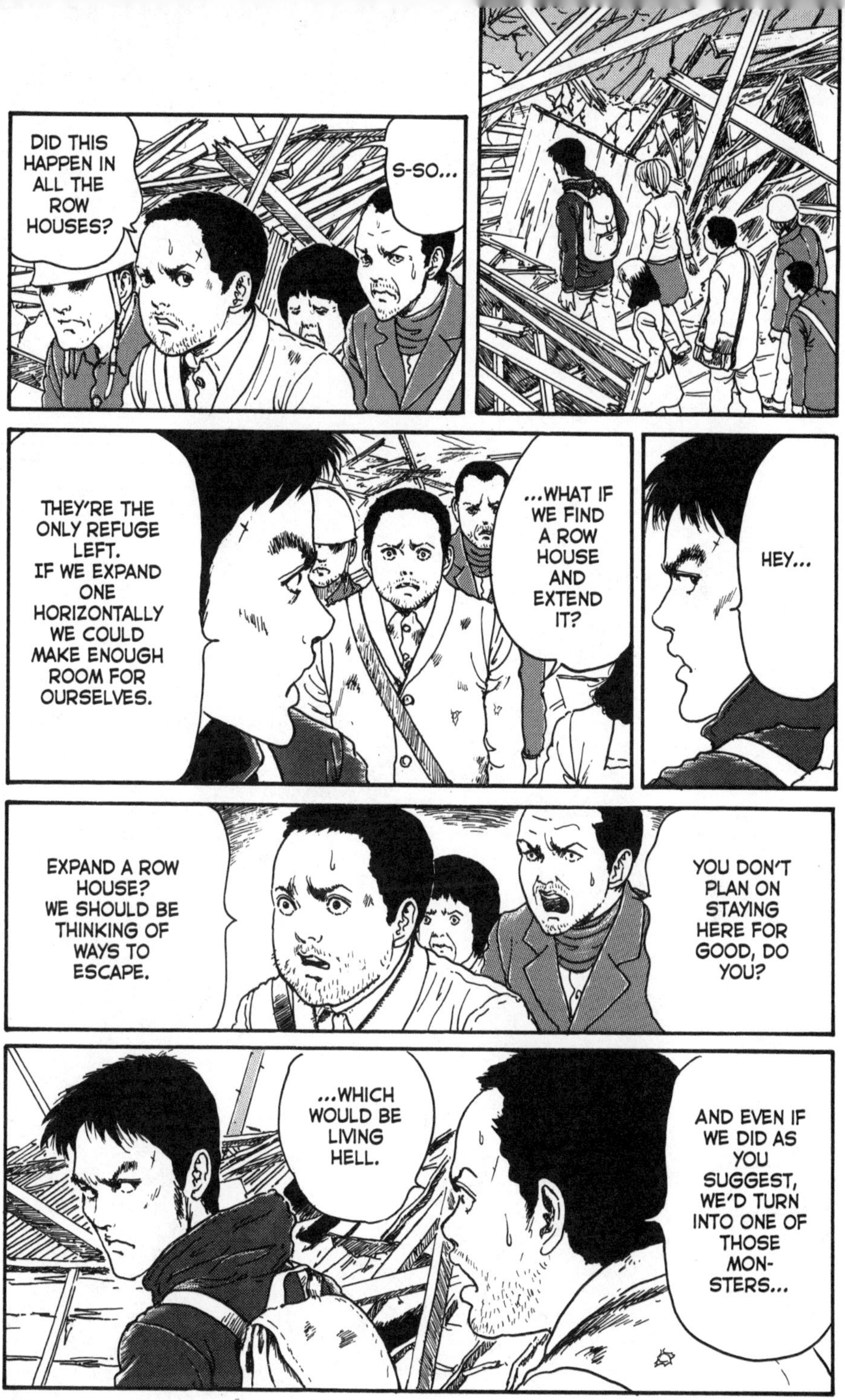
S-SO...
DID THIS HAPPEN IN ALL THE ROW HOUSES?
HEY...
...WHAT IF WE FIND A ROW HOUSE AND EXTEND IT?
THEY'RE THE ONLY REFUGE LEFT. IF WE EXPAND ONE HORIZONTALLY WE COULD MAKE ENOUGH ROOM FOR OURSELVES.
YOU DON'T PLAN ON STAYING HERE FOR GOOD, DO YOU?
EXPAND A ROW HOUSE? WE SHOULD BE THINKING OF WAYS TO ESCAPE.
AND EVEN IF WE DID AS YOU SUGGEST, WE'D TURN INTO ONE OF THOSE MON-STERS...
...WHICH WOULD BE LIVING HELL.

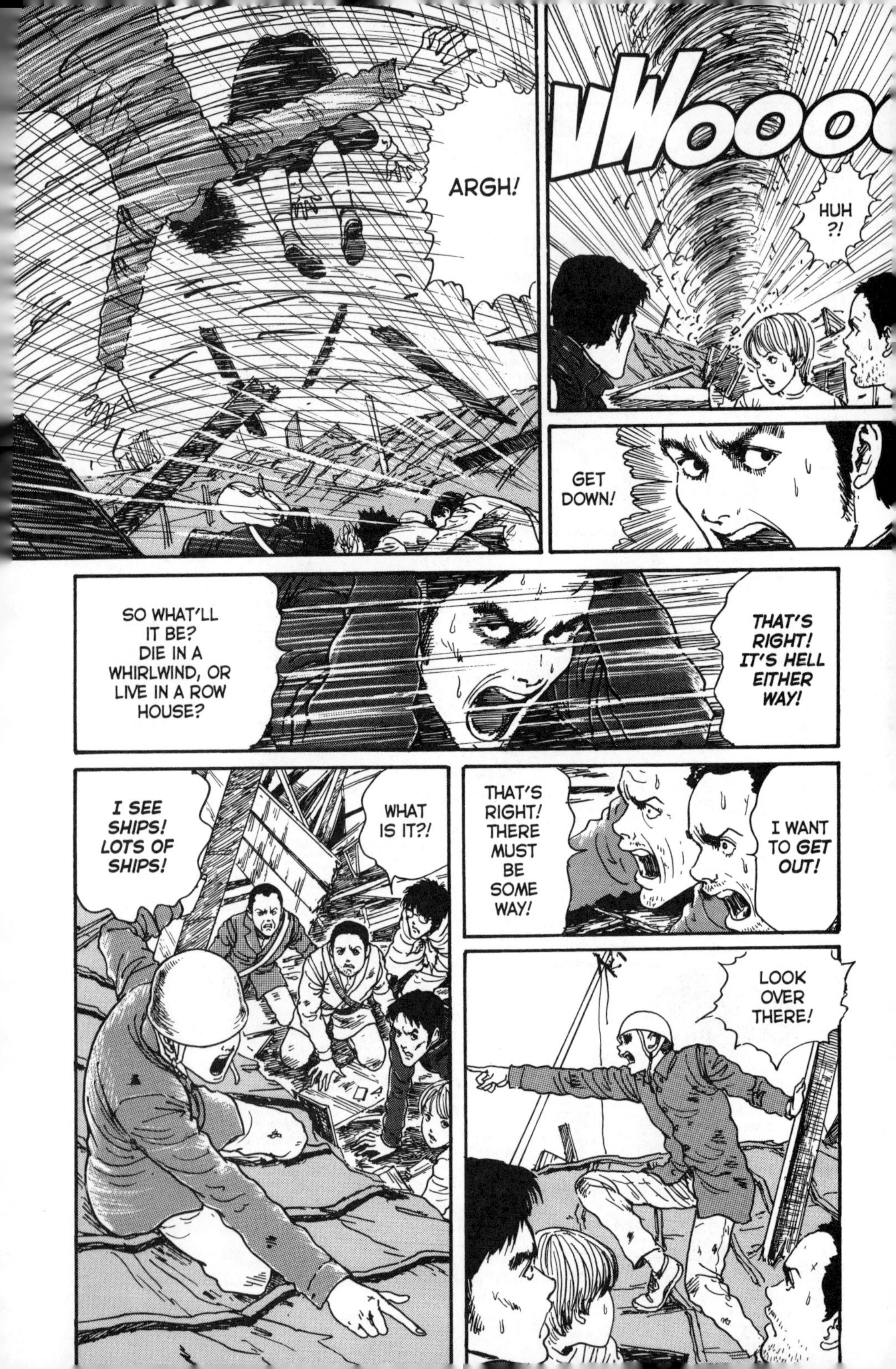
VWOOOO
HUH?!
GET DOWN!
ARGH!
THAT'S RIGHT! IT'S HELL EITHER WAY!
SO WHAT'LL IT BE? DIE IN A WHIRLWIND, OR LIVE IN A ROW HOUSE?
I WANT TO GET OUT!
THAT'S RIGHT! THERE MUST BE SOME WAY!
LOOK OVER THERE!
WHAT IS IT?!
I SEE SHIPS! LOTS OF SHIPS!

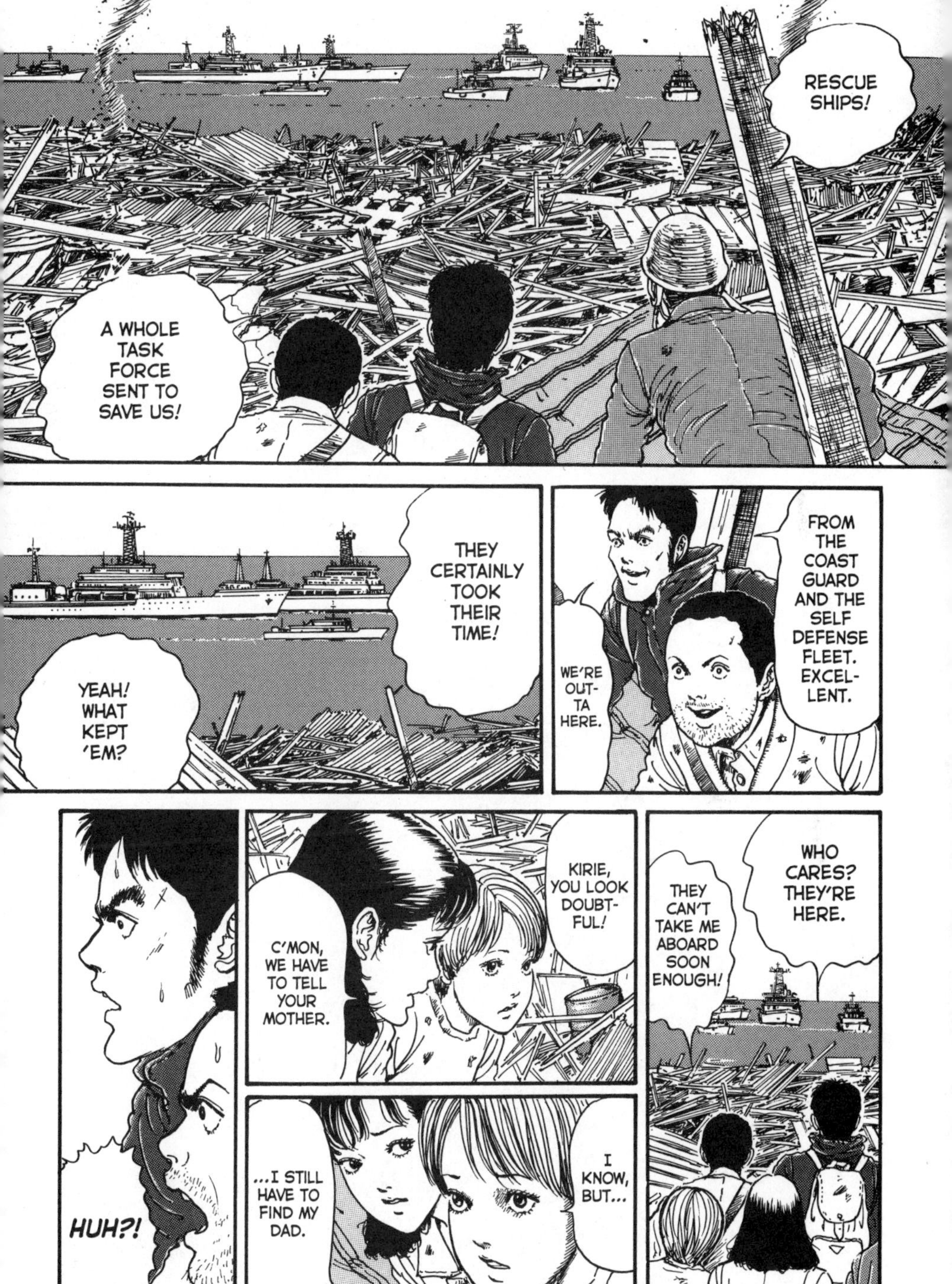
RESCUE SHIPS!
A WHOLE TASK FORCE SENT TO SAVE US!
FROM THE COAST GUARD AND THE SELF DEFENSE FLEET. EXCEL-LENT.
WE'RE OUT-TA HERE.
THEY CERTAINLY TOOK THEIR TIME!
YEAH! WHAT KEPT 'EM?
WHO CARES? THEY'RE HERE.
THEY CAN'T TAKE ME ABOARD SOON ENOUGH!
KIRIE, YOU LOOK DOUBT-FUL!
C'MON, WE HAVE TO TELL YOUR MOTHER.
I KNOW, BUT...
...I STILL HAVE TO FIND MY DAD.
HUH?!

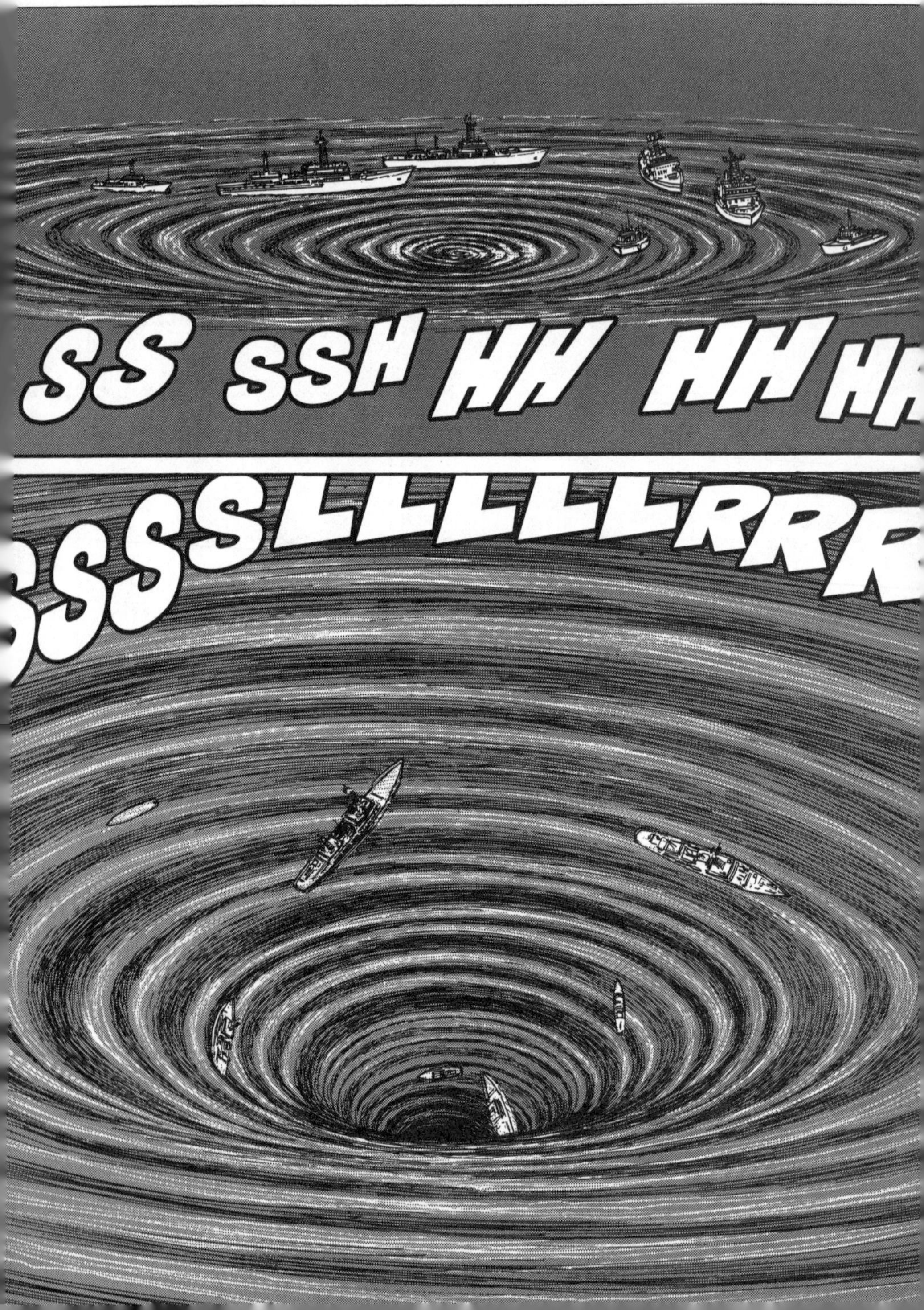
SS SSH HH HHH
SSSSLLLLLRRR

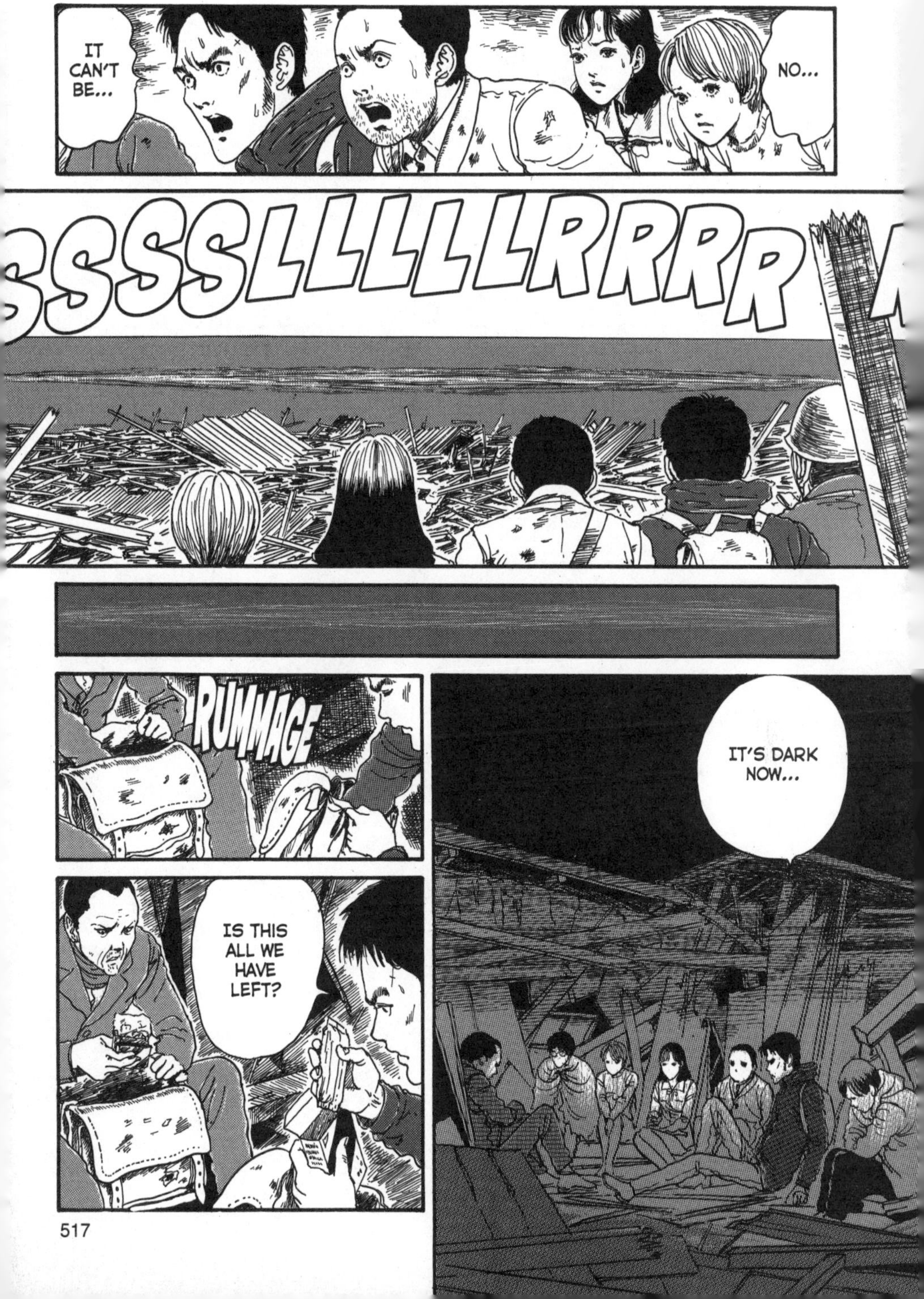
NO...
IT CAN'T BE...
SSSSLLLLLRRRR
IT'S DARK NOW...
RUMMAGE
IS THIS ALL WE HAVE LEFT?

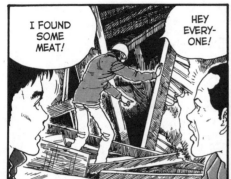

IT ISN'T ENOUGH TO SUSTAIN US.
RUMB
ISN'T THERE ANYTHING IN TOWN? SOME CANNED FOOD?
HEY EVERY-ONE!
I FOUND SOME MEAT!
WHAT? REALLY?!
SOMEONE COOKED ONE OF THOSE SNAIL PEO...SNAILS.
PROBABLY LEFT HERE BY A GANG.
S-SO THIS IS WHAT...
...YOU MEANT BY MEAT?
GULP
...

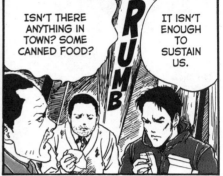

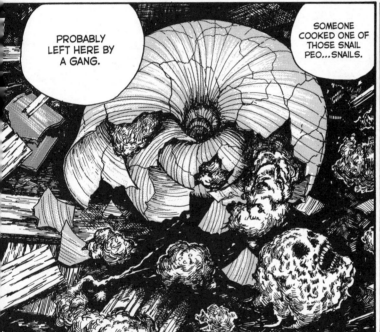

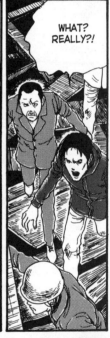

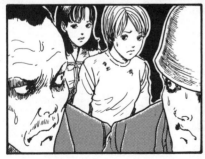

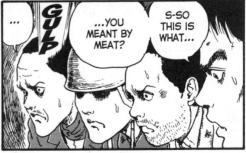

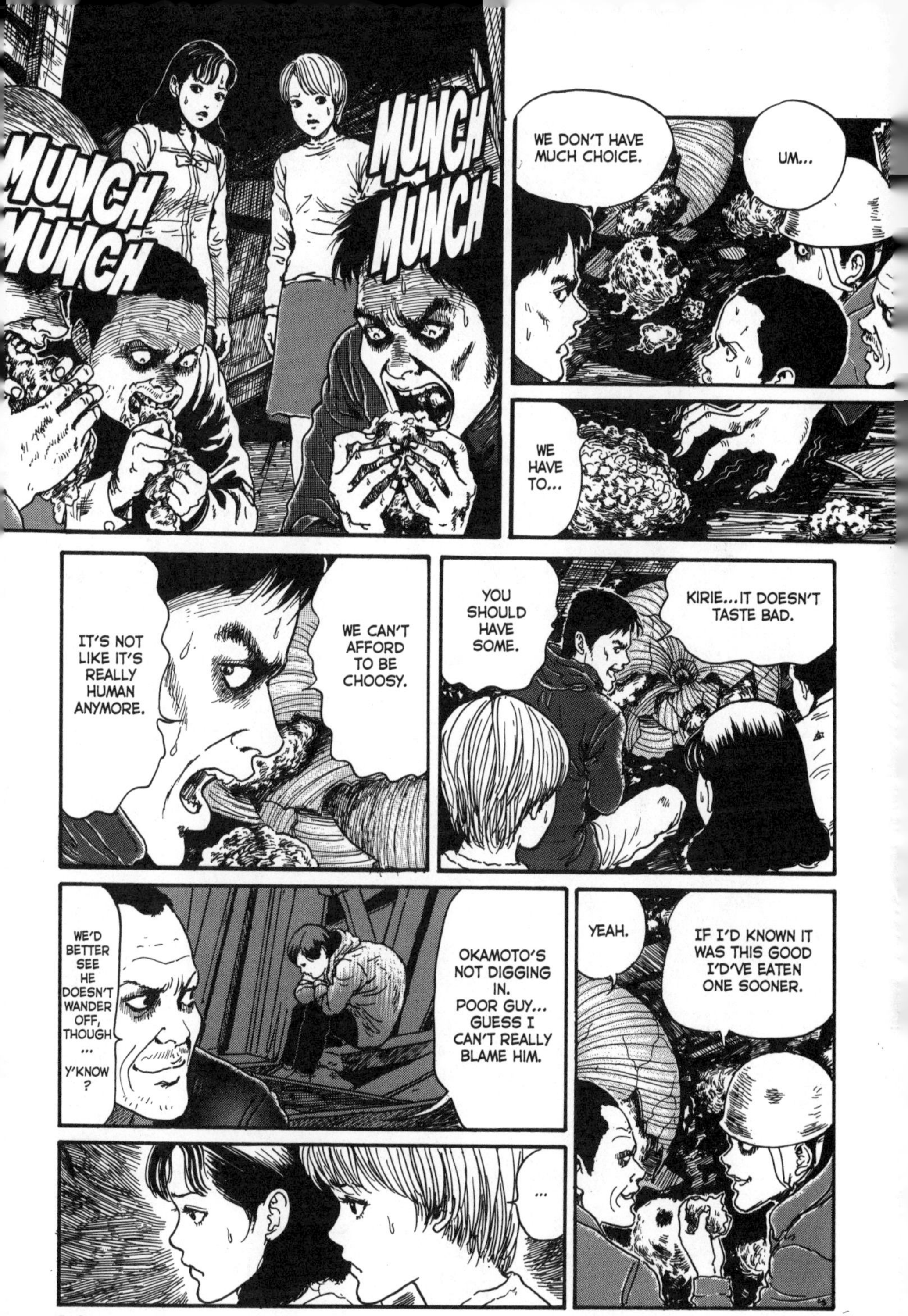
UM...
WE DON'T HAVE MUCH CHOICE.
WE HAVE TO...
MUNCH MUNCH
MUNCH MUNCH
KIRIE...IT DOESN'T TASTE BAD.
YOU SHOULD HAVE SOME.
WE CAN'T AFFORD TO BE CHOOSY.
IT'S NOT LIKE IT'S REALLY HUMAN ANYMORE.
IF I'D KNOWN IT WAS THIS GOOD I'D'VE EATEN ONE SOONER.
YEAH.
OKAMOTO'S NOT DIGGING IN. POOR GUY... GUESS I CAN'T REALLY BLAME HIM.
WE'D BETTER SEE HE DOESN'T WANDER OFF, THOUGH... Y'KNOW?
...

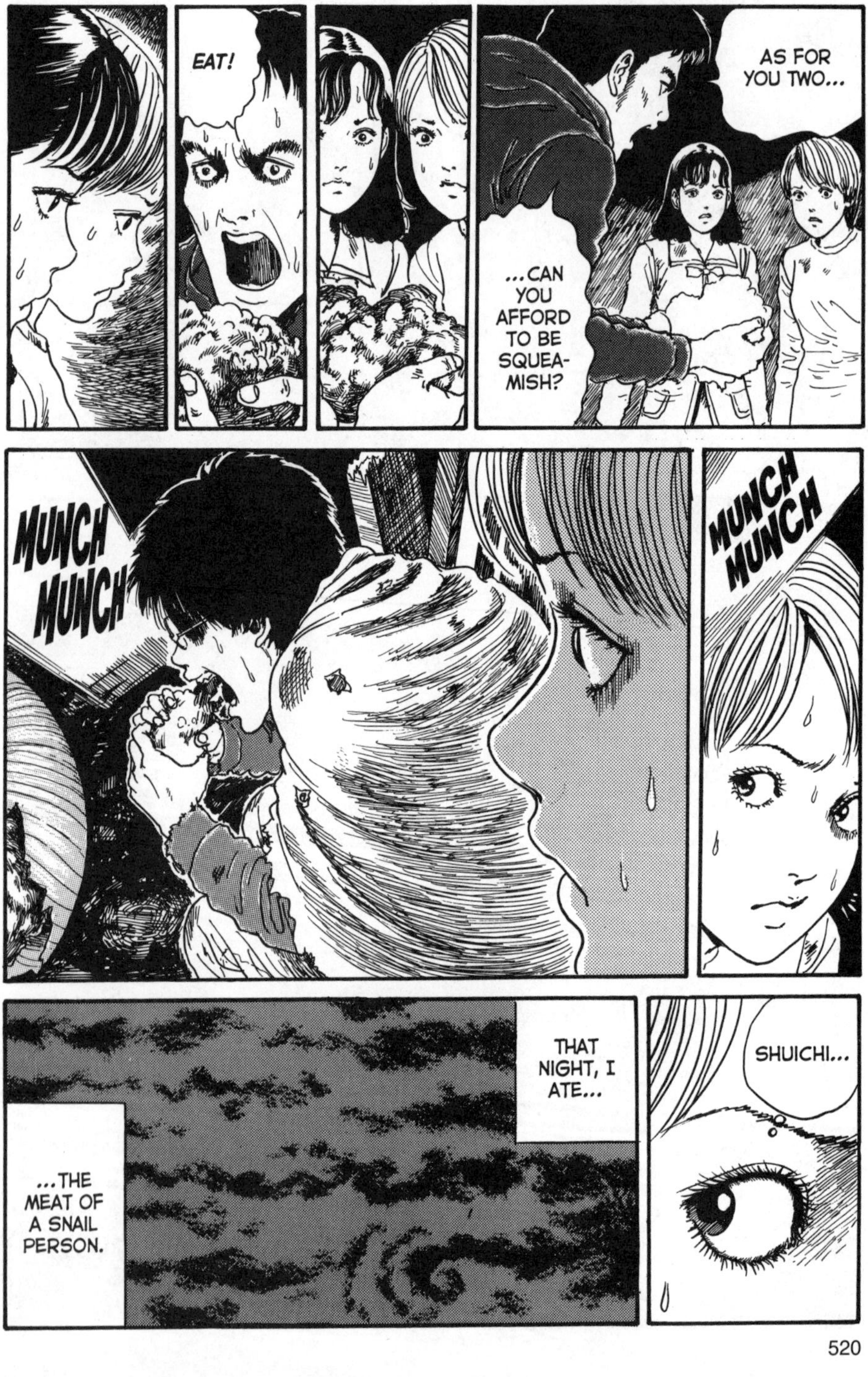
AS FOR YOU TWO...
...CAN YOU AFFORD TO BE SQUEAMISH?
EAT!
MUNCH MUNCH
MUNCH MUNCH
SHUICHI...
THAT NIGHT, I ATE...
...THE MEAT OF A SNAIL PERSON.

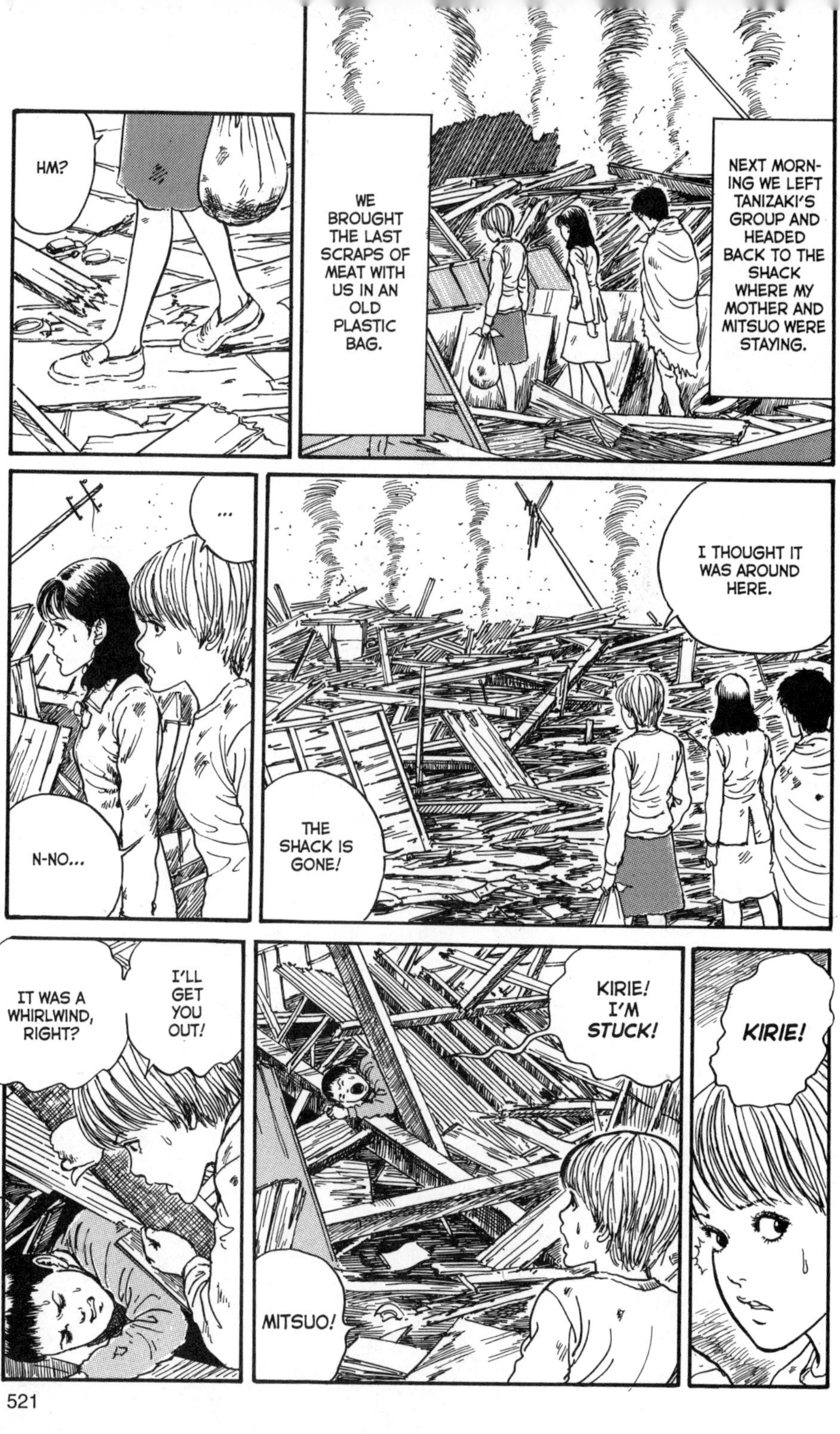
NEXT MORNING WE LEFT TANIZAKI'S GROUP AND HEADED BACK TO THE SHACK WHERE MY MOTHER AND MITSUO WERE STAYING.
WE BROUGHT THE LAST SCRAPS OF MEAT WITH US IN AN OLD PLASTIC BAG.
HM?
I THOUGHT IT WAS AROUND HERE.
THE SHACK IS GONE!
...
N-NO...
KIRIE!
KIRIE! I'M STUCK!
MITSUO!
I'LL GET YOU OUT!
IT WAS A WHIRLWIND, RIGHT?

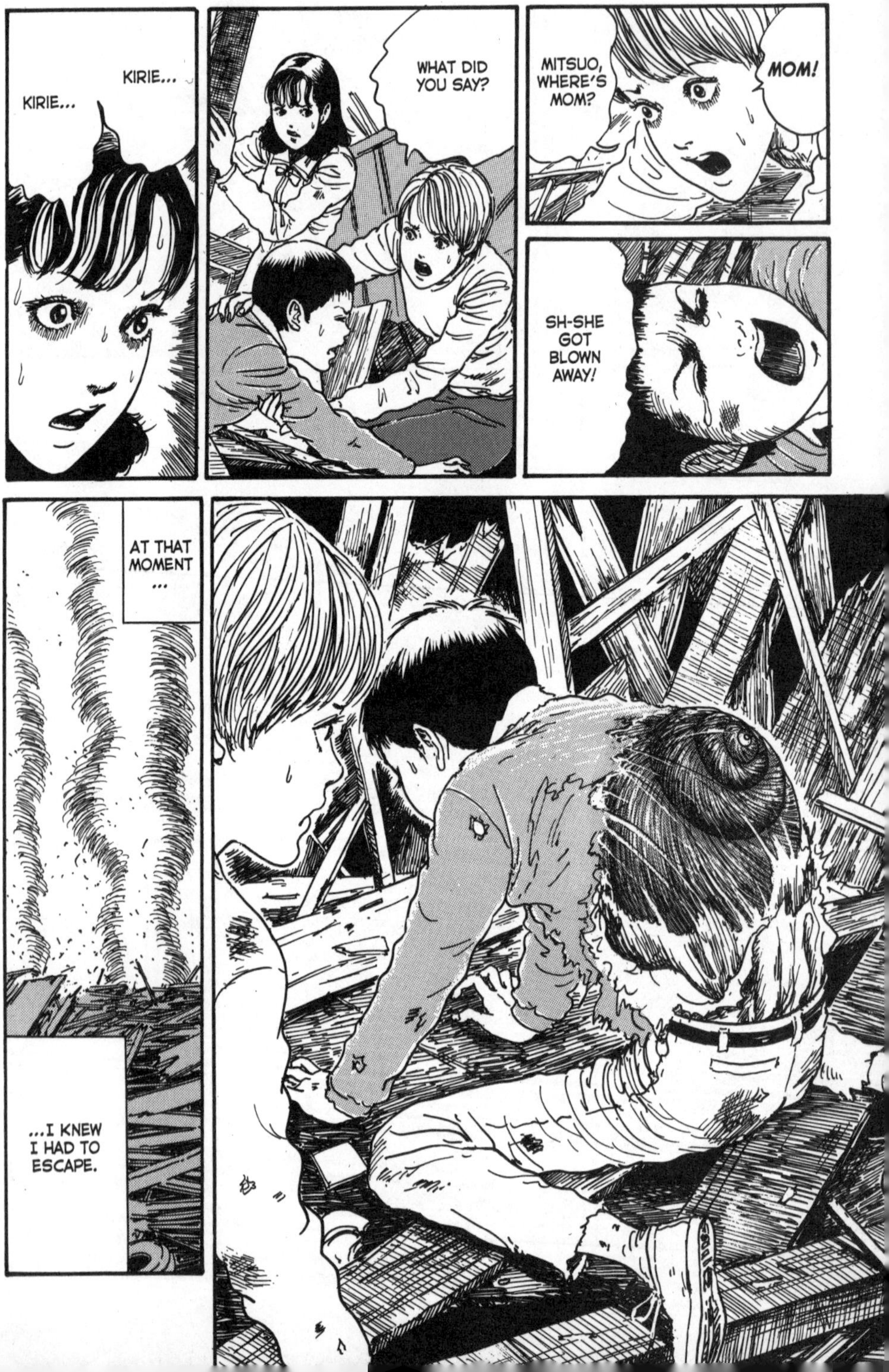
MOM!
MITSUO, WHERE'S MOM?
SH-SHE GOT BLOWN AWAY!
WHAT DID YOU SAY?
KIRIE...
KIRIE...
AT THAT MOMENT ...
...I KNEW I HAD TO ESCAPE.

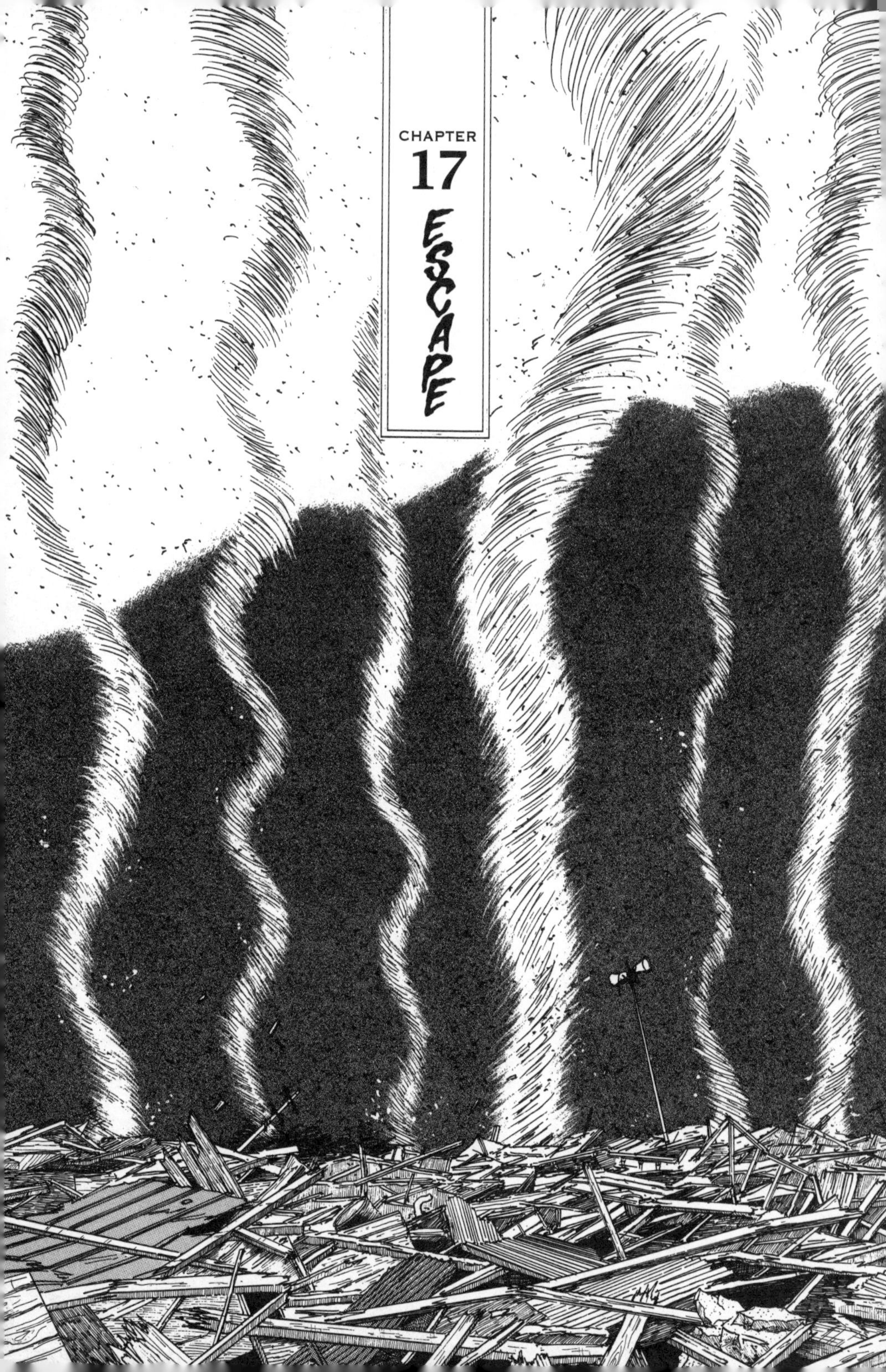
CHAPTER
17
ESCAPE

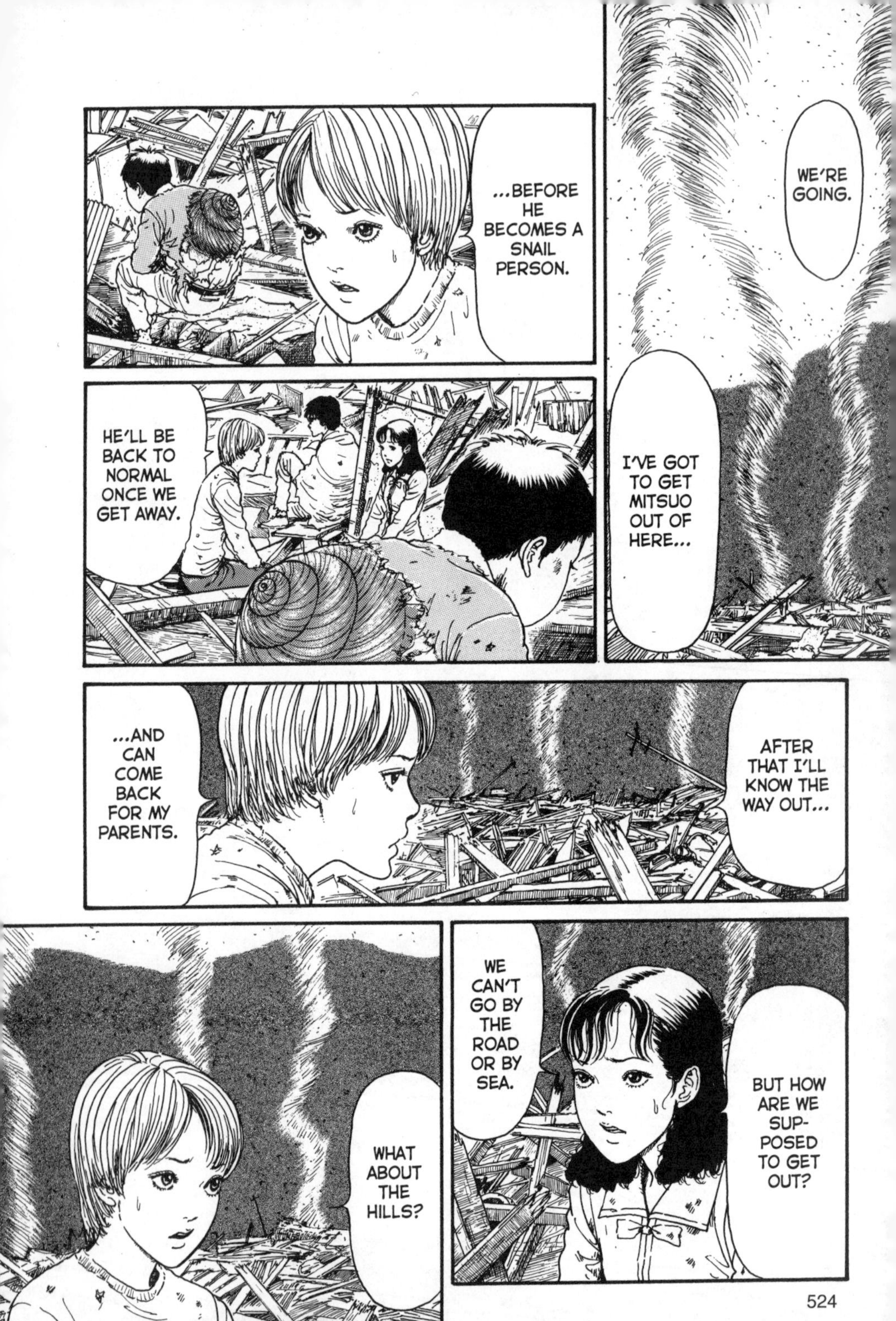
WE'RE GOING.
I'VE GOT TO GET MITSUO OUT OF HERE...
...BEFORE HE BECOMES A SNAIL PERSON.
HE'LL BE BACK TO NORMAL ONCE WE GET AWAY.
AFTER THAT I'LL KNOW THE WAY OUT...
...AND CAN COME BACK FOR MY PARENTS.
BUT HOW ARE WE SUP-POSED TO GET OUT?
WE CAN'T GO BY THE ROAD OR BY SEA.
WHAT ABOUT THE HILLS?

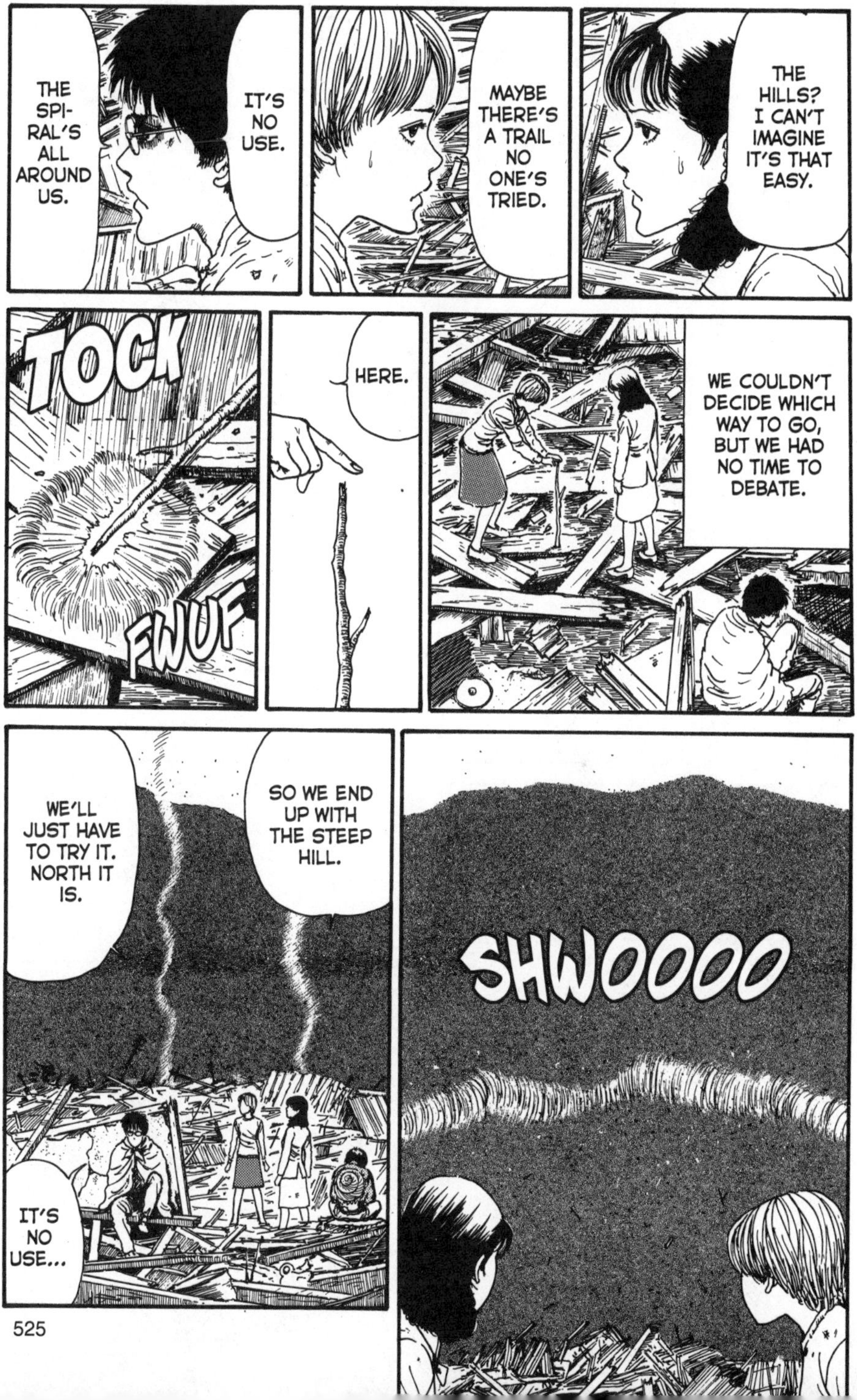
THE HILLS? I CAN'T IMAGINE IT'S THAT EASY.
MAYBE THERE'S A TRAIL NO ONE'S TRIED.
IT'S NO USE.
THE SPI-RAL'S ALL AROUND US.
WE COULDN'T DECIDE WHICH WAY TO GO, BUT WE HAD NO TIME TO DEBATE.
HERE.
TOCK
FWUF
SHWOOOO
SO WE END UP WITH THE STEEP HILL.
WE'LL JUST HAVE TO TRY IT. NORTH IT IS.
IT'S NO USE...

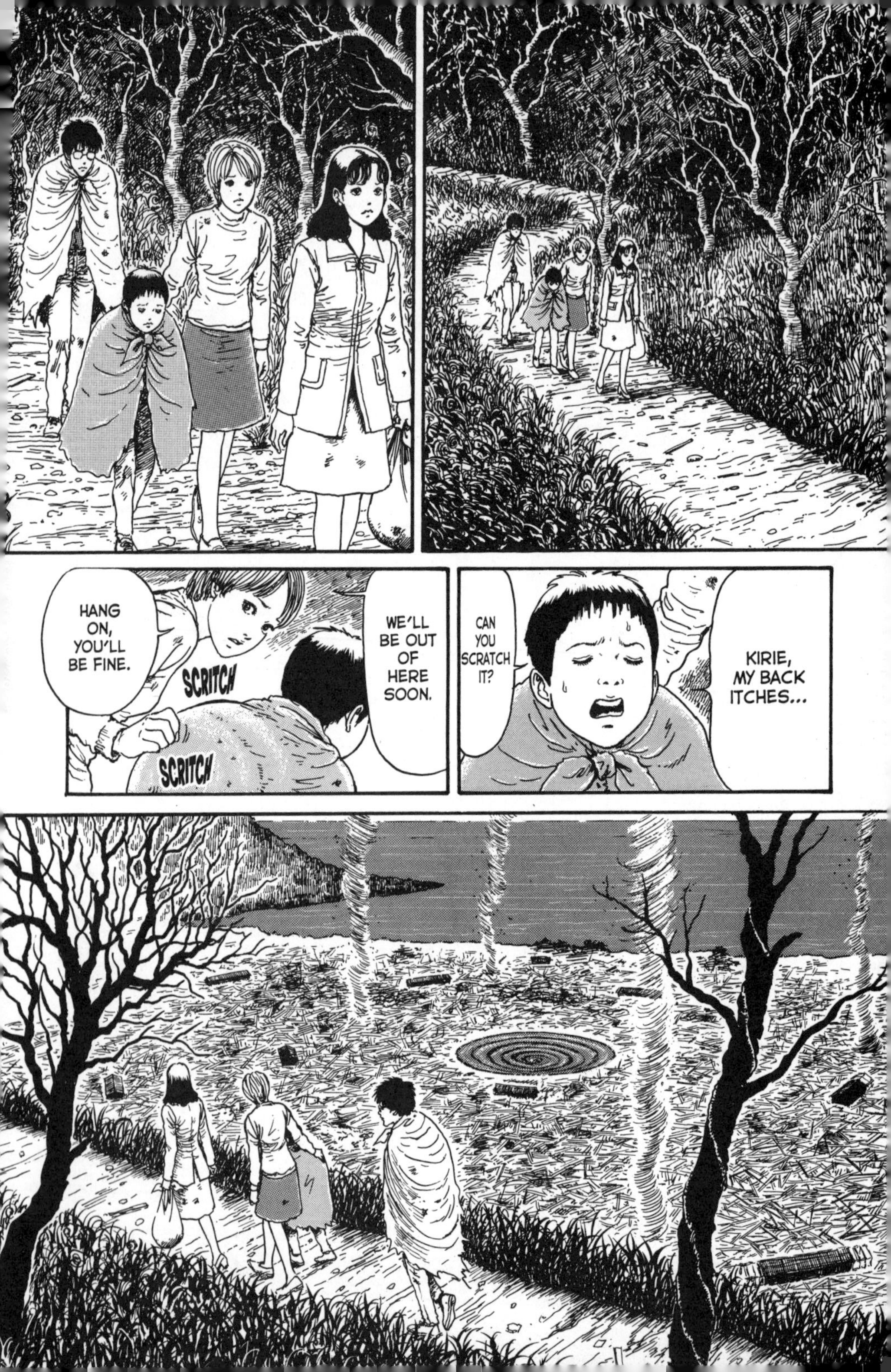
KIRIE, MY BACK ITCHES...
CAN YOU SCRATCH IT?
WE'LL BE OUT OF HERE SOON.
HANG ON, YOU'LL BE FINE.
SCRITCH
SCRITCH

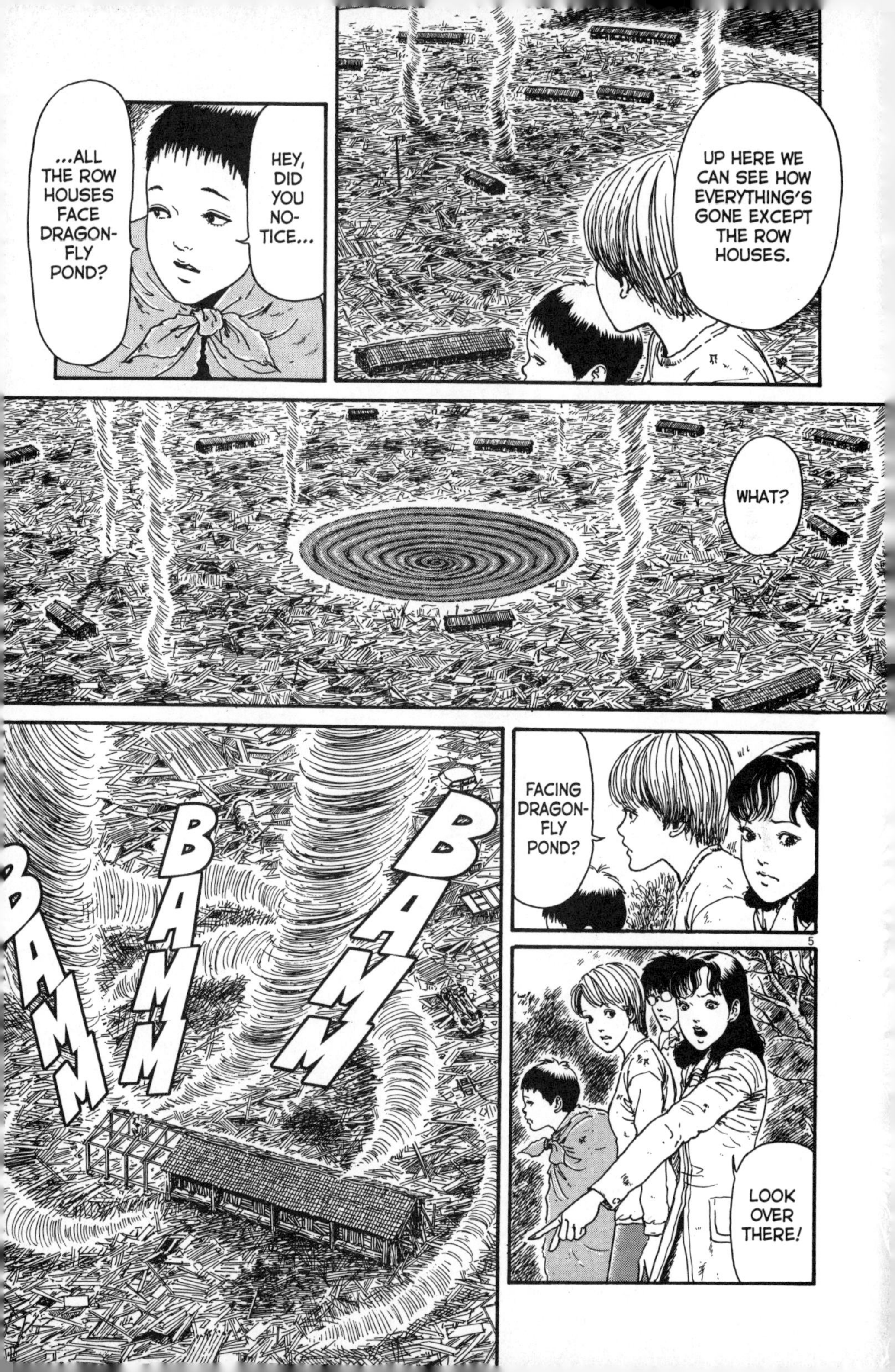
UP HERE WE CAN SEE HOW EVERYTHING'S GONE EXCEPT THE ROW HOUSES.
HEY, DID YOU NO-TICE...
...ALL THE ROW HOUSES FACE DRAGON-FLY POND?
WHAT?
FACING DRAGON-FLY POND?
LOOK OVER THERE!
BAMM
BAMM
BAMM

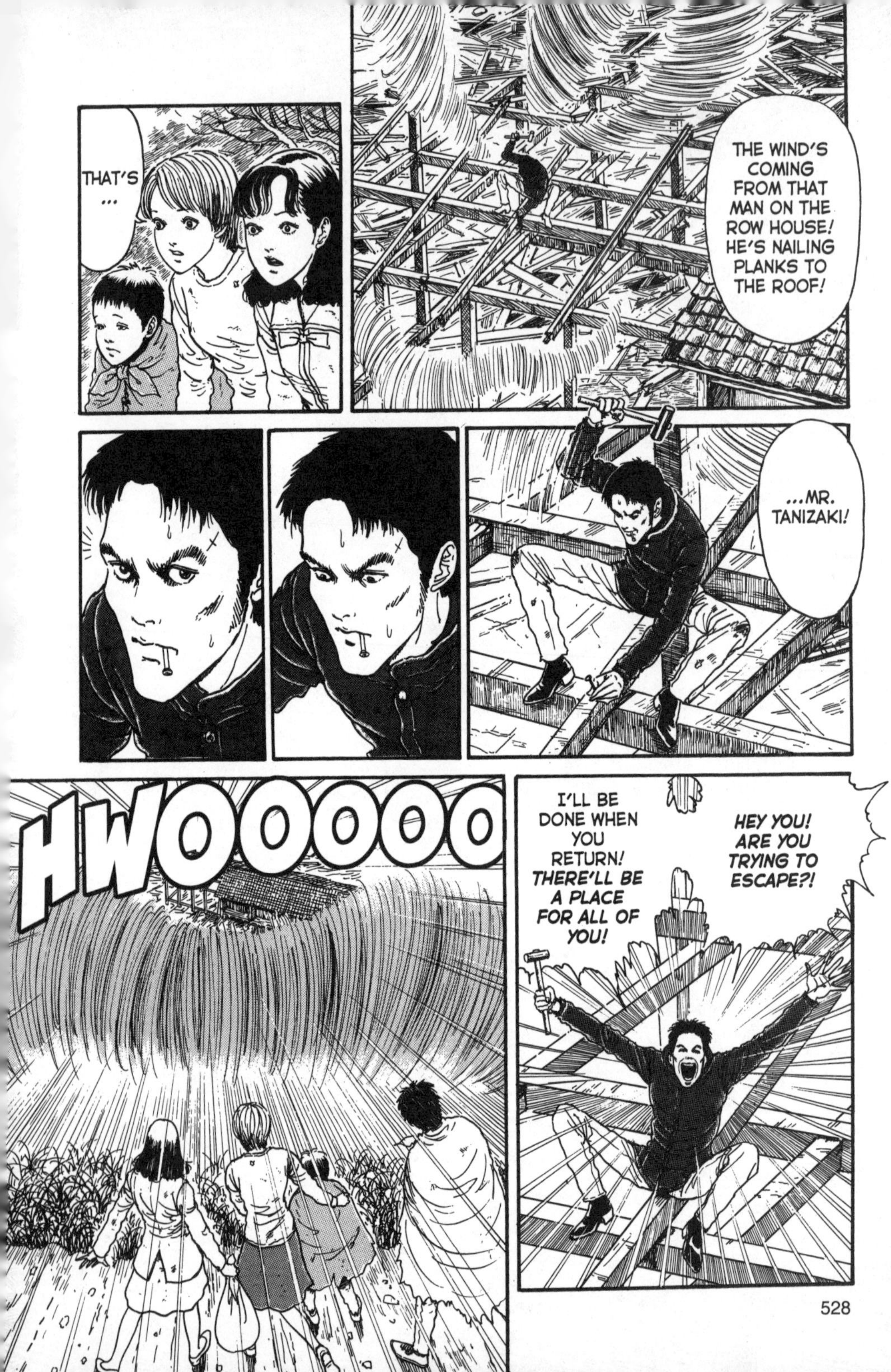
THE WIND'S COMING FROM THAT MAN ON THE ROW HOUSE! HE'S NAILING PLANKS TO THE ROOF!
THAT'S ...
...MR. TANIZAKI!
HEY YOU! ARE YOU TRYING TO ESCAPE?!
I'LL BE DONE WHEN YOU RETURN! THERE'LL BE A PLACE FOR ALL OF YOU!
HWOOOOOO

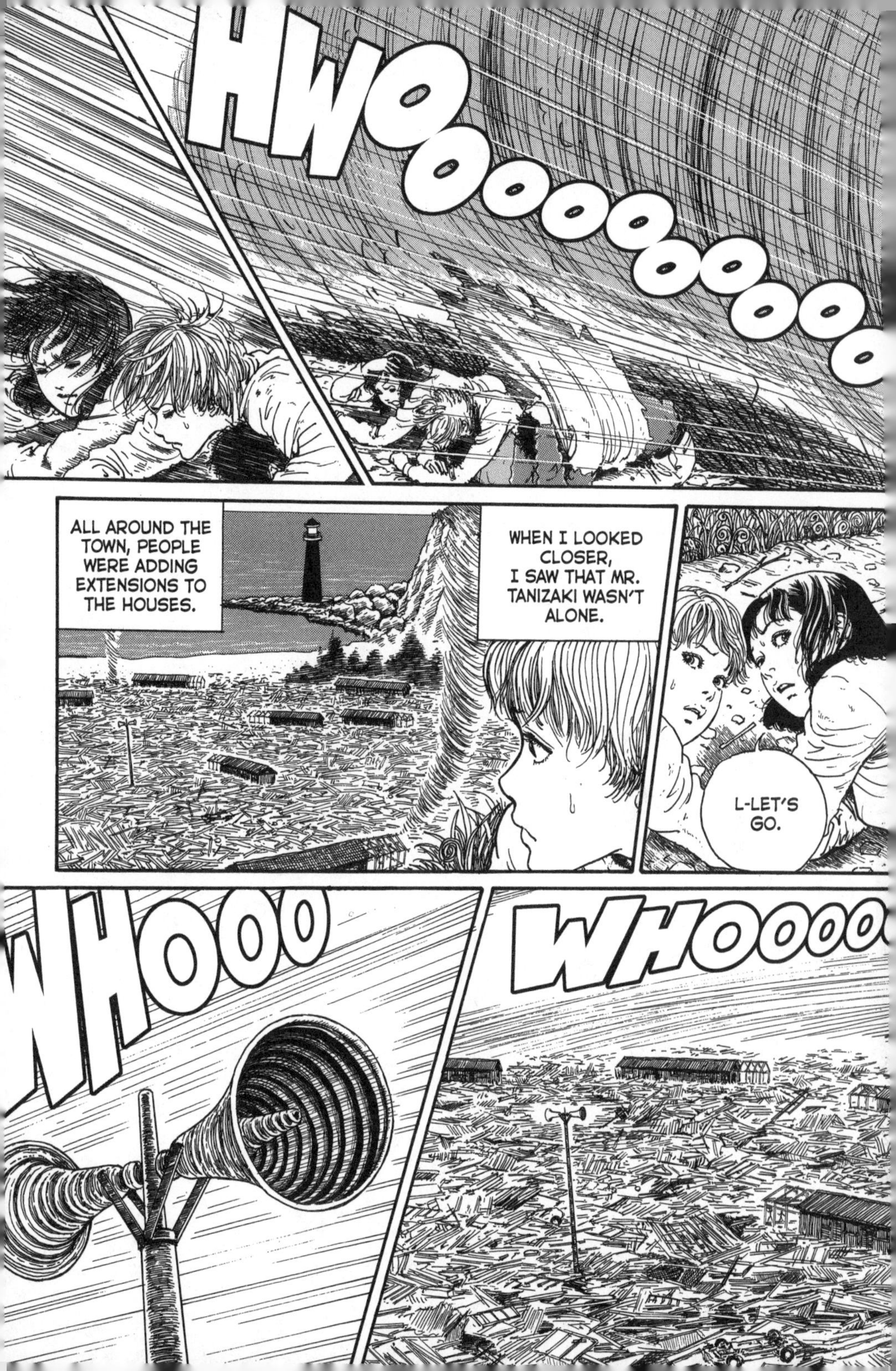
HWOOOOOOOOOO
L-LET'S GO.
WHEN I LOOKED CLOSER, I SAW THAT MR. TANIZAKI WASN'T ALONE.
ALL AROUND THE TOWN, PEOPLE WERE ADDING EXTENSIONS TO THE HOUSES.
WHOOOO
WHOOO

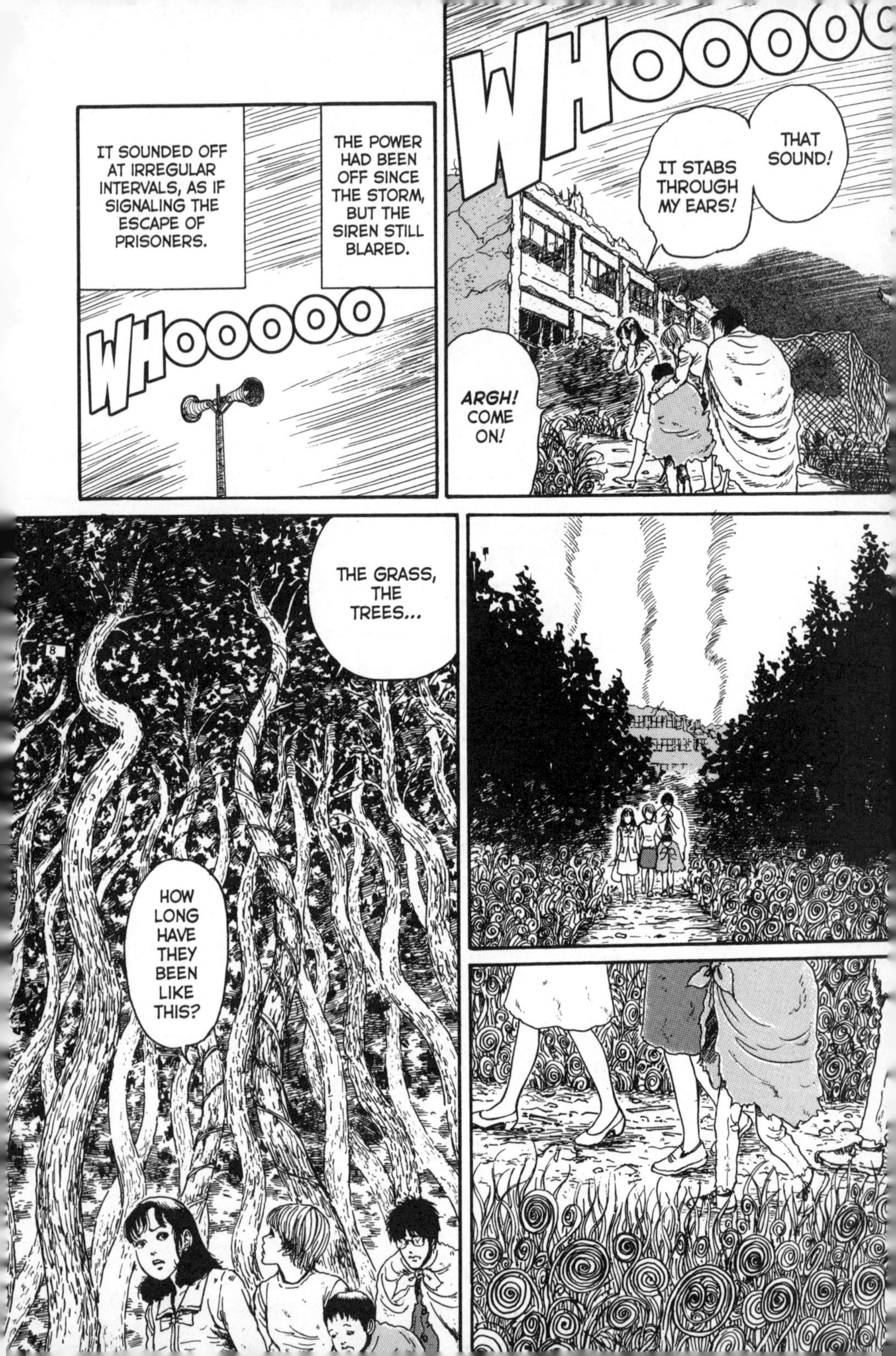
WHOOOOO
THAT SOUND!
IT STABS THROUGH MY EARS!
ARGH! COME ON!
THE POWER HAD BEEN OFF SINCE THE STORM, BUT THE SIREN STILL BLARED.
IT SOUNDED OFF AT IRREGULAR INTERVALS, AS IF SIGNALING THE ESCAPE OF PRISONERS.
WHOOOOO
THE GRASS, THE TREES...
HOW LONG HAVE THEY BEEN LIKE THIS?

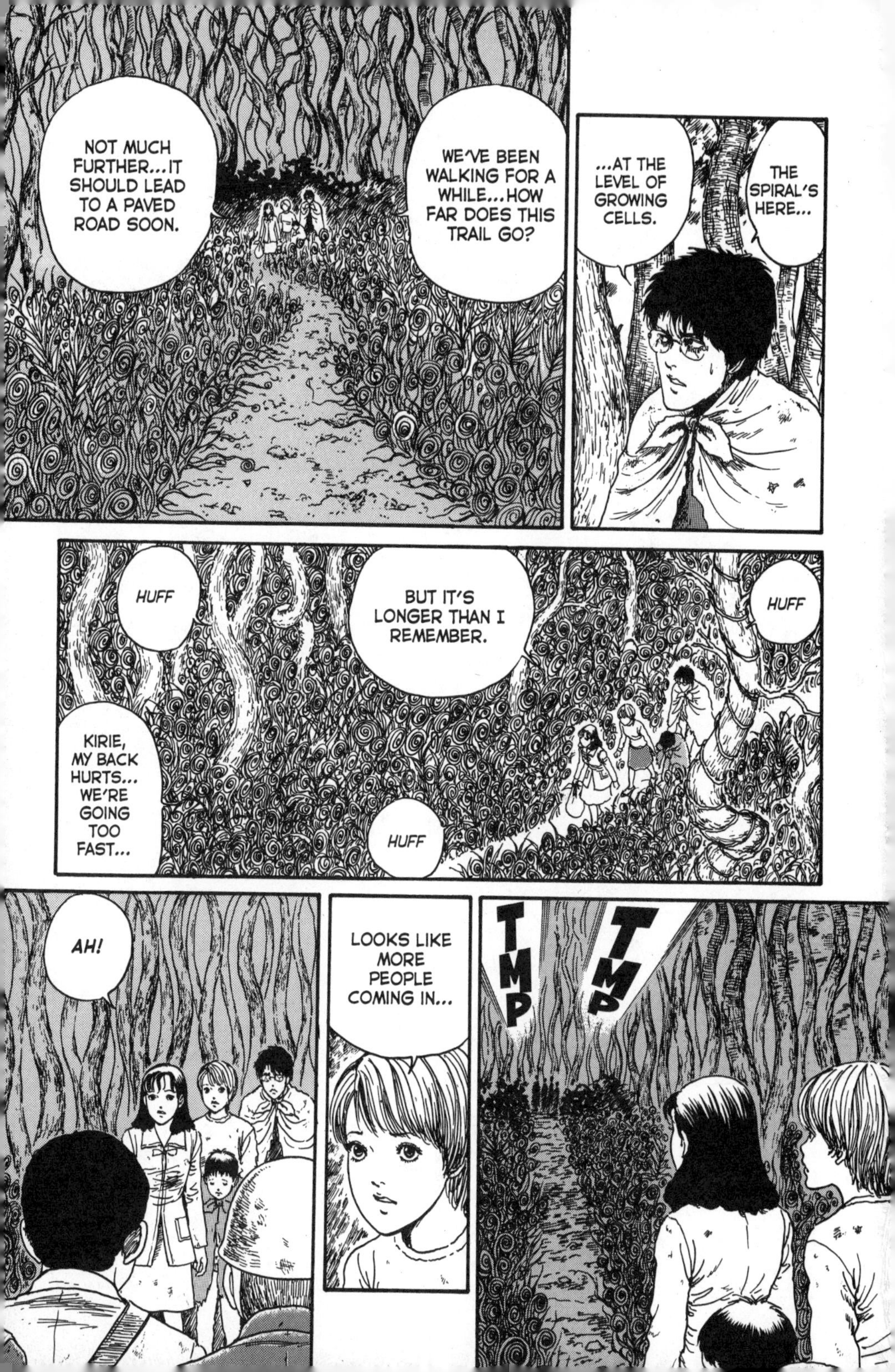
THE SPIRAL'S HERE...
...AT THE LEVEL OF GROWING CELLS.
WE'VE BEEN WALKING FOR A WHILE...HOW FAR DOES THIS TRAIL GO?
NOT MUCH FURTHER...IT SHOULD LEAD TO A PAVED ROAD SOON.
HUFF
BUT IT'S LONGER THAN I REMEMBER.
HUFF
KIRIE, MY BACK HURTS... WE'RE GOING TOO FAST...
HUFF
TMP
TMP
LOOKS LIKE MORE PEOPLE COMING IN...
AH!

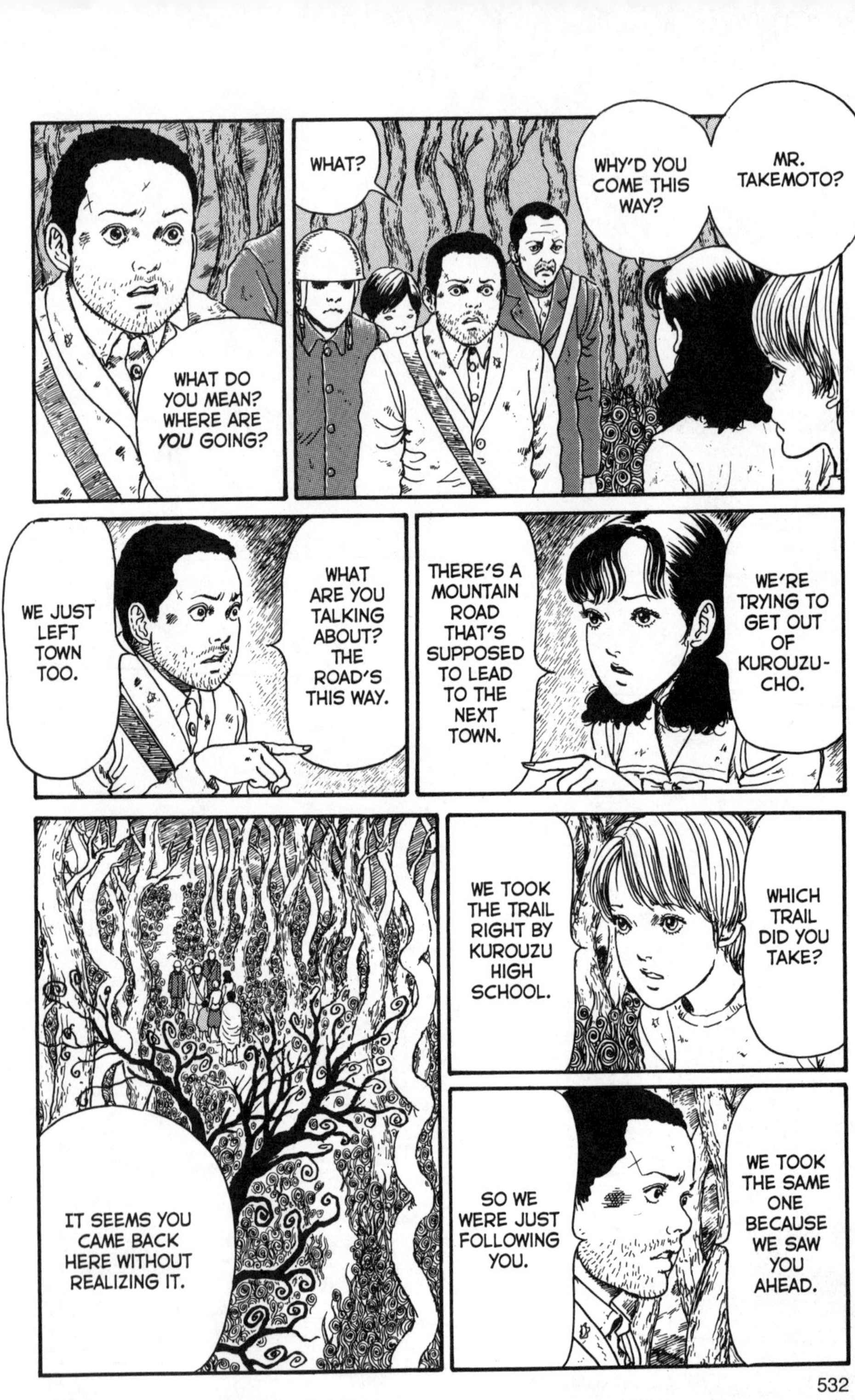
MR. TAKEMOTO?
WHY'D YOU COME THIS WAY?
WHAT?
WHAT DO YOU MEAN? WHERE ARE *YOU* GOING?
WE'RE TRYING TO GET OUT OF KUROUZU-CHO.
THERE'S A MOUNTAIN ROAD THAT'S SUPPOSED TO LEAD TO THE NEXT TOWN.
WHAT ARE YOU TALKING ABOUT? THE ROAD'S THIS WAY.
WE JUST LEFT TOWN TOO.
WHICH TRAIL DID YOU TAKE?
WE TOOK THE TRAIL RIGHT BY KUROUZU HIGH SCHOOL.
WE TOOK THE SAME ONE BECAUSE WE SAW YOU AHEAD.
SO WE WERE JUST FOLLOWING YOU.
IT SEEMS YOU CAME BACK HERE WITHOUT REALIZING IT.

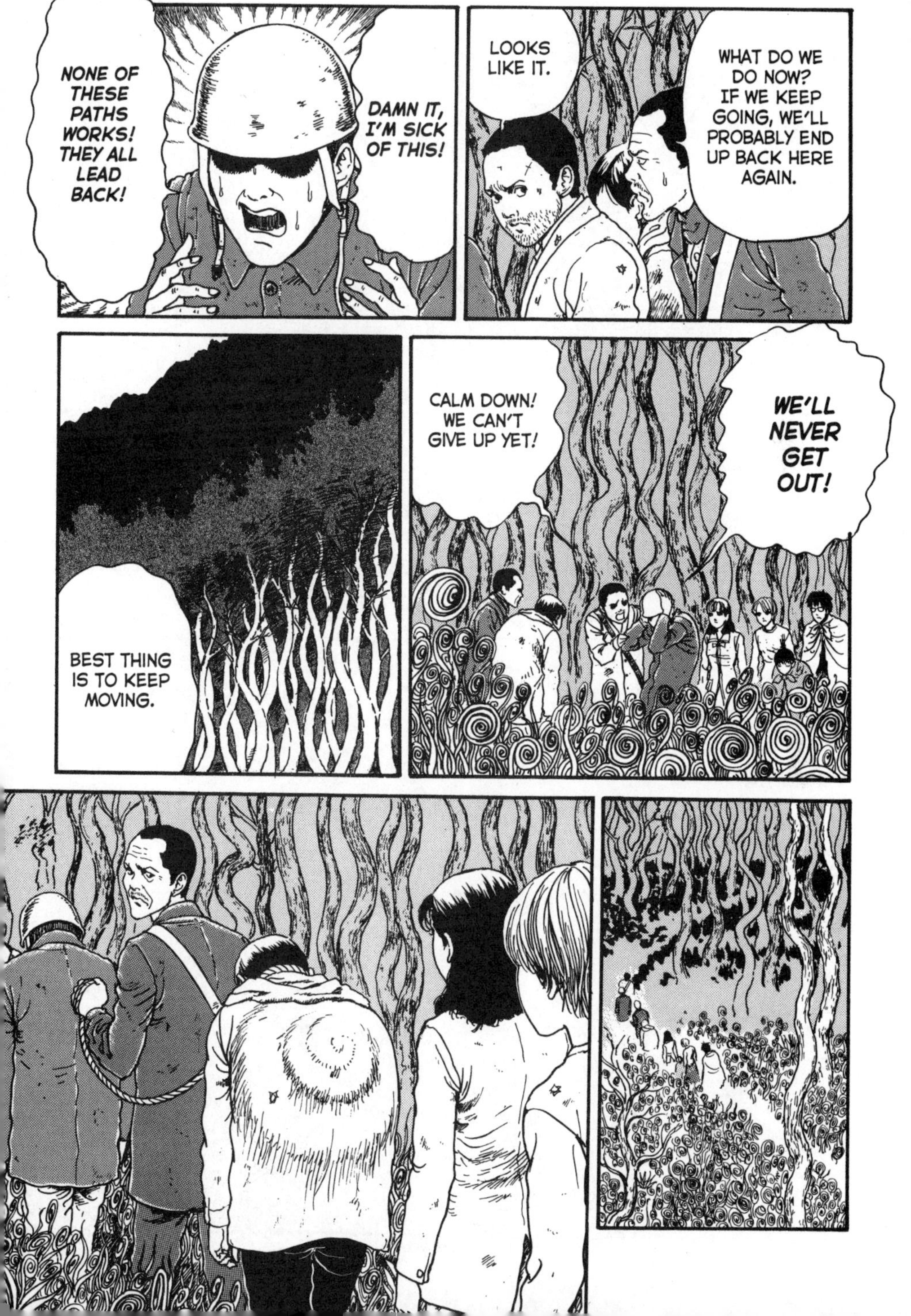
WHAT DO WE DO NOW? IF WE KEEP GOING, WE'LL PROBABLY END UP BACK HERE AGAIN.
LOOKS LIKE IT.
DAMN IT, I'M SICK OF THIS!
NONE OF THESE PATHS WORKS! THEY ALL LEAD BACK!
WE'LL NEVER GET OUT!
CALM DOWN! WE CAN'T GIVE UP YET!
BEST THING IS TO KEEP MOVING.

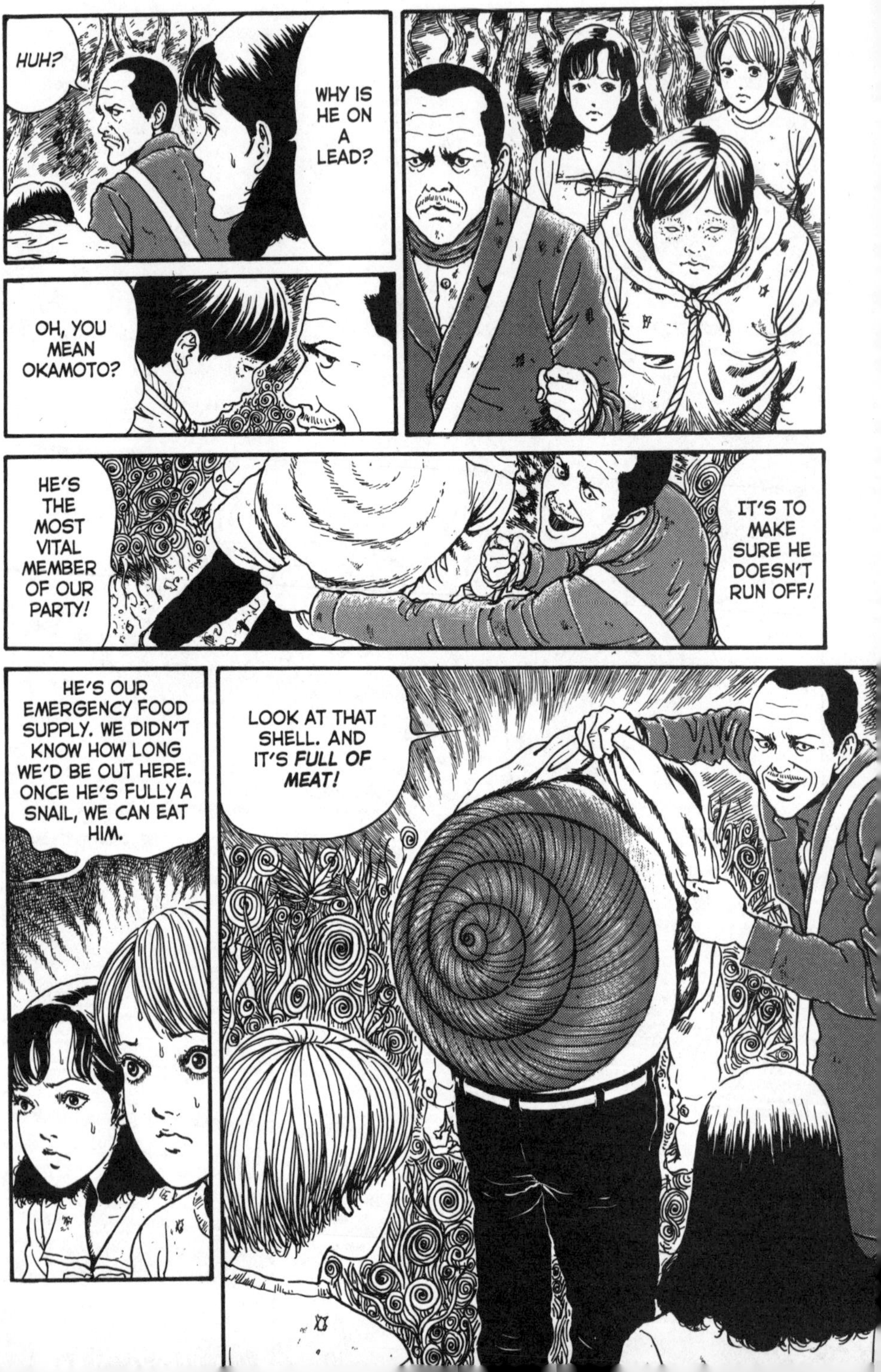
WHY IS HE ON A LEAD?
HUH?
OH, YOU MEAN OKAMOTO?
IT'S TO MAKE SURE HE DOESN'T RUN OFF!
HE'S THE MOST VITAL MEMBER OF OUR PARTY!
LOOK AT THAT SHELL. AND IT'S *FULL OF MEAT!*
HE'S OUR EMERGENCY FOOD SUPPLY. WE DIDN'T KNOW HOW LONG WE'D BE OUT HERE. ONCE HE'S FULLY A SNAIL, WE CAN EAT HIM.

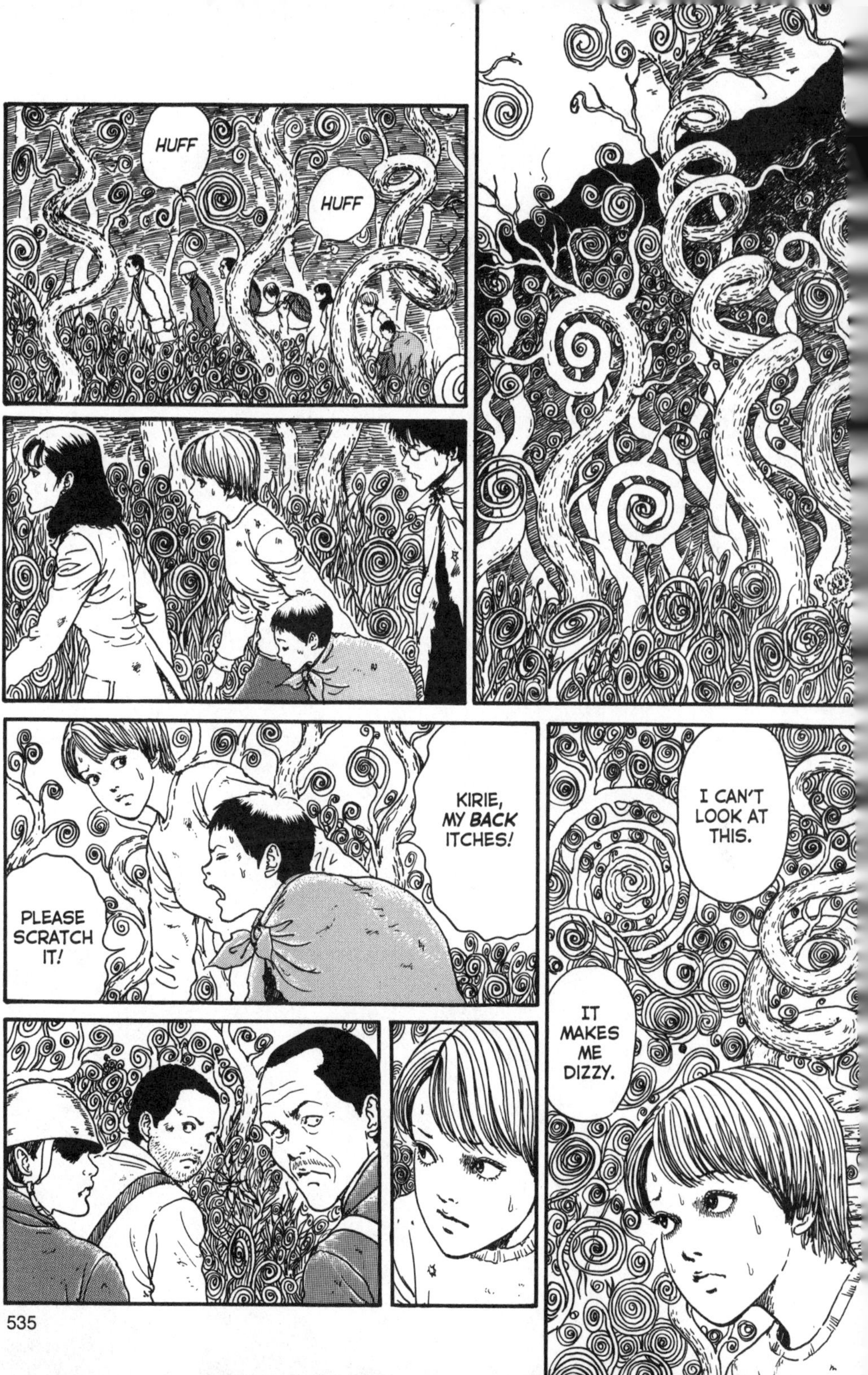
HUFF
HUFF
I CAN'T LOOK AT THIS.
IT MAKES ME DIZZY.
KIRIE, MY *BACK* ITCHES!
PLEASE SCRATCH IT!

SHLOOOP

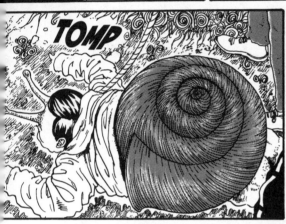

TOMP

SHUDDER SHUDDER

HA HA HA!

WELL... LOOK AT THAT!

SHUP

SHUP

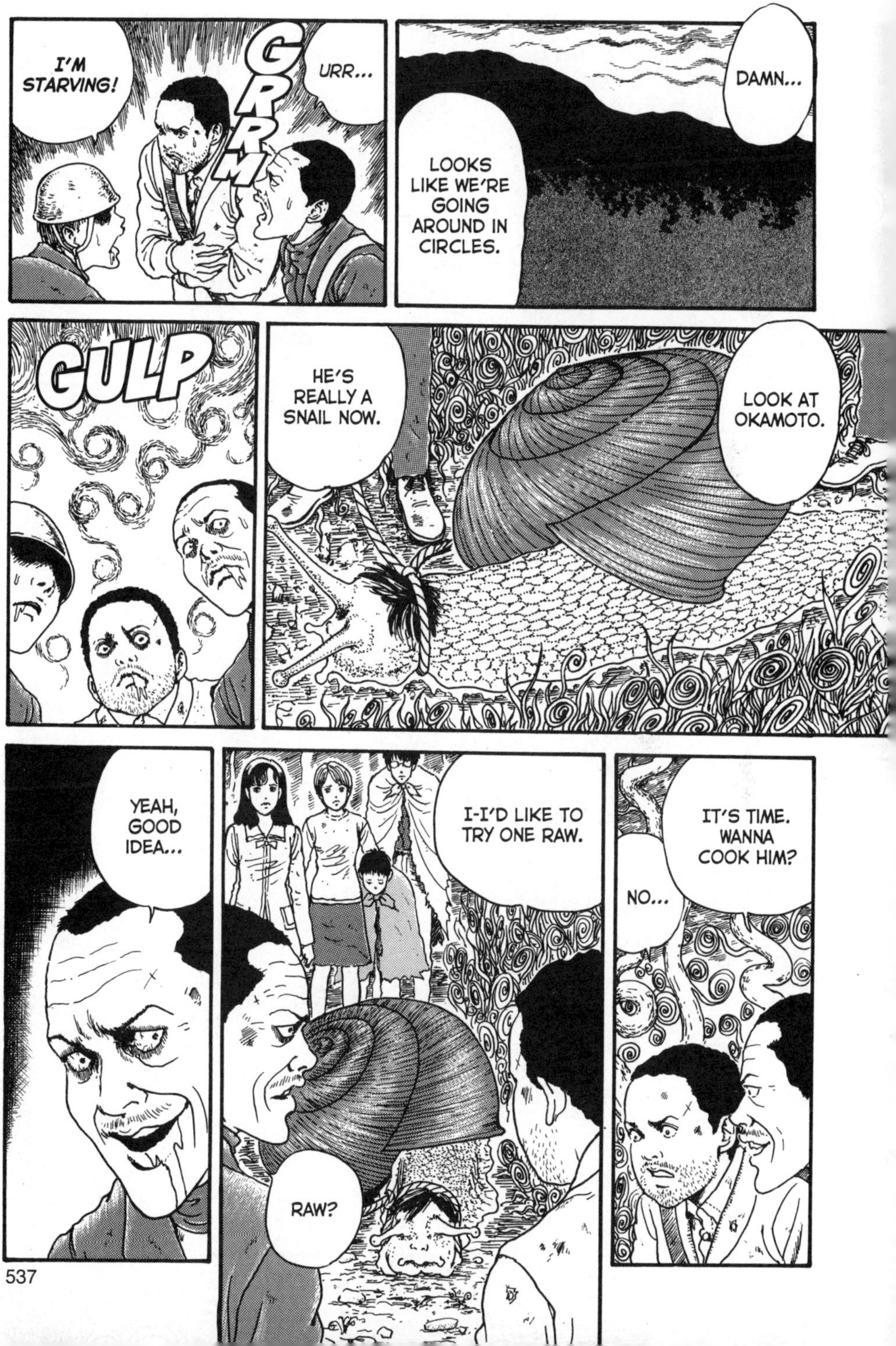
DAMN...
LOOKS LIKE WE'RE GOING AROUND IN CIRCLES.
URR...
GRRM
I'M STARVING!
LOOK AT OKAMOTO.
HE'S REALLY A SNAIL NOW.
GULP
IT'S TIME. WANNA COOK HIM?
NO...
I-I'D LIKE TO TRY ONE RAW.
RAW?
YEAH, GOOD IDEA...

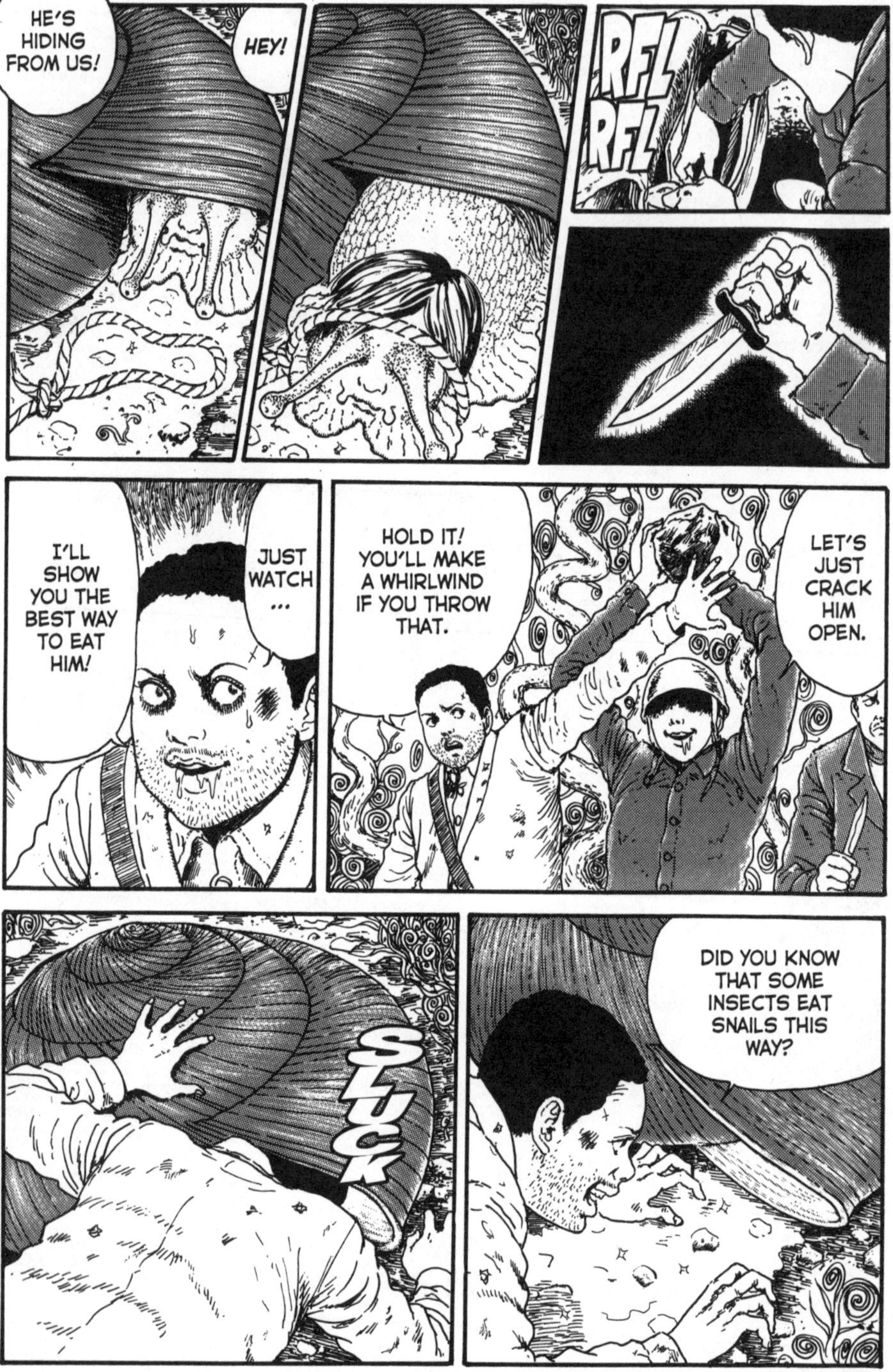
RFL RFL
HEY!
HE'S HIDING FROM US!
LET'S JUST CRACK HIM OPEN.
HOLD IT! YOU'LL MAKE A WHIRLWIND IF YOU THROW THAT.
JUST WATCH ...
I'LL SHOW YOU THE BEST WAY TO EAT HIM!
DID YOU KNOW THAT SOME INSECTS EAT SNAILS THIS WAY?
SLUCK

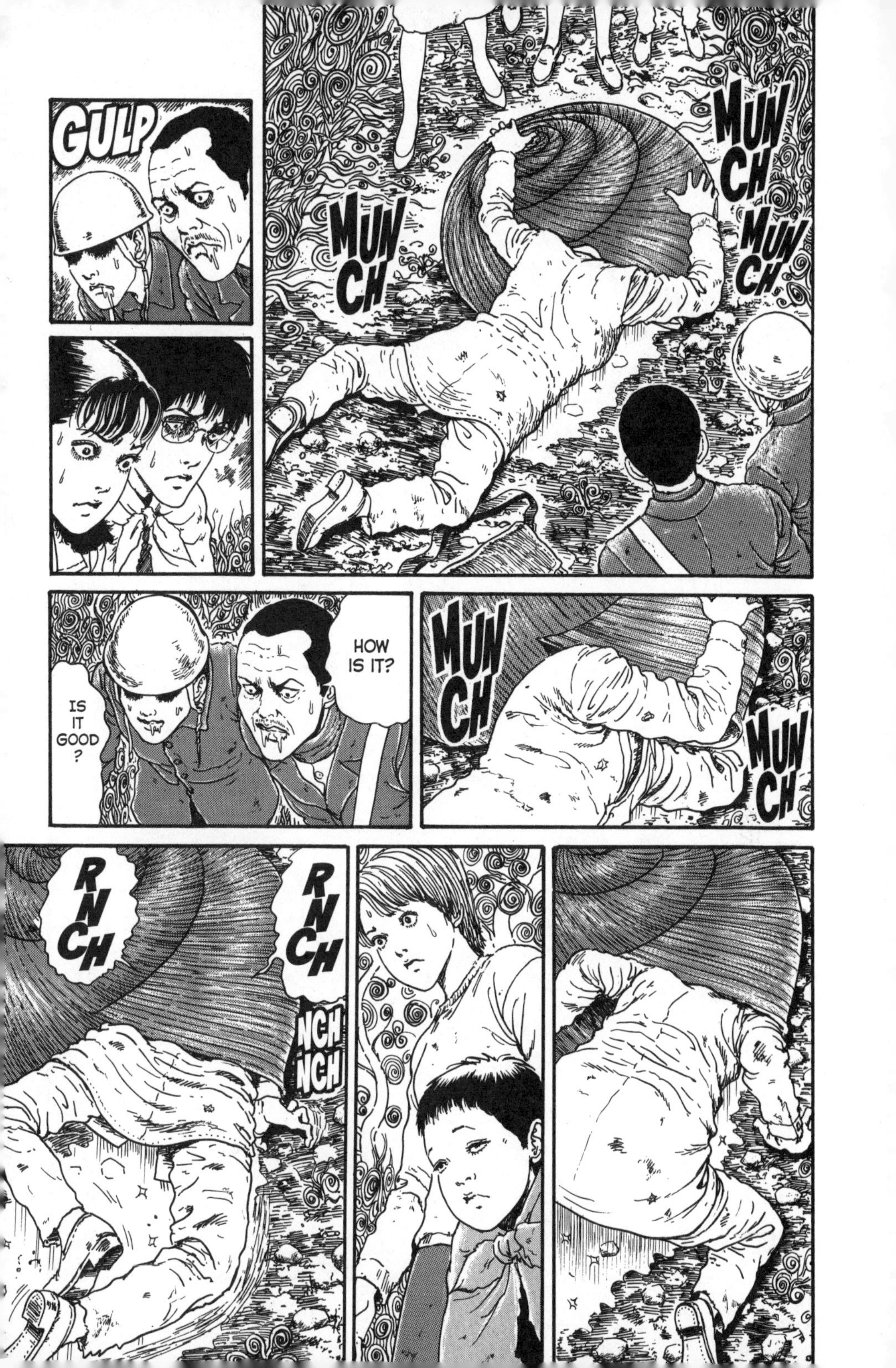
MUNCH
MUNCH
MUNCH
GULP
MUNCH
MUNCH
HOW IS IT?
IS IT GOOD?
RNCH
RNCH
NCH NCH

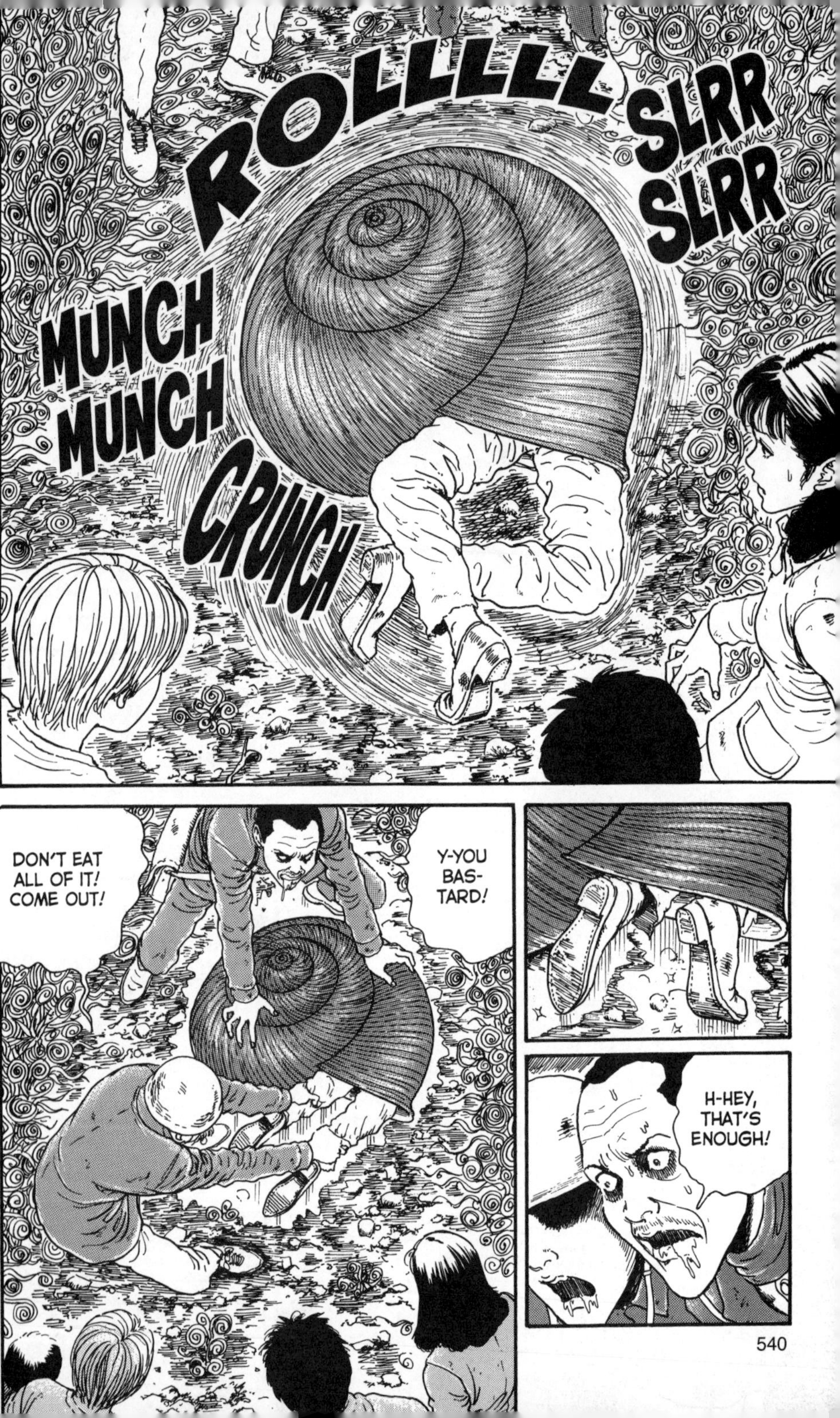
ROLLLLL
SLRR SLRR
MUNCH MUNCH
CRUNCH
H-HEY, THAT'S ENOUGH!
Y-YOU BAS-TARD!
DON'T EAT ALL OF IT! COME OUT!

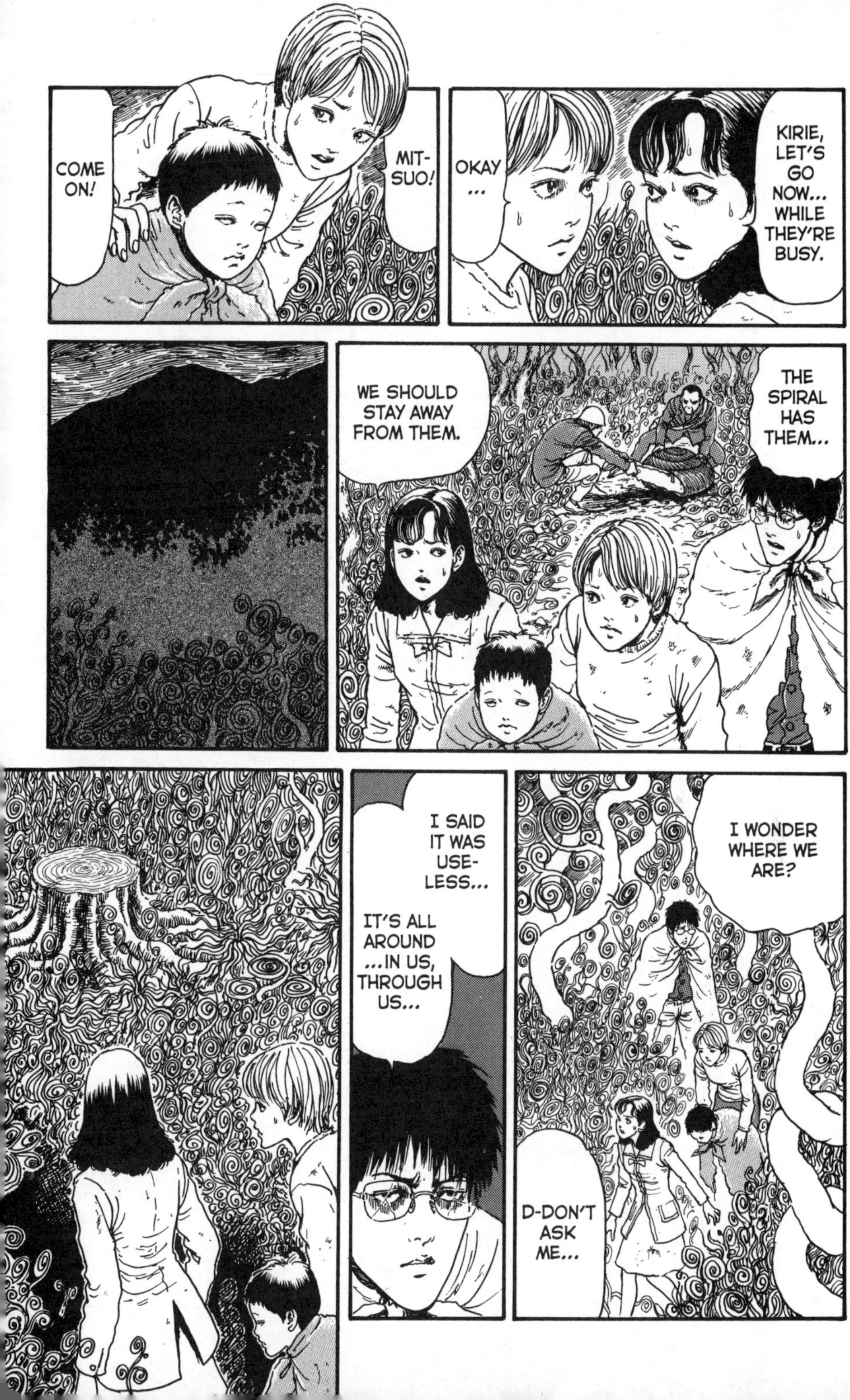
KIRIE, LET'S GO NOW... WHILE THEY'RE BUSY.
OKAY ...
MIT-SUO!
COME ON!
THE SPIRAL HAS THEM...
WE SHOULD STAY AWAY FROM THEM.
I WONDER WHERE WE ARE?
D-DON'T ASK ME...
I SAID IT WAS USE-LESS...
IT'S ALL AROUND ...IN US, THROUGH US...

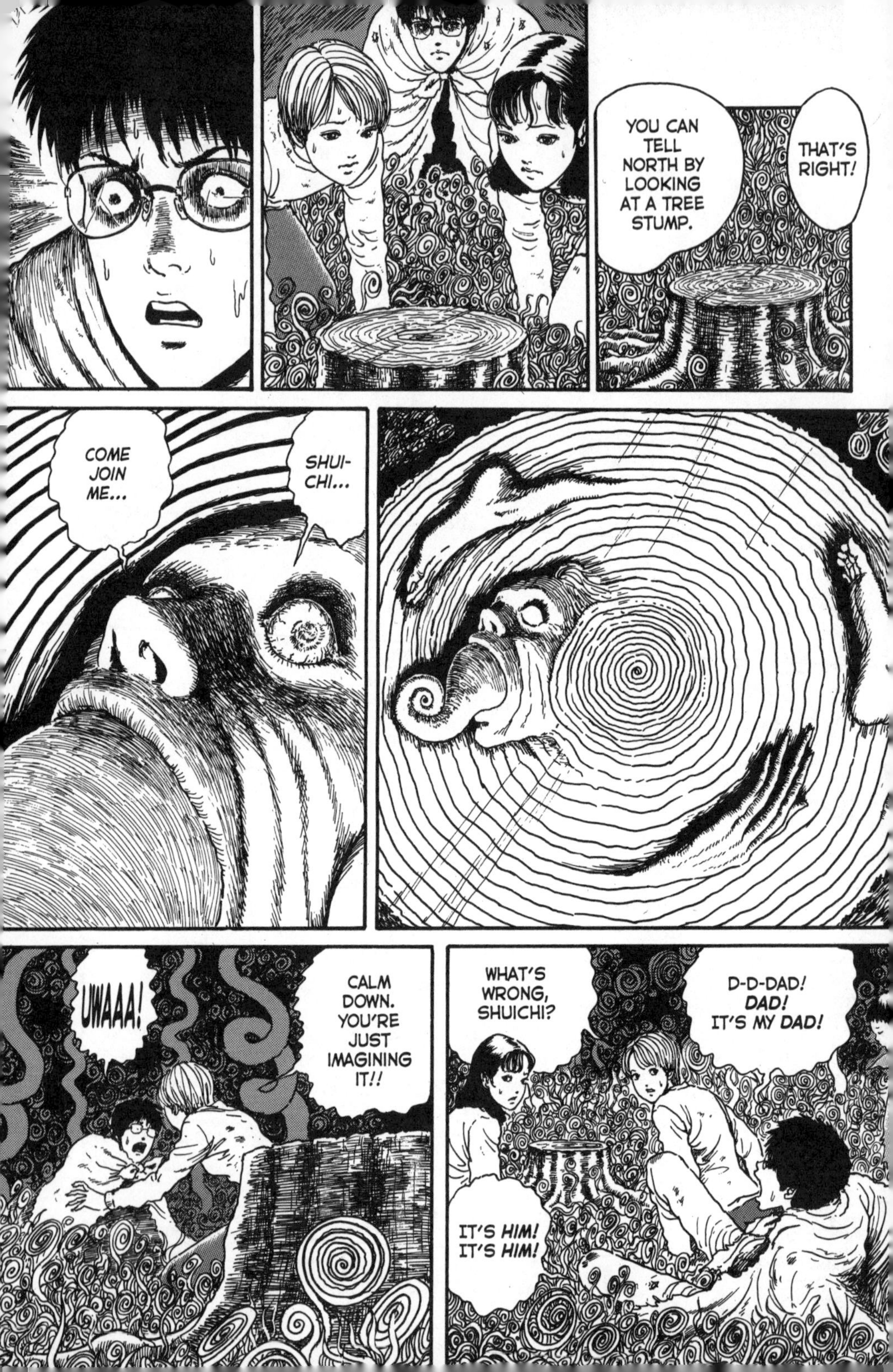
THAT'S RIGHT!
YOU CAN TELL NORTH BY LOOKING AT A TREE STUMP.
SHUI-CHI...
COME JOIN ME...
D-D-DAD! *DAD!* IT'S MY *DAD!*
WHAT'S WRONG, SHUICHI?
IT'S *HIM!* IT'S *HIM!*
CALM DOWN. YOU'RE JUST IMAGINING IT!!
UWAAA!

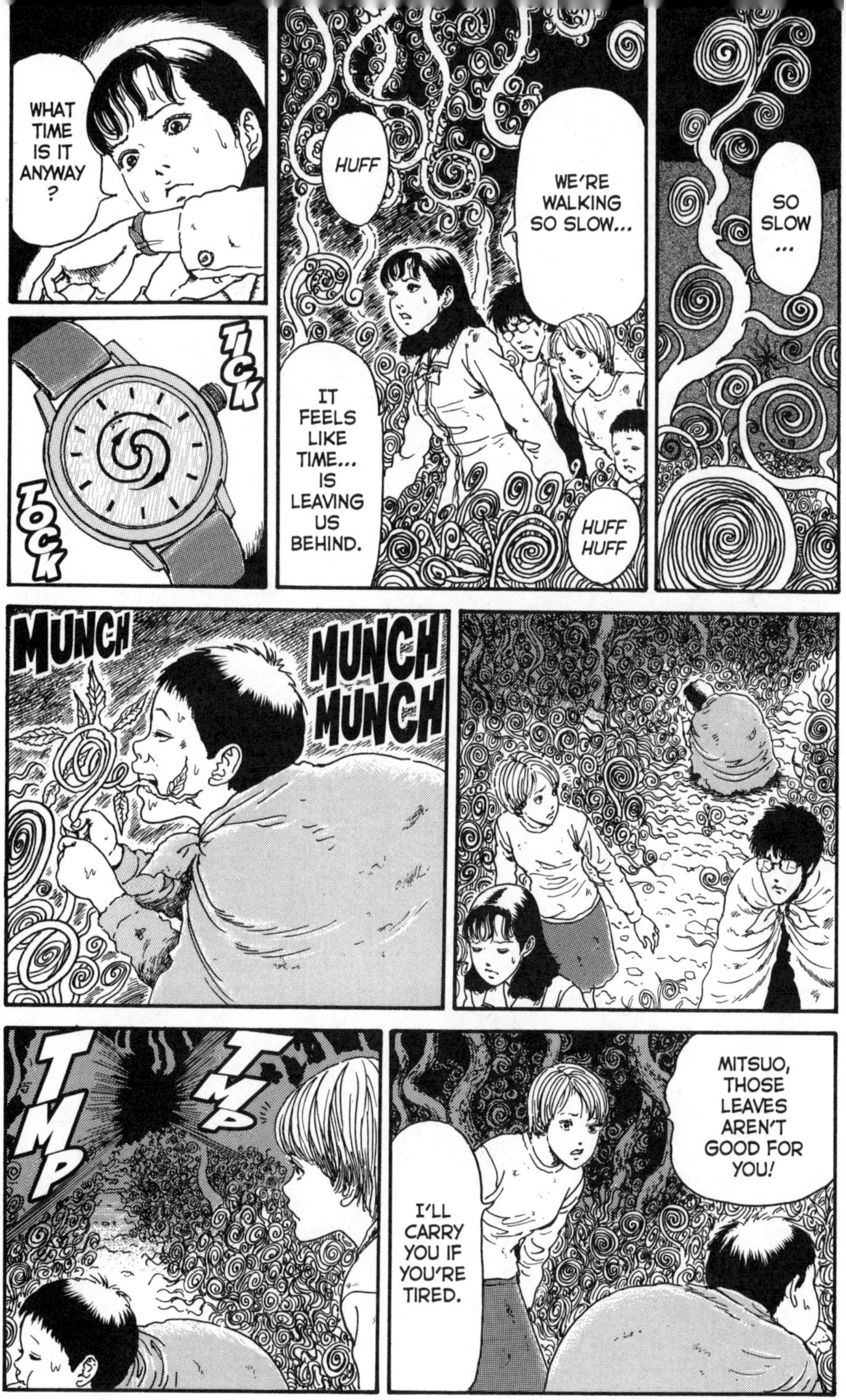
SO SLOW ...
WE'RE WALKING SO SLOW...
HUFF
IT FEELS LIKE TIME... IS LEAVING US BEHIND.
HUFF HUFF
WHAT TIME IS IT ANYWAY ?
TICK
TOCK
MUNCH MUNCH
MUNCH
MITSUO, THOSE LEAVES AREN'T GOOD FOR YOU!
I'LL CARRY YOU IF YOU'RE TIRED.
TMP
TMP

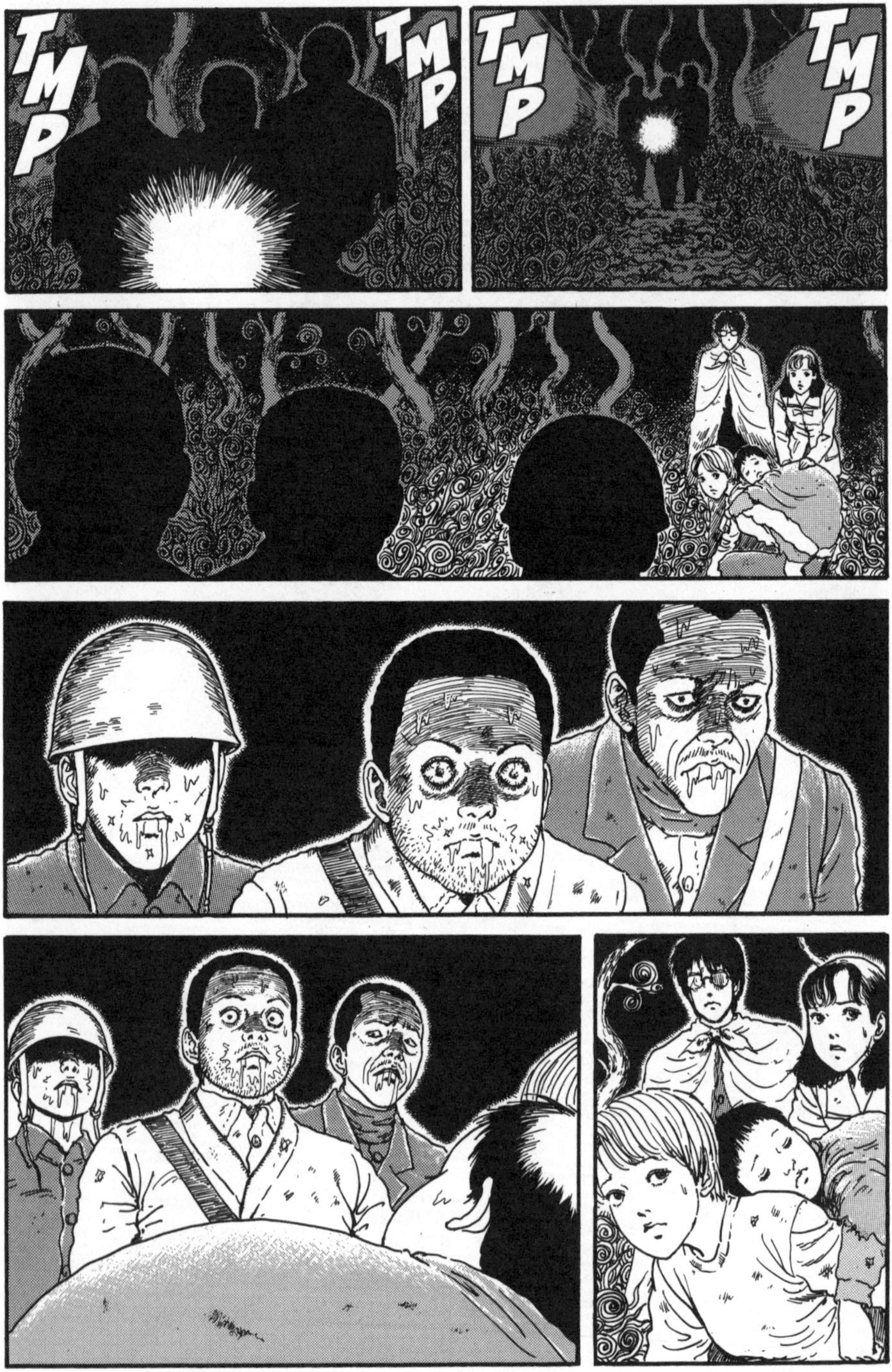
TMP
TMP
TMP
TMP

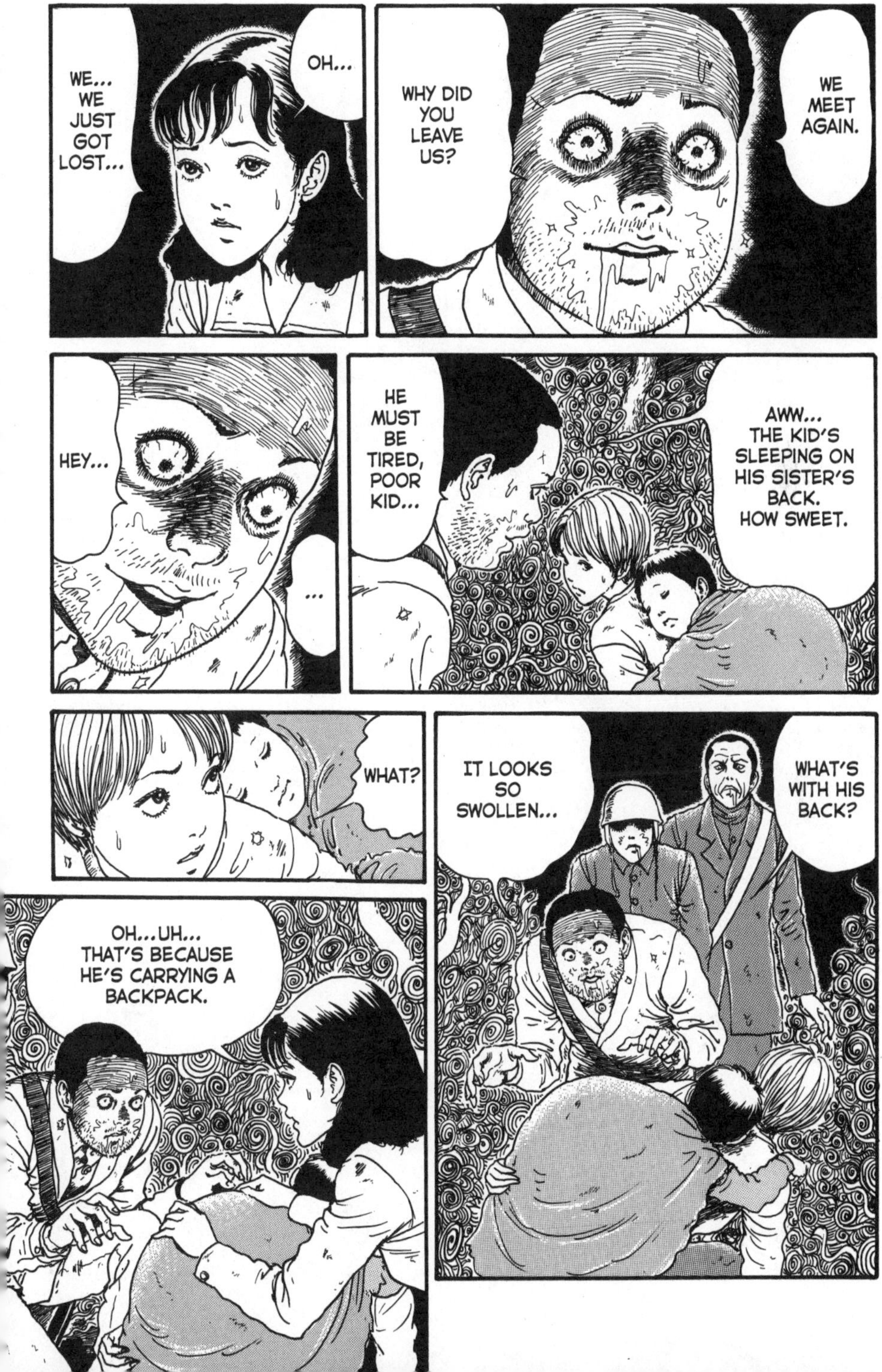
WE MEET AGAIN.
WHY DID YOU LEAVE US?
OH...
WE... WE JUST GOT LOST...
AWW... THE KID'S SLEEPING ON HIS SISTER'S BACK. HOW SWEET.
HE MUST BE TIRED, POOR KID...
HEY...
...
WHAT'S WITH HIS BACK?
IT LOOKS SO SWOLLEN...
WHAT?
OH...UH... THAT'S BECAUSE HE'S CARRYING A BACKPACK.

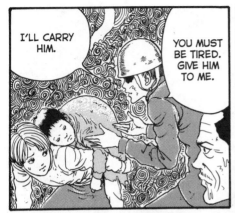

MM... I SEE...
WELL... LET'S GO ON TOGETHER, OKAY?
YOU MUST BE TIRED. GIVE HIM TO ME.
I'LL CARRY HIM.
NO, NO...I'M FINE.
NO YOU'RE NOT.
WE HAVE A WAYS TO GO. COME ON!
TUG
I'LL TAKE HIM.
O-OKAY.

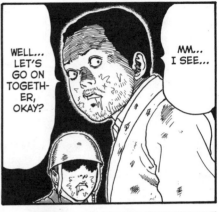

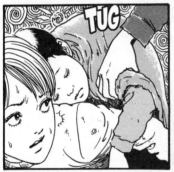

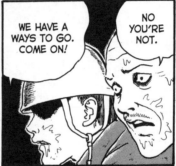

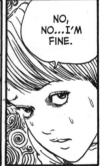

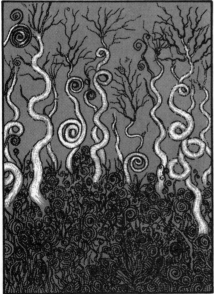

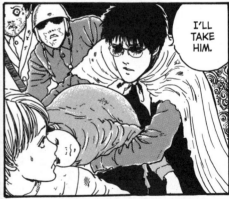

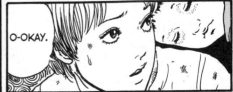

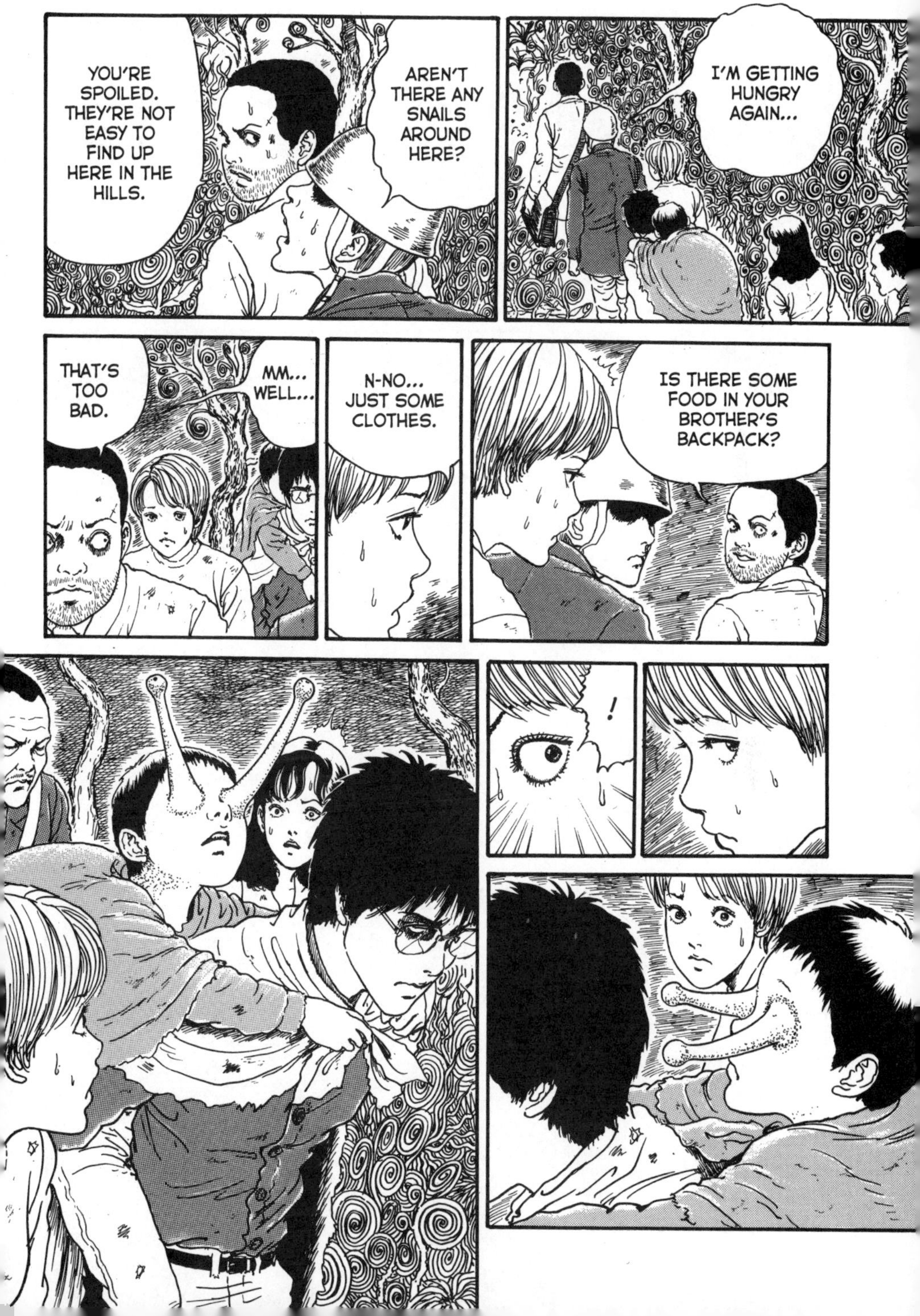
I'M GETTING HUNGRY AGAIN...
AREN'T THERE ANY SNAILS AROUND HERE?
YOU'RE SPOILED. THEY'RE NOT EASY TO FIND UP HERE IN THE HILLS.
IS THERE SOME FOOD IN YOUR BROTHER'S BACKPACK?
N-NO... JUST SOME CLOTHES.
MM... WELL...
THAT'S TOO BAD.
!

ANYWAY, I WAS THINK-ING...

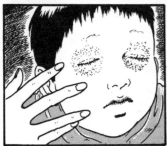

NOTH-ING'S WRONG.

WHAT'S WRONG?

AAH!

FWOO

PLOP

PLOP

?!

SHLUUP

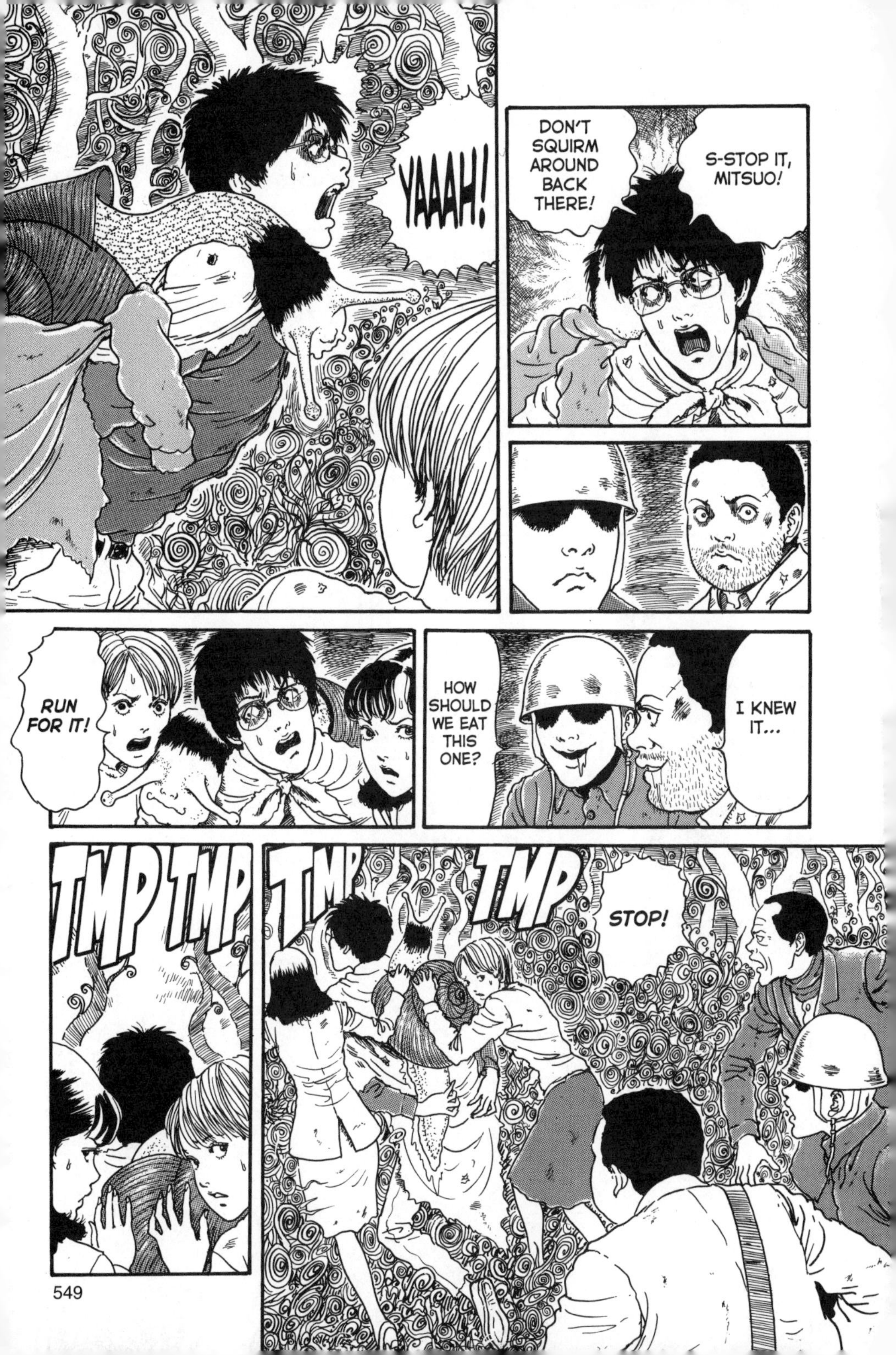
S-STOP IT, MITSUO!
DON'T SQUIRM AROUND BACK THERE!
YAAAH!
I KNEW IT...
HOW SHOULD WE EAT THIS ONE?
RUN FOR IT!
STOP!
TMP
TMP
TMP TMP

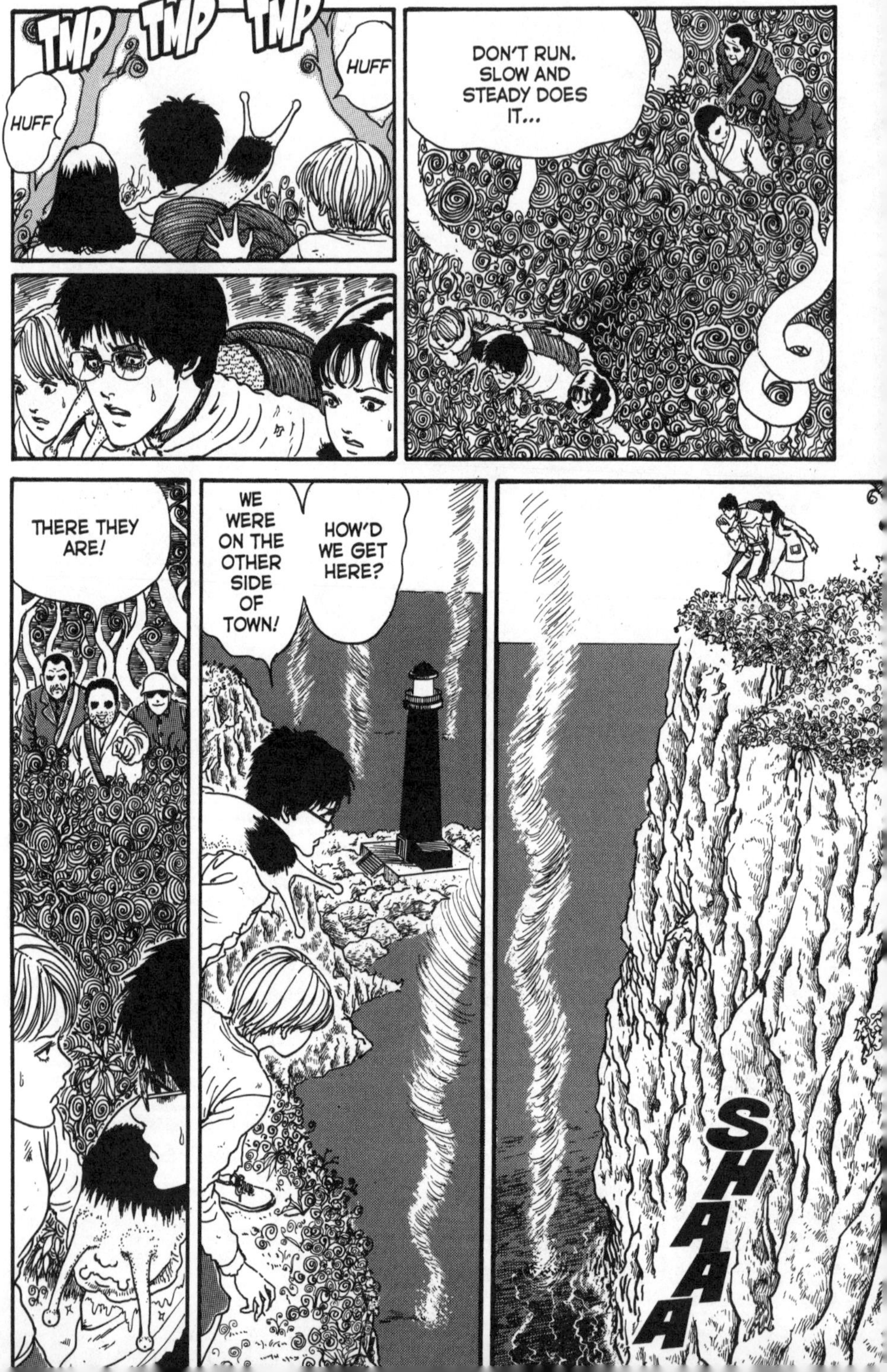
DON'T RUN. SLOW AND STEADY DOES IT...
TMP TMP TMP
HUFF
HUFF
SHAAAA
HOW'D WE GET HERE?
WE WERE ON THE OTHER SIDE OF TOWN!
THERE THEY ARE!

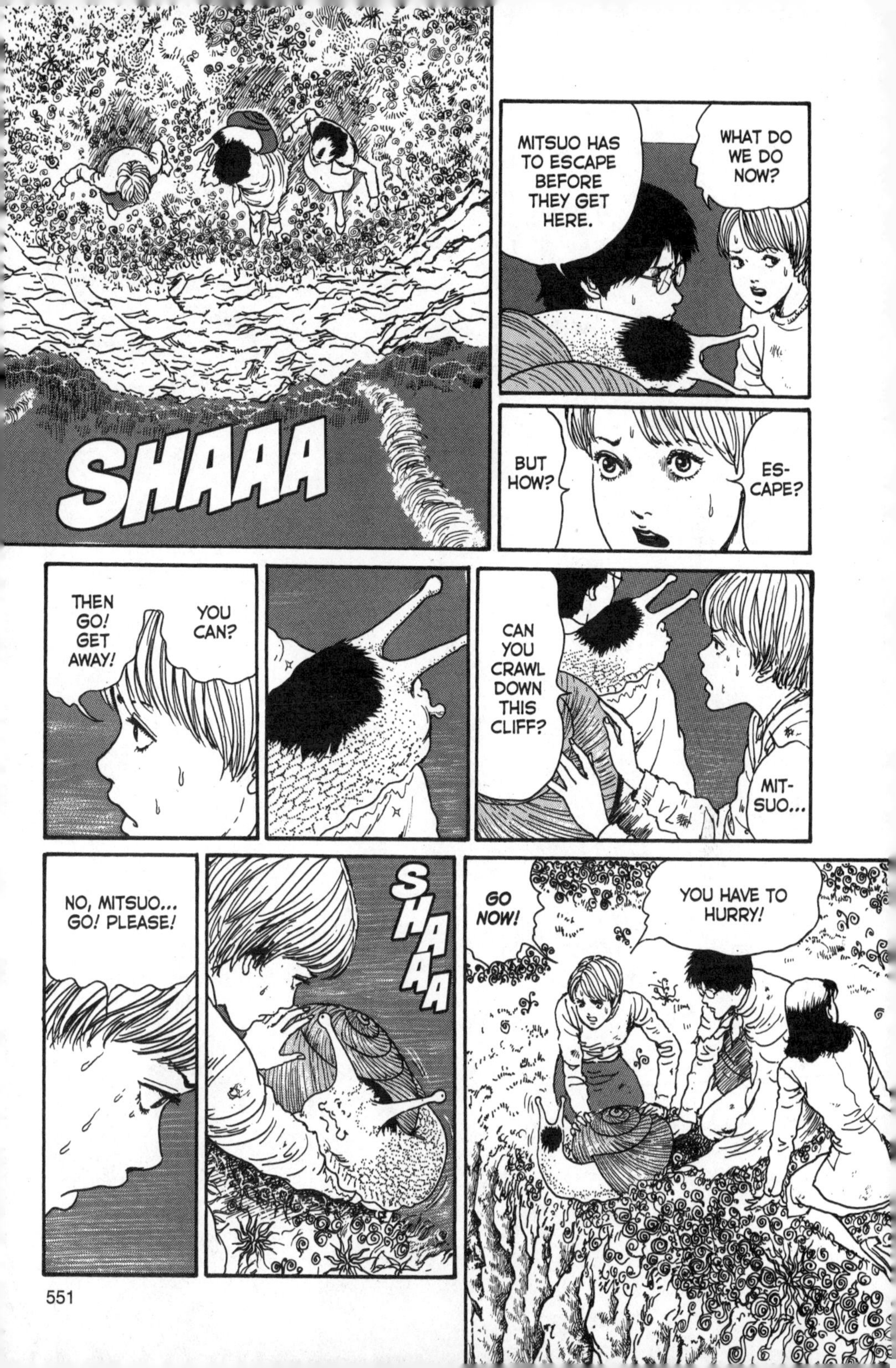
WHAT DO WE DO NOW?
MITSUO HAS TO ESCAPE BEFORE THEY GET HERE.
ES-CAPE?
BUT HOW?
SHAAA
MIT-SUO...
CAN YOU CRAWL DOWN THIS CLIFF?
YOU CAN?
THEN GO! GET AWAY!
YOU HAVE TO HURRY!
GO NOW!
SHAAA
NO, MITSUO... GO! PLEASE!

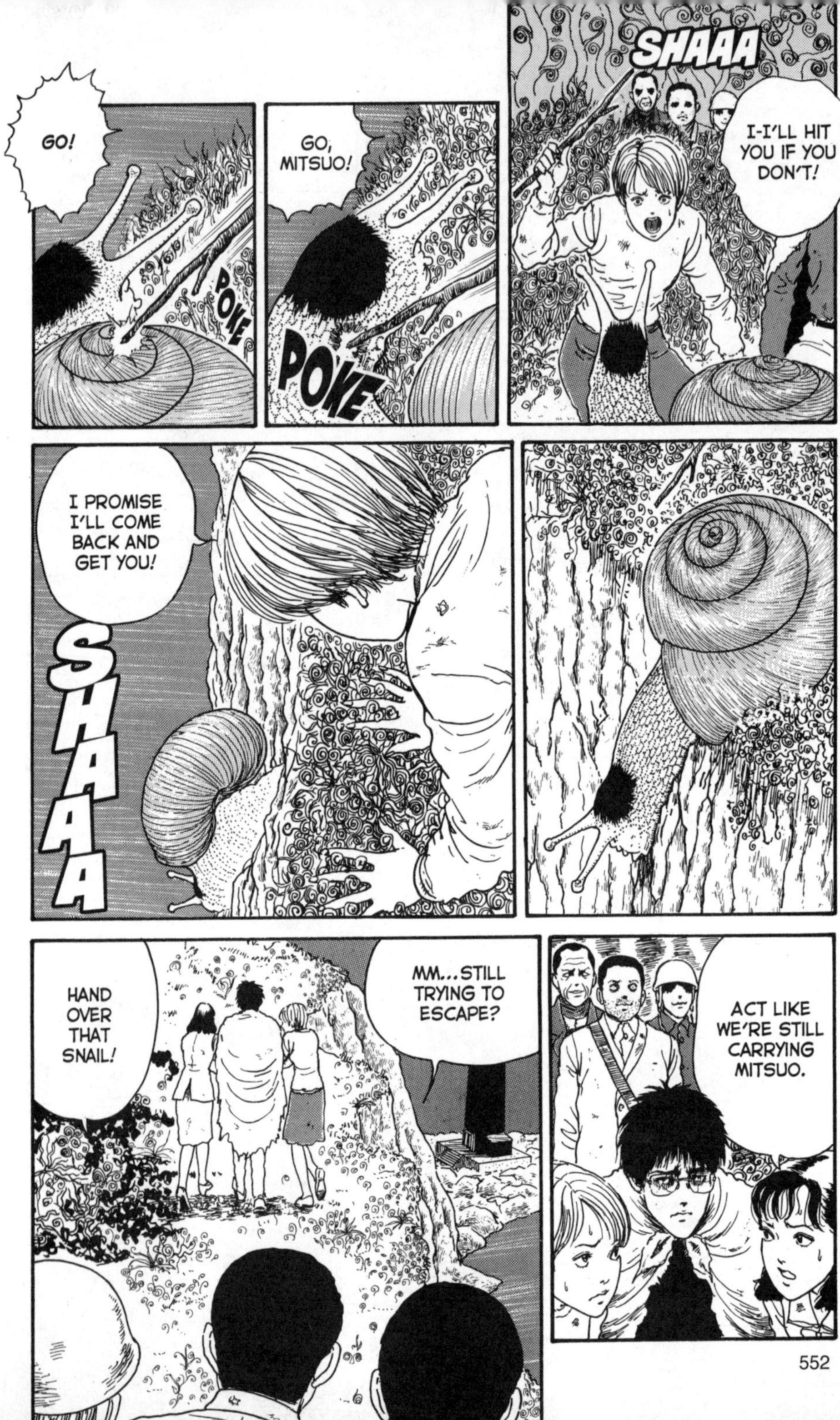
SHAAA
I-I'LL HIT YOU IF YOU DON'T!
GO, MITSUO!
POKE
GO!
POKE
I PROMISE I'LL COME BACK AND GET YOU!
SHAAAA
ACT LIKE WE'RE STILL CARRYING MITSUO.
MM...STILL TRYING TO ESCAPE?
HAND OVER THAT SNAIL!

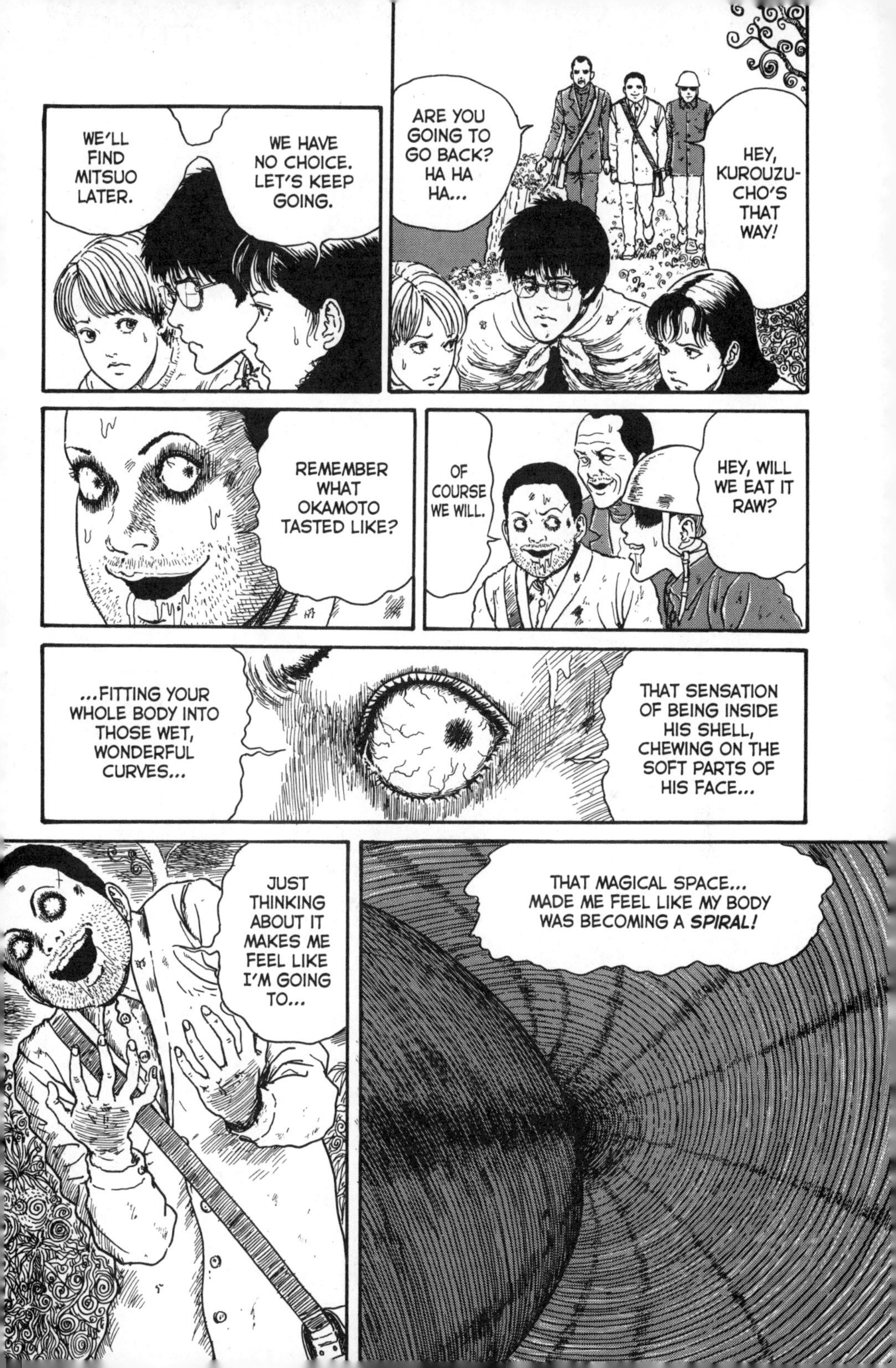
HEY, KUROUZU-CHO'S THAT WAY!
ARE YOU GOING TO GO BACK? HA HA HA...
WE HAVE NO CHOICE. LET'S KEEP GOING.
WE'LL FIND MITSUO LATER.
HEY, WILL WE EAT IT RAW?
OF COURSE WE WILL.
REMEMBER WHAT OKAMOTO TASTED LIKE?
THAT SENSATION OF BEING INSIDE HIS SHELL, CHEWING ON THE SOFT PARTS OF HIS FACE...
...FITTING YOUR WHOLE BODY INTO THOSE WET, WONDERFUL CURVES...
THAT MAGICAL SPACE... MADE ME FEEL LIKE MY BODY WAS BECOMING A SPIRAL!
JUST THINKING ABOUT IT MAKES ME FEEL LIKE I'M GOING TO...

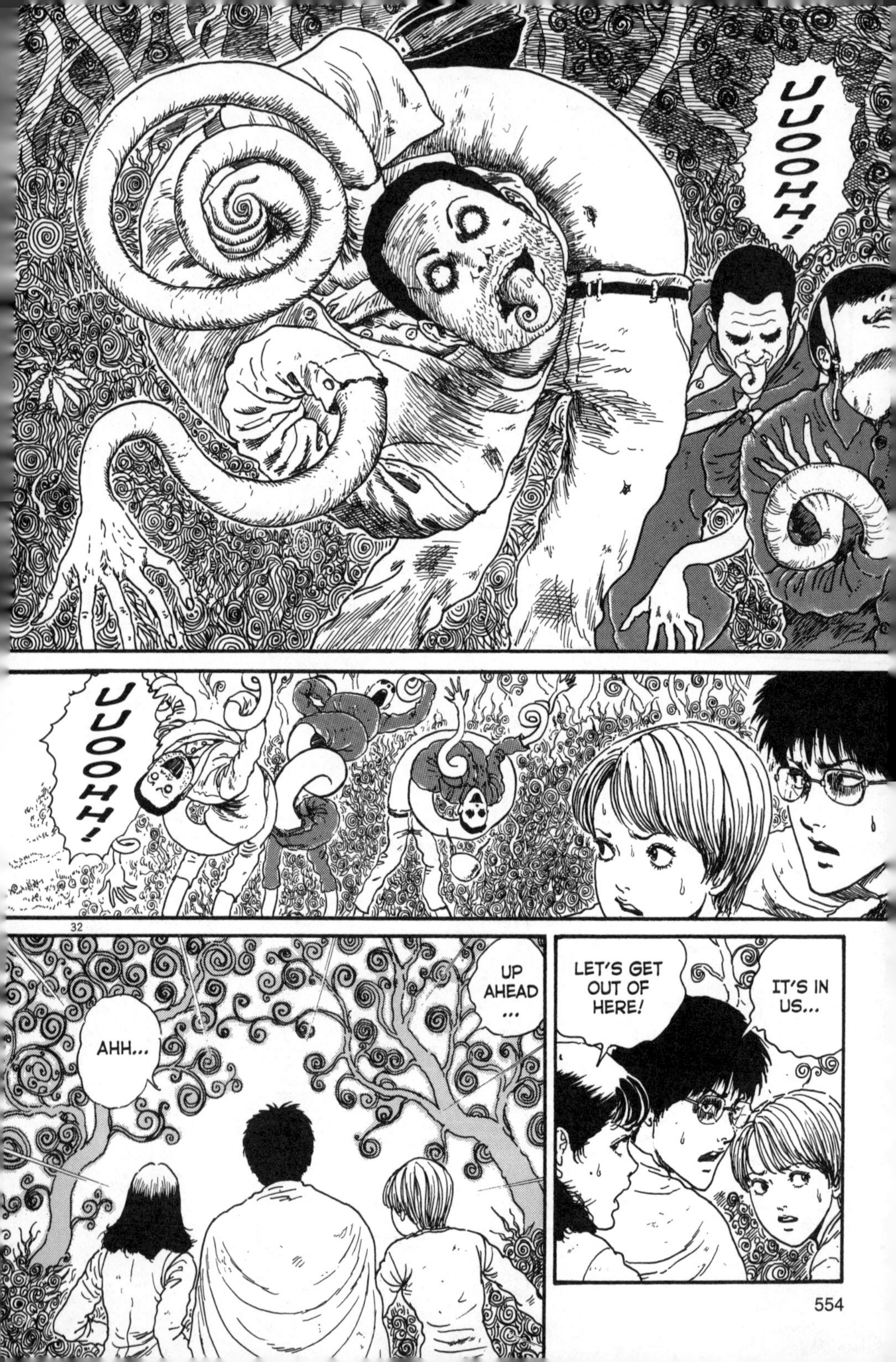
UUOOHH!
UUOOHH!
IT'S IN US...
LET'S GET OUT OF HERE!
UP AHEAD...
AHH...

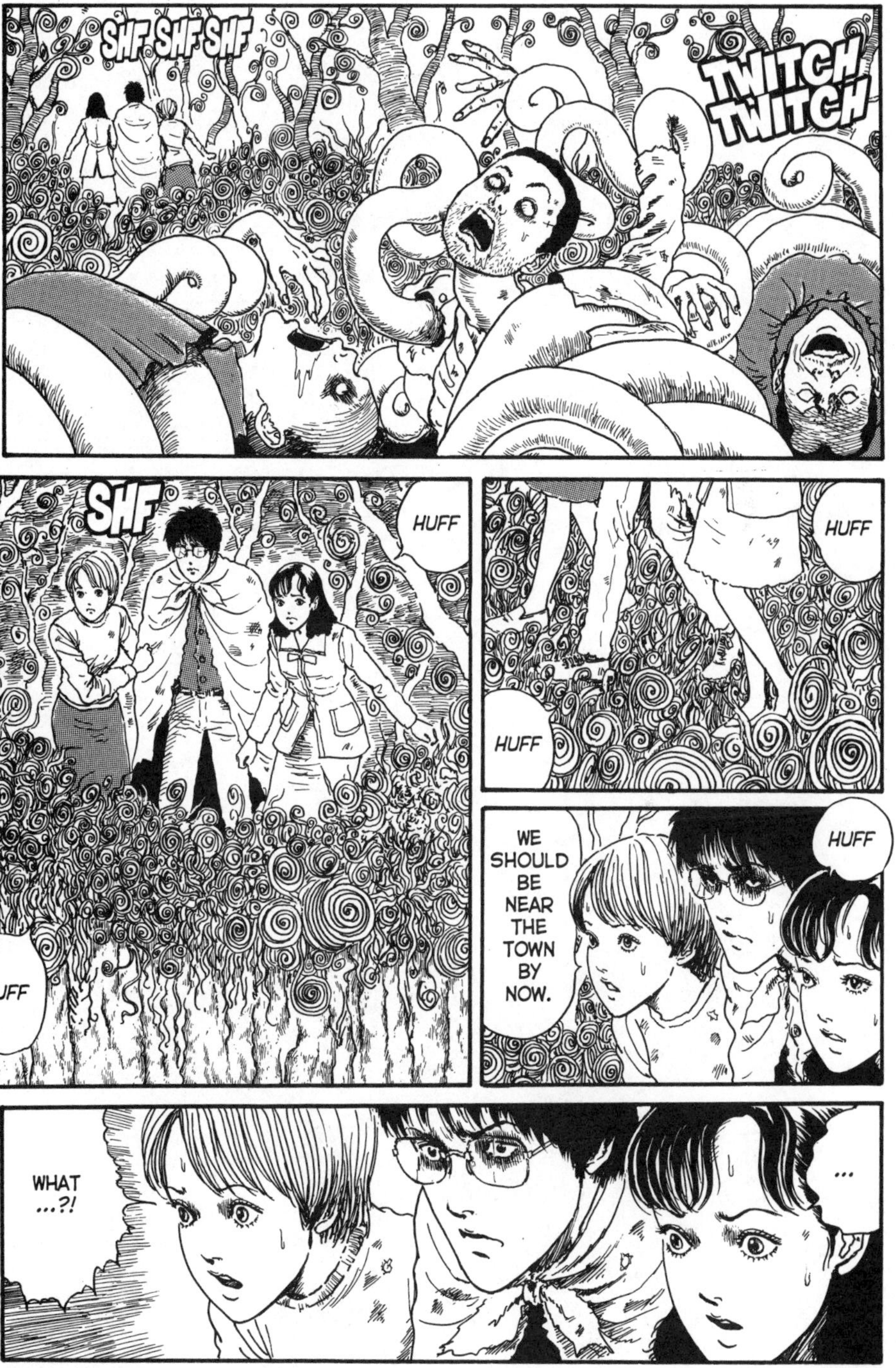
TWITCH
TWITCH
SHF SHF SHF
HUFF
HUFF
HUFF
WE SHOULD BE NEAR THE TOWN BY NOW.
SHF
HUFF
HUFF
...
WHAT ...?!

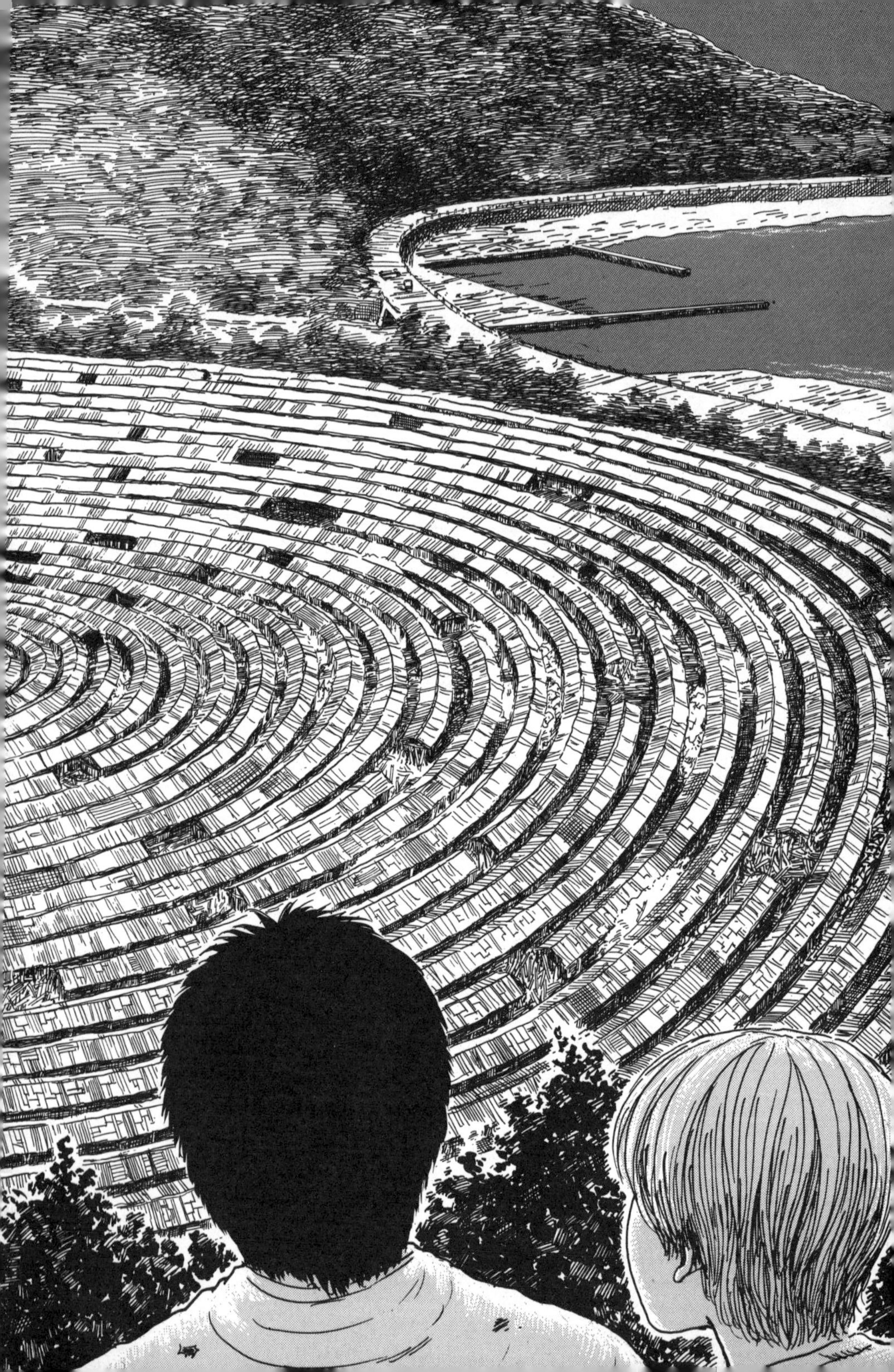

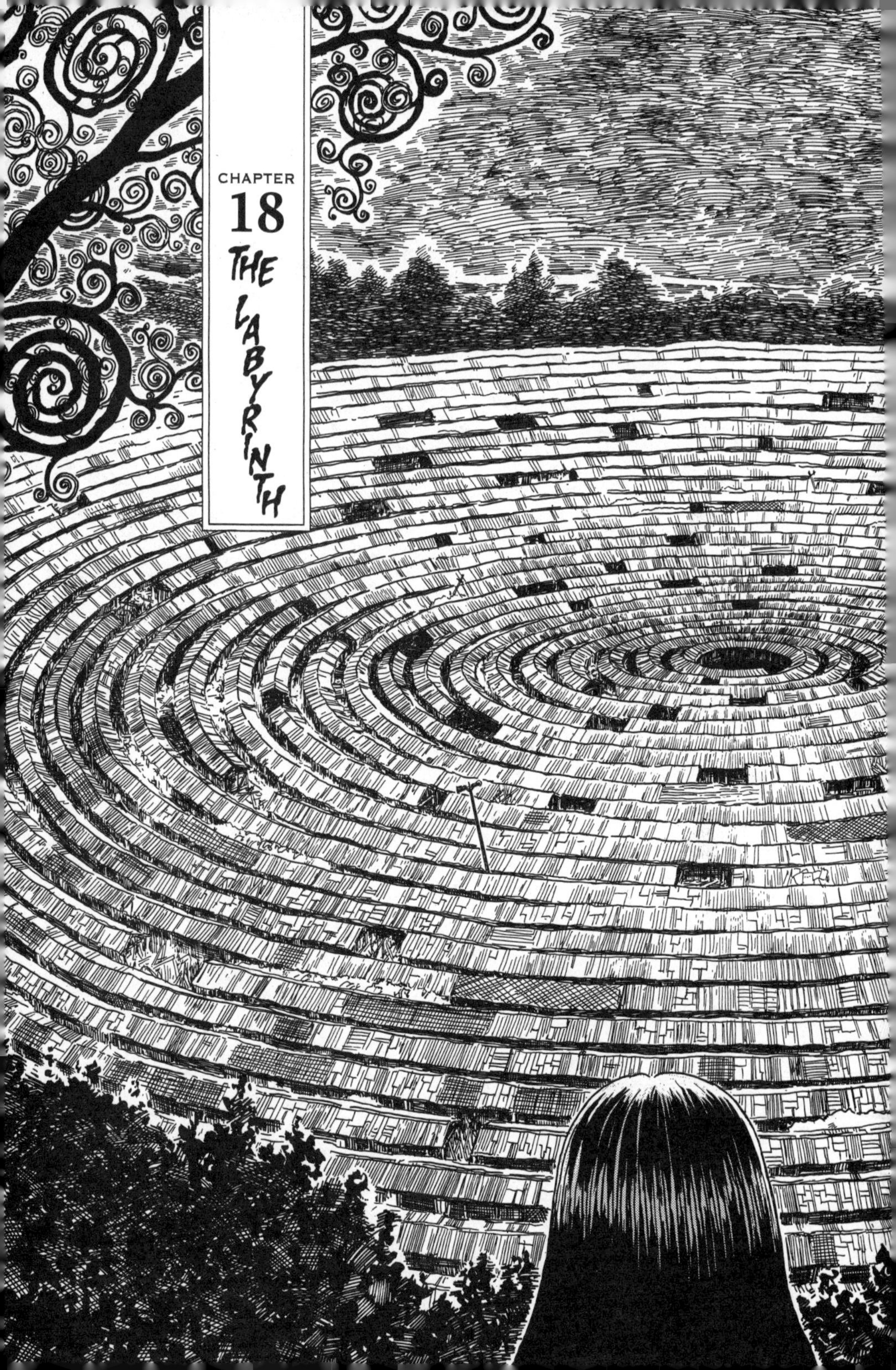
CHAPTER
18
THE LABYRINTH

WHERE ARE WE?
THIS ISN'T KUROUZU-CHO.
WE ENDED UP SOMEWHERE STRANGE AGAIN.
...
THIS *IS* KUROUZU-CHO. LOOK OVER THERE.
DOESN'T THAT BUILDING LOOK FAMILIAR?
HUH?

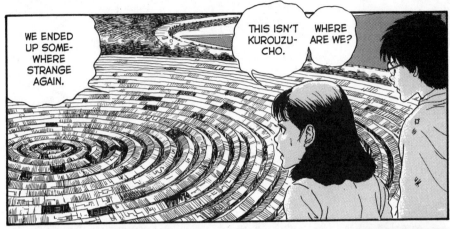

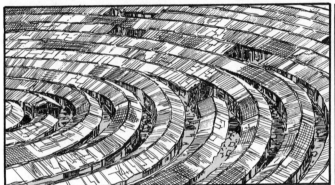

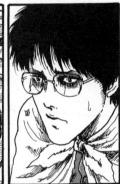

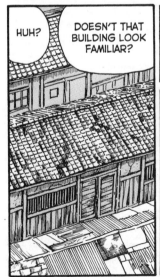

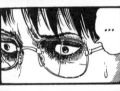

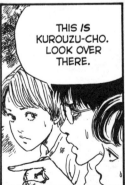

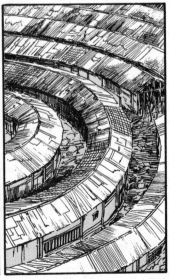

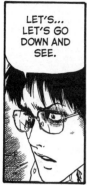

THAT'S THE ROW HOUSE?!
THAT'S *ALL* THE ROW HOUSES, EXTENDED AND JOINED TOGETHER.
B-BUT HOW?!
LET'S... LET'S GO DOWN AND SEE.
HUFF
HUFF
SHF SHF
HOW DID OUR TOWN TURN INTO THIS?
I FEEL LIKE I'M GOING MAD.
THEY *BUILT* THEM...
THE SURVIVORS, *THEY* DID ALL THIS.
WHAT?!
REMEMBER HOW PEOPLE ALL OVER TOWN WERE EXPANDING THE ROW HOUSES?
BUILDING THEM OUT ON BOTH SIDES RESULTED IN THEM CONNECTING UP LIKE THIS.

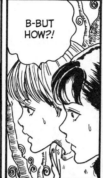

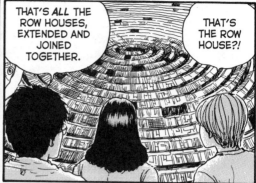

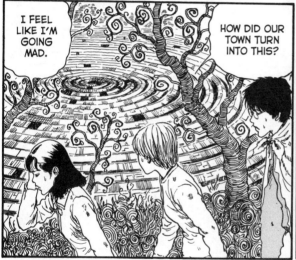

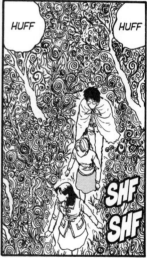

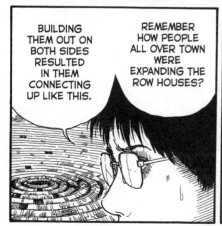

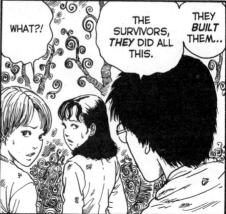

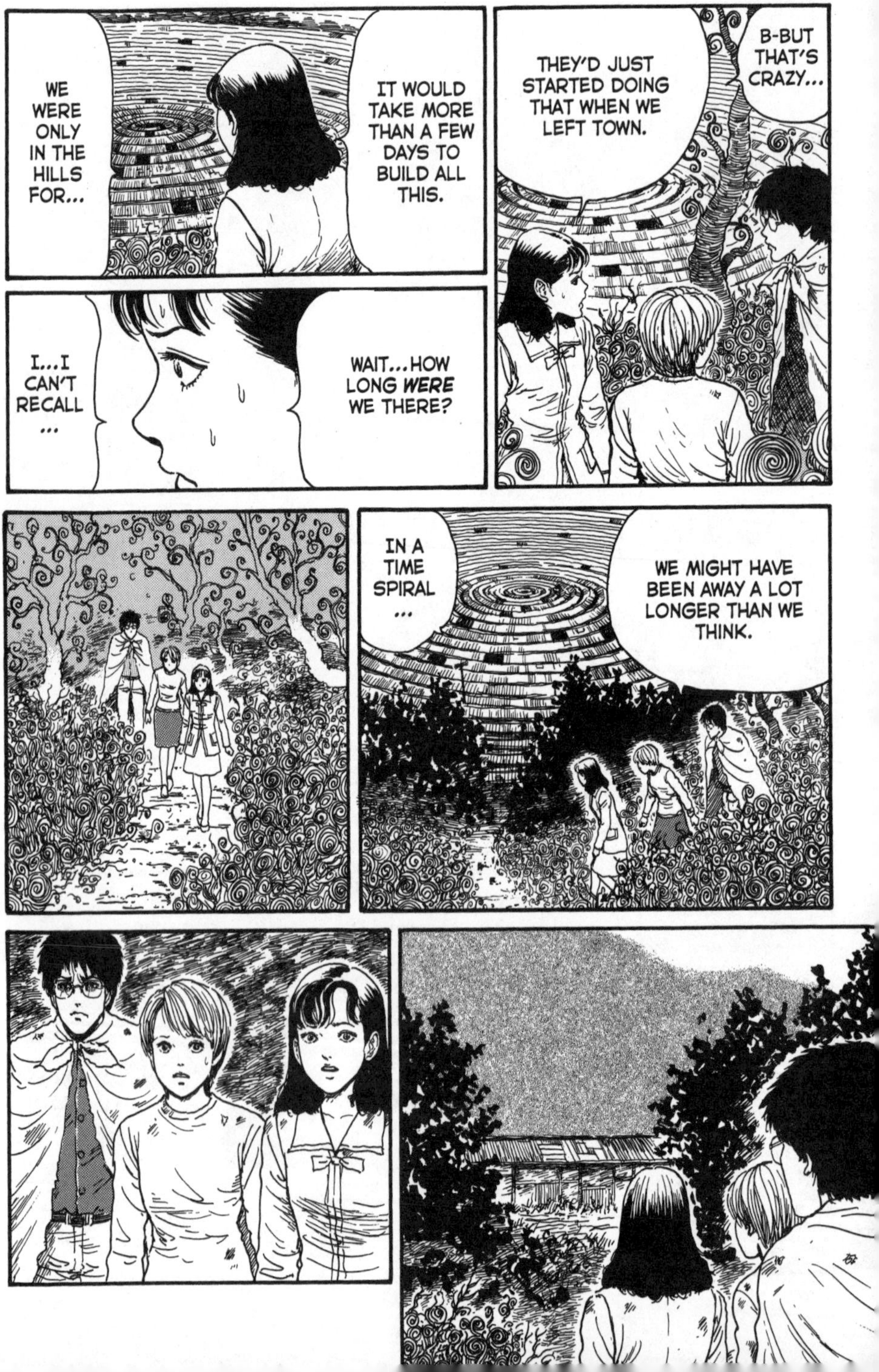
B-BUT THAT'S CRAZY...
THEY'D JUST STARTED DOING THAT WHEN WE LEFT TOWN.
IT WOULD TAKE MORE THAN A FEW DAYS TO BUILD ALL THIS.
WE WERE ONLY IN THE HILLS FOR...
WAIT...HOW LONG *WERE* WE THERE?
I...I CAN'T RECALL ...
WE MIGHT HAVE BEEN AWAY A LOT LONGER THAN WE THINK.
IN A TIME SPIRAL ...

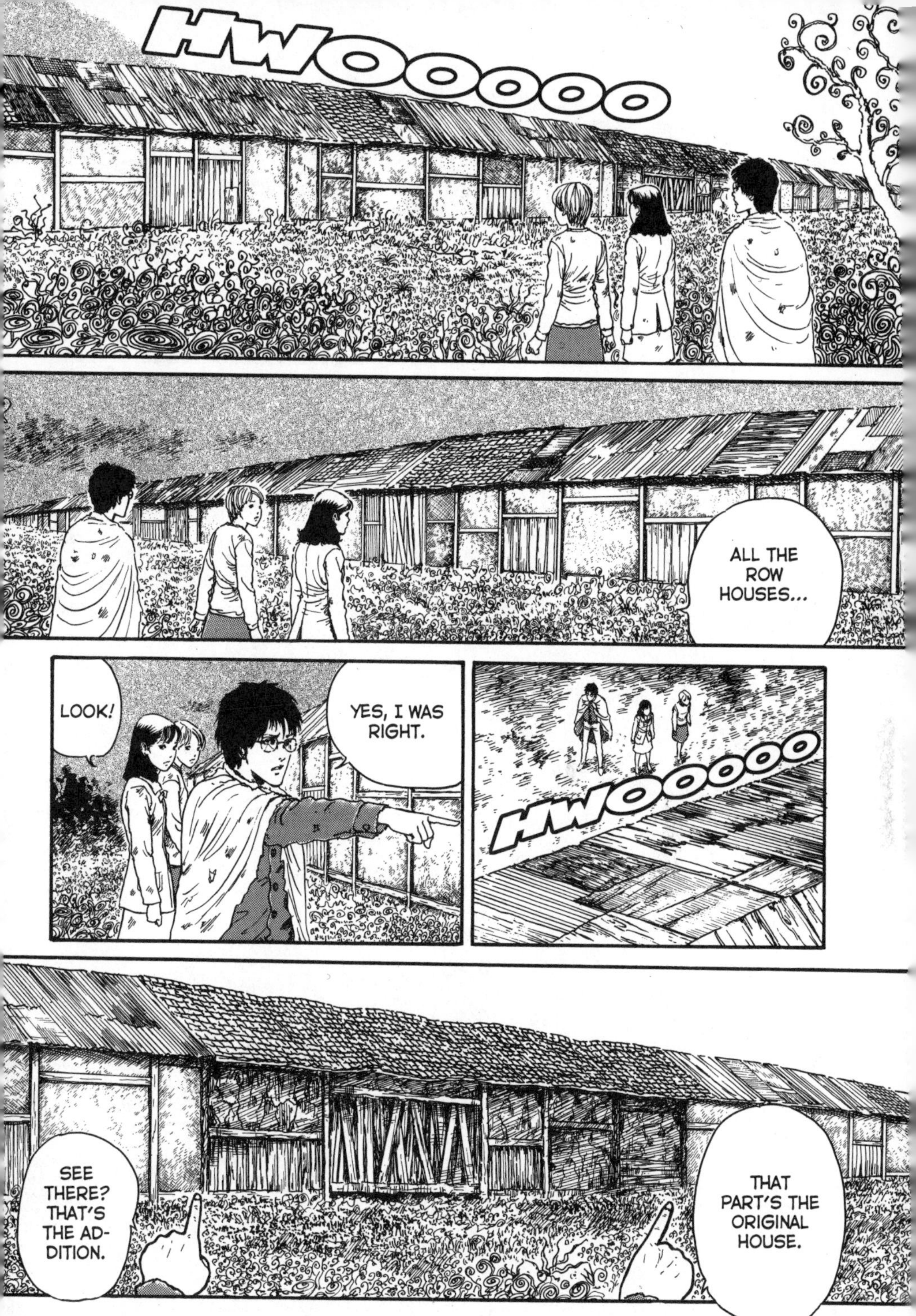
HWOOOOO
ALL THE ROW HOUSES...
HWOOOOO
YES, I WAS RIGHT.
LOOK!
THAT PART'S THE ORIGINAL HOUSE.
SEE THERE? THAT'S THE ADDITION.

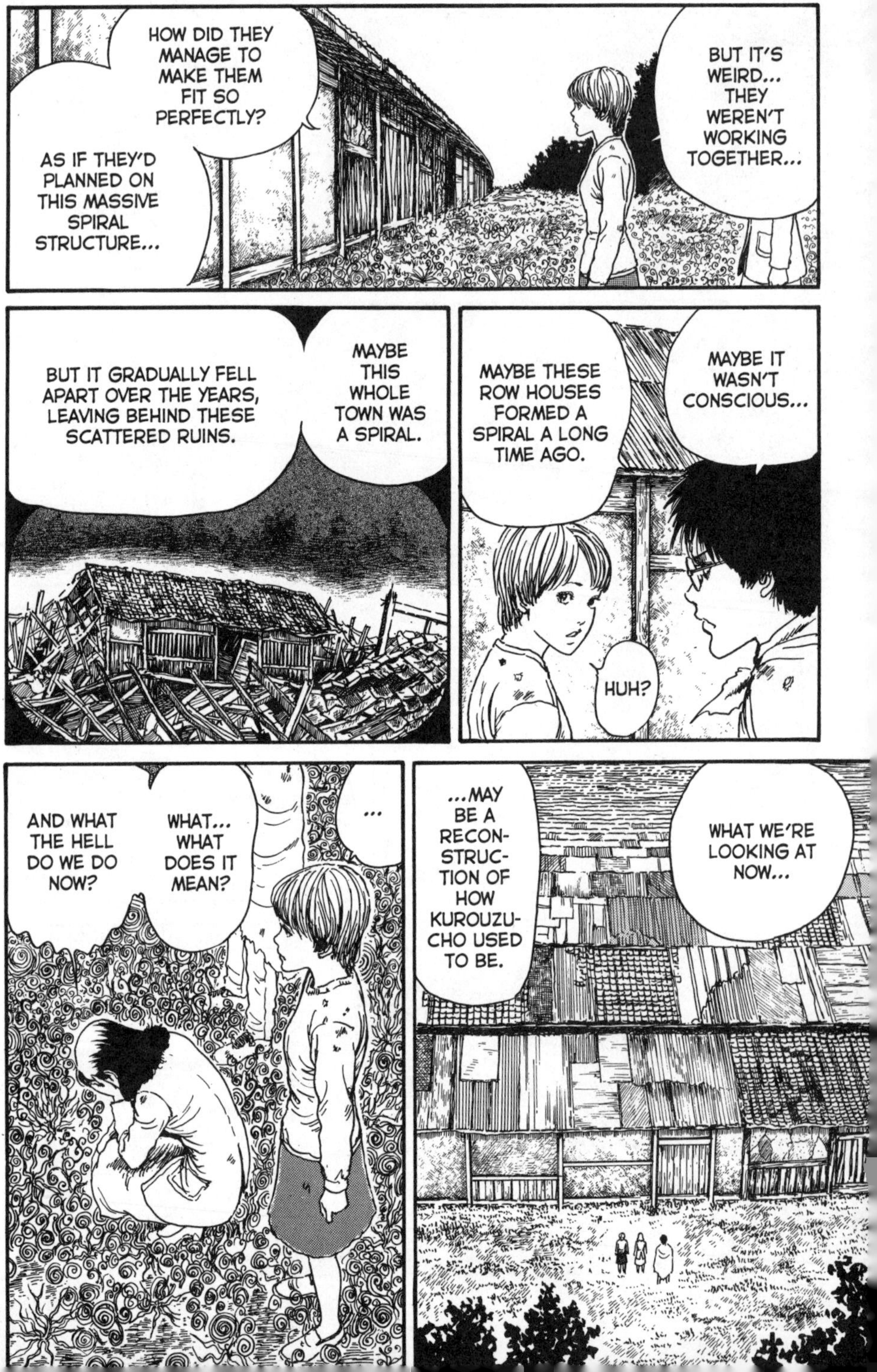
BUT IT'S WEIRD... THEY WEREN'T WORKING TOGETHER...
HOW DID THEY MANAGE TO MAKE THEM FIT SO PERFECTLY?
AS IF THEY'D PLANNED ON THIS MASSIVE SPIRAL STRUCTURE...
MAYBE IT WASN'T CONSCIOUS...
MAYBE THESE ROW HOUSES FORMED A SPIRAL A LONG TIME AGO.
HUH?
MAYBE THIS WHOLE TOWN WAS A SPIRAL.
BUT IT GRADUALLY FELL APART OVER THE YEARS, LEAVING BEHIND THESE SCATTERED RUINS.
WHAT WE'RE LOOKING AT NOW...
...MAY BE A RECON-STRUC-TION OF HOW KUROUZU-CHO USED TO BE.
...
WHAT... WHAT DOES IT MEAN?
AND WHAT THE HELL DO WE DO NOW?

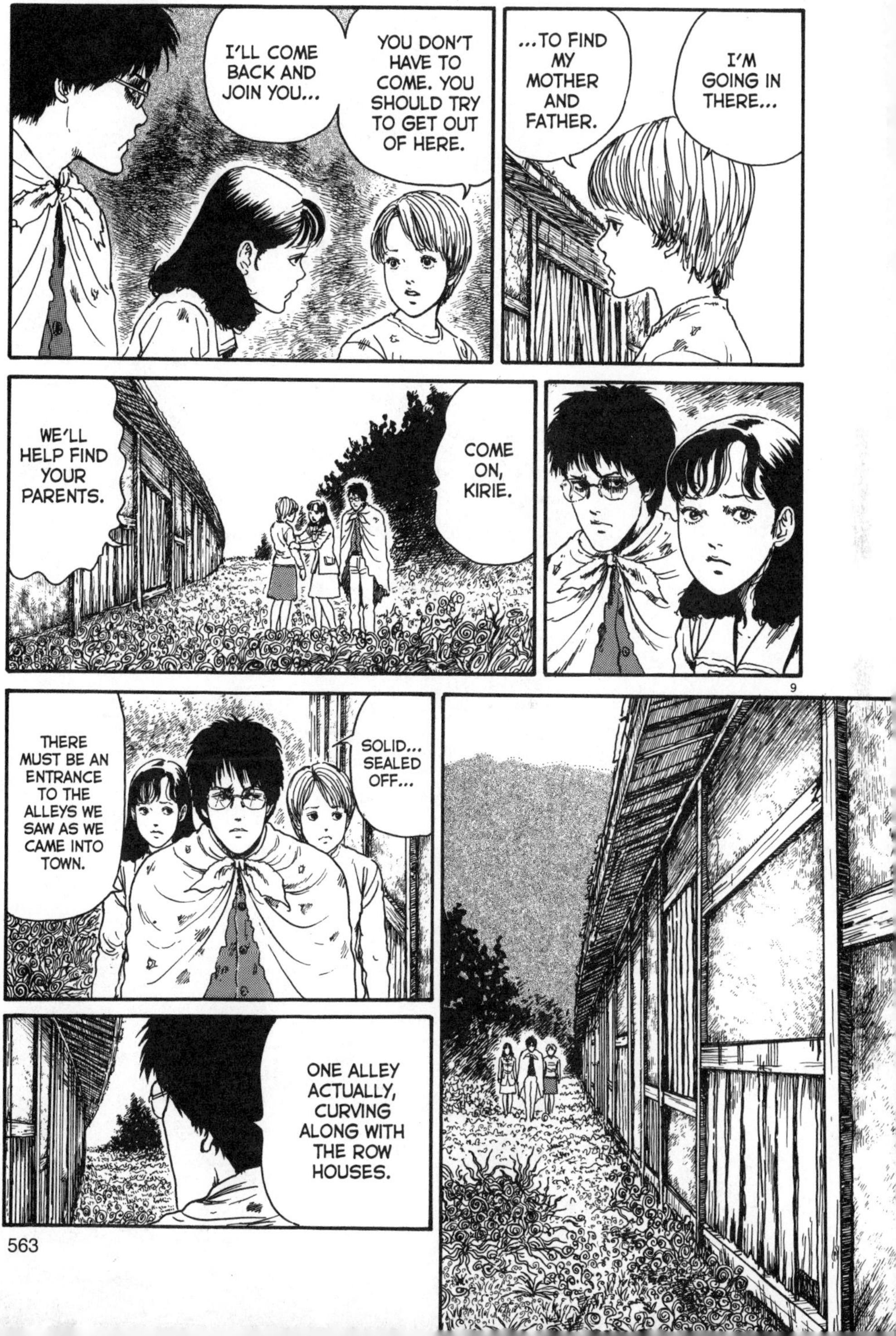
I'M GOING IN THERE...
...TO FIND MY MOTHER AND FATHER.
YOU DON'T HAVE TO COME. YOU SHOULD TRY TO GET OUT OF HERE.
I'LL COME BACK AND JOIN YOU...
COME ON, KIRIE.
WE'LL HELP FIND YOUR PARENTS.
SOLID... SEALED OFF...
THERE MUST BE AN ENTRANCE TO THE ALLEYS WE SAW AS WE CAME INTO TOWN.
ONE ALLEY ACTUALLY, CURVING ALONG WITH THE ROW HOUSES.

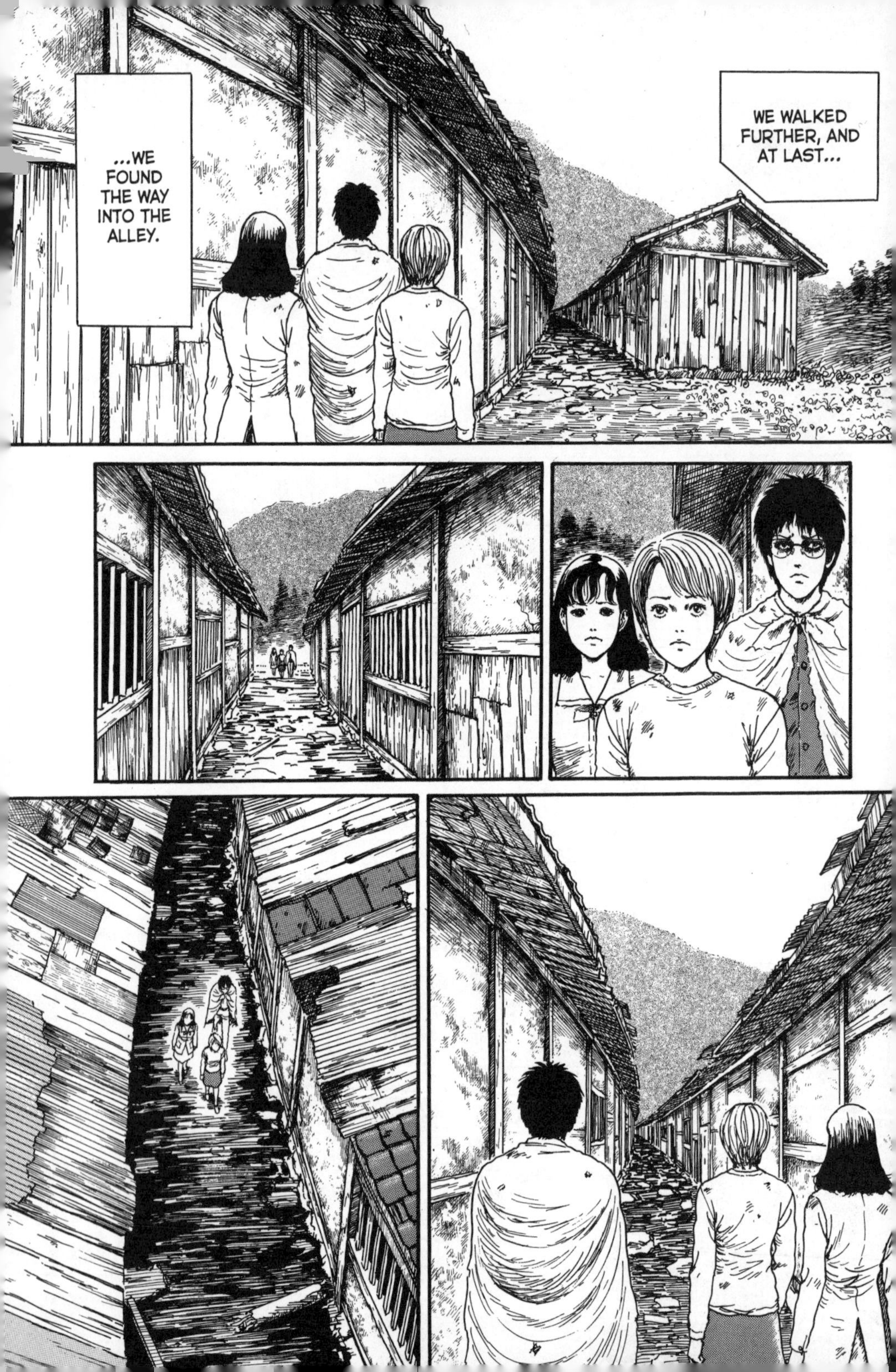
WE WALKED FURTHER, AND AT LAST...
...WE FOUND THE WAY INTO THE ALLEY.

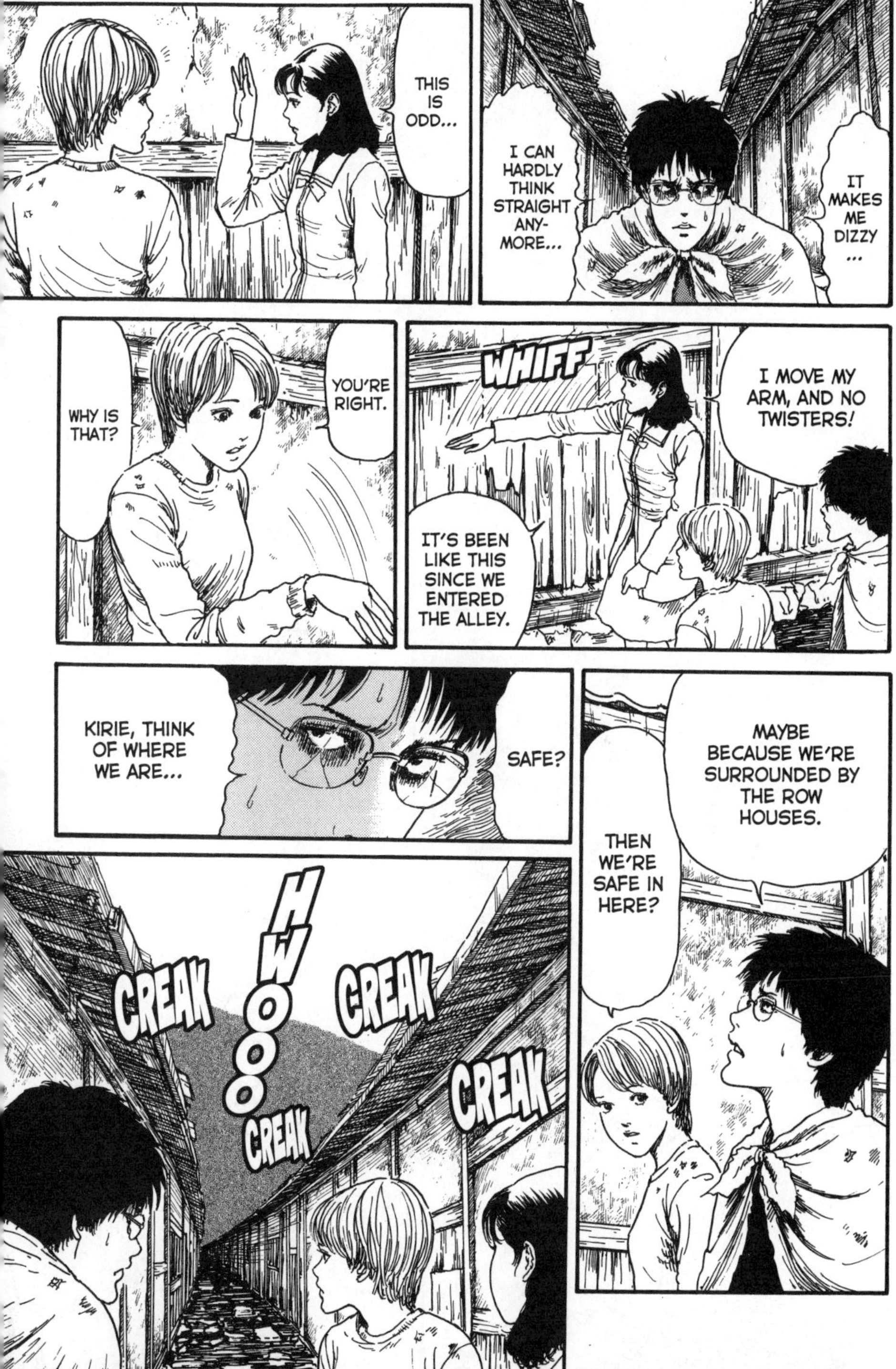
IT MAKES ME DIZZY ...
I CAN HARDLY THINK STRAIGHT ANY-MORE...
THIS IS ODD...
I MOVE MY ARM, AND NO TWISTERS!
WHIFF
IT'S BEEN LIKE THIS SINCE WE ENTERED THE ALLEY.
YOU'RE RIGHT.
WHY IS THAT?
MAYBE BECAUSE WE'RE SURROUNDED BY THE ROW HOUSES.
THEN WE'RE SAFE IN HERE?
SAFE?
KIRIE, THINK OF WHERE WE ARE...
CREAK
CREAK
HWOOOO
CREAK
CREAK

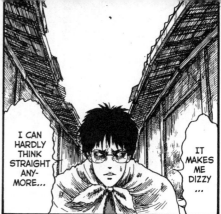

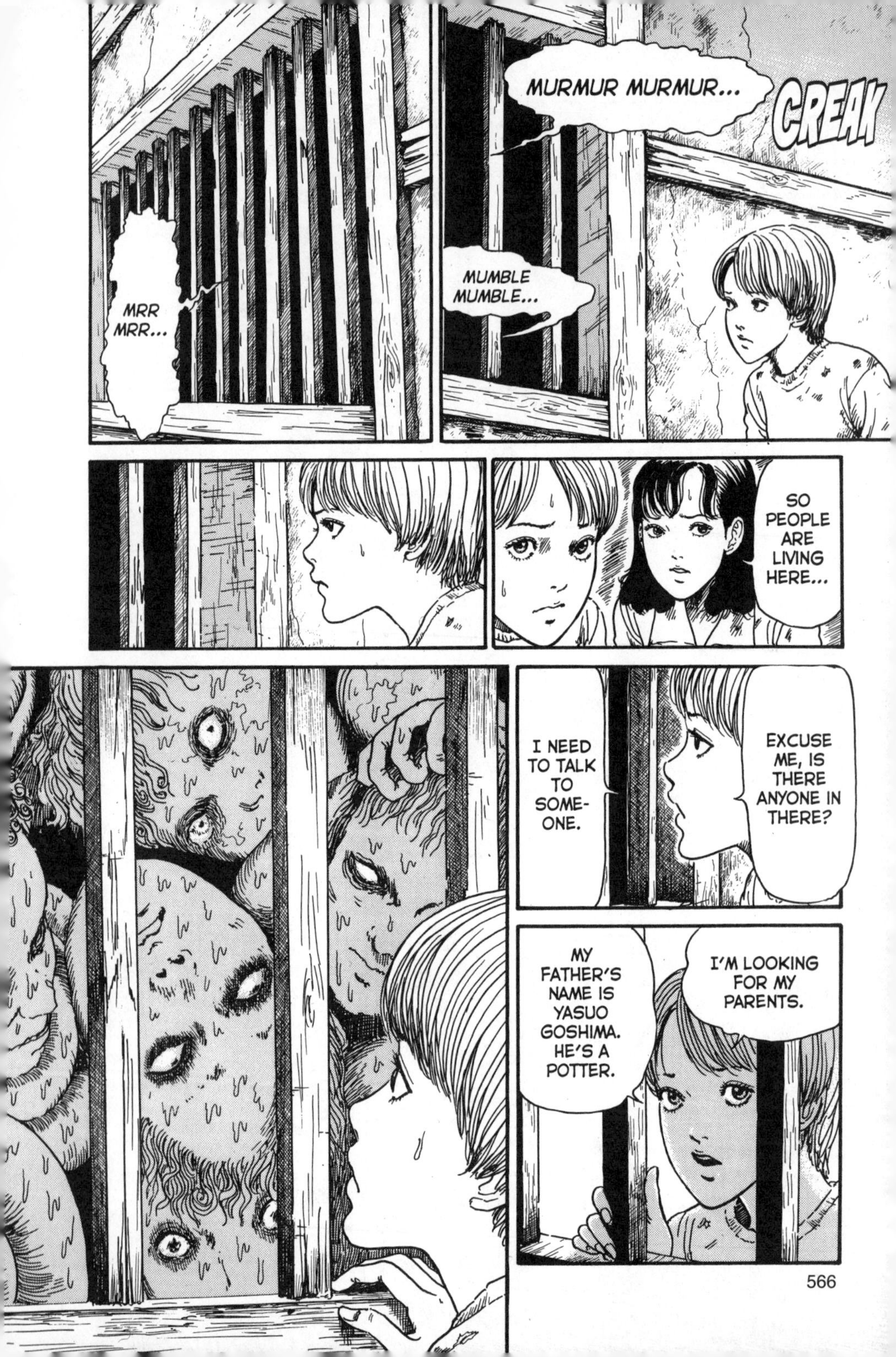
CREAK
MURMUR MURMUR...
MUMBLE MUMBLE...
MRR MRR...
SO PEOPLE ARE LIVING HERE...
EXCUSE ME, IS THERE ANYONE IN THERE?
I NEED TO TALK TO SOME-ONE.
I'M LOOKING FOR MY PARENTS.
MY FATHER'S NAME IS YASUO GOSHIMA. HE'S A POTTER.

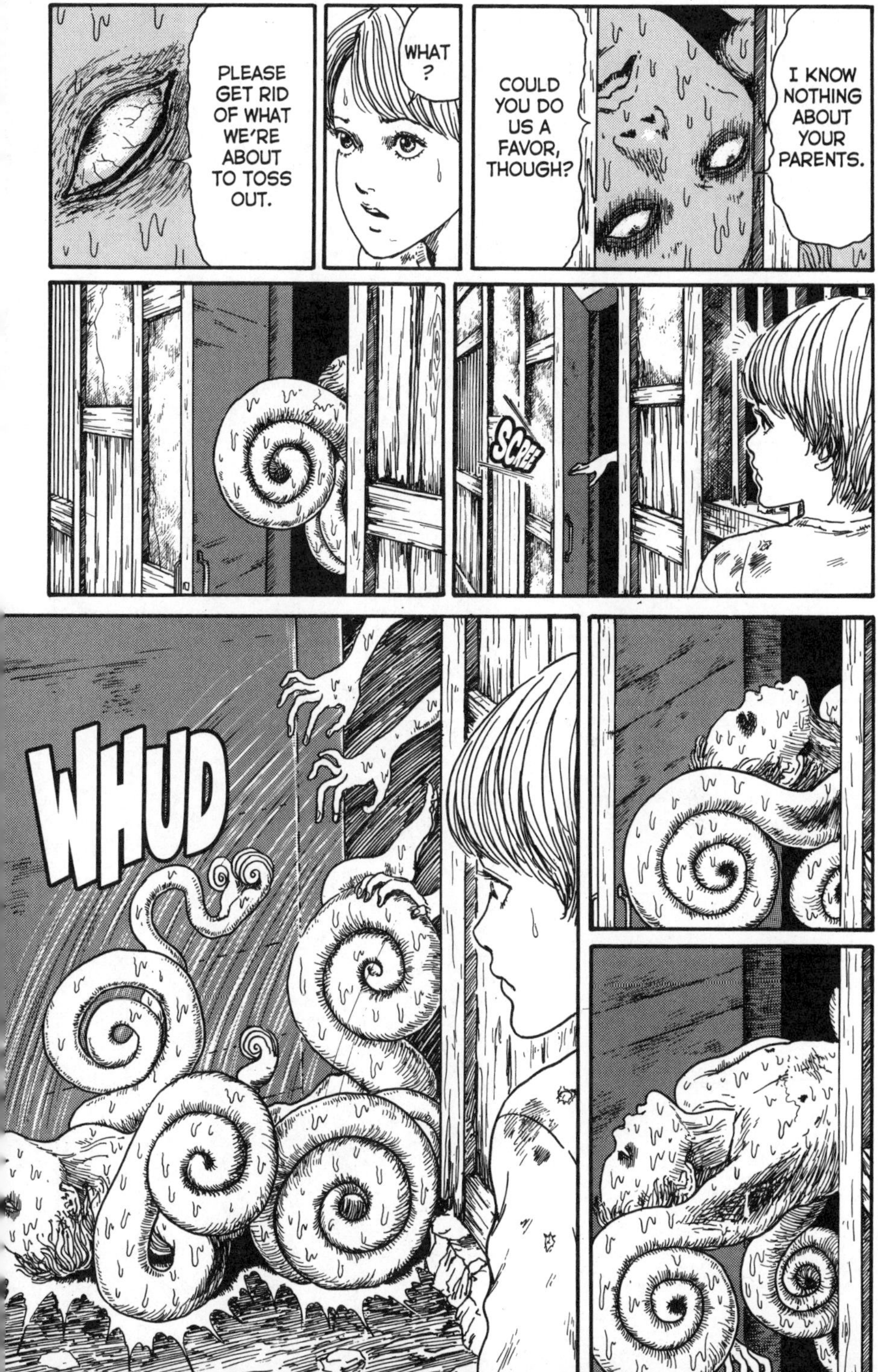
I KNOW NOTHING ABOUT YOUR PARENTS.
COULD YOU DO US A FAVOR, THOUGH?
WHAT ?
PLEASE GET RID OF WHAT WE'RE ABOUT TO TOSS OUT.
SCREE
WHUD

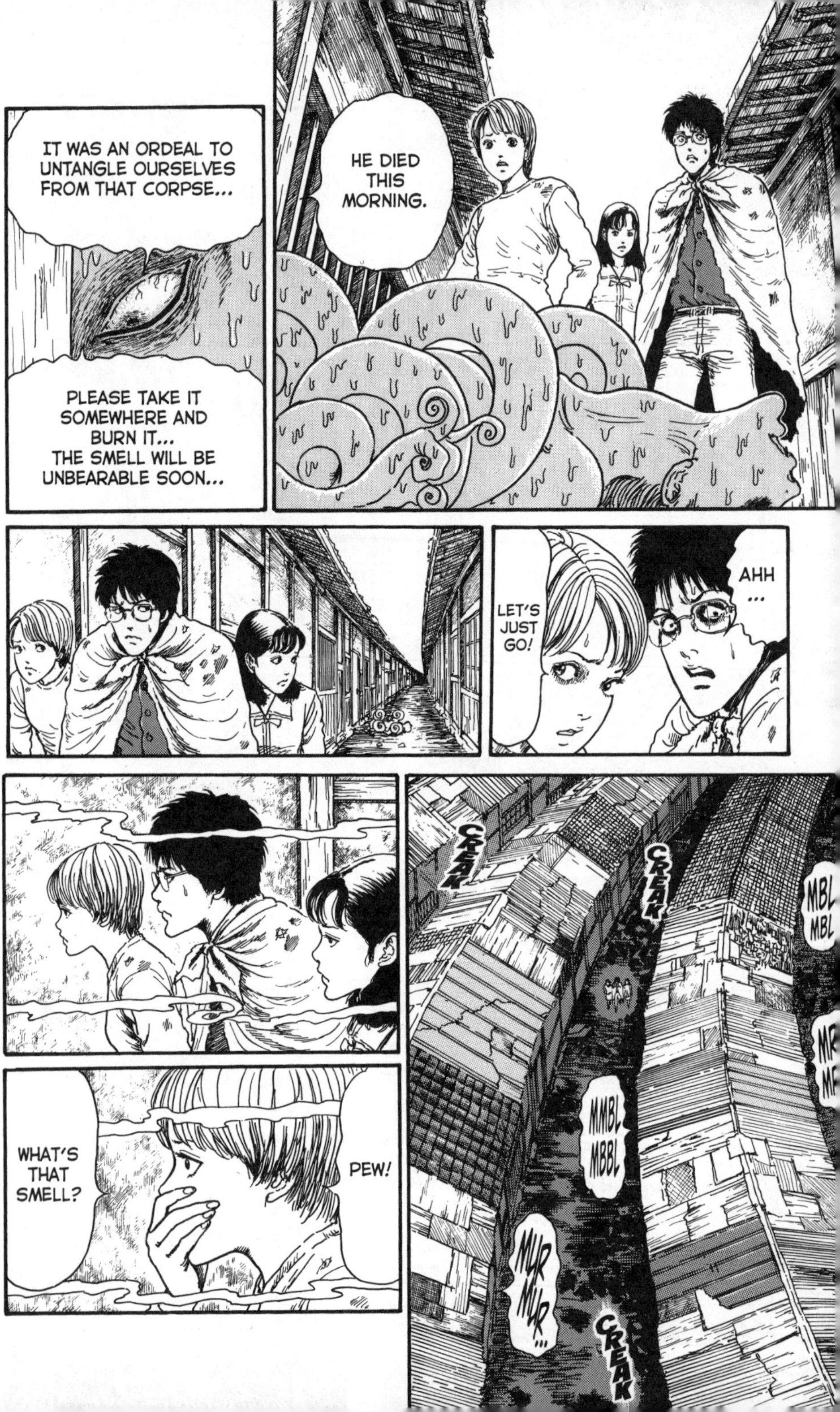
HE DIED THIS MORNING.
IT WAS AN ORDEAL TO UNTANGLE OURSELVES FROM THAT CORPSE...
PLEASE TAKE IT SOMEWHERE AND BURN IT... THE SMELL WILL BE UNBEARABLE SOON...
AHH...
LET'S JUST GO!
CREAK
CREAK
MBL MBL
MMBL MBBL
MUR MUR...
CREAK
PEW!
WHAT'S THAT SMELL?

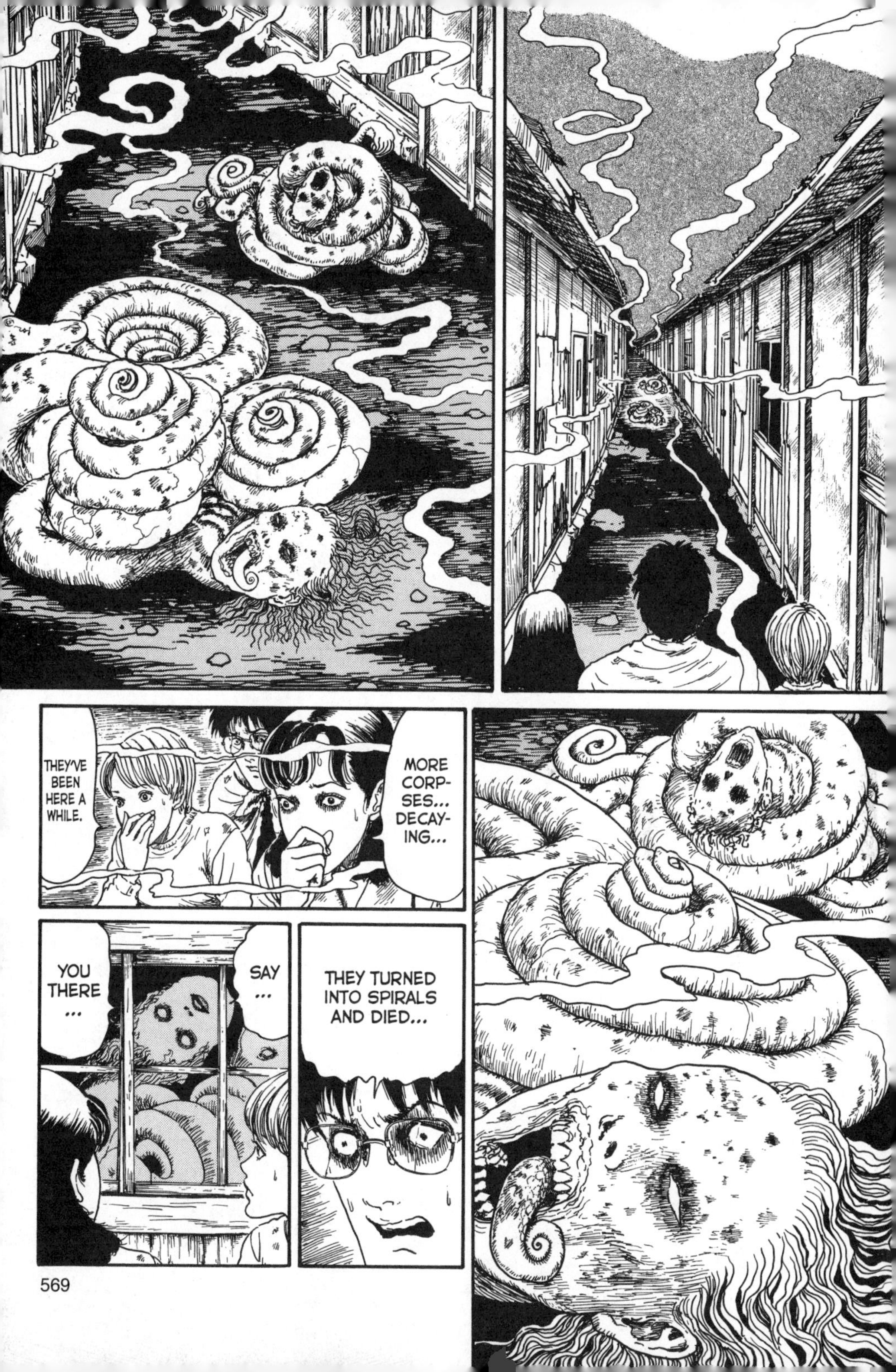
MORE CORP-SES... DECAY-ING...
THEY'VE BEEN HERE A WHILE.
THEY TURNED INTO SPIRALS AND DIED...
SAY ...
YOU THERE ...

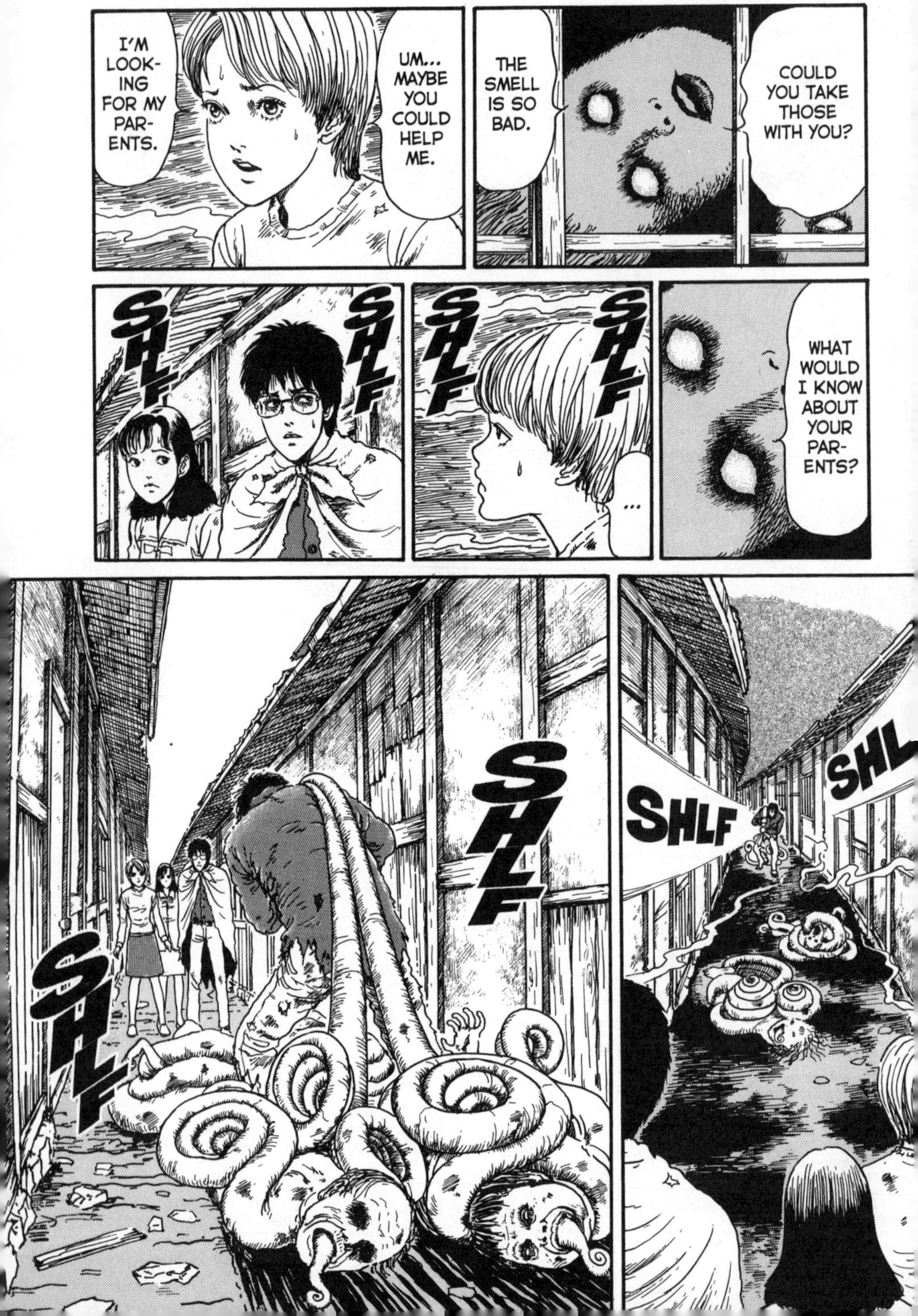
COULD YOU TAKE THOSE WITH YOU?
THE SMELL IS SO BAD.
UM... MAYBE YOU COULD HELP ME.
I'M LOOKING FOR MY PARENTS.
WHAT WOULD I KNOW ABOUT YOUR PARENTS?
SHLF
SHLF
...
SHLF
SHLF
SHL
SHLF
SHLF
SHLF

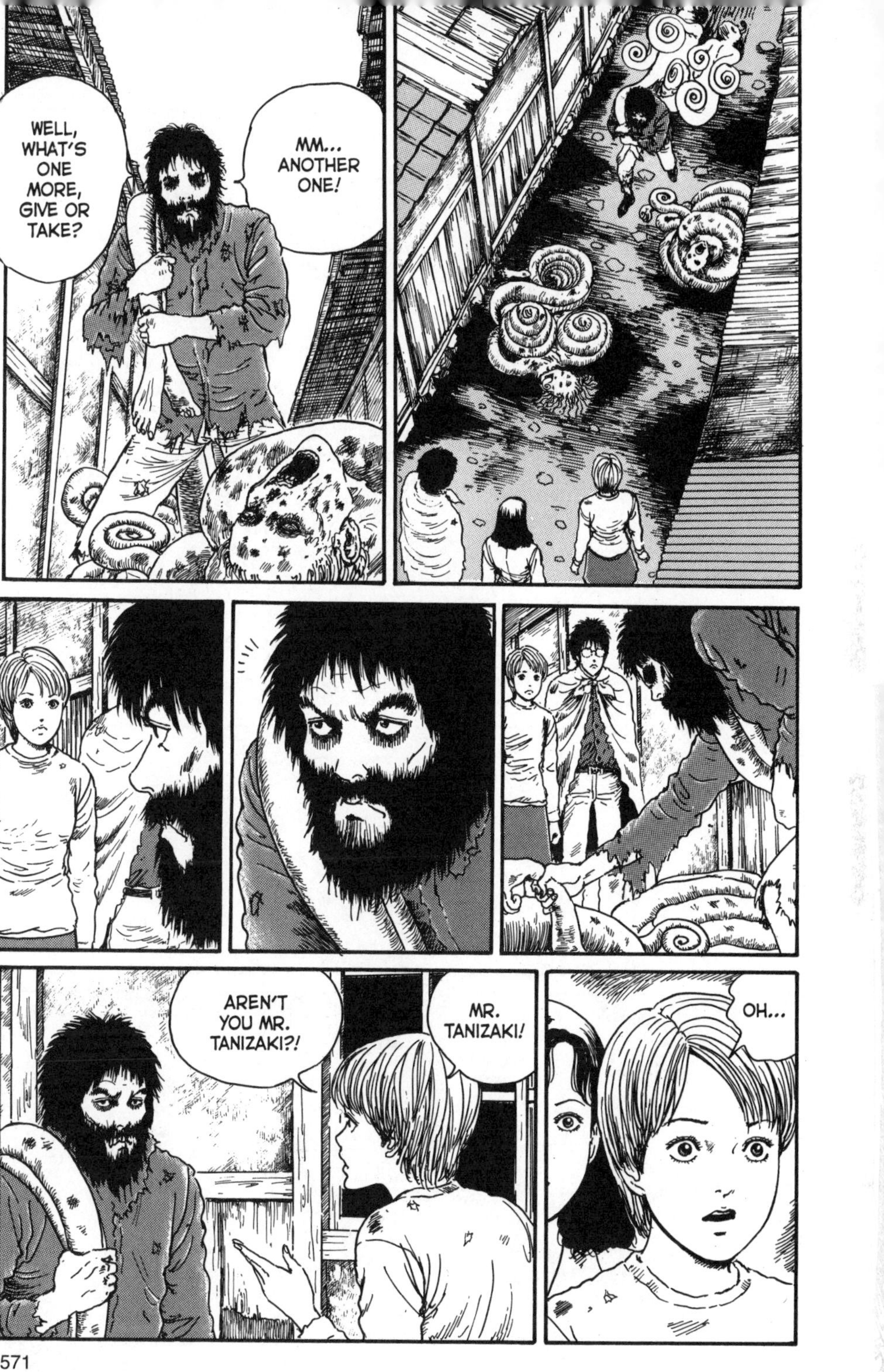
MM... ANOTHER ONE!
WELL, WHAT'S ONE MORE, GIVE OR TAKE?
OH...
MR. TANIZAKI!
AREN'T YOU MR. TANIZAKI?!

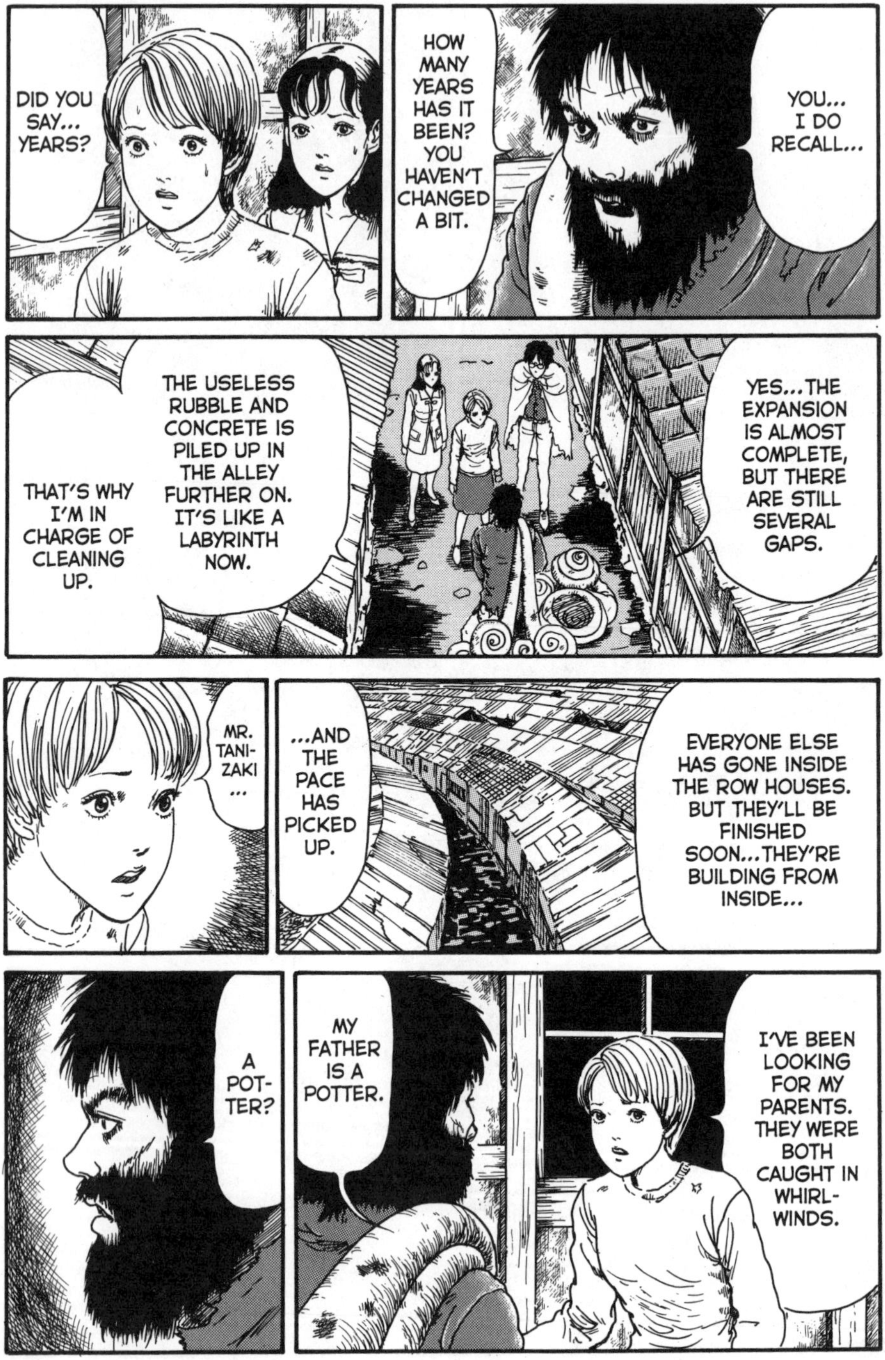
YOU... I DO RECALL...
HOW MANY YEARS HAS IT BEEN? YOU HAVEN'T CHANGED A BIT.
DID YOU SAY... YEARS?
YES...THE EXPANSION IS ALMOST COMPLETE, BUT THERE ARE STILL SEVERAL GAPS.
THE USELESS RUBBLE AND CONCRETE IS PILED UP IN THE ALLEY FURTHER ON. IT'S LIKE A LABYRINTH NOW.
THAT'S WHY I'M IN CHARGE OF CLEANING UP.
EVERYONE ELSE HAS GONE INSIDE THE ROW HOUSES. BUT THEY'LL BE FINISHED SOON...THEY'RE BUILDING FROM INSIDE...
...AND THE PACE HAS PICKED UP.
MR. TANI-ZAKI ...
I'VE BEEN LOOKING FOR MY PARENTS. THEY WERE BOTH CAUGHT IN WHIRL-WINDS.
MY FATHER IS A POTTER.
A POT-TER?

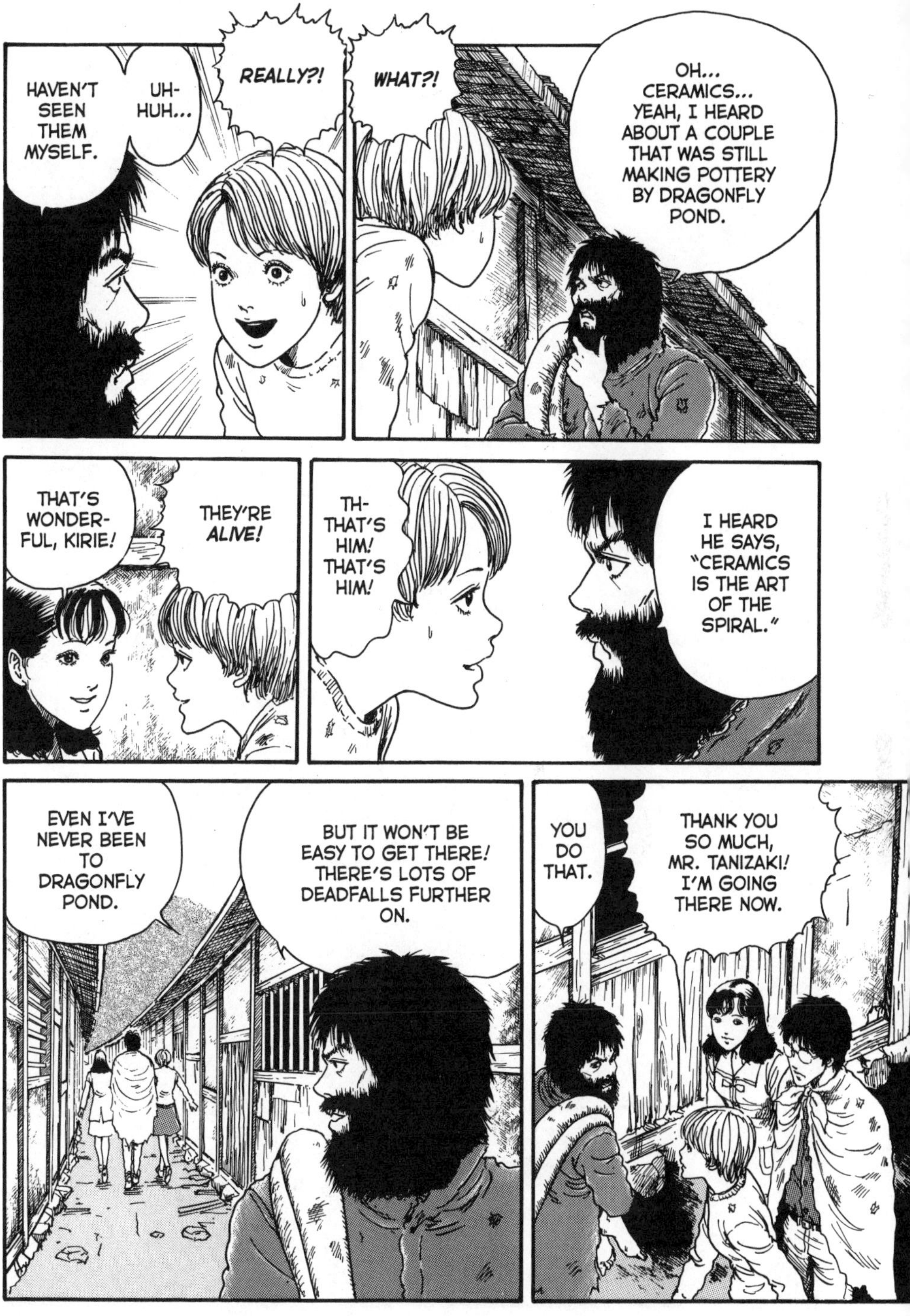
OH... CERAMICS... YEAH, I HEARD ABOUT A COUPLE THAT WAS STILL MAKING POTTERY BY DRAGONFLY POND.
WHAT?!
REALLY?!
UH-HUH...
HAVEN'T SEEN THEM MYSELF.
I HEARD HE SAYS, "CERAMICS IS THE ART OF THE SPIRAL."
TH-THAT'S HIM! THAT'S HIM!
THEY'RE *ALIVE!*
THAT'S WONDER-FUL, KIRIE!
THANK YOU SO MUCH, MR. TANIZAKI! I'M GOING THERE NOW.
YOU DO THAT.
BUT IT WON'T BE EASY TO GET THERE! THERE'S LOTS OF DEADFALLS FURTHER ON.
EVEN I'VE NEVER BEEN TO DRAGONFLY POND.

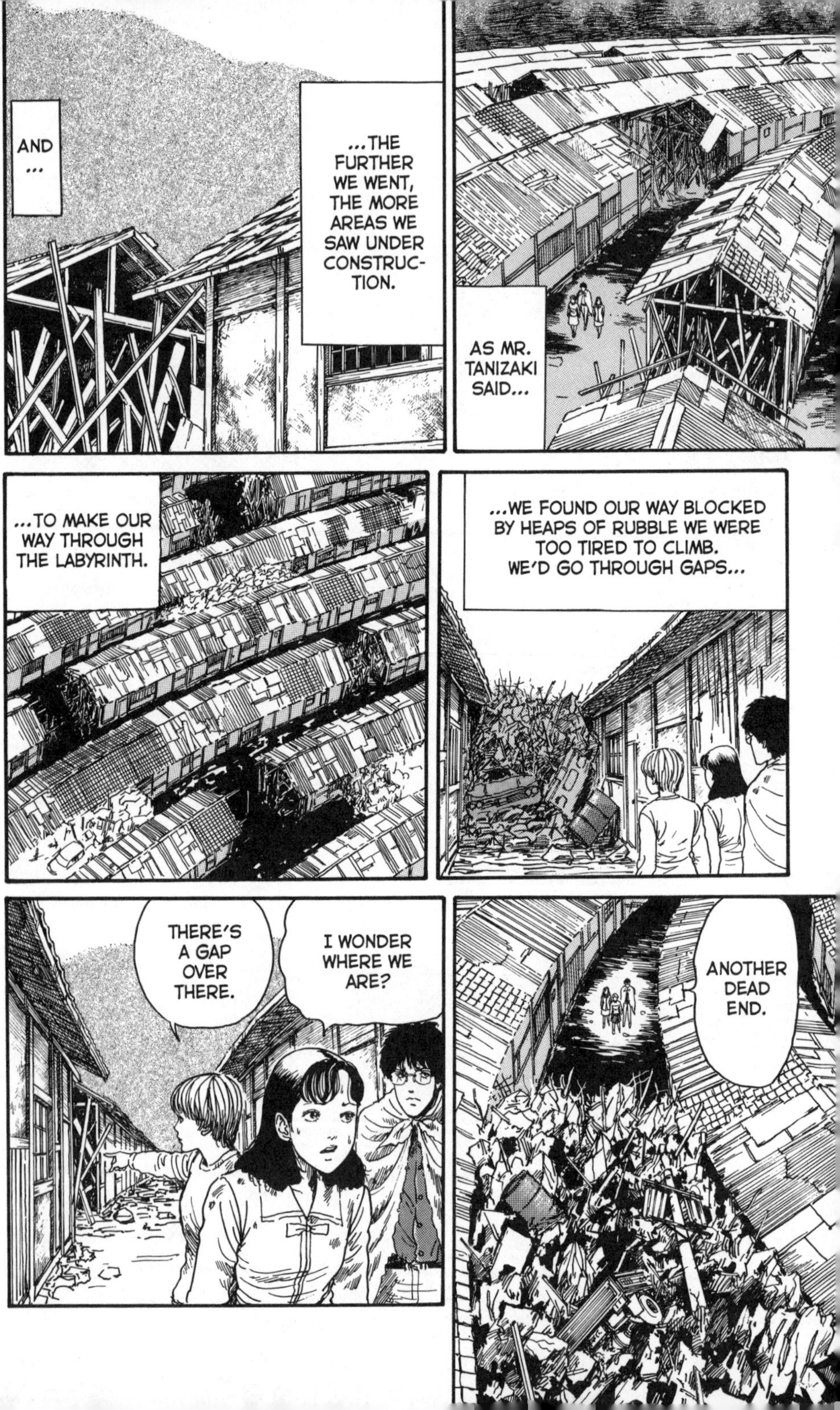
AS MR. TANIZAKI SAID...
...THE FURTHER WE WENT, THE MORE AREAS WE SAW UNDER CONSTRUCTION.
AND ...
...WE FOUND OUR WAY BLOCKED BY HEAPS OF RUBBLE WE WERE TOO TIRED TO CLIMB. WE'D GO THROUGH GAPS...
...TO MAKE OUR WAY THROUGH THE LABYRINTH.
ANOTHER DEAD END.
I WONDER WHERE WE ARE?
THERE'S A GAP OVER THERE.

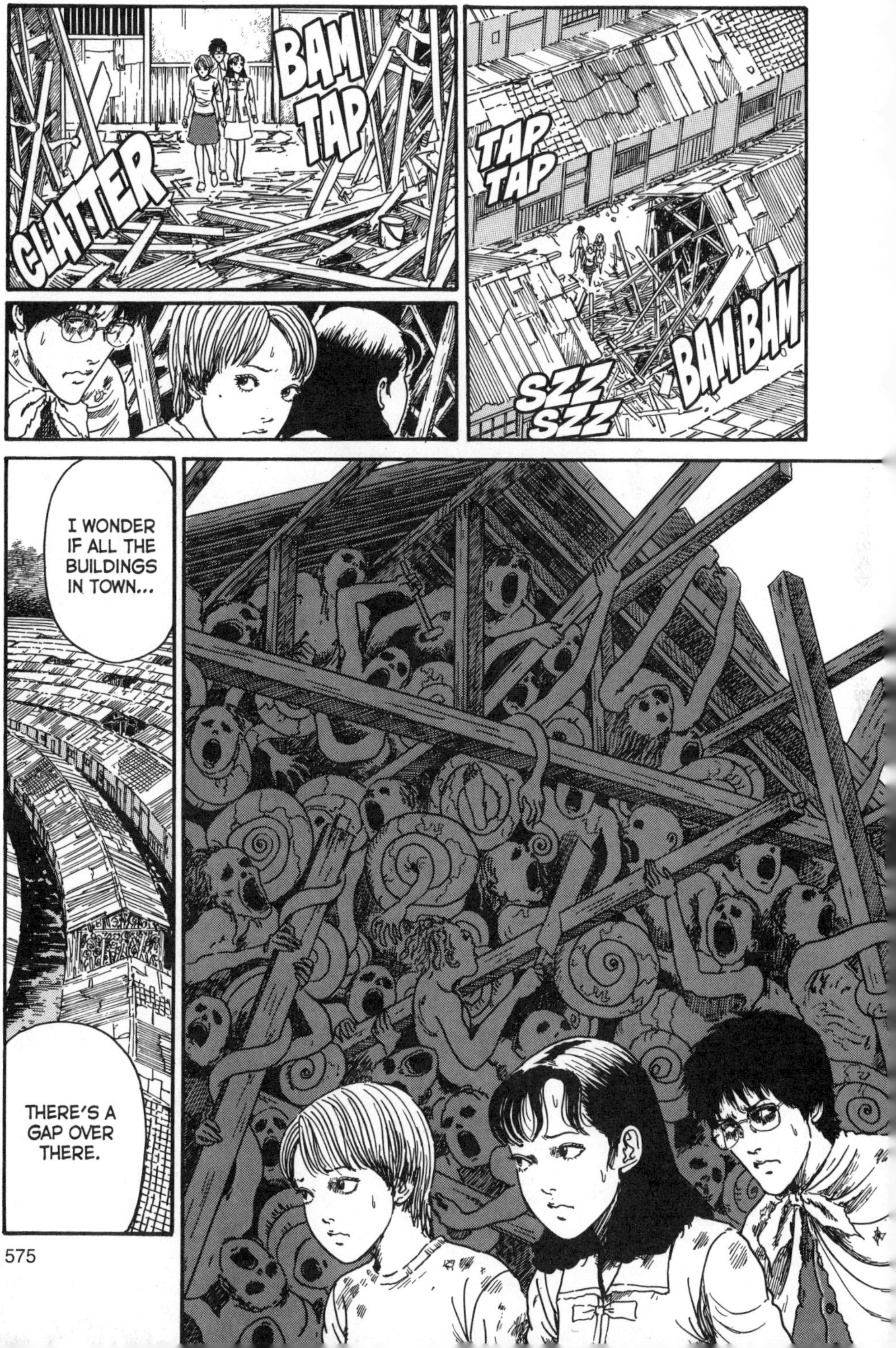

TAP TAP
BAM BAM
SZZ SZZ
BAM TAP
CLATTER
I WONDER IF ALL THE BUILDINGS IN TOWN...
THERE'S A GAP OVER THERE.

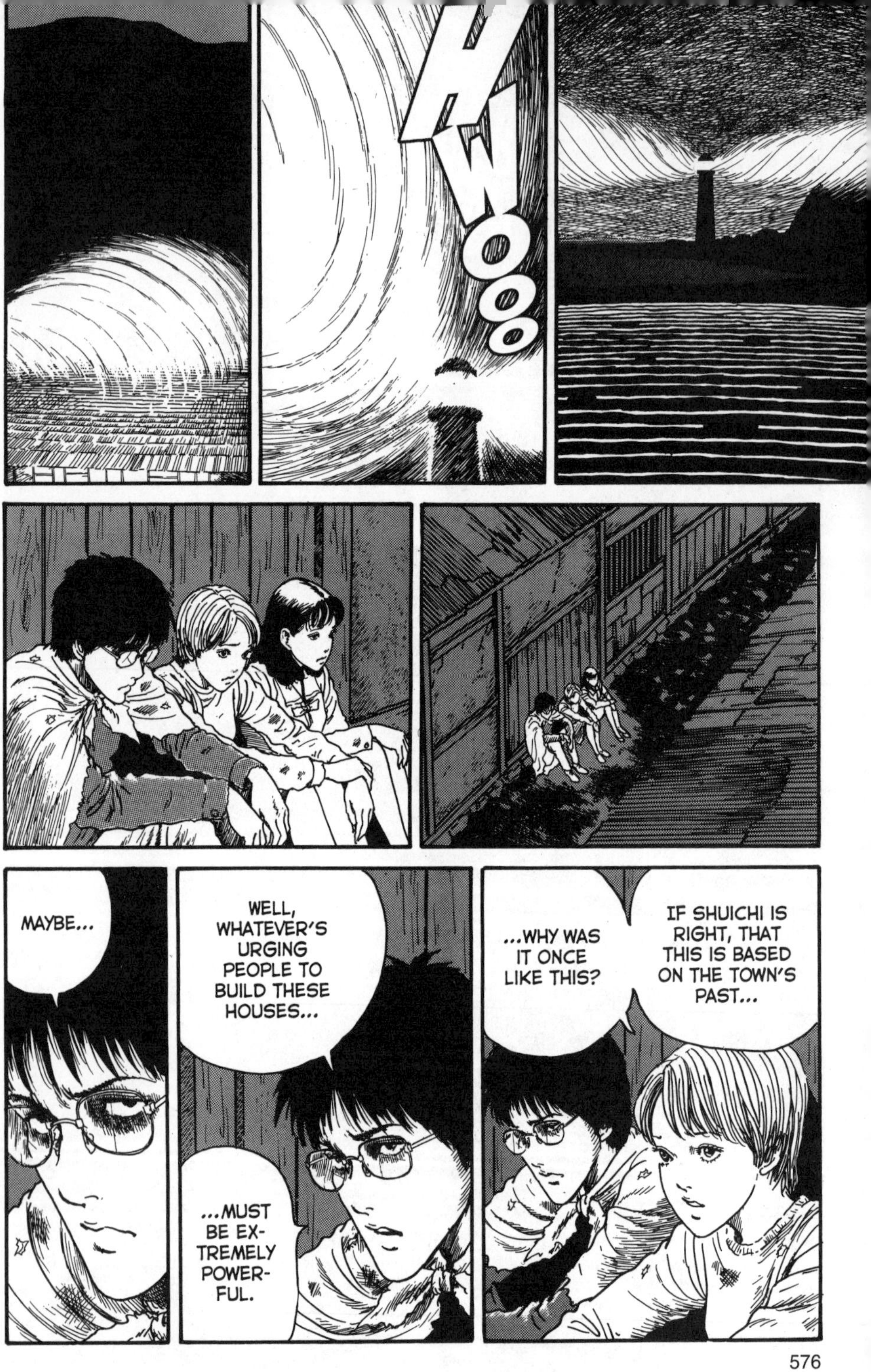
HWOOO
IF SHUICHI IS RIGHT, THAT THIS IS BASED ON THE TOWN'S PAST...
...WHY WAS IT ONCE LIKE THIS?
WELL, WHATEVER'S URGING PEOPLE TO BUILD THESE HOUSES...
...MUST BE EX-TREMELY POWER-FUL.
MAYBE...

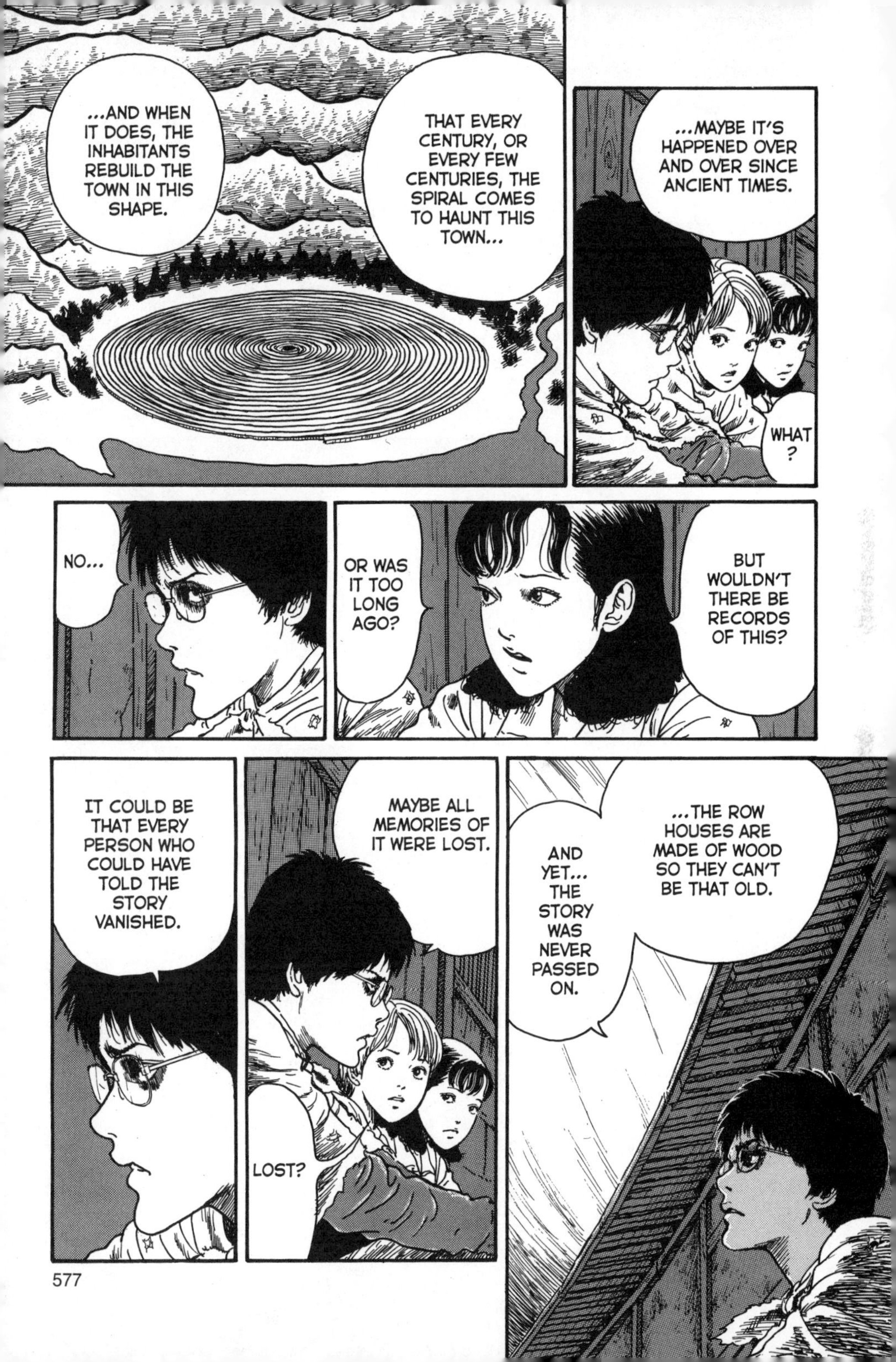
...MAYBE IT'S HAPPENED OVER AND OVER SINCE ANCIENT TIMES.
WHAT?
THAT EVERY CENTURY, OR EVERY FEW CENTURIES, THE SPIRAL COMES TO HAUNT THIS TOWN...
...AND WHEN IT DOES, THE INHABITANTS REBUILD THE TOWN IN THIS SHAPE.
BUT WOULDN'T THERE BE RECORDS OF THIS?
OR WAS IT TOO LONG AGO?
NO...
...THE ROW HOUSES ARE MADE OF WOOD SO THEY CAN'T BE THAT OLD.
AND YET... THE STORY WAS NEVER PASSED ON.
MAYBE ALL MEMORIES OF IT WERE LOST.
LOST?
IT COULD BE THAT EVERY PERSON WHO COULD HAVE TOLD THE STORY VANISHED.

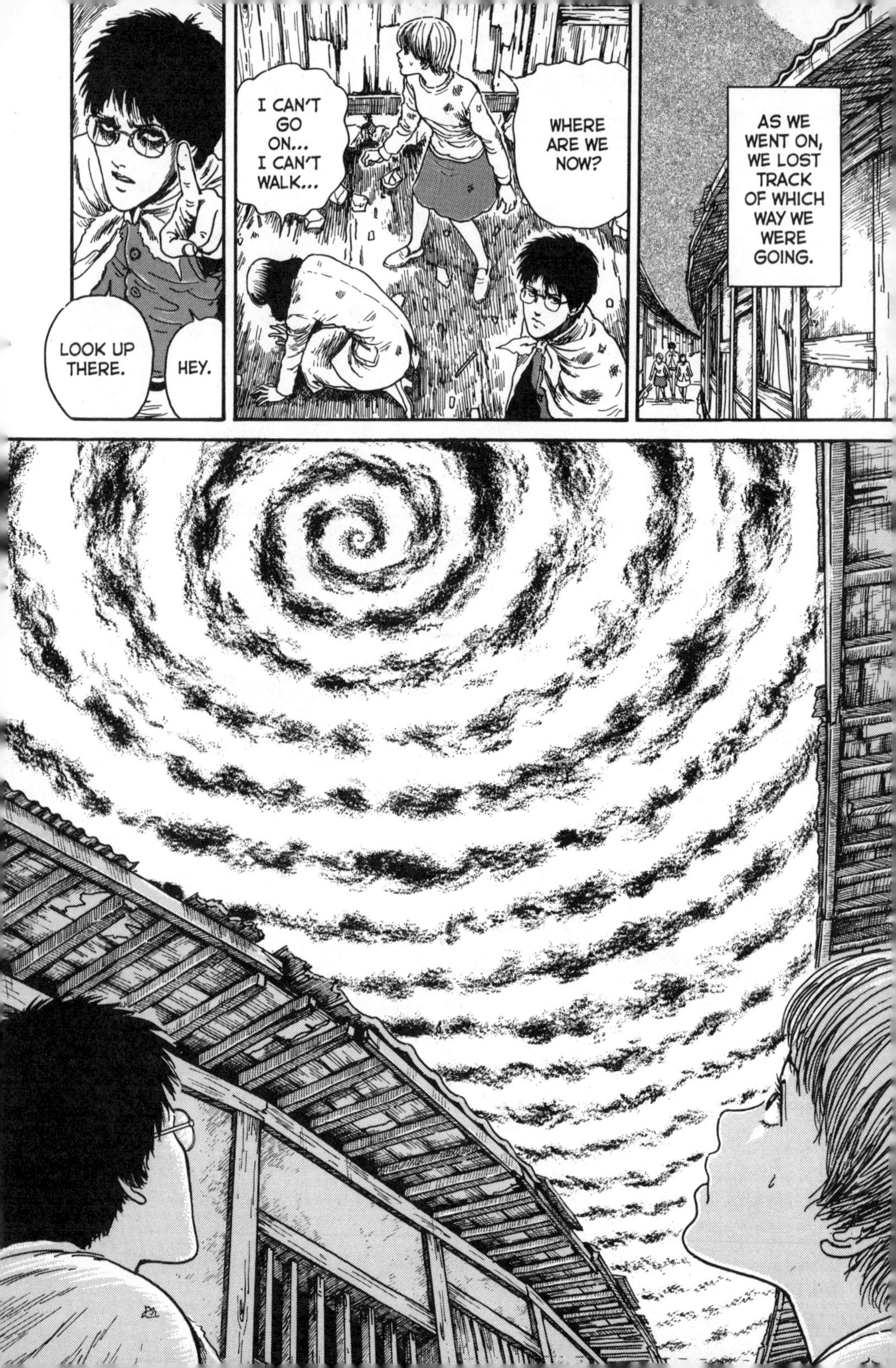
AS WE WENT ON, WE LOST TRACK OF WHICH WAY WE WERE GOING.
WHERE ARE WE NOW?
I CAN'T GO ON... I CAN'T WALK...
HEY.
LOOK UP THERE.

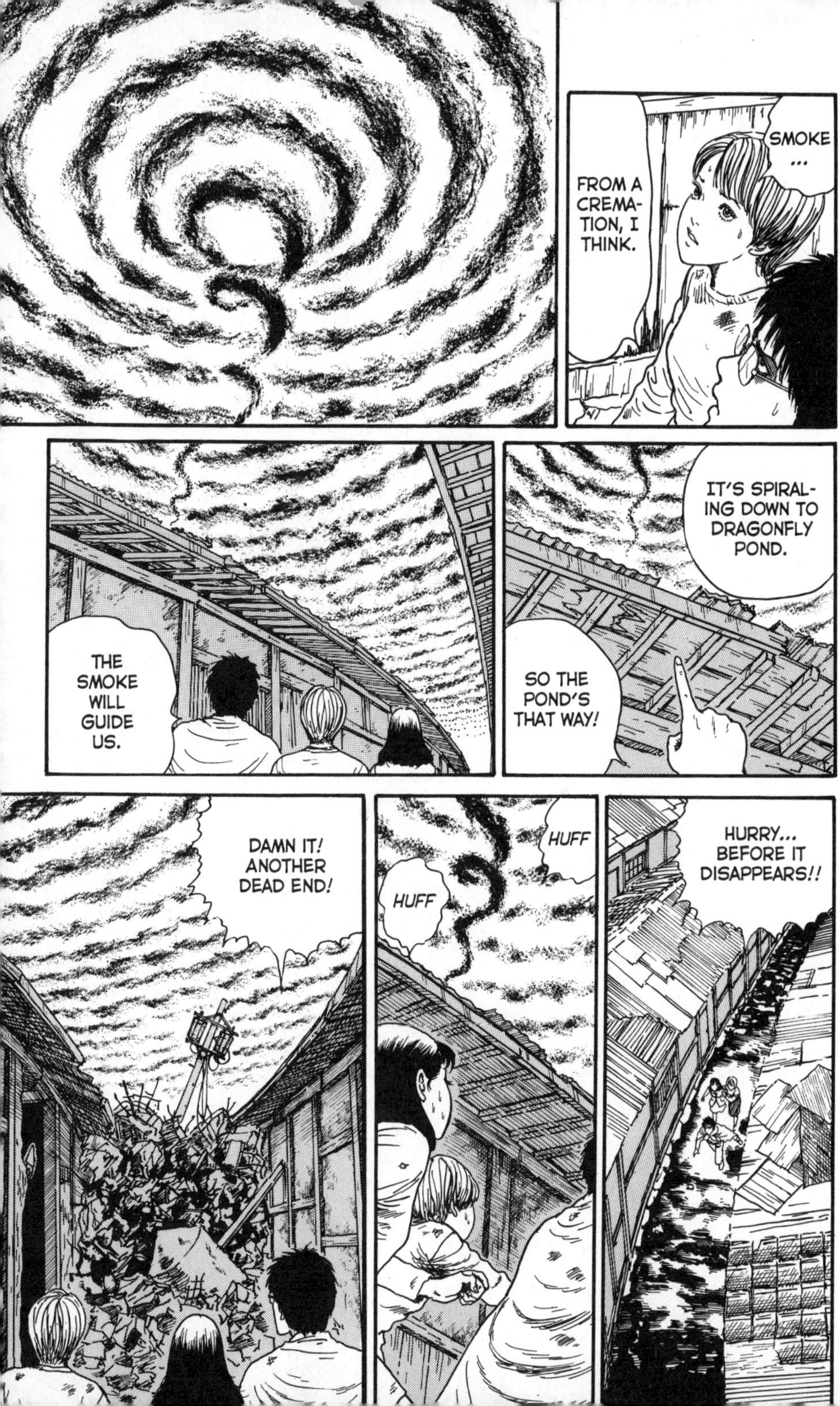
SMOKE...
FROM A CREMATION, I THINK.
IT'S SPIRALING DOWN TO DRAGONFLY POND.
SO THE POND'S THAT WAY!
THE SMOKE WILL GUIDE US.
HURRY... BEFORE IT DISAPPEARS!!
HUFF
HUFF
DAMN IT! ANOTHER DEAD END!

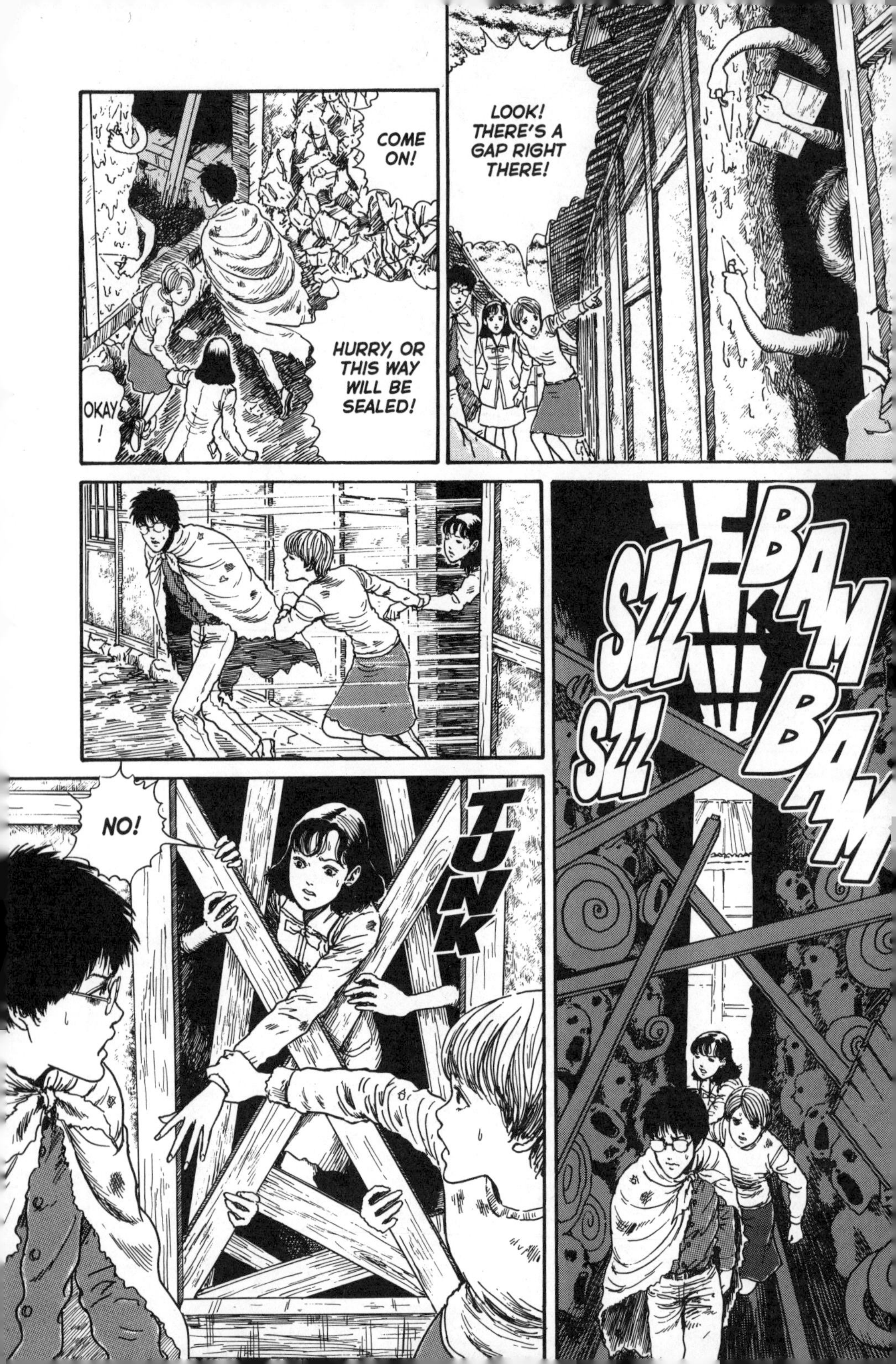
LOOK! THERE'S A GAP RIGHT THERE!
COME ON!
HURRY, OR THIS WAY WILL BE SEALED!
OKAY!
BAM BAM BAM
SZZ SZZ
TUNK
NO!

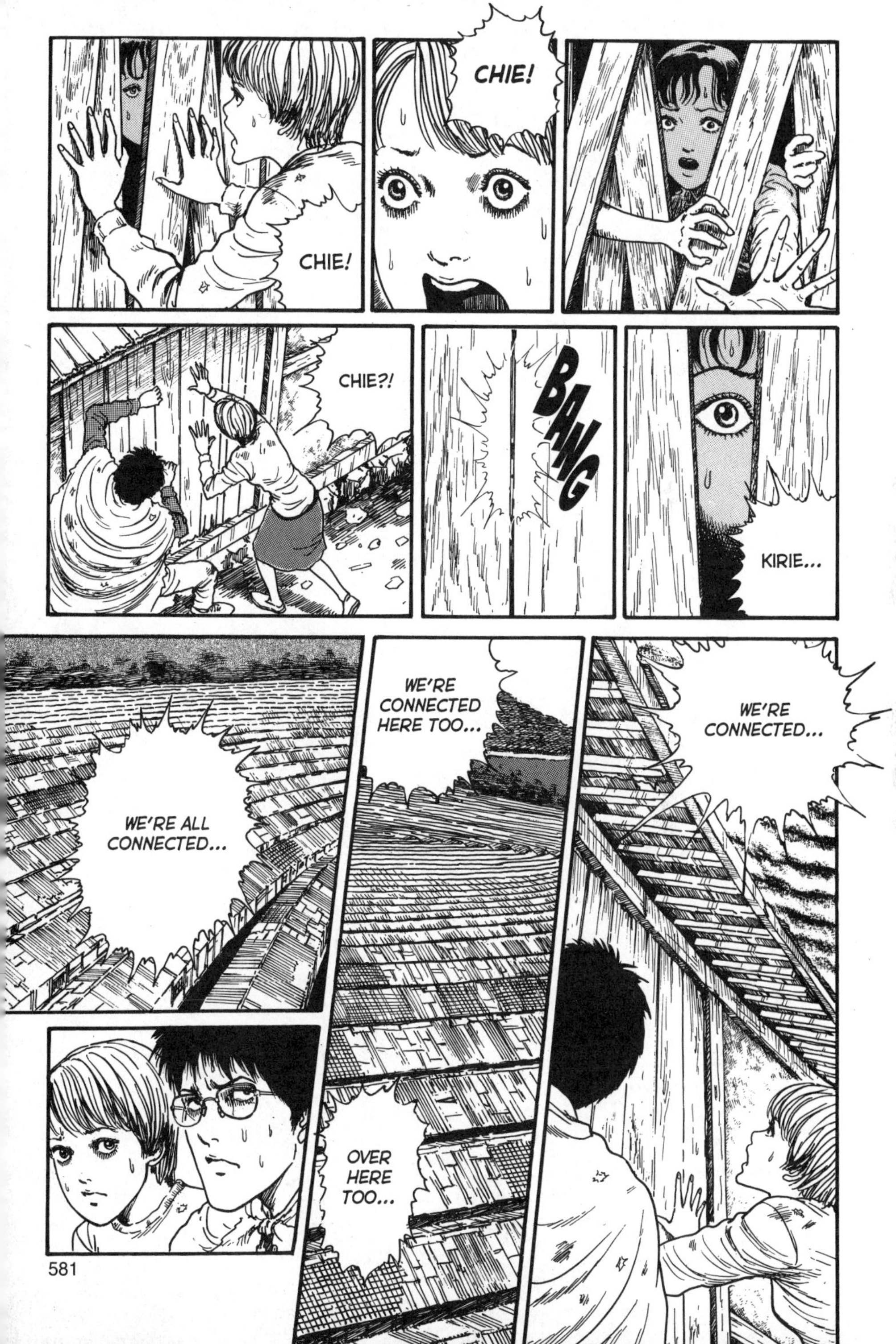
CHIE!
CHIE!
KIRIE...
BANG
CHIE?!
WE'RE CONNECTED...
WE'RE CONNECTED HERE TOO...
OVER HERE TOO...
WE'RE ALL CONNECTED...

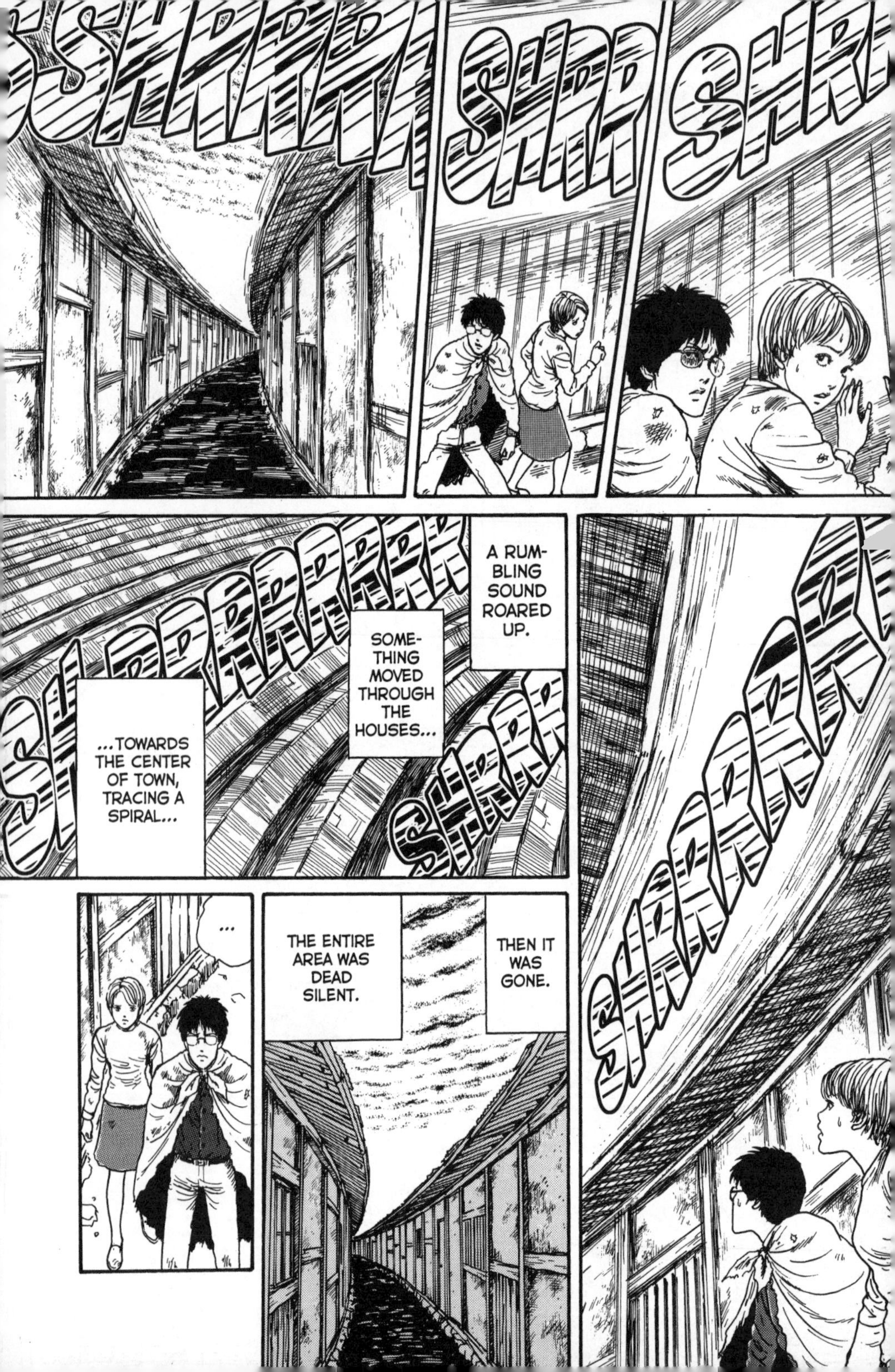

SHRR
SHRR
SHRRRR
SHRRRRR
A RUM-BLING SOUND ROARED UP.
SOME-THING MOVED THROUGH THE HOUSES...
SHRRRRRR
SHRRR
...TOWARDS THE CENTER OF TOWN, TRACING A SPIRAL...
THEN IT WAS GONE.
THE ENTIRE AREA WAS DEAD SILENT.
...

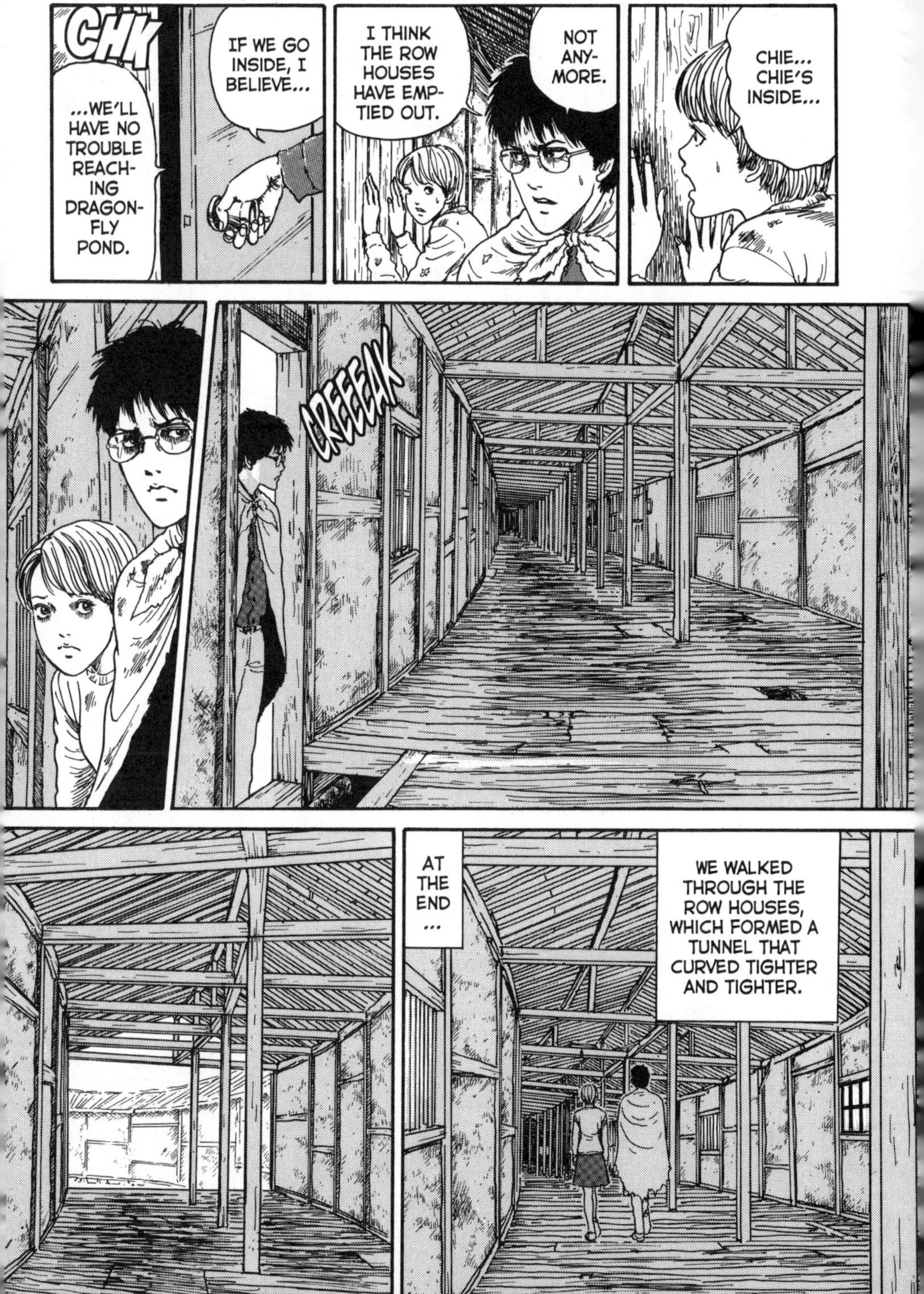
CHIE... CHIE'S INSIDE...
NOT ANY-MORE.
I THINK THE ROW HOUSES HAVE EMP-TIED OUT.
IF WE GO INSIDE, I BELIEVE...
CHK
...WE'LL HAVE NO TROUBLE REACH-ING DRAGON-FLY POND.
CREEEAK
WE WALKED THROUGH THE ROW HOUSES, WHICH FORMED A TUNNEL THAT CURVED TIGHTER AND TIGHTER.
AT THE END ...

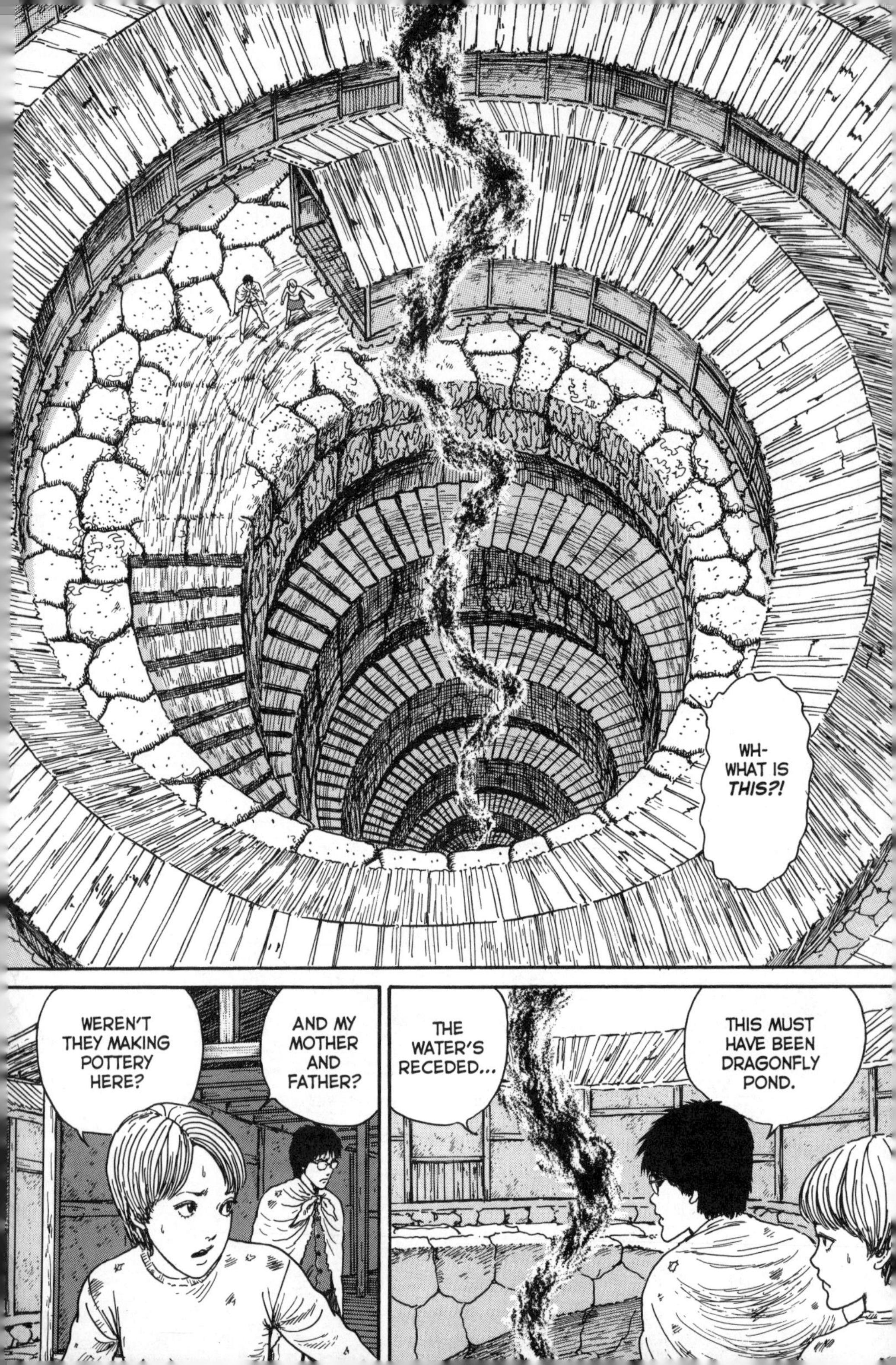
WH- WHAT IS *THIS?!*
THIS MUST HAVE BEEN DRAGONFLY POND.
THE WATER'S RECEDED...
AND MY MOTHER AND FATHER?
WEREN'T THEY MAKING POTTERY HERE?

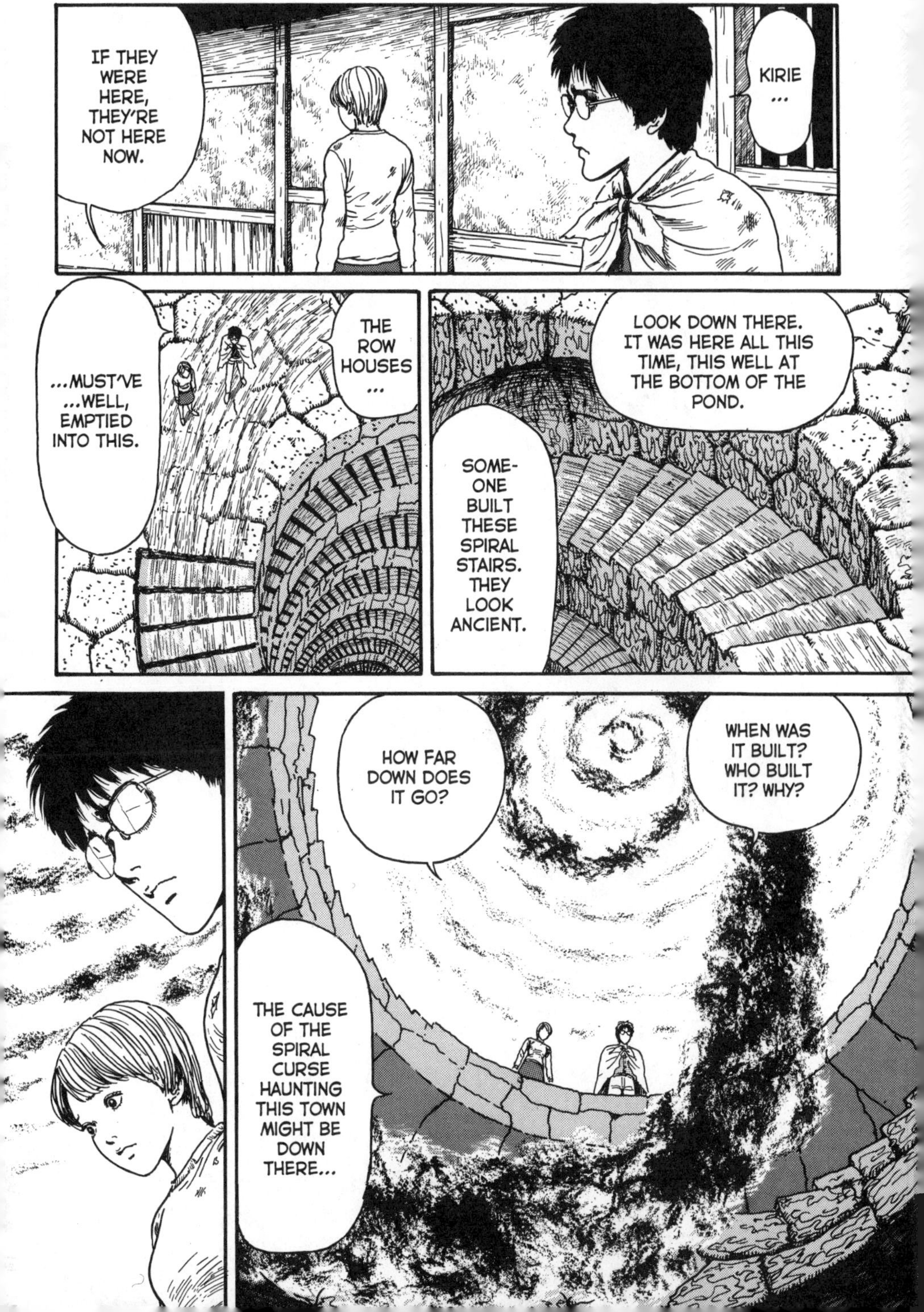
KIRIE ...
IF THEY WERE HERE, THEY'RE NOT HERE NOW.
LOOK DOWN THERE. IT WAS HERE ALL THIS TIME, THIS WELL AT THE BOTTOM OF THE POND.
SOME-ONE BUILT THESE SPIRAL STAIRS. THEY LOOK ANCIENT.
THE ROW HOUSES ...
...MUST'VE ...WELL, EMPTIED INTO THIS.
WHEN WAS IT BUILT? WHO BUILT IT? WHY?
HOW FAR DOWN DOES IT GO?
THE CAUSE OF THE SPIRAL CURSE HAUNTING THIS TOWN MIGHT BE DOWN THERE...

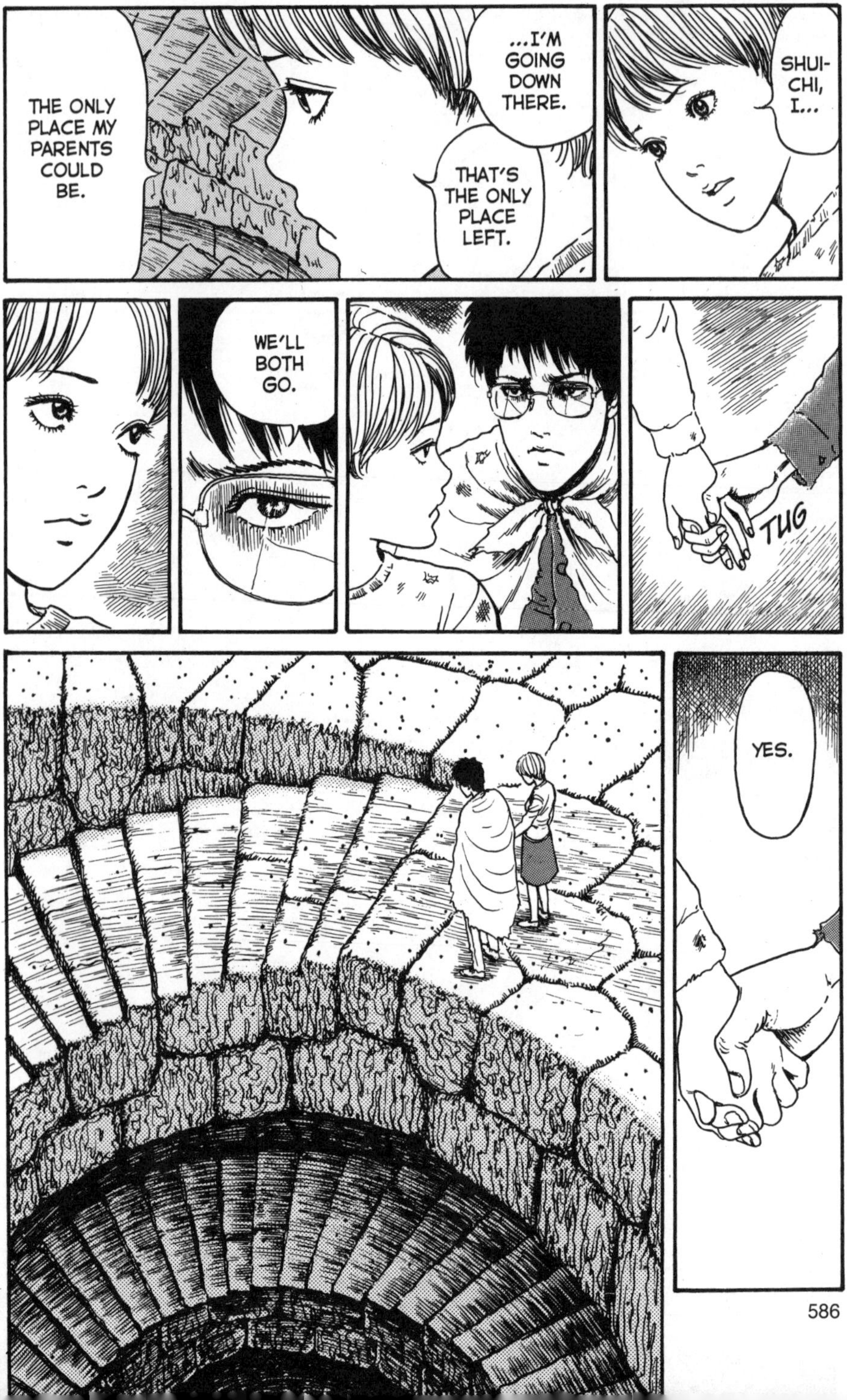
SHUI-CHI, I...
...I'M GOING DOWN THERE.
THAT'S THE ONLY PLACE LEFT.
THE ONLY PLACE MY PARENTS COULD BE.
TUG
WE'LL BOTH GO.
YES.

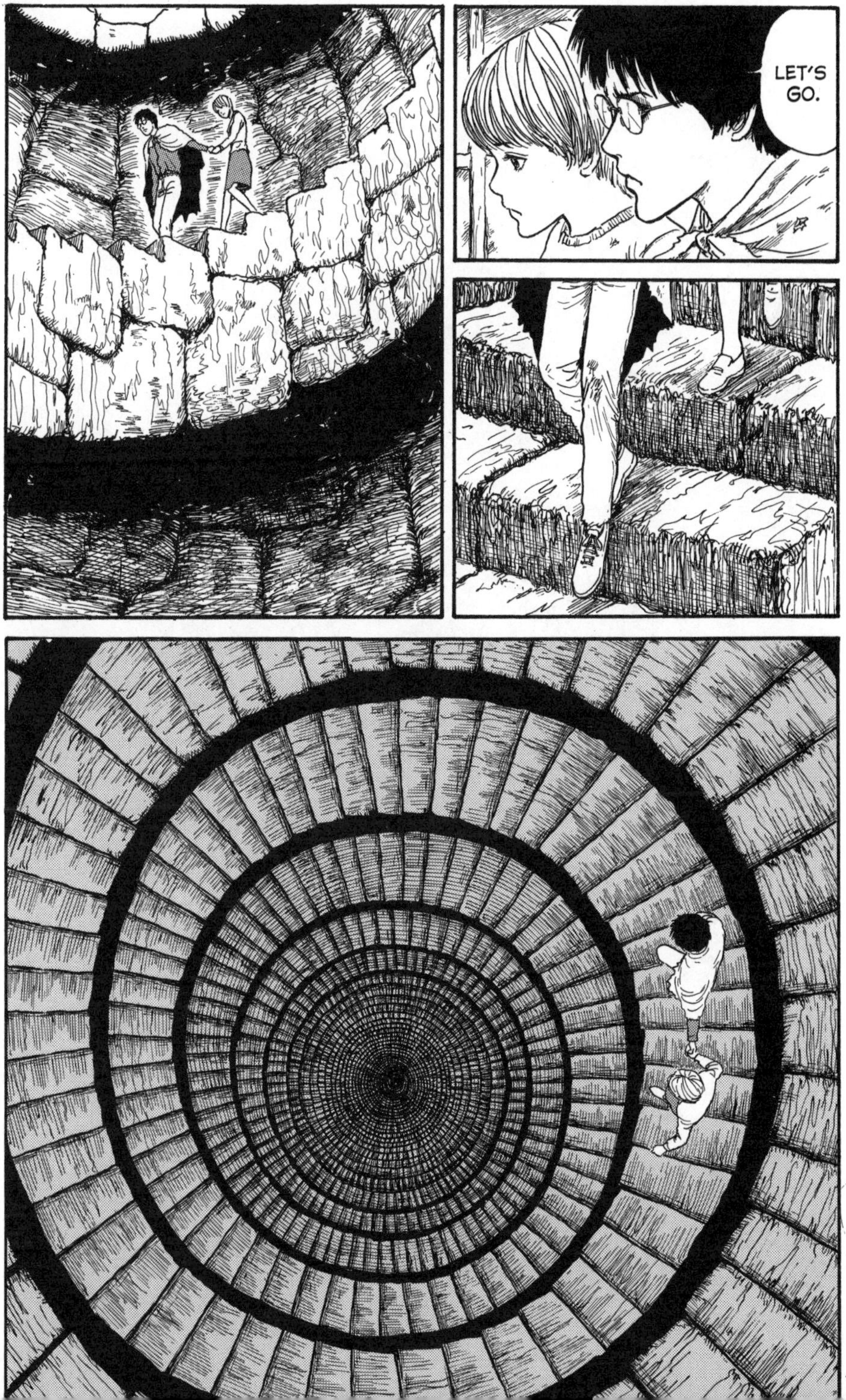
LET'S GO.

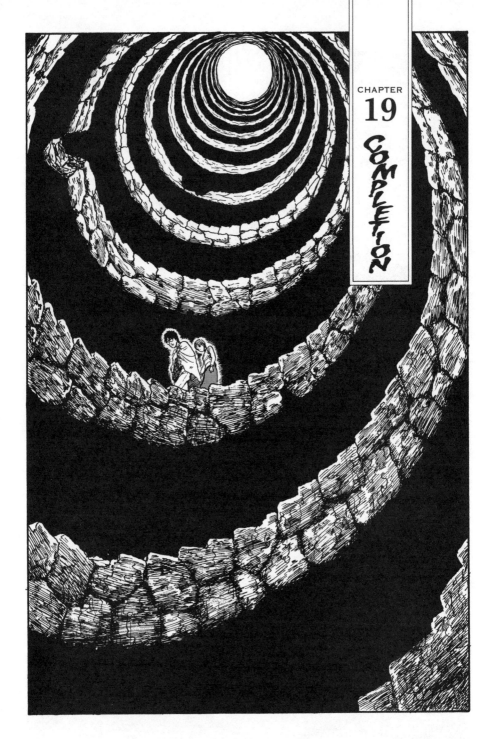

CHAPTER
19
COMPLETION

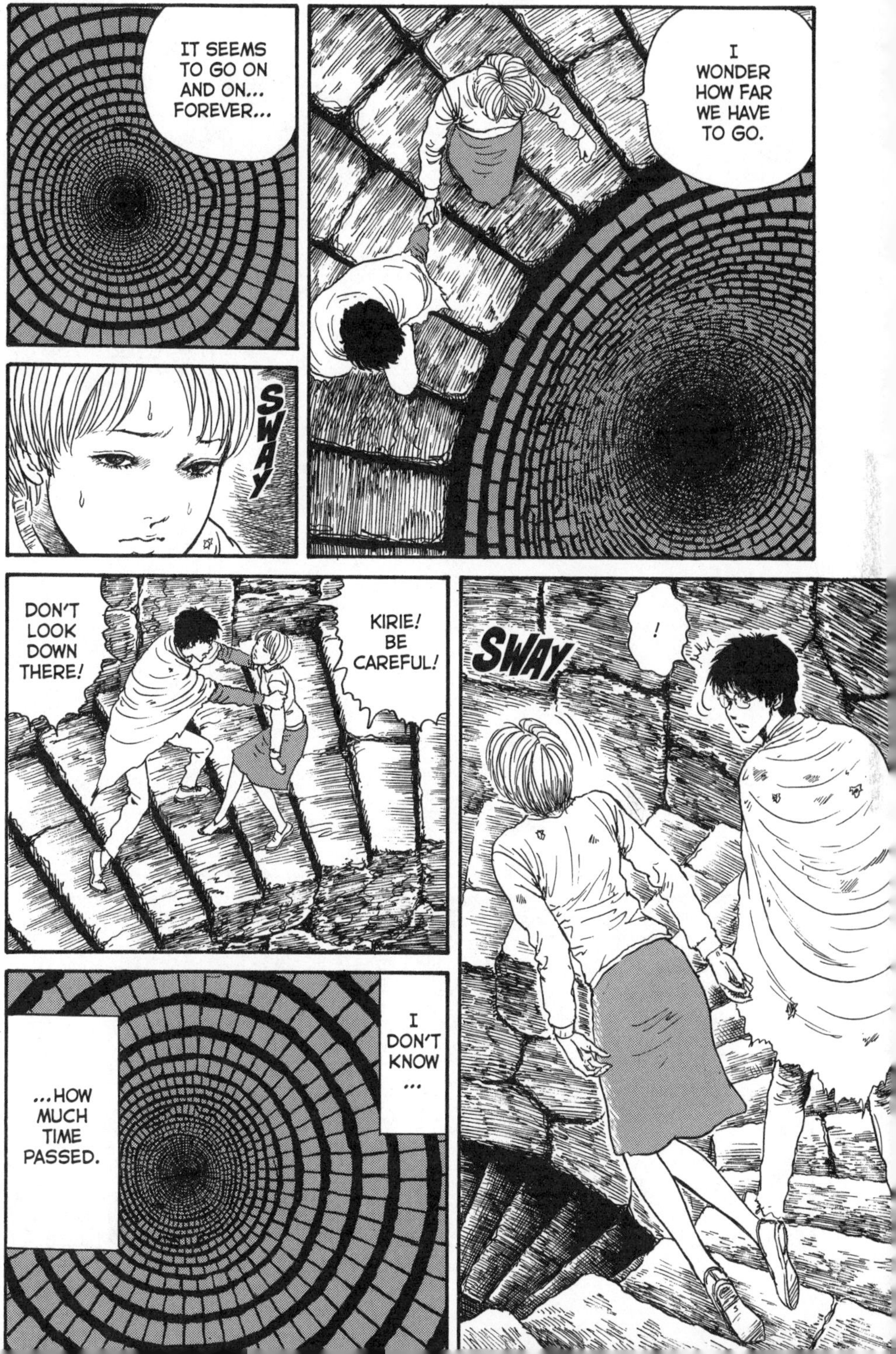
I WONDER HOW FAR WE HAVE TO GO.
IT SEEMS TO GO ON AND ON... FOREVER...
SWAY
SWAY
!
KIRIE! BE CAREFUL!
DON'T LOOK DOWN THERE!
I DON'T KNOW ...
...HOW MUCH TIME PASSED.

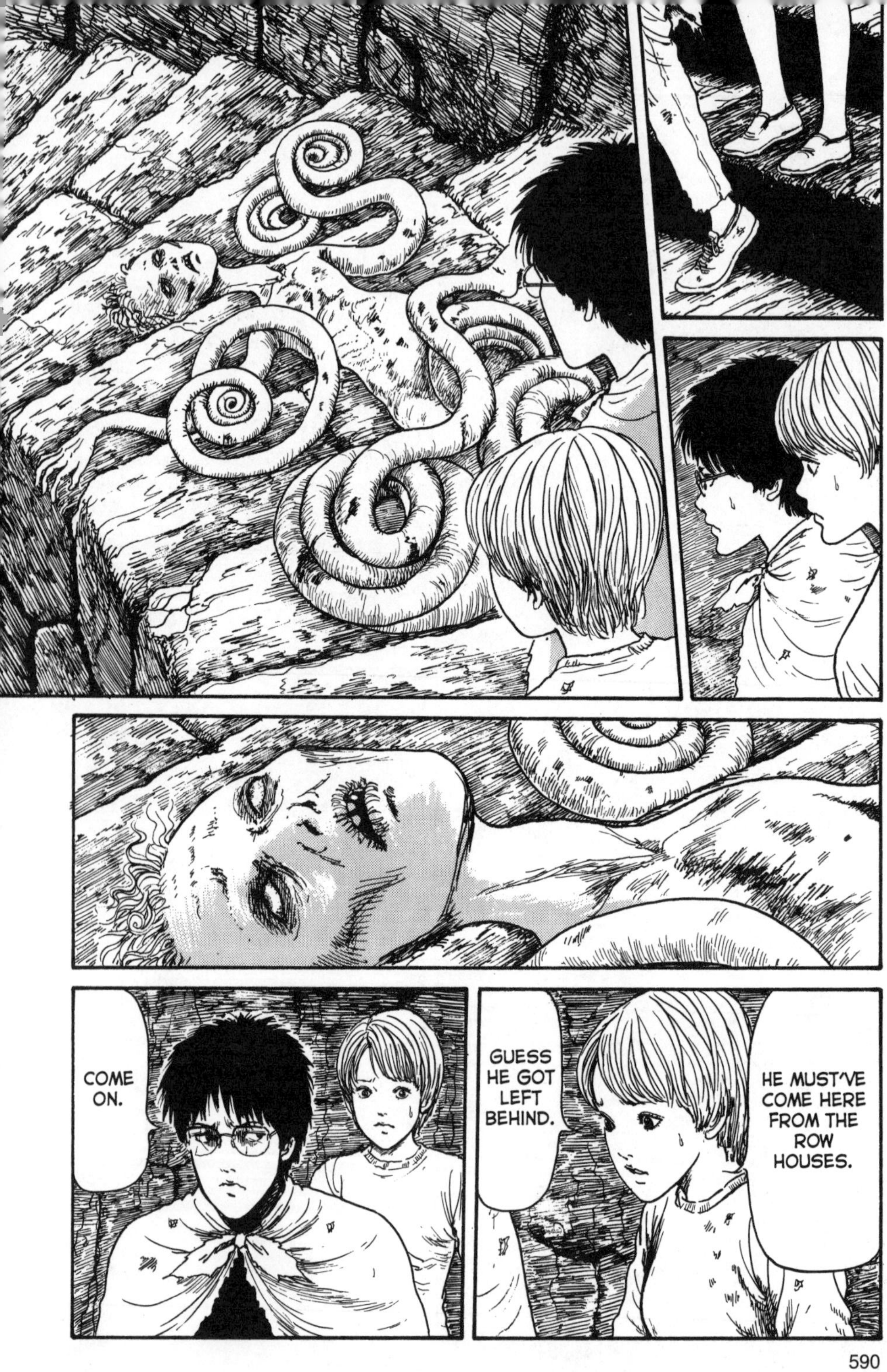
HE MUST'VE COME HERE FROM THE ROW HOUSES.
GUESS HE GOT LEFT BEHIND.
COME ON.

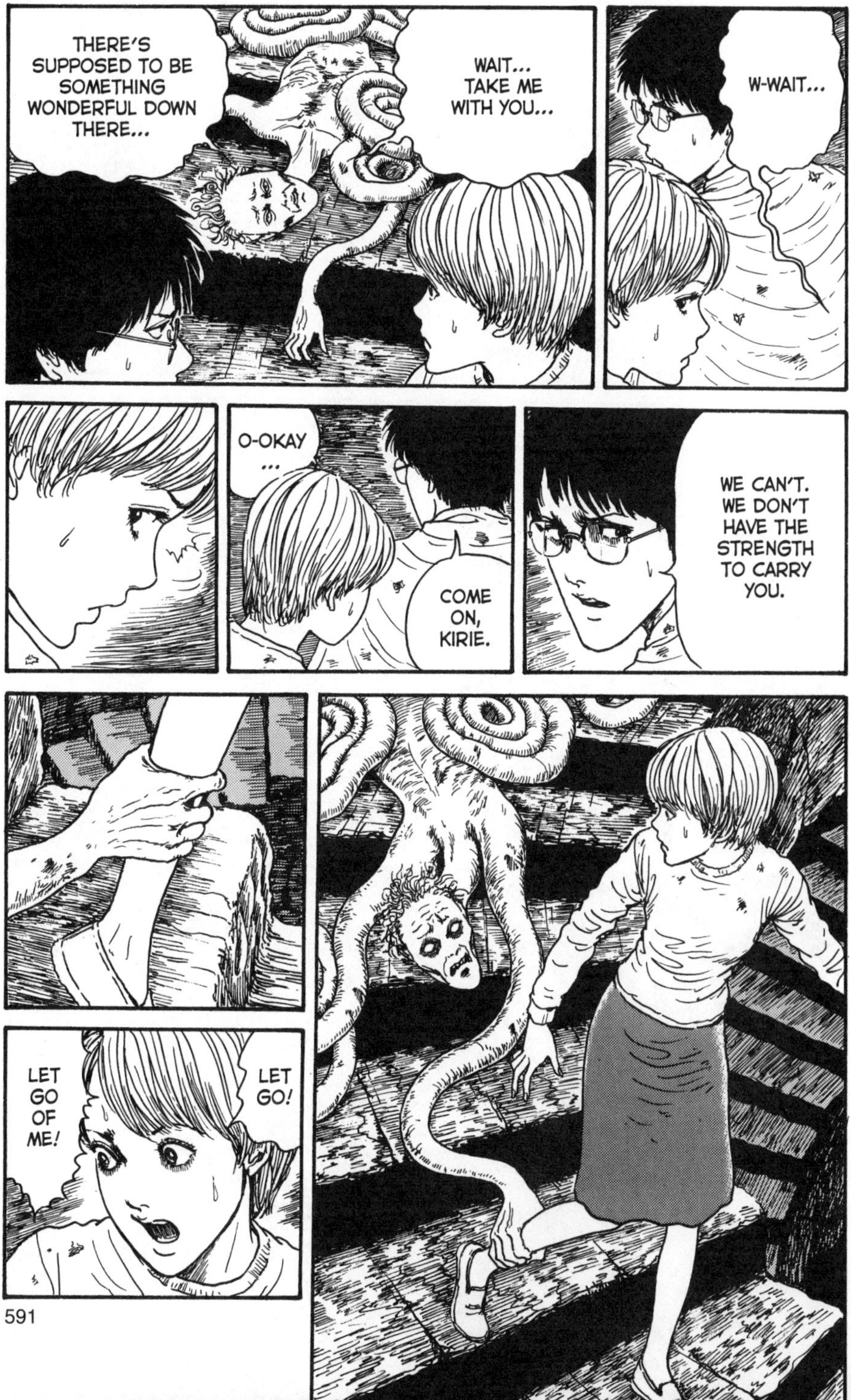
W-WAIT...
WAIT... TAKE ME WITH YOU...
THERE'S SUPPOSED TO BE SOMETHING WONDERFUL DOWN THERE...
WE CAN'T. WE DON'T HAVE THE STRENGTH TO CARRY YOU.
COME ON, KIRIE.
O-OKAY ...
LET GO!
LET GO OF ME!

TAKE ME WITH YOU!

LET GO OF ME!

STOP IT! LET GO OF HER!!

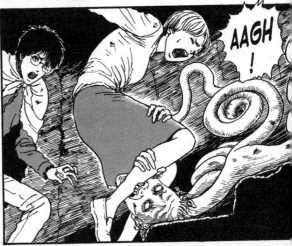

AAGH!

?!

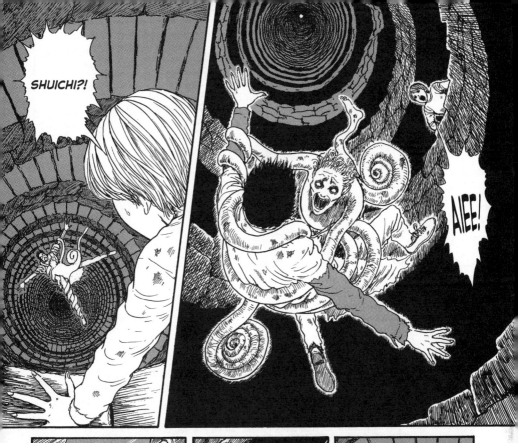

SHUICHI?!

AIEE!

HUFF

HUFF

SHUICHI!

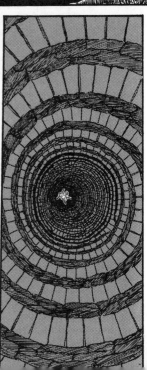

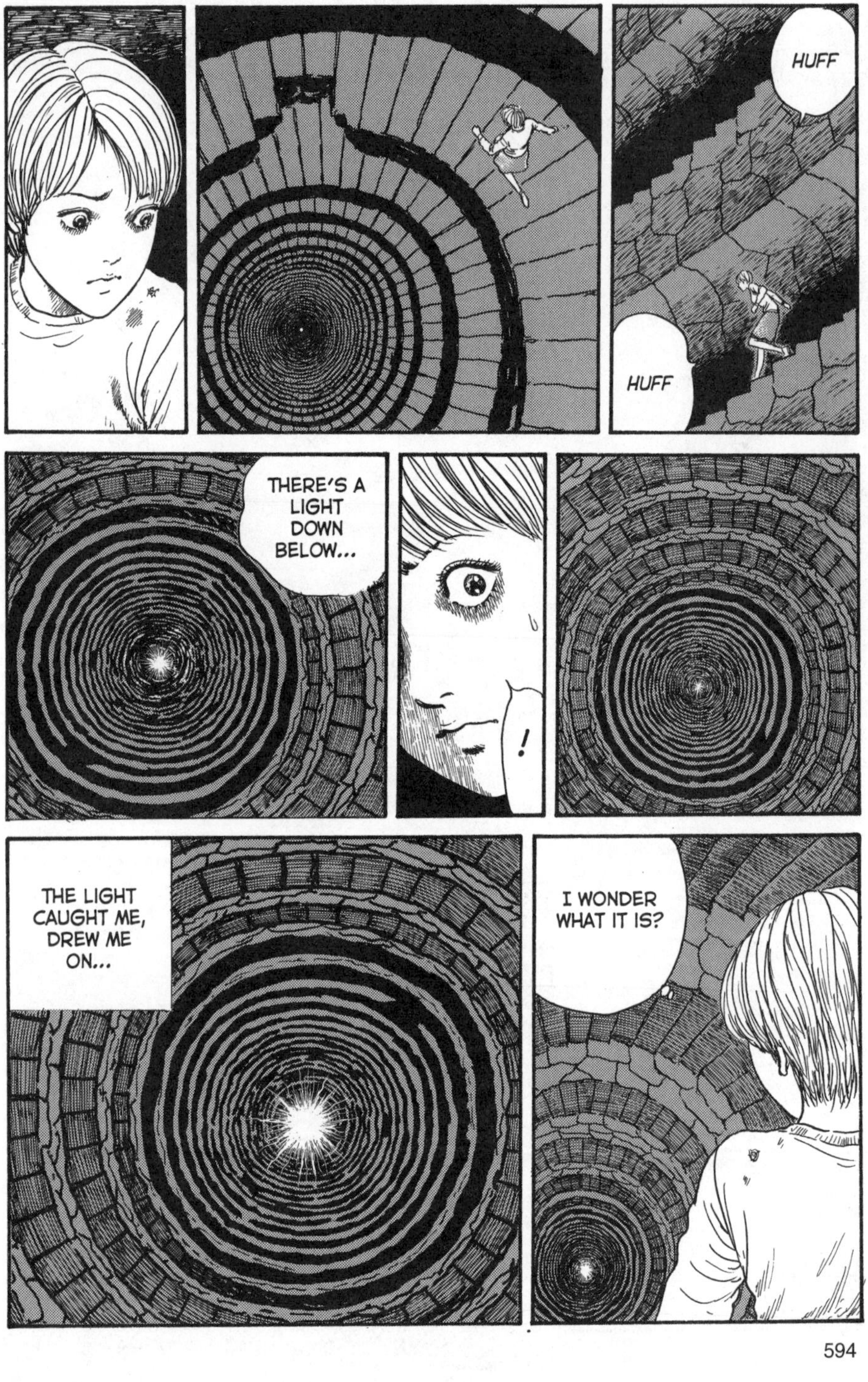
HUFF
HUFF
!
THERE'S A LIGHT DOWN BELOW...
I WONDER WHAT IT IS?
THE LIGHT CAUGHT ME, DREW ME ON...

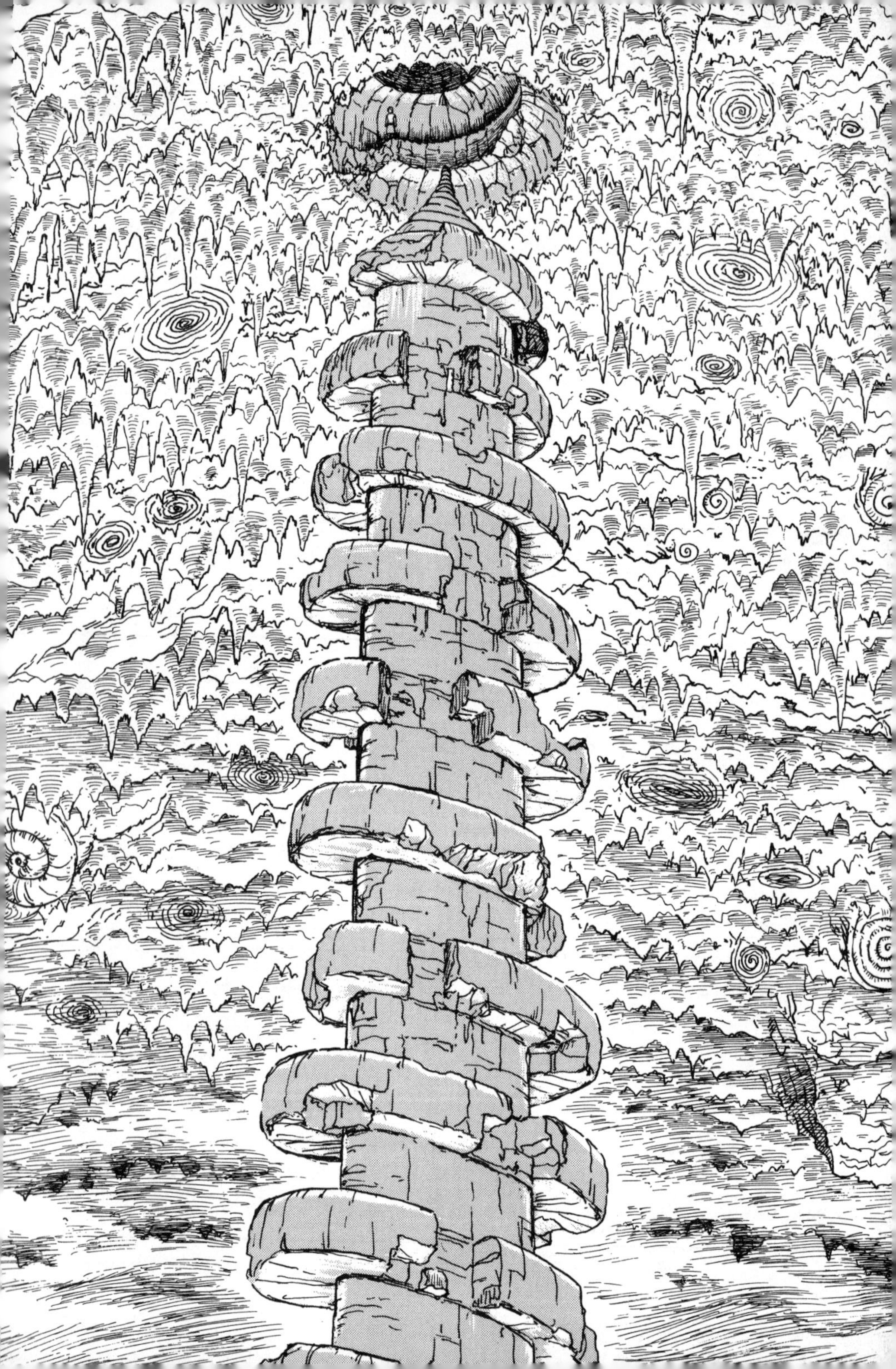

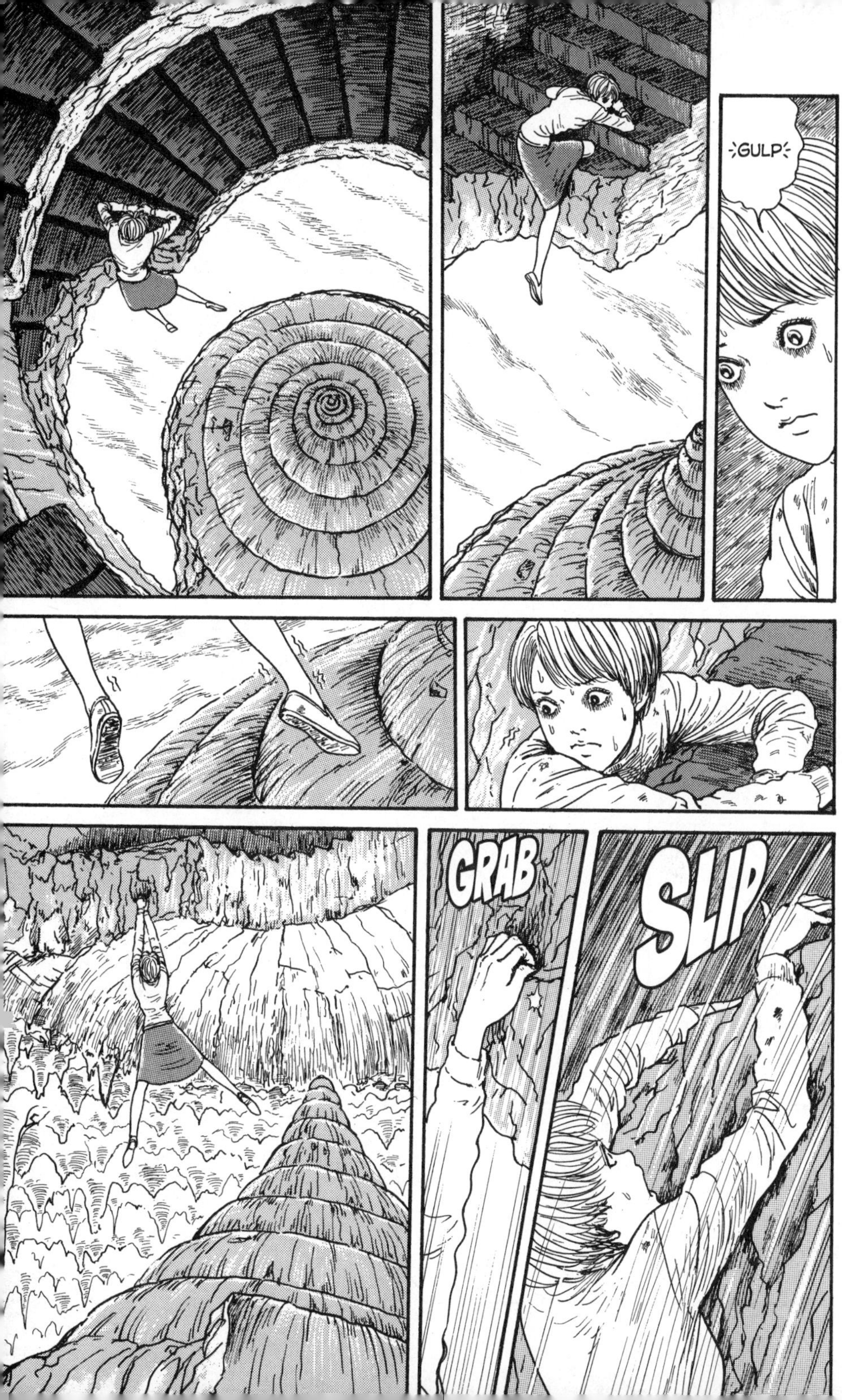
GULP
SLIP
GRAB

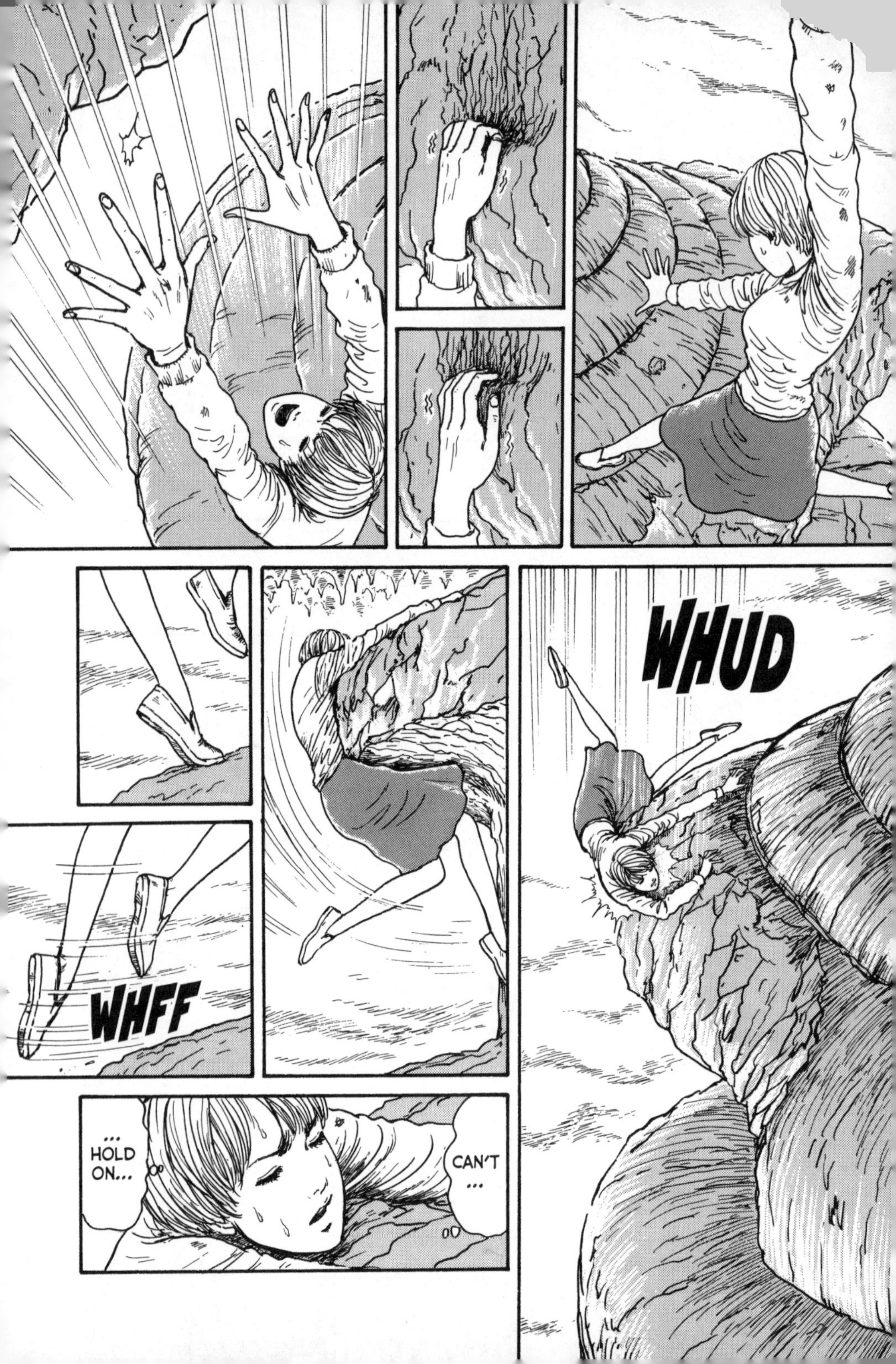
WHUD
WHFF
CAN'T ...
... HOLD ON...

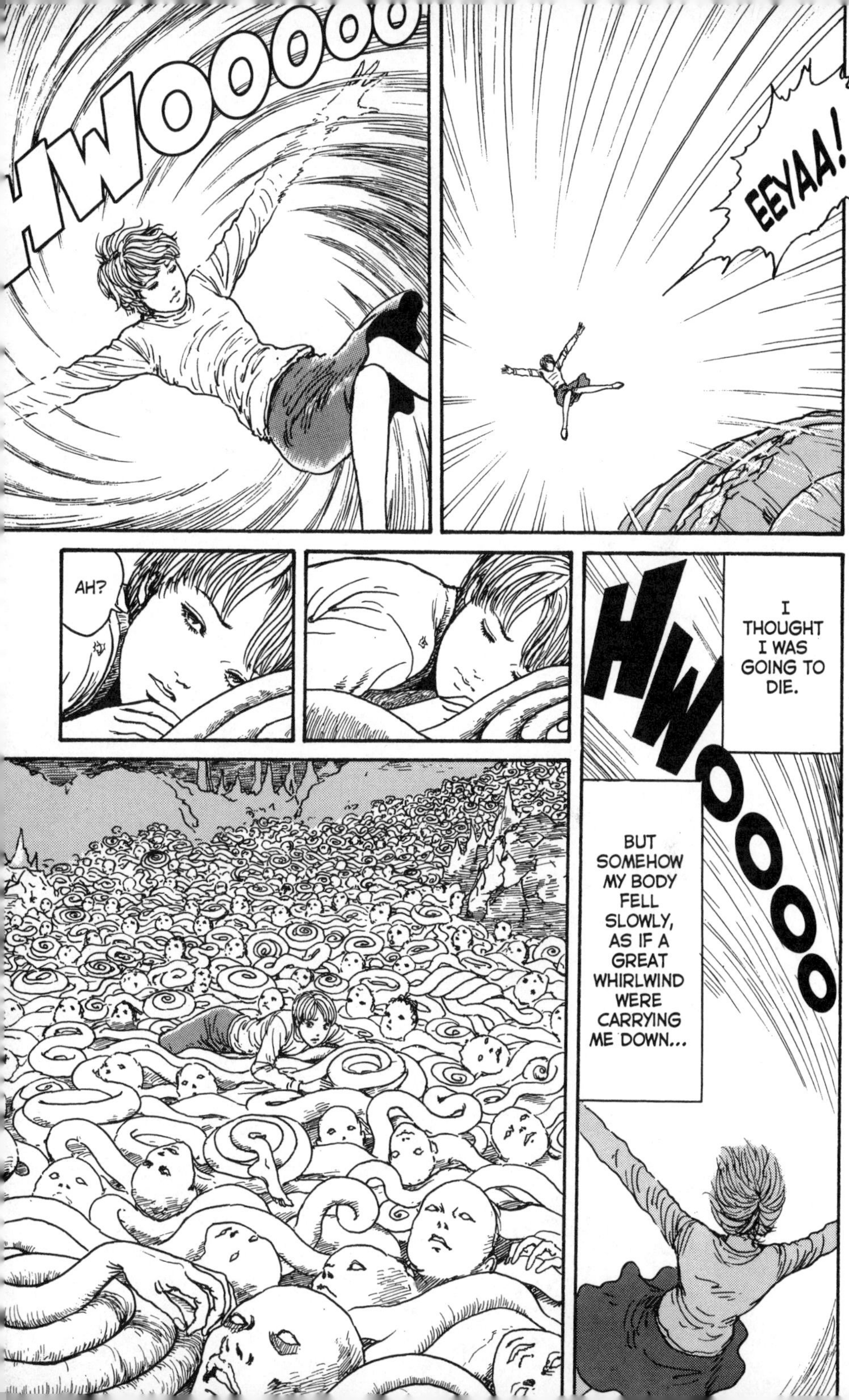
EEYAA!
HWOOOOOO
HWOOOOO
I THOUGHT I WAS GOING TO DIE.
BUT SOMEHOW MY BODY FELL SLOWLY, AS IF A GREAT WHIRLWIND WERE CARRYING ME DOWN...
AH?

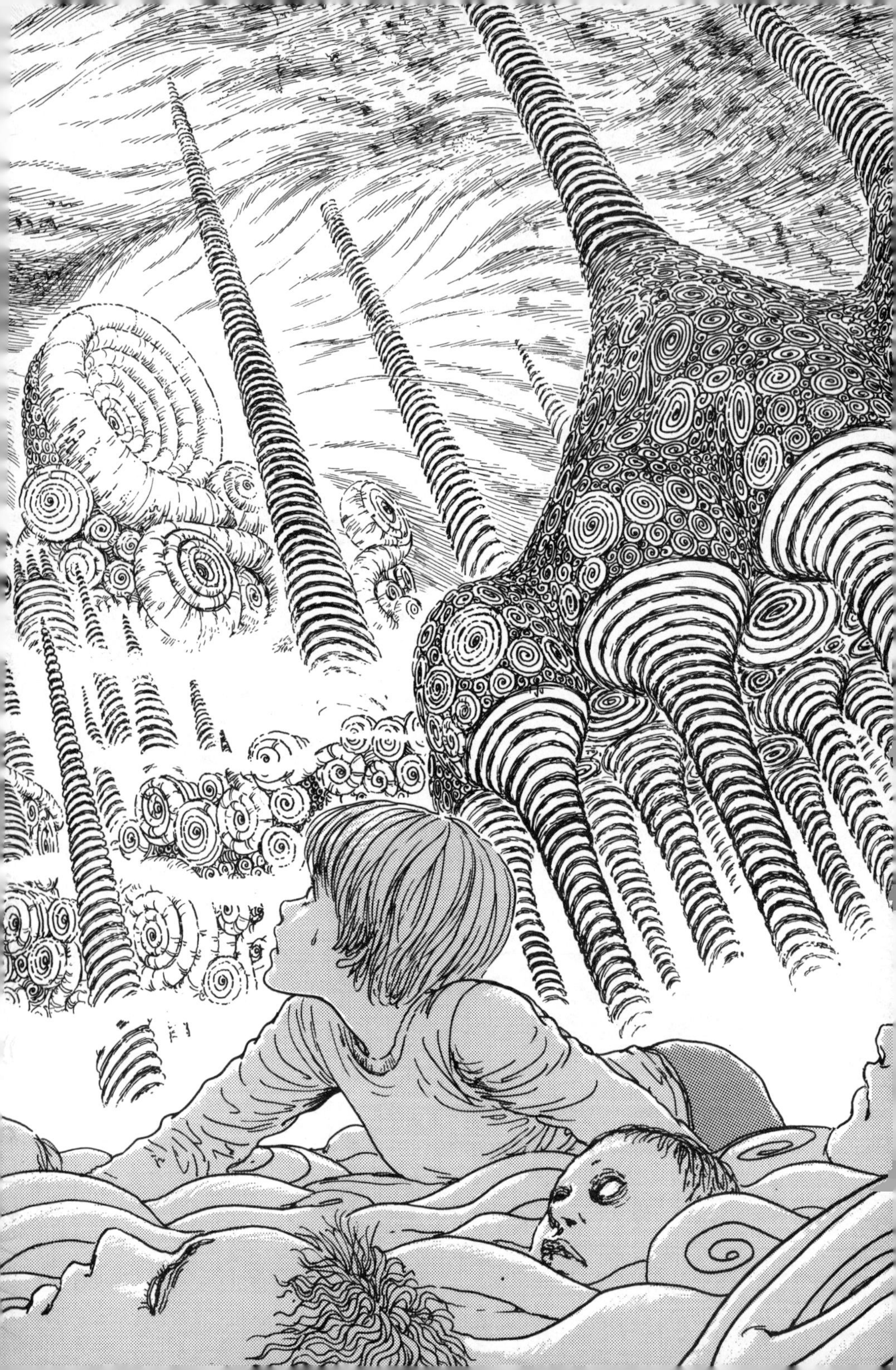

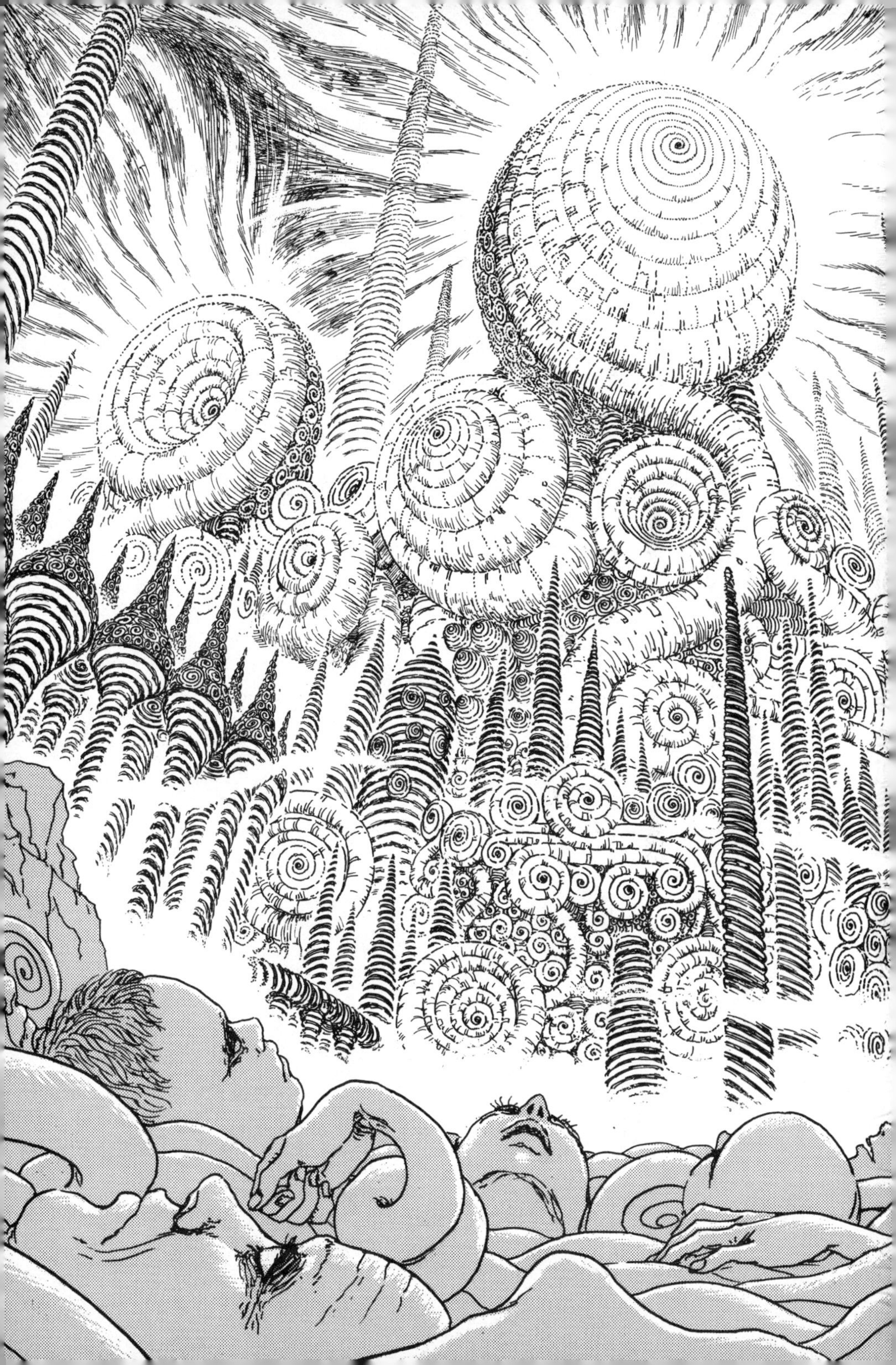

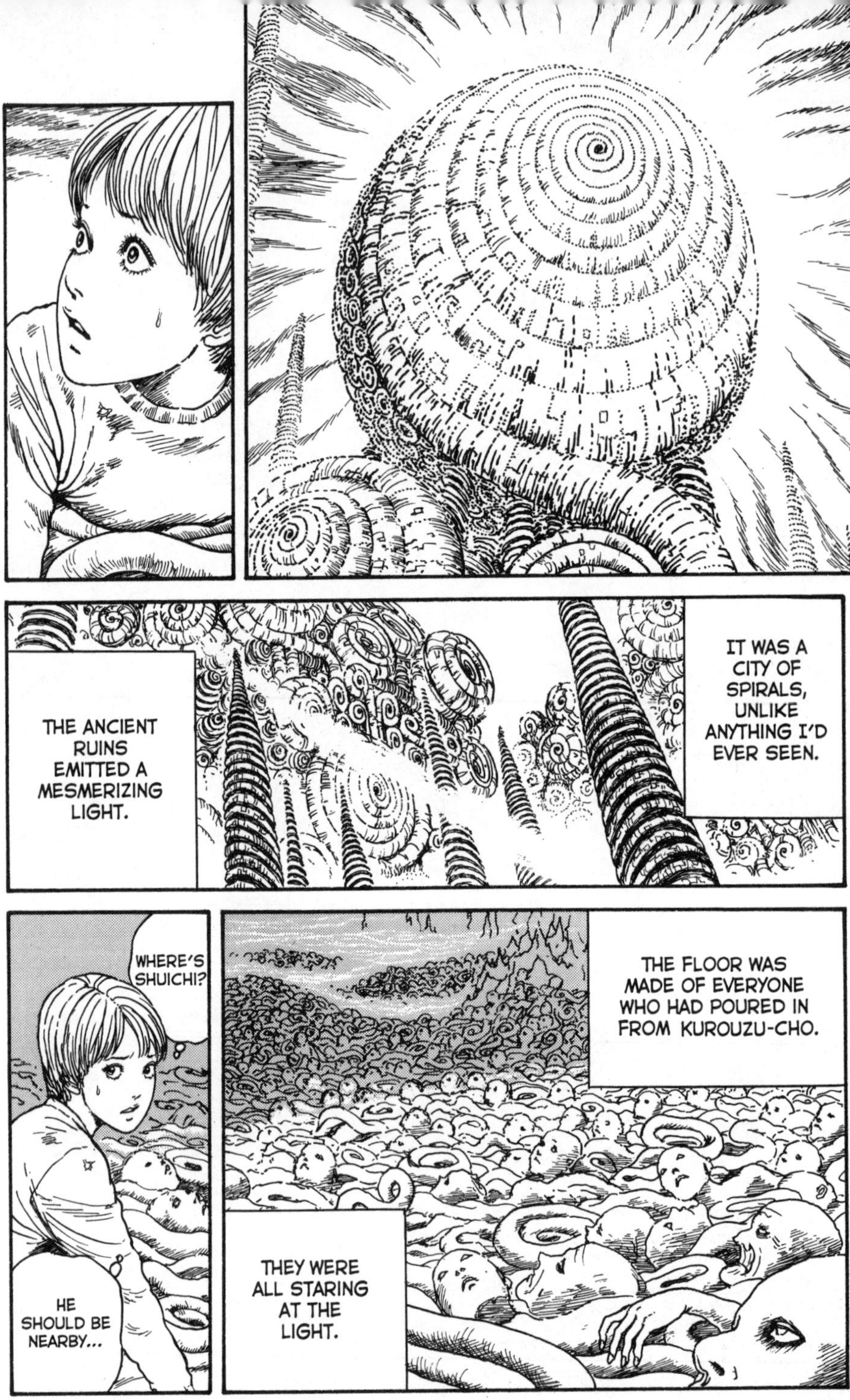
IT WAS A CITY OF SPIRALS, UNLIKE ANYTHING I'D EVER SEEN.
THE ANCIENT RUINS EMITTED A MESMERIZING LIGHT.
THE FLOOR WAS MADE OF EVERYONE WHO HAD POURED IN FROM KUROUZU-CHO.
THEY WERE ALL STARING AT THE LIGHT.
WHERE'S SHUICHI?
HE SHOULD BE NEARBY...

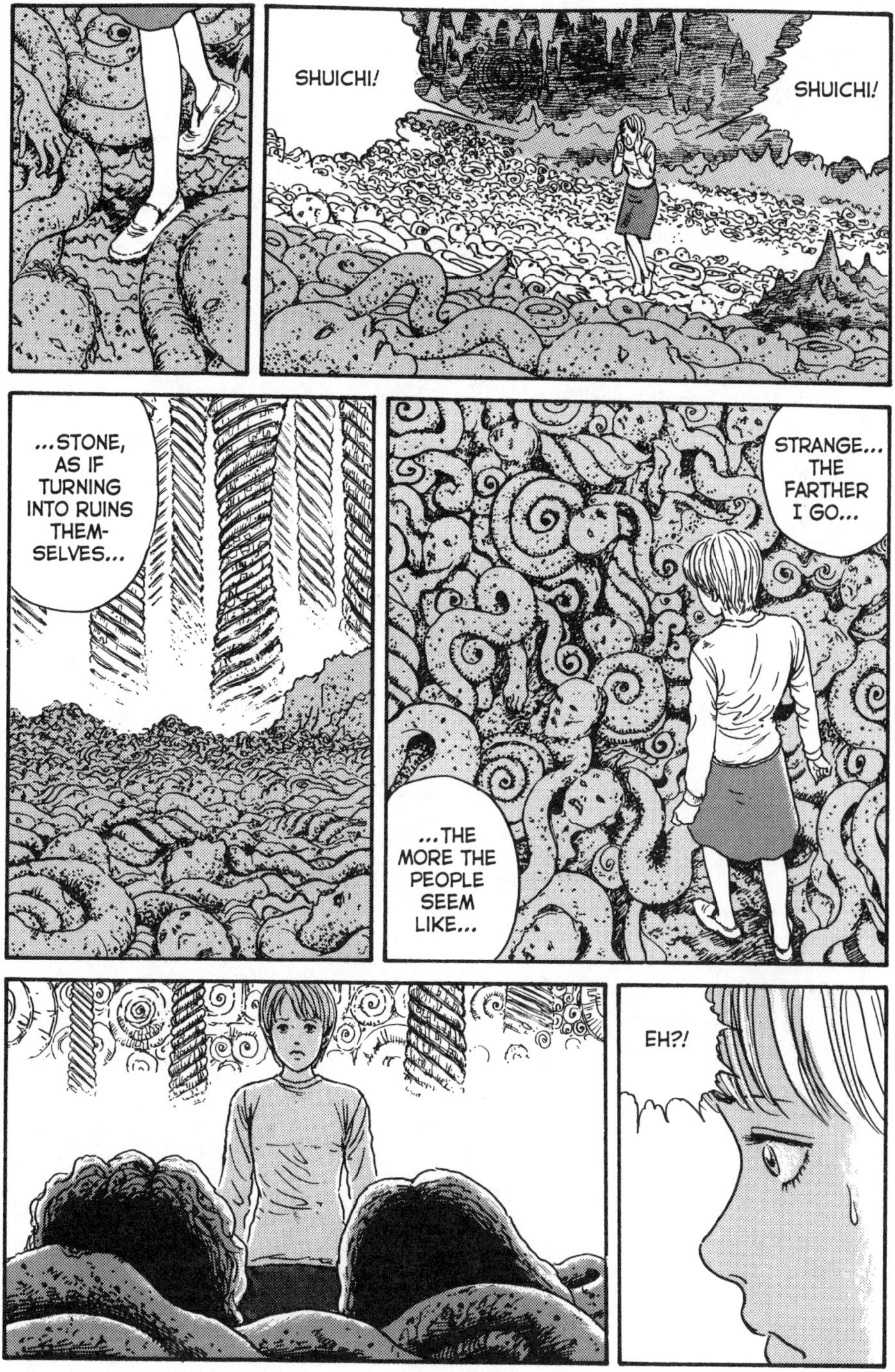
SHUICHI!
SHUICHI!
STRANGE... THE FARTHER I GO...
...THE MORE THE PEOPLE SEEM LIKE...
...STONE, AS IF TURNING INTO RUINS THEM-SELVES...
EH?!

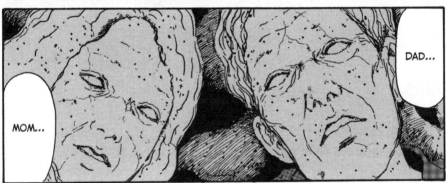

DAD...

MOM...

KIRIE...

KIRIE...

SO YOU WERE HERE...

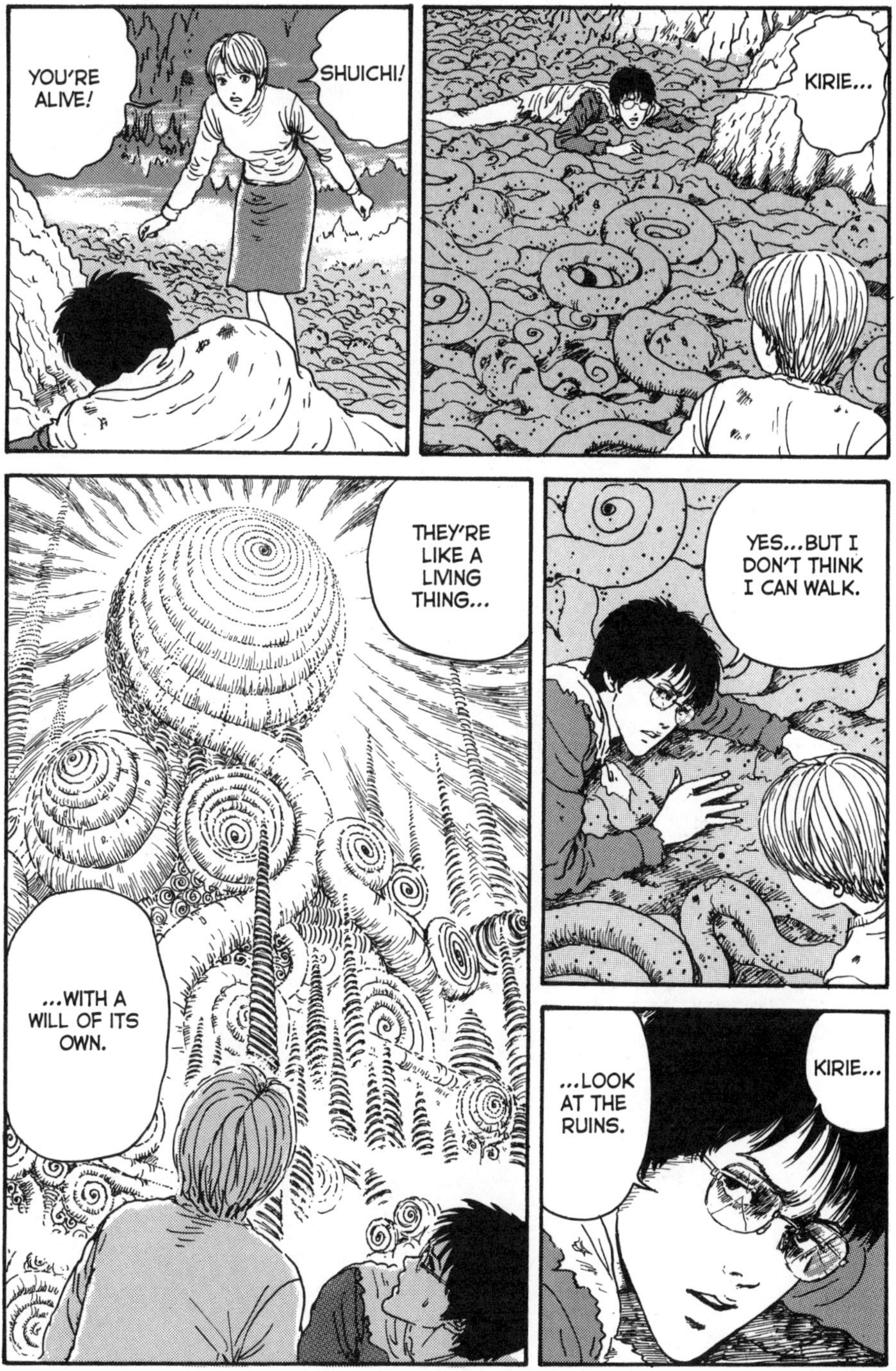
KIRIE...
SHUICHI!
YOU'RE ALIVE!
YES...BUT I DON'T THINK I CAN WALK.
KIRIE...
...LOOK AT THE RUINS.
THEY'RE LIKE A LIVING THING...
...WITH A WILL OF ITS OWN.

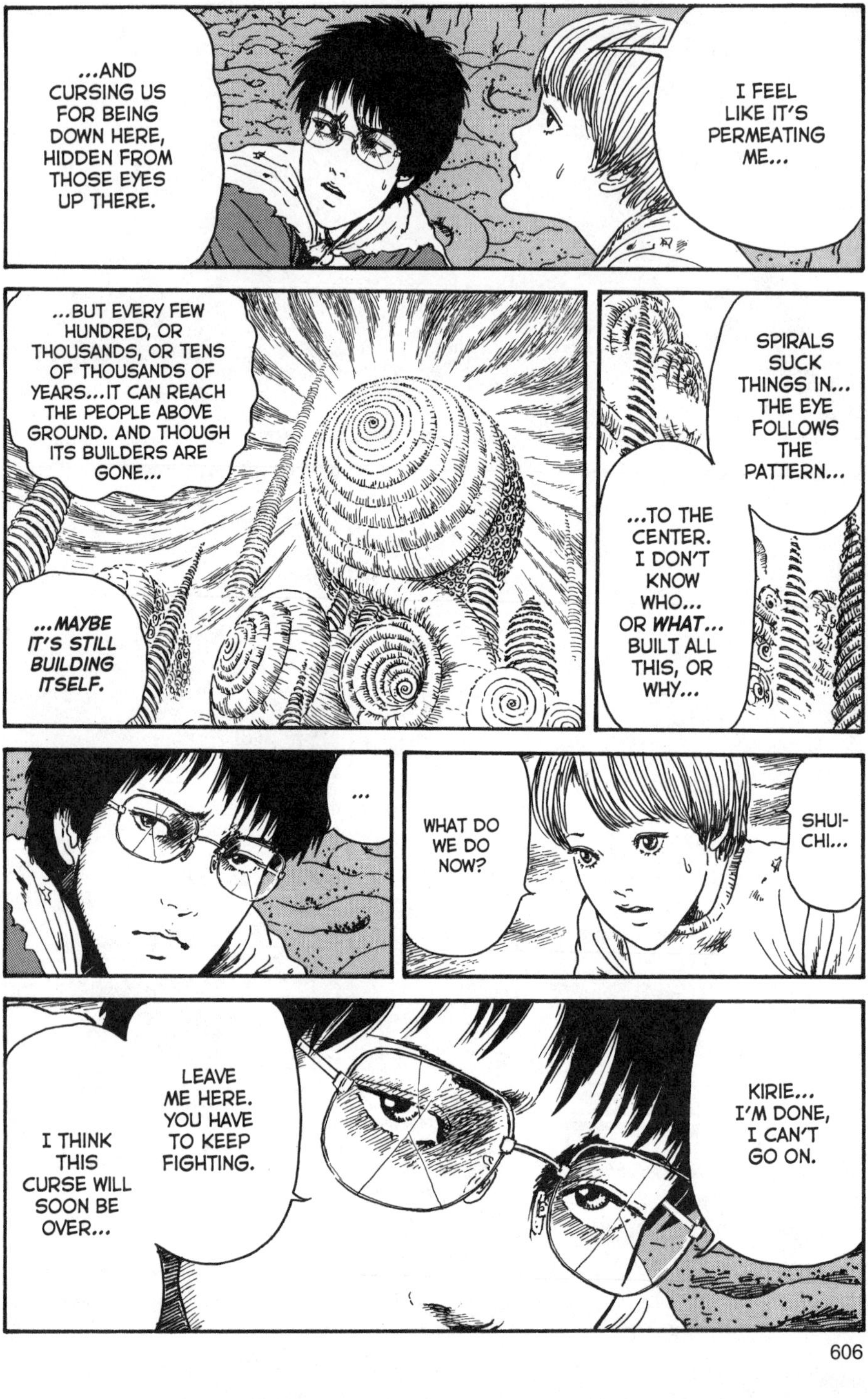
I FEEL LIKE IT'S PERMEATING ME...
...AND CURSING US FOR BEING DOWN HERE, HIDDEN FROM THOSE EYES UP THERE.
SPIRALS SUCK THINGS IN... THE EYE FOLLOWS THE PATTERN...
...TO THE CENTER. I DON'T KNOW WHO... OR *WHAT*... BUILT ALL THIS, OR WHY...
...BUT EVERY FEW HUNDRED, OR THOUSANDS, OR TENS OF THOUSANDS OF YEARS...IT CAN REACH THE PEOPLE ABOVE GROUND. AND THOUGH ITS BUILDERS ARE GONE...
...MAYBE IT'S STILL BUILDING ITSELF.
SHUI-CHI...
WHAT DO WE DO NOW?
...
KIRIE... I'M DONE, I CAN'T GO ON.
LEAVE ME HERE. YOU HAVE TO KEEP FIGHTING.
I THINK THIS CURSE WILL SOON BE OVER...

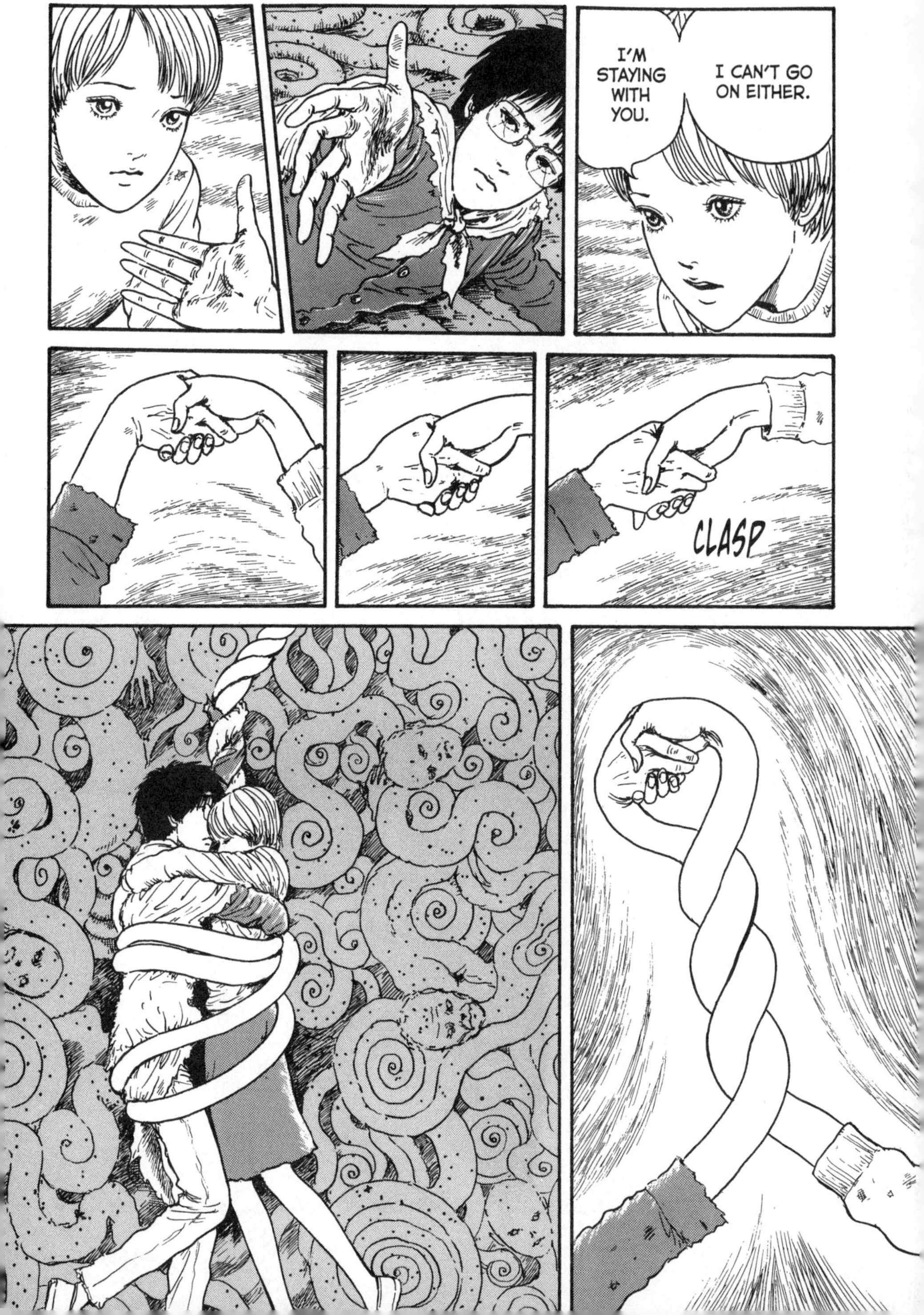
I CAN'T GO ON EITHER.
I'M STAYING WITH YOU.
CLASP

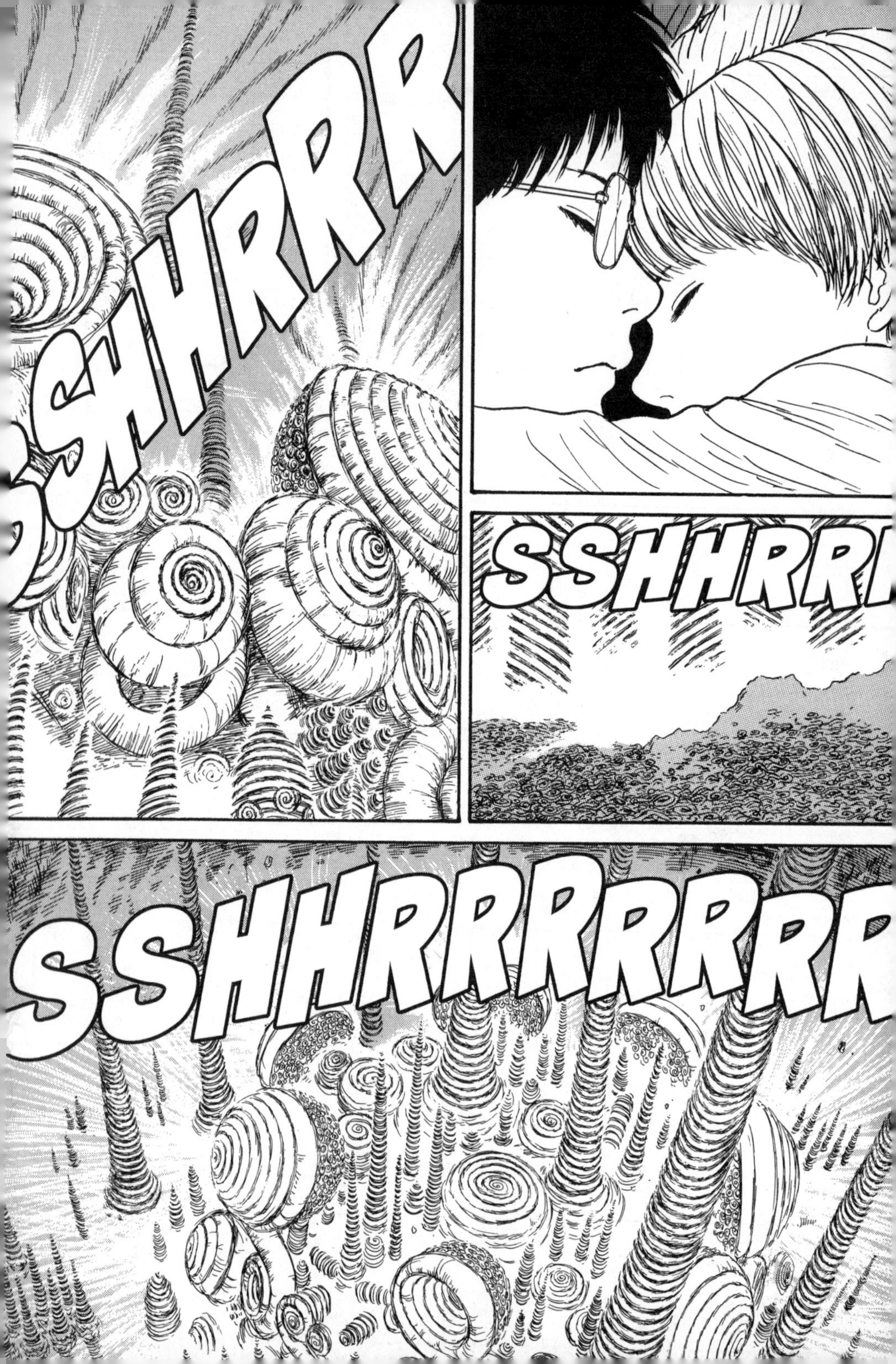
SSHHRRR
SSHHRRRR
SSHHRRRRRRR

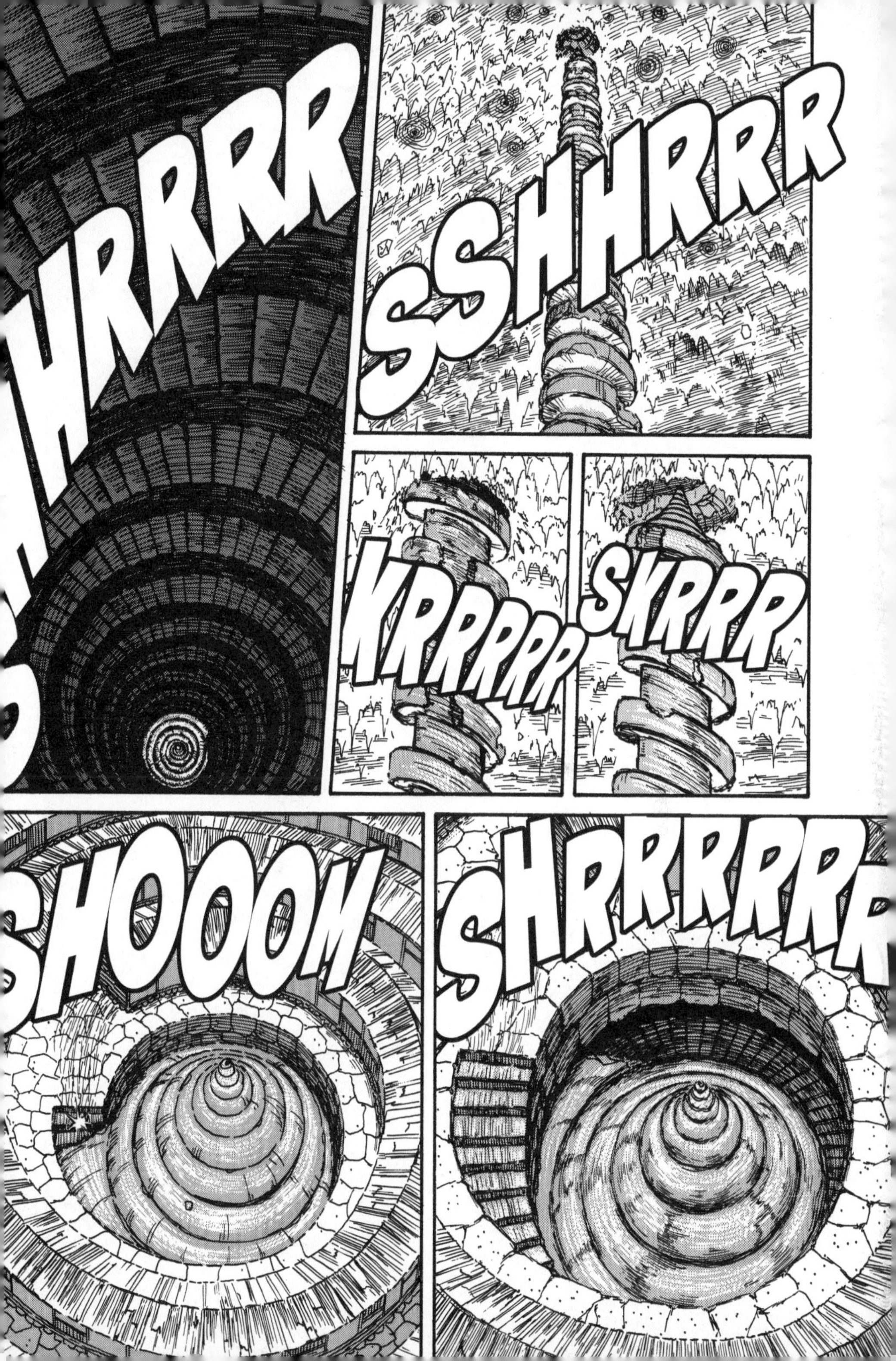
SSHHRRRR
SKRRRR
KRRRRRR
HRRRR
SHRRRRRR
SHOOOM

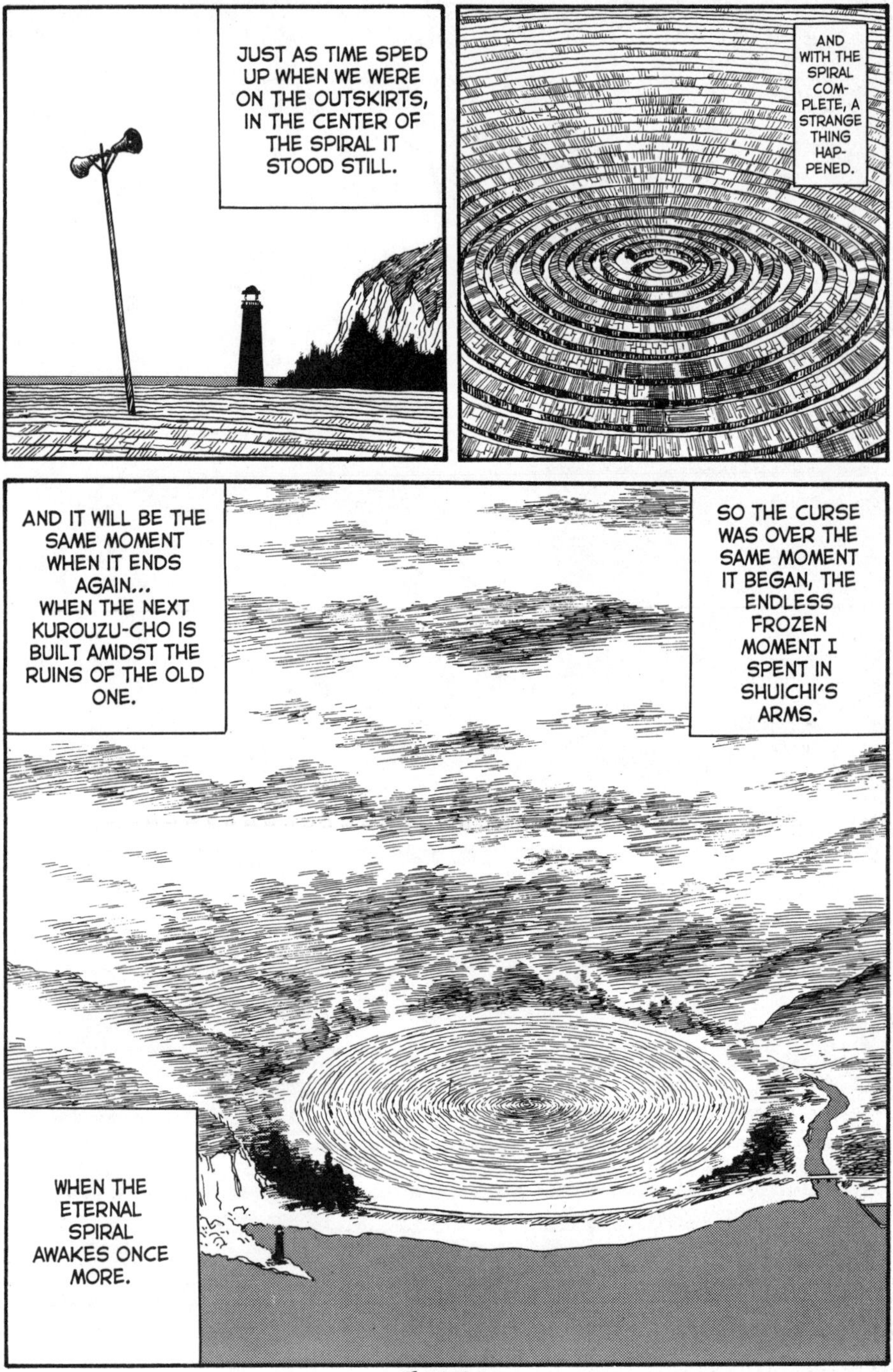
AND WITH THE SPIRAL COM- PLETE, A STRANGE THING HAP- PENED.
JUST AS TIME SPED UP WHEN WE WERE ON THE OUTSKIRTS, IN THE CENTER OF THE SPIRAL IT STOOD STILL.
SO THE CURSE WAS OVER THE SAME MOMENT IT BEGAN, THE ENDLESS FROZEN MOMENT I SPENT IN SHUICHI'S ARMS.
AND IT WILL BE THE SAME MOMENT WHEN IT ENDS AGAIN... WHEN THE NEXT KUROUZU-CHO IS BUILT AMIDST THE RUINS OF THE OLD ONE.
WHEN THE ETERNAL SPIRAL AWAKES ONCE MORE.

THE END

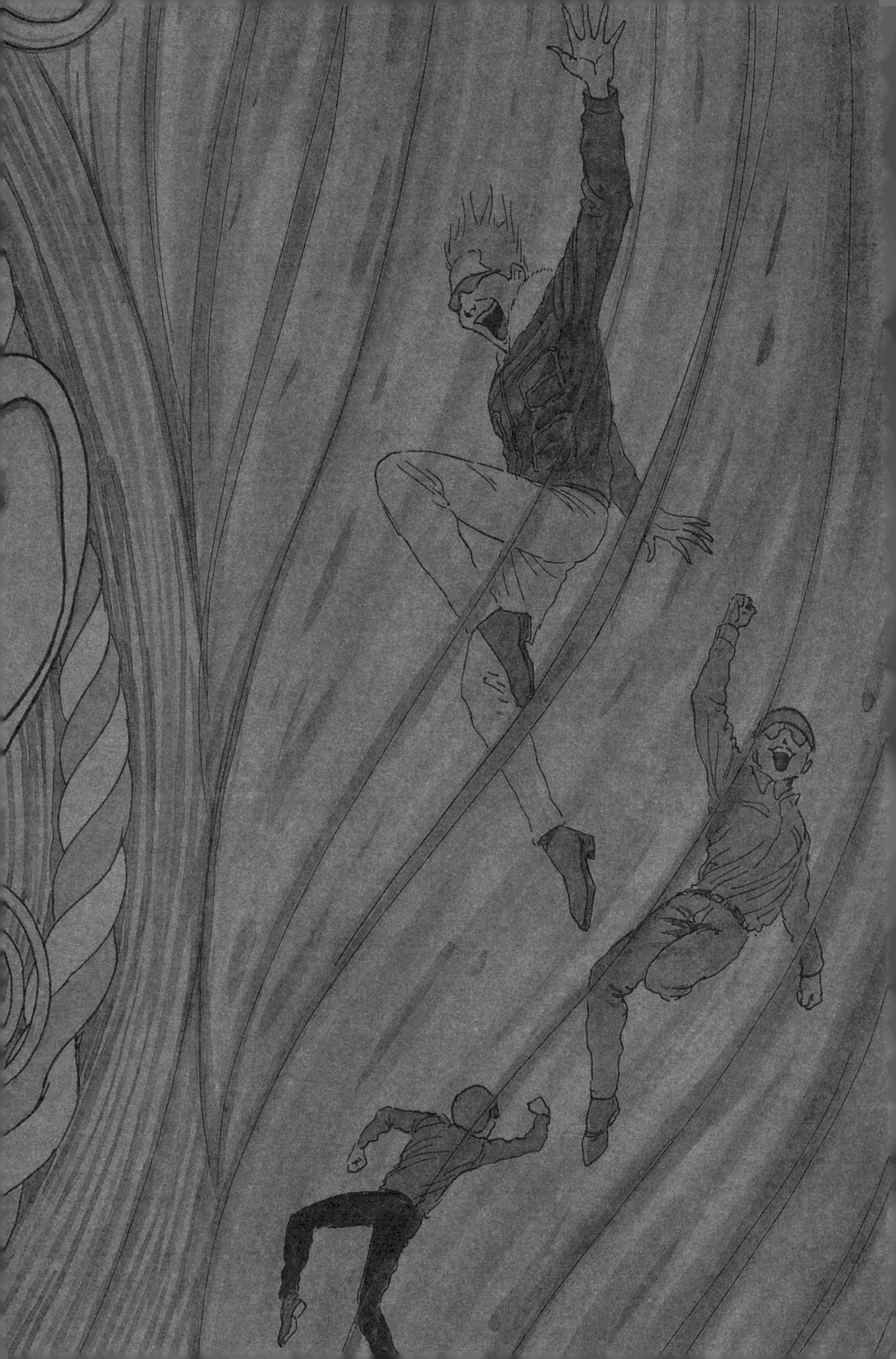

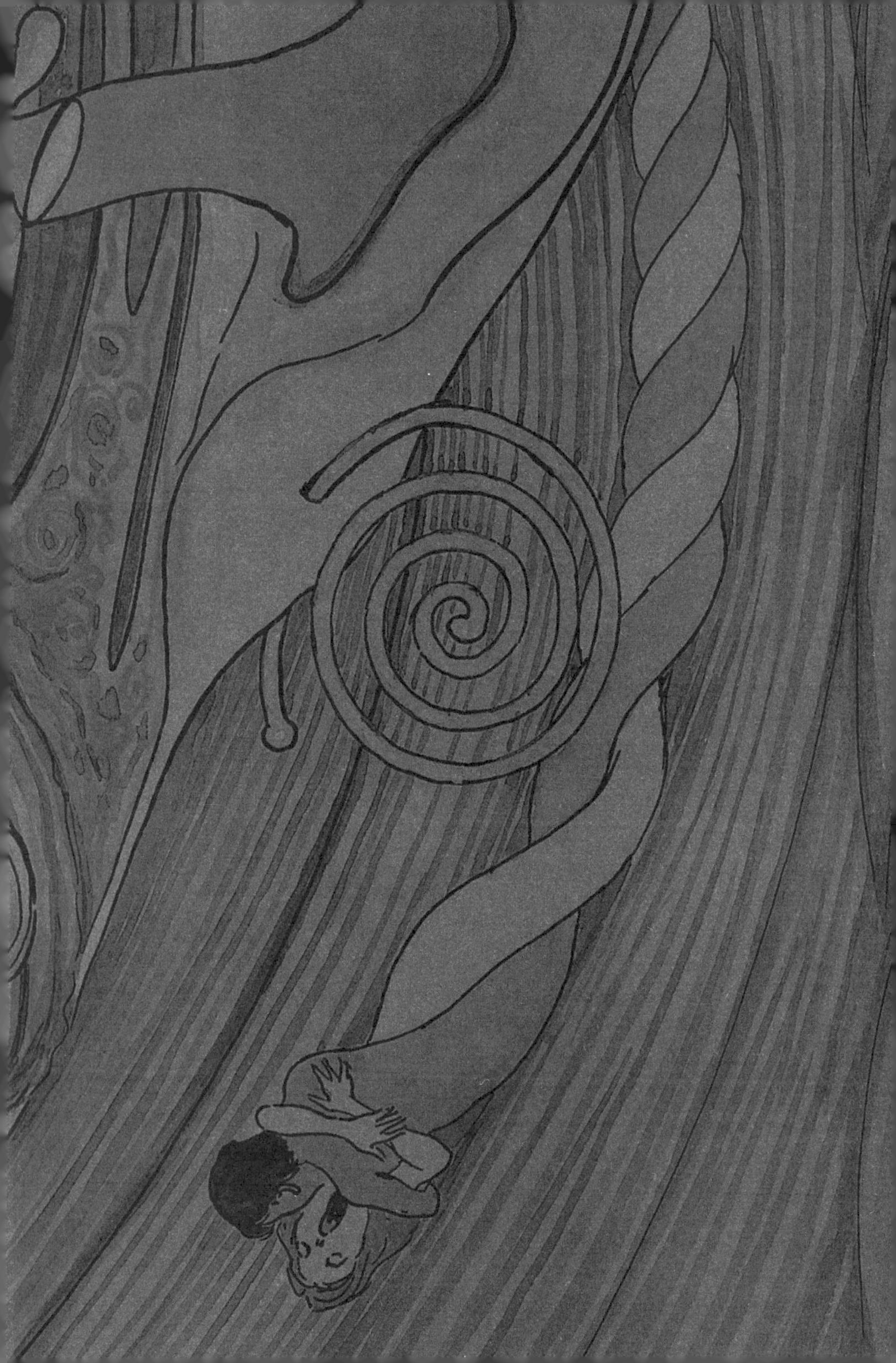

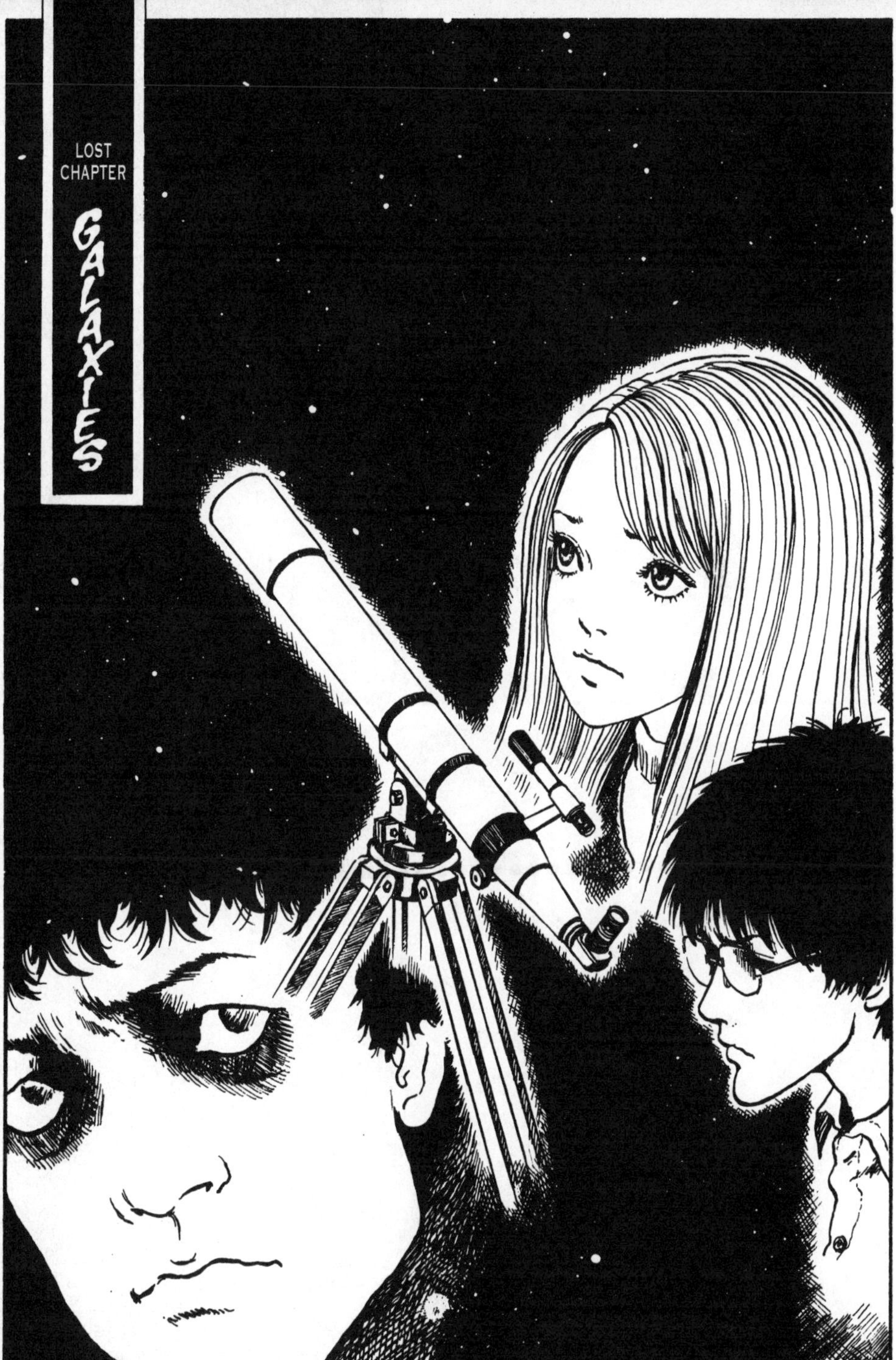
LOST
CHAPTER
GALAXIES

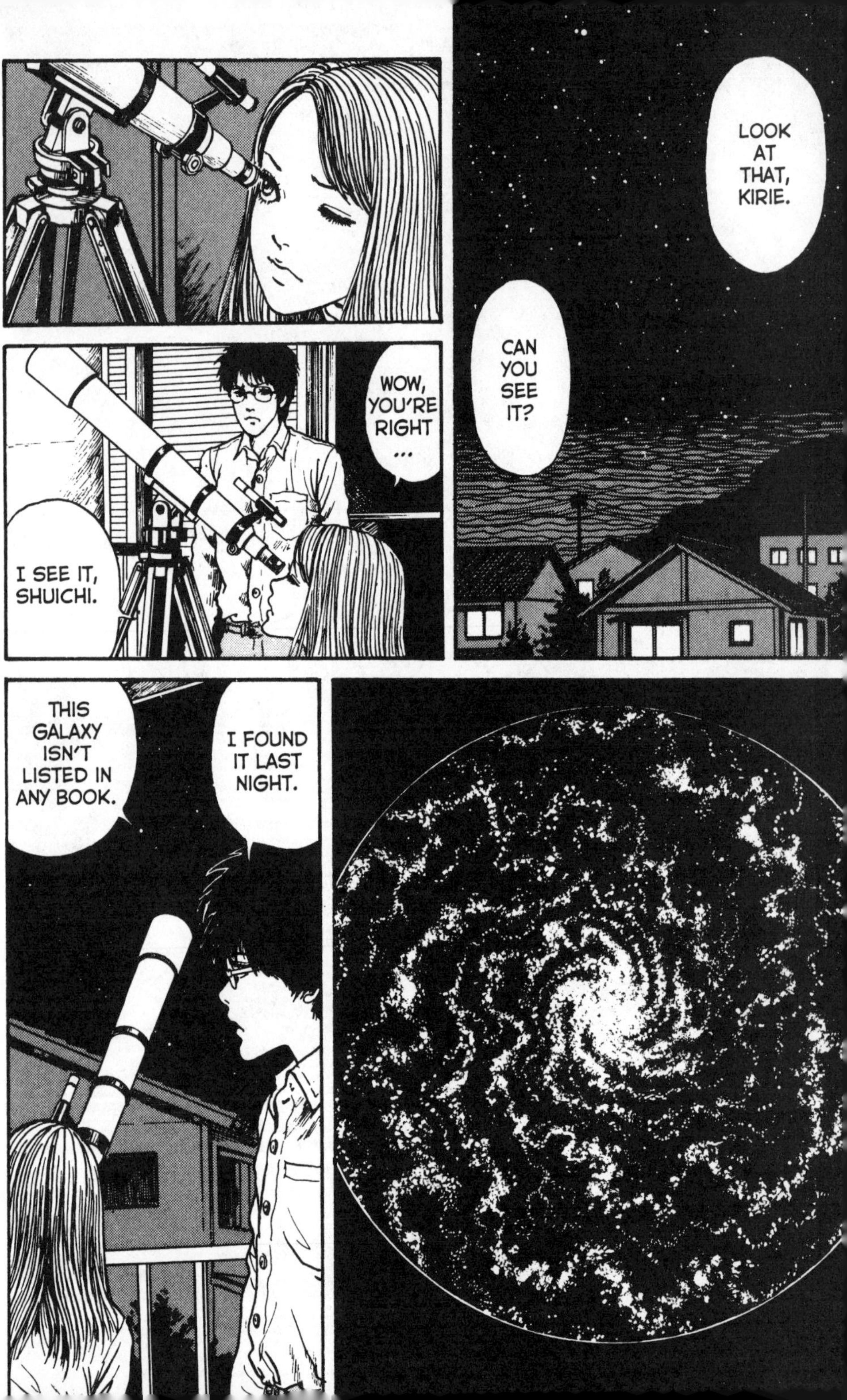
LOOK AT THAT, KIRIE.
CAN YOU SEE IT?
WOW, YOU'RE RIGHT ...
I SEE IT, SHUICHI.
I FOUND IT LAST NIGHT.
THIS GALAXY ISN'T LISTED IN ANY BOOK.

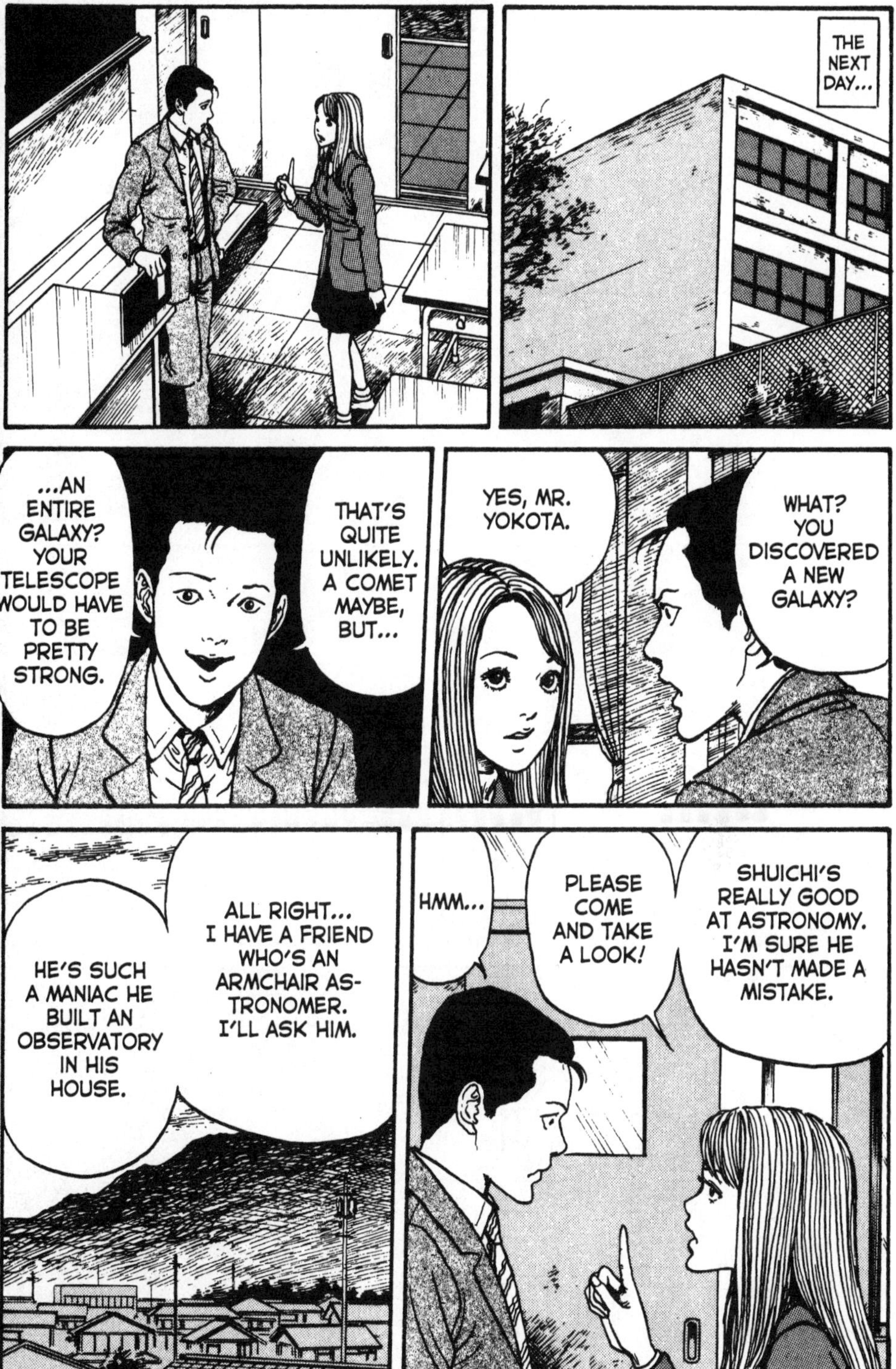
THE NEXT DAY...
WHAT? YOU DISCOVERED A NEW GALAXY?
YES, MR. YOKOTA.
THAT'S QUITE UNLIKELY. A COMET MAYBE, BUT...
...AN ENTIRE GALAXY? YOUR TELESCOPE WOULD HAVE TO BE PRETTY STRONG.
SHUICHI'S REALLY GOOD AT ASTRONOMY. I'M SURE HE HASN'T MADE A MISTAKE.
PLEASE COME AND TAKE A LOOK!
HMM...
ALL RIGHT... I HAVE A FRIEND WHO'S AN ARMCHAIR AS-TRONOMER. I'LL ASK HIM.
HE'S SUCH A MANIAC HE BUILT AN OBSERVATORY IN HIS HOUSE.

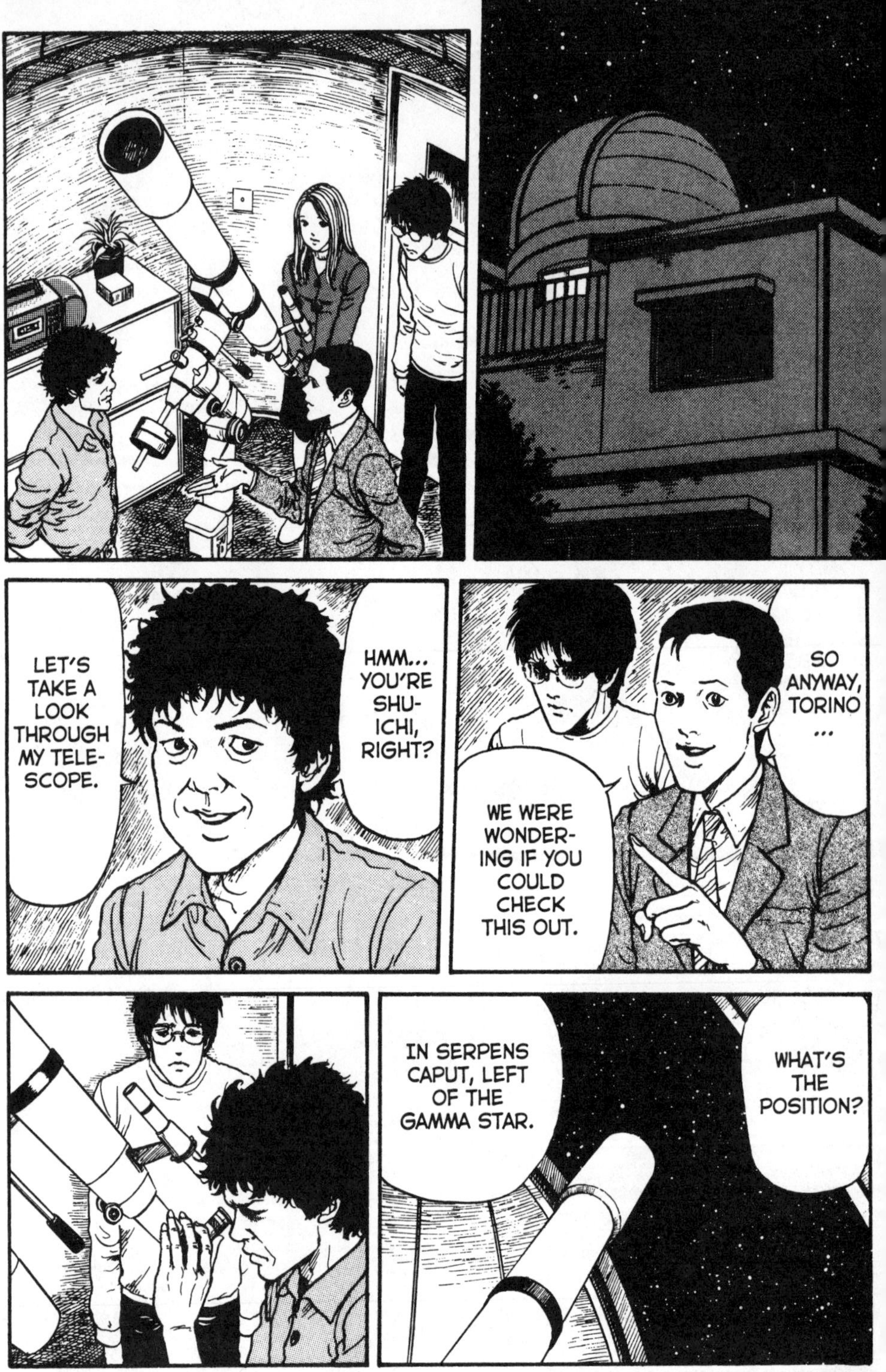
SO ANYWAY, TORINO ...
WE WERE WONDERING IF YOU COULD CHECK THIS OUT.
HMM... YOU'RE SHUICHI, RIGHT?
LET'S TAKE A LOOK THROUGH MY TELESCOPE.
WHAT'S THE POSITION?
IN SERPENS CAPUT, LEFT OF THE GAMMA STAR.

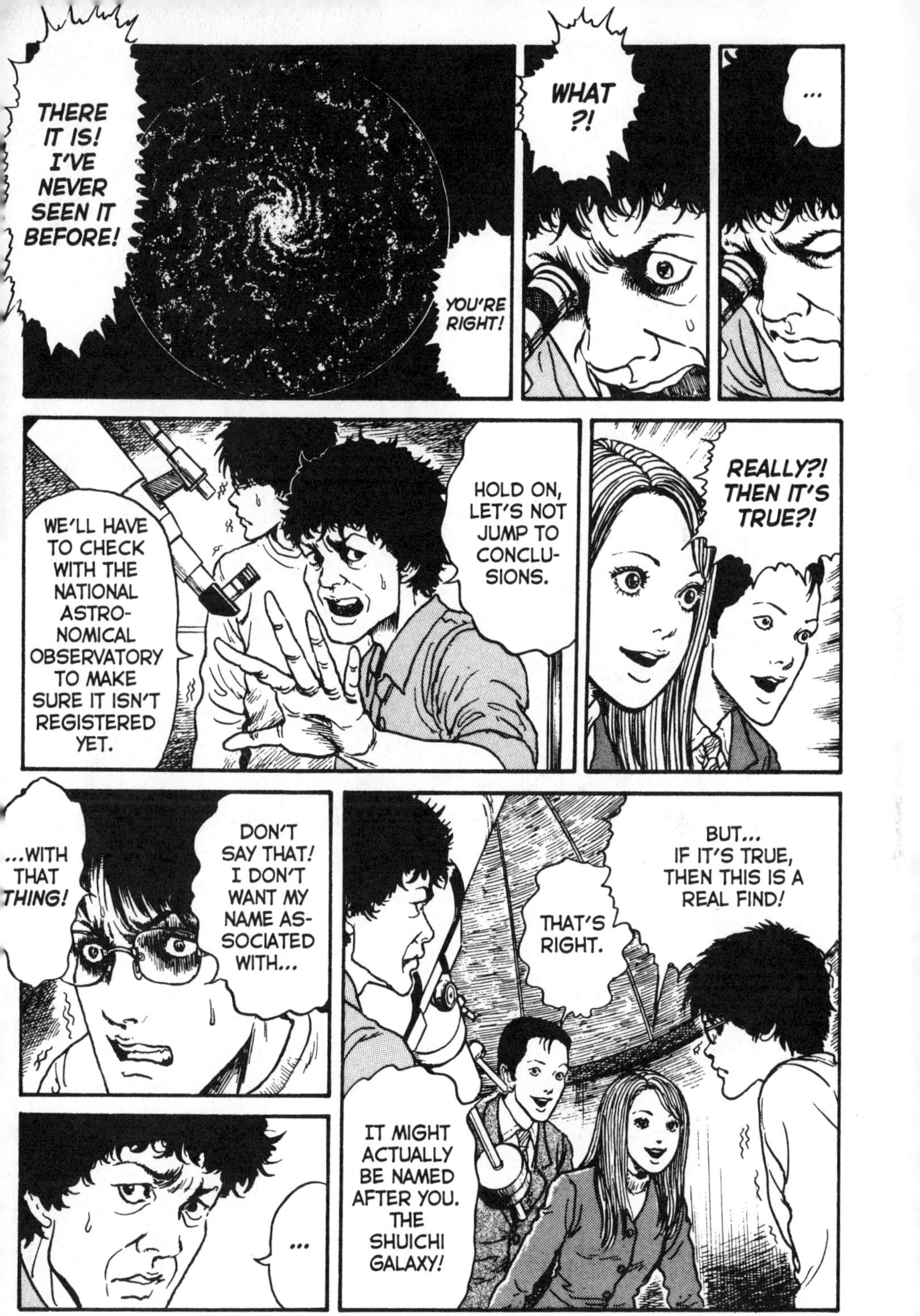
...
WHAT?!
THERE IT IS! I'VE NEVER SEEN IT BEFORE!
YOU'RE RIGHT!
REALLY?! THEN IT'S TRUE?!
HOLD ON, LET'S NOT JUMP TO CONCLU-SIONS.
WE'LL HAVE TO CHECK WITH THE NATIONAL ASTRO-NOMICAL OBSERVATORY TO MAKE SURE IT ISN'T REGISTERED YET.
BUT... IF IT'S TRUE, THEN THIS IS A REAL FIND!
THAT'S RIGHT.
IT MIGHT ACTUALLY BE NAMED AFTER YOU. THE SHUICHI GALAXY!
DON'T SAY THAT! I DON'T WANT MY NAME AS-SOCIATED WITH...
...WITH THAT THING!
...

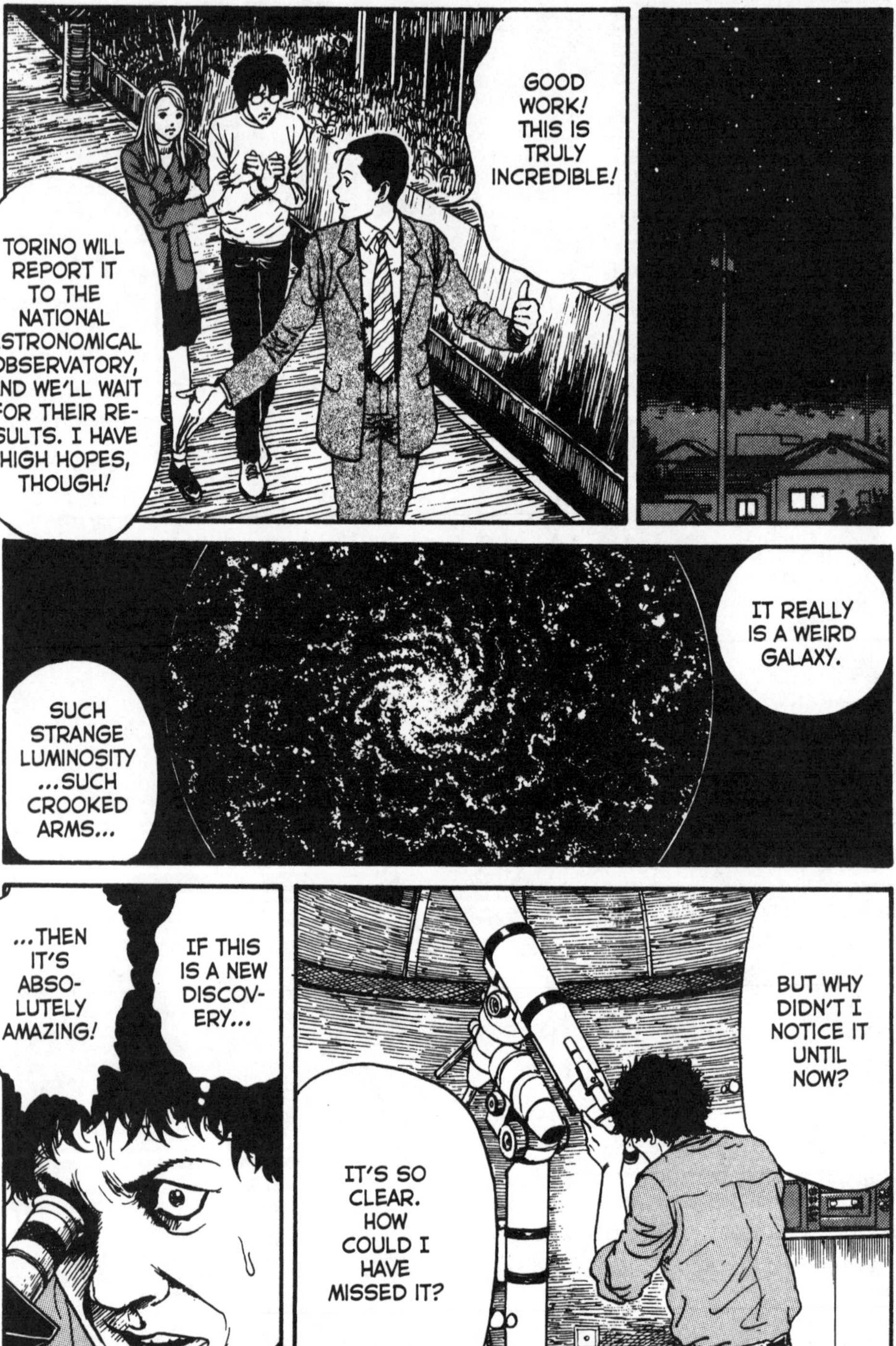
GOOD WORK! THIS IS TRULY INCREDIBLE!
TORINO WILL REPORT IT TO THE NATIONAL ASTRONOMICAL OBSERVATORY, AND WE'LL WAIT FOR THEIR RESULTS. I HAVE HIGH HOPES, THOUGH!
IT REALLY IS A WEIRD GALAXY.
SUCH STRANGE LUMINOSITY ...SUCH CROOKED ARMS...
BUT WHY DIDN'T I NOTICE IT UNTIL NOW?
IT'S SO CLEAR. HOW COULD I HAVE MISSED IT?
IF THIS IS A NEW DISCOVERY...
...THEN IT'S ABSOLUTELY AMAZING!

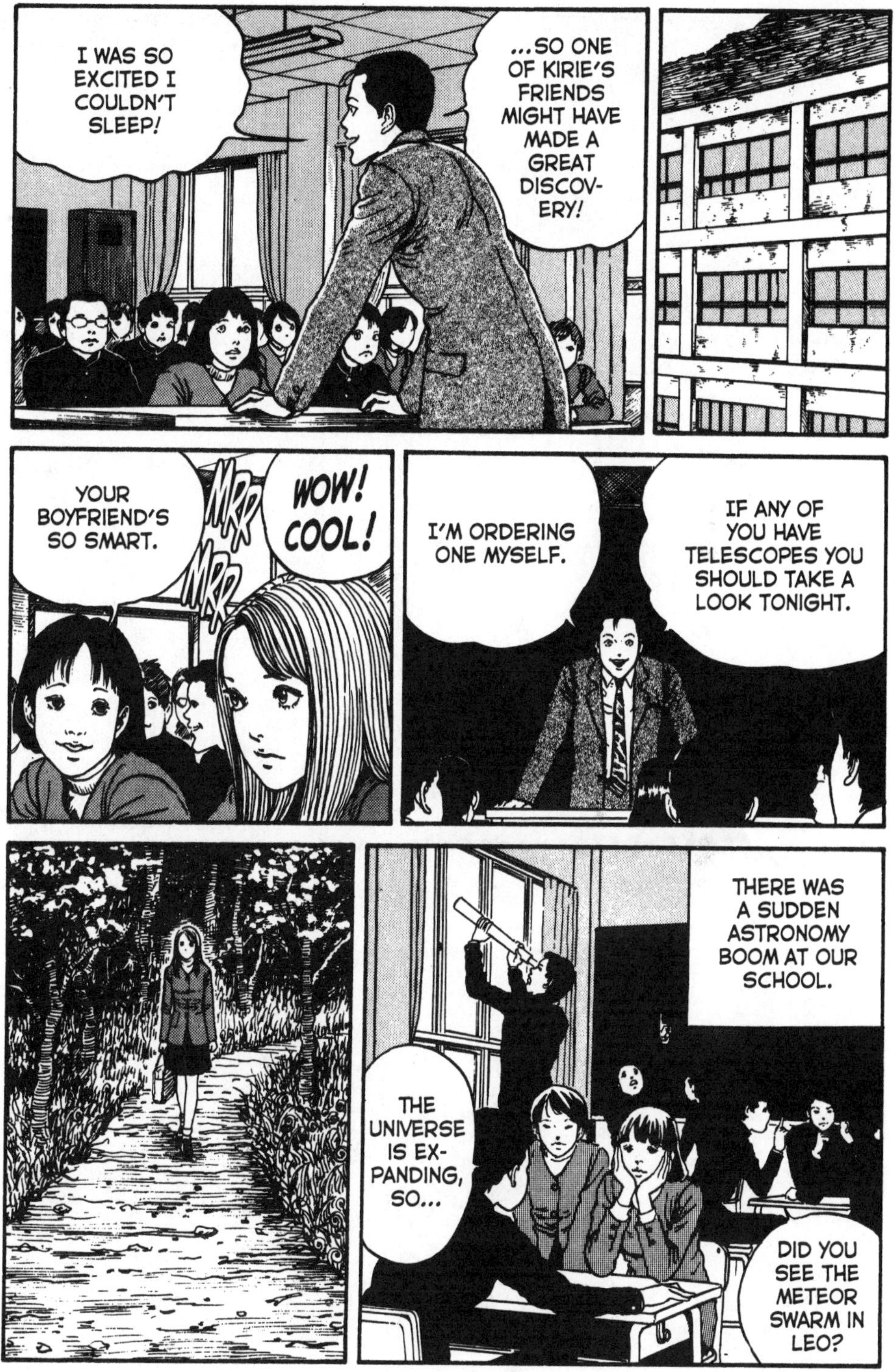
...SO ONE OF KIRIE'S FRIENDS MIGHT HAVE MADE A GREAT DISCOV-ERY!
I WAS SO EXCITED I COULDN'T SLEEP!
IF ANY OF YOU HAVE TELESCOPES YOU SHOULD TAKE A LOOK TONIGHT.
I'M ORDERING ONE MYSELF.
WOW! COOL!
MRR MRR
YOUR BOYFRIEND'S SO SMART.
THERE WAS A SUDDEN ASTRONOMY BOOM AT OUR SCHOOL.
THE UNIVERSE IS EX-PANDING, SO...
DID YOU SEE THE METEOR SWARM IN LEO?

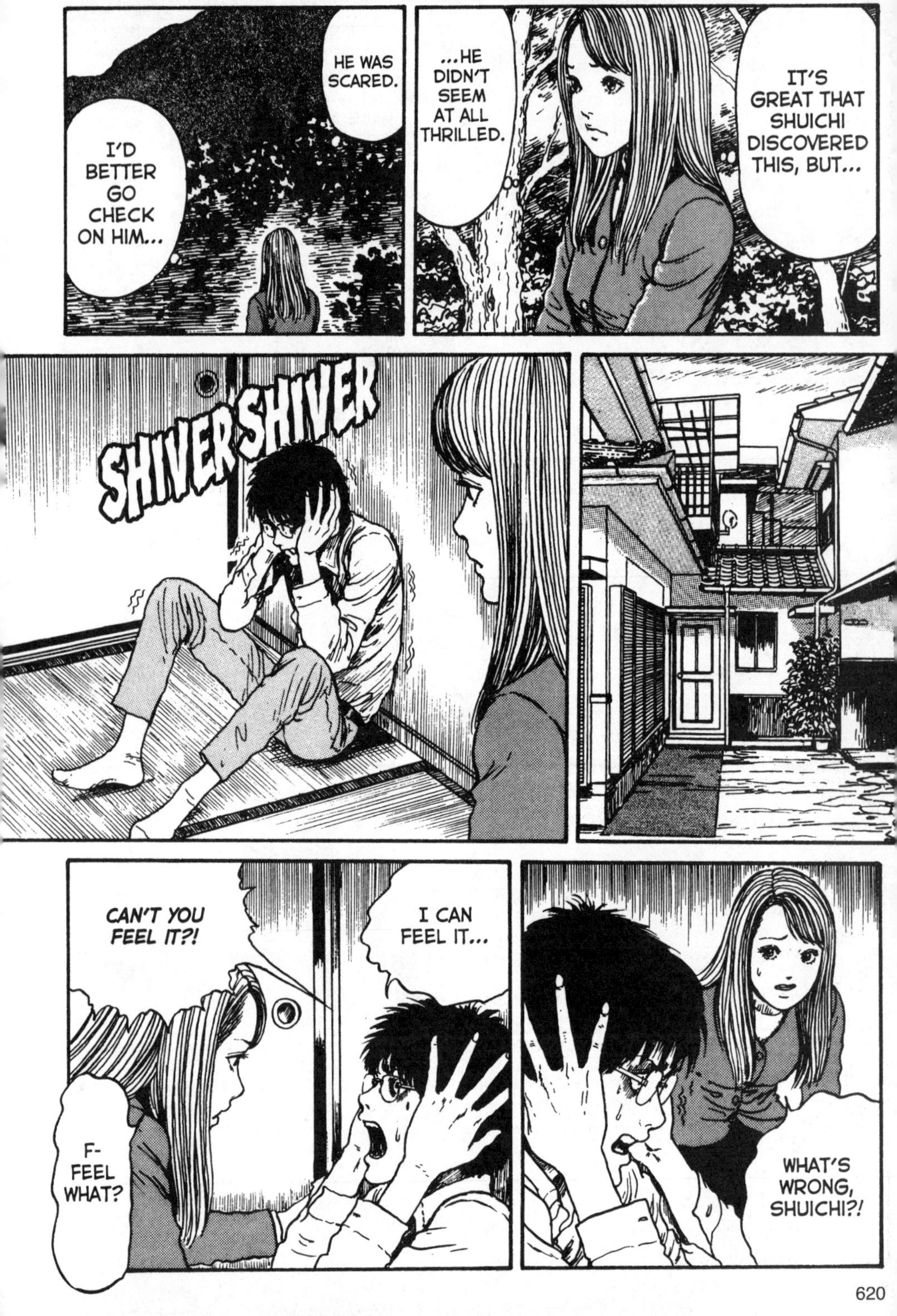
IT'S GREAT THAT SHUICHI DISCOVERED THIS, BUT...
...HE DIDN'T SEEM AT ALL THRILLED.
HE WAS SCARED.
I'D BETTER GO CHECK ON HIM...
SHIVER SHIVER
WHAT'S WRONG, SHUICHI?!
I CAN FEEL IT...
CAN'T YOU FEEL IT?!
F-FEEL WHAT?

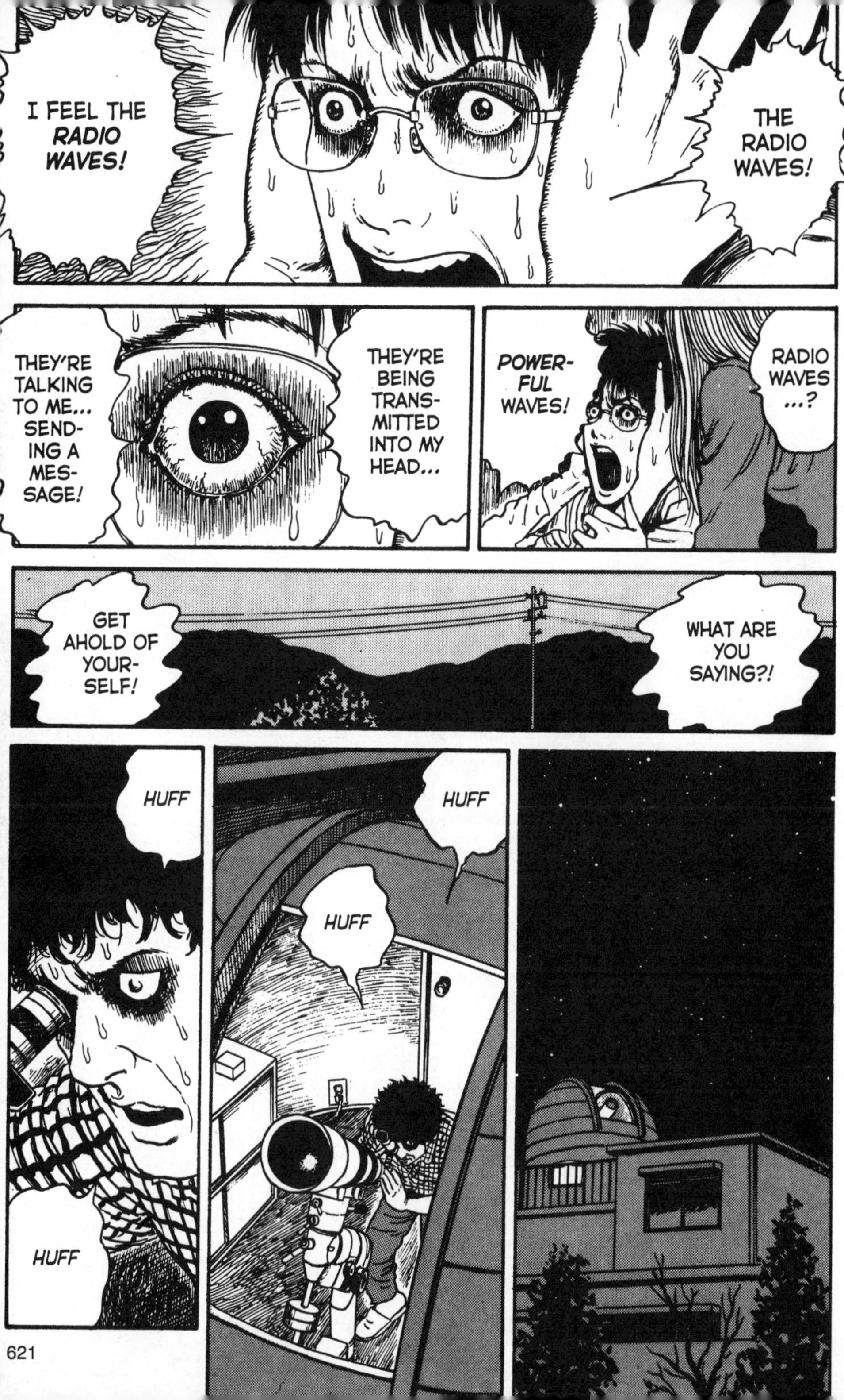

THE RADIO WAVES!
I FEEL THE RADIO WAVES!
RADIO WAVES ...?
POWERFUL WAVES!
THEY'RE BEING TRANSMITTED INTO MY HEAD...
THEY'RE TALKING TO ME... SENDING A MESSAGE!
WHAT ARE YOU SAYING?!
GET AHOLD OF YOURSELF!
HUFF
HUFF
HUFF
HUFF

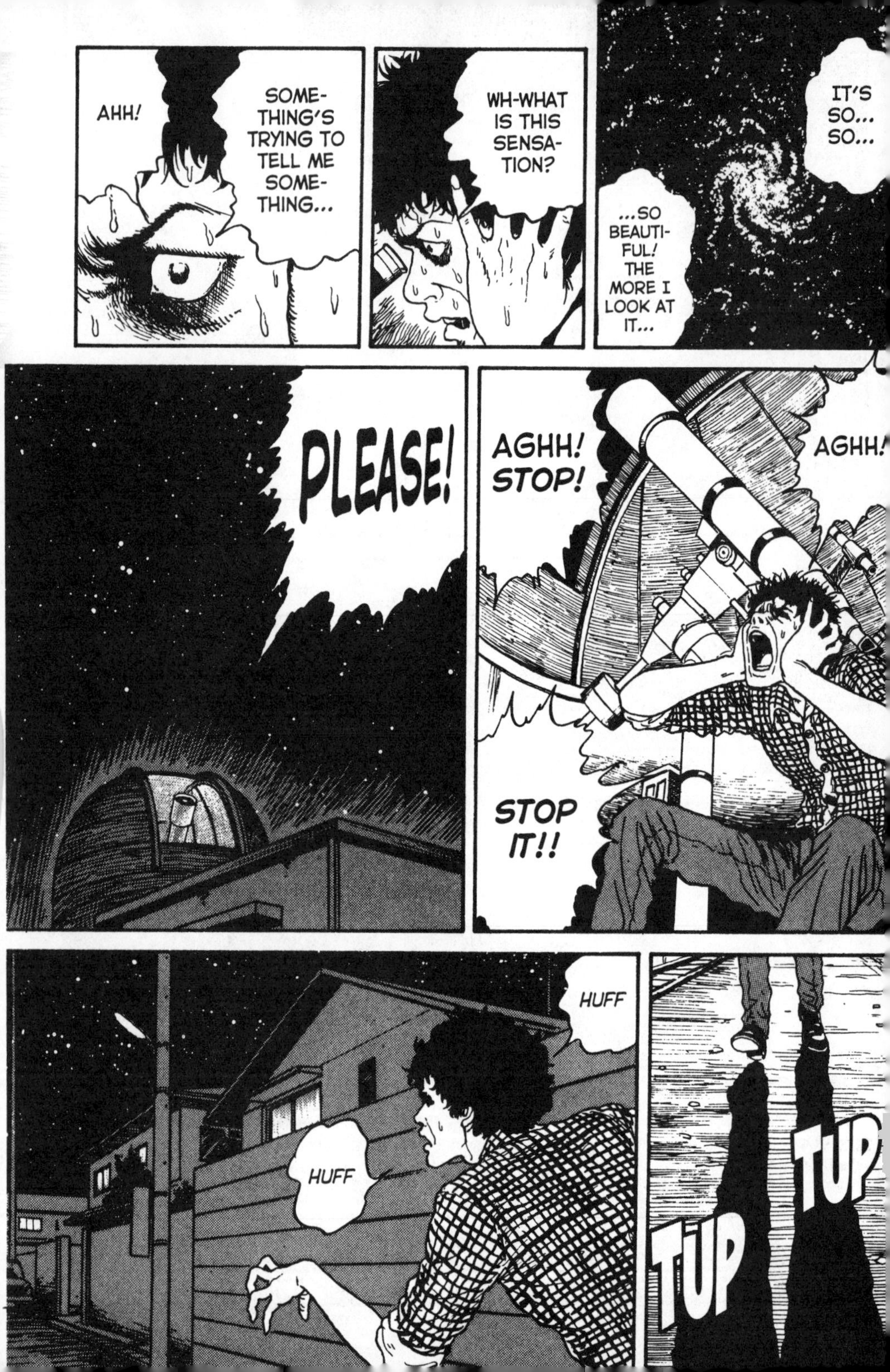
IT'S SO... SO...
...SO BEAUTI-FUL! THE MORE I LOOK AT IT...
WH-WHAT IS THIS SENSA-TION?
SOME-THING'S TRYING TO TELL ME SOME-THING...
AHH!
AGHH!
AGHH! STOP!
STOP IT!!
PLEASE!
TUP
TUP
HUFF
HUFF

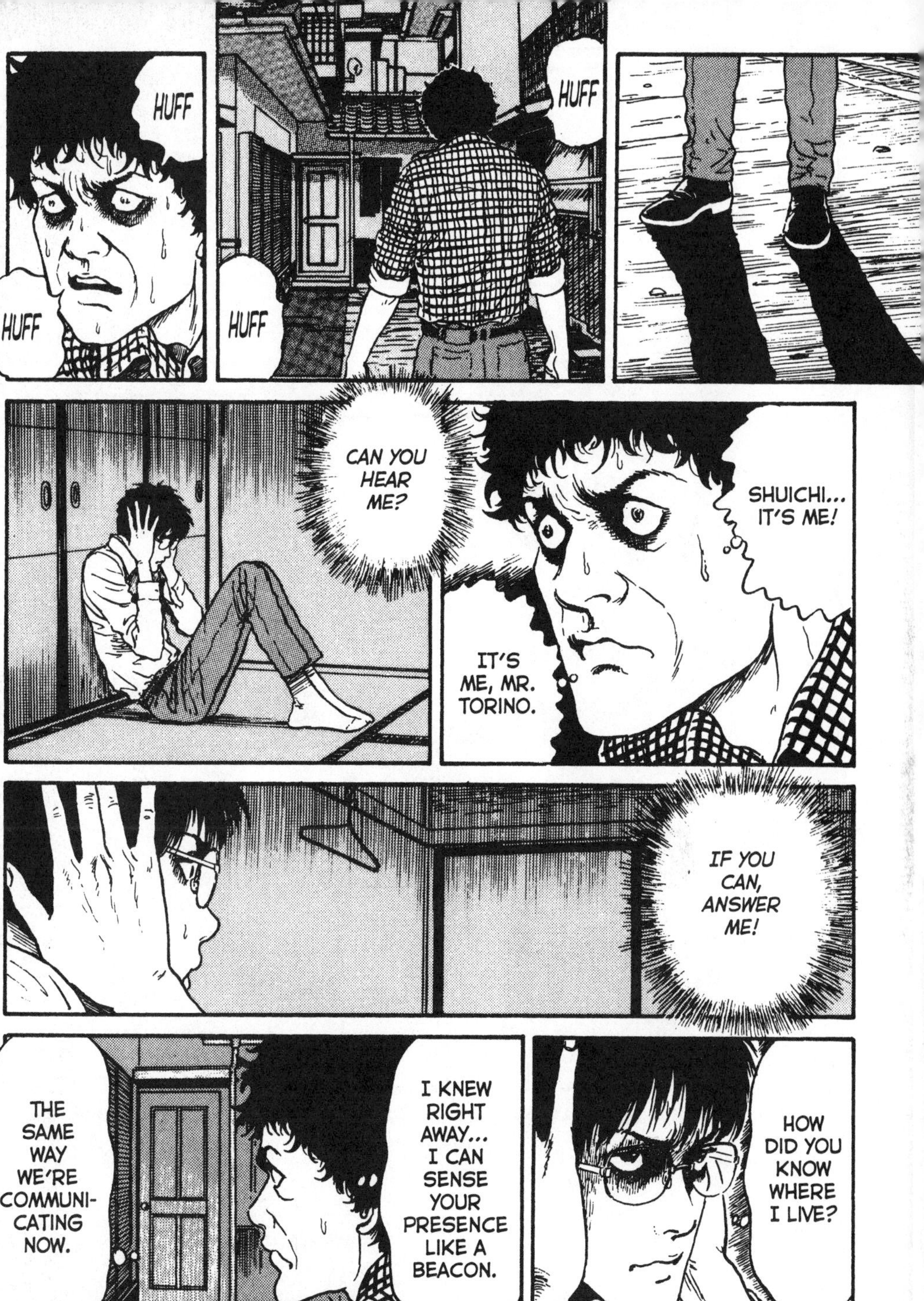
HUFF
HUFF
HUFF
HUFF
SHUICHI... IT'S ME!
IT'S ME, MR. TORINO.
CAN YOU HEAR ME?
IF YOU CAN, ANSWER ME!
HOW DID YOU KNOW WHERE I LIVE?
I KNEW RIGHT AWAY... I CAN SENSE YOUR PRESENCE LIKE A BEACON.
THE SAME WAY WE'RE COMMUNICATING NOW.

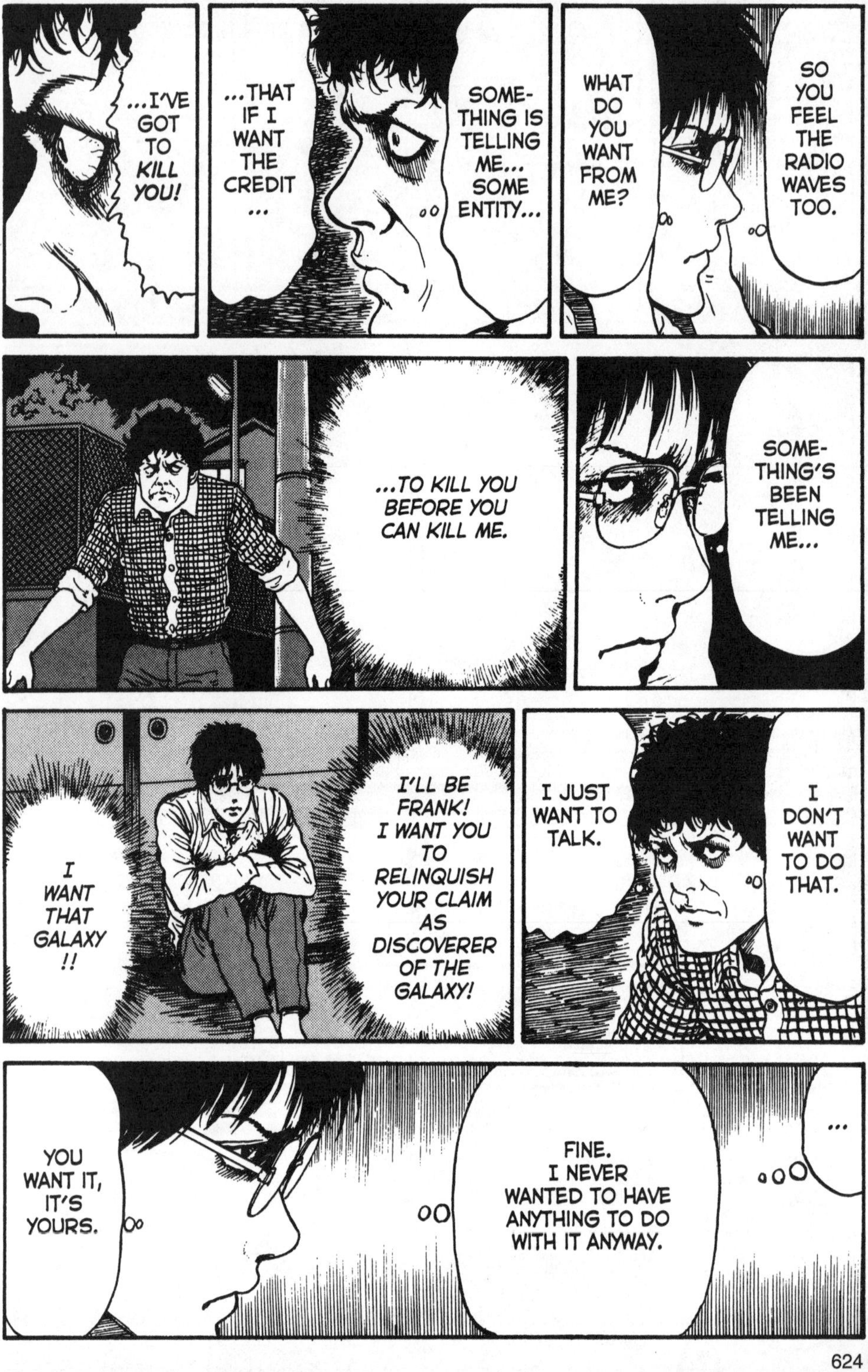
SO YOU FEEL THE RADIO WAVES TOO.
WHAT DO YOU WANT FROM ME?
SOME-THING IS TELLING ME... SOME ENTITY...
...THAT IF I WANT THE CREDIT ...
...I'VE GOT TO KILL YOU!
SOME-THING'S BEEN TELLING ME...
...TO KILL YOU BEFORE YOU CAN KILL ME.
I DON'T WANT TO DO THAT.
I JUST WANT TO TALK.
I'LL BE FRANK! I WANT YOU TO RELINQUISH YOUR CLAIM AS DISCOVERER OF THE GALAXY!
I WANT THAT GALAXY !!
...
FINE. I NEVER WANTED TO HAVE ANYTHING TO DO WITH IT ANYWAY.
YOU WANT IT, IT'S YOURS.

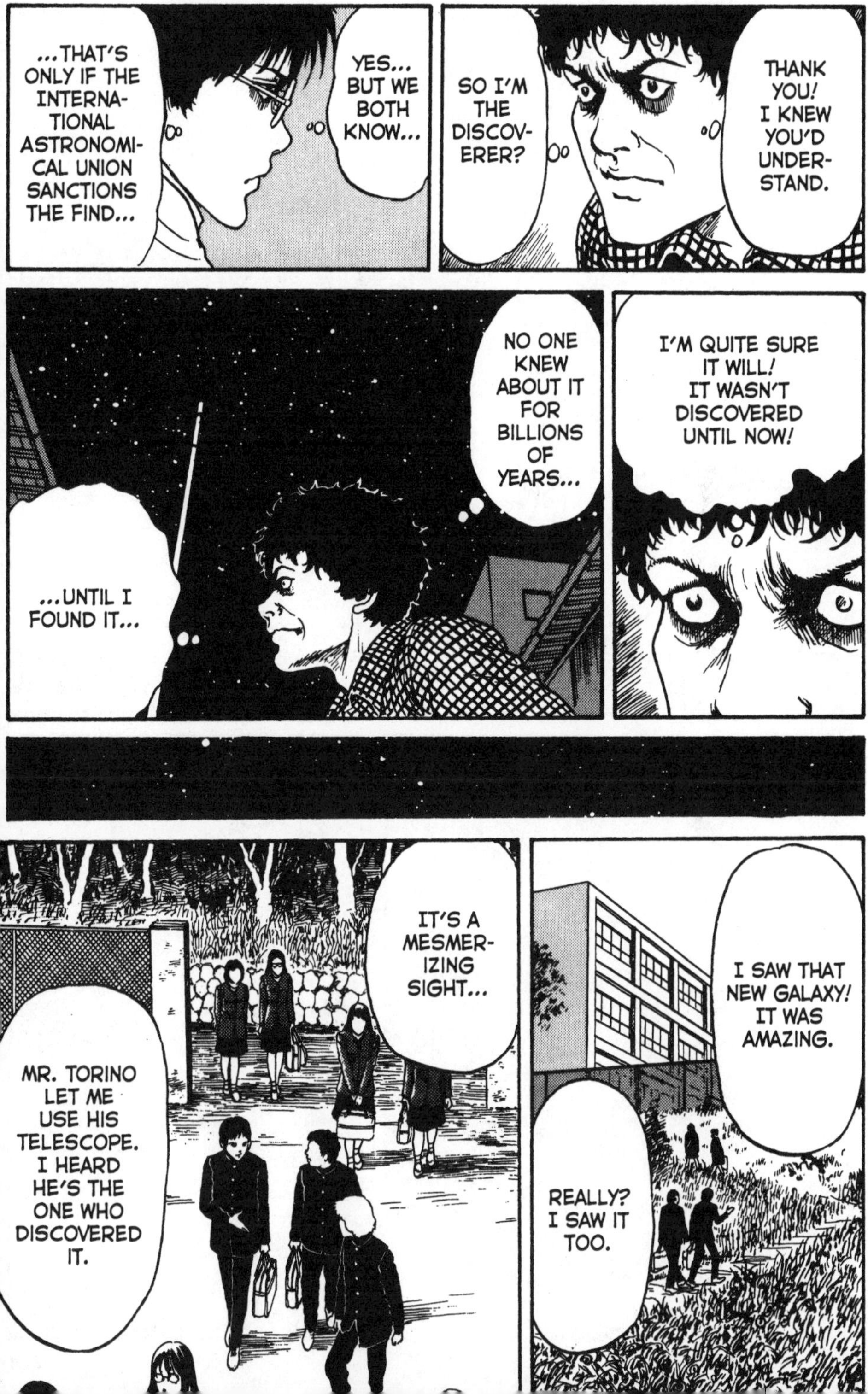
THANK YOU! I KNEW YOU'D UNDERSTAND.
SO I'M THE DISCOVERER?
YES... BUT WE BOTH KNOW...
...THAT'S ONLY IF THE INTERNATIONAL ASTRONOMICAL UNION SANCTIONS THE FIND...
I'M QUITE SURE IT WILL! IT WASN'T DISCOVERED UNTIL NOW!
NO ONE KNEW ABOUT IT FOR BILLIONS OF YEARS...
...UNTIL I FOUND IT...
I SAW THAT NEW GALAXY! IT WAS AMAZING.
REALLY? I SAW IT TOO.
IT'S A MESMERIZING SIGHT...
MR. TORINO LET ME USE HIS TELESCOPE. I HEARD HE'S THE ONE WHO DISCOVERED IT.

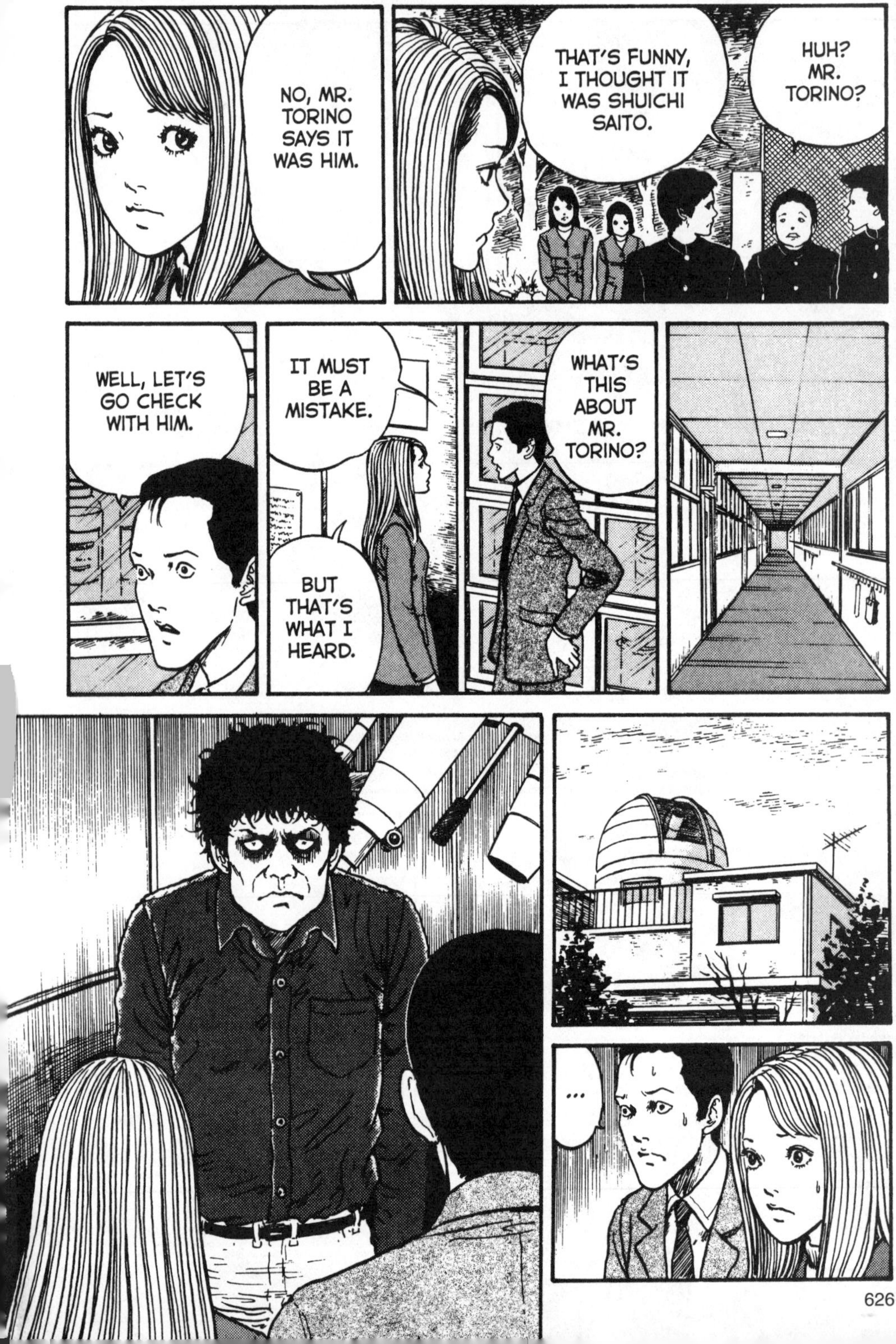
HUH? MR. TORINO?
THAT'S FUNNY, I THOUGHT IT WAS SHUICHI SAITO.
NO, MR. TORINO SAYS IT WAS HIM.
WHAT'S THIS ABOUT MR. TORINO?
IT MUST BE A MISTAKE.
BUT THAT'S WHAT I HEARD.
WELL, LET'S GO CHECK WITH HIM.
...

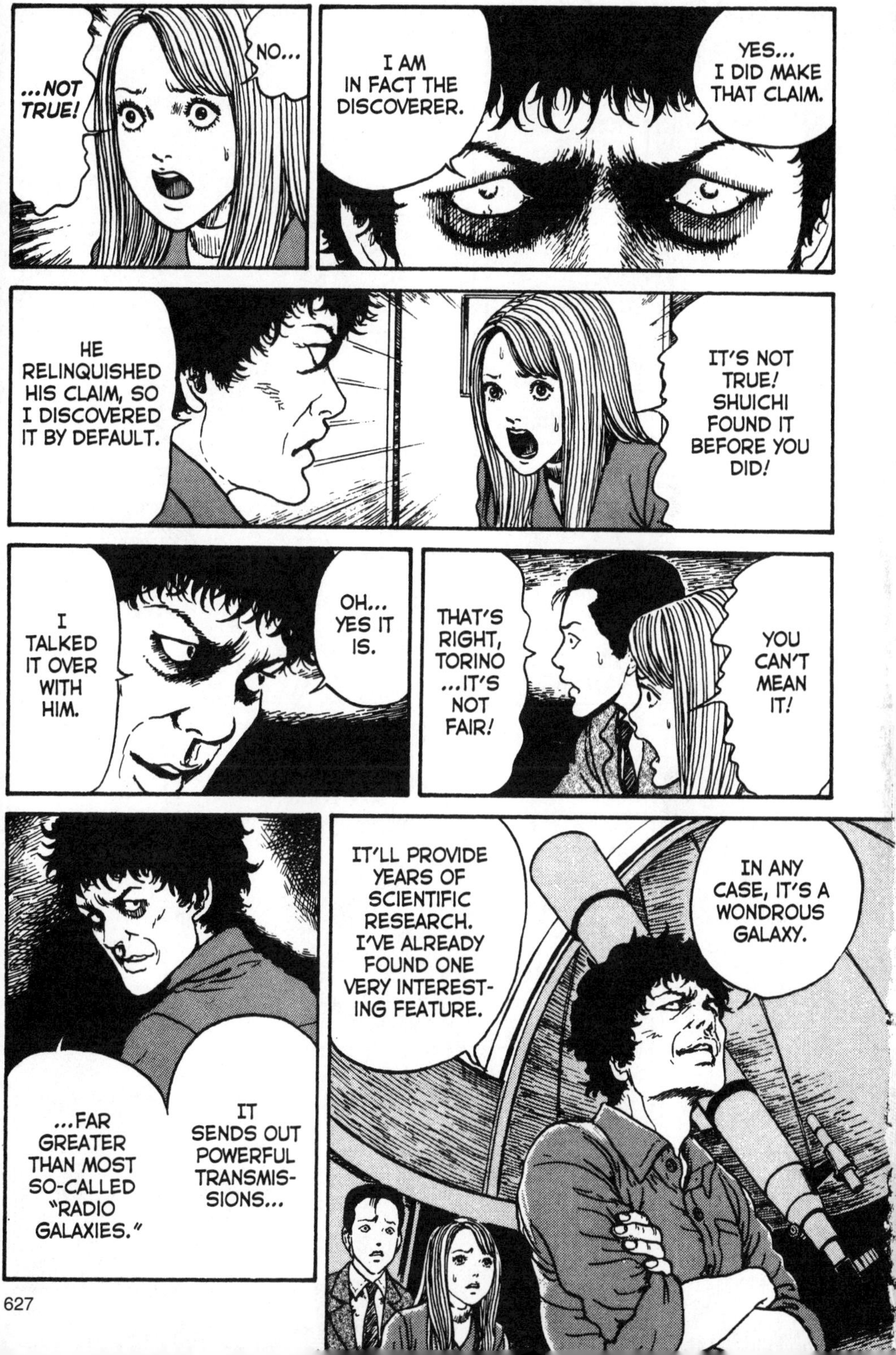
YES... I DID MAKE THAT CLAIM.
I AM IN FACT THE DISCOVERER.
NO...
...NOT TRUE!
IT'S NOT TRUE! SHUICHI FOUND IT BEFORE YOU DID!
HE RELINQUISHED HIS CLAIM, SO I DISCOVERED IT BY DEFAULT.
YOU CAN'T MEAN IT!
THAT'S RIGHT, TORINO ...IT'S NOT FAIR!
OH... YES IT IS.
I TALKED IT OVER WITH HIM.
IN ANY CASE, IT'S A WONDROUS GALAXY.
IT'LL PROVIDE YEARS OF SCIENTIFIC RESEARCH. I'VE ALREADY FOUND ONE VERY INTEREST-ING FEATURE.
IT SENDS OUT POWERFUL TRANSMIS-SIONS...
...FAR GREATER THAN MOST SO-CALLED "RADIO GALAXIES."

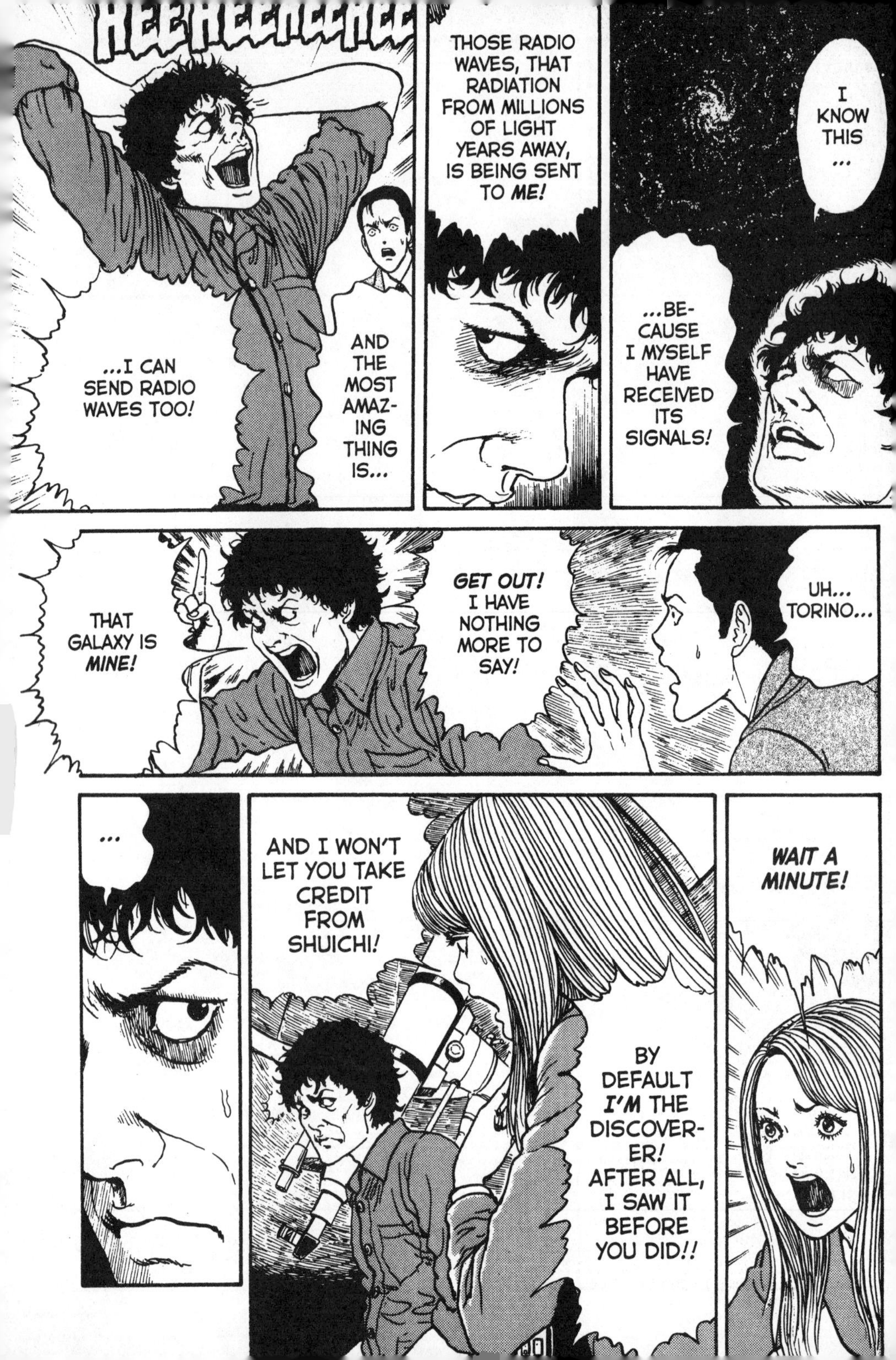
I KNOW THIS ...
...BE- CAUSE I MYSELF HAVE RECEIVED ITS SIGNALS!
THOSE RADIO WAVES, THAT RADIATION FROM MILLIONS OF LIGHT YEARS AWAY, IS BEING SENT TO *ME!*
HEEHEEHEEHEE
AND THE MOST AMAZ- ING THING IS...
...I CAN SEND RADIO WAVES TOO!
UH... TORINO...
GET OUT! I HAVE NOTHING MORE TO SAY!
THAT GALAXY IS *MINE!*
WAIT A MINUTE!
AND I WON'T LET YOU TAKE CREDIT FROM SHUICHI!
BY DEFAULT *I'M* THE DISCOVER- ER! AFTER ALL, I SAW IT BEFORE YOU DID!!
...

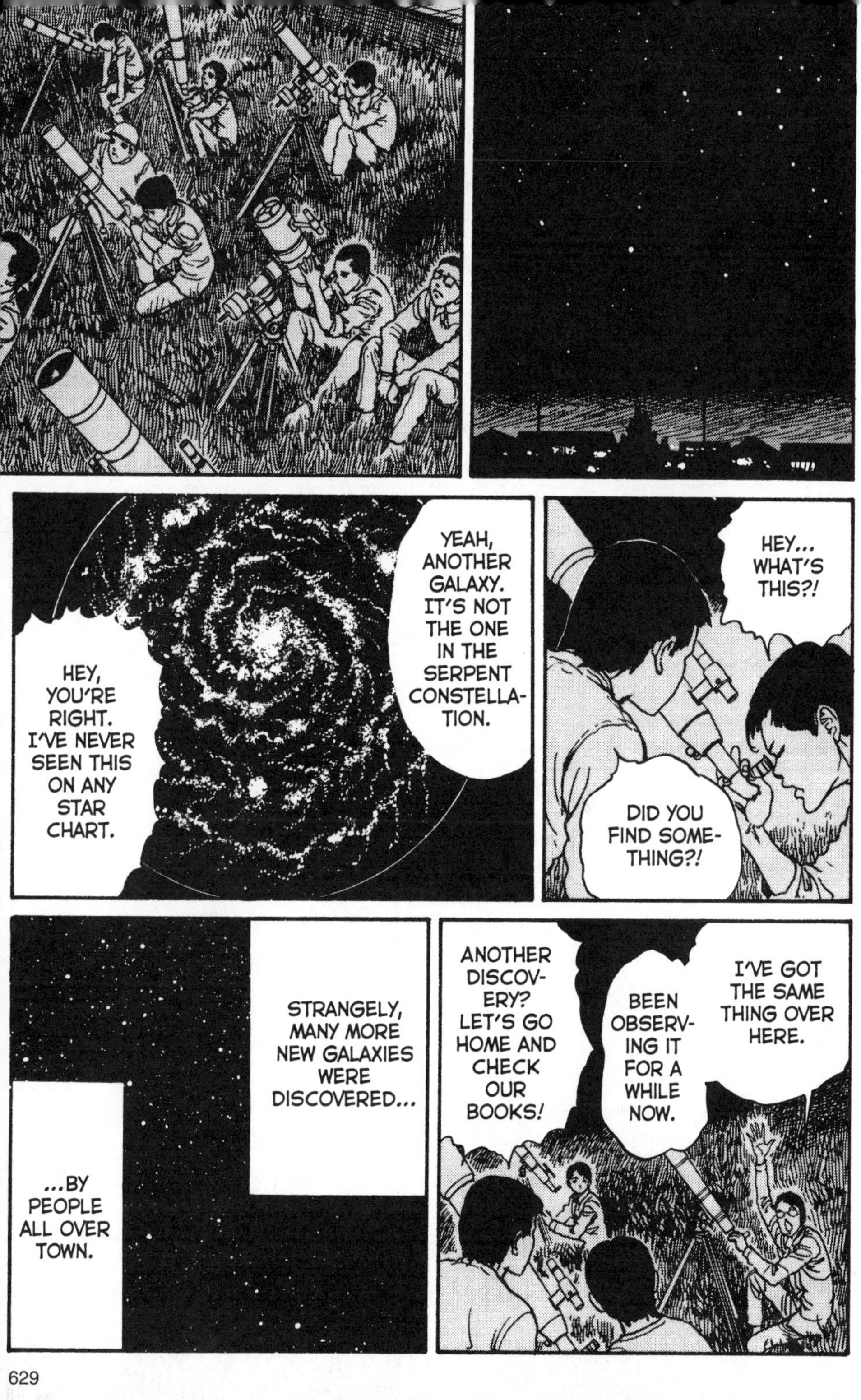
HEY... WHAT'S THIS?!
DID YOU FIND SOME-THING?!
YEAH, ANOTHER GALAXY. IT'S NOT THE ONE IN THE SERPENT CONSTELLA-TION.
HEY, YOU'RE RIGHT. I'VE NEVER SEEN THIS ON ANY STAR CHART.
I'VE GOT THE SAME THING OVER HERE.
BEEN OBSERV-ING IT FOR A WHILE NOW.
ANOTHER DISCOV-ERY? LET'S GO HOME AND CHECK OUR BOOKS!
STRANGELY, MANY MORE NEW GALAXIES WERE DISCOVERED...
...BY PEOPLE ALL OVER TOWN.

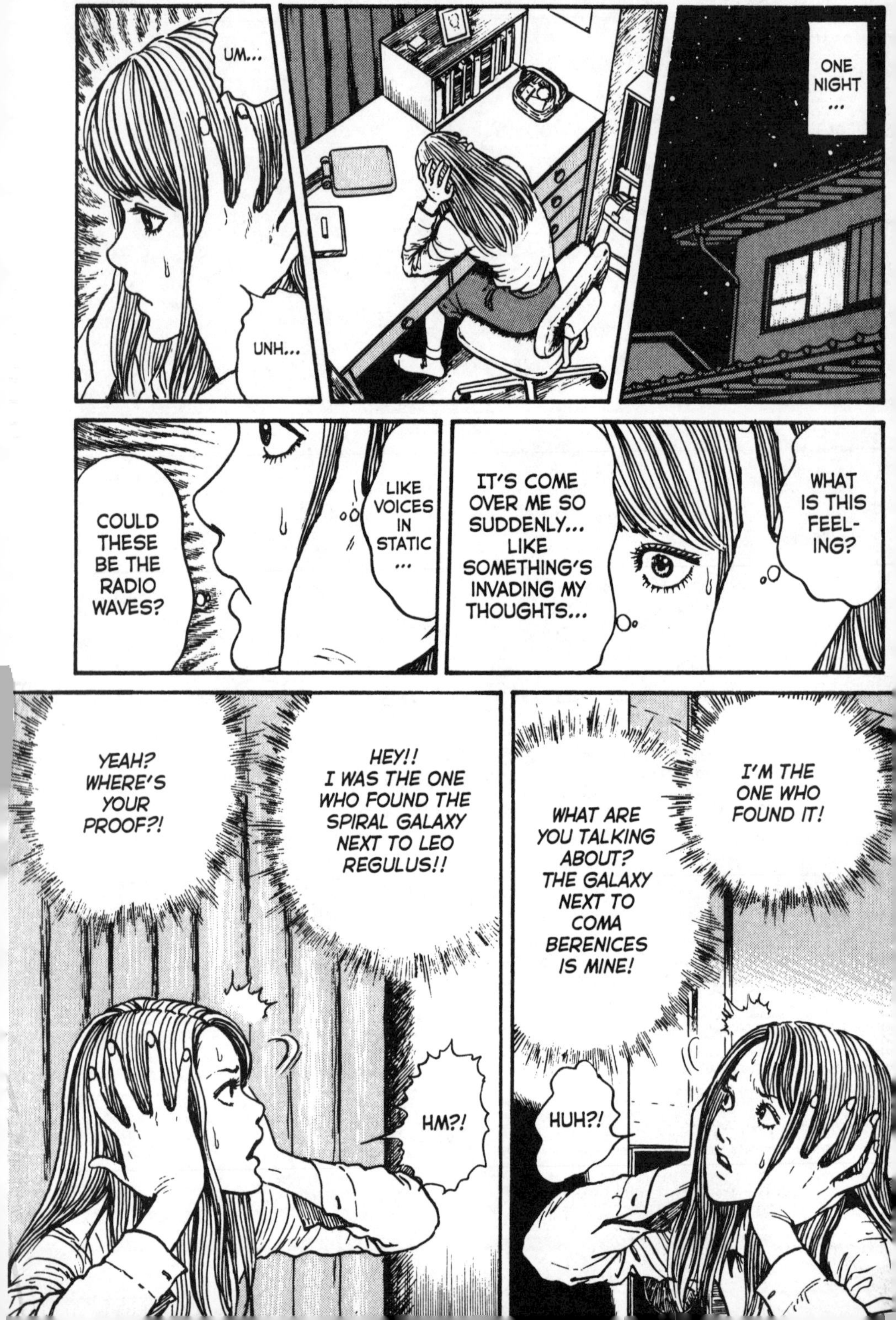
ONE NIGHT ...
UM...
UNH...
WHAT IS THIS FEEL-ING?
IT'S COME OVER ME SO SUDDENLY... LIKE SOMETHING'S INVADING MY THOUGHTS...
LIKE VOICES IN STATIC ...
COULD THESE BE THE RADIO WAVES?
I'M THE ONE WHO FOUND IT!
WHAT ARE YOU TALKING ABOUT? THE GALAXY NEXT TO COMA BERENICES IS MINE!
HUH?!
HEY!! I WAS THE ONE WHO FOUND THE SPIRAL GALAXY NEXT TO LEO REGULUS!!
YEAH? WHERE'S YOUR PROOF?!
HM?!

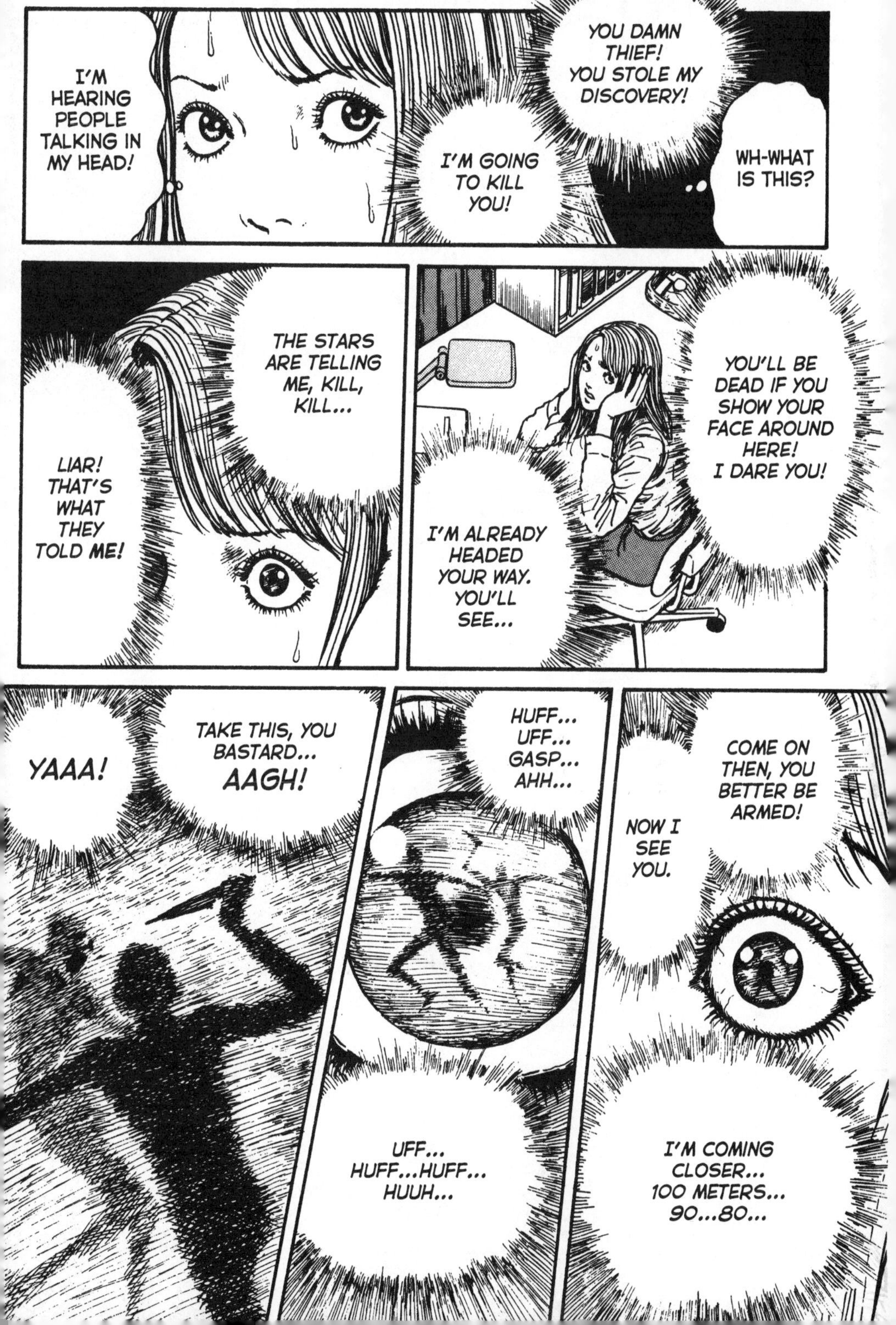
YOU DAMN THIEF! YOU STOLE MY DISCOVERY!
WH-WHAT IS THIS?
I'M GOING TO KILL YOU!
I'M HEARING PEOPLE TALKING IN MY HEAD!
YOU'LL BE DEAD IF YOU SHOW YOUR FACE AROUND HERE! I DARE YOU!
I'M ALREADY HEADED YOUR WAY. YOU'LL SEE...
THE STARS ARE TELLING ME, KILL, KILL...
LIAR! THAT'S WHAT THEY TOLD ME!
COME ON THEN, YOU BETTER BE ARMED!
NOW I SEE YOU.
I'M COMING CLOSER... 100 METERS... 90...80...
HUFF... UFF... GASP... AHH...
UFF... HUFF...HUFF... HUUH...
TAKE THIS, YOU BASTARD... AAGH!
YAAA!

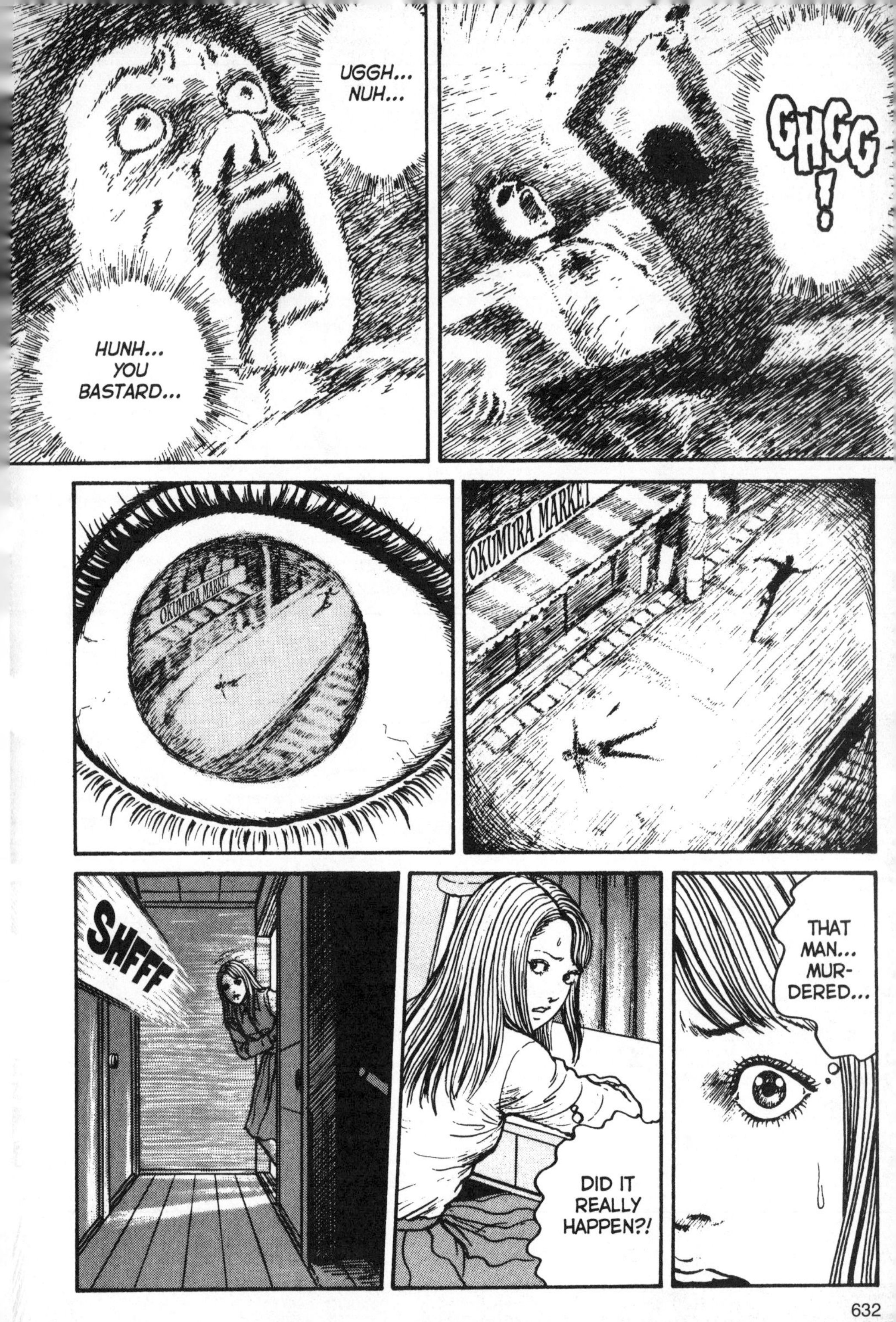
GHGG!
UGGH... NUH...
HUNH... YOU BASTARD...
OKUMURA MARKET
OKUMURA MARKET
THAT MAN... MUR-DERED...
DID IT REALLY HAPPEN?!
SHFFF

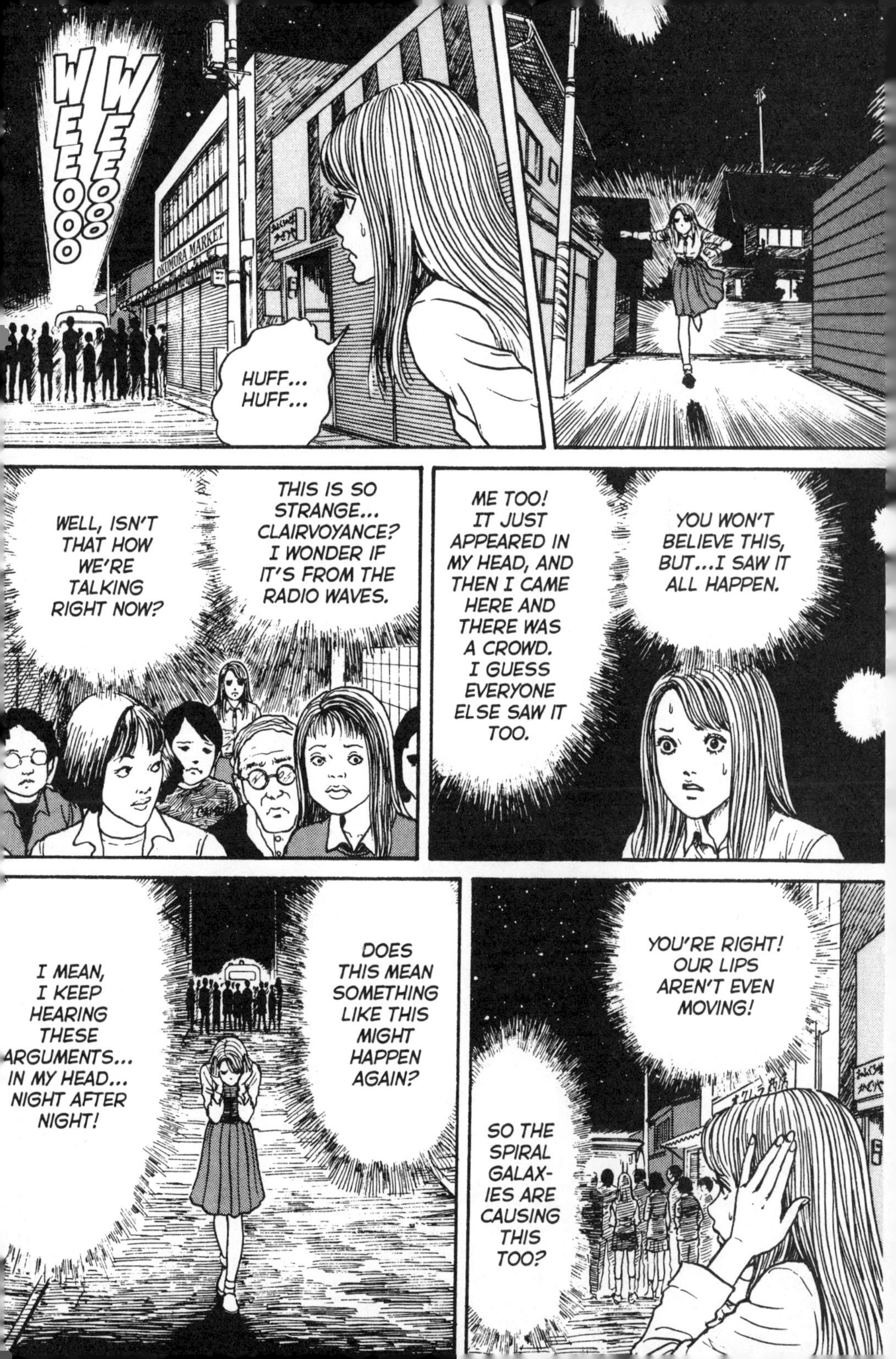
WEEEOOO
WEEEOOO
OKUMURA MARKET
HUFF... HUFF...
YOU WON'T BELIEVE THIS, BUT...I SAW IT ALL HAPPEN.
ME TOO! IT JUST APPEARED IN MY HEAD, AND THEN I CAME HERE AND THERE WAS A CROWD. I GUESS EVERYONE ELSE SAW IT TOO.
THIS IS SO STRANGE... CLAIRVOYANCE? I WONDER IF IT'S FROM THE RADIO WAVES.
WELL, ISN'T THAT HOW WE'RE TALKING RIGHT NOW?
YOU'RE RIGHT! OUR LIPS AREN'T EVEN MOVING!
SO THE SPIRAL GALAX-IES ARE CAUSING THIS TOO?
DOES THIS MEAN SOMETHING LIKE THIS MIGHT HAPPEN AGAIN?
I MEAN, I KEEP HEARING THESE ARGUMENTS... IN MY HEAD... NIGHT AFTER NIGHT!

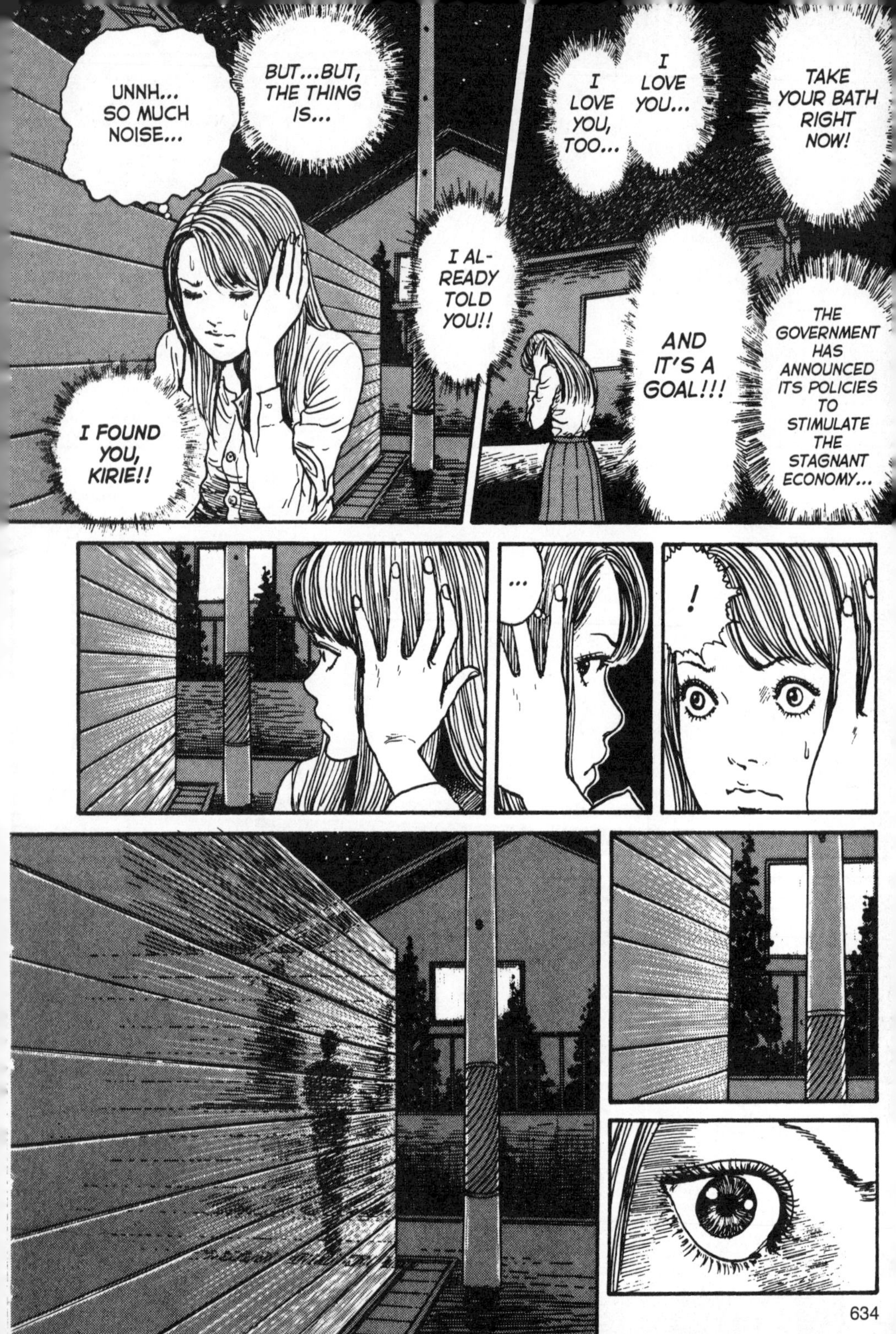
TAKE YOUR BATH RIGHT NOW!
I LOVE YOU...
I LOVE YOU, TOO...
THE GOVERNMENT HAS ANNOUNCED ITS POLICIES TO STIMULATE THE STAGNANT ECONOMY...
AND IT'S A GOAL!!!
I AL-READY TOLD YOU!!
BUT...BUT, THE THING IS...
UNNH... SO MUCH NOISE...
I FOUND YOU, KIRIE!!
!
...

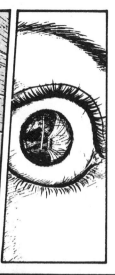

OH!

THAT'S MR. TORINO!

WHAT'S HE DOING BEHIND THAT CORNER...?

TMP

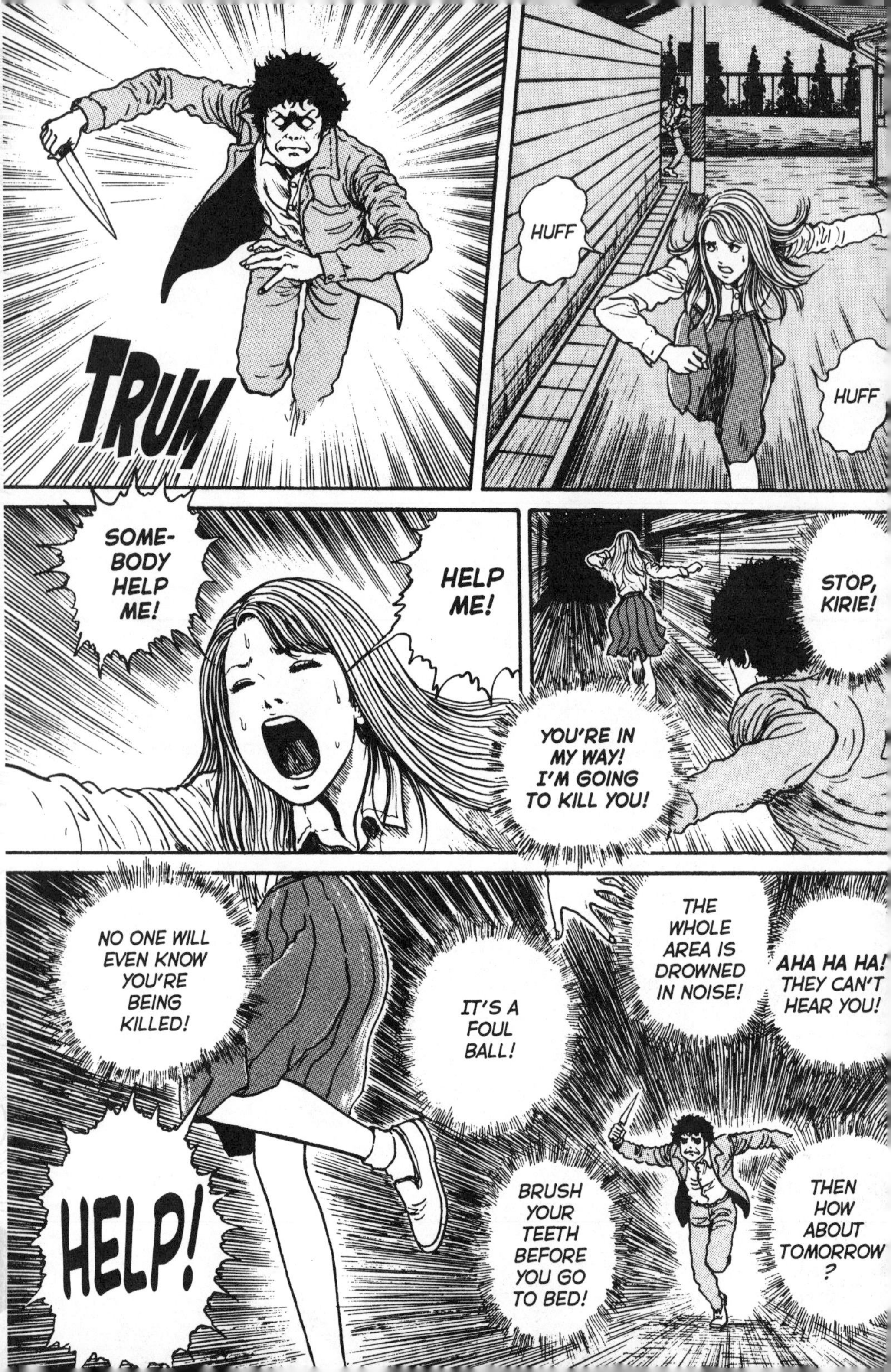
HUFF
HUFF
TRUM
STOP, KIRIE!
YOU'RE IN MY WAY! I'M GOING TO KILL YOU!
HELP ME!
SOME-BODY HELP ME!
AHA HA HA! THEY CAN'T HEAR YOU!
THE WHOLE AREA IS DROWNED IN NOISE!
IT'S A FOUL BALL!
NO ONE WILL EVEN KNOW YOU'RE BEING KILLED!
THEN HOW ABOUT TOMORROW?
BRUSH YOUR TEETH BEFORE YOU GO TO BED!
HELP!

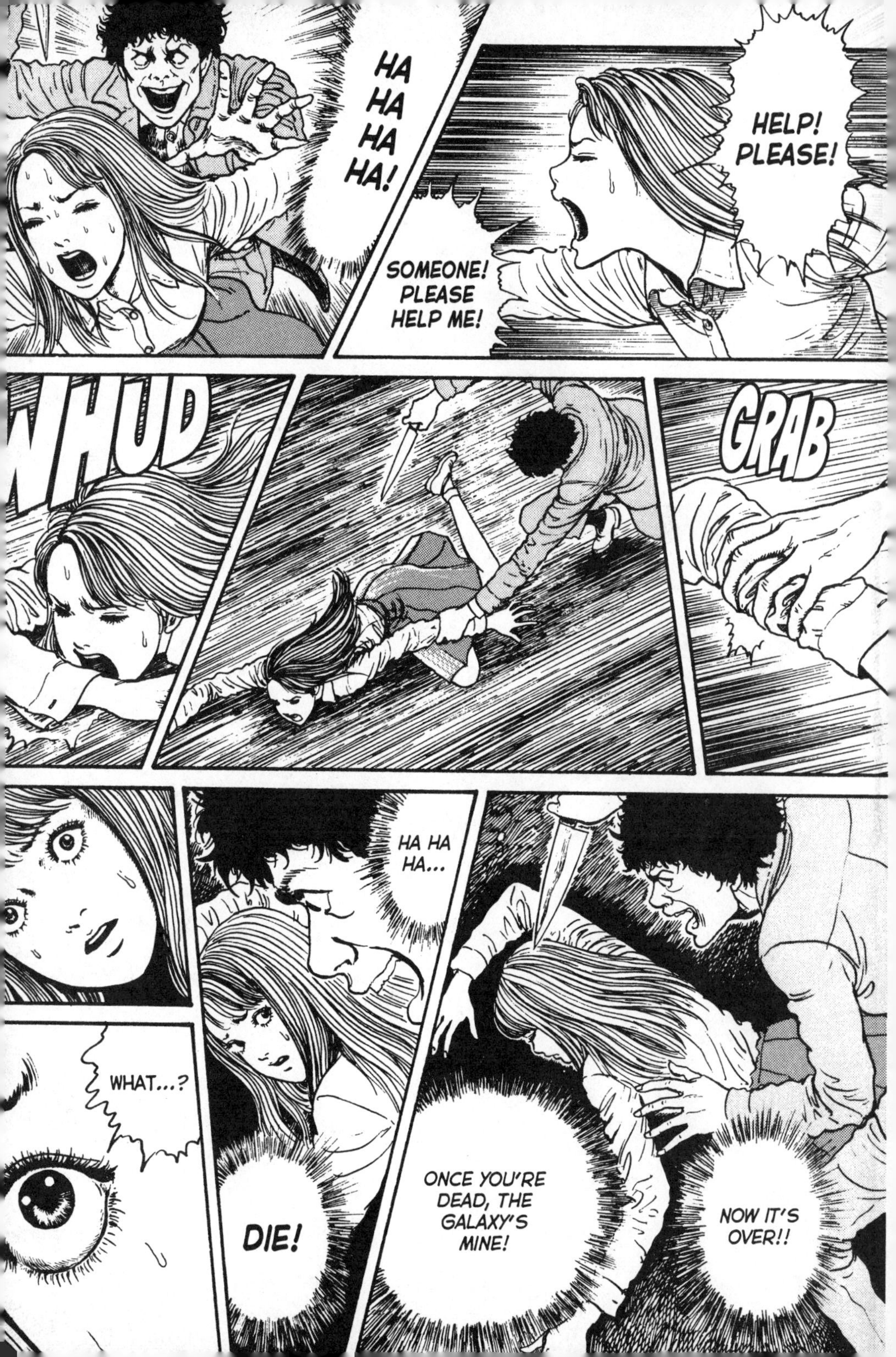
HELP! PLEASE!
SOMEONE! PLEASE HELP ME!
HA HA HA HA!
GRAB
WHUD
NOW IT'S OVER!!
ONCE YOU'RE DEAD, THE GALAXY'S MINE!
HA HA HA...
DIE!
WHAT...?

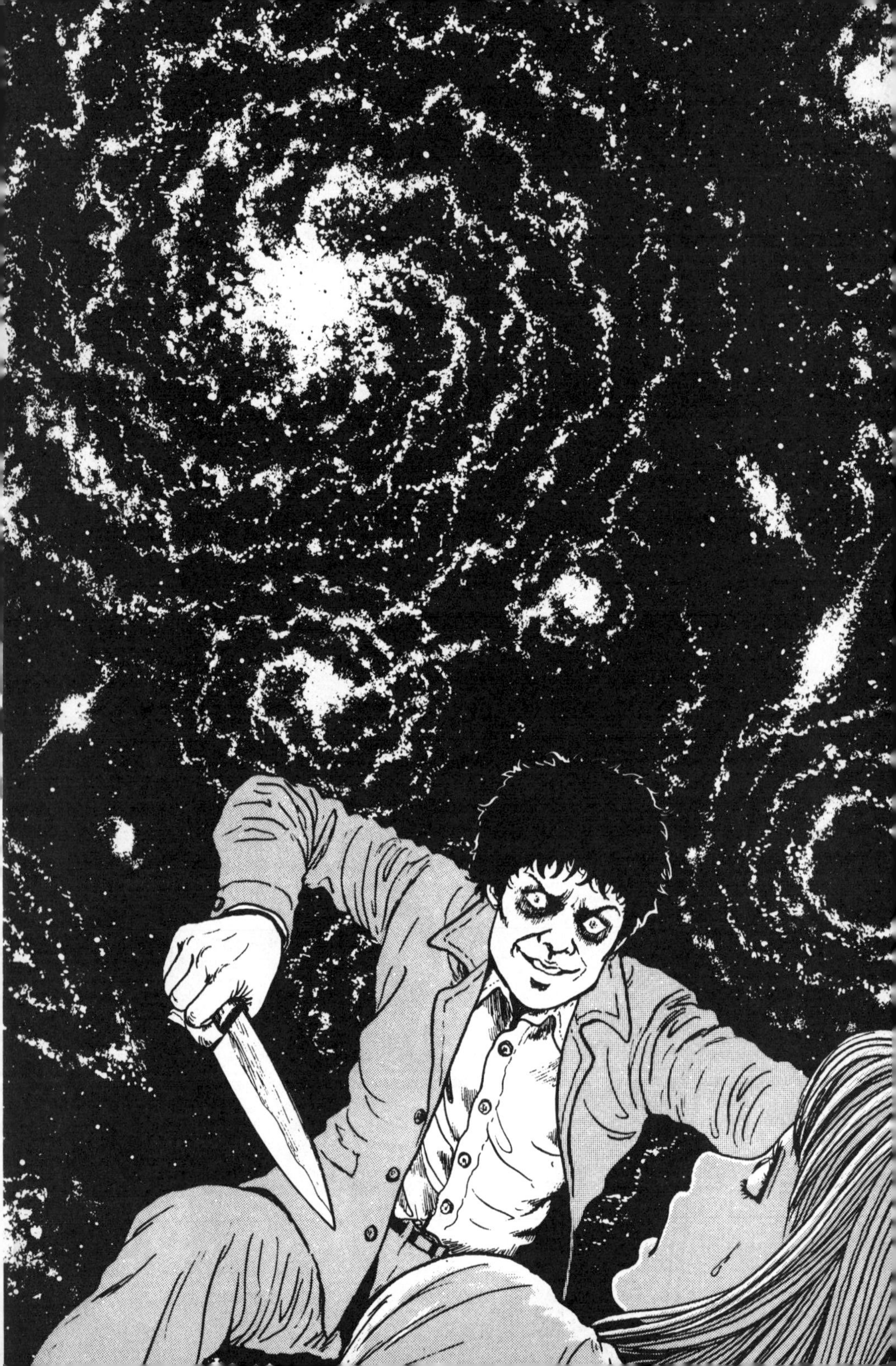

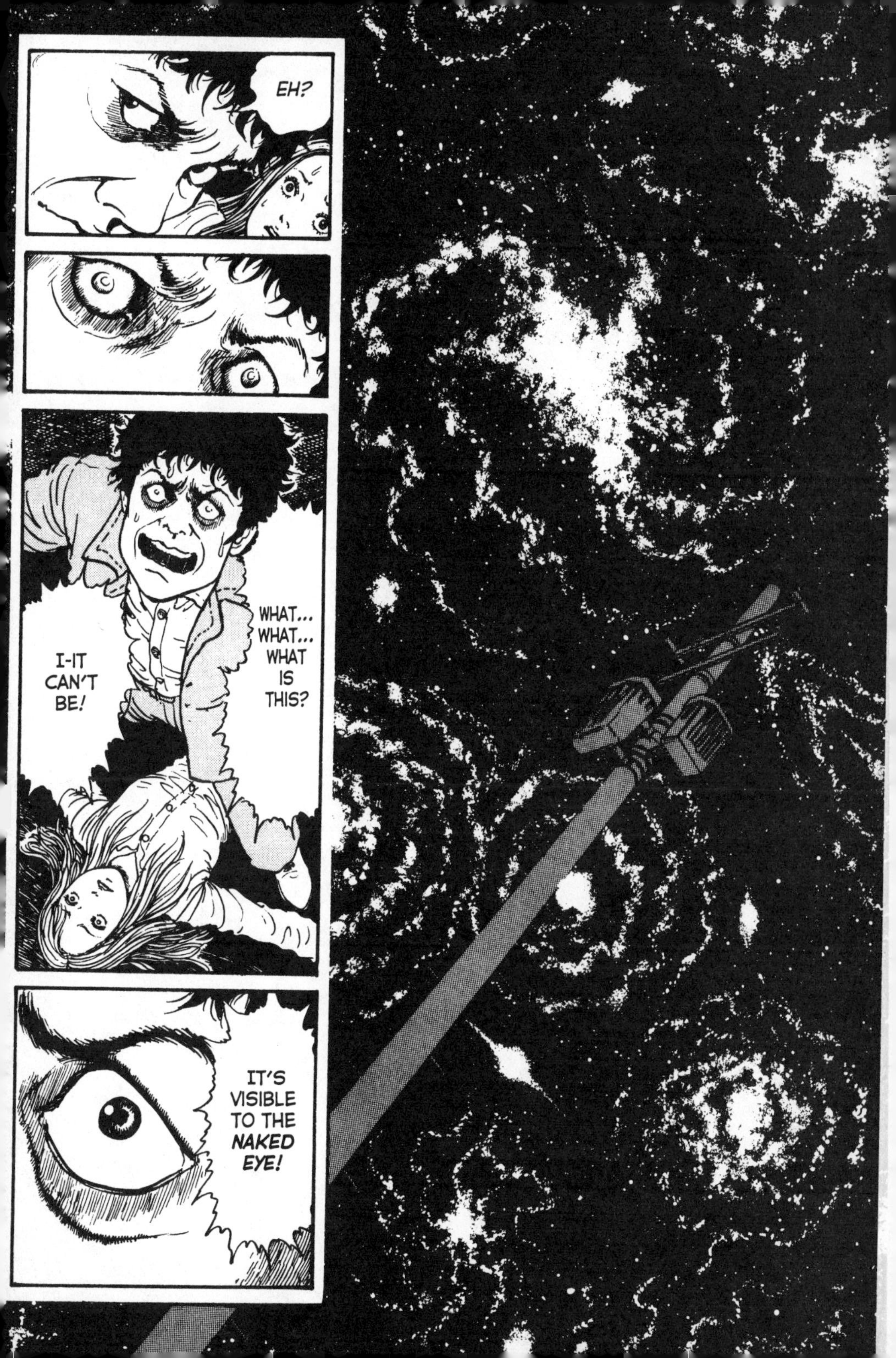
EH?
WHAT... WHAT... WHAT IS THIS?
I-IT CAN'T BE!
IT'S VISIBLE TO THE NAKED EYE!

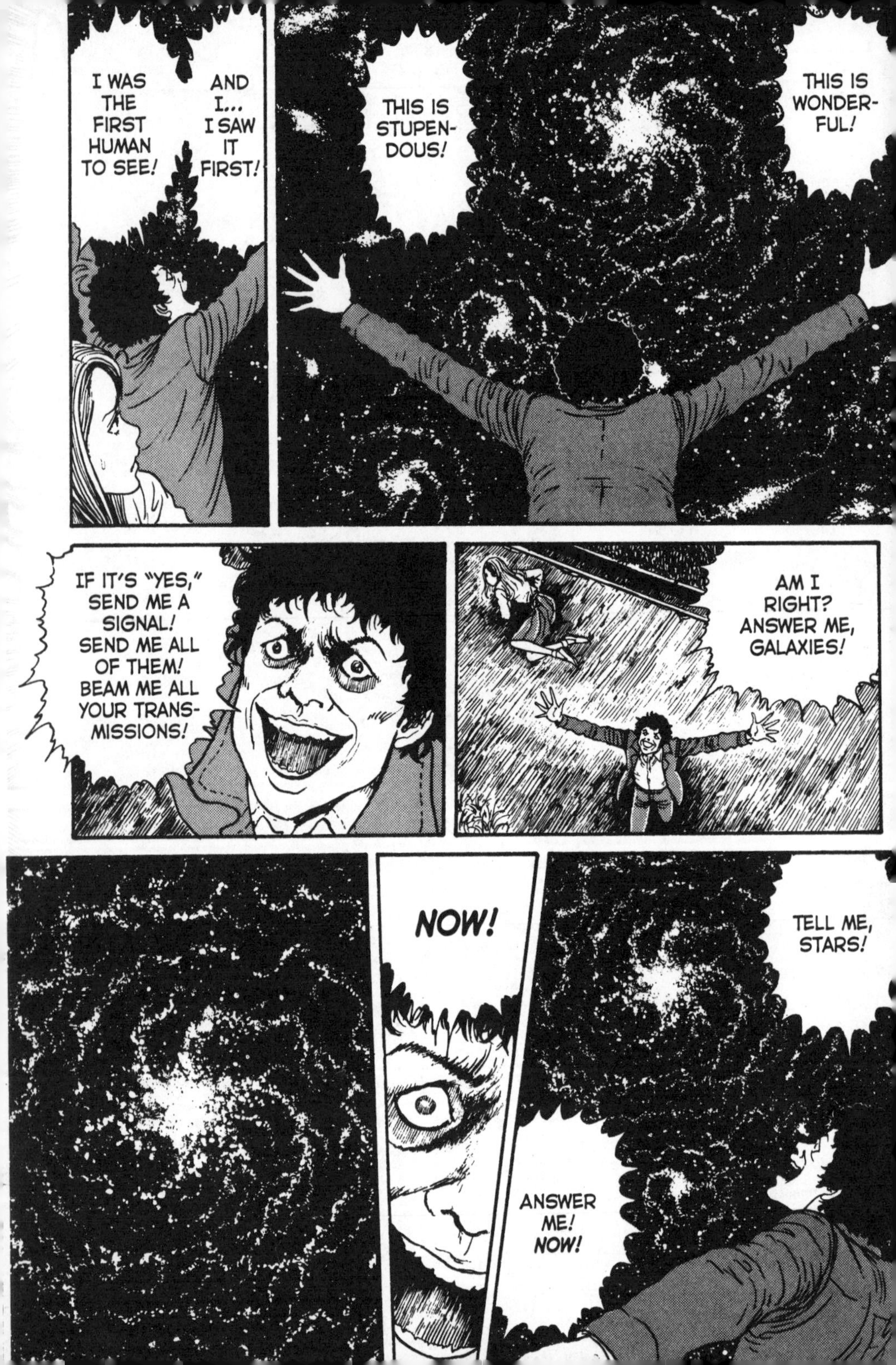
THIS IS WONDERFUL!
THIS IS STUPENDOUS!
AND I... I SAW IT FIRST!
I WAS THE FIRST HUMAN TO SEE!
AM I RIGHT? ANSWER ME, GALAXIES!
IF IT'S "YES," SEND ME A SIGNAL! SEND ME ALL OF THEM! BEAM ME ALL YOUR TRANSMISSIONS!
TELL ME, STARS!
ANSWER ME! NOW!
NOW!

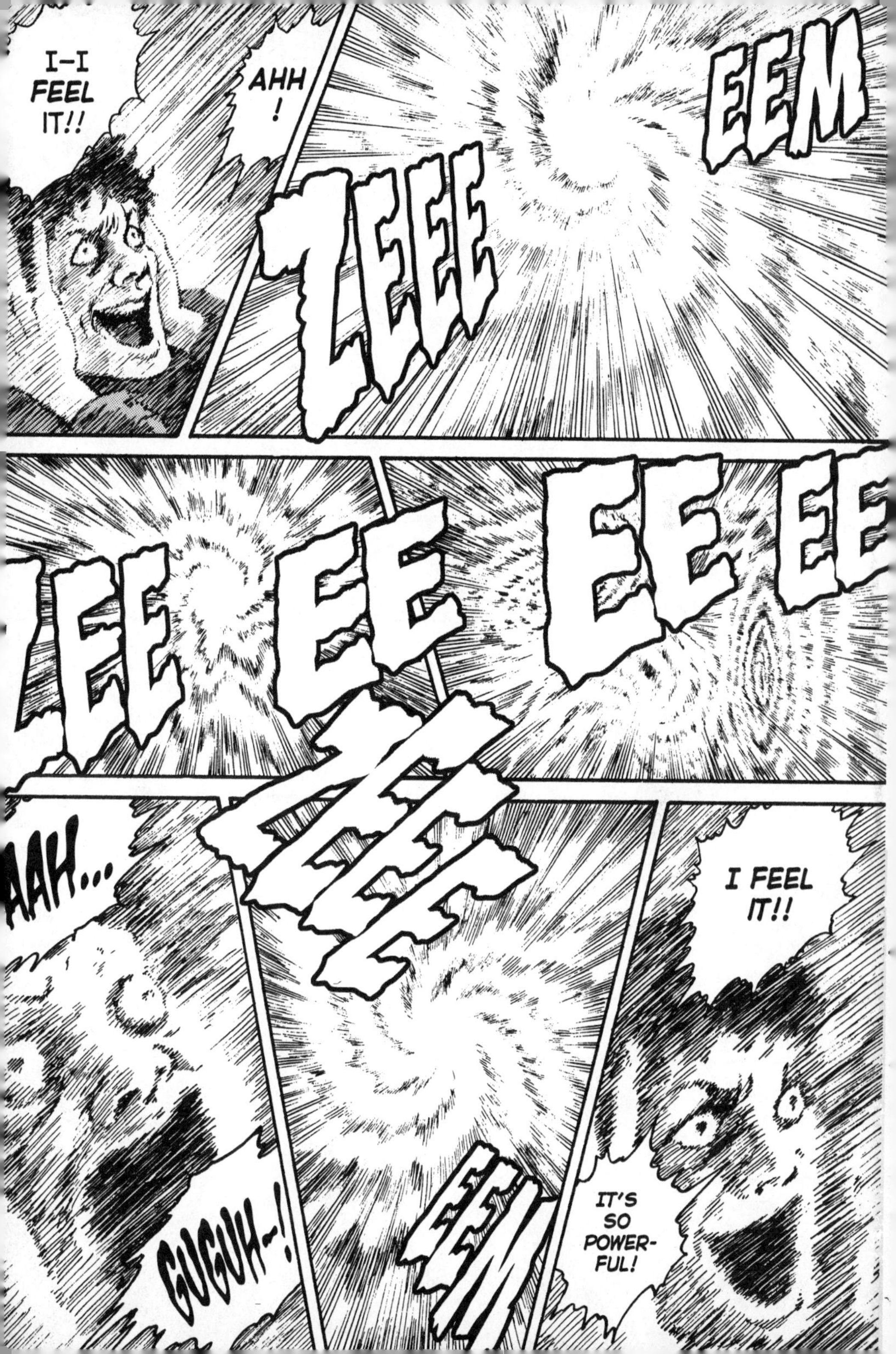
ZEEE
EEM
AHH!
I–I FEEL IT!!
EE
EE
EE
EE
I FEEL IT!!
IT'S SO POWER-FUL!
ZEEE
EEM
AAH...
GUGUH–!

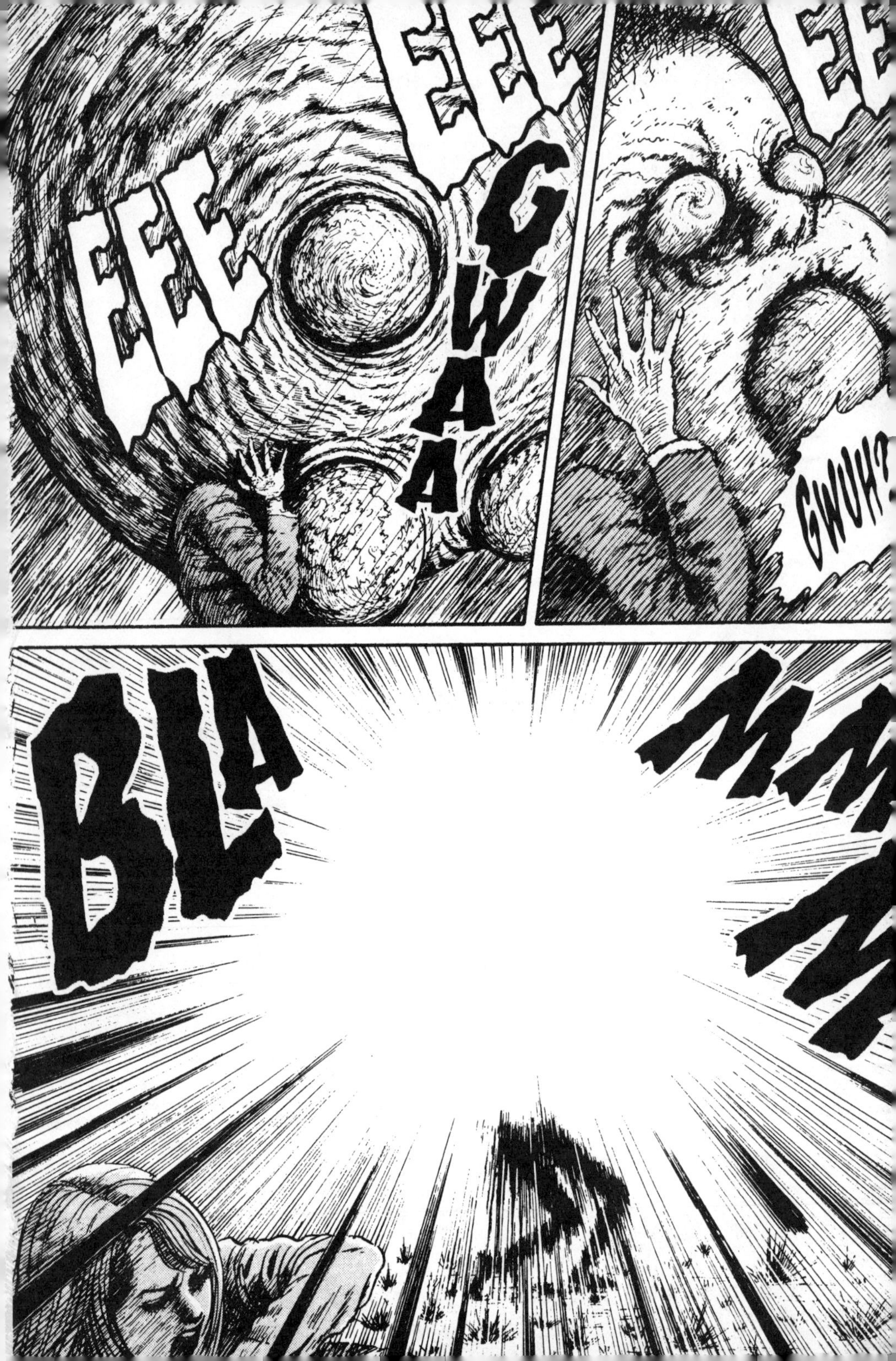
EE
GWUH?
EEE
EEE
GWAAA
BLA
MM

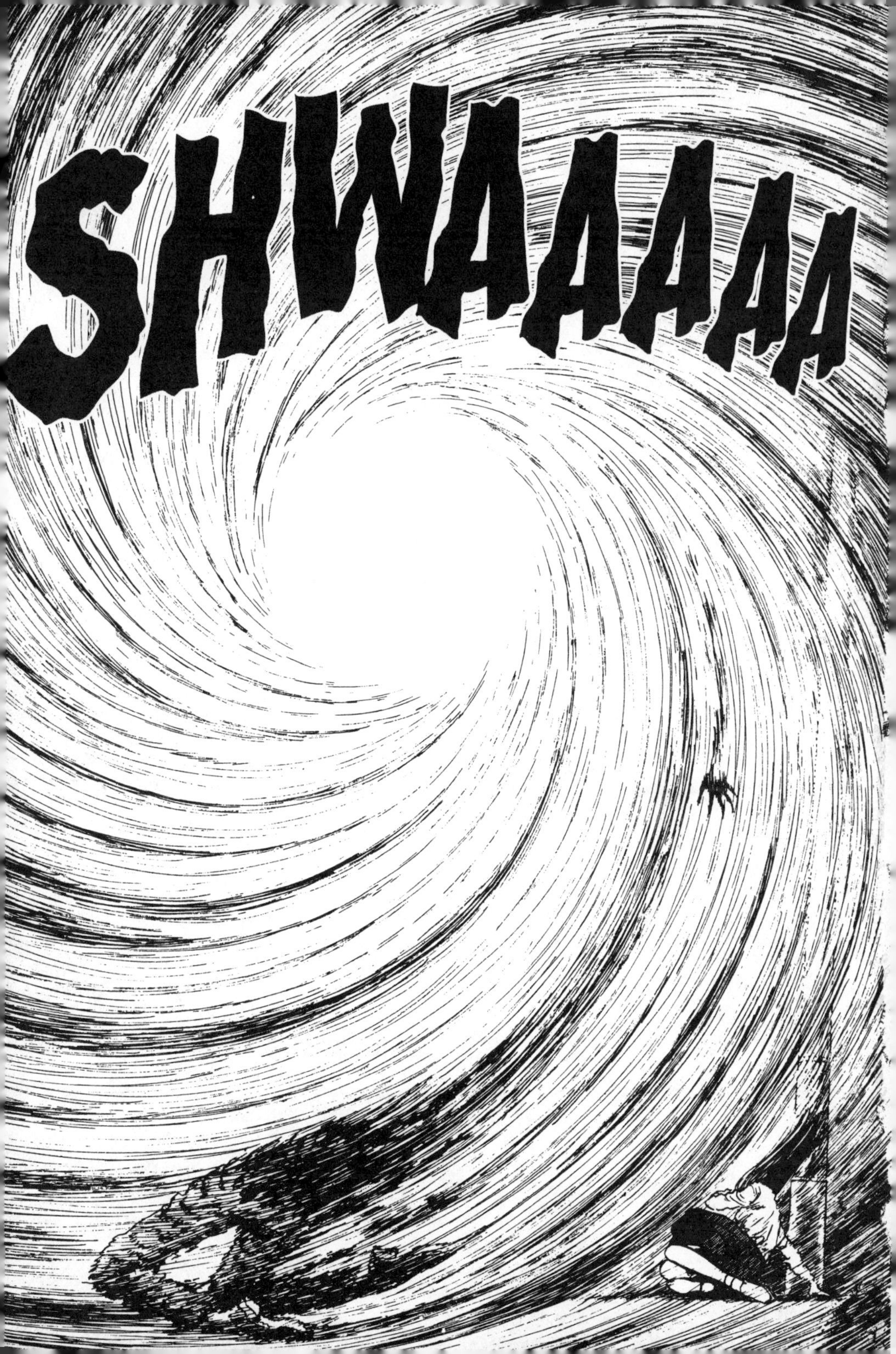
SHWAAAAAA

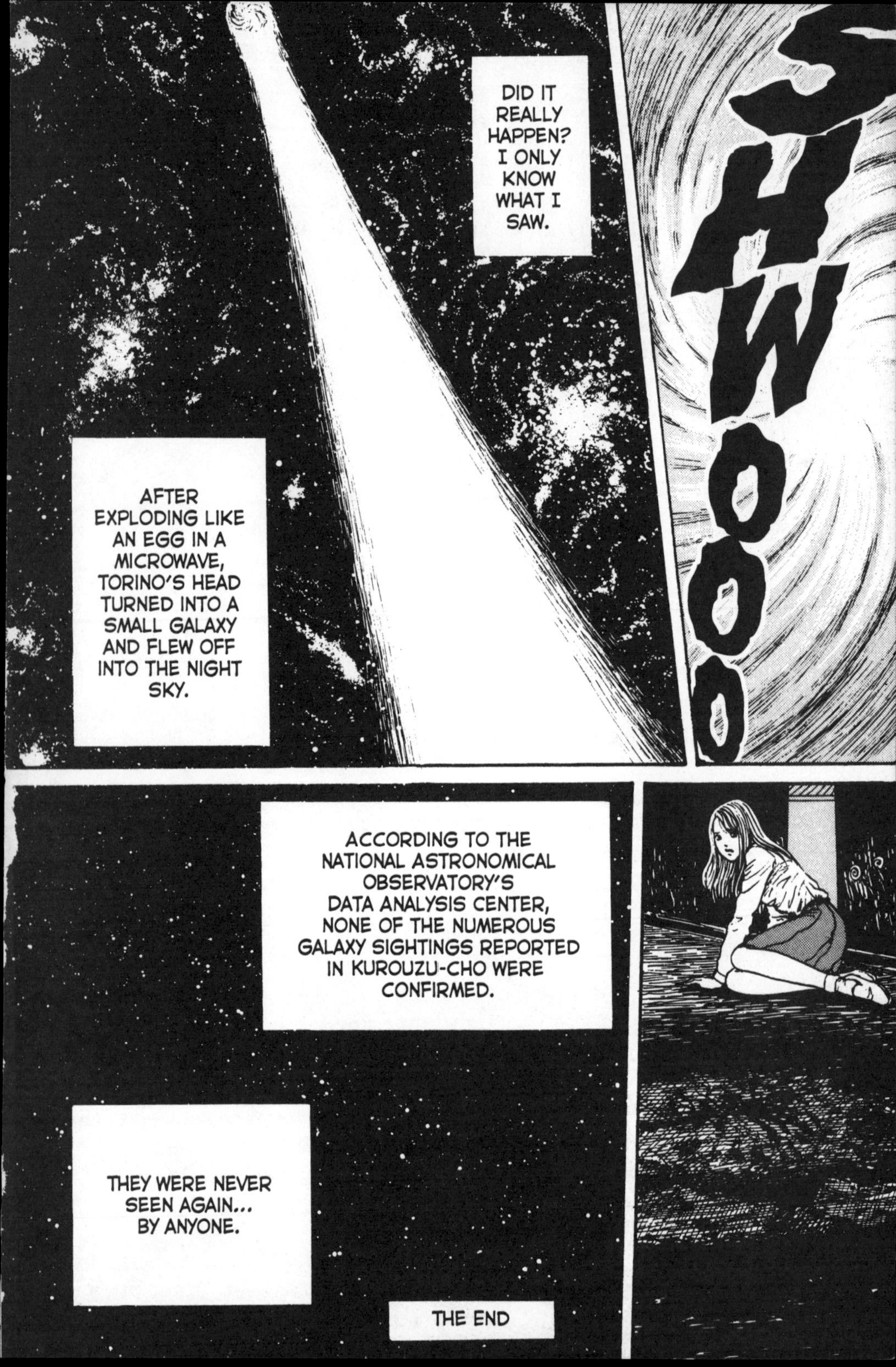
SHWOOO
DID IT REALLY HAPPEN? I ONLY KNOW WHAT I SAW.
AFTER EXPLODING LIKE AN EGG IN A MICROWAVE, TORINO'S HEAD TURNED INTO A SMALL GALAXY AND FLEW OFF INTO THE NIGHT SKY.
ACCORDING TO THE NATIONAL ASTRONOMICAL OBSERVATORY'S DATA ANALYSIS CENTER, NONE OF THE NUMEROUS GALAXY SIGHTINGS REPORTED IN KUROUZU-CHO WERE CONFIRMED.
THEY WERE NEVER SEEN AGAIN... BY ANYONE.
THE END

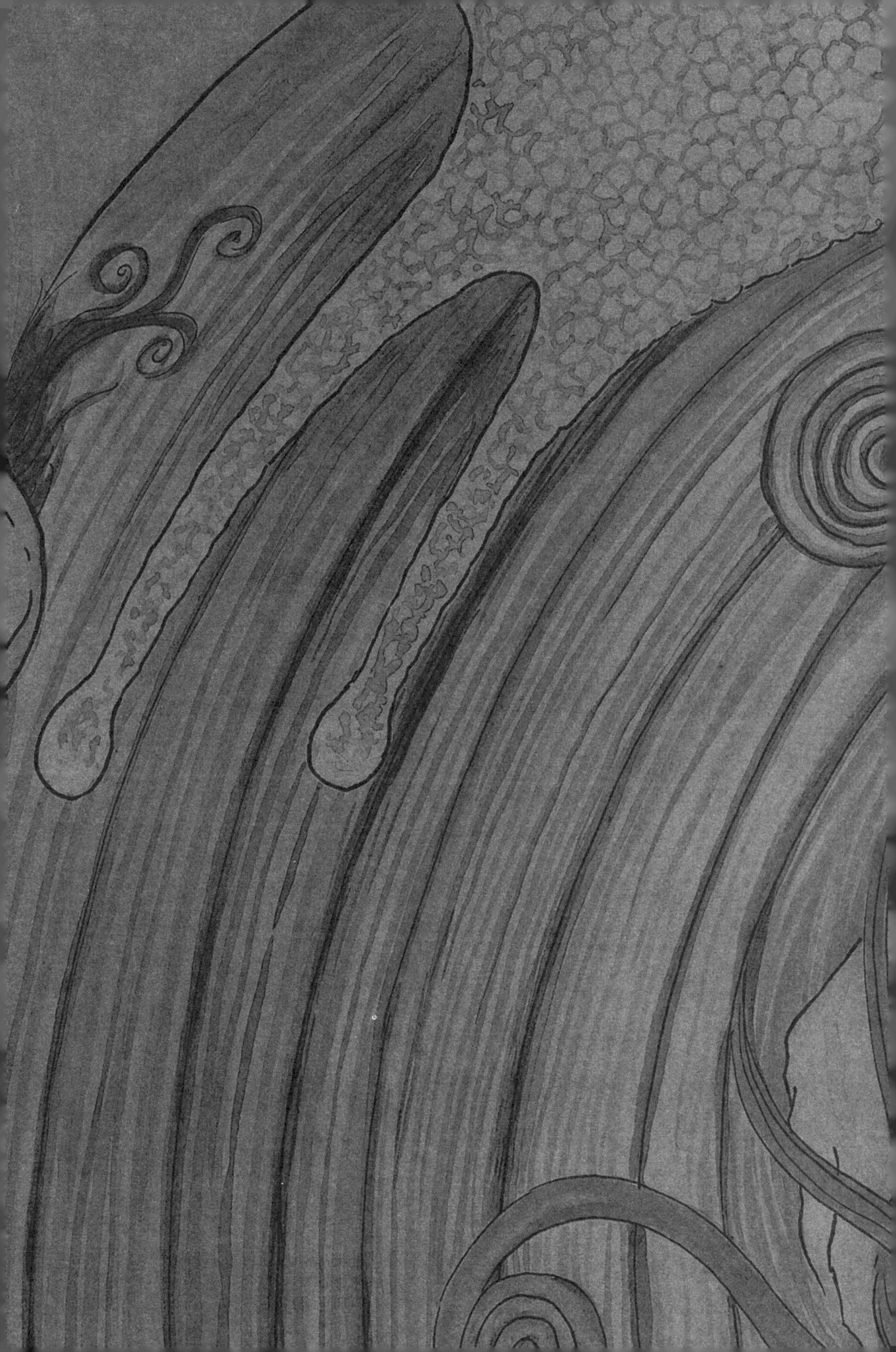

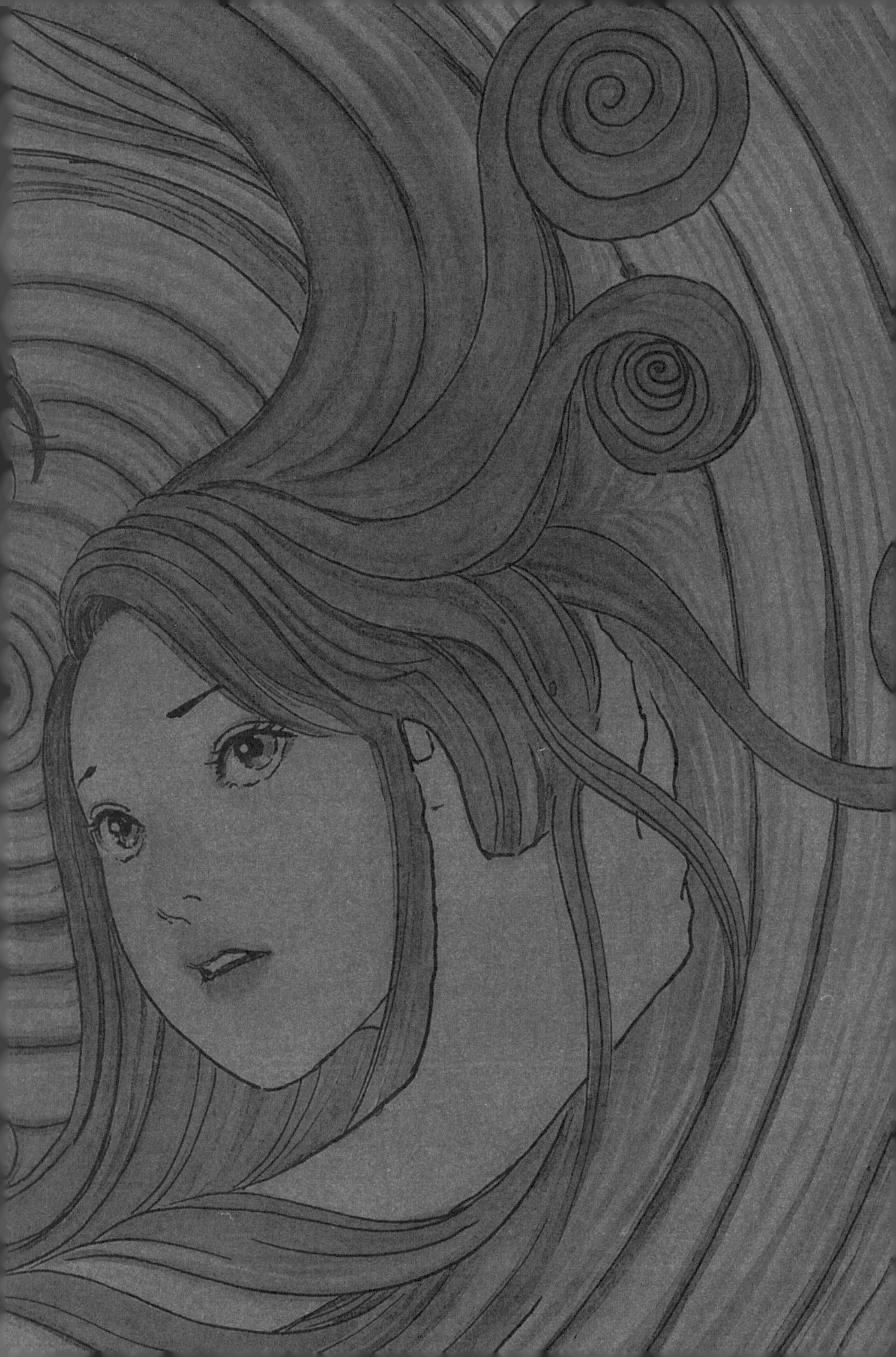

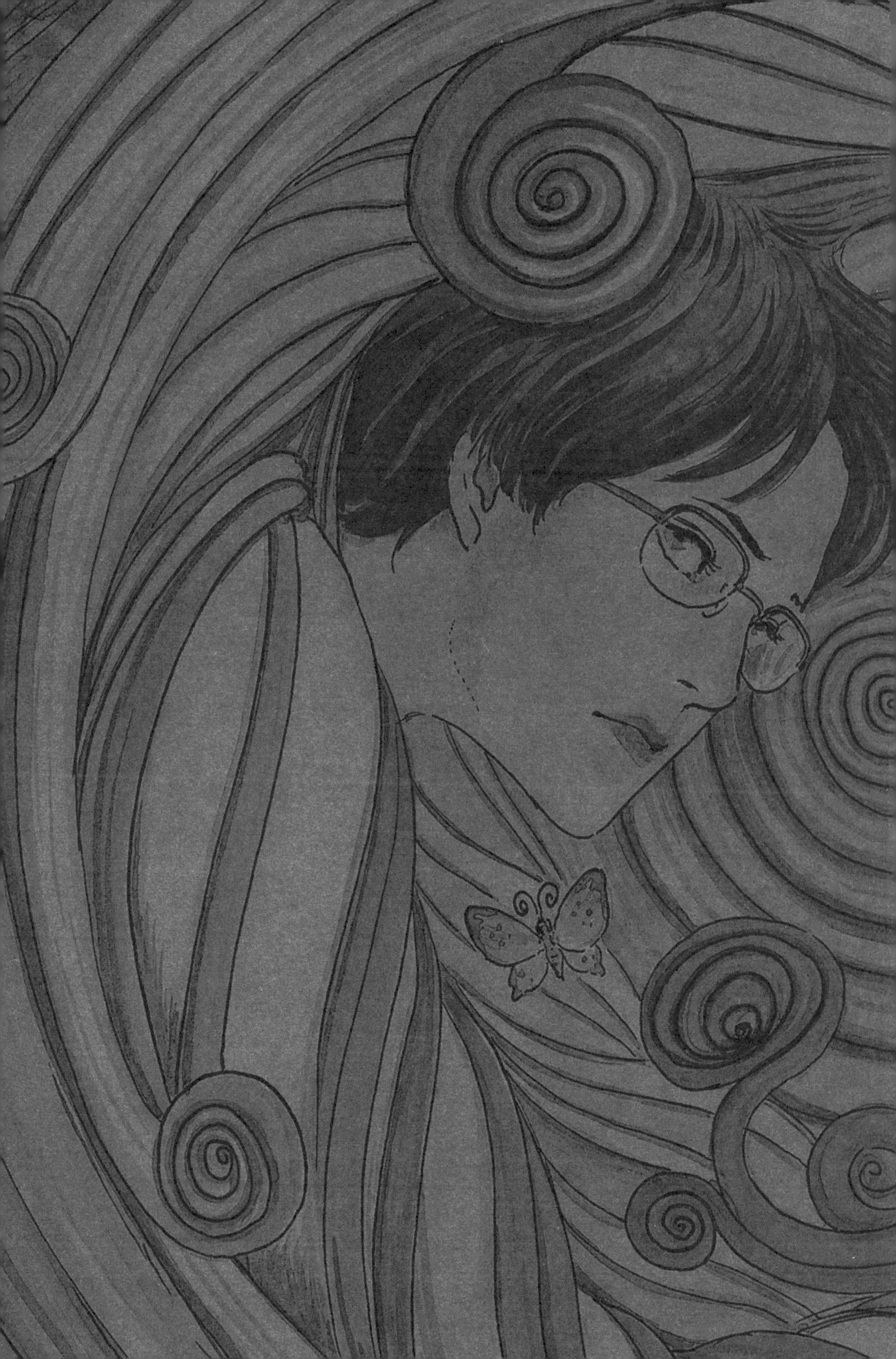

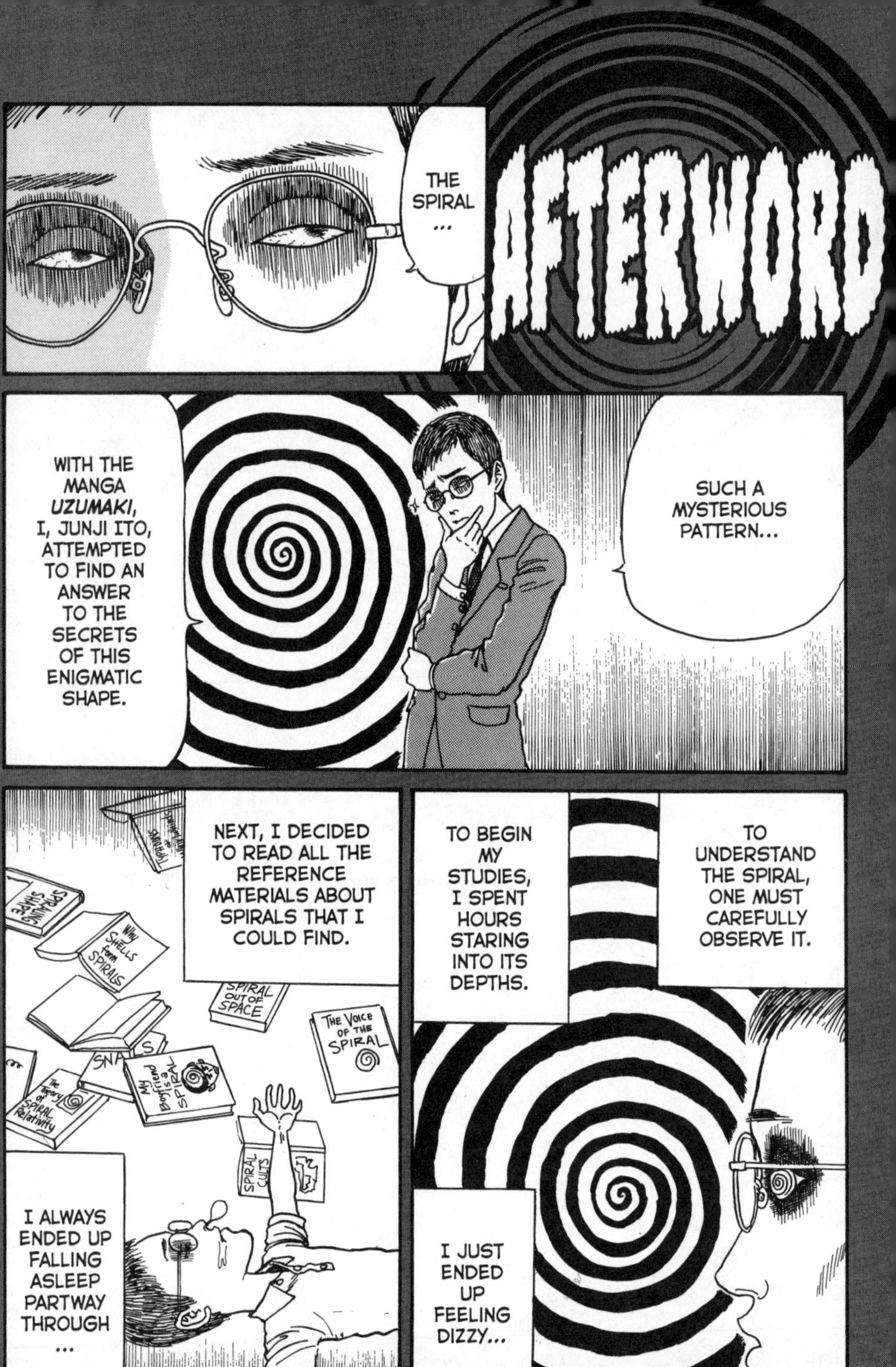
AFTERWORD
THE SPIRAL ...
SUCH A MYSTERIOUS PATTERN...
WITH THE MANGA *UZUMAKI*, I, JUNJI ITO, ATTEMPTED TO FIND AN ANSWER TO THE SECRETS OF THIS ENIGMATIC SHAPE.
TO UNDERSTAND THE SPIRAL, ONE MUST CAREFULLY OBSERVE IT.
TO BEGIN MY STUDIES, I SPENT HOURS STARING INTO ITS DEPTHS.
I JUST ENDED UP FEELING DIZZY...
NEXT, I DECIDED TO READ ALL THE REFERENCE MATERIALS ABOUT SPIRALS THAT I COULD FIND.
SPIRALING SHAPE
Why SHELLS form SPIRALS
SPIRAL OUT OF SPACE
THE VOICE OF THE SPIRAL
My Boyfriend is a SPIRAL
The Theory of SPIRAL Relativity
SPIRAL CULTS
I ALWAYS ENDED UP FALLING ASLEEP PARTWAY THROUGH ...

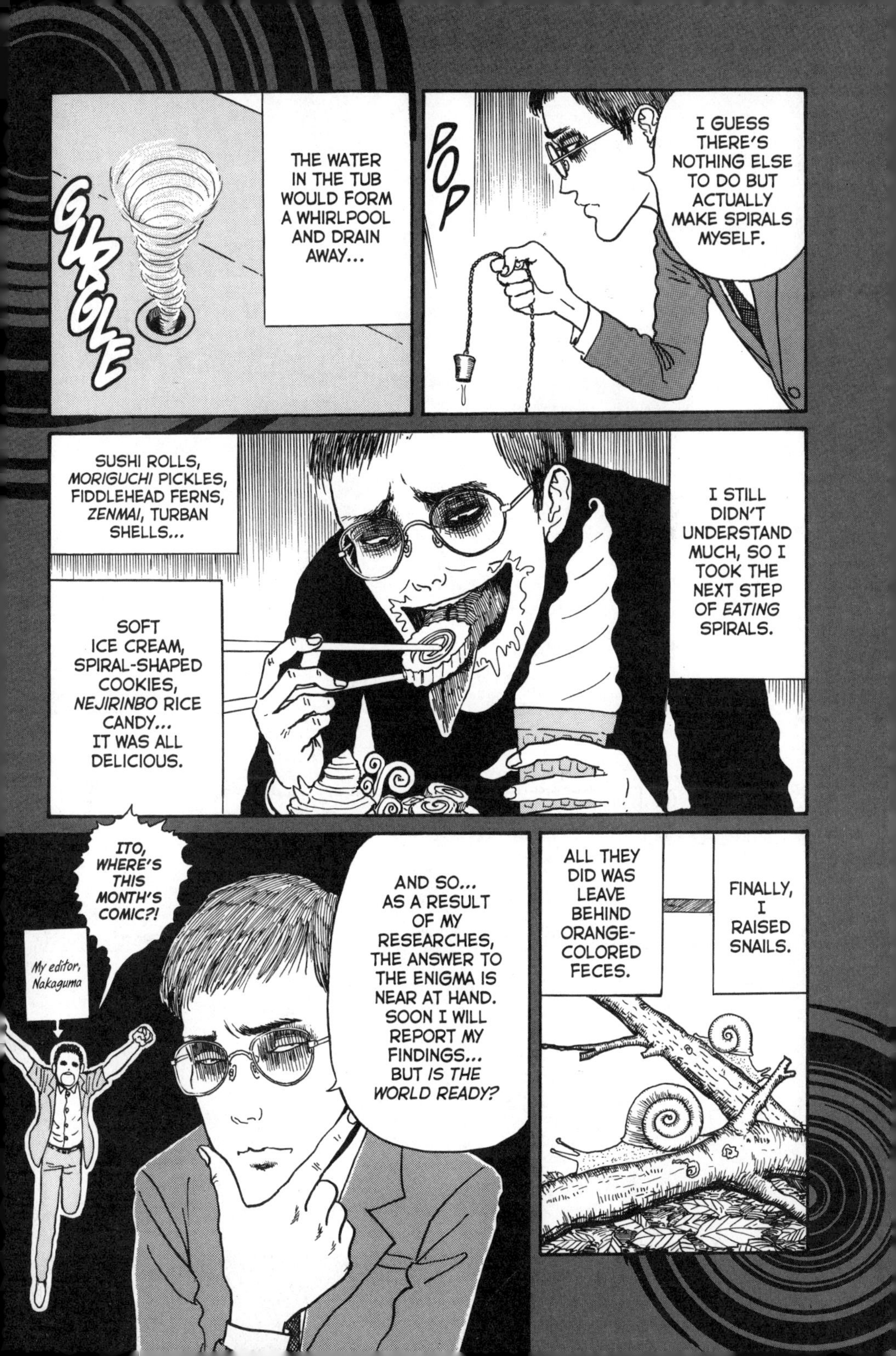
I GUESS THERE'S NOTHING ELSE TO DO BUT ACTUALLY MAKE SPIRALS MYSELF.
POP
THE WATER IN THE TUB WOULD FORM A WHIRLPOOL AND DRAIN AWAY...
GURGLE
I STILL DIDN'T UNDERSTAND MUCH, SO I TOOK THE NEXT STEP OF *EATING* SPIRALS.
SUSHI ROLLS, *MORIGUCHI* PICKLES, FIDDLEHEAD FERNS, *ZENMAI*, TURBAN SHELLS...
SOFT ICE CREAM, SPIRAL-SHAPED COOKIES, *NEJIRINBO* RICE CANDY... IT WAS ALL DELICIOUS.
FINALLY, I RAISED SNAILS.
ALL THEY DID WAS LEAVE BEHIND ORANGE-COLORED FECES.
AND SO... AS A RESULT OF MY RESEARCHES, THE ANSWER TO THE ENIGMA IS NEAR AT HAND. SOON I WILL REPORT MY FINDINGS... BUT *IS THE WORLD READY?*
ITO, WHERE'S THIS MONTH'S COMIC?!
My editor, Nakaguma

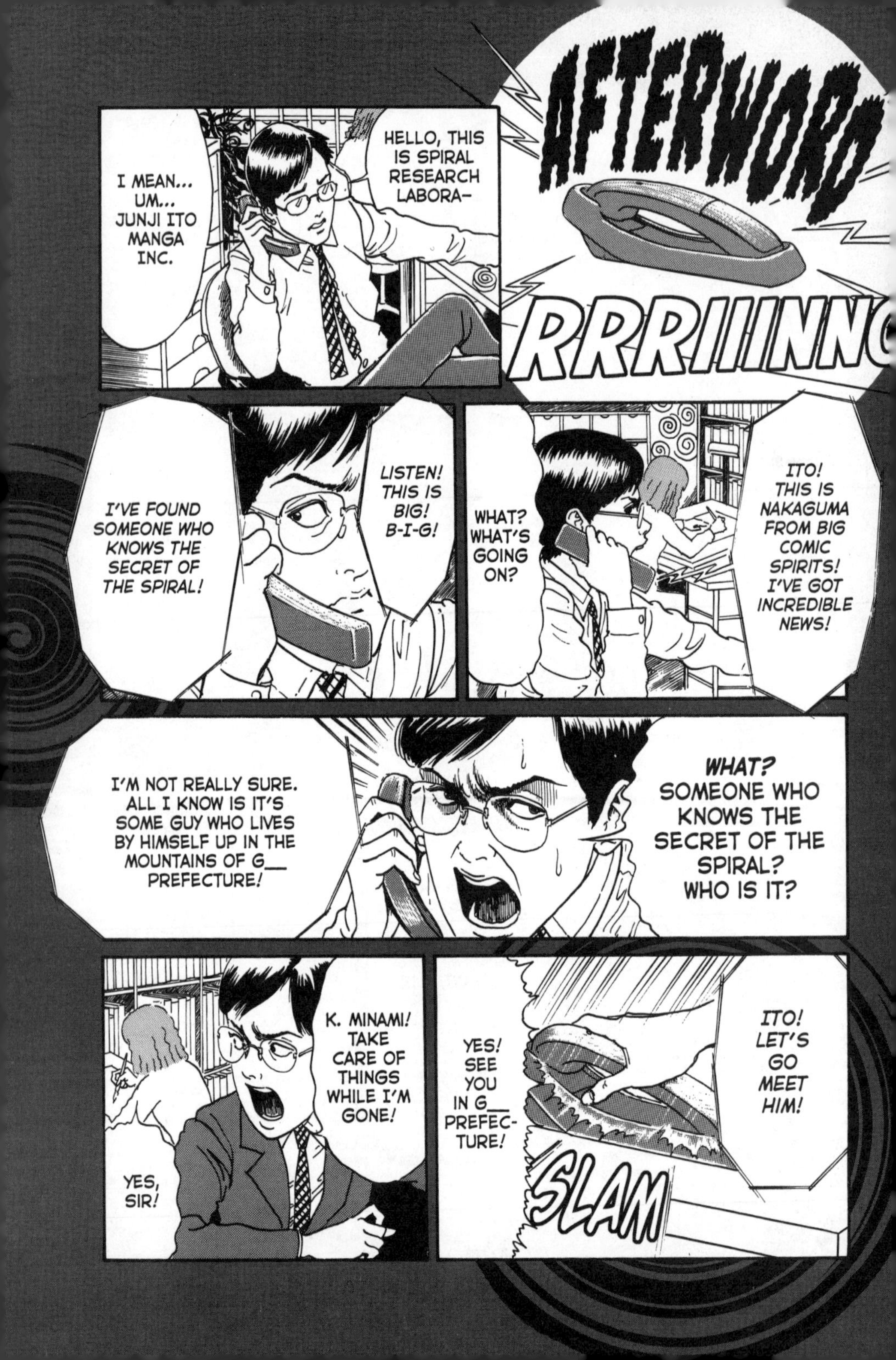
AFTERWORD
RRRIIINNG
HELLO, THIS IS SPIRAL RESEARCH LABORA-
I MEAN... UM... JUNJI ITO MANGA INC.
ITO! THIS IS NAKAGUMA FROM BIG COMIC SPIRITS! I'VE GOT INCREDIBLE NEWS!
WHAT? WHAT'S GOING ON?
LISTEN! THIS IS BIG! B-I-G!
I'VE FOUND SOMEONE WHO KNOWS THE SECRET OF THE SPIRAL!
WHAT? SOMEONE WHO KNOWS THE SECRET OF THE SPIRAL? WHO IS IT?
I'M NOT REALLY SURE. ALL I KNOW IS IT'S SOME GUY WHO LIVES BY HIMSELF UP IN THE MOUNTAINS OF G__ PREFECTURE!
ITO! LET'S GO MEET HIM!
YES! SEE YOU IN G__ PREFEC-TURE!
SLAM
K. MINAMI! TAKE CARE OF THINGS WHILE I'M GONE!
YES, SIR!

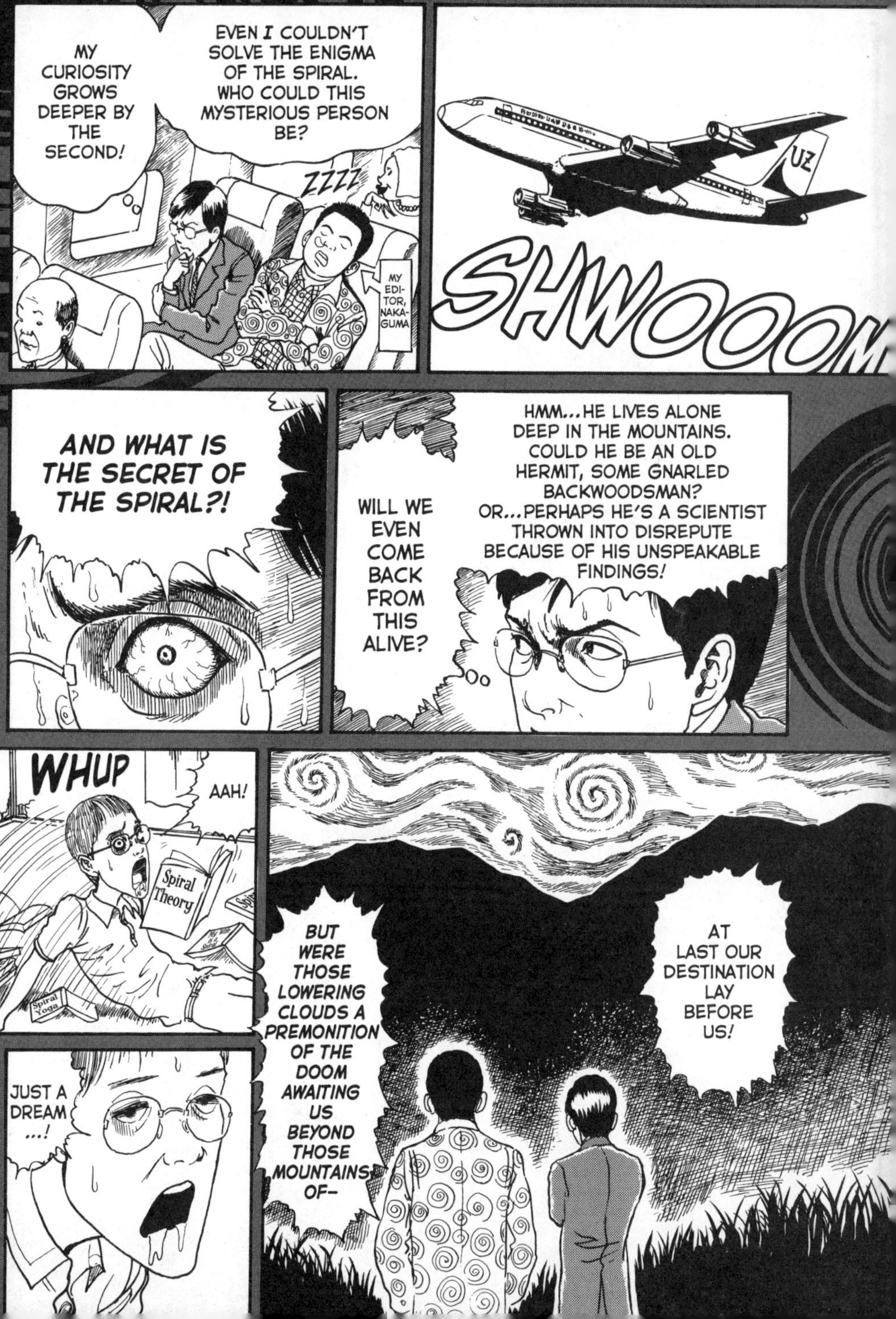
SHWOOOM
EVEN I COULDN'T SOLVE THE ENIGMA OF THE SPIRAL. WHO COULD THIS MYSTERIOUS PERSON BE?
MY CURIOSITY GROWS DEEPER BY THE SECOND!
ZZZZ
MY EDITOR, NAKAGUMA
HMM...HE LIVES ALONE DEEP IN THE MOUNTAINS. COULD HE BE AN OLD HERMIT, SOME GNARLED BACKWOODSMAN? OR...PERHAPS HE'S A SCIENTIST THROWN INTO DISREPUTE BECAUSE OF HIS UNSPEAKABLE FINDINGS!
WILL WE EVEN COME BACK FROM THIS ALIVE?
AND WHAT IS THE SECRET OF THE SPIRAL?!
AT LAST OUR DESTINATION LAY BEFORE US!
BUT WERE THOSE LOWERING CLOUDS A PREMONITION OF THE DOOM AWAITING US BEYOND THOSE MOUNTAINS OF–
WHUP
AAH!
Spiral Theory
Spiral Yoga
JUST A DREAM ...!

WHAT A RIP-OFF!

AFTER-WORD

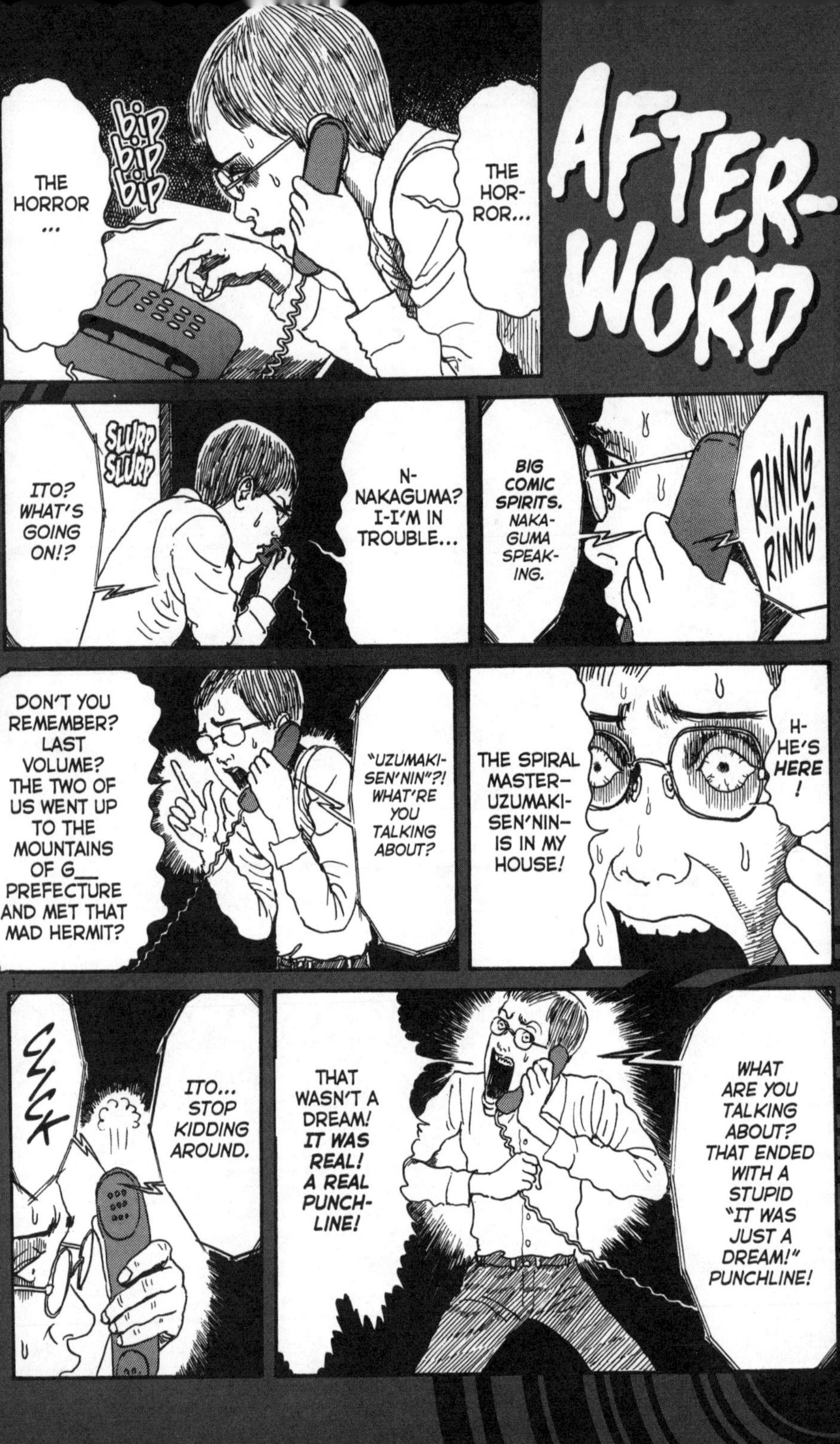
THE HORROR...
bip bip bip
THE HORROR...
RINNG RINNG
BIG COMIC SPIRITS. NAKAGUMA SPEAKING.
N-NAKAGUMA? I-I'M IN TROUBLE...
SLURP SLURP
ITO? WHAT'S GOING ON!?
H-HE'S HERE!
THE SPIRAL MASTER—UZUMAKI-SEN'NIN—IS IN MY HOUSE!
"UZUMAKI-SEN'NIN"?! WHAT'RE YOU TALKING ABOUT?
DON'T YOU REMEMBER? LAST VOLUME? THE TWO OF US WENT UP TO THE MOUNTAINS OF G__ PREFECTURE AND MET THAT MAD HERMIT?
WHAT ARE YOU TALKING ABOUT? THAT ENDED WITH A STUPID "IT WAS JUST A DREAM!" PUNCHLINE!
THAT WASN'T A DREAM! IT WAS REAL! A REAL PUNCHLINE!
ITO... STOP KIDDING AROUND.
CLICK

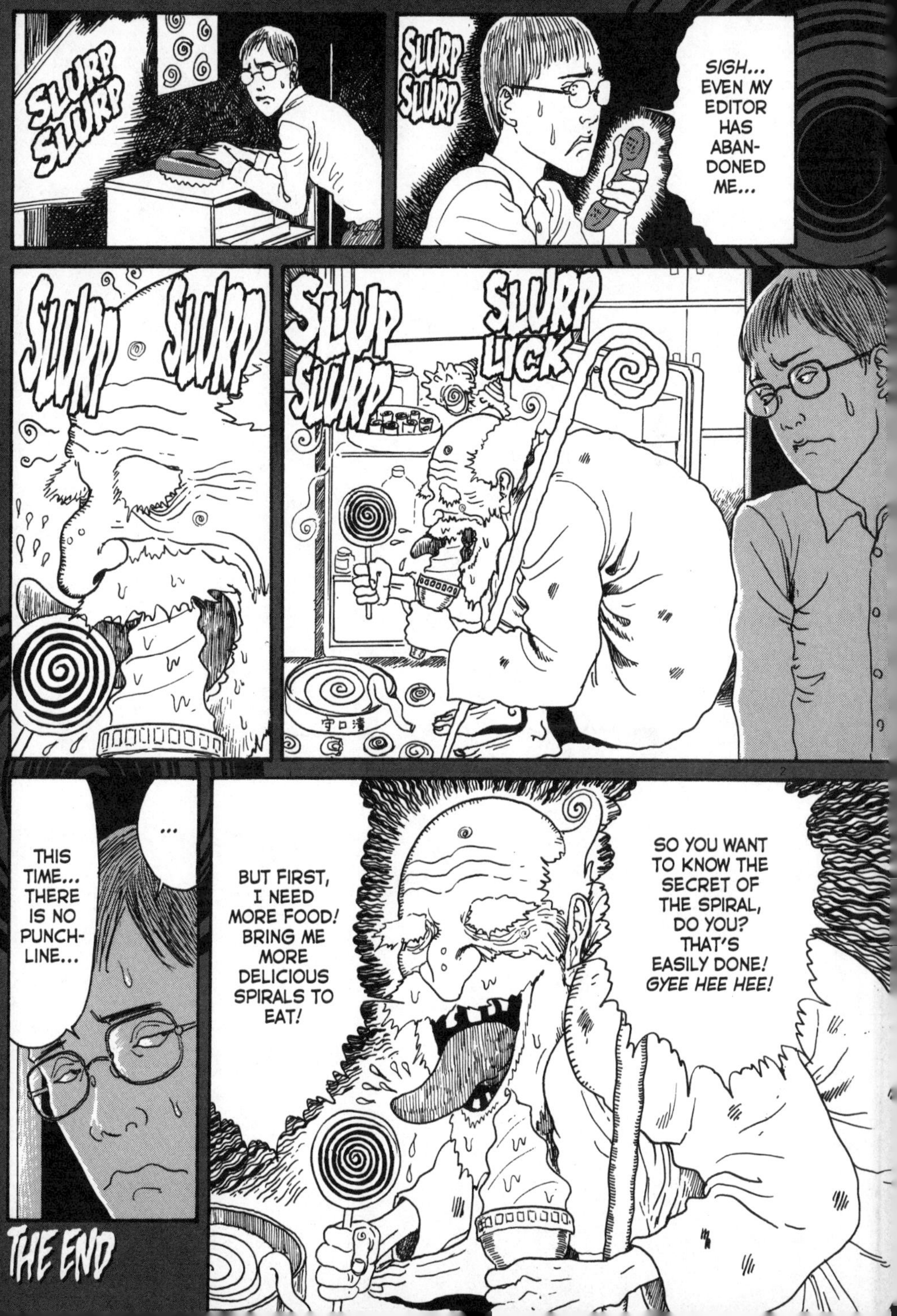
SIGH... EVEN MY EDITOR HAS ABANDONED ME...
SLURP SLURP
SLURP SLURP
SLURP LICK
SLUP SLURP
守口漬
SLURP SLURP
SO YOU WANT TO KNOW THE SECRET OF THE SPIRAL, DO YOU? THAT'S EASILY DONE! GYEE HEE HEE!
BUT FIRST, I NEED MORE FOOD! BRING ME MORE DELICIOUS SPIRALS TO EAT!
...
THIS TIME... THERE IS NO PUNCHLINE...
THE END

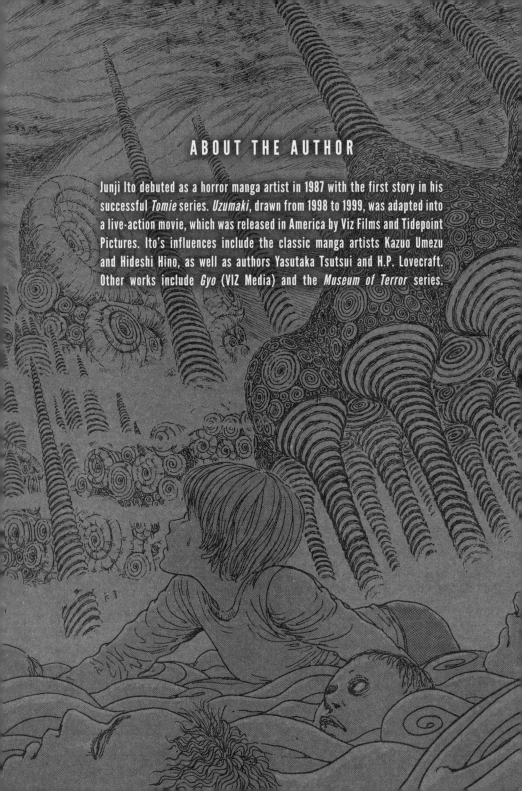

ABOUT THE AUTHOR

Junji Ito debuted as a horror manga artist in 1987 with the first story in his successful *Tomie* series. *Uzumaki*, drawn from 1998 to 1999, was adapted into a live-action movie, which was released in America by Viz Films and Tidepoint Pictures. Ito's influences include the classic manga artists Kazuo Umezu and Hideshi Hino, as well as authors Yasutaka Tsutsui and H.P. Lovecraft. Other works include *Gyo* (VIZ Media) and the *Museum of Terror* series.

UZUMAKI

UZUMAKI
Deluxe Edition

Story & Art by
JUNJI ITO

UZUMAKI
by Junji ITO
© 2010 JI Inc.
All rights reserved.
Original Japanese edition published by SHOGAKUKAN.
English translation rights in the United States of America, Canada, the United Kingdom,
Ireland, Australia and New Zealand arranged with SHOGAKUKAN.

Translation & English Adaptation/Yuji Oniki
Touch-up Art & Lettering/Susan Daigle-Leach
Editors/Jason Thompson, Alvin Lu (First Edition), Gary Leach (Signature Edition)

Deluxe Edition:
Design/Sam Elzway
Editor/Masumi Washington

Printed in the U.S.A.

Published by VIZ Media, LLC
P.O. Box 77010
San Francisco, CA 94107

First English edition published in 2002

Deluxe Edition
14
First printing, October 2013
Fourteenth printing, May 2021

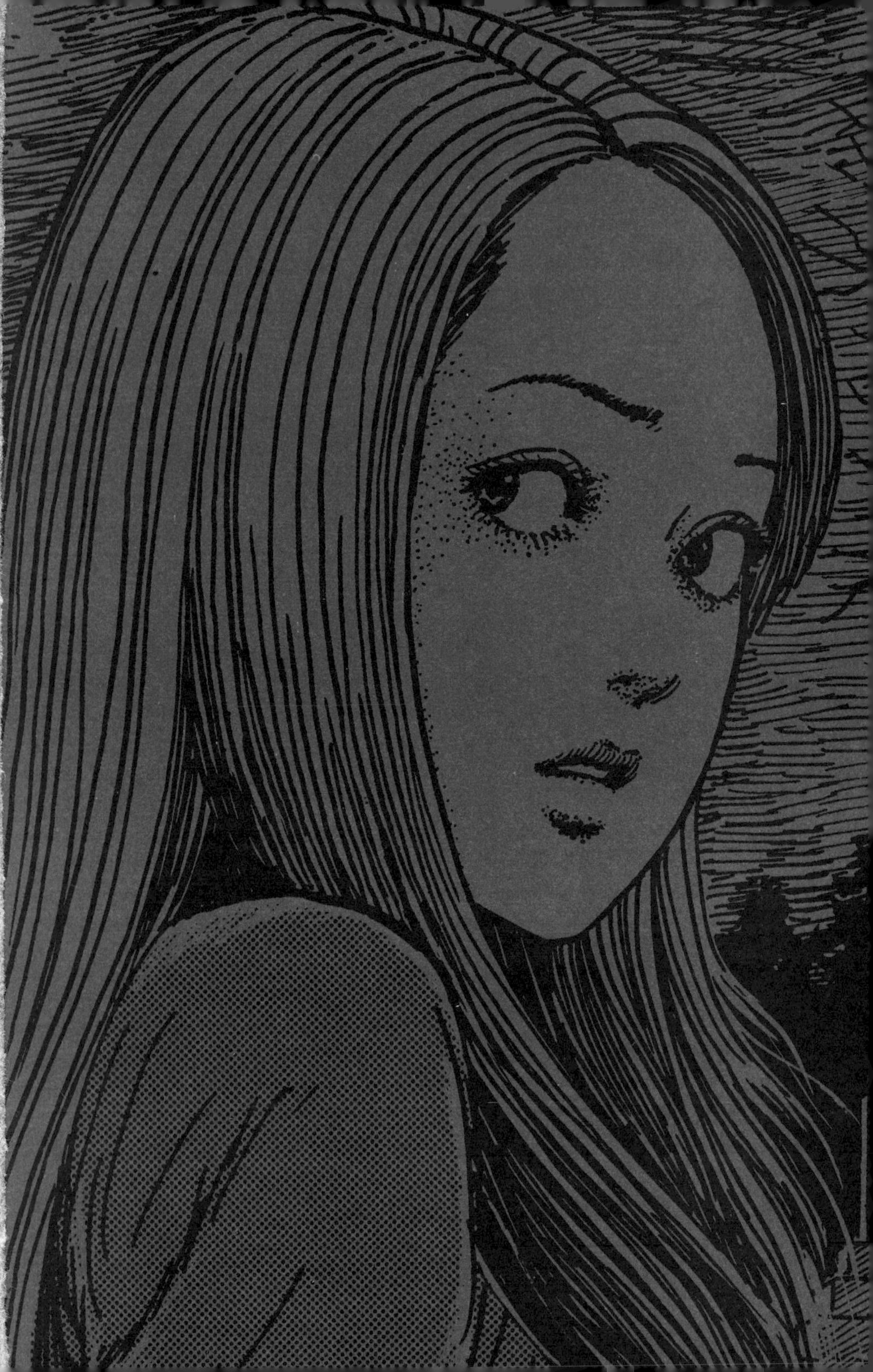

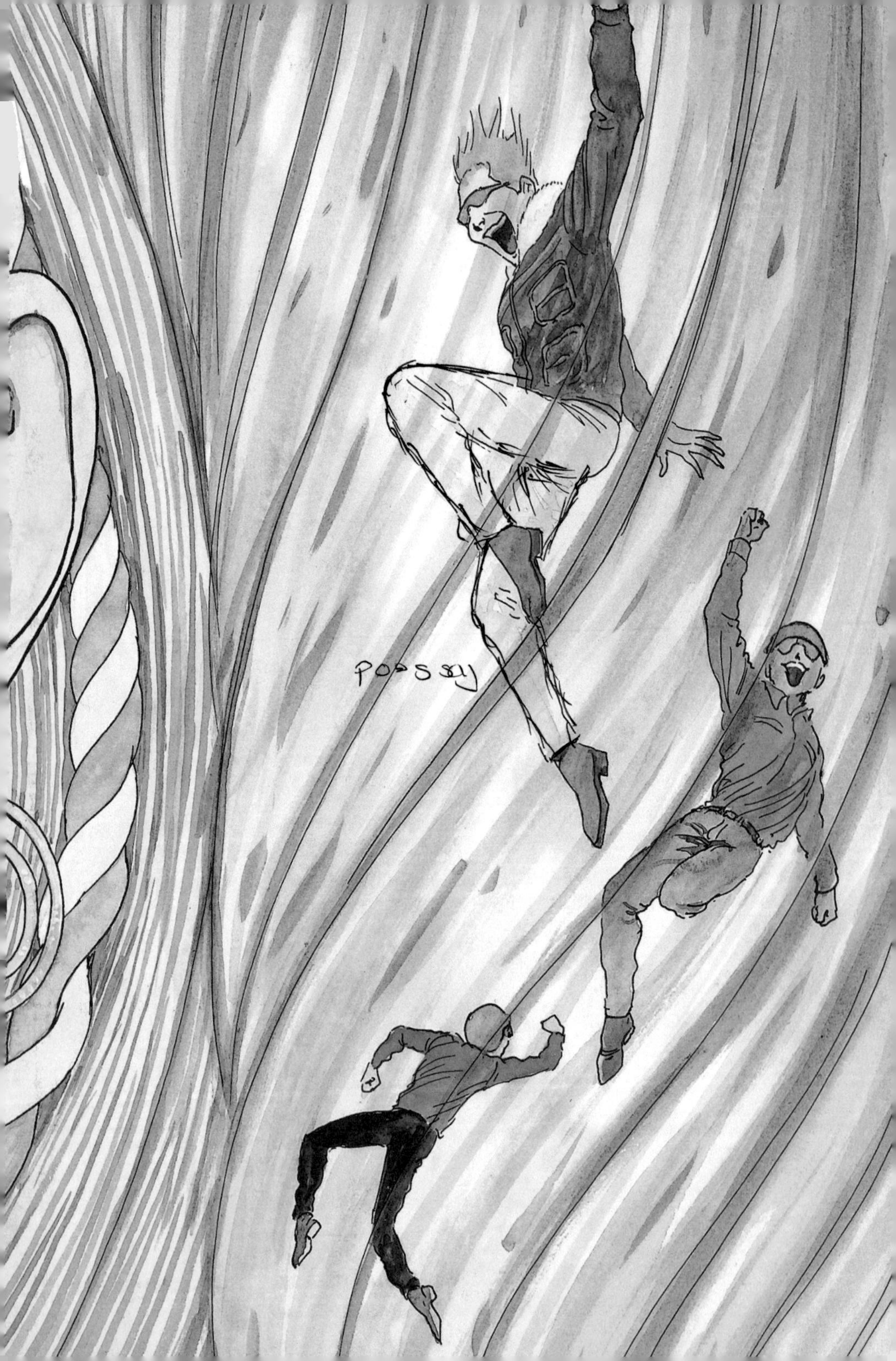